DIVISION H

Bankruptcy and other Mercantile Statutes

Statutes

Statutory Instruments

Notes by the Accountant of Court

Statutes

Mercantile Law Amendment Act Scotland 1856

(19 & 20 Vict. c. 60)

An Act to amend the laws of Scotland affecting trade and commerce. [21st July 1856]

1–5. [Repealed by the Sale of Goods Act 1893, s. 60.]

Guarantees, etc., to be in writing
6. All guarantees, securities, or cautionary obligations made or granted by any person for any other person, and all representations and assurances as to the character, conduct, credit, ability, trade, or dealings of any person, made or granted to the effect or for the purpose of enabling such person to obtain credit, money, goods, or postponement of payment of debt, or of any other obligation demandable from him, shall be in writing, and shall be subscribed by the person undertaking such guarantee, security, or cautionary obligation, or making such representations and assurances, or by some person duly authorised by him or them, otherwise the same shall have no effect.

7. [Repealed by the Partnership Act 1890, s. 48.]

Cautioners not to be entitled to benefit of discussion
8. Where any person shall become bound as cautioner for any principal debtor, it shall not be necessary for the creditor to whom such cautionary obligation shall be granted, before calling on the cautioner for payment of the debt to which such cautionary obligation refers, to discuss or do diligence against the principal debtor, as now required by law; but it shall be competent to such creditor to proceed against the principal debtor and the said cautioner, or against either of them, and to use all action or diligence against both or either of them which is competent according to the law of Scotland: Provided always, that nothing herein contained shall prevent any cautioner from stipulating in the instrument of caution that the creditor shall be bound before proceeding against him to discuss and do diligence against the principal debtor.

Discharge of one cautioner to operate as a discharge to all
9. Where two or more parties shall become bound as cautioners for any debtor, any discharge granted by the creditor in such debt or obligation to any one of such cautioners without the consent of the other cautioners shall be deemed and taken to be a discharge granted to all the cautioners; but nothing herein contained shall be deemed to extend to the case of a cautioner consenting to the discharge of a co-cautioner who may have become bankrupt.

10–16. [Repealed by the Bills of Exchange Act 1882, Sched. 2.]

Carriers to be liable for losses by accidental fires
17. All carriers for hire of goods within Scotland shall be liable to make

good to the owner of such goods all losses arising from accidental fire while such goods were in the custody or possession of such carriers.

Every port in the United Kingdom, etc., to be deemed a home port

18. In relation to the rights and remedies of persons having claims for repairs done to or supplies furnished to or for ships, every port within the United Kingdom of Great Britain and Ireland, the Islands of Man, Guernsey, Jersey, Alderney, and Sark, and the islands adjacent to any of them, being part of the dominions of Her Majesty, shall be deemed a home port.

Court of Session to make regulations for carrying Act into effect

19. The Court of Session is hereby empowered from time to time to make such regulations by Act or Acts of Sederunt as the said Court may deem meet for carrying into effect the purposes of this Act: Provided always, that within fourteen days from the commencement of any future session of Parliament there shall be transmitted to both Houses of Parliament copies of all Acts of Sederunt made and passed under the powers hereby given.

Title of Act

20. In citing this Act it shall be sufficient to use the expression " The Mercantile Law Amendment Act Scotland 1856 ".

Act to apply to Scotland only

21. Nothing in this Act contained shall apply to any part of the United Kingdom except Scotland.

Bills of Exchange Act 1882

(45 & 46 Vict. c. 61)

An Act to codify the law relating to bills of exchange, cheques, and promissory notes. [18th August 1882]

PART I

PRELIMINARY

Short title

1. This Act may be cited as the Bills of Exchange Act 1882.

Interpretation of terms

2. In this Act, unless the context otherwise requires,—

" Acceptance " means an acceptance completed by delivery or notification.

" Action " includes a counter claim and set off.

" Banker " includes a body of persons whether incorporated or not who carry on the business of banking.

" Bankrupt " includes any person whose estate is vested in a trustee or assignee under the law for the time being in force relating to bankruptcy.

" Bearer " means the person in possession of a bill or note which is payable to bearer.

" Bill " means bill of exchange, and " note " means promissory note.

" Delivery " means transfer of possession, actual or constructive, from one person to another.

" Holder " means the payee or indorsee of a bill or note who is in possession of it, or the bearer thereof.

" Indorsement " means an indorsement completed by delivery.

" Issue " means the first delivery of a bill or note, complete in form to a person who takes it as a holder.

" Person " includes a body of persons whether incorporated or not.

" Value " means valuable consideration.

" Written " includes printed, and " writing " includes print.

PART II

BILLS OF EXCHANGE

Form and Interpretation

Bill of exchange defined

[1]**3.**—(1) A bill of exchange is an unconditional order in writing, addressed by one person to another, signed by the person giving it, requiring the person to whom it is addressed to pay on demand or at a fixed or determinable future time a sum certain in money to or to the order of a specified person, or to bearer.

(2) An instrument which does not comply with these conditions, or which orders any act to be done in addition to the payment of money, is not a bill of exchange.

(3) An order to pay out of a particular fund is not unconditional within the meaning of this section; but an unqualified order to pay, coupled with (*a*) an indication of a particular fund out of which the drawee is to reimburse himself or a particular account to be debited with the amount, or (*b*) a statement of the transaction which gives rise to the bill, is unconditional.

(4) A bill is not invalid by reason—

(*a*) That it is not dated;

(*b*) That it does not signify the value given, or that any value has been given therefor;

(*c*) That it does not specify the place where it is drawn or the place where it is payable.

NOTE

[1] " (1) A bill of exchange or promissory note drawn or made on or after the appointed day shall be invalid if the sum payable is an amount of money wholly or partly in shillings or pence.

(2) A bill of exchange or promissory note for an amount wholly or partly in shillings or pence dated 15th February 1971 or later shall be deemed to have been drawn or made before 15th February 1971 if it bears a certificate in writing by a banker that it was so drawn or made."—Decimal Currency Act 1969, s. 2.

Inland and foreign bills

4.—(1) An inland bill is a bill which is or on the face of it purports to be (*a*) both drawn and payable within the British Islands, or (*b*) drawn within the British Islands upon some person resident therein. Any other bill is a foreign bill.

For the purposes of this Act " British Islands " mean any part of the United Kingdom of Great Britain and Ireland, the islands of Man, Guernsey, Jersey, Alderney, and Sark, and the islands adjacent to any of them being part of the dominions of Her Majesty.

(2) Unless the contrary appear on the face of the bill the holder may treat it as an inland bill.

Effect where different parties to bill are the same person

5.—(1) A bill may be drawn payable to, or to the order of, the drawer; or it may be drawn payable to, or to the order of, the drawee.

(2) Where in a bill drawer and drawee are the same person, or where the drawee is a fictitious person or a person not having capacity to contract, the holder may treat the instrument, at his option, either as a bill of exchange or as a promissory note.

Address to drawee

6.—(1) The drawee must be named or otherwise indicated in a bill with reasonable certainty.

(2) A bill may be addressed to two or more drawees whether they are partners or not, but an order addressed to two drawees in the alternative or to two or more drawees in succession is not a bill of exchange.

Certainty required as to payee

7.—(1) Where a bill is not payable to bearer, the payee must be named or otherwise indicated therein with reasonable certainty.

(2) A bill may be made payable to two or more payees jointly, or it may be made payable in the alternative to one of two, or one or some of several payees. A bill may also be made payable to the holder of an office for the time being.

(3) Where the payee is a fictitious or non-existing person the bill may be treated as payable to bearer.

What bills are negotiable

8.—(1) When a bill contains words prohibiting transfer, or indicating an intention that it should not be transferable, it is valid as between the parties thereto, but it is not negotiable.

(2) A negotiable bill may be payable either to order or to bearer.

(3) A bill is payable to bearer which is expressed to be so payable, or on which the only or last indorsement is an indorsement in blank.

(4) A bill is payable to order which is expressed to be so payable, or which is expressed to be payable to a particular person, and does not contain words prohibiting transfer or indicating an intention that it should not be transferable.

(5) Where a bill, either originally or by indorsement, is expressed to be payable to the order of a specified person, and not to him or his order, it is nevertheless payable to him or his order at his option.

Sum payable

9.—(1) The sum payable by a bill is a sum certain within the meaning of this Act, although it is required to be paid—

(*a*) With interest.

(*b*) By stated instalments.

(*c*) By stated instalments, with a provision that upon default in payment of any instalments the whole shall become due.

(*d*) According to an indicated rate of exchange or according to a rate of exchange to be ascertained as directed by the bill.

(2) Where the sum payable is expressed in words and also in figures, and there is a discrepancy between the two, the sum denoted by the words is the amount payable.

(3) Where a bill is expressed to be payable with interest, unless the instrument otherwise provides, interest runs from the date of the bill, and if the bill is undated from the issue thereof.

Bill payable on demand

10.—(1) A bill is payable on demand—

(*a*) Which is expressed to be payable on demand, or at sight, or on presentation; or

(*b*) In which no time for payment is expressed.

(2) Where a bill is accepted or indorsed when it is overdue, it shall, as regards the acceptor who so accepts, or any indorser who so indorses it, be deemed a bill payable on demand.

Bill payable at a future time

11. A bill is payable at a determinable future time within the meaning of this Act which is expressed to be payable—
(1) At a fixed period after date or sight.
(2) On or at a fixed period after the occurrence of a specified event which is certain to happen, though the time of happening may be uncertain.

An instrument expressed to be payable on a contingency is not a bill, and the happening of the event does not cure the defect.

Omission of date in bill payable after date

12. Where a bill expressed to be payable at a fixed period after date is issued undated, or where the acceptance of a bill payable at a fixed period after sight is undated, any holder may insert therein the true date of issue or acceptance, and the bill shall be payable accordingly.

Provided that (1) where the holder in good faith and by mistake inserts a wrong date, and (2) in every case where a wrong date is inserted, if the bill subsequently comes into the hands of a holder in due course the bill shall not be avoided thereby, but shall operate and be payable as if the date so inserted had been the true date.

Ante-dating and post-dating

13.—(1) Where a bill or an acceptance or any indorsement on a bill is dated, the date shall, unless the contrary be proved, be deemed to be the true date of the drawing, acceptance, or indorsement, as the case may be.
(2) A bill is not invalid by reason only that it is ante-dated or post-dated, or that it bears date on a Sunday.

Computation of time of payment

14. Where a bill is not payable on demand the day on which it falls due is determined as follows:—.
[1] (1) The bill is due and payable in all cases on the last day of the time of payment as fixed by the bill or, if that is a non-business day, on the succeeding business day.
(2) Where a bill is payable at a fixed period after date, or after the happening of a specified event, the time of payment is determined by excluding the day from which the time is to begin to run and by including the day of payment.
(3) Where a bill is payable at a fixed period after sight, the time begins to run from the date of the acceptance if the bill be accepted, and from the date of noting or protest if the bill be noted or protested for non-acceptance, or for non-delivery.
(4) The term " month " in a bill means calendar month.

NOTE
[1] As substituted by the Banking and Financial Dealings Act 1971, s. 3 (2).

Case of need

15. The drawer of a bill and any indorser may insert therein the name of a person to whom the holder may resort in case of need, that is to say, in case the bill is dishonoured by non-acceptance or non-payment. Such person is called the referee in case of need. It is in the option of the holder to resort to the referee in case of need or not as he may think fit.

Optional stipulations by drawer or indorser

16. The drawer of a bill, and any indorser, may insert therein an express stipulation—

(1) Negativing or limiting his own liability to the holder:

(2) Waiving as regards himself some or all of the holder's duties.

Definition and requisites of acceptance

17.—(1) The acceptance of a bill is the signification by the drawee of his assent to the order of the drawer.

(2) An acceptance is invalid unless it complies with the following conditions, namely:

(*a*) It must be written on the bill and be signed by the drawee. The mere signature of the drawee without additional words is sufficient.

(*b*) It must not express that the drawee will perform his promise by any other means than the payment of money.

Time for acceptance

18. A bill may be accepted—

(1) Before it has been signed by the drawer, or while otherwise incomplete:

(2) When it is overdue, or after it has been dishonoured by a previous refusal to accept, or by non-payment:

(3) When a bill payable after sight is dishonoured by non-acceptance, and the drawee subsequently accepts it, the holder, in the absence of any different agreement, is entitled to have the bill accepted as of the date of first presentment to the drawee for acceptance.

General and qualified acceptances

19.—(1) An acceptance is either (*a*) general, or (*b*) qualified.

(2) A general acceptance assents without qualification to the order of the drawer. A qualified acceptance in express terms varies the effect of the bill as drawn.

In particular an acceptance is qualified which is—.

(*a*) conditional, that is to say, which makes payment by the acceptor dependent on the fulfilment of a condition therein stated:

(*b*) partial, that is to say, an acceptance to pay part only of the amount for which the bill is drawn:

(*c*) local, that is to say, an acceptance to pay only at a particular specified place:

An acceptance to pay at a particular place is a general acceptance, unless it expressly states that the bill is to be paid there only and not elsewhere:

(*d*) qualified as to time:

(*e*) the acceptance of some one or more of the drawees, but not of all.

Inchoate instruments

[1] **20.**—(1) Where a simple signature on a blank paper is delivered by the signer in order that it may be converted into a bill, it operates as a *prima facie* authority to fill it up as a complete bill for any amount using the signature for that of the drawer, or the acceptor, or an indorser:

and, in like manner, when a bill is wanting in any material particular, the person in possession of it has a *prima facie* authority to fill up the omission in any way he thinks fit.

(2) In order that any such instrument when completed may be enforceable against any person who became a party thereto prior to its completion, it must be filled up within a reasonable time, and strictly in accordance with the authority given. Reasonable time for this purpose is a question of fact.

Provided that if any such instrument after completion is negotiated to a holder in due course it shall be valid and effectual for all purposes in his hands, and he may enforce it as if it had been filled up within a reasonable time and strictly in accordance with the authority given.

NOTE
[1] As amended by the Finance Act 1970, Sched. 8.

Delivery
   21.—(1) Every contract on a bill, whether it be the drawer's, the acceptor's, or an indorser's, is incomplete and revocable, until delivery of the instrument in order to give effect thereto.
   Provided that where an acceptance is written on a bill, and the drawee gives notice to or according to the directions of the person entitled to the bill that he has accepted it, the acceptance then becomes complete and irrevocable.
   (2) As between immediate parties, and as regards a remote party other than a holder in due course, the delivery—

   (*a*) in order to be effectual must be made either by or under the authority of the party drawing, accepting, or indorsing, as the case may be:

   (*b*) may be shown to have been conditional or for a special purpose only, and not for the purpose of transferring the property in the bill.

But if the bill be in the hands of a holder in due course a valid delivery of the bill by all parties prior to him so as to make them liable to him is conclusively presumed.
   (3) Where a bill is no longer in the possession of a party who has signed it as drawer, acceptor, or indorser, a valid and unconditional delivery by him is presumed until the contrary is proved.

Capacity and Authority of Parties

Capacity of parties
   22.—(1) Capacity to incur liability as a party to a bill is co-extensive with capacity to contract.
   Provided that nothing in this section shall enable a corporation to make itself liable as drawer, acceptor, or indorser of a bill unless it is competent to do so under the law for the time being in force relating to corporations.
   (2) Where a bill is drawn or indorsed by an infant, minor, or corporation having no capacity or power to incur liability on a bill, the drawing or indorsement entitles the holder to receive payment of the bill, and to enforce it against any other party thereto.

Signature essential to liability
   23. No person is liable as drawer, indorser, or acceptor of a bill who has not signed it as such: Provided that—
   (1) Where a person signs a bill in a trade or assumed name, he is liable thereon as if he had signed it in his own name:
   (2) The signature of the name of a firm is equivalent to the signature by the person so signing of the names of all persons liable as partners in that firm.

Forged or unauthorised signature
   24. Subject to the provisions of this Act, where a signature on a bill is forged or placed thereon without the authority of the person whose signature it purports to be, the forged or unauthorised signature is wholly inoperative, and no right to retain the bill or to give a discharge therefor or to enforce payment thereof against any party thereto can be acquired

through or under that signature, unless the party against whom it is sought to retain or enforce payment of the bill is precluded from setting up the forgery or want of authority.

Provided that nothing in this section shall affect the ratification of an unauthorised signature not amounting to a forgery.

Procuration signatures

25. A signature by procuration operates as notice that the agent has but a limited authority to sign, and the principal is only bound by such signature if the agent in so signing was acting within the actual limits of his authority.

Person signing as agent or in representative capacity

26.—(1) Where a person signs a bill as drawer, indorser, or acceptor, and adds words to his signature, indicating that he signs for or on behalf of a principal, or in a representative character, he is not personally liable thereon; but the mere addition to his signature of words describing him as an agent, or as filling a representative character, does not exempt him from personal liability.

(2) In determining whether a signature on a bill is that of the principal or that of the agent by whose hand it is written, the construction most favourable to the validity of the instrument shall be adopted.

The Consideration for a Bill

Value and holder for value

27.—(1) Valuable consideration for a bill may be constituted by—

(*a*) Any consideration sufficient to support a simple contract;

(*b*) An antecedent debt or liability. Such a debt or liability is deemed valuable consideration whether the bill is payable on demand or at a future time.

(2) Where value has at any time been given for a bill the holder is deemed to be a holder for value as regards the acceptor and all parties to the bill who became parties prior to such time.

(3) Where the holder of a bill has a lien on it, arising from contract or by implication of law, he is deemed to be a holder for value to the extent of the sum for which he has a lien.

Accommodation bill or party

28.—(1) An accommodation party to a bill is a person who has signed a bill as drawer, acceptor, or indorser, without receiving value therefor, and for the purpose of lending his name to some other person.

(2) An accommodation party is liable on the bill to a holder for value; and it is immaterial whether, when such holder took the bill, he knew such party to be an accommodation party or not.

Holder in due course

[1] **29.**—(1) A holder in due course is a holder who has taken a bill, complete and regular on the face of it, under the following conditions; namely—

(*a*) That he became the holder of it before it was overdue, and without notice that it had been previously dishonoured, if such was the fact;

(*b*) That he took the bill in good faith and for value, and that at the time the bill was negotiated to him he had no notice of any defect in the title of the person who negotiated it.

(2) In particular the title of a person who negotiates a bill is defective within the meaning of this Act when he obtained the bill, or the acceptance thereof, by fraud, duress, or force and fear, or other unlawful means, or for

an illegal consideration, or when he negotiates it in breach of faith, or under such cirumstances as amount to a fraud.

(3) A holder (whether for value or not), who derives his title to a bill through a holder in due course, and who is not himself a party to any fraud or illegality affecting it, has all the rights of that holder in due course as regards the acceptor and all parties to the bill prior to that holder.

NOTE

[1] See the Consumer Credit Act 1974, s. 125.

Presumption of value and good faith

30.—(1) Every party whose signature appears on a bill is *prima facie* deemed to have become a party thereto for value.

(2) Every holder of a bill is *prima facie* deemed to be a holder in due course; but if in an action on a bill it is admitted or proved that the acceptance, issue, or subsequent negotiation of the bill is affected with fraud, duress, or force and fear, or illegality, the burden of proof is shifted, unless and until the holder proves that, subsequent to the alleged fraud or illegality, value has in good faith been given for the bill.

Negotiation of Bills

Negotiation of bill

31.—(1) A bill is negotiated when it is transferred from one person to another in such a manner as to constitute the transferee the holder of the bill.

(2) A bill payable to bearer is negotiated by delivery.

(3) A bill payable to order is negotiated by the indorsement of the holder completed by delivery.

(4) Where the holder of a bill payable to his order transfers it for value without indorsing it the transfer gives the transferee such title as the transferor had in the bill, and the transferee in addition acquires the right to have the indorsement of the transferor.

(5) Where any person is under obligation to indorse a bill in a representative capacity, he may indorse the bill in such terms as to negative personal liability.

Requisites of a valid indorsement

32. An indorsement in order to operate as a negotiation must comply with the following conditions, namely:—

(1) It must be written on the bill itself and be signed by the indorser. The simple signature of the indorser on the bill, without additional words, is sufficient.

An indorsement written on an allonge, or on a " copy " of a bill issued or negotiated in a country where " copies " are recognised, is deemed to be written on the bill itself.

(2) It must be an indorsement of the entire bill. A partial indorsement, that is to say, an indorsement which purports to transfer to the indorsee a part only of the amount payable or which purports to transfer the bill to two or more indorsees severally does not operate as a negotiation of the bill.

(3) Where a bill is payable to the order of two or more payees or indorsees who are not partners all must indorse, unless the one indorsing has authority to indorse for the others.

(4) Where, in a bill payable to order, the payee or indorsee is wrongly designated, or his name is misspelt, he may indorse the bill as therein described, adding, if he think fit, his proper signature.

(5) Where there are two or more indorsements on a bill, each indorsement is deemed to have been made in the order in which it appears on the bill, until the contrary is proved.

(6) An indorsement may be made in blank or special. It may also contain terms making it restrictive.

Conditional indorsement

33. Where a bill purports to be indorsed conditionally the condition may be disregarded by the payer, and payment to the indorsee is valid whether the condition has been fulfilled or not.

Indorsement in blank and special indorsement

34.—(1) An indorsement in blank specifies no indorsee, and a bill so indorsed becomes payable to bearer.

(2) A special indorsement specifies the person to whom, or to whose order, the bill is to be payable.

(3) The provisions of this Act relating to a payee apply with the necessary modifications to an indorsee under a special indorsement.

(4) When a bill has been indorsed in blank, any holder may convert the blank indorsement into a special indorsement by writing above the indorser's signature a direction to pay the bill to or to the order of himself or some other person.

Restrictive indorsement

35.—(1) An indorsement is restrictive which prohibits the further negotiation of the bill, or which expresses that it is a mere authority to deal with the bill as thereby directed, and not a transfer of the ownership thereof, as, for example, if a bill be indorsed " Pay D. only ", or " Pay D. for the Account of X.", or " Pay D. or order for collection ".

(2) A restrictive indorsement gives the indorsee the right to receive payment of the bill and to sue any party thereto that his indorser could have sued, but gives him no power to transfer his rights as indorsee unless it expressly authorises him to do so.

(3) Where a restrictive indorsement authorises further transfer, all subsequent indorsees take the bill with the same rights and subject to the same liabilities as the first indorsee under the restrictive indorsement.

Negotiation of overdue or dishonoured bill

36.—(1) Where a bill is negotiable in its origin it continues to be negotiable until it has been (*a*) restrictively indorsed or (*b*) discharged by payment or otherwise.

(2) Where an overdue bill is negotiated, it can only be negotiated subject to any defect of title affecting it at its maturity, and thenceforward no person who takes it can acquire or give a better title than that which the person from whom he took it had.

(3) A bill payable on demand is deemed to be overdue within the meaning and for the purposes of this section when it appears on the face of it to have been in circulation for an unreasonable length of time. What is an unreasonable length of time for this purpose is a question of fact.

(4) Except where an indorsement bears date after the maturity of the bill, every negotiation is *prima facie* deemed to have been effected before the bill was overdue.

(5) Where a bill which is not overdue has been dishonoured any person who takes it with notice of the dishonour takes it subject to any defect of title attaching thereto at the time of dishonour, but nothing in this sub-section shall affect the rights of a holder in due course.

Negotiation of a bill to party already liable thereon

37. Where a bill is negotiated back to the drawer, or to a prior indorser or to the acceptor, such party may, subject to the provisions of this Act, re-issue and further negotiate the bill, but he is not entitled to enforce payment of the bill against any intervening party to whom he was previously liable.

Rights of the holder
38. The rights and powers of the holder of a bill are as follows:
(1) He may sue on the bill in his own name:
(2) Where he is a holder in due course, he holds the bill free from any defect of title of prior parties, as well as from mere personal defences available to prior parties among themselves, and may enforce payment against all parties liable on the bill.
(3) Where his title is defective (*a*) if he negotiates the bill to a holder in due course, that holder obtains a good and complete title to the bill; and (*b*) if he obtains payment of the bill the person who pays him in due course gets a valid discharge for the bill.

General Duties of the Holder

When presentment for acceptance is necessary
39.—(1) Where a bill is payable after sight, presentment for acceptance is necessary in order to fix the maturity of the instrument.
(2) Where a bill expressly stipulates that it shall be presented for acceptance, or where a bill is drawn payable elsewhere than at the residence or place of business of the drawee, it must be presented for acceptance before it can be presented for payment.
(3) In no other case is presentment for acceptance necessary in order to render liable any party to the bill.
(4) Where the holder of a bill, drawn payable elsewhere than at the place of business or residence of the drawee, has not time, with the exercise of reasonable diligence, to present the bill for acceptance before presenting it for payment on the day that it falls due, the delay caused by presenting the bill for acceptance before presenting it for payment is excused, and does not discharge the drawer and indorsers.

Time for presenting bill payable after sight
40.—(1) Subject to the provisions of this Act, when a bill payable after sight is negotiated, the holder must either present it for acceptance or negotiate it within a reasonable time.
(2) If he do not do so, the drawer and all indorsers prior to that holder are discharged.
(3) In determining what is a reasonable time within the meaning of this section, regard shall be had to the nature of the bill, the usage of trade with respect to similar bills, and the facts of the particular case.

Rules as to presentment for acceptance, and excuses for non-presentment
41.—(1) A bill is duly presented for acceptance which is presented in accordance with the following rules:
(*a*) The presentment must be made by or on behalf of the holder to the drawee or to some person authorised to accept or refuse acceptance on his behalf at a reasonable hour on a business day and before the bill is overdue:
(*b*) Where a bill is addressed to two or more drawees, who are not partners, presentment must be made to them all, unless one has authority to accept for all, then presentment may be made to him only:
(*c*) where the drawee is dead presentment may be made to his personal representative:

(*d*) Where the drawee is bankrupt, presentment may be made to him or to his trustee:

(*e*) Where authorised by agreement or usage, a presentment through the post office is sufficient.

(2) Presentment in accordance with these rules is excused, and a bill may be treated as dishonoured by non-acceptance—.

(*a*) Where the drawee is dead or bankrupt, or is a fictitious person or person not having capacity to contract by bill:

(*b*) Where, after the exercise of reasonable diligence, such presentment cannot be effected:

(*c*) Where although the presentment has been irregular, acceptance has been refused on some other ground.

(3) The fact that the holder has reason to believe that the bill, on presentment, will be dishonoured does not excuse presentment.

Non-acceptance

42. When a bill is duly presented for acceptance and is not accepted within the customary time, the person presenting it must treat it as dishonoured by non-acceptance. If he does not, the holder shall lose his right of recourse against the drawer and indorsers.

Dishonour by non-acceptance and its consequences

43.—(1) A bill is dishonoured by non-acceptance—.

(*a*) when it is duly presented for acceptance, and such an acceptance as is prescribed by this Act is refused or cannot be obtained; or

(*b*) when presentment for acceptance is excused and the bill is not accepted.

(2) Subject to the provisions of this Act when a bill is dishonoured by non-acceptance, an immediate right of recourse against the drawer and indorsers accrues to the holder, and no presentment for payment is necessary.

Duties as to qualified acceptances

44.—(1) The holder of a bill may refuse to take a qualified acceptance, and if he does not obtain an unqualified acceptance may treat the bill as dishonoured by non-acceptance.

(2) Where a qualified acceptance is taken and the drawer or an indorser has not expressly or impliedly authorised the holder to take a qualified acceptance, or does not subsequently assent thereto, such drawer or indorser is discharged from his liability on the bill.

The provisions of this sub-section do not apply to a partial acceptance, whereof due notice has been given. Where a foreign bill has been accepted as to part, it must be protested as to the balance.

(3) When the drawer or indorser of a bill receives notice of a qualified acceptance, and does not within a reasonable time express his dissent to the holder, he shall be deemed to have assented thereto.

Rules as to presentment for payment

45. Subject to the provisions of this Act a bill must be duly presented for payment. If it be not so presented the drawer and indorsers shall be discharged.

A bill is duly presented for payment which is presented in accordance with the following rules:—.

(1) Where the bill is not payable on demand, presentment must be made on the day it falls due.

(2) Where the bill is payable on demand, then, subject to the provisions of this Act, presentment must be made within a reasonable time after its issue in order to render the drawer liable, and within a reasonable time after its indorsement, in order to render the indorser liable.

In determining what is a reasonable time, regard shall be had to the nature of the bill, the usage of trade with regard to similar bills, and the facts of the particular case.

(3) Presentment must be made by the holder or by some person authorised to receive payment on his behalf at a reasonable hour on a business day, at the proper place as hereinafter defined, either to the person designated by the bill as payer, or to some person authorised to pay or refuse payment on his behalf, if with the exercise of reasonable diligence such person can there be found.

(4) A bill is presented at the proper place:—

  (*a*) Where a place of payment is specified in the bill and the bill is there presented.

  (*b*) Where no place of payment is specified, but the address of the drawee or acceptor is given in the bill, and the bill is there presented.

  (*c*) Where no place of payment is specified and no address given, and the bill is presented at the drawee's or acceptor's place of business if known, and if not, at his ordinary residence if known.

  (*d*) In any other case if presented to the drawee or acceptor wherever he can be found, or if presented at his last known place of business or residence.

(5) Where a bill is presented at the proper place, and after the exercise of reasonable diligence no person authorised to pay or refuse payment can be found there, no further presentment to the drawee or acceptor is required.

(6) Where a bill is drawn upon, or accepted by two or more persons who are not partners, and no place of payment is specified, presentment must be made to them all.

(7) Where the drawee or acceptor of a bill is dead, and no place of payment is specified, presentment must be made to a personal representative, if such there be, and with the exercise of reasonable diligence he can be found.

(8) Where authorised by agreement or usage a presentment through the post office is sufficient.

Excuses for delay or non-presentment for payment

46.—(1) Delay in making presentment for payment is excused when the delay is caused by circumstances beyond the control of the holder, and not imputable to his default, misconduct, or negligence. When the cause of delay ceases to operate presentment must be made with reasonable diligence.

(2) Presentment for payment is dispensed with—

  (*a*) Where, after the exercise of reasonable diligence presentment, as required by this Act, cannot be effected.

The fact that the holder has reason to believe that the bill will, on presentment, be dishonoured, does not dispense with the necessity for presentment.

  (*b*) Where the drawee is a fictitious person.

  (*c*) As regards the drawer where the drawee or acceptor is not bound, as between himself and the drawer, to accept or pay the bill, and the drawer has no reason to believe that the bill would be paid if presented.

  (*d*) As regards an indorser, where the bill was accepted or made for the accommodation of that indorser, and he has no reason to expect that the bill would be paid if presented.

  (*e*) By waiver of presentment, express or implied.

Dishonour by non-payment

47.—(1) A bill is dishonoured by non-payment (*a*) when it is duly presented for payment and payment is refused or cannot be obtained, or (*b*) when presentment is excused and the bill is overdue and unpaid.

(2) Subject to the provisions of this Act, when a bill is dishonoured by non-payment, an immediate right of recourse against the drawer and indorsers accrues to the holder.

Notice of dishonour and effect of non-notice

48. Subject to the provisions of this Act, when a bill has been dishonoured by non-acceptance or by non-payment, notice of dishonour must be given to the drawer and each indorser, and any drawer or indorser to whom such notice is not given is discharged: Provided that—

(1) Where a bill is dishonoured by non-acceptance, and notice of dishonour is not given, the rights of a holder in due course subsequent to the omission shall not be prejudiced by the omission.

(2) Where a bill is dishonoured by non-acceptance and due notice of dishonour is given, it shall not be necessary to give notice of a subsequent dishonour by non-payment unless the bill shall in the meantime have been accepted.

Rules as to notice of dishonour

49. Notice of dishonour in order to be valid and effectual must be given in accordance with the following rules:—

(1) The notice must be given by or on behalf of the holder, or by or on behalf of an indorser who, at the time of giving it, is himself liable on the bill.

(2) Notice of dishonour may be given by an agent either in his own name, or in the name of any party entitled to give notice, whether that party be his principal or not.

(3) Where the notice is given by or on behalf of the holder, it enures for the benefit of all subsequent holders and all prior indorsers who have a right of recourse against the party to whom it is given.

(4) Where notice is given by or on behalf of an indorser entitled to give notice as herein-before provided, it enures for the benefit of the holder and all indorsers subsequent to the party to whom notice is given.

(5) The notice may be given in writing or by personal communication, and may be given in any terms which sufficiently identify the bill, and intimate that the bill has been dishonoured by non-acceptance or non-payment.

(6) The return of a dishonoured bill to the drawer or an indorser is, in point of form, deemed a sufficient notice of dishonour.

(7) A written notice need not be signed, and an insufficient written notice may be supplemented and validated by verbal communication. A misdescription of the bill shall not vitiate the notice unless the party to whom the notice is given is in fact misled thereby.

(8) Where notice of dishonour is required to be given to any person, it may be given either to the party himself, or to his agent in that behalf.

(9) Where the drawer or indorser is dead, and the party giving notice knows it, the notice must be given to a personal representative, if such there be, and with the exercise of reasonable diligence he can be found.

(10) Where the drawer or indorser is bankrupt, notice may be given either to the party himself or to the trustee.

(11) Where there are two or more drawers or indorsers who are not partners, notice must be given to each of them, unless one of them has authority to receive such notice for the others.

(12) The notice may be given as soon as the bill is dishonoured, and must be given within a reasonable time thereafter.

In the absence of special circumstances notice is not deemed to have been given within a reasonable time, unless—

(*a*) Where the person giving and the person to receive notice reside in the same place, the notice is given or sent off in time to reach the latter on the day after the dishonour of the bill.

(*b*) Where the person giving and the person to receive notice reside in different places, the notice is sent off on the day after the dishonour of the bill, if there be a post at a convenient hour on that day, and if there be no such post on that day then by the next post thereafter.

(13) Where a bill when dishonoured is in the hands of an agent, he may either give notice to the parties liable on the bill, or he may give notice to his principal. If he give notice to his principal, he must do so within the same time as if he were the holder, and the principal upon receipt of such notice has himself the same time for giving notice as if the agent had been an independent holder.

(14) Where a party to a bill receives due notice of dishonour, he has after the receipt of such notice the same period of time for giving notice to antecedent parties that the holder has after the dishonour.

(15) Where a notice of dishonour is duly addressed and posted, the sender is deemed to have given due notice of dishonour notwithstanding any miscarriage by the post office.

Excuses for non-notice and delay

50.—(1) Delay in giving notice of dishonour is excused where the delay is caused by circumstances beyond the control of the party giving notice, and not imputable to his default, misconduct, or negligence. When the cause of delay ceases to operate the notice must be given with reasonable diligence.

(2) Notice of dishonour is dispensed with—.

(*a*) When, after the exercise of reasonable diligence, notice as required by this Act cannot be given to or does not reach the drawer or indorser sought to be charged:

(*b*) By waiver, express or implied. Notice of dishonour may be waived before the time of giving notice has arrived, or after the omission to give due notice:

(*c*) As regards the drawer in the following cases, namely, (1) where the drawer and drawee are the same person, (2) where the drawee is a fictitious person or a person not having capacity to contract, (3) where the drawer is the person to whom the bill is presented for payment, (4) where the drawee or acceptor is as between himself and the drawer under no obligation to accept or pay the bill, (5) where the drawer has countermanded payment:

(*d*) As regards the indorser in the following cases, namely (1) where the drawee is a fictitious person or a person not having capacity to contract and the indorser was aware of the fact at the time he indorsed the bill, (2) where the indorser is the person to whom the bill is presented for payment, (3) where the bill was accepted or made for his accommodation.

Noting or protest of bill

51.—(1) Where an inland bill has been dishonoured it may, if the holder thinks fit, be noted for non-acceptance or non-payment, as the case may be; but it shall not be necessary to note or protest any such bill in order to preserve the recourse against the drawer or indorser.

(2) Where a foreign bill, appearing on the face of it to be such, has been dishonoured by non-acceptance it must be duly protested for non-acceptance, and where such a bill, which has not been previously dishonoured by non-acceptance, is dishonoured by non-payment it must be duly protested for non-payment. If it be not so protested the drawer and indorsers are discharged. Where a bill does not appear on the face of it to be a foreign bill, protest thereof in case of dishonour is unnecessary.

(3) A bill which has been protested for non-acceptance may be subsequently protested for non-payment.

[1] (4) Subject to the provisions of this Act, when a bill is noted or protested, it may be noted on the day of its dishonour, and must be noted not later than the next succeeding business day. When a bill has been duly noted, the protest may be subsequently extended as of the date of the noting.

(5) Where the acceptor of a bill becomes bankrupt or insolvent or suspends payment before it matures, the holder may cause the bill to be protested for better security against the drawer and indorsers.

(6) A bill must be protested at the place where it is dishonoured: Provided that—.

(a) When a bill is presented through the post office, and returned by post dishonoured, it may be protested at the place to which it is returned and on the day of its return if received during business hours, and if not received during business hours, then not later than the next business day:

(b) When a bill drawn payable at the place of business or residence of some person other than the drawee has been dishonoured by non-acceptance, it must be protested for non-payment at the place where it is expressed to be payable, and no further presentment for payment to, or demand on, the drawee is necessary.

(7) A protest must contain a copy of the bill, and must be signed by the notary making it, and must specify—.

(a) The person at whose request the bill is protested:

(b) The place and date of protest, the cause or reason for protesting the bill, the demand made, and the answer is given, if any, or the fact that the drawee or acceptor could not be found.

(8) Where a bill is lost or destroyed, or is wrongly detained from the person entitled to hold it, protest may be made on a copy or written particulars thereof.

(9) Protest is dispensed with by any circumstance which would dispense with notice of dishonour. Delay in noting or protesting is excused when the delay is caused by circumstances beyond the control of the holder, and not imputable to his default, misconduct, or negligence. When the cause of delay ceases to operate the bill must be noted or protested with reasonable diligence.

NOTE
[1] As amended by the Bills of Exchange (Time of Noting) Act 1917, s. 1.

Duties of holder as regards drawee or acceptor

52.—(1) When a bill is accepted generally presentment for payment is not necessary in order to render the acceptor liable.

(2) When by the terms of a qualified acceptance presentment for payment is required, the acceptor, in the absence of an express stipulation to that effect, is not discharged by the omission to present the bill for payment on the day that it matures.

(3) In order to render the acceptor of a bill liable it is not necessary to protest it, or that notice of dishonour should be given to him.

(4) Where the holder of a bill presents it for payment, he shall exhibit the bill to the person from whom he demands payment, and when a bill is paid the holder shall forthwith deliver it up to the party paying it.

Liabilities of Parties

Funds in hands of drawee

53.—(1) A bill, of itself, does not operate as an assignment of funds in the hands of the drawee available for the payment thereof, and the drawee of a bill who does not accept as required by this Act is not liable on the instrument. This sub-section shall not extend to Scotland.

[1] (2) Subject to section 75A of this Act, in Scotland, where the drawee of a bill has in his hands funds available for the payment thereof, the bill operates as an assignment of the sum for which it is drawn in favour of the holder, from the time when the bill is presented to the drawee.

NOTE

[1] As amended by the Law Reform (Miscellaneous Provisions) (Scotland) Act 1985, s. 11(*a*), with effect from 30th December 1985.

Liability of acceptor

54. The acceptor of a bill, by accepting it—
(1) Engages that he will pay it according to the tenor of his acceptance:
(2) Is precluded from denying to a holder in due course:
   (*a*) The existence of the drawer, the genuineness of his signature, and his capacity and authority to draw the bill;
   (*b*) In the case of a bill payable to drawer's order, the then capacity of the drawer to indorse, but not the genuineness or validity of his indorsement;
   (*c*) In the case of a bill payable to the order of a third person, the existence of the payee and his then capacity to indorse, but not the genuineness or validity of his indorsement.

Liability of drawer or indorser

55.—(1) The drawer of a bill by drawing it—
   (*a*) Engages that on due presentment it shall be accepted and paid according to its tenor, and that if it be dishonoured he will compensate the holder or any indorser who is compelled to pay it, provided that the requisite proceedings on dishonour be duly taken;
   (*b*) Is precluded from denying to a holder in due course the existence of the payee and his then capacity to indorse.
(2) The indorser of a bill by indorsing it—
   (*a*) Engages that on due presentment it shall be accepted and paid according to its tenor, and that if it be dishonoured he will compensate the holder or a subsequent indorser who is compelled to pay it, provided that the requisite proceedings on dishonour be duly taken;
   (*b*) Is precluded from denying to a holder in due course the genuineness and regularity in all respects of the drawer's signature and all previous indorsements;
   (*c*) Is precluded from denying to his immediate or a subsequent indorsee that the bill was at the time of his indorsement a valid and subsisting bill, and that he had then a good title thereto.

Stranger signing bill liable as indorser

56. Where a person signs a bill otherwise than as a drawer or acceptor, he thereby incurs the liabilities of an indorser to a holder in due course.

Measure of damages against parties to dishonoured bill

[1] **57.** Where a bill is dishonoured, the measure of damages, which shall be deemed to be liquidated damages, shall be as follows:

(1) The holder may recover from any party liable on the bill, and the drawer who has been compelled to pay the bill may recover from the acceptor, and an indorser who has been compelled to pay the bill may recover from the acceptor or from the drawer, or from a prior indorser—

   (*a*) The amount of the bill;

   (*b*) Interest thereon from the time of presentment for payment if the bill is payable on demand, and from the maturity of the bill in any other case:

   (*c*) The expenses of noting, or, when protest is necessary, and the protest has been extended, the expenses of protest.

(2) [Repealed by the Administration of Justice Act 1977, Sched. 5, Pt. I.]

(3) Where by this Act interest may be recovered as damages, such interest may, if justice require it, be withheld wholly or in part, and where a bill is expressed to be payable with interest at a given rate, interest as damages may or may not be given at the same rate as interest proper.

NOTE

  [1] Saved: the Law Reform (Miscellaneous Provisions) Act 1934, s. 3(1) and proviso (*c*).

Transferor by delivery and transferee

58.—(1) Where the holder of a bill payable to bearer negotiates it by delivery without indorsing it, he is called a "transferor by delivery".

(2) A transferor by delivery is not liable on the instrument.

(3) A transferor by delivery who negotiates a bill thereby warrants to his immediate transferee being a holder for value that the bill is what it purports to be, that he has a right to transfer it, and that at the time of transfer he is not aware of any fact which renders it valueless.

Discharge of Bill

Payment in due course

59.—(1) A bill is discharged by payment in due course by or on behalf of the drawee or acceptor.

"Payment in due course" means payment made at or after the maturity of the bill to the holder thereof in good faith and without notice that his title to the bill is defective.

(2) Subject to the provisions herein-after contained, when a bill is paid by the drawer or an indorser it is not discharged; but

   (*a*) Where a bill payable to, or to the order of, a third party is paid by the drawer, the drawer may enforce payment thereof against the acceptor, but may not re-issue the bill.

   (*b*) Where a bill is paid by an indorser, or where a bill payable to drawer's order is paid by the drawer, the party paying it is remitted to his former rights as regards the acceptor or antecedent parties, and he may, if he thinks fit, strike out his own and subsequent indorsements, and again negotiate the bill.

(3) Where an accommodation bill is paid in due course by the party accommodated the bill is discharged.

Banker paying demand draft wherein indorsement is forged

60. When a bill payable to order on demand is drawn on a banker, and the banker on whom it is drawn pays the bill in good faith and in the ordinary course of business, it is not incumbent on the banker to show that the indorsement of the payee or any subsequent indorsement was made by or under the authority of the person whose indorsement it purports to be, and the banker is deemed to have paid the bill in due course, although such indorsement has been forged or made without authority.

Acceptor the holder at maturity

61. When the acceptor of a bill is or becomes the holder of it at or after its maturity, in his own right, the bill is discharged.

Express waiver

62.—(1) When the holder of a bill at or after its maturity absolutely and unconditionally renounces his rights against the acceptor the bill is discharged.

[THE NEXT PAGE IS H 21]

The renunciation must be in writing, unless the bill is delivered up to the acceptor.

(2) The liabilities of any party to a bill may in like manner be renounced by the holder before, at, or after its maturity; but nothing in this section shall affect the rights of a holder in due course without notice of the renunciation.

Cancellation

63.—(1) Where a bill is intentionally cancelled by the holder or his agent, and the cancellation is apparent thereon, the bill is discharged.

(2) In like manner any party liable on a bill may be discharged by the intentional cancellation of his signature by the holder or his agent. In such case any indorser who would have had a right of recourse against the party whose signature is cancelled, is also discharged.

(3) A cancellation made unintentionally, or under a mistake, or without the authority of the holder is inoperative; but where a bill or any signature thereon appears to have been cancelled the burden of proof lies on the party who alleges that the cancellation was made unintentionally, or under a mistake, or without authority.

Alteration of bill

[1] **64.**—(1) Where a bill or acceptance is materially altered without the assent of all parties liable on the bill, the bill is avoided except as against a party who has himself made, authorised, or assented to the alteration, and subsequent indorsers.

Provided that,

Where a bill has been materially altered, but the alteration is not apparent, and the bill is in the hands of a holder in due course, such holder may avail himself of the bill as if it had not been altered, and may enforce payment of it according to its original tenor.

(2) In particular the following alterations are material, namely, any alteration of the date, the sum payable, the time of payment, the place of payment, and, where a bill has been accepted generally, the addition of a place of payment without the acceptor's assent.

NOTE
[1] Explained by the Decimal Currency Act 1969, s. 3 (2).

Acceptance and Payment for Honour

Acceptance for honour supra protest

65.—(1) Where a bill of exchange has been protested for dishonour by non-acceptance, or protested for better security, and is not overdue, any person, not being a party already liable thereon, may, with the consent of the holder, intervene and accept the bill *supra* protest, for the honour of any party liable thereon, or for the honour of the person for whose account the bill is drawn.

(2) A bill may be accepted for honour for part only of the sum for which it is drawn.

(3) An acceptance for honour *supra* protest in order to be valid must—

(*a*) be written on the bill, and indicate that it is an acceptance for honour:

(*b*) be signed by the acceptor for honour.

(4) Where an acceptance for honour does not expressly state for whose honour it is made, it is deemed to be an acceptance for the honour of the drawer.

(5) Where a bill payable after sight is accepted for honour, its maturity is calculated from the date of the noting for non-acceptance and not from the date of the acceptance for honour.

Liability of acceptor for honour

66.—(1) The acceptor for honour of a bill by accepting it engages that he will, on due presentment, pay the bill according to the tenor of his acceptance, if it is not paid by the drawee, provided it has has been duly presented for payment, and protested for non-payment, and that he receives notice of these facts.

(2) The acceptor for honour is liable to the holder and to all parties to the bill subsequent to the party for whose honour he has accepted.

Presentment to acceptor for honour

67.—(1) Where a dishonoured bill has been accepted for honour *supra* protest, or contains a reference in case of need, it must be protested for non-payment before it is presented for payment to the acceptor for honour, or referee in case of need.

(2) Where the address of the acceptor for honour is in the same place where the bill is protested for non-payment, the bill must be presented to him not later than the day following its maturity; and where the address of the acceptor for honour is in some place other than the place where it was protested for non-payment, the bill must be forwarded not later than the day following its maturity for presentment to him.

(3) Delay in presentment or non-presentment is excused by any circumstance which would excuse delay in presentment for payment or non-presentment for payment.

(4) When a bill of exchange is dishonoured by the acceptor for honour it must be protested for non-payment by him.

Payment for honour supra protest

68.—(1) Where a bill has been protested for non-payment, any person may intervene and pay it *supra* protest for the honour of any party liable thereon, or for the honour of the person for whose account the bill is drawn.

(2) Where two or more persons offer to pay a bill for the honour of different parties, the person whose payment will discharge most parties to the bill shall have the preference.

(3) Payment for honour *supra* protest, in order to operate as such and not as a mere voluntary payment, must be attested by a notarial act of honour, which may be appended to the protest or form an extension of it.

(4) The notarial act of honour must be founded on a declaration made by the payer for honour, or his agent in that behalf, declaring his intention to pay the bill for honour, and for whose honour he pays.

(5) Where a bill has been paid for honour, all parties subsequent to the party for whose honour it is paid are discharged, but the payer for honour is subrogated for, and succeeds to both the rights and duties of, the holder as regards the party for whose honour he pays, and all parties liable to that party.

(6) The payer for honour on paying to the holder the amount of the bill and the notarial expenses incidental to its dishonour is entitled to receive both the bill itself and the protest. If the holder do not on demand deliver them up he shall be liable to the payer for honour in damages.

(7) Where the holder of a bill refuses to receive payment *supra* protest he shall lose his right of recourse against any party who would have been discharged by such payment.

Lost Instruments

Holder's right to duplicate of lost bill

69. Where a bill has been lost before it is overdue, the person who was the holder of it may apply to the drawer to give him another bill of the same tenor, giving security to the drawer if required to indemnify him against all persons whatever in case the bill alleged to have been lost shall be found again.

If the drawer on request as aforesaid refuses to give such duplicate bill, he may be compelled to do so.

Action on lost bill

70. In any action or proceeding upon a bill, the court or a judge may order that the loss of the instrument shall not be set up, provided an indemnity be given to the satisfaction of the court or judge against the claims of any other person upon the instrument in question.

Bill in a Set

Rules as to sets

71.—(1) Where a bill is drawn in a set, each part of the set being numbered, and containing a reference to the other parts, the whole of the parts constitute one bill.

(2) Where the holder of a set indorses two or more parts to different persons, he is liable on every such part, and every indorser subsequent to him is liable on the part he has himself indorsed as if the said parts were separate bills.

(3) Where two or more parts of a set are negotiated to different holders in due course, the holder whose title first accrues is as between such holders deemed the true owner of the bill; but nothing in this sub-section shall affect the rights of a person who in due course accepts or pays the part first presented to him.

(4) The acceptance may be written on any part, and it must be written on one part only.

If the drawee accepts more than one part, and such accepted parts get into the hands of different holders in due course, he is liable on every such part as if it were a separate bill.

(5) When the acceptor of a bill drawn in a set pays it without requiring the part bearing his acceptance to be delivered up to him, and that part at maturity is outstanding in the hands of a holder in due course, he is liable to the holder thereof.

(6) Subject to the preceding rules, where any one part of a bill drawn in a set is discharged by payment or otherwise, the whole bill is discharged.

Conflict of Laws

Rules where laws conflict

72. Where a bill drawn in one country is negotiated, accepted, or payable in another, the rights, duties, and liabilities of the parties thereto are determined as follows:

(1) The validity of a bill as regards requisites in form is determined by the law of the place of issue, and the validity as regards requisites in form of the supervening contracts, such as acceptance, or indorsement, or acceptance *supra* protest, is determined by the law of the place where such contract was made.

Provided that—

> (*a*) Where a bill is issued out of the United Kingdom it is not invalid by reason only that it is not stamped in accordance with the law of the place of issue:
>
> (*b*) Where a bill, issued out of the United Kingdom, conforms, as regards requisites in form, to the law of the United Kingdom, it may, for the purpose of enforcing payment thereof, be treated as valid as between all persons who negotiate, hold, or become parties to it in the United Kingdom.

(2) Subject to the provisions of this Act, the interpretation of the drawing, indorsement, acceptance, or acceptance *supra* protest of a bill, is determined by the law of the place where such contract is made.

Provided that where an inland bill is indorsed in a foreign country the indorsement shall as regards the payer be interpreted according to the law of the United Kingdom.

(3) The duties of the holder with respect to presentment for acceptance or payment and the necessity for or sufficiency of a protest or notice of dishonour, or otherwise, are determined by the law of the place where the act is done or the bill is dishonoured.

(4) [Repealed by the Administration of Justice Act 1977, Sched. 5, Pt. I.]

(5) Where a bill is drawn in one country and is payable in another, the due date thereof is determined according to the law of the place where it is payable.

Part III

Cheques of a Banker

Cheque defined

[1] **73.** A cheque is a bill of exchange drawn on a banker payable on demand.

Except as otherwise provided in this part, the provisions of this Act applicable to a bill of exchange payable on demand apply to a cheque.

NOTE
[1] Extended by the National Loans Act 1968, s. 14(7).

Presentment of cheque for payment

74. Subject to the provisions of this Act—

(1) Where a cheque is not presented for payment within a reasonable time of its issue, and the drawer or the person on whose account it is drawn had the right at the time of such presentment as between him and the banker to have the cheque paid and suffers actual damage through the delay, he is discharged to the extent of such damage, that is to say, to the extent to which such drawer or person is a creditor of such banker to a larger amount than he would have been had such cheque been paid.

(2) In determining what is a reasonable time regard shall be had to the nature of the instrument, the usage of trade and of bankers, and the facts of the particular case.

(3) The holder of such cheque as to which such drawer or person is discharged shall be a creditor, in lieu of such drawer or person, of such banker to the extent of such discharge, and entitled to recover the amount from him.

Revocation of banker's authority

75. The duty and authority of a banker to pay a cheque drawn on him by his customer are determined by—

(1) Countermand of payment:

(2) Notice of the customer's death.

[1] **75A.**—(1) On the countermand of payment of a cheque, the banker shall be treated as having no funds available for the payment of the cheque.

(2) This section applies to Scotland only.

NOTE
[1] As amended by the Law Reform (Miscellaneous Provisions) (Scotland) Act 1985, s. 11(*b*), with effect from 30th December 1985.

[1] *Crossed Cheques*

General and special crossings defined

76.—(1) Where a cheque bears across its face an addition of—

(*a*) The words "and company" or any abbreviation thereof between two parallel transverse lines, either with or without the words "not negotiable"; or

[THE NEXT PAGE IS H 25]

(*b*) Two parallel transverse lines simply either with or without the words " not negotiable ";
that addition constitutes a crossing, and the cheque is crossed generally.

(2) Where a cheque bears across its face an addition of the name of a banker, either with or without the words " not negotiable ", that addition constitutes a crossing, and the cheque is crossed specially and to that banker.

NOTE
¹ Provisions applied by the Cheques Act 1957, s. 5. See S.I. 1957 No. 1764 and 1972 Nos. 641, 764 and 765.

Crossing by drawer or after issue

77.—(1) A cheque may be crossed generally or specially by the drawer.

(2) Where a cheque is uncrossed, the holder may cross it generally or specially.

(3) Where a cheque is crossed generally the holder may cross it specially.

(4) Where a cheque is crossed generally or specially, the holder may add the words " not negotiable ".

(5) Where a cheque is crossed specially, the banker to whom it is crossed may again cross it specially to another banker for collection.

(6) Where an uncrossed cheque, or a cheque crossed generally, is sent to a banker for collection, he may cross it specially to himself.

Crossing a material part of cheque

78. A crossing authorised by this Act is a material part of the cheque; it shall not be lawful for any person to obliterate or, except as authorised by this Act, to add to or alter the crossing.

Duties of banker as to crossed cheques

79.—(1) Where a cheque is crossed specially to more than one banker, except when crossed to an agent for collection being a banker, the banker on whom it is drawn shall refuse payment thereof.

(2) Where the banker on whom a cheque is drawn which is so crossed nevertheless pays the same, or pays a cheque crossed generally otherwise than to a banker, or if crossed specially otherwise than to the banker to whom it is crossed, or his agent for collection being a banker, he is liable to the true owner of the cheque for any loss he may sustain owing to the cheque having been so paid.

Provided that where a cheque is presented for payment which does not at the time of presentment appear to be crossed, or to have had a crossing which has been obliterated, or to have been added to or altered otherwise than as authorised by this Act, the banker paying the cheque in good faith and without negligence shall not be responsible or incur any liability, nor shall the payment be questioned by reason of the cheque having been crossed, or of the crossing having been obliterated or having been added to or altered otherwise than as authorised by this Act, and of payment having been made otherwise than to a banker or to the banker to whom the cheque is or was crossed, or to his agent for collection being a banker, as the case may be.

Protection to banker and drawer where cheque is crossed

80. Where the banker, on whom a crossed cheque is drawn, in good faith and without negligence pays it, if crossed generally, to a banker, and if crossed specially, to the banker to whom it is crossed, or his agent for collection being a banker, the banker paying the cheque, and, if the cheque has come into the hands of the payee, the drawer, shall respectively be entitled to the same rights and be placed in the same position as if payment of the cheque had been made to the true owner thereof.

Effect of crossing on holder

81. When a person takes a crossed cheque which bears on it the words
" not negotiable ", he shall not have and shall not be capable of giving a
better title to the cheque than that which the person from whom he took it
had.

82. [Repealed by the Cheques Act 1957, Sched.]

PART IV

PROMISSORY NOTES

Promissory note defined

83.—(1) A promissory note is an unconditional promise in writing made
by one person to another signed by the maker, engaging to pay, on demand
or at a fixed or determinable future time, a sum certain in money, to, or to
the order of, a specified person or to bearer.

(2) An instrument in the form of a note payable to maker's order is not a
note within the meaning of this section unless and until it is indorsed by the
maker.

(3) A note is not invalid by reason only that it contains also a pledge of
collateral security with authority to sell or dispose thereof.

(4) A note which is, or on the face of it purports to be, both made and
payable within the British Islands is an inland note. Any other note is a
foreign note.

Delivery necessary

84. A promissory note is inchoate and incomplete until delivery thereof
to the payee or bearer.

Joint and several notes

85.—(1) A promissory note may be made by two or more makers, and
they may be liable thereon jointly, or jointly and severally, according to its
tenor.

(2) Where a note runs " I promise to pay ", and is signed by two or more
persons it is deemed to be their joint and several note.

Note payable on demand

86.—(1) Where a note payable on demand has been indorsed, it must be
presented for payment within a reasonable time of the indorsement. If it be
not so presented the indorser is discharged.

(2) In determining what is a reasonable time regard shall be had to the
nature of the instrument, the usage of trade, and the facts of the particular
case.

(3) Where a note payable on demand is negotiated, it is not deemed to
be overdue, for the purpose of affecting the holder with defects of title of
which he had no notice, by reason that it appears that a reasonable time for
presenting it for payment has elapsed since its issue.

Presentment of note for payment

87.—(1) Where a promissory note is in the body of it made payable at a
particular place, it must be presented for payment at that place in order to
render the maker liable. In any other case, presentment for payment is not
necessary in order to render the maker liable.

(2) Presentment for payment is necessary in order to render the
indorser of a note liable.

(3) Where a note is in the body of it made payable at a particular place,
presentment at that place is necessary in order to render an indorser liable;

but when a place of payment is indicated by way of memorandum only, presentment at that place is sufficient to render the indorser liable, but a presentment to the maker elsewhere, if sufficient in other respects, shall also suffice.

Liability of maker

88. The maker of a promissory note by making it—.

(1) Engages that he will pay it according to its tenor;

(2) Is precluded from denying to a holder in due course the existence of the payee and his then capacity to indorse.

Application of Part II to notes

89.—(1) Subject to the provisions in this part, and except as by this section provided, the provisions of this Act relating to bills of exchange apply, with the necessary modifications, to promissory notes.

(2) In applying those provisions the maker of a note shall be deemed to correspond with the acceptor of a bill, and the first indorser of a note shall be deemed to correspond with the drawer of an accepted bill payable to drawer's order.

(3) The following provisions as to bills do not apply to notes; namely, provisions relating to—.

(*a*) Presentment for acceptance;

(*b*) Acceptance;

(*c*) Acceptance *supra* protest;

(*d*) Bills in a set.

(4) Where a foreign note is dishonoured, protest thereof is unnecessary.

PART V

SUPPLEMENTARY

Good faith

90. A thing is deemed to be done in good faith, within the meaning of this Act, where it is in fact done honestly, whether it is done negligently or not.

Signature

91.—(1) Where, by this Act, any instrument or writing is required to be signed by any person, it is not necessary that he should sign it with his own hand, but it is sufficient if his signature is written thereon by some other person by or under his authority.

(2) In the case of a corporation, where, by this Act, any instrument or writing is required to be signed, it is sufficient if the instrument or writing be sealed with the corporate seal.

But nothing in this section shall be construed as requiring the bill or note of a corporation to be under seal.

Computation of time

[1] **92.** Where, by this Act, the time limited for doing any act or thing is less than three days, in reckoning time, non-business days are excluded.

[2] " Non-business days " for the purposes of this Act mean—

(*a*) Saturday, Sunday, Good Friday, Christmas Day:

(*b*) A bank holiday under the Banking and Financial Dealings Act 1971:

(*c*) A day appointed by royal proclamation as a public fast or thanksgiving day.

(*d*) A day declared by an order under section 2 of the Banking and
Financial Dealings Act 1971 to be a non-business day.

Any other day is a business day.

NOTES
  ¹ As amended by the Banking and Financial Dealings Act 1971, ss. 3 (1) and 4 (4). Applied:
see the Development Land Tax Act 1976, Sched. 8, para. 21 (4).
  ² Applied: see the Finance (No. 2) Act 1975, s. 46 (1) (3) (*b*) (4).

When noting equivalent to protest

93. For the purposes of this Act, where a bill or note is required to be
protested within a specified time or before some further proceeding is taken,
it is sufficient that the bill has been noted for protest before the expiration of
the specified time or the taking of the proceeding; and the formal protest
may be extended at any time thereafter as of the date of the noting.

Protest when notary not accessible

94. Where a dishonoured bill or note is authorised or required to be
protested, and the services of a notary cannot be obtained at the place where
the bill is dishonoured, any householder or substantial resident of the place
may, in the presence of two witnesses, give a certificate, signed by them,
attesting the dishonour of the bill, and the certificate shall in all respects
operate as if it were a formal protest of the bill.

The form given in Schedule 1 to this Act may be used with necessary
modifications, and if used shall be sufficient.

Dividend warrants may be crossed

95. The provisions of this Act as to crossed cheques shall apply to a
warrant for payment of dividend.

96. [Repealed by the Statute Law Revision Act 1898.]

Savings

 ¹ **97.**—(1) The rules in bankruptcy relating to bills of exchange, promissory notes, and cheques, shall continue to apply thereto notwithstanding
anything in this Act contained.

(2) The rules of common law including the law merchant, save in so far
as they are inconsistent with the express provisions of this Act, shall continue
to apply to bills of exchange, promissory notes, and cheques.

(3) Nothing in this Act or in any repeal effected thereby shall affect—

(*a*) Any law or enactment for the time being in force relating to the
revenue:

(*b*) The provisions of the Companies Act 1862, or Acts amending it, or
any Act relating to joint stock banks or companies:

(*c*) The provisions of any Act relating to or confirming the privileges of
the Bank of England or the Bank of Ireland respectively:

(*d*) The validity of any usage relating to dividend warrants, or the
indorsements thereof.

NOTE
  ¹ As amended by the Statute Law Revision Act 1898.

Saving of summary diligence in Scotland

98. Nothing in this Act or in any repeal effected thereby shall extend or
restrict, or in any way alter or affect the law and practice in Scotland in
regard to summary diligence.

Construction with other Acts, etc.
99. Where any Act or document refers to any enactment repealed by this Act, the Act or document shall be construed, and shall operate, as if it referred to the corresponding provisions of this Act.

Parole evidence allowed in certain judicial proceedings in Scotland
[1] **100.** In any judicial proceedings in Scotland, any fact relating to a bill of exchange, bank cheque, or promissory note, which is relevant to any question of liability thereon, may be proved by parole evidence: Provided that this enactment shall not in any way affect the existing law and practice whereby the party who is, according to the tenor of any bill of exchange, bank cheque, or promissory note, debtor to the holder in the amount thereof may be required, as a condition of obtaining a sist of diligence, or suspension of a charge, or threatened charge, to make such consignation, or to find such caution as the court or judge before whom the cause is depending may require.

NOTE
[1] As repealed in part by the Prescription and Limitation (Scotland) Act 1973, Sched. 5, Pt. I.

SCHEDULES

FIRST SCHEDULE

(Section 94)

Form of Protest which may be used when the services of a Notary cannot be obtained

Know all men that I, *A.B.* [householder], of   in the county of   , in the United Kingdom, at the request of *C.D.*, their being no notary public available, did on the   day of   188   at   demand payment [*or* acceptance] of the bill of exchange hereunder written, from *E.F.*, to which demand he made answer [state answer, if any], wherefore I now, in the presence of *G.H.* and *J.K.* do protest the said bill of exchange.

> (Signed) *A.B.*
>   *G.H.* } *Witnesses.*
>   *J.K.*

N.B.—The bill itself should be annexed, or a copy of the bill and all that is written thereon should be underwritten.

Factors Act 1889

(52 & 53 Vict. c. 45)

An Act to amend and consolidate the Factors Acts.

[26th August 1889]

Preliminary

Definitions
[1] **1.** For the purposes of this Act—
(1) The expression "mercantile agent" shall mean a mercantile agent having in the customary course of his business as such agent authority either to sell goods, or to consign goods for the purpose of sale, or to buy goods, or to raise money on the security of goods:

(2) A person shall be deemed to be in possession of goods or of the documents of title to goods, where the goods or documents are in his actual custody or are held by any other person subject to his control or for him or on his behalf:

(3) The expression "goods" shall include wares and merchandise;

(4) The expression "document of title" shall include any bill of lading, dock warrant, warehouse-keeper's certificate, and warrant or order for the

delivery of goods, and any other document used in the ordinary course of business as proof of the possession or control of goods, or authorising or purporting to authorise, either by endorsement or by delivery, the possessor of the document to transfer or receive goods thereby represented:

(5) The expression " pledge " shall include any contract pledging, or giving a lien or security on, goods, whether in consideration of an original advance or of any further or continuing advance or of any pecuniary liability:

(6) The expression " person " shall include any body of persons corporate or unincorporate.

NOTE

[1] " 1. Subject to the following provisions, the Factors Act 1889, shall apply to Scotland:—
(1) The expression " lien " shall mean and include right of retention; the expression " vendors lien " shall mean and include any right of retention competent to the original owner or vendor; and the expression " set off " shall mean and include compensation.
(2) In the application of section 5 of the recited Act, a sale, pledge, or other disposition of goods shall not be valid unless made for valuable consideration."—Factors (Scotland) Act 1890.

Dispositions by Mercantile Agents

Powers of mercantile agent with respect to disposition of goods

2.—(1) Where a mercantile agent is, with the consent of the owner, in possession of goods or of the documents of title to goods, any sale, pledge, or other disposition of the goods, made by him when acting in the ordinary course of business of a mercantile agent, shall, subject to the provisions of this Act, be as valid as if he were expressly authorised by the owner of the goods to make the same; provided that the person taking under the disposition acts in good faith, and has not at the time of the disposition notice that the person making the disposition has not authority to make the same.

(2) Where a mercantile agent has, with the consent of the owner, been in possession of goods or of the documents of title to goods, any sale, pledge, or other disposition, which would have been valid if the consent had continued, shall be valid notwithstanding the determination of the consent: provided that the person taking under the disposition has not at the time thereof notice that the consent has been determined.

(3) Where a mercantile agent has obtained possession of any documents of title to goods by reason of his being or having been, with the consent of the owner, in possession of the goods represented thereby, or of any other documents of title to the goods, his possession of the first-mentioned documents shall, for the purposes of this Act, be deemed to be with the consent of the owner.

(4) For the purposes of this Act the consent of the owner shall be presumed in the absence of evidence to the contrary.

Effect of pledges of documents of title

3. A pledge of the documents of title to goods shall be deemed to be a pledge of the goods.

Pledge for antecedent debt

4. Where a mercantile agent pledges goods as security for a debt or liability due from the pledgor to the pledgee before the time of the pledge, the pledgee shall acquire no further right to the goods than could have been enforced by the pledgor at the time of the pledge.

Rights acquired by exchange of goods or documents

5. The consideration necessary for the validity of a sale, pledge, or other disposition, of goods, in pursuance of this Act, may be either a payment in cash, or the delivery or transfer of other goods, or of a document

of title to goods, or of a negotiable security, or any other valuable consideration; but where goods are pledged by a mercantile agent in consideration of
the delivery or transfer of other goods, or of a document of title to goods, or
of a negotiable security, the pledgee shall acquire no right or interest in the
goods so pledged in excess of the value of the goods, documents, or security
when so delivered or transferred in exchange.

Agreements through clerks, etc.

6. For the purposes of this Act an agreement made with a mercantile
agent through a clerk or other person authorised in the ordinary course of
business to make contracts of sale or pledge on his behalf shall be deemed to
be an agreement with the agent.

Provisions as to consignors and consignees

7.—(1) Where the owner of goods has given possession of the goods to
another person for the purpose of consignment or sale, or has shipped the
goods in the name of another person, and the consignee of the goods has not
had notice that such person is not the owner of the goods, the consignee
shall, in respect of advances made to or for the use of such person, have the
same lien on the goods as if such person were the owner of the goods, and
may transfer any such lien to another person.

(2) Nothing in this section shall limit or affect the validity of any sale,
pledge, or disposition, by a mercantile agent.

Dispositions by Sellers and Buyers of Goods

Disposition by seller remaining in possession

8. Where a person, having sold goods, continues, or is, in possession of
the goods or of the documents of title to the goods, the delivery or transfer by
that person, or by a mercantile agent acting for him, of the goods or
documents of title under any sale, pledge, or other disposition thereof, or
under any agreement for sale, pledge, or other disposition thereof, to any
person receiving the same in good faith and without notice of the previous
sale, shall have the same effect as if the person making the delivery or
transfer were expressly authorised by the owner of the goods to make the
same.

Disposition by buyer obtaining possession

[1] **9.** Where a person, having bought or agreed to buy goods, obtains with
the consent of the seller possession of the goods or the documents of title to
the goods, the delivery or transfer, by that person or by a mercantile agent
acting for him, of the goods or documents of title, under any sale, pledge, or
other disposition thereof, or under any agreement for sale, pledge, or other
disposition thereof, to any person receiving the same in good faith and
without notice of any lien or other right of the original seller in respect of the
goods, shall have the same effect as if the person making the delivery or
transfer were a mercantile agent in possession of the goods or documents of
title with the consent of the owner.

For the purposes of this section—.
    (i) the buyer under a conditional sale agreement shall be deemed
        not to be a person who has bought or agreed to buy goods, and
    (ii) " conditional sale agreement " means an agreement for the sale
        of goods which is a consumer credit agreement within the mean-
        ing of the Consumer Credit Act 1974 under which the purchase
        price or part of it is payable by instalments, and the property in
        the goods is to remain in the seller (notwithstanding that the
        buyer is to be in possession of the goods) until such conditions as

to the payment of instalments or otherwise as may be specified in the agreement are fulfilled.

NOTE

[1] As amended by the Consumer Credit Act 1974, Sched. 4, para. 2: see also the Hire-Purchase (Scotland) Act 1965, ss. 50 and 55.

Effect of transfer of documents on vendor's lien or right of stoppage in transitu

10. Where a document of title to goods has been lawfully transferred to a person as a buyer or owner of the goods, and that person transfers the document to a person who takes the document in good faith and for valuable consideration, the last-mentioned transfer shall have the same effect for defeating any vendor's lien or right of stoppage in transitu as the transfer of a bill of lading has for defeating the right of stoppage in transitu.

Supplemental

Mode of transferring documents

11. For the purposes of this Act, the transfer of a document may be by endorsement, or, where the document is by custom or by its express terms transferable by delivery, or makes the goods deliverable to the bearer, then by delivery.

Saving for rights of true owner

12.—(1) Nothing in this Act shall authorise an agent to exceed or depart from his authority as between himself and his principal, or exempt him from any liability, civil or criminal, for so doing.

(2) Nothing in this Act shall prevent the owner of goods from recovering the goods from an agent or his trustee in bankruptcy at any time before the sale or pledge thereof, or shall prevent the owner of goods pledged by an agent from having the right to redeem the goods at any time before the sale thereof, on satisfying the claim for which the goods were pledged, and paying to the agent, if by him required, any money in respect of which the agent would by law be entitled to retain the goods or the documents of title thereto, or any of them, by way of lien as against the owner, or from recovering from any person with whom the goods have been pledged any balance of money remaining in his hands as the produce of the sale of the goods after deducting the amount of his lien.

(3) Nothing in this Act shall prevent the owner of goods sold by an agent from recovering from the buyer the price agreed to be paid for the same, or any part of that price, subject to any right of set off on the part of the buyer against the agent.

Saving for common law powers of agent

13. The provisions of this Act shall be construed in amplification and not in derogation of the powers exerciseable by an agent independently of this Act.

14–15. [Repealed by the Statute Law Revision Act 1908.]

. . . .

Short title

17. This Act may be cited as the Factors Act 1889.

[1] **Partnership Act 1890**

(53 & 54 Vict. c. 39)

An Act to declare and amend the law of partnership.

[14th August 1890]

NOTE
[1] Extended by the Limited Partnerships Act 1907, s. 7.

Definition of partnership

1.—(1) Partnership is the relation which subsists between persons carrying on a business in common with a view of profit.

(2) But the relation between members of any company or association which is—.

(a) Registered as a company under the Companies Act 1862, or any other Act of Parliament for the time being in force and relating to the registration of joint stock companies; or

(b) Formed or incorporated by or in pursuance of any other Act of Parliament or letters patent, or Royal Charter; or

(c) A company engaged in working mines within and subject to the jurisdiction of the Stannaries:

is not a partnership within the meaning of this Act.

Rules for determining existence of partnership

2. In determining whether a partnership does or does not exist, regard shall be had to the following rules:—.

(1) Joint tenancy, tenancy in common, joint property, common property, or part ownership does not of itself create a partnership as to anything so held or owned, whether the tenants or owners do or do not share any profits made by the use thereof.

(2) The sharing of gross returns does not of itself create a partnership, whether the persons sharing such returns have or have not a joint or common right or interest in any property from which or from the use of which the returns are derived.

(3) The receipt by a person of a share of the profits of a business is *prima facie* evidence that he is a partner in the business, but the receipt of such a share, or of a payment contingent on or varying with the profits of a business, does not of itself make him a partner in the business; and in particular—.

(a) The receipt by a person of a debt or other liquidated amount by instalments or otherwise out of the accruing profits of a business does not of itself make him a partner in the business or liable as such:

(b) A contract for the remuneration of a servant or agent of a person engaged in a business by a share of the profits of the business does not of itself make the servant or agent a partner in the business or liable as such:

(c) A person being the widow or child of a deceased partner, and receiving by way of annuity a portion of the profits made in the business in which the deceased person was a partner, is not by reason only of such receipt a partner in the business or liable as such:

(d) The advance of money by way of loan to a person engaged or about to engage in any business on a contract with that person that the lender shall receive a rate of interest varying with the profits, or shall receive a share of the profits arising from carrying on the business, does not of itself make the lender a partner with the person or persons carrying on the business or liable as such: Provided that the contract is in writing, and signed by or on behalf of all the parties thereto:

(*e*) A person receiving by way of annuity or otherwise a portion of the profits of a business in consideration of the sale by him of the goodwill of the business is not by reason only of such receipt a partner in the business or liable as such.

Postponement of rights of person lending or selling in consideration of share of profits in case of insolvency

[1] **3.** In the event of any person to whom money has been advanced by way of loan upon such a contract as is mentioned in the last foregoing section, or of any buyer of a goodwill in consideration of a share of the profits of the business, being adjudged a bankrupt, entering into an arrangement to pay his creditors less than 100p in the pound, or dying in insolvent circumstances, the lender of the loan shall not be entitled to recover anything in respect of his loan, and the seller of the goodwill shall not be entitled to recover anything in respect of the share of profits contracted for, until the claims of the other creditors of the borrower or buyer for valuable consideration in money or money's worth have been satisfied.

NOTE

[1] As amended by the Decimal Currency Act 1969, s. 10(1) and see the Bankruptcy (Scotland) Act 1985, s. 51(3).

Meaning of firm

4.—(1) Persons who have entered into partnership with one another are for the purposes of this Act called collectively a firm, and the name under which their business is carried on is called the firm-name.

[1] (2) In Scotland a firm is a legal person distinct from the partners of whom it is composed, but an individual partner may be charged on a decree or diligence directed against the firm, and on payment of the debts is entitled to relief *pro rata* from the firm and its other members.

NOTE

[1] See the Agricultural Holdings (Scotland) Act 1949, Sched. 9, para. 3(*b*), and the Capital Transfer Tax Act 1984, s. 119(2).

Relations of Partners to persons dealing with them

Power of partner to bind the firm

5. Every partner is an agent of the firm and his other partners for the purpose of the business of the partnership; and the acts of every partner who does any act for carrying on in the usual way business of the kind carried on by the firm of which he is a member bind the firm and his partners, unless the partner so acting has in fact no authority to act for the firm in the particular matter, and the person with whom he is dealing either knows that he has no authority, or does not know or believe him to be a partner.

Partners bound by acts on behalf of firm

6. An act or instrument relating to the business of the firm done or executed in the firm-name, or in any other manner showing an intention to bind the firm, by any person thereto authorised, whether a partner or not, is binding on the firm and all the partners.

Provided that this section shall not affect any general rule of law relating to the execution of deeds or negotiable instruments.

Partner using credit of firm for private purposes

7. Where one partner pledges the credit of the firm for a purpose apparently not connected with the firm's ordinary course of business, the firm is not bound, unless he is in fact specially authorised by the other partners; but this section does not affect any personal liability incurred by an individual partner.

Effect of notice that firm will not be bound by acts of partner

8. If it has been agreed between the partners that any restriction shall be placed on the power of any one or more of them to bind the firm, no act done in contravention of the agreement is binding on the firm with respect to persons having notice of the agreement.

Liability of partners

[1] **9.** Every partner in a firm is liable jointly with the other partners, and in Scotland severally also, for all debts and obligations of the firm incurred while he is a partner: and after his death his estate is also severally liable in a due course of administration for such debts and obligations, so far as they remain unsatisfied, but subject in England or Ireland to the prior payment of his separate debts.

NOTE
[1] See the Value Added Tax Act 1983, s. 30(5).

Liability of the firm for wrongs

10. Where, by any wrongful act or omission of any partner acting in the ordinary course of the business of the firm, or with the authority of his co-partners, loss or injury is caused to any person not being a partner in the firm, or any penalty is incurred, the firm is liable therefor to the same extent as the partner so acting or omitting to act.

Misapplication of money or property received for or in custody of the firm

11. In the following cases; namely—

(*a*) Where one partner acting within the scope of his apparent authority receives the money or property of a third person and misapplies it; and

(*b*) Where a firm in the course of its business receives money or property of a third person, and the money or property so received is misapplied by one or more of the partners while it is in the custody of the firm;

the firm is liable to make good the loss.

Liability for wrongs joint and several

12. Every partner is liable jointly with his co-partners and also severally for everything for which the firm while he is a partner therein becomes liable under either of the two last preceding sections.

Improper employment of trust-property for partnership purposes

13. If a partner, being a trustee, improperly employs trust-property in the business or on the account of the partnership, no other partner is liable for the trust-property to the persons beneficially interested therein:

Provided as follows:—

(1) This section shall not affect any liability incurred by any partner by reason of his having notice of a breach of trust; and

(2) Nothing in this section shall prevent trust-money from being followed and recovered from the firm if still in its possession or under its control.

Persons liable by "holding out"

14.—(1) Every one who by words spoken or written or by conduct represents himself, or who knowingly suffers himself to be represented, as a partner in a particular firm, is liable as a partner to any one who has on the faith of any such representation given credit to the firm, whether the representation has or has not been made or communicated to the person so giving credit by or with the knowledge of the apparent partner making the representation or suffering it to be made.

(2) Provided that where after a partner's death the partnership business is continued in the old firm-name, the continued use of that name or of the deceased partner's name as part thereof shall not of itself make his executors or administrators estate or effects liable for any partnership debts contracted after his death.

Admissions and representations of partners

15. An admission or representation made by any partner concerning the partnership affairs, and in the ordinary course of its business, is evidence against the firm.

Notice to acting partner to be notice to the firm

16. Notice to any partner who habitually acts in the partnership business of any matter relating to partnership affairs operates as notice to the firm, except in the case of a fraud on the firm committed by or with the consent of that partner.

Liabilities of incoming and outgoing partners

17.—(1) A person who is admitted as a partner into an existing firm does not thereby become liable to the creditors of the firm for anything done before he became a partner.

(2) A partner who retires from a firm does not thereby cease to be liable for partnership debts or obligations incurred before his retirement.

(3) A retiring partner may be discharged from any existing liabilities, by an agreement to that effect between himself and the members of the firm as newly constituted and the creditors, and this agreement may be either express or inferred as a fact from the course of dealing between the creditors and the firm as newly constituted.

Revocation of continuing guaranty by change in firm

18. A continuing guaranty or cautionary obligation given either to a firm or to a third person in respect of the transactions of a firm is, in the absence of agreement to the contrary, revoked as to future transactions by any change in the constitution of the firm to which, or of the firm in respect of the transactions of which, the guaranty or obligation was given.

Relations of Partners to one another

Variation by consent of terms of partnership

19. The mutual rights and duties of partners, whether ascertained by agreement or defined by this Act, may be varied by the consent of all the partners, and such consent may be either express or inferred from a course of dealing.

Partnership property

20.—(1) All property and rights and interests in property originally brought into the partnership stock or acquired, whether by purchase or otherwise, on account of the firm, or for the purposes and in the course of the partnership business, are called in this Act partnership property, and must be held and applied by the partners exclusively for the purposes of the partnership, and in accordance with the partnership agreement.

(2) Provided that the legal estate or interest in any land, or in Scotland the title to and interest in any heritable estate, which belongs to the partnership shall devolve according to the nature and tenure thereof, and the general rules of law thereto applicable, but in trust, so far as necessary, for the persons beneficially interested in the land under this section.

(3) Where co-owners of an estate or interest in any land, or in Scotland of any heritable estate, not being itself partnership property, are partners as to profits made by the use of that land or estate, and purchase other land or estate out of the profits to be used in like manner, the land or estate so purchased belongs to them, in the absence of an agreement to the contrary, not as partners, but as co-owners for the same respective estates and interests as are held by them in the land or estate first mentioned at the date of the purchase.

Property bought with partnership money

21. Unless the contrary intention appears, property bought with money belonging to the firm is deemed to have been bought on account of the firm.

Conversion into personal estate of land held as partnership property

22. Where land or any heritable interest therein has become partnership property, it shall, unless the contrary intention appears, be treated as be-tween the partners (including the representatives of a deceased partner), and also as between the heirs of a deceased partner and his executors or administrators, as personal or moveable and not real or heritable estate.

. . . .

Rules as to interests and duties of partners subject to special agreement

24. The interests of partners in the partnership property and their rights and duties in relation to the partnership shall be determined, subject to any agreement express or implied between the partners, by the following rules:

(1) All the partners are entitled to share equally in the capital and profits of the business, and must contribute equally towards the losses whether of capital or otherwise sustained by the firm.

(2) The firm must indemnify every partner in respect of payments made and personal liabilities incurred by him—.

(*a*) In the ordinary and proper conduct of the business of the firm; or

(*b*) In or about anything necessarily done for the preservation of the business or property of the firm.

(3) A partner making, for the purpose of the partnership, any actual payment or advance beyond the amount of capital which he has agreed to subscribe, is entitled to interest at the rate of five per cent. per annum from the date of the payment or advance.

(4) A partner is not entitled, before the ascertainment of profits, to interest on the capital subscribed by him.

(5) Every partner may take part in the management of the partnership business.

(6) No partner shall be entitled to remuneration for acting in the part-nership business.

(7) No person may be introduced as a partner without the consent of all existing partners.

(8) Any difference arising as to ordinary matters connected with the partnership business may be decided by a majority of the partners, but no change may be made in the nature of the partnership business without the consent of all existing partners.

(9) The partnership books are to be kept at the place of business of the partnership (or the principal place, if there is more than one), and every partner may, when he thinks fit, have access to and inspect and copy any of them.

Expulsion of partner

25. No majority of the partners can expel any partner unless a power to do so has been conferred by express agreement between the partners.

Retirement from partnership at will

26.—(1) Where no fixed term has been agreed upon for the duration of the partnership, any partner may determine the partnership at any time on giving notice of his intention so to do to all the other partners.

(2) Where the partnership has originally been constituted by deed, a notice in writing, signed by the partner giving it, shall be sufficient for this purpose.

Where partnership for term is continued over, a continuance on old terms presumed

27.—(1) Where a partnership entered into for a fixed term is continued after the term has expired, and without any express new agreement, the rights and duties of the partners remain the same as they were at the expiration of the term, so far as is consistent with the incidents of a partnership at will.

(2) A continuance of the business by the partners, or such of them as habitually acted therein during the term, without any settlement or liquidation of the partnership affairs, is presumed to be a continuance of the partnership.

Duty of partners to render accounts, etc.

28. Partners are bound to render true accounts and full information of all things affecting the partnership to any partner or his legal representatives.

Accountability of partners for private profits

29.—(1) Every partner must account to the firm for any benefit derived by him without the consent of the other partners from any transaction concerning the partnership, or from any use by him of the partnership property, name, or business connection.

(2) This section applies also to transactions undertaken after a partnership has been dissolved by the death of a partner, and before the affairs thereof have been completely wound up, either by any surviving partner or by the representatives of the deceased partner.

Duty of partner not to compete with firm

30. If a partner, without the consent of the other partners, carries on any business of the same nature as and competing with that of the firm, he must account for and pay over to the firm all profits made by him in that business.

Rights of assignee of share in partnership

31.—(1) An assignment by any partner of his share in the partnership, either absolute or by way of mortgage or redeemable charge, does not, as against the other partners, entitle the assignee, during the continuance of the partnership, to interfere in the management or administration of the partnership business or affairs, or to require any accounts of the partnership transactions, or to inspect the partnership books, but entitles the assignee only to receive the share of profits to which the assigning partner would otherwise be entitled, and the assignee must accept the account of profits agreed to by the partners.

(2) In case of a dissolution of the partnership, whether as respects all the partners or as respects the assigning partner, the assignee is entitled to receive the share of the partnership assets to which the assigning partner is entitled as between himself and the other partners, and, for the purpose of ascertaining that share, to an account as from the date of the dissolution.

Dissolution of Partnership, and its consequences

Dissolution by expiration or notice

32. Subject to any agreement between the partners, a partnership is dissolved—.

(*a*) If entered into for a fixed term, by the expiration of that term:

(*b*) If entered into for a single adventure or undertaking, by the termination of that adventure or undertaking:

(*c*) If entered into for an undefined time, by any partner giving notice to the other or others of his intention to dissolve the partnership.

In the last-mentioned case the partnership is dissolved as from the date mentioned in the notice as the date of dissolution, or, if no date is so mentioned, as from the date of the communication of the notice.

Dissolution by bankruptcy, death, or charge

33.—(1) Subject to any agreement between the partners, every partnership is dissolved as regards all the partners by the death or bankruptcy of any partner.

(2) A partnership may, at the option of the other partners, be dissolved if any partner suffers his share of the partnership property to be charged under this Act for his separate debt.

Dissolution by illegality of partnership

34. A partnership is in every case dissolved by the happening of any event which makes it unlawful for the business of the firm to be carried on or for the members of the firm to carry it on in partnership.

Dissolution by the Court

35. On application by a partner the court may decree a dissolution of the partnership in any of the following cases:

(*a*) When a partner is found lunatic by inquisition, or in Scotland by cognition, or is shown to the satisfaction of the court to be of permanently unsound mind, in either of which cases the application may be made as well on behalf of that partner by his committee or next friend or person having title to intervene as by any other partner:

(*b*) When a partner, other than the partner suing, becomes in any other way permanently incapable of performing his part of the partnership contract:

(*c*) When a partner, other than the partner suing, has been guilty of such conduct as, in the opinion of the court, regard being had to the nature of the business, is calculated to prejudicially affect the carrying on of the business:

(*d*) When a partner, other than the partner suing, wilfully or persistently commits a breach of the partnership agreement, or otherwise so conducts himself in matters relating to the partnership business that it is not reasonably practicable for the other partner or partners to carry on the business in partnership with him:

(*e*) When the business of the partnership can only be carried on at a loss:

[1] (*f*) Whenever in any case circumstances have arisen which, in the opinion of the court, render it just and equitable that the partnership be dissolved.

NOTE

[1] Amended. See the National Health Service (Amendment) Act 1949, s. 7 (4) (N.H.S. medical partnerships).

Rights of persons dealing with firm against apparent members of firm

36.—(1) Where a person deals with a firm after a change in its constitution he is entitled to treat all apparent members of the old firm as still being members of the firm until he has notice of the change.

(2) An advertisement in the *London Gazette* as to a firm whose principal place of business is in England or Wales, in the *Edinburgh Gazette* as to a firm whose principal place of business is in Scotland, and in the *Dublin Gazette* as to a firm whose principal place of business is in Ireland, shall be notice as to persons who had not dealings with the firm before the date of the dissolution or change so advertised.

(3) The estate of a partner who dies, or who becomes bankrupt, or of a partner who, not having been known to the person dealing with the firm to be a partner, retires from the firm, is not liable for partnership debts contracted after the date of the death, bankruptcy, or retirement respectively.

Right of partners to notify dissolution

37. On the dissolution of a partnership or retirement of a partner any partner may publicly notify the same, and may require the other partner or partners to concur for that purpose in all necessary or proper acts, if any, which cannot be done without his or their concurrence.

Continuing authority of partners for purposes of winding up

38. After the dissolution of a partnership the authority of each partner to bind the firm, and the other rights and obligations of the partners, continue notwithstanding the dissolution so far as may be necessary to wind up the affairs of the partnership, and to complete transactions begun but unfinished at the time of the dissolution, but not otherwise.

Provided that the firm is in no case bound by the acts of a partner who has become bankrupt; but this proviso does not affect the liability of any person who has after the bankruptcy represented himself or knowingly suffered himself to be represented as a partner of the bankrupt.

Rights of partners as to application of partnership property

39. On the dissolution of a partnership every partner is entitled, as against the other partners in the firm, and all persons claiming through them in respect of their interests as partners, to have the property of the partnership applied in payment of the debts and liabilities of the firm, and to have the surplus assets after such payment applied in payment of what may be due to the partners respectively after deducting what may be due from them as partners to the firm; and for that purpose any partner or his representatives may, on the termination of the partnership, apply to the court to wind up the business and affairs of the firm.

Apportionment of premium where partnership prematurely dissolved

40. Where one partner has paid a premium to another on entering into a partnership for a fixed term, and the partnership is dissolved before the expiration of that term otherwise than by the death of a partner, the court may order the repayment of the premium, or of such part thereof as it thinks just, having regard to the terms of the partnership contract and to the length of time during which the partnership has continued; unless

(*a*) the dissolution is, in the judgment of the court, wholly or chiefly due to the misconduct of the partner who paid the premium, or

(*b*) the partnership has been dissolved by an agreement containing no provision for a return of any part of the premium.

Rights where partnership dissolved for fraud or misrepresentation

41. Where a partnership contract is rescinded on the ground of the fraud or misrepresentation of one of the parties thereto, the party entitled to rescind is, without prejudice to any other right, entitled—.

(*a*) to a lien on, or right of retention of, the surplus of the partnership assets, after satisfying the partnership liabilities, for any sum of money paid by him for the purchase of a share in the partnership and for any capital contributed by him, and is

(*b*) to stand in the place of the creditors of the firm for any payments made by him in respect of the partnership liabilities, and

(*c*) to be indemnified by the person guilty of the fraud or making the representation against all the debts and liabilities of the firm.

Right of outgoing partner in certain cases to share profits made after dissolution

42.—(1) Where any member of a firm has died or otherwise ceased to be a partner, and the surviving or continuing partners carry on the business of the firm with its capital or assets without any final settlement of accounts as between the firm and the outgoing partner or his estate, then, in the absence of any agreement to the contrary, the outgoing partner or his estate is entitled at the option of himself or his representatives to such share of the profits made since the dissolution as the court may find to be attributable to the use of his share of the partnership assets, or to interest at the rate of five per cent. per annum on the amount of his share of the partnership assets.

(2) Provided that where by the partnership contract an option is given to surviving or continuing partners to purchase the interest of a deceased or outgoing partner, and that option is duly exercised, the estate of the deceased partner, or the outgoing partner or his estate, as the case may be, is not entitled to any further or other share of profits; but if any partner assuming to act in exercise of the option does not in all material respects comply with the terms thereof, he is liable to account under the foregoing provisions of this section.

Retiring or deceased partner's share to be a debt

43. Subject to any agreement between the partners, the amount due from surviving or continuing partners to an outgoing partner or the representatives of a deceased partner in respect of the outgoing or deceased partner's share is a debt accruing at the date of the dissolution or death.

Rule for distribution of assets on final settlement of accounts

44. In settling accounts between the partners after a dissolution of partnership, the following rules shall, subject to any agreement, be observed:

(*a*) Losses, including losses and deficiencies of capital, shall be paid first out of profits, next out of capital, and lastly, if necessary, by the partners individually in the proportion in which they were entitled to share profits:

(*b*) The assets of the firm including the sums, if any, contributed by the partners to make up losses or deficiencies of capital, shall be applied in the following manner and order:

1. In paying the debts and liabilities of the firm to persons who are not partners therein:

2. In paying to each partner rateably what is due from the firm to him for advances as distinguished from capital:

3. In paying to each partner rateably what is due from the firm to him in respect of capital:

4. The ultimate residue, if any, shall be divided among the partners in the proportion in which profits are divisible.

Supplemental

Definitions of "court" and "business"

45. In this Act, unless the contrary intention appears,—

The expression "court" includes every court and judge having jurisdiction in the case:

The expression "business" includes every trade, occupation, or profession.

Saving for rules of equity and common law

46. The rules of equity and of common law applicable to partnership shall continue in force except so far as they are inconsistent with the express provisions of this Act.

Provision as to bankruptcy in Scotland

47.—(1) In the application of this Act to Scotland the bankruptcy of a firm or of an individual shall mean sequestration under the Bankruptcy (Scotland) Acts, and also in the case of an individual the issue against him of a decree of cessio bonorum.

(2) Nothing in this Act shall alter the rules of the law of Scotland relating to the bankruptcy of a firm or of the individual partners thereof.

48, 49. [Repealed by the Statute Law Revision Act 1908.]

Short title

50. This Act may be cited as the Partnership Act 1890.

[THE NEXT PAGE IS H 105]

Cheques Act 1957

(5 & 6 Eliz. 2, c. 36)

An Act to amend the law relating to cheques and certain other instruments. [17th July 1957]

Protection of bankers paying unindorsed or irregularly indorsed cheques, etc.

1.—(1) Where a banker in good faith and in the ordinary course of business pays a cheque drawn on him which is not indorsed or is irregularly indorsed, he does not, in doing so, incur any liability by reason only of the absence of, or irregularity in, indorsement, and he is deemed to have paid it in due course.

(2) Where a banker in good faith and in the ordinary course of business pays any such instrument as the following, namely:—.

  (a) a document issued by a customer of his which, though not a bill of exchange, is intended to enable a person to obtain payment from him of the sum mentioned in the document;

  (b) a draft payable on demand drawn by him upon himself, whether payable at the head office or some other office of his bank;

he does not, in doing so, incur any liability by reason only of the absence of, or irregularity in, indorsement, and the payment discharges the instrument.

Rights of bankers collecting cheques not indorsed by holders

2. A banker who gives value for, or has a lien on, a cheque payable to order which the holder delivers to him for collection without indorsing it, has such (if any) rights as he would have had if, upon delivery, the holder had indorsed it in blank.

Unindorsed cheques as evidence of payment

3. An unindorsed cheque which appears to have been paid by the banker on whom it is drawn is evidence of the receipt by the payee of the sum payable by the cheque.

Protection of bankers collecting payment of cheques, etc.

[1] **4.**—(1) Where a banker, in good faith and without negligence:—

  (a) receives payment for a customer of an instrument to which this section applies; or

  (b) having credited a customer's account with the amount of such an instrument, receives payment thereof for himself;

and the customer has no title, or a defective title, to the instrument, the banker does not incur any liability to the true owner of the instrument by reason only of having received payment thereof.

(2) This section applies to the following instruments, namely:—.

  (a) cheques:

  (b) any document issued by a customer of a banker which, though not a bill of exchange, is intended to enable a person to obtain payment from that banker of the sum mentioned in the document;

  (c) any document issued by a public officer which is intended to enable a person to obtain payment from the Paymaster General or the Queen's and Lord Treasurer's Remembrancer of the sum mentioned in the document but is not a bill of exchange;

  (d) any draft payable on demand drawn by a banker upon himself, whether payable at the head office or some other office of his bank.

(3) A banker is not to be treated for the purposes of this section as having been negligent by reason only of his failure to concern himself with absence of, or irregularity in, indorsement of an instrument.

NOTE
  [1] See the Consumer Credit Act 1974, s. 83 (2), and the Banking Act 1979, s. 47.

Application of certain provisions of Bills of Exchange Act 1882, to instruments not being bills of exchange

5. The provisions of the Bills of Exchange Act 1882, relating to crossed cheques shall, so far as applicable, have effect in relation to instruments (other than cheques) to which the last foregoing section applies as they have effect in relation to cheques.

Construction, saving and repeal

6.—(1) This Act shall be construed as one with the Bills of Exchange Act 1882.

(2) The foregoing provisions of this Act do not make negotiable any instrument which, apart from them, is not negotiable.

(3) [Repealed by the Statute Law (Repeals) Act 1974.]

.   .   .   .   .   .

Short title and commencement

8.—(1) This Act may be cited as the Cheques Act 1957.

(2) This Act shall come into operation at the expiration of a period of three months beginning with the day on which it is passed.

Unfair Contract Terms Act 1977

(1977, c. 50)

An Act to impose further limits on the extent to which under the law of England and Wales and Northern Ireland civil liability for breach of contract, or for negligence or other breach of duty, can be avoided by means of contract terms and otherwise, and under the law of Scotland civil liability can be avoided by means of contract terms.   [26th October 1977]

.   .   .   .   .   .

Part II

Amendment of Law for Scotland

Scope of Part II

15.—(1) This Part of this Act applies only to contracts, is subject to Part III of this Act and does not affect the validity of any discharge or indemnity given by a person in consideration of the receipt by him of compensation in settlement of any claim which he has.

(2) Subject to subsection (3) below, sections 16 to 18 of this Act apply to any contract only to the extent that the contract—

    (*a*) relates to the transfer of the ownership or possession of goods from one person to another (with or without work having been done on them);

(*b*) constitutes a contract of service or apprenticeship;

(*c*) relates to services of whatever kind, including (without prejudice to the foregoing generality) carriage, deposit and pledge, care and custody, mandate, agency, loan and services relating to the use of land;

(*d*) relates to the liability of an occupier of land to persons entering upon or using that land;

(*e*) relates to a grant of any right or permission to enter upon or use land not amounting to an estate or interest in the land.

(3) Notwithstanding anything in subsection (2) above, sections 16 to 18—

(*a*) do not apply to any contract to the extent that the contract—

(i) is a contract of insurance (including a contract to pay an annuity on human life);

(ii) relates to the formation, constitution or dissolution of any body corporate or unincorporated association or partnership;

(*b*) apply to—

a contract of marine salvage or towage;

a charter party of a ship or hovercraft;

a contract for the carriage of goods by ship or hovercraft; or,

a contract to which subsection (4) below relates,

only to the extent that—

(i) both parties deal or hold themselves out as dealing in the course of a business (and then only in so far as the contract purports to exclude or restrict liability for breach of duty in respect of death or personal injury); or

(ii) the contract is a consumer contract (and then only in favour of the consumer).

(4) This subsection relates to a contract in pursuance of which goods are carried by ship or hovercraft and which either—

(*a*) specifies ship or hovercraft as the means of carriage over part of the journey to be covered; or

(*b*) makes no provision as to the means of carriage and does not exclude ship or hovercraft as that means,

in so far as the contract operates for and in relation to the carriage of the goods by that means.

Liability for breach of duty

16.—(1) Where a term of a contract purports to exclude or restrict liability for breach of duty arising in the course of any business or from the occupation of any premises used for business purposes of the occupier, that term—

(*a*) shall be void in any case where such exclusion or restriction is in respect of death or personal injury;

(*b*) shall, in any other case, have no effect if it was not fair and reasonable to incorporate the term in the contract.

(2) Subsection (1) (*a*) above does not affect the validity of any discharge and indemnity given by a person, on or in connection with an award to him of compensation for pneumoconiosis attributable to employment in the coal industry, in respect of any further claim arising from his contracting that disease.

(3) Where under subsection (1) above a term of a contract is void or has no effect, the fact that a person agreed to, or was aware of, the term shall not of itself be sufficient evidence that he knowingly and voluntarily assumed any risk.

Control of unreasonable exemptions in consumer or standard form contracts

17.—(1) Any term of a contract which is a consumer contract or a standard form contract shall have no effect for the purpose of enabling a party to the contract—

    (*a*) who is in breach of a contractual obligation, to exclude or restrict any liability of his to the consumer or customer in respect of the breach;

    (*b*) in respect of a contractual obligation, to render no performance, or to render a performance substantially different from that which the consumer or customer reasonably expected from the contract;

if it was not fair and reasonable to incorporate the term in the contract.

(2) In this section " customer " means a party to a standard form contract who deals on the basis of written standard terms of business of the other party to the contract who himself deals in the course of a business.

Unreasonable indemnity clauses in consumer contracts

18.—(1) Any term of a contract which is a consumer contract shall have no effect for the purpose of making the consumer indemnify another person (whether a party to the contract or not) in respect of liability which that other person may incur as a result of breach of duty or breach of contract, if it was not fair and reasonable to incorporate the term in the contract.

(2) In this section " liability " means liability arising in the course of any business or from the occupation of any premises used for business purposes of the occupier.

" Guarantee " of consumer goods

19.—(1) This section applies to a guarantee—

    (*a*) in relation to goods which are of a type ordinarily supplied for private use or consumption; and

    (*b*) which is not a guarantee given by one party to the other party to a contract under or in pursuance of which the ownership or possession of the goods to which the guarantee relates is transferred.

(2) A term of a guarantee to which this section applies shall be void in so far as it purports to exclude or restrict liability for loss or damage (including death or personal injury)—

    (*a*) arising from the goods proving defective while—

        (i) in use otherwise than exclusively for the purposes of a business; or

        (ii) in the possession of a person for such use; and

    (*b*) resulting from the breach of duty of a person concerned in the manufacture or distribution of the goods.

(3) For the purposes of this section, any document is a guarantee if it contains or purports to contain some promise or assurance (however worded or presented) that defects will be made good by complete or partial replacement, or by repair, monetary compensation or otherwise.

Obligations implied by law in sale and hire-purchase contracts

¹ **20.**—(1) Any term of a contract which purports to exclude or restrict liability for breach of the obligations arising from—

    (*a*) section 12 of the Sale of Goods Act 1979 (seller's implied undertakings as to title etc.);

    (*b*) section 8 of the Supply of Goods (Implied Terms) Act 1973 (implied terms as to title in hire-purchase agreements),

shall be void.

(2) Any term of a contract which purports to exclude or restrict liability for breach of the obligations arising from—

    (*a*) section 13, 14 or 15 of the said Act of 1979 (seller's implied undertakings as to conformity of goods with description or sample, or as to their quality or fitness for a particular purpose);

(*b*) section 9, 10 or 11 of the said Act of 1973 (the corresponding provisions in relation to hire-purchase),

shall—

    (i) in the case of a consumer contract, be void against the consumer;

    (ii) in any other case, have no effect if it was not fair and reasonable to incorporate the term in the contract.

NOTE

[1] As amended by the Sale of Goods Act 1979, Sched. 2, para. 21.

Obligations implied by law in other contracts for the supply of goods

21.—(1) Any term of a contract to which this section applies purporting to exclude or restrict liability for breach of an obligation—

    (*a*) such as is referred to in subsection (3) (*a*) below—

        (i) in the case of a consumer contract, shall be void against the consumer, and

        (ii) in any other case, shall have no effect if it was not fair and reasonable to incorporate the term in the contract;

    (*b*) such as is referred to in subsection (3) (*b*) below, shall have no effect if it was not fair and reasonable to incorporate the term in the contract.

(2) This section applies to any contract to the extent that it relates to any such matter as is referred to in section 15 (2) (*a*) of this Act, but does not apply to—

    (*a*) a contract of sale of goods or a hire-purchase agreement; or

    (*b*) a charterparty of a ship or hovercraft unless it is a consumer contract (and then only in favour of the consumer).

(3) An obligation referred to in this subsection is an obligation incurred under a contract in the course of a business and arising by implication of law from the nature of the contract which relates—

    (*a*) to the correspondence of goods with description or sample, or to the quality or fitness of goods for any particular purpose; or

    (*b*) to any right to transfer ownership or possession of goods, or to the enjoyment of quiet possession of goods.

(4) Nothing in this section applies to the supply of goods on a redemption of trading stamps within the Trading Stamps Act 1964.

Consequence of breach

22. For the avoidance of doubt, where any provision of this Part of this Act requires that the incorporation of a term in a contract must be fair and reasonable for that term to have effect—

    (*a*) if that requirement is satisfied, the term may be given effect to notwithstanding that the contract has been terminated in consequence of breach of that contract;

    (*b*) for the term to be given effect to, that requirement must be satisfied even where a party who is entitled to rescind the contract elects not to rescind it.

Evasion by means of secondary contract

23. Any term of any contract shall be void which purports to exclude or restrict, or has the effect of excluding or restricting—

    (*a*) the exercise, by a party to any other contract, of any right or remedy which arises in respect of that other contract in consequence of breach of duty, or of obligation, liability for which could not by virtue of the provisions of this Part of this Act be excluded or restricted by a term of that other contract;

    (*b*) the application of the provisions of this Part of this Act in respect of that or any other contract.

The " reasonableness " test

24.—(1) In determining for the purposes of this Part of this Act whether it was fair and reasonable to incorporate a term in a contract, regard shall be had only to the circumstances which were, or ought reasonably to have been, known to or in the contemplation of the parties to the contract at the time the contract was made.

(2) In determining for the purposes of section 20 or 21 of this Act whether it was fair and reasonable to incorporate a term in a contract, regard shall be had in particular to the matters specified in Schedule 2 to this Act; but this subsection shall not prevent a court or arbiter from holding, in accordance with any rule of law, that a term which purports to exclude or restrict any relevant liability is not a term of the contract.

(3) Where a term in a contract purports to restrict liability to a specified sum of money, and the question arises for the purposes of this Part of this Act whether it was fair and reasonable to incorporate the term in the contract, then, without prejudice to subsection (2) above, regard shall be had in particular to—

(*a*) the resources which the party seeking to rely on that term could expect to be available to him for the purpose of meeting the liability should it arise;

(*b*) how far it was open to that party to cover himself by insurance.

(4) The onus of proving that it was fair and reasonable to incorporate a term in a contract shall lie on the party so contending.

Interpretation of Part II

25.—(1) In this Part of this Act—

" breach of duty " means the breach—

(*a*) of any obligation, arising from the express or implied terms of a contract, to take reasonable care or exercise reasonable skill in the performance of the contract;

(*b*) of any common law duty to take reasonable care or exercise reasonable skill;

(*c*) of the duty of reasonable care imposed by section 2 (1) of the Occupiers' Liability (Scotland) Act 1960;

" business " includes a profession and the activities of any government department or local or public authority;

" consumer " has the meaning assigned to that expression in the definition in this section of " consumer contract ";

" consumer contract " means a contract (not being a contract of sale by auction or competitive tender) in which—

(*a*) one party to the contract deals, and the other party to the contract (" the consumer ") does not deal or hold himself out as dealing, in the course of a business, and

(*b*) in the case of a contract such as is mentioned in section 15 (2) (*a*) of this Act, the goods are of a type ordinarily supplied for private use or consumption;

and for the purposes of this Part of this Act the onus of proving that a contract is not to be regarded as a consumer contract shall lie on the party so contending;

¹ " goods " has the same meaning as in the Sale of Goods Act 1979;

" hire-purchase agreement " has the same meaning as in section 189 (1) of the Consumer Credit Act 1974;

" personal injury " includes any disease and any impairment of physical or mental condition.

(2) In relation to any breach of duty or obligation, it is immaterial for any purpose of this Part of this Act whether the act or omission giving rise to that breach was inadvertent or intentional, or whether liability for it arises directly or vicariously.

(3) In this Part of this Act, any reference to excluding or restricting any liability includes—

    (*a*) making the liability or its enforcement subject to any restrictive or onerous conditions;

    (*b*) excluding or restricting any right or remedy in respect of the liability, or subjecting a person to any prejudice in consequence of his pursuing any such right or remedy;

    (*c*) excluding or restricting any rule of evidence or procedure;

    (*d*) excluding or restricting any liability by reference to a notice having contractual effect,

but does not include an agreement to submit any question to arbitration.

(4) In subsection (3)(*d*) above "notice" includes an announcement, whether or not in writing, and any other communication or pretended communication.

(5) In sections 15 and 16 and 19 to 21 of this Act, any reference to excluding or restricting liability for breach of an obligation or duty shall include a reference to excluding or restricting the obligation or duty itself.

NOTE

[1] As amended by the Sale of Goods Act 1979, Sched. 2, para. 22.

Part III

Provisions applying to whole of United Kingdom

Miscellaneous

International supply contracts

26.—(1) The limits imposed by this Act on the extent to which a person may exclude or restrict liability by reference to a contract term do not apply to liability arising under such a contract as is described in subsection (3) below.

(2) The terms of such a contract are not subject to any requirement of reasonableness under section 3 or 4: and nothing in Part II of this Act shall require the incorporation of the terms of such a contract to be fair and reasonable for them to have effect.

(3) Subject to subsection (4), that description of contract is one whose characteristics are the following—

    (*a*) either it is a contract of sale of goods or it is one under or in pursuance of which the possession or ownership of goods passes; and

    (*b*) it is made by parties whose places of business (or, if they have none, habitual residences) are in the territories of different States (the Channel Islands and the Isle of Man being treated for this purpose as different States from the United Kingdom).

(4) A contract falls within subsection (3) above only if either—

    (*a*) the goods in question are, at the time of the conclusion of the contract, in the course of carriage, or will be carried, from the territory of one State to the territory of another; or

    (*b*) the acts constituting the offer and acceptance have been done in the territories of different States; or

    (*c*) the contract provides for the goods to be delivered to the territory of a State other than that within whose territory those acts were done.

Choice of law clauses

27.—(1) Where the proper law of a contract is the law of any part of the United Kingdom only by choice of the parties (and apart from that choice would be the law of some country outside the United Kingdom) sections 2 to 7 and 16 to 21 of this Act do not operate as part of the proper law.

(2) This Act has effect notwithstanding any contract term which applies or purports to apply the law of some country outside the United Kingdom, where (either or both)—

    (*a*) the term appears to the court, or arbitrator or arbiter to have been imposed wholly or mainly for the purpose of enabling the party imposing it to evade the operation of this Act; or

[1] (*b*) the contract is a consumer contract as defined in Part II of this Act, and the consumer at the date when the contract was made was habitually resident in the United Kingdom, and the essential steps necessary for the making of the contract were taken there, whether by him or by others on his behalf.

NOTE
[1] As applied to Scotland by subs. (3) of this section.

Temporary provision for sea carriage of passengers
[1] **28.**—(1) This section applies to a contract for carriage by sea of a passenger or of a passenger and his luggage where the provisions of the Athens Convention (with or without modification) do not have, in relation to the contract, the force of law in the United Kingdom.

(2) In a case where—

    (*a*) the contract is not made in the United Kingdom, and

    (*b*) neither the place of departure nor the place of destination under it is in the United Kingdom,

a person is not precluded by this Act from excluding or restricting liability for loss or damage, being loss or damage for which the provisions of the Convention would, if they had the force of law in relation to the contract, impose liability on him.

(3) In any other case, a person is not precluded by this Act from excluding or restricting liability for that loss or damage—

    (*a*) in so far as the exclusion or restriction would have been effective in that case had the provisions of the Convention had the force of law in relation to the contract; or

    (*b*) in such circumstances and to such extent as may be preyscribed, by reference to a prescribed term of the contract.

[2] (4) For the purposes of subsection (3)(*a*), the values which shall be taken to be the official values in the United Kingdom of the amounts (expressed in gold francs) by reference to which liability under the provisions of the Convention is limited shall be such amounts in sterling as the Secretary of State may from time to time by order made by statutory instrument specify.

(5) In this section,—

    (*a*) the references to excluding or restricting liability include doing any of those things in relation to the liability which are mentioned in section 13 or section 25(3) and (5); and

    (*b*) "the Athens Convention" means the Athens Convention relating to the Carriage of Passengers and their Luggage by Sea, 1974; and

    (*c*) "prescribed" means prescribed by the Secretary of State by regulations made by statutory instrument;

and a statutory instrument containing the regulations shall be subject to annulment in pursuance of a resolution of either House of Parliament.

NOTES
[1] See the Merchant Shipping Act 1979, s. 16(3).
[2] See S.I. 1985 No. 1430.

Saving for other relevant legislation

29.—[1] (1) Nothing in this Act removes or restricts the effect of, or prevents reliance upon, any contractual provision which—

(*a*) is authorised or required by the express terms or necessary implication of an enactment; or

(*b*) being made with a view to compliance with an international agreement to which the United Kingdom is a party, does not operate more restrictively than is contemplated by the agreement.

(2) A contract term is to be taken—

(*a*) the purposes of Part I of this Act, as satisfying the requirement of reasonableness; and

(*b*) those of Part II to have been unfair and reasonable to incorporate,

if it is incorporated or approved by, or incorporated pursuant to a decision or ruling of, a competent authority acting in the exercise of any statutory jurisdiction or function and is not a term in a contract to which the competent authority is itself a party.

(3) In this section—

"competent authority" means any court, arbitrator or arbiter, government department or public authority;

"enactment" means any legislation (including subordinate legislation) of the United Kingdom or Northern Ireland and any instrument having effect by virtue of such legislation; and

"statutory" means conferred by an enactment.

NOTE

[1] See the Telecommunications Act 1984, Sched. 5, para. 12(7).

30. [Repealed by the Consumer Safety Act 1978, Sched. 3.]

General

Commencement; amendments; repeals

31.—(1) This Act comes into force on 1st February 1978.

(2) Nothing in this Act applies to contracts made before the date on which it comes into force; but subject to this, it applies to liability for any loss or damage which is suffered on or after that date.

(3) The enactments specified in Schedule 3 to this Act are amended as there shown.

(4) The enactments specified in Schedule 4 to this Act are repealed to the extent specified in column 3 of that Schedule.

Citation and extent

32.—(1) This Act may be cited as the Unfair Contract Terms Act 1977.

(2) Part I of this Act extends to England and Wales and to Northern Ireland; but it does not extend to Scotland.

(3) Part II of this Act extends to Scotland only.

(4) This Part of this Act extends to the whole of the United Kingdom.

SCHEDULES

. . . . . .

Section 24(2)   SCHEDULE 2

"GUIDELINES" FOR APPLICATION OF REASONABLENESS TEST

The matters to which regard is to be had in particular for the purposes of sections 6(3), 7(3) and (4), 20 and 21 are any of the following which appear to be relevant—

(a) the strength of the bargaining positions of the parties relative to each other, taking into account (among other things) alternative means by which the customer's requirements could have been met;

(b) whether the customer received an inducement to agree to the term, or in accepting it had an opportunity of entering into a similar contract with other persons, but without having to accept a similar term;

(c) whether the customer knew or ought reasonably to have known of the existence and extent of the term (having regard, among other things, to any custom of the trade and any previous course of dealing between the parties);

(d) where the term excludes or restricts any relevant liability if some condition is not complied with, whether it was reasonable at the time of the contract to expect that compliance with that condition would be practicable;

(e) whether the goods were manufactured, processed or adapted to the special order of the customer.

Section 31(3)   SCHEDULE 3

[1] AMENDMENT OF ENACTMENTS

In the Supply of Goods (Implied Terms) Act 1973 (as originally enacted and as substituted by the Consumer Credit Act 1974)—

(a) in section 14(1) for the words from "conditional sale" to the end substitute "a conditional sale agreement where the buyer deals as consumer within Part I of the Unfair Contract Terms Act 1977";

(b) in section 15(1), in the definition of "business", for "local authority or statutory undertaker" substitute "or local or public authority".

NOTE

[1] As amended by the Sale of Goods Act 1979, Sched. 3, and the Statute Law (Repeals) Act 1981.

Sale of Goods Act 1979

(1979 c. 54)

An Act to consolidate the law relating to the sale of goods.

[6th December 1979]

PART I

CONTRACTS TO WHICH ACT APPLIES

Contracts to which Act applies

1.—(1) This Act applies to contracts of sale of goods made on or after (but not to those made before) 1st January 1894.

(2) In relation to contracts made on certain dates, this Act applies subject to the modification of certain of its sections as mentioned in Schedule 1 below.

(3) Any such modification is indicated in the section concerned by a reference to Schedule 1 below.

(4) Accordingly, where a section does not contain such a reference, this Act applies in relation to the contract concerned without such modification of the section.

PART II

FORMATION OF THE CONTRACT

Contract of sale

Contract of sale

2.—(1) A contract of sale of goods is a contract by which the seller transfers or agrees to transfer the property in goods to the buyer for a money consideration, called the price.

[THE NEXT PAGE IS H 115]

(2) There may be a contract of sale between one part owner and another.

(3) A contract of sale may be absolute or conditional.

(4) Where under a contract of sale the property in the goods is transferred from the seller to the buyer the contract is called a sale.

(5) Where under a contract of sale the transfer of the property in the goods is to take place at a future time or subject to some condition later to be fulfilled the contract is called an agreement to sell.

(6) An agreement to sell becomes a sale when the time elapses or the conditions are fulfilled subject to which the property in the goods is to be transferred.

Capacity to buy and sell

3.—(1) Capacity to buy and sell is regulated by the general law concerning capacity to contract and to transfer and acquire property.

(2) Where necessaries are sold and delivered to a minor or to a person who by reason of mental incapacity or drunkenness is incompetent to contract, he must pay a reasonable price for them.

(3) In subsection (2) above " necessaries " means goods suitable to the condition in life of the minor or other person concerned and to his actual requirements at the time of the sale and delivery.

Formalities of contract

How contract of sale is made

4.—(1) Subject to this and any other Act, a contract of sale may be made in writing (either with or without seal), or by word of mouth, or partly in writing and partly by word of mouth, or may be implied from the conduct of the parties.

(2) Nothing in this section affects the law relating to corporations.

Subject matter of contract

Existing or future goods

5.—(1) The goods which form the subject of a contract of sale may be either existing goods, owned or possessed by the seller, or goods to be manufactured or acquired by him after the making of the contract of sale, in this Act called future goods.

(2) There may be a contract for the sale of goods the acquisition of which by the seller depends on a contingency which may or may not happen.

(3) Where by a contract of sale the seller purports to effect a present sale of future goods, the contract operates as an agreement to sell the goods.

Goods which have perished   *relates to Specific Goods .   IMPOSSIBILITY*

6. Where there is a contract for the sale of specific goods, and the goods without the knowledge of the seller have perished at the time when the contract is made, the contract is void.

Goods perishing before sale but after agreement to sell *Specific Goods . FRUSTRATION .*

7. Where there is an agreement to sell specific goods and subsequently the goods, without any fault on the part of the seller or buyer, perish before the risk passes to the buyer, the agreement is avoided.

The price

Ascertainment of price

8.—(1) The price in a contract of sale may be fixed by the contract, or may be left to be fixed in a manner agreed by the contract, or may be determined by the course of dealing between the parties.

(2) Where the price is not determined as mentioned in subsection (1) above the buyer must pay a reasonable price.

(3) What is a reasonable price is a question of fact dependent on the circumstances of each particular case.

Agreement to sell at valuation

9.—(1) Where there is an agreement to sell goods on the terms that the price is to be fixed by the valuation of a third party, and he cannot or does not make the valuation, the agreement is avoided; but if the goods or any part of them have been delivered to and appropriated by the buyer he must pay a reasonable price for them.

(2) Where the third party is prevented from making the valuation by the fault of the seller or buyer, the party not at fault may maintain an action for damages against the party at fault.

Conditions and warranties

Stipulations about time

10.—(1) Unless a different intention appears from the terms of the contract, stipulations as to time of payment are not of the essence of a contract of sale.

(2) Whether any other stipulation as to time is or is not of the essence of the contract depends on the terms of the contract.

(3) In a contract of sale " month " *prima facie* means calendar month.

When condition to be treated as warranty

11.—(1) Subsections (2) to (4) and (7) below do not apply to Scotland and subsection (5) below applies only to Scotland.

. . . . . .

(5) In Scotland, failure by the seller to perform any material part of a contract of sale is a breach of contract, which entitles the buyer either within a reasonable time after delivery to reject the goods and treat the contract as repudiated, or to retain the goods and treat the failure to perform such material part as a breach which may give rise to a claim for compensation or damages.

(6) Nothing in this section affects a condition or warranty whose fulfilment is excused by law by reason of impossibility or otherwise.

. . . . . .

Implied terms about title, etc.

12.—(1) In a contract of sale, other than one to which subsection (3) below applies, there is an implied condition on the part of the seller that in the case of a sale he has a right to sell the goods, and in the case of an agreement to sell he will have such a right at the time when the property is to pass.

(2) In a contract of sale, other than one to which subsection (3) below applies, there is also an implied warranty that—

(a) the goods are free, and will remain free until the time when the property is to pass, from any charge or encumbrance not disclosed or known to the buyer before the contract is made, and

(b) the buyer will enjoy quiet possession of the goods except so far as it may be disturbed by the owner or other person entitled to the benefit of any charge or encumbrance so disclosed or known.

(3) This subsection applies to a contract of sale in the case of which there appears from the contract or is to be inferred from its circumstances an

intention that the seller should transfer only such title as he or a third person may have.

(4) In a contract to which subsection (3) above applies there is an implied warranty that all charges or encumbrances known to the seller and not known to the buyer have been disclosed to the buyer before the contract is made.

(5) In a contract to which subsection (3) above applies there is also an implied warranty that none of the following will disturb the buyer's quiet possession of the goods, namely—

    (*a*) the seller;

    (*b*) in a case where the parties to the contract intend that the seller should transfer only such title as a third person may have, that person;

    (*c*) anyone claiming through or under the seller or that third person otherwise than under a charge or encumbrance disclosed or known to the buyer before the contract is made.

(6) Paragraph 3 of Schedule 1 below applies in relation to a contract made before 18th May 1973.

Sale by description

13.—(1) Where there is a contract for the sale of goods by description, there is an implied condition that the goods will correspond with the description.

(2) If the sale is by sample as well as by description it is not sufficient that the bulk of the goods corresponds with the sample if the goods do not also correspond with the description.

(3) A sale of goods is not prevented from being a sale by description by reason only that, being exposed for sale or hire, they are selected by the buyer.

(4) Paragraph 4 of Schedule 1 below applies in relation to a contract made before 18th May 1973.

Implied terms about quality or fitness

14.—(1) Except as provided by this section and section 15 below and subject to any other enactment, there is no implied condition or warranty about the quality or fitness for any particular purpose of goods supplied under a contract of sale.

(2) Where the seller sells goods in the course of a business, there is an implied condition that the goods supplied under the contract are of merchantable quality, except that there is no such condition—

    (*a*) as regards defects specifically drawn to the buyer's attention before the contract is made; or

    (*b*) if the buyer examines the goods before the contract is made, as regards defects which that examination ought to reveal.

(3) Where the seller sells goods in the course of a business and the buyer, expressly or by implication, makes known—

    (*a*) to the seller, or

    (*b*) where the purchase price or part of it is payable by instalments and the goods were previously sold by a credit-broker to the seller, to that credit-broker,

any particular purpose for which the goods are being bought, there is an implied condition that the goods supplied under the contract are reasonably fit for that purpose, whether or not that is a purpose for which such goods are commonly supplied, except where the circumstances show that the buyer does not rely, or that it is unreasonable for him to rely, on the skill or judgment of the seller or credit-broker.

(4) An implied condition or warranty about quality or fitness for a particular purpose may be annexed to a contract of sale by usage.

(5) The preceding provisions of this section apply to a sale by a person who in the course of a business is acting as agent for another as they apply to a sale by a principal in the course of a business, except where that other is not selling in the course of a business and either the buyer knows that fact or reasonable steps are taken to bring it to the notice of the buyer before the contract is made.

(6) Goods of any kind are of merchantable quality within the meaning of subsection (2) above if they are as fit for the purpose or purposes for which goods of that kind are commonly bought as it is reasonable to expect having regard to any description applied to them, the price (if relevant) and all the other relevant circumstances.

[1] (7) Paragraph 5 of Schedule 1 below applies in relation to a contract made on or after 18th May 1973 and before the appointed day, and paragraph 6 in relation to one made before 18th May 1973.

[1] (8) In subsection (7) above and paragraph 5 of Schedule 1 below references to the appointed day are to the day appointed for the purposes of those provisions by an order of the Secretary of State made by statutory instrument.

NOTE
[1] The appointed day is 19th May 1985: S.I. 1983 No. 1572.

Sale by sample

Sale by sample

15.—(1) A contract of sale is a contract for sale by sample where there is an express or implied term to that effect in the contract.

(2) In the case of a contract for sale by sample there is an implied condition—

(*a*) that the bulk will correspond with the sample in quality;

(*b*) that the buyer will have a reasonable opportunity of comparing the bulk with the sample;

(*c*) that the goods will be free from any defect, rendering them unmerchantable, which would not be apparent on reasonable examination of the sample.

(3) In subsection (2)(*c*) above "unmerchantable" is to be construed in accordance with section 14(6) above.

(4) Paragraph 7 of Schedule 1 below applies in relation to a contract made before 18th May 1973.

PART III

EFFECTS OF THE CONTRACT

Transfer of property as between seller and buyer

Goods must be ascertained

16. Where there is a contract for the sale of unascertained goods no property in the goods is transferred to the buyer unless and until the goods are ascertained.

Property passes when intended to pass

17.—(1) Where there is a contract for the sale of specific or ascertained goods the property in them is transferred to the buyer at such time as the parties to the contract intend it to be transferred.

(2) For the purpose of ascertaining the intention of the parties regard shall be had to the terms of the contract, the conduct of the parties and the circumstances of the case.

Rules for ascertaining intention

18. Unless a different intention appears, the following are rules for ascertaining the intention of the parties as to the time at which the property in the goods is to pass to the buyer.

> *Rule* 1.—Where there is an unconditional contract for the sale of specific goods in a deliverable state the property in the goods passes to the buyer when the contract is made, and it is immaterial whether the time of payment or the time of delivery, or both, be postponed.

> *Rule* 2.—Where there is a contract for the sale of specific goods and the seller is bound to do something to the goods for the purpose of putting them into a deliverable state, the property does not pass until the thing is done and the buyer has notice that it has been done.

> *Rule* 3.—Where there is a contract for the sale of specific goods in a deliverable state but the seller is bound to weigh, measure, test, or do some other act or thing with reference to the goods for the purpose of ascertaining the price, the property does not pass until the act or thing is done and the buyer has notice that it has been done.

> *Rule* 4.—When goods are delivered to the buyer on approval or on sale or return or other similar terms the property in the goods passes to the buyer:—
>> (*a*) when he signifies his approval or acceptance to the seller or does any other act adopting the transaction;
>> (*b*) if he does not signify his approval or acceptance to the seller but retains the goods without giving notice of rejection, then, if a time has been fixed for the return of the goods, on the expiration of that time, and, if no time has been fixed, on the expiration of a reasonable time.

> *Rule* 5.—(1) Where there is a contract for the sale of unascertained or future goods by description, and goods of that description and in a deliverable state are unconditionally appropriated to the contract, either by the seller with the assent of the buyer or by the buyer with the assent of the seller, the property in the goods then passes to the buyer; and the assent may be express or implied, and may be given either before or after the appropriation is made.

> (2) Where, in pursuance of the contract, the seller delivers the goods to the buyer or to a carrier or other bailee or custodier (whether named by the buyer or not) for the purpose of transmission to the buyer, and does not reserve the right of disposal, he is to be taken to have unconditionally appropriated the goods to the contract.

Reservation of right of disposal

19.—(1) Where there is a contract for the sale of specific goods or where goods are subsequently appropriated to the contract, the seller may, by the terms of the contract or appropriation, reserve the right of disposal of the goods until certain conditions are fulfilled; and in such a case, notwithstanding the delivery of the goods to the buyer, or to a carrier or other bailee or custodier for the purpose of transmission to the buyer, the property in the goods does not pass to the buyer until the conditions imposed by the seller are fulfilled.

(2) Where goods are shipped, and by the bill of lading the goods are deliverable to the order of the seller or his agent, the seller is *prima facie* to be taken to reserve the right of disposal.

(3) Where the seller of goods draws on the buyer for the price, and transmits the bill of exchange and bill of lading to the buyer together to secure acceptance or payment of the bill of exchange, the buyer is bound to return the bill of lading if he does not honour the bill of exchange, and if he wrongfully retains the bill of lading the property in the goods does not pass to him.

Risk prima facie passes with property

20.—(1) Unless otherwise agreed, the goods remain at the seller's risk until the property in them is transferred to the buyer, but when the property in them is transferred to the buyer the goods are at the buyer's risk whether delivery has been made or not.

(2) But where delivery has been delayed through the fault of either buyer or seller the goods are at the risk of the party at fault as regards any loss which might not have occurred but for such fault.

(3) Nothing in this section affects the duties or liabilities of either seller or buyer as a bailee or custodier of the goods of the other party.

Transfer of title

Sale by person not the owner

21.—(1) Subject to this Act, where goods are sold by a person who is not their owner, and who does not sell them under the authority or with the consent of the owner, the buyer acquires no better title to the goods than the seller had, unless the owner of the goods is by his conduct precluded from denying the seller's authority to sell.

(2) Nothing in this Act affects—

    (*a*) the provisions of the Factors Acts or any enactment enabling the apparent owner of goods to dispose of them as if he were their true owner;

    (*b*) the validity of any contract of sale under any special common law or statutory power of sale or under the order of a court of competent jurisdiction.

exceptions to rule . . . .

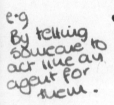

e·g By telling s'one to act like an agent for them.

● **Sale under voidable title**

23. When the seller of goods has a voidable title to them, but his title has not been avoided at the time of the sale, the buyer acquires a good title to the goods, provided he buys them in good faith and without notice of the seller's defect of title.

Seller in possession after sale

24. Where a person having sold goods continues or is in possession of the goods, or of the documents of title to the goods, the delivery or transfer by that person, or by a mercantile agent acting for him, of the goods or documents of title under any sale, pledge, or other disposition thereof, to any person receiving the same in good faith and without notice of the previous sale, has the same effect as if the person making the delivery or transfer were expressly authorised by the owner of the goods to make the same.

Buyer in possession after sale

25.—(1) Where a person having bought or agreed to buy goods obtains, with the consent of the seller, possession of the goods or the documents of title to the goods, the delivery or transfer by that person, or by a mercantile agent acting for him, of the goods or documents of title, under any sale, pledge, or other disposition thereof, to any person receiving the same in good faith and without notice of any lien or other right of the original seller in respect of the goods, has the same effect as if the person making the delivery or transfer were a mercantile agent in possession of the goods or documents of title with the consent of the owner.

(2) For the purposes of subsection (1) above—

    (*a*) the buyer under a conditional sale agreement is to be taken not to be a person who has bought or agreed to buy goods, and (*b*) "conditional sale agreement" means an agreement for the sale of goods which is a consumer credit agreement within the meaning of the Consumer Credit Act 1974 under which the purchase price or part of it is payable by instalments, and the property in the goods is to remain in the seller (notwithstanding that the buyer is to be in possession of the goods) until such conditions as to the payment of instalments or otherwise as may be specified in the agreement are fulfilled.

[1] (3) Paragraph 9 of Schedule 1 below applies in relation to a contract under which a person buys or agrees to buy goods and which is made before the appointed day.

[1] (4) In subsection (3) above and paragraph 9 of Schedule 1 below references to the appointed day are to the day appointed for the purposes of those provisions by an order of the Secretary of State made by statutory instrument.

NOTE

[1] The appointed day is 19th May 1985: S.I. 1983 No. 1572.

Supplementary to sections 24 and 25

26. In sections 24 and 25 above "mercantile agent" means a mercantile agent having in the customary course of his business as such agent authority either—

(*a*) to sell goods, or

(*b*) to consign goods for the purpose of sale, or

(*c*) to buy goods, or

(*d*) to raise money on the security of goods.

Part IV

Performance of the Contract

Duties of seller and buyer

27. It is the duty of the seller to deliver the goods, and of the buyer to accept and pay for them, in accordance with the terms of the contract of sale.

Payment and delivery are concurrent conditions

28. Unless otherwise agreed, delivery of the goods and payment of the price are concurrent conditions, that is to say, the seller must be ready and willing to give possession of the goods to the buyer in exchange for the price and the buyer must be ready and willing to pay the price in exchange for possession of the goods.

Rules about delivery

29.—(1) Whether it is for the buyer to take possession of the goods or for the seller to send them to the buyer is a question depending in each case on the contract, express or implied, between the parties.

(2) Apart from any such contract, express or implied, the place of delivery is the seller's place of business if he has one, and if not, his residence; except that, if the contract is for the sale of specific goods, which to the knowledge of the parties when the contract is made are in some other place, then that place is the place of delivery.

(3) Where under the contract of sale the seller is bound to send the goods to the buyer, but no time for sending them is fixed, the seller is bound to send them within a reasonable time.

(4) Where the goods at the time of sale are in the possession of a third person, there is no delivery by seller to buyer unless and until the third person acknowledges to the buyer that he holds the goods on his behalf; but nothing in this section affects the operation of the issue or transfer of any document of title to goods.

(5) Demand or tender of delivery may be treated as ineffectual unless made at a reasonable hour; and what is a reasonable hour is a question of fact.

(6) Unless otherwise agreed, the expenses of and incidental to putting the goods into a deliverable state must be borne by the seller.

Delivery of wrong quantity

30.—(1) Where the seller delivers to the buyer a quantity of goods less than he contracted to sell, the buyer may reject them, but if the buyer accepts the goods so delivered he must pay for them at the contract rate.

(2) Where the seller delivers to the buyer a quantity of goods larger than he contracted to sell, the buyer may accept the goods included in the contract and reject the rest, or he may reject the whole.

(3) Where the seller delivers to the buyer a quantity of goods larger than he contracted to sell and the buyer accepts the whole of the goods so delivered he must pay for them at the contract rate.

(4) Where the seller delivers to the buyer the goods he contracted to sell mixed with goods of a different description not included in the contract, the buyer may accept the goods which are in accordance with the contract and reject the rest, or he may reject the whole.

(5) This section is subject to any usage of trade, special agreement, or course of dealing between the parties.

Instalment deliveries

31.—(1) Unless otherwise agreed, the buyer of goods is not bound to accept delivery of them by instalments.

(2) Where there is a contract for the sale of goods to be delivered by stated instalments, which are to be separately paid for, and the seller makes defective deliveries in respect of one or more instalments, or the buyer neglects or refuses to take delivery of or pay for one or more instalments, it is a question in each case depending on the terms of the contract and the circumstances of the case whether the breach of contract is a repudiation of the whole contract or whether it is a severable breach giving rise to a claim for compensation but not to a right to treat the whole contract as repudiated.

Delivery to carrier

32.—(1) Where, in pursuance of a contract of sale, the seller is authorised or required to send the goods to the buyer, delivery of the goods to a carrier (whether named by the buyer or not) for the purpose of transmission to the buyer is prima facie deemed to be a delivery of the goods to the buyer.

(2) Unless otherwise authorised by the buyer, the seller must make such contract with the carrier on behalf of the buyer as may be reasonable having regard to the nature of the goods and the other circumstances of the case; and if the seller omits to do so, and the goods are lost or damaged in course of transit, the buyer may decline to treat the delivery to the carrier as a delivery to himself or may hold the seller responsible in damages.

(3) Unless otherwise agreed, where goods are sent by the seller to the buyer by a route involving sea transit, under circumstances in which it is usual to insure, the seller must give such notice to the buyer as may enable him to insure them during their sea transit; and if the seller fails to do so, the goods are at his risk during such sea transit.

Risk where goods are delivered at distant place

33. Where the seller of goods agrees to deliver them at his own risk at a place other than that where they are when sold, the buyer must nevertheless (unless otherwise agreed) take any risk of deterioration in the goods necessarily incident to the course of transit.

Buyer's right of examining the goods

34.—(1) Where goods are delivered to the buyer, and he has not previously examined them, he is not deemed to have accepted them until he has had a reasonable opportunity of examining them for the purpose of ascertaining whether they are in conformity with the contract.

(2) Unless otherwise agreed, when the seller tenders delivery of goods to the buyer, he is bound on request to afford the buyer a reasonable opportunity of examining the goods for the purpose of ascertaining whether they are in conformity with the contract.

Acceptance

35.—(1) The buyer is deemed to have accepted the goods when he intimates to the seller that he has accepted them, or (except where section 34 above otherwise provides) when the goods have been delivered to him and he does any act in relation to them which is inconsistent with the ownership of the seller, or when after the lapse of a reasonable time he retains the goods without intimating to the seller that he has rejected them.

(2) Paragraph 10 of Schedule 1 below applies in relation to a contract made before 22nd April 1967 or (in the application of this Act to Northern Ireland) 28th July 1967.

Buyer not bound to return rejected goods

36. Unless otherwise agreed, where goods are delivered to the buyer, and he refuses to accept them, having the right to do so, he is not bound to return them to the seller, but it is sufficient if he intimates to the seller that he refuses to accept them.

Buyer's liability for not taking delivery of goods

37.—(1) When the seller is ready and willing to deliver the goods, and requests the buyer to take delivery, and the buyer does not within a reasonable time after such request take delivery of the goods, he is liable to the seller for any loss occasioned by his neglect or refusal to take delivery, and also for a reasonable charge for the care and custody of the goods.

(2) Nothing in this section affects the rights of the seller where the neglect or refusal of the buyer to take delivery amounts to a repudiation of the contract.

PART V

RIGHTS OF UNPAID SELLER AGAINST THE GOODS

Preliminary

Unpaid seller defined

38.—(1) The seller of goods is an unpaid seller within the meaning of this Act—

(*a*) when the whole of the price has not been paid or tendered;

(*b*) when a bill of exchange or other negotiable instrument has been received as conditional payment, and the condition on which it was received has not been fulfilled by reason of the dishonour of the instrument or otherwise.

(2) In this Part of this Act "seller" includes any person who is in the position of a seller, as, for instance, an agent of the seller to whom the bill of lading has been indorsed, or a consignor or agent who has himself paid (or is directly responsible for) the price.

Unpaid seller's rights

39.—(1) Subject to this and any other Act, notwithstanding that the property in the goods may have passed to the buyer, the unpaid seller of goods, as such, has by implication of law—

(*a*) a lien on the goods or right to retain them for the price while he is in possession of them;

(*b*) in case of the insolvency of the buyer, a right of stopping the goods in transit after he has parted with the possession of them;

(*c*) a right of re-sale as limited by this Act.

(2) Where the property in goods has not passed to the buyer, the unpaid seller has (in addition to his other remedies) a right of withholding delivery similar to and co-extensive with his rights of lien or retention and stoppage in transit where the property has passed to the buyer.

40. [Repealed by the Debtors (Scotland) Act 1987, Sched. 8.]

Unpaid seller's lien

Seller's lien

41.—(1) Subject to this Act, the unpaid seller of goods who is in possession of them is entitled to retain possession of them until payment or tender of the price in the following cases:—

(*a*) where the goods have been sold without any stipulation as to credit;

(*b*) where the goods have been sold on credit but the term of credit has expired;

(*c*) where the buyer becomes insolvent.

(2) The seller may exercise his lien or right of retention notwithstanding that he is in possession of the goods as agent or bailee or custodier for the buyer.

Part delivery

42. Where an unpaid seller has made part delivery of the goods, he may exercise his lien or right of retention on the remainder, unless such part delivery has been made under such circumstances as to show an agreement to waive the lien or right of retention.

Termination of lien

43.—(1) The unpaid seller of goods loses his lien or right of retention in respect of them—

(*a*) when he delivers the goods to a carrier or other bailee or custodier for the purpose of transmission to the buyer without reserving the right of disposal of the goods;

(*b*) when the buyer or his agent lawfully obtains possession of the goods;

(*c*) by waiver of the lien or right of retention.

(2) An unpaid seller of goods who has a lien or right of retention in respect of them does not lose his lien or right of retention by reason only that he has obtained judgment or decree for the price of the goods.

Stoppage in transit

Right of stoppage in transit

44. Subject to this Act, when the buyer of goods becomes insolvent the unpaid seller who has parted with the possession of the goods has the right of stopping them in transit, that is to say, he may resume possession of the goods as long as they are in course of transit, and may retain them until payment or tender of the price.

Duration of transit

45.—(1) Goods are deemed to be in course of transit from the time when they are delivered to a carrier or other bailee or custodier for the purpose of transmission to the buyer, until the buyer or his agent in that behalf takes delivery of them from the carrier or other bailee or custodier.

(2) If the buyer or his agent in that behalf obtains delivery of the goods before their arrival at the appointed destination, the transit is at an end.

(3) If, after the arrival of the goods at the appointed destination, the carrier or other bailee or custodier acknowledges to the buyer or his agent that he holds the goods on his behalf and continues in possession of them as bailee or custodier for the buyer or his agent, the transit is at an end, and it is immaterial that a further destination for the goods may have been indicated by the buyer.

(4) If the goods are rejected by the buyer, and the carrier or other bailee or custodier continues in possession of them, the transit is not deemed to be at an end, even if the seller has refused to receive them back.

(5) When goods are delivered to a ship chartered by the buyer it is a question depending on the circumstances of the particular case whether they are in the possession of the master as a carrier or as agent to the buyer.

(6) Where the carrier or other bailee or custodier wrongfully refuses to deliver the goods to the buyer or his agent in that behalf, the transit is deemed to be at an end.

(7) Where part delivery of the goods has been made to the buyer or his agent in that behalf, the remainder of the goods may be stopped in transit, unless such part delivery has been made under such circumstances as to show an agreement to give up possession of the whole of the goods.

How stoppage in transit is effected

46.—(1) The unpaid seller may exercise his right of stoppage in transit either by taking actual possession of the goods or by giving notice of his claim to the carrier or other bailee or custodier in whose possession the goods are.

(2) The notice may be given either to the person in actual possession of the goods or to his principal.

(3) If given to the principal, the notice is ineffective unless given at such time and under such circumstances that the principal, by the exercise of reasonable diligence, may communicate it to his servant or agent in time to prevent a delivery to the buyer.

(4) When notice of stoppage in transit is given by the seller to the carrier or other bailee or custodier in possession of the goods, he must re-deliver the goods to, or according to the directions of, the seller; and the expenses of the re-delivery must be borne by the seller.

Re-sale, etc., by buyer

Effect of sub-sale, etc., by buyer

47.—(1) Subject to this Act, the unpaid seller's right of lien or retention or stoppage in transit is not affected by any sale or other disposition of the goods which the buyer may have made, unless the seller has assented to it.

(2) Where a document of title to goods has been lawfully transferred to any person as buyer or owner of the goods, and that person transfers the document to a person who takes it in good faith and for valuable consideration, then—

    (*a*) if the last-mentioned transfer was by way of sale the unpaid seller's right of lien or retention or stoppage in transit is defeated; and (*b*) if the last-mentioned transfer was made by way of pledge or other disposition for value, the unpaid seller's right of lien or retention or stoppage in transit can only be exercised subject to the rights of the transferee.

Rescission: and re-sale by seller

Rescission: and re-sale by seller

48.—(1) Subject to this section, a contract of sale is not rescinded by the mere exercise by an unpaid seller of his right of lien or retention or stoppage in transit.

(2) Where an unpaid seller who has exercised his right of lien or retention or stoppage in transit re-sells the goods, the buyer acquires a good title to them as against the original buyer.

(3) Where the goods are of a perishable nature, or where the unpaid seller gives notice to the buyer of his intention to re-sell, and the buyer does not within a reasonable time pay or tender the price, the unpaid seller may re-sell the goods and recover from the original buyer damages for any loss occasioned by his breach of contract.

(4) Where the seller expressly reserves the right of re-sale in case the buyer should make default, and on the buyer making default re-sells the goods, the original contract of sale is rescinded but without prejudice to any claim the seller may have for damages.

Part VI

Actions for Breach of the Contract

Seller's remedies

Action for price

49.—(1) Where, under a contract of sale, the property in the goods has passed to the buyer and he wrongfully neglects or refuses to pay for the goods according to the terms of the contract, the seller may maintain an action against him for the price of the goods.

(2) Where, under a contract of sale, the price is payable on a day certain irrespective of delivery and the buyer wrongfully neglects or refuses to pay such price, the seller may maintain an action for the price, although the property in the goods has not passed and the goods have not been appropriated to the contract.

(3) Nothing in this section prejudices the right of the seller in Scotland to recover interest on the price from the date of tender of the goods, or from the date on which the price was payable, as the case may be.

Damages for non-acceptance

50.—(1) Where the buyer wrongfully neglects or refuses to accept and pay for the goods, the seller may maintain an action against him for damages for non-acceptance.

(2) The measure of damages is the estimated loss directly and naturally resulting, in the ordinary course of events, from the buyer's breach of contract.

(3) Where there is an available market for the goods in question the measure of damages is *prima facie* to be ascertained by the difference between the contract price and the market or current price at the time or times when the goods ought to have been accepted or (if no time was fixed for acceptance) at the time of the refusal to accept.

Buyer's remedies

Damages for non-delivery

51.—(1) Where the seller wrongfully neglects or refuses to deliver the goods to the buyer, the buyer may maintain an action against the seller for damages for non-delivery.

(2) The measure of damages is the estimated loss directly and naturally resulting, in the ordinary course of events, from the seller's breach of contract.

(3) Where there is an available market for the goods in question the measure of damages is *prima facie* to be ascertained by the difference between the contract price and the market or current price of the goods at the time or times when they ought to have been delivered or (if no time was fixed) at the time of the refusal to deliver.

Specific performance

52.—(1) In any action for breach of contract to deliver specific or ascertained goods the court may, if it thinks fit, on the plaintiff's application, by its judgment or decree direct that the contract shall be performed specifically, without giving the defendant the option of retaining the goods on payment of damages.

(2) The plaintiff's application may be made at any time before judgment or decree.

(3) The judgment or decree may be unconditional, or on such terms and conditions as to damages, payment of the price and otherwise as seem just to the court.

(4) The provisions of this section shall be deemed to be supplementary to, and not in derogation of, the right of specific implement in Scotland.

Remedy for breach of warranty

53.—(1) Where there is a breach of warranty by the seller, or where the buyer elects (or is compelled) to treat any breach of a condition on the part of the seller as a breach of warranty, the buyer is not by reason only of such breach of warranty entitled to reject the goods; but he may—

   (*a*) set up against the seller the breach of warranty in diminution or extinction of the price, or

   (*b*) maintain an action against the seller for damages for the breach of warranty.

(2) The measure of damages for breach of warranty is the estimated loss directly and naturally resulting, in the ordinary course of events, from the breach of warranty.

(3) In the case of breach of warranty of quality such loss is *prima facie* the difference between the value of the goods at the time of delivery to the buyer and the value they would have had if they had fulfilled the warranty.

(4) The fact that the buyer has set up the breach of warranty in diminution or extinction of the price does not prevent him from maintaining an action for the same breach of warranty if he has suffered further damage.

(5) Nothing in this section prejudices or affects the buyer's right of rejection in Scotland as declared by this Act.

Interest, etc.

Interest, etc.

54. Nothing in this Act affects the right of the buyer or the seller to recover interest or special damages in any case where by law interest or special damages may be recoverable, or to recover money paid where the consideration for the payment of it has failed.

PART VII

SUPPLEMENTARY

Exclusion of implied terms

55.—(1) Where a right, duty or liability would arise under a contract of sale of goods by implication of law, it may (subject to the Unfair Contract Terms Act 1977) be negatived or varied by express agreement, or by the course of dealing between the parties, or by such usage as binds both parties to the contract.

(2) An express condition or warranty does not negative a condition or warranty implied by this Act unless inconsistent with it.

(3) Paragraph 11 of Schedule 1 below applies in relation to a contract made on or after 18th May 1973 and before 1st February 1978, and paragraph 12 in relation to one made before 18th May 1973.

Conflict of laws

56. Paragraph 13 of Schedule 1 below applies in relation to a contract made on or after 18th May 1973 and before 1st February 1978, so as to make provision about conflict of laws in relation to such a contract.

Auction sales

57.—(1) Where goods are put up for sale by auction in lots, each lot is prima facie deemed to be the subject of a separate contract of sale.

(2) A sale by auction is complete when the auctioneer announces its completion by the fall of the hammer, or in other customary manner; and until the announcement is made any bidder may retract his bid.

(3) A sale by auction may be notified to be subject to a reserve or upset price, and a right to bid may also be reserved expressly by or on behalf of the seller.

(4) Where a sale by auction is not notified to be subject to a right to bid by or on behalf of the seller, it is not lawful for the seller to bid himself or to employ any person to bid at the sale, or for the auctioneer knowingly to take any bid from the seller or any such person.

(5) A sale contravening subsection (4) above may be treated as fraudulent by the buyer.

(6) Where, in respect of a sale by auction, a right to bid is expressly reserved (but not otherwise) the seller or any one person on his behalf may bid at the auction.

Payment into court in Scotland

58. In Scotland where a buyer has elected to accept goods which he might have rejected, and to treat a breach of contract as only giving rise to a claim for damages, he may, in an action by the seller for the price, be required, in the discretion of the court before which the action depends, to consign or pay into court the price of the goods, or part of the price, or to give other reasonable security for its due payment.

Reasonable time a question of fact

59. Where a reference is made in this Act to a reasonable time the question what is a reasonable time is a question of fact.

Rights etc. enforceable by action

60. Where a right, duty or liability is declared by this Act, it may (unless otherwise provided by this Act) be enforced by action.

Interpretation

61.—(1) In this Act, unless the context or subject matter otherwise requires,—

"action" includes counterclaim and set-off, and in Scotland condescendence and claim and compensation;

"business" includes a profession and the activities of any government department (including a Northern Ireland department) or local or public authority;

"buyer" means a person who buys or agrees to buy goods;

"contract of sale" includes an agreement to sell as well as a sale;

"credit-broker" means a person acting in the course of a business of credit brokerage carried on by him, that is a business of effecting introductions of individuals desiring to obtain credit—

(*a*) to persons carrying on any business so far as it relates to the provision of credit, or

(*b*) to other persons engaged in credit brokerage;

"defendant" includes in Scotland defender, respondent, and claimant in a multiplepoinding;

"delivery" means voluntary transfer of possession from one person to another;

"document of title to goods" has the same meaning as it has in the Factors Acts;

"Factors Acts" means the Factors Act 1889, the Factors (Scotland) Act 1890, and any enactment amending or substituted for the same;

"fault" means wrongful act or default;

"future goods" means goods to be manufactured or acquired by the seller after the making of the contract of sale;

"goods" includes all personal chattels other than things in action and money, and in Scotland all corporeal moveables except money; and in particular "goods" includes emblements, industrial growing crops, and things attached to or forming part of the land which are agreed to be severed before sale or under the contract of sale;

"plaintiff" includes pursuer, complainer, claimant in a multiplepoinding and defendant or defender counterclaiming;

"property" means the general property in goods, and not merely a special property;

"quality", in relation to goods, includes their state or condition;

"sale" includes a bargain and sale as well as a sale and delivery;

"seller" means a person who sells or agrees to sell goods;

"specific goods" means goods identified and agreed on at the time a contract of sale is made;

"warranty" (as regards England and Wales and Northern Ireland) means an agreement with reference to goods which are the subject of a contract of sale, but collateral to the main purpose of such contract, the breach of which gives rise to a claim for damages, but not to a right to reject the goods and treat the contract as repudiated.

(2) As regards Scotland a breach of warranty shall be deemed to be a failure to perform a material part of the contract.

(3) A thing is deemed to be done in good faith within the meaning of this Act when it is in fact done honestly, whether it is done negligently or not.

[1] (4) A person is deemed to be insolvent within the meaning of this Act if he has either ceased to pay his debts in the ordinary course of business or he cannot pay his debts as they become due, whether he has committed an act of bankruptcy or not.

(5) Goods are in a deliverable state within the meaning of this Act when they are in such a state that the buyer would under the contract be bound to take delivery of them.

(6) As regards the definition of "business" in subsection (1) above,

paragraph 14 of Schedule 1 below applies in relation to a contract made on or after 18th May 1973 and before 1st February 1978, and paragraph 15 in relation to one made before 18th May 1973.

NOTE

[1] As amended by the Bankruptcy (Scotland) Act 1985, Sched. 8, with effect from 1st April 1986.

Savings: rules of law etc.

62.—(1) The rules in bankruptcy relating to contracts of sale apply to those contracts, notwithstanding anything in this Act.

(2) The rules of the common law, including the law merchant, except in so far as they are inconsistent with the provisions of this Act, and in particular the rules relating to the law of principal and agent and the effect of fraud, misrepresentation, duress or coercion, mistake, or other invalidating cause, apply to contracts for the sale of goods.

(3) Nothing in this Act or the Sale of Goods Act 1893 affects the enactments relating to bills of sale, or any enactment relating to the sale of goods which is not expressly repealed or amended by this Act or that.

(4) The provisions of this Act about contracts of sale do not apply to a transaction in the form of a contract of sale which is intended to operate by way of mortgage, pledge, charge, or other security.

(5) Nothing in this Act prejudices or affects the landlord's right of hypothec or sequestration for rent in Scotland.

Consequential amendments, repeals and savings

63.—(1) Without prejudice to section 17 of the Interpretation Act 1978 (repeal and re-enactment), the enactments mentioned in Schedule 2 below have effect subject to the amendments there specified (being amendments consequential on this Act).

(2) The enactments mentioned in Schedule 3 below are repealed to the extent specified in column 3, but subject to the savings in Schedule 4 below.

(3) The savings in Schedule 4 below have effect.

Short title and commencement

64.—(1) This Act may be cited as the Sale of Goods Act 1979.

(2) This Act comes into force on 1st January 1980.

SCHEDULES

Section 1   SCHEDULE 1

MODIFICATION OF ACT FOR CERTAIN CONTRACTS

Preliminary

1.—(1) This Schedule modifies this Act as it applies to contracts of sale of goods made on certain dates.

(2) In this Schedule references to sections are to those of this Act and references to contracts are to contracts of sale of goods.

(3) Nothing in this Schedule affects a contract made before 1st January 1894.

. . . . . .

Section 12: implied terms about title, etc.

3. In relation to a contract made before 18th May 1973, substitute the following for section 12:—

Implied terms about title, etc.

    12. In a contract of sale, unless the circumstances of the contract are such as to show a different intention, there is—

        (*a*) an implied condition on the part of the seller that in the case of a sale he has a right to sell the goods, and in the case of an agreement to sell he will have such a right at the time when the property is to pass;

[THE NEXT PAGE IS H 131]

(*b*) an implied warranty that the buyer will have and enjoy quiet possession of the goods;

(*c*) an implied warranty that the goods will be free from any charge or encumbrance in favour of any third party, not declared or known to the buyer before or at the time when the contract is made.

Section 13: sale by description

4. In relation to a contract made before 18th May 1973, omit section 13(3).

Section 14: quality or fitness (i)

[1] 5. In relation to a contract made on or after 18th May 1973 and before the appointed day, substitute the following for section 14:—

Implied terms about quality or fitness

14.—(1) Except as provided by this section and section 15 below and subject to any other enactment, there is no implied condition or warranty about the quality or fitness for any particular purpose of goods supplied under a contract of sale.

(2) Where the seller sells goods in the course of a business, there is an implied condition that the goods supplied under the contract are of merchantable quality, except that there is no such condition—

(*a*) as regards defects specifically drawn to the buyer's attention before the contract is made; or

(*b*) if the buyer examines the goods before the contract is made, as regards defects which that examination ought to reveal.

(3) Where the seller sells goods in the course of a business and the buyer, expressly or by implication, makes known to the seller any particular purpose for which the goods are being bought, there is an implied condition that the goods supplied under the contract are reasonably fit for that purpose, whether or not that is a purpose for which such goods are commonly supplied, except where the circumstances show that the buyer does not rely, or that it is unreasonable for him to rely, on the seller's skill or judgment.

(4) An implied condition or warranty about quality or fitness for a particular purpose may be annexed to a contract of sale by usage.

(5) The preceding provisions of this section apply to a sale by a person who in the course of a business is acting as agent for another as they apply to a sale by a principal in the course of a business, except where that other is not selling in the course of a business and either the buyer knows that fact or reasonable steps are taken to bring it to the notice of the buyer before the contract is made.

(6) Goods of any kind are of merchantable quality within the meaning of subsection (2) above if they are as fit for the purpose or purposes for which goods of that kind are commonly bought as it is reasonable to expect having regard to any description applied to them, the price (if relevant) and all the other relevant circumstances.

(7) In the application of subsection (3) above to an agreement for the sale of goods under which the purchase price or part of it is payable by instalments any reference to the seller includes a reference to the person by whom any antecedent negotiations are conducted; and section 58(3) and (5) of the Hire-Purchase Act 1965, section 54(3) and (5) of the Hire-Purchase (Scotland) Act 1965 and section 65(3) and (5) of the Hire-Purchase Act (Northern Ireland) 1966 (meaning of antecedent negotiations and related expressions) apply in relation to this subsection as in relation to each of those Acts, but as if a reference to any such agreement were included in the references in subsection (3) of each of those sections to the agreements there mentioned.

NOTE

[1] The appointed day is 19th May 1985: S.I. 1983 No. 1572.

Section 14: quality or fitness (ii)

6. In relation to a contract made before 18th May 1973 substitute the following for section 14:—

Implied terms about quality or fitness

14.—(1) Subject to this and any other Act, there is no implied condition or warranty about the quality or fitness for any particular purpose of goods supplied under a contract of sale.

(2) Where the buyer, expressly or by implication, makes known to the seller the particular purpose for which the goods are required, so as to show that the buyer relies on

the seller's skill or judgment, and the goods are of a description which it is in the course of the seller's business to supply (whether he is the manufacturer or not), there is an implied condition that the goods will be reasonably fit for such purpose, except that in the case of a contract for the sale of a specified article under its patent or other trade name there is no implied condition as to its fitness for any particular purpose.

(3) Where goods are bought by description from a seller who deals in goods of that description (whether he is the manufacturer or not), there is an implied condition that the goods will be of merchantable quality; but if the buyer has examined the goods, there is no implied condition as regards defects which such examination ought to have revealed.

(4) An implied condition or warranty about quality or fitness for a particular purpose may be annexed by the usage of trade.

(5) An express condition or warranty does not negative a condition or warranty implied by this Act unless inconsistent with it.

Section 15: sale by sample

7. In relation to a contract made before 18th May 1973, omit section 15(3).

. . . .

Section 25: buyer in possession

[1] 9. In relation to a contract under which a person buys or agrees to buy goods and which is made before the appointed day, omit section 25(2).

NOTE

[1] The appointed day is 19th May 1985: S.I. 1983 No. 1572.

Section 35: acceptance

10. In relation to a contract made before 22nd April 1967 or (in the application of this Act to Northern Ireland) 28th July 1967, in section 35(1) omit "(except where section 34 above otherwise provides)".

Section 55: exclusion of implied terms (i)

11. In relation to a contract made on or after 18th May 1973 and before 1st February 1978 substitute the following for section 55:—

Exclusion of implied terms

55.—(1) Where a right, duty or liability would arise under a contract of sale of goods by implication of law, it may be negatived or varied by express agreement, or by the course of dealing between the parties or by such usage as binds both parties to the contract, but the preceding provision has effect subject to the following provisions of this section.

(2) An express condition or warranty does not negative a condition or warranty implied by this Act unless inconsistent with it.

(3) In the case of a contract of sale of goods, any term of that or any other contract exempting from all or any of the provisions of section 12 above is void.

(4) In the case of a contract of sale of goods, any term of that or any other contract exempting from all or any of the provisions of section 13, 14 or 15 above is void in the case of a consumer sale and is, in any other case, not enforceable to the extent that it is shown that it would not be fair or reasonable to allow reliance on the term.

(5) In determining for the purposes of subsection (4) above whether or not reliance on any such term would be fair or reasonable regard shall be had to all the circumstances of the case and in particular to the following matters—

    (*a*) the strength of the bargaining positions of the seller and buyer relative to each other, taking into account, among other things, the availability of suitable alternative products and sources of supply;

    (*b*) whether the buyer received an inducement to agree to the term or in accepting it had an opportunity of buying the goods or suitable alternatives without it from any source of supply;

    (*c*) whether the buyer knew or ought reasonably to have known of the existence and extent of the term (having regard, among other things, to any custom of the trade and any previous course of dealing between the parties);

(*d*) where the term exempts from all or any of the provisions of section 13, 14 or 15 above if some condition is not complied with, whether it was reasonable at the time of the contract to expect that compliance with that condition would be practicable;

(*e*) whether the goods were manufactured, processed, or adapted to the special order of the buyer.

(6) Subsection (5) above does not prevent the court from holding, in accordance with any rule of law, that a term which purports to exclude or restrict any of the provisions of section 13, 14 or 15 above is not a term of the contract.

(7) In this section " consumer sale " means a sale of goods (other than a sale by auction or by competitive tender) by a seller in the course of a business where the goods—

(*a*) are of a type ordinarily bought for private use or consumption; and

(*b*) are sold to a person who does not buy or hold himself out as buying them in the course of a business.

(8) The onus of proving that a sale falls to be treated for the purposes of this section as not being a consumer sale lies on the party so contending.

(9) Any reference in this section to a term exempting from all or any of the provisions of any section of this Act is a reference to a term which purports to exclude or restrict, or has the effect of excluding or restricting, the operation of all or any of the provisions of that section, or the exercise of a right conferred by any provision of that section, or any liability of the seller for breach of a condition or warranty implied by any provision of that section.

(10) It is hereby declared that any reference in this section to a term of a contract includes a reference to a term which although not contained in a contract is incorporated in the contract by any other term of the contract.

(11) Nothing in this section prevents the parties to a contract for the international sale of goods from negativing or varying any right, duty or liability which would otherwise arise by implication of law under sections 12 to 15 above.

(12) In subsection (11) above " contract for the international sale of goods " means a contract of sale of goods made by parties whose places of business (or, if they have none, habitual residences) are in the territories of different States (the Channel Islands and the Isle of Man being treated for this purpose as different States from the United Kingdom) and in the case of which one of the following conditions is satisfied:—

(*a*) the contract involves the sale of goods which are at the time of the conclusion of the contract in the course of carriage or will be carried from the territory of one State to the territory of another; or

(*b*) the acts constituting the offer and acceptance have been effected in the territories of different States; or

(*c*) delivery of the goods is to be made in the territory of a State other than that within whose territory the acts constituting the offer and the acceptance have been effected.

Section 55: exclusion of implied terms (ii)

12. In relation to a contract made before 18th May 1973 substitute the following for section 55:—

Exclusion of implied terms

55. Where a right, duty or liability would arise under a contract of sale by implication of law, it may be negatived or varied by express agreement, or by the course of dealing between the parties, or by such usage as binds both parties to the contract.

Section 56: conflict of laws

13.—(1) In relation to a contract made on or after 18th May 1973 and before 1st February 1978 substitute for section 56 the section set out in sub-paragraph (3) below.

(2) In relation to a contract made otherwise than as mentioned in sub-paragraph (1) above, ignore section 56 and this paragraph.

(3) The section mentioned in sub-paragraph (1) above is as follows:—

Conflict of laws

56.—(1) Where the proper law of a contract for the sale of goods would, apart from a term that it should be the law of some other country or a term to the like effect, be the law of any part of the United Kingdom, or where any such contract contains a term which purports to substitute, or has the effect of substituting, provisions of the law of some other country for all or any of the provisions of sections 12 to 15 and 55 above, those sections shall, notwithstanding that term but subject to subsection (2) below, apply to the contract.

(2) Nothing in subsection (1) above prevents the parties to a contract for the international sale of goods from negativing or varying any right, duty or liability which would otherwise arise by implication of law under sections 12 to 15 above.

(3) In subsection (2) above " contract for the international sale of goods " means a contract of sale of goods made by parties whose places of business (or, if they have none, habitual residences) are in the territories of different States (the Channel Islands and the Isle of Man being treated for this purpose as different States from the United Kingdom) and in the case of which one of the following conditions is satisfied:—

(*a*) the contract involves the sale of goods which are at the time of the conclusion of the contract in the course of carriage or will be carried from the territory of one State to the territory of another; or

(*b*) the acts constituting the offer and acceptance have been effected in the territories of different States; or

(*c*) delivery of the goods is to be made in the territory of a State other than that within whose territory the acts constituting the offer and the acceptance have been effected.

Section 61 (1): definition of " business " (i)

14. In relation to a contract made on or after 18th May 1973 and before 1st February 1978, in the definition of " business " in section 61 (1) for " or local or public authority " substitute ", local authority or statutory undertaker ".

Section 61 (1): definition of " business " (ii)

15. In relation to a contract made before 18th May 1973 omit the definition of " business " in section 61 (1).

SCHEDULES 2 AND 3

NOTE

The amendments contained in these Schedules have been given effect to in so far as they affect material included in *The Parliament House Book*.

Section 63   SCHEDULE 4

SAVINGS

Preliminary

1. In this Schedule references to the 1893 Act are to the Sale of Goods Act 1893.

Orders

2. An order under section 14 (8) or 25 (4) above may make provision that it is to have effect only as provided by the order (being provision corresponding to that which could, apart from this Act, have been made by an order under section 192 (4) of the Consumer Credit Act 1974 bringing into operation an amendment or repeal making a change corresponding to that made by the order under section 14 (8) or 25 (4) above).

Offences

3. Where an offence was committed in relation to goods before 1st January 1969 or (in the application of this Act to Northern Ireland) 1st August 1969, the effect of a conviction in respect of the offence is not affected by the repeal by this Act of section 24 of the 1893 Act.

1893 Act, section 26

4. The repeal by this Act of provisions of the 1893 Act does not extend to the following provisions of that Act in so far as they are needed to give effect to or interpret section 26 of that Act, namely, the definitions of " goods " and " property " in section 62 (1), section 62 (2) and section 63 (which was repealed subject to savings by the Statute Law Revision Act 1908).

Things done before 1st January 1894

5. The repeal by this Act of section 60 of and the Schedule to the 1893 Act (which effected repeals and which were themselves repealed subject to savings by the Statute Law Revision Act 1908) does not affect those savings, and accordingly does not affect things done or acquired before 1st January 1894.

6. In so far as the 1893 Act applied (immediately before the operation of the repeals made by this Act) to contracts made before 1st January 1894 (when the 1893 Act came into operation), the 1893 Act shall continue so to apply notwithstanding this Act.

[1] **Bankruptcy (Scotland) Act 1985**

(1985 c. 66)

An Act to reform the law of Scotland relating to sequestration and personal insolvency; and for connected purposes.

[30th October 1985]

NOTE
[1] See the Financial Services Act 1986, s.45(2) and (3).

ARRANGEMENT OF SECTIONS

Administration of bankruptcy

Administration of bankruptcy

Accountant in Bankruptcy

1.—(1) The Accountant in Bankruptcy shall have the following general functions in the administration of sequestration and personal insolvency—

(*a*) the supervision of the performance by interim trustees, permanent trustees and commissioners of the functions conferred on them by this Act and the investigation of any complaints made against them;

(*b*) the maintenance of a list of persons (in this Act referred to as the "list of interim trustees") from which interim trustees shall be appointed;

(*c*) the maintenance of a register (in this Act referred to as the "register of insolvencies"), in a form prescribed by the Court of Session by act of sederunt, which shall contain particulars of—

(i) estates which have been sequestrated; and

(ii) trust deeds which have been sent to him for registration under paragraph 5(*d*) of Schedule 5 to this Act; and

(*d*) the preparation of an annual report which shall be presented to the Court of Session and the Secretary of State and shall contain—

(i) statistical information relating to the state of all sequestrations of which particulars have been registered in the register of insolvencies during the year to which the report relates;

(ii) particulars of trust deeds registered as protected trust deeds in that year; and

(iii) particulars of the performance of the Accountant in Bankruptcy's functions under this Act.

(2) The Accountant of Court shall be the Accountant in Bankruptcy.

(3) If it appears to the Accountant in Bankruptcy that an interim trustee, permanent trustee or commissioner has failed without reasonable excuse to perform a duty imposed on him by any provision of this Act, he shall report the matter to the court which, after hearing the interim trustee, permanent trustee or commissioner on the matter, may remove him from office or censure him or make such other order as the circumstances of the case may require.

(4) If the Accountant in Bankruptcy has reasonable grounds to suspect that an interim trustee, permanent trustee or commissioner has committed an offence in the performance of his functions under this Act, or that an offence has been committed in relation to a sequestration—

(*a*) by the debtor, in respect of his assets, his dealings with them or his conduct in relation to his business or financial affairs; or

(*b*) by a person other than the debtor in that person's dealings with the debtor, the interim trustee or the permanent trustee in respect of the debtor's assets, business or financial affairs,

he shall report the matter to the Lord Advocate.

(5) The Accountant in Bankruptcy shall—

(*a*) make the register of insolvencies, at all reasonable times, available for inspection; and

(*b*) provide any person, on request, with a certified copy of any entry in the register.

(6) The power of the Secretary of State to regulate fees under section 2 of the Courts of Law Fees (Scotland) Act 1895 shall include power to prescribe the fees payable in respect of any matter relating to the functions of the Accountant in Bankruptcy.

Interim trustee

2.—(1) In every sequestration there shall be appointed under section 13 of this Act an interim trustee whose general functions shall be—

(*a*) to safeguard the debtor's estate pending the appointment of a permanent trustee under this Act;

(*b*) to ascertain the reasons for the debtor's insolvency and the circumstances surrounding it;

(*c*) to ascertain the state of the debtor's liabilities and assets;

(*d*) to administer the sequestration process pending the appointment of a permanent trustee; and

(*e*) whether or not he is still acting in the sequestration, to supply the Accountant in Bankruptcy with such information as the Accountant in Bankruptcy considers necessary to enable him to discharge his functions under this Act.

(2) A person shall be entitled to have his name included in the list of interim trustees if, but only if, he—

(*a*) resides within the jurisdiction of the Court of Session, and

(*b*) is qualified to act as an insolvency practitioner.

(3) The Accountant in Bankruptcy shall remove a person's name from the list of interim trustees—

(*a*) at the person's own request;

(*b*) if it appears to the Accountant in Bankruptcy that the person has ceased to meet either of the requirements mentioned in subsection (2) above; or

(*c*) if, on an application by the Accountant in Bankruptcy to the sheriff for the sheriffdom in which the person is habitually resident or his principal place of business is, or was last, situated, the sheriff is satisfied that the person is physically or mentally incapacitated from acting as interim trustee:

Provided that removal of a person's name in pursuance of paragraph (*a*) above shall not absolve that person, if he is acting as an interim or permanent trustee in a particular case, from continuing so to act until he has completed his duties in relation to that case:

Provided also that, until the coming into force of section 2 of the Insolvency Act 1985 (qualifications of insolvency practitioners), paragraph (*b*) above shall have effect as if at the end were added the words "or is not a fit and proper person to act as an interim trustee".

(4) Any person aggrieved by the exclusion or removal of his name from the list of interim trustees may appeal against that exclusion or removal to the Court of Session.

Permanent trustee

3.—(1) In every sequestration there shall be a permanent trustee whose general functions shall be—

(a) to recover, manage and realise the debtor's estate, whether situated in Scotland or elsewhere;

(b) to distribute the estate among the debtor's creditors according to their respective entitlements;

(c) to ascertain the reasons for the debtor's insolvency and the circumstances surrounding it;

(d) to ascertain the state of the debtor's liabilities and assets;

(e) to maintain a sederunt book during his term of office for the purpose of providing an accurate record of the sequestration process;

(f) to keep regular accounts of his intromissions with the debtor's estate, such accounts being available for inspection at all reasonable times by the commissioners (if any), the creditors and the debtor; and

(g) whether or not he is still acting in the sequestration, to supply the Accountant in Bankruptcy with such information as the Accountant in Bankruptcy considers necessary to enable him to discharge his functions under this Act.

(2) A permanent trustee in performing his functions under this Act shall have regard to advice offered to him by the commissioners (if any).

(3) If the permanent trustee has reasonable grounds to suspect that an offence has been committed in relation to a sequestration—

(a) by the debtor in respect of his assets, his dealings with them or his conduct in relation to his business or financial affairs; or

(b) by a person other than the debtor in that person's dealings with the debtor, the interim trustee or the permanent trustee in respect of the debtor's assets, business or financial affairs,

he shall report the matter to the Accountant in Bankruptcy.

(4) A report under subsection (3) above shall be absolutely privileged.

Commissioners

4. In any sequestration (other than one to which Schedule 2 to this Act applies) commissioners, whose general functions shall be to supervise the intromissions of the permanent trustee with the sequestrated estate and to advise him, may be elected in accordance with section 30 of this Act.

Petitions for sequestration

Sequestration of the estate of living or deceased debtor

5.—(1) The estate of a debtor may be sequestrated in accordance with the provisions of this Act.

(2) The sequestration of the estate of a living debtor shall be on the petition of—

(a) the debtor, with the concurrence of a qualified creditor or qualified creditors;

(b) a qualified creditor or qualified creditors, if the debtor is apparently insolvent; or

(c) the trustee acting under a voluntary trust deed granted by or on behalf of the debtor whereby his estate is conveyed to the trustee for the benefit of his creditors generally (in this Act referred to as a "trust deed").

(3) The sequestration of the estate of a deceased debtor shall be on the petition of—

(a) an executor or a person entitled to be appointed as executor on the estate;

(b) a qualified creditor or qualified creditors of the deceased debtor; or

(c) the trustee acting under a trust deed.

[1] (4) In this Act "qualified creditor" means a creditor who, at the date of the presentation of the petition, is a creditor of the debtor in respect of liquid or illiquid debts (other than contingent or future debts or amounts payable under a confiscation order), whether secured or unsecured, which amount (or of one such debt which amounts) to not less than £750 or such sum as may be prescribed; and "qualified creditors" means creditors who at the said date are creditors of the debtor in respect of such debts as aforesaid amounting in aggregate to not less than £750 or such sum as may be prescribed; and in the foregoing provisions of this subsection "confiscation order" has the meaning assigned by section 1(1) of the Criminal Justice (Scotland) Act 1987, by section 71(9)(*a*) of the Criminal Justice Act 1988 or by section 1(8) of the Drug Trafficking Offences Act 1986.

(5) Paragraphs 1(1) and (3), 2(1)(*a*) and (2) and 6 of Schedule 1 to this Act shall apply in order to ascertain the amount of the debt or debts for the purposes of subsection (4) above as they apply in order to ascertain the amount which a creditor is entitled to claim, but as if for any reference to the date of sequestration there were substituted a reference to the date of presentation of the petition.

(6) The petitioner shall send a copy of any petition presented under this section to the Accountant in Bankruptcy.

(7) Where, after a petition for sequestration has been presented but before the sequestration has been awarded, the debtor dies then—

(*a*) if the petitioner was the debtor, the petition shall fall;

(*b*) if the petitioner is a creditor, the proceedings shall continue in accordance with this Act so far as circumstances will permit.

(8) Where, after a petition for sequestration has been presented under this section but before the sequestration has been awarded, a creditor who—

(*a*) is the petitioner or concurs in a petition by the debtor; or

(*b*) has lodged answers to the petition,

withdraws or dies, there may be sisted in the place of—

(i) the creditor mentioned in paragraph (*a*) above, any creditor who was a qualified creditor at the date when the petition was presented and who remains so qualified at the date of the sist;

(ii) the creditor mentioned in paragraph (*b*) above, any other creditor.

NOTE

[1] As amended by the Criminal Justice (Scotland) Act 1987, s.45(5)(*a*) and the Criminal Justice Act 1988, Sched. 15, para. 107.

Sequestration of other estates

6.—(1) Subject to subsection (2) below, the estate belonging to or held for or jointly by the members of any of the following entities may be sequestrated—

(*a*) a trust in respect of debts incurred by it,

(*b*) a partnership, including a dissolved partnership;

(*c*) a body corporate or an unincorporated body;

(*d*) a limited partnership (including a dissolved partnership) within the meaning of the Limited Partnerships Act 1907.

(2) It shall not be competent to sequestrate the estate of any of the following entities—

(*a*) a company registered under the Companies Act 1985 or under the former Companies Acts (within the meaning of that Act); or

(*b*) an entity in respect of which an enactment provides, expressly or by implication, that sequestration is incompetent.

(3) The sequestration of a trust estate in respect of debts incurred by the trust shall be on the petition of—

(*a*) a majority of the trustees, with the concurrence of a qualified creditor or qualified creditors; or

(*b*) a qualified creditor or qualified creditors, if the trustees as such are apparently insolvent.

(4) The sequestration of the estate of a partnership shall be on the petition of—

    (*a*) the partnership, with the concurrence of a qualified creditor or qualified creditors; or

    (*b*) a qualified creditor or qualified creditors, if the partnership is apparently insolvent.

(5) A petition under subsection (4)(*b*) above may be combined with a petition for the sequestration of the estate of any of the partners as an individual where that individual is apparently insolvent.

(6) The sequestration of the estate of a body corporate or of an unincorporated body shall be on the petition of—

    (*a*) a person authorised to act on behalf of the body, with the concurrence of a qualified creditor or qualified creditors; or

    (*b*) a qualified creditor or qualified creditors, if the body is apparently insolvent.

(7) The application of this Act to the sequestration of the estate of a limited partnership shall be subject to such modifications as may be prescribed.

(8) Subsections (6) and (8) of section 5 of this Act shall apply for the purposes of this section as they apply for the purposes of that section.

Meaning of apparent insolvency

[1] **7.**—[2] (1) A debtor's apparent insolvency shall be constituted (or, where he is already apparently insolvent, constituted anew) whenever—

    (*a*) his estate is sequestrated, or he is adjudged bankrupt in England or Wales or Northern Ireland; or

    (*b*) not being a person whose property is for the time being affected by a restraint order or subject to a confiscation, or charging, order, he gives written notice to his creditors that he has ceased to pay his debts in the ordinary course of business; or

    (*c*) any of the following circumstances occurs—

        (i) he grants a trust deed;

        (ii) following the service on him of a duly executed charge for payment of a debt, the days of charge expire without payment;

        (iii) following a poinding or seizure of any of his moveable property in pursuance of a summary warrant for the recovery of rates or taxes, 14 days elapse without payment;

        (iv) a decree of adjudication of any part of his estate is granted, either for payment or in security;

        (v) his effects are sold under a sequestration for rent due by him; or

        (vi) a receiving order is made against him in England or Wales,

    unless it is shown that at the time when any such circumstance occurred, the debtor was able and willing to pay his debts as they became due or that but for his property being affected by a restraint order or subject to a confiscation, or charging, order he would be able to do so; or

    (*d*) a creditor of the debtor, in respect of a liquid debt which amounts (or liquid debts which in aggregate amount) to not less than £750 or such sum as may be prescribed, has served on the debtor, by personal service by an officer of court, a demand in the prescribed form requiring him either to pay the debt (or debts) or to find security for its (or their) payment, and within three weeks after the date of service of the demand the debtor has not—

        (i) complied with the demand; or

        (ii) intimated to the creditor, by recorded delivery, that he denies that there is a debt or that the sum claimed by the creditor as the debt is immediately payable.

In paragraph (*d*) above, "liquid debt" does not include a sum payable under a confiscation order; and in the foregoing provisions of this subsection—

"charging order" has the meaning assigned by section 9(2) of the Drug Trafficking Offences Act 1986 or by section 78(2) of the Criminal Justice Act 1988;

"confiscation order" has the meaning assigned by section 1(1) of the Criminal Justice (Scotland) Act 1987, by section 71(9)(*a*) of the said Act of 1988 or by section 1(8) of the said Act of 1986; and

"restraint order" has the meaning assigned by section 9 of the said Act of 1987, by section 77(1) of the said Act of 1988 or by section 8 of the said Act of 1986.

(2) A debtor's apparent insolvency shall continue, if constituted under—

(*a*) subsection (1)(*a*) above, until his discharge; or

(*b*) subsection (1)(*b*), (*c*) or (*d*) above, until he becomes able to pay his debts and pays them as they become due.

(3) The apparent insolvency of—

(*a*) a partnership shall be constituted either in accordance with the foregoing provisions of this section or if any of the partners is apparently insolvent for a debt of the partnership;

(*b*) an unincorporated body shall be constituted if a person representing the body is apparently insolvent, or a person holding property of the body in a fiduciary capacity is apparently insolvent, for a debt of the body.

(4) Notwithstanding subsection (2) of section 6 of this Act, the apparent insolvency of an entity such as is mentioned in paragraph (*a*) or (*b*) of that subsection may be constituted (or as the case may be constituted anew) under subsection (1) above; and any reference in the foregoing provisions of this section to a debtor shall, except where the context otherwise requires, be construed as including a reference to such an entity.

NOTES

[1] See the Debtors (Scotland) Act 1987, s.9(10)(*b*).

[2] As amended by the Criminal Justice (Scotland) Act 1987, s.45(5)(*b*) and the Criminal Justice Act 1988, Sched. 15, para. 108.

Further provisions relating to presentation of petitions

8.—(1) Subject to subsection (2) below, a petition for the sequestration of a debtor's estate (other than a deceased debtor's estate) may be presented—

(*a*) at any time by the debtor or by a trustee acting under a trust deed; but

(*b*) by a qualified creditor or qualified creditors, only if the apparent insolvency founded on in the petition was constituted within four months before the petition is presented.

(2) A petition for the sequestration of the estate of a limited partnership may be presented within such time as may be prescribed.

(3) A petition for the sequestration of the estate of a deceased debtor may be presented—

(*a*) at any time by an executor or a person entitled to be appointed as executor on the estate or a trustee acting under a trust deed;

(*b*) by a qualified creditor or qualified creditors of the deceased debtor—

(i) in a case where the apparent insolvency of the debtor was constituted within four months before his death, at any time;

(ii) in any other case (whether or not apparent insolvency has been constituted), not earlier than six months after the debtor's death.

(4) If an executor does not petition for sequestration of the deceased debtor's estate or for the appointment of a judicial factor to administer the estate within a reasonable period after he knew or ought to have known that the estate was absolutely insolvent and likely to remain so, any intromission by him with the estate after the expiry of that period shall be deemed to be an intromission without a title.

(5) The presentation of, or the concurring in, a petition for sequestration shall bar the effect of any enactment or rule of law relating to the limitation of actions in any part of the United Kingdom.

(6) Where before sequestration is awarded it becomes apparent that a

petitioning or concurring creditor was ineligible so to petition or concur he shall withdraw, or as the case may be withdraw from, the petition but another creditor may be sisted in his place.

Jurisdiction

9.—(1) The Court of Session shall have jurisdiction in respect of the sequestration of the estate of a living debtor or of a deceased debtor if the debtor has an established place of business in Scotland, or was habitually resident there, at the relevant time.

(2) The Court of Session shall have jurisdiction in respect of the sequestration of the estate of any entity which may be sequestrated by virtue of section 6 of this Act, if the entity—

   (*a*) had an established place of business in Scotland at the relevant time; or

[THE NEXT PAGE IS H 143]

(*b*) was constituted or formed under Scots law, and at any time carried on business in Scotland.

(3) Notwithstanding that the partner of a firm, whether alive or deceased, does not fall within subsection (1) above, the Court of Session shall have jurisdiction in respect of the sequestration of his estate if a petition has been presented for the sequestration of the estate of the firm of which he is, or was at the relevant time before his decease, a partner and the process of that sequestration is still current.

(4) The provisions of this section shall apply to the sheriff as they apply to the Court of Session but as if for the word "Scotland" wherever it occurs there were substituted the words "the sheriffdom" and in subsection (3) after the word "presented" there were inserted the words "in the sheriffdom".

(5) In this section "the relevant time" means at any time in the year immediately preceding the date of presentation of the petition or the date of death, as the case may be.

Concurrent proceedings for sequestration or analogous remedy

10.—(1) If, in the course of sequestration proceedings, the petitioner for sequestration, the debtor or a creditor concurring in the petition (the petition in such proceedings being hereafter in this section referred to as the "instant petition") is, or becomes, aware that—

(*a*) another petition for sequestration of the debtor's estate is before a court or such sequestration has been awarded; or

(*b*) a petition for the appointment of a judicial factor on the debtor's estate is before a court or such a judicial factor has been appointed; or

¹ (*c*) a petition is before a court for the winding up of the debtor under Part XX of the Companies Act 1985 or the debtor has been wound up under the said Part XX; or

(*d*) an application for an analogous remedy in respect of the debtor's estate is proceeding or such an analogous remedy is in force,

he shall as soon as possible bring that fact to the notice of the court to which the instant petition was presented.

(2) If a petitioner (not being the debtor) or a creditor concurring in the petition fails to comply with subsection (1) above, he may be made liable for the expenses of presenting the petition for sequestration; and, if the debtor fails to comply with subsection (1) above, he shall be guilty of an offence and liable, on summary conviction, to a fine not exceeding level 5 on the standard scale.

(3) Where in the course of sequestration proceedings any of the circumstances mentioned in paragraph (*a*), (*b*) or (*c*) of subsection (1) above exists then—

(*a*) the court to which the instant petition was presented may, on its own motion or at the instance of the debtor or any creditor or other person having an interest, allow that petition to proceed or may sist or dismiss it; or

(*b*) without prejudice to paragraph (*a*) above, the Court of Session may, on its own motion or on application by the debtor or any creditor or other person having an interest, direct the sheriff before whom the instant petition is pending, or the court before which the other petition is pending, to sist or dismiss the instant petition or, as the case may be, the other petition, or may order the petitions to be heard together.

(4) Where in respect of the same estate—

(*a*) a petition for sequestration is pending before a court; and

(*b*) an application for an analogous remedy is proceeding or an analogous remedy is in force, the court, in its own motion or at the instance of the debtor or any creditor or other person having an interest, may allow the petition for sequestration to proceed or may sist or dismiss it.

(5) In this section "analogous remedy" means a bankruptcy order under the Bankruptcy Act 1914 or under the Insolvency Act 1985 or an administration order under section 112 of the County Courts Act 1984 in England and Wales or under any enactment having the like effect in Northern Ireland or a remedy analogous to either of the aforesaid remedies, or to sequestration, in any other country.

NOTE
[1] Substituted (*prosp.*) by the Financial Services Act 1986, Sched. 16, para. 29.

Creditor's oath

11.—(1) Every creditor, being a petitioner for sequestration, a creditor who concurs in a petition by a debtor or a qualified creditor who becomes sisted under subsection (8)(i) of section 5 of this Act or under that subsection as applied by section 6(8) of this Act, shall produce an oath in the prescribed form made by him or on his behalf.

(2) The oath may be made—

(*a*) in the United Kingdom, before any person entitled to administer an oath there;

(*b*) outwith the United Kingdom, before a British diplomatic or consular officer or any person authorised to administer an oath or affirmation under the law of the place where the oath is made.

(3) The identity of the person making the oath and the identity of the person before whom the oath is made and their authority to make and to administer the oath respectively shall be presumed to be correctly stated, and any seal or signature on the oath shall be presumed to be authentic, unless the contrary is established.

(4) If the oath contains any error or has omitted any fact, the court to which the petition for sequestration was presented may, at any time before sequestration is awarded, allow another oath to be produced rectifying the original oath; and this section shall apply to the making of that other oath as it applies to the making of the original oath.

(5) Every creditor must produce along with the oath an account or voucher (according to the nature of the debt) which constitutes *prima facie* evidence of the debt; and a petitioning creditor shall in addition produce such evidence as is available to him to show the apparent insolvency of the debtor.

Award of sequestration and appointment and resignation of interim trustee

When sequestration is awarded

12.—(1) Where a petition for sequestration of his estate is presented by the debtor, the court shall award sequestration forthwith if the court is satisfied that the petition has been presented in accordance with the provisions of this Act unless cause is shown why sequestration cannot competently be awarded.

(2) Where a petition for sequestration of a debtor's estate is presented by a creditor or a trustee acting under a trust deed, the court to which the petition is presented shall grant warrant to cite the debtor to appear before it on such date as shall be specified in the warrant, being a date not less than six nor more than 14 days after the date of citation, to show cause why sequestration should not be awarded.

(3) If, on a petition for sequestration presented by a creditor or a trustee acting under a trust deed, the court is satisfied that, if the debtor has not appeared, proper citation has been made of the debtor, that the petition has been presented in accordance with the provisions of this Act and that, in the case of a petition by a creditor, the requirements of this Act relating to apparent insolvency have been fulfilled, it shall award sequestration forthwith unless—

(*a*) cause is shown why sequestration cannot competently be awarded; or

(*b*) the debtor forthwith pays or satisfies or produces written evidence of the payment or satisfaction of, or gives sufficient security for the payment of—

(i) the debt in respect of which he became apparently insolvent; and

(ii) any other debt due by him to the petitioner and any creditor concurring in the petition.

[1] (4) In this Act "the date of sequestration" means if the petition for sequestration is presented by—

(*a*) the debtor, the date on which sequestration is awarded;

(*b*) a creditor or a trustee acting under a trust deed, the date on which the court grants warrant under subsection (2) above.

NOTE

[1] Applied by the Debtors (Scotland) Act 1987, s.72(5) (*prosp.*).

Appointment and resignation of interim trustee

[1] **13.**—[2,3] (1) An interim trustee shall be appointed by the court from the list of interim trustees on sequestration being awarded or as soon as may be thereafter:

Provided that, where the petition for sequestration is presented by a creditor or a trustee acting under a trust deed, an interim trustee may be so appointed before sequestration is awarded if—

(*a*) the debtor consents, or

(*b*) the Accountant in Bankruptcy, the trustee acting under the trust deed or any creditor shows cause.

(2) The court may, on an application by an interim trustee, authorise the interim trustee to resign office and, if he does so, shall appoint another person from the list of interim trustees to act in his place; and an interim trustee shall not otherwise resign office.

(3) Without prejudice to section 1(3) of this Act or to subsection (4) below, where the court is satisfied that an interim trustee—

(*a*) is unable to act (whether by, under or by virtue of a provision of this Act or from any other cause whatsoever); or

(*b*) has had his name removed from the list of interim trustees; or

(*c*) has so conducted himself that he should no longer continue to act in the sequestration,

the court, on the application of the debtor, a creditor, the Accountant in Bankruptcy or, in respect of paragraph (*a*) above, the interim trustee, shall appoint another interim trustee from that list to act in his place.

(4) Where under section 1(3) of this Act the court removes an interim trustee from office, the court, on the application of the Accountant in Bankruptcy or, in respect of paragraph (*a*) above, the interim trustee, shall appoint another interim trustee from that list to act in his place.

(5) Subject to subsection (6) below, no one shall act as interim trustee in a sequestration if he would, by virtue of section 24(2) of this Act, be disqualified from acting as permanent trustee in that sequestration; but where an interim trustee is, by virtue of this subsection, prohibited from so acting he shall forthwith make an application under subsection (3)(*a*) above.

(6) No person appointed as interim trustee under this section shall be entitled to decline to accept his appointment.

(7) Notwithstanding the provisions of paragraph (*a*) of section 18(3) of this Act, the court may, if requested to do so in the petition for sequestration, empower the interim trustee to act as is mentioned in that paragraph.

(8) An order of the court making an appointment under this section shall be appealable only by the debtor, a creditor, the Accountant in Bankruptcy or the appointee and only on the ground that the person appointed is unable to act as mentioned in subsection (3)(*a*) above, or is not on the list of interim trustees:

Provided that such an order under subsection (3) above may also be appealed against by the displaced interim trustee on the ground that the court should not have been satisfied as is mentioned in that subsection.

(9) An interim trustee, as soon as may be after his appointment, shall notify the debtor and the Accountant in Bankruptcy of the appointment.

NOTES

[1] See the Debtors (Scotland) Act 1987, s.66(2)(*e*) (*prosp.*).

[2] See the Drug Trafficking Offences Act 1986, s.16(5).

[3] Excluded by the Criminal Justice (Scotland) Act 1987, s.33(4).

Registration of court order

14.—(1) The clerk of the court shall forthwith after the date of sequestration send—

> (*a*) a certified copy of the relevant court order to the keeper of the register of inhibitions and adjudications for recording in that register; and
>
> (*b*) a copy of the order to the Accountant in Bankruptcy.

(2) Recording under subsection (1)(*a*) above shall have the effect as from the date of sequestration of an inhibition and of a citation in an adjudication of the debtor's heritable estate at the instance of the creditors who subsequently have claims in the sequestration accepted under section 49 of this Act.

(3) The effect mentioned in subsection (2) above shall expire—

> (*a*) on the recording under section 15(5)(*a*) or 17(8)(*a*) of, or by virtue of paragraph 11 of Schedule 4 to, this Act of a certified copy of an order; or
>
> (*b*) subject to subsection (4) below, if the effect has not expired by virtue of paragraph (*a*) above, at the end of the period of three years beginning with the date of sequestration.

(4) The permanent trustee, if not discharged, shall before the end of the period of three years mentioned in subsection (3)(*b*) above send a memorandum in a form prescribed by the Court of Session by act of sederunt to the keeper of the register of inhibitions and adjudications for recording in that register, and such recording shall renew the effect mentioned in subsection (2) above; and thereafter the said effect shall continue to be preserved only if such a memorandum is so recorded before the expiry of every subsequent period of three years.

(5) In this section "relevant court order" means, if the petition for sequestration is presented by—

> (*a*) the debtor, the order of the court awarding sequestration; or
>
> (*b*) a creditor or the trustee acting under a trust deed, the order of the court granting warrant under section 12(2) of this Act.

Further provisions relating to award of sequestration

15.—(1) Where sequestration has been awarded by the Court of Session, it shall remit the sequestration to such sheriff as in all the circumstances of the case it considers appropriate.

(2) The Court of Session may at any time after sequestration has been awarded, on application being made to it, transfer the sequestration from the sheriff before whom it is depending or to whom it has been remitted to any other sheriff.

(3) Where the court makes an order refusing to award sequestration, the petitioner or a creditor concurring in the petition for sequestration may appeal against the order within 14 days of the date of making of the order.

(4) Without prejudice to any right to bring an action of reduction of an award of sequestration, such an award shall not be subject to review otherwise than by recall under sections 16 and 17 of this Act.

(5) Where a petition for sequestration is presented by a creditor or a trustee acting under a trust deed, the clerk of the court shall—

> (*a*) on the final determination or abandonment of any appeal under subsection (3) above in relation to the petitioner, or if there is no such appeal on the expiry of the 14 days mentioned in that subsec-

tion, send a certified copy of an order refusing to award sequestration to the keeper of the register of inhibitions and adjudications for recording in that register;

    (*b*) forthwith send a copy of an order awarding or refusing to award sequestration to the Accountant in Bankruptcy.

(6) The interim trustee, as soon as an award of sequestration has been granted, shall publish a notice in the prescribed form in the *Edinburgh Gazette* and the *London Gazette* stating that sequestration has been awarded and inviting the submission of claims to him.

(7) Where sequestration has been awarded, the process of sequestration shall not fall asleep.

(8) Where a debtor learns, whether before or after the date of sequestration, that he may derive benefit from another estate, he shall as soon as practicable after that date inform—

    (*a*) the permanent trustee or, if the permanent trustee has not yet been elected or appointed, the interim trustee of that fact; and

    (*b*) the person who is administering that other estate of the sequestration.

(9) If the debtor fails to comply with subsection (8) above, he shall be guilty of an offence and liable, on summary conviction, to a fine not exceeding level 5 on the standard scale.

Petitions for recall of sequestration

16.—(1) A petition for recall of an award of sequestration may be presented to the Court of Session by—

    (*a*) the debtor, any creditor or any other person having an interest (notwithstanding that he was a petitioner, or concurred in the petition, for the sequestration);

    (*b*) the interim trustee, the permanent trustee, or the Accountant in Bankruptcy.

(2) The petitioner shall serve upon the debtor, any person who was a petitioner, or concurred in the petition, for the sequestration, the interim trustee or permanent trustee and the Accountant in Bankruptcy, a copy of the petition along with a notice stating that the recipient of the notice may lodge answers to the petition within 14 days of the service of the notice.

(3) At the same time as service is made under subsection (2) above, the petitioner shall publish a notice in the *Edinburgh Gazette* stating that a petition has been presented under this section and that any person having an interest may lodge answers to the petition within 14 days of the publication of the notice.

(4) Subject to section 41(1)(*b*) of this Act, a petition under this section may be presented—

    (*a*) within 10 weeks after the date of sequestration; but

    (*b*) at any time if the petition is presented on any of the grounds mentioned in paragraphs (*a*) to (*c*) of section 17(1) of this Act.

(5) Notwithstanding that a petition has been presented under this section, the proceedings in the sequestration shall continue (subject to section 17(6) of this Act) as if that petition had not been presented until the recall is granted.

(6) Where—

    (*a*) a petitioner under this section; or

    (*b*) a person who has lodged answers to the petition,

withdraws or dies, any person entitled to present or, as the case may be, lodge answers to a petition under this section may be sisted in his place.

Recall of sequestration

17.—(1) The Court of Session may recall an award of sequestration if it is satisfied that in all the circumstances of the case (including those arising after the date of the award of sequestration) it is appropriate to do so and, without prejudice to the foregoing generality, may recall the award if it is satisfied that—

(*a*) the debtor has paid his debts in full or has given sufficient security for their payment;

(*b*) a majority in value of the creditors reside in a country other than Scotland and that it is more appropriate for the debtor's estate to be administered in that other country; or

(*c*) one or more other awards of sequestration of the estate or analogous remedies (as defined in section 10(5) of this Act) have been granted.

(2) Where one or more awards of sequestration of the debtor's estate have been granted, the court may, after such intimation as it considers necessary, recall an award whether or not the one in respect of which the petition for recall was presented.

(3) On recalling an award of sequestration, the court—

(*a*) shall make provision for the payment of the outlays and remuneration of the interim trustee and permanent trustee by directing that such payment shall be made out of the debtor's estate or by requiring any person who was a party to the petition for sequestration to pay the whole or any part of the said outlays and remuneration;

(*b*) without prejudice to subsection (7) below, may direct that payment of the expenses of a creditor who was a petitioner, or concurred in the petition, for sequestration shall be made out of the debtor's estate;

(*c*) may make any further order that it considers necessary or reasonable in all the circumstances of the case.

(4) Subject to subsection (5) below, the effect of the recall of an award of sequestration shall be, so far as practicable, to restore the debtor and any other person affected by the sequestration to the position he would have been in if the sequestration had not been awarded.

(5) A recall of an award of sequestration shall not—

(*a*) affect the interruption of prescription caused by the presentation of the petition for sequestration or the submission of a claim under section 22 or 48 of this Act;

(*b*) invalidate any transaction entered into before such recall by the interim trustee or permanent trustee with a person acting in good faith.

(6) Where the court considers that it is inappropriate to recall or to refuse to recall an award of sequestration forthwith, it may order that the proceedings in the sequestration shall continue but shall be subject to such conditions as it may think fit.

(7) The court may make such order in relation to the expenses in a petition for recall as it thinks fit.

(8) The clerk of court shall send—

(*a*) a certified copy of any order recalling an award of sequestration to the keeper of the register of inhibitions and adjudications for recording in that register; and

(*b*) a copy of any order recalling or refusing to recall an award of sequestration, or of any order under section 41(1)(*b*)(ii) of this Act, to—

    (i) the Accountant in Bankruptcy; and

    (ii) the permanent trustee (if any) who shall insert it in the sederunt book.

Period between award of sequestration and statutory meeting of creditors

Interim preservation of estate

18.—(1) The interim trustee may give general or particular directions to the debtor relating to the management of the debtor's estate.

(2) In exercising the functions conferred on him by section 2(1)(*a*) of this Act, an interim trustee may—

(*a*) require the debtor to deliver up to him any money or valuables, or any document relating to the debtor's business or financial affairs, belonging to or in the possession of the debtor or under his control;

(*b*) place in safe custody anything mentioned in paragraph (*a*) above;

(*c*) require the debtor to deliver up to him any perishable goods belonging to the debtor or under his control and may arrange for the sale or disposal of such goods;

(*d*) make or cause to be made an inventory or valuation of any property belonging to the debtor;

(*e*) require the debtor to implement any transaction entered into by the debtor;

(*f*) effect or maintain insurance policies in respect of the business or property of the debtor;

(*g*) close down the debtor's business.

(3) The court, on the application of the interim trustee, may—

(*a*) empower the interim trustee to—
   (i) carry on any business of the debtor;
   (ii) borrow money,
   in so far as it is necessary for the trustee to do so to safeguard the debtor's estate;

(*b*) on cause shown, grant a warrant authorising the interim trustee to enter the house where the debtor resides or his business premises and to search for and take possession of anything mentioned in paragraphs (*a*) and (*c*) of subsection (2) above, if need be by opening shut and lock-fast places; or

(*c*) make such other order to safeguard the debtor's estate as it thinks appropriate.

(4) The court, on an application by the debtor on the grounds that a direction under subsection (1) above is unreasonable, may—

(*a*) if it considers the direction to be unreasonable, set aside the direction; and

(*b*) in any event, give such directions to the debtor regarding the management of his estate as it considers appropriate;

but, subject to any interim order of the court, the debtor shall comply with the direction appealed against pending the final determination of the appeal.

(5) The debtor shall be guilty of an offence if—

(*a*) he fails without reasonable excuse to comply with—
   (i) a direction under subsection (1) or (4)(*b*) above; or
   (ii) a requirement under subsection (2)(*a*), (*c*) or (*e*) above; or

(*b*) he obstructs the interim trustee where the interim trustee is acting in pursuance of subsection (3)(*b*) above.

(6) A person convicted of an offence under subsection (5) above shall be liable—

(*a*) on summary conviction to a fine not exceeding the statutory maximum or—
   (i) to imprisonment for a term not exceeding three months; or
   (ii) if he has previously been convicted of an offence inferring dishonest appropriation of property or an attempt at such appropriation, to imprisonment for a term not exceeding six months,
   or (in the case of either sub-paragraph) to both such fine and such imprisonment; or

(*b*) on conviction on indictment to a fine or to imprisonment for a term not exceeding two years or to both.

Debtor's list of assets and liabilities

19.—(1) The debtor shall deliver to the interim trustee—

   (*a*) if the petitioner for sequestration is the debtor, within seven days of the appointment of the interim trustee;

   (*b*) if the petitioner for sequestration is a creditor or a trustee acting under a trust deed, within seven days of the interim trustee notifying the debtor of his appointment,

a list of the debtor's assets and liabilities in the prescribed form.

(2) If without reasonable excuse the debtor—

   (*a*) fails to deliver in accordance with subsection (1) above a list of assets and liabilities to the interim trustee; or

   (*b*) fails to disclose any material fact in it; or

   (*c*) makes a material misstatement in it,

he shall be guilty of an offence and liable on summary conviction to a fine not exceeding level 5 on the standard scale or to imprisonment for a term not exceeding three months or to both.

Trustee's duties on receipt of list of assets and liabilities

20.—(1) On receipt of the debtor's list of assets and liabilities, the interim trustee shall prepare a preliminary statement of the debtor's affairs so far as within the knowledge of the interim trustee and shall indicate in the statement whether, in his opinion, the debtor's assets are unlikely to be sufficient to pay any dividend whatsoever in respect of the debts mentioned in paragraphs (*e*) to (*h*) of section 51(1) of this Act.

(2) The interim trustee shall, not later than four days before the date fixed for the statutory meeting, send to the Accountant in Bankruptcy—

   (*a*) a copy of the debtor's list of assets and liabilities; and

   (*b*) a copy of the preliminary statement of the debtor's affairs; and

   (*c*) written comments by the interim trustee indicating what in his opinion are the causes of the insolvency and to what extent the conduct of the debtor may have contributed to the insolvency.

(3) The written comments made under subsection (2)(*c*) above shall be absolutely privileged.

(4) The interim trustee may request—

   (*a*) the debtor to appear before him and to give information relating to his assets, his dealings with them or his conduct in relation to his business or financial affairs; or

   (*b*) the debtor's spouse or any other person who the interim trustee believes can give such information to give that information,

and if the interim trustee considers it necessary he may apply to the sheriff for an order requiring the debtor, spouse or other person to appear before the sheriff for private examination.

(5) Subsections (2) to (4) of section 44 and sections 46 and 47 of this Act shall apply, subject to any necessary modifications, in respect of private examination under subsection (4) above as they apply in respect of private examination under the said subsection (2).

Statutory meeting of creditors and confirmation of permanent trustee

Calling of statutory meeting

21.—(1) The interim trustee shall call a meeting of creditors (in this Act referred to as "the statutory meeting") to be held within 28 days, or such longer period as the sheriff on cause shown may allow, after the date of the award of sequestration.

(2) Not less than seven days before the date fixed for the statutory meeting, the interim trustee shall notify—

   (*a*) every creditor known to him; and

   (*b*) the Accountancy [*sic*] in Bankruptcy,

of the date, time and place of the meeting, and shall in the notification to creditors invite the submission of such claims as have not already been submitted and inform them of his duties under section 23(3) and (5) of this Act.

(3) The creditors may continue the statutory meeting to a date not later than seven days after the end of the period—

(*a*) of 28 days mentioned in subsection (1) above; or (as the case may be),

(*b*) allowed by the sheriff under that subsection.

Submission of claims for voting purposes at statutory meeting

22.—(1) For the purposes of voting at the statutory meeting, a creditor shall submit a claim in accordance with this section to the interim trustee at or before the meeting.

(2) A creditor shall submit a claim under this section by producing to the interim trustee—

(*a*) a statement of claim in the prescribed form; and

(*b*) an account or voucher (according to the nature of the debt) which constitutes *prima facie* evidence of the debt:

Provided that the interim trustee may dispense with any requirement under this subsection in respect of any debt or any class of debt.

(3) Where a creditor neither resides nor has a place of business in the United Kingdom, the interim trustee—

(*a*) shall, if he knows where the creditor resides or has a place of business and if no notification has been given to that creditor under section 21(2) of this Act, write to him informing him that he may submit a claim under this section;

(*b*) may allow the creditor to submit an informal claim in writing.

(4) A creditor who has produced a statement of claim in accordance with subsection (2) above may at any time before the statutory meeting produce in place of that statement of claim another such statement of claim specifying a different amount for his claim.

(5) If a creditor produces under this section a statement of claim, account, voucher or other evidence which is false—

(*a*) the creditor shall be guilty of an offence unless he shows that he neither knew nor had reason to believe that the statement of claim, account, voucher or other evidence was false;

(*b*) the debtor shall be guilty of an offence if he—

(i) knew or became aware that the statement of claim, account, voucher or other evidence was false; and

(ii) failed as soon as practicable after acquiring such knowledge to report it to the interim trustee or permanent trustee.

(6) A creditor may, in such circumstances as may be prescribed, state the amount of his claim in foreign currency.

(7) The interim trustee shall, on production of any document to him under this section, initial the document and keep a record of it stating the date when it was produced to him, and, if requested by the sender, shall return it (if it is not a statement of claim) to him.

(8) The submission of a claim under this section shall bar the effect of any enactment or rule of law relating to the limitation of actions in any part of the United Kingdom.

(9) Schedule 1 to this Act shall have effect for determining the amount in respect of which a creditor shall be entitled to claim.

(10) A person convicted of an offence under subsection (5) above shall be liable—

(*a*) on summary conviction to a fine not exceeding the statutory maximum or—

(i) to imprisonment for a term not exceeding three months; or

(ii) if he has previously been convicted of an offence inferring dishonest appropriation of property or an attempt at such appropriation, to imprisonment for a term not exceeding six months, or (in the case of either sub-paragraph) to both such fine and such imprisonment; or

(b) on conviction on indictment to a fine or to imprisonment for a term not exceeding two years or to both.

Proceedings at statutory meeting before election of permanent trustee

23.—(1) At the commencement of the statutory meeting, the chairman shall be the interim trustee who as chairman shall—

(a) for the purposes of subsection (2) below, accept or reject in whole or in part the claim of each creditor, and, if the amount of a claim is stated in foreign currency, he shall convert that amount into sterling, in such manner as may be prescribed, at the rate of exchange prevailing at the close of business on the date of sequestration;

(b) invite the creditors thereupon to elect one of their number as chairman in his place and shall preside over the election:

Provided that if a chairman is not elected in pursuance of this paragraph, the interim trustee shall remain the chairman throughout the meeting; and

(c) arrange for a record to be made of the proceedings at the meeting.

(2) The acceptance of a claim in whole or in part under subsection (1) above shall, subject to section 24(3) of this Act, determine the entitlement of a creditor to vote at the statutory meeting.

(3) On the conclusion of the proceedings under subsection (1) above, the interim trustee—

(a) shall make the debtor's list of assets and liabilities and the preliminary statement under section 20(1) of this Act available for inspection;

(b) shall answer to the best of his ability any questions, and shall consider any representations, put to him by the creditors relating to the debtor's assets, business or financial affairs or his conduct in relation thereto;

(c) shall, after considering any such representations as are mentioned in paragraph (b) above, indicate whether, in his opinion, the debtor's assets are unlikely to be sufficient as mentioned in section 20(1) of this Act; and

(d) shall prepare (either at or as soon as possible after the statutory meeting), a final statement of the debtor's affairs.

(4) Where the interim trustee has indicated under subsection (3)(c) above that, in his opinion, the debtor's assets are unlikely to be sufficient as mentioned in section 20(1) of this Act, he shall forthwith make a report of the proceedings at the statutory meeting to the sheriff who shall thereupon appoint the interim trustee as the permanent trustee; and the provisions of this Act shall have effect as regards the sequestration subject to such modifications, and with such further provisions, as are set out in Schedule 2 to this Act.

(5) The interim trustee shall as soon as possible after the statutory meeting send a copy of the statement prepared by him under subsection (3)(d) above, together with an intimation as to whether or not he intends to apply under section 27(1) of this Act for a certificate of discharge, to—

(a) every creditor known to him; and

(b) the Accountant in Bankruptcy.

Election of permanent trustee

24.—(1) Where subsection (4) of section 23 of this Act is not applicable, the creditors shall, at the conclusion of the proceedings under subsection (3) of that section, proceed at the statutory meeting to the election of the permanent trustee.

(2) None of the following persons shall be eligible for election as perma-

nent trustee, nor shall anyone who becomes such a person after having been elected as permanent trustee be qualified to continue to act as permanent trustee—

(a) the debtor;

(b) a person who is not qualified to act as an insolvency practitioner or who, though qualified to act as an insolvency practitioner, is not qualified to act as such in relation to the debtor;

(c) a person who holds an interest opposed to the general interests of the creditors;

(d) a person who resides outwith the jurisdiction of the Court of Session.

(3) The following persons shall not be entitled to vote in the election of the permanent trustee—

(a) anyone acquiring a debt due by the debtor, otherwise than by succession, after the date of sequestration;

(b) any creditor to the extent that his debt is a postponed debt.

(4) If no creditor entitled to vote in the election of the permanent trustee attends the statutory meeting or if no permanent trustee is elected, the interim trustee shall forthwith—

(a) so notify the Accountant in Bankruptcy; and

(b) report the proceedings at the statutory meeting to the sheriff, who shall thereupon appoint the interim trustee as the permanent trustee.

(5) Where subsection (4) above applies, the provisions of this Act shall have effect as regards the sequestration subject to such modifications, and with such further provisions, as are set out in Schedule 2 to this Act.

Confirmation of permanent trustee

25.—(1) On the election of the permanent trustee—

(a) the interim trustee shall forthwith make a report of the proceedings at the statutory meeting to the sheriff; and

(b) the debtor, a creditor, the interim trustee, the permanent trustee or the Accountant in Bankruptcy may, within four days after the statutory meeting, object to any matter connected with the election; and such objection shall be by summary application to the sheriff, specifying the grounds on which the objection is taken.

(2) If there is no timeous objection under subsection (1)(b) above, the sheriff shall forthwith declare the elected person to be the permanent trustee; and the sheriff shall confirm his election and the sheriff clerk shall issue to him an act and warrant in a form prescribed by the Court of Session by act of sederunt and send a copy of the act and warrant to the Accountant in Bankruptcy.

(3) If there is a timeous objection under subsection (1)(b) above, the sheriff shall forthwith give parties an opportunity to be heard thereon and shall give his decision.

(4) If in his decision under subsection (3) above the sheriff—

(a) rejects the objection, subsection (2) above shall apply as if there had been no timeous objection;

(b) sustains the objection, he shall order the interim trustee to arrange a new meeting for the election of a permanent trustee; and sections 23 and 24 of this Act and this section shall apply in relation to such a meeting.

(5) Any declaration, confirmation or decision of the sheriff under this section shall be final, and no expense in objecting under this section shall fall on the debtor's estate.

(6) The permanent trustee shall—

(a) insert a copy of the said act and warrant in the sederunt book; and

(b) where he is not the same person as the interim trustee, publish a notice in the *Edinburgh Gazette* in the prescribed form stating that he has been confirmed in office as permanent trustee.

Provisions relating to termination of interim trustee's functions

26.—(1) Where the interim trustee does not himself become the permanent trustee, he shall, on confirmation of the permanent trustee in office, hand over to him everything in his possession which relates to the sequestration (including a copy of the debtor's list of assets and liabilities, of the statement prepared under section 23(3)(*d*), and of the written comments sent under section 20(2)(*c*) of this Act) and shall thereupon cease to act in the sequestration.

(2) Within three months of the confirmation in office of the permanent trustee, the interim trustee shall—

(*a*) submit to the Accountant in Bankruptcy—
  (i) his accounts of his intromissions (if any) with the debtor's estate; and
  (ii) a claim for outlays reasonably incurred, and for remuneration for work reasonably undertaken, by him; and

(*b*) send to the permanent trustee (unless the interim trustee has himself become the permanent trustee), a copy of what is submitted to the Accountant in Bankruptcy under paragraph (*a*) above.

(3) On a submission being made to him under subsection (2) above, the Accountant in Bankruptcy—

(*a*) shall—
  (i) audit the accounts; and
  (ii) issue a determination fixing the amount of the outlays and remuneration payable to the interim trustee; and

(*b*) shall send a copy of—
  (i) the said determination to the interim trustee (except where the interim trustee has himself become the permanent trustee); and
  (ii) the interim trustee's audited accounts and of the said determination to the permanent trustee, who shall insert the copies in the sederunt book.

(4) The interim trustee, the permanent trustee, the debtor or any creditor may appeal to the sheriff against a determination under subsection (3)(*a*)(ii) above within 14 days of its issue.

(5) The permanent trustee, on being confirmed in office, shall make such insertions in the sederunt book as are appropriate to provide a record of the sequestration process before his confirmation, but he shall make no insertion therein relating to the written comments made by the interim trustee under section 20(2)(*c*) of this Act.

Discharge of interim trustee

27.—(1) On receiving a copy of the Accountant in Bankruptcy's determination sent under subsection (3)(*b*)(i) of section 26 of this Act the interim trustee may apply to him for a certificate of discharge.

(2) The interim trustee shall send notice of an application under subsection (1) above to the debtor and to the permanent trustee and shall inform the debtor—

(*a*) that he, the permanent trustee or any creditor may make written representations relating to the application to the Accountant in Bankruptcy within a period of 14 days after such notification;

(*b*) that the audited accounts of his intromissions (if any) with the debtor's estate are available for inspection at the office of the interim trustee and that a copy of those accounts has been sent to the permanent trustee for insertion in the sederunt book; and

(*c*) of the effect mentioned in subsection (5) below.

(3) On the expiry of the period mentioned in subsection (2)(*a*) above the

Accountant in Bankruptcy, after considering any representations duly made to him, shall—

(a) grant or refuse to grant the certificate of discharge; and

(b) notify (in addition to the interim trustee) the debtor, the permanent trustee, and all creditors who have made such representations, accordingly.

(4) The interim trustee, the permanent trustee, the debtor or any creditor who has made representations under subsection (2)(a) above may, within 14 days after the issuing of the determination under subsection (3) above, appeal therefrom to the sheriff and if the sheriff determines that a certificate of discharge which has been refused should be granted he shall order the Accountant in Bankruptcy to grant it; and the sheriff clerk shall send a copy of the decree of the sheriff to the Accountant in Bankruptcy.

(5) The grant of a certificate of discharge under this section by the Accountant in Bankruptcy shall have the effect of discharging the interim trustee from all liability (other than any liability arising from fraud) to the creditors or to the debtor in respect of any act or omission of the interim trustee in exercising the functions conferred on him by this Act.

(6) Where a certificate of discharge is granted under this section, the permanent trustee shall make an appropriate entry in the sederunt book.

(7) Where the interim trustee has died, resigned office or been removed from office, then once the accounts of his intromissions (if any) with the debtor's estate are or have been submitted to and audited by the Accountant in Bankruptcy, the Accountant in Bankruptcy shall issue a determination fixing the amount of the outlays and remuneration payable to the interim trustee and the provisions of subsection (4) of section 26 of this Act and the foregoing provisions of this section shall, subject to any necessary modifications, apply in relation to that interim trustee or, if he has died, to his executor as they apply in relation to an interim trustee receiving a copy of such a determination under subsection (3)(b)(i) of that section.

Replacement of permanent trustee

Resignation and death of permanent trustee

28.—(1) The permanent trustee may resign office if—

(a) the creditors, at a meeting called for the purpose, accept his resignation and thereupon elect a new permanent trustee; or

(b) on an application by the permanent trustee, the sheriff is satisfied that he should be permitted to resign; but the sheriff may make the granting of an application under this paragraph subject to the election of a new permanent trustee and to such conditions as he thinks appropriate in all the circumstances of the case.

(2) Where the sheriff grants an application under paragraph (b) of subsection (1) above—

(a) except where paragraph (b) below applies, the commissioners, or if there are no commissioners, the Accountant in Bankruptcy, shall call a meeting of the creditors to be held not more than 28 days after the permanent trustee has resigned, for the election by them of a new permanent trustee;

(b) if the application has been granted subject to the election of a new permanent trustee, the resigning permanent trustee shall himself call a meeting of the creditors, to be held not more than 28 days after the granting of the application, for the purpose referred to in paragraph (a) above.

(3) Where the commissioners become, or if there are no commissioners the Accountant in Bankruptcy becomes, aware that the permanent trustee has died, they or as the case may be the Accountant in Bankruptcy shall as soon as practicable after becoming so aware call a meeting of creditors for the election by the creditors of a new permanent trustee.

(4) The foregoing provisions of this Act relating to the election and confirmation in office of the permanent trustee shall, subject to any necessary modifications, apply in relation to the election and confirmation in office of a new permanent trustee in pursuance of subsection (1), (2) or (3) above.

(5) Where no new permanent trustee is elected in pursuance of subsection (2) or (3) above, a person nominated by the Accountant in Bankruptcy from the list of interim trustees, not being a person ineligible for election as permanent trustee under section 24(2) of this Act, shall forthwith apply to the sheriff for appointment as permanent trustee, and the sheriff shall thereupon so appoint him; and the provisions of this Act shall have effect as regards the sequestration subject to such modifications and with such further provisions as are set out in Schedule 2 to this Act.

(6) The new permanent trustee may require—

(a) delivery to him of all documents relating to the sequestration in the possession of the former trustee or his representatives, except the former trustee's accounts of which he shall be entitled to delivery of only a copy;

(b) the former trustee or his representatives to submit the trustee's accounts for audit to the commissioners or, if there are no commissioners, to the Accountant in Bankruptcy, and the commissioners or the Accountant in Bankruptcy shall issue a determination fixing the amount of the outlays and remuneration payable to the trustee or representatives in accordance with section 53 of this Act.

(7) The former trustee or his representatives, the new permanent trustee, the debtor or any creditor may appeal against a determination issued under subsection (6)(b) above within 14 days after it is issued—

(a) where it is a determination of the commissioners, to the Accountant in Bankruptcy; and

(b) where it is a determination of the Accountant in Bankruptcy, to the sheriff;

and the determination of the Accountant in Bankruptcy under paragraph (a) above shall be appealable to the sheriff.

Removal of permanent trustee and trustee not acting

29.—(1) The permanent trustee may be removed from office—

(a) by the creditors (other than any such person as is mentioned in section 24(3) of this Act) at a meeting called for the purpose if they also elect forthwith a new permanent trustee; or

(b) without prejudice to section 1(3) of this Act, by order of the sheriff, on the application of—

    (i) the Accountant in Bankruptcy;

    (ii) the commissioners; or

    (iii) a person representing not less than one quarter in value of the creditors,

if the sheriff is satisfied that cause has been shown on the basis of circumstances other than those to which subsection (9) below applies.

(2) The sheriff shall order any application under subsection (1)(b) above to be served on the permanent trustee and intimated in the *Edinburgh Gazette*, and before disposing of the application shall give the permanent trustee an opportunity of being heard.

(3) On an application under subsection (1)(b) above, the sheriff may, in ordering the removal of the permanent trustee from office, make such further order as he thinks fit or may, instead of removing the permanent trustee from office, make such other order as he thinks fit.

(4) The permanent trustee, the Accountant in Bankruptcy, the commissioners or any creditor may appeal against the decision of the sheriff on

an application under subsection (1)(*b*) above within 14 days after the date of that decision.

(5) If the permanent trustee has been removed from office under subsection (1)(*b*) above or under section 1(3) of this Act or following an appeal under subsection (4) above, the commissioners or, if there are no commissioners, the Accountant in Bankruptcy shall call a meeting of creditors, to be held not more than 28 days after such removal, for the election by them of a new permanent trustee.

(6) Without prejudice to section 1(3) of this Act, where the sheriff is satisfied of any of the circumstances to which subsection (9) below applies he may, on the application of a commissioner, the debtor, a creditor or the Accountant in Bankruptcy, and after such intimation as the sheriff considers necessary—

(*a*) declare the office of permanent trustee to have become or to be vacant; and

(*b*) make any necessary order to enable the sequestration to proceed or to safeguard the estate pending the election of a new permanent trustee;

and thereafter the commissioners or, if there are no commissioners, the Accountant in Bankruptcy shall call a meeting of creditors, to be held not more than 28 days after such declaration, for the election by them of a new permanent trustee.

(7) The foregoing provisions of this Act relating to the election and confirmation in office of the permanent trustee shall, subject to any necessary modifications, apply in relation to the election and confirmation in office of a new permanent trustee in pursuance of subsection (5) or (6) above.

(8) Subsections (5) to (7) of section 28 of this Act shall apply for the purposes of this section as they apply for the purposes of that section.

(9) The circumstances to which this subsection applies are that the permanent trustee—

(*a*) is unable to act (whether by, under or by virtue of a provision of this Act or from any other cause whatsoever other than death); or

(*b*) has so conducted himself that he should no longer continue to act in the sequestration.

Election, resignation and removal of commissioners

Election, resignation and removal of commissioners

30.—(1) At the statutory meeting or any subsequent meeting of creditors, the creditors (other than any such person as is mentioned in section 24(3) of this Act) may, from among the creditors or their mandatories, elect one or more commissioners (or new or additional commissioners); but not more than five commissioners shall hold office in any sequestration at any one time.

(2) None of the following persons shall be eligible for election as a commissioner, nor shall anyone who becomes such a person after having been elected as a commissioner be entitled to continue to act as a commissioner—

(*a*) any person mentioned in paragraph (*a*) or (*c*) of section 24(2) of this Act as not being eligible for election;

(*b*) a person who is an associate of the debtor or of the permanent trustee.

(3) A commissioner may resign office at any time.

(4) Without prejudice to section 1(3) of this Act, a commissioner may be removed from office—

(*a*) if he is a mandatory of a creditor, by the creditor recalling the mandate and intimating in writing its recall to the permanent trustee;

(*b*) by the creditors (other than any such person as is mentioned in section 24(3) of this Act) at a meeting called for the purpose.

Vesting of estate in permanent trustee

Vesting of estate at date of sequestration

31.—(1) Subject to section 33 of this Act, the whole estate of the debtor shall vest as at the date of sequestration in the permanent trustee for the benefit of the creditors; and—

(*a*) the estate shall so vest by virtue of the act and warrant issued on confirmation of the permanent trustee's appointment; and

(*b*) the act and warrant shall, in respect of the heritable estate in Scotland of the debtor, have the same effect as if a decree of adjudication in implement of sale, as well as a decree of adjudication for payment and in security of debt, subject to no legal reversion, had been pronounced in favour of the permanent trustee.

(2) The exercise by the permanent trustee of any power conferred on him by this Act in respect of any heritable estate vested in him by virtue of the act and warrant shall not be challengeable on the ground of any prior inhibition (reserving any effect of such inhibition on ranking).

(3) Where the debtor has an uncompleted title to any heritable estate in Scotland, the permanent trustee may complete title thereto either in his own name or in the name of the debtor, but completion of title in the name of the debtor shall not validate by accretion any unperfected right in favour of any person other than the permanent trustee.

(4) Any moveable property, in respect of which but for this subsection—

(*a*) delivery or possession; or

(*b*) intimation of its assignation,

would be required in order to complete title to it, shall vest in the permanent trustee by virtue of the act and warrant as if at the date of sequestration the permanent trustee had taken delivery or possession of the property or had made intimation of its assignation to him, as the case may be.

(5) Any non-vested contingent interest which the debtor has shall vest in the permanent trustee as if an assignation of that interest had been executed by the debtor and intimation thereof made at the date of sequestration.

(6) Any person claiming a right to any estate claimed by the permanent trustee may apply to the court for the estate to be excluded from such vesting, a copy of the application being served on the permanent trustee; and the court shall grant the application if it is satisfied that the estate should not be so vested.

(7) Where any successor of a deceased debtor whose estate has been sequestrated has made up title to, or is in possession of, any part of that estate, the court may, on the application of the permanent trustee, order the successor to convey such estate to him.

[1] (8) In subsection (1) above the "whole estate of the debtor" means, subject to subsection (9) below, his whole estate at the date of sequestration, wherever situated, including—

(*a*) any income or estate vesting in the debtor on that date; and

(*b*) the capacity to exercise and to take proceedings for exercising, all such powers in, over, or in respect of any property as might have been exercised by the debtor for his own benefit as at, or on, the date of sequestration or might be exercised on a relevant date (within the meaning of section 32(10) of this Act).

[2] (9) Subject to subsection (10) below, the "whole estate of the debtor" does not include any interest of the debtor as tenant under any of the following tenancies—

(*a*) a tenancy which is an assured tenancy within the meaning of Part II of the Housing (Scotland) Act 1988, or

(*b*) a protected tenancy within the meaning of the Rent (Scotland) Act 1984 in respect of which, by virtue of any provision of Part VIII of that Act, no premium can lawfully be required as a condition of the assignation, or

(*c*) a secure tenancy within the meaning of Part III of the Housing (Scotland) Act 1987.

[2] (10) On the date on which the permanent trustee serves notice to that effect on the debtor, the interest of the debtor as tenant under any of the tenancies referred to in subsection (9) above shall form part of his estate and vest in the permanent trustee as if it had vested in him under section 32(6) of this Act.

NOTES

[1] See the Drug Trafficking Offences Act 1986, s.16(2) and the Criminal Justice Act 1988, s.85. As amended by the Housing Act 1988, s.118. Excluded by the Social Security Act 1989, Sched. 4, para. 8(2). Amended (*prosp.*) by *ibid.*, para. 23.

[2] Inserted by the Housing Act 1988, s.118.

Vesting of estate, and dealings of debtor, after sequestration

32.—(1) Subject to subsection (2) below, any income of whatever nature received by the debtor on a relevant date, other than income arising from the estate which is vested in the permanent trustee, shall vest in the debtor.

[1] (2) The sheriff, on the application of the permanent trustee, may, after

[THE NEXT PAGE IS H 159]

having regard to all the circumstances, determine a suitable amount to allow for—

 (*a*) aliment for the debtor; and

2 (*b*) the debtor's relevant obligations;

and if the debtor's income is in excess of the total amount so allowed the sheriff shall fix the amount of the excess and order it to be paid to the permanent trustee.

(3) The debtor's relevant obligations referred to in paragraph (*b*) of subsection (2) above are—

 (*a*) any obligation of aliment owed by him ("obligation of aliment" having the same meaning as in the Family Law (Scotland) Act 1985);

 (*b*) any obligation of his to make a periodical allowance to a former spouse;

but any amount allowed under that subsection for the relevant obligations need not be sufficient for compliance with a subsisting order or agreement as regards such aliment or periodical allowance.

(4) In the event of any change in the debtor's circumstances, the sheriff, on the application of the permanent trustee, the debtor or any other interested person, may vary or recall any order under subsection (2) above.

(5) Diligence in respect of a debt or obligation of which the debtor would be discharged under section 55 of this Act were he discharged under section 54 thereof shall not be competent against income vesting in him under subsection (1) above.

(6) Without prejudice to subsection (1) above, any estate, wherever situated, which—

 (*a*) is acquired by the debtor on a relevant date; and

 (*b*) would have vested in the permanent trustee if it had been part of the debtor's estate on the date of sequestration,

shall vest in the permanent trustee for the benefit of the creditors as at the date of acquisition; and any person who holds any such estate shall, on production to him of a copy of the act and warrant certified by the sheriff clerk confirming the permanent trustee's appointment, convey or deliver the estate to the permanent trustee:

Provided that—

 (i) if such a person has in good faith and without knowledge of the sequestration conveyed the estate to the debtor or to anyone on the instructions of the debtor, he shall incur no liability to the permanent trustee except to account for any proceeds of the conveyance which are in his hands; and

 (ii) this subsection shall be without prejudice to any right or interest acquired in the estate in good faith and for value.

(7) The debtor shall immediately notify the permanent trustee of any assets acquired by him on a relevant date or of any other substantial change in his financial circumstances; and, if the debtor fails to comply with this subsection, he shall be guilty of an offence and liable on summary conviction to a fine not exceeding level 5 on the standard scale or to imprisonment for a term not exceeding three months or to both.

(8) Subject to subsection (9) below, any dealing of or with the debtor relating to his estate vested in the permanent trustee under section 31 of this Act shall be of no effect in a question with the permanent trustee.

(9) Subsection (8) above shall not apply where the person seeking to uphold the dealing establishes—

 (*a*) that the permanent trustee—

  (i) has abandoned to the debtor the property to which the dealing relates;

  (ii) has expressly or impliedly authorised the dealing; or

  (iii) is otherwise personally barred from challenging the dealing, or

 (*b*) that the dealing is—

  (i) the performance of an obligation undertaken before the date of sequestration by a person obliged to the debtor in the obligation;

   (ii) the purchase from the debtor of goods for which the purchaser has given value to the debtor or is willing to give value to the permanent trustee; or

  (iii) a banking transaction in the ordinary course of business between the banker and the debtor,

and that the person dealing with the debtor was, at the time when the dealing occurred, unaware of the sequestration and had at that time no reason to believe that the debtor's estate had been sequestrated or was the subject of sequestration proceedings.

(10) In this section "a relevant date" means a date after the date of sequestration and before the date on which the debtor's discharge becomes effective.

NOTES
[1] See the Drug Trafficking Offences Act 1986, s.16(2).
[2] See the Criminal Justice (Scotland) Act 1987, s.33(2).

Limitations on vesting
   33.—(1) The following property of the debtor shall not vest in the permanent trustee—

   (*a*) property exempted from poinding for the purpose of protecting the debtor and his family;

   (*b*) property held on trust by the debtor for any other person.

(2) The vesting of a debtor's estate in a permanent trustee shall not affect the right of hypothec of a landlord.

(3) Sections 31 and 32 of this Act are without prejudice to the right of any secured creditor which is preferable to the rights of the permanent trustee.

Safeguarding of interests of creditors of insolvent persons

Gratuitous alienations
  [1,2] **34.**—(1) Where this subsection applies, an alienation by a debtor shall be challengeable by—

   (*a*) any creditor who is a creditor by virtue of a debt incurred on or before the date of sequestration, or before the granting of the trust deed or the debtor's death, as the case may be; or

   (*b*) the permanent trustee, the trustee acting under the trust deed or the judicial factor, as the case may be.

(2) Subsection (1) above applies where—

   (*a*) by the alienation, whether before or after the coming into force of this section, any of the debtor's property has been transferred or any claim or right of the debtor has been discharged or renounced; and

   (*b*) any of the following has occurred—

    (i) his estate has been sequestrated (other than, in the case of a natural person, after his death); or

   (ii) he has granted a trust deed which has become a protected trust deed; or

  (iii) he has died and within 12 months after his death, his estate has been sequestrated; or

  (iv) he has died and within the said 12 months, a judicial factor has been appointed under section 11A of the Judicial Factors (Scotland) Act 1889 to administer his estate and the estate was absolutely insolvent at the date of death; and

   (*c*) the alienation took place on a relevant day.

(3) For the purposes of paragraph (*c*) of subsection (2) above, the day on which an alienation took place shall be the day on which the alienation became completely effectual; and in that paragraph "relevant day" means, if the alienation has the effect of favouring—

(*a*) a person who is an associate of the debtor, a day not earlier than five years before the date of sequestration, the granting of the trust deed or the debtor's death, as the case may be; or

(*b*) any other person, a day not earlier than two years before the said date.

(4) On a challenge being brought under subsection (1) above, the court shall grant decree of reduction or for such restoration of property to the debtor's estate or other redress as may be appropriate, but the court shall not grant such a decree if the person seeking to uphold the alienation establishes—

(*a*) that immediately, or at any other time, after the alienation the debtor's assets were greater than his liabilities; or

(*b*) that the alienation was made for adequate consideration; or

(*c*) that the alienation—
   (i) was a birthday, Christmas or other conventional gift; or
   (ii) was a gift made, for a charitable purpose, to a person who is not an associate of the debtor,

which having regard to all the circumstances, it was reasonable for the debtor to make:

Provided that this subsection shall be without prejudice to any right or interest acquired in good faith and for the value from or through the transferee in the alienation.

(5) In subsection (4) above, "charitable purpose" means any charitable, benevolent or philanthropic purpose whether or not it is charitable within the meaning of any rule of law.

(6) For the purposes of the foregoing provisions of this section, an alienation in implementation of a prior obligation shall be deemed to be one for which there was no consideration or no adequate consideration to the extent that the prior obligation was undertaken for no consideration or no adequate consideration.

(7) This section is without prejudice to the operation of section 2 of the Married Women's Policies of Assurance (Scotland) Act 1880 (policy of assurance may be effected in trust for spouse, future spouse and children).

(8) A permanent trustee, the trustee acting under a protected trust deed and a judicial factor appointed under section 11A of the Judicial Factors (Scotland) Act 1889 shall have the same right as a creditor has under any rule of law to challenge an alienation of a debtor made for no consideration or for no adequate consideration.

(9) The permanent trustee shall insert in the sederunt book a copy of any decree under this section affecting the sequestrated estate.

NOTES

[1] See the Drug Trafficking Offences Act 1986, s.16(6).
[2] Restricted by the Criminal Justice (Scotland) Act 1987, s.33(5).

Recalling of order for payment of capital sum on divorce

35.—(1) This section applies where—

(*a*) a court has made an order, whether before or after the coming into force of this section, under section 5 of the Divorce (Scotland) Act 1976 or section 8(2) of the Family Law (Scotland) Act 1985, for the payment by a debtor of a capital sum or under the said section 8(2) for the transfer of property by him;

(*b*) on the date of the making of the order the debtor was absolutely insolvent or was rendered so by implementation of the order; and

(*c*) within five years after the making of the order—
   (i) the debtor's estate has been sequestrated other than after his death; or
   (ii) he has granted a trust deed which has (whether or not within the five years) become a protected trust deed; or
   (iii) he has died and, within 12 months after his death, his estate has been sequestrated; or

(iv) he has died and, within the said 12 months, a judicial factor has been appointed under section 11A of the Judicial Factors (Scotland) Act 1889 to administer his estate.

(2) Where this section applies, the court, on an application brought by the permanent trustee, the trustee acting under the trust deed or the judicial factor, may make an order for recall of the order made under the said section 5 or 8(2) and for the repayment to the applicant of the whole or part of any sum already paid, or as the case may be for the return to the applicant of all or part of any property already transferred, under that order, or, where such property has been sold, for payment to the applicant of all or part of the proceeds of sale:

Provided that before making an order under this subsection the court shall have regard to all the circumstances including, without prejudice to the generality of this proviso, the financial, and other, circumstances (in so far as made known to the court) of the person against whom the order would be made.

(3) Where an application is brought under this section in a case where the debtor's estate has been sequestrated, the permanent trustee shall insert a copy of the decree of recall in the sederunt book.

Unfair preferences
[1,2] **36.**—(1) Subject to subsection (2) below, subsection (4) below applies to a transaction entered into by a debtor, whether before or after the coming into force of this section, which has the effect of creating a preference in favour of a creditor to the prejudice of the general body of creditors, being a preference created not earlier than six months before—

(a) the date of sequestration of the debtor's estate (if, in the case of a natural person, a date within his lifetime); or

(b) the granting by him of a trust deed which has become a protected trust deed; or

(c) his death where, within 12 months after his death—
   (i) his estate has been sequestrated, or
   (ii) a judicial factor has been appointed under section 11A of the Judicial Factors (Scotland) Act 1889 to administer his estate and his estate was absolutely insolvent at the date of death.

(2) Subsection (4) below shall not apply to any of the following transactions—

(a) a transaction in the ordinary course of trade or business;

(b) a payment in cash for a debt which when it was paid had become payable unless the transaction was collusive with the purpose of prejudicing the general body of creditors;

(c) a transaction whereby the parties thereto undertake reciprocal obligations (whether the performance by the parties of their respective obligations occurs at the same time or at different times) unless the transaction was collusive as aforesaid;

(d) the granting of a mandate by a debtor authorising an arrestee to pay over the arrested funds or part thereof to the arrester where—
   (i) there has been a decree for payment or a warrant for summary diligence; and
   (ii) the decree or warrant has been preceded by an arrestment on the dependence of the action or followed by an arrestment in execution.

(3) For the purposes of subsection (1) above, the day on which a preference was created shall be the day on which the preference became completely effectual.

(4) A transaction to which this subsection applies shall be challengeable by—

(a) any creditor who is a creditor by virtue of a debt incurred on or before the date of sequestration, the granting of the protected trust deed or the debtor's death, as the case may be; or (*b*) the permanent trustee, the trustee acting under the protected trust deed, or the judicial factor, as the case may be.

(5) On a challenge being brought under subsection (4) above, the court, if satisfied that the transaction challenged is a transaction to which this section applies, shall grant decree of reduction or for such restoration of property to the debtor's estate or other redress as may be appropriate:

Provided that this subsection shall be without prejudice to any right or interest acquired in good faith and for value from or through the creditor in whose favour the preference was created.

(6) A permanent trustee, the trustee acting under a protected trust deed and a judicial factor appointed under section 11A of the Judicial Factors (Scotland) Act 1889 shall have the same right as a creditor has under any rule of law to challenge a preference created by a debtor.

(7) The permanent trustee shall insert in the sederunt book a copy of any decree under this section affecting the sequestrated estate.

NOTES
[1] See the Drug Trafficking Offences Act 1986, s.16(6).
[2] Restricted by the Criminal Justice (Scotland) Act 1987, s.33(5).

Effect of sequestration on diligence

Effect of sequestration on diligence
[1] **37.**—(1) The order of the court awarding sequestration shall as from the date of sequestration have the effect, in relation to diligence done (whether before or after the date of sequestration) in respect of any part of the debtor's estate, of—
(*a*) a decree of adjudication of the heritable estate of the debtor for payment of his debts which has been duly recorded in the register of inhibitions and adjudications on that date; and
(*b*) an arrestment in execution and decree of forthcoming, an arrestment in execution and warrant of sale, and a completed poinding, in favour of the creditors according to their respective entitlements.

(2) No inhibition on the estate of the debtor which takes effect within the period of 60 days before the date of sequestration shall be effectual to create a preference for the inhibitor and any relevant right of challenge shall, at the date of sequestration, vest in the permanent trustee as shall any right of the inhibitor to receive payment for the discharge of the inhibition:

Provided that this subsection shall neither entitle the trustee to receive any payment made to the inhibitor before the date of sequestration nor affect the validity of anything done before that date in consideration of such payment.

(3) In subsection (2) above, "any relevant right of challenge" means any right to challenge a deed voluntarily granted by the debtor if it is a right which vested in the inhibitor by virtue of the inhibition.

(4) No arrestment or poinding of the estate of the debtor (including any estate vesting in the permanent trustee under section 32(6) of this Act) executed—
(*a*) within the period of 60 days before the date of sequestration and whether or not subsisting at that date; or
(*b*) on or after the date of sequestration,
shall be effectual to create a preference for the arrester or poinder; and the estate so arrested or poinded, or the proceeds of sale thereof, shall be handed over to the permanent trustee.

(5) An arrester or poinder whose arrestment or poinding is executed within the said period of 60 days shall be entitled to payment, out of the arrested or poinded estate or out of the proceeds of the sale thereof, of the expenses incurred—
(*a*) in obtaining the extract of the decree or other document on which the arrestment or poinding proceeded;

(b) in executing the arrestment or poinding; and

(c) in taking any further action in respect of the diligence.

(6) No poinding of the ground in respect of the estate of the debtor (including any estate vesting in the permanent trustee under section 32(6) of this Act) executed within the period of 60 days before the date of sequestration or on or after that date shall be effectual in a question with the permanent trustee, except for the interest on the debt of a secured creditor, being interest for the current half-yearly term and arrears of interest for one year immediately before the commencement of that term.

(7) The foregoing provisions of this section shall apply to the estate of a deceased debtor which—

(a) has been sequestrated; or

(b) was absolutely insolvent at the date of death and in respect of which a judicial factor has been appointed under section 11A of the Judicial Factors (Scotland) Act 1889,

within 12 months after his death, but as if for any reference to the date of sequestration and the debtor there were substituted respectively a reference to the date of the deceased's death and to the deceased debtor.

(8) It shall be incompetent on or after the date of sequestration for any creditor to raise or insist in an adjudication against the estate of a debtor (including any estate vesting in the permanent trustee under section 32(6) of this Act) or to be confirmed as executor-creditor on the estate.

(9) Where—

(a) a deceased debtor's estate is sequestrated; or

(b) a judicial factor is appointed under section 11A of the Judicial Factors (Scotland) Act 1889 to administer his estate (in a case where the estate is absolutely insolvent),

within 12 months after the debtor's death, no confirmation as executor-creditor on that estate at any time after the debtor's death shall be effectual in a question with the permanent trustee or the judicial factor; but the executor-creditor shall be entitled out of that estate, or out of the proceeds of sale thereof, to the expenses incurred by him in obtaining the confirmation.

NOTE

[1] New subs. (5A) inserted (*prosp.*) by the Debtors (Scotland) Act 1987, Sched. 6, para. 27.

Administration of estate by permanent trustee

Taking possession of estate by permanent trustee

38.—(1) The permanent trustee shall—

(a) as soon as may be after his confirmation in office, for the purpose of recovering the debtor's estate under section 3(1)(a) of this Act, and subject to section 40 of this Act, take possession of the debtor's whole estate so far as vesting in the permanent trustee under sections 31 and 32 of this Act and any document in the debtor's possession or control relating to his assets or his business or financial affairs;

(b) make up and maintain an inventory and valuation of the estate which he shall record in the sederunt book; and

(c) forthwith thereafter send a copy of any such inventory and valuation to the Accountant in Bankruptcy.

(2) The permanent trustee shall be entitled to have access to all documents relating to the assets or the business or financial affairs of the debtor sent by or on behalf of the debtor to a third party and in that third party's hands and to make copies of any such documents.

(3) If any person obstructs a permanent trustee who is exercising, or attempting to exercise, a power conferred by subsection (2) above, the

sheriff, on the application of the permanent trustee, may order that person to cease so to obstruct the permanent trustee.

(4) The permanent trustee may require delivery to him of any title deed or other document of the debtor, notwithstanding that a right of lien is claimed over the title deed or document; but this subsection is without prejudice to any preference of the holder of the lien.

[THE NEXT PAGE IS H 165]

Management and realisation of estate

39.—[1] (1) As soon as may be after his confirmation in office, the permanent trustee shall consult with the commissioners or, if there are no commissioners, with the Accountant in Bankruptcy concerning the exercise of his functions under section 3(1)(*a*) of this Act; and, subject to subsection (6) below, the permanent trustee shall comply with any general or specific directions given to him, as the case may be—

(*a*) by the creditors;

(*b*) on the application under this subsection of the commissioners, by the court; or

(*c*) if there are no commissioners, by the Accountant in Bankruptcy,

as to the exercise by him of such functions.

[1] (2) The permanent trustee may, but if there are commissioners only with the consent of the commissioners, the creditors or the court, do any of the following things if he considers that its doing would be beneficial for the administration of the estate—

(*a*) carry on any business of the debtor;

(*b*) bring, defend or continue any legal proceedings relating to the estate of the debtor;

(*c*) create a security over any part of the estate;

(*d*) where any right, option or other power forms part of the debtor's estate, make payments or incur liabilities with a view to obtaining, for the benefit of the creditors, any property which is the subject of the right option or power.

(3) Any sale of the debtor's estate by the permanent trustee may be by either public sale or private bargain.

(4) The following rules shall apply to the sale of any part of the debtor's heritable estate over which a heritable security is held by a creditor or creditors if the rights of the secured creditor or creditors are preferable to those of the permanent trustee—

(*a*) the permanent trustee may sell that part only with the concurrence of every such creditor unless he obtains a sufficiently high price to discharge every such security;

(*b*) subject to paragraph (*c*) below, the following acts shall be precluded—

(i) the taking of steps by a creditor to enforce his security over that part after the permanent trustee has intimated to the creditor that he intends to sell it;

(ii) the commencement by the permanent trustee of the procedure for the sale of that part after a creditor has intimated to the permanent trustee that he intends to commence the procedure for its sale;

(*c*) where the permanent trustee or a creditor has given intimation under paragraph (*b*) above, but has unduly delayed in proceeding with the sale, then, if authorised by the court in the case of intimation under—

(i) sub-paragraph (i) of that paragraph, any creditor to whom intimation has been given may enforce his security; or

(ii) sub-paragraph (ii) of that paragraph, the permanent trustee may sell that part.

(5) The function of the permanent trustee under section 3(1)(*a*) of this Act to realise the debtor's estate shall include the function of selling, with or without recourse against the estate, debts owing to the estate.

(6) The permanent trustee may sell any perishable goods without complying with any directions given to him under subsection (1)(*a*) or (*c*) above if the permanent trustee considers that compliance with such directions would adversely affect the sale.

(7) The validity of the title of any purchaser shall not be challengeable on

the ground that there has been a failure to comply with a requirement of this section.

(8) It shall be incompetent for the permanent trustee or an associate of his or for any commissioner, to purchase any of the debtor's estate in pursuance in this section.

NOTE

[1] See also ss. 23(4), 24(5), 28(5) and Sched. 2, para. 7.

Power of permanent trustee in relation to the debtor's family home

40.—(1) Before the permanent trustee sells or disposes of any right or interest in the debtor's family home he shall—

(a) obtain the relevant consent; or

(b) where he is unable to do so, obtain the authority of the court in accordance with subsection (2) below.

(2) Where the permanent trustee requires to obtain the authority of the court in terms of subsection (1)(b) above, the court, after having regard to all the circumstances of the case, including—

(a) the needs and financial resources of the debtor's spouse or former spouse;

(b) the needs and financial resources of any child of the family;

(c) the interests of the creditors;

(d) the length of the period during which (whether before or after the relevant date) the family home was used as a residence by any of the persons referred to in paragraph (a) or (b) above,

may refuse to grant the application or may postpone the granting of the application for such period (not exceeding 12 months) as it may consider reasonable in the circumstances or may grant the application subject to such conditions as it may prescribe.

(3) Subsection (2) above shall apply—

(a) to an action for division and sale of the debtor's family home; or

(b) to an action for the purpose of obtaining vacant possession of the debtor's family home,

brought by the permanent trustee as it applies to an application under subsection (1)(b) above and, for the purposes of this subsection, any reference in the said subsction (2) to that granting of the application shall be construed as a reference to the granting of decree in the action.

(4) In this section—

(a) "family home" means any property in which, at the relevant date, the debtor had (whether alone or in common with any other person) a right or interest, being property which was occupied at that date as a residence by the debtor and his spouse or by the debtor's spouse or former spouse (in any case with or without a child of the family) or by the debtor with a child of the family;

(b) "child of the family" includes any child or grandchild of either the debtor or his spouse or former spouse, and any person who has been brought up or accepted by either the debtor or his spouse or former spouse as if he or she were a child of the debtor, spouse or former spouse whatever the age of such a child, grandchild or person may be;

(c) "relevant consent" means in relation to the sale or disposal of any right or interest in a family home—

(i) in a case where the family home is occupied by the debtor's spouse or former spouse, the consent of the spouse, or, as the case may be, the former spouse, whether or not the family home is also occupied by the debtor;

(ii) where sub-paragraph (i) above does not apply, in a case where the family home is occupied by the debtor with a child of the family, the consent of the debtor; and (*d*) "relevant date" means the day immediately preceding the date of sequestration.

Protection of rights of spouse against arrangements intended to defeat them

41.—(1) If a debtor's sequestrated estate includes a matrimonial home of which the debtor, immediately before the date of issue of the act and warrant of the permanent trustee (or, if more than one such act and warrant is issued in the sequestration, of the first such issued) was an entitled spouse and the other spouse is a non-entitled spouse—

(*a*) the permanent trustee shall, where he—
    (i) is aware that the entitled spouse is married to the non-entitled spouse; and
    (ii) knows where the non-entitled spouse is residing,
inform the non-entitled spouse, within the period of 14 days beginning with that date, of the fact that sequestration of the entitled spouse's estate has been awarded, of the right of petition which exists under section 16 of this Act and of the effect of paragraph (*b*) below; and

(*b*) the Court of Session, on the petition under section 16 of this Act of the non-entitled spouse presented either within the period of 40 days beginning with that date or within the period of 10 weeks beginning with the date of sequestration may—
    (i) under section 17 of this Act recall the sequestration; or
    (ii) make such order as it thinks appropriate to protect the occupancy rights of the non-entitled spouse;
if it is satisfied that the purpose of the petition for sequestration was wholly or mainly to defeat the occupancy rights of the non-entitled spouse.

(2) In subsection (1) above—

"entitled spouse" and "non-entitled spouse" have the same meanings as in section 6 of the Matrimonial Homes (Family Protection) (Scotland) Act 1981;

"matrimonial home" has the meaning assigned by section 22 of that Act as amended by the Law Reform (Miscellaneous Provisions) (Scotland) Act 1985; and

"occupancy rights" has the meaning assigned by section 1(4) of the said Act of 1981.

Contractual powers of permanent trustee

42.—(1) Subject to subsections (2) and (3) below, the permanent trustee may adopt any contract entered into by the debtor before the date of sequestration where he considers that its adoption would be beneficial to the administration of the debtor's estate, except where the adoption is precluded by the express or implied terms of the contract, or may refuse to adopt any such contract.

(2) The permanent trustee shall, within 28 days from the receipt by him of a request in writing from any party to a contract entered into by the debtor or within such longer period of that receipt as the court on application by the permanent trustee may allow, adopt or refuse to adopt the contract.

(3) If the permanent trustee does not reply in writing to the request under subsection (2) above within the said period of 28 days or longer period, as the case may be, he shall be deemed to have refused to adopt the contract.

(4) The permanent trustee may enter into any contract where he considers that this would be beneficial for the administration of the debtor's estate.

Money received by permanent trustee

43.—(1) Subject to subsection (2) below, all money received by the permanent trustee in the exercise of his functions shall be deposited by him in the name of the debtor's estate in an appropriate bank or institution.

(2) The permanent trustee may at any time retain in his hands a sum not exceeding £200 or such other sum as may be prescribed.

Examination of debtor

Private examination

[1] **44.**—(1) The permanent trustee may request—

(*a*) the debtor to appear before him and to give information relating to his assets, his dealings with them or his conduct in relation to his business or financial affairs; or

(*b*) the debtor's spouse or any other person who the permanent trustee believes can give such information (in this Act such spouse or other person being referred to as a "relevant person"), to give that information,

and, if he considers it necessary, the permanent trustee may apply to the sheriff for an order to be made under subsection (2) below.

(2) Subject to section 46(2) of this Act, on application to him under subsection (1) above the sheriff may make an order requiring the debtor or a relevant person to attend for private examination before him on a date (being not earlier than eight days nor later than 16 days after the date of the order) and at a time specified in the order.

(3) A person who fails without reasonable excuse to comply with an order made under subsection (2) above shall be guilty of an offence and liable on summary conviction to a fine not exceeding level 5 on the standard scale or to imprisonment for a term not exceeding three months or to both.

(4) Where the debtor is an entity whose estate may be sequestrated by virtue of section 6(1) of this Act, the references in this section and in sections 45 to 47 of this Act to the debtor shall be construed, unless the context otherwise requires, as references to a person representing the entity.

NOTE

[1] See also ss. 23(4), 24(5), 28(5) and Sched. 2, para. 8.

Public examination

[1] **45.**—(1) Not less than eight weeks before the end of the first accounting period, the permanent trustee—

(*a*) may; or

(*b*) if requested to do so by the Accountant in Bankruptcy or the commissioners (if any) or one quarter in value of the creditors, shall,

apply to the sheriff for an order for the public examination before the sheriff of the debtor or of a relevant person relating to the debtor's assets, his dealings with them or his conduct in relation to his business or financial affairs:

Provided that, on cause shown, such application may be made by the permanent trustee at any time.

(2) Subject to section 46(2) of this Act, the sheriff, on an application under subsection (1) above, shall make an order requiring the debtor or relevant person to attend for examination before him in open court on a date (being not earlier than eight days nor later than 16 days after the date of the order) and at a time specified in the order.

(3) On the sheriff making an order under subsection (2) above, the permanent trustee shall—

(*a*) publish in the *Edinburgh Gazette* a notice in such form and containing such particulars as may be prescribed; and

(*b*) send a copy of the said notice—
  (i) to every creditor known to the permanent trustee; and
  (ii) where the order is in respect of a relevant person, to the debtor, and

inform the creditor and, where applicable, the debtor that he may participate in the examination.

(4) A person who fails without reasonable excuse to comply with an order made under subsection (2) above shall be guilty of an offence and liable on summary conviction to a fine not exceeding level 5 on the standard scale or to imprisonment for a term not exceeding three months or to both.

NOTE
[1] See also ss. 23(4), 24(5), 28(5) and Sched. 2, para. 8.

Provisions ancillary to sections 44 and 45
46.—(1) If the debtor or relevant person is residing—
(*a*) in Scotland, the sheriff may, on the application of the permanent trustee, grant a warrant which may be executed by a messenger-at-arms or sheriff officer anywhere in Scotland; or
(*b*) in any other part of the United Kingdom, the Court of Session or the sheriff may, on the application of the permanent trustee, request any court having jurisdiction where the debtor or the relevant person, as the case may be, resides to take appropriate steps, which shall be enforceable by that court,
to apprehend the debtor or relevant person and have him taken to the place of the examination:

Provided that a warrant under paragraph (*a*) above shall not be granted nor a request under paragraph (*b*) above made unless the court is satisfied that it is necessary to do so to secure the attendance of the debtor or relevant person at the examination.

(2) If the debtor or a relevant person is for any good reason prevented from attending for examination, the sheriff may, without prejudice to subsection (3) below, grant a commission to take his examination (the commissioner being in this section and section 47 below referred to as an "examining commissioner").

(3) The sheriff or the examining commissioner may at any time adjourn the examination to such day as the sheriff or the examining commissioner may fix.

(4) The sheriff or the examining commissioner may order the debtor or a relevant person to produce for inspection any document in his custody or control relating to the debtor's assets, his dealings with them or his conduct in relation to his business or financial affairs, and to deliver the document or a copy thereof to the permanent trustee for further examination by him.

Conduct of examination
47.—(1) The examination, whether before the sheriff or an examining commissioner, shall be taken on oath.
(2) At the examination—
(*a*) the permanent trustee or a solicitor or counsel acting on his behalf and, in the case of public examination, any creditor may question the debtor or a relevant person; and
(*b*) the debtor may question a relevant person,
as to any matter relating to the debtor's assets, his dealings with them or his conduct in relation to his business or financial affairs.

(3) The debtor or a relevant person shall be required to answer any question relating to the debtor's assets, his dealings with them or his conduct in relation to his business or financial affairs and shall not be excused from answering any such question on the ground that the answer may incriminate or tend to incriminate him or on the ground of confidentiality:

Provided that—

(*a*) a statement made by the debtor or a relevant person in answer to such a question shall not be admissible in evidence in any subsequent criminal proceedings against the person making the statement, except where the proceedings are in respect of a charge of perjury relating to the statement;

(*b*) a person subject to examination shall not be required to disclose any information which he has received from a person who is not called for examination if the information is confidential between them.

[1] (4) The rules relating to the recording of evidence in ordinary causes specified in the First Schedule to the Sheriff Courts (Scotland) Act 1907 shall apply in relation to the recording of evidence at the examination before the sheriff or the examining commissioner.

(5) The debtor's deposition at the examination shall be subscribed by himself and by the sheriff (or, as the case may be, the examining commissioner) and shall be inserted in the sederunt book.

(6) The permanent trustee shall insert a copy of the record of the examination in the sederunt book and send a copy of the record to the Accountant in Bankruptcy.

(7) A relevant person shall be entitled to fees or allowances in respect of his attendance at the examination as if he were a witness in an ordinary civil cause in the sheriff court:

Provided that, if the sheriff thinks that it is appropriate in all the circumstances, he may disallow or restrict the entitlement to such fees or allowances.

NOTE
[1] As amended by S.I. 1986 No. 517.

Submission and adjudication of claims

Submission of claims to permanent trustee
[1] **48.**—(1) Subject to subsection (2) below and subsections (8) and (9) of section 52 of this Act, a creditor in order to obtain an adjudication as to his entitlement—

(*a*) to vote at a meeting of creditors other than the statutory meeting; or

(*b*) (so far as funds are available), to a dividend out of the debtor's estate in respect of any accounting period,

shall submit a claim in accordance with this section to the permanent trustee respectively—

(i) at or before the meeting; or

(ii) not later than eight weeks before the end of the accounting period.

(2) A claim submitted by a creditor—

(*a*) under section 22 of this Act and accepted in whole or in part by the interim trustee for the purpose of voting at the statutory meeting; or

(*b*) under this section and accepted in whole or in part by the permanent trustee for the purpose of voting at a meeting or of drawing a dividend in respect of any accounting period,

shall be deemed to have been re-submitted for the purpose of obtaining an adjudication as to his entitlement both to vote at any subsequent meeting and (so far as funds are available) to a dividend in respect of an accounting period, or, as the case may be, any subsequent accounting period.

(3) Subsections (2) and (3) of section 22 of this Act shall apply for the purposes of this section but as if in the proviso to subsection (2) for the words "interim trustee" there were substituted the words "permanent trustee with the consent of the commissioners, if any", and for any other reference to the interim trustee there were substituted a reference to the permanent trustee.

(4) A creditor who has submitted a claim under this section (or under section 22 of this Act, a statement of claim which has been deemed re-submitted as mentioned in subsection (2) above) may at any time submit a further claim under this section specifying a different amount for his claim:

Provided that a secured creditor shall not be entitled to produce a further claim specifying a different value for the security at any time after the permanent trustee requires the creditor to discharge, or convey or assign, the security under paragraph 5(2) of Schedule 1 to this Act.

(5) The permanent trustee, for the purpose of satisfying himself as to the validity or amount of a claim submitted by a creditor under this section, may require—

(*a*) the creditor to produce further evidence; or

(*b*) any other person who he believes can produce relevant evidence, to produce such evidence,

and, if the creditor or other person refuses or delays to do so, the permanent trustee may apply to the sheriff for an order requiring the creditor or other person to attend for his private examinatioₙ before the sheriff.

(6) Sections 44(2) and (3) and 47(1) of this Act shall apply, subject to any necessary modifications, to the examination of the creditor or other person as they apply to the examination of a relevant person; and references in this subsection and subsection (5) above to a creditor in a case where the creditor is an entity mentioned in section 6(1) of this Act shall be construed, unless the context otherwise requires, as references to a person representing the entity.

(7) Subsections (5) to (10) of section 22 of this Act shall apply for the purposes of this section but as if—

(*a*) in subsection (5) the words "interim trustee or" were omitted;

(*b*) in subsection (7) for the words "interim" and "keep a record of it" there were substituted respectively the words "permanent" and "make an insertion relating thereto in the sederunt book".

(8) At any private examination under subsection (5) above, a solicitor or counsel may act on behalf of the permanent trustee or he may appear himself.

NOTE

[1] See the Criminal Justice (Scotland) Act 1987, s.33(2).

Adjudication of claims

49.—(1) At the commencement of every meeting of creditors (other than the statutory meeting), the permanent trustee shall, for the purposes of section 50 of this Act so far as it relates to voting at that meeting, accept or reject the claim of each creditor.

(2) Where funds are available for payment of a dividend out of the debtor's estate in respect of an accounting period, the permanent trustee for the purpose of determining who is entitled to such a dividend shall, not later than four weeks before the end of the period, accept or reject every claim submitted or deemed to have been re-submitted to him under this Act; and shall at the same time make a decision on any matter requiring to be specified under paragraph (*a*) or (*b*) of subsection (5) below.

(3) If the amount of a claim is stated in foreign currency the permanent trustee in adjudicating on the claim under subsection (1) or (2) above shall convert the amount into sterling, in such manner as may be prescribed, at the rate of exchange prevailing at the close of business on the date of sequestration.

(4) Where the permanent trustee rejects a claim, he shall forthwith notify the creditor giving reasons for the rejection.

(5) Where the permanent trustee accepts or rejects a claim, he shall record in the sederunt book his decision on the claim specifying—

(*a*) the amount of the claim accepted by him,

(*b*) the category of debt, and the value of any security, as decided by him, and

(*c*) if he is rejecting the claim, his reasons therefor.

(6) The debtor or any creditor may, if dissatisfied with the acceptance or rejection of any claim (or, in relation to such acceptance or rejection, with a decision in respect of any matter requiring to be specified under subsection (5)(*a*) or (*b*) above), appeal therefrom to the sheriff—

(*a*) if the acceptance or rejection is under subsection (1) above, within two weeks of that acceptance or rejection;

(*b*) if the acceptance or rejection is under subsection (2) above, not later than two weeks before the end of the accounting period,

and the permanent trustee shall record the sheriff's decision in the sederunt book.

(7) Any reference in this section to the acceptance or rejection of a claim shall be construed as a reference to the acceptance or rejection of the claim in whole or in part.

Entitlement to vote and draw dividend

Entitlement to vote and draw dividend

50. A creditor who has had his claim accepted in whole or in part by the permanent trustee or on appeal under subsection (6) of section 49 of this Act shall be entitled—

(*a*) subject to sections 29(1)(*a*) and 30(1) and (4)(*b*) of this Act, in a case where the acceptance is under (or on appeal arising from) subsection (1) of the said section 49, to vote on any matter at the meeting of creditors for the purpose of voting at which the claim is accepted; and

(*b*) in a case where the acceptance is under (or on appeal arising from) subsection (2) of the said section 49, to payment out of the debtor's estate of a dividend in respect of the accounting period for the purposes of which the claim is accepted; but such entitlement to payment shall arise only in so far as that estate has funds available to make that payment, having regard to section 51 of this Act.

Distribution of debtor's estate

Order of priority in distribution

51.—[1] (1) The funds of the debtor's estate shall be distributed by the permanent trustee to meet the following debts in the order in which they are mentioned—

(*a*) the outlays and remuneration of the interim trustee in the administration of the debtor's estate;

(*b*) the outlays and remuneration of the permanent trustee in the administration of the debtor's estate;

(*c*) where the debtor is a deceased debtor, deathbed and funeral expenses reasonably incurred and expenses reasonably incurred in administering the deceased's estate;

(*d*) the expenses reasonably incurred by a creditor who is a petitioner, or concurs in the petition, for sequestration;

(*e*) preferred debts (excluding any interest which has accrued thereon to the date of sequestration);

(*f*) ordinary debts, that is to say a debt which is neither a secured debt nor a debt mentioned in any other paragraph of this subsection;

(*g*) interest at the rate specified in subsection (7) below on—
   (i) the preferred debts;
   (ii) the ordinary debts,
between the date of sequestration and the date of payment of the debt;

(*h*) any postponed debt.

[2] (2) In this Act "preferred debt" means a debt listed in Part I of Schedule 3 to this Act; and Part II of that Schedule shall have effect for the interpretation of the said Part I.

(3) In this Act "postponed debt" means—

(*a*) a loan made to the debtor, in consideration of a share of the profits in his business, which is postponed under section 3 of the Partnership Act 1890 to the claims of other creditors;

(b) a loan made to the debtor by the debtor's spouse;

(c) a creditor's right to anything vesting in the permanent trustee by virtue of a successful challenge under section 34 of this Act or to the proceeds of sale of such a thing.

(4) Any debt falling within any of paragraphs (c) to (h) of subsection (1) above shall have the same priority as any other debt falling within the same paragraph and, where the funds of the estate are inadequate to enable the debts mentioned in the paragraph to be paid in full, they shall abate in equal proportions.

(5) Any surplus remaining, after all the debts mentioned in this section have been paid in full, shall be made over to the debtor or to his successors or assignees; and in this subsection "surplus" includes any kind of estate but does not include any unclaimed dividend.

(6) Nothing in this section shall affect—

(a) the right of a secured creditor which is preferable to the rights of the permanent trustee; or

(b) any preference of the holder of a lien over a title deed or other document which has been delivered to the permanent trustee in accordance with a requirement under section 38(4) of this Act.

(7) The rate of interest referred to in paragraph (g) of subsection (1) above shall be whichever is the greater of—

(a) the prescribed rate at the date of sequestration; and

(b) the rate applicable to that debt apart from the sequestration.

NOTES
[1] See the Prevention of Terrorism (Temporary Provisions) Act 1989, Sched. 4, para. 31(5)(b).
[2] Applied by the Criminal Justice (Scotland) Act 1987, s.5(8)(b).

Estate to be distributed in respect of accounting periods
52.—(1) Subject to subsection (6) below, the permanent trustee, until the funds of the estate are exhausted, shall make up accounts of his intromissions with the debtor's estate in respect of periods of 26 weeks, the first such period commencing with the date of sequestration.

(2) In this Act "accounting period" shall be construed in accordance with subsections (1) above and (6) below.

(3) Subject to the following provisions of this section, the permanent trustee shall, if the funds of the debtor's estate are sufficient and after making allowance for future contingencies, pay under section 53(7) of this Act a dividend out of the estate to the creditors in respect of each accounting period.

(4) The permanent trustee may pay—

(a) the debts mentioned in subsection (1)(a) to (d) of section 51 of this Act, other than his own remuneration, at any time;

(b) the preferred debts at any time but only with the consent of the commissioners or, if there are no commissioners, of the Accountant in Bankruptcy.

(5) If the permanent trustee—

(a) is not ready to pay a dividend in respect of an accounting period; or

(b) considers it would be inappropriate to pay such a dividend because the expense of doing so would be disproportionate to the amount of the dividend,

he may, with the consent of the commissioners, or if there are no commissioners of the Accountant in Bankruptcy, postpone such payment to a date not later than the time for payment of a dividend in respect of the next accounting period.

(6) Where the permanent trustee considers that it would be expedient to accelerate payment of a dividend other than a dividend in respect of the first accounting period, the accounting period shall be shortened so as to end on such date as the permanent trustee, with the consent of the

commissioners (if any), may specify and the next accounting period shall run from the end of that shortened period; and the permanent trustee shall record in the sederunt book the date so specified.

(7) Where an appeal is taken under section 49(6)(*b*) of this Act against the acceptance or rejection of a creditor's claim, the permanent trustee shall, at the time of payment of dividends and until the appeal is determined, set aside an amount which would be sufficient, if the determination in the appeal were to provide for the claim being accepted in full, to pay a dividend in respect of that claim.

(8) Where a creditor—

(*a*) has failed to produce evidence in support of his claim earlier than eight weeks before the end of an accounting period on being required by the permanent trustee to do so under section 48(5) of this Act; and

(*b*) has given a reason for such failure which is acceptable to the permanent trustee,

the permanent trustee shall set aside, for such time as is reasonable to enable him to produce that evidence or any other evidence that will enable the permanent trustee to be satisfied under the said section 48(5), an amount which would be sufficient, if the claim were accepted in full, to pay a dividend in respect of that claim.

(9) Where a creditor submits a claim to the permanent trustee later than eight weeks before the end of an accounting period but more than eight weeks before the end of a subsequent accounting period in respect of which, after making allowance for contingencies, funds are available for the payment of a dividend, the permanent trustee shall, if he accepts the claim in whole or in part, pay to the creditor—

(*a*) the same dividend or dividends as has or have already been paid to creditors of the same class in respect of any accounting period or periods; and

(*b*) whatever dividend may be payable to him in respect of the said subsequent accounting period:

Provided that paragraph (*a*) above shall be without prejudice to any dividend which has already been paid.

Procedure after end of accounting period

53.—[1] (1) Within two weeks after the end of an accounting period, the permanent trustee shall in respect of that period submit to the commissioners or, if there are no commissioners, to the Accountant in Bankruptcy—

(*a*) his accounts of his intromissions with the debtor's estate for audit and, where funds are available after making allowance for contingencies, a scheme of division of the divisible funds; and

(*b*) a claim for the outlays reasonably incurred by him and for his remuneration;

and, where the said documents are submitted to the commissioners, he shall send a copy of them to the Accountant in Bankruptcy.

(2) All accounts in respect of legal services incurred by the permanent trustee shall, before payment thereof by him, be submitted for taxation to the auditor of the court before which the sequestration is pending:

Provided that the permanent trustee may be authorised by the Accountant in Bankruptcy to pay any such account without taxation.

(3) Within six weeks after the end of an accounting period—

(*a*) the commissioners or, as the case may be, the Accountant in Bankruptcy shall—

(i) audit the accounts; and

(ii) issue a determination fixing the amount of the outlays and the remuneration payable to the permanent trustee; and

(*b*) the permanent trustee shall make the audited accounts, scheme of division and the said determination available for inspection by the debtor and the creditors.

(4) The basis for fixing the amount of the remuneration payable to the permanent trustee may be a commission calculated by reference to the value of the debtor's estate which has been realised by the permanent trustee, but there shall in any event be taken into account—

    (*a*) the work which, having regard to that value, was reasonably undertaken by him; and

    (*b*) the extent of his responsibilities in administering the debtor's estate.

(5) In fixing the amount of such remuneration in respect of the final accounting period, the commissioners or, as the case may be, the Accountant in Bankruptcy may take into account any adjustment which the commissioners or the Accountant in Bankruptcy may wish to make in the amount of the remuneration fixed in respect of any earlier accounting period.

(6) Not later than eight weeks after the end of an accounting period, the permanent trustee, the debtor or any creditor may appeal against a determination issued under subsection (3)(*a*)(ii) above—

    (*a*) where it is a determination of the commissioners, to the Accountant in Bankruptcy; and

    (*b*) where it is a determination of the Accountant in Bankruptcy, to the sheriff;

and the determination of the Accountant in Bankruptcy under paragraph (*a*) above shall be appealable to the sheriff.

(7) On the expiry of the period within which an appeal may be taken under subsection (6) above or, if an appeal is so taken, on the final determination of the last such appeal, the permanent trustee shall pay to the creditors their dividends in accordance with the scheme of division.

(8) Any dividend—

    (*a*) allocated to a creditor which is not cashed or uplifted; or

    (*b*) dependent on a claim in respect of which an amount has been set aside under subsection (7) or (8) of section 52 of this Act,

shall be deposited by the permanent trustee in an appropriate bank or institution.

(9) If a creditor's claim is revalued, the permanent trustee may—

    (*a*) in paying any dividend to that creditor, make such adjustment to it as he considers necessary to take account of that revaluation; or

    (*b*) require the creditor to repay him the whole or part of a dividend already paid to him.

(10) The permanent trustee shall insert in the sederunt book the audited accounts, the scheme of division and the final determination in relation to the permanent trustee's outlays and remuneration.

NOTE
[1] See also ss. 23(4), 24(5), 28(5) and Sched. 2, para. 9.

Discharge of debtor

Automatic discharge after three years

54.—(1) Subject to the following provisions of this section the debtor shall be discharged on the expiry of three years from the date of sequestration.

(2) Every debtor who has been discharged under or by virtue of this section or section 75(4) of this Act may apply to the Accountant in Bankruptcy for a certificate that he has been so discharged; and the Accountant in Bankruptcy, if satisfied of such discharge, shall grant a certificate of discharge in the prescribed form.

(3) The permanent trustee or any creditor may, not later than two years

and nine months after the date of sequestration, apply to the sheriff for a deferment of the debtor's discharge by virtue of subsection (1) above.

(4) On an application being made to him under subsection (3) above, the sheriff shall order—

    (*a*) the applicant to serve the application on the debtor and (if he is not himself the applicant and is not discharged) the permanent trustee; and

    (*b*) the debtor to lodge in court a declaration—

       (i) that he has made a full and fair surrender of his estate and a full disclosure of all claims which he is entitled to make against other persons; and

      (ii) that he has delivered to the interim or permanent trustee every document under his control relating to his estate or his business or financial affairs;

and, if the debtor fails to lodge such a declaration in court within 14 days of being required to do so, the sheriff shall defer his discharge without a hearing for a period not exceeding two years.

(5) If the debtor lodges the declaration in court within the said period of 14 days, the sheriff shall—

    (*a*) fix a date for a hearing not earlier than 28 days after the date of the lodging of the declaration; and

    (*b*) order the applicant to notify the debtor and the permanent trustee or (if he has been discharged) the Accountant in Bankruptcy of the date of the hearing;

and the permanent trustee or (if he has been discharged) the Accountant in Bankruptcy shall, not later than seven days before the date fixed under paragraph (*a*) above, lodge in court a report upon the debtor's assets and liabilities, his financial and business affairs and his conduct in relation thereto and upon the sequestration and his conduct in the course of it.

(6) After considering at the hearing any representations made by the applicant, the debtor or any creditor, the sheriff shall make an order either deferring the discharge for such period not exceeding two years as he thinks appropriate or dismissing the application:

Provided that the applicant or the debtor may appeal against an order under this subsection within 14 days after it is made.

(7) Where the discharge is deferred under subsections (4) or (6) above, the clerk of the court shall send—

    (*a*) a certified copy of the order of the sheriff deferring discharge to the keeper of the register of inhibitions and adjudications for recording in that register; and

    (*b*) a copy of such order to—

      (i) the Accountant in Bankruptcy; and

      (ii) the permanent trustee (if not discharged) for insertion in the sederunt book.

(8) A debtor whose discharge has been deferred under subsection (4) or (6) above may, at any time thereafter and provided that he lodges in court a declaration as to the matters mentioned in sub-paragraphs (i) and (ii) of paragraph (*b*) of the said subsection (4), petition the sheriff for his discharge; and subsections (5) to (7) above shall, with any necessary modifications, apply in relation to the proceedings which shall follow the lodging of a declaration under this subsection as they apply in relation to the proceedings which follow the timeous lodging of a declaration under the said paragraph (*b*).

(9) The permanent trustee or any creditor may, not later than three months before the end of a period of deferment, apply to the sheriff for a further deferment of the discharge; and subsections (4) to (8) above and this subsection shall apply in relation to that further deferment.

Effect of discharge under section 54

55.—(1) Subject to subsection (2) below, on the debtor's discharge under section 54 of this Act, the debtor shall be discharged within the United Kingdom of all debts and obligations contracted by him, or for which he was liable, at the date of sequestration.

[1,2] (2) The debtor shall not be discharged by virtue of subsection (1) above from—

(*a*) any liability to pay a fine or other penalty due to the Crown;

(*b*) any liability to forfeiture of a sum of money deposited in court under section 1(3) of the Bail etc. (Scotland) Act 1980;

(*c*) any liability incurred by reason of fraud or breach of trust;

(*d*) any obligation to pay aliment or any sum of an alimentary nature under any enactment or rule of law or any periodical allowance payable on divorce by virtue of a court order or under an obligation, not being aliment or a periodical allowance which could be included in the amount of a creditor's claim under paragraph 2 of Schedule 1 to this Act;

(*e*) the obligation imposed on him by section 64 of this Act.

NOTES

[1] See the Drug Trafficking Offences Act 1986, s.39(6) and the Criminal Justice Act 1988, Sched. 15, para. 109.

[2] Applied by the Criminal Justice (Scotland) Act 1987, s.45(5)(*c*).

Discharge on composition

56. Schedule 4 to this Act shall have effect in relation to an offer of composition by or on behalf of the debtor to the permanent trustee in respect of his debts and his discharge and the discharge of the permanent trustee where the offer is approved.

Discharge of permanent trustee

Discharge of permanent trustee

57.—(1) After the permanent trustee has made a final division of the debtor's estate and has inserted his final audited accounts in the sederunt book, he—

(*a*) shall deposit any unclaimed dividends and any unapplied balances in an appropriate bank or institution;

(*b*) shall thereafter send to the Accountant in Bankruptcy the sederunt book, a copy of the audited accounts and a receipt for the deposit of the unclaimed dividends and unapplied balances; and

(*c*) may at the same time as sending the said documents apply to the Accountant in Bankruptcy for a certificate of discharge.

(2) The permanent trustee shall send notice of an application under subsection (1)(*c*) above to the debtor and to all the creditors known to the permanent trustee and shall inform the debtor and such creditors—

(*a*) that they may make written representations relating to the application to the Accountant in Bankruptcy within a period of 14 days after such notification;

(*b*) that the sederunt book is available for inspection at the office of the Accountant in Bankruptcy and contains the audited accounts of, and scheme of division in, the sequestration; and

(*c*) of the effect mentioned in subsection (5) below.

(3) On the expiry of the period mentioned in subsection (2)(*a*) above, the Accountant in Bankruptcy, after examining the documents sent to him and considering any representations duly made to him, shall—

(*a*) grant or refuse to grant the certificate of discharge; and

(*b*) notify (in addition to the permanent trustee) the debtor and all creditors who have made such representations accordingly.

(4) The permanent trustee, the debtor or any creditor who has made representations under subsection (2)(*a*) above, may within 14 days after the

issuing of the determination under subsection (3) above, appeal therefrom to the sheriff and if the sheriff determines that a certificate of discharge which has been refused should be granted he shall order the Accountant in Bankruptcy to grant it; and the sheriff clerk shall send a copy of the decree of the sheriff to the Accountant in Bankruptcy.

(5) The grant of a certificate of discharge under this section by the Accountant in Bankruptcy shall have the effect of discharging the permanent trustee from all liability (other than any liability arising from fraud) to the creditors or to the debtor in respect of any act or omission of the permanent trustee in exercising the functions conferred on him by this Act including, where he was also the interim trustee, the functions conferred on him as interim trustee.

(6) Where a certificate of discharge is granted under this section, the Accountant in Bankruptcy shall make an appropriate entry in the register of insolvencies and in the sederunt book.

(7) Where the permanent trustee has died, resigned office or been removed from office, the provisions of this section shall, subject to any necessary modifications, apply in relation to that permanent trustee or, if he has died, to his executor as they apply to a permanent trustee who has made a final division of the debtor's estate in accordance with the foregoing provisions of this Act.

Unclaimed dividends

58.—(1) Any person, producing evidence of his right, may apply to the Accountant in Bankruptcy to receive a dividend deposited under section 57(1)(*a*) of this Act, if the application is made not later than seven years after the date of such deposit.

(2) If the Accountant in Bankruptcy is satisfied of the applicant's right to the dividend, he shall authorise the appropriate bank or institution to pay to the applicant the amount of that dividend and of any interest which has accrued thereon.

(3) The Accountant in Bankruptcy shall, at the expiry of seven years from the date of deposit of any unclaimed dividend or unapplied balance under section 57(1)(*a*) of this Act, hand over the deposit receipt or other voucher relating to such dividend or balance to the Secretary of State, who shall thereupon be entitled to payment of the amount due, principal and interest, from the bank or institution in which the deposit was made.

Voluntary trust deeds for creditors

Voluntary trust deeds for creditors

59. Schedule 5 to this Act shall have effect in relation to trust deeds executed after the commencement of this section.

Miscellaneous and supplementary

Liabilities and rights of co-obligants

60.—(1) Where a creditor has an obligant (in this section referred to as the "co-obligant") bound to him along with the debtor for the whole or part of the debt, the co-obligant shall not be freed or discharged from his liability for the debt by reason of the discharge of the debt or by virtue of the creditor's voting or drawing a dividend or assenting to, or not opposing—

　(*a*) the discharge of the debtor; or
　(*b*) any composition.
(2) Where—
　(*a*) a creditor has had a claim accepted in whole or in part; and
　(*b*) a co-obligant holds a security over any part of the debtor's estate,
the co-obligant shall account to the permanent trustee so as to put the estate in the same position as if the co-obligant had paid the debt to the

creditor and thereafter had had his claim accepted in whole or in part in the sequestration after deduction of the value of the security.

(3) Without prejudice to any right under any rule of law of a co-obligant who has paid the debt, the co-obligant may require and obtain at his own expense from the creditor an assignation of the debt on payment of the amount thereof, and thereafter may in respect of that debt submit a claim, and vote and draw a dividend, if otherwise legally entitled to do so.

(4) In this section a "co-obligant" includes a cautioner.

Extortionate credit transactions

61.—(1) This section applies where the debtor is or has been a party to a transaction for, or involving, the provision to him of credit and his estate is sequestrated.

(2) The court may, on the application of the permanent trustee, make an order with respect to the transaction if the transaction is or was extortionate and was not entered into more than three years before the date of sequestration.

(3) For the purposes of this section a transaction is extortionate if, having regard to the risk accepted by the person providing the credit—

(a)   the terms of it are or were such as to require grossly exorbitant payments to be made (whether unconditionally or in certain contingencies) in respect of the provision of the credit; or

(b)   it otherwise grossly contravened ordinary principles of fair dealing;
and it shall be presumed, unless the contrary is proved, that a transaction with respect to which an application is made under this section is, or as the case may be was, extortionate.

(4) An order under this section with respect to any transaction may contain such one or more of the following as the court thinks fit—

(a)   provision setting aside the whole or part of any obligation created by the transaction;

(b)   provision otherwise varying the terms of the transaction or varying the terms on which any security for the purposes of the transaction is held;

(c)   provision requiring any person who is a party to the transaction to pay to the permanent trustee any sums paid to that person, by virtue of the transaction, by the debtor;

(d)   provision requiring any person to surrender to the permanent trustee any property held by him as security for the purposes of the transaction;

(e)   provision directing accounts to be taken between any persons.

(5) Any sums or property required to be paid or surrendered to the permanent trustee in accordance with an order under this section shall vest in the permanent trustee.

(6) Neither—

(a)   the permanent trustee; nor

(b)   a debtor who has not been discharged,

shall be entitled to make an application under section 139(1)(a) of the Consumer Credit Act 1974 (re-opening of extortionate credit agreements) for any agreement by which credit is or has been provided to the debtor to be re-opened; but the powers conferred by this section shall be exercisable in relation to any transaction concurrently with any powers exercisable under this Act in relation to that transaction as a gratuitous alienation or unfair preference.

(7) In this section "credit" has the same meaning as in the said Act of 1974.

Sederunt book and other documents

62.—(1) Subject to subsection (2) below, whoever by virtue of this Act for the time being holds the sederunt book shall make it available for inspection at all reasonable hours by any interested person.

(2) As regards any case in which the person on whom a duty is imposed by subsection (1) above is the Accountant in Bankruptcy, the Court of Session may by act of sederunt—

(*a*) limit the period for which the duty is so imposed; and

(*b*) prescribe conditions in accordance with which the duty shall be carried out.

(3) Any entry in the sederunt book shall be sufficient evidence of the facts stated therein, except where it is founded on by the permanent trustee in his own interest.

(4) Notwithstanding any provision of this Act, the permanent trustee shall not be bound to insert in the sederunt book any document of a confidential nature.

(5) The permanent trustee shall not be bound to exhibit to any person other than a commissioner or the Accountant in Bankruptcy any document in his possession of a confidential nature.

(6) An extract from the register of insolvencies bearing to be signed by the Accountant in Bankruptcy shall be sufficient evidence of the facts stated therein.

Power to cure defects in procedure

63.—(1) The sheriff may, on the application of any person having an interest—

(*a*) if there has been a failure to comply with any requirement of this Act or any regulations made under it, make an order waiving any such failure and, so far as practicable, restoring any person prejudiced by the failure to the position he would have been in but for the failure;

(*b*) if for any reason anything required or authorised to be done in, or in connection with, the sequestration process cannot be done, make such order as may be necessary to enable that thing to be done.

(2) The sheriff, in an order under subsection (1) above, may impose such conditions, including conditions as to expenses, as he thinks fit and may—

(*a*) authorise or dispense with the performance of any act in the sequestration process;

(*b*) appoint as permanent trustee on the debtor's estate a person who would be eligible to be elected under section 24 of this Act, whether or not in place of an existing trustee;

(*c*) extend or waive any time limit specified in or under this Act.

(3) An application under subsection (1) above—

(*a*) may at any time be remitted by the sheriff to the Court of Session, of his own accord or on an application by any person having an interest;

(*b*) shall be so remitted, if the Court of Session so directs on an application by any such person,

if the sheriff or the Court of Session, as the case may be, considers that the remit is desirable because of the importance or complexity of the matters raised by the application.

(4) The permanent trustee shall record in the sederunt book the decision of the sheriff or the Court of Session under this section.

Debtor to co-operate with permanent trustee

64.—(1) The debtor shall take every practicable step, and in particular shall execute any document, which may be necessary to enable the permanent trustee to perform the functions conferred on him by this Act.

(2) If the sheriff, on the application of the permanent trustee, is satisfied that the debtor has failed—

(a) to execute any document in compliance with subsection (1) above, he may authorise the sheriff clerk to do so; and the execution of a document by the sheriff clerk under this paragraph shall have the like force and effect in all respects as if the document had been executed by the debtor;

(b) to comply in any other respect with subsection (1) above, he may order the debtor to do so.

(3) If the debtor fails to comply with an order of the sheriff under subsection (2) above, he shall be guilty of an offence.

(4) In this section "debtor" includes a debtor discharged under this Act.

(5) A person convicted of an offence under subsection (3) above shall be liable—

(a) on summary conviction, to a fine not exceeding the statutory maximum or—
  (i) to imprisonment for a term not exceeding three months; or
  (ii) if he has previously been convicted of an offence inferring dishonest appropriation of property or an attempt at such appropriation, to imprisonment for a term not exceeding six months,
or (in the case of either sub-paragraph) to both such fine and such imprisonment; or

(b) on conviction on indictment to a fine or to imprisonment for a term not exceeding two years or to both.

Arbitration and compromise

65.—(1) The permanent trustee may (but if there are commissioners only with the consent of the commissioners, the creditors or the court)—

(a) refer to arbitration any claim or question of whatever nature which may arise in the course of the sequestration; or

(b) make a compromise with regard to any claim of whatever nature made against or on behalf of the sequestrated estate;

and the decree arbitral or comprise shall be binding on the creditors and the debtor.

(2) Where any claim or question is referred to arbitration under this section, the Accountant in Bankruptcy may vary any time limit in respect of which any procedure under this Act has to be carried out.

(3) The permanent trustee shall insert a copy of the decree arbitral, or record the compromise, in the sederunt book.

Meetings of creditors and commissioners

66. Part I of Schedule 6 to this Act shall have effect in relation to meetings of creditors other than the statutory meeting; Part II of that Schedule shall have effect in relation to all meetings of creditors under this Act; and Part III of that Schedule shall have effect in relation to meetings of commissioners.

General offences by debtor etc.

67.—(1) A debtor who during the relevant period makes a false statement in relation to his assets or his business or financial affairs to any creditor or to any person concerned in the administration of his estate shall be guilty of an offence, unless he shows that he neither knew nor had reason to believe that his statement was false.

(2) A debtor, or other person acting in his interest whether with or without his authority, who during the relevant period destroys, damages, conceals or removes from Scotland any part of the debtor's estate or any document relating to his assets or his business or financial affairs shall be guilty of an offence, unless the debtor or other person shows that he did not do so with intent to prejudice the creditors.

(3) A debtor who is absent from Scotland and who after the date of sequestration of his estate fails, when required by the court, to come to Scotland for any purpose connected with the administration of his estate, shall be guilty of an offence.

(4) A debtor, or other person acting in his interest whether with or without his authority, who during the relevant period falsifies any document relating to the debtor's assets or his business or financial affairs, shall be guilty of an offence, unless the debtor or other person shows that he had no intention to mislead the permanent trustee, a commissioner or any creditor.

(5) If a debtor whose estate is sequestrated—

(*a*) knows that a person has falsified any document relating to the debtor's assets or his business or financial affairs; and

(*b*) fails, within one month of the date of acquiring such knowledge, to report his knowledge to the interim or permanent trustee,

he shall be guilty of an offence.

(6) A person who is absolutely insolvent and who during the relevant period transfers anything to another person for an inadequate consideration or grants any unfair preference to any of his creditors shall be guilty of an offence, unless the transferor or grantor shows that he did not do so with intent to prejudice the creditors.

(7) A debtor who is engaged in trade or business shall be guilty of an offence if at any time in the period of one year ending with the date of sequestration of his estate, he pledges or disposes of, otherwise than in the ordinary course of his trade or business, any property which he has obtained on credit and has not paid for unless he shows that he did not intend to prejudice his creditors.

(8) A debtor who is engaged in trade or business shall be guilty of an offence if at any time in the period of two years ending with the date of sequestration, he has failed to keep or preserve such records as are necessary to give a fair view of the state of his assets or his business and financial affairs and to explain his transactions, unless he shows that such failure was neither reckless nor dishonest:

Provided that a debtor shall not be guilty of an offence under this subsection if, at the date of sequestration, his unsecured liabilities did not exceed the prescribed amount; but, for the purposes of this proviso, if at any time the amount of a debt (or part of a debt) over which a security is held exceeds the value of the security, that debt (or part) shall be deemed at that time to be unsecured to the extent of the excess.

(9) If a debtor, either alone or jointly with another person, obtains credit to the extent of £100 (or such other sum as may be prescribed) or more without giving the person from whom he obtained it the relevant information about his status he shall be guilty of an offence.

(10) For the purpose of subsection (9) above—

(*a*) "debtor" means—

(i) a debtor whose estate has been sequestrated, or

(ii) a person who has been adjudged bankrupt in England and Wales or Northern Ireland,

and who, in either case, has not been discharged;

(*b*) the reference to the debtor obtaining credit includes a reference to a case where goods are hired to him under a hire-purchase agreement or agreed to be sold to him under a conditional sale agreement; and

(*c*) the relevant information about the status of the debtor is the information that his estate has been sequestrated and that he has not received his discharge or, as the case may be, that he is an undischarged bankrupt in England and Wales or Northern Ireland.

(11) In this section—

(*a*) "the relevant period" means the period commencing one year immediately before the date of sequestration of the debtor's estate and ending with his discharge;

(*b*) references to intent to prejudice creditors shall include references to intent to prejudice an individual creditor.

(12) A person convicted of any offence under this section shall be liable—

(*a*) on summary conviction, to a fine not exceeding the statutory maximum or—

(i) to imprisonment for a term not exceeding three months; or

(ii) if he has previously been convicted of an offence inferring dishonest appropriation of property or an attempt at such appropriation, to imprisonment for a term not exceeding six months,

or (in the case of either sub-paragraph) to both such fine and such imprisonment; or

(*b*) on conviction on indictment to a fine or—

(i) in the case of an offence under subsection (1), (2), (4) or (7) above to imprisonment for a term not exceeding two years,

(ii) in any other case to imprisonment for a term not exceeding two years,

or (in the case of either sub-paragraph) to both such fine and such imprisonment.

Summary proceedings

68.—(1) Summary proceedings for an offence under this Act may be commenced at any time within the period of six months after the date on which evidence sufficient in the opinion of the Lord Advocate to justify the proceedings comes to his knowledge.

(2) Subsection (3) of section 331 of the Criminal Procedure (Scotland) Act 1975 (date of commencement of summary proceedings) shall have effect for the purposes of subsection (1) above as it has effect for the purposes of that section.

(3) For the purposes of subsection (1) above, a certificate of the Lord Advocate as to the date on which the evidence in question came to his knowledge is conclusive evidence of the date on which it did so.

Outlays of interim and permanent trustee

69. The Secretary of State may, by regulations, provide for the premium (or a proportionate part thereof) of any bond of caution or other security required, for the time being, to be given by an insolvency practitioner to be taken into account as part of the outlays of the insolvency practitioner in his actings as an interim trustee or permanent trustee.

Supplies by utilities

70.—(1) This section applies where on any day ("the relevant day")—

(*a*) sequestration is awarded in a case where the petition was presented by the debtor,

(*b*) a warrant is granted under section 12(2) of this Act in a case where the petition was presented by a creditor or a trustee acting under a trust deed; or

(*c*) the debtor grants a trust deed,

and in this section "the office holder" means the interim trustee, the permanent trustee or the trustee acting under a trust deed, as the case may be.

(2) If a request falling within subsection (3) below is made for the giving after the relevant day of any of the supplies mentioned in subsection (4) below, the supplier—

(*a*) may make it a condition of the giving of the supply that the office holder personally guarantees the payment of any charges in respect of the supply; and (*b*) shall not make it a condition of the giving of the supply, or do anything which has the effect of making it a condition of the giving of the supply, that any outstanding charges in respect of a supply given to the debtor before the relevant day are paid.

(3) A request falls within this subsection if it is made—

(*a*) by or with the concurrence of the officer holder; and

(*b*) for the purposes of any business which is or has been carried on by or on behalf of the debtor.

(4) The supplies referred to in subsection (2) above are—

[1] (*a*) a supply of gas by a public gas supplier within the meaning of Part I of the Gas Act 1986;

[2] (*b*) a supply of electricity by an Electricity Board (within the meaning of the Energy Act 1983);

(*c*) a supply of water by a water authority (within the meaning of the Water (Scotland) Act 1980);

(*d*) a supply of telecommunication services (within the meaning of the Telecommunications Act 1984) by a public telecommunications operator (within the meaning of that Act).

(5) In subsection (4) above the reference to telecommunication services does not include a reference to services consisting in the conveyance of cable programmes, that is to say programmes included in cable programme services (within the meaning of the Cable and Broadcasting Act 1984).

NOTES

[1] As amended by the Gas Act 1986, Sched. 7, para. 32.

[2] Amended (*prosp.*) by the Electricity Act 1989, Sched. 16, para. 32.

Edinburgh Gazette

71. The keeper of the *Edinburgh Gazette* shall, on each day of its publication, send a free copy of it to—

(*a*) the Accountant in Bankruptcy; and

(*b*) the petition department of the Court of Session.

Regulations

72. Any power to make regulations under this Act shall be exercisable by statutory instrument subject to annulment in pursuance of a resolution of either House of Parliament; and the regulations may make different provision for different cases or classes of case.

Interpretation

73.—[1] (1) In this Act, unless the context otherwise requires—

"Accountant in Bankruptcy" shall be construed in accordance with section 1 of this Act;

"accounting period" shall be construed in accordance with section 52(1) and (6) of this Act;

"apparent insolvency" and "apparently insolvent" shall be construed in accordance with section 7 of this Act;

"appropriate bank or institution" means the Bank of England, an institution authorised under the Banking Act 1987 or a person for the time being specified in Schedule 2 to that Act;

"act and warrant" means an act and warrant issued under section 25(2) of, or paragraph 2(2) of Schedule 2 to, this Act;

"associate" shall be construed in accordance with section 74 of this Act;

"business" means the carrying on of any activity, whether for profit or not;

"commissioner", except in the expression "examining commissioner", shall be construed in accordance with section 30(1) of this Act;

"court" means Court of Session or sheriff;

"date of sequestration" has the meaning assigned by section 12(4) of this Act;

"debtor" includes, without prejudice to the expression's generality, an entity whose estate may be sequestrated by virtue of section 6 of this Act, a deceased debtor or his executor or a person entitled to be appointed as executor to a deceased debtor;

"examination" means a public examination under section 45 of this Act or a private examination under section 44 of this Act;

"examining commissioner" shall be construed in accordance with section 46(2) of this Act;

"interim trustee" shall be construed in accordance with section 2 of this Act;

"list of interim trustees" has the meaning assigned by section 1(1)(*b*) of this Act;

"ordinary debt" shall be construed in accordance with section 51(1)(*f*) of this Act;

"permanent trustee" shall be construed in accordance with section 3 of this Act;

"postponed debt" has the meaning assigned by section 51(3) of this Act;

"preferred debt" has the meaning assigned by section 51(2) of this Act;

"prescribed" means prescribed by regulations made by the Secretary of State;

"protected trust deed" shall be construed in accordance with paragraph 8 of Schedule 5 to this Act;

"qualified creditor" and "qualified creditors" shall be construed in accordance with section 5(4) of this Act;

"qualified to act as an insolvency practitioner" means being, in accordance with section 2 of the Insolvency Act 1985 (qualifications of insolvency practitioners), so qualified:
 Provided that, until the coming into force of that section the expression shall instead mean satisfying such requirements (which, without prejudice to the generality of this definition, may include requirements as to the finding of caution) as may be prescribed for the purposes of this Act;

"register of insolvencies" has the meaning assigned by section 1(1)(*c*) of this Act;

"relevant person" has the meaning assigned by section 44(1)(*b*) of this Act;

"secured creditor" means a creditor who holds a security for his debt over any part of the debtor's estate;

"security" means any security, heritable or moveable, or any right of lien, retention or preference;

"sederunt book" means the sederunt book maintained under section 3(1)(*e*) of this Act;

"standard scale" means the standard scale as defined in section 75(*b*) of the Criminal Justice Act 1982;

"statutory meeting" has the meaning assigned by section 21(1) of this Act;

"statutory maximum" has the meaning assigned by section 74(2) of the Criminal Justice Act 1982;

"trust deed" has the meaning assigned by section 5(2)(*c*) of this Act; and

"unfair preference" means a preference created as is mentioned in subsection (1) of section 36 of this Act by a transaction to which subsection (4) of that section applies.

(2) Any reference in this Act to a debtor being absolutely insolvent shall be construed as a reference to his liabilities being greater than his assets, and any reference to a debtor's estate being absolutely insolvent shall be construed accordingly.

(3) Any reference in this Act to value of the creditors is, in relation to any matter, a reference to the value of their claims as accepted for the purposes of that matter.

(4) Any reference in this Act to "the creditors" in the context of their giving consent or doing any other thing shall, unless the context otherwise requires, be construed as a reference to the majority in value of such creditors as vote in that context at a meeting of creditors.

(5) Any reference in this Act to any of the following acts by a creditor barring the effect of any enactment or rule of law relating to the limitation of actions in any part of the United Kingdom, namely—

    (*a*)   the presentation of a petition for sequestration;

    (*b*)   the concurrence in such a petition; and

    (*c*)   the submission of a claim,

shall be construed as a reference to that act having the same effect, for the purposes of any such enactment or rule of law, as an effective acknowledgement of the creditor's claim; and any reference in this Act to any such enactment shall not include a reference to an enactment which implements or gives effect to any international agreement or obligation.

NOTE

[1] As amended by the Banking Act 1987, Sched. 6, para. 20.

Meaning of "associate"

[1] **74.**—(1) Subject to subsection (7) below, for the purposes of this Act any question whether a person is an associate of another person shall be determined in accordance with the following provisions of this section (any reference, whether in those provisions or in regulations under the said subsection (7), to a person being an associate of another person being taken to be a reference to their being associates of each other).

(2) A person is an associate of an individual if that person is the individual's husband or wife, or is a relative, or the husband or wife of a relative, of the individual or of the individual's husband or wife.

(3) A person is an associate of any person with whom he is in partnership, and of any person who is an associate of any person with whom he is in partnership; and a firm is an associate of any person who is a member of the firm.

(4) For the purposes of this section a person is a relative of an individual if he is that individual's brother, sister, uncle, aunt, nephew, niece, lineal ancestor or lineal descendant treating—

    (*a*)   any relationship of the half blood as a relationship of the whole blood and the stepchild or adopted child of any person as his child; and

    (*b*)   an illegitimate child as the legitimate child of his mother and reputed father,

and references in this section to a husband or wife include a former husband or wife and a reputed husband or wife.

(5) A person is an associate of any person whom he employs or by whom he is employed; and for the purposes of this subsection any director or other officer of a company shall be treated as employed by that company.

(5A) A company is an associate of another company—

    (*a*)   if the same person has control of both, or a person has control of one and persons who are his associates, or he and persons who are his associates, have control of the other; or

    (*b*)   if a group of two or more persons has control of each company, and the groups either consist of the same persons or could be regarded as consisting of the same persons by treating (in one or more cases) a member of either group as replaced by a person of whom he is an associate.

(5B) A company is an associate of another person if that person has control of it or if that person and persons who are his associates together have control of it.

(5C) For the purposes of this section a person shall be taken to have control of a company if—

(*a*) the directors of the company or of another company which has control of it (or any of them) are accustomed to act in accordance with his directions or instructions; or

(*b*) he is entitled to exercise, or control the exercise of, one third or more of the voting power at any general meeting of the company or of another company which has control of it:

and where two or more persons together satisfy either of the above conditions, they shall be taken to have control of the company.

(6) In subsections (5), (5A), (5B) and (5C) above, "company" includes any body corporate (whether incorporated in Great Britain or elsewhere).

(7) The Secretary of State may be regulations—

(*a*) amend the foregoing provisions of this section so as to provide further categories of persons who, for the purposes of this Act, are to be associates of other persons; and

(*b*) provide that any or all of subsections (2) to (6) above (or any subsection added by virtue of paragraph (*a*) above) shall cease to apply, whether in whole or in part, or shall apply subject to such modifications as he may specify in the regulations;

and he may in the regulations make such incidental or transitional provision as he considers appropriate.

NOTE
[1] As amended by S.I. 1985 No. 1925.

Amendments, repeals and transitional provisions
  75.—(1) Subject to subsection (3) below—

[THE NEXT PAGE IS H 187]

(*a*) the enactments mentioned in Part I of Schedule 7 to this Act shall have effect subject to the amendments respectively specified in that Schedule, being amendments consequential on the provisions of this Act;

(*b*) Part II of that Schedule, which re-enacts certain provisions of the Bankruptcy (Scotland) Act 1913 repealed by this Act, shall have effect.

(2) The enactments set out in columns 1 and 2 of Schedule 8 to this Act are, subject to subsection (3) below, hereby repealed to the extent specified in the third column of that Schedule.

(3) Subject to subsections (4) and (5) below, nothing in this Act shall affect any of the enactments repealed or amended by this Act in their operation in relation to a sequestration as regards which the award was made before the coming into force of this section.

(4) Where a debtor's estate has been sequestrated before the coming into force of this section but he has not been discharged, the debtor shall be discharged on the expiry of—

(*a*) two years after such coming into force; or

(*b*) three years after the date of sequestration,

whichever expires later:

Provided that, not later than three months before the date on which the debtor is due to be discharged under this subsection, the trustee in the sequestration or any creditor may apply to the sheriff for a deferment of that discharge; and subsections (4) to (8) of section 54 of this Act shall apply in relation to that application by the trustee as they apply in relation to an application under subsection (3) of that section by the permanent trustee.

(5) Section 63 of this Act shall apply in a case where before the coming into force of this section sequestration of a debtor's estate has been awarded under the Bankruptcy (Scotland) Act 1913 but the debtor has not yet been discharged, subject to the following modifications—

(*a*) in subsections (1)(*a*) and (2)(*c*) for the words "this Act" there shall be substituted the words "the Bankruptcy (Scotland) Act 1913";

(*b*) in subsections (2)(*b*) and (4) the word "permanent" shall be omitted; and

(*c*) in subsection (2)(*b*) for the words "24 of this Act" there shall be substituted the words "64 of the Bankruptcy (Scotland) Act 1913".

(6) The apparent insolvency of a debtor may be constituted for the purposes of this Act notwithstanding that the circumstance founded upon to constitute the apparent insolvency occurred on a date before the coming into force of section 7 of this Act; and, for those purposes, the apparent insolvency shall be deemed to have been constituted on that date:

Provided that apparent insolvency shall be constituted by virtue of this subsection only on grounds which would have constituted notour bankruptcy under the Bankruptcy (Scotland) Act 1913.

(7) Where a debtor whose estate is sequestrated after the commencement of this subsection is liable, by virtue of a transaction entered into before that date, to pay royalties or a share of the profits to any person in respect of any copyright or interest in copyright comprised in the sequestrated estate, section 102 of the Bankruptcy (Scotland) Act 1913 (trustee's powers in relation to copyright) shall apply in relation to the permanent trustee as it applied before its repeal in relation to a trustee in bankruptcy under the said Act of 1913.

(8) Where sequestration of a debtor's estate is awarded under this Act a person shall not be guilty of an offence under any provision of this Act in respect of anything done before the date of commencement of that provision but, notwithstanding the repeal by this Act of the Bankruptcy (Scotland) Act 1913, he shall be guilty of an offence under that Act in respect of anything done before that date which would have been an offence under that Act if the award of sequestration had been made under that Act.

(9) Unless the context otherwise requires, any reference in any enactment or document to notour bankruptcy, or to a person being notour bankrupt, shall be construed as a reference to apparent insolvency, or to a person being apparently insolvent, within the meaning of section 7 of this Act.

(10) Unless the context otherwise requires, any reference in any enactment or document to a person's estate being sequestrated under the Bankruptcy (Scotland) Act 1913 shall be construed as, or as including, a reference to its being sequestrated under this Act; and analogous references shall be construed accordingly.

(11) Unless the context otherwise requires, any reference in any enactment or document to a trustee in sequestration or to a trustee in bankruptcy shall be construed as a reference to a permanent trustee, or in a case where no permanent trustee has been elected or appointed an interim trustee, within the meaning of this Act; and analogous expressions shall be construed accordingly.

(12) Unless the context otherwise requires, any reference in any enactment or document—

(*a*) to a "gratuitous alienation" shall be construed as including a reference to an alienation challengeable under section 34(1) of this Act or under section 615A(1) of the Companies Act 1985;

(*b*) to a "fraudulent preference" or to an "unfair preference" shall be construed as including a reference to—

  (i) an unfair preference within the meaning of this Act;

  (ii) a preference created as is mentioned in subsection (1) of section 36 of this Act (as applied by section 615B of the said Act of 1985), by a transaction to which subsection (4) of the said section 36 (as so applied) applies.

Receipts and expenses

76.—(1) Any—

(*a*) payments received by the Secretary of State under section 58(3) of this Act; or

(*b*) amounts handed over to him in accordance with section 53 of this Act by virtue of the insertion provided for in paragraph 9 of Schedule 2 to this Act,

shall be paid by him into the Consolidated Fund.

(2) There shall be paid out of moneys provided by Parliament—

(*a*) any amount of outlays and remuneration payable in accordance with section 53 of this Act by virtue of the insertion mentioned in subsection (1)(*b*) above;

(*b*) any administrative expenses incurred by the Secretary of State under this Act; and

(*c*) any increase attributable to this Act in the sums so payable under any other Act.

Crown application

77. The application of this Act to the Crown is to the Crown as creditor only.

Short title, commencement and extent

78.—(1) This Act may be cited as the Bankruptcy (Scotland) Act 1985.

[1](2) This Act, except this section, shall come into force on such day as the Secretary of State may by order made by statutory instrument appoint; and different days may be so appointed for different purposes and for different provisions.

(3) An order under subsection (2) above may contain such transitional provisions and savings as appear to the Secretary of State necessary or

expedient in connection with the provisions brought into force (whether wholly or partly) by the order.

(4) Without prejudice to section 75(3) to (5) of this Act, this Act applies to sequestrations as regards which the petition—

(*a*) is presented on or after the date of coming into force of section 5 of this Act; or

(*b*) was presented before, but in respect of which no award of sequestration has been made by, that date.

(5) This Act, except the provisions mentioned in subsection (6) below, extends to Scotland only.

(6) The provisions referred to in subsection (5) above are sections 8(5), 22(8) (including that subsection as applied by section 48(7)), 46, 55 and 73(5), paragraph 16(*b*) of Schedule 4 and paragraph 3 of Schedule 5.

NOTE [1] See Release Bulletin for commencement details.

SCHEDULES

Sections 5(5) and 22(9)   SCHEDULE 1

DETERMINATION OF AMOUNT OF CREDITOR'S CLAIM

Amount which may be claimed generally

1.—(1) Subject to the provisions of this Schedule, the amount in respect of which a creditor shall be entitled to claim shall be the accumulated sum of principal and any interest which is due on the debt as at the date of sequestration.

(2) If a debt does not depend on a contingency but would not be payable but for the sequestration until after the date of sequestration, the amount of the claim shall be calculated as if the debt were payable on the date of sequestration but subject to the deduction of interest at the rate specified in section 51(7) of this Act from the said date until the date for payment of the debt.

(3) In calculating the amount of his claim, a creditor shall deduct any discount (other than any discount for payment in cash) which is allowable by contract or course of dealing between the creditor and the debtor or by the usage of trade.

Claims for aliment and periodical allowance on divorce

2.—(1) A person entitled to aliment, however arising, from a living debtor as at the date of sequestration, or from a deceased debtor immediately before his death, shall not be entitled to include in the amount of his claim—

(*a*) any unpaid aliment for any period before the date of sequestration unless the amount of the aliment has been quantified by court decree or by any legally binding obligation which is supported by evidence in writing, and, in the case of spouses (or, where the aliment is payable to a divorced person in respect of a child, former spouses) they were living apart during that period;

(*b*) any aliment for any period after the date of sequestration.

(2) Sub-paragraph (1) above shall apply to a periodical allowance payable on divorce—

(*a*) by virtue of a court order; or

(*b*) under any legally binding obligation which is supported by evidence in writing,

as it applies to aliment and as if for the words from "in the case" to "they" there were substituted the words "the payer and payee".

Debts depending on contingency

3.—(1) Subject to sub-paragraph (2) below, the amount which a creditor shall be entitled to claim shall not include a debt in so far as its existence or amount depends upon a contingency.

(2) On an application by the creditor—

(*a*) to the permanent trustee; or

(*b*) if there is no permanent trustee, to the sheriff,

the permanent trustee or sheriff shall put a value on the debt in so far as it is contingent, and the amount in respect of which the creditor shall then be entitled to claim shall be that value but no more; and, where the contingent debt is an annuity, a cautioner may not then be sued for more than that value.

(3) Any interested person may appeal to the sheriff against a valuation under sub-paragraph (2) above by the permanent trustee, and the sheriff may affirm or vary that valuation.

Debts due under composition contracts

4. Where in the course of a sequestration the debtor is discharged following approval by the sheriff of a composition offered by the debtor but the sequestration is subsequently revived, the amount in respect of which a creditor shall be entitled to claim shall be the same amount as if the composition had not been so approved less any payment already made to him under the composition contract.

Secured debts

5.—(1) In calculating the amount of his claim, a secured creditor shall deduct the value of any security as estimated by him:
Provided that if he surrenders, or undertakes in writing to surrender, a security for the benefit of the debtor's estate, he shall not be required to make a deduction of the value of that security.
(2) The permanent trustee may, at any time after the expiry of 12 weeks from the date of sequestration, require a secured creditor at the expense of the debtor's estate to discharge the security or convey or assign it to the permanent trustee on payment to the creditor of the value specified by the creditor; and the amount in respect of which the creditor shall then be entitled to claim shall be any balance of his debt remaining after receipt of such payment.
(3) In calculating the amount of his claim, a creditor whose security has been realised shall deduct the amount (less the expenses of realisation) which he has received, or is entitled to receive, from the realisation.

Valuation of claims against partners for debts of the partnership

6. Where a creditor claims in respect of a debt of a partnership, against the estate of one of its partners, the creditor shall estimate the value of—
    (a) the debt to the creditor from the firm's estate where that estate has not been sequestrated; or
    (b) the creditor's claim against that estate where it has been sequestrated,
and deduct that value from his claim against the partner's estate; and the amount in respect of which he shall be entitled to claim on the partner's estate shall be the balance remaining after that deduction has been made.

Sections 23(4), 24(5) and 28(5)   SCHEDULE 2

ADAPTATION OF PROCEDURE ETC. UNDER THIS ACT WHERE PERMANENT TRUSTEE NOT ELECTED

1. Section 24(2) shall, in so far as it relates to qualifications for continuing to act as permanent trustee, apply to a permanent trustee appointed, as it applies to one elected, under this Act.
2.—(1) In place of sections 25 and 26, sub-paragraphs (2) and (3) below shall have effect.
(2) The sheriff clerk shall issue to the permanent trustee an act and warrant in such form as shall be prescribed by the Court of Session by act of sederunt.
(3) The permanent trustee, on appointment, shall make such insertions in the sederunt book as are appropriate to provide a record of the sequestration process before his appointment, but he shall make no insertion therein relating to the written comments made by the interim trustee under section 20(2)(c) of this Act.
3.—(1) In place of subsections (1) to (5) of section 28 sub-paragraphs (2) and (3) below shall have effect.
(2) The permanent trustee may resign office with the consent of the Accountant in Bankruptcy or the sheriff.
(3) Where the permanent trustee resigns under sub-paragraph (2) above, or dies, a person nominated by the Accountant in Bankruptcy from the list of interim trustees, not being a person ineligible for election as permanent trustee under section 24(2) of this Act, shall forthwith apply to the sheriff for appointment as permanent trustee, and the sheriff shall thereupon so appoint him.
4. In section 29—
    (a) subsection (5) shall not have effect but sub-paragraph (3) of paragraph 3 above shall apply where the permanent trustee has been removed from office under subsection (1)(b) of section 29 of this Act or following an appeal under subsection (4) of that section as that sub-paragraph applies where he resigns or dies;
    (b) subsection (6) shall have effect as if for the words from "(b)" to the end there were substituted the words—
       "(b) appoint as permanent trustee a person nominated by the Accountant in Bank-

ruptcy from the list of interim trustees, not being a person ineligible for election as permanent trustee under section 24(2) of this Act.";

(c) subsection (7) shall not have effect; and

(d) subsection (8) shall have effect as if for the word "(4)" there were substituted the word "(5)".

5. Where an appointment is made under paragraph 3(3), or by virtue of paragraph 4(a) or (b) above, the provisions of this Act shall continue to have effect as regards the sequestration subject to such modifications and with such further provisions as are set out in this Schedule.

6. Section 30 shall not have effect, and, in any sequestration to which this Schedule applies by virtue of section 28(5) of this Act, any commissioners already holding office shall cease to do so.

7. In section 39—

(a) in subsection (1), the reference to the permanent trustee's confirmation in office shall be construed as a reference to his receiving the act and warrant issued under paragraph 2(2) of this Schedule;

(b) subsection (2) shall have effect as if for the words "if there are commissioners only with the consent of the commissioners, the creditors or the court" there were substituted the words "only with the consent of the Accountant in Bankruptcy".

8. Any power under section 44 or 45 to apply to the sheriff for an order requiring attendance shall be exercisable only with the consent of the Accountant in Bankruptcy (unless, in the case of section 45(1), the Accountant in Bankruptcy has requested the application).

9. In subsection (1) of section 53 the reference to the period in respect of which submission is to be made by the permanent trustee shall, where that period is the first accounting period, be construed as including a reference to any period during which he has acted as interim trustee in the sequestration; and that section shall have effect as if after that subsection there were inserted the following subsection—

"(1A) Where the funds of the debtor's estate are in~~fficient to meet the amount of the outlays and remuneration of both the interim trustee and the permanent trustee—

(a) that amount to the extent of the insufficiency shall be met by the Accountant in Bankruptcy out of money provided under section 76(2)(a) of this Act; and

(b) the Accountant in Bankruptcy in his determination under subsection (3)(a)(ii) below shall specify the respective sums to be met out of the debtor's estate and out of the money so provided:

Provided that—

(i) no amount shall be payable by virtue of paragraph (a) above if any dividend has been paid to creditors in the sequestration; and

(ii) if any amount is paid by virtue of that paragraph and a subsequent distribution of the estate is proposed, that amount shall be handed over to the Secretary of State before such distribution is made.".

Section 51

SCHEDULE 3

PREFERRED DEBTS

Part I

List of Preferred Debts

Debts to Inland Revenue

[1] 1.—(1) Sums due at the relevant date from the debtor on account of deductions of income tax from emoluments paid during the period of 12 months next before that date, being deductions which the debtor was liable to make under section 203 of the Income and Corporation Taxes Act 1988 (pay as you earn), less the amount of the repayments of income tax which the debtor was liable to make during that period.

(2) Sums due at the relevant date from the debtor in respect of such deductions as are required to be made by the debtor for that period under section 559 of the Income and Corporation Taxes Act 1988 (subcontractors in the construction industry).

NOTE
[1] As amended by the Income and Corporation Taxes Act 1988, Sched. 29.

Debts due to Customs and Excise

2.—(1) Any value added tax which is referable to the period of six months next before the relevant date.

(2) The amount of any car tax which is due at the relevant date from the debtor and which became due within a period of 12 months next before that date.

(3) Any amount which is due—

(a) by way of general betting duty or bingo duty, or

(b) under section 12(1) of the Betting and Gaming Duties Act 1981 (general betting duty and pool betting duty recoverable from agent collecting stakes), or

(c) under section 14 of, or Schedule 2 to, that Act (gaming licence duty),

from the debtor at the relevant date and which became due within the period of 12 months next before that date.

Social Security contributions

3.—(1) All sums which on the relevant date are due from the debtor on account of Class 1 or Class 2 contributions under the Social Security Act 1975 or the Social Security (Northern Ireland) Act 1975 and which became due from the debtor in the 12 months next before the relevant date.

(2) All sums which on the relevant date have been assessed on and are due from the debtor on account of Class 4 contributions under either of the said Acts of 1975, being sums which—

(a) are due to the Commissioners of Inland Revenue (rather than to the Secretary of State or a Northern Ireland department); and

(b) are assessed on the debtor up to 5th April next before the relevant date,

but not exceeding, in the whole, any one year's assessment.

Contributions to occupational pension schemes, etc.

4. Any sum which is owed by the debtor and is a sum to which Schedule 3 to the Social Security Pensions Act 1975 (contributions to occupational pension scheme and state scheme premiums) applies.

Remuneration of employees, etc.

5.—(1) So much of any amount which—

(a) is owed by the debtor to a person who is or has been an employee of the debtor, and

(b) is payable by way of remuneration in respect of the whole or any part of the period of four months next before the relevant date,

as does not exceed the prescribed amount.

(2) An amount owed by way of accrued holiday remuneration, in respect of any period of employment before the relevant date, to a person whose employment by the debtor has been terminated, whether before, on or after that date.

(3) So much of any sum owed in respect of money advanced for the purpose as has been applied for the payment of a debt which, if it had not been paid, would have been a debt falling within sub-paragraph (1) or (2) above.

6. So much of any amount which—

(a) is ordered, whether before or after the relevant date, to be paid by the debtor under the Reserve Forces (Safeguard of Employment) Act 1985; and

(b) is so ordered in respect of a default made by the debtor before that date in the discharge of his obligations under that Act,

as does not exceed such amount as may be prescribed.

Levies on coal and steel production

[1] 6A. Any sums due at the relevant date from the debtor in respect of—

(a) the levies on the production of coal and steel referred to in Articles 49 and 50 of the E.C.S.C. Treaty, or

(b) any surcharge for delay provided for in Article 50(3) of that Treaty and Article 6 of Decision 3/52 of the High Authority of the Coal and Steel Community.

NOTE

[1] Inserted by S.I. 1987 No. 2093. This paragraph does not affect any declaration or payment of a dividend made before 1st January 1988: *ibid.*, para. 3(2).

PART II

INTERPRETATION OF PART I

Meaning of "the relevant date"

7. In Part I of this Schedule "the relevant date" means—

(*a*) in relation to a debtor (other than a deceased debtor), the date of sequestration; and

(*b*) in relation to a deceased debtor, the date of his death.

Periods to which value added tax referable

8.—(1) For the purpose of paragraph 2(1) of Part I of this Schedule—

(*a*) where the whole of the prescribed accounting period to which any value added tax is attributable falls within the period of six months next before the relevant date ("the relevant period"), the whole amount of that tax shall be referable to the relevant period; and

(*b*) in any other case the amount of any value added tax which shall be referable to the relevant period shall be the proportion of the tax which is equal to such proportion (if any) of the accounting reference period in question as falls within the relevant period.

[THE NEXT PAGE IS H 193]

(2) In sub-paragraph (1) above "prescribed accounting period" has the same meaning as in the Value Added Tax Act 1983.

Amounts payable by way of remuneration

9.—(1) For the purposes of paragraph 5 of Part I of this Schedule a sum is payable by the debtor to a person by way of remuneration in respect of any period if—
  (*a*) it is paid as wages or salary (whether payable for time or for piece work or earned wholly or partly by way of commission) in respect of services rendered to the debtor in that period; or
  (*b*) it is an amount falling within sub-paragraph (2) below and is payable by the debtor in respect of that period.
(2) An amount falls within this sub-paragraph if it is—
  (*a*) a guarantee payment under section 12(1) of the Employment Protection (Consolidation) Act 1978 (employee without work to do for a day or part of a day),
  (*b*) remuneration on suspension on medical grounds under section 19 of that Act,
  (*c*) any payment for the time off under section 27(3) (trade-union duties), 31(3) (looking for work, etc.) or 31A(4) (ante-natal care) of that Act,
  (*d*) [Repealed by the Social Security Act 1986, Sched. 10, para. 80 and Sched. 11.]
  (*e*) remuneration under a protective award made by an industrial tribunal under section 101 of the Employment Protection Act 1975 (redundancy dismissal with compensation).
(3) For the purposes of paragraph 5(2) of Part I of this Schedule, holiday remuneration shall be deemed, in the case of a person whose employment has been terminated by or in consequence of the award of sequestration of his employer's estate, to have accrued to that person in respect of any period of employment if, by virtue of that person's contract of employment or of any enactment (including an order made or direction given under any enactment), that remuneration would have accrued in respect of that period if that person's employment had continued until he became entitled to be allowed the holiday.
(4) Without prejudice to the preceding provisions of this paragraph—
  (*a*) any remuneration payable by the debtor to a person in respect of a period of holiday or of absence from work through sickness or other good cause is deemed to be wages or, as the case may be, salary in respect of services rendered to the debtor in that period; and
  (*b*) references in this paragraph to remuneration in respect of a period of holiday include references to any sums which, if they had been paid, would have been treated for the purposes of the enactments relating to social services as earnings in respect of that period.

Transitional provisions

10. Regulations under paragraph 5 or 6 of Part I of this Schedule may contain such transitional provisions as may appear to the Secretary of State necessary or expedient.

Section 56   SCHEDULE 4

DISCHARGE ON COMPOSITION

1.—(1) At any time after the sheriff clerk issues the act and warrant to the permanent trustee, an offer of composition may be made by or on behalf of the debtor, in respect of his debts, to the permanent trustee.
(2) Any offer of composition shall specify caution or other security to be provided for its implementation.
2. The permanent trustee shall submit the offer of composition along with a report thereon to the commissioners or, if there are no commissioners, to the Accountant in Bankruptcy.
3. The commissioners or, if there are no commissioners, the Accountant in Bankruptcy—
  (*a*) if they consider (or he considers) that the offer of composition will be timeously implemented and that, if the rules set out in section 51 of, and Schedule 1 to, this Act were applicable, its implementation would secure payment of a dividend of at least 25p in the £ in respect of the ordinary debts; and
  (*b*) if satisfied with the caution or other security specified in the offer,
shall recommend that the offer should be placed before the creditors.
4. Where a recommendation is made that the offer of composition should be placed before the creditors, the permanent trustee shall—

(*a*) intimate the recommendation to the debtor and record it in the sederunt book;

(*b*) publish in the *Edinburgh Gazette* a notice stating that an offer of composition has been made and where its terms may be inspected;

(*c*) invite every creditor known to him to accept or reject the offer by completing a prescribed form sent by the permanent trustee with the invitation and returning the completed form to him; and

(*d*) send along with the prescribed form a report—

(i) summarising the offer and the present state of the debtor's affairs and the progress in realising his estate; and

(ii) estimating, if the offer is accepted, the expenses to be met in concluding the sequestration proceedings and the dividend which would be payable in respect of the ordinary debts if the rules set out in section 51 of, and Schedule 1 to, this Act were applied.

5.—(1) The permanent trustee shall determine from the completed prescribed forms duly received by him that the offer of composition has been accepted by the creditors, if a majority in number and not less than two-thirds in value of the creditors known to him have accepted it, and otherwise shall determine that they have rejected it.

(2) For the purposes of this paragraph, a prescribed form shall be deemed to be duly received by the permanent trustee if it is received by him not later than 14 days after the date on which it was sent to the creditor.

(3) The permanent trustee shall intimate in writing his determination under this paragraph to the debtor and any other person by whom the offer of composition was made and shall insert his determination in the sederunt book.

6. Where the permanent trustee determines that the creditors have accepted the offer of composition, he shall submit to the sheriff—

(*a*) a statement that he has so determined;

(*b*) a copy of the report mentioned in paragraph 4(*d*) of this Schedule; and

(*c*) a declaration by the debtor as to the matters mentioned in sub-paragraphs (i) and (ii) of section 54(4)(*b*) of this Act.

7.—(1) The sheriff shall, on the receipt by him of the documents mentioned in paragraph 6 of this Schedule, fix a date and time for a hearing to consider whether or not to approve the offer of composition.

(2) The permanent trustee shall then send to every creditor known to him a notice in writing stating—

(*a*) that he had determined that the creditors have accepted the offer of composition;

(*b*) that a hearing has been fixed by the sheriff to consider whether or not to approve the offer;

(*c*) the place, date and time of the hearing; and

(*d*) that the recipient of the notice may make representations at the hearing as to whether or not the offer of composition should be approved.

8.—(1) At the hearing the sheriff shall examine the documents and hear any representations and thereafter shall make an order—

(*a*) if he is satisfied that a majority in number and not less than two-thirds in value of the creditors known to the permanent trustee have accepted the offer of composition and that the terms of the offer are reasonable, approving the offer; and

(*b*) if he is not so satisfied, refusing to approve the offer of composition.

(2) The sheriff may make an order approving the offer of composition, notwithstanding that there has been a failure to comply with any provision of this Schedule.

(3) The debtor or any creditor may within 14 days of the order being made appeal against an order approving or refusing to approve the offer of composition.

9.—(1) Where the offer of composition is approved, the permanent trustee shall—

(*a*) submit to the commissioners or, if there are no commissioners, to the Accountant in Bankruptcy, his accounts of his intromissions with the debtor's estate for audit and a claim for the outlays reasonably incurred by him and for his remuneration; and where the said documents are submitted to the commissioners, he shall send a copy of them to the Accountant in Bankruptcy;

(*b*) take all reasonable steps to ensure that the interim trustee (where he is a different person) has submitted, or submits, to the Accountant in Bankruptcy his accounts and his claim for his outlays and remuneration.

(2) Subsections (3), (4), (6) and (10) of section 53 of this Act shall apply, subject to any necessary modifications, in respect of the accounts and claim submitted under sub-paragraph (1)(*a*) above as they apply in respect of the accounts and claim submitted under section 53(1) of this Act.

10. As soon as the procedure under paragraph 9 of this Schedule has been completed, there shall be lodged with the sheriff clerk—

(*a*) by the permanent trustee, a declaration that all necessary charges in connection with the sequestration have been paid or that satisfactory provision has been made in respect of the payment of such charges;

(b) by or on behalf of the debtor, the bond of caution or other security for payment of the composition.

11. Once the documents have been lodged under paragraph 10 of this Schedule, the sheriff shall make an order discharging the debtor and the permanent trustee; and subsection (7) of section 54 of this Act shall apply in relation to an order under this paragraph as it applies in relation to an order under subsection (6) of that section.

12. An order under paragraph 11 of this Schedule discharging the permanent trustee shall have the effect of discharging him from all liability (other than any liability arising from fraud) to the creditors or to the debtor in respect of any act or omission of the permanent trustee in exercising the functions conferred on him by this Act.

13. Notwithstanding that an offer of composition has been made, the sequestration shall proceed as if no such offer of composition has been made until the discharge of the debtor becomes effective; and the sequestration shall thereupon cease.

14. A creditor who has not submitted a claim under section 48 of this Act before the sheriff makes an order approving an offer of composition shall not be entitled to make any demand against a person offering the composition on behalf of the debtor or against a cautioner in the offer; but this paragraph is without prejudice to any right of such a creditor to a dividend out of the debtor's estate equal to the dividend which creditors of the same class are entitled to receive under the composition.

15. A debtor may make two, but no more than two, offers of composition in the course of a sequestration.

16. On an order under paragraph 11 of this Schedule discharging the debtor becoming effective—

(a) the debtor shall be re-invested in his estate as existing at the date of the order;

(b) the debtor shall, subject to paragraph 14 of this Schedule, be discharged of all debts for which he was liable at the date of sequestration (other than any debts mentioned in section 55(2) of this Act); and

(c) the claims of creditors in the sequestration shall be converted into claims for their respective shares in the composition.

17.—(1) Without prejudice to any rule of law relating to the reduction of court decrees, the Court of Session, on the application of any creditor, may recall the order of the sheriff approving the offer of composition and discharging the debtor and the permanent trustee where it is satisfied—

(a) that there has been, or is likely to be, default in payment of the composition or of any instalment thereof; or

(b) that for any reason the composition cannot be proceeded with or cannot be proceeded with without undue delay or without injustice to the creditors.

(2) The effect of a decree of recall under this paragraph where the debtor has already been discharged shall be to revive the sequestration:

Provided that the revival of the sequestration shall not affect the validity of any transaction which has been entered into by the debtor since his discharge with a person who has given value and has acted in good faith.

(3) Where the permanent trustee has been discharged, the Court may, on pronouncing a decree of recall under this paragraph, appoint a judicial factor to administer the debtor's estate, and give the judicial fact such order as it thinks fit as to that administration.

(4) The clerk of court shall send a copy of a decree of recall under this paragraph to the permanent trustee or judicial factor for insertion in the sederunt book.

18.—(1) Without prejudice to any rule of law relating to the reduction of court decrees, the Court of Session, on the application of any creditor, may reduce an order under paragraph 11 of this Schedule discharging a debtor where it is satisfied that a payment was made or a preference granted or that a payment or preference was promised for the purpose of facilitating the obtaining of the debtor's discharge.

(2) The Court may, whether or not it pronounces a decree of reduction under this paragraph, order a creditor who has received a payment or preference in connection with the debtor's discharge to surrender the payment or the value of the preference to the debtor's estate.

(3) Where the permanent trustee has been discharged, the Court may, on pronouncing a decree of reduction under this paragraph, appoint a judicial factor to administer the debtor's estate, and give the judicial factor such order as it thinks fit as to that administration.

(4) The clerk of court shall send a copy of a decree of reduction under this paragraph to the permanent trustee or judicial factor for insertion in the sederunt book.

Section 59   [1] SCHEDULE 5

NOTE

[1] See the Debtors (Scotland) Act 1987, s.93(4) (*prosp.*).

Voluntary Trust Deeds for Creditors

Remuneration of trustee

1. Whether or not provision is made in the trust deed for auditing the trustee's accounts and for determining the method of fixing the trustee's remuneration or whether or not the trustee and the creditors have agreed on such auditing and the method of fixing the remuneration, the debtor, the trustee or any creditor may, at any time before the final distribution of the debtor's estate among the creditors, have the trustee's accounts audited by and his remuneration fixed by the Accountant in Bankruptcy.

Registration of notice of inhibition

2.—(1) The trustee, from time to time after the trust deed has been delivered to him, may cause a notice in such form as shall be prescribed the Court of Session by act of sederunt to be recorded in the register of inhibitions and adjudications; and such recording shall have the same effect as the recording in that register of letters of inhibition against the debtor.

(2) The trustee, after the debtor's estate has been finally distributed among his creditors or the trust deed has otherwise ceased to be operative, shall cause to be so recorded a notice in such form as shall be prescribed as aforesaid recalling the notice recorded under sub-paragraph (1) above.

Lodging of claim to bar effect of limitation of actions

3. The submission of a claim by a creditor to the trustee acting under a trust deed shall bar the effect of any enactment or rule of law relating to limitation of actions in any part of the United Kingdom.

Valuation of claims

4. Unless the trust deed otherwise provides, Schedule 1 to this Act shall apply in relation to a trust deed as it applies in relation to a sequestration but subject to the following modifications—
   (*a*) in paragraphs 1, 2 and 5 for the word "sequestration" wherever it occurs there shall be substituted the words "granting of the trust deed";
   (*b*) in paragraph 3—
      (i) in sub-paragraph (2), for the words from the beginning of paragraph (*a*) to "or sheriff" there shall be substituted the words "the trustee"; and
      (ii) in sub-paragraph (3), for the reference to the permanent trustee there shall be substituted a reference to the trustee;
   (*c*) paragraph 4 shall be omitted; and
   (*d*) in paragraph 5(2) for the references to the permanent trustee there shall be substituted references to the trustee.

Protected trust deeds

5. Paragraphs 6 and 7 of this Schedule shall apply in respect of a trust deed if—
   (*a*) the trustee is a person who would not be disqualified under section 24(2) of this Act from acting as permanent trustee if the debtor's estate were being sequestrated;
   (*b*) the trustee, forthwith after the trust deed has been delivered to him, both publishes in the *Edinburgh Gazette* and sends to every creditor known to him a notice in the prescribed form—
      (i) stating that the trust deed has been granted by the debtor; and
      (ii) inviting creditors, in order that paragraphs 6 and 7 of this Schedule may apply, to accede to the trust deed within four weeks of the date of which the notice is so published;
   (*c*) within the said period of four weeks a majority in number and not less than two-thirds in value of the creditors accede to the trust deed; and
   (*d*) the trustee immediately after the expiry of the said period sends to the Accountant in Bankruptcy for registration in the register of insolvencies a copy of the trust deed with a certificate endorsed thereon that it is a true copy and the accession of creditors as required by sub-paragraph (*c*) above has been obtained.

6. Where the provisions of paragraph 5 of this Schedule have been fulfilled, then—
   (*a*) subject to paragraph 7 of this Schedule, a creditor who has not acceded to the trust

deed shall have no higher right to recover his debt than a creditor who has so acceded; and

(*b*) the debtor may not petition for the sequestration of his estate while the trust deed subsists.

7.—(1) A qualified creditor who has not acceded to the trust deed may present a petition for sequestration of the debtor's estate—

(*a*) not later than six weeks after the date of publication of the notice under paragraph 5(*b*) of this Schedule; but

(*b*) subject to section 8(1)(*b*) of this Act, at any time if he avers that the provision for distribution of the estate is or is likely to be unduly prejudicial to a creditor or class of creditors.

(2) The court may award sequestration in pursuance of sub-paragraph (1)(*a*) above if it considers that to do so would be in the best interests of the creditors.

(3) The court shall award sequestration in pursuance of sub-paragraph (1)(*b*) above if, but only if, it is satisfied that the creditor's said averment is correct.

8. In this Act a trust deed in respect of which paragraphs 6 and 7 of this Schedule apply is referred to as a "protected trust deed".

9. Where the trustee under a protected trust deed has made the final distribution of the estate among the creditors, he shall, not more than 28 days after the final distribution, send to the Accountant in Bankruptcy for registration if the register of insolvencies—

(*a*) a statement in the prescribed form indicating how the estate was realised and distributed; and

(*b*) a certificate to the effect that the distribution was in accordance with the trust deed.

10. Where the trustee under a protected trust deed has obtained a discharge from the creditors who have acceded to the trust deed he shall forthwith give notice of the discharge—

(*a*) by sending the notice by recorded delivery to every creditor known to him who has not acceded to the trust deed; and

(*b*) by sending the notice to the Accountant in Bankruptcy who shall register the fact of the discharge in the register of insolvencies,

and, except where the court makes an order under paragraph 12 below, the sending of such notice to a creditor who has not acceded to the trust deed shall be effective to make the discharge binding upon that creditor.

Creditors not acceding to protected trust deed

11. A creditor who has not acceded to a protected trust deed may, not more than 28 days after notice has been sent under paragraph 10 above, apply to the court for an order under paragraph 12 below.

12. Where, on an application by a creditor under paragraph 11 above, the court is satisfied (on grounds other than those on which a petition under paragraph 7(1)(*b*) above was or could have been presented by that creditor) that the intromissions of the trustee under the protected trust deed with the estate of the debtor have been so unduly prejudicial to that creditor's claim that he should not be bound by the discharge it may order that he shall not be so bound.

13. Where the court makes an order under paragraph 12 above, the clerk of court shall send a copy of the order to—

(*a*) the trustee; and

(*b*) the Accountant in Bankruptcy who shall register the copy of the order in the register of insolvencies.

Section 66   SCHEDULE 6

MEETINGS OF CREDITORS AND COMMISSIONERS

PART I

MEETINGS OF CREDITORS OTHER THAN THE STATUTORY MEETING

Calling of meeting

1. The permanent trustee shall call a meeting of creditors if required to do so by—

(*a*) order of the court;

(*b*) one-tenth in number or one-third in value of the creditors;

(*c*) a commissioner; or

(*d*) the Accountant in Bankruptcy.

2. A meeting called under paragraph 1 above shall be held not later than 28 days after the

issuing of the order of the court under sub-paragraph (*a*) of that paragraph or the receipt by the permanent trustee of the requirement under sub-paragraph (*b*), (*c*) or (*d*) thereof.

3. The permanent trustee or a commissioner who has given written notice to him may at any time call a meeting of creditors.

4. The permanent trustee or a commissioner calling a meeting under paragraph 1 or 3 above shall, not less than seven days before the date fixed for the meeting, notify—
(*a*) every creditor known to him; and
(*b*) the Accountant in Bankruptcy,
of the date, time and place fixed for the holding of the meeting and its purpose.

5.—(1) Where a requirement has been made under paragraph 1 above but no meeting has been called by the permanent trustee, the Accountant in Bankruptcy may, of his own accord or on the application of any creditor, call a meeting of creditors.

(2) The Accountant in Bankruptcy calling a meeting under this paragraph shall, not less than seven days before the date fixed for the meeting, take reasonable steps to notify the creditors of the date, time and place fixed for the holding of the meeting and its purpose.

6. It shall not be necessary to notify under paragraph 4 or 5 of this Schedule any creditor whose accepted claim is less than £50 or such sum as may be prescribed, unless the creditor has requested in writing such notification.

Role of permanent trustee at meeting

7.—(1) At the commencement of a meeting, the chairman shall be the permanent trustee who as chairman shall, after carrying out his duty under section 49(1) of this Act, invite the creditors to elect one of their number as chairman in his place and shall preside over the election.

(2) If a chairman is not elected in pursuance of this paragraph, the permanent trustee shall remain the chairman throughout the meeting.

(3) The permanent trustee shall arrange for a record to be made of the proceedings at the meeting and he shall insert the minutes of the meeting in the sederunt book.

Appeals

8. The permanent trustee, a creditor or any other person having an interest may, within 14 days after the date of a meeting called under paragraph 1 or 3 above, appeal to the sheriff against a resolution of the creditors at the meeting.

Part II

All Meetings of Creditors

Validity of proceedings

9. No proceedings at a meeting shall be invalidated by reason only that any notice or other document relating to the calling of the meeting which is required to be sent or given under any provision of this Act has not been received by, or come to the attention of, any creditor before the meeting.

Locus of meeting

10. Every meeting shall be held in such place (whether or not in the sheriffdom) as is, in the opinion of the person calling the meeting, the most convenient for the majority of the creditors.

Mandatories

11.—(1) A creditor may authorise in writing any person to represent him at at meeting.

(2) A creditor shall lodge any authorisation given under sub-paragraph (1) above with the interim trustee or, as the case may be, the permanent trustee before the commencement of the meeting.

(3) Any reference in paragraph 7(1) of this Schedule and the following provisions of this Part of this Schedule to a creditor shall include a reference to a person authorised by him under this paragraph.

Quorum

12. The quorum at any meeting shall be one creditor.

Voting at meeting

13. Any question at a meeting shall be determined by a majority in value of the creditors who vote on that question.

Objections by creditors

14.—(1) The chairman at any meeting may allow or disallow any objection by a creditor, other than (if the chairman is not the permanent trustee) an objection relating to a creditor's claim.

(2) Any person aggrieved by the determination of the chairman in respect of an objection may appeal therefrom to the sheriff.

(3) If the chairman is in doubt whether to allow or disallow an objection, the meeting shall proceed as if no objection had been made, except that for the purposes of appeal the objection shall be deemed to have been disallowed.

Adjournment of meeting

15.—(1) If no creditor has appeared at a meeting at the expiry of a period of half an hour after the time appointed for the commencement of the meeting, the chairman shall adjourn the meeting to such other day as the chairman shall appoint, being not less than seven nor more than 21 days after the day on which the meeting was adjourned.

(2) The chairman may, with the consent of a majority in value of the creditors who vote on the matter, adjourn a meeting.

(3) Any adjourned meeting shall be held at the same time and place as the original meeting, unless in the resolution for the adjournment of the meeting another time or place is specified.

Minutes of meeting

16. The minutes of every meeting shall be signed by the chairman and within 14 days of the meeting a copy of the minutes shall be sent to the Accountant in Bankruptcy.

PART III

MEETINGS OF COMMISSIONERS

17. The permanent trustee may call a meeting of commissioners at any time, and shall call a meeting of commissioners—

(*a*) on being required to do so by order of the court; or
(*b*) on being requested to do so by the Accountant in Bankruptcy or any commissioner.

18. If the permanent trustee fails to call a meeting of commissioners within 14 days of being required or requested to do so under paragraph 17 of this Schedule, a commissioner may call a meeting of commissioners.

19. The permanent trustee shall give the commissioners at least seven days notice of a meeting called by him, unless the commissioners decide that they do not require such notice.

20. The permanent trustee shall act as clerk at meetings and shall insert a record of the deliberations of the commissioners in the sederunt book.

21. If the commissioners are considering the performance of the functions of the permanent trustee under any provision of this Act, he shall withdraw from the meeting if requested to do so by the commissioners; and in such a case a commissioner shall act as clerk, shall transmit a record of the deliberations of the commissioners to the permanent trustee for insertion in the sederunt book and shall authenticate the insertion when made.

22. The quorum at a meeting of commissioners shall be one commissioner and the commissioners may act by a majority of the commissioners present at the meeting.

23. Any matter may be agreed by the commissioners without a meeting if such agreement is unanimous and is subsequently recorded in a minute signed by the commissioners; and that minute shall be inserted by the permanent trustee in the sederunt book.

Section 75(1) ¹ SCHEDULE 7

PART I

CONSEQUENTIAL AMENDMENTS

———

NOTE
¹ Amendments to Acts printed in *The Parliament House Book* have been given effect.

———

. . . . . .

PART II

RE-ENACTMENT OF CERTAIN PROVISIONS OF BANKRUPTCY (SCOTLAND) ACT 1913 (c. 20)

Arrestments and poindings

[1] 24.—(1) Subject to sub-paragraph (2) below, all arrestments and poindings which have been executed within 60 days prior to the constitution of the apparent insolvency of the debtor, or within four months thereafter, shall be ranked *pari passu* as if they had all been executed on the same date.

(2) Any such arrestment which is executed on the dependence of an action shall be followed up without undue delay.

(3) Any creditor judicially producing in a process relative to the subject of such arrestment or poinding liquid grounds of debt or decree of payment within the 60 days or four months referred to in sub-paragraph (1) above shall be entitled to rank as if he had executed an arrestment or a poinding; and if the first or any subsequent arrester obtains in the meantime a decree of furthcoming, and recovers payment, or a poinding creditor carries through a sale, he shall be accountable for the sum recovered to those who, by virtue of this Act, may be eventually found to have a right to a ranking *pari passu* thereon, and shall be liable in an action at their instance for payment to them proportionately, after allowing out of the fund the expense of such recovery.

(4) Arrestments executed for attaching the same effects of the debtor after the period of four months subsequent to the constitution of his apparent insolvency shall not compete with those within the said periods prior or subsequent thereto, but may rank with each other on any reversion of the fund attached in accordance with any enactment or rule of law relating thereto.

(5) Any reference in the foregoing provisions of this paragraph to a debtor shall be construed as including a reference to an entity whose apparent insolvency may, by virtue of subsection (5) of section 7 of this Act, be constituted under subsection (1) of that section.

(6) This paragraph shall apply in respect of arrestments and poindings which have been executed either before or after the coming into force of this paragraph.

(7) The repeal of the Bankruptcy (Scotland) Act 1913 shall not affect the equalisation of arrestments and poindings (whether executed before or after the coming into force of this paragraph) in consequence of the constitution of notour bankruptcy under that Act.

———

NOTE
[1] See the Debtors (Scotland) Act 1987, ss.13(2)(*b*) and 67 (*prosp.*). Amended (*prosp.*) by *ibid.* Sched. 6, para. 28.

———

Exemptions from stamp or other duties for conveyances, deeds etc. relating to sequestrated estates

25. Any—
(*a*) conveyance, assignation, instrument, discharge, writing, or deed relating solely to the estate of a debtor which has been or may be sequestrated, either under this or any former Act, being estate which after the execution of such conveyance, assignation, instrument, discharge, writing, or deed, shall be and remain the property of such debtor, for the benefit of his creditors, or the interim or permanent trustee appointed or chosen under or by virtue of such sequestration,
(*b*) discharge to such debtor,
(*c*) deed, assignation, instrument, or writing for reinvesting the debtor in the estate,
(*d*) article of roup or sale, or submission,
(*e*) other instrument or writing whatsoever relating solely to the estate of any such debtor; and
(*f*) other deed or writing forming part of the proceedings ordered under such sequestration,
shall be exempt from all stamp duties or other Government duty.

Section 75(2)   SCHEDULE 8

REPEALS

[Repeals to Acts printed in *The Parliament House Book* have been given effect.]

[THE NEXT PAGE IS H 205]

[1] **Law Reform (Miscellaneous Provisions) (Scotland) Act 1985**

(1985 c. 73)

An Act to amend the law of Scotland in respect of certain . . . contracts and obligations; . . .   [30th October 1985]

NOTE

[1] These provisions in force on 30th December 1985: see s. 60(3), reprinted in Division E, *supra*.

. . . .

Provisions relating to other contracts and obligations

Rectification of defectively expressed documents

8.—(1) Subject to section 9 of this Act, where the court is satisfied, on an application made to it, that—

(a) a document intended to express or to give effect to an agreement fails to express accurately the common intention of the parties to the agreement at the date when it was made; or

(b) a document intended to create. transfer, vary or renounce a right, not being a document falling within paragraph (a) above, fails to express accurately the intention of the grantor of the document at the date when it was executed,

it may order the document to be rectified in any manner that it may specify in order to give effect to that intention.

(2) For the purposes of subsection (1) above, the court shall be entitled to have regard to all relevant evidence, whether written or oral.

(3) Subject to section 9 of this Act, in ordering the rectification of a document under subsection (1) above (in this subsection referred to as "the original document"), the court may, at its own instance or on an application made to it, order the rectification of any other document intended for any of the purposes mentioned in paragraph (a) or (b) of subsection (1) above which is defectively expressed by reason of the defect in the original document.

(4) Subject to section 9(4) of this Act, a document ordered to be rectified under this section shall have effect as if it had always been so rectified.

(5) Subject to section 9(5) of this Act, where a document recorded in the Register of Sasines is ordered to be rectified under this section and the order is likewise recorded, the document shall be treated as having been always so recorded as rectified.

(6) Nothing in this section shall apply to a document of a testamentary nature.

(7) It shall be competent to register in the Register of Inhibitions and Adjudications a notice of an application under this section for the rectification of a deed relating to land, being an application in respect of which authority for service or citation has been granted; and the land to which the application relates shall be rendered litigious as from the date of registration of such a notice.

(8) A notice under subsection (7) above shall specify the names and designations of the parties to the application and the date when authority for service or citation was granted and contain a description of the land to which the application relates.

(9) In this section and section 9 of this Act "the court" means the Court of Session or the sheriff.

Provisions supplementary to section 8: protection of other interest

9.—(1) The court shall order a document to be rectified under section 8 of this Act only where it is satisfied—

(*a*) that the interests of a person to whom this section applies would not be adversely affected to a material extent by the rectification; or

(*b*) that that person has consented to the proposed rectification.

(2) Subject to subsection (3) below, this section applies to a person (other than a party to the agreement or the grantor of the document) who has acted or refrained from acting in reliance on the terms of the document or on the title sheet of an interest in land registered in the Land Register of Scotland being an interest to which the document relates, with the result that his position has been affected to a material extent.

(3) This section does not apply to a person—

(*a*) who, at the time when he acted or refrained from acting as mentioned in subsection (2) above, knew, or ought in the circumstances known to him at that time to have been aware, that the document or (as the case may be) the title sheet failed accurately to express the common intention of the parties to the agreement or, as the case may be, the intention of the grantor of the document; or

(*b*) whose reliance on the terms of the document or on the title sheet was otherwise unreasonable.

(4) Notwithstanding subsection (4) of section 8 of this Act and without prejudice to subsection (5) below, the court may, for the purpose of protecting the interests of a person to whom this section applies, order that the rectification of a document shall have effect as at such date as it may specify, being a date later than that as at which it would have effect by virtue of the said subsection (4).

(5) Notwithstanding subsection (5) of section 8 of this Act and without prejudice to subsection (4) above, the court may, for the purpose of protecting the interests of a person to whom this section applies, order that a document as rectified shall be treated as having been recorded as mentioned in the said subsection (5) at such date as it may specify, being a date later than that as at which it would be treated by virtue of that subsection as having been so recorded.

(6) For the purposes of subsection (1) above, the court may require the Keeper of the Registers of Scotland to produce such information as he has in his possession relating to any persons who have asked him to supply details with regard to a title sheet mentioned in subsection (2) above; and any expense incurred by the Keeper under this subsection shall be borne by the applicant for the order.

(7) Where a person to whom this section applies was unaware, before a document was ordered to be rectified under section 8 of this Act, that an application had been made under that section for the rectification of the document, the Court of Session, on an application made by that person within the time specified in subsection (8) below, may—

(*a*) reduce the rectifying order; or

(*b*) order the applicant for the rectifying order to pay such compensation to that person as it thinks fit in respect of his reliance on the terms of the document or on the title sheet.

(8) The time referred to in subsection (7) above is whichever is the earlier of the following—

(*a*) the expiry of five years after the making of the rectifying order;

(*b*) the expiry of two years after the making of that order first came to the notice of the person referred to in that subsection.

Negligent misrepresentation

10.—(1) A party to a contract who has been induced to enter into it by negligent misrepresentation made by or on behalf of another party to the contract shall not be disentitled, by reason only that the misrepresentation is not fraudulent, from recovering damages from the other party in respect of any loss or damage he has suffered as a result of the misrepresentation; and any rule of law that such damages cannot be recovered unless fraud is proved shall cease to have effect.

(2) Subsection (1) applies to any proceedings commenced on or after the date on which it comes into force, whether or not the negligent misrepresentation was made before or after that date, but does not apply to any proceedings commenced before that date.

·   ·   ·   ·   ·   ·

[THE NEXT PAGE IS H 301]

Statutory Instruments

Bankruptcy (Scotland) Regulations 1985

(S.I. 1985 No. 1925)

[4th December 1985]

The Secretary of State, in exercise of the powers conferred on him by sections 6(7), 7(1)(*d*), 8(2), 11(1), 15(6), 19(1), 22(2)(*a*) and (6), 23(1)(*a*), 25(6)(*b*), 45(3)(*a*), 48(7), 49(3), 51(7)(*a*), 54(2), 67(8), 69, 73 and 74 of, and paragraph 4(*c*) of Schedule 4 and paragraphs 5(*b*) and 9(*a*) of Schedule 5 to, the Bankruptcy (Scotland) Act 1985 (c. 66) and of all other powers enabling him in that behalf, hereby makes the following regulations:—

Citation and commencement
1. These regulations may be cited as the Bankruptcy (Scotland) Regulations 1985 and shall come into operation, for the purposes of regulations 3 and 4 of these regulations, on 1st February 1986 and for all other purposes, on 1st April 1986.

Interpretation
2. In these regulations,
  "the Act" means the Bankruptcy (Scotland) Act 1985; and
  "the 1907 Act" means the Limited Partnerships Act 1907;

Qualification to act as insolvency practitioner
3.—(1) A person shall be qualified to act as an insolvency practitioner for the purposes of the Act, until the coming into force of section 2 of the Insolvency Act 1985 only if he satisfies the following requirement:—
  (*a*) he is an individual;
  (*b*) he holds a certificate entitling him, or is otherwise entitled, at the relevant time, to practise as a member of a relevant professional body or, in any other case, he has, at the relevant time, a minimum of 5 years' experience as an insolvency practitioner;
  (*c*) he finds caution in accordance with the provisions of regulation 4 of these regulations; and
  (*d*) he is not an undischarged bankrupt.
  (2) For the purposes of paragraph (1) above—
  (*a*) the expression "the relevant time" means any time at which a person acts as an insolvency practitioner or has, or seeks to have, his name included in the list of interim trustees;
  (*b*) the expression "a relevant professional body" means—
    The Law Society of Scotland
    The Institute of Chartered Accountants of Scotland
    The Insolvency Practitioners Association
    The Chartered Association of Certified Accountants
    The Law Society
    The Institute of Chartered Accountants in England and Wales
    The Institute of Chartered Accountants in Ireland;
  (*c*) a person shall be treated as having a minimum of 5 years' experience as an insolvency practitioner if he has, in not less that 10 cases in the previous 5 years, acted—
    (i) as a liquidator, receiver or trustee in bankruptcy or trustee under a trust deed or other voluntary arrangement for the

benefit of creditors or a judicial factor under section 163 of the Bankruptcy (Scotland) Act 1913, or under section 11A of the Judicial Factors (Scotland) Act 1889 or in any similar capacity in any member state of the European Communities; or

(ii) as a senior assistant or deputy to any of those persons; and

(d) an undischarged bankrupt means a person who has not been discharged after his estate has been sequestrated or he has been adjudged bankrupt or he has granted a trust deed for the benefit of his creditors or he has been subject, in any other country, to any procedure similar to sequestration, bankruptcy or the granting of a trust deed for creditors.

4.—(1) For the purposes of regulation 3(1)(c) of these regulations, a person shall be qualified to act as an insolvency practioner in the circumstances set out in the following paragraphs if he finds caution in accordance with the following provisions of this regulation.

(2) A person shall be qualified to act as an interim trustee if he lodges with the Accountant in Bankruptcy at the time of his application for his name to be included in the list of interim trustees and, for as long as his name remains on that list, maintains in force a bond (hereinafter referred to as "a global bond") in terms of which it is provided that, whenever he is appointed as an interim trustee in a sequestration, the amount of caution in respect of his actings or omissions as interim trustee shall be not less than the net value of the debtor's assets in the sequestration as estimated by the interim trustee.

(3) Subject to paragraph (4) below, a person shall be qualified to act as a permanent trustee in a sequestration, if, for as long as he acts as such trustee, he has and maintains in force

(a) in the case where he has acted as the interim trustee in the sequestration, the global bond referred to in paragraph (2) above, which provides for caution, or

(b) a bond of caution, which he lodges with the sheriff clerk, before the issue of the act and warrant in his favour,

in respect of his actings or omissions as a permanent trustee for such amount as shall be not less than the net value of the debtor's assets in the final statement of the debtor's affairs prepared by the interim trustee under section 23(3)(d) of the Act.

(4) A person shall be qualified to act as a trustee under a protected trust deed, if, for as long as he acts as such trustee, he has and maintains in force a bond of caution or a global bond referred to in paragraph (2) above which provides for caution in respect of his actings or omissions as such trustee for such amount as shall not be less than the value of the debtor's assets conveyed to him under the trust deed.

(5) In this regulation, the expression "net value of the debtor's assets" means the value of the debtor's assets under deduction of any security which is not surrendered to the insolvency practitioner.

Forms
5. The forms set out in the Schedule to these regulations are the forms prescribed for the purposes of the provisions of the Act referred to therein.

Claims in foreign currency
6. A creditor may state the amount of his claim in foreign currency for the purposes of section 22(6), or that section as applied by section 48(7), of the Act, where—

(a) his claim is constituted by decree or other order made by a court ordering the debtor to pay to the creditor a sum expressed in foreign currency; or, where it is not so constituted, (*b*) his claim arises from a contract or bill of exchange in terms of which payment is or may be required to be made by the debtor to the creditor in foreign currency.

Conversion of foreign currency claims

7. For the purposes of sections 23(1)(*a*) and 49(3) of the Act, the manner of conversion into Sterling of the amount of a claim stated in foreign currency shall be at the rate of exchange for that currency at the mean of the buying and selling spot rates prevailing at the close of business on the date of sequestration in the London market as published in any national newspaper.

Interest on claims in sequestration

8. The prescribed rate of interest for the purposes of section 51(7) of the Act (interest on preferred debts and ordinary debts between the date of sequestration and the date of payment of the debt) is 15 *per centum per annum*.

Amount of unsecured liabilities

9. The amount of the unsecured liabilities of the debtor, for the purposes of section 67(8) of the Act (the offence of failing to keep proper records), shall be £20,000.

Premium of bond of caution

10. Any premium (or a proportionate part thereof) of any bond of caution or other security required to be given by an insolvency practitioner in respect of his actings as an interim trustee or a permanent trustee in any sequestration in which he is elected or appointed may be taken into account as part of his outlays in that sequestration.

Definition of "associate"

11.—(1) Section 74 of the Act (meaning of "associate") shall be amended or modified in accordance with the following paragraphs:—

(2) Subsection (3) shall be amended by substituting for the words—

"and of the husband or wife or a relative of any individual with whom he is in partnership;"

the words

"and of any person who is an associate of any person with whom he is in partnership;".

(3) After subsection (5), there shall be inserted the following subsections:—

"(5A) A company is an associate of another company—

(*a*) if the same person has control of both, or a person has control of one and persons who are his associates, or he and person who are his associates, have control of the other; or

(*b*) if a group of two or more persons has control of each company, and the groups either consist of the same persons or could be regarded as consisting of the same persons by treating (in one or more cases) a member of either group as replaced by a person of whom he is an associate.

(5B) A company is an associate of another person if that person has control of it or if that person and persons who are his associates together have control of it.

(5C) For the purposes of this section a person shall be taken to have control of a company if—

(*a*) the directors of the company or of another company which has control of it (or any of them) are accustomed to act in accordance with his directions or instructions; or

(*b*) he is entitled to exercise, or control the exercise of, one third or
more of the voting power at any general meeting of the company or
of another company which has control of it;

and where two or more persons together satisfy either of the above conditions, they shall be taken to have control of the company.''

(4) Subsection (6) shall apply subject to the modification that, for the
words "In subsection (5) above,", there shall be substituted the words "In
subsections (5), (5A), (5B) and (5C) above,".

Application of the Act to limited partnerships

12.—(1) The application of the Act to the sequestration of the estate of a
limited partnership shall be subject to the modifications specified in this
regulation.

(2) Any reference in the Act to a partnership (other than in section 6(1)
or to a firm shall be construed as including a reference to a limited partnership.

(3) In the application of section 9 of the Act to limited partnerships, the
Court of Session and the Sheriff shall have jurisdiction in respect of the
sequestration of the estate of a limited partnership if it is registered in Scotland for the purposes of the 1907 Act and, in the case of the sheriff, if it has
an established place of business within the sheriffdom.

(4) For the purposes of section 8(2) of the Act, a petition for the sequestration of the estate of a limited partnership may be presented—

(*a*) by a qualified creditor or qualified creditors only if the apparent
insolvency founded on in the petition was constituted within four
months before the date of presentation of the petition; or

(*b*) at any time by any other person.

(5) Without prejudice to the provisions of sections 14(1), 15(5) and 17(8)
of the Act, the clerk of court shall send a copy of every court order mentioned in those sections to the Registrar of Limited Partnerships in Scotland.

| Regulation 5 | SCHEDULE |
| | LIST OF FORMS |

Form No.	Purpose
1.	Statutory demand for payment of debt.
2.	Oath by creditor.
3.	Notice by the interim trustee in the *Edinburgh Gazette* and the *London Gazette*.
4.	List of the assets and liabilities of the debtor.
5.	Statement of claim by creditor.
6.	Notice by permanent trustee in the *Edinburgh Gazette* of confirmation in office.
7.	Notice by permanent trustee in the *Edinburgh Gazette* of public examination of the debtor or a relevant person.
8.	Certificate of discharge of debtor.
9.	Acceptance or rejection by creditor of an offer of compo-sition.
10.	Notice in *Edinburgh Gazette* by trustee under a trust deed for the benefit of creditors.
11.	Statement of realisation and distribution of estate under a protected trust deed.

FORM 1

STATUTORY DEMAND FOR PAYMENT OF DEBT
Bankruptcy (Scotland) Act 1985: Section 7(1)(*d*)

Warning to person receiving Demand
If you do nothing in response to this demand, you could be made bankrupt and your property and goods taken away from you. Please read **carefully** this Demand and Notes for Debtors.

Please do not ignore this form
If you are in any doubt about what to do, you should seek advice **immediately** from a solicitor or a Citizens Advice Bureau.

Notes for Creditors

This form must be served personally on the debtor by a sheriff officer or messenger-at-arms. An additional copy of the Demand should also be given to the debtor at the same time.

Insert name and address of debtor

Insert name and address of creditor

(a) Insert name and address of authorised person, but

* Delete if creditor is completing demand

(b) Insert name of creditor

(c) Insert name of debtor
* Delete as appropriate

(d) Insert amount of debt(s) claimed. The total of the debt(s) must not be less than £750.
(e) Describe the matters which led to the debt(s). If more space is needed please use a separate sheet of paper.

(f) Insert the reasons why it is claimed that the debt(s) forming the subject of the Demand are liquid. A debt is liquid where it is for a certain settled amount and is immediately payable by the debtor. There must also be clear evidence of the existence of the debt, for example, a written admission by the debtor or a document which establishes the debt (such as a court decree or contract).

The Demand

To _____

_____

From _____

_____

1. I, [(a) _____

_____

being a person authorised to act on behalf of]*

(b) _____
(the creditor) claim that as at the date of this Demand you

(c) _____
owe [me] [the creditor]* the sum of
(d) £ _____
    (the sum demanded)

2. The sum demanded is in respect of (e)

_____

_____

3. The sum demanded is immediately payable and consists of a liquid debt or debts in that

(f) _____

_____

4. If you believe

—that you do not owe the creditor the sum demanded or any part of it, or

—that you do not have to pay the sum demanded or any part of it immediately to the creditor

you must **IMMEDIATELY** fill in the **DENIAL SLIP** at the end of this form (or a copy of it) and post it, or a letter to the same effect to the creditor by **RECORDED DELIVERY POST** so as to arrive within 3 weeks after the date of service of this Demand on you (this date is shown in the Docquet of Service below).

5. If however you accept

   —that you owe the creditor the sum demanded <u>and</u>

   that you have to pay the sum demanded immediately to the creditor

you must, within the 3 week period mentioned in paragraph 4 above, pay it to the creditor or find security for its payment.

6. If, within the 3 week period mentioned in paragraph 4 above, you have not taken the steps mentioned in either paragraph 4 or 5 above, you may be made bankrupt by the court, and your property and goods put into the hands of a trustee for the benefit of all your creditors.

* Delete whichever does not apply

Signed _____

Creditor*/on behalf of creditor

Date _____

DOCQUET OF SERVICE

Note

This Docquet of Service should be completed by the messenger-at-arms or sheriff officer and witness at the time of serving the demand upon the debtor. The Docquet of Service on the duplicate demand, which is also to be given to the debtor, should also be completed.

(a) Insert name of debtor
(b) Insert date of service. This is the date after which the period of 3 weeks mentioned in paragraphs 4–6 of the above Demand starts to run.
(c) Insert name and address of messenger-at-arms or sheriff officer

To *(a)* _____

You are served with the above Demand on *(b)* _____

      by me,

(c) _____

* Delete whichever is inapplicable

in the presence of the witness who also signs below.

Signed _____

      Messenger-at-Arms*/
      Sheriff Officer

Date _____

Name and address of witness in BLOCK LETTERS

_____
_____

_____

Signed _____
      Witness

NOTES FOR DEBTOR—READ CAREFULLY

1. If you do nothing in response to this Demand you could be made bankrupt. **Please do not ignore this form**

2. *(a)* If you deny that you owe the sum demanded or any part of it; or

   (b) If you accept that you owe the sum demanded but deny that you have to pay it or any part of it immediately (even though you may admit that you must pay it at some time),

   you must fill in the attached Denial Slip (or a copy of it) and post it, or a letter to the same effect, to the creditor by **RECORDED DELIVERY POST**. This should be done **immediately** and before the end of the 3 week period mentioned in paragraph 4 of the form. If you do not do so, you could be made bankrupt.

   You should keep a copy of what you send to the creditor and the recorded delivery slip.

3. If, however, you accept—

   (a) that you owe the sum demanded; and

   (b) that you have to pay the sum demanded immediately to the creditor,

   you should either pay the sum demanded or find security for such payment. If you cannot do either you should get in touch with the creditor **immediately** and try to agree with him a way of paying off the sum demanded perhaps by paying by instalments.

   Even if the creditor agrees that the sum demanded or any part of it need not be paid immediately to him, you should still send the **Denial Slip** as in Note 2 above, to protect you from the possibility of being made bankrupt.

4. If you are in any doubt as to—

   (a) whether you owe the sum demanded or any part of it; or

   (b) whether the sum demanded or any part of it must be paid immediately; or

   (c) whether any of the details mentioned in connection with the debt(s) in paragraphs 2 and 3 of the form are correct; or

   (d) about what you should do with this form or its implications,

   you should seek advice **immediately** from a solicitor or from a Citizens Advice Bureau.

DENIAL SLIP

To be completed in the circumstances described in paragraph 4 of the Demand Form or in the notes for Debtor 2 and 3.

Note You must fill in and sign this Denial Slip. Tear it off and post it **immediately** to the creditor by **RECORDED DELIVERY POST** to arrive within the 3 week period mentioned in paragraph 4 of the Demand Form.

(a) Insert name and address of creditor

To *(a)* _____

_____

_____

_____

I refer to the demand served on me on

(b) Insert date of service of Demand as shown in the docquet of service

(b) _____

*Delete if inapplicable

I DENY

(c) and *(d)*

(c) that I owe you the sum demanded

Only delete *(c)* if you accept that you owe the whole of the sum demanded but retain *(d)* if you are denying that you have to pay that sum immediately

**(d)* that I have to pay you the sum demanded immediately.

Signature of debtor

Date _____

Name of debtor in BLOCK CAPITALS

_____
_____

Address of debtor

FORM 2

OATH BY CREDITOR

Bankruptcy (Scotland) Act 1985; Section 11(1)

This oath must be sworn by the creditor or a person authorised to act on his behalf before a person entitled to administer the oath, eg. in the U.K. a Notary Public (usually a Solicitor) or a Justice of the Peace.

In the case of an oath administered outside the U.K. see section 11(2)*(b)* of the Act.

(a) Insert name and address of creditor

(a) _____

(b) If applicable, insert name and address of authorised person acting on behalf of creditor

(b) _____

**Delete as appropriate*

I do solemnly and sincerely swear*/affirm that to the best of my knowledge and belief

(c) Insert name and address of debtor

(c) _____

**Delete as appropriate*

owes me*/the creditor ther sum of

(d) Insert total amount of the debt or debts amounting in aggregate, to not less than £750.

(d) £——— which is now payable and that the particulars of the debt or debts making up that sum, which are set out overleaf, are correct.

**Delete as appropriate*

Sworn*/Affirmed at (e) _____

(e) Insert name of place where oath is sworn

(f) Insert date

on (f) _____

(g) Name and address and designation of person administering the oath or affirmation

before (g) _____

Signed _____
           creditor*/on behalf of creditor

Signature of person administering the oath*/affirmation

**Delete as appropriate*

PARTICULARS OF EACH DEBT

Notes	
A separate set of particulars should be made out in respect of each debt.	
(1) Insert total amount of the debt which is now payable, showing separately the amount of principal and interest claimed. Interest may be claimed only where the creditor is entitled to it. Do not deduct the value of any security held at this stage (see Note 4).	**(1) Amount of debt**
(2) Specify what the debt is in respect of, the date or dates when it was incurred and when it became payable.	**(2) Details of debt**
(3) Attach any evidence of the debt, such as an extract decree (or copy of it certified by the Clerk of Court) or any voucher or other supporting evidence of the debt.	**(3) Evidence of debt**
(4) Specify the nature and value of any security held in respect of the debt or debts. For the purposes of the petition for sequestration, the value of any such security need not be deducted from the amount of the debt claimed.	**(4) Security for debt**
Security is defined for the purposes of the Bankruptcy (Scotland) Act 1985 as meaning "any security, heritable or moveable, or any right of lien, retention or preference".	

FORM 3

NOTICE BY THE INTERIM TRUSTEE IN THE EDINBURGH GAZETTE AND THE
LONDON GAZETTE

Bankruptcy (Scotland) Act 1985: Section 15(6)

Notes	Sequestration of the estate of *(a)*
(a) Insert name of debtor	
(b) Insert the name, designation and address of the debtor and, if he trades under a different name, state also his trading name and address	The estate of *(b)*————————
(c) Insert either "Court of Session" or "Sheriff"	was sequestrated by the *(c)* ————
(d) Insert name of sheriff court where applicable	at *(d)* ————————————
(e) Insert date of award of sequestration	on *(e)* ————————————
(f) Insert name, designation and business address of the interim trustee	and *(f)* ————————————
	has been appointed by the court to act as interim trustee on the sequestrated estate.
	Any creditor of the debtor named above is invited to submit his statement of claim in the prescribed form, with any supporting accounts or vouchers, to the interim trustee.

Any creditor known to the interim trustee will be notified of the date, time and place of the statutory meeting of creditors to elect a permanent trustee.

Signature of interim trustee

_____

Date _____

FORM 4

LIST OF THE ASSETS AND LIABILITIES OF THE DEBTOR

Bankruptcy (Scotland) Act 1985: Section 19(1)

WARNING TO THE DEBTOR

It is a criminal offence under section 19(2) of the Act for you, without reasonable excuse to—

• fail to submit a list of your assets and liabilities to the interim trustee within 7 days of his appointment in the case where you petitioned for the sequestration of your own estate, or,

• fail, in any other case, to submit a list within 7 days of being notified of the appointment of the interim trustee;

• fail to disclose any material fact in the list; or
• make a material mis-statement in the list.
On summary conviction you may be liable to a maximum fine of £1,000 or to imprisonment for a maximum period of 3 months or to both.

(a) Insert your name and adddress

I *(a)*

_____

_____

_____

have listed overleaf all my assets and liabilities as at the date of sequestration of my estate on *(b)* _____

(b) Insert date of sequestration. In the case where you petitioned for the sequestration of your estate it is the date of the court order awarding that sequestration. In any other case, it is the date on which the court granted warrant to cite you to appear before it.

I certify that the details in that list are true, complete and accurate to the best of my knowledge and belief.

Signature of debtor

_____

Date _____

LIST OF ASSETS AND LIABILITIES

Notes for debtor

1. You must list <u>separately</u> **all** *your assets as at the date of sequestration of your estate and*
(a) give a short description of each asset e.g. house, insurance policy, business assets etc.;
(b) state whether you own or lease each asset or what right you have to it. Also state whether it is held jointly with any other person, such as a house held jointly with your spouse;

1. **Assets**

(c) state whether the asset is subject to any security (e.g. a mortgage over your house) and give the amount of the debt secured by the security;

2. *You must list separately all your debts and other liabilities as at the date of sequestration of your estate and*
(a) *give a short description of each debt and attach any relevant bills or accounts. If the creditor holds a decree or has arrested or done other diligence for the debt, attach any relevant papers and copy decrees etc.; and*
(b) *state the name and address of the creditor.*

Use additional sheets of paper as necessary

2. Liabilities

FORM 5

STATEMENT OF CLAIM BY CREDITOR

Bankruptcy (Scotland) Act 1985: Sections 22(2)*(a)* and 48

WARNING

It is a criminal offence
● for a creditor to produce a statement of claim, account, voucher or other evidence which is false, unless he shows that he neither knew nor had reason to believe that it was false; or

● for a debtor who knows or becomes aware that it is false to fail to report it to the interim or permanent trustee within one month of acquiring such knowledge.
On conviction either creditor or debtor may be liable to a fine and/or imprisonment.

Notes

(a) *Insert name and address of debtor*

(b) *Insert name and address of creditor*

(c) *Insert name and address, if applicable, of authorised person acting on behalf of the creditor*

(d) *Insert total amount claimed in respect of all the debts, the particulars of which are set out overleaf.*

*Delete as appropriate

Sequestration of the estate of

(a) _____
_____
_____

(b) _____
_____

(c) _____
_____
_____
_____

I submit a claim of *(d)* £_____
in the above sequestration and certify that the particulars of the debt or debts making up that claim, which are set out overleaf, are true, complete and accurate, to the best of my knowledge and belief.

Signed _____
Creditor*/person acting on behalf of creditor

Date _____

PARTICULARS OF EACH DEBT

Notes

A separate set of particulars should be made out in respect of each debt.

1. Describe briefly the debt, giving details of its nature, the date when it was incurred and when payment became due.

Attach any documentary evidence of the debt, if available.

2. Insert total amount of the debt, showing separately the amount of principal and any interest which is due on the debt as at the date of sequestration. Interest may only be claimed if the creditor is entitled to it. Show separately the V.A.T. on the debt and indicate whether the V.A.T. is being claimed back from H.M. Customs and Excise

3. Specify and give details of the nature of any security held in respect of the debt including—

(a) the subjects covered and the date when it was given;

(b) the value of the security.

Note: The permanent trustee may, at any time after 12 weeks from the date of sequestration, require a creditor to discharge a security or to convey or assign it to him on payment of the value specified by the creditor.

(c) whether the creditor is surrendering or undertakes to surrender the security.

Security is defined for the purposes of the Bankruptcy (Scotland) Act 1985 as meaning "any security, heritable or moveable, or any right of lien, retention or preference".

4. In calculating the total amount of his claim, a secured creditor must deduct the value of any security as estimated by him, unless he surrenders it (see note 3(c) above).

1. **Particulars of debt**

2. **Amount of debt**

3. **Security for debt**

4. **Total amount of the debt**

FORM 6

NOTICE BY PERMANENT TRUSTEE IN THE EDINBURGH GAZETTE OF
CONFIRMATION IN OFFICE

Bankruptcy (Scotland) Act 1985: Section 25(6)(b)

Notes	
(a) Insert name of debtor	Sequestration of the estate of
	(a) _____
(b) Insert name and address of permanent trustee	I (b) _____
	_____
	_____
	_____
	give notice that I have been confirmed as permanent trustee on the sequestrated estate of *(c)*
(c) Insert name and address of debtor	
	_____
(d) Insert Sheriff Court	by the Sheriff at *(d)* _____
	_____
(e) Insert date	on *(e)* _____
	Signature of permanent trustee
	Date _____

FORM 7

NOTICE BY PERMANENT TRUSTEE IN THE EDINBURGH GAZETTE OF PUBLIC
EXAMINATION OF THE DEBTOR OR A RELEVANT PERSON

Bankruptcy (Scotland) Act 1985: Section 45(3)(a)

Notes	
(a) Insert name of debtor	Sequestration of the estate of *(a)*
(b) Insert name of Sheriff Court	The Sheriff at *(b)* _____ has ordered that a public examination of
(c) Insert name and address of person(s) to be examined	(c) _____
	_____
	_____
(d) Insert address of place of examination	will take place at *(d)* _____
	_____
(e) Insert day, date and time of examination	on *(e)* _____
	Signature of permanent trustee
	Date _____

FORM 8

CERTIFICATE OF DISCHARGE OF DEBTOR

Bankruptcy (Scotland) Act 1985: Section 54(2)

Notes

The effect of this discharge is stated in Section 55 of the Act which is in the following terms:—

"55.—(1) Subject to subsection (2) below, on the debtor's discharge under section 54 of this Act, the debtor shall be discharged within the United Kingdom of all debts and obligations contracted by him, or for which he was liable, at the date of sequestration.

(2) The debtor shall be discharged by virtue of subsection (1) above from—

(a) any liability to pay a fine or other penalty due to the Crown;

(b) any liability to forfeiture of a sum of money deposited in court under section 1(3) of the Bail etc. (Scotland) Act 1980;

(c) any liability incurred by reason of fraud or breach of trust;

(d) any obligation to pay aliment or any sum of an alimentary nature under any enactment or rule of law or any periodical allowance payable on divorce by virtue of a court order or under an obligation, not being aliment or a periodical allowance which could be included in the amount of a creditor's claim under paragraph 2 of Schedule 1 to this Act;

(e) the obligation imposed on him by section 64 of this Act.".

Section 64(1)of the Act requires the debtor to take every practical step, and in particular to execute any document, which may be necessary to enable the permanent trustee to perform the functions conferred upon him by the Act.

Notes

(a) *Insert name of debtor*

(b) *Insert name and address of debtor*

(c) *Insert date of sequestration*

**Delete whichever is inappropriate. A discharge is granted under or by virtue of section 54 where the debtor's estate was sequestrated on or after 1st April 1986 and under or by virtue of section 75(4) if it was sequestrated before that date.*

(d) *Insert date of discharge.*

Sequestration of the estate of
(a)_____

I certify that (b) _____
_____
_____
_____

whose estate was sequestrated on

(c) _____
was discharged under or by virtue of section 54*/75(4) of the Bankruptcy (Scotland) Act 1985 on

(d) _____

Signature of
Accountant in Bankruptcy

_____
Date _____

FORM 9

ACCEPTANCE OR REJECTION BY CREDITOR OF AN OFFER OF COMPOSITION

Bankruptcy (Scotland) Act 1985: Schedule 4 paragraph 4*(c)*

Notes	Sequestration of the estate of
(a) Insert name of debtor	*(a)* _____
(b) Insert name and address of permanent trustee	To *(b)* _____ _____ _____ _____
(c) Insert name and address of creditor	I *(c)* _____ _____ _____
*Delete whichever is inappropriate	accept*/reject the offer of composition made by or on behalf of
(d) Insert name and address of debtor	*(d)* _____ _____ _____
(f) Insert date	which was summarised in the report which you sent me on *(f)* _____
	Signature of Creditor _____ Date _____

FORM 10

NOTICE IN EDINBURGH GAZETTE BY TRUSTEE UNDER A TRUST DEED FOR THE BENEFIT OF CREDITORS

Bankruptcy (Scotland) Act 1985: Schedule 5 paragraph 5*(b)*

Notes

If within the 4 week period referred to in the notice a majority in number and not less than two thirds in value of the creditors accede to the trust deed and a certified copy of the trust deed is then sent by the trustee to the Accountant in Bankruptcy for registration in the Register of Insolvencies, then the trust deed will become a protected trust deed.

The effect of this is that paragraphs 6 and 7 of Schedule 5 to the Act will apply to the trust deed. Briefly, this has the effect of restricting the rights of non-acceding creditors and to confer certain protection upon the trust deed from being superseded by the sequestration of the debtor's estate.

Notes	Trust deed for creditors by
(a) Insert name of debtor	*(a)* _____
(b) Insert name, designation and address of debtor, and if he trades under a different name, state also his trading name and address	A trust deed has been granted by *(b)* _____ _____ _____ _____
(c) Insert date of granting of trust deed	on *(c)*
(d) Insert name and address of trustee	conveying his estate to me *(d)* _____ _____ _____ _____

as trustee for the benefit of his creditors generally.

In order that the trust deed may become a protected trust deed (see notes), all creditors of the debtor are invited to accede to the trust deed within 4 weeks of the date of publication of this notice in the *Edinburgh Gazette*.

Signature of
trustee _____

Date _____

FORM 11

STATEMENT OF REALISATION AND DISTRIBUTION OF ESTATE UNDER A PROTECTED TRUST DEED

Bankruptcy (Scotland) Act 1985: Schedule 5 paragraph 9*(a)*

Notes	Protected trust deed of
(a) Insert name of debtor	*(a)* _____
	The statement overleaf is a true and accurate account of my realisation and distribution of the estate of
(b) Insert name and address of debtor	*(b)* _____
	_____
	_____
	_____
	under the trust deed granted in my favour for the benefit of his creditors dated
(c) Insert date of trust deed	*(c)* _____
	Signature of trustee _____
	Name and address _____
	_____
	_____
	Date _____

STATEMENT

Notes

Receipts

Item   Book value   Sum realised

Total sum realised £ _____

Other receipts (e.g. Bank interest)

Total receipts £ _____

Distribution of estate

(a) *Give details of all the expenses connected with the administration of the estate including your outlays and remuneration.*

(a) Administrative expenses

(b) *Give details of any payments made to secured creditors*

(b) Secured creditors

(c) *Give details of any payments made to preferred creditors*

(c) Preferred creditors

(d) *State the rate of dividend paid, the total amount of the claims of ordinary creditors and the total amount paid to them. List in an annex the amounts paid to individual ordinary creditors and their claims.*

(d) Ordinary creditors

A dividend of   p. in the £   on claims lodged of   , as per annex.

Total sum distributed £ _____

Act of Sederunt (Bankruptcy) 1986

(S.I. 1986 No. 517)

[11th March 1986]

The Lords of Council and Session, under and by virtue of the powers conferred on them by section 32 of the Sheriff Courts (Scotland) Act 1971 (c. 58), sections 1, 14, 25 of, and paragraph 2(2) of Schedule 2 and paragraph 2(1) and 2(2) of Schedule 5 to, the Bankruptcy (Scotland) Act 1985 (c. 66), and of all other powers competent to them in that behalf, do hereby enact and declare—

Citation, commencement and interpretation
1.—(1) This Act of Sederunt may be cited as the Act of Sederunt (Bankruptcy) 1986 and shall come into operation on 1st April 1986.
(2) This Act of Sederunt shall be inserted in the Books of Sederunt.
(3) In this Act of Sederunt—
"the 1985 Act" means the Bankruptcy (Scotland) Act 1985.

Revocation
2. The Act of Sederunt (Summary Sequestrations) 1937 is revoked.

Appeals
3.—(1) An appeal under section 13(8) (against appointment by court of interim trustee), 15(3) (against order refusing to award sequestration), 29(4) (against order of the sheriff removing a permanent trustee), 54(6) (against order deferring discharge of debtor or dismissal of an application to defer discharge) or under paragraph 8(3) of Schedule 4 (against order approving or refusing to approve offer of compensation) of the 1985 Act shall be taken by note of appeal which shall be written by the appellant on the interlocutor sheet, or other written record containing the interlocutor appealed against, or on a separate sheet lodged with the sheriff clerk; and such note of appeal shall be as nearly as may be in the following terms:-
"The (*state appellant*) appeals to the (*Sheriff Principal/Court of Session*),"
and such note of appeal shall be signed by the appellant or his solicitor and shall bear the date on which it is signed.
(2) Where the 1985 Act does not specify the time within which an appeal shall be taken, such appeal shall be taken within fourteen days of the date of the interlocutor appealed against.
(3) Where the appeal is an appeal to the Court of Session the note of appeal shall specify the name and address of the solicitors in Edinburgh who will be acting for the appellant in the appeal.
(4) On an appeal being taken to the Sheriff Principal the sheriff clerk shall transmit the process within four days to the Sheriff Principal, and on an appeal to the Court of Session he shall transmit the process within four days to the Deputy Principal Clerk of Session.
(5) Within the period of four days referred to in sub-paragraph (4) the sheriff clerk shall send written notice of the appeal—
    (*a*) in the case of any appeal under section 13(8) of the 1985 Act, to such other party as shall be specified by the court from which the appeal is made;
    (*b*) in the case of an appeal under section 15(3) of the 1985 Act, to any concurring creditor and the debtor, as the case may be;
    (*c*) in the case of an appeal under section 29(4) of the 1985 Act, to the permanent trustee, the Accountant in Bankruptcy, the commissioners

and any person representing not less than one quarter in value of the creditors, as the case may be;

(*d*) in the case of an appeal under section 54(6) of the 1985 Act, to the applicant creditor, the permanent trustee and the debtor, as the case may be;

(*e*) in the case of an appeal under paragraph 8(3) of Schedule 4 of the 1985 Act, to the permanent trustee, the debtor and the creditors to whom notice of the hearing fixed by the sheriff was given, as the case may be,

and shall certify on the interlocutor that he has done so.

(6) Failure by the sheriff clerk to give notice prescribed in sub-paragraph (5) shall not invalidate the appeal.

Forms

4.—(1) The register of insolvencies maintained by the Accountant in Bankruptcy under section 1(1)(*c*) of the 1985 Act shall be as nearly as may be in accordance with Form 1 as set out in the Schedule to this Act of Sederunt.

(2) The memorandum to be sent by a permanent trustee to the Keeper of the register of inhibitions and adjudications under section 14(4) of the 1985 Act shall be as nearly as may be in accordance with Form 2 as set out in the Schedule to this Act of Sederunt.

(3) The act and warrant issued by the sheriff clerk under section 25(2) or paragraph 2(2) of Schedule 2 to the 1985 Act shall be as nearly as may be in accordance with Form 3 as set out in the Schedule to this Act of Sederunt.

(4) A notice by a trustee under a trust deed for creditors to be recorded in the register of inhibitions and adjudications under paragraph 2(1) of Schedule 5 to the 1985 Act shall be as nearly as may be in accordance with Form 4 as set out in the Schedule to this Act of Sederunt.

(5) A notice under paragraph 2(2) of Schedule 5 to the 1985 Act recalling a notice referred to in sub-paragraph (4) shall be as nearly as may be in accordance with Form 5 as set out in the Schedule to this Act of Sederunt.

Amendment

5. [Amendment to the Bankruptcy (Scotland) Act 1985, s. 47(4) is incorporated in the print of that Act.]

SCHEDULE

Paragraph 4(1) FORM 1
Form of register of insolvencies

A. Sequestrations

Name of debtor

Debtor's residence and his principal place of business (if any) at date of sequestration or date of death

Date of death in case of deceased debtor

Occupation of debtor

Name and address of petitioner for sequestration

Court by which sequestration awarded

Sheriff court to which sequestration remitted (where applicable)

Date of first order

Date of award of sequestration

Date of recall of sequestration (where applicable)

Name and address of interim trustee and date of appointment

Name and address of permanent trustee and date of confirmation of appointment

Date of debtor's discharge and whether on composition or by operation of law

Date of interim trustee's discharge

Date of permanent trustee's discharge

B. Protected Trust Deeds for Creditors

Name and address of granter of trust deed

Name and address of trustee under the deed

Date (or dates) of execution of deed

Date on which copy deed and certificate of accession were registered

Date of registration of statement indicating how the estate was realised and distributed and certificate to the effect that the distribution was in accordance with the trust deed

Date of trustee's discharge

Date of registration of copy of order of court that non-acceding creditor is not bound by trustee's discharge

Paragraph 4(2)   **FORM 2**

Form of memorandum by permanent trustee to be recorded in the register of inhibitions and adjudications under section 14(4) of the Bankruptcy (Scotland) Act 1985

From: A.B. (*name and address*) trustee in the sequestration of C.D. (*name and address*)

To: Keeper of register of inhibitions and adjudications

A certified copy of the order of the court awarding sequestration on (*date*) in respect of C.D. is recorded in your Register on (*date*).

Record this memorandum to renew the effect of that recording for a further period of 3 years.

                     (*Signed*) A.B. [*or* E.F., Solicitor for A.B.]

(*Date*)

Paragraph 4(3)   **FORM 3**

Form of Act and Warrant on confirmation or appointment of the trustee under section 25(2) or paragraph 2(2) of Schedule 2 respectively to the Bankruptcy (Scotland) Act 1985

                         (*Place and Date**)

The Sheriff of the Sheriffdom of (*insert Sheriffdom*) has *[confirmed/appointed] and hereby *[confirms/appoints] A.B. (*insert name and designation*) as permanent trustee on the sequestrated estate of C.D. (*insert name and designation*); and the whole estate wherever situated of C.D. at (*insert date of sequestration*) is vested in and now belongs to A.B. as trustee for the benefit of the creditors of C.D. in terms of the Bankruptcy (Scotland) Act 1985.

                         (*Signed*) E.F. Sheriff Clerk

*Delete as appropriate

Paragraph 4(4)   FORM 4

Form of notice of inhibition by trustee under trust deed to be recorded in register of inhibitions and adjudications under paragraph 2(1) of Schedule 5 to the Bankruptcy (Scotland) Act 1985

A trust deed within the meaning of the Bankruptcy (Scotland) Act 1985 has been granted by C.D. (*name and address*) and delivered to A.B. (*name and address*) as trustee acting under the trust deed.

Under the trust deed the estate of C.D. has been conveyed to A.B. as trustee for the benefit of the creditors generally of C.D.

         (*Signed*) A.B. [*or* E.F., Solicitor for A.B.]

(*Date*)

Paragraph 4(5)   FORM 5

Form of notice of recall of inhibition under paragraph 2(2) of Schedule 5 to the Bankruptcy (Scotland) Act 1985 to be recorded in the register of inhibitions and adjudications

The notice by A.B. (*name and address*) as trustee under the trust deed for creditors of C.D. (*name and address*) recorded on (*date*) is now recalled.

         (*Signed* A.B. [*or* E.F., Solicitor for A.B.]

(*Date*)

[THE NEXT PAGE IS H 401]

Notes by the Accountant of Court

**Notes by the Accountant of Court for the
Guidance of Trustees in Sequestrations**

With Note of Fees Payable and Appendix

I.—*Preliminary*

The Act of Parliament, applicable to the administration of estates in bankruptcy, the duties of trustees and commissioners, and the supervision thereof by the Accountant of Court, is *The Bankruptcy (Scotland) Act 1913*.

It is to be observed that the Accountant has no right to interfere with the *administration and management* of estates in bankruptcy; his power is one of *control* of trustees and commissioners, to the effect of providing for the performance of their duties. This power is *official*, rather than *judicial*. It is exercised subject to the directions of the court.

II.—*Noting of Claims by Trustee*

The Act provides (section 46) that the trustee shall, on production of the oaths and grounds of debt by creditors, mark them with his initials, and make an entry of them in the sederunt book, and of the date when the same were produced.

III.—*Taking Possession of, Managing, and Realising the Estate*

Under section 76 of the Act, it is the duty of the trustee to take possession of the bankrupt's estate and effects, and of his title deeds, books, bills, vouchers, and other papers and documents. He is next required to make up an inventory of the estate and effects, and a valuation showing the estimated value, and the annual revenue thereof, and forthwith to transmit a copy of such inventory and valuation to the Accountant. See form of inventory and notes applicable to it (Appendix I).

Under section 78, the trustee " shall manage, realise, and recover the estate belonging to the bankrupt, wherever situated " (including non-vested contingent rights) " and convert the same into money, according to the directions given by the creditors at any meeting; and, if no such directions are given, he shall do so with the advice of the commissioners ".

(The duties of the commissioners in relation to the trustee are to audit his accounts, fix his commission, superintend his proceedings, and give advice and assistance relative to his management. See sections 81 and 121.)

A power is given to the trustee, with the consent of the commissioners, to compound and transact and refer to arbitration, questions regarding the estate, or claims made thereon. See section 172.

IV.—*Examination of the Bankrupt, and of Others who can give Information Relative to the Estate*

The trustee's duties in regard to the bankrupt's examination will be found stated in sections 83 to 91 inclusive. The 83rd section provides that the trustee shall advertise his election, and the examination of the bankrupt, etc., in the *Edinburgh Gazette*, and shall send special notices to the creditors. A copy of this and of all other circulars must be sent to the Accountant (section 80). In the case of a deceased bankrupt the Accountant suggests that intimation of the trustee's election, etc., should be made within eight days of the date of the trustee's Act and Warrant.

Besides affording all necessary information in regard to the position of the bankrupt's affairs at the date of the sequestration, the examination ought to disclose the causes of the bankruptcy, where these are not set forth by the bankrupt in his state of affairs, so that parties interested may be able to ascertain, from one or other of these sources, whether the bankruptcy has arisen from innocent misfortunes or losses in business, or from culpable or undue conduct (see section 143). If more than one of these causes have operated to bring about the result of bankruptcy, the examination and state ought to make it clear, in so far as practicable, to what extent the deficiency has been created by the separate operation of these respective causes.

The following example may be given to illustrate the foregoing observations:—

Assets, say	£500·00
Liabilities, say	1,000·00
Amount of Deficiency	£500·00

Arising as follows:—

From losses in business arising from bad debts, say   £100·00

From losses on raising money by accommodation bills, say ....100·00

From losses on speculation in dealing in stocks and shares, say ....100·00

From losses arising from pawning or selling goods by auction, out of the ordinary course of trade ....100·00

Extravagance arising from expense of living, not met by the returns or profits of business, say ....100·00

——— £500.00.

Where it is impossible to give an account of the deficiency in figures by reason of the failure of the bankrupt to keep books, this should be brought out distinctly in the examination.

Where the causes of bankruptcy have been satisfactorily disclosed by the bankrupt by explanations given to the trustee personally, it may not be necessary to bring out these explanations in the public examination of the bankrupt, BUT THE TRUSTEE OUGHT TO MINUTE SUCH EXPLANATIONS, EITHER IN HIS REPORT TO THE SECOND MEETING OF CREDITORS OR OTHERWISE, SO THAT THEY MAY APPEAR IN THE RECORD OF THE SEDERUNT BOOK.

It occurs in some sequestrations that the bankrupt has been engaged in concocting claims by false entries in books, or by fictitious accounts and vouchers. It also not infrequently occurs that the bankrupt has given fraudulent preferences to creditors, which may be set aside. In either of these cases the examination ought to bear fully and distinctly upon such transactions.

The examination, state of affairs, and explanations are of the utmost importance, as forming the foundation of the trustee's report to the second meeting of creditors (section 92), and of his report on the bankrupt's conduct (section 143).

If the bankrupt has been guilty of fraudulent conduct for which he may be prosecuted criminally, these documents ought to disclose the particulars of the offences with which he is chargeable. They ought also to bear evidence on the subject of fraudulent concealment of effects, or other elements in the bankrupt's trading or conduct, which are material in the consideration of his right to discharge.

The trustee, in conducting the examination, is bound to keep in view the provision as regards fraudulent bankruptcy contained in the Act, section 178.

V.—*The Trustee's Report to the Second Meeting of Creditors*

This report is required under the 92nd section. It is an appropriate medium for communicating with the creditors on the subject of any matters relating to the administration and management in regard to which the trustee may require their directions under the 78th section, or for submitting to them any facts connected with the bankrupt's conduct, which he desires to bring before them.

It is in the trustee's report to the second meeting of creditors, under the 92nd section of the Act, that the state of the bankrupt's affairs is set forth by the trustee. In this report the trustee is required to submit an estimate of what the estate may produce. This estimate may be brought out by stating the *gross* estate as in the inventory, and deducting therefrom the secured and preferable debts, and the expenses as estimated, and bringing out the net assets available for division amongst the ordinary or unsecured creditors, at so much per £ on the amount of their debts, so far as then known to the trustee.

VI.—*Making up Accounts, Audit thereof, and Transmission of Copies to Accountant*

It is enacted (section 80) that the trustee " shall also keep regular accounts of the affairs of the estate, and transmit to the Accountant, before each of the periods herein assigned for payment of a dividend, a *copy*, certified by himself, of such accounts, in so far as not previously transmitted ".

In sections 121, 127, and 129 the accounts, and the periods at which these are to be made up, are specified. These periods are:—

1st.   At the end of four months from date of award of sequestration.
2nd.   At the end of eights months   „   „   „
3rd.   At the end of eleven months   „   „   „   , and

Each succeeding account at the end of three months from the close of the immediately preceding account. It should be specially noted that the closing dates are calculated from the date of the actual award and not from the date of the first deliverance on the petition for sequestration.

Trustees should present their accounts in a form which will show the whole estate of the bankrupt, the funds recovered by the trustee, and the property outstanding (V, section 121). A form of account charge and discharge (see Appendix II (*a*)) indicates how this may be done. In addition, it is important that an account-current should be prepared, showing the daily balances in bank and in the trustee's hands (see Appendix II (*b*)); this will show at a glance whether the provisions of section 79 have been properly observed (see also paragraph VII below).

Where a dividend is paid, the account must show in detail the date of the payment, the name of the creditor, and the amount paid to him.

The duties of the commissioners, in relation to the audit of the accounts, are set forth in separate notes issued by the accountant for their guidance. In particular, trustees should note that the commissioners must meet to audit the accounts within fourteen days of the respective closing dates, whether a dividend is to be declared or not.

Trustees are directed by the Act to transmit to the accountant *copies, certified by themselves,* of their accounts *before* each of the periods assigned for payment of a dividend. The periods for payment of dividends are assigned in sections 126, 128, and 129, *i.e.* two months after the respective closing dates of the accounts, and copies of the accounts ought to be transmitted before these periods, WHETHER A DIVIDEND HAS BEEN DECLARED OR POSTPONED. The periods before which copies of the trustee's accounts ought to be transmitted to the Accountant, unless these periods are altered as aftermentioned (see Note VIII), are therefore:—

First Account, before the end of six months from the date of *awarding* sequestration.

Second Account, before the end of ten months from the date of *awarding* sequestration.

Third Account, before the end of thirteen months from the date of *awarding* sequestration, and

Each succeeding account before the end of three months from the preceding period for transmission.

A copy of the commissioners' docquet of audit must be appended to the copy account lodged with the Accountant.

Where the sequestration embraces both the company's and individual partner's estates, it is *essential* that the intromissions with these be kept separate and distinct.

It is provided by the 80th section that the accounts shall be patent to the commissioners and to the creditors or their agents, at all times.

Re procedure in summary sequestrations, see paragraph XXI.

VII.—*Deposit of Money in Bank*

It is enacted (section 78) " The trustee shall lodge all money which he shall receive in such bank as the majority of the creditors in number and value, at any general meeting, shall appoint, and failing such appointment, in any joint-stock bank of issue in Scotland (provided that the bank be not one in which the trustee shall be an acting partner, manager, agent, or cashier); and the money shall be lodged in the name of the trustee, in his official character under this Act ".

The penalties for failure in this duty are: (1) (by section 79 as amended by the Insolvency Act 1976) " If the trustee shall keep in his hands any sum exceeding £100 belonging to the estate for more than ten days, he shall pay interest to the creditors at the rate of £20 per centum per annum on the excess of such sum above £100, for such time as the same shall be in his hands beyond ten days; and unless the money has been so kept from innocent causes, the trustee shall be dismissed from his office upon petition to the Lord Ordinary or sheriff, by any creditor, and have no claim to remuneration, and shall be liable in expenses "; and (2) by the 158th section, the failure in duty may be reported by the Accountant to the Lord Ordinary or the sheriff, who shall have power to censure such trustees, or remove them from their office, or otherwise deal with them as the justice of the case may require.

The Court of Session has found (*Freyd's Trustee*, 29th June 1864, 2 M. 1293) that the fund set apart by the commissioners for the payment of a dividend forms part of the funds of the sequestrated estate, and is subject to the provisions before quoted as to the lodging of the moneys of the estate in bank. According to this decision, the trustee is not entitled to withdraw from bank the amount set apart for payment of a dividend at the time at which it is payable, but only to draw from time to time such sums as may be required to meet the payments to the creditors, as they claim their dividends. If a trustee hold in his hands moneys of the estate (whether set apart for dividends or not) beyond the limit prescribed by the section of the Act before quoted, he is liable to the penalties thereby imposed.

VIII.—*Adjudication on Claims and Payment of Dividends*

By the 118th section the trustee may, with the consent of the commissioners, dispense with the necessity for lodging oaths relative to certain preferable debts, and may pay such debts before the period for payment of the first dividend.

By the 123rd section the trustee may, *at any time after a claim has been lodged*, require further evidence in support thereof, and, where a dividend is to be paid, the trustee shall, within fourteen days after the expiry of the first four months, examine the oaths and grounds of debt, and in writing reject or admit them, or require further evidence, and he shall complete the list of creditors entitled to draw a dividend (see sections 119 and 120). The trustee ought not to proceed to adjudicate on the claims until he is in a position to declare a dividend (*Monkhouse* v. *Mackinnon* (1881) 8 R. 454).

By the 124th section the trustee shall give notice of the dividend in the *Gazette*, and by circular; and, when he has rejected any claim, he shall notify the same by letter with a copy of his deliverance.

By the 125th section the trustee shall, before the expiration of six months from the date of award, make up a scheme of division, and send notice to each creditor of the amount of his dividend.

By the 126th section the trustee shall pay the dividend on the first lawful day after the expiration of the six months, and shall lodge in bank dividends under appeal, or on contingent claims.

The 127th, 128th, and 129th sections provide for similar procedure in the case of subsequent dividends.

The 130th section authorises the acceleration of dividends, if found to be expedient. When application is made to the Accountant under this section there should be sent with it a certified copy minute by the commissioners authorising the trustee to make the appliocation.

The 131st section provides for the postponement of dividends, and for the disposing with the *Gazette* notice thereof, if the commissioners think fit.

The 132nd section authorises the alteration of the statutory periods in cases in which the winding up is necessarily postponed. In this way the statutory periods may be extended and reduced in number, and the expenses consequently diminished.

The trustee must keep in view that a fee of 5 per cent. is payable to the Accountant in respect of dividends declared on the preferable and ordinary claims as ranked.

The total amount to be distributed should be intimated to the Accountant in order that the appropriate note of fee may be issued. The dividends on the preferable claims should be shown separately in the trustee's accounts.

IX.—*Annual Returns to the Sheriff-Clerks*

The provisions of section 157 regarding these returns are now in abeyance.

X.—*The Sequestration Sederunt Book*

It is the duty of the trustee to keep the sederunt book, which it is provided shall be patent to the commissioners and to the creditors or their agents, at all times (see section 80).

The sederunt book must contain a complete record of the case. Among the documents and records which the Act requires to be engrossed in it, the following should be specially noted, *viz.*:

1. The election of the commissioners, which is to be declared by a deliverance of the sheriff in the sederunt book (section 72).

2. An entry is to be made by the trustee of the production to him by creditors of their oaths and grounds of debt (section 46).

3. The intimation of the recall of a mandate by a creditor in favour of a commissioner is to be recorded (section 72).

4. The state of affairs made up by the bankrupt is to be engrossed with A COPY OF THE DOCQUET STATING THAT THIS IS THE STATE SIGNED BY THE BANKRUPT AND THE SHERIFF IN RELATION TO THE STATUTORY OATH (section 77).

5. The oath which the bankrupt is required to make before the close of his examination must be engrossed (section 91).

6. The minutes of creditors and of commissioners, states of accounts, reports, circulars sent by trustee, and certificates of their having been posted, and all proceedings necessary to give a correct view of the management of the estate, must be recorded (section 80).

7. The commissioners are required to certify, by a writing under their hands, engrossed or copied in the sederunt book, the balance due to or by the trustee in his account with the estate, as at the expiration of the periods at which the trustee's accounts are ordered to be made up (section 121).

8. A COPY OF THE TRUSTEE'S REPORT ON THE BANKRUPT'S CONDUCT MUST BE ENGROSSED (section 143).

9. A complete list of the documents which the Accountant requires to be affixed in the sederunt book is shown in Appendix III (*a*) (Ordinary Sequestrations).

The Accountant is empowered (section 159) to require *exhibition* of the sederunt book.

XI.—Final Meeting of Creditors and Trustee's Discharge

It is provided by the 152nd section, that after a final division of the funds, the trustee shall, by advertisement in the *Gazette* and by letters to the creditors, call a meeting of the creditors, to be held not sooner than fourteen days after such publication in the *Gazette*, to consider as to an application for his discharge, and he shall lay before the creditors the sederunt book, accounts, and a list of unclaimed dividends, and the creditors may declare their opinion of his conduct.

(*Note.*—This provision does not apply to summary sequestrations.) *See also paragraph XX.*

The trustee must, before his discharge, transmit the sederunt book to the Accountant (section 153).

He must also transmit a continuation of his accounts from the statutory period immediately preceding, down to the actual close of his accounts.

The trustee on being directed by the Accountant must deposit the unclaimed dividends and any unapplied balance in bank, on consignation receipt and transmit said consignation receipt to him, in terms of section 153. A fee of £3.00 is payable on each consignation receipt lodged with the Accountant. Forms of consignation receipts for unclaimed dividends and unapplied balances are subjoined. The money should be consigned in the principal Edinburgh office of the bank.

Form of Consignation Receipt for Unclaimed Dividend

Received on account of the Accountant of Court by the hands of A.B. (*design*), Trustee in the Sequestration of C.D. (*design*), the sum of   , being the amount of dividends unclaimed in said Sequestration, conform to list annexed, lodged in terms of section 153 of the Bankruptcy (Scotland) Act 1913.

List of Unclaimed Dividends referred to in the foregoing Receipt

Names, Designations and last known addresses of Creditors entitled to Dividends.	Amount of Claim.	Particulars of Dividends.	Amount Deposited.
E.F., Merchant in G…	£	3rd Dividend being at the rate of per pound on ordinary claims.	£

Form of Consignation Receipt for Unapplied Balance

Received on account of the Accountant of Court, by the hands of A.B. (*design*), Trustee in the Sequestration of C.D. (*design*), the sum of   , being amount of unapplied balance in said Sequestration lodged in terms of section 153 of the Bankruptcy (Scotland) Act 1913.

The expenses of the trustee's discharge should not exceed £90.00 (exclusive of VAT) in an ordinary sequestration, or £26.00 (exclusive of VAT) in a summary sequestration, and the trustee should reserve the appropriate sum before making a final division of the estate. The Accountant does not call for the exhibition of law accounts charged within these limits.

The transmission of the sederunt book, before the trustee's discharge, is required from *every* trustee in any sequestration (section 153). There is no distinction made regarding this duty between sequestrations wound up by composition, including deed of arrangement, and those wound up by a division of the funds.

A fee of £14.00 is payable to the Accountant for the examination of the sederunt book and the issue of the certificate which entitles the trustee to apply for his discharge. This fee applies to both ordinary and summary sequestrations and the trustee should keep in view to make reservation therefor in his final scheme of division. Where a certificate is issued in terms of section 176(8–2) no such fee is exigible.

On the trustee's discharge being granted an extract thereof will be transmitted to the Accountant by the clerk of court (sections 152 and 176(15)). Accordingly no charge is allowed in the account of expenses of discharge for agency transmitting extract to the Accountant.

XII.—*Composition Settlements*

Sections 134 to 142 and section 145 detail the trustee's duties in sequestrations in which a composition settlement is carried through. The Accountant does not think it necessary to detail these, but he wishes to point out that section 135 provides that the Lord Ordinary or sheriff if he shall find that the offer has been duly made and assented to, and "is *reasonable*", shall pronounce a deliverance approving thereof.

In cases of sequestrations wound up under composition-contracts, the trustee ought to transmit to the Accountant at the proper periods as above—

1. Copies of his accounts, certified by himself, brought down to the statutory periods (for making up such accounts), which may have occurred before the composition shall have been approved of; and

2. Copy of his final account.

It is provided (section 137) that the judge, on discharging the bankrupt, shall declare the sequestration at an end, and (section 139) exoner and discharge the trustee.

The trustee, however, in order to obtain delivery of his bond of caution, must transmit the sederunt book to the Accountant in terms of the 153rd section, having engrossed in it (in addition to the documents necessary both in composition and division cases): (1) the circular letter and abstract state of affairs, and valuation of the estate (sections 134 and 136) sent to the creditors previous to the meeting at which the composition was decided on, with certificate of postage thereof; (2) the bond of caution for the composition; and (3) the trustee's report to the sheriff as to the composition.

XIII.—*Trustee's Report on the Bankrupt's Conduct*

The trustee is required to prepare this report *as soon as may be after the bankrupt's examination*, and to engross a copy of it in the sederunt book under the provisions of the 143rd section. It must be produced in the proceedings for the bankrupt's discharge, in terms of that section, and it is also evidence which may be founded on under the provisions of the 149th section of the Act. The 143rd section specifies the particulars of the bankrupt's conduct upon which the trustee is required to report. It may be possible, in some cases, to adopt in this report the very words of the Act; but these words ought to be employed with caution, and where there are any peculiar circumstances connected with the conduct of the bankrupt, or the causes of the bankruptcy (such as fraudulent concealment of estates or effects, refusal to comply with the provisions of the Bankruptcy Act, reckless trading, betting, gambling, extravagance, or failure to keep proper books), these ought to be clearly brought out. If the trustee should report generally in the words of the statute, in a case where there were, in point of fact, elements which ought to have been set forth specially for the information of the judge in dealing with the bankrupt's application for discharge, he may be called on afterwards in court to justify his report.

It has already been suggested in these notes that the examination of the bankrupt, and of others who can give information relative to the estate, the bankrupt's state of affairs, and the explanations which the bankrupt may have given the trustee, afford the materials upon which this report ought to be based.

Even though the bankrupt should die during the course of the sequestration a report must be prepared in all cases where he has been examined in court, as the bankrupt's representatives may apply for his discharge.

The trustee is not entitled to any fee for his report on the bankrupt's conduct. (See *White* v. *Robertson*, 19th March 1879, 6. R. 854.)

XIV.—*Recording Abbreviate of Sequestration*

By section 44 of the Act the effect of the recorded abbreviate of sequestration expires on the lapse of five years, unless it is renewedq by memorandum in the form of Schedule A, No. 4, of the Act; and the trustee is required, unless he has been discharged, so to record it anew.

XV.—*Public Sale of Heritable Estate*

The trustee may sell the heritable estate publicly:—
1. With concurrence of the heritable creditors (section 109); or
2. Without such concurrence, on certain conditions (section 110).

XVI.—*Sale of Heritable Estate by Private Bargain*

It is provided by section 111 that "It shall be competent for the trustee, with concurrence of a majority of the creditors in number and value, and of the heritable creditors, if any, and of the Accountant, to sell the heritable estate by private bargain, on such terms and conditions regarding price and otherwise, as the trustee, with concurrence of these parties, may fix ".

The Accountant in these cases requires the trustee (1) to exhibit the missives of sale showing the terms and conditions of the proposed sale; (2) to exhibit a valuation or other satisfactory evidence of the value of the subjects proposed to be sold; (3) to exhibit minutes of creditors and commissioners or other evidence that the creditors and commissioners approve of the proposed sale; (4) to lodge with the Accountant a list of creditors, with the amount of their claims, showing those who have concurred, and a certificate by the trustee in the following terms:— I certify that the above list is a complete and correct one, and that the whole creditors holding heritable securities *affecting the subjects for sale*, and that a majority, in number and value, of the ordinary creditors have concurred in the proposed sale, and in its terms and conditions. (The trustee may obtain the consents of the creditors by issuing a circular narrating the circumstances under which a private sale is considered advisable, and appending to the circular a form of consent for signature and return.)

If the foregoing requirements are met and the Accountant is satisfied that the sale is appropriate he will pronounce an order granting his concurrence, which may be used as part of the title. The Accountant does not consider it expedient that he should become a party to the disposition to the purchaser.

Note.—In computing majorities, all claims count in value, but only those of £20 or over in number. Where the offer or missives of sale are in respect of both heritable and moveable estate, the sum applicable to heritage alone must be stated.

XVII.—*Cases of Fraudulent Conduct on the Part of Bankrupts*

Section 180 of the Act provides that it shall be the duty of the trustee to report all offences under the Act to the Lord Advocate, who shall direct such inquiry and take such proceedings as he shall think fit.

XVIII.—*Law Agency in Sequestrations*

As there appears to be in some places a misunderstanding as to the duties which a trustee is bound to perform himself, and for which he is remunerated by his commission, as distinct from those which he is entitled to employ an agent to perform at the expense of the sequestrated estate, the Accountant thinks it right to note the distinction as he understands it.

In the foregoing notes he has endeavoured to point out the duties which the Act directs the trustee to perform, and for which duties he is remunerated by his commission. A person accepting the office of trustee is expected to understand these duties, and to be able to perform them personally, and if he requires any assistance he should obtain it at his own expense.

The trustee is only entitled to have the services of a law agent in matters properly pertaining to that profession, *i.e.* in conducting litigation, in conveyancing, and in giving or procuring advice on legal difficulties which may occur. Where a trustee conducts a litigation or carries through a conveyance himself, he is entitled to the outlays applicable thereto, but not to fees for legal business, his whole remuneration being limited to commission.

It is the trustee's duty to examine the law accounts before they are taxed, to submit them, if necessary, to the commissioners, and, if necessary, to appear, or to be represented, before the Auditor of Court at the taxation.

The duties of the commissioners in relation to the taxation and payment of the business accounts are pointed out in the Accountant's Notes for the Guidance of Commissioners.

The Lord Ordinary on the Bills decided (in *Geddes' Trustee*, 6th April 1865) that where the law agent in a sequestration is one of the commissioners he is entitled to out-of-pocket expenses only while so acting. In the case cited all professional charges of the agent while he acted as commissioner were disallowed.

Trustees should note that the accountant acts upon this decision and holds the trustee personally liable to make good to the estate a sum equal to the amount of fees paid to any such commissioner. This rule is also applied where the commissioner's firm or any partner thereof acts as law agent.

XIX.—*Trustee's Commission*

The only remuneration for his services to which a trustee is entitled is his commission, as the same may be fixed by the commissioners, subject to an appeal to the Accountant in terms of section 122 of the Act.

By section 121 the commissioners are required to " settle the amount " of the commission or fee, and by section 122 the trustee is required to intimate by circular to every creditor on the estate, and to the bankrupt, the deliverance of the commissioners fixing such, and a right of appeal follows thereon. *The actual sum* allowed should therefore be recorded in the minute and repeated in the circular.

Section 122 also provides that in the event of an appeal no credit for the commission can be taken in the trustee's accounts until such time as the appeal has been finally disposed of. It is the evident intention of this section that the circular should be issued promptly and that no credit should be taken for commission until the days of appeal have expired. In these circumstances, the Accountant (under section 80), requires trustees to send him a copy of every such circular immediately after it has been issued.

The Accountant holds that the commission for the period under review must be " settled "—*i.e.* its precise amount must be fixed—and that the commissioners cannot authorise the trustee to take a " payment to account ", or to retain as extra commission any subsequent unapplied balance. (Vide *Lindsay* v. *Hendrie*, 15th June 1880, 7 R. 911, at p. 923.)

XX.—*Mandatories*

A trustee, or his partner, cannot act as mandatory at a meeting of creditors. (See *Maxwell Witham* v. *Teenan's Trustee*, 20th March 1884, 11 R. 776.)

Notwithstanding this, trustees or their partners sometimes hold mandates from creditors, and occasionally at the final meeting there are no creditors present, but only the trustee, or his partner, as a mandatory, who cannot constitute a meeting. The Accountant considers that when a trustee has duly called the final meeting and no creditor appears, instead of trying to constitute a meeting he ought to prepare a certificate to the effect that the meeting was duly called, that he attended at the time and place intimated, produced the *Gazette* containing the notice of the meeting, copy of the circular calling it, certificate of postage thereof, list of unclaimed dividends and the sederunt book, but that no creditor appeared. This certificate ought to be lodged with the petition for discharge, and a copy of it engrossed in the sederunt book.

XXI.—*Summary Sequestration Procedure—(Principal Specialties of)*

Subject to certain special provisions set out in sections 175 and 176 of the Act, the provisions of the Act as to ordinary sequestrations apply also to summary sequestrations, which are defined by section 174. The principal specialties of summary sequestration procedure prescribed by the said sections are as follows, *viz*:—

State of Affairs

Where a debtor petitions, he must lodge a state of his affairs subscribed by himself with the sheriff-clerk. Where a creditor petitions, the first deliverance shall ordain the debtor to lodge such a state within six days. (Section 175 (3) and (4).)

Bankrupt's Examination

Trustee to apply *orally* within seven days for bankrupt's examination. No time limit prescribed for date of examination. (Section 176 (1).)

Intimation of Trustee's Appointment, Second Meeting and Payment of Dividends

Section 176 (5) and (7) of the Bankruptcy Act contemplates that a dividend may generally be declared at the second meeting of creditors. In the circular intimating the trustee's appointment no specified time is therefore given for holding this meeting; but a reasonable time must elapse between the date of issue of the circular and the latest date for lodging claims, *i.e.* twenty-one days prior to the second meeting. (Section 176 (4).)

Not less than fourteen days prior to the second meeting, the trustee issues his adjudications on the claims. If any claims are rejected, the creditors concerned are notified by post ten days at least prior to the second meeting. There is no provision for the other creditors receiving any notification until their dividends are actually remitted to them; the trustee, however, is required to prepare a list of the claims admitted and rejected, which may be inspected by any creditor or the bankrupt. (Section 176 (5).) No provision is made for advertising payment of the first dividend in the *Gazette*.

The bankrupt, or any creditor, may appeal against any deliverance by the trustee, who must be notified by registered letter posted at least three days prior to the second meeting. If the bankrupt is objecting to an adjudication, or a creditor is objecting to an adjudication on another creditor's claim, the creditor whose claim is in question must also receive notification as above. (Section 176 (6a).)

Section 176 (6a–b–c–d) indicates the procedure in the event of appeals against the trustee's adjudications. If the court has not disposed of the appeals by the date of the second meeting, the dividend may be postponed until such time as the appeals have been disposed of. (Section 176 (8–1).)

At the second meeting the trustee and commissioners may fix a date for payment of a dividend; no specified time is provided for. The commissioners must audit the trustee's accounts at least ten days prior to the payment of the dividend, and at the same time fix his commission. Appeals against the amount of commission fixed may be lodged with the Accountant of Court within six days of the date of the commissioner's deliverance; it is therefore obvious that the commission must be intimated to the creditors in order to give them an opportunity of appealing, although no circular is provided for in section 176 (9). The Accountant's decision on the appeal is final.

The scheme of division of the dividend will apparently fall to be made up as soon as the time for appeals against the trustee's commission has expired. On the due date the trustee pays the dividend to the creditors; this is normally the first statutory notification which the creditors receive, as already indicated, although trustees often intimate payment of the dividend at the same time as they intimate their commission.

If a dividend cannot be declared at the second meeting, the trustee and commissioners may postpone payment of a dividend to a date not later than three months after the second meeting. (Section 176 (7).) If a dividend can be declared within that time, the procedure will be as follows:—

A date is fixed for the meeting of the commissioners for the purpose of declaring a dividend.

Fourteen days prior to the commissioners' meeting, the trustee issues his adjudications and prepares a list of claims admitted and rejected. (Claims may of course have been lodged prior to the second meeting of creditors, but it would be in accordance with practice for the trustee to admit any further claims lodged twenty-one days prior to the commissioners' meeting.)

If any claims are rejected, intimation is given to the creditors concerned at least ten days prior to the meeting of commissioners.

Appeals against adjudications may be posted to the trustee (and/or creditors as the case may be) not later than three days prior to the meeting of commissioners.

(If these appeals have not been disposed of by the time the commissioners meet, the dividend may be postponed until such time as the court has disposed of them.)

At the meeting of commissioners, a date is fixed for payment of the dividend. The audit of the trustee's accounts, and the fixing of his commission, are then undertaken, as previously indicated.

It will be seen from the above that, when a dividend cannot be declared at the second meeting, trustees should apply section 176 (5), substituting, for the second meeting, the meeting of commissioners called to fix a date for payment of a dividend.

The Act is silent as regards cases where it is not possible to declare a dividend within three months of the date of the second meeting. Trustees in such cases should apply section 176 (5) as shown above.

Second Dividend

Where a second dividend is contemplated, the trustee and commissioners fix a date for payment. Not less than thirty days prior to payment, a notice must be inserted in the *Gazette*, specifying, as the last date for lodging claims, a date not less than fourteen and not more than twenty-one days prior to payment. A circular to that effect should also be issued to creditors who have not previously lodged claims. (Section 176 (10).) The trustee's accounts must presumably be audited, and his remuneration fixed by the commissioners, before publication of the *Gazette* notice and circular, if not at the meeting at which the dividend was declared.

Section 176 (10) provides that, as regards the remaining procedure, the provisions of section 176 (5) and (6) shall apply, with the substitution of the date of payment in place of that of the second meeting, *i.e.*:—

Fourteen days before payment of the dividend, the trustee issues his adjudications on any new claims lodged.

If any claims are rejected, intimation is given to the creditors concerned at least ten days prior to the date of payment.

Appeals against adjudications must be posted to the trustee (and creditors, as the case may be) not later than three days prior to payment of the dividend. (If these appeals have not been disposed of by the date fixed for payment, the dividend may be postponed until the court has disposed of the appeals.)

Reports to Accountant

Within ten days after expiry of six months from date of Act and Warrant, and *every three months thereafter*, the trustee must lodge with the Accountant reports *in duplicate*. Accounts will be accepted in lieu of reports if they embody (by notes or otherwise) all the information required by subsection 176(13).

No Final Meeting of Creditors—Equivalent Procedure

The trustee must send completed sederunt book and any unclaimed dividends to the Accountant, who, when satisfied, certifies that trustee is entitled to his discharge. (See Appendix III (*b*) for the engrossments in the sederunt book which the Accountant requires.)

Trustee makes *oral* application for his discharge, and sheriff fixes a diet for hearing objections, if any. Intimation to be made in *Gazette* seven days prior to date of diet.

XXII.—Fees

The following are the fees in bankruptcy proceedings payable in this department. (S.I. 1986 No. 450.)

In Bankruptcies

For registering case, and related work	£10.00
For supervising proceedings in sequestration 5 per cent. on amount to be divided amongst preferable and ordinary creditors	
For report on bankrupt's petition for discharge	14.00
For concurrence in private sale of heritage, if £1,000 or under plus £5.00 extra for each additional £1,000 or part thereof, but not to exceed £180 ...	10.00
For special report	16.00 to 65.00
For report on appeal against trustee's commission	4.00
plus 5 per cent on the trustee's commission as fixed, but not to exceed £180.	
For auditing the accounts and fixing the commission of trustee under voluntary trust deed, plus 17½per cent. on commission allowed to trustee.	5.00
For examining sederunt book	14.00
For issuing acknowledgment for sederunt book	4.00

In Consignations

For lodging consignation	3.00
For producing or delivering up	6.00
plus 50p for every £100 or part thereof uplifted, but not to exceed 25.00	

Miscellaneous

Certifying copy of any other document (plus copying charges if necessary)	£3.50
Recording, engrossing, extracting or copying—all documents:	
(a) By manuscript or typescript per page of 250 words	2.50
(b) By copying by electrical or mechanical means first page	1.00
subsequent pages	0.25
Searches—for any search of records or archives:	
(a) For first half hour of time taken	3.50
(b) For more than one-half hour of time up to a maximum two hours ...	8.50
(c) For each hour or part of an hour in excess of two hours	2.50
(d) Plus correspondence fee where applicable	2.50

G. L. KERR
Accountant of Court.

2 PARLIAMENT SQUARE,
EDINBURGH, 17 April 1986.

APPENDIX 1

Form of Inventory and Valuation

INVENTORY AND VALUATION of the estate and effects belonging to C.D. (*designation*) made up by A.B. (*designation*), trustee on the sequestrated estate showing also the annual revenue thereof, in terms of the Bankruptcy (Scotland) Act 1913, section 76.

I. Real or heritable estate in Scotland:—

Dwelling-house with Shops in   Street, Glasgow, yielding a
gross rental of £100 per annum, conform to rental annexed, and valued
    by   (*designation*) as per valuation dated 30th December 1976, at   **£1,200.00**
This property is burdened with a bond amounting to £800.

II. Stock-in-trade, *viz.*:—

Stationery, per Inventory and Valuation of
dated 30th December 1976 .... £580.83
Books, per   do.   do. 360.37
Tools and other Materials used in Binding, per do. ...... <u>255.87</u>   **1,197.07**

Note.—Messrs. G. and H.,   , claim a security or lien over
part of the stock. The amount of the debt in respect of
which they claim this security or lien has not been ascertained.

III. Book debts, as appearing in the bankrupt's book, *viz.*:—

	Considered by trustees to be		
	Bad	Doubtful	Good
John Thomson, Merchant in			£275.83
William Jones, Grocer in			5.13
Thomas Johnstone, Bookseller ...		£3.06	
Andrew Smith, Bookseller	£15.00		
Thomas Brown, Merchant in			30.13
Thomas Thomson, Bookseller in		16.42	
W. Anderson, Grocer in		8.12	
Alexander Forbes, Innkeeper in	6.41		
William M'Leod, Grocer in	3.27		
Amount of debts considered good, valued at £1.00 per £ .			£311.09
Amount of debts considered doubtful		£27.60	
Value at £0.50 per £			£13.80
Amount of debts considered bad and of no value	£24.68		

324.89

IV. Other assets which do not appear in the bankrupt's records, but which have
been discovered by the trustee, *viz.*:—

Arrears of rent due at Whitsunday last by James Johnstone   £25.00
Balance due to the bankrupt on current account in his name
with the Royal Bank   as at the date of sequest-
ration 139.73
Cash in the bankrupt's shop till .... <u>5.00</u>   169.73

V. Stock and shares of joint-stock companies:—
   £100 ordinary £1 shares in the Edinburgh Gas Company Ltd. valued at
   £1·20 each ....   120·00

VI. Household furniture in the bankrupt's house, No.   Street, conform to
   Inventory and Valuation by (*designation*) dated 30th
   December 1976 ....   165·42

                                                    Amount   £3,177·11

(Date)   (Signed)   A. B., *Trustee.*

STATEMENT of the annual revenue derivable from the estate belonging to the said C.D.
I. Gross rental of dwelling-house and shops included in the foregoing inventory and valuation
   for the year now current, ending at Whitsunday 1976, and payable at Martinmas 1975 and
   Whitsunday 1976 in equal portions, *viz.:*—
   Dwelling-house No. 17   Street, Glasgow, con-
   sisting of second flat, let to James Johnstone ...   £35·00
   Large Shop, etc., let to William George, Grocer   55·00
   Cellar below Shop occupied by John Williams ..   10·00
                                                            £100·00
II. Revenue derivable from shares in joint-stock companies:—
   Estimated dividend from £100 shares of Gas Company, at 6 per cent.
   on the paid-up capital (£5 per share), being the rate of dividend
   declared for previous year ....   6·00
   The other estate and effects of the bankrupt yield no revenue.

                                                    Amount   £106·00

                                (Signed)   A. B., *Trustee.*

Observations by the Accountant.—When separate inventories and valuations of particular
portions of the estate, such as household furniture, stock-in-trade, etc., have been obtained, it
will be sufficient, in preparing the inventory and valuation of the whole estate, if such valuations
are referred to for the particulars embraced in them. Reference to subsidiary inventories and
valuations should show the name and designation of the party by whom they were made, and
also their dates. It will be observed that the book debts must be shown in detail.

   The trustee is directed " forthwith to transmit copies of such inventory and valuation to the
Accountant ". The copies transmitted ought to be certified by the trustee.

   When the sequestration embraces the estates of a company and the estates of individual
partners, it is necessary that these estates should be kept distinct in the inventory and valuation.

   The inventory and valuation required is an inventory and valuation of the whole estate and
effects of the bankrupt, whether affected by special securities or burdened by the mass of his
debts. The bonded subject should be shown at gross values and the amounts secured thereon
stated separately as part of the debts.

APPENDIX II (a)

Form of ACCOUNT CHARGE AND DISCHARGE of the Intromissions of A.B.
(*designation*), Trustee in the Sequestration of C.D. (*designation*)

From 14th December 1976 (date of award of sequestration) to 14th April 1977

CHARGE

I. ESTATE AS PER TRUSTEE'S INVENTORY.
   Dwelling-house and shops valued at ....   £1,200·00
   Stock-in-trade valued at ....   1,197·00
   Book Debts (as detailed in Trustee's Inventory)—estimated to realise   324·89
   One hundred Shares in Edinburgh Gas Co. Ltd., valued at ....   120·00
   Household furniture valued at ....   165·42
   Other assets not shown in Bankrupt's records:—
   Arrears of rent due by James Johnstone ....   £25·00
   Balance on current account with Royal Bank ....   139·73
   Cash in shop till ....   5·00
                                                            169·73

                                                            £3,177·11

II. ESTATE ACCRUED SINCE TRUSTEE'S INVENTORY WAS MADE UP.

1977

Feb. 1.   Rents of Property for half-year to Martin-
         mas 1976 ....   £50·00

     9.   Dividend on Cash Shares at December
         1976—£2·54 less tax £0·89 ....   1·65

Mar. 13.   Interest on Deposit Receipt p. £50 dated
         2nd February 1977 ....   0·42   52·07

(In the case of a business carried on by the Trustee,
the business receipts—*i.e.* sales, shop drawings,
etc.—should be shown here.)

III. ESTATE REALISED.

		Value in Inventory	Amount Realised
1976			
Dec. 29.	Cash in till	£5·00	£5·00
1977			
Jan. 3.	Balance on current account with Royal Bank	139·73	139·73
Feb. 1.	Arrears of rent due by James Johnstone	25·00	25·00
10.	Debt due by John Thomson .	275·83	275·83
16.	Debt due by Wm. Jones ...	5·13	5·13
28.	Household furniture, per J. Williams, Auctioneer	165·42	150·42
Mar. 6.	Debt due by W. Anderson ..	4·06	8·12
28.	Gas shares	120·00	125·62
		£740·17	£734·85

Loss on realisation—carried to branch I of
     discharge ....   5·32

                                     £740·17

                 SUM OF THE CHARGE   £3,229·18

DISCHARGE

I. LOSS ON REALISATION.
              Amount carried from branch III of charge ....   £5·32

II. ALLOWANCE TO BANKRUPT.

1977

Mar. 6.   Paid to account ....   £20·00

     20.   Paid balance ....   13·60   33·60

III. SEQUESTRATION EXPENSES, AND EXPENSES OF REALISATION.

1977

Jan. 13.   Law agents' account of expenses as taxed   56·60

1976

Dec. 29.   Accountant of Court—fee for lodging copy
         act and warrant ....   5·00

1977

Jan. 6.   J. Williams—fee for valuation of furniture   6·00

Apr. 14.   Trustee's posts and incidents to close of
         account ....   2·50   70·10

IV. EXPENSES IN CONNECTION WITH HERITABLE PROPERTY (AND/OR CARRYING
     ON BANKRUPT'S BUSINESS).

1977

Jan. 17.   Interest on bond p. £800 to Martinmas
         1976—£44, less tax £15·40 ....   28·60

Mar. 6.   Feuduty, rates, taxes, etc. (details) ......   109·06
         (In the case of a business carried on by the
         trustee, payments in connection with the
         business—*i.e.* purchases, wages, lighting,
         cleaning, etc.—should be shown here.)

                                        137·66

V. PAYMENTS TO CREDITORS.
   (a) *Preferable claims.*
   1977
   Mar. 21. Messrs. G. & H. ....   10·00

   (b) Dividend of   per £1 to ordinary creditors.
   (Enter date of payment and amount paid to each
   creditor, if a dividend has been paid during the
   period of the account.) ....   0·00

                                                  10·00

VI. ESTATE AT CLOSE OF THIS ACCOUNT.
   A. *Funds at credit of estate.*
     Balance on current account with Royal Bank ....   50·00
     Sums on deposit receipt with Royal Bank:—
     Dated 10th February 1977 .... £200·00
     Dated 28th February 1977 .... 150·00
     Dated 28th March 1977 .... 30·00
     Dated 3rd April 1977 .... 100·00
                                         480·00
     Balance in trustee's hands ....   5·56

                        Carried forward   535·56   256·68

                        Brought forward   £535·56   256·68

   B. *Ownership Outstanding.*
     Dwelling-house and shops—valued as
       before at .... £1,200·00
     This property was exposed for public
     sale on 15th March 1977, but no
     offerer appeared. It will again be
     exposed on 30th April, at a reduced
     upset price.
     Stock-in-trade—valued as before at ..   1,197·07
     This asset has since been sold for
     £1,303, and the proceeds will be
     brought into next account.
     Book Debts outstanding.
      Good—Thomas Brown   £30·13
      Payment is expected at
      an early date.
      Doubtful.
      T. Thomson   £16·42
      T. Johnstone   3·06

                  £19·48

     The trustee proposes to
     take action for recovery
     of these debts.
     Valued before at £·50 per £   9·75
     Bad.
     As per trustee's inventory
                £24·68½
     It is not anticipated that
     any of these debts will be
     recovered ....   0·00
                              39·87
                                  2,436·94

                                               2,972·50

SUM OF THE DISCHARGE EQUAL TO THE CHARGE   £3,229·18

                    (Signed)   A. B., *Trustee.*

APPENDIX II (b)

Form of ACCOUNT CURRENT, or progressive state of the intromissions of A.B. (*designation*), trustee in the sequestration of C.D. (*designation*)

From 14th December 1976 (date of award of sequestration) to 14th April 1977

			State of Bank Account		State of
			Deposit Receipt	Current Account	Trustee's Account
1976					
Dec.	29.	Received in cash in till			£5·00
		Paid Accountant, of Court—fee for lodging copy act and warrant			5·00
1977					
Jan.	3.	Received balance on bankrupt's account with Royal Bank			£139·73
		Paid into bank (C/A)		£100·00	Dr. 139·73 100·00
					Dr. 39·73
	6.	Paid J. Williams—fee for valuation of furniture			6·00
					Dr. 33·73
	13.	Paid law agents' account of expenses as taxed			56·60
					Cr. 22·87
	16.	Withdrawn from bank (C/A)		30·00	30·00
				70·00	Dr. 7·13
	17.	Paid interest on bond p. £800— £44 less tax £15·40			28·60
Feb.	1.	Received arrears of rent			Cr. 21·47
		due by James Johnstone £25·00			
		Half-year's rent to Martinmas 1976 from James Johnstone ..... 17·50			
		Half-year's rent to Martinmas 1976 from Wm. George for shop ..... 27·50			
		Half-year's rent from John Williams for cellar 5·00			75·00
					Dr. 53·53
	2.	Paid into bank (D/R)	50·00		50·00
					Dr. 3·53
	9.	Received dividend on gas shares—due Dec. 1976—£2·54 less tax £0·89 ...			1·65
					Dr. 5·18
	10.	Received debt due by John Thomson .			275·83
					Dr. 281·01
		Paid into bank (D/R) and (C/A)	200·00	80·00	280·00
				150·00	Dr. 1·01
	16.	Received debt due by William Jones ..			5·13
					Dr. 6·14
	28.	Received per J. Williams proceeds of household furniture sold			150·42
					Dr. 156·56
		Paid into bank (D/R)	150·00		150·00
		Carried forward	400·00	150·00	Dr. 6·56

		State of Bank Account		State of Trustee's Account	
		Deposit Receipt	Current Account		
	Brought forward	400·00	150·00	Dr.	6·56
Mar. 6. Received debt due by W. Anderson ..					8·12
				Dr.	14·68
Paid to account of allowance to bankrupt					20·00
				Cr.	5·32
Paid feuduty, rates and taxes on heritable property					109·06
				Cr.	114·38
13. Uplift deposit receipt dated 2nd February 1977, p. £50, with interest thereon—£0·42		50·00			50·42
		350·00		Cr.	63·96
20. Paid balance of allowance to bankrupt					13·60
				Cr.	77·56
21. Paid G. & H. Preferable claim					10·00
				Cr.	87·56
28. Received price of gas shares sold					125·62
				Dr.	38·06
Paid into bank (D/R)		30·00			30·00
		380·00		Dr.	80·06
Apr. 3. Withdrawn from bank (C/A)			100·00		100·00
			50·00	Dr.	108·06
Paid into bank (D/R)		100·00			100·00
		480·00		Dr.	8·06
Apr. 14. Paid trustee's posts and incidents to close of account					2·50
Balances at credit of estate at 14th April 1977		£480·00	50·00	Dr.	5·56

(Signed)   A.B., *Trustee.*

EDINBURGH, *20th April 1977.*—We, the Commissioners on the Sequestrated Estate of C.D., hereby certify that the balance due by the trustee as at 14th April 1977 amounts to £1·51, that the balance in bank is £402 (on deposit receipt, £390, on current account, £12) and that the trustee has regularly deposited the money of the estate in bank, in terms of section 78 of the Bankrupty (Scotland) Act 1913.

(Signed)   U.V., *Commissioner.*
  „   W.X., *Commissioner.*
  „   Y.Z., *Commissioner.*

APPENDIX III (a)

ORDINARY SEQUESTRATION

1. Petition for sequestration.
2. First deliverance (if not at debtor's instance).
3. Deliverance awarding sequestration.
4. Minute of first meeting of creditors.
5. Account and report of interim J.F. if any appointed.

6. Principal deliverance confirming election of commissioners.
7. Trustee's Act and warrant.
8. Bankrupt's state of affairs—docquet by bankrupt and sheriff *re* statutory oath.
9. Circular intimating trustee's appointment.
10. Certificate of posting of trustee's appointment.
11. Note of claims lodged if not otherwise shown by scheme of division.
12. Petition for bankrupt's examination with deliverance.
13. Record of examination signed by bankrupt and sheriff or certified by shorthand writer, or
13A. If no examination a note of circumstances obviating it.
14. Principal oath by bankrupt.
15. Minute of second meeting of creditors.
16. Trustee's report to second meeting.
17. Trustee's state of affairs, submitted to second meeting of creditors with list of debtors and creditors if any referred to.
18. Principal deliverance confirming any commissioners elected at second meeting.
19. Inventory and valuation of estate.
20. Trustee's accounts for all periods.
21. If dividend paid (a) adjudication on claims.
                (b) scheme of division.
                (c) circular intimating payment of dividend and trustee's commission.
22. Report on bankrupt's conduct.
23. Circular calling final meeting.
24. Certificate of posting of circular calling final meeting.
25. Minute of final meeting.

APPENDIX III (b)

SUMMARY SEQUESTRATION

1. Petition for sequestration.
2. First deliverance (if not at debtor's instance).
3. Deliverance awarding sequestration.
4. Minute of first meeting of creditors.
5. Account and report of interim J.F. if any appointed.
6. Principal deliverance confirming election of commissioners.
7. Trustee's act and warrant.
8. Bankrupt's state of affairs—Docquet by bankrupt and sheriff *re* statutory oath.
9. Circular intimating trustee's appointment.
10. Certificate of posting of trustee's appointment.
11. Note of claims lodged if not otherwise shown by a scheme of division.
12. Record of examination signed by bankrupt and sheriff or certified by shorthand writer, or
12A. If no examination a note of circumstances obviating it.
13. Principal oath by bankrupt.
14. Minute of second meeting of creditors.
15. Trustee's report to second meeting of creditors.
16. Trustee's state of affairs submitted to second meeting of creditors, with list of debtors and creditors.
17. Principal deliverance confirming any commissioners elected at second meeting.
18. Inventory and valuation of estate.
19. Trustee's accounts.
20. If no assets realised, note of outlays of trustee.
21. If dividend paid (a) adjudication on claims.
                (b) scheme of division.
                (c) circular intimating trustee's commission.
22. Report on bankrupt's conduct.

Notes by the Accountant of Court for the Guidance of Commissioners in Sequestrations under the Bankruptcy (Scotland) Act 1913

N.B.—These notes are generally applicable to all processes of sequestration, except that in cases of summary sequestration awarded and regulated by sections 174, 175, and 176 of the Act, the periods for making up accounts are not fixed by statute as in ordinary sequestration, but are left to be fixed by the commissioners themselves, separate provision being made in these sections for the audit of the accounts, the fixing of commission, and the declaration of dividends.

The duties and powers of the commissioners are thus clearly and succinctly described in the 81st section of the Bankruptcy (Scotland) Act 1913:—

1. They shall superintend the proceedings of the trustee [1];
2. Concur with him in submissions and transactions [2];
3. Give their advice and assistance relative to the management of the estate;
4. Decide as to paying or postponing payment of a dividend;
5. Assemble at any time to ascertain the situation of the bankrupt estate; and
6. Any one of them may make such report as he may think proper to a general meeting of creditors.

NOTES

[1] By the 78th section of the Act it is enacted: " The trustee shall manage, realise, and recover the estate belonging to the bankrupt, wherever situated, and convert the same into money, according to the directions given by the creditors at any meeting, and if no such directions are given, he shall do so with the advice of the commissioners."

[2] By the 172nd section of the Act, the trustee, with the consent of the commissioners, may compound, transact, or refer to arbitration any question arising regarding the estate, or any demand or claim made thereon.

It is enacted by the 121st section of the said Act: " Immediately on the expiration of four months from the date of the deliverance actually awarding sequestration, unless the dividend is accelerated as hereinafter provided (section 130), the trustee shall proceed to make up a state of the whole estate of the bankrupt, of the funds recovered by him, and of the property outstanding (specifying the cause why it has not been recovered), and also an account of his intromissions, and generally of his management; and within fourteen days after the expiration of the said four months, the commissioners shall meet and examine such state and account, and ascertain whether the trustee has lodged the moneys recovered by him in bank or not; and if he has failed to do so, they shall debit him with a sum at the rate of £20 per annum on every £100 not so lodged, and so after that rate on any larger or smaller sum, being not less than £100; and they shall (1) audit his accounts; and (2) settle the amount of his commission or fee; and (3) authorise him to take credit for such commission or fee in his accounts with the estate; and (4) they shall certify by a writing under their hands engrossed or copied in the sederunt book, the balance due to or by the trustee in his account with the estate as at the expiration of the said four months, and they shall declare whether any, and what part, of the net produce of the estate, after making a reasonable deduction for future contingencies, shall be divided among the creditors ".

By section 121 the commissioners are required to " settle the amount " of the commission or fee, and by section 122 the trustee is required to intimate by circular to every creditor on the estate, and to the bankrupt, the deliverance of the commissioners fixing such, and a right of appeal follows thereon. The actual sum allowed, and the realisations to which it applies, should therefore be recorded in the minute and repeated in the circular.

The actual amount of the commission for the period under review must be fixed: the commissioners cannot authorise the trustee to take a " payment to account ", or to retain as extra commission any unapplied balance, after payment of expenses of unspecified amount.

Provision is made in sections 127 and 129 of the Act for similar procedure at the end of eight months from the date of the deliverance actually awarding sequestration, and thereafter at intervals of three months from the close of the immediately preceding account, until the whole funds shall be divided.

The commissioners will observe that it is thus the trustee's duty to close his accounts as follows:—

First Account, on the expiration of four months from the date of the deliverance *actually awarding* sequestration.

Second Account, on the expiration of eight months from date of awarding.

Third Account, on the expiration of eleven months from date of awarding.

Fourth Account, on the expiration of fourteen months; and each succeeding account thereafter on the expiration of three months from the date at which the preceding account was closed. The commissioners will also observe that it is their duty, within fourteen days of the period when each of these accounts is closed, to meet and examine such accounts, etc., and perform the other duties specified in the 121st section, whether a dividend is to be declared or not.

If the trustee fails to submit the accounts for audit at the statutory periods above mentioned, the commissioners are entitled to call on him to do so; and if he refuse or delay to answer their call, they should represent the matter to the Accountant, who will give them the assistance and directions proper in the circumstances.

Note.—It should be kept in view that the above-noted periods for closing accounts do not apply to summary sequestrations.

It is further enacted, in the event of a composition being offered, that before it is approved of, " the commissioners shall audit the accounts of the trustee, and ascertain the balance due to or by him, and fix the remuneration for his trouble, subject to the review of the Lord Ordinary or the sheriff, if complained of by the trustee, the bankrupt, or any of the creditors". (Section 138 of the Act.)

The commissioners are thus constituted the proper auditors of the trustee's accounts, and it is their duty to audit these accounts, deduct any entries to which they object, and certify the correct balance, in their opinion, by minute.

In particular, it is their duty to ascertain that the trustee has lodged the money of the estate in bank, in terms of the Act. In addition to what is provided on this subject by the 121st section of the Act, provisions applicable to the lodging of the money in bank are contained in the 78th and 79th sections. The 78th section provides that the trustee " shall lodge all money which he shall receive in the course of such management, realisation, and recovery, in such bank as the majority of the creditors in number and value at any general meeting shall appoint, and failing such appointment, in any joint-stock bank of issue in Scotland (provided that the bank be not one in which the trustee shall be an acting partner, manager, agent or cashier); and the money shall be lodged in the name of the trustee, in his official character under this Act, and such bank shall once yearly at least balance such account ". The 79th section enacts: " If the trustee shall keep in his hands any sum exceeding £100 belonging to the estate, for more than ten days, he shall pay interest to the creditors at the rate of £20 per centum per annum on the excess of such sum above £100, for such time as the same shall be in his hands beyond ten days; and unless the money has been so kept from innocent causes, the trustee shall be dismissed from his office, upon petition to the Lord Ordinary or sheriff by any creditor, and have no claim to remuneration, and shall be liable in expenses."

The Court of Session has found (*Freyd's Trustee*, 29th June 1864, 2 M. 1293) that the fund set apart by the commissioners for the payment of a dividend forms part of the funds of the sequestrated estate, and is subject to the provisions before quoted, as to the lodging of the money of the estate in bank. According to this decision, the trustee is not entitled to withdraw from bank the amount set apart for payment of a dividend at the time at which it is payable, but only to draw from time to time such sums as may be required to meet the payments to the creditors as they claim their dividends. If a trustee hold in his hand moneys of the estate (whether set apart for dividends or not) beyond the limit prescribed by the Act, he is liable to the penalties thereby imposed.

The Accountant begs to impress upon the commissioners the necessity of their satisfying themselves at each period of audit, by examination of deposit-receipts or of bank accounts (duly certified by the bank officials), that the money is in bank, as represented in the accounts. Cases have occurred in which trustees have made false representations in their accounts regarding their bank transactions; and commissioners have, without examining these transactions and checking them with the bank vouchers, certified falsely in their docquets that the accounts were correct, and the money lodged in bank as represented. The Accountant has power to submit to the Lord Advocate all such cases of misrepresentation, for the purpose of having the parties prosecuted criminally, under the provisions of the 161st section of the Act.

It is provided (section 154): " All accounts for law business incurred by the trustee shall, before payment thereof by the trustee, be submitted for taxation to the Auditor of the Court of Session, or to the Auditor of the Sheriff Court of the county in which the sequestration was carried on, as may be directed by a general meeting of the creditors ". The commissioners ought to ascertain that all accounts for law business have been so taxed, before passing the payments thereof by the trustee, in their audit of his accounts, and they ought also to satisfy themselves that the accounts have been incurred for work which the trustee is entitled to employ a law agent to do at the expense of the estate, *e.g.* litigation, conveyancing, or for giving or procuring proper legal advice where required, and not incurred for the performance of duties which the Bankruptcy Act requires the trustee to do in virtue of his office, and for which he is remunerated by his commission. The deliverance of the commissioners on this subject may, if wrong, be corrected on appeal to the proper court (section 165).

The Lord Ordinary on the Bills has decided (*Geddes's Trustee*, 6th April 1865) that where the law agent in a sequestration is one of the commissioners he is not entitled to charge more than his costs out of pocket while so acting. In the case quoted, all the professional charges of the agent while he acted as a commissioner were disallowed.

Any commissioner who is a law agent should note that the Accountant acts upon this decision, and holds the trustee personally liable to make good to the estate a sum equal to the amount of fees paid to any such commissioner. This rule is also applied where the commissioner's firm or any partner thereof acts as law agent.

W. L. O'CONNOR,
Accountant of Court

DIVISION I

Companies

Statutes

Notes

Statutory Instruments

Statutes

Business Names Act 1985

(1985 c. 7)

An Act to consolidate certain enactments relating to the names under which persons may carry on business in Great Britain.

[11th March 1985]

ARRANGEMENT OF SECTIONS

Persons subject to this Act

1.—(1) This Act applies to any person who has a place of business in Great Britain and who carries on business in Great Britain under a name which—

   (a) in the case of a partnership, does not consist of the surnames of all partners who are individuals and the corporate names of all partners who are bodies corporate without any addition other than an addition permitted by this Act;

   (b) in the case of an individual, does not consist of his surname without any addition other than one so permitted;

   (c) in the case of a company, being a company which is capable of being wound up under the Companies Act 1985, does not consist of its corporate name without any addition other than one so permitted.

(2) The following are permitted additions for the purposes of subsection (1)—

   (a) in the case of a partnership, the forenames of individual partners or the initials of those forenames or, where two or more individual partners have the same surname, the addition of "s" at the end of that surname; or

   (b) in the case of an individual, his forename or its initial;

   (c) in any case, any addition merely indicating that the business is carried on in succession to a former owner of the business.

Prohibition of use of certain business names

2.—(1) Subject to the following subsections, a person to whom this Act applies shall not, without the written approval of the Secretary of State, carry on business in Great Britain under a name which—

   (a) would be likely to give the impression that the business is connected with Her Majesty's Government or with any local authority; or

   (b) includes any word or expression for the time being specified in regulations made under this Act.

(2) Subsection (1) does not apply to the carrying on of a business by a person—

   (*a*) to whom the business has been transferred on or after 26th February 1982; and

   (*b*) who carries on the business under the name which was its lawful business name immediately before that transfer,

during the period of 12 months beginning with the date of that transfer.

(3) Subsection (1) does not apply to the carrying on of a business by a person who—

   (*a*) carried on that business immediately before 26th February 1982; and

   (*b*) continues to carry it on under the name which immediately before that date was its lawful business name.

(4) A person who contravenes subsection (1) is guilty of an offence.

Words and expressions requiring Secretary of State's approval

3.—(1) The Secretary of State may by regulations—

   (*a*) specify words or expressions for the use of which as or as part of a business name his approval is required by section 2(1)(*b*); and

   (*b*) in relation to any such word or expression, specify a government department or other body as the relevant body for purposes of the following subsection.

(2) Where a person to whom this Act applies proposes to carry on a business under a name which is or includes any such word or expression, and a government department or other body is specified under subsection (1)(*b*) in relation to that word or expression, that person shall—

   (*a*) request (in writing) the relevant body to indicate whether (and if so why) it has any objections to the proposal; and

   (*b*) submit to the Secretary of State a statement that such a request has been made and a copy of any response received from the relevant body.

Disclosure required of persons using business names

4.—(1) A person to whom this Act applies shall—

   (*a*) subject to subsection (3), state in legible characters on all business letters, written orders for goods or services to be supplied to the business, invoices and receipts issued in the course of the business and written demands for payment of debts arising in the course of the business—

      (i) in the case of a partnership, the name of each partner,

      (ii) in the case of an individual, his name,

      (iii) in the case of a company, its corporate name, and

      (iv) in relation to each person so named, an address in Great Britain at which service of any document relating in any way to the business will be effective; and

   (*b*) in any premises where the business is carried on and to which the customers of the business or suppliers of any goods or services to the business have access, display in a prominent position so that it may easily be read by such customers or suppliers a notice containing such names and addresses.

(2) A person to whom this Act applies shall secure that the names and addresses required by subsection (1)(*a*) to be stated on his business letters, or which would have been so required but for the subsection next following, are immediately given, by written notice to any person with whom anything is done or discussed in the course of the business and who asks for such names and addresses.

(3) Subsection (1)(*a*) does not apply in relation to any document issued

by a partnership of more than 20 persons which maintains at its principal place of business a list of the names of all the partners if—

    (*a*) none of the names of the partners appears in the document otherwise than in the text or as a signatory; and

    (*b*) the document states in legible characters the address of the partnership's principal place of business and that the list of the partners' names is open to inspection at that place.

(4) Where a partnership maintains a list of the partners' names for purposes of subsection (3), any person may inspect the list during office hours.

(5) The Secretary of State may by regulations require notices under subsection (1)(*b*) or (2) to be displayed or given in a specified form.

(6) A person who without reasonable excuse contravenes subsection (1) or (2), or any regulations made under subsection (5), is guilty of an offence.

(7) Where an inspection required by a person in accordance with subsection (4) is refused, any partner of the partnership concerned who without reasonable excuse refused that inspection, or permitted it to be refused, is guilty of an offence.

Civil remedies for breach of s.4

5.—(1) Any legal proceedings brought by a person to whom this Act applies to enforce a right arising out of a contract made in the course of a business in respect of which he was, at the time the contract was made, in breach of subsection (1) or (2) of section 4 shall be dismissed if the defendant (or, in Scotland, the defender) to the proceedings shows—

    (*a*) that he has a claim against the plaintiff (pursuer) arising out of that contract which he has been unable to pursue by reason of the latter's breach of section 4(1) or (2), or

    (*b*) that he has suffered some financial loss in connection with the contract by reason of the plaintiff's (pursuer's) breach of section 4(1) or (2),

unless the court before which the proceedings are brought is satisfied that it is just and equitable to permit the proceedings to continue.

(2) This section is without prejudice to the right of any person to enforce such rights as he may have against another person in any proceedings brought by that person.

Regulations

6.—(1) Regulations under this Act shall be made by statutory instrument and may contain such transitional provisions and savings as the Secretary of State thinks appropriate, and may make different provision for different cases or classes of case.

(2) In the case of regulations made under section 3, the statutory instrument containing them shall be laid before Parliament after the regulations are made and shall cease to have effect at the end of the period of 28 days beginning with the day on which they were made (but without prejudice to anything previously done by virtue of them or to the making of new regulations) unless during that period they are approved by a resolution of each House of Parliament.

In reckoning this period of 28 days, no account is to be taken of any time during which Parliament is dissolved or prorogued, or during which both Houses are adjourned for more than four days.

(3) In the case of regulations made under section 4, the statutory instrument containing them is subject to annulment in pursuance of a resolution of either House of Parliament.

Offences

7.—(1) Offences under this Act are punishable on summary conviction.

(2) A person guilty of an offence under this Act is liable to a fine not exceeding one-fifth of the statutory maximum.

(3) If after a person has been convicted summarily of an offence under section 2 or 4(6) the original contravention is continued, he is liable on a second or subsequent summary conviction of the offence to a fine not exceeding one-fiftieth of the statutory maximum for each day on which the contravention is continued (instead of to the penalty which may be imposed on the first conviction of the offence).

(4) Where an offence under section 2 or 4(6) or (7) committed by a body corporate is proved to have been committed with the consent or connivance of, or to be attributable to any neglect on the part of, any director, manager, secretary or other similar officer of the body corporate, or any person who was purporting to act in any such capacity, he as well as the body corporate is guilty of the offence and liable to be proceeded against and punished accordingly.

(5) Where the affairs of a body corporate are managed by its members, subsection (4) applies in relation to the acts and defaults of a member in connection with his functions of management as if he were a director of the body corporate.

(6) For purposes of the following provisions of the Companies Act 1985—

   (*a*) section 731 (summary proceedings under the Companies Acts), and
   (*b*) section 732(3) (legal professional privilege),

this Act is to be treated as included in those Acts.

Interpretation
   8.—(1) The following definitions apply for purposes of this Act—
   "business" includes a profession;
   "initial" includes any recognised abbreviation of a name;
   "lawful business name", in relation to a business, means a name under which the business was carried on without contravening section 2(1) of this Act or section 2 of the Registration of Business Names Act 1916;
   "local authority" means any local authority within the meaning of the Local Government Act 1972 or the Local Government (Scotland) Act 1973, the Common Council of the City of London or the Council of the Isles of Scilly;
   "partnership" includes a foreign partnership;
   "statutory maximum" means—
      (*a*) in England and Wales the prescribed sum under section 32 of the Magistrates' Courts Act 1980, and
      (*b*) in Scotland, the prescribed sum under section 289B of the Criminal Procedure (Scotland) Act 1975;
   and "surname", in relation to a peer or person usually known by a British title different from his surname, means the title by which he is known.

(2) Any expression used in this Act and also in the Companies Act 1985 has the same meaning in this Act as in that.

Northern Ireland
   9. This Act does not extend to Northern Ireland.

Commencement
   10. This Act comes into force on 1st July 1985.

Citation
   11. This Act may be cited as the Business Names Act 1985.

Company Securities (Insider Dealing) Act 1985

(1985 c. 8)

An Act to consolidate the enactments relating to insider dealing in company securities.   [11th March 1985]

ARRANGEMENT OF SECTIONS

Regulation of insider dealing

Prohibition on stock exchange deals by insiders, etc.

¹ **1.**—(1) Subject to section 3, an individual who is, or at any time in the preceding six months has been, knowingly connected with a company shall not deal on a recognised stock exchange in securities of that company if he has information which—

(a) he holds by virtue of being connected with the company,

(b) it would be reasonable to expect a person so connected, and in the position by virtue of which he is so connected, not to disclose except for the proper performance of the functions attaching to that position, and

(c) he knows is unpublished price sensitive information in relation to those securities.

(2) Subject to section 3, an individual who is, or at any time in the preceding six months has been, knowingly connected with a company shall not deal on a recognised stock exchange in securities of any other company if he has information which—

(a) he holds by virtue of being connected with the first company,

(b) it would be reasonable to expect a person so connected, and in the position by virtue of which he is so connected, not to disclose except for the proper performance of the functions attaching to that position,

(c) he knows is unpublished price sensitive information in relation to those securities of that other company, and (*d*) relates to any transaction (actual or contemplated) involving both the first company and that other company, or involving one of them and securities of the other, or to the fact that any such transaction is no longer contemplated.

(3) The next subsection applies where—

(*a*) an individual has information which he knowingly obtained (directly or indirectly) from another individual who—

(i) is connected with a particular company, or was at any time in the six months preceding the obtaining of the information so connected, and

(ii) the former individual knows or has reasonable cause to believe held the information by virtue of being so connected, and

(*b*) the former individual knows or has reasonable cause to believe that, because of the latter's connection and position, it would be reasonable to expect him not to disclose the information except for the proper performance of the functions attaching to that position.

(4) Subject to section 3, the former individual in that case—

(*a*) shall not himself deal on a recognised stock exchange in securities of that company if he knows that the information is unpublished price sensitive information in relation to those securities, and

(*b*) shall not himself deal on a recognised stock exchange in securities of any other company if he knows that the information is unpublished price sensitive information in relation to those securities and it relates to any transaction (actual or contemplated) involving the first company and the other company, or involving one of them and securities of the other, or to the fact that any such transaction is no longer contemplated.

(5) Subject to section 3, where an individual is contemplating, or has contemplated, making (whether with or without another person) a take-over offer for a company in a particular capacity, that individual shall not deal on a recognised stock exchange in securities of that company in another capacity if he knows that information that the offer is contemplated, or is no longer contemplated, is unpublished price sensitive information in relation to those securities.

(6) Subject to section 3, where an individual has knowingly obtained (directly or indirectly), from an individual to whom subsection (5) applies, information that the offer referred to in that subsection is being contemplated or is no longer contemplated, the former individual shall not himself deal on a recognised stock exchange in securities of that company if he knows that the information is unpublished price sensitive information in relation to those securities.

(7) Subject to section 3, an individual who is for the time being prohibited by any provision of this section from dealing on a recognised stock exchange in any securities shall not counsel or procure any other person to deal in those securities, knowing or having reasonable cause to believe that that person would deal in them on a recognised stock exchange.

(8) Subject to section 3, an individual who is for the time being prohibited as above-mentioned from dealing on a recognised stock exchange in any securities by reason of his having any information, shall not communicate that information to any other person if he knows or has reasonable cause to believe that that or some other person will make use of the information for the purpose of dealing, or of counselling or procuring any other person to deal, on a recognised stock exchange in those securities.

NOTE
[1] See the Financial Services Act 1986, ss.177 and 178.

Abuse of information obtained in official capacity
[1] **2.**—(1) This section applies to any information which—

(*a*) is held by a public servant or former public servant by virtue of his position or former position as a Crown servant, or is knowingly obtained by an individual (directly or indirectly) from a public servant or former public servant who he knows or has reasonable cause to believe held the information by virtue of any such position,

(b) it would be reasonable to expect an individual in the position of the public servant or former position of the former public servant not to disclose except for the proper performance of the functions attaching to that position, and

(c) the individual holding it knows is unpublished price sensitive information in relation to securities of a particular company ("relevant securities").

(2) This section applies to a public servant or former public servant holding information to which this section applies and to any individual who knowingly obtained any such information (directly or indirectly) from a public servant or former public servant who that individual knows or has reasonable cause to believe held the information by virtue of his position or former position as a public servant.

(3) Subject to section 3, an individual to whom this section applies—

(a) shall not deal on a recognised stock exchange in any relevant securities,

(b) shall not counsel or procure any other person to deal in any such securities, knowing or having reasonable cause to believe that that other person would deal in them on a recognised stock exchange, and

(c) shall not communicate to any other person the information held or (as the case may be) obtained by him as mentioned in subsection (2) if he knows or has reasonable cause to believe that that or some other person will make use of the information for the purpose of dealing, or of counselling or procuring any other person to deal, on a recognised stock exchange in any such securities.

(4) "Public servant" means—

(a) a Crown servant;

(b) a member, officer or servant of a designated agency, competent authority or transferee body (within the meaning of the Financial Services Act 1986);

(c) an officer or servant of a recognised self-regulating organisation, recognised investment exchange or recognised clearing house (within the meaning of that Act);

(d) any person declared by an order for the time being in force under subsection (5) to be a public servant for the purposes of this section.

(5) If it appears to the Secretary of State that the members, officers or employees of or persons otherwise connected with any body appearing to him to exercise public functions may have access to unpublished price sensitive information relating to securities, he may by order declare that those persons are to be public servants for the purposes of this section.

(6) The power to make an order under subsection (5) shall be exercisable by statutory instrument and an instrument containing such an order shall be subject to annulment in pursuance of a resolution of either House of Parliament.

NOTE
[1] As amended by the Financial Services Act 1986, s.173. See also *ibid.*, ss.177 and 178.

Actions not prohibited by ss. 1, 2

3.—[1] (1) Sections 1 and 2 do not prohibit an individual by reason of his having any information from—

(a) doing any particular thing otherwise than with a view to the making of a profit or the avoidance of a loss (whether for himself or another person) by the use of that information;

  (*b*) entering into a transaction in the course of the exercise in good faith of his functions as liquidator, receiver or trustee in bankruptcy;

  (*c*) doing any particular thing if the information—

    (i) was obtained by him in the course of a business of a jobber in which he was engaged or employed, and

    (ii) was of a description which it would be reasonable to expect him to obtain in the ordinary course of that business,

  and he does that thing in good faith in the course of that business; or

  (*d*) doing any particular thing in relation to any particular securities if the information—

    (i) was obtained by him in the course of a business of a market maker in those securities in which he was engaged or employed, and

    (ii) was of a description which it would be reasonable to expect him to obtain in the ordinary course of that business,

  and he does that thing in good faith in the course of that business.

"Jobber" means an individual, partnership or company dealing in securities on a recognised stock exchange and recognised by the Council of The Stock Exchange as carrying on the business of a jobber.

"Market maker" means a person (whether an individual, partnership or company) who—

  (*a*) holds himself out at all normal times in compliance with the rules of a recognised stock exchange as willing to buy and sell securities at prices specified by him; and

  (*b*) is recognised as doing so by that recognised stock exchange.

(2) An individual is not, by reason only of his having information relating to any particular transaction, prohibited—

  (*a*) by section 1(2), 4(*b*), (5) or (6) from dealing on a recognised stock exchange in any securities, or

  (*b*) by section 1(7) or (8) from doing any other thing in relation to securities which he is prohibited from dealing in by any of the provisions mentioned in paragraph (*a*), or

  (*c*) by section 2 from doing anything,

if he does that thing in order to facilitate the completion or carrying out of the transaction.

NOTE
[1] As amended by the Financial Services Act 1986, s.174(1) and (2) and Sched. 17.

Off-market deals in advertised securities
 [1] **4.**—(1) Subject to section 6, sections 1 to 3 apply in relation to—

  (*a*) dealing otherwise than on a recognised stock exchange in the advertised securities of any company—

    (i) through an off-market dealer who is making a market in those securities, in the knowledge that he is an off-market dealer, that he is making a market in those securities and that the securities are advertised securities, or

    (ii) as an off-market dealer who is making a market in those securities or as an officer, employee or agent of such a dealer acting in the course of the dealer's business;

  (*b*) counselling or procuring a person to deal in advertised securities in the knowledge or with reasonable cause to believe that he would deal in them as mentioned in paragraph (*a*);

  (*c*) communicating any information in the knowledge or with reasonable cause to believe that it would be used for such dealing or for such counselling or procuring,

as they apply in relation to dealing in securities on a recognised stock exchange and to counselling or procuring or communicating any information in connection with such dealing.

(2) In its application by virtue of this section the definition of "market

maker" in section 3(1) shall have effect as if the references to a recognised stock exchange were references to a recognised investment exchange (other than an overseas investment exchange) within the meaning of the Financial Services Act 1986.

NOTE
[1] As amended by the Financial Services Act 1986, s.174(3). See also *ibid.*, ss.177 and 178.

Restriction on promoting off-market deals abroad
[1] **5.**—(1) An individual who, by reason of his having information, is for the time being prohibited by any provision of section 1 or 2 from dealing in any securities shall not—

(a) counsel or procure any other person to deal in those securities in the knowledge or with reasonable cause to believe that that person would deal in the securities outside Great Britain on any stock exchange other than a recognised stock exchange, or

(b) communicate that information to any other person in the knowledge or with reasonable cause to believe that that or some other person will make use of the information for the purpose of dealing, or of counselling or procuring any other person to deal, in the securities outside Great Britain on any stock exchange other than a recognised stock exchange.

(2) Subsection (1) does not prohibit an individual by reason of his having any information from acting as mentioned in any of paragraphs (a) to (c) of section 3(1).

(3) An individual is not, by reason only of having information relating to a particular transaction, prohibited by any provision of this section from doing anything if he does that thing in order to facilitate the completion or carrying out of the transaction.

NOTE
[1] See the Financial Services Act 1986, ss.177 and 178.

Price stabilisation
[1] **6.**—(1) No provision of section 1, 2, 4 or 5 prohibits an individual from doing anything for the purpose of stabilising the price of securities if it is done in conformity with rules made under section 48 of the Financial Services Act 1986 and—

(a) in respect of securities which fall within any of paragraphs 1 to 5 of Schedule 1 to that Act and are specified by the rules; and

(b) during such period before or after the issue of those securities as is specified by the rules.

(2) Any order under subsection (8) of section 48 of that Act shall apply also in relation to subsection (1) of this section.

NOTE
[1] Substituted by the Financial Services Act 1986, s.175.

Trustees and personal representatives
7.—(1) Where a trustee or personal representative or, where a trustee or personal representative is a body corporate, an individual acting on behalf of that trustee or personal representative who, apart from paragraph (a) of section 3(1) or, as the case may be, subsection (2) of section 5, would be prohibited by any of sections 1 to 5 from dealing, or counselling or procuring any other person to deal, in any securities deals in those securities or counsels or procures any other person to deal in them, he is presumed to have acted with propriety if he acted on the advice of a person who—

(a) appeared to him to be an appropriate person from whom to seek such advice, and

(b) did not appear to him to be prohibited by section 1, 2, 4 or 5 from dealing in those securities.

(2) "With propriety" means otherwise than with a view to the making of a profit or the avoidance of a loss (whether for himself or another person) by the use of the information in question.

Punishment of contraventions

8.—(1) An individual who contravenes section 1, 2, 4 or 5 is liable—

[1] (a) on conviction on indictment to imprisonment for a term not exceeding seven years or a fine, or both, and

(b) on summary conviction to imprisonment for a term not exceeding six months or a fine not exceeding the statutory maximum, or both.

[2] (2) Proceedings for an offence under this section shall not be instituted in England and Wales except by, or with the consent of, the Secretary of State or the Director of Public Prosecutions.

(3) No transaction is void or voidable by reason only that it was entered into in contravention of section 1, 2, 4 or 5.

NOTES

[1] As amended by the Criminal Justice Act 1988, s.48(1).

[2] As amended by the Companies Act 1989, s.209.

Interpretation for ss. 1–8

"Connected with a company"

9. For purposes of this Act, an individual is connected with a company if, but only if—

(a) he is a director of that company or a related company, or

(b) he occupies a position as an officer (other than a director) or employee of that company or a related company or a position involving a professional or business relationship between himself (or his employer or a company of which he is a director) and the first company or a related company which in either case may reasonably be expected to give him access to information which, in relation to securities of either company, is unpublished price sensitive information, and which it would be reasonable to expect a person in his position not to disclose except for the proper performance of his functions.

"Unpublished price sensitive information"

10. Any reference in this Act to unpublished price sensitive information in relation to any securities of a company is a reference to information which—

(a) relates to specific matters relating or of concern (directly or indirectly) to that company, that is to say, is not of a general nature relating or of concern to that company, and

(b) is not generally known to those persons who are accustomed or would be likely to deal in those securities but which would if it were generally known to them be likely materially to affect the price of those securities.

"Company"; "related company"

11. In this Act—

(a) "company" means any company, whether or not a company within the meaning of the Companies Act 1985, and

(b) "related company", in relation to a company, means any body corporate which is that company's subsidiary or holding company, or a subsidiary of that company's holding company.

"Securities", etc.

12. In this Act—

(a) "securities" means listed securities and, in the case of a company within the meaning of the Companies Act 1985, or a company registered under Chapter II of Part XXII of that Act or an unregistered company, the following securities (whether or not listed), that is to say, any shares, any debentures, or any right to subscribe for, call for or make delivery of a share or debenture;

(*b*) "listed securities", in relation to a company, means any securities of the company listed on a recognised stock exchange; and

(*c*) "advertised securities", in relation to a particular occurrence, means listed securities or securities in respect of which, not more than six months before that occurrence, information indicating the prices at which persons have dealt or were willing to deal in those securities has been published for the purpose of facilitating deals in those securities.

"Deals in securities"; "off-market dealer", etc.

13.—(1) For purposes of this Act, a person deals in securities if (whether as principal or agent) he buys or sells or agrees to buy or sell any securities; and references to dealing in securities on a recognised stock exchange include dealing in securities through an investment exchange.

¹ (1A) For the purposes of this Act a person who (whether as principal or agent) buys or sells or agrees to buy or sell investments within paragraph 9 of Schedule 1 to the Financial Services Act 1986 (contracts for differences etc.) where the purpose or pretended purpose mentioned in that paragraph is to secure a profit or avoid a loss wholly or partly by reference to fluctuations in the value or price of securities shall be treated as if he were dealing in those securities.

(2) "Investment exchange" means an organisation maintaining a system whereby an offer to deal in securities made by a subscriber to the organisation is communicated, without his identity being revealed, to other subscribers to the organisation, and whereby any acceptance of that offer by any of those other subscribers is recorded and confirmed.

² (3) "Off-market dealer" means a person who is an authorised person within the meaning of the Financial Services Act 1986.

(4) An off-market dealer is taken—

(*a*) to deal in advertised securities, if he deals in such securities or acts as an intermediary in connection with deals made by other persons in such securities (references to such a dealer's officer, employee or agent dealing in such securities to be construed accordingly), and

(*b*) to make a market in any securities, if in the course of his business as an off-market dealer he holds himself out both to prospective buyers and to prospective sellers of those securities (other than particular buyers or sellers) as willing to deal in them otherwise than on a recognised stock exchange.

(5) For purposes of section 4, an individual is taken to deal through an off-market dealer if the latter is a party to the transaction, is an agent for either party to the transaction or is acting as an intermediary in connection with the transaction.

NOTES

¹ Inserted by the Financial Services Act 1986, s.176. For (*prosp.*) amendments to s.13 see the 1986 Act, ss.174(4) and Sched. 17.

² Substituted by the Financial Services Act 1976, s.174(4)(*b*).

"Take-over offer"

14. In this Act, "take-over offer for a company" means an offer made to all the holders (or all the holders other than the person making the offer and his nominees) of the shares in the company to acquire those shares or a specified proportion of them or to all the holders (or all the holders other than the person making the offer and his nominees) of a particular class of those shares to acquire the shares of that class or a specified proportion of them.

15. [Repealed by the Financial Services Act 1986, Sched. 17.]

General interpretation provisions

16.—(1) In this Act—

"Crown servant" means an individual who holds office under, or is employed by, the Crown;

"debenture" has the same meaning in relation to companies not incorporated under the Companies Act 1985 as it has in relation to companies so incorporated;

[1] "recognised stock exchange" means The Stock Exchange and any other investment exchange which is declared by an order of the Secretary of State for the time being in force to be a recognised stock exchange for the purposes of this Act;

"share" has the same meaning in relation to companies not incorporated under the Companies Act 1985 as it has in relation to companies so incorporated;

"statutory maximum" means—

    (*a*) in England and Wales, the prescribed sum within section 32 of the Magistrates' Courts Act 1980, and

    (*b*) in Scotland, the prescribed sum within section 289B of the Criminal Procedure (Scotland) Act 1975;

"unregistered company" means any body corporate to which the provisions of the Companies Act 1985 specified in Schedule 22 to that Act apply by virtue of section 718 of that Act.

[2] (1A) The power to make an order under subsection (1) above shall be exercisable by statutory instrument.

[3] (2) Subject to sections 9 to 14 and this section, expressions used in this Act and the Companies Act 1985 have the same meaning in this Act as in that.

(3) The definitions in sections 11, 12(*a*) and (*b*), 13(2) and 14, and in subsection (1) above, apply except where the context otherwise requires.

NOTES

[1] As amended by the Financial Services Act 1986, Sched. 16, para. 28(*a*).

[2] Inserted by the Financial Services Act 1986, Sched. 16, para. 28(*b*).

[3] As amended by the Financial Services Act 1986, Sched. 16, para. 28(*c*).

General

Northern Ireland

17. This Act does not extend to Northern Ireland.

Commencement

18. This Act comes into force on 1st July 1985.

Citation

19. This Act may be cited as the Company Securities (Insider Dealing) Act 1985.

**Companies Consolidation
(Consequential Provisions)
Act 1985**

(1985 c. 9)

An Act to make, in connection with the consolidation of the Companies Acts 1948 to 1983 and other enactments relating to companies, provision for transitional matters and savings, repeals (including the repeal, in accordance with recommendations of the Law Commission, of certain provisions of the Companies Act 1984 which are no longer of practical utility) and consequential amendments of other Acts.   [11th March 1985]

ARRANGEMENT OF SECTIONS

General

Old public companies

Meaning of "old public company"

1.—(1) For the purposes of the Companies Act 1985 ("the principal Act") and this Act, an "old public company" is a company limited by shares or by guarantee and having a share capital in respect of which the following conditions are satisfied—

(*a*) the company either existed on 22nd December 1980 or was incorporated after that date pursuant to an application made before that date.

(*b*) on that date or, if later, on the day of the company's incorporation the company was not or (as the case may be) would not have been a private company within section 28 of the Companies Act 1948, and

(*c*) the company has not since that date or the day of the company's incorporation (as the case may be) either been re-registered as a public company or become a private company.

(2) References in the principal Act (other than so much of it as is derived from Part I of the Companies Act 1980, and other than section 33 (penalty for trading under misleading name)) to a public company or a company other than a private company are to be read as including (unless the context otherwise requires) references to an old public company, and references in that Act to a private company are to be read accordingly.

Re-registration as public company

2.—(1) An old public company may be re-registered as a public company if—

(*a*) the directors pass a resolution, complying with the following subsection, that it should be so re-registered, and

(*b*) an application for the purpose in the prescribed form and signed by a director or secretary of the company is delivered to the registrar of companies together with the documents mentioned in subsection (4) below, and

(*c*) at the time of the resolution, the conditions specified in section 3 below are satisfied.

(2) The resolution must alter the company's memorandum so that it states that the company is to be a public company and make such other alterations in it as are necessary to bring it in substance and in form into conformity with the requirements of the principal Act with respect to the memorandum of a public company.

(3) A resolution of the directors under this section is subject to section 380 of the principal Act (copy of resolution to be forwarded to registrar of companies within 15 days).

(4) The documents referred to in subsection (1)(*b*) are—

(*a*) a printed copy of the memorandum as altered in pursuance of the resolution, and

(*b*) a statutory declaration in the prescribed form by a director or secretary of the company that the resolution has been passed and that the conditions specified in section 3 of this Act were satisfied at the time of the resolution.

(5) The registrar may accept a declaration under subsection (4)(*b*) as sufficient evidence that the resolution has been passed and the necessary conditions were satisfied.

(6) Section 47(1) and (3) to (5) of the principal Act apply on an application for re-registration under this section as they apply on an application under section 43 of that Act.

Conditions for re-registering under s. 2

3.—(1) The following are the conditions referred to in section 2(1)(*c*) (being conditions also relevant under section 4).

(2) At the time concerned, the nominal value of the company's allotted share capital must not be less than the authorised minimum (defined in section 118 of the principal Act).

(3) In the case of all the shares of the company, or of all those of its shares which are comprised in a portion of the share capital which satisfies the condition in subsection (2)—

(*a*) each share must be paid up at least as to one-quarter of the nominal value of that share and the whole of any premium on it;

(*b*) where any of the shares in question or any premium payable on them has been fully or partly paid up by an undertaking given by any person that he or another should do work or perform services for the company or another, the undertaking must have been performed or otherwise discharged; and

(*c*) where any of the shares in question has been allotted as fully or partly paid up as to its nominal value or any premium payable on it otherwise than in cash, and the consideration for the allotment consists of or includes an undertaking (other than one to which paragraph (*b*) applies) to the company, then either—

(i) that undertaking must have been either performed or otherwise discharged, or

(ii) there must be a contract between the company and some person pursuant to which the undertaking is to be performed within five years from the time of the resolution.

Old public company becoming private

4.—(1) An old public company may pass a special resolution not to be re-registered under section 2 as a public company; and section 54 of the principal Act (litigated objection by shareholders) applies to the resolution as it would apply to a special resolution by a public company to be re-registered as private.

(2) If either—

(*a*) 28 days from the passing of the resolution elapse without an application being made under section 54 of the principal Act (as applied), or

(*b*) such an application is made and proceedings are concluded on the application without the court making an order for the cancellation of the resolution,

the registrar of companies shall issue the company with a certificate stating that it is a private company; and the company then becomes a private company by virtue of the issue of the certificate.

(3) For the purposes of subsection (2)(*b*), proceedings on the application are concluded—

(*a*) except in a case within the following paragraph, when the period mentioned in section 54(7) of the principal Act (as applied) for delivering an office copy of the court's order under that section to the registrar of companies has expired, or (*b*) when the company has been notified that the application has been withdrawn.

(4) If an old public company delivers to the registrar of companies a statutory declaration in the prescribed form by a director or secretary of the company that the company does not at the time of the declaration satisfy the conditions specified in section 3 for the company to be re-registered as public, the registrar shall issue the company with a certificate stating that it is a private company; and the company then becomes a private company by virtue of the issue of the certificate.

(5) A certificate issued to a company under subsection (2) or (4) is conclusive evidence that the requirements of that subsection have been complied with and that the company is a private company.

Failure by old public company to obtain new classification

5.—(1) If at any time a company which is an old public company has not delivered to the registrar of companies a declaration under section 4(4), the company and any officer of it who is in default is guilty of an offence unless at that time the company—

(*a*) has applied to be re-registered under section 2, and the application has not been refused or withdrawn, or

(*b*) has passed a special resolution not to be re-registered under that section, and the resolution has not been revoked, and has not been cancelled under section 54 of the principal Act as applied by section 4 above.

(2) A person guilty of an offence under subsection (1) is liable on summary conviction to a fine not exceeding one-fifth of the statutory maximum or, on conviction after continued contravention, to a daily default fine not exceeding one-fiftieth of the statutory maximum for every day on which the subsection is contravened.

Shares of old public company held by itself; charges on own shares

6.—(1) The following has effect notwithstanding section 1(2).

(2) References to a public company in sections 146 to 149 of the principal Act (treatment of a company's shares when acquired by itself) do not include an old public company; and references in those sections to a private company are to be read accordingly.

(3) In the case of a company which after 22nd March 1982 remained an old public company and did not before that date apply to be re-registered under section 8 of the Act of 1980 as a public company, any charge on its own shares which was in existence on or immediately before that date is a permitted charge for the purposes of Chapter V of Part V of the principal Act and accordingly not void under section 150 of that Act.

7. [Repealed by the Financial Services Act 1986, Sched. 17.]

Trading under misleading name

8.—(1) An old public company is guilty of an offence if it carries on any trade, profession or business under a name which includes, as its last part, the words "public limited company" or "cwmni cyfyngedig cyhoeddus".

(2) A company guilty of an offence under this section, and any officer of the company who is in default, is liable on summary conviction as for an offence under section 33 of the principal Act.

Payment for share capital

9.—(1) Subject as follows, sections 99, 101 to 103, 106, 108 and 110 to 115 in Part IV of the principal Act apply to a company whose directors have passed and not revoked a resolution to be re-registered under section 2 of this Act, as those sections apply to a public company.

(2) Sections 99, 101 to 103, 108 and 112 of the principal Act do not apply to the allotment of shares by a company, other than a public company registered as such on its original incorporation, where the contract for the allotment was entered into—

(*a*) except in a case falling within the following paragraph, on or before 22nd June 1982;

(*b*) in the case of a company re-registered or registered as a public company in pursuance of—

(i) a resolution to be re-registered under section 43 of the principal Act,

(ii) a resolution to be re-registered under section 2 of this Act, or

(iii) a resolution by a joint stock company that the company be a public company,

being a resolution that was passed on or before 22nd June 1982, before the date on which the resolution was passed.

Miscellaneous savings

Pre-1901 companies limited by guarantee
10. Section 15 of the principal Act does not apply in the case of companies registered before 1st January 1901.

Company official seal
11.—(1) A company which was incorporated before 12th February 1979 and which has such an official seal as is mentioned in section 40 of the principal Act may use the seal for sealing such securities and documents as are there mentioned, notwithstanding anything in any instrument constituting or regulating the company or in any instrument made before that date which relates to any securities issued by the company.

(2) Any provision of such an instrument which requires any such securities or documents to be signed shall not apply to the securities or documents if they are sealed with that seal.

Share premiums: retrospective relief
12.—(1) The relief given by this section (being a replacement of section 39 of the Companies Act 1981) applies only where a company has issued shares in circumstances to which this section applies before 4th February 1981.

(2) Subject as follows, this section applies where the issuing company (that is, the company issuing shares as mentioned in section 130 of the principal Act) has issued at a premium shares which were allotted in pursuance of any arrangement providing for the allotment of shares in the issuing company on terms that the consideration for the shares allotted was to be provided by the issue or transfer to the issuing company of shares in another company or by the cancellation of any shares in that other company not held by the issuing company.

(3) The other company in question must either have been at the time of the arrangement a subsidiary of the issuing company or of any company which was then the issuing company's holding company or have become such a subsidiary on the acquisition or cancellation of its shares in pursuance of the arrangement.

(4) Any part of the premiums on the shares so issued which was not transferred to the company's share premium account in accordance with section 56 of the Act of 1948 shall be treated as if that section had never applied to those premiums (and may accordingly be disregarded in determining the sum to be included in the company's share premium account).

(5) Section 133(2) and (3) of the principal Act apply for the interpretation of this section; and for the purposes of this section—

(a) "company" (except in references to the issuing company) includes any body corporate, and

(b) the definition of "arrangement" in section 131(7) of the principal Act applies.

(6) This section is deemed included in Chapter III of Part V of the principal Act for the purpose of the Secretary of State's power under section 134 of that Act to make regulations in respect of relief from the requirements of section 130 of that Act.

Saving, in case of re-issued debentures, of rights of certain mortgagees

13. Whereas by section 104 of the Companies (Consolidation) Act 1908 it was provided that, upon the re-issue of redeemed debentures, the person entitled to the debentures should have the same rights and priorities as if the debentures had not previously been issued:

And whereas section 45 of the Companies Act 1928 amended section 104 of the Act of 1908 so as to provide (among other things) that the said person should have the same priorities as if the debentures had never been redeemed, but saved, in the case of debentures redeemed before, but re-issued after, 1st November 1929, the rights and priorities of persons under mortgages and charges created before that date:

Now, therefore, where any debentures which were redeemed before the date last mentioned have been re-issued after that date and before the commencement of the Act of 1948 (1st July 1948), or are or have been re-issued after that commencement, the re-issue of the debentures does not prejudice, and is deemed never to have prejudiced, any right or priority which any person would have had under or by virtue of any such mortgage or charge as above referred to if section 104 of the Act of 1908, as originally enacted, had been enacted in the Act of 1948 instead of section 90 of that Act, and in the principal Act instead of section 194 of that Act.

Removal of directors appointed for life pre-1945

14. Section 303(1) of the principal Act does not, in the case of a private company, authorise the removal of a director holding office for life on 18th July 1945, whether or not subject to retirement under an age limit by virtue of the articles or otherwise.

Tax-free payments to directors

15. Section 311(1) of the principal Act does not apply to remuneration under a contract which was in force on 18th July 1945 and provides expressly (and not by reference to the articles) for payment of remuneration as mentioned in that subsection; and section 311(2) does not apply to any provision contained in such a contract.

Statutory declaration of solvency in voluntary winding up

16. In relation to a winding up commenced before 22nd December 1981, section 577 of the principal Act applies in the form of section 283 of the Act of 1948, without the amendment of that section made by section 105 of the Act of 1981.

Court's power to control proceedings

17. Nothing in section 603 of the principal Act affects the practice or powers of the court as existing immediately before 1st November 1929, with respect to the staying of proceedings against a company registered in England and Wales and in course of being wound up.

Effect of floating charge in winding up

18. In relation to a charge created on or before 31st December 1947, section 617(1) of the principal Act has effect with the substitution of "six months" for "12 months".

Saving from s.649 of principal Act
19. Nothing in section 649 of the principal Act affects the practice or powers of the court as existing immediately before 1st November 1929, with respect to the costs of an application for leave to proceed with an action or proceeding against a company which is being wound up in England and Wales.

20. [Repealed by the Banking Act 1987, Sched. 7, Pt. I.]

Priority of old debts in winding up
21. Nothing in this Act affects the priority to which any person may have been entitled under section 319 of the 1948 Act in respect of a debt of any of the descriptions specified in paragraph (*a*)(ii) of subsection (1) of that section (which included references to profits tax and excess profits tax), or in paragraph (*f*) or (*g*) of that subsection (old workmen's compensation cases).

Saving as to certain old liquidations
22.—(1) The provisions of the principal Act with respect to winding up (other than sections 635, 658 and 620 as applied for the purposes of section 620 and subsection (2) below) shall not apply to any company of which the winding up commenced before 1st November 1929; but every such company shall be wound up in the same manner and with the same incidents as if the Companies Act 1929, the Act of 1948 and the principal Act (apart from the sections above-mentioned) had not passed; and, for the purposes of the winding up, the Act or Acts under which the winding up commenced shall be deemed to remain in full force.

(2) A copy of every order staying or sisting the proceedings in a winding up commenced as above shall forthwith be forwarded by the company, or otherwise as may be prescribed, to the registrar of companies, who shall enter the order in his records relating to the company.

Restrictions on shares imposed pre-1982
23. Where before 3rd December 1981 shares in a company were directed by order of the Secretary of State to be subject to the restrictions imposed by section 174 of the Act of 1948, and the order remains in force at the commencement date, nothing in this Act prevents the continued application of the order with such effect as it had immediately before the repeal of section 174 took effect.

Saving for conversion of winding up under 1981 s.107
24.—(1) The repeal of section 107 of the 1981 Act (conversion of creditors' winding up into members' voluntary winding up, due to circumstances arising in the period April to August 1981) does not affect the enablement for such a conversion by means of a statutory declaration (complying with subsection (2) of the section) delivered to the registrar of companies after the commencement date.

(2) For the purposes of sections 577(4) and 583 of the principal Act (consequences of actual or prospective failure to pay debts in full within the period stated by the directors in the declaration of solvency), the period

stated in the declaration in the case of a winding up converted under section 107 is taken to have been 12 months from the commencement of the winding up, unless the contrary is shown.

Miscellaneous amendments

. . . . . .

Repeal of obsolete provisions

. . . . . .

Repeals, etc. consequential on Companies Acts consolidation; continuity of law

Repeals

29. The enactments specified in the second column of Schedule 1 to this Act are repealed to the extent specified in the third column of the Schedule.

Amendment of post-1948 statutes

30. The enactments specified in the first column of Schedule 2 to this Act (being enactments passed after the Act of 1948 and containing references to that Act or others of the Companies Acts 1948 to 1983) are amended as shown in the second column of the Schedule.

Continuity of law

31.—(1) In this section—

(*a*) "the new Acts" means the principal Act, the Company Securities (Insider Dealing) Act 1985, the Business Names Act 1985 and this Act;

(*b*) "the old Acts" means the Companies Act 1948 to 1983 and any other enactment which is repealed by this Act and replaced by a corresponding provision in the new Acts; and

(*c*) "the commencement date" means 1st July 1985.

(2) So far as anything done or treated as done under or for the purposes of any provision of the old Acts could have been done under or for the purposes of the corresponding provision of the new Acts, it is not invalidated by the repeal of that provision but has effect as if done under or for the purposes of the corresponding provision; and any order, regulation or other instrument made or having effect under any provision of the old Acts shall, in so far as its effect is preserved by this subsection, be treated for all purposes as made and having effect under the corresponding provision.

(3) Where any period of time specified in a provision of the old Acts is current immediately before the commencement date, the new Acts have effect as if the corresponding provision had been in force when the period began to run; and (without prejudice to the foregoing) any period of time so specified and current is deemed for the purposes of the new Acts—

(*a*) to run from the date or event from which it was running immediately before the commencement date, and

(*b*) to expire (subject to any provision of the new Acts for its extension) whenever it would have expired if the new Acts had not been passed;

and any rights, priorities, liabilities, reliefs, obligations, requirements, powers, duties or exemptions dependent on the beginning, duration or end of such a period as above mentioned shall be under the new Acts as they were or would have been under the old.

(4) Where in any provision of the new Acts there is a reference to another provision of those Acts, and the first-mentioned provision operates, or is capable of operating, in relation to things done or omitted, or events occurring or not occurring, in the past (including in particular past acts of compliance with any enactment, failures of compliance, contraventions, offences and convictions of offences), the reference to that other provision is to be read as including a reference to the corresponding provision of the old Acts.

(5) A contravention of any provision of the old Acts committed before the commencement date shall not be visited with any severer punishment under or by virtue of the new Acts than would have been applicable under that provision at the time of the contravention; but—

   (a) where an offence for the continuance of which a penalty was provided has been committed under any provision of the old Acts, proceedings may be taken under the new Acts in respect of the continuance of the offence after the commencement date in the like manner as if the offence had been committed under the corresponding provision of the new Acts; and

   (b) the repeal of any transitory provision of the old Acts (not replaced by any corresponding provision of the new Acts) requiring a thing to be done within a certain time does not affect a person's continued liability to be prosecuted and punished in respect of the failure, or continued failure, to do that thing.

(6) A reference in any enactment, instrument or document (whether express or implied, and in whatever phraseology) to a provision (whether first in force before or after the Act of 1948 or contained in that Act) which is replaced by a corresponding provision of the new Acts is to be read, where necessary to retain for the enactment, instrument or document the same force and effect as it would have had but for the passing of the new Acts, as, or as including, a reference to that corresponding provision.

(7) The generality of subsection (6) is not affected by any specific conversion of references made by this Act, nor by the inclusion in any provision of the new Acts of a reference (whether express or implied, and in whatever phraseology) to the provision of the old Acts corresponding to that provision, or to a provision of the old Acts which is replaced by a corresponding provision of the new.

(8) Nothing in the new Acts affects—

   (a) the registration or re-registration of any company under the former Companies Acts, or the continued existence of any company by virtue of such registration or re-registration; or

   (b) the application of—

      (i) Table B in the Joint Stock Companies Act 1856, or

      (ii) Table A in the Companies Act 1862, the Companies (Consolidation) Act 1908, the Companies Act 1929 or the Companies Act 1948,

   to any company existing immediately before the commencement date; or

   (c) the operation of any enactment providing for any partnership, association or company being wound up, or being wound up as a company or as an unregistered company under any of the former Companies Acts.

(9) Anything saved from repeal by section 459 of the Act of 1948 and still in force immediately before the commencement date remains in force notwithstanding the repeal of the whole of that Act.

(10) Where any provision of the new Acts was, immediately before the commencement date, contained in or given effect by a statutory instrument (whether or not made under a power in any of the old Acts), then—

   (a) the foregoing provisions of this section have effect as if that provision was contained in the old Acts, and (*b*) insofar as the provision was, immediately before that date, subject to a power (whether or not under the old Acts) of variation or revocation, nothing in the new Acts is to be taken as prejudicing any future exercise of the power.

(11) The provisions of this section are without prejudice to the operation of sections 16 and 17 of the Interpretation Act 1978 (savings from, and effect of, repeals); and for the purposes of section 17(2) of that Act (construction of references to enactments repealed and replaced; continuity of powers preserved in repealing enactment), any provision of the old Acts which is replaced by a provision of the principal Act, the Company Securities (Insider Dealing) Act 1985 or the Business Names Act 1985 is deemed to have been repealed and re-enacted by that one of the new Acts and not by this Act.

General

Interpretation
32. In this Act—
  "the Act of 1948" means the Companies Act 1948,
  "the Act of 1980" means the Companies Act 1980,
  "the Act of 1981" means the Companies Act 1981, and
  "the principal Act" means the Companies Act 1985;
and expressions used in this Act and also in the principal Act have the same meanings in this Act as in that (the provisions of Part XXVI of that Act to apply accordingly).

Northern Ireland
33. Except in so far as it has effect for maintaining the continuity of the law, or—
  (*a*) repeals any enactment which extends to Northern Ireland, or
  (*b*) amends any enactment which extends to Northern Ireland (otherwise than by the insertion of provisions expressed not so to extend),
nothing in this Act extends to Northern Ireland.

Commencement
34. This Act comes into force on 1st July 1985.

Citation
35. This Act may be cited as the Companies Consolidation (Consequential Provisions) Act 1985.

SCHEDULES

Section 29   SCHEDULE 1

ENACTMENTS REPEALED

[Repeals to Acts reprinted in *The Parliament House Book* have been given effect.]

Section 30   SCHEDULE 2

AMENDMENTS OF ENACTMENTS CONSEQUENTIAL ON CONSOLIDATION OF COMPANIES ACTS

[Amendments to Acts reprinted in *The Parliament House Book* have been given effect.]

¹ **Companies Act 1985**

(1985 c. 6)

An Act to consolidate the greater part of the Companies Acts.
[11th March 1985]

NOTE
¹ The extensive amendments to this Act by the Companies Act 1989 will be given effect as that Act is brought into force. For forms see S.I. 1985 No. 854, as amended by S.I. 1986 No. 2097, 1987 No. 752 and 1988 No. 1359.

ARRANGEMENT OF SECTIONS

PART I

FORMATION AND REGISTRATION OF COMPANIES; JURIDICAL STATUS AND MEMBERSHIP

CHAPTER I
COMPANY FORMATION

Memorandum of association

Section

Chapter III
A Company's Capacity; Formalities of
Carrying on Business

Part II

Re-registration as a Means of Altering a
Company's Status

Private company becoming public

Limited company becoming unlimited

Unlimited company becoming limited

Public company becoming private

Part III

Capital Issues

[Repealed]

PART IV

ALLOTMENT OF SHARES AND DEBENTURES

General provisions as to allotment

Pre-emption rights

Commissions and discounts

Amount to be paid for shares; the means of payment

Valuation provisions

Other matters arising out of allotment, etc.

PART V

SHARE CAPITAL, ITS INCREASE, MAINTENANCE AND
REDUCTION

CHAPTER I
GENERAL PROVISIONS ABOUT SHARE CAPITAL

CHAPTER II
CLASS RIGHTS

CHAPTER III
SHARE PREMIUMS

CHAPTER IV
REDUCTION OF SHARE CAPITAL

CHAPTER V
MAINTENANCE OF CAPITAL

PART VI

DISCLOSURE OF INTERESTS IN SHARES

PART VII

ACCOUNTS AND AUDIT

CHAPTER I
PROVISIONS APPLYING TO COMPANIES GENERALLY

PART IX

A COMPANY'S MANAGEMENT; DIRECTORS AND SECRETARIES; THEIR QUALIFICATIONS, DUTIES AND RESPONSIBILITIES

PART X

ENFORCEMENT OF FAIR DEALING BY DIRECTORS

PART XI

COMPANY ADMINISTRATION AND PROCEDURE

CHAPTER I
COMPANY IDENTIFICATION

PART XII

REGISTRATION OF CHARGES

CHAPTER I
REGISTRATION OF CHARGES (ENGLAND AND WALES)

CHAPTER II
REGISTRATION OF CHARGES (SCOTLAND)

PART XIII

ARRANGEMENTS AND RECONSTRUCTIONS

PART XIIIA

Part XIV

Investigation of Companies and their Affairs; Requisition of Documents

Appointment and functions of inspectors

Other powers of investigation available to Secretary of State

Requisition and seizure of books and papers

Supplementary

Part XV

Orders Imposing Restrictions on Shares
(Sections 210, 216, 445)

Part XVI

Fraudulent Trading by a Company

Part XVII

Protection of Company's Members against Unfair Prejudice

PART XVIII

FLOATING CHARGES AND RECEIVERS
(SCOTLAND)

CHAPTER I
FLOATING CHARGES

CHAPTER II
RECEIVERS

CHAPTER III
GENERAL

PART XIX

RECEIVERS AND MANAGERS
(ENGLAND AND WALES)

PART XX

WINDING UP OF COMPANIES REGISTERED
UNDER THIS ACT OR THE FORMER COMPANIES ACTS

CHAPTER I
PRELIMINARY

CHAPTER II
WINDING UP BY THE COURT

CHAPTER III
VOLUNTARY WINDING UP

CHAPTER IV
WINDING UP SUBJECT TO SUPERVISION OF COURT

CHAPTER V
*PROVISIONS APPLICABLE TO EVERY MODE OF
WINDING UP*

[THE NEXT PAGE IS I 41]

Part XXVI

Interpretation

Part XXVII

Final Provisions

[1] PART I

FORMATION AND REGISTRATION OF COMPANIES; JURIDICAL STATUS AND MEMBERSHIP

NOTE

[1] For interpretation of "public company", "private company" etc., see s. 1(3) and the Companies Consolidation (Consequential Provisions) Act 1985, s. 1.

CHAPTER I
COMPANY FORMATION

Memorandum of association

Mode of forming incorporated company

1.—(1) Any two or more persons associated for a lawful purpose may, by subscribing their names to a memorandum of association and otherwise complying with the requirements of this Act in respect of registration, form an incorporated company, with or without limited liability.

(2) A company so formed may be either—

(*a*) a company having the liability of its members limited by the memorandum to the amount, if any, unpaid on the shares respectively held by them ("a company limited by shares");

(*b*) a company having the liability of its members limited by the memorandum to such amount as the members may respectively thereby undertake to contribute to the assets of the company in the event of its being wound up ("a company limited by guarantee"); or

(*c*) a company not having any limit on the liability of its members ("an unlimited company").

(3) A "public company" is a company limited by shares or limited by guarantee and having a share capital, being a company—

(*a*) the memorandum of which states that it is to be a public company, and

(*b*) in relation to which the provisions of this Act or the former Companies Acts as to the registration or re-registration of a company as a public company have been complied with on or after 22nd December 1980;

and a "private company" is a company that is not a public company.

(4) With effect from 22nd December 1980, a company cannot be formed as, or become, a company limited by guarantee with a share capital.

Requirements with respect to memorandum

2.—(1) The memorandum of every company must state—

(*a*) the name of the company;

(*b*) whether the registered office of the company is to be situated in England and Wales, or in Scotland;

(*c*) the objects of the company.

(2) Alternatively to subsection (1)(*b*), the memorandum may contain a statement that the company's registered office is to be situated in Wales; and a company whose registered office is situated in Wales may by special resolution alter its memorandum so as to provide that its registered office is to be so situated.

(3) The memorandum of a company limited by shares or by guarantee must also state that the liability of its members is limited.

(4) The memorandum of a company limited by guarantee must also state that each member undertakes to contribute to the assets of the company if it should be wound up while he is a member, or within one year after he ceases to be a member, for payment of the debts and liabilities of the company contracted before he ceases to be a member, and of the costs, charges and expenses of winding up, and for adjustment of the rights of the contributories among themselves, such amount as may be required, not exceeding a specified amount.

(5) In the case of a company having a share capital—

(*a*) the memorandum must also (unless it is an unlimited company) state the amount of the share capital with which the company proposes to be registered and the division of the share capital into shares of a fixed amount;

(*b*) no subscriber of the memorandum may take less than one share; and

(*c*) there must be shown in the memorandum against the name of each subscriber the number of shares he takes.

(6) The memorandum must be signed by each subscriber in the presence of at least one witness, who must attest the signature; and that attestation is sufficient in Scotland as well as in England and Wales.

(7) A company may not alter the conditions contained in its memorandum except in the cases, in the mode and to the extent, for which express provision is made by this Act.

Forms of memorandum

3.—(1) Subject to the provisions of sections 1 and 2, the form of the memorandum of association of—

(*a*) a public company, being a company limited by shares,

(*b*) a public company, being a company limited by guarantee and having a share capital,

(*c*) a private company limited by shares,

(*d*) a private company limited by guarantee and not having a share capital,

(*e*) a private company limited by guarantee and having a share capital, and

(*f*) an unlimited company having a share capital,

shall be as specified respectively for such companies by regulations made by the Secretary of State, or as near to that form as circumstances admit.

(2) Regulations under this section shall be made by statutory instrument subject to annulment in pursuance of a resolution of either House of Parliament.

Resolution to alter objects

4. A company may by special resolution alter its memorandum with respect to the objects of the company, so far as may be required to enable it—

(*a*) to carry on its business more economically or more efficiently; or

(*b*) to attain its main purpose by new or improved means; or

(*c*) to enlarge or change the local area of its operations; or

(*d*) to carry on some business which under existing circumstances may conveniently or advantageously be combined with the business of the company; or

(*e*) to restrict or abandon any of the objects specified in the memorandum; or

(*f*) to sell or dispose of the whole or any part of the undertaking of the company; or

(*g*) to amalgamate with any other company or body of persons;

but if an application is made under the following section, the alteration does not have effect except in so far as it is confirmed by the court.

Procedure for objecting to alteration

5.—(1) Where a company's memorandum has been altered by special resolution under section 4, application may be made to the court for the alteration to be cancelled.

(2) Such an application may be made—

(*a*) by the holders of not less in the aggregate than 15 per cent. in nominal value of the company's issued share capital or any class of it or, if the company is not limited by shares, not less than 15 per cent. of the company's members; or

(*b*) by the holders of not less than 15 per cent. of the company's debentures entitling the holders to object to an alteration of its objects;

but an application shall not be made by any person who has consented to or voted in favour of the alteration.

(3) The application must be made within 21 days after the date on which the resolution altering the company's objects was passed, and may be made on behalf of the persons entitled to make the application by such one or more of their number as they may appoint in writing for the purpose.

(4) The court may on such an application make an order confirming the alteration either wholly or in part and on such terms and conditions as it thinks fit, and may—

(*a*) if it thinks fit, adjourn the proceedings in order that an arrangement may be made to its satisfaction for the purchase of the interests of dissentient members, and

(*b*) give such directions and make such orders as it thinks expedient for facilitating or carrying into effect any such arrangement.

(5) The court's order may (if the court thinks fit) provide for the purchase by the company of the shares of any members of the company, and for the reduction accordingly of its capital, and may make such alterations in the company's memorandum and articles as may be required in consequence of that provision.

(6) If the court's order requires the company not to make any, or any specified, alteration in its memorandum or articles, the company does not then have power without the leave of the court to make any such alteration in breach of that requirement.

(7) An alteration in the memorandum or articles of a company made by virtue of an order under this section, other than one made by resolution of the company, is of the same effect as if duly made by resolution; and this Act applies accordingly to the memorandum or articles as so altered.

(8) The debentures entitling the holders to object to an alteration of a company's objects are any debentures secured by a floating charge which were issued or first issued before 1st December 1947 or form part of the same series as any debentures so issued; and a special resolution altering a company's objects requires the same notice to the holders of any such debentures as to members of the company.

In the absence of provisions regulating the giving of notice to any such debenture holders, the provisions of the company's articles regulating the giving of notice to members apply.

Provisions supplementing ss. 4, 5

6.—(1) Where a company passes a resolution altering its objects, then—

(*a*) if with respect to the resolution no application is made under section 5, the company shall within 15 days from the end of the period for making such an application deliver to the registrar of companies a printed copy of its memorandum as altered; and

(*b*) if such an application is made, the company shall—

(i) forthwith give notice (in the prescribed form) of that fact to the registrar, and

(ii) within 15 days from the date of any order cancelling or confirming the alteration, deliver to the registrar an office copy of the order and, in the case of an order confirming the alteration, a printed copy of the memorandum as altered.

(2) The court may by order at any time extend the time for the delivery of documents to the registrar under subsection (1)(*b*) for such period as the court may think proper.

(3) If a company makes default in giving notice or delivering any document to the registrar of companies as required by subsection (1), the company and every officer of it who is in default is liable to a fine and, for continued contravention, to a daily default fine.

(4) The validity of an alteration of a company's memorandum with respect to the objects of the company shall not be questioned on the ground that it was not authorised by section 4, except in proceedings taken for the purpose (whether under section 5 or otherwise) before the expiration of 21 days after the date of the resolution in that behalf.

(5) Where such proceedings are taken otherwise than under section 5, subsections (1) to (3) above apply in relation to the proceedings as if they had been taken under that section, and as if an order declaring the alteration invalid were an order cancelling it, and as if an order dismissing the proceedings were an order confirming the alteration.

Articles of association

Articles prescribing regulations for companies

7.—(1) There may in the case of a company limited by shares, and there shall in the case of a company limited by guarantee or unlimited, be registered with the memorandum articles of association signed by the subscribers to the memorandum and prescribing regulations for the company.

(2) In the case of an unlimited company having a share capital, the articles must state the amount of share capital with which the company proposes to be registered.

(3) Articles must—
  (*a*) be printed,
  (*b*) be divided into paragraphs numbered consecutively, and
  (*c*) be signed by each subscriber of the memorandum in the presence of at least one witness who must attest the signature (which attestation is sufficient in Scotland as well as in England and Wales).

Tables A, C, D and E

8.—(1) Table A is as prescribed by regulations made by the Secretary of State[1]; and a company may for its articles adopt the whole or any part of that Table.

(2) In the case of a company limited by shares, if articles are not registered or, if articles are registered, in so far as they do not exclude or modify Table A, that Table (so far as applicable, and as in force at the date of the company's registration) constitutes the company's articles, in the same manner and to the same extent as if articles in the form of that Table had been duly registered.

(3) If in consequence of regulations under this section Table A is altered, the alteration does not affect a company registered before the alteration takes effect, or repeal as respects that company any portion of the Table.

(4) The form of the articles of association of—
  (*a*) a company limited by guarantee and not having a share capital,
  (*b*) a company limited by guarantee and having a share capital, and
  (*c*) an unlimited company having a share capital,
shall be respectively in accordance with Table C, D or E prescribed by regulations made by the Secretary of State[1], or as near to that form as circumstances admit.

(5) Regulations under this section shall be made by statutory instrument

subject to annulment in pursuance of a resolution of either House of Parliament.

NOTE
[1] See S.I. 1985 No. 805.

Alteration of articles by special resolution

9.—(1) Subject to the provisions of this Act and to the conditions contained in its memorandum, a company may by special resolution alter its articles.

(2) Alterations so made in the articles are (subject to this Act) as valid as if originally contained in them, and are subject in like manner to alteration by special resolution.

Registration and its consequences

Documents to be sent to registrar

10.—(1) The company's memorandum and articles (if any) shall be delivered—

    (*a*) to the registrar of companies for England and Wales, if the memorandum states that the registered office of the company is to be situated in England and Wales, or that it is to be situated in Wales; and

    (*b*) to the registrar of companies for Scotland, if the memorandum states that the registered office of the company is to be situated in Scotland.

(2) With the memorandum there shall be delivered a statement in the prescribed form containing the names and requisite particulars of—

    (*a*) the person who is, or the persons who are, to be the first director or directors of the company; and

    (*b*) the person who is, or the persons who are, to be the first secretary or joint secretaries of the company;

and the requisite particulars in each case are those set out in Schedule 1.

(3) The statement shall be signed by or on behalf of the subscribers of the memorandum and shall contain a consent signed by each of the persons named in it as a director, as secretary or as one of joint secretaries, to act in the relevant capacity.

(4) Where a memorandum is delivered by a person as agent for the subscribers, the statement shall specify that fact and the person's name and address.

(5) An appointment by any articles delivered with the memorandum of a person as director or secretary of the company is void unless he is named as a director or secretary in the statement.

(6) There shall in the statement be specified the intended situation of the company's registered office on incorporation.

Minimum authorised capital (public companies)

11. When a memorandum delivered to the registrar of companies under section 10 states that the association to be registered is to be a public company, the amount of the share capital stated in the memorandum to be that with which the company proposes to be registered must not be less than the authorised minimum (defined in section 118).

Duty of registrar

12.—(1) The registrar of companies shall not register a company's memorandum delivered under section 10 unless he is satisfied that all the requirements of this Act in respect of registration and of matters precedent and incidental to it have been complied with.

(2) Subject to this, the registrar shall retain and register the memorandum and articles (if any) delivered to him under that section.

(3) A statutory declaration in the prescribed form by—

(*a*) a solicitor engaged in the formation of a company, or

(*b*) a person named as a director or secretary of the company in the statement delivered under section 10(2),

that those requirements have been complied with shall be delivered to the registrar of companies, and the registrar may accept such a declaration as sufficient evidence of compliance.

Effect of registration

[1] **13.**—(1) On the registration of a company's memorandum, the registrar of companies shall give a certificate that the company is incorporated and, in the case of a limited company, that it is limited.

(2) The certificate may be signed by the registrar, or authenticated by his official seal.

(3) From the date of incorporation mentioned in the certificate, the subscribers of the memorandum, together with such other persons as may from time to time become members of the company, shall be a body corporate by the name contained in the memorandum.

(4) That body corporate is then capable forthwith of exercising all the functions of an incorporated company, but with such liability on the part of its members to contribute to its assets in the event of its being wound up as is provided by this Act and the Insolvency Act.

This is subject, in the case of a public company, to section 117 (additional certificate as to amount of allotted share capital).

(5) The persons named in the statement under section 10 as directors, secretary or joint secretaries are, on the company's incorporation, deemed to have been respectively appointed as its first directors, secretary or joint secretaries.

(6) Where the registrar registers an association's memorandum which states that the association is to be a public company, the certificate of incorporation shall contain a statement that the company is a public company.

(7) A certificate of incorporation given in respect of an association is conclusive evidence—

(*a*) that the requirements of this Act in respect of registration and of matters precedent and incidental to it have been complied with, and that the association is a company authorised to be registered, and is duly registered, under this Act, and

(*b*) if the certificate contains a statement that the company is a public company, that the company is such a company.

NOTE
[1] As amended by the Insolvency Act 1986, Sched. 13, Pt. I.

Effect of memorandum and articles

14.—(1) Subject to the provisions of this Act, the memorandum and articles, when registered, bind the company and its members to the same extent as if they respectively had been signed and sealed by each member, and contained covenants on the part of each member to observe all the provisions of the memorandum and of the articles.

(2) Money payable by a member to the company under the memorandum or articles is a debt due from him to the company, and in England and Wales is of the nature of a specialty debt.

Memorandum and articles of company limited by guarantee

[1] **15.**—(1) In the case of a company limited by guarantee and not having a share capital, every provision in the memorandum or articles, or in any resolution of the company purporting to give any person a right to participate in the divisible profits of the company otherwise than as a member, is void.

(2) For purposes of provisions of this Act relating to the memorandum of a company limited by guarantee, and for those of section 1(4) and this section, every provision in the memorandum or articles, or in any resolution, of a company so limited purporting to divide the company's undertaking into shares or interests is to be treated as a provision for a share capital, notwithstanding that the nominal amount or number of the shares or interests is not specified by the provision.

NOTE
[1] Excluded by the Companies Consolidation (Consequential Provisions) Act 1985, s.10.

Effect of alteration on company's members

16.—(1) A member of a company is not bound by an alteration made in the memorandum or articles after the date on which he became a member, if and so far as the alteration—

(*a*) requires him to take or subscribe for more shares than the number held by him at the date on which the alteration is made; or

(*b*) in any way increases his liability as at that date to contribute to the company's share capital or otherwise to pay money to the company.

(2) Subsection (1) operates notwithstanding anything in the memorandum or articles; but it does not apply in a case where the member agrees in writing, either before or after the alteration is made, to be bound by the alteration.

Conditions in memorandum which could have been in articles

17.—(1) A condition contained in a company's memorandum which could lawfully have been contained in articles of association instead of in the memorandum may be altered by the company by special resolution; but if an application is made to the court for the alteration to be cancelled, the alteration does not have effect except in so far as it is confirmed by the court.

(2) This section—

(*a*) is subject to section 16, and also to Part XVII (court order protecting minority), and

(*b*) does not apply where the memorandum itself provides for or prohibits the alteration of all or any of the conditions above referred to, and does not authorise any variation or abrogation of the special rights of any class of members.

(3) Section 5 (except subsections (2)(*b*) and (8)) and section 6(1) to (3) apply in relation to any alteration and to any application made under this section as they apply in relation to alterations and applications under sections 4 to 6.

Amendments of memorandum or articles to be registered

18.—(1) Where an alteration is made in a company's memorandum or articles by any statutory provision, whether contained in an Act of Parliament or in an instrument made under an Act, a printed copy of the Act or instrument shall, not later than 15 days after that provision comes into force, be forwarded to the registrar of companies and recorded by him.

(2) Where a company is required (by this section or otherwise) to send to the registrar any document making or evidencing an alteration in the company's memorandum or articles (other than a special resolution under section 4), the company shall send with it a printed copy of the memorandum or articles as altered.

(3) If a company fails to comply with this section, the company and any officer of it who is in default is liable to a fine and, for continued contravention, to a daily default fine.

Copies of memorandum and articles to be given to members

19.—(1) A company shall, on being so required by any member, send to him a copy of the memorandum and of the articles (if any), and a copy of any Act of Parliament which alters the memorandum, subject to payment—

    (*a*) in the case of a copy of the memorandum and of the articles, of 5 pence or such less sum as the company may prescribe, and

    (*b*) in the case of a copy of an Act, of such sum not exceeding its published price as the company may require.

(2) If a company makes default in complying with this section, the company and every officer of it who is in default is liable for each offence to a fine.

Issued copy of memorandum to embody alterations

20.—(1) Where an alteration is made in a company's memorandum, every copy of the memorandum issued after the date of the alteration shall be in accordance with the alteration.

(2) If, where any such alteration has been made, the company at any time after the date of the alteration issues any copies of the memorandum which are not in accordance with the alteration, it is liable to a fine, and so too is every officer of the company who is in default.

Registered documentation of Welsh companies

21.—(1) Where a company is to be registered with a memorandum stating that its registered office is to be situated in Wales, the memorandum and articles to be delivered for registration under section 10 may be in Welsh; but, if they are, they shall be accompanied by a certified translation into English.

(2) Where a company whose registered office is situated in Wales has altered its memorandum as allowed by section 2(2), it may deliver to the registrar of companies for registration a certified translation into Welsh of its memorandum and articles.

(3) A company whose memorandum states that its registered office is to be situated in Wales may comply with any provision of this Act requiring it to deliver any document to the register of companies by delivering to him that document in Welsh (or, if it consists of a prescribed form, completed in Welsh), together with a certified translation into English.

But any document making or evidencing an alteration in the company's memorandum or articles, and any copy of a company's memorandum or articles as altered, shall be in the same language as the memorandum and articles originally registered and, if that language is Welsh, shall be accompanied by a certified translation into English.

(4) Where a company has under subsection (2) delivered a translation into Welsh of its memorandum and articles, it may, when delivering to the registrar of companies a document making or evidencing an alteration in the memorandum or articles or a copy of the memorandum or articles as altered, deliver with it a certified translation into Welsh.

(5) In this section "certified translation" means a translation certified in the prescribed manner to be a correct translation; and a reference to delivering a document includes sending, forwarding, producing or (in the case of a notice) giving it.

A company's membership

Definition of "member"

22.—(1) The subscribers of a company's memorandum are deemed to have agreed to become members of the company, and on its registration shall be entered as such in its register of members.

(2) Every other person who agrees to become a member of a company, and whose name is entered in its register of members, is a member of the company.

Membership of holding company

23.—(1) Except in the cases mentioned below in this section, a body corporate cannot be a member of a company which is its holding company; and any allotment or transfer of shares in a company to its subsidiary is void.

(2) This does not prevent a subsidiary which was, on 1st July 1948, a member of its holding company, from continuing to be a member; but (subject to subsection (4)) the subsidiary has no right to vote at meetings of the holding company or any class of its members.

(3) Subject as follows, subsections (1) and (2) apply in relation to a nominee for a body corporate which is a subsidiary, as if references to such a body corporate included a nominee for it.

(4) Nothing in this section applies where the subsidiary is concerned as personal representative, or where it is concerned as trustee, unless the holding company or a subsidiary of it is beneficially interested under the trust and is not so interested only by way of security for the purposes of a transaction entered into by it in the ordinary course of a business which includes the lending of money.

Schedule 2 has effect for the interpretation of the reference in this subsection to a company or its subsidiary being beneficially interested.

(5) In relation to a company limited by guarantee or unlimited which is a holding company, the reference in subsection (1) to shares (whether or not the company has a share capital) includes the interest of its members as such, whatever the form of that interest.

Minimum membership for carrying on business

24. If a company carries on business without having at least two members and does so for more than six months, a person who, for the whole or any part of the period that it so carries on business after those six months—

　　(*a*)　is a member of the company, and

　　(*b*)　knows that it is carrying on business with only one member,

is liable (jointly and severally with the company) for the payment of the company's debts contracted during the period or, as the case may be, that part of it.

CHAPTER II
COMPANY NAMES

Name as stated in memorandum

25.—(1) The name of a public company must end with the words "public limited company" or, if the memorandum states that the company's registered office is to be situated in Wales, those words or their equivalent in Welsh ("cwmni cyfyngedig cyhoeddus"); and those words or that equivalent may not be preceded by the word "limited" or its equivalent in Welsh ("cyfyngedig").

(2) In the case of a company limited by shares or by guarantee (not being a public company), the name must have "limited" as its last word, except that—

　　(*a*)　this is subject to section 30 (exempting, in certain circumstances, a company from the requirement to have "limited" as part of the name), and

　　(*b*)　if the company is to be registered with a memorandum stating that its registered office is to be situated in Wales, the name may have "cyfyngedig" as its last word.

Prohibition on registration of certain names

26.—(1) A company shall not be registered under this Act by a name—

　　(*a*)　which includes, otherwise than at the end of the name, any of the following words or expressions, that is to say, "limited", "unlimited" or "public limited company" or their Welsh equivalents ("cyfyngedig", "anghyfyngedig" and "cwmni cyfyngedig cyhoeddus" respectively);

(b) which includes, otherwise than at the end of the name, an abbreviation of any of those words or expressions;

(c) which is the same as a name appearing in the registrar's index of company names;

(d) the use of which by the company would in the opinion of the Secretary of State constitute a criminal offence; or

(e) which in the opinion of the Secretary of State is offensive.

(2) Except with the approval of the Secretary of State, a company shall not be registered under this Act by a name which—

(a) in the opinion of the Secretary of State would be likely to give the impression that the company is connected in any way with Her Majesty's Government or with any local authority; or

(b) includes any word or expression for the time being specified in regulations under section 29.

"Local authority" means any local authority within the meaning of the Local Government Act 1972 or the Local Government (Scotland) Act 1973, the Common Council of the City of London or the Council of the Isles of Scilly.

(3) In determining for purposes of subsection (1)(c) whether one name is the same as another, there are to be disregarded—

(a) the definite article, where it is the first word of the name;

(b) the following words and expressions where they appear at the end of the name, that is to say—

"company" or its Welsh equivalent ("cwmni"),

"and company" or its Welsh equivalent ("a'r cwmni"),

"company limited" or its Welsh equivalent ("cwmni cyfyngedig"),

"and company limited" or its Welsh equivalent ("a'r cwmni cyfyngedig"),

"limited" or its Welsh equivalent ("cyfyngedig"),

"unlimited" or its Welsh equivalent ("anghyfyngedig"), and

"public limited company" or its Welsh equivalent ("cwmni cyfyngedig cyhoeddus");

(c) abbreviations of any of those words or expressions where they appear at the end of the name; and

(d) type and case of letters, accents, spaces between letters and punctuation marks;

and "and" and "&" are to be taken as the same.

Alternatives of statutory designations

27.—(1) A company which by any provision of this Act is either required or entitled to include in its name, as its last part, any of the words specified in subsection (4)below may, instead of those words, include as the last part of the name the abbreviations there specified as alternatives in relation to those words.

(2) A reference in this Act to the name of a company or to the inclusion of any of those words in a company's name includes a reference to the name including (in place of any of the words so specified) the appropriate alternative, or to the inclusion of the appropriate alternative, as the case may be.

(3) A provision of this Act requiring a company not to include any of those words in its name also requires it not to include the abbreviated alternative specified in subsection (4).

(4) For the purposes of this section—

(a) the alternative of "limited" is "ltd.";

(b) the alternative of "public limited company" is "p.l.c.";

(*c*) the alternative of "cyfyngedig" is "cyf."; and

(*d*) the alternative of "cwmni cyfyngedig cyhoeddus" is "c.c.c.".

Change of name

28.—(1) A company may by special resolution change its name (but subject to section 31 in the case of a company which has received a direction under subsection (2) of that section from the Secretary of State).

(2) Where a company has been registered by a name which—

(*a*) is the same as or, in the opinion of the Secretary of State, too like a name appearing at the time of the registration in the registrar's index of company names, or

(*b*) is the same as or, in the opinion of the Secretary of State, too like a name which should have appeared in that index at that time,

the Secretary of State may within 12 months of that time, in writing, direct the company to change its name within such period as he may specify.

Section 26(3) applies in determining under this subsection whether a name is the same as or too like another.

(3) If it appears to the Secretary of State that misleading information has been given for the purpose of a company's registration with a particular name, or that undertakings or assurances have been given for that purpose and have not been fulfilled, he may within five years of the date of its registration with that name in writing direct the company to change its name within such period as he may specify.

(4) Where a direction has been given under subsection (2) or (3), the Secretary of State may by a further direction in writing extend the period within which the company is to change its name, at any time before the end of that period.

(5) A company which fails to comply with a direction under this section, and any officer of it who is in default, is liable to a fine and, for continued contravention, to a daily default fine.

(6) Where a company changes its name under this section, the registrar of companies shall (subject to section 26) enter the new name on the register in place of the former name, and shall issue a certificate of incorporation altered to meet the circumstances of the case; and the change of name has effect from the date on which the altered certificate is issued.

(7) A change of name by a company under this section does not affect any rights or obligations of the company or render defective any legal proceedings by or against it; and any legal proceedings that might have been continued or commenced against it by its former name may be continued or commenced against it by its new name.

Regulations about names

29.—(1) The Secretary of State may by regulations—

(*a*) specify words or expressions for the registration of which as or as part of a company's corporate name his approval is required under section 26(2)(*b*), and

(*b*) in relation to any such word or expression, specify a government department or other body as the relevant body for purposes of the following subsection.

(2) Where a company proposes to have as, or as part of, its corporate name any such word or expression and a government department or other body is specified under subsection (1)(*b*) in relation to that word or expression, a request shall be made (in writing) to the relevant body to indicate whether (and if so why) it has any objections to the proposal; and the person to make the request is—

(*a*) in the case of a company seeking to be registered under this Part, the person making the statutory declaration required by section 12(3),

(b) in the case of a company seeking to be registered under section 680, the persons making the statutory declaration required by section 686(2), and

(c) in any other case, a director or secretary of the company concerned.

(3) The person who has made that request to the relevant body shall submit to the registrar of companies a statement that it has been made and a copy of any response received from that body, together with—

(a) the requisite statutory declaration, or

(b) a copy of the special resolution changing the company's name,

according as the case is one or other of those mentioned in subsection (2).

(4) Sections 709 and 710 (public rights of inspection of documents kept by registrar of companies) do not apply to documents sent under subsection (3) of this section.

(5) Regulations under this section may contain such transitional provisions and savings as the Secretary of State thinks appropriate and may make different provision for different cases or classes of case.

(6) The regulations shall be made by statutory instrument, to be laid before Parliament after it is made; and the regulations shall cease to have effect at the end of 28 days beginning with the day on which the regulations were made (but without prejudice to anything previously done by virtue of them or to the making of new regulations), unless during that period they are approved by resolution of each House. In reckoning that period, no account is to be taken of any time during which Parliament is dissolved or prorogued or during which both Houses are adjourned for more than four days.

Exemption from requirement of "limited" as part of the name

[1] **30.**—(1) Certain companies are exempt from requirements of this Act relating to the use of "limited" as part of the company name.

(2) A private company limited by guarantee is exempt from those requirements, and so too is a company which on 25th February 1982 was a private company limited by shares with a name which, by virtue of a licence under section 19 of the Companies Act 1948, did not include "limited"; but in either case the company must, to have the exemption, comply with the requirements of the following subsection.

(3) Those requirements are that—

(a) the objects of the company are (or, in the case of a company about to be registered, are to be) the promotion of commerce, art, science, education, religion, charity or any profession, and anything incidental or conductive to any of those objects; and

(b) the company's memorandum or articles—

(i) require its profits (if any) or other income to be applied in promoting its objects,

(ii) prohibit the payment of dividends to its members, and

(iii) require all the assets which would otherwise be available to its members generally to be transferred on its winding up either to another body with objects similar to its own or to another body the objects of which are the promotion of charity and anything incidental or conducive thereto (whether or not the body is a member of the company).

(4) A statutory declaration that a comany complies with the requirements of subsection (3) may be delivered to the registrar of companies, who may accept the declaration as sufficient evidence of the matters stated in it; and the registrar may refuse to register a company by a name which does not include the word "limited" unless such a declaration has been delivered to him.

(5) The statutory declaration must be in the prescribed form and be made—

(a) in the case of a company to be formed, by a solicitor engaged in its formation or by a person named as director or secretary in the statement delivered under section 10(2);

(*b*) in the case of a company to be registered in pursuance of section 680, by two or more directors or other principal officers of the company; and

(*c*) in the case of a company proposing to change its name so that it ceases to have the word "limited" as part of its name, by a director or secretary of the company.

(6) References in this section to the word "limited" include (in an appropriate case) its Welsh equivalent ("cyfyngedig"), and the appropriate alternative ("ltd." or "cyf.", as the case may be).

(7) A company which is exempt from requirements relating to the use of "limited" and does not include that word as part of its name, is also exempt from the requirements of this Act relating to the publication of its name and the sending of lists of members to the registrar of companies.

NOTE
[1] Extended by the Financial Services Act 1986, Sched. 9, para. 2.

Provisions applying to company exempt under s. 30
[1] **31.**—(1) A company which is exempt under section 30 and whose name does not include "limited" shall not alter its memorandum or articles of association so that it ceases to comply with the requirements of subsection (3) of that section.

(2) If it appears to the Secretary of State that such a company—

(*a*) has carried on any business other than the promotion of any of the objects mentioned in that subsection, or

(*b*) has applied any of its profits or other income otherwise than in promoting such objects, or

(*c*) has paid a dividend to any of its members,

he may, in writing, direct the company to change its name by resolution of the directors within such period as may be specified in the direction, so that its name ends with "limited".

A resolution passed by the directors in compliance with a direction under this subsection is subject to section 380 of this Act (copy to be forwarded to the registrar of companies within 15 days).

(3) A company which has received a direction under subsection (2) shall not thereafter be registered by a name which does not include "limited", without the approval of the Secretary of State.

(4) References in this section to the word "limited" include (in an appropriate case) its Welsh equivalent ("cyfyngedig"), and the appropriate alternative ("ltd." or "cyf.", as the case may be).

(5) A company which contravenes subsection (1), and any officer of it who is in default, is liable to a fine and, for continued contravention, to a daily default fine.

(6) A company which fails to comply with a direction by the Secretary of State under subsection (2), and any officer of the company who is in default, is liable to a fine and, for continued contravention, to a daily default fine.

NOTE
[1] Extended by the Financial Services Act 1986, Sched. 9, para. 2.

Power to require company to abandon misleading name
32.—(1) If in the Secretary of State's opinion the name by which a company is registered gives so misleading an indication of the nature of its activities as to be likely to cause harm to the public, he may direct it to change its name.

(2) The direction must, if not duly made the subject of an application to the court under the following subsection, be complied with within a period of six weeks from the date of the direction or such longer period as the Secretary of State may think fit to allow.

(3) The company may, within a period of three weeks from the date of the direction, apply to the court to set it aside; and the court may set the

direction aside or confirm it and, if it confirms the direction, shall specify a period within which it must be complied with.

(4) If a company makes default in complying with a direction under this section, it is liable to a fine and, for continued contravention, to a daily default fine.

(5) Where a company changes its name under this section, the registrar shall (subject to section 26) enter the new name on the register in place of the former name, and shall issue a certificate of incorporation altered to meet the circumstances of the case; and the change of name has effect from the date on which the altered certificate is issued.

(6) A change of name by a company under this section does not affect any of the rights or obligations of the company, or render defective any legal proceedings by or against it; and any legal proceedings that might have been continued or commenced against it by its former name may be continued or commenced against it by its new name.

Prohibition on trading under misleading name

33.—(1) A person who is not a public company is guilty of an offence if he carries on any trade, profession or business under a name which includes, as its last part, the words "public limited company" or their equivalent in Welsh ("cwmni cyfyngedig cyhoeddus").

(2) A public company is guilty of an offence if, in circumstances in which the fact that it is a public company is likely to be material to any person, it uses a name which may reasonably be expected to give the impression that it is a private company.

(3) A person guilty of an offence under subsection (1) or (2) and, if that person is a company, any officer of the company who is in default, is liable to a fine and, for continued contravention, to a daily default fine.

Penalty for improper use of "limited" or "cyfyngedig"

34. If any person trades or carries on business under a name or title of which "limited" or "cyfyngedig", or any contraction or imitation of either of those words, is the last word, that person, unless duly incorporated with limited liability, is liable to a fine and, for continued contravention, to a daily default fine.

CHAPTER III
A COMPANY'S CAPACITY; FORMALITIES OF CARRYING ON BUSINESS

Company's capacity: power of directors to bind it

35.—(1) In favour of a person dealing with a company in good faith, any transaction decided on by the directors is deemed to be one which it is within the capacity of the company to enter into, and the power of the directors to bind the company is deemed to be free of any limitation under the memorandum or articles.

(2) A party to a transaction so decided on is not bound to enquire as to the capacity of the company to enter into it or as to any such limitation on the powers of the directors, and is presumed to have acted in good faith unless the contrary is proved.

Form of company contracts

36.—(1) Contracts on behalf of a company may be made as follows—

(*a*) a contract which if made between private persons would be by law required to be in writing, and if made according to the law of England and Wales to be under seal, may be made on behalf of the company in writing under the company's common seal;

(*b*) a contract which if made between private persons would be by law required to be in writing, signed by the parties to be charged therewith, may be made on behalf of the company in writing signed by any person acting under its authority, express or implied;

(*c*) a contract which if made between private persons would by law be valid although made by parol only, and not reduced into writing, may be made by parol on behalf of the company by any person acting under its authority, express or implied.

(2) A contract made according to this section—

(*a*) is effectual in law, and binds the company and its successors and all other parties to it;

(*b*) may be varied or discharged in the same manner in which it is authorised by this section to be made.

(3) A deed to which a company is a party is held to be validly executed according to the law of Scotland on behalf of the company if it is executed in accordance with this Act or is sealed with the company's common seal and subscribed on behalf of the company by two of the directors, or by a director and the secretary; and such subscription on behalf of the company is binding whether attested by witnesses or not.

(4) Where a contract purports to be made by a company, or by a person as agent for a company, at a time when the company has not been formed, then subject to any agreement to the contrary the contract has effect as one entered into by the person purporting to act for the company or as agent for it, and he is personally liable on the contract accordingly.

Bills of exchange and promissory notes

37. A bill of exchange or promissory note is deemed to have been made, accepted or endorsed on behalf of a company if made, accepted or endorsed in the name of, or by or on behalf or on account of, the company by a person acting under its authority.

Execution of deeds abroad

38.—(1) A company may, by writing under its common seal, empower any person, either generally or in respect of any specified matters, as its attorney, to execute deeds on its behalf in any place elsewhere than in the United Kingdom.

(2) A deed signed by such an attorney on behalf of the company and under his seal binds the company and has the same effect as if it were under the company's common seal.

Power of company to have official seal for use abroad

39.—(1) A company whose objects require or comprise the transaction of business in foreign countries may, if authorised by its articles, have for use in any territory, district or place elsewhere than in the United Kingdom, an official seal, which shall be a facsimile of the common seal of the company, with the addition on its face of the name of every territory, district or place where it is to be used.

(2) A deed or other document to which the official seal is duly affixed binds the company as if it had been sealed with the company's common seal.

(3) A company having an official seal for use in any such territory, district or place may, by writing under its common seal, authorise any person appointed for the purpose in that that territory, district or place to affix the official seal to any deed or other document to which the company is party in that territory, district or place.

(4) As between the company and a person dealing with such an agent, the agent's authority continues during the period (if any) mentioned in the instrument conferring the authority, or if no period is there mentioned, then until notice of the revocation or determination of the agent's authority has been given to the person dealing with him.

(5) The person affixing the official seal shall certify in writing on the deed or other instrument to which the seal is affixed the date on which and the place at which it is affixed.

Official seal for share certificates, etc.

40. A company may have, for use for sealing securities issued by the company and for sealing documents creating or evidencing securities so issued, an official seal which is a facsimile of the company's common seal with the addition on its face of the word "Securities".

Authentication of documents

41. A document or proceeding requiring authentication by a company may be signed by a director, secretary or other authorised officer of the company, and need not be under the company's common seal.

Events affecting a company's status

42.—(1) A company is not entitled to rely against other persons on the happening of any of the following events—

(a) the making of a winding-up order in respect of the company, or the appointment of a liquidator in a voluntary winding up of the company, or

(b) any alteration of the company's memorandum or articles, or

(c) any change among the company's directors, or

(d) (as regards service of any document on the company) any change in the situation of the company's registered office,

if the event had not been officially notified at the material time and is not shown by the company to have been known at that time to the person concerned, or if the material time fell on or before the 15th day after the date of official notification (or, where the 15th day was a non-business day, on or before the next day that was not) and it is shown that the person concerned was unavoidably prevented from knowing of the event at that time.

(2) In subsection (1)—

(a) "official notification" and "officially notified" have the meanings given by section 711(2) (registrar of companies to give public notice of the issue or receipt by him of certain documents), and

(b) "non-business day" means a Saturday or Sunday, Christmas Day, Good Friday and any other day which is a bank holiday in the part of Great Britain where the company is registered.

[1] PART II

RE-REGISTRATION AS A MEANS OF ALTERING A COMPANY'S STATUS

NOTE
[1] For interpretation of "public company", "private company" etc., see s. 1(3) and the Companies Consolidation (Consequential Provisions) Act 1985, s. 1.

Private company becoming public

Re-registration of private company as public

43.—(1) Subject to this and the following five sections, a private company (other than a company not having a share capital) may be re-registered as a public company if—

(a) a special resolution that it should be so re-registered is passed; and

(b) an application for re-registration is delivered to the registrar of companies, together with the necessary documents.

A company cannot be re-registered under this section if it has previously been re-registered as unlimited.

(2) The special resolution must—

(a) alter the company's memorandum so that it states that the company is to be a public company; and

(b) make such other alterations in the memorandum as are necessary to bring it (in substance and in form) into conformity with the require-ments of this Act with respect to the memorandum of a public com-pany (the alterations to include compliance with section 25(1) as regards the company's name); and

(c) make such alterations in the company's articles as are requisite in the circumstances.

(3) The application must be in the prescribed form and be signed by a director or secretary of the company; and the documents to be delivered with it are the following—

(a) a printed copy of the memorandum and articles as altered in pur-suance of the resolution;

(b) a copy of a written statement by the company's auditors that in their opinion the relevant balance sheet shows that at the balance sheet date the amount of the company's net assets (within the meaning given to that expression by section 264(2)) was not less than the aggregate of its called-up share capital and undistributable reserves;

(c) a copy of the relevant balance sheet, together with a copy of an unqualified report (defined in section 46) by the company's auditors in relation to that balance sheet;

(d) if section 44 applies, a copy of the valuation report under subsection (2)(b) of that section; and

(e) a statutory declaration in the prescribed form by a director or sec-retary of the company—

(i) that the special resolution required by this section has been passed and that the conditions of the following two sections (so far as applicable) have been satisfied, and

(ii) that, between the balance sheet date and the application for re-registration, there has been no change in the company's finan-cial position that has resulted in the amount of its net assets becoming less than the aggregate of its called-up share capital and undistributable reserves.

(4) "Relevant balance sheet" means a balance sheet prepared as at a date not more than seven months before the company's application under this section.

(5) A resolution that a company be re-registered as a public company may change the company name by deleting the word "company" or the words "and company", or its or their equivalent in Welsh ("cwmni", "a'r cwmni"), including any abbreviation of them.

Consideration for shares recently alloted to be valued

44.—(1) The following applies if shares have been allotted by the com-pany between the date as at which the relevant balance sheet was prepared and the passing of the special resolution under section 43, and those shares were allotted as fully or partly paid up as to their nominal value or any pre-mium on them otherwise than in cash.

(2) Subject to the following provisions, the registrar of companies shall not entertain an application by the company under section 43 unless beforehand—

(a) the consideration for the allotment has been valued in accordance with section 108, and

(b) a report with respect to the value of the consideration has been made to the company (in accordance with that section) during the six months immediately preceding the allotment of the shares.

(3) Where an amount standing to the credit of any of the company's reserve accounts, or of its profit and loss account, has been applied in pay-ing up (to any extent) any of the shares allotted or any premium on those shares, the amount applied does not count as consideration for the allot-ment, and accordingly subsection (2) does not apply to it.

(4) Subsection (2) does not apply if the allotment is in connection with an arrangement providing for it to be on terms that the whole or part of the consideration for the shares allotted is to be provided by the transfer to the company or the cancellation of all or some of the shares, or of all or some of the shares of a particular class, in another company (with or without the issue to the company applying under section 43 of shares, or of shares of any particular class, in that other company).

(5) But subsection (4) does not exclude the application of subsection (2), unless under the arrangement it is open to all the holders of the shares of the other company in question (or, where the arrangement applies only to shares of a particular class, all the holders of the other company's shares of that class) to take part in the arrangement.

In determining whether that is the case, shares held by or by a nominee of the company allotting shares in connection with the arrangement, or by or by a nominee of a company which is that company's holding company or subsidiary or a company which is a subsidiary of its holding company, are to be disregarded.

(6) Subsection (2) does not apply to preclude an application under section 43, if the allotment of the company's shares is in connection with its proposed merger with another company; that is, where one of the companies concerned proposes to acquire all the assets and liabilities of the other in exchange for the issue of shares or other securities of that one to shareholders of the other, with or without any cash payment to shareholders.

[1] (7) In this section—

> (*a*) "arrangement" means any agreement, scheme or arrangement, including an arrangement sanctioned in accordance with section 425 (company compromise with creditors and members) or section 110 of the Insolvency Act (liquidator in winding up accepting shares as consideration for sale of company's property), and
>
> (*b*) "another company" includes any body corporate and any body to which letters patent have been issued under the Chartered Companies Act 1837.

NOTE
[1] As amended by the Insolvency Act 1986, Sched. 13, Pt. I.

Additional requirements relating to share capital

45.—(1) For a private company to be re-registered under section 43 as a public company, the following conditions with respect to its share capital must be satisfied at the time the special resolution under that section is passed.

(2) Subject to subsections (5) to (7) below—

> (*a*) the nominal value of the company's allotted share capital must be not less than the authorised minimum, and
>
> (*b*) each of the company's allotted shares must be paid up at least as to one-quarter of the nominal value of that share and the whole of any premium on it.

(3) Subject to subsection (5), if any shares in the company or any premium on them have been fully or partly paid up by an undertaking given by any person that he or another should do work or perform services (whether for the company or any other person), the undertaking must have been performed or otherwise discharged.

(4) Subject to subsection (5), if shares have been allotted as fully or partly paid up as to their nominal value or any premium on them otherwise than in cash, and the consideration for the allotment consists of or includes an undertaking to the company (other than one to which subsection (3) applies), then either—

> (*a*) the undertaking must have been performed or otherwise discharged, or

(*b*) there must be a contract between the company and some person pursuant to which the undertaking is to be performed within five years from the time the resolution under section 43 is passed.

(5) For the purpose of determining whether subsections (2)(*b*), (3) and (4) are complied with, certain shares in the company may be disregarded; and these are—

(*a*) subject to the next subsection, any share which was allotted before 22nd June 1982, and

(*b*) any share which was allotted in pursuance of an employees' share scheme and by reason of which the company would, but for this subsection, be precluded under subsection (2)(*b*) (but not otherwise) from being re-registered as a public company.

(6) A share is not to be disregarded under subsection (5)(*a*) if the aggregate in nominal value of that share and other shares proposed to be so disregarded is more than one-tenth of the nominal value of the company's allotted share capital; but for this purpose the allotted share capital is treated as not including any shares disregarded under subsection (5)(*b*).

(7) Any shares disregarded under subsection (5) are treated as not forming part of the allotted share capital for the purposes of subsection (2)(*a*).

Meaning of "unqualified report" in s. 43(3)

46.—(1) The following subsections explain the reference in section 43(3)(*c*) to an unqualified report of the company's auditors on the relevant balance sheet.

[1] (2) If the balance sheet was prepared for a financial year of the company, the reference is to an auditors' report stating without material qualification the auditors' opinion that the balance sheet has been properly prepared in accordance with this Act.

[1] (3) If the balance sheet was not prepared for a financial year of the company, the reference is to an auditors' report stating without material qualification the auditors' opinion that the balance sheet has been properly prepared in accordance with the provisions of this Act which would have applied if it had been so prepared.

For the purposes of an auditors' report under this subsection the provisions of this Act shall be deemed to apply with such modifications as are necessary by reason of the fact that the balance sheet is not prepared for a financial year of the company.

[1] (4) A qualification shall be regarded as material unless the auditors state in their report that the matter giving rise to the qualification is not material for the purpose of determining (by reference to the company's balance sheet) whether at the balance sheet date the amount of the company's net assets was not less than the aggregate of its called up share capital and undistributable reserves.

In this subsection "net assets" and "undistributable reserves" have the meaning given by section 264(2) and (3).

NOTE

[1] Substituted by the Companies Act 1989, s.23 and Sched. 10, para. 1.

Certificate of re-registration under s. 43

47.—(1) If the registrar of companies is satisfied, on an application under section 43, that a company may be re-registered under that section as a public company, he shall—

   (*a*) retain the application and other documents delivered to him under the section; and

   (*b*) issue the company with a certificate of incorporation stating that the company is a public company.

(2) The registrar may accept a declaration under section 43(3)(*e*) as sufficient evidence that the special resolution required by that section has been passed and the other conditions of re-registration satisfied.

(3) The registrar shall not issue the certificate if it appears to him that the court has made an order confirming a reduction of the company's capital which has the effect of bringing the nominal value of the company's allotted share capital below the authorised minimum.

(4) Upon the issue to a company of a certificate of incorporation under this section—

   (*a*) the company by virtue of the issue of that certificate becomes a public company; and

   (*b*) any alterations in the memorandum and articles set out in the resolution take effect accordingly.

(5) The certificate is conclusive evidence—

   (*a*) that the requirements of this Act in respect of re-registration and of matters precedent and incidental thereto have been complied with; and

   (*b*) that the company is a public company.

Modification for unlimited company re-registering

48.—(1) In their application to unlimited companies, sections 43 to 47 are modified as follows.

(2) The special resolution required by section 43(1) must, in addition to the matters mentioned in subsection (2) of that section—

   (*a*) state that the liability of the members is to be limited by shares, and what the company's share capital is to be; and

   (*b*) make such alterations in the company's memorandum as are necessary to bring it in substance and in form into conformity with the requirements of this Act with respect to the memorandum of a company limited by shares.

(3) The certificate of incorporation issued under section 47(1) shall, in addition to containing the statement required by paragraph (*b*) of that subsection, state that the company has been incorporated as a company limited by shares; and—

   (*a*) the company by virtue of the issue of the certificate becomes a public company so limited; and

   (*b*) the certificate is conclusive evidence of the fact that it is such a company.

Limited company becoming unlimited

Re-registration of limited company as unlimited

49.—(1) Subject as follows, a company which is registered as limited may be re-registered as unlimited in pursuance of an application in that behalf complying with the requirements of this section.

(2) A company is excluded from re-registering under this section if it is limited by virtue of re-registration under section 44 of the Companies Act 1967 or section 51 of this Act.

(3) A public company cannot be re-registered under this section; nor can a company which has previously been re-registered as unlimited.

(4) An application under this section must be in the prescribed form and be signed by a director or the secretary of the company, and be lodged with the registrar of companies, together with the documents specified in subsection (8) below.

(5) The application must set out such alterations in the company's memorandum as—

(*a*) if it is to have a share capital, are requisite to bring it (in substance and in form) into conformity with the requirements of this Act with respect to the memorandum of a company to be formed as an unlimited company having a share capital; or

(*b*) if it is not to have a share capital, are requisite in the circumstances.

(6) If articles have been registered, the application must set out such alterations in them as—

(*a*) if the company is to have a share capital, are requisite to bring the articles (in substance and in form) into conformity with the requirements of this Act with respect to the articles of a company to be formed as an unlimited company having a share capital; or

(*b*) if the company is not to have a share capital, are requisite in the circumstances.

(7) If articles have not been registered, the application must have annexed to it, and request the registration of, printed articles; and these must, if the company is to have a share capital, comply with the requirements mentioned in subsection (6)(*a*) and, if not, be articles appropriate to the circumstances.

(8) The documents to be lodged with the registrar are—

(*a*) the prescribed form of assent to the company's being registered as unlimited, subscribed by or on behalf of all the members of the company;

(*b*) a statutory declaration made by the directors of the company—

(i) that the persons by whom or on whose behalf the form of assent is subscribed constitute the whole membership of the company, and

(ii) if any of the members have not subscribed that form themselves, that the directors have taken all reasonable steps to satisfy themselves that each person who subscribed it on behalf of a member was lawfully empowered to do so;

(*c*) a printed copy of the memorandum incorporating the alterations in it set out in the application; and

(*d*) if articles have been registered, a printed copy of them incorporating the alterations set out in the application.

(9) For purposes of this section—

(*a*) subscription to a form of assent by the legal personal representative of a deceased member of a company is deemed subscription by him; and

(*b*) a trustee in bankruptcy of a member of a company is, to the exclusion of the latter, deemed a member of the company.

Certificate of re-registration under s. 49

50.—(1) The registrar of companies shall retain the application and other documents lodged with him under section 49 and shall—

(*a*) if articles are annexed to the application, register them; and

(*b*) issue to the company a certificate of incorporation appropriate to the status to be assumed by it by virtue of that section.

(2) On the issue of the certificate—

(*a*) the status of the company, by virtue of the issue, is changed from limited to unlimited; and

(*b*) the alterations in the memorandum set out in the application and (if articles have been previously registered) any alterations to the articles so set out take effect as if duly made by resolution of the company; and

(c) the provisions of this Act apply accordingly to the memorandum and articles as altered.

(3) The certificate is conclusive evidence that the requirements of section 49 in respect of re-registration and of matters precedent and incidental to it have been complied with, and that the company was authorised to be re-registered under this Act in pursuance of that section and was duly so re-registered.

Unlimited company becoming limited

Re-registration of unlimited company as limited

51.—(1) Subject as follows, a company which is registered as unlimited may be re-registered as limited if a special resolution that it should be so re-registered is passed, and the requirements of this section are complied with in respect of the resolution and otherwise.

(2) A company cannot under this section be re-registered as a public company; and a company is excluded from re-registering under it if it is unlimited by virtue of re-registration under section 43 of the Companies Act 1967 or section 49 of this Act.

(3) The special resolution must state whether the company is to be limited by shares or by guarantee and—

(a) if it is to be limited by shares, must state what the share capital is to be and provide for the making of such alterations in the memorandum as are necessary to bring it (in substance and in form) into conformity with the requirements of this Act with respect to the memorandum of a company so limited, and such alterations in the articles as are requisite in the circumstances;

(b) if it is to be limited by guarantee, must provide for the making of such alterations in its memorandum and articles as are necessary to bring them (in substance and in form) into conformity with the requirements of this Act with respect to the memorandum and articles of a company so limited.

(4) The special resolution is subject to section 380 of this Act (copy to be forwarded to registrar within 15 days); and an application for the company to be re-registered as limited, framed in the prescribed form and signed by a director or by the secretary of the company, must be lodged with the registrar of companies, together with the necessary documents, not earlier than the day on which the copy of the resolution forwarded under section 380 is received by him.

(5) The documents to be lodged with the registrar are—

(a) a printed copy of the memorandum as altered in pursuance of the resolution; and

(b) a printed copy of the articles as so altered.

(6) This section does not apply in relation to the re-registration of an unlimited company as a public company under section 43.

Certification of re-registration under s. 51

52.—(1) The registrar shall retain the application and other documents lodged with him under section 51, and shall issue to the company a certificate of incorporation appropriate to the status to be assumed by the company by virtue of that section.

(2) On the issue of the certificate—

(a) the status of the company is, by virtue of the issue, changed from unlimited to limited; and

(b) the alterations in the memorandum specified in the resolution and the alterations in, and additions to, the articles so specified take effect.

(3) The certificate is conclusive evidence that the requirements of section 51 in respect of re-registration and of matters precedent and incidental to it have been complied with, and that the company was authorised to be re-registered in pursuance of that section and was duly so re-registered.

Public company becoming private

Re-registration of public company as private

53.—(1) A public company may be re-registered as a private company if—

  (*a*) a special resolution complying with subsection (2) below that it should be so re-registered is passed and has not been cancelled by the court under the following section;

  (*b*) an application for the purpose in the prescribed form and signed by a director or the secretary of the company is delivered to the registrar of companies, together with a printed copy of the memorandum and articles of the company as altered by the resolution; and

  (*c*) the period during which an application for the cancellation of the resolution under the following section may be made has expired without any such application having been made; or

  (*d*) where such an application has been made, the application has been withdrawn or an order has been made under section 54(5) confirming the resolution and a copy of that order has been delivered to the registrar.

(2) The special resolution must alter the company's memorandum so that it no longer states that the company is to be a public company and must make such other alterations in the company's memorandum and articles as are requisite in the circumstances.

(3) A company cannot under this section be re-registered otherwise than as a company limited by shares or by guarantee.

Litigated objection to resolution under s. 53

54.—(1) Where a special resolution by a public company to be re-registered under section 53 as a private company has been passed, an application may be made to the court for the cancellation of that resolution.

(2) The application may be made—

  (*a*) by the holders of not less in the aggregate than 5 per cent. in nominal value of the company's issued share capital or any class thereof;

  (*b*) if the company is not limited by shares, by not less than 5 per cent. of its members; or

  (*c*) by not less than 50 of the company's members;

but not by a person who has consented to or voted in favour of the resolution.

(3) The application must be made within 28 days after the passing of the resolution and may be made on behalf of the persons entitled to make the application by such one or more of their number as they may appoint in writing for the purpose.

(4) If such an application is made, the company shall forthwith give notice in the prescribed form of that fact to the registrar of companies.

(5) On the hearing of the application, the court shall make an order either cancelling or confirming the resolution and—

  (*a*) may make that order on such terms and conditions as it thinks fit, and may (if it thinks fit) adjourn the proceedings in order that an arrangement may be made to the satisfaction of the court for the purchase of the interests of dissentient members; and

  (*b*) may give such directions and make such orders as it thinks expedient for facilitating or carrying into effect any such arrangement.

(6) The court's order may, if the court thinks fit, provide for the purchase by the company of the shares of any of its members and for the reduction accordingly of the company's capital, and may make such alterations in the company's memorandum and articles as may be required in consequence of that provision.

(7) The company shall, within 15 days from the making of the court's order, or within such longer period as the court may at any time by order direct, deliver to the registrar of companies an office copy of the order.

(8) If the court's order requires the company not to make any, or any specified, alteration in its memorandum or articles, the company has not then power without the leave of the court to make any such alteration in breach of the requirement.

(9) An alteration in the memorandum or articles made by virtue of an order under this section, if not made by resolution of the company, is of the same effect as if duly made by resolution; and this Act applies accordingly to the memorandum or articles as so altered.

(10) A company which fails to comply with subsection (4) or subsection (7), and any officer of it who is in default, is liable to a fine and, for continued contravention, to a daily default fine.

Certificate of re-registration under s.53

55.—(1) If the registrar of companies is satisfied that a company may be re-registered under section 53, he shall—
  (*a*) retain the application and other documents delivered to him under that section; and
  (*b*) issue the company with a certificate of incorporation appropriate to a private company.

(2) On the issue of the certificate—
  (*a*) the company by virtue of the issue becomes a private company; and
  (*b*) the alterations in the memorandum and articles set out in the resolution under section 53 take effect accordingly.

(3) The certificate is conclusive evidence—
  (*a*) that the requirements of section 53 in respect of re-registration and of matters precedent and incidental to it have been complied with; and
  (*b*) that the company is a private company.

PART III

CAPITAL ISSUES

[Repealed by the Financial Services Act 1986, Sched. 17.]

[1] PART IV

ALLOTMENT OF SHARES AND DEBENTURES

NOTE
  [1] Applied by the Companies Consolidation (Consequential Provisions) Act 1985, s.9. For interpretation of "public company", "private company" etc., see *ibid.*, s.1, and s.1(3), *supra*.

General provisions as to allotment

Authority of company required for certain allotments

80.—(1) The directors of a company shall not exercise any power of the company to allot relevant securities, unless they are, in accordance with this section, authorised to do so by—

(*a*) the company in general meeting; or

(*b*) the company's articles.

(2) In this section "relevant securities" means—

(*a*) shares in the company other than shares shown in the memorandum to have been taken by the subscribers to it or shares allotted in pursuance of an employees' share scheme, and

(*b*) any right to subscribe for, or to convert any security into, shares in the company (other than shares so allotted);

and a reference to the allotment of relevant securities includes the grant of such a right but (subject to subsection (6) below), not the allotment of shares pursuant to such a right.

(3) Authority under this section may be given for a particular exercise of the power or for its exercise generally, and may be unconditional or subject to conditions.

(4) The authority must state the maximum amount of relevant securities that may be allotted under it and the date on which it will expire, which must be not more than five years from whichever is relevant of the following dates—

(*a*) in the case of an authority contained in the company's articles at the time of its original incorporation, the date of that incorporation; and

(*b*) in any other case, the date on which the resolution is passed by virtue of which the authority is given;

but such an authority (including an authority contained in the articles) may be previously revoked or varied by the company in general meeting.

(5) The authority may be renewed or further renewed by the company in general meeting for a further period not exceeding five years; but the resolution must state (or restate) the amount of relevant securities which may be allotted under the authority or, as the case may be, the amount remaining to be allotted under it, and must specify the date on which the renewed authority will expire.

(6) In relation to authority under this section for the grant of such rights as are mentioned in subsection (2)(*b*), the reference in subsection (4) (as also the corresponding reference in subsection (5)) to the maximum amount of relevant securities that may be allotted under the authority is to the maximum amount of shares which may be allotted pursuant to the rights.

(7) The directors may allot relevant securities, notwithstanding that authority under this section has expired, if they are allotted in pursuance of an offer or agreement made by the company before the authority expired and the authority allowed it to make an offer or agreement which would or might require relevant securities to be allotted after the authority expired.

(8) A resolution of a company to give, vary, revoke or renew such an authority may, notwithstanding that it alters the company's articles, be an ordinary resolution; but it is in any case subject to section 380 of this Act (copy to be forwarded to registrar within 15 days).

(9) A director who knowingly and wilfully contravenes, or permits or authorises a contravention of, this section is liable to a fine.

(10) Nothing in this section affects the validity of any allotment.

(11) This section does not apply to any allotment of relevant securities by a company, other than a public company registered as such on its original incorporation, if it is made in pursuance of an offer or agreement made before the earlier of the following two dates—

(*a*) the date of the holding of the first general meeting of the company after its registration or re-registration as a public company, and

(*b*) 22nd June 1982;

but any resolution to give, vary or revoke an authority for the purposes of section 14 of the Companies Act 1980 or this section has effect for those purposes if passed at any time after the end of April 1980.

Election by private company as to duration of authority

[1] **80A.**—(1) A private company may elect (by elective resolution in accordance with section 379A) that the provisions of this section shall apply, instead of the provisions of section 80(4) and (5), in relation to the giving or renewal, after the election, of an authority under that section.

(2) The authority must state the maximum amount of relevant securities that may be allotted under it and may be given—

(*a*) for an indefinite period, or

(*b*) for a fixed period, in which case it must state the date on which it will expire.

(3) In either case an authority (including an authority contained in the articles) may be revoked or varied by the company in general meeting.

(4) An authority given for a fixed period may be renewed or further renewed by the company in general meeting.

(5) A resolution renewing an authority—

(*a*) must state, or re-state, the amount of relevant securities which may be allotted under the authority or, as the case may be, the amount remaining to be allotted under it, and

(*b*) must state whether the authority is renewed for an indefinite period or for a fixed period, in which case it must state the date on which the renewed authority will expire.

(6) The references in this section to the maximum amount of relevant securities that may be allotted shall be construed in accordance with section 80(6).

(7) If an election under this section ceases to have effect, an authority then in force which was given for an indefinite period or for a fixed period of more than five years—

(*a*) if given five years or more before the election ceases to have effect, shall expire forthwith, and

(*b*) otherwise, shall have effect as if it had been given for a fixed period of five years.

NOTE

[1] Inserted by the Companies Act 1989, s.115(1).

81–83. [Repealed by the Financial Services Act 1986, Sched. 17.]

[THE NEXT PAGE IS I 81]

Allotment where issue not fully subscribed

[1] **84.**—(1) No allotment shall be made of any share capital of a public company offered for subscription unless—

(*a*) that capital is subscribed for in full; or

(*b*) the offer states that, even if the capital is not subscribed for in full, the amount of that capital subscribed for may be allotted in any event or in the event of the conditions specified in the offer being satisfied;

and, where conditions are so specified, no allotment of the capital shall be made by virtue of paragraph (*b*) unless those conditions are satisfied.

(2) If shares are prohibited from being allotted by subsection (1) and 40 days have elapsed after the first issue of the prospectus, all money received from applicants for shares shall be forthwith repaid to them without interest.

(3) If any of the money is not repaid within 48 days after the issue of the prospectus, the directors of the company are jointly and severally liable to repay it with interest at the rate of 5 per cent. per annum from the expiration of the 48th day; except that a director is not so liable if he proves that the default in repayment was not due to any misconduct or negligence on his part.

(4) This section applies in the case of shares offered as wholly or partly payable otherwise than in cash as it applies in the case of shares offered for subscription (the word "subscribed" in subsection (1) being construed accordingly).

(5) In subsections (2) and (3) as they apply to the case of shares offered as wholly or partly payable otherwise than in cash, references to the repayment of money received from applicants for shares include—

(*a*) the return of any other consideration so received (including, if the case so requires, the release of the applicant from any undertaking), or

(*b*) if it is not reasonably practicable to return the consideration, the payment of money equal to its value at the time it was so received,

and references to interest apply accordingly.

(6) Any condition requiring or binding an applicant for shares to waive compliance with any requirement of this section is void.

NOTE

[1] As amended by the Financial Services Act 1986, Sched. 17.

Effect of irregular allotment

85.—[1] (1) An allotment made by a company to an applicant in contravention of section 84 is voidable at the instance of the applicant within one month after the date of the allotment, and not later, and is so voidable notwithstanding that the company is in the course of being wound up.

(2) If a director of a company knowingly contravenes, or permits or authorises the contravention of, any provision of either of those sections with respect to allotment, he is liable to compensate the company and the allottee respectively for any loss, damages or costs which the company or the allottee may have sustained or incurred by the contravention.

(3) But proceedings to recover any such loss, damages or costs shall not be commenced after the expiration of two years from the date of the allotment.

NOTE

[1] As amended by the Financial Services Act 1986, Sched. 17.

86, 87. [Repealed by the Financial Services Act 1986, Sched. 17.]

Return as to allotments, etc.

88.—(1) This section applies to a company limited by shares and to a company limited by guarantee and having a share capital.

(2) When such a company makes an allotment of its shares, the company shall within one month thereafter deliver to the registrar of companies for registration—

    (*a*) a return of the allotments (in the prescribed form) stating the number and nominal amount of the shares comprised in the allotment, the names and addresses of the allottees, and the amount (if any) paid or due and payable on each share, whether on account of the nominal value of the share or by way of premium; and

    (*b*) in the case of shares allotted as fully or partly paid up otherwise than in cash—

        (i) a contract in writing constituting the title of the allottee to the allotment together with any contract of sale, or for services or other consideration in respect of which that allotment was made (such contracts being duly stamped), and

        (ii) a return stating the number and nominal amount of shares so allotted, the extent to which they are to be treated as paid up, and the consideration for which they have been allotted.

(3) Where such a contract as above mentioned is not reduced to writing, the company shall within one month after the allotment deliver to the registrar of companies for registration the prescribed particulars of the contract stamped with the same stamp duty as would have been payable if the contract had been reduced to writing.

(4) Those particulars are deemed an instrument within the meaning of the Stamp Act 1891; and the registrar may, as a condition of filing the particulars, require that the duty payable on them be adjudicated under section 12 of that Act.

(5) If default is made in complying with this section, every officer of the company who is in default is liable to a fine and, for continued contravention, to a daily default fine, but subject as follows.

(6) In the case of default in delivering to the registrar within one month after the allotment any document required by this section to be delivered, the company, or any officer liable for the default, may apply to the court for relief; and the court, if satisfied that the omission to deliver the docu-

ment was accidental or due to inadvertence, or that it is just and equitable
to grant relief, may make an order extending the time for the delivery of
the document for such period as the court thinks proper.

Pre-emption rights

Offers to shareholders to be on pre-emptive basis
89.—(1) Subject to the provisions of this section and the seven sections
next following, a company proposing to allot equity securities (defined in
section 94)—

> (*a*) shall not allot any of them on any terms to a person unless it has
> made an offer to each person who holds relevant shares or relevant
> employee shares to allot to him on the same or more favourable
> terms a proportion of those securities which is as nearly as practi-
> cable equal to the proportion in nominal value held by him of the
> aggregate of relevant shares and relevant employee shares, and
>
> (*b*) shall not allot any of those securities to a person unless the period
> during which any such offer may be accepted has expired or the
> company has received notice of the acceptance or refusal of every
> offer so made.

(2) Subsection (3) below applies to any provision of a company's memorandum or articles which requires the company, when proposing to allot
equity securities consisting of relevant shares of any particular class, not to
allot those securities on any terms unless it has complied with the condition
that it makes such an offer as is described in subsection (1) to each person
who holds relevant shares or relevant employee shares of that class.

(3) If in accordance with a provision to which this subsection applies—

> (*a*) a company makes an offer to allot securities to such a holder, and
>
> (*b*) he or anyone in whose favour he has renounced his right to their
> allotment accepts the offer,

subsection (1) does not apply to the allotment of those securities, and the
company may allot them accordingly; but this is without prejudice to the
application of subsection (1) in any other case.

(4) Subsection (1) does not apply to a particular allotment of equity
securities if these are, or are to be, wholly or partly paid up otherwise than
in cash; and securities which a company has offered to allot to a holder of
relevant shares or relevant employee shares may be allotted to him, or
anyone in whose favour he has renounced his right to their allotment, without contravening subsection (1)(*b*).

(5) Subsection (1) does not apply to the allotment of securities which
would, apart from a renunciation or assignment of the right to their allotment, be held under an employees' share scheme.

Communication of pre-emption offers to shareholders
90.—(1) This section has effect as to the manner in which offers required
by section 89(1), or by a provision to which section 89(3) applies, are to be
made to holders of a company's shares.

(2) Subject to the following subsections, an offer shall be in writing and
shall be made to a holder of shares either personally or by sending it by
post (that is to say, prepaying and posting a letter containing the offer) to
him or to his registered address or, if he has no registered address in the
United Kingdom, to the address in the United Kingdom supplied by him to
the company for the giving of notice to him.

If sent by post, the offer is deemed to be made at the time at which the
letter would be delivered in the ordinary course of post.

(3) Where shares are held by two or more persons jointly, the offer may
be made to the joint holder first named in the register of members in
respect of the shares.

(4) In the case of a holder's death or bankruptcy, the offer may be made—

(*a*) by sending it by post in a prepaid letter addressed to the persons claiming to be entitled to the shares in consequence of the death or bankruptcy by name, or by the title of representatives of the deceased, or trustee of the bankrupt, or by any like description, at the address in the United Kingdom supplied for the purpose by those so claiming, or

(*b*) (until such an address has been so supplied) by giving the notice in any manner in which it might have been given if the death or bankruptcy had not occurred.

(5) If the holder—

(*a*) has no registered address in the United Kingdom and has not given to the company an address in the United Kingdom for the service of notices on him, or

(*b*) is the holder of a share warrant,

the offer may be made by causing it, or a notice specifying where a copy of it can be obtained or inspected, to be published in the *Gazette*.

(6) The offer must state a period of not less than 21 days during which it may be accepted; and the offer shall not be withdrawn before the end of that period.

(7) This section does not invalidate a provision to which section 89(3) applies by reason that that provision requires or authorises an offer under it to be made in contravention of any of subsections (1) to (6) above; but, to the extent that the provision requires or authorises such an offer to be so made, it is of no effect.

Exclusion of ss. 89, 90 by private company

91.—(1) Section 89(1), section 90(1) to (5) or section 90(6) may, as applying to allotments by a private company of equity securities or to such allotments of a particular description, be excluded by a provision contained in the memorandum or articles of that company.

(2) A requirement or authority contained in the memorandum or articles of a private company, if it is inconsistent with any of those subsections, has effect as a provision excluding that subsection; but a provision to which section 89(3) applies is not to be treated as inconsistent with section 89(1).

Consequences of contravening ss. 89, 90

92.—(1) If there is a contravention of section 89(1), or of section 90(1) to (5) or section 90(6), or of a provision to which section 89(3) applies, the company, and every officer of it who knowingly authorised or permitted the contravention, are jointly and severally liable to compensate any person to whom an offer should have been made under the subsection or provision contravened for any loss, damage, costs or expenses which the person has sustained or incurred by reason of the contravention.

(2) However, no proceedings to recover any such loss, damage, costs or expenses shall be commenced after the expiration of two years from the delivery to the registrar of companies of the return of allotments in question or, where equity securities other than shares are granted, from the date of the grant.

Saving for other restrictions as to offers

93.—(1) Sections 89 to 92 are without prejudice to any enactment by virtue of which a company is prohibited (whether generally or in specified circumstances) from offering or allotting equity securities to any person.

(2) Where a company cannot by virtue of such an enactment offer or allot equity securities to a holder of relevant shares or relevant employee shares, those sections have effect as if the shares held by that holder were not relevant shares or relevant employee shares.

Definitions for ss. 89–96

94.—(1) The following subsections apply for the interpretation of sections 89 to 96.

(2) "Equity security", in relation to a company, means a relevant share in the company (other than a share shown in the memorandum to have been taken by a subscriber to the memorandum or a bonus share), or a right to subscribe for, or to convert securities into, relevant shares in the company.

(3) A reference to the allotment of equity securities or of equity securities consisting of relevant shares of a particular class includes the grant of a right to subscribe for, or to convert any securities into, relevant shares in the company or (as the case may be) relevant shares of a particular class; but such a reference does not include the allotment of any relevant shares pursuant to such a right.

(4) "Relevant employee shares", in relation to a company, means shares of the company which would be relevant shares in it but for the fact that they are held by a person who acquired them in pursuance of an employees' share scheme.

(5) "Relevant shares", in relation to a company, means shares in the company other than—

    (*a*) shares which as respects dividends and capital carry a right to participate only up to a specified amount in a distribution, and

    (*b*) shares which are held by a person who acquired them in pursuance of an employees' share scheme or, in the case of shares which have not been allotted, are to be allotted in pursuance of such a scheme.

(6) A reference to a class of shares is to shares to which the same rights are attached as to voting and as to participation, both as respects dividends and as respects capital, in a distribution.

(7) In relation to an offer to allot securities required by section 89(1) or by any provision to which section 89(3) applies, a reference in sections 89 to 94 (however expressed) to the holder of shares of any description is to whoever was at the close of business on a date, to be specified in the offer and to fall in the period of 28 days immediately before the date of the offer, the holder of shares of that description.

Disapplication of pre-emption rights

95.—(1) Where the directors of a company are generally authorised for purposes of section 80, they may be given power by the articles, or by a special resolution of the company, to allot equity securities pursuant to that authority as if—

    (*a*) section 89(1) did not apply to the allotment, or

    (*b*) that subsection applied to the allotment with such modifications as the directors may determine;

and where the directors make an allotment under this subsection, sections 89 to 94 have effect accordingly.

(2) Where the directors of a company are authorised for purposes of section 80 (whether generally or otherwise), the company may by special resolution resolve either—

    (*a*) that section 89(1) shall not apply to a specified allotment of equity securities to be made pursuant to that authority, or

    (*b*) that that subsection shall apply to the allotment with such modifications as may be specified in the resolution;

and where such a resolution is passed, sections 89 to 94 have effect accordingly.

(3) The power conferred by subsection (1) or a special resolution under subsection (2) ceases to have effect when the authority to which it relates is revoked or would (if not renewed) expire; but if the authority is renewed, the power or (as the case may be) the resolution may also be renewed, for a

period not longer than that for which the authority is renewed, by a special resolution of the company.

(4) Notwithstanding that any such power or resolution has expired, the directors may allot equity securities in pursuance of an offer or agreement previously made by the company, if the power or resolution enabled the company to make an offer or agreement which would or might require equity securities to be allotted after it expired.

(5) A special resolution under subsection (2), or a special resolution to renew such a resolution, shall not be proposed unless it is recommended by the directors and there has been circulated, with the notice of the meeting at which the resolution is proposed, to the members entitled to have that notice a written statement by the directors setting out—

(a) their reasons for making the recommendation,
(b) the amount to be paid to the company in respect of the equity securities to be allotted, and
(c) the directors' justification of that amount.

(6) A person who knowingly or recklessly authorises or permits the inclusion in a statement circulated under subsection (5) of any matter which is misleading, false or deceptive in a material particular is liable to imprisonment or a fine, or both.

Saving for company's pre-emption procedure operative before 1982

96.—(1) Where a company which is re-registered or registered as a public company is or, but for the provisions of the Companies Act 1980 and the enactments replacing it, would be subject at the time of re-registration or (as the case may be) registration to a pre-1982 pre-emption requirement, sections 89 to 95 do not apply to an allotment of the equity securities which are subject to that requirement.

(2) A "pre-1982 pre-emption requirement" is a requirement imposed (whether by the company's memorandum or articles, or otherwise) before the relevant date in 1982 by virtue of which the company must, when making an allotment of equity securities, make an offer to allot those securities or some of them in a manner which (otherwise than because involving a contravention of section 90(1) to (5) or 90(6)) is inconsistent with sections 89 to 94; and "the relevant date in 1982" is—

(a) except in a case falling within the following paragraph, 22nd June in that year, and
(b) in the case of a company which was re-registered or registered as a public company on an application made before that date, the date on which the application was made.

(3) A requirement which—

(a) is imposed on a private company (having been so imposed before the relevant date in 1982) otherwise than by the company's memorandum or articles, and
(b) if contained in the company's memorandum or articles, would have effect under section 91 to the exclusion of any provisions of sections 89 to 94,

has effect, so long as the company remains a private company, as if it were contained in the memorandum or articles.

(4) If on the relevant date in 1982 a company, other than a public company registered as such on its original incorporation, was subject to such a requirement as is mentioned in section 89(2) imposed otherwise than by the memorandum or articles, the requirement is to be treated for purposes of sections 89 to 94 as if it were contained in the memorandum or articles.

Commissions and discounts

Power of company to pay commissions

97.—(1) It is lawful for a company to pay a commission to any person in consideration of his subscribing or agreeing to subscribe (whether absolutely or conditionally) for any shares in the company, or procuring or agreeing to procure subscriptions (whether absolute or conditional) for any shares in the company, if the following conditions are satisfied.

(2) The payment of the commission must be authorised by the company's articles; and—

    (*a*) the commission paid or agreed to be paid must not exceed 10 per cent. of the price at which the shares are issued or the amount or rate authorised by the articles, whichever is the less.

NOTE

As amended by the Financial Services Act 1986, Sched. 17. Amended (*prosp.*) by *ibid.*, Sched. 16, para. 16.

Apart from s.97, commissions and discounts barred

98.—(1) Except as permitted by section 97, no company shall apply any of its shares or capital money, either directly or indirectly in payment of any commission, discount or allowance to any person in consideration of his subscribing or agreeing to subscribe (whether absolutely or conditionally) for any shares in the company, or procuring or agreeing to procure subscriptions (whether absolute or conditional) for any shares in the company.

(2) This applies whether the shares or money be so applied by being added to the purchase money of any property acquired by the company or to the contract price of any work to be executed for the company, or the money be paid out of the nominal purchase money or contract price, or otherwise.

(3) Nothing in section 97 or this section affects the power of a company to pay such brokerage as has previously been lawful.

(4) A vendor to, or promoter of, or other person who receives payment in money or shares from, a company has, and is deemed always to have had, power to apply any part of the money or shares so received in payment of any commission, the payment of which, if made directly by the company, would have been lawful under section 97 of this section.

Amount to be paid for shares;
the means of payment

General rules as to payment for shares on allotment

99.—(1) Subject to the following provisions of this Part, shares allotted by a company, and any premium on them, may be paid up in money or money's worth (including goodwill and know-how).

(2) A public company shall not accept at any time, in payment up of its shares or any premium on them, an undertaking given by any person that he or another should do work or perform services for the company or any other person.

(3) If a public company accepts such an undertaking in payment up of its shares or any premium on them, the holder of the shares when they or the premium are treated as paid up (in whole or in part) by the undertaking is liable—

(*a*) to pay the company in respect of those shares an amount equal to their nominal value, together with the whole of any premium or, if the case so requires, such proportion of that amount as is treated as paid up by the undertaking; and

(*b*) to pay interest at the appropriate rate on the amount payable under paragraph (*a*) above.

(4) This section does not prevent a company from allotting bonus shares to its members or from paying up, with sums available for the purpose, any amounts for the time being unpaid on any of its shares (whether on account of the nominal value of the shares or by way of premium).

(5) The reference in subsection (3) to the holder of shares includes any person who has an unconditional right to be included in the company's register of members in respect of those shares or to have an instrument of transfer of them executed in his favour.

Prohibition on allotment of shares at a discount

100.—(1) A company's shares shall not be allotted at a discount.

(2) If shares are allotted in contravention of this section, the allottee is liable to pay the company an amount equal to the amount of the discount, with interest at the appropriate rate.

Shares to be allotted as at least one-quarter paid-up

101.—(1) A public company shall not allot a share except as paid up at least as to one-quarter of its nominal value and the whole of any premium on it.

(2) Subsection (1) does not apply to shares allotted in pursuance of an employees' share scheme.

(3) If a company allots a share in contravention of subsection (1), the share is to be treated as if one-quarter of its nominal value, together with the whole of any premium on it, had been received.

(4) But the allottee is liable to pay the company the minimum amount which should have been received in respect of the share under subsection (1) (less the value of any consideration actually applied in payment up, to any extent, of the share and any premium on it), with interest at the appropriate rate.

(5) Subsections (3) and (4) do not apply to the allotment of bonus shares, unless the allottee knew or ought to have known the shares were allotted in contravention of subsection (1).

Restriction on payment by long-term undertaking

102.—(1) A public company shall not allot shares as fully or partly paid up (as to their nominal value or any premium on them) otherwise than in cash if the consideration for the allotment is or includes an undertaking which is to be, or may be, performed more than five years after the date of the allotment.

(2) If a company allots shares in contravention of subsection (1), the allottee is liable to pay the company an amount equal to the aggregate of their nominal value and the whole of any premium (or, if the case so requires, so much of that aggregate as is treated as paid up by the undertaking), with interest at the appropriate rate.

(3) Where a contract for the allotment of shares does not contravene subsection (1), any variation of the contract which has the effect that the contract would have contravened the subsection, if the terms of the contract as varied had been its original terms, is void.

(4) Subsection (3) applies also to the variation by a public company of the terms of a contract entered into before the company was re-registered as a public company.

(5) The following subsection applies where a public company allots shares for a consideration which consists of or includes (in accordance with subsection (1)) an undertaking which is to be performed within five years of the allotment, but the undertaking is not performed within the period allowed by the contract for the allotment of the shares.

(6) The allottee is then liable to pay the company, at the end of the period so allowed, an amount equal to the aggregate of the nominal value of the shares and the whole of any premium (or, if the case so requires, so much of that aggregate as is treated as paid up by the undertaking), with interest at the appropriate rate.

(7) A reference in this section to a contract for the allotment of shares includes an ancillary contract relating to payment in respect of them.

Non-cash consideration to be valued before allotment
103.—(1) A public company shall not allot shares as fully or partly paid up (as to their nominal value or any premium on them) otherwise than in cash unless—

    (a) the consideration for the allotment has been independently valued under section 108; and

    (b) a report with respect to its value has been made to the company by a person appointed by the company (in accordance with that section) during the six months immediately preceding the allotment of the shares; and

    (c) a copy of the report has been sent to the proposed allottee.

(2) Where an amount standing to the credit of any of a company's reserve accounts, or of its profit and loss account is applied in paying up (to any extent) any shares allotted to members of the company or any premiums on shares so allotted, the amount applied does not count as consideration for the allotment, and accordingly subsection (1) does not apply in that case.

(3) Subsection (1) does not apply to the allotment of shares by a company in connection with an arrangement providing for the allotment of shares in that company on terms that the whole or part of the consideration for the shares allotted is to be provided by the transfer to that company (or the cancellation) of all or some of the shares, or of all or some of the shares of a particular class, in another company (with or without the issue to that company of shares, or of shares of any particular class, in that other company).

(4) But subsection (3) does not exclude the application of subsection (1) unless under the arrangement it is open to all the holders of the shares in the other company in question (or, where the arrangement applies only to shares of a particular class, to all the holders of shares in that other company, being holders of shares of that class) to take part in the arrangement.

In determining whether that is the case, shares held by or by a nominee of the company proposing to allot the shares in connection with the arrangement, or by or by a nominee of a company which is that company's holding company or subsidiary or a company which is a subsidiary of its holding company, shall be disregarded.

(5) Subsection (1) also does not apply to the allotment of shares by a company in connection with its proposed merger with another company; that is, where one of the companies proposes to acquire all the assets and liabilities of the other in exchange for the issue of shares or other securities of that one to shareholders of the other, with or without any cash payment to shareholders.

(6) If a company allots shares in contravention of subsection (1) and either—

    (a) the allottee has not received the valuer's report required by that subsection to be sent to him; or

(*b*) there has been some other contravention of this section or section
108 which the allottee knew or ought to have known amounted to a
contravention,

the allottee is liable to pay the company an amount equal to the aggregate
of the nominal value of the shares and the whole of any premium (or, if the
case so requires, so much of that aggregate as is treated as paid up by the
consideration), with interest at the appropriate rate.

[1] (7) In this section—

(*a*) "arrangement" means any agreement, scheme or arrangement
(including an arrangement sanctioned in accordance with section
425 (company compromise with creditors and members) or section
110 of the Insolvency Act (liquidator in winding up accepting shares
as consideration for sale of company property)), and

(*b*) any reference to a company, except where it is or is to be construed
as a reference to a public company, includes any body corporate and
any body to which letters patent have been issued under the Chartered Companies Act 1837.

NOTE
[1] As amended by the Insolvency Act 1986, Sched. 13, Pt. I.

Transfer to public company of non-cash asset in initial preriod
104.—(1) A public company formed as such shall not, unless the conditions of this section have been complied with, enter into an agreement
with a person for the transfer by him during the initial period of one or
more non-cash assets to the company or another, if—

(*a*) that person is a subscriber to the company's memorandum, and

(*b*) the consideration for the transfer to be given by the company is
equal in value at the time of the agreement to one-tenth or more of
the company's nominal share capital issued at that time.

(2) The "initial period" for this purpose is two years beginning with the
date of the company being issued with a certificate under section 117 (or
the previous corresponding provision) that it was entitled to do business.

(3) This section applies also to a company re-registered as a public company (except one re-registered under section 8 of the Companies Act 1980
or section 2 of the Consequential Provisions Act), or registered under section 685 (joint stock company) or the previous corresponding provision;
but in that case—

(*a*) there is substituted a reference in subsection (1)(*a*) to a person who
is a member of the company on the date of registration or re-registration, and

(*b*) the initial period is then two years beginning with that date.

In this subsection the reference to a company re-registered as a public
company includes a private company so re-registered which was a public
company before it was a private company.

(4) The conditions of this section are as follows—

(*a*) the consideration to be received by the company, and any consideration other than cash to be given by the company, must have been
independently valued under section 109;

(*b*) a report with respect to the consideration to be so received and
given must have been made to the company in accordance with that
section during the six months immediately preceding the date of the
agreement;

(*c*) the terms of the agreement must have been approved by an ordinary
resolution of the company; and

(*d*) not later than the giving of the notice of the meeting at which the
resolution is proposed, copies of the resolution and report must
have been circulated to the members of the company entitled to
receive the notice and, if the person with whom the agreement in

question is proposed to be made is not then a member of the company so entitled, to that person.

(5) In subsection (4)(*a*)—

(*a*) the reference to the consideration to be received by the company is to the asset to be transferred to it or the advantage to the company of the asset's transfer to another person; and

(*b*) the specified condition is without prejudice to any requirement to value any consideration for purposes of section 103.

(6) In the case of the following agreements, this section does not apply—

(*a*) where it is part of the company's ordinary business to acquire, or arrange for other persons to acquire, assets of a particular description, an agreement entered into by the company in the ordinary course of its business for the transfer of an asset of that description to it or to such a person, as the case may be;

(*b*) an agreement entered into by the company under the supervision of the court, or of an officer authorised by the court for the purpose, for the transfer of an asset to the company or to another.

Agreements contravening s. 104

105.—(1) The following subsection applies if a public company enters into an agreement contravening section 104, the agreement being made with the person referred to in subsection (1)(*a*) or (as the case may be) subsection (3) of that section, and either—

(*a*) that person has not received the valuer's report required for compliance with the conditions of the section, or

(*b*) there has been some other contravention of the section or of section 108(1), (2) or (5) or section 109, which he knew or ought to have known amounted to a contravention.

(2) The company is then entitled to recover from that person any consideration given by it under the agreement, or an amount equal to the value of the consideration at the time of the agreement; and the agreement, so far as not carried out, is void.

(3) However, if the agreement is or includes an agreement for the allotment of shares in the company, then—

(*a*) whether or not the agreement also contravenes section 103, subsection (2) above does not apply to it in so far as it is for the allotment of shares; and

(*b*) the allottee is liable to pay the company an amount equal to the aggregate of the nominal value of the shares and the whole of any premium (or, if the case so requires, so much of that aggregate as is treated as paid up by the consideration), with interest at the appropriate rate.

Shares issued to subscribers of memorandum

106. Shares taken by a subscriber to the memorandum of a public company in pursuance of an undertaking of his in the memorandum, and any premium on the shares, shall be paid up in cash.

Meaning of "the appropriate rate"

107. In sections 99 to 105 "the appropriate rate", in relation to interest, means 5 per cent. per annum or such other rate as may be specified by order made by the Secretary of State by statutory instrument subject to annulment in pursuance of a resolution of either House of Parliament.

Valuation provisions

Valuation and report (s. 103)

108.—(1) The valuation and report required by section 103 (or, where applicable, section 44) shall be made by an independent person, that is to say a person qualified at the time of the report to be appointed, or continue to be, an auditor of the company.

(2) However, where it appears to the independent person (from here on referred to as "the valuer") to be reasonable for the valuation of the consideration, or part of it, to be made (or for him to accept such a valuation) by another person who—

(*a*) appears to him to have the requisite knowledge and experience to value the consideration or that part of it; and

(*b*) is not an officer or servant of the company or any other body corporate which is that company's subsidiary or holding company or a subsidiary of that company's holding company or a partner or employee of such an officer or servant,

he may arrange for or accept such a valuation, together with a report which will enable him to make his own report under this section and provide the note required by subsection (6) below.

(3) The reference in subsection (2)(*b*) to an officer or servant does not include an auditor.

(4) The valuer's report shall state—

(*a*) the nominal value of the shares to be wholly or partly paid for by the consideration in question;

(*b*) the amount of any premium payable on the shares;

(*c*) the description of the consideration and, as respects so much of the consideration as he himself has valued, a description of that part of the consideration, the method used to value it and the date of the valuation;

(*d*) the extent to which the nominal value of the shares and any premium are to be treated as paid up—

(i) by the consideration;

(ii) in cash.

(5) Where the consideration or part of it is valued by a person other than the valuer himself, the latter's report shall state that fact and shall also—

(*a*) state the former's name and what knowledge and experience he has to carry out the valuation, and

(*b*) describe so much of the consideration as was valued by the other person, and the method used to value it, and specify the date of the valuation.

(6) The valuer's report shall contain or be accompanied by a note by him—

(*a*) in the case of a valuation made by a person other than himself, that it appeared to himself reasonable to arrange for it to be so made or to accept a valuation so made;

(*b*) whoever made the valuation, that the method of valuation was reasonable in all the circumstances;

(*c*) that it appears to the valuer that there has been no material change in the value of the consideration in question since the valuation; and

(*d*) that on the basis of the valuation the value of the consideration, together with any cash by which the nominal value of the shares or any premium payable on them is to be paid up, is not less than so much of the aggregate of the nominal value and the whole of any such premium as is treated as paid up by the consideration and any such cash.

(7) Where the consideration to be valued is accepted partly in payment up of the nominal value of the shares and any premium and partly for some other consideration given by the company, section 103 (and, where applicable, section 44) and the foregoing provisions of this section apply as if references to the consideration accepted by the company included the proportion of that consideration which is properly attributable to the payment up of that value and any premium; and—

(*a*) the valuer shall carry out, or arrange for, such other valuations as will enable him to determine that proportion; and

(*b*) his report shall state what valuations have been made under this subsection and also the reason for, and method and date of, any such valuation and any other matters which may be relevant to that determination.

Valuation and report (s. 104)

109.—(1) Subsections (1) to (3) and (5) of section 108 apply also as respects the valuation and report for the purposes of section 104.

(2) The valuer's report for those purposes shall—

(*a*) state the consideration to be received by the company, describing the asset in question (specifying the amount to be received in cash) and the consideration to be given by the company (specifying the amount to be given in cash);

(*b*) state the method and date of valuation;

(*c*) contain or be accompanied by a note as to the matters mentioned in section 108(6)(*a*) to (*c*); and

(*d*) contain or be accompanied by a note that on the basis of the valuation the value of the consideration to be received by the company is not less than the value of the consideration to be given by it.

(3) A reference in section 104 or this section to consideration given for the transfer of an asset includes consideration given partly for its transfer; but—

(*a*) the value of any consideration partly so given is to be taken as the proportion of the consideration properly attributable to its transfer;

(*b*) the valuer shall carry out or arrange for such valuations of anything else as will enable him to determine that proportion; and

(*c*) his report for purposes of section 104 shall state what valuation has been made under this subsection and also the reason for and method and date of any such valuation and any other matters which may be relevant to that determination.

Entitlement of valuer to full disclosure

110.—(1) A person carrying out a valuation or making a report under section 103 or 104, with respect to any consideration proposed to be accepted or given by a company, is entitled to require from the officers of the company such information and explanation as he thinks necessary to enable him to carry out the valuation or make the report and provide a note under section 108(6) or (as the case may be) section 109(2)(*c*).

(2) A person who knowingly or recklessly makes a statement which—

(*a*) is misleading, false or deceptive in a material particular, and

(*b*) is a statement to which this subsection applies,

is guilty of an offence and liable to imprisonment or a fine, or both.

(3) Subsection (2) applies to any statement made (whether orally or in writing) to a person carrying out a valuation or making a report under section 108 or 109, being a statement which conveys or purports to convey any information or explanation which that person requires, or is entitled to require, under subsection (1) of this section.

Matters to be communicated to registrar

111.—(1) A company to which a report is made under section 108 as to the value of any consideration for which, or partly for which, it proposes to allot shares shall deliver a copy of the report to the registrar of companies for registration at the same time that it files the return of the allotments of those shares under section 88.

(2) A company which has passed a resolution under section 104 with respect to the transfer of an asset shall, within 15 days of so doing, deliver to the registrar of companies a copy of the resolution together with the valuer's report required by that section.

(3) If default is made in complying with subsection (1), every officer of the company who is in default is liable to a fine and, for continued contravention, to a daily default fine; but this is subject to the same exception as is made by section 88(6) (relief on application to the court) in the case of default in complying with that section.

(4) If a company fails to comply with subsection (2), it and every officer of it who is in default is liable to a fine and, for continued contravention, to a daily default fine.

Right to damages, &c. not affected
[1] **111A.** A person is not debarred from obtaining damages or other compensation from a company by reason only of his holding or having held shares in the company or any right to apply or subscribe for shares or to be included in the company's register in respect of shares.

NOTE
[1] Inserted by the Companies Act 1989, s.131(1).

Other matters arising out of allotment etc.

Liability of subsequent holders of shares allotted
112.—(1) If a person becomes a holder of shares in respect of which—
 (a) there has been a contravention of section 99, 100, 101 or 103; and
 (b) by virtue of that contravention, another is liable to pay any amount under the section contravened,
that person is also liable to pay that amount (jointly and severally with any other person so liable), unless he is exempted from liability by subsection (3) below.

(2) If a company enters into an agreement in contravention of section 104 and—
 (a) the agreement is or includes an agreement for the allotment of shares in the company; and
 (b) a person becomes a holder of shares allotted under the agreement; and
 (c) by virtue of the agreement and allotment under it, another person is liable to pay any amount under section 105,
the person who becomes the holder of the shares is also liable to pay that amount (jointly and severally with any other person so liable), unless he is exempted from liability by the following subsection; and this applies whether or not the agreement also contravenes section 103.

(3) A person otherwise liable under subsection (1) or (2) is exempted from that liability if either—
 (a) he is a purchaser for value and, at the time of the purchase, he did not have actual notice of the contravention concerned; or
 (b) he derived title to the shares (directly or indirectly) from a person who became a holder of them after the contravention and was not liable under subsection (1) or (as the case may be) subsection (2).

(4) References in this section to a holder, in relation to shares in a company, include any person who has an unconditional right to be included in the company's register of members in respect of those shares or to have an instrument of transfer of the shares executed in his favour.

(5) As subsections (1) and (3) apply in relation to the contraventions there mentioned, they also apply—
 (a) to a contravention of section 102; and
 (b) to a failure to carry out a term of a contract as mentioned in subsections (5) and (6) of that section.

Relief in respect of certain liabilities under ss. 99 et seq.
113.—(1) Where a person is liable to a company under—
 (a) section 99, 102, 103 or 105;

(*b*) section 112(1) by reference to a contravention of section 99 or 103; or

(*c*) section 112(2) or (5),

in relation to payment in respect of any shares in the company, or is liable by virtue of an undertaking given to it in, or in connection with, payment for any such shares, the person so liable may make an application to the court to be exempted in whole or in part from the liability.

(2) If the liability mentioned in subsection (1) arises in relation to payment in respect of any shares, the court may, on an application under that subsection, exempt the applicant from the liability only—

(*a*) if and to the extent that it appears to the court just and equitable to do so having regard to the matters mentioned in the following subsection,

(*b*) if and to the extent that it appears to the court just and equitable to do so in respect of any interest which he is liable to pay the company under any of the relevant sections.

(3) The matters to be taken into account by the court under subsection (2)(*a*) are—

(*a*) whether the applicant has paid, or is liable to pay, any amount in respect of any other liability arising in relation to those shares under any of the relevant sections, or of any liability arising by virtue of any undertaking given in or in connection with payment for those shares;

(*b*) whether any person other than the applicant has paid or is likely to pay (whether in pursuance of an order of the court or otherwise) any such amount; and

(*c*) whether the applicant or any other person has performed in whole or in part, or is likely so to perform, any such undertaking, or has done or is likely to do any other thing in payment or part payment for the shares.

(4) Where the liability arises by virtue of an undertaking given to the company in, or in connection with, payment for shares in it, the court may, on an application under subsection (1), exempt the applicant from the liability only if and to the extent that it appears to the court just and equitable to do so having regard to—

(*a*) whether the applicant has paid or is liable to pay any amount in respect of liability arising in relation to the shares under any of the provisions mentioned in that subsection; and

(*b*) whether any person other than the applicant has paid or is likely to pay (whether in pursuance of an order of the court or otherwise) any such amount.

(5) In determining whether it should exempt the applicant in whole or in part from any liability, the court shall have regard to the following overriding principles, namely—

(*a*) that a company which has allotted shares should receive money or money's worth at least equal in value to the aggregate of the nominal value of those shares and the whole of any premium or, if the case so requires, so much of that aggregate as is treated as paid up; and

(*b*) subject to this, that where such a company would, if the court did not grant the exemption, have more than one remedy against a particular person, it should be for the company to decide which remedy it should remain entitled to pursue.

(6) If a person brings proceedings against another ("the contributor") for a contribution in respect of liability to a company arising under any of sections 99 to 105 or 112, and it appears to the court that the contributor is liable to make such a contribution, the court may exercise the powers of the following subsection.

(7) The court may, if and to the extent that it appears to it, having regard to the respective culpability (in respect of the liability to the company) of the contributor and the person bringing the proceedings, that it is just and equitable to do so—

(*a*) exempt the contributor in whole or in part from his liability to make such a contribution; or

(*b*) order the contributor to make a larger contribution than, but for this subsection, he would be liable to make.

(8) Where a person is liable to a company under section 105(2), the court may, on application, exempt him in whole or in part from that liability if and to the extent that it appears to the court just and equitable to do so having regard to any benefit accruing to the company by virtue of anything done by him towards the carrying out of the agreement mentioned in that subsection.

Penalty for contravention

114. If a company contravenes any of the provisions of sections 99 to 104 and 106 the company and any officer of it who is in default is liable to a fine.

Undertakings to do work, etc.

115.—(1) Subject to section 113, an undertaking given by any person, in or in connection with payment for shares in a company, to do work or perform services or to do any other thing, if it is enforceable by the company apart from this Act, is so enforceable notwithstanding that there has been a contravention in relation to it of section 99, 102 or 103.

(2) Where such an undertaking is given in contravention of section 104 in respect of the allotment of shares, it is so enforceable notwithstanding the contravention.

Application of ss. 99 et seq. to special cases

[1] **116.** Except as provided by section 9 of the Consequential Provisions Act (transitional cases dealt with by section 31 of the Companies Act 1980), sections 99, 101 to 103, 106, 108, 110, 111 and 112 to 115 apply—

(*a*) to a company which has passed and not revoked a resolution to be re-registered under section 43 as a public company, and

(*b*) to a joint stock company which has passed, and not revoked, a resolution that the company be a public company,

as those sections apply to a public company.

NOTE
[1] As amended by the Companies Act 1989, s.131(2).

[1] PART V

SHARE CAPITAL, ITS INCREASE, MAINTENANCE
AND REDUCTION

NOTE
[1] For interpretation of "public company", "private company" etc., see s. 1(3) and the Companies Consolidation (Consequential Provisions) Act 1985, s. 1.

CHAPTER I
GENERAL PROVISIONS ABOUT SHARE CAPITAL

Public company share capital requirements

117.—(1) A company registered as a public company on its original incorporation shall not do business or exercise any borrowing powers unless the registrar of companies has issued it with a certificate under this section or the company is re-registered as a private company.

(2) The registrar shall issue a company with such a certificate if, on an application made to him by the company in the prescribed form, he is satisfied that the nominal value of the company's allotted share capital is not less than the authorised minimum, and there is delivered to him a statutory declaration complying with the following subsection.

(3) The statutory declaration must be in the prescribed form and be signed by a director or secretary of the company; and it must—

(*a*) state that the nominal value of the company's allotted share capital is not less than the authorised minimum;

(*b*) specify the amount paid up, at the time of the application, on the allotted share capital of the company;

(*c*) specify the amount, or estimated amount, of the company's preliminary expenses and the persons by whom any of those expenses have been paid or are payable; and

(*d*) specify any amount or benefit paid or given, or intended to be paid or given, to any promoter of the company, and the consideration for the payment or benefit.

(4) For the purposes of subsection (2), a share allotted in pursuance of an employees' share scheme may not be taken into account in determining the nominal value of the company's allotted share capital unless it is paid up at least as to one-quarter of the nominal value of the share and the whole of any premium on the share.

(5) The registrar may accept a statutory declaration delivered to him under this section as sufficient evidence of the matters stated in it.

(6) A certificate under this section in respect of a company is conclusive evidence that the company is entitled to do business and exercise any borrowing powers.

(7) If a company does business or exercises borrowing powers in contravention of this section, the company and any officer of it who is in default is liable to a fine.

(8) Nothing in this section affects the validity of any transaction entered into by a company; but, if a company enters into a transaction in contravention of this section and fails to comply with its obligations in that connection within 21 days from being called upon to do so, the directors of the company are jointly and severally liable to indemnify the other party to the transaction in respect of any loss or damage suffered by him by reason of the company's failure to comply with those obligations.

The authorised minimum

118.—(1) In this Act, "the authorised minimum" means £50,000, or such other sum as the Secretary of State may by order made by statutory instrument specify instead.

(2) An order under this section which increases the authorised minimum may—

(*a*) require any public company having an allotted share capital of which the nominal value is less than the amount specified in the order as the authorised minimum to increase that value to not less than that amount or make application to be re-registered as a private company;

(*b*) make, in connection with any such requirement, provision for any of the matters for which provision is made by this Act relating to a company's registration, re-registration or change of name, to payment for any share comprised in a company's capital and to offers of shares in or debentures of a company to the public, including provision as to the consequences (whether in criminal law or otherwise) of a failure to comply with any requirement of the order; and

(*c*) contain such supplemental and transitional provisions as the Secretary of State thinks appropriate, make different provision for different cases and, in particular, provide for any provision of the order to come into operation on different days for different purposes.

(3) An order shall not be made under this section unless a draft of it has been laid before Parliament and approved by resolution of each House.

Provision for different amounts to be paid on shares

119. A company, if so authorised by its articles, may do any one or more of the following things—

(a) make arrangements on the issue of shares for a difference between the shareholders in the amounts and times of payment of calls on their shares;

(b) accept from any member the whole or a part of the amount remaining unpaid on any shares held by him, although no part of that amount has been called up;

(c) pay dividend in proportion to the amount paid up on each share where a larger amount is paid up on some shares than on others.

Reserve liability of limited company

120. A limited company may by special resolution determine that any portion of its share capital which has not been already called up shall not be capable of being called up except in the event and for the purposes of the company being wound up; and that portion of its share capital is then not capable of being called up except in that event and for those purposes.

Alteration of share capital (limited companies)

121.—(1) A company limited by shares or a company limited by guarantee and having a share capital, if so authorised by its articles, may alter the conditions of its memorandum in any of the following ways.

(2) The company may—

(a) increase its share capital by new shares of such amount as it thinks expedient;

(b) consolidate and divide all or any of its share capital into shares of larger amount than its existing shares;

(c) convert all or any of its paid-up shares into stock, and re-convert that stock into paid-up shares of any denomination;

(d) sub-divide its shares, or any of them, into shares of smaller amount than is fixed by the memorandum (but subject to the following subsection);

(e) cancel shares which, at the date of the passing of the resolution to cancel them, have not been taken or agreed to be taken by any person, and diminish the amount of the company's share capital by the amount of the shares so cancelled.

(3) In any sub-division under subsection (2)(d) the proportion between the amount paid and the amount, if any, unpaid on each reduced share must be the same as it was in the case of the share from which the reduced share is derived.

(4) The powers conferred by this section must be exercised by the company in general meeting.

(5) A cancellation of shares under this section does not for purposes of this Act constitute a reduction of share capital.

Notice to registrar of alteration

122.—(1) If a company having a share capital has—

(a) consolidated and divided its share capital into shares of larger amount than its existing shares; or

(b) converted any shares into stock; or

(c) re-converted stock into shares; or

(d) sub-divided its shares or any of them; or

(e) redeemed any redeemable shares; or

(f) cancelled any shares (otherwise than in connection with a reduction of share capital under section 135),

it shall within one month after so doing give notice in the prescribed form to the registrar of companies, specifying (as the case may be) the shares consolidated, divided, converted, sub-divided, redeemed or cancelled, or the stock re-converted.

(2) If default is made in complying with this section, the company and every officer of it who is in default is liable to a fine and, for continued contravention, to a daily default fine.

Notice to registrar of increased share capital

123.—(1) If a company having a share capital (whether or not its shares have been converted into stock) increases its share capital beyond the registered capital, it shall within 15 days after the passing of the resolution authorising the increase, give to the registrar of companies notice of the increase, and the registrar shall record the increase.

(2) The notice must include such particulars as may be prescribed with respect to the classes of shares affected and the conditions subject to which the new shares have been or are to be issued.

(3) There shall be forwarded to the registrar together with the notice a printed copy of the resolution authorising the increase, or a copy of the resolution in some other form approved by the registrar.

(4) If default is made in complying with this section, the company and every officer of it who is in default is liable to a fine and, for continued contravention, to a daily default fine.

Reserve capital of unlimited company

124. An unlimited company having a share capital may by its resolution for re-registration as a public company under section 43, or as a limited company under section 51—

(*a*) increase the nominal amount of its share capital by increasing the nominal amount of each of its shares (but subject to the condition that no part of the increased capital is to be capable of being called up except in the event and for the purpose of the company being wound up), and

(*b*) alternatively or in addition, provide that a specified portion of its uncalled share capital is not to be capable of being called up except in that event and for that purpose.

CHAPTER II
CLASS RIGHTS

Variation of class rights

125.—(1) This section is concerned with the variation of the rights attached to any class of shares in a company whose share capital is divided into shares of different classes.

(2) Where the rights are attached to a class of shares otherwise than by the company's memorandum, and the company's articles do not contain provision with respect to the variation of the rights, those rights may be varied if, but only if—

(*a*) the holders of three-quarters in nominal value of the issued shares of that class consent in writing to the variation; or

(*b*) an extraordinary resolution passed at a separate general meeting of the holders of that class sanctions the variation;

and any requirement (howsoever imposed) in relation to the variation of those rights is complied with to the extent that it is not comprised in paragraphs (*a*) and (*b*) above.

(3) Where—

(*a*) the rights are attached to a class of shares by the memorandum or otherwise;

(*b*) the memorandum or articles contain provision for the variation of those rights; and

(c) the variation of those rights is connected with the giving, variation, revocation or renewal of an authority for allotment under section 80 or with a reduction of the company's share capital under section 135;

those rights shall not be varied unless—

(i) the condition mentioned in subsection (2)(a) or (b) above is satisfied; and

(ii) any requirement of the memorandum or articles in relation to the variation of rights of that class is complied with to the extent that it is not comprised in that condition.

(4) If the rights are attached to a class of shares in the company by the memorandum or otherwise and—

(a) where they are so attached by the memorandum, the articles contain provision with respect to their variation which had been included in the articles at the time of the company's original incorporation; or

(b) where they are so attached otherwise, the articles contain such provision (whenever first so included),

and in either case the variation is not connected as mentioned in subsection (3)(c), those rights may only be varied in accordance with that provision of the articles.

(5) If the rights are attached to a class of shares by the memorandum, and the memorandum and articles do not contain provision with respect to the variation of those rights, those rights may be varied if all the members of the company agree to the variation.

(6) The provisions of section 369 (length of notice for calling company meetings), section 370 (general provisions as to meetings and votes), and sections 376 and 377 (circulation of members' resolutions) and the provisions of the articles relating to general meetings shall, so far as applicable, apply in relation to any meeting of shareholders required by this section or otherwise to take place in connection with the variation of the rights attached to a class of shares, and shall so apply with the necessary modifications and subject to the following provisions, namely—

(a) the necessary quorum at any such meeting other than an adjourned meeting shall be two persons holding or representing by proxy at least one-third in nominal value of the issued shares of the class in question and at an adjourned meeting one person holding shares of the class in question or his proxy;

(b) any holder of shares of the class in question present in person or by proxy may demand a poll.

(7) Any alteration of a provision contained in a company's articles for the variation of the rights attached to a class of shares, or the insertion of any such provision into the articles, is itself to be treated as a variation of those rights.

(8) In this section and (except where the context otherwise requires) in any provision for the variation of the rights attached to a class of shares contained in a company's memorandum or articles, references to the variation of those rights are to be read as including references to their abrogation.

Saving for court's powers under other provisions

126. Nothing in subsections (2) to (5) of section 125 derogates from the powers of the court under the following sections of this Act, namely—

  sections 4 to 6 (company resolution to alter objects),

  section 54 (litigated objection to public company becoming private by re-registration),

  section 425 (court control of company compromising with members and creditors),

section 427 (company reconstruction or amalgamation),
sections 459 to 461 (protection of minorities).

Shareholders' right to object to variation

127.—(1) This section applies if, in the case of a company whose share capital is divided into different classes of shares—

    (*a*) provision is made by the memorandum or articles for authorising the variation of the rights attached to any class of shares in the company, subject to—

        (i) the consent of any specified proportion of the holders of the issued shares of that class, or

        (ii) the sanction of a resolution passed at a separate meeting of the holders of those shares,

    and in pursuance of that provision the rights attached to any such class of shares are at any time varied; or

    (*b*) the rights attached to any class of shares in the company are varied under section 125(2).

(2) The holders of not less in the aggregate than 15 per cent. of the issued shares of the class in question (being persons who did not consent to or vote in favour of the resolution for the variation), may apply to the court to have the variation cancelled; and if such an application is made, the variation has no effect unless and until it is confirmed by the court.

(3) Application to the court must be made within 21 days after the date on which the consent was given or the resolution was passed (as the case may be), and may be made on behalf of the shareholders entitled to make the application by such one or more of their number as they may appoint in writing for the purpose.

(4) The court, after hearing the applicant and any other persons who apply to the court to be heard and appear to the court to be interested in the application, may, if satisfied having regard to all the circumstances of the case, that the variation would unfairly prejudice the shareholders of the class represented by the applicant, disallow the variation and shall, if not so satisfied, confirm it.

The decision of the court on any such application is final.

(5) The company shall within 15 days after the making of an order by the court on such an application forward a copy of the order to the registrar of companies; and, if default is made in complying with this provision, the company and every officer of it who is in default is liable to a fine and, for continued contravention, to a daily default fine.

(6) "Variation", in this section, includes abrogation; and "varied" is to be construed accordingly.

Registration of particulars of special rights

128.—(1) If a company allots shares with rights which are not stated in its memorandum or articles, or in any resolution or agreement which is required by section 380 to be sent to the registrar of companies, the company shall deliver to the registrar of companies, within one month from allotting the shares, a statement in the prescribed form containing particulars of those rights.

(2) This does not apply if the shares are in all respects uniform with shares previously allotted; and shares are not for this purpose to be treated as different from shares previously allotted by reason only that the former do not carry the same rights to dividends as the latter during the 12 months immediately following the former's allotment.

(3) Where the rights attached to any shares of a company are varied otherwise than by an amendment of the company's memorandum or articles or by a resolution or agreement subject to section 380, the com-

pany shall within one month from the date on which the variation is made deliver to the registrar of companies a statement in the prescribed form containing particulars of the variation.

(4) Where a company (otherwise than by any such amendment, resolution or agreement as is mentioned above) assigns a name or other designation, or a new name or other designation, to any class of its shares, it shall within one month from doing so deliver to the registrar of companies a notice in the prescribed form giving particulars of the name or designation so assigned.

(5) If a company fails to comply with this section, the company and every officer of it who is in default is liable to a fine and, for continued contravention, to a daily default fine.

Registration of newly created class rights

129.—(1) If a company not having a share capital creates a class of members with rights which are not stated in its memorandum or articles or in a resolution or agreement to which section 380 applies, the company shall deliver to the registrar of companies within one month from the date on which the new class is created a statement in the prescribed form containing particulars of the rights attached to that class.

(2) If the rights of any class of members of the company are varied otherwise than by an amendment of the memorandum or articles or by a resolution or agreement subject to section 380, the company shall within one month from the date on which the variation is made deliver to the registrar a statement in the prescribed form containing particulars of the variation.

(3) If a company (otherwise than by such an amendment, resolution or agreement as is mentioned above) assigns a name or other designation, or a new name or other designations, to any class of its members, it shall within one month from doing so deliver to the registrar a notice in the prescribed form giving particulars of the name or designation so assigned.

(4) If a company fails to comply with this section, the company and every officer of it who is in default is liable to a fine and, for continued contravention, to a daily default fine.

[1] CHAPTER III
SHARE PREMIUMS

NOTE
[1] See the Companies Consolidation (Consequential Provisions) Act 1985, s. 12(6).

Application of share premiums

[1] **130.**—(1) If a company issues shares at a premium, whether for cash or otherwise, a sum equal to the aggregate amount or value of the premiums on those shares shall be transferred to an account called "the share premium account".

(2) The share premium account may be applied by the company in paying up unissued shares to be allotted to members as fully paid bonus shares, or in writing off—

(*a*) the company's preliminary expenses; or
(*b*) the expenses of, or the commission paid or discount allowed on, any issue of shares or debentures of the company,

or in providing for the premium payable on redemption of debentures of the company.

(3) Subject to this, the provisions of this Act relating to the reduction of a company's share capital apply as if the share premium account were part of its paid-up share capital.

(4) Sections 131 and 132 below give relief from the requirements of this section, and in those sections references to the issuing company are to the company issuing shares as above mentioned.

NOTE
[1] See the Companies Consolidation (Consequential Provisions) Act 1985, s. 12, in relation to shares issued before 4th February 1981.

Merger relief

131.—(1) With the exception made by section 132(4) (group reconstruction) this section applies where the issuing company has secured at least a 90 per cent. equity holding in another company in pursuance of an arrangement providing for the allotment of equity shares in the issuing company on terms that the consideration for the shares allotted is to be provided—

(a) by the issue or transfer to the issuing company of equity shares in the other company, or

(b) by the cancellation of any such shares not held by the issuing company.

(2) If the equity shares in the issuing company allotted in pursuance of the arrangement in consideration for the acquisition or cancellation of equity shares in the other company are issued at a premium, section 130 does not apply to the premiums on those shares.

(3) Where the arrangement also provides for the allotment of any shares in the issuing company on terms that the consideration for those shares is to be provided by the issue or transfer to the issuing company of non-equity shares in the other company or by the cancellation of any such shares in that company not held by the issuing company, relief under subsection (2) extends to any shares in the issuing company allotted on those terms in pursuance of the arrangement.

(4) Subject to the next subsection, the issuing comany is to be regarded for purposes of this section as having secured at least a 90 per cent. equity holding in another company in pursuance of such an arrangement as is mentioned in subsection (1) if in consequence of an acquisition or cancellation of equity shares in that company (in pursuance of that arrangement) it holds equity shares in that company (whether all or any of those shares were acquired in pursuance of that arrangement, or not) of an aggregate nominal value equal to 90 per cent. or more of the nominal value of that company's equity share capital.

(5) Where the equity share capital of the other company is divided into different classes of shares, this section does not apply unless the requirements of subsection (1) are satisfied in relation to each of those classes of shares taken separately.

(6) Shares held by a company which is the issuing company's holding company or subsidiary, or a subsidiary of the issuing company's holding company, or by its or their nominees, are to be regarded for purposes of this section as held by the issuing company.

[1] (7) In relation to a company and its shares and capital, the following definitions apply for purposes of this section—

(a) "equity shares" means shares comprised in the company's equity share capital; and

(b) "non-equity shares" means shares (of any class) not so comprised; and "arrangement" means any agreement, scheme or arrangement (including an arrangement sanctioned under section 425 (company compromise with members and creditors) or section 110 of the Insolvency Act (liquidator accepting shares etc. as consideration for sale of company property)).

(8) The relief allowed by this section does not apply if the issue of shares took place before 4th February 1981.

NOTE
[1] As amended by the Insolvency Act 1986, Sched. 13, Pt. I.

Relief in respect of group reconstructions

132.—(1) This section applies where the issuing company—

(a) is a wholly-owned subsidiary of another company ("the holding company"), and (*b*) allots shares to the holding company or to another wholly-owned subsidiary of the holding company in consideration for the transfer to the issuing company of assets other than cash, being assets of any company ("the transferor company") which is a member of the group of companies which comprises the holding company and all its wholly-owned subsidiaries.

(2) Where the shares in the issuing company allotted in consideration for the transfer are issued at a premium, the issuing company is not required by section 130 to transfer any amount in excess of the minimum premium value to the share premium account.

(3) In subsection (2), "the minimum premium value" means the amount (if any) by which the base value of the consideration for the shares allotted exceeds the aggregate nominal value of those shares.

(4) For the purposes of subsection (3), the base value of the consideration for the shares allotted is the amount by which the base value of the assets transferred exceeds the base value of any liabilities of the transferor company assumed by the issuing company as part of the consideration for the assets transferred.

(5) For the purposes of subsection (4)—

(*a*) the base value of the assets transferred is to be taken as—

   (i) the cost of those assets to the transferor company, or

   (ii) the amount at which those assets are stated in the transferor company's accounting records immediately before the transfer, whichever is the less; and

(*b*) the base value of the liabilities assumed is to be taken as the amount at which they are stated in the transferor company's accounting records immediately before the transfer.

(6) The relief allowed by this section does not apply (subject to the next subsection) if the issue of shares took place before the date of the coming into force of the Companies (Share Premium Account) Regulations 1984 (which were made on 21st December 1984).

(7) To the extent that the relief allowed by this section would have been allowed by section 38 of the Companies Act 1981 as originally enacted (the text of which section is set out in Schedule 25 to this Act), the relief applies where the issue of shares took place before the date of the coming into force of those regulations, but not if the issue took place before 4th February 1981.

(8) Section 131 does not apply in a case falling within this section.

Provisions supplementing ss. 131, 132

133.—(1) An amount corresponding to one representing the premiums or part of the premiums on shares issued by a company which by virtue of sections 131 or 132 of this Act, or section 12 of the Consequential Provisions Act, is not included in the company's share premium account may also be disregarded in determining the amount at which any shares or other consideration provided for the shares issued is to be included in the company's balance sheet.

(2) References in this Chapter (however expressed) to—

(*a*) the acquisition by a company of shares in another company; and

(*b*) the issue or allotment of shares to, or the transfer of shares to or by, a company,

include (respectively) the acquisition of any of those shares by, and the issue or allotment or (as the case may be) the transfer of any of those shares to or by, nominees of that company; and the reference in section 132 to the company transferring the shares is to be construed accordingly.

(3) References in this Chapter to the transfer of shares in a company include the transfer of a right to be included in the company's register of members in respect of those shares.

(4) In sections 131 to 133 "company", except in references to the issuing company, includes any body corporate.

Provision for extending or restricting relief from s. 130

134.—(1) The Secretary of State may by regulations in a statutory instrument make such provision as appears to him to be appropriate—

 (*a*) for relieving companies from the requirements of section 130 in relation to premiums other than cash premiums, or

 (*b*) for restricting or otherwise modifying any relief from those requirements provided by this Chapter.

(2) Regulations under this section may make different provision for different cases or classes of case and may contain such incidental and supplementary provisions as the Secretary of State thinks fit.

(3) No such regulations shall be made unless a draft of the instrument containing them has been laid before Parliament and approved by a resolution of each House.

CHAPTER *IV*
REDUCTION OF *SHARE CAPITAL*

Special resolution for reduction of share capital

135.—(1) Subject to confirmation by the court, a company limited by shares or a company limited by guarantee and having a share capital may, if so authorised by its articles, by special resolution reduce its share capital in any way.

(2) In particular, and without prejudice to subsection (1), the company may—

 (*a*) extinguish or reduce the liability on any of its shares in respect of share capital not paid up; or

 (*b*) either with or without extinguishing or reducing liability on any of its shares, cancel any paid-up share capital which is lost or unrepresented by available assets; or

 (*c*) either with or without extinguishing or reducing liability on any of its shares, pay off any paid-up share capital which is in excess of the company's wants;

and the company may, if and so far as is necessary, alter its memorandum by reducing the amount of its share capital and of its shares accordingly.

(3) A special resolution under this section is in this Act referred to as "a resolution for reducing share capital".

Application to court for order of confirmation

136.—(1) Where a company has passed a resolution for reducing share capital, it may apply to the court for an order confirming the reduction.

(2) If the proposed reduction of share capital involves either—

 (*a*) diminution of liability in respect of unpaid share capital; or

 (*b*) the payment to a shareholder of any paid-up share capital,

and in any other case if the court so directs, the next three subsections have effect, but subject throughout to subsection (6).

(3) Every creditor of the company who at the date fixed by the court is entitled to any debt or claim which, if that date were the commencement of the winding up of the company, would be admissible in proof against the company is entitled to object to the reduction of capital.

(4) The court shall settle a list of creditors entitled to object, and for that purpose—

 (*a*) shall ascertain, as far as possible without requiring an application from any creditor, the names of those creditors and the nature and amount of their debts or claims; and

 (*b*) may publish notices fixing a day or days within which creditors not entered on the list are to claim to be so entered or are to be excluded from the right of objecting to the reduction of capital.

(5) If a creditor entered on the list whose debt or claim is not discharged or has not determined does not consent to the reduction, the court may, if

it thinks fit, dispense with the consent of that creditor, on the company securing payment of his debt or claim by appropriating (as the court may direct) the following amount—

(*a*) if the company admits the full amount of the debt or claim or, though not admitting it, is willing to provide for it, then the full amount of the debt or claim;

(*b*) if the company does not admit, and is not willing to provide for, the full amount of the debt or claim, or if the amount is contingent or not ascertained, then an amount fixed by the court after the like enquiry and adjudication as if the company were being wound up by the court.

(6) If a proposed reduction of share capital involves either the diminution of any liability in respect of unpaid share capital or the payment to any shareholder of any paid-up share capital, the court may, if having regard to any special circumstances of the case it thinks proper to do so, direct that subsections (3) to (5) of this section shall not apply as regards any class or any classes of creditors.

Court order confirming reduction

137.—(1) The court, if satisfied with respect to every creditor of the company who under section 136 is entitled to object to the reduction of capital that either—

(*a*) his consent to the reduction has been obtained; or

(*b*) his debt or claim has been discharged or has determined, or has been secured,

may make an order confirming the reduction on such terms and conditions as it thinks fit.

(2) Where the court so orders, it may also—

(*a*) if for any special reason it thinks proper to do so, make an order directing that the company shall, during such period (commencing on or at any time after the date of the order) as is specified in the order, add to its name as its last words the words "and reduced"; and

(*b*) make an order requiring the company to publish (as the court directs) the reasons for reduction of capital or such other information in regard to it as the court thinks expedient with a view to giving proper information to the public and (if the court thinks fit) the causes which led to the reduction.

(3) Where a company is ordered to add to its name the words "and reduced", those words are, until the expiration of the period specified in the order, deemed to be part of the company's name.

Registration of order and minute of reduction

138.—(1) The registrar of companies, on production to him of an order of the court confirming the reduction of a company's share capital, and the delivery to him of a copy of the order and of a minute (approved by the court) showing, with respect to the company's share capital as altered by the order—

(*a*) the amount of the share capital;

(*b*) the number of shares into which it is to be divided, and the amount of each share; and

(*c*) the amount (if any) at the date of the registration deemed to be paid up on each share,

shall register the order and minute (but subject to section 139).

(2) On the registration of the order and minute, and not before, the resolution for reducing share capital as confirmed by the order so registered takes effect.

(3) Notice of the registration shall be published in such manner as the court may direct.

(4) The registrar shall certify the registration of the order and minute; and the certificate—

(*a*) may be either signed by the registrar, or authenticated by his official seal;

(*b*) is conclusive evidence that all the requirements of this Act with respect to the reduction of share capital have been complied with, and that the company's share capital is as stated in the minute.

(5) The minute when registered is deemed to be substituted for the corresponding part of the company's memorandum, and is valid and alterable as if it had been originally contained therein.

(6) The substitution of such a minute for part of the company's memorandum is deemed an alteration of the memorandum for purposes of section 20.

Public company reducing capital below authorised minimum

139.—(1) This section applies where the court makes an order confirming a reduction of a public company's capital which has the effect of bringing the nominal value of its allotted share capital below the authorised minimum.

(2) The registrar of companies shall not register the order under section 138 unless the court otherwise directs, or the company is first re-registered as a private company.

(3) The court may authorise the company to be so re-registered without its having passed the special resolution required by section 53; and where that authority is given, the court shall specify in the order the alterations in the company's memorandum and articles to be made in connection with that re-registration.

(4) The company may then be re-registered as a private company, if an application in the prescribed form and signed by a director or secretary of the company is delivered to the registrar, together with a printed copy of the memorandum and articles as altered by the court's order.

(5) On receipt of such an application, the registrar shall retain it and the other documents delivered with it and issue the company with a certificate of incorporation appropriate to a company that is not a public company; and—

(*a*) the company by virtue of the issue of the certificate becomes a private company, and the alterations in the memorandum and articles set out in the court's order take effect; and

(*b*) the certificate is conclusive evidence that the requirements of this section in respect of re-registration and of matters precedent and incidental thereto have been complied with, and that the company is a private company.

Liability of members on reduced shares

140.—(1) Where a company's share capital is reduced, a member of the company (past or present) is not liable in respect of any share to any call or contribution exceeding in amount the difference (if any) between the amount of the share as fixed by the minute and the amount paid on the share or the reduced amount (if any), which is deemed to have been paid on it, as the case may be.

[1] (2) But the following two subsections apply if—

(*a*) a creditor, entitled in respect of a debt or claim to object to the reduction of share capital, by reason of his ignorance of the proceedings for reduction of share capital, or of their nature and effect with respect to his claim, is not entered on the list of creditors; and

(*b*) after the reduction of capital, the company is unable (within the meaning of section 123 of the Insolvency Act) to pay the amount of his debt or claim.

(3) Every person who was a member of the company at the date of the registration of the order for reduction and minute is then liable to contribute for the payment of the debt or claim in question an amount not

exceeding that which he would have been liable to contribute if the company had commenced to be wound up on the day before that date.

(4) If the company is wound up, the court, on the application of the creditor in question and proof of ignorance referred to in subsection (2)(*a*), may (if it thinks fit) settle accordingly a list of persons so liable to contribute, and make and enforce calls and orders on the contributories settled on the list, as if they were ordinary contributories in a winding up.

(5) Nothing in this section affects the rights of the contributories among themselves.

NOTE
[1] As amended by the Insolvency Act 1986, Sched. 13, Pt. I.

Penalty for concealing name of creditor, etc.
    141. If an officer of the company—
    (*a*) wilfully conceals the name of a creditor entitled to object to the reduction of capital; or
    (*b*) wilfully misrepresents the nature or amount of the debt or claim of any creditor; or
    (*c*) aids, abets or is privy to any such concealment or misrepresentation as is mentioned above,
he is guilty of an offence and liable to a fine.

[1] CHAPTER V
MAINTENANCE OF CAPITAL

NOTE
[1] See the Companies Consolidation (Consequential Provisions) Act 1985, s. 6, in relation to old public companies.

Duty of directors on serious loss of capital
    142.—(1) Where the net assets of a public company are half or less of its called-up share capital, the directors shall, not later than 28 days from the earliest day on which that fact is known to a director of the company, duly convene an extraordinary general meeting of the company for a date not later than 56 days from that day for the purpose of considering whether any, and if so what, steps should be taken to deal with the situation.

(2) If there is a failure to convene an extraordinary general meeting as required by subsection (1), each of the directors of the company who—
    (*a*) knowingly and wilfully authorises or permits the failure, or
    (*b*) after the expiry of the period during which that meeting should have been convened, knowingly and wilfully authorises or permits the failure to continue,
is liable to a fine.

(3) Nothing in this section authorises the consideration, at a meeting convened in pursuance of subsection (1), of any matter which could not have been considered at that meeting apart from this section.

General rule against company acquiring own shares
    143.—(1) Subject to the following provisions, a company limited by shares or limited by guarantee and having a share capital shall not acquire its own shares, whether by purchase, subscription or otherwise.

(2) If a company purports to act in contravention of this section, the company is liable to a fine, and every officer of the company who is in default is liable to imprisonment or a fine, or both; and the purported acquisition is void.

(3) A company limited by shares may acquire any of its own fully paid shares otherwise than for valuable consideration; and subsection (1) does not apply in relation to—
    (*a*) the redemption or purchase of shares in accordance with Chapter VII of this Part,

(*b*) the acquisition of shares in a reduction of capital duly made,

(*c*) the purchase of shares in pursuance of an order of the court under section 5 (alteration of objects), section 54 (litigated objection to resolution for company to be re-registered as private) or Part XVII (relief to members unfairly prejudiced), or

(*d*) the forfeiture of shares, or the acceptance of shares surrendered in lieu, in pursuance of the articles, for failure to pay any sum payable in respect of the shares.

Acquisition of shares by company's nominee

144.—(1) Subject to section 145, where shares are issued to a nominee of a company mentioned in section 143(1), or are acquired by a nominee of such a company from a third person as partly paid up, then, for all purposes—

(*a*) the shares are to be treated as held by the nominee on his own account; and

(*b*) the company is to be regarded as having no beneficial interest in them.

(2) Subject to that section, if a person is called on to pay any amount for the purpose of paying up, or paying any premium on, any shares in such a company which were issued to him, or which he otherwise acquired, as the company's nominee and he fails to pay that amount within 21 days from being called on to do so, then—

(*a*) if the shares were issued to him as subscriber to the memorandum by virtue of an undertaking of his in the memorandum, the other subscribers to the memorandum, or

(*b*) if the shares were otherwise issued to or acquired by him, the directors of the company at the time of the issue or acquisition,

are jointly and severally liable with him to pay that amount.

(3) If in proceedings for the recovery of any such amount from any such subscriber or director under this section it appears to the court—

(*a*) that he is or may be liable to pay that amount, but

(*b*) that he has acted honestly and reasonably and, having regard to all the circumstances of the case, he ought fairly to be excused from liability,

the court may relieve him, either wholly or partly, from his liability on such terms as the court thinks fit.

(4) Where any such subscriber or director has reason to apprehend that a claim will or might be made for the recovery of any such amount from him, he may apply to the court for relief; and the court has the same power to relieve him as it would have had in proceedings for the recovery of that amount.

Exceptions from s. 144

145.—(1) Section 144(1) does not apply to shares acquired otherwise than by subscription by a nominee of a public company, where a person acquires shares in the company with financial assistance given to him directly or indirectly by the company for the purpose of or in connection with the acquisition, and the company has a beneficial interest in the shares.

(2) Section 144(1) and (2) do not apply—

(*a*) to shares acquired by a nominee of a company when the company has no beneficial interest in those shares, or

(*b*) to shares issued in consequence of an application made before 22nd December 1980, or transferred in pursuance of an agreement to acquire them made before that date.

(3) Schedule 2 to this Act has effect for the interpretation of references in this section to a company having, or not having, a beneficial interest in shares.

Treatment of shares held by or for public company

146.—(1) Except as provided by section 148, the following applies to a public company—

(*a*) where shares in the company are forfeited, or surrendered to the company in lieu, in pursuance of the articles, for failure to pay any sum payable in respect of the shares;

(*b*) where shares in the company are acquired by it (otherwise than by any of the methods mentioned in section 143(3)(*a*) to (*d*)) and the company has a beneficial interest in the shares;

(*c*) where the nominee of the company acquires shares in the company from a third person without financial assistance being given directly or indirectly by the company and the company has a beneficial interest in the shares; or

(*d*) where a person acquires shares in the company with financial assistance given to him directly or indirectly by the company for the purpose of or in connection with the acquisition, and the company has a beneficial interest in the shares.

Schedule 2 to this Act has effect for the interpretation of references in this subsection to the company having a beneficial interest in shares.

(2) Unless the shares or any interest of the company in them are previously disposed of, the company must, not later than the end of the relevant period from their forfeiture or surrender or, in a case within subsection (1)(*b*), (*c*) or (*d*), their acquisition—

(*a*) cancel them and diminish the amount of the share capital by the nominal value of the shares cancelled, and

(*b*) where the effect of cancelling the shares will be that the nominal value of the company's allotted share capital is brought below the authorised minimum, apply for re-registration as a private company, stating the effect of the cancellation.

(3) For this purpose "the relevant period" is—

(*a*) three years in the case of shares forfeited or surrendered to the company in lieu of forfeiture, or acquired as mentioned in subsection (1)(*b*) or (*c*);

(*b*) one year in the case of shares acquired as mentioned in subsection (1)(*d*).

(4) The company and, in a case within subsection (1)(*c*) or (*d*), the company's nominee or (as the case may be) the other shareholder must not exercise any voting rights in respect of the shares; and any purported exercise of those rights is void.

Matters arising out of compliance with s. 146(2)

147.—(1) The directors may take such steps as are requisite to enable the company to carry out its obligations under section 146(2) without complying with sections 135 and 136 (resolution to reduce share capital; application to court for approval).

(2) The steps taken may include the passing of a resolution to alter the company's memorandum so that it no longer states that the company is to be a public company; and the resolution may make such other alterations in the memorandum as are requisite in the circumstances.

Such a resolution is subject to section 380 (copy to be forwarded to registrar within 15 days).

(3) The application for re-registration required by section 146(2)(*b*) must be in the prescribed form and be signed by a director or secretary of the company, and must be delivered to the registrar of companies together with a printed copy of the memorandum and articles of the company as altered by the resolution.

(4) If the registrar is satisfied that the company may be re-registered under section 146, he shall retain the application and other documents

delivered with it and issue the company with a certificate of incorporation appropriate to a company that is not a public company; and—

    (a)   the company by virtue of the issue of the certificate becomes a private company, and the alterations in the memorandum and articles set out in the resolution take effect accordingly, and

    (b)   the certificate is conclusive evidence that the requirements of sections 146 to 148 in respect of re-registration and of matters precedent and incidental to it have been complied with, and that the company is a private company.

Further provisions supplementing ss. 146, 147

    148.—(1) Where, after shares in a private company—

    (a)   are forfeited in pursuance of the company's articles or are surrendered to the company in lieu of forfeiture, or

    (b)   are acquired by the company (otherwise than by such surrender for forfeiture, and otherwise than by any of the methods mentioned in section 143(3)), the company having a beneficial interest in the shares, or

    (c)   are acquired by the nominee of a company in the circumstances mentioned in section 146(1)(c), or

    (d)   are acquired by any person in the circumstances mentioned in section 146(1)(d),

the company is re-registered as a public company, sections 146 and 147, and also section 149, apply to the company as if it had been a public company at the time of the forfeiture, surrender or acquisition, but with the modification required by the following subsection.

    (2) That modification is to treat any reference to the relevant period from the forfeiture, surrender or acquisition as referring to the relevant period from the re-registration of the company as a public company.

    (3) Schedule 2 to this Act has effect for the interpretation of the reference in subsection (1)(b) to the company having a beneficial interest in shares.

    (4) Where a public company or a nominee of a public company acquires shares in the company or an interest in such shares, and those shares are (or that interest is) shown in a balance sheet of the company as an asset, an amount equal to the value of the shares or (as the case may be) the value to the company of its interest in them shall be transferred out of profits available for dividend to a reserve fund and are not then available for distribution.

Sanctions for non-compliance

    149.—(1) If a public company required by section 146(2) to apply to be re-registered as a private company fails to do so before the end of the relevant period referred to in that subsection, section 81 (restriction on public offers) applies to it as if it were a private company such as is mentioned in that section; but, subject to this, the company continues to be treated for the purpose of this Act as a public company until it is so re-registered.

    (2) If a company when required to do so by section 146(2) (including that subsection as applied by section 148(1)) fails to cancel any shares in accordance with paragraph (a) of that subsection or to make an application for re-registration in accordance with paragraph (b) of it, the company and every officer of it who is in default is liable to a fine and, for continued contravention, to a daily default fine.

Charges of public companies on own shares

    150.—(1) A lien or other charge of a public company on its own shares (whether taken expressly or otherwise), except a charge permitted by any of the following subsections, is void.

This is subject to section 6 of the Consequential Provisions Act (saving for charges of old public companies on their own shares).

(2) In the case of any description of company, a charge on its own shares is permitted if the shares are not fully paid and the charge is for any amount payable in respect of the shares.

(3) In the case of a company whose ordinary business—

(*a*) includes the lending of money, or

(*b*) consists of the provision of credit or the bailment (in Scotland, hiring) of goods under a hire purchase agreement, or both,

a charge of the company on its own shares is permitted (whether the shares are fully paid or not) if it arises in connection with a transaction entered into by the company in the ordinary course of its business.

(4) In the case of a company which is re-registered or is registered under section 680 as a public company, a charge on its own shares is permitted if the charge was in existence immediately before the company's application for re-registration or (as the case may be) registration.

This subsection does not apply in the case of such a company as is referred to in section 6(3) of the Consequential Provisions Act (old public company remaining such after 22nd March 1982, not having applied to be re-registered as public company).

CHAPTER VI

FINANCIAL ASSISTANCE BY A COMPANY FOR ACQUISITION OF ITS
OWN SHARES

Provisions applying to both public and private companies

Financial assistance generally prohibited

151.—(1) Subject to the following provisions of this Chapter, where a person is acquiring or is proposing to acquire shares in a company, it is not lawful for the company or any of its subsidiaries to give financial assistance directly or indirectly for the purpose of that acquisition before or at the same time as the acquisition takes place.

(2) Subject to those provisions, where a person has acquired shares in a company and any liability has been incurred (by that or any other person), for the purpose of that acquisition, it is not lawful for the company or any of its subsidiaries to give financial assistance directly or indirectly for the purpose of reducing or discharging the liability so incurred.

(3) If a company acts in contravention of this section, it is liable to a fine, and every officer of it who is in default is liable to imprisonment or a fine, or both.

Definitions for this Chapter

152.—(1) In this Chapter—

(*a*) "financial assistance" means—

   (i) financial assistance given by way of gift,

   (ii) financial assistance given by way of guarantee, security or indemnity, other than an indemnity in respect of the indemnifier's own neglect or default, or by way of release or waiver,

   (iii) financial assistance given by way of a loan or any other agreement under which any of the obligations of the person giving the assistance are to be fulfilled at a time when in accordance with the agreement any obligation of another party to the agreement remains unfulfilled, or by way of the novation of, or the assignment of rights arising under, a loan or such other agreement, or

   (iv) any other financial assistance given by a company the net assets of which are thereby reduced to a material extent or which has no net assets;

(*b*) "distributable profits", in relation to the giving of any financial assistance—

    (i) means those profits out of which the company could lawfully make a distribution equal in value to that assistance, and

    (ii) includes, in a case where the financial assistance is or includes a non-cash asset, any profit which, if the company were to make a distribution of that asset, would under section 276 (distributions in kind) be available for that purpose,

    and

(*c*) "distribution" has the meaning given by section 263(2).

(2) In subsection (1)(*a*)(iv), "net assets" means the aggregate of the company's assets, less the aggregate of its liabilities ("liabilities" to include any provision for liabilities or charges within paragraph 89 of Schedule 4).

(3) In this Chapter—

(*a*) a reference to a person incurring a liability includes his changing his financial position by making an agreement or arrangement (whether enforceable or unenforceable, and whether made on his own account or with any other person) or by any other means, and

(*b*) a reference to a company giving financial assistance for the purpose of reducing or discharging a liability incurred by a person for the purpose of the acquisition of shares includes its giving such assistance for the purpose of wholly or partly restoring his financial position to what it was before the acquisition took place.

Transactions not prohibited by s. 151

153.—(1) Section 151(1) does not prohibit a company from giving financial assistance for the purpose of an acquisition of shares in it or its holding company if—

(*a*) the company's principal purpose in giving that assistance is not to give it for the purpose of any such acquisition, or the giving of the assistance for that purpose is but an incidental part of some larger purpose of the company, and

(*b*) the assistance is given in good faith in the interests of the company.

(2) Section 151(2) does not prohibit a company from giving financial assistance if—

(*a*) the company's principal purpose in giving the assistance is not to reduce or discharge any liability incurred by a person for the purpose of the acquisition of shares in the company or its holding company, or the reduction or discharge of any such liability is but an incidental part of some larger purpose of the company, and

(*b*) the assistance is given in good faith in the interests of the company.

(3) Section 151 does not prohibit—

(*a*) a distribution of a company's assets by way of dividend lawfully made or a distribution made in the course of the company's winding up,

(*b*) the allotment of bonus shares,

(*c*) a reduction of capital confirmed by order of the court under section 137,

(*d*) a redemption or purchase of shares made in accordance with Chapter VII of this Part,

(*e*) anything done in pursuance of an order of the court under section 425 (compromises and arrangements with creditors and members),

(*f*) anything done under an arrangement made in pursuance of section 110 of the Insolvency Act (acceptance of shares by liquidator in winding up as consideration for sale of property), or

(*g*) anything done under an arrangement made between a company and its creditors which is binding on the creditors by virtue of Part I of the Insolvency Act.

(4) Section 151 does not prohibit—

  (*a*) where the lending of money is part of the ordinary business of the company, the lending of money by the company in the ordinary course of its business,

[2] (*b*) the provision by a company, in good faith in the interests of the company, of financial assistance for the purposes of an employees' share scheme,

(*bb*) without prejudice to paragraph (*b*), the provision of financial assistance by a company or any of its subsidiaries for the purposes of or in connection with anything done by the company (or a company connected with it) for the purpose of enabling or facilitating transactions in shares in the first-mentioned company between, and involving the acquisition of beneficial ownership of those shares by, any of the following persons—

    (i) the bona fide employees or former employees of that company or of another company in the same group; or

    (ii) the wives, husbands, widows, widowers, children or step-children under the age of 18 of any such employees or former employees.

  (*c*) the making by a company of loans to persons (other than directors) employed in good faith by the company with a view to enabling those persons to acquire fully paid shares in the company or its holding company to be held by them by way of beneficial ownership.

(5) For the purposes of subsection (4)(*bb*) a company is connected with another company if—

  (*a*) they are in the same group; or

  (*b*) one is entitled, either alone or with any other company in the same group, to exercise or control the exercise of a majority of the voting rights attributable to the share capital which are exerciseable in all circumstances at any general meeting of the other company or of its holding company;

and in this section "group", in relation to a company, means that company, any other company which is its holding company or subsidiary and any other company which is a subsidiary of that holding company.

NOTES

[1] As amended by the Insolvency Act 1985, Sched. 6, para. 8, the Insolvency Act 1986, Sched. 13, Pt. I, and the Financial Services Act 1986, s.196.

[2] As amended by the Companies Act 1989, s. 132.

Special restriction for public companies

154.—(1) In the case of a public company, section 153(4) authorises the giving of financial assistance only if the company has net assets which are not thereby reduced or, to the extent that those assets are thereby reduced, if the assistance is provided out of distributable profits.

(2) For this purpose the following definitions apply—

  (*a*) "net assets" means the amount by which the aggregate of the company's assets exceeds the aggregate of its liabilities (taking the amount of both assets and liabilities to be as stated in the company's accounting records immediately before the financial assistance is given);

  (*b*) "liabilities" includes any amount retained as reasonably necessary for the purpose of providing for any liability or loss which is either likely to be incurred, or certain to be incurred but uncertain as to amount or as to the date on which it will arise.

Private companies

Relaxation of s. 151 for private companies

155.—(1) Section 151 does not prohibit a private company from giving financial assistance in a case where the acquisition of shares in question is or was an acquisition of shares in the company or, if it is a subsidiary of another private company, in that other company if the following provisions of this section, and sections 156 to 158, are complied with as respects the giving of that assistance.

(2) The financial assistance may only be given if the company has net assets which are not thereby reduced or, to the extent that they are reduced, if the assistance is provided out of distributable profits.

Section 154(2) applies for the interpretation of this subsection.

(3) This section does not permit financial assistance to be given by a subsidiary, in a case where the acquisition of shares in question is or was an acquisition of shares in its holding company, if it is also a subsidiary of a public company which is itself a subsidiary of that holding company.

(4) Unless the company proposing to give the financial assistance is a wholly-owned subsidiary, the giving of assistance under this section must be approved by special resolution of the company in general meeting.

(5) Where the financial assistance is to be given by the company in a case where the acquisition of shares in question is or was an acquisition of shares in its holding company, that holding company and any other company which is both the company's holding company and a subsidiary of that other holding company (except, in any case, a company which is a wholly-owned subsidiary) shall also approve by special resolution in general meeting the giving of the financial assistance.

(6) The directors of the company proposing to give the financial assistance and, where the shares acquired or to be acquired are shares in its holding

[THE NEXT PAGE IS I 115]

company, the directors of that company and of any other company which is both the company's holding company and a subsidiary of that other holding company shall before the financial assistance is given make a statutory declaration in the prescribed form complying with the section next following.

Statutory declaration under s. 155

156.—(1) A statutory declaration made by a company's directors under section 155(6) shall contain such particulars of the financial assistance to be given, and of the business of the company of which they are directors, as may be prescribed, and shall identify the person to whom the assistance is to be given.

(2) The declaration shall state that the directors have formed the opinion, as regards the company's initial situation immediately following the date on which the assistance is proposed to be given, that there will be no grounds on which it could then be found to be unable to pay its debts; and either—

    (*a*) if it is intended to commence the winding up of the company within 12 months of that date, that the company will be able to pay its debts in full within 12 months of the commencement of the winding up, or

    (*b*) in any other case, that the company will be able to pay its debts as they fall due during the year immediately following that date.

[1] (3) In forming their opinion for purposes of subsection (2), the directors shall take into account the same liabilities (including contingent and prospective liabilities) as would be relevant under section 122 of the Insolvency Act (winding up by the court) to the question whether the company is unable to pay its debts.

(4) The directors' statutory declaration shall have annexed to it a report addressed to them by their company's auditors stating that—

    (*a*) they have enquired into the state of affairs of the company, and

    (*b*) they are not aware of anything to indicate that the opinion expressed by the directors in the declaration as to any of the matters mentioned in subsection (2) of this section is unreasonable in all the circumstances.

(5) The statutory declaration and auditors' report shall be delivered to the registrar of companies—

    (*a*) together with a copy of any special resolution passed by the company under section 155 and delivered to the registrar in compliance with section 380, or

    (*b*) where no such resolution is required to be passed, within 15 days after the making of the declaration.

(6) If a company fails to comply with subsection (5), the company and every officer of it who is in default is liable to a fine and, for continued contravention, to a daily default fine.

(7) A director of a company who makes a statutory declaration under section 155 without having reasonable grounds for the opinion expressed in it is liable to imprisonment or a fine, or both.

NOTE
[1] As amended by the Insolvency Act 1986, Sched. 13, Pt. I.

Special resolution under s. 155

157.—(1) A special resolution required by section 155 to be passed by a company approving the giving of financial assistance must be passed on the date on which the directors of that company make the statutory declaration required by that section in connection with the giving of that assistance, or within the week immediately following that date.

(2) Where such a resolution has been passed, an application may be made to the court for the cancellation of the resolution—

    (*a*) by the holders of not less in the aggregate than 10 per cent. in nominal value of the company's issued share capital or any class of it, or

    (*b*) if the company is not limited by shares, by not less than 10 per cent. of the company's members;

but the application shall not be made by a person who has consented to or voted in favour of the resolution.

(3) Subsections (3) to (10) of section 54 (litigation to cancel resolution under section 53) apply to applications under this section as to applications under section 54.

(4) A special resolution passed by a company is not effective for purposes of section 155—

(*a*) unless the declaration made in compliance with subsection (6) of that section by the directors of the company, together with the auditors' report annexed to it, is available for inspection by members of the company at the meeting at which the resolution is passed,

(*b*) if it is cancelled by the court on an application under this section.

Time for giving financial assistance under s. 155

158.—(1) This section applies as to the time before and after which financial assistance may not be given by a company in pursuance of section 155.

(2) Where a special resolution is required by that section to be passed approving the giving of the assistance, the assistance shall not be given before the expiry of the period of four weeks beginning with—

(*a*) the date on which the special resolution is passed, or

(*b*) where more than one such resolution is passed, the date on which the last of them is passed,

unless, as respects that resolution (or, if more than one, each of them), every member of the company which passed the resolution who is entitled to vote at general meetings of the company voted in favour of the resolution.

(3) If application for the cancellation of any such resolution is made under section 157, the financial assistance shall not be given before the final determination of the application unless the court otherwise orders.

(4) The assistance shall not be given after the expiry of the period of eight weeks beginning with—

(*a*) the date on which the directors of the company proposing to give the assistance made their statutory declaration under section 155, or

(*b*) where that company is a subsidiary and both its directors and the directors of any of its holding companies made such a declaration, the date on which the earliest of the declarations is made,

unless the court, on an application under section 157, otherwise orders.

CHAPTER VII
REDEEMABLE SHARES; PURCHASE BY A COMPANY
OF ITS OWN SHARES

Redemption and purchase generally

Power to issue redeemable shares

159.—(1) Subject to the provisions of this Chapter, a company limited by shares or limited by guarantee and having a share capital may, if authorised to do so by its articles, issue shares which are to be redeemed or are liable to be redeemed at the option of the company or the shareholder.

(2) No redeemable shares may be issued at a time when there are no issued shares of the company which are not redeemable.

(3) Redeemable shares may not be redeemed unless they are fully paid; and the terms of redemption must provide for payment on redemption.

Financing etc. of redemption

160.—(1) Subject to the next subsection and to sections 171 (private companies redeeming or purchasing own shares out of capital) and 178(4) (terms of redemption or purchase enforceable in a winding up)—

(*a*) redeemable shares may only be redeemed out of distributable profits of the company or out of the proceeds of a fresh issue of shares made for the purposes of the redemption; and

(*b*) any premium payable on redemption must be paid out of distributable profits of the company.

(2) If the redeemable shares were issued at a premium, any premium payable on their redemption may be paid out of the proceeds of a fresh issue of shares made for the purposes of the redemption, up to an amount equal to—

(*a*) the aggregate of the premiums received by the company on the issue of the shares redeemed, or

(*b*) the current amount of the company's share premium account (including any sum transferred to that account in respect of premiums on the new shares),

whichever is the less; and in that case the amount of the company's share premium account shall be reduced by a sum corresponding (or by sums in the aggregate corresponding) to the amount of any payment made by virtue of this subsection out of the proceeds of the issue of the new shares.

(3) Subject to the following provisions of this Chapter, redemption of shares may be effected on such terms and in such manner as may be provided by the company's articles.

(4) Shares redeemed under this section shall be treated as cancelled on redemption, and the amount of the company's issued share capital shall be diminished by the nominal value of those shares accordingly; but the redemption of shares by a company is not to be taken as reducing the amount of the company's authorised share capital.

(5) Without prejudice to subsection (4), where a company is about to redeem shares, it has power to issue shares up to the nominal value of the shares to be redeemed as if those shares had never been issued.

Stamp duty on redemption of shares

161. [Repealed by the Finance Act 1988, Sched. 14, Pt. XI.]

Power of company to purchase own shares

[1] **162.**—(1) Subject to the following provisions of this Chapter, a company limited by shares or limited by guarantee and having a share capital may, if authorised to do so by its articles, purchase its own shares (including any redeemable shares).

(2) Sections 159 to 161 apply to the purchase by a company under this section of its own shares as they apply to the redemption of redeemable shares, save that the terms and manner of purchase need not be determined by the articles as required by section 160(3).

(3) A company may not under this section purchase its shares if as a result of the purchase there would no longer be any member of the company holding shares other than redeemable shares.

NOTE
[1] See the Finance Act 1986, s.66.

Definitions of "off-market" and "market" purchase

[1] **163.**—(1) A purchase by a company of its own shares is "off-market" if the shares either—

(*a*) are purchased otherwise than on a recognised investment exchange, or

(*b*) are purchased on a recognised investment exchange but are not subject to a marketing arrangement on that investment exchange.

(2) For this purpose, a company's shares are subject to a marketing arrangement on a recognised investment exchange if either—

(*a*) they are listed under Part IV of the Financial Services Act 1986; or (*b*) the company has been afforded facilities for dealings in those shares to take place on that investment exchange without prior permission for individual transactions from the authority governing that investment exchange and without limit as to the time during which those facilities are to be available.

(3) A purchase by a company of its own shares is a "market purchase" if it is a purchase made on a recognised investment exchange, other than a purchase which is an off-market purchase by virtue of subsection (1)(*b*).

(4) In this section "recognised investment exchange" means a recognised investment exchange other than an overseas investment exchange within the meaning of the Financial Services Act 1986.

NOTE
[1] As amended by the Financial Services Act 1986, Sched. 16, para. 17.

Authority for off-market purchase
164.—(1) A company may only make an off-market purchase of its own shares in pursuance of a contract approved in advance in accordance with this section or under section 165 below.

(2) The terms of the proposed contract must be authorised by a special resolution of the company before the contract is entered into; and the following subsections apply with respect to that authority and to resolutions conferring it.

(3) Subject to the next subsection, the authority may be varied, revoked or from time to time renewed by special resolution of the company.

(4) In the case of a public company, the authority conferred by the resolution must specify a date on which the authority is to expire; and in a resolution conferring or renewing authority that date must not be later than 18 months after that on which the resolution is passed.

(5) A special resolution to confer, vary, revoke or renew authority is not effective if any member of the company holding shares to which the resolution relates exercises the voting rights carried by any of those shares in voting on the resolution and the resolution would not have been passed if he had not done so.

For this purpose—
(*a*) a member who holds shares to which the resolution relates is regarded as exercising the voting rights carried by those shares not

only if he votes in respect of them on a poll on the question whether the resolution shall be passed, but also if he votes on the resolution otherwise than on a poll;

(*b*) notwithstanding anything in the company's articles, any member of the company may demand a poll on that question; and

(*c*) a vote and a demand for a poll by a person as proxy for a member are the same respectively as a vote and a demand by the member.

[THE NEXT PAGE IS I 119]

(6) Such a resolution is not effective for the purposes of this section unless (if the proposed contract is in writing) a copy of the contract or (if not) a written memorandum of its terms is available for inspection by members of the company both—

(*a*) at the company's registered office for not less than 15 days ending with the date of the meeting at which the resolution is passed, and

(*b*) at the meeting itself.

A memorandum of contract terms so made available must include the names of any members holding shares to which the contract relates; and a copy of the contract so made available must have annexed to it a written memorandum specifying any such names which do not appear in the contract itself.

(7) A company may agree to a variation of an existing contract so approved, but only if the variation is authorised by a special resolution of the company before it is agreed to; and subsections (3) to (6) above apply to the authority for a proposed variation as they apply to the authority for a proposed contract, save that a copy of the original contract or (as the case may require) a memorandum of its terms, together with any variations previously made, must also be available for inspection in accordance with subsection (6).

Authority for contingent purchase contract

165.—(1) A contingent purchase contract is a contract entered into by a company and relating to any of its shares—

(*a*) which does not amount to a contract to purchase those shares, but

(*b*) under which the company may (subject to any conditions) become entitled or obliged to purchase those shares.

(2) A company may only make a purchase of its own shares in pursuance of a contingent purchase contract if the contract is approved in advance by a special resolution of the company before the contract is entered into; and subsections (3) to (7) of section 164 apply to the contract and its terms.

Authority for market purchase

166.—(1) A company shall not make a market purchase of its own shares unless the purchase has first been authorised by the company in general meeting.

(2) That authority—

(*a*) may be general for that purpose, or limited to the purchase of shares of any particular class or description, and

(*b*) may be unconditional or subject to conditions.

(3) The authority must—

(*a*) specify the maximum number of shares authorised to be acquired,

(*b*) determine both the maximum and the minimum prices which may be paid for the shares, and

(*c*) specify a date on which it is to expire.

(4) The authority may be varied, revoked or from time to time renewed by the company in general meeting, but this is subject to subsection (3) above; and in a resolution to confer or renew authority, the date on which the authority is to expire must not be later than 18 months after that on which the resolution is passed.

(5) A company may under this section make a purchase of its own shares after the expiry of the time limit imposed to comply with subsection (3)(*c*), if the contract of purchase was concluded before the authority expired and the terms of the authority permitted the company to make a contract of purchase, which would or might be executed wholly or partly after its expiration.

(6) A resolution to confer or vary authority under this section may determine either or both the maximum and minimum prices for purchase by—

(*a*) specifying a particular sum, or

(b)   providing a basis or formula for calculating the amount of the price in question without reference to any person's discretion or opinion.

(7) A resolution of a company conferring, varying, revoking or renewing authority under this section is subject to section 380 (resolution to be sent to registrar of companies within 15 days).

Assignment or release of company's right to purchase own shares

167.—(1) The rights of a company under a contract approved under section 164 or 165, or under a contract for a purchase authorised under section 166, are not capable of being assigned.

(2) An agreement by a company to release its rights under a contract approved under section 164 or 165 is void unless the terms of the release agreement are approved in advance by a special resolution of the company before the agreement is entered into; and subsections (3) to (7) of section 164 apply to approval for a proposed release agreement as to authority for a proposed variation of an existing contract.

Payments apart from purchase price to be made out of distributable profits

168.—(1) A payment made by a company in consideration of—

(a)   acquiring any right with respect to the purchase of its own shares in pursuance of a contract approved under section 165, or

(b)   the variation of a contract approved under section 164 or 165, or

(c)   the release of any of the company's obligations with respect to the purchase of any of its own shares under a contract approved under section 164 or 165 or under a contract for a purchase authorised under section 166,

must be made out of the company's distributable profits.

(2) If the requirements of subsection (1) are not satisfied in relation to a contract—

(a)   in a case within paragraph (a) of the subsection, no purchase by the company of its own shares in pursuance of that contract is lawful under this Chapter.

(b)   in a case within paragraph (b), no such purchase following the variation is lawful under this Chapter, and

(c)   in a case within paragraph (c), the purported release is void.

Disclosure by company of purchase of own shares

169.—(1) Within the period of 28 days beginning with the date on which any shares purchased by a company under this Chapter are delivered to it, the company shall deliver to the registrar of companies for registration a return in the prescribed form stating with respect to shares of each class purchased the number and nominal value of those shares and the date on which they were delivered to the company.

(2) In the case of a public company, the return shall also state—

(a)   the aggregate amount paid by the company for the shares; and

(b)   the maximum and minimum prices paid in respect of shares of each class purchased.

(3) Particulars of shares delivered to the company on different dates and under different contracts may be included in a single return to the registrar; and in such a case the amount required to be stated under subsection (2)(a) is the aggregate amount paid by the company for all the shares to which the return relates.

(4) Where a company enters into a contract approved under section 164 or 165, or a contract for a purchase authorised under section 166, the company shall keep at its registered office—

(a)   if the contract is in writing, a copy of it; and

(b)   if not, a memorandum of its terms,

from the conclusion of the contract until the end of the period of 10 years beginning with the date on which the purchase of all the shares in pursuance of the contract is completed or (as the case may be) the date on which the contract otherwise determines.

(5) Every copy and memorandum so required to be kept shall, during business hours (subject to such reasonable restrictions as the company may in general meeting impose, provided that not less than two hours in each day are allowed for inspection) be open to inspection without charge—

(*a*) by any member of the company, and

(*b*) if it is a public company, by any other person.

(6) If default is made in delivering to the registrar any return required by this section, every officer of the company who is in default is liable to a fine and, for continued contravention, to a daily default fine.

(7) If default is made in complying with subsection (4), or if an inspection required under subsection (5) is refused, the company and every officer of it who is in default is liable to a fine and, for continued contravention, to a daily default fine.

(8) In the case of a refusal of an inspection required under subsection (5) of a copy or memorandum, the court may by order compel an immediate inspection of it.

(9) The obligation of a company under subsection (4) to keep a copy of any contract or (as the case may be) a memorandum of its terms applies to any variation of the contract so long as it applies to the contract.

NOTE
See the Finance Act 1986, s.66.

The capital redemption reserve

170.—(1) Where under this Chapter shares of a company are redeemed or purchased wholly out of the company's profits, the amount by which the company's issued share capital is diminished in accordance with section 160(4) on cancellation of the shares redeemed or purchased shall be transferred to a reserve, called "the capital redemption reserve".

(2) If the shares are redeemed or purchased wholly or partly out of the proceeds of a fresh issue and the aggregate amount of those proceeds is less than the aggregate nominal value of the shares redeemed or purchased, the amount of the difference shall be transferred to the capital redemption reserve.

(3) But subsection (2) does not apply if the proceeds of the fresh issue are applied by the company in making a redemption or purchase of its own shares in addition to a payment out of capital under section 171.

(4) The provisions of this Act relating to the reduction of a company's share capital apply as if the capital redemption reserve were paid-up share capital of the company, except that the reserve may be applied by the company in paying up its unissued shares to be allotted to members of the company as fully paid bonus shares.

Redemption or purchase of own shares out of capital (private companies only)

Power of private companies to redeem or purchase own shares out of capital

171.—(1) Subject to the following provisions of this Chapter, a private company limited by shares or limited by guarantee and having a share capital may, if so authorised by its articles, make a payment in respect of the redemption or purchase under section 160 or (as the case may be) section 162, of its own shares otherwise than out of its distributable profits or the proceeds of a fresh issue of shares.

(2) References below in this Chapter to payment out of capital are (subject to subsection (6)) to any payment so made, whether or not it would be regarded apart from this section as a payment out of capital.

(3) The payment which may (if authorised in accordance with the following provisions of this Chapter) be made by a company out of capital in

respect of the redemption or purchase of its own shares is such an amount as, taken together with—

(a) any available profits of the company, and

(b) the proceeds of any fresh issue of shares made for the purposes of the redemption or purchase,

is equal to the price of redemption or purchase; and the payment permissible under this subsection is referred to below in this Chapter as the permissible capital payment for the shares.

(4) Subject to subsection (6), if the permissible capital payment for shares redeemed or purchased is less than their nominal amount, the amount of the difference shall be transferred to the company's capital redemption reserve.

(5) Subject to subsection (6), if the permissible capital payment is greater than the nominal amount of the shares redeemed or purchased—

(a) the amount of any capital redemption reserve, share premium account or fully paid share capital or the company, and

(b) any amount representing unrealised profits of the company for the time being standing to the credit of any reserve maintained by the company in accordance with paragraph 34 of Schedule 4 (revaluation reserve),

may be reduced by a sum not exceeding (or by sums not in the aggregate exceeding) the amount by which the permissible capital payment exceeds the nominal amount of the shares.

(6) Where the proceeds of a fresh issue are applied by a company in making any redemption or purchase of its own shares in addition to a payment out of capital under this section, the references in subsections (4) and (5) to the permissible capital payment are to be read as referring to the aggregate of that payment and those proceeds.

Availability of profits for purposes of s. 171

172.—(1) The reference in section 171(3)(a) to available profits of the company is to the company's profits which are available for distribution (within the meaning of Part VIII); but the question whether a company has any profits so available and the amount of any such profits are to be determined for purposes of that section in accordance with the following subsections, instead of sections 270 to 275 in that Part.

(2) Subject to the next subsection, that question is to be determined by reference to—

(a) profits, losses, assets and liabilities,

(b) provisions of any of the kinds mentioned in paragraphs 88 and 89 of Schedule 4 (depreciation, diminution in value of assets, retentions to meet liabilities, etc.), and

(c) share capital and reserves (including undistributable reserves),

as stated in the relevant accounts for determining the permissible capital payment for shares.

(3) The relevant accounts for this purpose are such accounts, prepared as at any date within the period for determining the amount of the permissible capital payment, as are necessary to enable a reasonable judgment to be made as to the amounts of any of the items mentioned in subsection (2)(a) to (c) above.

(4) For purposes of determining the amount of the permissible capital payment for shares, the amount of the company's available profits (if any) determined in accordance with subsections (2) and (3) is treated as reduced by the amount of any distributions lawfully made by the company after the date of the relevant accounts and before the end of the period for determining the amount of that payment.

(5) The reference in subsection (4) to distributions lawfully made by the company includes—

(a) financial assistance lawfully given out of distributable profits in a case falling within section 154 or 155,

(b) any payment lawfully made by the company in respect of the purchase by it of any shares in the company (except a payment lawfully made otherwise than out of distributable profits), and

(c) a payment of any description specified in section 168(1) lawfully made by the company.

(6) References in this section to the period for determining the amount of the permissible capital payment for shares are to the period of three months ending with the date on which the statutory declaration of the directors purporting to specify the amount of that payment is made in accordance with subsection (3) of the section next following.

Conditions for payment out of capital

173.—(1) Subject to any order of the court under section 177, a payment out of capital by a private company for the redemption or purchase of its own shares is not lawful unless the requirements of this and the next two sections are satisfied.

(2) The payment out of capital must be approved by a special resolution of the company.

(3) The company's directors must make a statutory declaration specifying the amount of the permissible capital payment for the shares in question and stating that, having made full inquiry into the affairs and prospects of the company, they have formed the opinion—

(a) as regards its initial situation immediately following the date on which the payment out of capital is proposed to be made, that there will be no grounds on which the company could then be found unable to pay its debts, and

(b) as regards its prospects for the year immediately following that date, that, having regard to their intentions with respect to the management of the company's business during that year and to the amount and character of the financial resources which will in their view be available to the company during that year, the company will be able to continue to carry on business as a going concern (and will accordingly be able to pay its debts as they fall due) throughout that year.

[1] (4) In forming their opinion for purposes of subsection (3)(a), the directors shall take into account the same liabilities (including prospective and contingent liabilities) as would be relevant under section 122 of the Insolvency Act (winding up by the court) to the question whether a company is unable to pay its debts.

(5) The directors' statutory declaration must be in the prescribed form and contain such information with respect to the nature of the company's business as may be prescribed, and must in addition have annexed to it a report addressed to the directors by the company's auditors stating that—

(a) they have inquired into the company's state of affairs; and

(b) the amount specified in the declaration as the permissible capital payment for the shares in question is in their view properly determined in accordance with sections 171 and 172; and

(c) they are not aware of anything to indicate that the opinion expressed by the directors in the declaration as to any of the matters mentioned in subsection (3) is unreasonable in all the circumstances.

(6) A director who makes a declaration under this section without having reasonable grounds for the opinion expressed in the declaration is liable to imprisonment or a fine, or both.

NOTE
[1] As amended by the Insolvency Act 1986, Sched. 13, Pt. I.

Procedure for special resolution under s. 173

174.—(1) The resolution required by section 173 must be passed on, or within the week immediately following, the date on which the directors make the statutory declaration required by that section; and the payment out of capital must be made no earlier than five nor more than seven weeks after the date of the resolution.

(2) The resolution is ineffective if any member of the company holding shares to which the resolution relates exercises the voting rights carried by any of those shares in voting on the resolution and the resolution would not have been passed if he had not done so.

(3) For purposes of subsection (2), a member who holds such shares is to be regarded as exercising the voting rights carried by them in voting on the resolution not only if he votes in respect of them on a poll on the question whether the resolution shall be passed, but also if he votes on the resolution otherwise than on a poll; and, notwithstanding anything in a company's articles, any member of the company may demand a poll on that question.

(4) The resolution is ineffective unless the statutory declaration and auditors' report required by the section are available for inspection by members of the company at the meeting at which the resolution is passed.

(5) For purposes of this section a vote and a demand for a poll by a person as proxy for a member are the same (respectively) as a vote and demand by the member.

Publicity for proposed payment out of capital
175.—(1) Within the week immediately following the date of the resolution for payment out of capital the company must cause to be published in the *Gazette* a notice—

   (a) stating that the company has approved a payment out of capital for the purpose of acquiring its own shares by redemption or purchase or both (as the case may be);

   (b) specifying the amount of the permissible capital payment for the shares in question and the date of the resolution under section 173;

   (c) stating that the statutory declaration of the directors and the auditors' report required by that section are available for inspection at the company's registered office; and

   (d) stating that any creditor of the company may at any time within the five weeks immediately following the date of the resolution for payment out of capital apply to the court under section 176 for an order prohibiting the payment.

(2) Within the week immediately following the date of the resolution the company must also either cause a notice to the same effect as that required by subsection (1) to be published in an appropriate national newspaper or give notice in writing to that effect to each of its creditors.

(3) "An appropriate national newspaper" means a newspaper circulating throughout England and Wales (in the case of a company registered in England and Wales), and a newspaper circulating throughout Scotland (in the case of a company registered in Scotland).

(4) References below in this section to the first notice date are to the day on which the company first publishes the notice required by subsection (1) or first publishes or gives the notice required by subsection (2) (whichever is the earlier).

(5) Not later than the first notice date the company must deliver to the registrar of companies a copy of the statutory declaration of the directors and of the auditors' report required by section 173.

(6) The statutory declaration and auditors' report—

   (a) shall be kept at the company's registered office throughout the period beginning with the first notice date and ending five weeks after the date of the resolution for payment out of capital, and

   (b) shall during business hours on any day during that period be open to the inspection of any member or creditor of the company without charge.

(7) If an inspection required under subsection (6) is refused, the company and every officer of it who is in default is liable to a fine and, for continued contravention, to a daily default fine.

(8) In the case of refusal of an inspection required under subsection (6) of a declaration or report, the court may by order compel an immediate inspection of that declaration or report.

Objections by company's members or creditors
176.—(1) Where a private company passes a special resolution approving for purposes of this Chapter any payment out of capital for the redemption or purchase of any of its shares—

    (*a*) any member of the company other than one who consented to or voted in favour of the resolution; and

    (*b*) any creditor of the company,

may within five weeks of the date on which the resolution was passed apply to the court for cancellation of the resolution.

(2) The application may be made on behalf of the persons entitled to make it by such one or more of their number as they may appoint in writing for the purpose.

(3) If an application is made, the company shall—

    (*a*) forthwith give notice in the prescribed form of that fact to the registrar of companies; and

    (*b*) within 15 days from the making of any order of the court on the hearing of the application, or such longer period as the court may by order direct, deliver an office copy of the order to the registrar.

(4) A company which fails to comply with subsection (3), and any officer of it who is in default, is liable to a fine and for continued contravention, to a daily default fine.

Powers of court on application under s. 176
177.—(1) On the hearing of an application under section 176 the court may, if it thinks fit, adjourn the proceedings in order that an arrangement may be made to the court's satisfaction for the purchase of the interests of dissentient members or for the protection of dissentient creditors (as the case may be); and the court may give such directions and make such orders as it thinks expedient for facilitating or carrying into effect any such arrangement.

(2) Without prejudice to its powers under subsection (1), the court shall make an order on such terms and conditions as it thinks fit either confirming or cancelling the resolution; and, if the court confirms the resolution, it may in particular by order alter or extend any date or period of time specified in the resolution or in any provision in this Chapter which applies to the redemption or purchase of shares to which the resolution refers.

(3) The court's order may, if the court thinks fit, provide for the purchase by the company of the shares of any of its members and for the reduction accordingly of the company's capital, and may make such alterations in the company's memorandum and articles as may be required in consequence of that provision.

(4) If the court's order requires the company not to make any, or any specified, alteration in its memorandum or articles, the company has not then power without leave of the court to make any such alteration in breach of the requirement.

(5) An alteration in the memorandum or articles made by virtue of an order under this section, if not made by resolution of the company, is of the same effect as if duly made by resolution; and this Act applies accordingly to the memorandum or articles as so altered.

Supplementary

Effect of company's failure to redeem or purchase

178.—(1) This section has effect where a company has, on or after 15th June 1982,—

(*a*) issued shares on terms that they are or are liable to be redeemed, or

(*b*) agreed to purchase any of its own shares.

(2) The company is not liable in damages in respect of any failure on its part to redeem or purchase any of the shares.

(3) Subsection (2) is without prejudice to any right of the holder of the shares other than his right to sue the company for damages in respect of its failure; but the court shall not grant an order for specific performance of the terms of redemption or purchase if the company shows that it is unable to meet the costs of redeeming or purchasing the shares in question out of distributable profits.

(4) If the company is wound up and at the commencement of the winding up any of the shares have not been redeemed or purchased, the terms of redemption or purchase may be enforced against the company; and when shares are redeemed or purchased under this subsection, they are treated as cancelled.

(5) However, subsection (4) does not apply if—

(*a*) the terms provided for the redemption or purchase to take place at a date later than that of the commencement of the winding up, or

(*b*) during the period beginning with the date on which the redemption or purchase was to have taken place and ending with the commencement of the winding up the company could not at any time have lawfully made a distribution equal in value to the price at which the shares were to have been redeemed or purchased.

(6) There shall be paid in priority to any amount which the company is liable under subsection (4) to pay in respect of any shares—

(*a*) all other debts and liabilities of the company (other than any due to members in their character as such),

(*b*) if other shares carry rights (whether as to capital or as to income) which are preferred to the rights as to capital attaching to the first-mentioned shares, any amount due in satisfaction of those preferred rights;

but, subject to that, any such amount shall be paid in priority to any amounts due to members in satisfaction of their rights (whether as to capital or income) as members.

(7) [Repealed by the Insolvency Act 1985, Sched. 10, Pt. II.]

Power for Secretary of State to modify this Chapter

179.—(1) The Secretary of State may by regulations made by statutory instrument modify the provisions of this Chapter with respect to any of the following matters—

(*a*) the authority required for a purchase by a company of its own shares,

(*b*) the authority required for the release by a company of its rights under a contract for the purchase of its own shares or a contract under which the company may (subject to any conditions) become entitled or obliged to purchase its own shares,

(*c*) the information to be included in a return delivered by a company to the registrar of companies in accordance with section 169(1),

(*d*) the matters to be dealt with in the statutory declaration of the directors under section 173 with a view to indicating their opinion of their company's ability to make a proposed payment out of capital with due regard to its financial situation and prospects, and

(e) the contents of the auditors' report required by that section to be annexed to that declaration.

(2) The Secretary of State may also by regulations so made make such provision (including modification of the provisions of this Chapter) as appears to him to be appropriate—

(a) for wholly or partly relieving companies from the requirement of section 171(3)(a) that any available profits must be taken into account in determining the amount of the permissible capital payment for shares under that section, or

(b) for permitting a company's share premium account to be applied, to any extent appearing to the Secretary of State to be appropriate, in providing for the premiums payable on the redemption or purchase by the company of any of its own shares.

(3) Regulations under this section—

(a) may make such further modification of any provisions of this Chapter as appears to the Secretary of State to be reasonably necessary in consequences of any provision made under such regulations by virtue of subsection (1) or (2),

(b) may make different provision for different cases or classes of case, and

(c) may contain such further consequential provisions, and such incidental and supplementary provisions, as the Secretary of State thinks fit.

(4) No regulations shall be made under this section unless a draft of the instrument containing them has been laid before Parliament and approved by resolution of each House.

Transitional cases arising under this Chapter; and savings

180.—(1) Any preference shares issued by a company before 15th June 1982 which could but for the repeal by the Companies Act 1981 of section 58 of the Companies Act 1948 (power to issue redeemable preference shares) have been redeemed under that section are subject to redemption in accordance with the provisions of this Chapter.

(2) In a case to which sections 159 and 160 apply by virtue of this section, any premium payable on redemption may, notwithstanding the repeal by the 1981 Act of any provision of the 1948 Act, be paid out of the share premium account instead of out of profits, or partly out of that account and partly out of profits (but subject to the provisions of this Chapter so far as payment is out of profits).

(3) Any capital redemption reserve fund established before 15th June 1982 by a company for the purposes of section 58 of the Act of 1948 is to be known as the company's capital redemption reserve and be treated as if it had been established for the purposes of section 170 of this Act; and accordingly, a reference in any enactment or in the articles of any company, or in any other instrument, to a company's capital redemption reserve fund is to be construed as a reference to the company's capital redemption reserve.

Definitions for Chapter VII

181. In this Chapter—

(a) "distributable profits", in relation to the making of any payment by a company, means those profits out of which it could lawfully make a distribution (within the meaning given by section 263(2)) equal in value to the payment, and

(b) "permissible capital payment" means the payment permitted by section 171;

and references to payment out of capital are to be construed in accordance with section 171.

CHAPTER VIII
MISCELLANEOUS PROVISIONS ABOUT SHARES AND DEBENTURES

Share and debenture certificates, transfers and warrants

Nature, transfer and numbering of shares

182.—(1) The shares or other interest of any member in a company—

(*a*) are personal estate or, in Scotland, moveable property and are not in the nature of real estate or heritage,

(*b*) are transferable in manner provided by the company's articles, but subject to the Stock Transfer Act 1963 (which enables securities of certain descriptions to be ransferred by a simplified process).

(2) Each share in a company having a share capital shall be distinguished by its appropriate number; except that, if at any time all the issued shares in a company, or all the issued shares in it of a particular class, are fully paid up and rank *pari passu* for all purposes, none of those shares need thereafter have a distinguishing number so long as it remains fully paid up and ranks *pari passu* for all purposes with all shares of the same class for the time being issued and fully paid up.

Transfer and registration

183.—(1) It is not lawful for a company to register a transfer of shares in or debentures of the company unless a proper instrument of transfer has been delivered to it, or the transfer is an exempt transfer within the Stock Transfer Act 1982.

This applies notwithstanding anything in the company's articles.

(2) Subsection (1) does not prejudice any power of the company to register as shareholder or debenture holder a person to whom the right to any shares in or debentures of the company has been transmitted by operation of law.

(3) A transfer of the share or other interest of a deceased member of a company made by his personal representative, although the personal representative is not himself a member of the company, is as valid as if he had been such a member at the time of the execution of the instrument of transfer.

(4) On the application of the transferor of any share or interest in a company, the company shall enter in its register of members the name of the transferee in the same manner and subject to the same conditions as if the application for the entry were made by the transferee.

(5) If a company refuses to register a transfer of shares or debentures, the company shall, within two months after the date on which the transfer was lodged with it, send to the transferee notice of the refusal.

(6) If default is made in complying with subsection (5), the company and every officer of it who is in default is liable to a fine and, for continued contravention, to a daily default fine.

Certification of transfers

184.—(1) The certification by a company of any instrument of transfer of any shares in, or debentures of, the company is to be taken as a representation by the company to any person acting on the faith of the certification that there have been produced to the company such documents as on their face show a *prima facie* title to the shares or debentures in the transferor named in the instrument.

However, the certification is not to be taken as a representation that the transferor has any title to the shares or debentures.

(2) Where a person acts on the faith of a false certification by a company made negligently, the company is under the same liability to him as if the certification had been made fraudulently.

(3) For purposes of this section—

(*a*) an instrument of transfer is deemed certificated if it bears the words "certificate lodged" (or words to the like effect);

(*b*) the certification of an instrument of transfer is deemed made by a company if—

(i) the person issuing the instrument is a person authorised to issue certificated instruments of transfer on the company's behalf, and

(ii) the certification is signed by a person authorised to certificate transfers on the company's behalf or by an officer or servant either of the company or of a body corporate so authorised;

(*c*) a certification is deemed signed by a person if—

(i) it purports to be authenticated by his signature or initials (whether handwritten or not), and

(ii) it is not shown that the signature or initials was or were placed there neither by himself nor by a person authorised to use the signature or initials for the purpose of certificating transfers on the company's behalf.

Duty of company as to issue of certificates

185.—(1) Subject to the following provisions, every company shall—

(*a*) within two months after the allotment of any of its shares, debentures or debenture stock, and

(*b*) within two months after the date on which a transfer of any such shares, debentures or debenture stock is lodged with the company,

complete and have ready for delivery the certificates of all shares, the debentures and the certificates of all debenture stock allotted or transferred (unless the conditions of issue of the shares, debentures or debenture stock otherwise provide).

(2) For this purpose, "transfer" means a transfer duly stamped and otherwise valid, or an exempt transfer within the Stock Transfer Act 1982, and does not include such a transfer as the company is for any reason entitled to refuse to register and does not register.

(3) Subsection (1) does not apply in the case of a transfer to any person where, by virtue of regulations under section 3 of the Stock Transfer Act 1982, he is not entitled to a certificate or other document of or evidencing title in respect of the securities transferred; but if in such a case the transferee—

(*a*) subsequently becomes entitled to such a certificate or other document by virtue of any provision of those regulations, and

(*b*) gives notice in writing of that fact to the company,

this section has effect as if the reference in subsection (1)(*b*) to the date of the lodging of the transfer were a reference to the date of the notice.

[1] (4) A company of which shares or debentures are allotted or debenture stock is allotted to a recognised clearing house or a nominee of a recognised clearing house or of a recognised investment exchange, or with which a transfer is lodged for transferring any shares, debentures or debenture stock of the company to such a clearing house or nominee, is not required, in consequence of the allotment or the lodging of the transfer, to comply with subsection (1); but no person shall be a nominee for the purposes of this section unless he is a person designated for the purposes of this section in the rules of the recognised investment exchange in question.

"Recognised clearing house" means a recognised clearing house within the meaning of the Financial Services Act 1986 acting in relation to a recognised investment exchange and "recognised investment exchange" has the same meaning as in that Act.

(5) If default is made in complying with subsection (1), the company and every officer of it who is in default is liable to a fine and, for continued contravention, to a daily default fine.

(6) If a company on which a notice has been served requiring it to make good any default in complying with subsection (1) fails to make good the default within 10 days after service of the notice, the court may, on the application of the person entitled to have the certificates or the debentures delivered to him, exercise the power of the following subsection.

(7) The court may make an order directing the company and any officer of it to make good the default within such time as may be specified in the order; and the order may provide that all costs of and incidental to the application shall be borne by the company or by an officer of it responsible for the default.

NOTE
[1] As amended by the Financial Services Act 1986, s.194(5).

Certificate to be evidence of title

186. A certificate, under the common seal of the company or the seal kept by the company by virtue of section 40, specifying any shares held by a member, is *prima facie* evidence of his title to the shares.

Evidence of grant of probate or confirmation as executor

187. The production to a company of any document which is by law sufficient evidence of probate of the will, or letters of administration of the estate, or confirmation as executor, of a deceased person having been granted to some person shall be accepted by the company as sufficient evidence of the grant.

This has effect notwithstanding anything in the company's articles.

Issue and effect of share warrant to bearer

188.—(1) A company limited by shares, if so authorised by its articles, may, with respect to any fully paid-up shares, issue under its common seal a warrant stating that the bearer of the warrant is entitled to the shares specified in it, and may provide (by coupons or otherwise) for the payment of the future dividends on the shares included in the warrant.

(2) Such a warrant is termed a "share warrant" and entitles the bearer to the shares specified in it; and the shares may be transferred by delivery of the warrant.

Offences in connection with share warrants (Scotland)

189.—(1) If in Scotland a person—

(*a*) with intent to defraud, forges or alters, or offers, utters, disposes of, or puts off, knowing the same to be forged or altered, any share warrant or coupon, or any document purporting to be a share warrant or coupon, issued in pursuance of this Act; or

(*b*) by means of any such forged or altered share warrant, coupon, or document, purporting as aforesaid, demands or endeavours to obtain or receive any share or interest in any company under this Act, or to receive any dividend or money payable in respect thereof, knowing the warrant, coupon, or document to be forged or altered;

he is on conviction thereof liable to imprisonment or a fine, or both.

(2) If in Scotland a person without lawful authority or excuse (proof whereof lies on him)—

(*a*) engraves or makes on any plate, wood, stone, or other material, any share warrant or coupon purporting to be—

(i) a share warrant or coupon issued or made by any particular company in pursuance of this Act; or

(ii) a blank share warrant or coupon so issued or made; or

(iii) a part of such a share warrant or coupon; or

(*b*) uses any such plate, wood, stone, or other material, for the making or printing of any such share warrant or coupon, or of any such blank share warrant or coupon, or any part thereof respectively; or (*c*) knowingly has in his custody or possession any such plate, wood, stone, or other material;

he is on conviction thereof liable to imprisonment or a fine, or both.

Debentures

Register of debenture holders

190.—(1) A company registered in England and Wales shall not keep in Scotland any register of holders of debentures of the company or any duplicate of any such register or part of any such register which is kept outside Great Britain.

(2) A company registered in Scotland shall not keep in England and Wales any such register or duplicate as above-mentioned.

(3) Neither a register of holders of debentures of a company nor a duplicate of any such register or part of any such register which is kept outside Great Britain shall be kept in England and Wales (in the case of a company registered in England and Wales) or in Scotland (in the case of a company registered in Scotland) elsewhere than—

(*a*) at the company's registered office; or

(*b*) at any office of the company at which the work of making it up is done; or

(*c*) if the company arranges with some other person for the making up of the register or duplicate to be undertaken on its behalf by that other person, at the office of that other person at which the work is done.

(4) Where a company keeps (in England and Wales or in Scotland, as the case may be) both such a register and such a duplicate, it shall keep them at the same place.

(5) Every company which keeps any such register or duplicate in England and Wales or Scotland shall send to the registrar of companies notice (in the prescribed form) of the place where the register or duplicate is kept and of any change in that place.

(6) But a company is not bound to send notice under subsection (5) where the register or duplicate has, at all times since it came into existence, been kept at the company's registered office.

Right to inspect register

191.—(1) Every register of holders of debentures of a company shall, except when duly closed (but subject to such reasonable restrictions as the company may impose in general meeting, so that not less than two hours in each day shall be allowed for inspection) be open to the inspection—

(*a*) of the registered holder of any such debentures or any holder of shares in the company without fee; and

(*b*) of any other person on payment of a fee of 5 pence or such less sum as may be prescribed by the company.

(2) Any such registered holder of debentures or holder of shares, or any other person, may require a copy of the register of the holders of debentures of the company or any part of it, on payment of 10 pence (or such less sum as may be prescribed by the company) for every 100 words, or fractional part of 100 words, required to be copied.

(3) A copy of any trust deed for securing an issue of debentures shall be forwarded to every holder of any such debentures at his request on payment—

(*a*) in the case of a printed trust deed, of 20 pence (or such less sum as may be prescribed by the company), or

(*b*) where the trust deed has not been printed, of 10 pence (or such less sum as may be so prescribed), for every 100 words, or fractional part of 100 words, required to be copied.

(4) If inspection is refused, or a copy is refused or not forwarded, the company and every officer of it who is in default is liable to a fine and, for continued contravention, to a daily default fine.

(5) Where a company is in default as above mentioned, the court may by order compel an immediate inspection of the register or direct that the copies required be sent to the person requiring them.

(6) For purposes of this section, a register is deemed to be duly closed if closed in accordance with provisions contained in the articles or in the debentures or, in the case of debenture stock, in the stock certificates, or in the trust deed or other document securing the debentures or debenture stock, during such period or periods, not exceeding in the whole 30 days in any year, as may be therein specified.

(7) Liability incurred by a company from the making or deletion of an entry in its register of debenture holders, or from a failure to make or delete any such entry, is not enforceable more than 20 years after the date on which the entry was made or deleted or, in the case of any such failure, the failure first occurred.

This is without prejudice to any lesser period of limitation.

Liability of trustees of debentures

192.—(1) Subject to this section, any provision contained—

(*a*) in a trust deed for securing an issue of debentures, or

(*b*) in any contract with the holders of debentures secured by a trust deed,

is void in so far as it would have the effect of exempting a trustee of the deed from, or indemnifying him against, liability for breach of trust where he fails to show the degree of care and diligence required of him as trustee, having regard to the provisions of the trust deed conferring on him any powers, authorities or discretions.

(2) Subsection (1) does not invalidate—

(*a*) a release otherwise validly given in respect of anything done or omitted to be done by a trustee before the giving of the release; or

(*b*) any provision enabling such a release to be given—

(i) on the agreement thereto of a majority of not less than three-fourths in value of the debenture holders present and voting in person or, where proxies are permitted, by proxy at a meeting summoned for the purpose, and

(ii) either with respect to specific acts or omissions or on the trustee dying or ceasing to act.

(3) Subsection (1) does not operate—

(*a*) to invalidate any provision in force on 1st July 1948 so long as any person then entitled to the benefit of that provision or afterwards given the benefit of that provision under the following subsection remains a trustee of the deed in question; or

(*b*) to deprive any person of any exemption or right to be indemnified in respect of anything done or omitted to be done by him while any such provision was in force.

(4) While any trustee of a trust remains entitled to the benefit of a provision saved by subsection (3), the benefit of that provision may be given either—

(*a*) to all trustees of the deed, present and future; or

(*b*) to any named trustees or proposed trustees of it,

by a resolution passed by a majority of not less than three-fourths in value of the debenture holders present in person or, where proxies are permitted, by proxy at a meeting summoned for the purpose in accordance with the provisions of the deed or, if the deed makes no provision for summoning meetings, a meeting summoned for the purpose in any manner approved by the court.

Perpetual debentures

193. A condition contained in debentures, or in a deed for securing debentures, is not invalid by reason only that the debentures are thereby made irredeemable or redeemable only on the happening of a contingency (however remote), or on the expiration of a period (however long), any rule of equity to the contrary notwithstanding.

This applies to debentures whenever issued, and to deeds whenever executed.

Power to re-issue redeemed debentures

194.—(1) Where (at any time) a company has redeemed debentures previously issued, then—

    (*a*) unless provision to the contrary, whether express or implied, is contained in the articles or in any contract entered into by the company; or

    (*b*) unless the company has, by passing a resolution to that effect or by some other act, manifested its intention that the debentures shall be cancelled,

the company has, and is deemed always to have had, power to re-issue the debentures, either by re-issuing the same debentures or by issuing other debentures in their place.

(2) On a re-issue of redeemed debentures, the person entitled to the debentures has, and is deemed always to have had, the same priorities as if the debentures had never been redeemed.

(3) Where a company has (at any time) deposited any of its debentures to secure advances from time to time on current account or otherwise, the debentures are not deemed to have been redeemed by reason only of the company's account having ceased to be in debit while the debentures remained so deposited.

(4) The re-issue of a debenture or the issue of another debenture in its place under the power which by this section is given to or deemed to be possessed by a company is to be treated as the issue of a new debenture for purposes of stamp duty; but it is not to be so treated for the purposes of any provision limiting the amount or number of debentures to be issued.

This applies whenever the issue or re-issue was made.

(5) A person lending money on the security of a debenture re-issued under this section which appears to be duly stamped may give the debenture in evidence in any proceedings for enforcing his security without payment of the stamp duty or any penalty in respect of it, unless he had notice (or, but for his negligence, might have discovered) that the debenture was not duly stamped; but in that case the company is liable to pay the proper stamp duty and penalty.

Contract to subscribe for debentures

195. A contract with a company to take up and pay for debentures of the company may be enforced by an order for specific performance.

Payment of debts out of assets subject to floating charge (England and Wales)

[1] **196.**—(1) The following applies in the case of a company registered in England and Wales, where debentures of the company are secured by a charge which, as created, was a floating charge.

(2) If possession is taken, by or on behalf of the holders of any of the debentures, of any property comprised in or subject to the charge, and the company is not at that time in course of being wound up, the company's preferential debts shall be paid out of assets coming to the hands of the person taking possession in priority to any claims for principal or interest in respect of the debentures.

(3) "Preferential debts" means the categories of debts listed in Schedule 6 to the Insolvency Act; and for the purposes of that Schedule "the relevant date" is the date of possession being taken as above mentioned.

(4) Payments made under this section shall be recouped, as far as may be, out of the assets of the company available for payment of general creditors.

NOTE
[1] As amended by the Insolvency Act 1985, Sched. 6, para. 15 and the Insolvency Act 1986, Sched. 13, Pt. I.

Debentures to bearer (Scotland)

197. Notwithstanding anything in the statute of the Scots Parliament of 1696, chapter 25, debentures to bearer issued in Scotland are valid and binding according to their terms.

[1] PART VI

DISCLOSURE OF INTERESTS IN SHARES

NOTE
[1] For interpretation of "public company", "private company" etc., see s. 1(3) and the Companies Consolidation (Consequential Provisions) Act 1985, s. 1.

Individual and group acquisitions

Obligation of disclosure: the cases in which it may arise and "the relevant time"

198.—(1) Where a person either—

(*a*) to his knowledge acquires an interest in shares comprised in a public company's relevant share capital, or ceases to be interested in shares so comprised (whether or not retaining an interest in other shares so comprised), or

(*b*) becomes aware that he has acquired an interest in shares so comprised or that he has ceased to be interested in shares so comprised in which he was previously interested,

then in certain circumstances he comes under an obligation ("the obligation of disclosure") to make notification to the company of the interests which he has, or had, in its shares.

(2) In relation to a public company, "relevant share capital" means the company's issued share capital of a class carrying rights to vote in all circumstances at general meetings of the company; and it is hereby declared for the avoidance of doubt that—

(*a*) where a company's share capital is divided into different classes of shares, references in this Part to a percentage of the nominal value of its relevant share capital are to a percentage of the nominal value of the issued shares comprised in each of the classes taken separately, and

(*b*) the temporary suspension of voting rights in respect of shares comprised in issued share capital of a company of any such class does not affect the application of this Part in relation to interests in those or any other shares comprised in that class.

(3) Where, otherwise than in circumstances within subsection (1), a person—

(*a*) is aware at the time when it occurs of any change of circumstances affecting facts relevant to the application of the next following section to an existing interest of his in shares comprised in a company's share capital of any description, or

(*b*) otherwise becomes aware of any such facts (whether or not arising from any such change of circumstances),

then in certain circumstances he comes under the obligation of disclosure.

(4) The existence of the obligation in a particular case depends (in part) on circumstances obtaining before and after whatever is in that case the relevant time; and that is—

(*a*) in a case within subsection (1)(*a*) or (3)(*a*), the time of the event or change of circumstances there mentioned, and

(*b*) in a case within subsection (1)(*b*) or (3)(*b*), the time at which the person became aware of the facts in question.

Interests to be disclosed

199.—(1) For purposes of the obligation of disclosure, the interests to be taken into account are those in relevant share capital of the company concerned.

[1] (2) A person has a notifiable interest at any time when he is interested in shares comprised in that share capital of an aggregate nominal value equal to or more than 3 per cent. of the nominal value of that share capital.

(3) All facts relevant to determining whether a person has a notifiable interest at any time (or the percentage level of his interest) are taken to be what he knows the facts to be at that time.

(4) The obligation of disclosure arises under section 198(1) or (3) where the person has a notifiable interest immediately after the relevant time, but did not have such an interest immediately before that time.

(5) The obligation also arises under section 198(1) where—

(*a*) the person had a notifiable interest immediately before the relevant time, but does not have such an interest immediately after it, or

(*b*) he had a notifiable interest immediately before that time, and has such an interest immediately after it, but the percentage levels of his interest immediately before and immediately after that time are not the same.

NOTE

[1] As amended by the Companies Act 1989, s. 134(2).

"Percentage level" in relation to notifiable interests

200.—(1) Subject to the qualification mentioned below, "percentage level", in section 199(5)(*b*), means the percentage figure found by expressing the aggregate nominal value of all the shares comprised in the share capital concerned in which the person is interested immediately before or (as the case may be) immediately after the relevant time as a percentage of the nominal value of that share capital and rounding that figure down, if it is not a whole number, to the next whole number.

(2) Where the nominal value of the share capital is greater immediately after the relevant time than it was immediately before, the percentage level of the person's interest immediately before (as well as immediately after) that time is determined by reference to the larger amount.

201. [Repealed by the Companies Act 1989, Sched. 24.]

Particulars to be contained in notification

[1] **202.**—(1) Where notification is required by section 198 with respect to a person's interest (if any) in shares comprised in relevant share capital of a public company, the obligation to make the notification must be performed within the period of 2 days next following the day on which that obligation arises; and the notification must be in writing to the company.

(2) The notification must specify the share capital to which it relates, and must also—

(*a*) state the number of shares comprised in that share capital in which the person making the notification knows he was interested immediately after the time when the obligation arose, or

(*b*) in a case where the person no longer has a notifiable interest in shares comprised in that share capital, state that he no longer has that interest.

(3) A notification with respect to a person's interest in a company's relevant share capital (other than one stating that he no longer has a notifiable interest in shares comprised in that share capital) shall include particulars of—

(*a*) the identity of each registered holder of shares to which the notification relates, and

(*b*) the number of those shares held by each such registered holder,

so far as known to the person making the notification at the date when the notification is made.

(4) A person who has an interest in shares comprised in a company's relevant share capital, that interest being notifiable, is under obligation to notify the company in writing—

(*a*) of any particulars in relation to those shares which are specified in subsection (3), and

(*b*) of any change in those particulars,

of which in either case he becomes aware at any time after any interest notification date and before the first occasion following that date on which he comes under any further obligation of disclosure with respect to his interest in shares comprised in that share capital.

An obligation arising under this subsection must be performed within the period of 2 days next following the day on which it arises.

(5) The reference in subsection (4) to an interest notification date, in relation to a person's interest in shares comprised in a public company's relevant share capital, is to either of the following—

(*a*) the date of any notification made by him with respect to his interest under this Part, and

(*b*) where he has failed to make a notification, the date on which the period allowed for making it came to an end.

(6) A person who at any time has an interest in shares which is notifiable is to be regarded under subsection (4) as continuing to have a notifiable interest in them unless and until he comes under obligation to make a notification stating that he no longer has such an interest in those shares.

NOTE
[1] As amended by the Companies Act 1989, s. 134(3), and Sched. 24. Subs. (3) substituted (*prosp.*) by *ibid.*, s. 134(4).

Notification of family and corporate interests

203.—(1) For purposes of sections 198 to 202, a person is taken to be interested in any shares in which his spouse or any infant child or step-child of his is interested; and "infant" means, in relation to Scotland, pupil or minor.

(2) For those purposes, a person is taken to be interested in shares if a body corporate is interested in them and—

   (*a*) that body or its directors are accustomed to act in accordance with his directions or instructions, or

   (*b*) he is entitled to exercise or control the exercise of one-third or more of the voting power at general meetings of that body corporate.

(3) Where a person is entitled to exercise or control the exercise of one-third or more of the voting power at general meetings of a body corporate and that body corporate is entitled to exercise or control the exercise of any of the voting power at general meetings of another body corporate ("the effective voting power") then, for purposes of subsection (2)(*b*), the effective voting power is taken as exercisable by that person.

(4) For purposes of subsections (2) and (3), a person is entitled to exercise or control the exercise of voting power if—

   (*a*) he has a right (whether subject to conditions or not) the exercise of which would make him so entitled, or

   (*b*) he is under an obligation (whether or not so subject) the fulfilment of which would make him so entitled.

Agreement to acquire interests in a particular company

204.—(1) In certain circumstances the obligation of disclosure may arise from an agreement between two or more persons which includes provision for the acquisition by any one or more of them of interests in shares of a particular public company ("the target company"), being shares comprised in the relevant share capital of that company.

(2) This section applies to such an agreement if—

   (*a*) the agreement also includes provisions imposing obligations or restrictions on any one or more of the parties to it with respect to their use, retention or disposal of their interests in that company's shares acquired in pursuance of the agreement (whether or not together with any other interests of theirs in the company's shares to which the agreement relates), and

   (*b*) any interest in the company's shares is in fact acquired by any of the parties in pursuance of the agreement;

and in relation to such an agreement references below in this section, and in sections 205 and 206, to the target company are to the company which is the target company for that agreement in accordance with this and the previous subsection.

(3) The reference in subsection (2)(*a*) to the use of interests in shares in the target company is to the exercise of any rights or of any control or influence arising from those interests (including the right to enter into any agreement for the exercise, or for control of the exercise, of any of those rights by another person).

(4) Once any interest in shares in the target company has been acquired in pursuance of such an agreement as is mentioned above, this section continues to apply to that agreement irrespective of—

   (*a*) whether or not any further acquisitions of interests in the company's shares take place in pursuance of the agreement, and

   (*b*) any change in the persons who are for the time being parties to it, and

   (*c*) any variation of the agreement,

so long as the agreement continues to include provisions of any description mentioned in subsection (2)(*a*).

References in this subsection to the agreement include any agreement having effect (whether directly or indirectly) in substitution for the original agreement.

(5) In this section, and also in references elsewhere in this Part to an agreement to which this section applies, "agreement" includes any agreement or arrangement; and references in this section to provisions of an agreement—

(a) accordingly include undertakings, expectations or understandings operative under any arrangement, and

(b) (without prejudice to the above) also include any provisions, whether express or implied and whether absolute or not.

(6) However, this section does not apply to an agreement which is not legally binding unless it involves mutuality in the undertakings, expectations or understandings of the parties to it; nor does the section apply to an agreement to underwrite or sub-underwrite any offer of shares in a company, provided the agreement is confined to that purpose and any matters incidental to it.

Obligation of disclosure arising under s. 204

205.—(1) In the case of an agreement to which section 204 applies, each party to the agreement is taken (for purposes of the obligation of disclosure) to be interested in all shares in the target company in which any other party to it is interested apart from the agreement (whether or not the interest of the other party in question was acquired, or includes any interest which was acquired, in pursuance of the agreement).

(2) For those purposes, and also for those of the next section, an interest of a party to such an agreement in shares in the target company is an interest apart from the agreement if he is interested in those shares otherwise than by virtue of the application of section 204 and this section in relation to the agreement.

(3) Accordingly, any such interest of the person (apart from the agreement) includes for those purposes any interest treated as his under section 203 or by the application of section 204 and this section in relation to any other agreement with respect to shares in the target company to which he is a party.

(4) A notification with respect to his interest in shares in the target company made to that company under this Part by a person who is for the time being a party to an agreement to which section 204 applies shall—

(a) state that the person making the notification is a party to such an agreement,

(b) include the names and (so far as known to him) the addresses of the other parties to the agreement, identifying them as such, and

(c) state whether or not any of the shares to which the notification relates are shares in which he is interested by virtue of section 204 and this section and, if so, the number of those shares.

(5) Where a person makes a notification to a company under this Part in consequence of ceasing to be interested in any shares of that company by virtue of the fact that he or any other person has ceased to be a party to an agreement to which section 204 applies, the notification shall include a statement that he or that other person has ceased to be a party to the agreement (as the case may require) and also (in the latter case) the name and (if known to him) the address of that other.

Obligation of persons acting together to keep each other informed

206.—(1) A person who is a party to an agreement to which section 204 applies is subject to the requirements of this section at any time when—

(a) the target company is a public company, and he knows it to be so, and

(b) the shares in that company to which the agreement relates consist of or include shares comprised in relevant share capital of the company, and he knows that to be the case; and

(c) he knows the facts which make the agreement one to which section 204 applies.

(2) Such a person is under obligation to notify every other party to the agreement, in writing, of the relevant particulars of his interest (if any) apart from the agreement in shares comprised in relevant share capital of the target company—

(a) on his first becoming subject to the requirements of this section, and

(b) on each occurrence after that time while he is still subject to those requirements of any event or circumstances within section 198(1) (as it applies to his case otherwise than by reference to interests treated as his under section 205 as applying to that agreement).

(3) The relevant particulars to be notified under subsection (2) are—

(a) the number of shares (if any) comprised in the target company's relevant share capital in which the person giving the notice would be required to state his interest if he were under the obligation of disclosure with respect to that interest (apart from the agreement) immediately after the time when the obligation to give notice under subsection (2) arose, and

(b) the relevant particulars with respect to the registered ownership of those shares, so far as known to him at the date of the notice.

(4) A person who is for the time being subject to the requirements of this section is also under obligation to notify every other party to the agreement, in writing—

(a) of any relevant particulars with respect to the registered ownership of any shares comprised in relevant share capital of the target company in which he is interested apart from the agreement, and

(b) of any change in those particulars,

of which in either case he becomes aware at any time after any interest notification date and before the first occasion following that date on which he becomes subject to any further obligation to give notice under subsection (2) with respect to his interest in shares comprised in that share capital.

(5) The reference in subsection (4) to an interest notification date, in relation to a person's interest in shares comprised in the target company's relevant share capital, is to either of the following—

(a) the date of any notice given by him with respect to his interest under subsection (2), and

(b) where he has failed to give that notice, the date on which the period allowed by this section for giving the notice came to an end.

(6) A person who is a party to an agreement to which section 204 applies is under an obligation to notify each other party to the agreement, in writing, of his current address—

(a) on his first becoming subject to the requirements of this section, and

(b) on any change in his address occurring after that time and while he is still subject to those requirements.

(7) A reference to the relevant particulars with respect to the registered ownership of shares is to such particulars in relation to those shares as are mentioned in section 202(3)(a) or (b).

[1] (8) A person's obligation to give any notice required by this section to any other person must be performed within the period of 2 days next following the day on which that obligation arose.

NOTE
[1] As amended by the Companies Act 1989, s. 134(3).

Interests in shares by attribution

207.—(1) Where section 198 or 199 refers to a person acquiring an interest in shares or ceasing to be interested in shares, that reference in certain cases includes his becoming or ceasing to be interested in those shares by virtue of another person's interest.

(2) Such is the case where he becomes or ceases to be interested by virtue of section 203 or (as the case may be) section 205 whether—

    (*a*) by virtue of the fact that the person who is interested in the shares becomes or ceases to be a person whose interests (if any) fall by virtue of either section to be treated as his, or

    (*b*) in consequence of the fact that such a person has become or ceased to be interested in the shares, or

    (*c*) in consequence of the fact that he himself becomes or ceases to be a party to an agreement to which section 204 applies to which the person interested in the shares is for the time being a party, or

    (*d*) in consequence of the fact that an agreement to which both he and that person are parties becomes or ceases to be one to which that section applies.

(3) The person is then to be treated as knowing he has acquired an interest in the shares or (as the case may be) that he has ceased to be interested in them, if and when he knows both—

    (*a*) the relevant facts with respect to the other person's interest in the shares, and

    (*b*) the relevant facts by virtue of which he himself has become or ceased to be interested in them in accordance with section 203 or 205.

(4) He has the knowledge referred to in subsection (3)(*a*) if he knows (whether contemporaneously or not) either of the subsistence of the other person's interest at any material time or of the fact that the other has become or ceased to be interested in the shares at any such time; and "material time" is any time at which the other's interests (if any) fall or fell to be treated as his under section 203 or 205.

(5) A person is to be regarded as knowing of the subsistence of another's interest in shares or (as the case may be) that another has become or ceased to be interested in shares if he has been notified under section 206 of facts with respect to the other's interest which indicate that he is or has become or ceased to be interested in the shares (whether on his own account or by virtue of a third party's interest in them).

Interests in shares which are to be notified

208.—(1) This section applies, subject to the section next following, in determining for purposes of sections 198 to 202 whether a person has a notifiable interest in shares.

(2) A reference to an interest in shares is to be read as including an interest of any kind whatsoever in the shares; and accordingly there are to be disregarded any restraints or restrictions to which the exercise of any right attached to the interest is or may be subject.

(3) Where property is held on trust and an interest in shares is comprised in the property, a beneficiary of the trust who apart from this subsection does not have an interest in the shares is to be taken as having such an interest.

(4) A person is taken to have an interest in shares if—

    (*a*) he enters into a contract for their purchase by him (whether for cash or other consideration), or

    (*b*) not being the registered holder, he is entitled to exercise any right conferred by the holding of the shares or is entitled to control the exercise of any such right.

(5) A person is taken to have an interest in shares if, otherwise than by virtue of having an interest under a trust—

    (*a*) he has a right to call for delivery of the shares to himself or to his order, or

(*b*) he has a right to acquire an interest in shares or is under an obligation to take an interest in shares,
whether in any case the right or obligation is conditional or absolute.

(6) For purposes of subsection (4)(*b*), a person is entitled to exercise or
control the exercise of any right conferred by the holding of shares if he—

(*a*) has a right (whether subject to conditions or not) the exercise of
which would make him so entitled, or
(*b*) is under an obligation (whether so subject or not) the fulfilment of
which would make him so entitled.

(7) Persons having a joint interest are taken each of them to have that
interest.

(8) It is immaterial that shares in which a person has an interest are
unidentifiable.

Interests to be disregarded

209.—(1) The following interests in shares are disregarded for purposes
of sections 198 to 202—

(*a*) where property is held on trust according to the law of England and
Wales and an interest in shares is comprised in that property, an
interest in reversion or remainder or of a bare trustee or a custodian
trustee, and any discretionary interest;
(*b*) where property is held on trust according to the law of Scotland and
an interest in shares is comprised in that property, an interest in fee
or of a simple trustee and any discretionary interest;
¹ (*c*) an interest which subsists by virtue of an authorised unit trust
scheme within the meaning of the Financial Services Act 1986, a
scheme made under section 22 of the Charities Act 1960, section 11
of the Trustee Investments Act 1961 or section 1 of the Administration of Justice Act 1965 or the scheme set out in the Schedule to the
Church Funds Investment Measure 1958;
(*d*) an interest of the Church of Scotland General Trustees or of the
Church of Scotland Trust in shares held by them or of any other person in shares held by those trustees or that trust otherwise than as
simple trustees;
(*e*) an interest for the life of himself or another of a person under a
settlement in the case of which the property comprised in the settlement consists of or includes shares, and the conditions mentioned in
subsection (3) below are satisfied;
(*f*) an exempt interest held by a recognised jobber or market maker;
(*g*) an exempt security interest;
(*h*) an interest of the President of the Family Division of the High Court
subsisting by virtue of section 9 of the Administration of Estates Act
1925;
(*i*) an interest of the Accountant General of the Supreme Court in
shares held by him;
(*j*) [Repealed by the Companies Act 1989, Sched. 24. See also *ibid*.,
s. 134(6).]

(2) A person is not by virtue of section 208(4)(*b*) taken to be interested
in shares by reason only that he has been appointed a proxy to vote at a
specified meeting of a company or of any class of its members and at any
adjournment of that meeting, or has been appointed by a corporation to
act as its representative at any meeting of a company or of any class of its
members.

(3) The conditions referred to in subsection (1)(*e*) are, in relation to a
settlement—

(*a*) that it is irrevocable, and
³ (*b*) that the settlor (within the meaning of section 670 of the Income and
Corporation Taxes Act 1988) has no interest in any income arising
under, or property comprised in, the settlement.

(4) A person is a recognised jobber for purposes of subsection (1)(*f*) if he is a member of The Stock Exchange recognised by the Council of The Stock Exchange as carrying on the business of a jobber; and an interest of such a person in shares is an exempt interest for those purposes if—

   (*a*) he carries on that business in the United Kingdom, and

   (*b*) he holds the interest for the purposes of that business.

⁴ (4A) A person is a market maker for the purposes of subsection (1)(*f*) if—

   (*a*) he holds himself out at all normal times in compliance with the rules of a recognised investment exchange other than an overseas investment exchange (within the meaning of the Financial Services Act 1986) as willing to buy and sell securities at prices specified by him; and

   (*b*) is recognised as doing so by that investment exchange;

and an interest of such a person in shares is an exempt interest if he carries on business as a market maker in the United Kingdom, is subject to such rules in the carrying on of that business and holds the interest for the purposes of that business.

(5) An interest in shares is an exempt security interest for purposes of subsection (1)(*g*) if—

⁵ (*a*) it is held by a person who is—

     (i) a banking company, or an insurance company to which Part II of the Insurance Companies Act 1982 applies, or

     (ii) a trustee savings bank (within the Trustee Savings Banks Act 1981), or

     (iii) a member of The Stock Exchange carrying on business in the United Kingdom as a stockbroker,

     and

   (*b*) it is held by way of security only for the purposes of a transaction entered into in the ordinary course of his business as such a person,

or if it is held by way of security only either by the Bank of England or by the Post Office for the purposes of a transaction entered into in the ordinary course of that part of the business of the Post Office which consists of the provision of banking services.

NOTES

  ¹ As amended by the Financial Services Act 1986, s.197 and Sched. 16, para. 18.

  ³ As amended by the Income and Corporation Taxes Act 1988, Sched. 29.

  ⁴ Inserted by the Financial Services Act 1986, s.197.

  ⁵ As amended by the Banking Act 1987, Sched. 6, para. 8, and the Companies Act 1989, s. 23 and Sched. 10, para. 2.

Other provisions about notification under this Part

210.—(1) Where a person authorises another ("the agent") to acquire or dispose of, on his behalf, interests in shares comprised in relevant share capital of a public company, he shall secure that the agent notifies him immediately of acquisitions or disposals effected by the agent which will or may give rise to any obligation of disclosure imposed on him by this Part with respect to his interest in that share capital.

(2) An obligation of disclosure imposed on a person by any provision of sections 198 to 202 is treated as not being fulfilled unless the notice by means of which it purports to be fulfilled identifies him and gives his address and, in a case where he is a director of the company, is expressed to be given in fulfilment of that obligation.

(3) A person who—

   (*a*) fails to fulfil, within the proper period, an obligation of disclosure imposed on him by this Part, or

   (*b*) in purported fulfilment of any such obligation makes to a company a statement which he knows to be false, or recklessly makes to a company a statement which is false, or (*c*) fails to fulfil, within the proper period, an obligation to give another person a notice required by section 206, or

(*d*) fails without reasonable excuse to comply with subsection (1) of this section.

is guilty of an offence and liable to imprisonment or a fine, or both.

(4) It is a defence for a person charged with an offence under subsection (3)(*c*) to prove that it was not possible for him to give the notice to the other person required by section 206 within the proper period, and either—

(*a*) that it has not since become possible for him to give the notice so required, or

(*b*) that he gave the notice as soon after the end of that period as it became possible for him to do so.

(5) Where a person is convicted of an offence under this section (other than an offence relating to his ceasing to be interested in a company's shares), the Secretary of State may by order direct that the shares in relation to which the offence was committed shall, until further order, be subject to the restrictions of Part XV of this Act; and such an order may be made notwithstanding any power in the company's memorandum or articles enabling the company to impose similar restrictions on those shares.

(6) Sections 732 (restriction on prosecutions) and 733(2) and (3) (liability of directors, etc.) apply to offences under this section.

Power to make further provision by regulations

¹ **210A.**—(1) The Secretary of State may by regulations amend—

(*a*) the definition of "relevant share capital" (section 198(2)),

(*b*) the percentage giving rise to a "notifiable interest" (section 199(2)),

(*c*) the periods within which an obligation of disclosure must be fulfilled or a notice must be given (sections 202(1) and (4) and 206(8)),

(*d*) the provisions as to what is taken to be an interest in shares (section 208) and what interests are to be disregarded (section 209), and

(*e*) the provisions as to company investigations (section 212);

and the regulations may amend, replace or repeal the provisions referred to above and make such other consequential amendments or repeals of provisions of this Part as appear to the Secretary of State to be appropriate.

(2) The regulations may in any case make different provision for different descriptions of company; and regulations under subsection (1)(*b*), (*c*) or (*d*) may make different provision for different descriptions of person, interest or share capital.

(3) The regulations may contain such transitional and other supplementary and incidental provisions as appear to the Secretary of State to be appropriate, and may in particular make provision as to the obligations of a person whose interest in a company's shares becomes or ceases to be notifiable by virtue of the regulations.

(4) Regulations under this section shall be made by statutory instrument.

[THE NEXT PAGE IS I 143]

(5) No regulations shall be made under this section unless a draft of the regulations has been laid before and approved by a resolution of each House of Parliament.

NOTE
[1] Inserted by the Companies Act 1989, s. 136(5).

Registration and investigation of share acquisitions and disposals

Register of interests in shares
211.—(1) Every public company shall keep a register for purposes of sections 198 to 202, and whenever the company receives information from a person in consequence of the fulfilment of an obligation imposed on him by any of those sections, it is under obligation to inscribe in the register, against that person's name, that information and the date of the inscription.

(2) Without prejudice to subsection (1), where a company receives a notification under this Part which includes a statement that the person making the notification, or any other person, has ceased to be a party to an agreement to which section 204 applies, the company is under obligation to record that information against the name of that person in every place where his name appears in the register as a party to that agreement (including any entry relating to him made against another person's name).

(3) An obligation imposed by subsection (1) or (2) must be fulfilled within the period of three days next following the day on which it arises.

(4) The company is not, by virtue of anything done for the purposes of this section, affected with notice of, or put upon enquiry as to, the rights of any person in relation to any shares.

(5) The register must be so made up that the entries against the several names entered in it appear in chronological order.

(6) Unless the register is in such form as to constitute in itself an index, the company shall keep an index of the names entered in the register which shall in respect of each name contain a sufficient indication to enable the information entered against it to be readily found; and the company shall, within 10 days after the date on which a name is entered in the register, make any necessary alteration in the index.

(7) If the company ceases to be a public company it shall continue to keep the register and any associated index until the end of the period of six years beginning with the day next following that on which it ceases to be such a company.

(8) The register and any associated index—
(a) shall be kept at the place at which the register required to be kept by the company by section 325 (register of directors' interests) is kept, and
(b) subject to the next subsection, shall be available for inspection in accordance with section 219 below.

[1] (9) Neither the register nor any associated index shall be available for inspection in accordance with that section in so far as it contains information with respect to a company for the time being entitled to avail itself of the benefit conferred by section 231(3) (disclosure of shareholdings not required if it would be harmful to company's business).

(10) If default is made in complying with subsection (1) or (2), or with any of subsections (5) to (7), the company and every officer of it who is in default is liable to a fine and, for continued contravention, to a daily default fine.

(11) Any register kept by a company immediately before 15th June 1982 under section 34 of the Companies Act 1967 shall continue to be kept by the company under and for the purposes of this section.

NOTE
[1] As amended by the Companies Act 1989, s. 23 and Sched. 10, para. 3.

Company investigations

212.—(1) A public company may by notice in writing require a person whom the company knows or has reasonable cause to believe to be or, at any time during the three years immediately preceding the date on which the notice is issued, to have been interested in shares comprised in the company's relevant share capital—

(a) to confirm that fact or (as the case may be) to indicate whether or not it is the case, and

(b) where he holds or has during that time held an interest in shares so comprised, to give such further information as may be required in accordance with the following subsection.

(2) A notice under this section may require the person to whom it is addressed—

(a) to give particulars of his own past or present interest in shares comprised in relevant share capital of the company (held by him at any time during the three-year period mentioned in subsection (1)),

(b) where the interest is a present interest and any other interest in the shares subsists or, in any case, where another interest in the shares subsisted during that three-year period at any time when his own interest subsisted, to give (so far as lies within his knowledge) such particulars with respect to that other interest as may be required by the notice,

(c) where his interest is a past interest, to give (so far as lies within his knowledge) particulars of the identity of the person who held that interest immediately upon his ceasing to hold it.

(3) The particulars referred to in subsection (2)(a) and (b) include particulars of the identity of persons interested in the shares in question and of whether persons interested in the same shares are or were parties to any agreement to which section 204 applies or to any agreement or arrangement relating to the exercise of any rights conferred by the holding of the shares.

(4) A notice under this section shall require any information given in response to the notice to be given in writing within such reasonable time as may be specified in the notice.

(5) Sections 203 to 205 and 208 apply for the purpose of construing references in this section to persons interested in shares and to interests in shares respectively, as they apply in relation to sections 198 to 201 (but with the omission of any reference to section 209).

(6) This section applies in relation to a person who has or previously had, or is or was entitled to acquire, a right to subscribe for shares in a public company which would on issue be comprised in relevant share capital of that company as it applies in relation to a person who is or was interested in shares so comprised; and references above in this section to an interest in shares so comprised and to shares so comprised are to be read accordingly in any such case as including respectively any such right and shares which would on issue be so comprised.

Registration of interests disclosed under s. 212

213.—(1) Whenever in pursuance of a requirement imposed on a person under section 212 a company receives information to which this section applies relating to shares comprised in its relevant share capital, it is under obligation to enter against the name of the registered holder of those shares, in a separate part of its register of interests in shares—

(a) the fact that the requirement was imposed and the date on which it was imposed, and

(b) any information to which this section applies received in pursuance of the requirement.

(2) This section applies to any information received in pursuance of a requirement imposed by section 212 which relates to the present interests

held by any persons in shares comprised in relevant share capital of the company in question.

(3) Subsections (3) to (10) of section 211 apply in relation to any part of the register maintained in accordance with subsection (1) of this section as they apply in relation to the remainder of the register, reading references to subsection (1) of that section to include subsection (1) of this.

(4) In the case of a register kept by a company immediately before 15th June 1982 under section 34 of the Companies Act 1967, any part of the register so kept for the purposes of section 27 of the Companies Act 1976 shall continue to be kept by the company under and for the purposes of this section.

Company investigation on requisition by members

214.—(1) A company may be required to exercise its powers under section 212 on the requisition of members of the company holding at the date of the deposit of the requisition not less than one-tenth of such of the paid-up capital of the company as carries at that date the right of voting at general meetings of the company.

(2) The requisition must—
  (a) state that the requisitionists are requiring the company to exercise its powers under section 212,
  (b) specify the manner in which they require those powers to be exercised, and
  (c) give reasonable grounds for requiring the company to exercise those powers in the manner specified,
and must be signed by the requisitionists and deposited at the company's resitered office.

(3) The requisition may consist of several documents in like form each signed by one or more requisitionists.

(4) On the deposit of a requisition complying with this section it is the company's duty to exercise its powers under section 212 in the manner specified in the requisition.

(5) If default is made in complying with subsection (4), the company and every officer of it who is in default is liable to a fine.

Company report to members

215.—(1) On the conclusion of an investigation carried out by a company in pursuance of a requisition under section 214, it is the company's duty to cause a report of the information received in pursuance of that investigation to be prepared, and the report shall be made available at the company's registered office within a reasonable period after the conclusion of that investigation.

(2) Where—
  (a) a company undertakes an investigation in pursuance of a requisition under section 214, and
  (b) the investigation is not concluded before the end of three months beginning with the date immediately following the date of the deposit of the requisition,
it is the duty of the company to cause to be prepared, in respect of that period and each successive period of three months ending before the conclusion of the investigation, an interim report of the information received during that period in pursuance of the investigation. Each such report shall be made available at the company's registered office within a reasonable period after the end of the period to which it relates.

(3) The period for making any report prepared under this section available as required by subsection (1) or (2) shall not exceed 15 days.

[1] (4) Such a report shall not include any information with respect to a company entitled to avail itself of the benefit conferred by section 231(3) (disclosure of shareholdings not required if it would be harmful

to company's business); but where any such information is omitted, that fact shall be stated in the report.

(5) The company shall, within three days of making any report prepared under this section available at its registered office, notify the requisitionists that the report is so available.

(6) An investigation carried out by a company in pursuance of a requisition under section 214 is regarded for purposes of this section as concluded when the company has made all such inquiries as are necessary or expedient for the purposes of the requisition and in the case of each such inquiry, either a response has been received by the company or the time allowed for a response has elapsed.

(7) A report prepared under this section—

(a) shall be kept at the company's registered office from the day on which it is first available there in accordance with subsection (1) or (2) until the expiration of six years beginning with the day next following that day, and

(b) shall be available for inspection in accordance with section 219 below so long as it is so kept.

(8) If default is made in complying with subsection (1), (2), (5) or (7)(a), the company and every officer of it who is in default is liable to a fine.

NOTE
[1] As amended by the Companies Act 1989, s. 23 and Sched. 10, para. 3.

Penalty for failure to provide information

216.—(1) Where notice is served by a company under section 212 on a person who is or was interested in shares of the company and that person fails to give the company any information required by the notice within the time specified in it, the company may apply to the court for an order directing that the shares in question be subject to the restrictions of Part XV of this Act.

(2) Such an order may be made by the court notwithstanding any power contained in the applicant company's memorandum or articles enabling the company itself to impose similar restrictions on the shares in question.

(3) Subject to the following subsections, a person who fails to comply with a notice under section 212 or who, in purported compliance with such a notice, makes any statement which he knows to be false in a material particular or recklessly makes any statement which is false in a material particular is guilty of an offence and liable to imprisonment or a fine, or both.

Section 733(2) and (3) of this Act (liability of individuals for corporate default) apply to offences under this subsection.

(4) A person is not guilty of an offence by virtue of failing to comply with a notice under section 212 if he proves that the requirement to give the information was frivolous or vexatious.

(5) A person is not obliged to comply with a notice under section 212 if he is for the time being exempted by the Secretary of State from the operation of that section; but the Secretary of State shall not grant any such exemption unless—

(a) he had consulted with the Governor of the Bank of England, and

(b) he (the Secretary of State) is satisfied that, having regard to any undertaking given by the person in question with respect to any interest held or to be held by him in any shares, there are special reasons why that person should not be subject to the obligations imposed by that section.

Removal of entries from register

217.—(1) A company may remove an entry against a person's name from its register of interests in shares if more than six years have elapsed since the date of the entry being made, and either—

(a) that entry recorded the fact that the person in question had ceased

to have an interest notifiable under this Part in relevant share capital
of the company, or

(*b*) it has been superseded by a later entry made under section 211
against the same person's name;

and in a case within paragraph (*a*) the company may also remove that person's name from the register.

(2) If a person in pursuance of an obligation imposed on him by any provision of this Part gives to a company the name and address of another person as being interested in shares in the company, the company shall, within 15 days of the date on which it was given that information, notify the other person that he has been so named and shall include in that notification—

(*a*) particulars of any entry relating to him made, in consequence of its
being given that information, by the company in its register of interests in shares, and

(*b*) a statement informing him of his right to apply to have the entry
removed in accordance with the following provisions of this section.

(3) A person who has been notified by a company in pursuance of subsection (2) that an entry relating to him has been made in the company's register of interests in shares may apply in writing to the company for the removal of that entry from the register; and the company shall remove the entry if satisfied that the information in pursuance of which the entry was made was incorrect.

(4) If a person who is identified in a company's register of interests in shares as being a party to an agreement to which section 204 applies (whether by an entry against his own name or by an entry relating to him made against another person's name as mentioned in subsection (2)(*a*)) ceases to be a party to that agreement, he may apply in writing to the company for the inclusion of that information in the register; and if the company is satisfied that he has ceased to be a party to the agreement, it shall record that information (if not already recorded) in every place where his name appears as a party to that agreement in the register.

(5) If an application under subsection (3) or (4) is refused (in a case within subsection (4), otherwise than on the ground that the information has already been recorded) the applicant may apply to the court for an order directing the company to remove the entry in question from the register or (as the case may be) to include the information in question in the register; and the court may, if it thinks fit, make such an order.

(6) Where a name is removed from a company's register of interests in shares in pursuance of subsection (1) or (3) or an order under subsection (5), the company shall within 14 days of the date of that removal make any necessary alteration in any associated index.

(7) If default is made in complying with subsection (2) or (6), the company and every officer of it who is in default is liable to a fine and, for continued contravention, to a daily default fine.

Otherwise, entries not to be removed

218.—(1) Entries in a company's register of interests in shares shall not be deleted except in accordance with section 217.

(2) If an entry is deleted from a company's register of interests in shares in contravention of subsection (1), the company shall restore that entry to the register as soon as is reasonably practicable.

(3) If default is made in complying with subsection (1) or (2), the company and every officer of it who is in default is liable to a fine and, for continued contravention of subsection (2), to a daily default fine.

Inspection of register and reports

219.—(1) Any register of interests in shares and any report which is required by section 215(7) to be available for inspection in accordance with this section shall, during business hours (subject to such reasonable restrictions as the company may in general meeting impose, but so that not less than two hours in each day are allowed for inspection) be open to the inspection of any member of the company or of any other person without charge.

(2) Any such member or other person may require a copy of any such register or report, or any part of it, on payment of 10 pence or such less sum as the company may prescribe, for every 100 words or fractional part of 100 words required to be copied; and the company shall cause any copy so required by a person to be sent to him before the expiration of the period of 10 days beginning with the day next following that on which the requirement is received by the company.

(3) If an inspection required under this section is refused or a copy so required is not sent within the proper period, the company and every officer of it who is in default is liable to a fine and, for continued contravention, to a daily default fine.

(4) In the case of a refusal of an inspection required under this section of any register or report, the court may by order compel an immediate inspection of it; and in the case of failure to send a copy required under this section, the court may by order direct that the copy required shall be sent to the person requiring it.

(5) The Secretary of State may by regulations made by statutory instrument substitute a sum specified in the regulations for the sum for the time being mentioned in subsection (2).

Supplementary

Definitions for Part VI

220.—(1) In this Part of this Act—

"associated index", in relation to a register, means the index kept in relation to that register in pursuance of section 211(6),

"register of interests in shares" means the register kept in pursuance of section 211 including, except where the context otherwise requires, that part of the register kept in pursuance of section 213, and

"relevant share capital" has the meaning given by section 198(2).

(2) Where the period allowed by any provision of this Part for fulfilling an obligation is expressed as a number of days, any day that is a Saturday or Sunday or a bank holiday in any part of Great Britain is to be disregarded in reckoning that period.

[1] PART VII

ACCOUNTS AND AUDIT

NOTE
[1] For interpretation of "public company", "private company" etc., see s. 1(3) and the Companies Consolidation (Consequential Provisions) Act 1985, s. 1.

[1] CHAPTER I
PROVISIONS APPLYING TO COMPANIES GENERALLY

NOTE
[1] Ss. 221–244 inclusive substituted by the Companies Act 1989, ss. 1–11.

Accounting records

Duty to keep accounting records

221.—(1) Every company shall keep accounting records which are sufficient to show and explain the company's transactions and are such as to—

    (*a*) disclose with reasonable accuracy, at any time, the financial position of the company at that time, and (*b*) enable the directors to ensure that any balance sheet and profit and loss account prepared under this Part complies with the requirements of this Act.

(2) The accounting records shall in particular contain—

   (*a*) entries from day to day of all sums of money received and expended by the company, and the matters in respect of which the receipt and expenditure takes place, and

   (*b*) a record of the assets and liabilities of the company.

(3) If the company's business involves dealing in goods, the accounting records shall contain—

   (*a*) statements of stock held by the company at the end of each financial year of the company,

   (*b*) all statements of stocktakings from which any such statement of stock as is mentioned in paragraph (*a*) has been or is to be prepared, and

   (*c*) except in the case of goods sold by way of ordinary retail trade, statements of all goods sold and purchased, showing the goods and the buyers and sellers in sufficient detail to enable all these to be identified.

(4) A parent company which has a subsidiary undertaking in relation to which the above requirements do not apply shall take reasonable steps to secure that the undertaking keeps such accounting records as to enable the directors of the parent company to ensure that any balance sheet and profit and loss account prepared under this Part complies with the requirements of this Act.

(5) If a company fails to comply with any provision of this section, every officer of the company who is in default is guilty of an offence unless he shows that he acted honestly and that in the circumstances in which the company's business was carried on the default was excusable.

(6) A person guilty of an offence under this section is liable to imprisonment or a fine, or both.

Where and for how long records to be kept

222.—(1) A company's accounting records shall be kept at its registered office or such other place as the directors think fit, and shall at all times be open to inspection by the company's officers.

(2) If accounting records are kept at a place outside Great Britain, accounts and returns with respect to the business dealt with in the accounting records so kept shall be sent to, and kept at, a place in Great Britain, and shall at all times be open to such inspection.

(3) The accounts and returns to be sent to Great Britain shall be such as to—

   (*a*) disclose with reasonable accuracy the financial position of the business in question at intervals of not more than six months, and

   (*b*) enable the directors to ensure that the company's balance sheet and profit and loss account comply with the requirements of this Act.

(4) If a company fails to comply with any provision of subsections (1) to (3), every officer of the company who is in default is guilty of an offence, and liable to imprisonment or a fine or both, unless he shows that he acted honestly and that in the circumstances in which the company's business was carried on the default was excusable.

(5) Accounting records which a company is required by section 221 to keep shall be preserved by it—

   (*a*) in the case of a private company, for three years from the date on which they are made, and

   (*b*) in the case of a public company, for six years from the date on which they are made.

This is subject to any provision contained in rules made under section 411 of the Insolvency Act 1986 (company insolvency rules).

(6) An officer of a company is guilty of an offence, and liable to imprisonment or a fine or both, if he fails to take all reasonable steps for securing compliance by the company with subsection (5) or intentionally causes any default by the company under that subsection.

A company's financial year and accounting reference periods

A company's financial year

223.—(1) A company's "financial year" is determined as follows.

(2) Its first financial year begins with the first day of its first accounting reference period and ends with the last day of that period or such other date, not more than seven days before or after the end of that period, as the directors may determine.

(3) Subsequent financial years begin with the day immediately following the end of the company's previous financial year and end with the last day of its next accounting reference period or such other date, not more than seven days before or after the end of that period, as the directors may determine.

(4) In relation to an undertaking which is not a company, references in this Act to its financial year are to any period in respect of which a profit and loss account of the undertaking is required to be made up (by its constitution or by the law under which it is established), whether that period is a year or not.

(5) The directors of a parent company shall secure that, except where in their opinion there are good reasons against it, the financial year of each of its subsidiary undertakings coincides with the company's own financial year.

Accounting reference periods and accounting reference date

224.—(1) A company's accounting reference periods are determined according to its accounting reference date.

(2) A company may, at any time before the end of the period of nine months beginning with the date of its incorporation, by notice in the prescribed form given to the registrar specify its accounting reference date, that is, the date on which its accounting reference period ends in each calendar year.

[1] (3) Failing such notice, a company's accounting reference date is—

(*a*) in the case of a company incorporated before 1st April 1990;

(*b*) in the case of a company incorporated after 1st April 1990, the last day of the month in which the anniversary of its incorporation falls.

(4) A company's first accounting reference period is the period of more than six months, but not more than 18 months, beginning with the date of its incorporation and ending with its accounting reference date.

(5) Its subsequent accounting reference periods are successive periods of 12 months beginning immediately after the end of the previous accounting reference period and ending with its accounting reference date.

(6) This section has effect subject to the provisions of section 225 relating to the alteration of accounting reference dates and the consequences of such alteration.

NOTE

[1] As amended by S.I. 1990 No. 355, art. 15.

Alteration of accounting reference date

225.—(1) A company may by notice in the prescribed form given to the registrar specify a new accounting reference date having effect in relation to the company's current accounting reference period and subsequent periods.

(2) A company may by notice in the prescribed form given to the registrar specify a new accounting reference date having effect in relation to the company's previous accounting reference period and subsequent periods if—

(*a*) the company is a subsidiary undertaking or parent undertaking of another company and the new accounting reference date coincides with the accounting reference date of that other company, or (*b*) an administration order under Part II of the Insolvency Act 1986 is in force.

A company's "previous accounting reference period" means that immediately preceding its current accounting reference period.

(3) The notice shall state whether the current or previous accounting reference period—

(*a*) is to be shortened, so as to come to an end on the first occasion on which the new accounting reference date falls or fell after the beginning of the period, or

(*b*) is to be extended, so as to come to an end on the second occasion on which that date falls or fell after the beginning of the period.

(4) A notice under subsection (1) stating that the current accounting reference period is to be extended is ineffective, except as mentioned below, if given less than five years after the end of an earlier accounting reference period of the company which was extended by virtue of this section.

This subsection does not apply—

(*a*) to a notice given by a company which is a subsidiary undertaking or parent undertaking of another company and the new accounting reference date coincides with that of the other company, or

(*b*) where an administration order is in force under Part II of the Insolvency Act 1986,

or where the Secretary of State directs that it should not apply, which he may do with respect to a notice which has been given or which may be given.

(5) A notice under subsection (2)(*a*) may not be given if the period allowed for laying and delivering accounts and reports in relation to the previous accounting reference period has already expired.

(6) An accounting reference period may not in any case, unless an administration order is in force under Part II of the Insolvency Act 1986, be extended so as to exceed 18 months and a notice under this section is ineffective if the current or previous accounting reference period as extended in accordance with the notice would exceed that limit.

Annual accounts

Duty to prepare individual company accounts

226.—(1) The directors of every company shall prepare for each financial year of the company—

(*a*) a balance sheet as at the last day of the year, and

(*b*) a profit and loss account.

Those accounts are referred to in this Part as the company's "individual accounts."

(2) The balance sheet shall give a true and fair view of the state of affairs of the company as at the end of the financial year; and the profit and loss account shall give a true and fair view of the profit or loss of the company for the financial year.

(3) A company's individual accounts shall comply with the provisions of Schedule 4 as to the form and content of the balance sheet and profit and loss account and additional information to be provided by way of notes to the accounts.

(4) Where compliance with the provisions of that Schedule, and the other provisions of this Act as to the matters to be included in a company's individual accounts or in notes to those accounts, would not be sufficient to give a true and fair view, the necessary additional information shall be given in the accounts or in a note to them.

(5) If in special circumstances compliance with any of those provisions is inconsistent with the requirement to give a true and fair view, the directors shall depart from that provision to the extent necessary to give a true and fair view.

Particulars of any such departure, the reasons for it and its effect shall be given in a note to the accounts.

Duty to prepare group accounts

227.—(1) If at the end of a financial year a company is a parent company the directors shall, as well as preparing individual accounts for the year, prepare group accounts.

(2) Group accounts shall be consolidated accounts comprising—

(*a*) a consolidated balance sheet dealing with the state of affairs of the parent company and its subsidiary undertakings, and

(*b*) a consolidated profit and loss account dealing with the profit or loss of the parent company and its subsidiary undertakings.

(3) The accounts shall give a true and fair view of the state of affairs as at the end of the financial year, and the profit or loss for the financial year, of the undertakings included in the consolidation as a whole, so far as concerns members of the company.

(4) A company's group accounts shall comply with the provisions of Schedule 4A as to the form and content of the consolidated balance sheet and consolidated profit and loss account and additional information to be provided by way of notes to the accounts.

(5) Where compliance with the provisions of that Schedule, and the other provisions of this Act, as to the matters to be included in a company's group accounts or in notes to those accounts, would not be sufficient to give a true and fair view, the necessary additional information shall be given in the accounts or in a note to them.

(6) If in special circumstances compliance with any of those provisions is inconsistent with the requirement to give a true and fair view, the directors shall depart from that provision to the extent necessary to give a true and fair view.

Particulars of any such departure, the reasons for it and its effect shall be given in a note to the accounts.

Exemption for parent companies included in accounts of larger group

228.—(1) A company is exempt from the requirement to prepare group accounts if it is itself a subsidiary undertaking and its immediate parent undertaking is established under the law of a member State of the European Economic Community, in the following cases—

(*a*) where the company is a wholly-owned subsidiary of that parent undertaking;

(*b*) where that parent undertaking holds more than 50 per cent. of the shares in the company and notice requesting the preparation of group accounts has not been served on the company by shareholders holding in aggregate—

(i) more than half of the remaining shares in the company, or

(ii) 5 per cent. of the total shares in the company.

Such notice must be served not later than six months after the end of the financial year before that to which it relates.

(2) Exemption is conditional upon compliance with all of the following conditions—

(*a*) that the company is included in consolidated accounts for a larger group drawn up to the same date, or to an earlier date in the same financial year, by a parent undertaking established under the law of a member State of the European Economic Community;

(*b*) that those accounts are drawn up and audited, and that parent undertaking's annual report is drawn up, according to that law, in accordance with the provisions of the Seventh Directive (83/349/EEC);

(*c*) that the company discloses in its individual accounts that it is exempt from the obligation to prepare and deliver group accounts;

(*d*) that the company states in its individual accounts the name of the parent undertaking which draws up the group accounts referred to above and—
  (i) if it is incorporated outside Great Britain, the country in which it is incorporated,
  (ii) if it is incorporated in Great Britain, whether it is registered in England and Wales or in Scotland, and
  (iii) if it is unincorporated, the address of its principal place of business;
(*e*) that the company delivers to the registrar, within the period allowed for delivering its individual accounts, copies of those group accounts and of the parent undertaking's annual report, together with the auditors' report on them; and
(*f*) that if any document comprised in accounts and reports delivered in accordance with paragraph (*e*) is in a language other than English, there is annexed to the copy of that document delivered a translation of it into English, certified in the prescribed manner to be a correct translation.

(3) The exemption does not apply to a company any of whose securities are listed on a stock exchange in any member State of the European Economic Community.

(4) Shares held by directors of a company for the purpose of complying with any share qualification requirement shall be disregarded in determining for the purposes of subsection (1)(*a*) whether the company is a wholly-owned subsidiary.

(5) For the purposes of subsection (1)(*b*) shares held by a wholly-owned subsidiary of the parent undertaking, or held on behalf of the parent undertaking or a wholly-owned subsidiary, shall be attributed to the parent undertaking.

(6) In subsection (3) "securities" includes—
(*a*) shares and stock,
(*b*) debentures, including debenture stock, loan stock, bonds, certificates of deposit and other instruments creating or acknowledging indebtedness,
(*c*) warrants or other instruments entitling the holder to subscribe for securities falling within paragraph (*a*) or (*b*), and
(*d*) certificates or other instruments which confer—
  (i) property rights in respect of a security falling within paragraph (*a*), (*b*) or (*c*),
  (ii) any right to acquire, dispose of, underwrite or convert a security, being a right to which the holder would be entitled if he held any such security to which the certificate or other instrument relates, or
  (iii) a contractual right (other than an option) to acquire any such security otherwise than by subscription.

Subsidiary undertakings included in the consolidation
229.—(1) Subject to the exceptions authorised or required by this section, all the subsidiary undertakings of the parent company shall be included in the consolidation.

(2) A subsidiary undertaking may be excluded from consolidation if its inclusion is not material for the purpose of giving a true and fair view; but two or more undertakings may be excluded only if they are not material taken together.

(3) In addition, a subsidiary undertaking may be excluded from consolidation where—
(*a*) severe long-term restrictions substantially hinder the exercise of the rights of the parent company over the assets or management of that undertaking, or

(*b*) the information necessary for the preparation of group accounts cannot be obtained without disproportionate expense or undue delay, or

(*c*) the interest of the parent company is held exclusively with a view to subsequent resale and the undertaking has not previously been included in consolidated group accounts prepared by the parent company.

The reference in paragraph (*a*) to the rights of the parent company and the reference in paragraph (*c*) to the interest of the parent company are, respectively, to rights and interests held by or attributed to the company for the purposes of section 258 (definition of "parent undertaking") in the absence of which it would not be the parent company.

(4) Where the activities of one or more subsidiary undertakings are so different from those of other undertakings to be included in the consolidation that their inclusion would be incompatible with the obligation to give a true and fair view, those undertakings shall be excluded from consolidation.

This subsection does not apply merely because some of the undertakings are industrial, some commercial and some provide services, or because they carry on industrial or commercial activities involving different products or provide different services.

(5) Where all the subsidiary undertakings of a parent company fall within the above exclusions, no group accounts are required.

Treatment of individual profit and loss account where group accounts prepared
230.—(1) The following provisions apply with respect to the individual profit and loss account of a parent company where—

(*a*) the company is required to prepare and does prepare group accounts in accordance with this Act, and

(*b*) the notes to the company's individual balance sheet show the company's profit or loss for the financial year determined in accordance with this Act.

(2) The profit and loss account need not contain the information specified in paragraphs 52 to 57 of Schedule 4 (information supplementing the profit and loss account).

(3) The profit and loss account must be approved in accordance with section 233(1) (approval by board of directors) but may be omitted from the company's annual accounts for the purposes of the other provisions below in this Chapter.

(4) The exemption conferred by this section is conditional upon its being disclosed in the company's annual accounts that the exemption applies.

Disclosure required in notes to accounts: related undertakings
231.—(1) The information specified in Schedule 5 shall be given in notes to a company's annual accounts.

(2) Where the company is not required to prepare group accounts, the information specified in Part I of that Schedule shall be given; and where the company is required to prepare group accounts, the information specified in Part II of that Schedule shall be given.

(3) The information required by Schedule 5 need not be disclosed with respect to an undertaking which—

(*a*) is established under the law of a country outside the United Kingdom, or

(*b*) carries on business outside the United Kingdom,

if in the opinion of the directors of the company the disclosure would be seriously prejudicial to the business of that undertaking, or to the business of the company or any of its subsidiary undertakings, and the Secretary of State agrees that the information need not be disclosed.

This subsection does not apply in relation to the information required under paragraph 5(2), 6 or 20 of that Schedule.

(4) Where advantage is taken of subsection (3), that fact shall be stated in a note to the company's annual accounts.

(5) If the directors of the company are of the opinion that the number of undertakings in respect of which the company is required to disclose information under any provision of Schedule 5 to this Act is such that compliance with that provision would result in information of excessive length being given, the information need only be given in respect of—

(*a*) the undertakings whose results or financial position, in the opinion of the directors, principally affected the figures shown in the company's annual accounts, and

(*b*) undertakings excluded from consolidation under section 229(3) or (4).

This subsection does not apply in relation to the information required under paragraph 10 or 29 of that Schedule.

(6) If advantage is taken of subsection (5)—

(*a*) there shall be included in the notes to the company's annual accounts a statement that the information is given only with respect to such undertakings as are mentioned in that subsection, and

(*b*) the full information (both that which is disclosed in the notes to the accounts and that which is not) shall be annexed to the company's next annual return.

For this purpose the "next annual return" means that next delivered to the registrar after the accounts in question have been approved under section 233.

(7) If a company fails to comply with subsection (6)(*b*), the company and every officer of it who is in default is liable to a fine and, for continued contravention, to a daily default fine.

Disclosure required in notes to accounts: emoluments and other benefits of directors and others

232.—(1) The information specified in Schedule 6 shall be given in notes to a company's annual accounts.

(2) In that Schedule—

Part I relates to the emoluments of directors (including emoluments waived), pensions of directors and past directors, compensation for loss of office to directors and past directors and sums paid to third parties in respect of directors' services,

Part II relates to loans, quasi-loans and other dealings in favour of directors and connected persons, and

Part III relates to transactions, arrangements and agreements made by the company or a subsidiary undertaking for officers of the company other than directors.

(3) It is the duty of any director of a company, and any person who is or has at any time in the preceding five years been an officer of the company, to give notice to the company of such matters relating to himself as may be necessary for the purposes of Part I of Schedule 6.

(4) A person who makes default in complying with subsection (3) commits an offence and is liable to a fine.

Approval and signing of accounts

Approval and signing of accounts

233.—(1) A company's annual accounts shall be approved by the board of directors and signed on behalf of the board by a director of the company.

(2) The signature shall be on the company's balance sheet.

(3) Every copy of the balance sheet which is laid before the company in general meeting, or which is otherwise circulated, published or issued,

shall state the name of the person who signed the balance sheet on behalf of the board.

(4) The copy of the company's balance sheet which is delivered to the registrar shall be signed on behalf of the board by a director of the company.

(5) [Not yet in force.]

(6) If a copy of the balance sheet—

(*a*) is laid before the company, or otherwise circulated, published or issued, without the balance sheet having been signed as required by this section or without the required statement of the signatory's name being included, or

(*b*) is delivered to the registrar without being signed as required by this section,

the company and every officer of it who is in default is guilty of an offence and liable to a fine.

Directors' report

Duty to prepare directors' report

234.—(1) The directors of a company shall for each financial year prepare a report—

(*a*) containing a fair review of the development of the business of the company and its subsidiary undertakings during the financial year and of their position at the end of it, and

(*b*) stating the amount (if any) which they recommend should be paid as dividend and the amount (if any) which they propose to carry to reserves.

(2) The report shall state the names of the persons who, at any time during the financial year, were directors of the company, and the principal activities of the company and its subsidiary undertakings in the course of the year and any significant change in those activities in the year.

(3) The report shall also comply with Schedule 7 as regards the disclosure of the matters mentioned there.

(4) In Schedule 7—

Part I relates to matters of a general nature, including changes in asset values, directors' shareholdings and other interests and contributions for political and charitable purposes,

Part II relates to the acquisition by a company of its own shares or a charge on them,

Part III relates to the employment, training and advancement of disabled persons,

Part IV relates to the health, safety and welfare at work of the company's employees, and

Part V relates to the involvement of employees in the affairs, policy and performance of the company.

(5) In the case of any failure to comply with the provisions of this Part as to the preparation of a directors' report and the contents of the report, every person who was a director of the company immediately before the end of the period for laying and delivering accounts and reports for the financial year in question is guilty of an offence and liable to a fine.

(6) In proceedings against a person for an offence under this section it is a defence for him to prove that he took all reasonable steps for securing compliance with the requirements in question.

Approval and signing of directors' report

234A.—(1) The directors' report shall be approved by the board of directors and signed on behalf of the board by a director or the secretary of the company.

(2) Every copy of the directors' report which is laid before the company in general meeting, or which is otherwise circulated, published or issued, shall state the name of the person who signed it on behalf of the board.

(3) The copy of the directors' report which is delivered to the registrar shall be signed on behalf of the board by a director or the secretary of the company.

(4) If a copy of the directors' report—

(a) is laid before the company, or otherwise circulated, published or issued, without the report having been signed as required by this section or without the required statement of the signatory's name being included, or

(b) is delivered to the registrar without being signed as required by this section,

the company and every officer of it who is in default is guilty of an offence and liable to a fine.

Auditors' report

Auditors' report

235.—(1) A company's auditors shall make a report to the company's members on all annual accounts of the company of which copies are to be laid before the company in general meeting during their tenure of office.

(2) The auditors' report shall state whether in the auditors' opinion the annual accounts have been properly prepared in accordance with this Act, and in particular whether a true and fair view is given—

(a) in the case of an individual balance sheet, of the state of affairs of the company as at the end of the financial year,

(b) in the case of an individual profit and loss account, of the profit or loss of the company for the financial year,

(c) in the case of group accounts, of the state of affairs as at the end of the financial year, and the profit or loss for the financial year, of the undertakings included in the consolidation as a whole, so far as concerns members of the company.

(3) The auditors shall consider whether the information given in the directors' report for the financial year for which the annual accounts are prepared is consistent with those accounts; and if they are of opinion that it is not they shall state that fact in their report.

Signature of auditors' report

236.—(1) The auditors' report shall state the names of the auditors and be signed by them.

(2) Every copy of the auditors' report which is laid before the company in general meeting, or which is otherwise circulated, published or issued, shall state the names of the auditors.

(3) The copy of the auditors' report which is delivered to the registrar shall state the names of the auditors and be signed by them.

(4) If a copy of the auditors' report—

(a) is laid before the company, or otherwise circulated, published or issued, without the required statement of the auditors' names, or

(b) is delivered to the registrar without the required statement of the auditors' names or without being signed as required by this section,

the company and every officer of it who is in default is guilty of an offence and liable to a fine.

(5) References in this section to signature by the auditors are, where the office of auditor is held by a body corporate or partnership, to signature in the name of the body corporate or partnership by a person authorised to sign on its behalf.

Duties of auditors

237.—(1) A company's auditors shall, in preparing their report, carry out such investigations as will enable them to form an opinion as to—

(*a*) whether proper accounting records have been kept by the company and proper returns adequate for their audit have been received from branches not visited by them, and

(*b*) whether the company's individual accounts are in agreement with the accounting records and returns.

(2) If the auditors are of opinion that proper accounting records have not been kept, or that proper returns adequate for their audit have not been received from branches not visited by them, or if the company's individual accounts are not in agreement with the accounting records and returns, the auditors shall state that fact in their report.

(3) If the auditors fail to obtain all the information and explanations which, to the best of their knowledge and belief, are necessary for the purposes of their audit, they shall state that fact in their report.

(4) If the requirements of Schedule 6 (disclosure of information: emoluments and other benefits of directors and others) are not complied with in the annual accounts, the auditors shall include in their report, so far as they are reasonably able to do so, a statement giving the required particulars.

Publication of accounts and reports

Persons entitled to receive copies of accounts and reports

238.—(1) A copy of the company's annual accounts, together with a copy of the directors' report for that financial year and of the auditors' report on those accounts, shall be sent to—

(*a*) every member of the company,

(*b*) every holder of the company's debentures, and

(*c*) every person who is entitled to receive notice of general meetings,

not less than 21 days before the date of the meeting at which copies of those documents are to be laid in accordance with section 241.

(2) Copies need not be sent—

(*a*) to a person who is not entitled to receive notices of general meetings and of whose address the company is unaware, or

(*b*) to more than one of the joint holders of shares or debentures none of whom is entitled to receive such notices, or

(*c*) in the case of joint holders of shares or debentures some of whom are, and some not, entitled to receive such notices, to those who are not so entitled.

(3) In the case of a company not having a share capital, copies need not be sent to anyone who is not entitled to receive notices of general meetings of the company.

(4) If copies are sent less than 21 days before the date of the meeting, they shall, notwithstanding that fact, be deemed to have been duly sent if it is so agreed by all the members entitled to attend and vote at the meeting.

(5) If default is made in complying with this section, the company and every officer of it who is in default is guilty of an offence and liable to a fine.

(6) Where copies are sent out under this section over a period of days, references elsewhere in this Act to the day on which copies are sent out shall be construed as references to the last day of that period.

Right to demand copies of accounts and reports

239.—(1) Any member of a company and any holder of a company's debentures is entitled to be furnished, on demand and without charge, with a copy of the company's last annual accounts and directors' report and a copy of the auditors' report on those accounts.

(2) The entitlement under this section is to a single copy of those documents, but that is in addition to any copy to which a person may be entitled under section 238.

(3) If a demand under this section is not complied with within seven days, the company and every officer of it who is in default is guilty of an offence and liable to a fine and, for continued contravention, to a daily default fine.

(4) If in proceedings for such an offence the issue arises whether a person had already been furnished with a copy of the relevant document under this section, it is for the defendant to prove that he had.

Requirements in connection with publication of accounts
240.—(1) If a company publishes any of its statutory accounts, they must be accompanied by the relevant auditors' report under section 235.

(2) A company which is required to prepare group accounts for a financial year shall not publish its statutory individual accounts for that year without also publishing with them its statutory group accounts.

(3) If a company publishes non-statutory accounts, it shall publish with them a statement indicating—

(*a*) that they are not the company's statutory accounts,

(*b*) whether statutory accounts dealing with any financial year with which the non-statutory accounts purport to deal have been delivered to the registrar,

(*c*) whether the company's auditors have made a report under section 235 on the statutory accounts for any such financial year, and

(*d*) whether any report so made was qualified or contained a statement under section 237(2) or (3) (accounting records or returns inadequate, accounts not agreeing with records and returns or failure to obtain necessary information and explanations);

and it shall not publish with the non-statutory accounts any auditors' report under section 235.

(4) For the purposes of this section a company shall be regarded as publishing a document if it publishes, issues or circulates it or otherwise makes it available for public inspection in a manner calculated to invite members of the public generally, or any class of members of the public, to read it.

(5) References in this section to a company's statutory accounts are to its individual or group accounts for a financial year as required to be delivered to the registrar under section 242; and references to the publication by a company of "non-statutory accounts" are to the publication of—

(*a*) any balance sheet or profit and loss account relating to, or purporting to deal with, a financial year of the company, or

(*b*) an account in any form purporting to be a balance sheet or profit and loss account for the group consisting of the company and its subsidiary undertakings relating to, or purporting to deal with, a financial year of the company,

otherwise than as part of the company's statutory accounts.

(6) A company which contravenes any provision of this section, and any officer of it who is in default, is guilty of an offence and liable to a fine.

Laying and delivering of accounts and reports

Accounts and reports to be laid before company in general meeting
241.—(1) The directors of a company shall in respect of each financial year lay before the company in general meeting copies of the company's annual accounts, the directors' report and the auditors' report on those accounts.

(2) If the requirements of subsection (1) are not complied with before the end of the period allowed for laying and delivering accounts and reports, every person who immediately before the end of that period was a director of the company is guilty of an offence and liable to a fine and, for continued contravention, to a daily default fine.

(3) It is a defence for a person charged with such an offence to prove that he took all reasonable steps for securing that those requirements would be complied with before the end of that period.

(4) It is not a defence to prove that the documents in question were not in fact prepared as required by this Part.

Accounts and reports to be delivered to the registrar

242.—(1) The directors of a company shall in respect of each financial year deliver to the registrar a copy of the company's annual accounts together with a copy of the directors' report for that year and a copy of the auditors' report on those accounts.

If any document comprised in those accounts or reports is in a language other than English, the directors shall annex to the copy of that document delivered a translation of it into English, certified in the prescribed manner to be a correct translation.

(2) If the requirements of subsection (1) are not complied with before the end of the period allowed for laying and delivering accounts and reports, every person who immediately before the end of that period was a director of the company is guilty of an offence and liable to a fine and, for continued contravention, to a daily default fine.

(3) Further, if the directors of the company fail to make good the default within 14 days after the service of a notice on them requiring compliance, the court may on the application of any member or creditor of the company or of the registrar, make an order directing the directors (or any of them) to make good the default within such time as may be specified in the order.

The court's order may provide that all costs of and incidental to the application shall be borne by the directors.

(4) It is a defence for a person charged with an offence under this section to prove that he took all reasonable steps for securing that the requirements of subsection (1) would be complied with before the end of the period allowed for laying and delivering accounts and reports.

(5) It is not a defence in any proceedings under this section to prove that the documents in question were not in fact prepared as required by this Part.

242A. [Not yet in force.]

Accounts of subsidiary undertakings to be appended in certain cases

243.—(1) The following provisions apply where at the end of the financial year a parent company has as a subsidiary undertaking—

    (*a*) a body corporate incorporated outside Great Britain which does not have an established place of business in Great Britain, or

    (*b*) an unincorporated undertaking,

which is excluded from consolidation in accordance with section 229(4) (undertaking with activities different from the undertakings included in the consolidation).

(2) There shall be appended to the copy of the company's annual accounts delivered to the registrar in accordance with section 242 a copy of the undertaking's latest individual accounts and, if it is a parent undertaking, its latest group accounts.

If the accounts appended are required by law to be audited, a copy of the auditors' report shall also be appended.

(3) The accounts must be for a period ending not more than 12 months before the end of the financial year for which the parent company's accounts are made up.

(4) If any document required to be appended is in a language other than English, the directors shall annex to the copy of that document delivered a translation of it into English, certified in the prescribed manner to be a correct translation.

(5) The above requirements are subject to the following qualifications—

    (*a*) an undertaking is not required to prepare for the purposes of this section accounts which would not otherwise be prepared, and if no accounts satisfying the above requirements are prepared none need be appended;

(*b*) a document need not be appended if it would not otherwise be required to be published, or made available for public inspection, anywhere in the world, but in that case the reason for not appending it shall be stated in a note to the company's accounts;

(*c*) where an undertaking and all its subsidiary undertakings are excluded from consolidation in accordance with section 229(4), the accounts of such of the subsidiary undertakings of that undertaking as are included in its consolidated group accounts need not be appended.

(6) Subsections (2) to (4) of section 242 (penalties, etc. in case of default) apply in relation to the requirements of this section as they apply in relation to the requirements of subsection (1) of that section.

Period allowed for laying and delivering accounts and reports

244.—(1) The period allowed for laying and delivering accounts and reports is—

(*a*) for a private company, 10 months after the end of the relevant accounting reference period, and

(*b*) for a public company, seven months after the end of that period.

This is subject to the following provisions of this section.

(2) If the relevant accounting reference period is the company's first and is a period of more than 12 months, the period allowed is—

(*a*) 10 months or 7 months, as the case may be, from the first anniversary of the incorporation of the company, or

(*b*) 3 months from the end of the accounting reference period,

whichever last expires.

(3) Where a company carries on business, or has interests, outside the United Kingdom, the Channel Islands and the Isle of Man, the directors may, in respect of any financial year, give to the registrar before the end of the period allowed by subsection (1) or (2) a notice in the prescribed form—

(*a*) stating that the company so carries on business or has such interests, and

(*b*) claiming a 3 month extension of the period allowed for laying and delivering accounts and reports;

and upon such a notice being given the period is extended accordingly.

(4) If the relevant accounting period is treated as shortened by virtue of a notice given by the company under section 225 (alteration of accounting reference date), the period allowed for laying and delivering accounts is that applicable in accordance with the above provisions or 3 months from the date of the notice under that section, whichever last expires.

(5) If for any special reason the Secretary of State thinks fit he may, on an application made before the expiry of the period otherwise allowed, by notice in writing to a company extend that period by such further period as may be specified in the notice.

(6) In this section "the relevant accounting reference period" means the accounting reference period by reference to which the financial year for the accounts in question was determined.

Penalty for laying or delivering defective accounts

[1] **245.**—(1) If any accounts of a company of which a copy is laid before the company in general meeting or delivered to the registrar of companies do not comply with the requirements of this Act as to the matters to be included in, or in a note to, those accounts, every person who at the time when the copy is so laid or delivered is a director of the company is guilty of an offence and, in respect of each offence, liable to a fine.

This subsection does not apply to a company's group accounts.

(2) If any group accounts of which a copy is laid before a company in general meeting or delivered to the registrar of companies do not comply with section 229(5) to (7) or section 230, and with the other requirements of this Act as to the matters to be included in or in a note to those accounts,

every person who at the time when the copy was so laid or delivered was a director of the company is guilty of an offence and liable to a fine.

(3) In proceedings against a person for an offence under this section, it is a defence for him to prove that he took all reasonable steps for securing compliance with the requirements in question.

NOTE
[1] Substituted (*prosp.*) by the Companies Act 1989, s. 12.

[1]Chapter II
Exemptions, Exceptions and Special Provisions

NOTE
[1] Ss. 246–255D substituted by the Companies Act 1989, ss. 13–18.

Small and medium-sized companies and groups

Exemptions for small and medium-sized companies

246.—(1) A company which qualifies as a small or medium-sized company in relation to a financial year—

(*a*) is exempt from the requirements of paragraph 36A of Schedule 4 (disclosure with respect to compliance with accounting standards), and

(*b*) is entitled to the exemptions provided by Schedule 8 with respect to the delivery to the registrar under section 242 of individual accounts and other documents for that financial year.

(2) In that Schedule—

Part I relates to small companies,

Part II relates to medium-sized companies, and

Part III contains supplementary provisions.

(3) A company is not entitled to the exemptions mentioned in subsection (1) if it is, or was at any time within the financial year to which the accounts relate—

(*a*) a public company,

(*b*) a banking or insurance company, or

(*c*) an authorised person under the Financial Services Act 1986,

or if it is or was at any time during that year a member of an ineligible group.

(4) A group is ineligible if any of its members is—

(*a*) a public company or a body corporate which (not being a company) has power under its constitution to offer its shares or debentures to the public and may lawfully exercise that power,

(*b*) an authorised institution under the Banking Act 1987,

(*c*) an insurance company to which Part II of the Insurance Companies Act 1982 applies, or

(*d*) an authorised person under the Financial Services Act 1986.

(5) A parent company shall not be treated as qualifying as a small company in relation to a financial year unless the group headed by it qualifies as a small group, and shall not be treated as qualifying as a medium-sized company in relation to a financial year unless that group qualifies as a medium-sized group (see section 249).

Qualification of company as small or medium-sized

247.—(1) A company qualifies as small or medium-sized in relation to a financial year if the qualifying conditions are met—

(*a*) in the case of the company's first financial year, in that year, and

(*b*) in the case of any subsequent financial year, in that year and the preceding year.

(2) A company shall be treated as qualifying as small or medium-sized in relation to a financial year—

(*a*) if it so qualified in relation to the previous financial year under subsection (1); or (*b*) if it was treated as so qualifying in relation to the previous year by virtue of paragraph (*a*) and the qualifying conditions are met in the year in question.

(3) The qualifying conditions are met by a company in a year in which it satisfies two or more of the following requirements—

Small company

1. Turnover   Not more than £2 million
2. Balance sheet total   Not more than £975,000
3. Number of employees   Not more than 50

Medium-sized company

1. Turnover   Not more than £8 million
2. Balance sheet total   Not more than £3.9 million
3. Number of employees   Not more than 250.

(4) For a period which is a company's financial year but not in fact a year the maximum figures for turnover shall be proportionately adjusted.

(5) The balance sheet total means—

(*a*) where in the company's accounts Format 1 of the balance sheet formats set out in Part I of Schedule 4 is adopted, the aggregate of the amounts shown in the balance sheet under the headings corresponding to items A to D in that Format, and

(*b*) where Format 2 is adopted, the aggregate of the amounts shown under the general heading "Assets".

(6) The number of employees means the average number of persons employed by the company in the year (determined on a weekly basis).

That number shall be determined by applying the method of calculation prescribed by paragraph 56(2) and (3) of Schedule 4 for determining the corresponding number required to be stated in a note to the company's accounts.

Exemption for small and medium-sized groups

248.—(1) A parent company need not prepare group accounts for a financial year in relation to which the group headed by that company qualifies as a small or medium-sized group and is not an ineligible group.

(2) A group is ineligible if any of its members is—

(*a*) a public company or a body corporate which (not being a company) has power under its constitution to offer its shares or debentures to the public and may lawfully exercise that power,

(*b*) an authorised institution under the Banking Act 1987,

(*c*) an insurance company to which Part II of the Insurance Companies Act 1982 applies, or

(*d*) an authorised person under the Financial Services Act 1986.

(3) If the directors of a company propose to take advantage of the exemption conferred by this section, it is the auditors' duty to provide them with a report stating whether in their opinion the company is entitled to the exemption.

(4) The exemption does not apply unless—

(*a*) the auditors' report states that in their opinion the company is so entitled, and

(*b*) that report is attached to the individual accounts of the company.

Qualification of group as small or medium-sized

249.—(1) A group qualifies as small or medium-sized in relation to a financial year if the qualifying conditions are met—

(*a*) in the case of the parent company's first financial year, in that year, and

(*b*) in the case of any subsequent financial year, in that year and the preceding year.

(2) A group shall be treated as qualifying as small or medium-sized in relation to a financial year—

  (*a*) if it so qualified in relation to the previous financial year under subsection (1); or
  (*b*) if it was treated as so qualifying in relation to the previous year by virtue of paragraph (*a*) and the qualifying conditions are met in the year in question.

(3) The qualifying conditions are met by a group in a year in which it satisfies two or more of the following requirements—

Small group

1. Aggregate turnover	Not more than £2 million net (or £2.4 million gross)
2. Aggregate balance sheet total	Not more than £1 million net (or £1.2 million gross)
3. Aggregate number of employees	Not more than 50

Medium-sized group

1. Aggregate turnover	Not more than £8 million net (or £9.6 million gross)
2. Aggregate balance sheet total	Not more than £3.9 million net (or £4.7 million gross)
3. Aggregate number of employees	Not more than 250

(4) The aggregate figures shall be ascertained by aggregating the relevant figures determined in accordance with section 247 for each member of the group.

In relation to the aggregate figures for turnover and balance sheet total, "net" means with the set-offs and other adjustments required by Schedule 4A in the case of group accounts and "gross" means without those set-offs and other adjustments; and a company may satisfy the relevant requirement on the basis of either the net or the gross figure.

(5) The figures for each subsidiary undertaking shall be those included in its accounts for the relevant financial year, that is—

  (*a*) if its financial year ends with that of the parent company, that financial year, and
  (*b*) if not, its financial year ending last before the end of the financial year of the parent company.

(6) If those figures cannot be obtained without disproportionate expense or undue delay, the latest available figures shall be taken.

Dormant companies

Resolution not to appoint auditors

250.—(1) A company may by special resolution make itself exempt from the provisions of this Part relating to the audit of accounts in the following cases—

  (*a*) if the company has been dormant from the time of its formation, by a special resolution passed before the first general meeting of the company at which annual accounts are laid;
  (*b*) if the company has been dormant since the end of the previous financial year and—
    (i)   is entitled in respect of its individual accounts for that year to the exemptions conferred by section 246 on a small company, or would be so entitled but for being a member of an ineligible group, and
    (ii) is not required to prepare group accounts for that year,
  by a special resolution passed at a general meeting of the company at which the annual accounts for that year are laid.

(2) A company may not pass such a resolution if it is—

(*a*) a public company,

(*b*) a banking or insurance company, or

(*c*) an authorised person under the Financial Services Act 1986.

(3) A company is "dormant" during a period in which no significant accounting transaction occurs, that is, no transaction which is required by section 221 to be entered in the company's accounting records; and a company ceases to be dormant on the occurrence of such a transaction.

For this purpose there shall be disregarded any transaction arising from the taking of shares in the company by a subscriber to the memorandum in pursuance of an undertaking of his in the memorandum.

(4) Where a company is, at the end of a financial year, exempt by virtue of this section from the provisions of this Part relating to the audit of accounts—

(*a*) sections 238 and 239 (right to receive or demand copies of accounts and reports) have effect with the omission of references to the auditors' report;

(*b*) no copies of an auditors' report need be laid before the company in general meeting;

(*c*) no copy of an auditors' report need be delivered to the registrar, and if none is delivered, the copy of the balance sheet so delivered shall contain a statement by the directors, in a position immediately above the signature required by section 233(4), that the company was dormant throughout the financial year; and

(*d*) the company shall be treated as entitled in respect of its individual accounts for that year to the exemptions conferred by section 246 on a small company notwithstanding that it is a member of an ineligible group.

(5) Where a company which is exempt by virtue of this section from the provisions of this Part relating to the audit of accounts—

(*a*) ceases to be dormant, or

(*b*) would no longer qualify (for any other reason) to make itself exempt by passing a resolution under this section,

it shall thereupon cease to be so exempt.

Listed public companies

Provision of summary financial statement to shareholders

[1] **251.**—(1) A public company whose shares, or any class of whose shares, are listed need not, in such cases as may be specified by regulations made by the Secretary of State, and provided any conditions so specified are complied with, send copies of the documents referred to in section 238(1) to members of the company, but may instead send them a summary financial statement.

In this subsection "listed" means admitted to the Official List of The International Stock Exchange of the United Kingdom and the Republic of Ireland Limited.

(2) Copies of the documents referred to in section 238(1) shall, however, be sent to any member of the company who wishes to receive them; and the Secretary of State may by regulations make provision as to the manner in which it is to be ascertained whether a member of the company wishes to receive them.

(3) The summary financial statement shall be derived from the company's annual accounts and the directors' report and shall be in such form and contain such information as may be specified by regulations made by the Secretary of State.

(4) Every summary financial statement shall—

(*a*) state that it is only a summary of information in the company's annual accounts and the directors' report;

(b) contain a statement by the company's auditors of their opinion as to whether the summary financial statement is consistent with those accounts and that report and complies with the requirements of this section and regulations made under it;

(c) state whether the auditors' report on the annual accounts was unqualified or qualified, and if it was qualified set out the report in full together with any further material needed to understand the qualification;

(d) state whether the auditors' report on the annual accounts contained a statement under—

   (i) section 237(2) (accounting records or returns inadequate or accounts not agreeing with records and returns), or

   (ii) section 237(3) (failure to obtain necessary information and explanations),

and if so, set out the statement in full.

(5) Regulations under this section shall be made by statutory instrument which shall be subject to annulment in pursuance of a resolution of either House of Parliament.

(6) If default is made in complying with this section or regulations made under it, the company and every officer of it who is in default is guilty of an offence and liable to a fine.

(7) Section 240 (requirements in connection with publication of accounts) does not apply in relation to the provision to members of a company of a summary financial statement in accordance with this section.

NOTE

[1] See S.I. 1990 No. 515.

Private companies

Election to dispense with laying of accounts and reports before general meeting

252.—(1) A private company may elect (by elective resolution in accordance with section 379A) to dispense with the laying of accounts and reports before the company in general meeting.

(2) An election has effect in relation to the accounts and reports in respect of the financial year in which the election is made and subsequent financial years.

(3) Whilst an election is in force, the references in the following provisions of this Act to the laying of accounts before the company in general meeting shall be read as references to the sending of copies of the accounts to members and others under section 238(1)—

(a) section 235(1) (accounts on which auditors are to report),

(b) section 270(3) and (4) (accounts by reference to which distributions are justified), and

(c) section 320(2) (accounts relevant for determining company's net assets for purposes of ascertaining whether approval required for certain transactions);

and the requirement in section 271(4) that the auditors' statement under that provision be laid before the company in general meeting shall be read as a requirement that it be sent to members and others along with the copies of the accounts sent to them under section 238(1).

(4) If an election under this section ceases to have effect, section 241 applies in relation to the accounts and reports in respect of the financial year in which the election ceases to have effect and subsequent financial years.

Right of shareholder to require laying of accounts

253.—(1) Where an election under section 252 is in force, the copies of the accounts and reports sent out in accordance with section 238(1)—

(a) shall be sent not less than 28 days before the end of the period allowed for laying and delivering accounts and reports, and

(b) shall be accompanied, in the case of a member of the company, by a notice informing him of his right to require the laying of the accounts and reports before a general meeting;

and section 238(5) (penalty for default) applies in relation to the above requirements as to the requirements contained in that section.

(2) Before the end of the period of 28 days beginning with the day on which the accounts and reports are sent out in accordance with section 238(1), any member or auditor of the company may by notice in writing deposited at the registered office of the company require that a general meeting be held for the purpose of laying the accounts and reports before the company.

(3) If the directors do not within 21 days from the date of the deposit of such a notice proceed duly to convene a meeting, the person who deposited the notice may do so himself.

(4) A meeting so convened shall not be held more than three months from that date and shall be convened in the same manner, as nearly as possible, as that in which meetings are to be convened by directors.

(5) Where the directors do not duly convene a meeting, any reasonable expenses incurred by reason of that failure by the person who deposited the notice shall be made good to him by the company, and shall be recouped by the company out of any fees, or other remuneration in respect of their services, due or to become due to such of the directors as were in default.

(6) The directors shall be deemed not to have duly convened a meeting if they convene a meeting for a date more than 28 days after the date of the notice convening it.

Unlimited companies

Exemption from requirement to deliver accounts and reports

254.—(1) The directors of an unlimited company are not required to deliver accounts and reports to the registrar in respect of a financial year if the following conditions are met.

(2) The conditions are that at no time during the relevant accounting reference period—

(*a*) has the company been, to its knowledge, a subsidiary undertaking of an undertaking which was then limited, or

(*b*) have there been, to its knowledge, exercisable by or on behalf of two or more undertakings which were then limited, rights which if exercisable by one of them would have made the company a subsidiary undertaking of it, or

(*c*) has the company been a parent company of an undertaking which was then limited.

The references above to an undertaking being limited at a particular time are to an undertaking (under whatever law established) the liability of whose members is at that time limited.

(3) The exemption conferred by this section does not apply if at any time during the relevant accounting period the company carried on business as the promoter of a trading stamp scheme within the Trading Stamps Act 1964.

(4) Where a company is exempt by virtue of this section from the obligation to deliver accounts, section 240 (requirements in connection with publication of accounts) has effect with the following modifications—

(*a*) in subsection (3)(*b*) for the words from "whether statutory accounts" to "have been delivered to the registrar" substitute "that the company is exempt from the requirement to deliver statutory accounts", and

(*b*) in subsection (5) for "as required to be delivered to the registrar under section 242" substitute "as prepared in accordance with this Part and approved by the board of directors".

Banking and insurance companies and groups

Special provisions for banking and insurance companies

255.—(1) A banking or insurance company may prepare its individual accounts in accordance with Part I of Schedule 9 rather than Schedule 4.

(2) Accounts so prepared shall contain a statement that they are prepared in accordance with the special provisions of this Part relating to banking companies or insurance companies, as the case may be.

(3) In relation to the preparation of individual accounts in accordance with the special provisions of this Part relating to banking or insurance companies, the references to the provisions of Schedule 4 in section 226(4) and (5) (relationship between specific requirements and duty to give true and fair view) shall be read as references to the provisions of Part I of Schedule 9.

(4) The Secretary of State may, on the application or with the consent of the directors of a company which prepares individual accounts in accordance with the special provisons of this Part relating to banking or insurance companies, modify in relation to the company any of the requirements of this Part for the purpose of adapting them to the circumstances of the company.

This does not affect the duty to give a true and fair view.

Special provisions for banking and insurance groups

255A.—(1) The parent company of a banking or insurance group may prepare group accounts in accordance with the provisions of this Part as modified by Part II of Schedule 9.

(2) Accounts so prepared shall contain a statement that they are prepared in accordance with the special provisions of this Part relating to banking groups or insurance groups, as the case may be.

(3) References in this Part to a banking group are to a group where—

(*a*) the parent company is a banking company, or

(*b*) at least one of the undertakings in the group is an authorised institution under the Banking Act 1987 and the predominant activities of the group are such as to make it inappropriate to prepare group accounts in accordance with the formats in Part I of Schedule 4.

(4) References in this Part to an insurance group are to a group where—

(*a*) the parent company is an insurance company, or

(*b*) the predominant activity of the group is insurance business and activities which are a direct extension of or ancillary to insurance business.

(5) In relation to the preparation of group accounts in accordance with the special provisions of this Part relating to banking or insurance groups, the references to the provisions of Schedule 4A in section 227(5) and (6) (relationship between specific requirements and duty to give true and fair view) shall be read as references to those provisions as modified by Part II of Schedule 9.

(6) The Secretary of State may, on the application or with the consent of the directors of a company which prepares group accounts in accordance with the special provisions of this Part relating to banking or insurance groups, modify in relation to the company any of the requirements of this Part for the purpose of adapting them to the circumstances of the company.

Modification of disclosure requirements in relation to banking company or group

255B.—(1) In relation to a company which prepares accounts in accordance with the special provisions of this Part relating to banking companies or groups, the provisions of Schedule 5 (additional disclosure: related undertakings) have effect subject to Part III of Schedule 9.

(2) In relation to a banking company, or the parent company of a banking company, the provisions of Schedule 6 (disclosure: emoluments and

other benefits of directors and others) have effect subject to Part IV of
Schedule 9.

Directors' report where accounts prepared in accordance with special provisions
255C.—(1) The following provisions apply in relation to the directors'
report of a company for a financial year in respect of which it prepares
accounts in accordance with the special provisions of this Part relating to
banking or insurance companies or groups.

(2) The information required to be given by paragraph 6, 8 or 13 of Part I
of Schedule 9 (which is allowed to be given in a statement or report
annexed to the accounts), may be given in the directors' report instead.

Information so given shall be treated for the purposes of audit as forming
part of the accounts.

(3) The reference in section 234(1)(*b*) to the amount proposed to be carried to reserves shall be construed as a reference to the amount proposed
to be carried to reserves within the meaning of Part I of Schedule 9.

(4) If the company takes advantage, in relation to its individual or group
accounts, of the exemptions conferred by paragraph 27 or 28 of Part I of
Schedule 9, paragraph 1 of Schedule 7 (disclosure of asset values) does not
apply.

(5) The directors' report shall, in addition to complying with Schedule 7,
also comply with Schedule 10 (which specifies additional matters to be disclosed).

Power to apply provisions to banking partnerships
255D.—(1) The Secretary of State may by regulations apply to banking
partnerships, subject to such exceptions, adaptations and modifications as
he considers appropriate, the provisions of this Part applying to banking
companies.

(2) A "banking partnership" means a partnership which is an authorised
institution under the Banking Act 1987.

(3) Regulations under this section shall be made by statutory instrument.

(4) No regulations under this section shall be made unless a draft of the
instrument containing the regulations has been laid before Parliament and
approved by a resolution of each House.

[1] CHAPTER III
SUPPLEMENTARY PROVISIONS

NOTE
[1] Ss. 256–262A substituted by the Companies Act 1989, ss. 19–22.

Accounting standards

Accounting standards
256.—(1) In this Part "accounting standards" means statements of standard accounting practice issued by such body or bodies as may be prescribed by regulations.

(2) References in this Part to accounting standards applicable to a company's annual accounts are to such standards as are, in accordance with
their terms, relevant to the company's circumstances and to the accounts.

(3) The Secretary of State may make grants to or for the purposes of
bodies concerned with—
    (*a*) issuing accounting standards,
    (*b*) overseeing and directing the issuing of such standards, or
    (*c*) investigating departures from such standards or from the accounting
        requirements of this Act and taking steps to secure compliance with
        them.

(4) Regulations under this section may contain such transitional and other supplementary and incidental provisions as appear to the Secretary of State to be appropriate.

Power to alter accounting requirements

Power of Secretary of State to alter accounting requirements

257.—(1) The Secretary of State may by regulations made by statutory instrument modify the provisions of this Part.

(2) Regulations which—

(*a*) add to the classes of documents required to be prepared, laid before the company in general meeting or delivered to the registrar,

(*b*) restrict the classes of company which have the benefit of any exemption, exception or special provision,

(*c*) require additional matter to be included in a document of any class, or

(*d*) otherwise render the requirements of this Part more onerous,

shall not be made unless a draft of the instrument containing the regulations has been laid before Parliament and approved by a resolution of each House.

(3) Otherwise, a statutory instrument containing regulations under this section shall be subject to annulment in pursuance of a resolution of either House of Parliament.

(4) Regulations under this section may—

(*a*) make different provision for different cases or classes of case,

(*b*) repeal and re-enact provisions with modifications of form or arrangement, whether or not they are modified in substance,

(*c*) make consequential amendments or repeals in other provisions of this Act, or in other enactments, and

(*d*) contain such transitional and other incidental and supplementary provisions as the Secretary of State thinks fit.

(5) Any modification by regulations under this section of section 258 or Schedule 10A (parent and subsidiary undertakings) does not apply for the purposes of enactments outside the Companies Acts unless the regulations so provide.

Parent and subsidiary undertakings

Parent and subsidiary undertakings

258.—(1) The expressions "parent undertaking" and "subsidiary undertaking" in this Part shall be construed as follows; and a "parent company" means a parent undertaking which is a company.

(2) An undertaking is a parent undertaking in relation to another undertaking, a subsidiary undertaking, if—

(*a*) it holds a majority of the voting rights in the undertaking, or

(*b*) it is a member of the undertaking and has the right to appoint or remove a majority of its board of directors, or

(*c*) it has the right to exercise a dominant influence over the undertaking—

    (i) by virtue of provisions contained in the undertaking's memorandum or articles, or

    (ii) by virtue of a control contract, or

(*d*) it is a member of the undertaking and controls alone, pursuant to an agreement with other shareholders or members, a majority of the voting rights in the undertaking.

(3) For the purposes of subsection (2) an undertaking shall be treated as a member of another undertaking—

(*a*) if any of its subsidiary undertakings is a member of that undertaking, or (*b*) if any shares in that other undertaking are held by a person acting on behalf of the undertaking or any of its subsidiary undertakings.

(4) An undertaking is also a parent undertaking in relation to another undertaking, a subsidiary undertaking, if it has a participating interest in the undertaking and—

(*a*) it actually exercises a dominant influence over it, or

(*b*) it and the subsidiary undertaking are managed on a unified basis.

(5) A parent undertaking shall be treated as the parent undertaking of undertakings in relation to which any of its subsidiary undertakings are, or are to be treated as, parent undertakings; and references to its subsidiary undertakings shall be construed accordingly.

(6) Schedule 10A contains provisions explaining expressions used in this section and otherwise supplementing this section.

Other interpretation provisions

Meaning of "undertaking" and related expressions

259.—(1) In this Part "undertaking" means—

(*a*) a body corporate or partnership, or

(*b*) an unincorporated association carrying on a trade or business, with or without a view to profit.

(2) In this Part references to shares—

(*a*) in relation to an undertaking with a share capital, are to allotted shares;

(*b*) in relation to an undertaking with capital but no share capital, are to rights to share in the capital of the undertaking; and

(*c*) in relation to an undertaking without capital, are to interests—

(i) conferring any right to share in the profits or liability to contribute to the losses of the undertaking, or

(ii) giving rise to an obligation to contribute to the debts or expenses of the undertaking in the event of a winding up.

(3) Other expressions appropriate to companies shall be construed, in relation to an undertaking which is not a company, as references to the corresponding persons, officers, documents or organs, as the case may be, appropriate to undertakings of that description.

This is subject to provision in any specific context providing for the translation of such expressions.

(4) References in this Part to "fellow subsidiary undertakings" are to undertakings which are subsidiary undertakings of the same parent undertaking but are not parent undertakings or subsidiary undertakings of each other.

(5) In this Part "group undertaking", in relation to an undertaking, means an undertaking which is—

(*a*) a parent undertaking or subsidiary undertaking of that undertaking, or

(*b*) a subsidiary undertaking of any parent undertaking of that undertaking.

Participating interests

260.—(1) In this Part a "participating interest" means an interest held by an undertaking in the shares of another undertaking which it holds on a long-term basis for the purpose of securing a contribution to its activities by the exercise of control or influence arising from or related to that interest.

(2) A holding of 20 per cent. or more of the shares of an undertaking shall be presumed to be a participating interest unless the contrary is shown.

(3) The reference in subsection (1) to an interest in shares includes—

(*a*) an interest which is convertible into an interest in shares, and

(*b*) an option to acquire shares or any such interest;

and an interest or option falls within paragraph (*a*) or (*b*) notwithstanding that the shares to which it relates are, until the conversion or the exercise of the option, unissued.

(4) For the purposes of this section an interest held on behalf of an undertaking shall be treated as held by it.

(5) For the purposes of this section as it applies in relation to the expression "participating interest" in section 258(4) (definition of "subsidiary undertaking")—

(*a*) there shall be attributed to an undertaking any interests held by any of its subsidiary undertakings, and

(*b*) the references in subsection (1) to the purpose and activities of an undertaking include the purposes and activities of any of its subsidiary undertakings and of the group as a whole.

(6) In the balance sheet and profit and loss formats set out in Part I of Schedule 4, "participating interest" does not include an interest in a group undertaking.

(7) For the purposes of this section as it applies in relation to the expression "participating interest"—

(*a*) in those formats as they apply in relation to group accounts, and

(*b*) in paragraph 20 of Schedule 4A (group accounts: undertakings to be accounted for as associated undertakings),

the references in subsections (1) to (4) to the interest held by, and the purposes and activities of, the undertaking concerned shall be construed as references to the interest held by, and the purposes and activities of, the group (within the meaning of paragraph 1 of that Schedule).

Notes to the accounts

261.—(1) Information required by this Part to be given in notes to a company's annual accounts may be contained in the accounts or in a separate document annexed to the accounts.

(2) References in this Part to a company's annual accounts, or to a balance sheet or profit and loss account, include notes to the accounts giving information which is required by any provision of this Act, and required or allowed by any such provision to be given in a note to company accounts.

Minor definitions

262.—(1) In this Part—

"annual accounts" means—

(*a*) the individual accounts required by section 226, and

(*b*) any group accounts required by section 227,

      (but see also section 230 (treatment of individual profit and loss account where group accounts prepared));

"annual report", in relation to a company, means the directors' report required by section 234;

"balance sheet date" means the date as at which the balance sheet was made up;

"capitalisation", in relation to work or costs, means treating that work or those costs as a fixed asset;

"credit institution" means an undertaking carrying on a deposit-taking business within the meaning of the Banking Act 1987;

"fixed assets" means assets of a company which are intended for use on a continuing basis in the company's activities, and "current assets" means assets not intended for such use;

"group" means a parent undertaking and its subsidiary undertakings;

"included in the consolidation", in relation to group accounts, or "included in consolidated group accounts", means that the undertaking is included in the accounts by the method of full (and not proportional) consolidation, and references to an undertaking excluded from consolidation shall be construed accordingly;

"purchase price", in relation to an asset of a company or any raw materials or consumables used in the production of such an asset, includes any consideration (whether in cash or otherwise) given by the company in respect of that asset or those materials or consumables, as the case may be;

"qualified", in relation to an auditors' report, means that the report does not state the auditors' unqualified opinion that the accounts have been properly prepared in accordance with this Act or, in the case of an undertaking not required to prepare accounts in accordance with this Act, under any corresponding legislation under which it is required to prepare accounts;

"true and fair view" refers—

    (*a*) in the case of individual accounts, to the requirement of section 226(2), and

    (*b*) in the case of group accounts, to the requirement of section 227(3);

"turnover", in relation to a company, means the amounts derived from the provision of goods and services falling within the company's ordinary activities, after deduction of—

    (i) trade discounts,

    (ii) value added tax, and

    (iii) any other taxes based on the amounts so derived.

(2) In the case of an undertaking not trading for profit, any reference in this Part to a profit and loss account is to an income an expenditure account; and references to profit and loss and, in relation to group accounts, to a consolidated profit and loss account shall be construed accordingly.

(3) References in this Part to "realised profits" and "realised losses", in relation to a company's accounts, are to such profits or losses of the company as fall to be treated as realised in accordance with principles generally accepted, at the time when the accounts are prepared, with respect to the determination for accounting purposes of realised profits or losses.

This is without prejudice to—

    (*a*) the construction of any other expression (where appropriate) by reference to accepted accounting principles or practice, or

    (*b*) any specific provision for the treatment of profits or losses of any description as realised.

Index of defined expressions

262A. The following Table shows the provisions of this Part defining or otherwise explaining expressions used in this Part (other than expressions used only in the same section or paragraph)—

accounting reference date and accounting reference period	section 224
accounting standards and applicable accounting standards	section 256
annual accounts	
(generally)	section 262(1)
(includes notes to the accounts)	section 261(2)
annual report	section 262(1)
associated undertaking (in Schedule 4A)	paragraph 20 of that Schedule
balance sheet (includes notes)	section 261(2)
balance sheet date	section 262(1)
banking group	section 255A(3)
capitalisation (in relation to work or costs)	section 262(1)

credit institution	section 262(1)
current assets	section 262(1)
fellow subsidiary undertaking	section 259(4)
financial year	section 223
fixed assets	section 262(1)
group	section 262(1)
group undertaking	section 259(5)
historical cost accounting rules (in Schedule 4)	paragraph 29 of that Schedule
included in the consolidation and related expressions	section 262(1)
individual accounts	section 262(1)
insurance group	section 255A(4)
land of freehold tenure and land of leasehold tenure (in relation to Scotland)	
—in Schedule 4	paragraph 93 of that Schedule
—in Schedule 9	paragraph 36 of that Schedule
lease, long lease and short lease	
—in Schedule 4	paragraph 83 of that Schedule
in Schedule 9	paragraph 34 of that Schedule
listed investment	
—in Schedule 4	paragraph 84 of that Schedule
—in Schedule 9	paragraph 33 of that Schedule
notes to the accounts	section 261(1)
parent undertaking (and parent company)	section 258 and Schedule 10A
participating interest	section 260
pension costs (in Schedule 4)	paragraph 94(2) and (3) of that Schedule
period allowed for laying and delivering accounts and reports	section 244
profit and loss account	
(includes notes)	section 261(2)
(in relation to a company not trading for profit)	section 262(2)
provision	
—in Schedule 4	paragraphs 88 and 89 of that Schedule
—in Schedule 9	paragraph 32 of that Schedule
purchase price	section 262(1)
qualified	section 262(1)
realised losses and realised profits	section 262(3)
reserve (in Schedule 9)	paragraph 32 of that Schedule
shares	section 259(2)
social security costs (in Schedule 4)	paragraph 94(1) and (3) of that Schedule
special provisions for banking and insurance companies and groups	sections 255 and 255A
subsidiary undertaking	section 258 and Schedule 10A
true and fair view	section 262(1)
turnover	section 262(1)
undertaking and related expressions	section 259(1) to (3).

[1] PART VIII

DISTRIBUTION OF PROFITS AND ASSETS

NOTE

[1] For interpretation of "public company", "private company" etc., see s. 1(3) and the Companies Consolidation (Consequential Provisions) Act 1985, s. 1.

Limits of company's power of distribution

Certain distributions prohibited

263.—(1) A company shall not make a distribution except out of profits available for the purpose.

(2) In this Part, "distribution" means every description of distribution of a company's assets to its members, whether in cash or otherwise, except distribution by way of—

  (*a*) an issue of shares as fully or partly paid bonus shares, (*b*) the redemption or purchase of any of the company's own shares out of capital (including the proceeds of any fresh issue of shares) or out of unrealised profits in accordance with Chapter VII of Part V,

    (*c*) the reduction of share capital by extinguishing or reducing the liability of any of the members on any of the company's shares in respect of share capital not paid up, or by paying off paid-up share capital, and

    (*d*) a distribution of assets to members of the company on its winding up.

(3) For purposes of this Part, a company's profits available for distribution are its accumulated, realised profits, so far as not previously utilised by distribution or capitalisation, less its accumulated, realised losses, so far as not previously written off in a reduction or reorganisation of capital duly made.

This is subject to the provision made by sections 265 and 266 for investment and other companies.

(4) A company shall not apply an unrealised profit in paying up debentures, or any amounts unpaid on its issued shares.

(5) Where the directors of a company are, after making all reasonable enquiries, unable to determine whether a particular profit made before 22nd December 1980 is realised or unrealised, they may treat the profit as realised; and where after making such enquiries they are unable to determine whether a particular loss so made is realised or unrealised, they may treat the loss as unrealised.

Restriction on distribution of assets

    264.—(1) A public company may only make a distribution at any time—

    (*a*) if at that time the amount of its net assets is not less than the aggregate of its called-up share capital and undistributable reserves, and

    (*b*) if, and to the extent that, the distribution does not reduce the amount of those assets to less than that aggregate.

This is subject to the provision made by sections 265 and 266 for investment and other companies.

(2) In subsection (1), "net assets" means the aggregate of the company's assets less the aggregate of its liabilities ("liabilities" to include any provision for liabilities or charges within paragraph 89 of Schedule 4).

    [1](3) A company's undistributable reserves are—

    (*a*) the share premium account,

    (*b*) the capital redemption reserve,

    (*c*) the amount by which the company's accumulated, unrealised profits, so far as not previously utilised by capitalisation of a description to which this paragraph applies, exceed its accumulated, unrealised losses (so far as not previously written off in a reduction or reorganisation of capital duly made), and

    (*d*) any other reserve which the company is prohibited from distributing by any enactment (other than one contained in this Part) or by its memorandum or articles;

and paragraph (*c*) applies to every description of capitalisation except a transfer of profits of the company to its capital redemption reserve on or after 22nd December 1980.

(4) A public company shall not include any uncalled share capital as an asset in any accounts relevant for purposes of this section.

NOTE
[1] See the Telecommunications Act 1984, s. 66(3), as amended. See also the Gas Act 1986, s. 55(3), and the Electricity Act 1989, s. 75(3).

Other distributions by investment companies

    265.—(1) Subject to the following provisions of this section, an investment company (defined in section 266) may also make a distribution at any time out of its accumulated, realised revenue profits, so far as not previously utilised by distribution or capitalisation, less its accumulated revenue losses (whether realised or unrealised), so far as not previously written off in a reduction or reorganisation of capital duly made—

(a) if at that time the amount of its assets is at least equal to one-and-a-half times the aggregate of its liabilities, and

(b) if, and to the extent that, the distribution does not reduce that amount to less than one-and-a-half times that aggregate.

(2) In subsection (1)(a), "liabilities" includes any provision for liabilities or charges (within the meaning of paragraph 89 of Schedule 4).

[THE NEXT PAGE IS I 171]

(3) The company shall not include any uncalled share capital as an asset in any accounts relevant for purposes of this section.

[1] (4) An investment company may not make a distribution by virtue of subsection (1) unless—

(*a*) its shares are listed on a recognised investment exchange other than an overseas investment exchange within the meaning of the Financial Services Act 1986, and

(*b*) during the relevant period it has not—

(i) distributed any of its capital profits, or

(ii) applied any unrealised profits or any capital profits (realised or unrealised) in paying up debentures or amounts unpaid on its issued shares.

(5) The "relevant period" under subsection (4) is the period beginning with—

(*a*) the first day of the accounting reference period immediately preceding that in which the proposed distribution is to be made, or

(*b*) where the distribution is to be made in the company's first accounting reference period, the first day of that period,

and ending with the date of the distribution.

(6) An investment company may not make a distribution by virtue of subsection (1) unless the company gave to the registrar of companies the requisite notice (that is, notice under section 266(1)) of the company's intention to carry on business as an investment company—

(*a*) before the beginning of the relevant period under subsection (4), or

(*b*) in the case of a company incorporated on or after 22nd December 1980, as soon as may have been reasonably practicable after the date of its incorporation.

NOTE

[1] As amended by the Financial Services Act 1986, Sched. 16, para. 19.

Meaning of "investment company"

266.—(1) In section 265 "investment company" means a public company which has given notice in the prescribed form (which has not been revoked) to the registrar of companies of its intention to carry on business as an investment company, and has since the date of that notice complied with the requirements specified below.

(2) Those requirements are—

(*a*) that the business of the company consists of investing its funds mainly in securities, with the aim of spreading investment risk and giving members of the company the benefit of the results of the management of its funds,

(*b*) that none of the company's holdings in companies (other than those which are for the time being in investment companies) represents more than 15 per cent by value of the investing company's investments,

(*c*) that distribution of the company's capital profits is prohibited by its memorandum or articles of association,

(*d*) that the company has not retained, otherwise than in compliance with this Part, in respect of any accounting reference period more than 15 per cent of the income it derives from securities.

(3) Notice to the registrar of companies under subsection (1) may be revoked at any time by the company on giving notice in the prescribed form to the registrar that it no longer wishes to be an investment company within the meaning of this section; and, on giving such notice, the company ceases to be such a company.

[1] (4) Section 842(2) and (3) of the Income and Corporation Taxes Act 1988 and section 93(6)(*b*) of the Finance Act 1972 apply for purposes of subsection (2)(*b*) as for those of section 842(1)(*b*) of the Act first mentioned.

NOTE
¹ As amended by the Income and Corporation Taxes Act 1988, Sched. 29.

Extension of ss.265, 266 to other companies

267.—(1) The Secretary of State may by regulations in a statutory instrument extend the provisions of sections 265 and 266 (with or without modifications) to companies whose principal business consists of investing their funds in securities, land or other assets with the aim of spreading investment risk and giving their members the benefit of the results of the management of the assets.

(2) Regulations under this section—

(a) may make different provision for different classes of companies and may contain such transitional and supplemental provisions as the Secretary of State considers necessary, and

(b) shall not be made unless a draft of the statutory instrument containing them has been laid before Parliament and approved by a resolution of each House.

Realised profits of insurance company with long term business

268.—(1) Where an insurance company to which Part II of the Insurance Companies Act 1982 applies carries on long term business—

(a) any amount properly transferred to the profit and loss account of the company from a surplus in the fund or funds maintained by it in respect of that business, and

(b) any deficit in that fund or those funds,

are to be (respectively) treated, for purposes of this Part, as a realised profit and a realised loss; and, subject to this, any profit or loss arising in that business is to be left out of account for those purposes.

(2) In subsection (1)—

(a) the reference to a surplus in any fund or funds of an insurance company is to an excess of the assets representing that fund or those funds over the liabilities of the company attributable to its long term business, as shown by an actuarial investigation, and

(b) the reference to a deficit in any such fund or funds is to the excess of those liabilities over those assets, as so shown.

(3) In this section—

(a) "actuarial investigation" means an investigation to which section 18 of the Insurance Companies Act 1982 (periodic actuarial investigation of company with long term business) applies or which is made in pursuance of a requirement imposed by section 42 of that Act (actuarial investigation required by Secretary of State); and

(b) "long term business" has the same meaning as in that Act.

Treatment of development costs

269.—(1) Subject as follows, where development costs are shown as an asset in a company's accounts, any amount shown in respect of those costs is to be treated—

(a) under section 263, as a realised loss, and

(b) under section 265, as a realised revenue loss.

(2) This does not apply to any part of that amount representing an unrealised profit made on revaluation of those costs; nor does it apply if—

(a) there are special circumstances in the company's case justifying the directors in deciding that the amount there mentioned is not to be treated as required by subsection (1), and

(b) the note to the accounts required by paragraph 20 of Schedule 4 (reasons for showing development costs as an asset) states that the amount is not to be so treated and explains the circumstances relied upon to justify the decision of the directors to that effect.

Relevant accounts

Distribution to be justified by reference to company's accounts

270.—(1) This section and sections 271 to 276 below are for determining the question whether a distribution may be made by a company without contravening sections 263, 264 or 265.

[THE NEXT PAGE IS I 173]

(2) The amount of a distribution which may be made is determined by reference to the following items as stated in the company's accounts—

(*a*) profits, losses, assets and liabilities,

(*b*) provisions of any of the kinds mentioned in paragraphs 88 and 89 of Schedule 4 (depreciation, diminution in value of assets, retentions to meet liabilities, etc.), and

(*c*) share capital and reserves (including undistributable reserves).

(3) Except in a case falling within the next subsection, the company's accounts which are relevant for this purpose are its last annual accounts, that is to say those prepared under Part VII which were laid in respect of the last preceding accounting reference period in respect of which accounts so prepared were laid; and for this purpose accounts are laid if section 241 (1) has been complied with in relation to them.

(4) In the following two cases—

(*a*) where the distribution would be found to contravene the relevant section if reference were made only to the company's last annual accounts, or

(*b*) where the distribution is proposed to be declared during the company's first accounting reference period, or before any accounts are laid in respect of that period,

the accounts relevant under this section (called "interim accounts" in the first case, and "initial accounts" in the second) are those necessary to enable a reasonable judgment to be made as to the amounts of the items mentioned in subsection (2) above.

(5) The relevant section is treated as contravened in the case of a distribution unless the statutory requirements about the relevant accounts (that is, the requirements of this and the following three sections, as and where applicable) are complied with in relation to that distribution.

NOTE
[1] See the Gas Act 1986, Sched. 8, para. 41.

Requirements for last annual accounts

[1] **271.**—(1) If the company's last annual accounts constitute the only accounts relevant under section 270, the statutory requirements in respect of them are as follows.

(2) The accounts must have been properly prepared in accordance with this Act, or have been so prepared subject only to matters which are not material for determining, by reference to items mentioned in section 270(2), whether the distribution would contravene the relevant section; and, without prejudice to the foregoing—

(*a*) so much of the accounts as consists of a balance sheet must give a true and fair view of the state of the company's affairs as at the balance sheet date, and

(*b*) so much of the accounts as consists of a profit and loss account must give a true and fair view of the company's profit or loss for the period in respect of which the accounts were prepared.

[2] (3) The auditors must have made their report on the accounts under section 235; and the following subsection applies if the report is a qualified report, that is to say, it is not a report without qualification to the effect that in the auditors' opinion the accounts have been properly prepared in accordance with this Act.

(4) The auditors must in that case also have stated in writing (either at the time of their report or subsequently) whether, in their opinion, the matter in respect of which their report is qualified is material for determining, by reference to items mentioned in section 270(2), whether the distribution would contravene the relevant section; and a copy of the statement must have been laid before the company in general meeting.

(5) A statement under subsection (4) suffices for purposes of a particular distribution not only if it relates to a distribution which has been proposed

but also if it relates to distributions of any description which includes that particular distribution, notwithstanding that at the time of the statement it has not been proposed.

NOTES

[1] See the Gas Act 1986, Sched. 8, para. 41.

[2] As amended by the Companies Act 1989, s. 23 and Sched. 10, para. 4.

Requirements for interim accounts

[1] **272.**—(1) The following are the statutory requirements in respect of interim accounts prepared for a proposed distribution by a public company.

(2) The accounts must have been properly prepared, or have been so prepared subject only to matters which are not material for determining, by reference to items mentioned in section 270(2), whether the proposed distribution would contravene the relevant section.

[2] (3) "Properly prepared" means that the accounts must comply with section 226 (applying that section and Schedule 4 with such modifications as are necessary because the accounts are prepared otherwise than in respect of an accounting reference period) and any balance sheet comprised in the accounts must have been signed in accordance with section 233; and, without prejudice to the foregoing—

(a) so much of the accounts as consists of a balance sheet must give a true and fair view of the state of the company's affairs as at the balance sheet date, and

(b) so much of the accounts as consists of a profit and loss account must give a true and fair view of the company's profit or loss for the period in respect of which the accounts were prepared.

(4) A copy of the accounts must have been delivered to the registrar of companies.

(5) If the accounts are in a language other than English and the second sentence of section 242(1) (translation) does not apply, a translation into English of the accounts, certified in the prescribed manner to be a correct translation, must also have been delivered to the registrar.

NOTES

[1] See the Gas Act 1986, Sched. 8, para. 41.

[2] As amended by the Companies Act 1989, s. 23 and Sched. 10, paras. 5 and 6.

Requirements for initial accounts

[1] **273.**—(1) The following are the statutory requirements in respect of initial accounts prepared for a proposed distribution by a public company.

(2) The accounts must have been properly prepared, or they must have been so prepared subject only to matters which are not material for determining, by reference to items mentioned in section 270(2), whether the proposed distribution would contravene the relevant section.

(3) Section 272(3) applies as respects the meaning of "properly prepared".

(4) The company's auditors must have made a report stating whether, in their opinion, the accounts have been properly prepared; and the following subsection applies if their report is a qualified report, that is to say it is not a report without qualification to the effect that in the auditors' opinion the accounts have been so prepared.

(5) The auditors must in that case also have stated in writing whether, in their opinion, the matter in respect of which their report is qualified is material for determining, by reference to items mentioned in section 270(2), whether the distribution would contravene the relevant section.

(6) A copy of the accounts, of the auditors' report under subsection (4) and of the auditors' statement (if any) under subsection (5) must have been delivered to the registrar of companies.

[2] (7) If the accounts are, or the auditors' report under subsection (4) or their statement (if any) under subsection (5) is, in a language other than English and the second sentence of section 242(1) (translation) does not apply, a

translation into English of the accounts, the report or the statement (as the case may be), certified in the prescribed manner to be a correct translation, must also have been delivered to the registrar.

NOTES
[1] See the Gas Act 1986, Sched. 8, para. 41.
[2] As amended by the Companies Act 1989, s. 23 and Sched. 10, para. 6.

Method of applying s. 270 to successive distributions
[1] **274.**—(1) For the purpose of determining by reference to particular accounts whether a proposed distribution may be made by a company, section 270 has effect, in a case where one or more distributions have already been made in pursuance of determinations made by reference to those same accounts, as if the amount of the proposed distribution was increased by the amount of the distributions so made.

(2) Subsection (1) of this section applies (if it would not otherwise do so) to—

(*a*) financial assistance lawfully given by a public company out of its distributable profits in a case where the assistance is required to be so given by section 154,

(*b*) financial assistance lawfully given by a private company out of its distributable profits in a case where the assistance is required to be so given by section 155(2),

(*c*) financial assistance given by a company in contravention of section 151, in a case where the giving of that assistance reduces the company's net assets or increases its net liabilities,

(*d*) a payment made by a company in respect of the purchase by it of shares in the company (except a payment lawfully made otherwise than out of distributable profits), and

(*e*) a payment of any description specified in section 168 (company's purchase of right to acquire its own shares, etc.),

being financial assistance given or payment made since the relevant accounts were prepared, as if any such financial assistance or payment were a distribution already made in pursuance of a determination made by reference to those accounts.

(3) In this section the following definitions apply—
"financial assistance" means the same as in Chapter VI of Part V;
"net assets" has the meaning given by section 154(2)(*a*); and
"net liabilities", in relation to the giving of financial assistance by a company, means the amount by which the aggregate amount of the company's liabilities (within the meaning of section 154(2)(*b*)) exceeds the aggregate amount of its assets, taking the amount of the assets and liabilities to be as stated in the company's accounting records immediately before the financial assistance is given.

(4) Subsections (2) and (3) of this section are deemed to be included in Chapter VII of Part V for purposes of the Secretary of State's power to make regulations under section 179.

NOTE
[1] See the Gas Act 1986, Sched. 8, para. 41.

Treatment of assets in the relevant accounts
[1] **275.**—(1) For purposes of sections 263 and 264, a provision of any kind mentioned in paragraphs 88 and 89 of Schedule 4, other than one in respect of a diminution in value of a fixed asset appearing on a revaluation of all the fixed assets of the company, or of all of its fixed assets other than goodwill, is treated as a realised loss.

(2) If, on the revaluation of a fixed asset, an unrealised profit is shown to have been made and, on or after the revaluation, a sum is written off or retained for depreciation of that asset over a period, then an amount equal to the amount by which that sum exceeds the sum which would have been

so written off or retained for the depreciation of that asset over that period, if that profit had not been made, is treated for purposes of sections 263 and 264 as a realised profit made over that period.

(3) Where there is no record of the original cost of an asset, or a record cannot be obtained without unreasonable expense or delay, then for the purpose of determining whether the company has made a profit or loss in respect of that asset, its cost is taken to be the value ascribed to it in the earliest available record of its value made on or after its acquisition by the company.

(4) Subject to subsection (6), any consideration by the directors of the value at a particular time of a fixed asset is treated as a revaluation of the asset for the purposes of determining whether any such revaluation of the company's fixed assets as is required for purposes of the exception from subsection (1) has taken place at that time.

(5) But where any such assets which have not actually been revalued are treated as revalued for those purposes under subsection (4), that exception applies only if the directors are satisfied that their aggregate value at the time in question is not less than the aggregate amount at which they are for the time being stated in the company's accounts.

(6) Where section 271(2), 272(2) or 273(2) applies to the relevant accounts, subsections (4) and (5) above do not apply for the purpose of determining whether a revaluation of the company's fixed assets affecting the amount of the relevant items (that is, the items mentioned in section 270(2)) as stated in those accounts has taken place, unless it is stated in a note to the accounts—

(*a*) that the directors have considered the value at any time of any fixed assets of the company, without actually revaluing those assets,

(*b*) that they are satisfied that the aggregate value of those assets at the time in question is or was not less than the aggregate amount at which they are or were for the time being stated in the company's accounts, and

(*c*) that the relevant items in question are accordingly stated in the relevant accounts on the basis that a revaluation of the company's fixed assets which by virtue of subsections (4) and (5) included the assets in question took place at that time.

NOTE
[1] See the Gas Act 1986, Sched. 8, para. 41.

Distributions in kind
[1] **276.** Where a company makes a distribution of or including a non-cash asset, and any part of the amount at which that asset is stated in the accounts relevant for the purposes of the distribution in accordance with sections 270 to 275 represents an unrealised profit, that profit is to be treated as a realised profit—

(*a*) for the purpose of determining the lawfulness of the distribution in accordance with this Part (whether before or after the distribution takes place), and

[2](*b*) for the purpose of the application of paragraphs 12(*a*) and 34(3)(*a*) of Schedule 4 (only realised profits to be included in or transferred to the profit and loss account) in relation to anything done with a view to or in connection with the making of that distribution.

NOTES
[1] See the Gas Act 1986, Sched. 8, para. 41.
[2] As amended by the Companies Act 1989, s. 23 and Sched. 10, para. 7.

Supplementary

Consequences of unlawful distribution
277.—(1) Where a distribution, or part of one, made by a company to one of its members is made in contravention of this Part and, at the time of

the distribution, he knows or has reasonable grounds for believing that it is so made, he is liable to repay it (or that part of it, as the case may be) to the company or (in the case of a distribution made otherwise than in cash) to pay the company a sum equal to the value of the distribution (or part) at that time.

(2) The above is without prejudice to any obligation imposed apart from this section on a member of a company to repay a distribution unlawfully made to him; but this section does not apply in relation to—

(a) financial assistance given by a company in contravention of section 151, or

(b) any payment made by a company in respect of the redemption or purchase by the company of shares in itself.

(3) Subsection (2) of this section is deemed included in Chapter VII of Part V for purposes of the Secretary of State's power to make regulations under section 179.

Saving for provision in articles operative before Act of 1980

278. Where immediately before 22nd December 1980 a company was authorised by a provision of its articles to apply its unrealised profits in paying up in full or in part unissued shares to be allotted to members of the company as fully or partly paid bonus shares, that provision continues (subject to any alteration of the articles) as authority for those profits to be so applied after that date.

Distributions by banking or insurance companies

[1] **279.** Where a company's accounts relevant for the purposes of this Part are prepared in accordance with the special provisions of Part VII relating to banking or insurance companies, sections 264 to 275 apply with the modifications shown in Schedule 11.

NOTE

[1] Substituted by the Companies Act 1989, s. 23 and Sched. 10, para. 8.

Definitions for Part VIII

280.—(1) The following has effect for the interpretation of this Part.

(2) "Capitalisation", in relation to a company's profits, means any of the following operations (whenever carried out)—

(a) applying the profits in wholly or partly paying up unissued shares in the company to be allotted to members of the company as fully or partly paid bonus shares, or

(b) transferring the profits to capital redemption reserve.

(3) References to profits and losses of any description are (respectively) to profits and losses of that description made at any time and, except where the context otherwise requires, are (respectively) to revenue and capital profits and revenue and capital losses.

Saving for other restraints on distribution

281. The provisions of this Part are without prejudice to any enactment or rule of law, or any provision of a company's memorandum or articles, restricting the sums out of which, or the cases in which, a distribution may be made.

[1] PART IX

A COMPANY'S MANAGEMENT; DIRECTORS AND SECRETARIES; THEIR
QUALIFICATIONS, DUTIES AND RESPONSIBILITIES

NOTE

[1] For interpretation of "public company", "private company" etc., see s. 1(3) and the Companies Consolidation (Consequential Provisions) Act 1985, s. 1.

Officers and registered office

Directors

282.—(1) Every company registered on or after 1st November 1929 (other than a private company) shall have at least two directors.

(2) Every company registered before that date (other than a private company) shall have at least one director.

(3) Every private company shall have at least one director.

Secretary

283.—(1) Every company shall have a secretary.

(2) A sole director shall not also be secretary.

(3) Anything required or authorised to be done by or to the secretary may, if the office is vacant or there is for any other reason no secretary capable of acting, be done by or to any assistant or deputy secretary or, if there is no assistant or deputy secretary capable of acting, by or to any officer of the company authorised generally or specially in that behalf by the directors.

(4) No company shall—

(*a*) have as secretary to the company a corporation the sole director of which is a sole director of the company;

(*b*) have as sole director of the company a corporation the sole director of which is secretary to the company.

Acts done by person in dual capacity

284. A provision requiring or authorising a thing to be done by or to a director and the secretary is not satisfied by its being done by or to the same person acting both as director and as, or in place of, the secretary.

Validity of acts of directors

285. The acts of a director or manager are valid notwithstanding any defect that may afterwards be discovered in his appointment or qualification; and this provision is not excluded by section 292(2) (void resolution to appoint).

Qualifications of company secretaries

286.—(1) It is the duty of the directors of a public company to take all reasonable steps to secure that the secretary (or each joint secretary) of the company is a person who appears to them to have the requisite knowledge and experience to discharge the functions of secretary of the company and who—

(*a*) on 22nd December 1980 held the office of secretary or assistant or deputy secretary of the company; or

(*b*) for at least three of the five years immediately preceding his appointment as secretary held the office of secretary of a company other than a private company; or

(*c*) is a member of any of the bodies specified in the following subsection; or

(*d*) is a barrister, advocate or solicitor called or admitted in any part of the United Kingdom; or

(*e*) is a person who, by virtue of his holding or having held any other position or his being a member of any other body, appears to the directors to be capable of discharging those functions.

(2) The bodies referred to in subsection (1)(*c*) are—

(*a*)   the Institute of Chartered Accountants in England and Wales;

(*b*)   the Institute of Chartered Accountants of Scotland;

(*c*)   the Chartered Association of Certified Accountants;

(*d*)   the Institute of Chartered Accountants in Ireland;

(*e*)   the Institute of Chartered Secretaries and Administrators;

(*f*) the Institute of Cost and Management Accountants;

(*g*) the Chartered Institute of Public Finance and Accountancy.

Registered office

[1] **287.**—(1) A company shall at all times have a registered office to which all communications and notices may be addressed.

(2) On incorporation the situation of the company's registered office is that specified in the statement sent to the registrar under section 10.

(3) The company may change the situation of its registered office from time to time by giving notice in the prescribed form to the registrar.

(4) The change takes effect upon the notice being registered by the registrar, but until the end of the period of 14 days beginning with the date on which it is registered a person may validly serve any document on the company at its previous registered office.

(5) For the purposes of any duty of a company—

(*a*) to keep at its registered office, or make available for public inspection there, any register, index or other document, or

(*b*) to mention the address of its registered office in any document,

a company which has given notice to the registrar of a change in the situation of its registered office may act on the change as from such date, not more than 14 days after the notice is given, as it may determine.

(6) Where a company unavoidably ceases to perform at its registered office any such duty as is mentioned in subsection (5)(*a*) in circumstances in which it was not practicable to give prior notice to the registrar of a change in the situation of its registered office, but—

(*a*) resumes performance of that duty at other premises as soon as practicable, and

(*b*) gives notice accordingly to the registrar of a change in the situation of its registered office within 14 days of doing so,

it shall not be treated as having failed to comply with that duty.

(7) In proceedings for an offence of failing to comply with any such duty as is mentioned in subsection (5), it is for the person charged to show that by reason of the matters referred to in that subsection or subsection (6) no offence was committed.

NOTE
[1] Substituted by the Companies Act 1989, s. 136.

Register of directors and secretaries

288.—(1) Every company shall keep at its registered office a register of its directors and secretaries; and the register shall, with respect to the particulars to be contained in it of those persons, comply with sections 289 and 290 below.

(2) The company shall, within the period of 14 days from the occurrence of—

(*a*) any change among its directors or in its secretary, or

(*b*) any change in the particulars contained in the register,

send to the registrar of companies a notification in the prescribed form of the change and of the date on which it occurred; and a notification of a person having become a director or secretary, or one of joint secretaries, of the company shall contain a consent, signed by that person, to act in the relevant capacity.

(3) The register shall during business hours (subject to such reasonable restrictions as the company may by its articles or in general meeting impose, so that not less than two hours in each day be allowed for inspection) be open to the inspection of any member of the company without charge and of any other person on payment of 5 pence or such less sum as the company may prescribe, for each inspection.

(4) If an inspection required under this section is refused, or if default is made in complying with subsection (1) or (2), the company and every officer

of it who is in default is liable to a fine and, for continued contravention, to a daily default fine.

(5) In the case of a refusal of inspection of the register, the court may by order compel an immediate inspection of it.

(6) For purposes of this and the next section, a shadow director of a company is deemed a director and officer of it.

Particulars of directors to be registered under s. 288

289.—(1) Subject to the provisions of this section, the register kept by a company under section 288 shall contain the following particulars with respect to each director—

(*a*) in the case of an individual—

    (i) his present Christian name and surname,

    (ii) any former Christian name or surname,

    (iii) his usual residential address,

    (iv) his nationality,

    (v) his business occupation (if any),

    (vi) particulars of any other directorships held by him or which have been held by him, and

    (vii) in the case of a company subject to section 293 (age-limit), the date of his birth;

(*b*) in the case of a corporation, its corporate name and registered or principal office.

(2) In subsection (1)—

(*a*) "Christian name" includes a forename,

(*b*) "surname", in the case of a peer or a person usually known by a title different from his surname, means that title, and

(*c*) the reference to a former Christian name or surname does not include—

    (i) in the case of a peer or a person usually known by a British title different from his surname, the name by which he was known previous to the adoption of or succession to the title, or

    (ii) in the case of any person, a former Christian name or surname where that name or surname was changed or disused before the person bearing the name attained the age of 18, or has been changed or disused for a period of not less than 20 years, or

    (iii) in the case of a married woman, the name or surname by which she was known previous to the marriage.

(3) It is not necessary for the register to contain on any day particulars of a directorship—

(*a*) which has not been held by a director at any time during the five years preceding that day,

(*b*) which is held by a director in a company which—

    (i) is dormant or grouped with the company keeping the register, and

    (ii) if he also held that directorship for any period during those five years, was for the whole of that period either dormant or so grouped,

(*c*) which was held by a director for any period during those five years in a company which for the whole of that period was either dormant or grouped with the company keeping the register.

[1] (4) For purposes of subsection (3), "company" includes any body corporate incorporated in Great Britain; and—

(*a*) section 250(3) applies as regards whether and when a company is or has been dormant, and

(*b*) a company is to be regarded as being, or having been, grouped with another at any time if at that time it is or was a company of which the other is or was a wholly-owned subsidiary, or if it is or was a wholly-owned subsidiary of the other or of another company of which that other is or was a wholly-owned subsidiary.

NOTE
[1] As amended by the Companies Act 1989, s. 23 and Sched. 10, para. 9.

Particulars of secretaries to be registered under s. 288

290.—(1) The register to be kept by a company under section 288 shall contain the following particulars with respect to the secretary or, where there are joint secretaries, with respect to each of them—

(*a*) in the case of an individual, his present Christian name and surname, any former Christian name or surname and his usual residential address, and

(*b*) in the case of a corporation or a Scottish firm, its corporate or firm name and registered or principal office.

(2) Where all the partners in a firm are joint secretaries, the name and principal office of the firm may be stated instead of the particular specified above.

(3) Section 289(2) applies as regards the meaning of "Christian name", "surname" and "former Christian name or surname".

Provisions governing appointment of directors

Share qualification of directors

291.—(1) It is the duty of every director who is by the company's articles required to hold a specified share qualification, and who is not already qualified, to obtain his qualification within two months after his appointment, or such shorter time as may be fixed by the articles.

(2) For the purpose of any provision of the articles requiring a director or manager to hold any specified share qualification, the bearer of a share warrant is not deemed the holder of the shares specified in the warrant.

(3) The office of director of a company is vacated if the director does not within two months from the date of his appointment (or within such shorter time as may be fixed by the articles) obtain his qualification, or if after the expiration of that period or shorter time he ceases at any time to hold his qualification.

(4) A person vacating office under this section is incapable of being reappointed to be a director of the company until he has obtained his qualification.

(5) If after the expiration of that period or shorter time any unqualified person acts as a director of the company, he is liable to a fine and, for continued contravention, to a daily default fine.

Appointment of directors to be voted on individually

292.—(1) At a general meeting of a public company, a motion for the appointment of two or more persons as directors of the company by a

[THE NEXT PAGE IS I 181]

single resolution shall not be made, unless a resolution that it shall be so made has first been agreed to by the meeting without any vote being given against it.

(2) A resolution moved in contravention of this section is void, whether or not its being so moved was objected to at the time; but where a resolution so moved is passed, no provision for the automatic reappointment of retiring directors in default of another appointment applies.

(3) For purposes of this section, a motion for approving a person's appointment, or for nominating a person for appointment, is to be treated as a motion for his appointment.

(4) Nothing in this section applies to a resolution altering the company's articles.

Age limit for directors

293.—(1) A company is subject to this section if—

  (*a*) it is a public company, or

  (*b*) being a private company, it is a subsidiary of a public company or of a body corporate registered under the law relating to companies for the time being in force in Northern Ireland as a public company.

(2) No person is capable of being appointed a director of a company which is subject to this section if at the time of his appointment he has attained the age of 70.

(3) A director of such a company shall vacate his office at the conclusion of the annual general meeting commencing next after he attains the age of 70; but acts done by a person as director are valid notwithstanding that it is afterwards discovered that his appointment had terminated under this subsection.

(4) Where a person retires under subsection (3), no provision for the automatic reappointment of retiring directors in default of another appointment applies; and if at the meeting at which he retires the vacancy is not filled, it may be filled as a casual vacancy.

(5) Nothing in subsections (2) to (4) prevents the appointment of a director at any age, or requires a director to retire at any time, if his appointment is or was made or approved by the company in general meeting; but special notice is required of a resolution appointing or approving the appointment of a director for it to have effect under this subsection, and the notice of the resolution given to the company, and by the company to its members, must state, or have stated, the age of the person to whom it relates.

(6) A person reappointed director on retiring under subsection (3), or appointed in place of a director so retiring, is to be treated, for the purpose of determining the time at which he or any other director is to retire, as if he had become director on the day on which the retiring director was last appointed before his retirement.

Subject to this, the retirement of a director out of turn under subsection (3) is to be disregarded in determining when any other directors are to retire.

(7) In the case of a company first registered after the beginning of 1947, this section has effect subject to the provisions of the company's articles; and in the case of a company first registered before the beginning of that year—

  (*a*) this section has effect subject to any alterations of the company's articles made after the beginning of that year; and

  (*b*) if at the beginning of that year the company's articles contained provision for retirement of directors under an age limit, or for preventing or restricting appointments of directors over a given age, this section does not apply to directors to whom that provision applies.

Duty of director to disclose his age

294.—(1) A person who is appointed or to his knowledge proposed to be appointed director of a company subject to section 293 at a time when he has attained any retiring age applicable to him under that section or under the company's articles shall give notice of his age to the company.

(2) For purposes of this section, a company is deemed subject to section 293 notwithstanding that all or any of the section's provisions are excluded or modified by the company's articles.

(3) Subsection (1) does not apply in relation to a person's reappointment on the termination of a previous appointment as director of the company.

(4) A person who—

(*a*)   fails to give notice of his age as required by this section; or

(*b*)   acts as director under any appointment which is invalid or has terminated by reason of his age,

is liable to a fine and, for continued contravention, to a daily default fine.

(5) For purposes of subsection (4), a person who has acted as director under an appointment which is invalid or has terminated is deemed to have continued so to act throughout the period from the invalid appointment or the date on which the appointment terminated (as the case may be), until the last day on which he is shown to have acted thereunder.

Disqualification

295–299. [Repealed by the Company Directors Disqualification Act 1986, Sched. 4.]

300. [Repealed by the Insolvency Act 1985, Sched. 10, Pt. II.]

[THE NEXT PAGE IS I 185]

301 and **302.** [Repealed by the Company Directors Disqualification Act 1986, Sched. 4.]

Removal of directors

Resolution to remove director

303.—[1] (1) A company may by ordinary resolution remove a director before the expiration of his period of office, notwithstanding anything in its articles or in any agreement between it and him.

(2) Special notice is required of a resolution to remove a director under this section or to appoint somebody instead of a director so removed at the meeting at which he is removed.

(3) A vacancy created by the removal of a director under this section, if not filled at the meeting at which he is removed, may be filled as a casual vacancy.

(4) A person appointed director in place of a person removed under this section is treated, for the purpose of determining the time at which he or

any other director is to retire, as if he had become director on the day on which the person in whose place he is appointed was last appointed a director.

(5) This section is not to be taken as depriving a person removed under it of compensation or damages payable to him in respect of the termination of his appointment as director or of any appointment terminating with that as director, or as derogating from any power to remove a director which may exist apart from this section.

NOTE

[1] Excluded by the Companies Consolidation (Consequential Provisions) Act 1985, s. 14.

Director's right to protest removal

304.—(1) On receipt of notice of an intended resolution to remove a director under section 303, the company shall forthwith send a copy of the notice to the director concerned; and he (whether or not a member of the company) is entitled to be heard on the resolution at the meeting.

(2) Where notice is given of an intended resolution to remove a director under that section, and the director concerned makes with respect to it representations in writing to the company (not exceeding a reasonable length) and requests their notification to members of the company, the company shall, unless the representations are received by it too late for it to do so—

(a) in any notice of the resolution given to members of the company state the fact of the representations having been made; and

(b) send a copy of the representations to every member of the company to whom notice of the meeting is sent (whether before or after receipt of the representations by the company).

(3) If a copy of the representations is not sent as required by subsection (2) because received too late or because of the company's default, the director may (without prejudice to his right to be heard orally) require that the representations shall be read out at the meeting.

(4) But copies of the representations need not be sent out and the representations need not be read out at the meeting if, on the application either of the company or of any other person who claims to be aggrieved, the court is satisfied that the rights conferred by this section are being abused to secure needless publicity for defamatory matter.

(5) The court may order the company's costs on an application under this section to be paid in whole or in part by the director, notwithstanding that he is not a party to the application.

Other provisions about directors and officers

Directors' names on company correspondence, etc.

305.—(1) A company to which this section applies shall not state, in any form, the name of any of its directors (otherwise than in the text or as a signatory) on any business letter on which the company's name appears unless it states on the letter in legible characters the Christian name (or its initials) and surname of every director of the company who is an individual and the corporate name of every corporate director.

(2) This section applies to—

(a) every company registered under this Act or under the former Companies Acts (except a company registered before 23rd November 1916); and

(b) every company incorporated outside Great Britain which has an established place of business within Great Britain, unless it had established such a place of business before that date.

(3) If a company makes default in complying with this section, every officer of the company who is in default is liable for each offence to a fine; and for this purpose, where a corporation is an officer of the company, any officer of the corporation is deemed an officer of the company.

(4) For purposes of this section—
(*a*) "director" includes shadow director, and "officer" is to be construed accordingly;
(*b*) "Christian name" includes a forename;
(*c*) "initials" includes a recognised abbreviation of a Christian name; and
(*d*) in the case of peer or a person usually known by a title different from his surname, "surname" means that title.

Limited company may have directors with unlimited liability

306.—(1) In the case of a limited company the liability of the directors or managers, or of the managing director, may, if so provided by the memorandum, be unlimited.

(2) In the case of a limited company in which the liability of a director or manager is unlimited, the directors and any managers of the company and the member who proposes any person for election or appointment to the office of director or manager, shall add to that proposal a statement that the liability of the person holding that office will be unlimited.

(3) Before the person accepts the office or acts in it, notice in writing that his liability will be unlimited shall be given to him by the following or one of the following persons, namely—
(*a*) the promoters of the company,
(*b*) the directors of the company,
(*c*) any managers of the company,
(*d*) the company secretary.

(4) If a director, manager or proposer makes default in adding such a statement, or if a promoter, director, manager or secretary makes default in giving the notice required by subsection (3), then—
(*a*) he is liable to a fine, and
(*b*) he is also liable for any damage which the person so elected or appointed may sustain from the default;

but the liability of the person elected or appointed is not affected by the default.

Special resolution making liability of directors unlimited

307.—(1) A limited company, if so authorised by its articles, may by special resolution alter its memorandum so as to render unlimited the liability of its directors or managers, or of any managing director.

(2) When such a special resolution is passed, its provisions are as valid as if they had been originally contained in the memorandum.

Assignment of office by directors

308. If provision is made by a company's articles, or by any agreement entered into between any person and the company, for empowering a director or manager of the company to assign his office as such to another person, any assignment of office made in pursuance of that provision is (notwithstanding anything to the contrary contained in the provision) of no effect unless and until it is approved by a special resolution of the company.

Directors to have regard to interests of employees

309.—(1) The matters to which the directors of a company are to have regard in the performance of their functions include the interests of the company's employees in general, as well as the interests of its members.

(2) Accordingly, the duty imposed by this section on the directors is owed by them to the company (and the company alone) and is enforceable in the same way as any other fiduciary duty owed to a company by its directors.

(3) This section applies to shadow directors as it does to directors.

Provisions exempting officers and auditors from liability

310.—(1) This section applies to any provision, whether contained in a company's articles or in any contract with the company or otherwise, for exempting any officer of the company or any person (whether an officer or not) employed by the company as auditor from, or indemnifying him against, any liability which by virtue of any rule of law would otherwise attach to him in respect of any negligence, default, breach of duty or breach of trust of which he may be guilty in relation to the company.

(2) Except as provided by the following subsection, any such provision is void.
[1] (3) This section does not prevent a company—

(a) from purchasing and maintaining for any such officer or auditor insurance against any such liability, or

(b) from indemnifying any such officer or auditor against any liability incurred by him—

   (i) in defending any proceedings (whether civil or criminal) in which judgment is given in his favour or he is acquitted, or

   (ii) in connection with any application under section 144(3) or (4) (acquisition of shares by innocent nominee) or section 727 (general power to grant relief in case of honest and reasonable conduct) in which relief is granted to him by the court.

NOTE
[1] Substituted by the Companies Act 1989, s. 137(1).

PART X

ENFORCEMENT OF FAIR DEALING BY DIRECTORS

Restrictions on directors taking financial advantage

Prohibition on tax-free payments to directors
311.—[1] (1) It is not lawful for a company to pay a director remuneration (whether as director or otherwise) free of income tax, or otherwise calculated by reference to or varying with the amount of his income tax, or to or with any rate of income tax.

(2) Any provision contained in a company's articles, or in any contract, or in any resolution of a company or a company's directors, for payment to a director of remuneration as above mentioned has effect as if it provided for payment, as a gross sum subject to income tax, of the net sum for which it actually provides.

NOTE
[1] Excluded by the Companies Consolidation (Consequential Provisions) Act 1985, s. 15.

Payment to director for loss of office etc.
312. It is not lawful for a company to make to a director of the company any payment by way of compensation for loss of office, or as consideration for or in connection with his retirement from office, without particulars of the proposed payment (including its amount) being disclosed to members of the company and the proposal being approved by the company.

Company approval for property transfer
313.—(1) It is not lawful, in connection with the transfer of the whole or any part of the undertaking or property of a company, for any payment to be made to a director of the company by way of compensation for loss of office, or as consideration for or in connection with his retirement from office, unless particulars of the proposed payment (including its amount) have been disclosed to members of the company and the proposal approved by the company.

(2) Where a payment unlawful under this section is made to a director, the amount received is deemed to be received by him in trust for the company.

Director's duty of disclosure on takeover, etc.
314.—(1) This section applies where, in connection with the transfer to any persons of all or any of the shares in a company, being a transfer resulting from—

(*a*) an offer made to the general body of shareholders; or

(*b*) an offer made by or on behalf of some other body corporate with a view to the company becoming its subsidiary or a subsidiary of its holding company; or

(*c*) an offer made by or on behalf of an individual with a view to his obtaining the right to exercise or control the exercise of not less than one-third of the voting power at any general meeting of the company; or

(*d*) any other offer which is conditional on acceptance to a given extent,

a payment is to be made to a director of the company by way of compensation for loss of office, or as consideration for or in connection with his retirement from office.

(2) It is in those circumstances the director's duty to take all reasonable steps to secure that particulars of the proposed payment (including its amount) are included in or sent with any notice of the offer made for their shares which is given to any shareholders.

(3) If—

(*a*) the director fails to take those steps, or

(*b*) any person who has been properly required by the director to include those particulars in or send them with the notice required by subsection (2) fails to do so,

he is liable to a fine.

Consequences of non-compliance with s. 314

315.—(1) If in the case of any such payment to a director as is mentioned in section 314(1)—

(*a*) his duty under that section is not complied with, or

(*b*) the making of the proposed payment is not, before the transfer of any shares in pursuance of the offer, approved by a meeting (summoned for the purpose) of the holders of the shares to which the offer relates and of other holders of shares of the same class as any of those shares,

any sum received by the director on account of the payment is deemed to have been received by him in trust for persons who have sold their shares as a result of the offer made; and the expenses incurred by him in distributing that sum amongst those persons shall be borne by him and not retained out of that sum.

(2) Where—

(*a*) the shareholders referred to in subsection (1)(*b*) are not all the members of the company, and

(*b*) no provision is made by the articles for summoning or regulating the meeting referred to in that paragraph,

the provisions of this Act and of the company's articles relating to general meetings of the company apply (for that purpose) to the meeting either without modification or with such modifications as the Secretary of State on the application of any person concerned may direct for the purpose of adapting them to the circumstances of the meeting.

(3) If at a meeting summoned for the purpose of approving any payment as required by subsection (1)(*b*) a quorum is not present and, after the meeting has been adjourned to a later date, a quorum is again not present, the payment is deemed for the purposes of that subsection to have been approved.

Provisions supplementing ss. 312 to 315

316.—(1) Where in proceedings for the recovery of any payment as having, by virtue of section 313(2) or 315(1), been received by any person in trust, it is shown that—

(*a*) the payment was made in pursuance of any arrangement entered into as part of the agreement for the transfer in question, or within one year before or two years after that agreement or the offer leading to it; and

(b) the company or any person to whom the transfer was made was privy to that arrangement,

the payment is deemed, except in so far as the contrary is shown, to be one to which the provisions mentioned above in this subsection apply.

(2) If in connection with any such transfer as is mentioned in any of sections 313 to 315—

(a) the price to be paid to a director of the company whose office is to be abolished or who is to retire from office for any shares in the company held by him is in excess of the price which could at the time have been obtained by other holders of the like shares; or

(b) any valuable consideration is given to any such director,

the excess or the money value of the consideration (as the case may be) is deemed for the purposes of that section to have been a payment made to him by way of compensation for loss of office or as consideration for or in connection with his retirement from office.

(3) References in sections 312 to 315 to payments made to a director by way of compensation for loss of office or as consideration for or in connection with his retirement from office, do not include any *bona fide* payment by way of damages for breach of contract or by way of pension in respect of past services.

"Pension" here includes any superannuation allowance, superannuation gratuity or similar payment.

(4) Nothing in sections 313 to 315 prejudices the operation of any rule of law requiring disclosure to be made with respect to such payments as are there mentioned, or with respect to any other like payments made or to be made to a company's directors.

Directors to disclose interest in contracts

317.—(1) It is the duty of a director of a company who is in any way, whether directly or indirectly, interested in a contract or proposed contract with the company to declare the nature of his interest at a meeting of the directors of the company.

(2) In the case of a proposed contract, the declaration shall be made—

(a) at the meeting of the directors at which the question of entering into the contract is first taken into consideration; or

(b) if the director was not at the date of that meeting interested in the proposed contract, at the next meeting of the directors held after he became so interested;

and, in a case where the director becomes interested in a contract after it is made, the declaration shall be made at the first meeting of the directors held after he becomes so interested.

(3) For purposes of this section, a general notice given to the directors of a company by a director to the effect that—

(a) he is a member of a specified company or firm and is to be regarded as interested in any contract which may, after the date of the notice, be made with that company or firm; or

(b) he is to be regarded as interested in any contract which may after the date of the notice be made with a specified person who is connected with him (within the meaning of section 346 below),

is deemed a sufficient declaration of interest in relation to any such contract.

(4) However, no such notice is of effect unless either it is given at a meeting of the directors or the director takes reasonable steps to secure that it is brought up and read at the next meeting of the directors after it is given.

(5) A reference in this section to a contract includes any transaction or arrangement (whether or not constituting a contract) made or entered into on or after 22nd December 1980.

(6) For purposes of this section, a transaction or arrangement of a kind described in section 330 (prohibition of loans, quasi-loans etc. to directors) made by a company for a director of the company or a person connected with such a director is treated (if it would not otherwise be so treated, and whether or not it is prohibited by that section) as a transaction or arrangement in which that director is interested.

(7) A director who fails to comply with this section is liable to a fine.

(8) This section applies to a shadow director as it applies to a director, except that a shadow director shall declare his interest, not at a meeting of the directors, but by a notice in writing to the directors which is either—

  (*a*) a specific notice given before the date of the meeting at which, if he had been a director, the declaration would be required by subsection (2) to be made; or

  (*b*) a notice which under subsection (3) falls to be treated as a sufficient declaration of that interest (or would fall to be so treated apart from subsection (4)).

(9) Nothing in this section prejudices the operation of any rule of law restricting directors of a company from having an interest in contracts with the company.

Directors' service contracts to be open to inspection
   318.—(1) Subject to the following provisions, every company shall keep at an appropriate place—

  (*a*) in the case of each director whose contract of service with the company is in writing, a copy of that contract;

  (*b*) in the case of each director whose contract of service with the company is not in writing, a written memorandum setting out its terms; and

  (*c*) in the case of each director who is employed under a contract of service with a subsidiary of the company, a copy of that contract or, if it is not in writing, a written memorandum setting out its terms.

(2) All copies and memoranda kept by a company in pursuance of subsection (1) shall be kept at the same place.

(3) The following are appropriate places for the purposes of subsection (1)—

  (*a*) the company's registered office;

  (*b*) the place where its register of members is kept (if other than its registered office);

  (*c*) its principal place of business, provided that is situated in that part of Great Britain in which the company is registered.

(4) Every company shall send notice in the prescribed form to the registrar of companies of the place where copies and memoranda are kept in compliance with subsection (1), and of any change in that place, save in a case in which they have at all times been kept at the company's registered office.

(5) Subsection (1) does not apply to a director's contract of service with the company or with a subsidiary of it if that contract required him to work wholly or mainly outside the United Kingdom; but the company shall keep a memorandum—

  (*a*) in the case of a contract of service with the company, giving the director's name and setting out the provisions of the contract relating to its duration;

  (*b*) in the case of a contract of service with a subsidiary, giving the director's name and the name and place of incorporation of the subsidiary, and setting out the provisions of the contract relating to its duration,

at the same place as copies and memoranda are kept by the company in pursuance of subsection (1).

(6) A shadow director is treated for purposes of this section as a director.

(7) Every copy and memorandum required by subsection (1) or (5) to be kept shall, during business hours (subject to such reasonable restrictions as the company may in general meeting impose, so that not less than two hours in each day be allowed for inspection), be open to inspection of any member of the company without charge.

(8) If—

(*a*) default is made in complying with subsection (1) or (5), or

(*b*) an inspection required under subsection (7) is refused, or

(*c*) default is made for 14 days in complying with subsection (4),

the company and every officer of it who is in default is liable to a fine and, for continued contravention, to a daily default fine.

(9) In the case of a refusal of an inspection required under subsection (7) of a copy or memorandum, the court may by order compel an immediate inspection of it.

(10) Subsections (1) and (5) apply to a variation of a director's contract of service as they apply to the contract.

(11) This section does not require that there be kept a copy of, or memorandum setting out the terms of, a contract (or its variation) at a time when the unexpired portion of the term for which the contract is to be in force is less than 12 months, or at a time at which the contract can, within the next ensuing 12 months, be terminated by the company without payment of compensation.

Director's contract of employment for more than five years

319.—(1) This section applies in respect of any term of an agreement whereby a director's employment with the company of which he is a director or, where he is the director of a holding company, his employment within the group is to continue, or may be continued, otherwise than at the instance of the company (whether under the original agreement or under a new agreement entered into in pursuance of it), for a period of more than five years during which the employment—

(*a*) cannot be terminated by the company by notice; or

(*b*) can be so terminated only in specified circumstances.

(2) In any case where—

(*a*) a person is or is to be employed with a company under an agreement which cannot be terminated by the company by notice or can be so terminated only in specified circumstances; and

(*b*) more than six months before the expiration of the period for which he is or is to be so employed, the company enters into a further agreement (otherwise than in pursuance of a right conferred by or under the original agreement on the other party to it) under which he is to be employed with the company or, where he is a director of a holding company, within the group,

this section applies as if to the period for which he is to be employed under that further agreement there were added a further period equal to the unexpired period of the original agreement.

(3) A company shall not incorporate in an agreement such a term as is mentioned in subsection (1), unless the term is first approved by a resolution of the company in general meeting and, in the case of a director of a holding company, by a resolution of that company in general meeting.

(4) No approval is required to be given under this section by any body corporate unless it is a company within the meaning of this Act, or is registered under section 680, or if it is a wholly-owned subsidiary of any body corporate, wherever incorporated.

(5) A resolution of a company approving such a term as is mentioned in subsection (1) shall not be passed at a general meeting of the company unless a written memorandum setting out the proposed agreement incorporating the term is available for inspection by members of the company both—

(*a*) at the company's registered office for not less than 15 days ending with the date of the meeting; and

(*b*) at the meeting itself.

(6) A term incorporated in an agreement in contravention of this section is, to the extent that it contravenes the section, void; and that agreement and, in a case where subsection (2) applies, the original agreement are deemed to contain a term entitling the company to terminate it at any time by the giving of reasonable notice.

(7) In this section—

(*a*) "employment" includes employment under a contract for services; and

(*b*) "group", in relation to a director of a holding company, means the group which consists of that company and its subsidiaries;

and for purposes of this section a shadow director is treated as a director.

Substantial property transactions involving directors, etc.

320.—(1) With the exceptions provided by the section next following, a company shall not enter into an arrangement—

(*a*) whereby a director of the company or its holding company, or a person connected with such a director, acquires or is to acquire one or more non-cash assets of the requisite value from the company; or

(*b*) whereby the company acquires or is to acquire one or more non-cash assets of the requisite value from such a director or a person so connected,

unless the arrangement is first approved by a resolution of the company in general meeting and, if the director or connected person is a director of its holding company or a person connected with such a director, by a resolution in general meeting of the holding company.

(2) For this purpose a non-cash asset is of the requisite value if at the time the arrangement in question is entered into its value is not less than £1,000 but (subject to that) exceeds £50,000 or 10 per cent of the company's asset value, that is—

(*a*) except in a case falling within paragraph (*b*) below, the value of the company's net assets determined by reference to the accounts prepared and laid under Part VII in respect of the last preceding financial year in respect of which such accounts were so laid; and

(*b*) where no accounts have been so prepared and laid before that time, the amount of the company's called-up share capital.

(3) For purposes of this section and sections 321 and 322, a shadow director is treated as a director.

Exceptions from s. 320

321.—(1) No approval is required to be given under section 320 by any body corporate unless it is a company within the meaning of this Act or registered under section 680 or, if it is a wholly-owned subsidiary of any body corporate, wherever incorporated.

(2) Section 320(1) does not apply to an arrangement for the acquisition of a non-cash asset—

(*a*) if the asset is to be acquired by a holding company from any of its wholly-owned subsidiaries or from a holding company by any of its wholly-owned subsidiaries, or by one wholly-owned subsidiary of a holding company from another wholly-owned subsidiary of that same holding company, or

(*b*) if the arrangement is entered into by a company which is being wound up, unless the winding up is a members' voluntary winding up.

(3) Section 320(1)(a) does not apply to an arrangement whereby a person is to acquire an asset from a company of which he is a member, if the arrangement is made with that person in his character as a member.

Liabilities arising from contravention of s. 320

322.—(1) An arrangement entered into by a company in contravention of section 320, and any transaction entered into in pursuance of the arrangement (whether by the company or any other person) is voidable at the instance of the company unless one or more of the conditions specified in the next subsection is satisfied.

(2) Those conditions are that—

(*a*) restitution of any money or other asset which is the subject-matter of the arrangement or transaction is no longer possible or the company has been indemnified in pursuance of this section by any other person for the loss or damage suffered by it; or

(*b*) any rights acquired *bona fide* for value and without actual notice of the contravention by any person who is not a party to the arrangement or transaction would be affected by its avoidance; or

(*c*) the arrangement is, within a reasonable period, affirmed by the company in general meeting and, if it is an arrangement for the transfer of an asset to or by a director of its holding company or a person who is connected with such a director, is so affirmed with the approval of the holding company given by a resolution in general meeting.

(3) If an arrangement is entered into with a company by a director of the company or its holding company or a person connected with him in contravention of section 320, that director and the person so connected, and any other director of the company who authorised the arrangement or any transaction entered into in pursuance of such an arrangement, is liable—

(*a*) to account to the company for any gain which he has made directly or indirectly by the arrangement or transaction, and

(*b*) (jointly and severally with any other person liable under this subsection) to indemnify the company for any loss or damage resulting from the arrangement or transaction.

(4) Subsection (3) is without prejudice to any liability imposed otherwise than by that subsection, and is subject to the following two subsections; and the liability under subsection (3) arises whether or not the arrangement or transaction entered into has been avoided in pursuance of subsection (1).

(5) If an arrangement is entered into by a company and a person connected with a director of the company or its holding company in contravention of section 320, that director is not liable under subsection (3) if he shows that he took all reasonable steps to secure the company's compliance with that section.

(6) In any case, a person so connected and any such other director as is mentioned in subsection (3) is not so liable if he shows that, at the time the arrangement was entered into, he did not know the relevant circumstances constituting the contravention.

Share dealings by directors and their families

Prohibition on directors dealing in share options

323.—(1) It is an offence for a director of a company to buy—

(*a*) a right to call for delivery at a specified price and within a specified time of a specified number of relevant shares or a specified amount of relevant debentures; or

(*b*) a right to make delivery at a specified price and within a specified time of a specified number of relevant shares or a specified amount of relevant debentures; or

(*c*) a right (as he may elect) to call for delivery at a specified price and within a specified time or to make delivery at a specified price and within a specified time of a specified number of relevant shares or a specified amount of relevant debentures.

(2) A person guilty of an offence under subsection (1) is liable to imprisonment or a fine, or both.

(3) In subsection (1)—

(*a*) "relevant shares", in relation to a director of a company, means shares in the company or in any other body corporate, being the company's subsidiary or holding company, or a subsidiary of the company's holding company, being shares as respects which there has been granted a listing on a stock exchange (whether in Great Britain or elsewhere);

(*b*) "relevant debentures", in relation to a director of a company, means debentures of the company or of any other body corporate, being the company's subsidiary or holding company or a subsidiary of the company's holding company, being debentures as respects which there has been granted such a listing; and

(*c*) "price" includes any consideration other than money.

(4) This section applies to a shadow director as to a director.

(5) This section is not to be taken as penalising a person who buys a right to subscribe for shares in, or debentures of, a body corporate or buys debentures of a body corporate that confer upon the holder of them a right to subscribe for, or to convert the debentures (in whole or in part) into, shares of that body.

Duty of director to disclose shareholdings in own company

324.—(1) A person who becomes a director of a company and at the time when he does so is interested in shares in, or debentures of, the company or any other body corporate, being the company's subsidiary or holding company or a subsidiary of the company's holding company, is under obligation to notify the company in writing—

(*a*) of the subsistence of his interests at that time; and

(*b*) of the number of shares of each class in, and the amount of debentures of each class of, the company or other such body corporate in which each interest of his subsists at that time.

(2) A director of a company is under obligation to notify the company in writing of the occurrence, while he is a director, of any of the following events—

(*a*) any event in consequence of whose occurrence he becomes, or ceases to be, interested in shares in, or debentures of, the company or any other body corporate, being the company's subsidiary or holding company or a subsidiary of the company's holding company;

(*b*) the entering into by him of a contract to sell any such shares or debentures;

(*c*) the assignment by him of a right granted to him by the company to subscribe for shares in, or debentures of, the company; and

(*d*) the grant to him by another body corporate, being the company's subsidiary or holding company or a subsidiary of the company's holding company, of a right to subscribe for shares in, or debentures of, that other body corporate, the exercise of such a right granted to him and the assignment by him of such a right so granted;

and notification to the company must state the number or amount, and class, of shares or debentures involved.

(3) Schedule 13 has effect in connection with subsections (1) and (2) above; and of that Schedule—

(*a*) Part I contains rules for the interpretation of, and otherwise in relation to, those subsections and applies in determining, for purposes of those subsections, whether a person has an interest in shares or debentures;

(*b*) Part II applies with respect to the periods within which obligations imposed by the subsections must be fulfilled; and

(c) Part III specifies certain circumstances in which obligations arising from subsection (2) are to be treated as not discharged;

and subsections (1) and (2) are subject to any exceptions for which provision may be made by regulations made by the Secretary of State by statutory instrument.[1]

(4) Subsection (2) does not require the notification by a person of the occurrence of an event whose occurrence comes to his knowledge after he has ceased to be a director.

(5) An obligation imposed by this section is treated as not discharged unless the notice by means of which it purports to be discharged is expressed to be given in fulfilment of that obligation.

(6) This section applies to shadow directors as to directors; but nothing in it operates so as to impose an obligation with respect to shares in a body corporate which is the wholly-owned subsidiary of another body corporate.

(7) A person who—

(a) fails to discharge, within the proper period, an obligation to which he is subject under subsection (1) or (2), or

(b) in purported discharge of an obligation to which he is so subject, makes to the company a statement which he knows to be false, or recklessly makes to it a statement which is false,

is guilty of an offence and liable to imprisonment or a fine, or both.

(8) Section 732 (restriction on prosecutions) applies to an offence under this section.

NOTE
[1] See S.I. 1985 No. 802.

Register of directors' interests notified under s. 324

325.—(1) Every company shall keep a register for the purposes of section 324.

(2) Whenever a company receives information from a director given in fulfilment of an obligation imposed on him by that section, it is under obligation to enter in the register, against the director's name, the information received and the date of the entry.

(3) The company is also under obligation, whenever it grants to a director a right to subscribe for shares in, or debentures of, the company to enter in the register against his name—

(a) the date on which the right is granted,

(b) the period during which, or time at which, it is exercisable,

(c) the consideration for the grant (or, if there is no consideration, that fact), and

(d) the description of shares or debentures involved and the number or amount of them, and the price to be paid for them (or the consideration, if otherwise than in money).

(4) Whenever such a right as is mentioned above is exercised by a director, the company is under obligation to enter in the register against his name that fact (identifying the right), the number or amount of shares or debentures in respect of which it is exercised and, if they were registered in his name, that fact and, if not, the name or names of the person or persons in whose name or names they were registered, together (if they were registered in the names of two persons or more) with the number or amount of the shares or debentures registered in the name of each of them.

(5) Part IV of Schedule 13 has effect with respect to the register to be kept under this section, to the way in which entries in it are to be made, to the right of inspection, and generally.

(6) For purposes of this section, a shadow director is deemed a director.

Sanctions for non-compliance

326.—(1) The following applies with respect to defaults in complying with, and to contraventions of, section 325 and Part IV of Schedule 13.

(2) If default is made in complying with any of the following provisions—

(*a*) section 325(1), (2), (3) or (4), or

(*b*) Schedule 13, paragraph 21, 22 or 28,

the company and every officer of it who is in default is liable to a fine and, for continued contravention, to a daily default fine.

(3) If an inspection of the register required under paragraph 25 of the Schedule is refused, or a copy required under paragraph 26 is not sent within the proper period, the company and every officer of it who is in default is liable to a fine and, for continued contravention, to a daily default fine.

(4) If default is made for 14 days in complying with paragraph 27 of the Schedule (notice to registrar of where register is kept), the company and every officer of it who is in default is liable to a fine and, for continued contravention, to a daily default fine.

(5) If default is made in complying with paragraph 29 of the Schedule (register to be produced at annual general meeting), the company and every officer of it who is in default is liable to a fine.

(6) In the case of a refusal of an inspection of the register required under paragraph 25 of the Schedule, the court may by order compel an immediate inspection of it; and in the case of failure to send within the proper period a copy required under paragraph 26, the court may by order direct that the copy be sent to the person requiring it.

Extension of s. 323 to spouses and children

327.—(1) Section 323 applies to—

(*a*) the wife or husband of a director of a company (not being herself or himself a director of it), and

(*b*) an infant son or infant daughter of a director (not being himself or herself a director of the company),

as it applies to the director; but it is a defence for a person charged by virtue of this section with an offence under section 323 to prove that he (she) had no reason to believe that his (her) spouse or, as the case may be, parent was a director of the company in question.

(2) For purposes of this section—

(*a*) "son" includes step-son, and "daughter" includes step-daughter ("parent" being construed accordingly),

(*b*) "infant" means, in relation to Scotland, pupil or minor, and

(*c*) a shadow director of a company is deemed a director of it.

Extension of s. 324 to spouses and children

328.—(1) For the purposes of section 324—

(*a*) an interest of the wife or husband of a director of a company (not being herself or himself a director of it) in shares or debentures is to be treated as the director's interest; and

(*b*) the same applies to an interest of an infant son or infant daughter of a director of a company (not being himself or herself a director of it) in shares or debentures.

(2) For those purposes—

(*a*) a contract, assignment or right of subscription entered into, exercised or made by, or a grant made to, the wife or husband of a director of a company (not being herself or himself a director of it) is to be treated as having been entered into, exercised or made by, or (as the case may be) as having been made to, the director; and

(*b*) the same applies to a contract, assignment or right of subscription entered into, exercised or made by, or grant made to, an infant son or infant daughter of a director of a company (not being himself or herself a director of it).

(3) A director of a company is under obligation to notify the company in writing of the occurrence while he or she is a director, of either of the following events, namely—

(a) the grant by the company to his (her) spouse, or to his or her infant son or infant daughter, of a right to subscribe for shares in, or debentures of, the company; and

(b) the exercise by his (her) spouse or by his or her infant son or infant daughter of such a right granted by the company to the wife, husband, son or daughter.

(4) In a notice given to the company under subsection (3) there shall be stated—

(a) in the case of the grant of a right, the like information as is required by section 324 to be stated by the director on the grant to him by another body corporate of a right to subscribe for shares in, or debentures of, that other body corporate; and

(b) in the case of the exercise of a right, the like information as is required by that section to be stated by the director on the exercise of a right granted to him by another body corporate to subscribe for shares in, or debentures of, that other body corporate.

(5) An obligation imposed by subsection (3) on a director must be fulfilled by him before the end of five days beginning with the day following that on which the occurrence of the event giving rise to it comes to his knowledge; but in reckoning that period of days there is disregarded any Saturday or Sunday, and any day which is a bank holiday in any part of Great Britain.

(6) A person who—

(a) fails to fulfil, within the proper period, an obligation to which he is subject under subsection (3), or

(b) in purported fulfilment of such an obligation, makes to a company a statement which he knows to be false, or recklessly makes to a company a statement which is false,

is guilty of an offence and liable to imprisonment or a fine, or both.

(7) The rules set out in Part I of Schedule 13 have effect for the interpretation of, and otherwise in relation to, subsections (1) and (2); and subsections (5), (6) and (8) of section 324 apply with any requisite modification.

(8) In this section, "son" includes step-son, "daughter" includes step-daughter, and "infant" means, in relation to Scotland, pupil or minor.

(9) For purposes of section 325, an obligation imposed on a director by this section is to be treated as if imposed by section 324.

Duty to notify stock exchange of matters notified under preceding sections

329.—[1] (1) Whenever a company whose shares or debentures are listed on a recognised investment exchange other than an overseas investment exchange within the meaning of the Financial Services Act 1986 is notified of any matter by a director in consequence of the fulfilment of an obligation imposed by section 324 or 328, and that matter relates to shares or debentures so listed, the company is under obligation to notify that investment exchange of that matter; and the investment exchange may publish, in such manner as it may determine, any information received by it under this subsection.

(2) An obligation imposed by subsection (1) must be fulfilled before the end of the day next following that on which it arises; but there is disregarded for this purpose a day which is a Saturday or a Sunday or a bank holiday in any part of Great Britain.

(3) If default is made in complying with this section, the company and every officer of it who is in default is guilty of an offence and liable to a fine and, for continued contravention, to a daily default fine.

Section 732 (restriction on prosecutions) applies to an offence under this section.

NOTE

[1] As amended by the Financial Services Act 1986, Sched. 16, para. 20.

Restrictions on a company's power to make loans, etc., to directors and persons connected with them

General restriction on loans etc. to directors and persons connected with them

330.—(1) The prohibitions listed below in this section are subject to the exceptions in sections 332 to 338.

(2) A company shall not—

(*a*) make a loan to a director of the company or of its holding company;

(*b*) enter into any guarantee or provide any security in connection with a loan made by any person to such a director.

(3) A relevant company shall not—

(*a*) make a quasi-loan to a director of the company or of its holding company;

(*b*) make a loan or a quasi-loan to a person connected with such a director;

(*c*) enter into a guarantee or provide any security in connection with a loan or quasi-loan made by any other person for such a director or a person so connected.

(4) A relevant company shall not—

(*a*) enter into a credit transaction as creditor for such a director or a person so connected;

(*b*) enter into any guarantee or provide any security in connection with a credit transaction made by any other person for such a director or a person so connected.

(5) For purposes of sections 330 to 346, a shadow director is treated as a director.

(6) A company shall not arrange for the assignment to it, or the assumption by it, of any rights, obligations or liabilities under a transaction which, if it had been entered into by the company, would have contravened subsection (2), (3) or (4); but for the purposes of sections 330 to 347 the transaction is to be treated as having been entered into on the date of the arrangement.

(7) A company shall not take part in any arrangement whereby—

(*a*) another person enters into a transaction which, if it had been entered into by the company, would have contravened any of subsections (2), (3), (4) or (6); and

(*b*) that other person, in pursuance of the arrangement, has obtained or is to obtain any benefit from the company or its holding company or a subsidiary of the company or its holding company.

Definitions for ss.330 et seq.

331.—(1) The following subsections apply for the interpretation of sections 330 to 346.

(2) "Guarantee" includes indemnity, and cognate expressions are to be construed accordingly.

(3) A quasi-loan is a transaction under which one party ("the creditor") agrees to pay, or pays otherwise than in pursuance of an agreement, a sum for another ("the borrower") or agrees to reimburse, or reimburses otherwise than in pursuance of an agreement, expenditure incurred by another party for another ("the borrower")—

(*a*) on terms that the borrower (or a person on his behalf) will reimburse the creditor; or

(*b*) in circumstances giving rise to a liability on the borrower to reimburse the creditor.

(4) Any reference to the person to whom a quasi loan is made is a reference to the borrower; and the liabilities of a borrower under a quasi-loan include the liabilities of any person who has agreed to reimburse the creditor on behalf of the borrower.

(5) [Repealed by the Banking Act 1987, Sched. 7, Pt. 1.]

[1] (6) "Relevant company" means a company which—

(a) is a public company, or

(b) is a subsidiary of a public company, or

(c) is a subsidiary of a company which has as another subsidiary a public company, or

(d) has a subsidiary which is a public company.

(7) A credit transaction is a transaction under which one party ("the creditor")—

(a) supplies any goods or sells any land under a hire-purchase agreement or a conditional sale agreement;

(b) leases or hires any land or goods in return for periodical payments;

(c) otherwise disposes of land or supplies goods or services on the understanding that payment (whether in a lump sum or instalments or by way of periodical payments or otherwise) is to be deferred.

(8) "Services" means anything other than goods or land.

(9) A transaction or arrangement is made "for" a person if—

(a) in the case of a loan or quasi-loan, it is made to him;

(b) in the case of a credit transaction, he is the person to whom goods or services are supplied, or land is sold or otherwise disposed of, under the transaction;

(c) in the case of a guarantee or security, it is entered into or provided in connection with a loan or quasi-loan made to him or a credit transaction made for him;

(d) in the case of an arrangement within subsection (6) or (7) of section 330, the transaction to which the arrangement relates was made for him; and

(e) in the case of any other transaction or arrangement for the supply or transfer of, or of any interest in, goods, land or services, he is the person to whom the goods, land or services (or the interest) are supplied or transferred.

(10) "Conditional sale agreement" means the same as in the Consumer Credit Act 1974.

NOTE

[1] For interpretation of "public company", see s.1(3) and the Companies Consolidation (Consequential Provisions) Act 1985, s.1.

Short-term quasi-loans

332.—(1) Subsection (3) of section 330 does not prohibit a company ("the creditor") from making a quasi-loan to one of its directors or to a director of its holding company if—

(a) the quasi-loan contains a term requiring the director or a person on his behalf to reimburse the creditor his expenditure within two months of its being incurred; and

(b) the aggregate of the amount of that quasi-loan and of the amount outstanding under each relevant quasi-loan does not exceed £1,000.

(2) A quasi-loan is relevant for this purpose if it was made to the director by virtue of this section by the creditor or its subsidiary or, where the director is a director of the creditor's holding company, any other subsidiary of that company; and "the amount outstanding" is the amount of the outstanding liabilities of the person to whom the quasi-loan was made.

Inter-company loans in same group

333. In the case of a relevant company which is a member of a group of companies (meaning a holding company and its subsidiaries), paragraphs (b) and (c) of section 330(3) do not prohibit the company from—

(a) making a loan or quasi-loan to another member of that group; or (*b*) entering into a guarantee or providing any security in connection with a loan or quasi-loan made by any person to another member of the group,

by reason only that a director of one member of the group is associated with another.

Loans of small amounts

334. Without prejudice to any other provision of sections 332 to 338, paragraph (*a*) of section 330(2) does not prohibit a company from making a loan to a director of the company or of its holding company if the aggregate of the relevant amounts does not exceed £2,500.

Minor and business transactions

335.—(1) Section 330(4) does not prohibit a company from entering into a transaction for a person if the aggregate of the relevant amounts does not exceed £5,000.

(2) Section 330(4) does not prohibit a company from entering into a transaction for a person if—

(*a*) the transaction is entered into by the company in the ordinary course of its business; and

(*b*) the value of the transaction is not greater, and the terms on which it is entered into are no more favourable, in respect of the person for whom the transaction is made, than that or those which it is reasonable to expect the company to have offered to or in respect of a person of the same financial standing but unconnected with the company.

Transactions at behest of holding company

336. The following transactions are excepted from the prohibitions of section 330—

(*a*) a loan or quasi-loan by a company to its holding company, or a company entering into a guarantee or providing any security in connection with a loan or quasi-loan made by any person to its holding company;

(*b*) a company entering into a credit transaction as creditor for its holding company, or entering into a guarantee or providing any security in connection with a credit transaction made by any other person for its holding company.

Funding of director's expenditure on duty to company

337.—(1) A company is not prohibited by section 330 from doing anything to provide a director with funds to meet expenditure incurred or to be incurred by him for the purposes of the company or for the purpose of enabling him properly to perform his duties as an officer of the company.

(2) Nor does the section prohibit a company from doing anything to enable a director to avoid incurring such expenditure.

(3) Subsections (1) and (2) apply only if one of the following conditions is satisfied—

(*a*) the thing in question is done with prior approval of the company given at a general meeting at which there are disclosed all the matters mentioned in the next subsection;

(*b*) that thing is done on condition that, if the approval of the company is not so given at or before the next annual general meeting, the loan is to be repaid, or any other liability arising under any such transaction discharged, within six months from the conclusion of that meeting;

but those subsections do not authorise a relevant company to enter into any transaction if the aggregate of the relevant amounts exceeds £10,000.

(4) The matters to be disclosed under subsection (3)(*a*) are—

(*a*) the purpose of the expenditure incurred or to be incurred, or which would otherwise be incurred, by the director, (*b*) the amount of the funds to be provided by the company, and

(*c*) the extend of the company's liability under any transaction which is or is connected with the thing in question.

Loan or quasi-loan by money-lending company

338.—(1) There is excepted from the prohibitions in section 330—

(*a*) a loan or quasi-loan made by a money-lending company to any person; or

(*b*) a money-lending company entering into a guarantee in connection with any other loan or quasi-loan.

(2) "Money-lending company" means a company whose ordinary business includes the making of loans or quasi-loans, or the giving of guarantees in connection with loans or quasi-loans.

(3) Subsection (1) applies only if both the following conditions are satisfied—

(*a*) the loan or quasi-loan in question is made by the company, or it enters into the guarantee, in the ordinary course of the company's business; and

(*b*) the amount of the loan or quasi-loan, or the amount guaranteed, is not greater, and the terms of the loan, quasi-loan or guarantee are not more favourable, in the case of the person to whom the loan or quasi-loan is made or in respect of whom the guarantee is entered into, than that or those which it is reasonable to expect that company to have offered to or in respect of a person of the same financial standing but unconnected with the company.

[1] (4) But subsection (1) does not authorise a relevant company (unless it is a banking company) to enter into any transaction if the aggregate of the relevant amounts exceeds £50,000.

(5) In determining that aggregate, a company which a director does not control is deemed not to be connected with him.

(6) The condition specified in subsection (3)(*b*) does not of itself prevent a company from making a loan to one of its directors or a director of its holding company—

(*a*) for the purpose of facilitating the purchase, for use as that director's only or main residence, of the whole or part of any dwelling-house together with any land to be occupied and enjoyed with it;

(*b*) for the purpose of improving a dwelling-house or part of a dwelling-house so used or any land occupied and enjoyed with it;

(*c*) in substitution for any loan made by any person and falling within paragraph (*a*) or (*b*) of this subsection, if loans of that description are ordinarily made by the company to its employees and on terms no less favourable than those on which the transaction in question is made, and the aggregate of the relevant amounts does not exceed £50,000.

NOTE

[1] As amended by the Banking Act 1987, Sched. 6, para. 18, and the Companies Act 1989, s. 23 and Sched. 10, para. 10.

"Relevant amounts" for purposes of ss.334 et seq.

339.—(1) This section has effect for defining the "relevant amounts" to be aggregated under sections 334, 335(1), 337(3) and 338(4); and in relation to any proposed transaction or arrangement and the question whether it falls within one or other of the exceptions provided by those sections, "the relevant exception" is that exception; but where the relevant exception is the one provided by section 334 (loan of small amount), references in this section to a person connected with a director are to be disregarded.

(2) Subject as follows, the relevant amounts in relation to a proposed transaction or arrangement are—

    (*a*) the value of the proposed transaction or arrangement,
    (*b*) the value of any existing arrangement which—
        (i) falls within subsection (6) or (7) of section 330, and
        (ii) also falls within subsection (3) of this section, and
        (iii) was entered into by virtue of the relevant exception by the company or by a subsidiary of the company or, where the proposed transaction or arrangement is to be made for a director of its holding company or a person connected with such a director, by that holding company or any of its subsidiaries;
    (*c*) the amount outstanding under any other transaction—
        (i) falling within subsection (3) below, and
        (ii) made by virtue of the relevant exception, and
        (iii) made by the company or by a subsidiary of the company or, where the proposed transaction or arrangement is to be made for a director of its holding company or a person connected with such a director, by that holding company or any of its subsidiaries.

(3) A transaction falls within this subsection if it was made—
    (*a*) for the director for whom the proposed transaction or arrangement is to be made, or for any person connected with that director; or
    (*b*) where the proposed transaction or arrangement is to be made for a person connected with a director of a company, for that director or any person connected with him;

and an arrangement also falls within this subsection if it relates to a transaction which does so.

[1] (4) But where the proposed transaction falls within section 338 and is one which a banking company proposes to enter into under subsection (6) of that section (housing loans, etc.), any other transaction or arrangement which apart from this subsection would fall within subsection (3) of this section does not do so unless it was entered into in pursuance of section 338(6).

(5) A transaction entered into by a company which is (at the time of that transaction being entered into) a subsidiary of the company which is to make the proposed transaction, or is a subsidiary of that company's holding company, does not fall within subsection (3) if at the time when the question arises (that is to say, the question whether the proposed transaction or arrangement falls within any relevant exception), it no longer is such a subsidiary.

(6) Values for purposes of subsection (2) of this section are to be determined in accordance with the section next following; and "the amount outstanding" for purposes of subsection (2)(*c*) above is the value of the transaction less any amount by which that value has been reduced.

NOTE

[1] As amended by the Banking Act 1987, Sched. 6, para. 18, and the Companies Act 1989, s. 23 and Sched. 10, para. 10.

"Value" of transactions and arrangements

340.—(1) This section has effect for determining the value of a transaction or arrangement for purposes of sections 330 to 339.

(2) The value of a loan is the amount of its principal.

(3) The value of a quasi-loan is the amount, or maximum amount, which the person to whom the quasi-loan is made is liable to reimburse the creditor.

(4) The value of a guarantee or security is the amount guaranteed or secured.

(5) The value of an arrangement to which section 330(6) or (7) applies is the value of the transaction to which the arrangement relates less any amount by which the liabilities under the arrangement or transaction of the person for whom the transaction was made have been reduced.

(6) The value of a transaction or arrangement not falling within subsections (2) to (5) above is the price which it is reasonable to expect could be obtained for the goods, land or services to which the transaction or

arrangement relates if they had been supplied (at the time the transaction or arrangement is entered into) in the ordinary course of business and on the same terms (apart from price) as they have been supplied, or are to be supplied, under the transaction or arrangement in question.

(7) For purposes of this section, the value of a transaction or arrangement which is not capable of being expressed as a specific sum of money (because the amount of any liability arising under the transaction or arrangement is unascertainable, or for any other reason), whether or not any liability under the transaction or arrangement has been reduced, is deemed to exceed £50,000.

Civil remedies for breach of s. 330

341.—(1) If a company enters into a transaction or arrangement in contravention of section 330, the transaction or arrangement is voidable at the instance of the company unless—

> (a) restitution of any money or any other asset which is the subject-matter of the arrangement or transaction is no longer possible, or the company has been indemnified in pursuance of subsection (2)(b) below for the loss or damage suffered by it, or
>
> (b) any rights acquired *bona fide* for value and without actual notice of the contravention by a person other than the person for whom the transaction or arrangement was made would be affected by its avoidance.

(2) Where an arrangement or transaction is made by a company for a director of the company or its holding company or a person connected with such a director in contravention of section 330, that director and the person so connected and any other director of the company who authorised the transaction or arrangement (whether or not it has been avoided in pursuance of subsection (1)) is liable—

> (a) to account to the company for any gain which he has made directly or indirectly by the arrangement or transaction; and
>
> (b) (jointly and severally with any other person liable under this subsection) to indemnify the company for any loss or damage resulting from the arrangement or transaction.

(3) Subsection (2) is without prejudice to any liability imposed otherwise than by that subsection, but is subject to the next two subsections.

(4) Where an arrangement or transaction is entered into by a company and a person connected with a director of the company or its holding company in contravention of section 330, that director is not liable under subsection (2) of this section if he shows that he took all reasonable steps to secure the company's compliance with that section.

(5) In any case, a person so connected and any such other director as is mentioned in subsection (2) is not so liable if he shows that, at the time the arrangement or transaction was entered into, he did not know the relevant circumstances constituting the contravention.

Criminal penalties for breach of s. 330

342.—(1) A director of a relevant company who authorises or permits the company to enter into a transaction or arrangement knowing or having reasonable cause to believe that the company was thereby contravening section 330 is guilty of an offence.

(2) A relevant company which enters into a transaction or arrangement for one of its directors or for a director of its holding company in contravention of section 330 is guilty of an offence.

(3) A person who procures a relevant company to enter into a transaction or arrangement knowing or having reasonable cause to believe that the company was thereby contravening section 330 is guilty of an offence.

(4) A person guilty of an offence under this section is liable to imprisonment or a fine, or both.

(5) A relevant company is not guilty of an offence under subsection (2) if

Companies Act 1985

I 205

it shows that, at the time the transaction or arrangement was entered into, it did not know the relevant circumstances.

Record of transactions not disclosed in company accounts

343.—(1) The following provisions of this section—

[1] (a) apply in the case of a company which is, or is the holding company of, a banking company, and

(b) are subject to the exceptions provided by section 344.

[2] (2) Such a company shall maintain a register containing a copy of every transaction, arrangement or agreement of which particulars would, but for paragraph 2 of Part IV of Schedule 9, be required to be disclosed in the company's accounts or group accounts for the current financial year and for each of the preceding 10 financial years.

(3) In the case of a transaction, arrangement or agreement which is not in writing, there shall be contained in the register a written memorandum setting out its terms.

[2] (4) Such a company shall before its annual general meeting make available at its registered office for not less than 15 days ending with the date of the meeting a statement containing the particulars of transactions, arrangements and agreements which the company would, but for paragraph 2 of Part IV of Schedule 9, be required to disclose in its accounts or group accounts for the last complete financial year preceding that meeting.

(5) The statement shall be so made available for inspection by members of the company; and such a statement shall also be made available for their inspection at the annual general meeting.

(6) It is the duty of the company's auditors to examine the statement before it is made available to members of the company and to make a report to the members on it; and the report shall be annexed to the statement before it is made so available.

(7) The auditors' report shall state whether in their opinion the statement contains the particulars required by subsection (4); and, where their opinion is that it does not, they shall include in the report, so far as they are reasonably able to do so, a statement giving the required particulars.

(8) If a company fails to comply with any provision of subsections (2) to (5), every person who at the time of the failure is a director of it is guilty of an offence and liable to a fine; but—

(a) it is a defence in proceedings against a person for this offence to prove that he took all reasonable steps for securing compliance with the subsection concerned, and

(b) a person is not guilty of the offence by virtue only of being a shadow director of the company.

(9) For purposes of the application of this section to loans and quasi-loans made by a company to persons connected with a person who at any time is a director of the company or of its holding company, a company which a person does not control is not connected with him.

NOTES

[1] As amended by the Banking Act 1987, Sched. 6, para. 18, and the Companies Act 1989, s. 23 and Sched. 10, para. 10.

[2] As amended by the Companies Act 1989, s. 23 and Sched. 10, para. 11.

Exceptions from s.343

344.—(1) Section 343 does not apply in relation to—

(a) transactions or arrangements made or subsisting during a financial year by a company or by a subsidiary of a company for a person who was at any time during that year a director of the company or of its holding company or was connected with such a director, or

(b) an agreement made or subsisting during that year to enter into such a transaction or arrangement,

if the aggregate of the values of each transaction or arrangement made for that person, and of each agreement for such a transaction or arrangement,

[Release 19: 1 - vi - 90.]

less the amount (if any) by which the value of those transactions, arrangements and agreements has been reduced, did not exceed £1,000 at any time during the financial year.

For purposes of this subsection, values are to be determined as under section 340.

[1] (2) Section 343(4) and (5) do not apply to a banking company which is the wholly-owned subsidiary of a company incorporated in the United Kingdom.

NOTE

[1] As amended by the Banking Act 1987, Sched. 6, para. 18, and the Companies Act 1989, s. 23 and Sched. 10, para. 10.

Supplementary

Power to increase financial limits

345.—(1) The Secretary of State may by order in a statutory instrument substitute for any sum of money specified in this Part a larger sum specified in the order.

(2) An order under this section is subject to annulment in pursuance of a resolution of either House of Parliament.

(3) Such an order does not have effect in relation to anything done or not done before its coming into force; and accordingly, proceedings in respect of any liability (whether civil or criminal) incurred before that time may be continued or instituted as if the order had not been made.

"Connected persons", etc.

346.—(1) This section has effect with respect to references in this Part to a person being "connected" with a director of a company, and to a director being "associated with" or "controlling" a body corporate.

(2) A person is connected with a director of a company if, but only if, he (not being himself a director of it) is—

(*a*) that director's spouse, child or step-child; or

(*b*) except where the context otherwise requires, a body corporate with which the director is associated; or

(*c*) a person acting in his capacity as trustee of any trust the beneficiaries of which include—

(i) the director, his spouse or any children or step-children of his, or

(ii) a body corporate with which he is associated, or of a trust whose terms confer a power on the trustees that may be exercised for the benefit of the director, his spouse, or any children or step-children of his, or any such body corporate; or

(*d*) a person acting in his capacity as partner of that director or of any person who, by virtue of paragraph (*a*), (*b*) or (*c*) of this subsection, is connected with that director; or

(*e*) a Scottish firm in which—

(i) that director is a partner,

(ii) a partner is a person who, by virtue of paragraph (*a*), (*b*) or (*c*) above, is connected with that director, or

(iii) a partner is a Scottish firm in which that director is a partner or in which there is a partner who, by virtue of paragraph (*a*), (*b*) or (*c*) above, is connected with that director.

(3) In subsection (2)—

(*a*) a reference to the child or step-child of any person includes an illegitimate child of his, but does not include any person who has attained the age of 18; and

(*b*) paragraph (*c*) does not apply to a person acting in his capacity as trustee under an employees' share scheme or a pension scheme.

(4) A director of a company is associated with a body corporate if, but only if, he and the persons connected with him, together—

(*a*) are interested in shares comprised in the equity share capital of that body corporate of a nominal value equal to at least one-fifth of that share capital; or (*b*) are entitled to exercise or control the exercise of more than one-fifth of the voting power at any general meeting of that body.

(5) A director of a company is deemed to control a body corporate if, but only if—

(*a*) he or any person connected with him is interested in any part of the equity share capital of that body or is entitled to exercise or control the exercise of any part of the voting power at any general meeting of that body; and

(*b*) that director, the persons connected with him and the other directors of that company, together, are interested in more than one-half of that share capital or are entitled to exercise or control the exercise of more than one-half of that voting power.

(6) For purposes of subsections (4) and (5)—

(*a*) a body corporate with which a director is associated is not to be treated as connected with that director unless it is also connected with him by virtue of subsection (2)(*c*) or (*d*); and

(*b*) a trustee of a trust the beneficiaries of which include (or may include) a body corporate with which a director is associated is not to be treated as connected with a director by reason only of that fact.

(7) The rules set out in Part I of Schedule 13 apply for the purposes of subsections (4) and (5).

(8) References in those subsections to voting power the exercise of which is controlled by a director include voting power whose exercise is controlled by a body corporate controlled by him; but this is without prejudice to other provisions of subsections (4) and (5).

Transactions under foreign law

347. For purposes of sections 319 to 322 and 330 to 343, it is immaterial whether the law which (apart from this Act) governs any arrangement or transaction is the law of the United Kingdom, or of a part of it, or not.

PART XI

COMPANY ADMINISTRATION AND PROCEDURE

CHAPTER I
COMPANY IDENTIFICATION

Company name to appear outside place of business

348.—(1) Every company shall paint or affix, and keep painted or affixed, its name on the outside of every office or place in which its business is carried on, in a conspicuous position and in letters easily legible.

(2) If a company does not paint or affix its name as required above, the company and every officer of it who is in default is liable to a fine; and if a company does not keep its name painted or affixed as so required, the company and every officer of it who is in default is liable to a fine and, for continued contravention, to a daily default fine.

Company's name to appear in its correspondence, etc.

349.—(1) Every company shall have its name mentioned in legible characters—

(*a*) in all business letters of the company,
(*b*) in all its notices and other official publications,
(*c*) in all bills of exchange, promissory notes, endorsements, cheques and orders for money or goods purporting to be signed by or on behalf of the company, and
(*d*) in all its bills of parcels, invoices, receipts and letters of credit.

(2) If a company fails to comply with subsection (1) it is liable to a fine.

(3) If an officer of a company or a person on its behalf—

(*a*) issues or authorises the issue of any business letter of the company, or any notice or other official publication of the company, in which the company's name is not mentioned as required by subsection (1), or

(*b*) issues or authorises the issue of any bill of parcels, invoice, receipt or letter of credit of the company in which its name is not so mentioned,

he is liable to a fine.

(4) If an officer of a company or a person on its behalf signs or authorises to be signed on behalf of the company any bill of exchange, promissory note, endorsement, cheque or order for money or goods in which the company's name is not mentioned as required by subsection (1), he is liable to a fine; and he is further personally liable to the holder of the bill of exchange, promissory note, cheque or order for money or goods for the amount of it (unless it is duly paid by the company).

Company seal

350.—(1) Every company shall have its name engraved in legible characters on its seal; and if a company fails to comply with this subsection, it is liable to a fine.

(2) If an officer of a company or a person on its behalf uses or authorises the use of any seal purporting to be a seal of the company on which its name is not engraved as required by subsection (1), he is liable to a fine.

Particulars in correspondence, etc.

351.—(1) Every company shall have the following particulars mentioned in legible characters in all business letters and order forms of the company, that is to say—

(*a*) the company's place of registration and the number with which it is registered,

(*b*) the address of its registered office,

(*c*) in the case of an investment company (as defined in section 266), the fact that it is such a company, and

(*d*) in the case of a limited company exempt from the obligation to use the word "limited" as part of its name, the fact that it is a limited company.

(2) If in the case of a company having a share capital there is on the stationery used for any such letters, or on the company's order forms, a reference to the amount of share capital, the reference must be to paid-up share capital.

(3) Where the name of a public company includes, as its last part, the equivalent in Welsh of the words "public limited company" ("cwmni cyfyngedig cyhoeddus"), the fact that the company is a public limited company shall be stated in English and in legible characters—

(*a*) in all prospectuses, bill-heads, letter paper, notices and other official publications of the company, and

(*b*) in a notice conspicuously displayed in every place in which the company's business is carried on.

(4) Where the name of a limited company has "cyfyngedig" as the last word, the fact that the company is a limited company shall be stated in English and in legible characters—

(*a*) in all prospectuses, bill-heads, letter paper, notices and other official publications of the company, and

(*b*) in a notice conspicuously displayed in every place in which the company's business is carried on.

(5) As to contraventions of this section, the following applies—

(*a*) if a company fails to comply with subsection (1) or (2), it is liable to a fine, (*b*) if an officer of a company or a person on its behalf issues or author-ises the issue of any business letter or order form not complying with those subsections, he is liable to a fine, and

(*c*) if subsection (3) or (4) is contravened, the company and every offi-cer of it who is in default is liable to a fine and, in the case of subsec-tion (3), to a daily default fine for continued contravention.

CHAPTER II
REGISTER OF MEMBERS

Obligation to keep and enter up register

352.—(1) Every company shall keep a register of its members and enter in it the particulars required by this section.

(2) There shall be entered in the register—

(*a*) the names and addresses of the members;

(*b*) the date on which each person was registered as a member; and

(*c*) the date at which any person ceased to be a member.

(3) The following applies in the case of a company having a share capi-tal—

(*a*) with the names and addresses of the members there shall be entered a statement—

(i) of the shares held by each member, distinguishing each share by its number (so long as the share has a number) and, where the company has more than one class of issued shares, by its class, and

(ii) of the amount paid or agreed to be considered as paid on the shares of each member;

(*b*) where the company has converted any of its shares into stock and given notice of the conversion to the registrar of companies, the register shall show the amount and class of stock held by each mem-ber, instead of the amount of shares and the particulars relating to shares specified in paragraph (*a*).

(4) In the case of a company which does not have a share capital but has more than one class of members, there shall be entered in the register, with the names and addresses of the members, the class to which each member belongs.

(5) If a company makes default in complying with this section, the com-pany and every officer of it who is in default is liable to a fine and, for con-tinued contravention, to a daily default fine.

(6) An entry relating to a former member of the company may be removed from the register after the expiration of 20 years from the date on which he ceased to be a member.

(7) Liability incurred by a company from the making or deletion of an entry in its register of members, or from a failure to make or delete any such entry, is not enforceable more than 20 years after the date on which the entry was made or deleted or, in the case of any such failure, the failure first occurred.

This is without prejudice to any lesser period of limitation.

Location of register

353.—(1) A company's register of members shall be kept at its registered office, except that—

(*a*) if the work of making it up is done at another office of the company, it may be kept there; and

(*b*) if the company arranges with some other person for the making up of the register to be undertaken on its behalf by that other, it may be kept at the office of the other at which the work is done;

but it must not be kept, in the case of a company registered in England and

Wales, at any place elsewhere than in England and Wales or, in the case of a company registered in Scotland, at any place elsewhere than in Scotland.

(2) Subject as follows, every company shall send notice in the prescribed form to the registrar of companies of the place where its register of members is kept, and of any change in that place.

(3) The notice need not be sent if the register has, at all times since it came into existence (or, in the case of a register in existence on 1st July 1948, at all times since then) been kept at the company's registered office.

(4) If a company makes default for 14 days in complying with subsection (2), the company and every officer of it who is in default is liable to a fine and, for continued contravention, to a daily default fine.

Index of members

354.—(1) Every company having more than 50 members shall, unless the register of members is in such a form as to constitute in itself an index, keep an index of the names of the members of the company and shall, within 14 days after the date on which any alteration is made in the register of members, make any necessary alteration in the index.

(2) The index shall in respect of each member contain a sufficient indication to enable the account of that member in the register to be readily found.

(3) The index shall be at all times kept at the same place as the register of members.

(4) If default is made in complying with this section, the company and every officer of it who is in default is liable to a fine and, for continued contravention, to a daily default fine.

Entries in register in relation to share warrants

355.—(1) On the issue of a share warrant the company shall strike out of its register of members the name of the member then entered in it as holding the shares specified in the warrant as if he had ceased to be a member, and shall enter in the register the following particulars, namely—

(a) the fact of the issue of the warrant;

(b) a statement of the shares included in the warrant, distinguishing each share by its number so long as the share has a number; and

(c) the date of the issue of the warrant.

(2) Subject to the company's articles, the bearer of a share warrant is entitled, on surrendering it for cancellation, to have his name entered as a member in the register of members.

(3) The company is responsible for any loss incurred by any person by reason of the company entering in the register the name of a bearer of a share warrant in respect of the shares specified in it without the warrant being surrendered and cancelled.

(4) Until the warrant is surrendered, the particulars specified in subsection (1) are deemed to be those required by this Act to be entered in the register of members; and, on the surrender, the date of the surrender must be entered.

(5) Except as provided by section 291(2) (director's share qualification), the bearer of a share warrant may, if the articles of the company so provide, be deemed a member of the company within the meaning of this Act, either to the full extent or for any purposes defined in the articles.

Inspection of register and index

356.—(1) Except when the register of members is closed under the provisions of this Act, the register and the index of members' names shall during business hours be open to the inspection of any member of the company without charge, and of any other person on payment of the appropriate charge.

(2) The reference to business hours is subject to such reasonable restric-

tions as the company in general meeting may impose, but so that not less than two hours in each day is to be allowed for inspection.

(3) Any member of the company or other person may require a copy of the register, or of any part of it, on payment of the appropriate charge; and the company shall cause any copy so required by a person to be sent to him within 10 days beginning with the day next following that on which the requirement is received by the company.

(4) The appropriate charge is—

(*a*) under subsection (1), 5 pence or such less sum as the company may prescribe, for each inspection; and

(*b*) under subsection (3), 10 pence or such less sum as the company may prescribe, for every 100 words (or fraction of 100 words) required to be copied.

(5) If an inspection required under this section is refused, or if a copy so required is not sent within the proper period, the company and every officer of it who is in default is liable in respect of each offence to a fine.

(6) In the case of such refusal or default, the court may by order compel an immediate inspection of the register and index, or direct that the copies required be sent to the persons requiring them.

Non-compliance with ss. 353, 354, 356; agent's default

357. Where under section 353(1)(*b*), the register of members is kept at the office of some person other than the company, and by reason of any default of his the company fails to comply with—

   section 353(2) (notice to registrar),
   section 354(3) (index to be kept with register), or
   section 356 (inspection),

or with any requirement of this Act as to the production of the register, that other person is liable to the same penalties as if he were an officer of the company who was in default, and the power of the court under section 356(6) extends to the making of orders against that other and his officers and servants.

Power to close register

358. A company may, on giving notice by advertisement in a newspaper circulating in the district in which the company's registered office is situated, close the register of members for any time or times not exceeding in the whole 30 days in each year.

Power of court to rectify register

359.—(1) If—

(*a*) the name of any person is, without sufficient cause, entered in or omitted from a company's register of members, or

(*b*) default is made or unnecessary delay takes place in entering on the register the fact of any person having ceased to be a member,

the person aggrieved, or any member of the company, or the company, may apply to the court for rectification of the register.

(2) The court may either refuse the application or may order rectification of the register and payment by the company of any damages sustained by any party aggrieved.

(3) On such an application the court may decide any question relating to the title of a person who is a party to the application to have his name entered in or omitted from the register, whether the question arises between members or alleged members, or between members or alleged members on the one hand and the company on the other hand, and generally may decide any question necessary or expedient to be decided for rectification of the register.

(4) In the case of a company required by this Act to send a list of its members to the registrar of companies, the court, when making an order for rectification of the register, shall by its order direct notice of the rectification to be given to the registrar.

Trusts not to be entered on register in England and Wales

360. No notice of any trust, expressed, implied or constructive, shall be entered on the register, or be receivable by the registrar, in the case of companies registered in England and Wales.

Register to be evidence

361. The register of members is *prima facie* evidence of any matters which are by this Act directed or authorised to be inserted in it.

Overseas branch registers

362.—(1) A company having a share capital whose objects comprise the transaction of business in any of the countries or territories specified in Part I of Schedule 14 to this Act may cause to be kept in any such country or territory in which it transacts business a branch register of members resident in that country or territory.

(2) Such a branch register is to be known as an "overseas branch register"; and—

(a) any dominion register kept by a company under section 119 of the Companies Act 1948 is to become known as an overseas branch register of the company;

(b) where any Act or instrument (including in particular a company's articles) refers to a company's dominion register, that reference is to be read (unless the context otherwise requires) as being to an overseas branch register kept under this section; and

(c) references to a colonial register occurring in articles registered before 1st November 1929 are to be read as referring to an overseas branch register.

(3) Part II of Schedule 14 has effect with respect to overseas branch registers kept under this section; and Part III of the Schedule enables corresponding facilities in Great Britain to be accorded to companies incorporated in other parts of the world.

(4) The Foreign Jurisdiction Act 1890 has effect as if subsection (1) of this section, and Part II of Schedule 14, were included among the enactments which by virtue of section 5 of that Act may be applied by Order in Council to foreign countries in which for the time being Her Majesty has jurisdiction.

(5) Her Majesty may by Order in Council direct that subsection (1) above and Part II of Schedule 14 shall extend, with such exceptions, modifications or adaptations (if any) as may be specified in the Order, to any territories under Her Majesty's protection to which those provisions cannot be extended under the Foreign Jurisdiction Act 1890.

CHAPTER III
ANNUAL RETURN

Annual return (company having a share capital)

363.—(1) Subject to the provisions of this section, every company having a share capital shall, at least once in every year, make a return containing with respect to the company's registered office, registers of members and debenture holders, shares and debentures, indebtedness, past and present members and directors and secretary, the matters specified in Schedule 15.

(2) The annual return shall be in the prescribed form.

(3) A company need not make a return under subsection (1) either in the year of its incorporation or, if it is not required by this Act to hold an annual general meeting during the following year, in that year.

(4) Where the company has converted any of its shares into stock and given notice of the conversion to the registrar of companies, the list referred to in paragraph 5 of Schedule 15 must state the amount of stock held by each of the existing members instead of the amount of shares and the particulars relating to shares required by that paragraph.

(5) The return may, in any year, if the return for either of the two immediately preceding years has given (as at the date of that return) the full particulars required by that paragraph of the Schedule, give only such of those particulars as relate to persons ceasing to be or becoming members since the date of the last return and to shares transferred since that date or to changes as compared with that date in the amount of stock held by a member.

(6) The following applies to a company keeping an overseas branch register—

(*a*) references in subsection (5) to the particulars required by paragraph 5 are to be taken as not including any such particulars contained in the overseas branch register, in so far as copies of the entries containing those particulars are not received at the company's registered office before the date when the return in question is made;

(*b*) if an annual return is made between the date when entries are made in the overseas branch register and the date when copies of those entries are received at the company's registered office, the particulars contained in those entries (so far as relevant to an annual return) shall be included in the next or a subsequent annual return, as may be appropriate having regard to the particulars included in that return with respect to the company's register of members.

(7) If a company fails to comply with this section, the company and every officer of it who is in default is liable to a fine and, for continued contravention, to a daily default fine.

(8) For purposes of this section and Schedule 15, a shadow director is deemed a director and officer.

Annual return (company not having a share capital)

364.—(1) Every company not having a share capital shall once at least in every calendar year make a return in the prescribed form stating—

(*a*) the address of the company's registered office;

(*b*) if the register of members is under provisions of this Act kept elsewhere than at that office, the address of the place where it is kept;

(*c*) if any register of holders of debentures of the company or any duplicate of any such register or part of it is under provisions of this Act kept elsewhere than at the company's registered office, the address of the place where it is kept;

(*d*) all such particulars with respect to the persons who at the date of the return are the directors of the company, and any person who at that date is its secretary, as are by this Act required to be contained (with respect to directors and the secretary respectively) in the company's register of directors and secretaries.

(2) A company need not make a return under subsection (1) either in the year of its incorporation or, if it is not required by this Act to hold an annual general meeting during the following year, in that year.

(3) There shall be included in the return a statement containing particulars of the total amount of the company's indebtedness in respect of all mortgages and charges (whenever created) of any description specified in section 396(1) or, in the case of a company registered in Scotland, section 410(4).

(4) If a company fails to comply with this section, the company and every officer of it who is in default is liable to a fine and, for continued contravention, to a daily default fine.

(5) For purposes of this section, a shadow director is deemed a director and officer.

Time for completion of annual return

365.—(1) A company's annual return must be completed within 42 days after the annual general meeting for the year, whether or not that meeting is the first or only ordinary general meeting, or the first or only general meeting of the company in that year.

(2) The company must forthwith forward to the registrar of companies a copy of the return signed both by a director and by the secretary of the company.

(3) If a company fails to comply with this section, the company and every officer of it who is in default is liable to a fine and, for continued contravention, to a daily default fine; and for this purpose a shadow director is deemed an officer.

CHAPTER IV
MEETINGS AND RESOLUTIONS

Meetings

Annual general meeting

366.—(1) Every company shall in each year hold a general meeting as its annual general meeting in addition to any other meetings in that year, and shall specify the meeting as such in the notices calling it.

(2) However, so long as a company holds its first annual general meeting within 18 months of its incorporation, it need not hold it in the year of its incorporation or in the following year.

(3) Not more than 15 months shall elapse between the date of one annual general meeting of a company and that of the next.

(4) If default is made in holding a meeting in accordance with this section, the company and every officer of it who is in default is liable to a fine.

Election by private company to dispense with annual general meetings

[1] **366A.**—(1) A private company may elect (by elective resolution in accordance with section 379A) to dispense with the holding of annual general meetings.

(2) An election has effect for the year in which it is made and subsequent years, but does not affect any liability already incurred by reason of default in holding an annual general meeting.

(3) In any year in which an annual general meeting would be required to be held but for the election, and in which no such meeting has been held, any member of the company may, by notice to the company not later than three months before the end of the year, require the holding of an annual general meeting in that year.

(4) If such a notice is given, the provisions of section 366(1) and (4) apply with respect to the calling of the meeting and the consequences of default.

(5) If the election ceases to have effect, the company is not obliged under section 366 to hold an annual general meeting in that year if, when the election ceases to have effect, less than three months of the year remains.

This does not affect any obligation of the company to hold an annual general meeting in that year in pursuance of a notice given under subsection (3).

NOTE
[1] Inserted by the Companies Act 1989, s. 115(2).

Secretary of State's power to call meeting in default

367.—(1) If default is made in holding a meeting in accordance with section 366, the Secretary of State may, on the application of any member of the company, call, or direct the calling of, a general meeting of the company and give such ancillary or consequential directions as he thinks expedient, including directions modifying or supplementing, in relation to the calling, holding and conduct of the meeting, the operation of the company's articles.

(2) The directions that may be given under subsection (1) include a direction that one member of the company present in person or by proxy shall be deemed to constitute a meeting.

(3) If default is made in complying with directions of the Secretary of State under subsection (1), the company and every officer of it who is in default is liable to a fine.

(4) A general meeting held under this section shall, subject to any directions of the Secretary of State, be deemed to be an annual general meeting of the company; but, where a meeting so held is not held in the year in which the default in holding the company's annual general meeting occurred, the meeting so held shall not be treated as the annual general meeting for the year in which it is held unless at that meeting the company resolves that it be so treated.

(5) Where a company so resolves, a copy of the resolution shall, within 15 days after its passing, be forwarded to the registrar of companies and recorded by him; and if default is made in complying with this subsection, the company and every officer of it who is in default is liable to a fine and, for continued contravention, to a daily default fine.

Extraordinary general meeting on members' requisition

368.—(1) The directors of a company shall, on a members' requisition, forthwith proceed duly to convene an extraordinary general meeting of the company.

This applies notwithstanding anything in the company's articles.

(2) A members' requisition is a requisition of—

(*a*) members of the company holding at the date of the deposit of the requisition not less than one-tenth of such of the paid-up capital of the company as at that date carries the right of voting at general meetings of the company; or

(*b*) in the case of a company not having a share capital, members of it representing not less than one-tenth of the total voting rights of all the members having at the date of deposit of the requisition a right to vote at general meetings.

(3) The requisition must state the objects of the meeting, and must be signed by the requisitionists and deposited at the registered office of the company, and may consist of several documents in like form each signed by one or more requisitionists.

(4) If the directors do not within 21 days from the date of the deposit of the requisition proceed duly to convene a meeting, the requisitionists, or any of them representing more than one-half of the total voting rights of all of them, may themselves convene a meeting, but any meeting so convened shall not be held after the expiration of three months from that date.

(5) A meeting convened under this section by requisitionists shall be convened in the same manner, as nearly as possible, as that in which meetings are to be convened by directors.

(6) Any reasonable expenses incurred by the requisitionists by reason of the failure of the directors duly to convene a meeting shall be repaid to the requisitionists by the company, and any sum so repaid shall be retained by the company out of any sums due or to become due from the company by way of fees or other remuneration in respect of their services to such of the directors as were in default.

(7) In the case of a meeting at which a resolution is to be proposed as a special resolution, the directors are deemed not to have duly convened the

meeting if they do not give the notice required for special resolutions by section 378(2).

Length of notice for calling meetings

369.—(1) A provision of a company's articles is void in so far as it provides for the calling of a meeting of the company (other than an adjourned meeting) by a shorter notice than—

    (*a*) in the case of the annual general meeting, 21 days' notice in writing; and

    (*b*) in the case of a meeting other than an annual general meeting or a meeting for the passing of a special resolution—

        (i) seven days' notice in writing in the case of an unlimited company, and

        (ii) otherwise, 14 days' notice in writing.

(2) Save in so far as the articles of a company make other provision in that behalf (not being a provision avoided by subsection (1)), a meeting of the company (other than an adjourned meeting) may be called—

    (*a*) in the case of the annual general meeting, by 21 days' notice in writing; and

    (*b*) in the case of a meeting other than an annual general meeting or a meeting for the passing of a special resolution—

        (i) by seven days' notice in writing in the case of an unlimited company, and

        (ii) otherwise, 14 days' notice in writing.

(3) Notwithstanding that a meeting is called by shorter notice than that specified in subsection (2) or in the company's articles (as the case may be), it is deemed to have been duly called if it is so agreed—

    (*a*) in the case of a meeting called as the annual general meeting, by all the members entitled to attend and vote at it; and

    (*b*) otherwise, by the requisite majority.

(4) The requisite majority for this purpose is a majority in number of the members having a right to attend and vote at the meeting, being a majority—

    (*a*) together holding not less than 95 per cent. in nominal value of the shares giving a right to attend and vote at the meeting; or

    (*b*) in the case of a company not having a share capital, together representing not less than 95 per cent. of the total voting rights at that meeting of all the members.

[1] A private company may elect (by elective resolution in accordance with section 379A) that the above provisions shall have effect in relation to the company as if for the references to 95 per cent. there were substituted references to such lesser percentage, but not less than 90 per cent., as may be specified in the resolution or subsequently determined by the company in general meeting.

NOTE

[1] Inserted by the Companies Act 1989, s. 115(3).

General provisions as to meetings and votes

370.—(1) The following provisions have effect in so far as the articles of the company do not make other provision in that behalf.

(2) Notice of the meeting of a company shall be served on every member of it in the manner in which notices are required to be served by Table A (as for the time being in force).

(3) Two or more members holding not less than one-tenth of the issued share capital or, if the company does not have a share capital, not less than 5 per cent. in number of the members of the company may call a meeting.

(4) Two members personally present are a quorum.

(5) Any member elected by the members present at a meeting may be chairman of it.

(6) In the case of a company originally having a share capital, every member has one vote in respect of each share or each £10 of stock held by him; and in any other case every member has one vote.

Power of court to order meeting

371.—(1) If for any reason it is impracticable to call a meeting of a company in any manner in which meetings of that company may be called, or to conduct the meeting in manner prescribed by the articles or this Act, the court may, either of its own motion or on the application—

(*a*) of any director of the company, or

(*b*) of any member of the company who would be entitled to vote at the meeting,

order a meeting to be called, held and conducted in any manner the court thinks fit.

(2) Where such an order is made, the court may give such ancillary or consequential directions as it thinks expedient; and these may include a direction that one member of the company present in person or by proxy be deemed to constitute a meeting.

(3) A meeting called, held and conducted in accordance with an order under subsection (1) is deemed for all purposes a meeting of the company duly called, held and conducted.

Proxies

[1] **372.**—(1) Any member of a company entitled to attend and vote at a meeting of it is entitled to appoint another person (whether a member or not) as his proxy to attend and vote instead of him; and in the case of a private company a proxy appointed to attend and vote instead of a member has also the same right as the member to speak at the meeting.

(2) But, unless the articles otherwise provide—

(*a*) subsection (1) does not apply in the case of a company not having a share capital; and

(*b*) a member of a private company is not entitled to appoint more than one proxy to attend on the same occasion; and

[THE NEXT PAGE IS I 217]

(*c*) a proxy is not entitled to vote except on a poll.

(3) In the case of a company having a share capital, in every notice calling a meeting of the company there shall appear with reasonable prominence a statement that a member entitled to attend and vote is entitled to appoint a proxy or, where that is allowed, one or more proxies to attend and vote instead of him, and that a proxy need not also be a member.

(4) If default is made in complying with subsection (3) as respects any meeting, every officer of the company who is in default is liable to a fine.

(5) A provision contained in a company's articles is void in so far as it would have the effect of requiring the instrument appointing a proxy, or any other document necessary to show the validity of, or otherwise relating to, the appointment of a proxy, to be received by the company or any other person more than 48 hours before a meeting or adjourned meeting in order that the appointment may be effective.

(6) If for the purpose of any meeting of a company invitations to appoint as proxy a person or one of a number of persons specified in the invitations are issued at the company's expense to some only of the members entitled to be sent a notice of the meeting and to vote at it by proxy, then every officer of the company who knowingly and wilfully authorises or permits their issue in that manner is liable to a fine.

However, an officer is not so liable by reason only of the issue to a member at his request in writing of a form of appointment naming the proxy, or of a list of persons willing to act as proxy, if the form or list is available on request in writing to every member entitled to vote at the meeting by proxy.

(7) This section applies to meetings of any class of members of a company as it applies to general meetings of the company.

NOTE
[1] For interpretation of "private company", see s. 1(3) and the Companies Consolidation (Consequential Provisions) Act 1985, s. 1.

Right to demand a poll

373.—(1) A provision contained in a company's articles is void in so far as it would have the effect either—

(*a*) of excluding the right to demand a poll at a general meeting on any question other than the election of the chairman of the meeting or the adjournment of the meeting; or

(*b*) of making ineffective a demand for a poll on any such question which is made either—

(i) by not less than five members having the right to vote at the meeting; or

(ii) by a member or members representing not less than one-tenth of the total voting rights of all the members having the right to vote at the meeting; or

(iii) by a member or members holding shares in the company conferring a right to vote at the meeting, being shares on which an aggregate sum has been paid up equal to not less than one-tenth of the total sum paid up on all the shares conferring that right.

(2) The instrument appointing a proxy to vote at a meeting of a company is deemed also to confer authority to demand or join in demanding a poll; and for the purposes of subsection (1) a demand by a person as proxy for a member is the same as a demand by the member.

Voting on a poll

374. On a poll taken at a meeting of a company or a meeting of any class of members of a company, a member entitled to more than one vote need not, if he votes, use all his votes or cast all the votes he uses in the same way.

Representation of corporations at meetings

375.—(1) A corporation, whether or not a company within the meaning of this Act, may—

    (*a*) if it is a member of another corporation, being such a company, by resolution of its directors or other governing body authorise such person as it thinks fit to act as its representative at any meeting of the company or at any meeting of any class of members of the company;

    (*b*) if it is a creditor (including a holder of debentures) of another corporation, being such a company, by resolution of its directors or other governing body authorise such person as it thinks fit to act as its representative at any meeting of creditors of the company held in pursuance of this Act or of rules made under it, or in pursuance of the provisions contained in any debenture or trust deed, as the case may be.

(2) A person so authorised is entitled to exercise the same powers on behalf of the corporation which he represents as that corporation could exercise if it were an individual shareholder, creditor or debenture-holder of the other company.

Resolutions

Circulation of members' resolutions

376.—(1) Subject to the section next following, it is the duty of a company, on the requisition in writing of such number of members as is specified below and (unless the company otherwise resolves) at the expense of the requisitionists—

    (*a*) to give to members of the company entitled to receive notice of the next annual general meeting notice of any resolution which may properly be moved and is intended to be moved at that meeting;

    (*b*) to circulate to members entitled to have notice of any general meeting sent to them any statement of not more than 1,000 words with respect to the matter referred to in any proposed resolution or the business to be dealt with at that meeting.

(2) The number of members necessary for a requisition under subsection (1) is—

    (*a*) any number representing not less than one-twentieth of the total voting rights of all the members having at the date of the requisition a right to vote at the meeting to which the requisition relates; or

    (*b*) not less than 100 members holding shares in the company on which there has been paid up an average sum, per member, of not less than £100.

(3) Notice of any such resolution shall be given, and any such statement shall be circulated, to members of the company entitled to have notice of the meeting sent to them, by serving a copy of the resolution or statement on each such member in any manner permitted for service of notice of the meeting.

(4) Notice of any such resolution shall be given to any other member of the company by giving notice of the general effect of the resolution in any manner permitted for giving him notice of meetings of the company.

(5) For compliance with subsections (3) and (4), the copy must be served, or notice of the effect of the resolution be given (as the case may be), in the same manner and (so far as practicable) at the same time as notice of the meeting; and, where it is not practicable for it to be served or given at the same time, it must be served or given as soon as practicable thereafter.

(6) The business which may be dealt with at an annual general meeting includes any resolution of which notice is given in accordance with this section; and for purposes of this subsection notice is deemed to have been so

given notwithstanding the accidental omission, in giving it, of one or more members. This has effect notwithstanding anything in the company's articles.

(7) In the event of default in complying with this section, every officer of the company who is in default is liable to a fine.

In certain cases, compliance with s. 376 not required

377.—(1) A company is not bound under section 376 to give notice of a resolution or to circulate a statement unless—

(*a*) a copy of the requisition signed by the requisitionists (or two or more copies which between them contain the signatures of all the requisitionists) is deposited at the registered office of the company—

    (i) in the case of a requisition requiring notice of a resolution, not less than six weeks before the meeting, and

    (ii) otherwise, not less than one week before the meeting; and

(*b*) there is deposited or tendered with the requisition a sum reasonably sufficient to meet the company's expenses in giving effect to it.

(2) But if, after a copy of a requisition requiring notice of a resolution has been deposited at the company's registered office, an annual general meeting is called for a date six weeks or less after the copy has been deposited, the copy (though not deposited within the time required by subsection (1)) is deemed properly deposited for the purposes of that subsection.

(3) The company is also not bound under section 376 to circulate a statement if, on the application either of the company or of any other person who claims to be aggrieved, the court is satisfied that the rights conferred by that section are being abused to secure needless publicity for defamatory matter; and the court may order the company's costs on such an application to be paid in whole or in part by the requisitionists notwithstanding that they are not parties to the application.

Extraordinary and special resolutions

378.—(1) A resolution is an extraordinary resolution when it has been passed by a majority of not less than three-fourths of such members as (being entitled to do so) vote in person or, where proxies are allowed, by proxy, at a general meeting of which notice specifying the intention to propose the resolution as an extraordinary resolution has been duly given.

(2) A resolution is a special resolution when it has been passed by such a majority as is required for the passing of an extraordinary resolution and at a general meeting of which not less than 21 days' notice, specifying the intention to propose the resolution as a special resolution, has been duly given.

(3) If it is so agreed by a majority in number of the members having the right to attend and vote at such a meeting, being a majority—

(*a*) together holding not less than 95 per cent. in nominal value of the shares giving that right; or

(*b*) in the case of a company not having a share capital, together representing not less than 95 per cent. of the total voting rights at that meeting of all the members,

a resolution may be proposed and passed as a special resolution at a meeting of which less than 21 days' notice has been given.

A private company may elect (by elective resolution in accordance with section 379A) that the above provisions shall have effect in relation to the company as if for the references to 95 per cent. there were substituted references to such lesser percentage, but not less than 90 per cent., as may be specified in the resolution or subsequently determined by the company in general meeting.

(4) At any meeting at which an extraordinary resolution or a special resolution is submitted to be passed, a declaration by the chairman that the

resolution is carried is, unless a poll is demanded, conclusive evidence of the fact without proof of the number or proportion of the votes recorded in favour of or against the resolution.

(5) In computing the majority on a poll demanded on the question that an extraordinary resolution or a special resolution be passed, reference is to be had to the number of votes cast for and against the resolution.

(6) For purposes of this section, notice of a meeting is deemed duly given, and the meeting duly held, when the notice is given and the meeting held in the manner provided by this Act or the company's articles.

NOTE
[1] Inserted by the Companies Act 1989, s. 115(3).

Resolution requiring special notice

379.—(1) Where by any provision of this Act special notice is required of a resolution, the resolution is not effective unless notice of the intention to move it has been given to the company at least 28 days before the meeting at which it is moved.

(2) The company shall give its members notice of any such resolution at the same time and in the same manner as it gives notice of the meeting or, if that is not practicable, shall give them notice either by advertisement in a newspaper having an appropriate circulation or in any other mode allowed by the company's articles, at least 21 days before the meeting.

(3) If, after notice of the intention to move such a resolution has been given to the company, a meeting is called for a date 28 days or less after the notice has been given, the notice is deemed properly given, though not given within the time required.

Elective resolution of private company

[1] **379A.**—(1) An election by a private company for the purposes of—

  (*a*) section 80A (election as to duration of authority to allot shares),

  (*b*) section 252 (election to dispense with laying of accounts and reports before general meeting),

  (*c*) section 366A (election to dispense with holding of annual general meeting),

  (*d*) section 369(4) or 378(3) (election as to majority required to authorise short notice of meeting), or

  (*e*) section 386 (election to dispense with appointment of auditors annually),

shall be made by resolution of the company in general meeting in accordance with this section.

Such a resolution is referred to in this Act as an "elective resolution".

(2) An elective resolution is not effective unless—

  (*a*) at least 21 days' notice in writing is given of the meeting, stating that an elective resolution is to be proposed and stating the terms of the resolution, and

  (*b*) the resolution is agreed to at the meeting, in person or by proxy, by all the members entitled to attend and vote at the meeting.

(3) The company may revoke an elective resolution by passing an ordinary resolution to that effect.

(4) An elective resolution shall cease to have effect if the company is re-registered as a public company.

(5) An elective resolution may be passed or revoked in accordance with this section, and the provisions referred to in subsection (1) have effect, notwithstanding any contrary provision in the company's articles of association.

NOTE
[1] Inserted by the Companies Act 1989, s. 116(2).

Registration, etc. of resolutions and agreements

380.—(1) A copy of every resolution or agreement to which this section applies shall, within 15 days after it is passed or made, be forwarded to the registrar of companies and recorded by him; and it must be either a printed copy or else a copy in some other form approved by the registrar.

(2) Where articles have been registered, a copy of every such resolution or agreement for the time being in force shall be embodied in or annexed to every copy of the articles issued after the passing of the resolution or the making of the agreement.

(3) Where articles have not been registered, a printed copy of every such resolution or agreement shall be forwarded to any member at his request on payment of 5 pence or such less sum as the company may direct.

[1] (4) This section applies to—

(*a*) special resolutions;

(*b*) extraordinary resolutions;

[2](*bb*) an elective resolution or a resolution revoking such a resolution;

(*c*) resolutions or agreements which have been agreed to by all the members of a company but which, if not so agreed to, would not have been effective for their purpose unless (as the case may be) they had been passed as special resolutions or as extraordinary resolutions;

(*d*) resolutions or agreements which have been agreed to by all the members of some class of shareholders but which, if not so agreed to, would not have been effective for their purpose unless they had been passed by some particular majority or otherwise in some particular manner, and all resolutions or agreements which effectively bind all the members of any class of shareholders though not agreed to by all those members;

(*e*) a resolution passed by the directors of a company in compliance with a direction under section 31(2) (change of name on Secretary of State's direction);

(*f*) a resolution of a company to give, vary, revoke or renew an authority to the directors for the purposes of section 80 (allotment of relevant securities);

(*g*) a resolution of the directors passed under section 147(2) (alteration of memorandum on company ceasing to be a public company, following acquisition of its own shares);

(*h*) a resolution conferring, varying, revoking or renewing authority under section 166 (market purchase of company's own shares);

(*j*) a resolution for voluntary winding up, passed under section 84(1)(*a*) of the Insolvency Act;

[THE NEXT PAGE IS I 221]

    (*k*) a resolution passed by the directors of an old public company, under section 2(1) of the Consequential Provisions Act, that the company should be re-registered as a public company.

    (5) If a company fails to comply with subsection (1), the company and every officer of it who is in default is liable to a fine and, for continued contravention, to a daily default fine.

    (6) If a company fails to comply with subsection (2) or (3), the company and every officer of it who is in default is liable to a fine.

    (7) For purposes of subsections (5) and (6), a liquidator of a company is deemed an officer of it.

NOTES

[1] As amended by the Insolvency Act 1986, Sched. 13, Pt. I.

[2] Inserted by the Companies Act 1989, s. 116(3).

Resolution passed at adjourned meeting

    381. Where a resolution is passed at an adjourned meeting of—

    (*a*) a company;

    (*b*) the holders of any class of shares in a company;

    (*c*) the directors of a company;

the resolution is for all purposes to be treated as having been passed on the date on which it was in fact passed, and is not to be deemed passed on any earlier date.

Written resolutions of private companies

Written resolutions of private companies

    [1] **381A.**—(1) Anything which in the case of a private company may be done—

    (*a*) by resolution of the company in general meeting, or

    (*b*) by resolution of a meeting of any class of members of the company,

may be done, without a meeting and without any previous notice being required, by resolution in writing signed by or on behalf of all the members of the company who at the date of the resolution would be entitled to attend and vote at such meeting.

    (2) The signatures need not be on a single document provided each is on a document which accurately states the terms of the resolution.

    (3) The date of the resolution means when the resolutiuon is signed by or on behalf of the last member to sign.

    (4) A resolution agreed to in accordance with this section has effect as if passed—

    (*a*) by the company in general meeting, or

    (*b*) by a meeting of the relevant class of members of the company,

as the case may be; and any reference in any enactment to a meeting at which a resolution is passed or to members voting in favour of a resolution shall be construed accordingly.

    (5) Any reference in any enactment to the date of passing of a resolution is, in relation to a resolution agreed to in accordance with this section, a reference to the date of the resolution, unless section 381B(4) applies in which case it shall be construed as a reference to the date from which the resolution has effect.

    (6) A resolution may be agreed to in accordance with this section which would otherwise be required to be passed as a special, extraordinary or elective resolution; and any reference in any enactment to a special, extraordinary or elective resolution includes such a resolution.

    (7) This section has effect subject to the exceptions specified in Part I of Schedule 15A; and in relation to certain descriptions of resolution under this section the procedural requirements of this Act have effect with the adaptations specified in Part II of that Schedule.

NOTE
[1] Inserted by the Companies Act 1989, s. 113(2).

Rights of auditors in relation to written resolution
[1] **381B.**—(1) A copy of any written resolution proposed to be agreed to in accordance with section 381A shall be sent to the company's auditors.

(2) If the resolution concerns the auditors as auditors, they may within seven days from the day on which they receive the copy give notice to the company stating their opinion that the resolution should be considered by the company in general meeting or, as the case may be, by a meeting of the relevant class of members of the company.

(3) A written resolution shall not have effect unless—
(*a*) the auditors notify the company that in their opinion the resolution—
  (i) does not concern them as auditors, or
  (ii) does so concern them but need not be considered by the company in general meeting or, as the case may be, by a meeting of the relevant class of members of the company, or
(*b*) the period for giving a notice under subsection (2) expires without any notice having been given in accordance with that subsection.

(4) A written resolution previously agreed to in accordance with section 381A shall not have effect until that notification is given or, as the case may be, that period expires.

NOTE
[1] Inserted by the Companies Act 1989, s. 113(2).

Written resolutions: supplementary provisions
[1] **381C.**—(1) Sections 381A and 381B have effect notwithstanding any provision of the company's memorandum or articles.

(2) Nothing in those sections affects any enactment or rule of law as to—
(*a*) things done otherwise than by passing a resolution, or
(*b*) cases in which a resolution is treated as having been passed, or a person is precluded from alleging that a resolution has not been duly passed.

NOTE
[1] Inserted by the Companies Act 1989, s. 113(2).

Records of proceedings

Minutes of meetings
382.—(1) Every company shall cause minutes of all proceedings of general meetings, all proceedings at meetings of its directors and, where there are managers, all proceedings at meetings of its managers to be entered in books kept for that purpose.

(2) Any such minute, if purporting to be signed by the chairman of the meeting at which the proceedings were had, or by the chairman of the next succeeding meeting, is evidence of the proceedings.

(3) Where a shadow director by means of a notice required by section 317(8) declares an interest in a contract or proposed contract, this section applies—
(*a*) if it is a specific notice under paragraph (*a*) of that subsection, as if the declaration had been made at the meeting there referred to, and
(*b*) otherwise, as if it had been made at the meeting of the directors next following the giving of the notice;
and the making of the declaration is in either case deemed to form part of the proceedings at the meeting.

(4) Where minutes have been made in accordance with this section of the proceedings at any general meeting of the company or meeting of directors or managers, then, until the contrary is proved, the meeting is deemed duly held and convened, and all proceedings had at the meeting to have been duly had; and all appointments of directors, managers or liquidators are deemed valid.

(5) If a company fails to comply with subsection (1), the company and every officer of it who is in default is liable to a fine and, for continued contravention, to a daily default fine.

Recording of written resolutions

[1] **382A.**—(1) Where a written resolution is agreed to in accordance with section 381A which has effect as if agreed by the company in general meeting, the company shall cause a record of the resolution (and of the signatures) to be entered in a book in the same way as minutes of proceedings of a general meeting of the company.

(2) Any such record, if purporting to be signed by a director of the company or by the company secretary, is evidence of the proceedings in agreeing to the resolution; and where a record is made in accordance with this section, then, until the contrary is proved, the requirements of this Act with respect to those proceedings shall be deemed to be complied with.

(3) Section 382(5) (penalties) applies in relation to a failure to comply with subsection (1) above as it applies in relation to a failure to comply with subsection (1) of that section; and section 383 (inspection of minute books) applies in relation to a record made in accordance with this section as it applies in relation to the minutes of a general meeting.

NOTE

[1] Inserted by the Companies Act 1989, s. 113(3).

Inspection of minute books

383.—(1) The books containing the minutes of proceedings of any general meeting of a company held on or after 1st November 1929 shall be kept at the company's registered office, and shall during business hours be open to the inspection of any member without charge.

(2) The reference to business hours is subject to such reasonable restrictions as the company may by its articles or in general meeting impose, but so that not less than two hours in each day be allowed for inspection.

(3) Any member shall be entitled to be furnished, within seven days after he has made a request in that behalf to the company, with a copy of any such minutes as are referred to above, at a charge of not more than $2\frac{1}{2}$ pence for every 100 words.

(4) If an inspection required under this section is refused or if a copy required under this section is not sent within the proper time, the company and every officer of it who is in default is liable in respect of each offence to a fine.

(5) In the case of any such refusal or default, the court may by order compel an immediate inspection of the books in respect of all proceedings of general meetings, or direct that the copies required be sent to the persons requiring them.

[1]CHAPTER V
AUDITORS

NOTE

[1] Ss. 384–388 and 389A–394A substituted by the Companies Act 1989, ss. 119–123(1).

Appointment of auditors

Duty to appoint auditors

[1] **384.**—(1) Every company shall appoint an auditor or auditors in accordance with this Chapter.

This is subject to section 388A (dormant company exempt from obligation to appoint auditors).

(2) Auditors shall be appointed in accordance with section 385 (appointment at general meeting at which accounts are laid), except in the case of a

private company which has elected to dispense with the laying of accounts in which case the appointment shall be made in accordance with section 385A.

(3) References in this Chapter to the end of the time for appointing auditors are to the end of the time within which an appointment must be made under section 385(2) or 385A(2), according to whichever of those sections applies.

(4) Sections 385 and 385A have effect subject to section 386 under which a private company may elect to dispense with the obligation to appoint auditors annually.

Appointment at general meeting at which accounts laid

385.—(1) This section applies to every public company and to a private company which has not elected to dispense with the laying of accounts.

(2) The company shall, at each general meeting at which accounts are laid, appoint an auditor or auditors to hold office from the conclusion of that meeting until the conclusion of the next general meeting at which accounts are laid.

(3) The first auditors of the company may be appointed by the directors at any time before the first general meeting of the company at which accounts are laid; and auditors so appointed shall hold office until the conclusion of that meeting.

(4) If the directors fail to exercise their powers under subsection (3), the powers may be exercised by the company in general meeting.

Appointment by private company which is not obliged to lay accounts

385A.—(1) This section applies to a private company which has elected in accordance with section 252 to dispense with the laying of accounts before the company in general meeting.

(2) Auditors shall be appointed by the company in general meeting before the end of the period of 28 days beginning with the day on which copies of the company's annual accounts for the previous financial year are sent to members under section 238 or, if notice is given under section 253(2) requiring the laying of the accounts before the company in general meeting, the conclusion of that meeting.

Auditors so appointed shall hold office from the end of that period or, as the case may be, the conclusion of that meeting until the end of the time for appointing auditors for the next financial year.

(3) The first auditors of the company may be appointed by the directors at any time before—

(*a*) the end of the period of 28 days beginning with the day on which copies of the company's first annual accounts are sent to members under section 238, or

(*b*) if notice is given under section 253(2) requiring the laying of the accounts before the company in general meeting, the beginning of that meeting;

and auditors so appointed shall hold office until the end of that period or, as the case may be, the conclusion of that meeting.

(4) If the directors fail to exercise their powers under subsection (3), the powers may be exercised by the company in general meeting.

(5) Auditors holding office when the election is made shall, unless the company in general meeting determines otherwise, continue to hold office until the end of the time for appointing auditors for the next financial year; and auditors holding office when an election ceases to have effect shall continue to hold office until the conclusion of the next general meeting of the company at which accounts are laid.

Election by private company to dispense with annual appointment

386.—(1) A private company may elect (by elective resolution in accordance with section 379A) to dispense with the obligation to appoint auditors annually.

(2) When such an election is in force the company's auditors shall be deemed to be re-appointed for each succeeding financial year on the expiry of the time for appointing auditors for that year, unless—

(a) a resolution has been passed under section 250 by virtue of which the company is exempt from the obligation to appoint auditors, or

(b) a resolution has been passed under section 393 to the effect that their appointment should be brought to an end.

(3) If the election ceases to be in force, the auditors then holding office shall continue to hold office—

(a) where section 385 then applies, until the conclusion of the next general meeting of the company at which accounts are laid;

(b) where section 385A then applies, until the end of the time for appointing auditors for the next financial year under that section.

(4) No account shall be taken of any loss of the opportunity of further deemed re-appointment under this section in ascertaining the amount of any compensation or damages payable to an auditor on his ceasing to hold office for any reason.

Appointment by Secretary of State in default of appointment by company

387.—(1) If in any case no auditors are appointed, re-appointed or deemed to be re-appointed before the end of the time for appointing auditors, the Secretary of State may appoint a person to fill the vacancy.

(2) In such a case the company shall within one week of the end of the time for appointing auditors give notice to the Secretary of State of his power having become exercisable.

If a company fails to give the notice required by this subsection, the company and every officer of it who is in default is guilty of an offence and liable to a fine and, for continued contravention, to a daily default fine.

Filling of casual vacancies

388.—(1) The directors, or the company in general meeting, may fill a casual vacancy in the office of auditor.

(2) While such a vacancy continues, any surviving or continuing auditor or auditors may continue to act.

(3) Special notice is required for a resolution at a general meeting of a company—

(a) filling a casual vacancy in the office of auditor, or

(b) re-appointing as auditor a retiring auditor who was appointed by the directors to fill a casual vacancy.

(4) On receipt of notice of such an intended resolution the company shall forthwith send a copy of it—

(a) to the person proposed to be appointed, and

(b) if the casual vacancy was caused by the resignation of an auditor, to the auditor who resigned.

Dormant company exempt from obligation to appoint auditors

388A.—(1) A company which by virtue of section 250 (dormant companies: exemption from provisions as to audit of accounts) is exempt from the provisions of Part VII relating to the audit of accounts is also exempt from the obligation to appoint auditors.

(2) The following provisions apply if the exemption ceases.

(3) Where section 385 applies (appointment at general meeting at which accounts are laid), the directors may appoint auditors at any time before the next meeting of the company at which accounts are to be laid; and auditors so appointed shall hold office until the conclusion of that meeting.

(4) Where section 385A applies (appointment by private company not obliged to lay accounts), the directors may appoint auditors at any time before—

(*a*) the end of the period of 28 days beginning with the day on which copies of the company's annual accounts are next sent to members under section 238, or

(*b*) if notice is given under section 253(2) requiring the laying of the accounts before the company in general meeting, the beginning of that meeting;

and auditors so appointed shall hold office until the end of that period or, as the case may be, the conclusion of that meeting.

(5) If the directors fail to exercise their powers under subsection (3) or (4), the powers may be exercised by the company in general meeting.

Qualification for appointment as auditor
  [1] **389.**—(1) Subject to the next subsection, a person is not qualified for appointment as auditor of a company unless either—

(*a*) he is a member of a body of accountants established in the United Kingdom and for the time being recognised for the purposes of this provision by the Secretary of State; or

(*b*) he is for the time being authorised by the Secretary of State to be so appointed, as having similar qualifications obtained outside the United Kingdom or else he retains an authorisation formerly granted by the Board of Trade or the Secretary of State under section 161(1)(*b*) of the Companies Act 1948 (adequate knowledge and experience, or pre-1947 practice).

(2) Subject to subsections (6) to (8) below, a person is qualified for appointment as auditor of an unquoted company if he retains an authorisation granted by the Board of Trade or the Secretary of State under section 13(1) of the Companies Act 1967.

In this subsection—

(*a*) "unquoted company" means a company in the case of which, at the time of the person's appointment, the following condition is satisfied, namely, that no shares or debentures of the company, or of a body corporate of which it is the subsidiary, have been quoted on a stock exchange (whether in Great Britain or elsewhere) to the public for subscription or purchase, and

(*b*) "company" does not include a company that carries on business as the promoter of a trading stamp scheme within the meaning of the Trading Stamps Act 1964.

(3) Subject to the next subsection, the bodies of accountants recognised for the purposes of subsection (1)(*a*) are—

(*a*) the Institute of Chartered Accountants in England and Wales,
(*b*) the Institute of Chartered Accountants of Scotland,
(*c*) the Chartered Association of Certified Accountants, and
(*d*) the Institute of Chartered Accountants in Ireland.

(4) The Secretary of State may by regulations in a statutory instrument amend subsection (3) by adding or deleting any body, but shall not make regulations—

(*a*) adding any body, or
(*b*) deleting any body which has not considered [sic] in writing to its deletion,

unless he has published notice of his intention to do so in the London and Edinburgh *Gazettes* at least four months before making the regulations.

(5) The Secretary of State may refuse an authorisation under subsection (1)(*b*) to a person as having qualifications obtained outside the United Kingdom if it appears to him that the country in which the qualifications were obtained does not confer on persons qualified in the United Kingdom privileges corresponding to those conferred by that subsection.

(6) None of the following persons is qualified for appointment as auditor of a company—

(*a*) an officer or servant of the company;

(*b*) a person who is a partner of or in the employment of an officer or servant of the company;

(*c*) a body corporate;

and for this purpose an auditor of a company is not to be regarded as either officer or servant of it.

(7) A person is also not qualified for appointment as auditor of a company if he is, under subsection (6), disqualified for appointment as auditor of any other body corporate which is that company's subsidiary or holding company or a subsidiary of that company's holding company, or would be so disqualified if the body corporate were a company.

(8) Notwithstanding subsections (1), (6) and (7), a Scottish firm is qualified for appointment as auditor of a company if, but only if, all the partners are qualified for appointment as auditors of it.

(9) No person shall act as auditor of a company at a time when he knows that he is disqualified for appointment to that office; and if an auditor of a company to his knowledge becomes so disqualified during his term of office he shall thereupon vacate his office and give notice in writing to the company that he has vacated it by reason of that disqualification.

(10) A person who acts as auditor in contravention of subsection (9), or fails without reasonable excuse to give notice of vacating his office as required by that subsection, is guilty of an offence and liable to a fine and, for continued contravention, to a daily default fine.

NOTE

[1] Repealed (*prosp.*) by the Companies Act 1989, Sched. 24.

Rights of auditors

Rights to information

389A.—(1) The auditors of a company have a right of access at all times to the company's books, accounts and vouchers, and are entitled to require from the company's officers such information and explanations as they think necessary for the performance of their duties as auditors.

(2) An officer of a company commits an offence if he knowingly or recklessly makes to the company's auditors a statement (whether written or oral) which—

(*a*) conveys or purports to convey any information or explanations which the auditors require, or are entitled to require, as auditors of the company, and

(*b*) is misleading, false or deceptive in a material particular.

A person guilty of an offence under this subsection is liable to imprisonment or a fine, or both.

(3) A subsidiary undertaking which is a body corporate incorporated in Great Britain, and the auditors of such an undertaking, shall give to the auditors of any parent company of the undertaking such information and explanations as they may reasonably require for the purposes of their duties as auditors of that company.

If a subsidiary undertaking fails to comply with this subsection, the undertaking and every officer of it who is in default is guilty of an offence and liable to a fine; and if an auditor fails without reasonable excuse to comply with this subsection he is guilty of an offence and liable to a fine.

(4) A parent company having a subsidiary undertaking which is not a body corporate incorporated in Great Britain shall, if required by its auditors to do so, take all such steps as are reasonably open to it to obtain from the subsidiary undertaking such information and explanations as they may reasonably require for the purposes of their duties as auditors of that company.

If a parent company fails to comply with this subsection, the company and every officer of it who is in default is guilty of an offence and liable to a fine.

(5) Section 734 (criminal proceedings against unincorporated bodies) applies to an offence under subsection (3).

Right to attend company meetings, etc.

390.—(1) A company's auditors are entitled—

  (a) to receive all notices of, and other communications relating to, any general meeting which a member of the company is entitled to receive;
  (b) to attend any general meeting of the company; and
  (c) to be heard at any general meeting which they attend on any part of the business of the meeting which concerns them as auditors.

(2) In relation to a written resolution proposed to be agreed to by a private company in accordance with section 381A, the company's auditors are entitled—

  (a) to receive all such communications relating to the resolution as, by virtue of any provision of Schedule 15A, are required to be supplied to a member of the company,
  (b) to give notice in accordance with section 381B of their opinion that the resolution concerns them as auditors and should be considered by the company in general meeting or, as the case may be, by a meeting of the relevant class of members of the company,
  (c) to attend any such meeting, and
  (d) to be heard at any such meeting which they attend on any part of the business of the meeting which concerns them as auditors.

(3) The right to attend or be heard at a meeting is exercisable in the case of a body corporate or partnership by an individual authorised by it in writing to act as its representative at the meeting.

Remuneration of auditors

Remuneration of auditors

390A.—(1) The remuneration of auditors appointed by the company in general meeting shall be fixed by the company in general meeting or in such manner as the company in general meeting may determine.

(2) The remuneration of auditors appointed by the directors or the Secretary of State shall be fixed by the directors or the Secretary of State, as the case may be.

(3) There shall be stated in a note to the company's annual accounts the amount of the remuneration of the company's auditors in their capacity as such.

(4) For the purposes of this section "remuneration" includes sums paid in respect of expenses.

(5) This section applies in relation to benefits in kind as to payments in cash, and in relation to any such benefit references to its amount are to its estimated money value.

The nature of any such benefit shall also be disclosed.

Remuneration of auditors or their associates for non-audit work

390B.—(1) The Secretary of State may make provision by regulations for securing the disclosure of the amount of any remuneration received or receivable by a company's auditors or their associates in respect of services other than those of auditors in their capacity as such.

(2) The regulations may—

(*a*) provide that "remuneration" includes sums paid in respect of expenses,

(*b*) apply in relation to benefits in kind as to payments in cash, and in relation to any such benefit require disclosure of its nature and its estimated money value,

(*c*) define "associate" in relation to an auditor,

(*d*) require the disclosure of remuneration in respect of services rendered to associated undertakings of the company, and

(*e*) define "associated undertaking" for that purpose.

(3) The regulations may require the auditors to disclose the relevant information in their report or require the relevant information to be disclosed in a note to the company's accounts and require the auditors to supply the directors of the company with such information as is necessary to enable that disclosure to be made.

(4) The regulations may make different provision for different cases.

(5) Regulations under this section shall be made by statutory instrument which shall be subject to annulment in pursuance of a resolution of either House of Parliament.

Removal, resignation, etc. of auditors

Removal of auditors

391.—(1) A company may by ordinary resolution at any time remove an auditor from office, notwithstanding anything in any agreement between it and him.

(2) Where a resolution removing an auditor is passed at a general meeting of a company, the company shall within 14 days give notice of that fact in the prescribed form to the registrar.

If a company fails to give the notice required by this subsection, the company and every officer of it who is in default is guilty of an offence and liable to a fine and, for continued contravention, to a daily default fine.

(3) Nothing in this section shall be taken as depriving a person removed under it of compensation or damages payable to him in respect of the termination of his appointment as auditor or of any appointment terminating with that as auditor.

(4) An auditor of a company who has been removed has, notwithstanding his removal, the rights conferred by section 390 in relation to any general meeting of the company—

(*a*) at which his term of office would otherwise have expired, or

(*b*) at which it is proposed to fill the vacancy caused by his removal.

In such a case the references in that section to matters concerning the auditors as auditors shall be construed as references to matters concerning him as a former auditor.

Rights of auditors who are removed or not re-appointed

391A.—(1) Special notice is required for a resolution at a general meeting of a company—

(*a*) removing an auditor before the expiration of his term of office, or

(*b*) appointing as auditor a person other than a retiring auditor.

(2) On receipt of notice of such an intended resolution the company shall forthwith send a copy of it to the person proposed to be removed or, as the case may be, to the person proposed to be appointed and to the retiring auditor.

(3) The auditor proposed to be removed or (as the case may be) the retiring auditor may make with respect to the intended resolution representations in writing to the company (not exceeding a reasonable length) and request their notification to members of the company.

(4) The company shall (unless the representations are received by it too late for it to do so)—

(*a*) in any notice of the resolution given to members of the company, state the fact of the representations having been made, and

(*b*) send a copy of the representations to every member of the company to whom notice of the meeting is or has been sent.

(5) If a copy of any such representations is not sent out as required because received too late or because of the company's default, the auditor may (without prejudice to his right to be heard orally) require that the representations be read out at the meeting.

(6) Copies of the representations need not be sent out and the representations need not be read at the meeting if, on the application either of the company or of any other person claiming to be aggrieved, the court is satisfied that the rights conferred by this section are being abused to secure needless publicity for defamatory matter; and the court may order the company's costs on the application to be paid in whole or in part by the auditor, notwithstanding that he is not a party to the application.

Resignation of auditors

392.—(1) An auditor of a company may resign his office by depositing a notice in writing to that effect at the company's registered office.

The notice is not effective unless it is accompanied by the statement required by section 394.

(2) An effective notice of resignation operates to bring the auditor's term of office to an end as of the date on which the notice is deposited or on such later date as may be specified in it.

(3) The company shall within 14 days of the deposit of a notice of resignation send a copy of the notice to the registrar of companies.

If default is made in complying with this subsection, the company and every officer of it who is in default is guilty of an offence and liable to a fine and, for continued contravention, a daily default fine.

Rights of resigning auditors

392A.—(1) This section applies where an auditor's notice of resignation is accompanied by a statement of circumstances which he considers should be brought to the attention of members or creditors of the company.

(2) He may deposit with the notice a signed requisition calling on the directors of the company forthwith duly to convene an extraordinary general meeting of the company for the purpose of receiving and considering such explanation of the circumstances connected with his resignation as he may wish to place before the meeting.

(3) He may request the company to circulate to its members—

(*a*) before the meeting convened on his requisition, or

(*b*) before any general meeting at which his term of office would otherwise have expired or at which it is proposed to fill the vacancy caused by his resignation,

a statement in writing (not exceeding a reasonable length) of the circumstances connected with his resignation.

(4) The company shall (unless the statement is received too late for it to comply)—

(a) in any notice of the meeting given to members of the company, state the fact of the statement having been made, and

(b) send a copy of the statement to every member of the company to whom notice of the meeting is or has been sent.

(5) If the directors do not within 21 days from the date of the deposit of a requisition under this section proceed duly to convene a meeting for a day not more than 28 days after the date on which the notice convening the meeting is given, every director who failed to take all reasonable steps to secure that a meeting was convened as mentioned above is guilty of an offence and liable to a fine.

(6) If a copy of the statement mentioned above is not sent out as required because received too late or because of the company's default, the auditor may (without prejudice to his right to be heard orally) require that the statement be read out at the meeting.

(7) Copies of a statement need not be sent out and the statement need not be read out at the meeting if, on the application either of the company or of any other person who claims to be aggrieved, the court is satisfied that the rights conferred by this section are being abused to secure needless publicity for defamatory matter; and the court may order the company's costs on such an application to be paid in whole or in part by the auditor, notwithstanding that he is not a party to the application.

(8) An auditor who has resigned has, notwithstanding his resignation, the rights conferred by section 390 in relation to any such general meeting of the company as is mentioned in subsection (3)(a) or (b).

In such a case the references in that section to matters concerning the auditors as auditors shall be construed as references to matters concerning him as a former auditor.

Termination of appointment of auditors not appointed annually

393.—(1) When an election is in force under section 386 (election by private company to dispense with annual appointment), any member of the company may deposit notice in writing at the company's registered office proposing that the appointment of the company's auditors be brought to an end.

No member may deposit more than one such notice in any financial year of the company.

(2) If such a notice is deposited it is the duty of the directors—

(a) to convene a general meeting of the company for a date not more than 28 days after the date on which the notice was given, and

(b) to propose at the meeting a resolution in a form enabling the company to decide whether the appointment of the company's auditors should be brought to an end.

(3) If the decision of the company at the meeting is that the appointment of the auditors should be brought to an end, the auditors shall not be deemed to be re-appointed when next they would be and, if the notice was deposited within the period immediately following the distribution of accounts, any deemed re-appointment for the financial year following that to which those accounts relate which has already occurred shall cease to have effect.

The period immediately following the distribution of accounts means the period beginning with the day on which copies of the company's annual accounts are sent to members of the company under section 238 and ending 14 days after that day.

(4) If the directors do not within 14 days from the date of the deposit of the notice proceed duly to convene a meeting, the member who deposited the notice (or, if there was more than one, any of them) may himself convene the meeting; but any meeting so convened shall not be held after the expiration of three months from that date.

(5) A meeting convened under this section by a member shall be convened in the same manner, as nearly as possible, as that in which meetings are to be convened by directors.

(6) Any reasonable expenses incurred by a member by reason of the failure of the directors duly to convene a meeting shall be made good to him by the company; and any such sums shall be recouped by the company from such of the directors as were in default out of any sums payable, or to become payable, by the company by way of fees or other remuneration in respect of their services.

(7) This section has effect notwithstanding anything in any agreement between the company and its auditors; and no compensation or damages shall be payable by reason of the auditors' appointment being terminated under this section.

Statement by person ceasing to hold office as auditor

394.—(1) Where an auditor ceases for any reason to hold office, he shall deposit at the company's registered office a statement of any circumstances connected with his ceasing to hold office which he considers should be brought to the attention of the members or creditors of the company or, if he considers that there are no such circumstances, a statement that there are none.

(2) In the case of resignation, the statement shall be deposited along with the notice of resignation; in the case of failure to seek re-appointment, the statement shall be deposited not less than 14 days before the end of the time allowed for next appointing auditors; in any other case, the statement shall be deposited not later than the end of the period of 14 days beginning with the date on which he ceases to hold office.

(3) If the statement is of circumstances which the auditor considers should be brought to the attention of the members or creditors of the company, the company shall within 14 days of the deposit of the statement either—

   (a) send a copy of it to every person who under section 238 is entitled to be sent copies of the accounts, or

   (b) apply to the court.

(4) The company shall if it applies to the court notify the auditor of the application.

(5) Unless the auditor receives notice of such an application before the end of the period of 21 days beginning with the day on which he deposited the statement, he shall within a further seven days send a copy of the statement to the registrar.

(6) If the court is satisfied that the auditor is using the statement to secure needless publicity for defamatory matter—

   (a) it shall direct that copies of the statement need not be sent out, and

   (b) it may further order the company's costs on the application to be paid in whole or in part by the auditor, notwithstanding that he is not a party to the application;

and the company shall within 14 days of the court's decision send to the persons mentioned in subsection (3)(a) a statement setting out the effect of the order.

(7) If the court is not so satisfied, the company shall within 14 days of the court's decision—

   (a) send copies of the statement to the persons mentioned in subsection (3)(a), and

   (b) notify the auditor of the court's decision;

and the auditor shall within seven days of receiving such notice send a copy of the statement to the registrar.

Offences of failing to comply with s. 394

394A.—(1) If a person ceasing to hold office as auditor fails to comply with section 394 he is guilty of an offence and liable to a fine.

(2) In proceedings for an offence under subsection (1) it is a defence for the person charged to show that he took all reasonable steps and exercised all due diligence to avoid the commission of the offence.

(3) Sections 733 (liability of individuals for corporate default) and 734 (criminal proceedings against unincorporated bodies) apply to an offence under subsection (1).

(4) If a company makes default in complying with section 394, the company and every officer of it who is in default is guilty of an offence and liable to a fine and, for continued contravention, to a daily default fine.

PART XII

REGISTRATION OF CHARGES

CHAPTER I
REGISTRATION OF CHARGES (ENGLAND AND WALES)

Certain charges void if not registered

395.—[1] (1) Subject to the provisions of this Chapter, a charge created by a company registered in England and Wales and being a charge to which this section applies is, so far as any security on the company's property or undertaking is conferred by the charge, void against the liquidator or administrator and any creditor of the company, unless the prescribed particulars of the charge together with the instrument (if any) by which the charge is created or evidenced, are delivered to or received by the registrar of companies for registration in the manner required by this Chapter within 21 days after the date of the charge's creation.

(2) Subsection (1) is without prejudice to any contract or obligation for repayment of the money secured by the charge; and when a charge becomes void under this section, the money secured by it immediately becomes payable.

NOTE
[1] As amended by the Insolvency Act 1985, Sched. 6, para. 10.

Charges which have to be registered

396.—(1) Section 395 applies to the following charges—
(a) a charge for the purpose of securing any issue of debentures,
(b) a charge on uncalled share capital of the company,
(c) a charge created or evidenced by an instrument which, if executed by an individual, would require registration as a bill of sale,
(d) a charge on land (wherever situated) or any interest in it, but not including a charge for any rent or other periodical sum issuing out of the land,
(e) a charge on book debts of the company,
(f) a floating charge on the company's undertaking or property,
(g) a charge on calls made but not paid,
(h) a charge on a ship or aircraft, or any share in a ship,
(j) a charge on goodwill, on a patent or a licence under a patent, on a trademark or on a copyright or a licence under a copyright.

(2) Where a negotiable instrument has been given to secure the payment of any book debts of a company, the deposit of the instrument for the purpose of securing an advance to the company is not, for purposes of section 395, to be treated as a charge on those book debts.

(3) The holding of debentures entitling the holder to a charge on land is not for purposes of this section deemed to be an interest in land.

[1] (3A) The following are "intellectual property" for the purposes of this section—

(*a*) any patent, trade mark, service mark, registered design, copyright or design right;

(*b*) any licence under or in respect of any such right.

(4) In this Chapter, "charge" includes mortgage.

NOTE

[1] Inserted by the Copyright, Designs and Patents Act 1988, Sched. 7, para. 31(2).

Formalties of registration (debentures)

397.—(1) Where a series of debentures containing, or giving by reference to another instrument, any charge to the benefit of which the debenture holders of that series are entitled *pari passu* is created by a company, it is for purposes of section 395 sufficient if there are delivered to or received by the registrar, within 21 days after the execution of the deed containing the charge (or, if there is no such deed, after the execution of any debentures of the series), the following particulars in the prescribed form—

(*a*) the total amount secured by the whole series, and

(*b*) the dates of the resolutions authorising the issue of the series and the date of the covering deed (if any) by which the security is created or defined, and

(*c*) a general description of the property charged, and

(*d*) the names of the trustees (if any) for the debenture holders,

together with the deed containing the charge or, if there is no such deed, one of the debentures of the series:

Provided that there shall be sent to the registrar of companies, for entry in the register, particulars in the prescribed form of the date and amount of each issue of debentures of the series, but any omission to do this does not affect the validity of any of those debentures.

(2) Where any commission, allowance or discount has been paid or made either directly or indirectly by a company to a person in consideration of his—

(*a*) subscribing or agreeing to subscribe, whether absolutely or conditionally, for debentures of the company, or

(*b*) procuring or agreeing to procure subscriptions, whether absolute or conditional, for such debentures,

the particulars required to be sent for registration under section 395 shall include particulars as to the amount or rate per cent. of the commission, discount or allowance so paid or made, but omission to do this does not affect the validity of the debentures issued.

(3) The deposit of debentures as security for a debt of the company is not, for the purposes of subsection (2), treated as the issue of the debentures at a discount.

Verification of charge on property outside United Kingdom

398.—(1) In the case of a charge created out of the United Kingdom comprising property situated outside the United Kingdom, the delivery to and the receipt by the registrar of companies of a copy (verified in the prescribed manner) of the instrument by which the charge is created or evidenced has the same effect for purposes of sections 395 to 398 as the delivery and receipt of the instrument itself.

(2) In that case, 21 days after the date on which the instrument or copy could, in due course of post (and if despatched with due diligence), have been received in the United Kingdom are substituted for the 21 days mentioned in section 395(1) (or as the case may be, section 397(1)) as the time within which the particulars and instrument or copy are to be delivered to the registrar.

(3) Where a charge is created in the United Kingdom but comprises property outside the United Kingdom, the instrument creating or purporting to create the charge may be sent for registration under section 395 not-

[THE NEXT PAGE IS 229]

withstanding that further proceedings may be necessary to make the charge valid or effectual according to the law of the country in which the property is situated.

(4) Where a charge comprises property situated in Scotland or Northern Ireland and registration in the country where the property is situated is necessary to make the charge valid or effectual according to the law of that country, the delivery to and the receipt by the registrar of a copy (verified in the prescribed manner) of the instrument by which the charge is created or evidenced, together with a certificate in the prescribed form stating that the charge was presented for registration in Scotland or Northern Ireland (as the case may be) on the date on which it was so presented has, for purposes of sections 395 to 398, the same effect as the delivery and receipt of the instrument itself.

Company's duty to register charges it creates

399.—(1) It is a company's duty to send to the registrar of companies for registration the particulars of every charge created by the company and of the issues of debentures of a series requiring registration under sections 395 to 398; but registration of any such charge may be effected on the application of any person interested in it.

(2) Where registration is effected on the application of some person other than the company, that person is entitled to recover from the company the amount of any fees properly paid by him to the registrar on the registration.

(3) If a company fails to comply with subsection (1), then, unless the registration has been effected on the application of some other person, the company and every officer of it who is in default is liable to a fine and, for continued contravention, to a daily default fine.

Charges existing on property acquired

400.—(1) This section applies where a company registered in England and Wales acquires property which is subject to a charge of any such kind as would, if it had been created by the company after the acquisition of the property, have been required to be registered under this Chapter.

(2) The company shall cause the prescribed particulars of the charge, together with a copy (certified in the prescribed manner to be a correct copy) of the instrument (if any) by which the charge was created or is evidenced, to be delivered to the registrar of companies for registration in the manner required by this Chapter within 21 days after the date on which the acquisition is completed.

(3) However, if the property is situated and the charge was created outside Great Britain, 21 days after the date on which the copy of the instrument could in due course of post, and if despatched with due diligence, have been received in the United Kingdom is substituted for the 21 days above-mentioned as the time within which the particulars and copy of the instrument are to be delivered to the registrar.

(4) If default is made in complying with this section, the company and every officer of it who is in default is liable to a fine and, for continued contravention, to a daily default fine.

Register of charges to be kept by registrar of companies

401.—(1) The registrar of companies shall keep, with respect to each company, a register in the prescribed form of all the charges requiring registration under this Chapter; and he shall enter in the register with respect to such charges the following particulars—

(a) in the case of a charge to the benefit of which the holders of a series of debentures are entitled, the particulars specified in section 397(1), (*b*) in the case of any other charge—

    (i) if it is a charge created by the company, the date of its creation, and if it is a charge which was existing on property acquired by the company, the date of the acquisition of the property, and

    (ii) the amount secured by the charge, and

    (iii) short particulars of the property charged, and

    (iv) the persons entitled to the charge.

(2) The registrar shall give a certificate of the registration of any charge registered in pursuance of this Chapter, stating the amount secured by the charge.

The certificate—

(*a*) shall be either signed by the registrar, or authenticated by his official seal, and

(*b*) is conclusive evidence that the requirements of this Chapter as to registration have been satisfied.

(3) The register kept in pursuance of this section shall be open to inspection by any person.

Endorsement of certificate on debentures

402.—(1) The company shall cause a copy of every certificate of registration given under section 401 to be endorsed on every debenture or certificate of debenture stock which is issued by the company, and the payment of which is secured by the charge so registered.

(2) But this does not require a company to cause a certificate of registration of any charge so given to be endorsed on any debenture or certificate of debenture stock issued by the company before the charge was created.

(3) If a person knowingly and wilfully authorises or permits the delivery of a debenture or certificate of debenture stock which under this section is required to have endorsed on it a copy of a certificate of registration, without the copy being so endorsed upon it, he is liable (without prejudice to any other liability) to a fine.

Entries of satisfaction and release

403.—(1) The registrar of companies, on receipt of a statutory declaration in the prescribed form verifying, with respect to a registered charge,—

(*a*) that the debt for which the charge was given has been paid or satisfied in whole or in part, or

(*b*) that part of the property or undertaking charged has been released from the charge or has ceased to form part of the company's property or undertaking,

may enter on the register a memorandum of satisfaction in whole or in part, or of the fact that part of the property or undertaking has been released from the charge or has ceased to form part of the company's property or undertaking (as the case may be).

(2) Where the registrar enters a memorandum of satisfaction in whole, he shall if required furnish the company with a copy of it.

Rectification of register of charges

404.—(1) The following applies if the court is satisfied that the omission to register a charge within the time required by this Chapter or that the omission or mis-statement of any particular with respect to any such charge or in a memorandum of satisfaction was accidental, or due to inadvertence or to some other sufficient cause, or is not of a nature to prejudice the position of creditors or shareholders of the company, or that on other grounds it is just and equitable to grant relief.

(2) The court may, on the application of the company or a person interested, and on such terms and conditions as seem to the court just and expedient, order that the time for registration shall be extended or, as the case may be, that the omission or mis-statement shall be rectified.

Registration of enforcement of security

405.—(1) If a person obtains an order for the appointment of a receiver or manager of a company's property, or appoints such a receiver or manager under powers contained in an instrument, he shall within seven days of the order or of the appointment under those powers, give notice of the fact to the registrar of companies; and the registrar shall enter the fact in the register of charges.

(2) Where a person appointed receiver or manager of a company's property under powers contained in an instrument ceases to act as such receiver or manager, he shall, on so ceasing, give the registrar notice to that effect, and the registrar shall enter the fact in the register of charges.

(3) A notice under this section shall be in the prescribed form.

(4) If a person makes default in complying with the requirements of this section, he is liable to a fine and, for continued contravention, to a daily default fine.

Companies to keep copies of instruments creating charges

406.—(1) Every company shall cause a copy of every instrument creating a charge requiring registration under this Chapter to be kept at its registered office.

(2) In the case of a series of uniform debentures, a copy of one debenture of the series is sufficient.

Company's register of charges

407.—(1) Every limited company shall keep at its registered office a register of charges and enter in it all charges specifically affecting property of the company and all floating charges on the company's undertaking or any of its property.

(2) The entry shall in each case give a short description of the property charged, the amount of the charge and, except in the case of securities to bearer, the names of the persons entitled to it.

(3) If an officer of the company knowingly and wilfully authorises or permits the omission of an entry required to be made in pursuance of this section, he is liable to a fine.

Right to inspect instruments which create charges, etc.

408.—(1) The copies of instruments creating any charge requiring registration under this Chapter with the registrar of companies, and the register of charges kept in pursuance of section 407, shall be open during business hours (but subject to such reasonable restrictions as the company in general meeting may impose, so that not less than two hours in each day be allowed for inspection) to the inspection of any creditor or member of the company without fee.

(2) The register of charges shall also be open to the inspection of any other person on payment of such fee, not exceeding 5 pence, for each inspection, as the company may prescribe.

(3) If inspection of the copies referred to, or of the register, is refused, every officer of the company who is in default is liable to a fine and, for continued contravention, to a daily default fine.

(4) If such a refusal occurs in relation to a company registered in England and Wales, the court may by order compel an immediate inspection of the copies or register.

Charges on property in England and Wales created by oversea company

409.—(1) This Chapter extends to charges on property in England and Wales which are created, and to charges on property in England and Wales which is acquired, by a company (whether a company within the meaning of this Act or not) incorporated outside Great Britain which has an established place of business in England and Wales.

(2) In relation to such a company, sections 406 and 407 apply with the

substitution, for the reference to the company's registered office, of a reference to its principal place of business in England and Wales.

CHAPTER II
REGISTRATION OF CHARGES (SCOTLAND)

Charges void unless registered

410.—(1) The following provisions of this Chapter have effect for the purpose of securing the registration in Scotland of charges created by companies.

[1] (2) Every charge created by a company, being a charge to which this section applies, is, so far as any security on the company's property or any part of it is conferred by the charge, void against the liquidator or administrator and any creditor of the company unless the prescribed particulars of the charge, together with a copy (certified in the prescribed manner to be a correct copy) of the instrument (if any) by which the charge is created or evidenced, are delivered to or received by the registrar of companies for registration in the manner required by this Chapter within 21 days after the date of the creation of the charge.

(3) Subsection (2) is without prejudice to any contract or obligation for repayment of the money secured by the charge; and when a charge becomes void under this section the money secured by it immediately becomes payable.

(4) This section applies to the following charges—

(*a*) a charge on land wherever situated, or any interest in such land (not including a charge for any rent, ground annual or other periodical sum payable in respect of the land, but including a charge created by a heritable security within the meaning of section 9(8) of the Conveyancing and Feudal Reform (Scotland) Act 1970),

(*b*) a security over the uncalled share capital of the company,

[2] (*c*) a security over incorporeal moveable property of any of the following categories—

  (i) the book debts of the company,
  (ii) calls made but not paid,
  (iii) goodwill,
  (iv) a patent or a licence under a patent,
  (v) a trademark,
  (vi) a copyright or a licence under a copyright,
  (vii) a registered design or a licence in respect of such a design,
  (viii) a design right or a licence under a design right,

(*d*) a security over a ship or aircraft or any share in a ship, and

(*e*) a floating charge.

(5) In this Chapter "company" (except in section 424) means an incorporated company registered in Scotland; "registrar of companies" means the registrar or other officer performing under this Act the duty of registration of companies in Scotland; and references to the date of creation of a charge are—

(*a*) in the case of a floating charge, the date on which the instrument creating the floating charge was executed by the company creating the charge, and

(*b*) in any other case, the date on which the right of the person entitled to the benefit of the charge was constituted as a real right.

NOTES

[1] As amended by the Insolvency Act 1985, Sched. 6, para. 10.

[2] As amended by the Copyright, Designs and Patents Act 1988, Sched. 7, para. 31(3), with effect from 1st August 1989. Extended by the Patents, Designs and Marks Act 1986, Sched. 2, Pt. I, para. 1(2)(*k*). Sub- para. (vi) extended (to protect topography) by S.I. 1987 No. 1497.

Charges on property outside United Kingdom

411.—(1) In the case of a charge created out of the United Kingdom comprising property situated outside the United Kingdom, the period of 21 days after the date on which the copy of the instrument creating it could (in due course of post, and if despatched with due diligence) have been received in the United Kingdom is substituted for the period of 21 days

[THE NEXT PAGE IS 233]

after the date of the creation of the charge as the time within which, under section 410(2), the particulars and copy are to be delivered to the registrar.

(2) Where a charge is created in the United Kingdom but comprises property outside the United Kingdom, the copy of the instrument creating or purporting to create the charge may be sent for registration under section 410 notwithstanding that further proceedings may be necessary to make the charge valid or effectual according to the law of the country in which the property is situated.

Negotiable instrument to secure book debts

412. Where a negotiable instrument has been given to secure the payment of any book debts of a company, the deposit of the instrument for the purpose of securing an advance to the company is not, for purposes of section 410, to be treated as a charge on those book debts.

Charges associated with debentures

413.—(1) The holding of debentures entitling the holder to a charge on land is not, for the purposes of section 410, deemed to be an interest in land.

(2) Where a series of debentures containing, or giving by reference to any other instrument, any charge to the benefit of which the debenture-holders of that series are entitled *pari passu*, is created by a company, it is sufficient for purposes of section 410 if there are delivered to or received by the registrar of companies within 21 days after the execution of the deed containing the charge or, if there is no such deed, after the execution of any debentures of the series, the following particulars in the prescribed form—

(a) the total amount secured by the whole series,
(b) the dates of the resolutions authorising the issue of the series and the date of the covering deed (if any) by which the security is created or defined,
(c) a general description of the property charged,
(d) the names of the trustees (if any) for the debenture holders, and
(e) in the case of a floating charge, a statement of any provisions of the charge and of any instrument relating to it which prohibit or restrict or regulate the power of the company to grant further securities ranking in priority to, or *pari passu* with, the floating charge, or which vary or otherwise regulate the order of ranking of the floating charge in relation to subsisting securities,

together with a copy of the deed containing the charge or, if there is no such deed, of one of the debentures of the series:

Provided that, where more than one issue is made of debentures in the series, there shall be sent to the registrar of companies for entry in the register particulars (in the prescribed form) of the date and amount of each issue of debentures of the series, but any omission to do this does not affect the validity of any of those debentures.

(3) Where any commission, allowance or discount has been paid or made, either directly or indirectly, by a company to any person in consideration of his subscribing or agreeing to subscribe, whether absolutely or conditionally, for any debentures of the company, or procuring or agreeing to procure subscriptions (whether absolute or conditional) for any such debentures, the particulars required to be sent for registration under section 410 include particulars as to the amount or rate per cent. of the commission, discount or allowance so paid or made; but any omission to do this does not affect the validity of the debentures issued.

The deposit of any debentures as security for any debt of the company is not, for purposes of this subsection, treated as the issue of the debentures at a discount.

Charge by way of ex facie **absolute disposition, etc.**

414.—(1) For the avoidance of doubt, it is hereby declared that, in the case of a charge created by way of an *ex facie* absolute disposition or assignation qualified by a back letter or other agreement, or by a standard security qualified by an agreement compliance with section 410(2) does not of itself render the charge unavailable as security for indebtedness incurred after the date of compliance.

(2) Where the amount secured by a charge so created is purported to be increased by a further back letter or agreement, a further charge is held to have been created by the *ex facie* absolute disposition or assignation or (as the case may be) by the standard security, as qualified by the further back letter or agreement; and the provisions of this Chapter apply to the further charge as if—

(*a*) references in this Chapter (other than in this section) to the charge were references to the further charge, and

(*b*) references to the date of the creation of the charge were references to the date on which the further back letter or agreement was executed.

Company's duty to register charges created by it

415.—(1) It is a company's duty to send to the registrar of companies for registration the particulars of every charge created by the company and of the issues of debentures of a series requiring registration under sections 410 to 414; but registration of any such charge may be effected on the application of any person interested in it.

(2) Where registration is effected on the application of some person other than the company, that person is entitled to recover from the company the amount of any fees properly paid by him to the registrar on the registration.

(3) If a company makes default in sending to the registrar for registration the particulars of any charge created by the company or of the issues of debentures of a series requiring registration as above mentioned, then, unless the registration has been effected on the application of some other person, the company and every officer of it who is in default is liable to a fine and, for continued contravention, to a daily default fine.

Duty to register charges existing on property acquired

416.—(1) Where a company acquires any property which is subject to a charge of any kind as would, if it had been created by the company after the acquisition of the property, have been required to be registered under this Chapter, the company shall cause the prescribed particulars of the charge, together with a copy (certified in the prescribed manner to be a correct copy) of the instrument (if any) by which the charge was created or is evidenced, to be delivered to the registrar of companies for registration in the manner required by this Chapter within 21 days after the date on which the transaction was settled.

(2) If, however, the property is situated and the charge was created outside Great Britain, 21 days after the date on which the copy of the instrument could (in due course of post, and if despatched with due diligence) have been received in the United Kingdom are substituted for 21 days after the settlement of the transaction as the time within which the particulars and the copy of the instrument are to be delivered to the registrar.

(3) If default is made in complying with this section, the company and every officer of it who is in default is liable to a fine and, for continued contravention, to a daily default fine.

Register of charges to be kept by registrar of companies

417.—(1) The registrar of companies shall keep, with respect to each company, a register in the prescribed form of all the charges requiring registration under this Chapter, and shall enter in the register with respect to such charges the particulars specified below.

(2) In the case of a charge to the benefit of which the holders of a series of debentures are entitled, there shall be entered in the register the particulars specified in section 413(2).

(3) In the case of any other charge, there shall be entered—

(a) if it is a charge created by the company, the date of its creation, and if it was a charge existing on property acquired by the company, the date of the acquisition of the property,

(b) the amount secured by the charge,

(c) short particulars of the property charged,

(d) the persons entitled to the charge, and

(e) in the case of a floating charge, a statement of any of the provisions of the charge and of any instrument relating to it which prohibit or restrict or regulate the company's power to grant further securities ranking in priority to, or *pari passu* with, the floating charge, or which vary or otherwise regulate the order of ranking of the floating charge in relation to subsisting securities.

(4) The register kept in pursuance of this section shall be open to inspection by any person.

Certificate of registration to be issued

418.—(1) The registrar of companies shall give a certificate of the registration of any charge registered in pursuance of this Chapter.

(2) The certificate—

(a) shall be either signed by the registrar, or authenticated by his official seal,

(b) shall state the name of the company and the person first-named in the charge among those entitled to the benefit of the charge (or, in the case of a series of debentures, the name of the holder of the first such debenture to be issued) and the amount secured by the charge, and

(c) is conclusive evidence that the requirements of this Chapter as to registration have been complied with.

Entries of satisfaction and relief

419.—(1) The registrar of companies, on application being made to him in the prescribed form, and on receipt of a statutory declaration in the prescribed form verifying, with respect to any registered charge,—

(a) that the debt for which the charge was given has been paid or satisfied in whole or in part, or

(b) that part of the property charged has been released from the charge or has ceased to form part of the company's property,

may enter on the register a memorandum of satisfaction (in whole or in part) regarding that fact.

(2) Where the registrar enters a memorandum of satisfaction in whole, he shall, if required, furnish the company with a copy of the memorandum.

(3) Without prejudice to the registrar's duty under this section to require to be satisfied as above mentioned, he shall not be so satisfied unless—

(a) the creditor entitled to the benefit of the floating charge, or a person authorised to do so on his behalf, certifies as correct the particulars submitted to the registrar with respect to the entry on the register of memorandum under this section, or

(b) the court, on being satisfied that such certification cannot readily be obtained, directs him accordingly.

(4) Nothing in this section requires the company to submit particulars with respect to the entry in the register of a memorandum of satisfaction where the company, having created a floating charge over all or any part of its property, disposes of part of the property subject to the floating charge.

(5) A memorandum or certification required for the purposes of this section shall be in such form as may be prescribed.

Rectification of register

420. The court, on being satisfied that the omission to register a charge within the time required by this Act or that the omission or mis-statement of any particular with respect to any such charge or in a memorandum of satisfaction was accidental, or due to inadvertence or to some other sufficient cause, or is not of a nature to prejudice the position of creditors or shareholders of the company, or that it is on other grounds just and equitable to grant relief, may, on the application of the company or any person interested, and on such terms and conditions as seem to the court just and expedient, order that the time for registration shall be extended or (as the case may be) that the omission or mis-statement shall be rectified.

Copies of instruments creating charges to be kept by company

421.—(1) Every company shall cause a copy of every instrument creating a charge requiring registration under this Chapter to be kept at the company's registered office.

(2) In the case of a series of uniform debentures, a copy of one debenture of the series is sufficient.

Company's register of charges

422.—(1) Every company shall keep at its registered office a register of charges and enter in it all charges specifically affecting property of the company, and all floating charges on any property of the company.

(2) There shall be given in each case a short description of the property charged, the amount of the charge and, except in the case of securities to bearer, the names of the persons entitled to it.

(3) If an officer of the company knowingly and wilfully authorises or permits the omission of an entry required to be made in pursuance of this section, he is liable to a fine.

Right to inspect copies of instruments and company's register

423.—(1) The copies of instruments creating charges requiring registration under this Chapter with the registrar of companies, and the register of charges kept in pursuance of section 422, shall be open during business hours (but subject to such reasonable restrictions as the company in general meeting may impose, so that not less than two hours in each day be allowed for inspection) to the inspection of any creditor or member of the company without fee.

(2) The register of charges shall be open to the inspection of any other person on payment of such fee, not exceeding 5 pence for each inspection, as the company may prescribe.

(3) If inspection of the copies or register is refused, every officer of the company who is in default is liable to a fine and, for continued contravention, to a daily default fine.

(4) If such a refusal occurs in relation to a company, the court may by order compel an immediate inspection of the copies or register.

Extension of Chapter II

424.—(1) This Chapter extends to charges on property in Scotland which are created, and to charges on property in Scotland which is acquired, by a company incorporated outside Great Britain which has a place of business in Scotland.

(2) In relation to such a company, sections 421 and 422 apply with the substitution, for the reference to the company's registered office, of a reference to its principal place of business in Scotland.

Part XIII

Arrangements and Reconstructions

Power of company to compromise with creditors and members

[1] **425.**—[2] (1) Where a compromise or arrangement is proposed between a company and its creditors, or any class of them, or between the company and its members, or any class of them, the court may on the application of the company or any creditor or member of it or, in the case of a company being wound up or an administration order being in force in relation to a company, of the liquidator or administrator, order a meeting of the creditors or class of creditors, or of the members of the company or class of members (as the case may be), to be summoned in such manner as the court directs.

(2) If a majority in number representing three-fourths in value of the creditors or class of creditors or members or class of members (as the case may be), present and voting either in person or by proxy at the meeting, agree to any compromise or arrangement, the compromise or arrangement, if sanctioned by the court, is binding on all creditors or the class of creditors or on the members or class of members (as the case may be), and also on the company or, in the case of a company in the course of being wound up, on the liquidator and contributories of the company.

(3) The court's order under subsection (2) has no effect until an office copy of it has been delivered to the registrar of companies for registration; and a copy of every such order shall be annexed to every copy of the company's memorandum issued after the order has been made or, in the case of a company not having a memorandum, of every copy so issued of the instrument constituting the company or defining its constitution.

(4) If a company makes default in complying with subsection (3), the company and every officer of it who is in default is liable to a fine.

[3] (5) An order under subsection (1) pronounced in Scotland by the judge acting as vacation judge is not subject to review, reduction, suspension or stay of execution.

(6) In this section and the next—

(*a*) "company" means any company liable to be wound up under this Act, and

(*b*) "arrangement" includes a reorganisation of the company's share capital by the consolidation of shares of different classes or by the division of shares into shares of different classes, or by both of those methods.

NOTES

[1] See also s.131.

[2] As amended by the Insolvency Act 1985, Sched. 6, para. 11.

[3] As amended by the Court of Session Act 1988, Sched. 2.

Information as to compromise to be circulated

426.—(1) The following applies where a meeting of creditors or any class of creditors, or of members or any class of members, is summoned under section 425.

(2) With every notice summoning the meeting which is sent to a creditor or member there shall be sent also a statement explaining the effect of the compromise or arrangement and in particular stating any material interests of the directors of the company (whether as directors or as members or as creditors of the company or otherwise) and the effect on those interests of the compromise or arrangement, in so far as it is different from the effect on the like interests of other persons.

(3) In every notice summoning the meeting which is given by advertisement there shall be included either such a statement as above-mentioned or a notification of the place at which, and the manner in which, creditors or members entitled to attend the meeting may obtain copies of the statement.

(4) Where the compromise or arrangement affects the rights of debenture holders of the company, the statement shall give the like explanation as respects the trustees of any deed for securing the issue of the debentures as it is required to give as respects the company's directors.

(5) Where a notice given by advertisement includes a notification that copies of a statement explaining the effect of the compromise or arrangement proposed can be obtained by creditors or members entitled to attend the meeting, every such creditor or member shall, on making application in the manner indicated by the notice, be furnished by the company free of charge with a copy of the statement.

[1] (6) If a company makes default in complying with any requirement of this section, the company and every officer of it who is in default is liable to a fine; and for this purpose a liquidator or administrator of the company and a trustee of a deed for securing the issue of debentures of the company is deemed an officer of it.

However, a person is not liable under this subsection if he shows that the default was due to the refusal of another person, being a director or trustee for debenture holders, to supply the necessary particulars of his interests.

(7) It is the duty of any director of the company, and of any trustee for its debenture holders, to give notice to the company of such matters relating to himself as may be necessary for purposes of this section; and any person who makes default in complying with this subsection is liable to a fine.

NOTE

[1] As amended by the Insolvency Act 1985, Sched. 6, para. 12.

Provisions for facilitating company reconstruction or amalgamation

427.—(1) The following applies where application is made to the court under section 425 for the sanctioning of a compromise or arrangement proposed between a company and any such persons as are mentioned in that section.

(2) If it is shown—

(*a*) that the compromise or arrangement has been proposed for the purposes of, or in connection with, a scheme for the reconstruction of any company or companies, or the amalgamation of any two or more companies, and

(*b*) that under the scheme the whole or any part of the undertaking or the property of any company concerned in the scheme ("a transferor company") is to be transferred to another company ("the transferee company"),

the court may, either by the order sanctioning the compromise or arrangement or by any subsequent order, make provision for all or any of the following matters.

(3) The matters for which the court's order may make provision are—

(*a*) the transfer to the transferee company of the whole or any part of the undertaking and of the property or liabilities of any transferor company,

(*b*) the allotting or appropriation by the transferee company of any shares, debentures, policies or other like interests in that company which under the compromise or arrangement are to be allotted or appropriated by that company to or for any person,

(*c*) the continuation by or against the transferee company of any legal proceedings pending by or against any transferor company,

(*d*) the dissolution, without winding up, of any transferor company,

(*e*) the provision to be made for any persons who, within such time and in such manner as the court directs, dissent from the compromise or arrangement,

(*f*) such incidental, consequential and supplemental matters as are necessary to secure that the reconstruction or amalgamation is fully and effectively carried out.

(4) If an order under this section provides for the transfer of property or liabilities, then—

    (*a*) that property is by virtue of the order transferred to, and vests in, the transferee company, and

    (*b*) those liabilities are, by virtue of the order, transferred to and become liabilities of that company;

and property (if the order so directs) vests freed from any charge which is by virtue of the compromise or arrangement to cease to have effect.

(5) Where an order is made under this section, every company in relation to which the order is made shall cause an office copy of the order to be delivered to the registrar of companies for registration within seven days after its making; and if default is made in complying with this subsection, the company and every officer of it who is in default is liable to a fine and, for continued contravention, to a daily default fine.

(6) In this section the expression "property" includes property, rights and powers of every description; the expression "liabilities" includes duties and "company" includes only a company as defined in section 735(1).

Application of ss.425–427 to mergers and divisions of public companies

  [1] **427A.**—(1) Where—

    (*a*) a compromise or arrangement is proposed between a public company and any such persons as are mentioned in section 425(1) for the purposes of, or in connection with, a scheme for the reconstruction of any company or companies or the amalgamation of any two or more companies,

    (*b*) the circumstances are as specified in any of the cases described in subsection (2), and

    (*c*) the consideration for the transfer or each of the transfers envisaged in the case in question is to be shares in the transferee company or any of the transferee companies receivable by members of the transferor company or transferor companies, with or without any cash payment to members,

sections 425 to 427 shall, as regards that compromise or arrangement, have effect subject to the provisons of this section and Schedule 15B.

(2) The cases referred to in subsection (1) are as follows—

Case 1

Where under the scheme the undertaking, property and liabilities of the company in respect of which the compromise or arrangement in question is proposed are to be transferred to another public company, other than one formed for the purpose of, or in connection with, the scheme.

Case 2

Where under the scheme the undertaking, property and liabilities of each of two or more public companies concerned in the scheme, including the company in respect of which the compromise or arrangement in question is proposed, are to be transferred to a company (whether or not a public company) formed for the purpose of, or in connection with, the scheme.

Case 3

Where under the scheme the undertaking, property and liabilities of the company in respect of which the compromise or arrangement in question is proposed are to be divided among and transferred to two or more companies each of which is either—

    (*a*) a public company, or

    (*b*) a company (whether or not a public company) formed for the purposes of, or in connection with, the scheme.

(3) Before sanctioning any compromise or arrangement under section 425(2) the court may, on the application of any pre-existing transferee company or any member or creditor of it or, an administration order being in force in relation to the company, the administrator, order a meeting of the members of the company or any class of them or of the creditors of the company or any class of them to be summoned in such manner as the court directs.

(4) This section does not apply where the company in respect of which the compromise or arrangement is proposed is being wound up.

(5) This section does not apply to compromises or arrangements in respect of which an application has been made to the court for an order under section 425(1) before 1st January 1988.

(6) Where section 427 would apply in the case of a scheme but for the fact that the transferee company or any of the transferee companies is a company within the meaning of article 3 of the Companies (Northern Ireland) Order 1986 (and thus not within the definition of "company" in subsection (6) of section 427), section 427 shall apply notwithstanding that fact.

(7) In the case of a scheme mentioned in subsection (1), for a company within the meaning of article 3 of the Companies (Northern Ireland) Order 1986, the reference in section 427(5) to the registrar of companies shall have effect as a reference to the registrar as defined in article 2 of that Order.

(8) In this section and Schedule 15B—

"transferor company" means a company whose undertaking, property and liabilities are to be transferred by means of a transfer envisaged in any of the cases specified in subsection (2);

"transferee company" means a company to which a transfer envisaged in any of those cases is to be made;

"pre-existing transferee company" means a transferee company other than one formed for the purpose of, or in connection with, the scheme;

"compromise or arrangement" means a compromise or arrangement to which subsection (1) applies;

"the scheme" means the scheme mentioned in subsection (1)(*a*);

"company" includes only a company as defined in section 735(1) except that, in the case of a transferee company, it also includes a company as defined in article 3 of the Companies (Northern Ireland) Order 1986 (referred to in these definitions as a "Northern Ireland company");

"public company" means, in relation to a transferee company which is a Northern Ireland company, a public company within the meaning of article 12 of the Companies (Northern Ireland) Order 1986;

"the registrar of companies" means, in relation to a transferee company which is a Northern Ireland company, the registrar as defined in article 2 of the Companies (Northern Ireland) Order 1986;

"the *Gazette*" means, in relation to a transferee company which is a Northern Ireland company, the *Belfast Gazette*;

"case 1 scheme", "case 2 scheme" and "case 3 scheme" mean a scheme of the kind described in cases 1, 2 and 3 of subsection (2) respectively;

"property" and "liabilities" have the same meaning as in section 427.

NOTE

[1] Inserted by S.I. 1987 No. 1991. As amended by the Companies Act 1989, s. 114(2).

[1] PART XIIIA

TAKEOVER OFFERS

NOTE

[1] Ss.428–430F substitute former ss.428–430 by the Financial Services Act 1986, s.172 and Sched. 12.

"Takeover offers"

428.—(1) In this Part of this Act "a takeover offer" means an offer to acquire all the shares, or all the shares of any class or classes, in a company (other than shares which at the date of the offer are already held by the offeror), being an offer on terms which are the same in relation to all the shares to which the offer relates or, where those shares include shares of different classes, in relation to all the shares of each class.

(2) In subsection (1) "shares" means shares which have been allotted on the date of the offer but a takeover offer may include among the shares to which it relates all or any shares that are subsequently allotted before a date specified in or determined in accordance with the terms of the offer.

(3) The terms offered in relation to any shares shall for the purposes of this section be treated as being the same in relation to all the shares or, as the case may be, all the shares of a class to which the offer relates notwithstanding any variation permitted by subsection (4).

(4) A variation is permitted by this subsection where—

(*a*) the law of a country or territory outside the United Kingdom precludes an offer of consideration in the form or any of the forms specified in the terms in question or precludes it except after compliance by the offeror with conditions with which he is unable to comply or which he regards as unduly onerous; and

(*b*) the variation is such that the persons to whom an offer of consideration in that form is precluded are able to receive consideration otherwise than in that form but of substantially equivalent value.

(5) The reference in subsection (1) to shares already held by the offeror includes a reference to shares which he has contracted to acquire but that shall not be construed as including shares which are the subject of a contract binding the holder to accept the offer when it is made, being a contract entered into by the holder either for no consideration and under seal or for no consideration other than a promise by the offeror to make the offer.

(6) In the application of subsection (5) to Scotland, the words "and under seal" shall be omitted.

(7) Where the terms of an offer make provision for their revision and for acceptances on the previous terms to be treated as acceptances on the revised terms, the revision shall not be regarded for the purposes of this Part of this Act as the making of a fresh offer and references in this Part of this Act to the date of the offer shall accordingly be construed as references to the date on which the original offer was made.

(8) In this Part of this Act "the offeror" means, subject to section 430D, the person making a takeover offer and "the company" means the company whose shares are the subject of the offer.

Right of offeror to buy out minority shareholders

429.—(1) If, in a case in which a takeover offer does not relate to shares of different classes, the offeror has by virtue of acceptances of the offer acquired or contracted to acquire not less than nine-tenths in value of the shares to which the offer relates he may give notice to the holder of any shares to which the offer relates which the offeror has not acquired or contracted to acquire that he desires to acquire those shares.

(2) If, in a case in which a takeover offer relates to shares of different classes, the offeror has by virtue of acceptances of the offer acquired or contracted to acquire not less than nine-tenths in value of the shares of any class to which the offer relates, he may give notice to the holder of any shares of that class which the offeror has not acquired or contracted to acquire that he desires to acquire those shares.

(3) No notice shall be given under subsection (1) or (2) unless the offeror has acquired or contracted to acquire the shares necessary to satisfy the minimum specified in that subsection before the end of the period of four

months beginning with the date of the offer; and no such notice shall be given after the end of the period of two months beginning with the date on which he has acquired or contracted to acquire shares which satisfy that minimum.

(4) Any notice under this section shall be given in the prescribed manner; and when the offeror gives the first notice in relation to an offer he shall send a copy of it to the company together with a statutory declaration by him in the prescribed form stating that the conditions for the giving of the notice are satisfied.

(5) Where the offeror is a company (whether or not a company within the meaning of this Act) the statutory declaration shall be signed by a director.

(6) Any person who fails to send a copy of a notice or a statutory declaration as required by subsection (4) or makes such a declaration for the purposes of that subsection knowing it to be false or without having reasonable grounds for believing it to be true shall be liable to imprisonment or a fine. or both, and for continued failure to send the copy or declaration. to a daily default fine.

(7) If any person is charged with an offence for failing to send a copy of a notice as required by subsection (4) it is a defence for him to prove that he took reasonable steps for securing compliance with that subsection.

(8) Where during the period within which a takeover offer can be accepted the offeror acquires or contracts to acquire any of the shares to which the offer relates but otherwise than by virtue of acceptances of the offer, then, if—

(*a*) the value of the consideration for which they are acquired or contracted to be acquired ("the acquisition consideration") does not at that time exceed the value of the consideration specified in the terms of the offer; or

(*b*) those terms are subsequently revised so that when the revision is announced the value of the acquisition consideration, at the time mentioned in paragraph (*a*) above, no longer exceeds the value of the consideration specified in those terms.

[THE NEXT PAGE IS I 240/1]

the offeror shall be treated for the purposes of this section as having acquired or contracted to acquire those shares by virtue of acceptances of the offer; but in any other case those shares shall be treated as excluded from those to which the offer relates.

Effect of notice under s.429

430.—(1) The following provisions shall, subject to section 430C, have effect where a notice is given in respect of any shares under section 429.

(2) The offeror shall be entitled and bound to acquire those shares on the terms of the offer.

(3) Where the terms of an offer are such as to give the holder of any shares a choice of consideration the notice shall give particulars of the choice and state—

(*a*) that the holder of the shares may within six weeks from the date of the notice indicate his choice by a written communication sent to the offeror at an address specified in the notice; and

(*b*) which consideration specified in the offer is to be taken as applying in default of his indicating a choice as aforesaid;

and the terms of the offer mentioned in subsection (2) shall be determined accordingly.

(4) Subsection (3) applies whether or not any time-limit or other conditions applicable to the choice under the terms of the offer can still be complied with; and if the consideration chosen by the holder of the shares—

(*a*) is not cash and the offeror is no longer able to provide it; or

(*b*) was to have been provided by a third party who is no longer bound or able to provide it,

the consideration shall be taken to consist of an amount of cash payable by the offeror which at the date of the notice is equivalent to the chosen consideration.

(5) At the end of six weeks from the date of the notice the offeror shall forthwith—

(*a*) send a copy of the notice to the company; and

(*b*) pay or transfer to the company the consideration for the shares to which the notice relates.

(6) If the shares to which the notice relates are registered the copy of the notice sent to the company under subsection (5)(*a*) shall be accompanied by an instrument of transfer executed on behalf of the shareholder by a person appointed by the offeror; and on receipt of that instrument the company shall register the offeror as the holder of those shares.

(7) If the shares to which the notice relates are transferable by the delivery of warrants or other instruments the copy of the notice sent to the company under subsection (5)(*a*) shall be accompanied by a statement to that effect; and the company shall on receipt of the statement issue the offeror with warrants or other instruments in respect of the shares and those already in issue in respect of the shares shall become void.

(8) Where the consideration referred to in paragraph (*b*) of subsection (5) consists of shares or securities to be allotted by the offeror the reference in that paragraph to the transfer of the consideration shall be construed as a reference to the allotment of the shares or securities to the company.

(9) Any sum received by a company under paragraph (*b*) of subsection (5) and any other consideration received under that paragraph shall be held by the company on trust for the person entitled to the shares in respect of which the sum or other consideration was received.

(10) Any sum received by a company under paragraph (*b*) of subsection (5), and any dividend or other sum accruing from any other consideration received by a company under that paragraph, shall be paid into a separate bank account, being an account the balance on which bears interest at an appropriate rate and can be withdrawn by such notice (if any) as is appropriate.

(11) Where after reasonable enquiry made at such intervals as are reasonable the person entitled to any consideration held on trust by virtue of subsection (9) cannot be found and twelve years have elapsed since the consideration was received or the company is wound up the consideration (together with any interest, dividend or other benefit that has accrued from it) shall be paid into court.

(12) In relation to a company registered in Scotland, subsections (13) and (14) shall apply in place of subsection (11).

(13) Where after reasonable enquiry made at such intervals as are reasonable the person entitled to any consideration held on trust by virtue of subsection (9) cannot be found and twelve years have elapsed since the consideration was received or the company is wound up—

    (*a*) the trust shall terminate;

    (*b*) the company or, as the case may be, the liquidator shall sell any consideration other than cash and any benefit other than cash that has accrued from the consideration; and

    (*c*) a sum representing—

        (i) the consideration so far as it is cash;

        (ii) the proceeds of any sale under paragraph (*b*) above; and

        (iii) any interest, dividend or other benefit that has accrued from the consideration,

shall be deposited in the name of the Accountant of Court in a bank account such as is referred to in subsection (10) and the receipt for the deposit shall be transmitted to the Accountant of Court.

(14) Section 58 of the Bankruptcy (Scotland) Act 1985 (so far as consistent with this Act) shall apply with any necessary modifications to sums deposited under subsection (13) as that section applies to sums deposited under section 57(1)(*a*) of that Act.

(15) The expenses of any such enquiry as is mentioned in subsection (11) or (13) may be defrayed out of the money or other property held on trust for the person or persons to whom the enquiry relates.

Right of minority shareholder to be bought out by offeror

430A.—(1) If a takeover offer relates to all the shares in a company and at any time before the end of the period within which the offer can be accepted—

    (*a*) the offeror has by virtue of acceptances of the offer acquired or contracted to acquire some (but not all) of the shares to which the offer relates; and

    (*b*) those shares, with or without any other shares in the company which he has acquired or contracted to acquire, amount to not less than nine-tenths in value of all the shares in the company,

the holder of any shares to which the offer relates who has not accepted the offer may by a written communication addressed to the offeror require him to acquire those shares.

(2) If a takeover offer relates to shares of any class or classes and at any time before the end of the period within which the offer can be accepted—

    (*a*) the offeror has by virtue of acceptances of the offer acquired or contracted to acquire some (but not all) of the shares of any class to which the offer relates; and

    (*b*) those shares, with or without any other shares of that class which he has acquired or contracted to acquire, amount to not less than nine-tenths in value of all the shares of that class,

the holder of any shares of that class who has not accepted the offer may by a written communication addressed to the offeror require him to acquire those shares.

(3) Within one month of the time specified in subsection (1) or, as the case may be, subsection (2) the offeror shall give any shareholder who has not accepted the offer notice in the prescribed manner of the rights that are

exercisable by him under that subsection; and if the notice is given before the end of the period mentioned in that subsection it shall state that the offer is still open for acceptance.

(4) A notice under subsection (3) may specify a period for the exercise of the rights conferred by this section and in that event the rights shall not be exercisable after the end of that period; but no such period shall end less than three months after the end of the period within which the offer can be accepted.

(5) Subsection (3) does not apply if the offeror has given the shareholder a notice in respect of the shares in question under section 429.

(6) If the offeror fails to comply with subsection (3) he and, if the offeror is a company, every officer of the company who is in default or to whose neglect the failure is attributable, shall be liable to a fine and, for continued contravention, to a daily default fine.

(7) If an offeror other than a company is charged with an offence for failing to comply with subsection (3) it is a defence for him to prove that he took all reasonable steps for securing compliance with that subsection.

Effect of requirement under s.430A

430B.—(1) The following provisions shall, subject to section 430C, have effect where a shareholder exercises his rights in respect of any shares under section 430A.

(2) The offeror shall be entitled and bound to acquire those shares on the terms of the offer or on such other terms as may be agreed.

(3) Where the terms of an offer are such as to give the holder of shares a choice of consideration the holder of the shares may indicate his choice when requiring the offeror to acquire them and the notice given to the holder under section 430A(3)—

   (a) shall give particulars of the choice and of the rights conferred by this subsection; and

   (b) may state which consideration specified in the offer is to be taken as applying in default of his indicating a choice;

and the terms of the offer mentioned in subsection (2) shall be determined accordingly.

(4) Subsection (3) applies whether or not any time-limit or other conditions applicable to the choice under the terms of the offer can still be complied with; and if the consideration chosen by the holder of the shares—

   (a) is not cash and the offeror is no longer able to provide it; or

   (b) was to have been provided by a third party who is no longer bound or able to provide it,

the consideration shall be taken to consist of an amount of cash payable by the offeror which at the date when the holder of the shares requires the offeror to acquire them is equivalent to the chosen consideration.

Applications to the court

430C.—(1) Where a notice is given under section 429 to the holder of any shares the court may, on an application made by him within six weeks from the date on which the notice was given—

   (a) order that the offeror shall not be entitled and bound to acquire the shares; or

   (b) specify terms of acquisition different from those of the offer.

(2) If an application to the court under subsection (1) is pending at the end of the period mentioned in subsection (5) of section 430 that subsection shall not have effect until the application has been disposed of.

(3) Where the holder of any shares exercises his rights under section 430A the court may, on an application made by him or the offeror, order that the terms on which the offeror is entitled and bound to acquire the shares shall be such as the court thinks fit.

(4) No order for costs or expenses shall be made against a shareholder making an application under subsection (1) or (3) unless the court considers—

(*a*) that the application was unnecessary, improper or vexatious; or

(*b*) that there has been unreasonable delay in making the application or unreasonable conduct on his part in conducting the proceedings on the application.

(5) Where a takeover offer has not been accepted to the extent necessary for entitling the offeror to give notices under subsection (1) or (2) of section 429 the court may, on the application of the offeror, make an order authorising him to give notices under that subsection if satisfied—

(*a*) that the offeror has after reasonable enquiry been unable to trace one or more of the persons holding shares to which the offer relates;

(*b*) that the shares which the offeror has acquired or contracted to acquire by virtue of acceptances of the offer, together with the shares held by the person or persons mentioned in paragraph (*a*), amount to not less than the minimum specified in that subsection; and

(*c*) that the consideration offered is fair and reasonable;

but the court shall not make an order under this subsection unless it considers that it is just and equitable to do so having regard, in particular, to the number of shareholders who have been traced but who have not accepted the offer.

Joint offers

430D.—(1) A takeover offer may be made by two or more persons jointly and in that event this Part of this Act has effect with the following modifications.

(2) The conditions for the exercise of the rights conferred by sections 429 and 430A shall be satisfied by the joint offerors acquiring or contracting to acquire the necessary shares jointly (as respects acquisitions by virtue of acceptance of the offer) and either jointly or separately (in other cases); and, subject to the following provisions, the rights and obligations of the offeror under those sections and sections 430 and 430B shall be respectively joint rights and joint and several obligations of the joint offerors.

(3) It shall be a sufficient compliance with any provision of those sections requiring or authorising a notice or other document to be given or sent by or to the joint offerors that it is given or sent by or to any of them; but the statutory declaration required by section 429(4) shall be made by all of them and, in the case of a joint offeror being a company, signed by a director of that company.

(4) In sections 428, 430(8) and 430E references to the offeror shall be construed as references to the joint offerors or any of them.

(5) In section 430(6) and (7) references to the offeror shall be construed as references to the joint offerors or such of them as they may determine.

(6) In sections 430(4)(*a*) and 430B(4)(*a*) references to the offeror being no longer able to provide the relevant consideration shall be construed as references to none of the joint offerors being able to do so.

(7) In section 430C references to the offeror shall be construed as references to the joint offerors except that any application under subsection (3) or (5) may be made by any of them and the reference in subsection (5)(*a*) to the offeror having been unable to trace one or more of the persons holding shares shall be construed as a reference to none of the offerors having been able to do so.

Associates

430E.—(1) The requirement in section 428(1) that a takeover offer must extend to all the shares, or all the shares of any class or classes, in a company shall be regarded as satisfied notwithstanding that the offer does not extend to shares which associates of the offeror hold or have contracted to acquire; but, subject to subsection (2), shares which any such associate holds or has contracted to acquire, whether at the time when the offer is made or subsequently, shall be disregarded for the purposes of any reference in this Part of this Act to the shares to which a takeover offer relates.

(2) Where during the period within which a takeover offer can be accepted any associate of the offeror acquires or contracts to acquire any of the shares to which the offer relates, then, if the condition specified in subsection (8)(*a*) or (*b*) of section 429 is satisfied as respects those shares they shall be treated for the purposes of that section as shares to which the offer relates.

(3) In section 430A(1)(*b*) and (2)(*b*) the reference to shares which the offeror has acquired or contracted to acquire shall include a reference to shares which any associate of his has acquired or contracted to acquire.

(4) In this section "associate", in relation to an offeror means—

(*a*) a nominee of the offeror;

(*b*) a holding company, subsidiary or fellow subsidiary of the offeror or a nominee of such a holding company, subsidiary or fellow subsidiary;

(*c*) a body corporate in which the offeror is substantially interested; or

(*d*) any person who is, or is a nominee of, a party to an agreement with the offeror for the acquisition of, or of an interest in, the shares which are the subject of the takeover offer, being an agreement which includes provisions imposing obligations or restrictions such as are mentioned in section 204(2)(*a*).

(5) For the purposes of subsection (4)(*b*) a company is a fellow subsidiary of another body corporate if both are subsidiaries of the same body corporate but neither is a subsidiary of the other.

(6) For the purposes of subsection (4)(*c*) an offeror has a substantial interest in a body corporate if—

(*a*) that body or its directors are accustomed to act in accordance with his directions or instructions; or

(*b*) he is entitled to exercise or control the exercise of one-third or more of the voting power at general meetings of that body.

(7) Subsections (5) and (6) of section 204 shall apply to subsection (4)(*d*) above as they apply to that section and subsections (3) and (4) of section 203 shall apply for the purposes of subsection (6) above as they apply for the purposes of subsection (2)(*b*) of that section.

(8) Where the offeror is an individual his associates shall also include his spouse and any minor child or step-child of his.

Convertible securities

430F.—(1) For the purposes of this Part of this Act securities of a company shall be treated as shares in the company if they are convertible into or entitle the holder to subscribe for such shares; and references to the holder of shares or a shareholder shall be construed accordingly.

(2) Subsection (1) shall not be construed as requiring any securities to be treated—

(*a*) as shares of the same class as those into which they are convertible or for which the holder is entitled to subscribe; or

(*b*) as shares of the same class as other securities by reason only that the shares into which they are convertible or for which the holder is entitled to subscribe are of the same class.

PART XIV

INVESTIGATION OF COMPANIES AND THEIR AFFAIRS; REQUISITION OF DOCUMENTS

Appointment and functions of inspectors

Investigation of a company on its own application or that of its members

431.—(1) The Secretary of State may appoint one or more competent inspectors to investigate the affairs of a company and to report on them in such manner as he may direct.

[THE NEXT PAGE IS I 241]

(2) The appointment may be made—
  (*a*) in the case of a company having a share capital, on the application either of not less than 200 members or of members holding not less than one-tenth of the shares issued,
  (*b*) in the case of a company not having a share capital, on the application of not less than one-fifth in number of the persons on the company's register of members, and
  (*c*) in any case, on application of the company.

(3) The application shall be supported by such evidence as the Secretary of State may require for the purpose of showing that the applicant or applicants have good reason for requiring the investigation.

(4) The Secretary of State may, before appointing inspectors, require the applicant or applicants to give security, to an amount not exceeding £5,000, or such other sum as he may by order specify, for payment of the costs of the investigation.

An order under this subsection shall be made by statutory instrument subject to annulment in pursuance of a resolution of either House of Parliament.

Other company investigations

432.—(1) The Secretary of State shall appoint one or more competent inspectors to investigate the affairs of a company and report on them in such manner as he directs, if the court by order declares that its affairs ought to be so investigated.

(2) The Secretary of State may make such an appointment if it appears to him that there are circumstances suggesting—
  (*a*) that the company's affairs are being or have been conducted with intent to defraud its creditors or the creditors of any other person, or otherwise for a fraudulent or unlawful purpose, or in a manner which is unfairly prejudicial to some part of its members, or
  (*b*) that any actual or proposed act or omission of the company (including an act or omission on its behalf) is or would be so prejudicial, or that the company was formed for any fraudulent or unlawful purpose, or
  (*c*) that persons concerned with the company's formation or the management of its affairs have in connection therewith been guilty of fraud, misfeasance or other misconduct towards it or towards its members, or
  (*d*) that the company's members have not been given all the information with respect to its affairs which they might reasonably expect.

[1] (2A) Inspectors may be appointed under subsection (2) on terms that any report they may make is not for publication; and in such a case, the provisions of section 437(3) (availability and publication of inspectors' reports) do not apply.

(3) Subsections (1) and (2) are without prejudice to the powers of the Secretary of State under section 431; and the power conferred by subsection (2) is exercisable with respect to a body corporate notwithstanding that it is in course of being voluntarily wound up.

(4) The reference in subsection (2)(*a*) to a company's members includes any person who is not a member but to whom shares in the company have been transferred or transmitted by operation of law.

NOTE
[1] Inserted by the Companies Act 1989, s. 55.

Inspectors' powers during investigation

433.—(1) If inspectors appointed under section 431 or 432 to investigate the affairs of a company think it necessary for the purposes of their investigation to investigate also the affairs of another body corporate which is or at any relevant time has been the company's subsidiary or holding company, or a subsidiary of its holding company or a holding company of its subsidiary, they have power to do so; and they shall report on the affairs of the other body corporate so far as they think that the results of their investigation of its affairs are relevant to the investigation of the affairs of the company first mentioned above.

(2) [Repealed by the Financial Services Act 1986, s.212(3) and Sched. 17.]

Production of documents and evidence to inspectors
    [1] **434.**—(1) When inspectors are appointed under section 431 or 432, it is the duty of all officers and agents of the company, and of all officers and agents of any other body corporate whose affairs are investigated under section 433(1)—

    (*a*) to produce to the inspectors all documents of or relating to the company or, as the case may be, the other body corporate which are in their custody or power,

    (*b*) to attend before the inspectors when required to do so, and

    (*c*) otherwise to give the inspectors all assistance in connection with the investigation which they are reasonably able to give.

    [2] (2) If the inspectors consider that an officer or agent of the company or other body corporate, or any other person, is or may be in possession of information relating to a matter which they believe to be relevant to the investigation, they may require him—

    (*a*) to produce to them any documents in his custody or power relating to that matter,

    (*b*) to attend before them, and

    (*c*) otherwise to give them all assistance in connection with the investigation which he is reasonably able to give;

and it is that person's duty to comply with the requirement.

    [3] (3) An inspector may for the purposes of the investigation examine any person on oath, and may administer an oath accordingly.

(4) In this section a reference to officers or to agents includes past, as well as present, officers or agents (as the case may be); and "agents", in relation to a company or other body corporate, includes its bankers and solicitors and persons employed by it as auditors, whether these persons are or are not officers of the company or other body corporate.

(5) An answer given by a person to a question put to him in exercise of powers conferred by this section (whether as it has effect in relation to an investigation under any of sections 431 to 433, or as applied by any other section in this Part) may be used in evidence against him.

    [4] (6) In this section "documents" includes information recorded in any form; and, in relation to information recorded otherwise than in legible form, the power to require its production includes power to require the production of a copy of the information in legible form.

NOTES
    [1] As amended by the Companies Act 1989, s. 56.
    [2] Substituted by the Companies Act 1989, s. 56(3).
    [3] Substituted by the Companies Act 1989, s. 56(4).
    [4] Inserted by the Companies Act 1989, s. 56(5).

Power of inspector to call for directors' bank accounts
    435. [Repealed by the Companies Act 1989, Sched. 24.]

Obstruction of inspectors treated as contempt of court
    436.—[1] (1) If any person—

    (*a*) fails to comply with section 434(1)(*a*) or (*c*),

    (*b*) refuses to comply with a requirement under section 434(1)(*b*) or (2), or

    (*c*) refuses to answer any question put to him by the inspectors for the purposes of the investigation,

the inspectors may certify that fact in writing to the court.

(3) The court may thereupon enquire into the case; and, after hearing any witnesses who may be produced against or on behalf of the alleged

offender and after hearing any statement which may be offered in defence, the court may punish the offender in like manner as if he had been guilty of contempt of the court.

NOTE

[1] Substituted for former subss. (1) and (2) by the Companies Act 1989, s. 56(6).

Inspectors' reports

437.—(1) The inspectors may, and if so directed by the Secretary of State shall, make interim reports to the Secretary of State, and on the conclusion of their investigation shall make a final report to him.

Any such report shall be written or printed, as the Secretary of State directs.

[1] (1A) Any persons who have been appointed under section 431 or 432 may at any time and, if the Secretary of State directs them to do so, shall inform him of any matters coming to their knowledge as a result of their investigations.

[2] (1B) If it appears to the Secretary of State that matters have come to light in the course of the inspectors' investigation which suggest that a criminal offence has been committed, and those matters have been referred to the appropriate prosecuting authority, he may direct the inspectors to take no further steps in the investigation or to take only such further steps as are specified in the direction.

[2] (1C) Where an investigation is the subject of a direction under subsection (1B), the inspectors shall make a final report to the Secretary of State only where—

    (a) they were appointed under section 432(1) (appointment in pursuance of an order of the court), or

    (b) the Secretary of State directs them to do so.

(2) If the inspectors were appointed under section 432 in pursuance of an order of the court, the Secretary of State shall furnish a copy of any report of theirs to the court.

(3) In any case the Secretary of State may, if he thinks fit—

    (a) forward a copy of any report made by the inspectors to the company's registered office,

    (b) furnish a copy on request and on payment of the prescribed fee to—

        (i) any member of the company or other body corporate which is the subject of the report,

        (ii) any person whose conduct is referred to in the report,

        (iii) the auditors of that company or body corporate,

        (iv) the applicants for the investigation,

        (v) any other person whose financial interests appear to the Secretary of State to be affected by the matters dealt with in the report, whether as a creditor of the company or body corporate, or otherwise, and

    (c) cause any such report to be printed and published.

NOTES

[1] Inserted by the Financial Services Act 1986, Sched. 13, para. 7.

[2] Inserted by the Companies Act 1989, s. 57.

Power to bring civil proceedings on company's behalf

[1] **438.**—(1) If from any report made or information obtained under this Part it appears to the Secretary of State that any civil proceedings ought in the public interest to be brought by any body corporate, he may himself bring such proceedings in the name and on behalf of the body corporate.

(2) The Secretary of State shall indemnify the body corporate against any costs or expenses incurred by it in or in connection with proceedings brought under this section.

NOTE

[1] As amended by the Companies Act 1989, s. 58.

Expenses of investigating a company's affairs

439.—[1] (1) The expenses of an investigation under any of the powers conferred by this Part shall be defrayed in the first instance by the Secretary of State, but he may recover those expenses from the persons liable in accordance with this section.

There shall be treated as expenses of the investigation, in particular, such reasonable sums as the Secretary of State may determine in respect of general staff costs and overheads.

(2) A person who is convicted on a prosecution instituted as a result of the investigation, or is ordered to pay the whole or any part of the costs of proceedings brought under section 438, may in the same proceedings be ordered to pay those expenses to such extent as may be specified in the order.

(3) A body corporate in whose name proceedings are brought under that section is liable to the amount or value of any sums or property recovered by it as a result of those proceedings; and any amount for which a body corporate is liable under this subsection is a first charge on the sums or property recovered.

[2] (4) A body corporate dealt with by an inspectors' report, where the inspectors were appointed otherwise than of the Secretary of State's own motion, is liable except where it was the applicant for the investigation, and except so far as the Secretary of State otherwise directs.

[3] (5) Where inspectors were appointed—

(*a*) under section 431, or

(*b*) on an application under section 442(3),

the applicant or applicants for the investigation is or are liable to such extent (if any) as the Secretary of State may direct.

(6) The report of inspectors appointed otherwise than of the Secretary of State's own motion may, if they think fit, and shall if the Secretary of State so directs, include a recommendation as to the directions (if any) which they think appropriate, in the light of their investigation, to be given under subsection (4) or (5) of this section.

(7) For purposes of this section, any costs or expenses incurred by the Secretary of State in or in connection with proceedings brought under section 438 (including expenses incurred under subsection (2) of it) are to be treated as expenses of the investigation giving rise to the proceedings.

(8) Any liability to repay the Secretary of State imposed by subsections (2) and (3) above is (subject to satisfaction of his right to repayment) a liability also to indemnify all persons against liability under subsections (4) and (5); and any such liability imposed by subsection (2) is (subject as mentioned above) a liability also to indemnify all persons against liability under subsection (3).

(9) A person liable under any one of those subsections is entitled to contribution from any other person liable under the same subsection, according to the amount of their respective liabilities under it.

(10) Expenses to be defrayed by the Secretary of State under this section shall, so far as not recovered under it, be paid out of money provided by Parliament.

NOTES

[1] Substituted by the Companies Act 1989, s. 59(2).

[2] As amended by the Companies Act 1989, s. 59(3).

[3] Substituted by the Companies Act 1989, s. 59(4).

Power of Secretary of State to present winding-up petition

440. [Repealed by the Companies Act 1989, s. 60 and Sched. 24. Re-enacted in the Insolvency Act 1986, s. 124A by the Companies Act 1989, s. 60(3).]

Inspectors' report to be evidence
441.—[1] (1) A copy of any report of inspectors appointed under this Part, certified by the Secretary of State to be a true copy, is admissible in any legal proceedings as evidence of the opinion of the inspectors in relation to any matter contained in the report, and, in proceedings on an application under section 8 of the Company Directors Disqualification Act 1986, as evidence of any fact stated therein.

[THE NEXT PAGE IS I 245]

(2) A document purporting to be such a certificate as is mentioned above shall be received in evidence and be deemed to be such a certificate, unless the contrary is proved.

NOTE

[1] As amended by the Insolvency Act 1985, Sched. 6, para. 3, and the Insolvency Act 1986, Sched. 13, Pt. I, and by the Companies Act 1989, s. 61.

Other powers of investigation available to the Secretary of State

Power to investigate company ownership

442.—(1) Where it appears to the Secretary of State that there is good reason to do so, he may appoint one or more competent inspectors to investigate and report on the membership of any company, and otherwise with respect to the company, for the purpose of determining the true persons who are or have been financially interested in the success or failure (real or apparent) of the company or able to control or materially to influence its policy.

(2) The appointment of inspectors under this section may define the scope of their investigation (whether as respects the matter or the period to which it is to extend or otherwise) and in particular may limit the investigation to matters connected with particular shares or debentures.

[1] (3) If an application for investigation under this section with respect to particular shares or debentures of a company is made to the Secretary of State by members of the company, and the number of applicants or the amount of the shares held by them is not less than that required for an application for the appointment of inspectors under section 431(2)(*a*) or (*b*), then, subject to the following provisions, the Secretary of State shall appoint inspectors to conduct the investigation applied for.

[1] (3A) The Secretary of State shall not appoint inspectors if he is satisfied that the application is vexatious; and where inspectors are appointed their terms of appointment shall exclude any matter in so far as the Secretary of State is satisfied that it is unreasonable for it to be investigated.

[1] (3B) The Secretary of State may, before appointing inspectors, require the applicant or applicants to give security, to an amount not exceeding £5,000, or such other sum as he may by order specify, for payment of the costs of the investigation.

An order under this subsection shall be made by statutory instrument which shall be subject to annulment in pursuance of a resolution of either House of Parliament.

[1] (3C) If on an application under subsection (3) it appears to the Secretary of State that the powers conferred by section 444 are sufficient for the purposes of investigating the matters which inspectors would be appointed to investigate, he may instead conduct the investigation under that section.

(4) Subject to the terms of their appointment, the inspectors' powers extend to the investigation of any circumstances suggesting the existence of an arrangement or understanding which, though not legally binding, is or was observed or likely to be observed in practice and which is relevant to the purposes of the investigation.

NOTE

[1] Substituted for former subs. (3) by the Companies Act 1989, s. 62.

Provisions applicable on investigation under s. 442

443.—(1) For purposes of an investigation under section 442, sections 433(1), 434, 436 and 437 apply with the necessary modifications of references to the affairs of the company or to those of any other body corporate, subject however to the following subsections.

(2) Those sections apply to—
  (*a*) all persons who are or have been, or whom the inspector has reasonable cause to believe to be or have been, financially interested in the success or failure or the apparent success or failure of the company

or any other body corporate whose membership is investigated with that of the company, or able to control or materially influence its policy (including persons concerned only on behalf of others), and

(b) any other person whom the inspector has reasonable cause to believe possesses information relevant to the investigation,

as they apply in relation to officers and agents of the company or the other body corporate (as the case may be).

(3) If the Secretary of State is of opinion that there is good reason for not divulging any part of a report made by virtue of section 442 and this section, he may under section 437 disclose the report with the omission of that part; and he may cause to be kept by the registrar of companies a copy of the report with that part omitted or, in the case of any other such report, a copy of the whole report.

(4) [Repealed by the Companies Act 1989, Sched. 24.]

Power to obtain information as to those interested in shares, etc.

444.—(1) If it appears to the Secretary of State that there is good reason to investigate the ownership of any shares in or debentures of a company and that it is unnecessary to appoint inspectors for the purpose, he may require any person whom he has reasonable cause to believe to have or to be able to obtain any information as to the present and past interests in those shares or debentures and the names and addresses of the persons interested and of any persons who act or have acted on their behalf in relation to the shares or debentures to give any such information to the Secretary of State.

(2) For this purpose a person is deemed to have an interest in shares or debentures if he has any right to acquire or dispose of them or of any interest in them, or to vote in respect of them, or if his consent is necessary for the exercise of any of the rights of other persons interested in them, or if other persons interested in them can be required, or are accustomed, to exercise their rights in accordance with his instructions.

(3) A person who fails to give information required of him under this section, or who in giving such information makes any statement which he knows to be false in a material particular, or recklessly makes any statement which is false in a material particular, is liable to imprisonment or a fine, or both.

Power to impose restrictions on shares and debentures

445.—(1) If in connection with an investigation under either section 442 or 444 it appears to the Secretary of State that there is difficulty in finding out the relevant facts about any shares (whether issued or to be issued), he may by order direct that the shares shall until further order be subject to the restrictions of Part XV of this Act.

(2) This section, and Part XV in its application to orders under it, apply in relation to debentures as in relation to shares.

Investigation of share dealings

446.—(1) If it appears to the Secretary of State that there are circumstances suggesting that contraventions may have occurred, in relation to a company's shares or debentures, of section 323 or 324 (taken with Schedule 13), or of subsections (3) to (5) of section 328 (restrictions on share dealings by directors and their families; obligation of director to disclose shareholding in his own company), he may appoint one or more competent inspectors to carry out such investigations as are requisite to establish whether or not such contraventions have occurred and to report the result of their investigations to him.

(2) The appointment of inspectors under this section may limit the period to which their investigation is to extend or confine it to shares or debentures of a particular class, or both.

[1] (3) For purposes of an investigation under this section, sections 434 to 437 apply—
  (*a*) with the substitution, for references to any other body corporate whose affairs are investigated under section 433(1), of a reference to any other body corporate which is, or has at any relevant time been, the company's subsidiary or holding company, or a subsidiary of its holding company.
[2] (4) Sections 434 to 436 apply under the preceding subsection—
  (*a*) to any individual who is an authorised person within the meaning of the Financial Services Act 1986;
  (*b*) to any individual who holds a permission granted under paragraph 23 of Schedule 1 to that Act;
  (*c*) to any officer (whether past or present) of a body corporate which is such an authorised person or holds such a permission;
  (*d*) to any partner (whether past or present) in a partnership which is such an authorised person or holds such a permission;
  (*e*) to any member of the governing body or officer (in either case whether past or present) of an unincorporated association which is such an authorised person or holds such a permission.
  (5) [Repealed by the Financial Services Act 1986, s.212(3) and Sched. 17.
  (6) [Repealed by the Financial Services Act 1986, s.212(3) and Sched. 17.]
  (7) [Repealed by the Companies Act 1989, Sched. 24.]

NOTES
[1] As amended by the Financial Services Act 1986, Sched. 13, para. 8, and the Companies Act 1989, Sched. 24.
[2] As amended by the Financial Services Act 1986, Sched. 16, para. 21.

Requisition and seizure of books and papers

Secretary of State's power to require production of documents
[1] **447.**—(1) [Repealed by the Companies Act 1989, Sched. 24.]
  (2) The Secretary of State may at any time, if he thinks there is good reason to do so, give directions to a company requiring it, at such time and place as may be specified in the directions, to produce such documents as may be so specified.
  (3) The Secretary of State may at any time, if he thinks there is good reason to do so, authorise an officer of his or any other competent person, on producing (if so required) evidence of his authority, to require a company to produce to him (the officer or other person) forthwith any documents which he (the officer or other person) may specify.
  (4) Where by virtue of subsection (2) or (3) the Secretary of State or an officer of his or other person has power to require the production of documents from a company, he or the officer or other person has the like power to require production of those documents from any person who appears to him or the officer or other person to be in possession of them; but where any such person claims a lien on documents produced by him, the production is without prejudice to the lien.
  (5) The power under this section to require a company or other person to produce documents includes power—
  (*a*) if the documents are produced—
    (i) to take copies of them or extracts from them, and
    (ii) to require that person, or any other person who is a present or past officer of, or is or was at any time employed by, the company in question, to provide an explanation of any of them;
  (*b*) if the documents are not produced, to require the person who was required to produce them to state, to the best of his knowledge and belief, where they are.

(6) If the requirement to produce documents or provide an explanation or make a statement is not complied with, the company or other person on whom the requirement was so imposed is guilty of an offence and liable to a fine.

Sections 732 (restriction on prosecutions), 733 (liability of individuals for corporate default) and 734 (criminal proceedings against unincorporated bodies) apply to this offence.

(7) However, where a person is charged with an offence under subsection (6) in respect of a requirement to produce any documents, it is a defence to prove that they were not in his possession or under his control and that it was not reasonably practicable for him to comply with the requirement.

(8) A statement made by a person in compliance with such a requirement may be used in evidence against him.

[2] (9) In this section "documents" includes information recorded in any form; and, in relation to information recorded otherwise than in legible form, the power to require its production includes power to require the production of a copy of it in legible form.

NOTES
[1] As amended by the Companies Act 1989, s. 63.
[2] Inserted by the Companies Act 1989, s. 63(7).

Entry and search of premises
[1] **448.**—(1) A justice of the peace may issue a warrant under this section if satisfied on information on oath given by or on behalf of the Secretary of State, or by a person appointed or authorised to exercise powers under this Part, that there are reasonable grounds for believing that there are on any premises documents whose production has been required under this Part and which have not been produced in compliance with the requirement.

(2) A justice of the peace may also issue a warrant under this section if satisfied on information on oath given by or on behalf of the Secretary of State, or by a person appointed or authorised to exercise powers under this Part—

(*a*) that there are reasonable grounds for believing that an offence has been committed for which the penalty on conviction on indictment is imprisonment for a term of not less than two years and that there are on any premises documents relating to whether the offence has been committed,

(*b*) that the Secretary of State, or the person so appointed or authorised, has power to require the production of the documents under this Part, and

(*c*) that there are reasonable grounds for believing that if production was so required the documents would not be produced but would be removed from the premises, hidden, tampered with or destroyed.

(3) A warrant under this section shall authorise a constable, together with any other person named in it and any other constables—

(*a*) to enter the premises specified in the information, using such force as is reasonably necessary for the purpose;

(*b*) to search the premises and take possession of any documents appearing to be such documents as are mentioned in subsection (1) or (2), as the case may be, or to take, in relation to any such documents, any other steps which may appear to be necessary for preserving them or preventing interference with them;

(*c*) to take copies of any such documents; and

(*d*) to require any person named in the warrant to provide an explanation of them or to state where they may be found.

(4) If in the case of a warrant under subsection (2) the justice of the peace is satisfied on information on oath that there are also on the premises other documents relevant

to the investigation, the warrant shall also authorise the actions mentioned in subsection (3) to be taken in relation to such documents.

(5) A warrant under this section shall continue in force until the end of the period of one month beginning with the day on which it is issued.

(6) Any documents of which possession is taken under this section may be retained—

(*a*) for a period of three months; or

(*b*) if within that period proceedings to which the documents are relevant are commenced against any person for any criminal offence, until the conclusion of those proceedings.

(7) Any person who intentionally obstructs the exercise of any rights conferred by a warrant issued under this section or fails without reasonable excuse to comply with any requirement imposed in accordance with subsection (3)(*d*) is guilty of an offence and liable to a fine.

Sections 732 (restriction on prosecutions), 733 (liability of individuals for corporate default) and 734 (criminal proceedings against unincorporated bodies) apply to this offence.

(8) For the purposes of sections 449 and 451A (provision for security of information) documents obtained under this section shall be treated as if they had been obtained under the provision of this Part under which their production was or, as the case may be, could have been required.

(9) In the application of this section to Scotland for the references to a justice of the peace substitute references to a justice of the peace or a sheriff, and for the references to information on oath substitute references to evidence on oath.

(10) In this section "document" includes information recorded in any form.

NOTE
[1] Substituted by the Companies Act 1989, s. 64(1).

Provision for security of information obtained

[0] **449.**—(1) No information or document relating to a company which has been obtained under section 447 shall, without the previous consent in writing of that company, be published or disclosed, except to a competent authority, unless the publication or disclosure is required—

[1] (*a*) with a view to the institution of or otherwise for the purposes of criminal proceedings,

[2](*ba*) with a view to the institution of, or otherwise for the purposes of, any proceedings, on an application under section 6, 7 or 8 of the Company Directors Disqualification Act 1986,

[3] (*c*) for the purposes of enabling or assisting any inspector appointed under this Part, or under section 94 or 177 of the Financial Services Act 1986, to discharge his functions;

[4](*cc*) for the purpose of enabling or assisting any person authorised to exercise powers under section 44 of the Insurance Companies Act 1982, section 447 of this Act, section 106 of the Financial Services Act 1986 or section 84 of the Companies Act 1989 to discharge his functions;

[5] (*d*) for the purpose of enabling or assisting the Secretary of State to exercise any of his functions under this Act, the Insider Dealing Act, the Prevention of Fraud (Investments) Act 1958, the Insurance Companies Act 1982, the Insolvency Act 1986, the Company Directors Disqualification Act 1986 or the Financial Services Act 1986,

[5](*dd*) for the purpose of enabling or assisting the Department of Economic Development for Northern Ireland to exercise any powers conferred on it by the enactments relating to companies or insolvency or for the purpose of enabling or assisting any inspector appointed by it under the enactments relating to companies to discharge his functions,

(*e*) [Repealed by the Companies Act 1989, s. 65(2)(*e*).]

6 (*f*) for the purpose of enabling or assisting the Bank of England to discharge its functions under the Banking Act 1987 or any other functions,

(*g*) for the purpose of enabling or assisting the Deposit Protection Board to discharge its functions under that Act,

(*h*) for any purpose mentioned in section 180(1)(*b*), (*e*), (*h*) or (*n*) of the Financial Services Act 1986,

(*i*) for the purpose of enabling or assisting the Industrial Assurance Commissioner or the Industrial Assurance Commissioner for Northern Ireland to discharge his functions under the enactments relating to industrial assurance,

(*j*) for the purpose of enabling or assisting the Insurance Brokers Registration Council to discharge its functions under the Insurance Brokers (Registration) Act 1977,

(*k*) for the purpose of enabling or assisting an official receiver to discharge his functions under the enactments relating to insolvency or for the purpose of enabling or assisting a body which is for the time being a recognised professional body for the purposes of section 391 of the Insolvency Act 1986 to discharge its functions as such,

(*l*) with a view to the institution of, or otherwise for the purposes of, any disciplinary proceedings relating to the exercise by a solicitor, auditor, accountant, valuer or actuary of his professional duties,

7(*ll*) with a view to the institution of, or otherwise for the purposes of, any disciplinary proceedings relating to the discharge by a public servant of his duties;

8(*m*) for the purpose of enabling or assisting an overseas regulatory authority to exercise its regulatory functions.

9 (1A) In subsection (1)—

(*a*) in paragraph (*ll*) "public servant" means an officer or servant of the Crown or of any public or other authority for the time being designated for the purposes of that paragraph by the Secretary of State by order made by statutory instrument; and

(*b*) in paragraph (*m*) "overseas regulatory authority" and "regulatory functions" have the same meaning as in section 82 of the Companies Act 1989.

10 (1B) Subject to subsection (1C), subsection (1) shall not preclude publication or disclosure for the purpose of enabling or assisting any public or other authority for the time being designated for the purposes of this subsection by the Secretary of State by an order in a statutory instrument to discharge any functions which are specified in the order.

10 (1C) An order under subsection (1B) designating an authority for the purpose of that subsection may—

(*a*) impose conditions subject to which the publication or disclosure of any information or document is permitted by that subsection; and

(*b*) otherwise restrict the circumstances in which that subsection permits publication or disclosure.

10a (1D) Subsection (1) shall not preclude the publication or disclosure of any such information as is mentioned in section 180(5) of the Financial Services Act 1986 by any person who by virtue of that section is not precluded by section 179 of that Act from disclosing it.

(2) A person who publishes or discloses any information or document in contravention of this section is guilty of an offence and liable to imprisonment or a fine, or both.

Section 732 (restriction on prosecutions), 733 (liability of individuals for corporate default) and 734 (criminal proceedings against unincorporated bodies) apply to this offence.

11 (3) For the purposes of this section each of the following is a competent authority—

(a) the Secretary of State,
(b) an inspector appointed under this Part or under section 94 or 177 of the Financial Services Act 1986,
(c) any person authorised to exercise powers under section 44 of the Insurance Companies Act 1982, section 447 of this Act, section 106 of the Financial Services Act 1986 or section 84 of the Companies Act 1989,
(d) the Department of Economic Development in Northern Ireland,
(e) the Treasury,
(f) the Bank of England,
(g) the Lord Advocate,
(h) the Director of Public Prosecutions, and the Director of Public Prosecutions for Northern Ireland,
(i) any designated agency or transferee body within the meaning of the Financial Services Act 1986, and any body administering a scheme under section 54 of or paragraph 18 of Schedule 11 to that Act (schemes for compensation of investors),
(j) the Chief Registrar of friendly societies and the Registrar of Friendly Societies for Northern Ireland,
(k) the Industrial Assurance Commissioner and the Industrial Assurance Commissioner for Northern Ireland,
(l) any constable,
(m) any procurator fiscal.

[12] (3A) Any information which may by virtue of this section be disclosed to a competent authority may be disclosed to any officer or servant of the authority.

(4) A statutory instrument containing an order under subsection (1A)(a) or (1B) is subject to annulment in pursuance of a resolution of either House of Parliament.

NOTES

[0] Excluded by the Building Societies Act 1986, s. 54(1)(a). See also s. 54(3) of that Act. See the Banking Act 1987, s. 87(2). As amended by ibid., Sched. 6, para. 18, and the Companies Act 1989, s. 65.

[1] As substituted for former paras. (a) and (b) by the Financial Services Act 1986, Sched. 13, para. 9.

[2] Inserted by the Insolvency Act 1985, Sched. 6, para. 4 and amended by the Insolvency Act 1986, Sched. 13, Pt. I.

[3] Substituted by the Companies Act 1989, s. 65(2)(b).

[4] Inserted by the Companies Act 1989, s. 65(2)(c).

[5] As substituted by the Financial Services Act 1986, Sched. 13, para. 9.

[6] Paras. (f) to (m) inserted by the Financial Services Act, 1986, Sched. 13, para. 9.

[7] Inserted by the Companies Act 1989, s. 65(2)(h).

[8] Substituted by the Companies Act 1989, s. 65(2)(i).

[9] Inserted by the Financial Services Act 1986, Sched. 13, para. 9. Substituted by the Companies Act 1989, s. 65(3).

[10] Inserted by the Financial Services Act 1986, Sched. 13, para. 9. See S.I. 1988 No. 1334.

[10a] Inserted by the Financial Services Act 1986, Sched. 13, para. 9.

[11] Substituted by the Companies Act 1989, s.65(6).

[12] Inserted by the Companies Act 1989, s. 65(6).

Punishment for destroying, mutilating etc. company documents

450.—[1] (1) An officer of a company, or of an insurance company to which Part II of the Insurance Companies Act 1982 applies, who—
(a) destroys, mutilates or falsifies, or is privy to the destruction, mutilation or falsification of a document affecting or relating to the company's property or affairs, or
(b) makes, or is privy to the making of, a false entry in such a document,

is guilty of an offence, unless he proves that he had no intention to conceal the state of affairs of the company or to defeat the law.

(2) Such a person as above mentioned who fraudulently either parts with, alters or makes an omission in any such document or is privy to fraudulent parting with, fraudulent altering or fraudulent making of an omission in, any such document, is guilty of an offence.

(3) A person guilty of an offence under this section is liable to imprisonment or a fine, or both.

[2] (4) Sections 732 (restriction on prosecutions), 733 (liability of individuals for corporate default) and 734 (criminal proceedings against unincorporated bodies) apply to an offence under this section.

[3] (5) In this section "document" includes information recorded in any form.

NOTES

[1] As amended by the Companies Act 1989, s. 66.

[2] Substituted by the Companies Act 1989, s. 66(3).

[3] Inserted by the Companies Act 1989, s. 66(4).

Punishment for furnishing false information

[1] **451.** A person who, in purported compliance with a requirement imposed under section 447 to provide an explanation or make a statement, provides or makes an explanation or statement which he knows to be false in a material particular or recklessly provides or makes an explanation or statement which is so false, is guilty of an offence and liable to imprisonment or a fine, or both.

Sections 732 (restriction on prosecutions), 733 (liability of individuals for corporate default) and 734 (criminal proceedings against unincorporated bodies) apply to this offence.

NOTE

[1] As amended by the Companies Act 1989, s. 67.

Disclosure of information by Secretary of State

[1] **451A.**—(1) This section applies to information obtained under sections 434 to 446.

(2) The Secretary of State may, if he thinks fit—

(a) disclose any information to which this section applies to any person to whom, or for any purpose for which, disclosure is permitted under section 449, or

(b) authorise or require an inspector appointed under this Part to disclose such information to any such person or for any such purpose.

(3) Information to which this section applies may also be disclosed by an inspector appointed under this Part to—

(a) another inspector appointed under this Part or an inspector appointed under section 94 or 177 of the Financial Services Act 1986, or

(b) a person authorised to exercise powers under section 44 of the Insurance Companies Act 1982, section 447 of this Act, section 106 of the Financial Services Act 1986 or section 84 of the Companies Act 1989.

(4) Any information which may by virtue of subsection (3) be disclosed to any person may be disclosed to any officer or servant of that person.

(5) The Secretary of State may, if he thinks fit, disclose any information obtained under section 444 to—

(a) the company whose ownership was the subject of the investigation,

(b) any member of the company,

(c) any person whose conduct was investigated in the course of the investigation,

(d) the auditors of the company, or

(e) any person whose financial interests appear to the Secretary of State to be affected by matters covered by the investigation.

NOTE

[1] Substituted by the Companies Act 1989, s. 68.

Supplementary

Privileged information
   [1] **452.**—(1) Nothing in sections 431 to 446 requires the disclosure to the Secretary of State or to an inspector appointed by him—
   (*a*) by any person of information which he would in an action in the High Court or the Court of Session be entitled to refuse to disclose on grounds of legal professional privilege except, if he is a lawyer, the name and address of his client.
   [2] (1A) Nothing in section 434, 443 or 446 requires a person (except as mentioned in subsection (1B) below) to disclose information or produce documents in respect of which he owes an obligation of confidence by virtue of carrying on the business of banking unless—
   (*a*) the person to whom the obligation of confidence is owed is the company or other body corporate under investigation,
   (*b*) the person to whom the obligation of confidence is owed consents to the disclosure or production, or
   (*c*) the making of the requirement is authorised by the Secretary of State.
   [2] (1B) Subsection (1A) does not apply where the person owing the obligation of confidence is the company or other body corporate under investigation under section 431, 432 or 433.
   (2) Nothing in sections 447 to 451 compels the production by any person of a document which he would in an action in the High Court or the Court of Session be entitled to refuse to produce on grounds of legal professional privilege, or authorises the taking of possession of any such document which is in the person's possession.
   (3) The Secretary of State shall not under section 447 require, or authorise an officer of his or other person to require, the production by a person carrying on the business of banking of a document relating to the affairs of a customer of his unless either it appears to the Secretary of State that it is necessary to do so for the purpose of investigating the affairs of the first-mentioned person, or the customer is a person on whom a requirement has been imposed under that section, or under section 44(2) to (4) of the Insurance Companies Act 1982 (provision corresponding to section 447).

NOTES
   [1] As amended by the Companies Act 1989, s. 69 and Sched. 24.
   [2] Inserted by the Companies Act 1989, s. 69(3).

Investigation of oversea companies
   453.—[1] (1) The provisions of this Part apply to bodies corporate incorporated outside Great Britain which are carrying on business in Great Britain, or have at any time carried on business there, as they apply to companies under this Act; but subject to the following exceptions, adaptations and modifications.
   [2] (1A) The following provisions do not apply to such bodies—
   (*a*) section 431 (investigation on application of company or its members),
   (*b*) section 438 (power to bring civil proceedings on the company's behalf),
   (*c*) sections 442 to 445 (investigation of company ownership and power to obtain information as to those interested in shares, etc.), and
   (*d*) section 446 (investigation of share dealings).
   [2] (1B) The other provisions of this Part apply to such bodies subject to such adaptations and modifications as may be specified by regulations made by the Secretary of State.

(2) Regulations under this section shall be made by statutory instrument subject to annulment in pursuance of a resolution of either House of Parliament.

NOTES

[1] Substituted by the Companies Act 1989, s. 70.

[2] Inserted by the Companies Act 1989, s. 70.

[THE NEXT PAGE IS I 251]

PART XV

ORDERS IMPOSING RESTRICTIONS
ON SHARES (SECTIONS 210, 216, 445)

Consequence of order imposing restrictions

454.—(1) So long as any shares are directed to be subject to the restrictions of this Part—

(*a*) any transfer of those shares or, in the case of unissued shares, any transfer of the right to be issued with them, and any issue of them, is void;

(*b*) no voting rights are exercisable in respect of the shares;

(*c*) no further shares shall be issued in right of them or in pursuance of any offer made to their holder; and

(*d*) except in a liquidation, no payment shall be made of any sums due from the company on the shares, whether in respect of capital or otherwise.

(2) Where shares are subject to the restrictions of subsection (1)(*a*), any agreement to transfer the shares or, in the case of unissued shares, the right to be issued with them is void (except an agreement to sell the shares on the making of an order under section 456(3)(*b*) below).

(3) Where shares are subject to the restrictions of subsection (1)(*c*) or (*d*), an agreement to transfer any right to be issued with other shares in right of those shares, or to receive any payment on them (otherwise than in a liquidation) is void (except an agreement to transfer any such right on the sale of the shares on the making of an order under section 456(3)(*b*) below).

Punishment for attempted evasion of restrictions

455.—(1) A person is liable to a fine if he—

(*a*) exercises or purports to exercise any right to dispose of any shares which, to his knowledge, are for the time being subject to the restrictions of this Part or of any right to be issued with any such shares, or

(*b*) votes in respect of any such shares (whether as holder or proxy), or appoints a proxy to vote in respect of them, or

(*c*) being the holder of any such shares, fails to notify of their being subject to those restrictions any person whom he does not know to be aware of that fact but does know to be entitled (apart from the restrictions) to vote in respect of those shares whether as holder or as proxy, or

(*d*) being the holder of any such shares, or being entitled to any right to be issued with other shares in right of them, or to receive any payment on them (otherwise than in a liquidation), enters into any agreement which is void under section 454(2) or (3).

(2) If shares in a company are issued in contravention of the restrictions, the company and every officer of it who is in default is liable to a fine.

(3) Section 732 (restriction on prosecutions) applies to an offence under this section.

Relaxation and removal of restrictions

456.—(1) Where shares in a company are by order made subject to the restrictions of this Part, application may be made to the court for an order directing that the shares be no longer so subject.

(2) If the order applying the restrictions was made by the Secretary of State, or he has refused to make an order disapplying them, the application may be made by any person aggrieved; and if the order was made by the court under section 216 (non-disclosure of share holding), it may be made by any such person or by the company.

(3) Subject as follows, an order of the court or the Secretary of State directing that shares shall cease to be subject to the restrictions may be made only if—

    (*a*) the court or (as the case may be) the Secretary of State is satisfied that the relevant facts about the shares have been disclosed to the company and no unfair advantage has accrued to any person as a result of the earlier failure to make that disclosure, or

    (*b*) the shares are to be sold and the court (in any case) or the Secretary of State (if the order was made under section 210 or 445) approves the sale.

(4) Where shares in a company are subject to the restrictions, the court may on application order the shares to be sold, subject to the court's approval as to the sale, and may also direct that the shares shall cease to be subject to the restrictions.

An application to the court under this subsection may be made by the Secretary of State (unless the restrictions were imposed by court order under section 216), or by the company.

(5) Where an order has been made under subsection (4), the court may on application make such further order relating to the sale or transfer of the shares as it thinks fit.

An application to the court under this subsection may be made—

    (*a*) by the Secretary of State (unless the restrictions on the shares were imposed by court order under section 216), or

    (*b*) by the company, or

    (*c*) by the person appointed by or in pursuance of the order to effect the sale, or

    (*d*) by any person interested in the shares.

(6) An order (whether of the Secretary of State or the court) directing that shares shall cease to be subject to the restrictions of this Part, if it is—

    (*a*) expressed to be made with a view to permitting a transfer of the shares, or

    (*b*) made under subsection (4) of this section,

may continue the restrictions mentioned in paragraphs (*c*) and (*d*) of section 454(1), either in whole or in part, so far as they relate to any right acquired or offer made before the transfer.

(7) Subsection (3) does not apply to an order directing that shares shall cease to be subject to any restrictions which have been continued in force in relation to those shares under subsection (6).

Further provisions on sale by court order of restricted shares

457.—(1) Where shares are sold in pursuance of an order of the court under section 456(4) the proceeds of sale, less the costs of the sale, shall be paid into court for the benefit of the persons who are beneficially interested in the shares; and any such person may apply to the court for the whole or part of those proceeds to be paid to him.

(2) On application under subsection (1) the court shall (subject as provided below) order the payment to the applicant of the whole of the proceeds of sale together with any interest thereon or, if any other person had a beneficial interest in the shares at the time of their sale, such proportion of those proceeds and interest as is equal to the proportion which the value of the applicant's interest in the shares bears to the total value of the shares.

(3) On granting an application for an order under section 456(4) or (5) the court may order that the applicant's costs be paid out of the proceeds of sale; and if that order is made, the applicant is entitled to payment of his costs out of those proceeds before any person interested in the shares in question receives any part of those proceeds.

PART XVI

FRAUDULENT TRADING BY A
COMPANY

Punishment for fraudulent trading
458. If any business of a company is carried on with intent to defraud creditors of the company or creditors of any other person, or for any fraudulent purpose, every person who was knowingly a party to the carrying on of the business in that manner is liable to imprisonment or a fine, or both.

This applies whether or not the company has been, or is in the course of being, wound up.

PART XVII

PROTECTION OF COMPANY'S MEMBERS AGAINST
UNFAIR PREJUDICE

Order on application of company member
459.—(1) A member of a company may apply to the court by petition for an order under this Part on the ground that the company's affairs are being or have been conducted in a manner which is unfairly prejudicial to the interests of some part of the members (including at least himself) or that any actual or proposed act or omission of the company (including an act or omission on its behalf) is or would be so prejudicial.

(2) The provisions of this Part apply to a person who is not a member of a company but to whom shares in the company have been transferred or transmitted by operation of law, as those provisions apply to a member of the company; and references to a member or members are to be construed accordingly.

Order on application of Secretary of State
460.—(1) If in the case of any company—
  (*a*) the Secretary of State has received a report under section 437, or exercised his powers under section 447 or 448 of this Act or section 44(2) to (6) of the Insurance Companies Act 1982 (inspection of company's books and papers), and
  (*b*) it appears to him that the company's affairs are being or have been conducted in a manner which is unfairly prejudicial to the interests of some part of the members, or that any actual or proposed act or omission of the company (including an act or omission on its behalf) is or would be so prejudicial,
he may himself (in addition to or instead of presenting a petition under section 440 for the winding up of the company) apply to the court by petition for an order under this Part.

(2) In this section (and, so far as applicable for its purposes, in the section next following) "company" means any body corporate which is liable to be wound up under this Act.

Provisions as to petitions and orders under this Part
461.—(1) If the court is satisfied that a petition under this Part is well founded, it may make such order as it thinks fit for giving relief in respect of the matters complained of.

(2) Without prejudice to the generality of subsection (1), the court's order may—
  (*a*) regulate the conduct of the company's affairs in the future,
  (*b*) require the company to refrain from doing or continuing an act complained of by the petitioner or to do an act which the petitioner has complained it has omitted to do,

(*c*) authorise civil proceedings to be brought in the name and on behalf of the company by such person or persons and on such terms as the court may direct,

(*d*) provide for the purchase of the shares of any members of the company by other members or by the company itself and, in the case of a purchase by the company itself, the reduction of the company's capital accordingly.

(3) If an order under this Part requires the company not to make any, or any specified, alteration in the memorandum or articles, the company does not then have power without leave of the court to make any such alteration in breach of that requirement.

(4) Any alteration in the company's memorandum or articles made by virtue of an order under this Part is of the same effect as if duly made by resolution of the company, and the provisions of this Act apply to the memorandum or articles as so altered accordingly.

(5) An office copy of an order under this Part altering, or giving leave to alter, a company's memorandum or articles shall, within 14 days from the making of the order or such longer period as the court may allow, be delivered by the company to the registrar of companies for registration; and if a company makes default in complying with this subsection, the company and every officer of it who is in default is liable to a fine and, for continued contravention, to a daily default fine.

[1] (6) The power under section 411 of the Insolvency Act to make rules shall, so far as it relates to a winding up petition, apply for the purposes of a petition under this Part.

NOTE

[1] As amended by the Insolvency Act 1985, Sched. 6, para. 24 and the Insolvency Act 1986, Sched. 13, Pt. I.

Part XVIII

Floating Charges and Receivers (Scotland)

Chapter I
Floating Charges

Power of incorporated company to create floating charge

462.—(1) It is competent under the law of Scotland for an incorporated company (whether a company within the meaning of this Act or not), for the purpose of securing any debt or other obligation (including a cautionary obligation) incurred or to be incurred by, or binding upon, the company or any other person to create in favour of the creditor in the debt or obligation a charge, in this Part referred to as a floating charge, over all or any part of the property (including uncalled capital) which may from time to time be comprised in its property and undertaking.

(2) A floating charge may be created, in the case of a company which the Court of Session has jurisdiction to wind up, only by the execution, under the seal of the company, of an instrument or bond or other written acknowledgment of debt or obligation which purports to create such a charge.

(3) Execution in accordance with this section includes execution by an attorney authorised for such purpose by the company by writing under its common seal; and any such execution on behalf of the company binds the company.

(4) References in this Part to the instrument by which a floating charge was created are, in the case of a floating charge created by words in a bond or other written acknowledgment, references to the bond or, as the case may be, the other written acknowledgment.

[1] (5) Subject to this Act, a floating charge has effect in accordance with this Part and Part III of the Insolvency Act 1986 in relation to any heritable property in Scotland to which it relates, notwithstanding that the instrument creating it is not recorded in the Register of Sasines or, as appropriate, registered in accordance with the Land Registration (Scotland) Act 1979.

NOTE
[1] As amended by the Insolvency Act 1986, Sched. 13, Pt. I.

Effect of floating charge on winding up
[1] **463.**—(1) On the commencement of the winding up of a company, a floating charge created by the company attaches to the property then comprised in the company's property and undertaking or, as the case may be, in part of that property and undertaking, but does so subject to the rights of any person who—

(a) has effectually executed diligence on the property or any part of it; or

(b) holds a fixed security over the property or any part of it ranking in priority to the floating charge; or

(c) holds over the property or any part of it another floating charge so ranking.

(2) The provisions of Part IV of the Insolvency Act (except section 185) have effect in relation to a floating charge, subject to subsection (1), as if the charge were a fixed security over the property to which it has attached in respect of the principal of the debt or obligation to which it relates and any interest due or to become due thereon.

(3) Nothing in this section derogates from the provisions of sections 53(7) and 54(6) of the Insolvency Act (attachment of floating charge on appointment of receiver), or prejudices the operation of sections 175 and 176 of that Act (payment of preferential debts in winding up).

(4) Interest accrues, in respect of a floating charge which after 16th November 1972 attaches to the property of the company, until payment of the sum due under the charge is made.

NOTE
[1] As amended by the Insolvency Act 1985, Sched. 6, para. 18 and the Insolvency Act 1986, Scheds. 12 and 13, Pt. I.

Ranking of floating charges
[1] **464.**—(1) Subject to subsection (2), the instrument creating a floating charge over all or any part of the company's property under section 462 may contain—

(a) provisions prohibiting or restricting the creation of any fixed security or any other floating charge having priority over, or ranking *pari passu* with, the floating charge; or

(b) provisions regulating the order in which the floating charge shall rank with any other subsisting or future floating charges or fixed securities over that property or any part of it.

(2) Where all or any part of the property of a company is subject both to a floating charge and to a fixed security arising by operation of law, the fixed security has priority over the floating charge.

(3) Where the order of ranking of the floating charge with any other subsisting or future floating charges or fixed securities over all or any part of the company's property is not regulated by provisions contained in the instrument creating the floating charge, the order of ranking is determined in accordance with the following provisions of this section.

(4) Subject to the provisions of this section—

(a) a fixed security, the right to which has been constituted as a real right before a floating charge has attached to all or any part of the property of the company, has priority of ranking over the floating charge;

(b) floating charges rank with one another according to the time of registration in accordance with Chapter II of Part XII;

(c) floating charges which have been received by the registrar for registration by the same postal delivery rank with one another equally.

(5) Where the holder of a floating charge over all or any part of the company's property which has been registered in accordance with Chapter II of Part XII has received intimation in writing of the subsequent registration in accordance with that Chapter of another floating charge over the same property or any part thereof, the preference in ranking of the first-mentioned floating charge is restricted to security for—

(a) the holder's present advances;

(b) future advances which he may be required to make under the instrument creating the floating charge or under any ancillary document;

(c) interest due or to become due on all such advances; and

(d) any expenses or outlays which may reasonably be incurred by the holder.

(6) This section is subject to sections 175 and 176 of the Insolvency Act.

NOTE
[1] As amended by the Insolvency Act 1985, Sched. 6, para. 19 and the Insolvency Act 1986, Sched. 13, Pt. I.

Continued effect of certain charges validated by Act of 1972

465.—(1) Any floating charge which—

(a) purported to subsist as a floating charge on 17th November 1972, and

(b) if it had been created on or after that date, would have been validly created by virtue of the Companies (Floating Charges and Receivers) (Scotland) Act 1972,

is deemed to have subsisted as a valid floating charge as from the date of its creation.

(2) Any provision which—

(a) is contained in an instrument creating a floating charge or in any ancillary document executed prior to, and still subsisting at, the commencement of that Act,

(b) relates to the ranking of charges, and

(c) if it had been made after the commencement of that Act, would have been a valid provision,

is deemed to have been a valid provision as from the date of its making.

Alteration of floating charges

466.—(1) The instrument creating a floating charge under section 462 or any ancillary document may be altered by the execution of an instrument of alteration by the company, the holder of the charge and the holder of any other charge (including a fixed security) which would be adversely affected by the alteration.

(2) Such an instrument of alteration is validly executed if it is executed—

(a) in the case of a company, under its common seal or by an attorney authorised for such purpose by the company by a writing under its common seal;

(b) where trustees for debenture-holders are acting under and in accordance with a trust deed, by those trustees;

(c) where, in the case of a series of secured debentures, no such trustees are acting, by or on behalf of—

(i) a majority in nominal value of those present or represented by proxy and voting at a meeting of debenture-holders at which the holders of at least one-third in nominal value of the outstanding debentures of the series are present or so represented; or

(ii) where no such meeting is held, the holders of at least one-half in nominal value of the outstanding debentures of the series; or (*d*) in such manner as may be provided for in the instrument creating the floating charge or any ancillary document.

(3) Section 464 applies to an instrument of alteration under this section as it applies to an instrument creating a floating charge.

(4) Subject to the next subsection, section 410(2) and (3) and section 420 apply to an instrument of alteration under this section which—

(*a*) prohibits or restricts the creation of any fixed security or any other floating charge having priority over, or ranking *pari passu* with, the floating charge; or

(*b*) varies, or otherwise regulates the order of, the ranking of the floating charge in relation to fixed securities or to other floating charges; or

(*c*) releases property from the floating charge; or

(*d*) increases the amount secured by the floating charge.

(5) Section 410(2) and (3) and section 420 apply to an instrument of alteration falling under subsection (4) of this section as if references in the said sections to a charge were references to an alteration to a floating charge, and as if in section 410(2) and (3)—

(*a*) references to the creation of a charge were references to the execution of such alteration; and

(*b*) for the words from the beginning of subsection (2) to the word "applies" there were substituted the words "Every alteration to a floating charge created by a company".

(6) Any reference (however expressed) in any enactment, including this Act, to a floating charge is, for the purposes of this section and unless the context otherwise requires, to be construed as including a reference to the floating charge as altered by an instrument of alteration falling under subsection (4) of this section.

CHAPTER II
RECEIVERS

[Repealed by the Insolvency Act 1986, Sched. 12.]

[THE NEXT PAGE IS I 267]

CHAPTER III
GENERAL

Interpretation for Part XVIII generally

[1] **486.**—(1) In this Part, unless the context otherwise requires the following expressions have the following meanings respectively assigned to them, that is to say—

"ancillary document" means—

(a) a document which relates to the floating charge and which was executed by the debtor or creditor in the charge before the registration of the charge in accordance with Chapter II of Part XII; or

(b) an instrument of alteration such as is mentioned in section 466 in this Part;

"company" means an incorporated company (whether a company within the meaning of this Act or not);

"fixed security", in relation to any property of a company, means any security, other than a floating charge or a charge having the nature of a floating charge, which on the winding up of the company in Scotland would be treated as an effective security over that property, and (without prejudice to that generality) includes a security over that property, being a heritable security within the meaning of section 9(8) of the Conveyancing and Feudal Reform (Scotland) Act 1970;

"Register of Sasines" means the appropriate division of the General Register of Sasines.

NOTE
[1] As amended by the Insolvency Act 1986, Sched. 12.

Extent of Part XVIII

487. This Part extends to Scotland only.

PART XIX

RECEIVERS AND MANAGERS

[Repealed by the Insolvency Act 1986, Sched. 12.]

[THE NEXT PAGE IS I 317]

PART XX

WINDING UP OF COMPANIES REGISTERED UNDER THIS ACT OR THE FORMER COMPANIES ACTS

CHAPTER I
PRELIMINARY

[Repealed by the Insolvency Act 1986, Sched. 12.]

CHAPTER II
WINDING UP BY THE COURT

[Repealed by the Insolvency Act 1986, Sched. 12.]

CHAPTER III
VOLUNTARY WINDING UP

[Repealed by the Insolvency Act 1986, Sched. 12.]

CHAPTER IV
WINDING UP SUBJECT TO SUPERVISION OF COURT

[Repealed by the Insolvency Act 1986, Sched. 12.]

CHAPTER V
PROVISIONS APPLICABLE TO EVERY MODE OF WINDING UP

[Repealed by the Insolvency Act 1986, Sched. 12.]

CHAPTER VI
MATTERS ARISING SUBSEQUENT TO WINDING UP

Power of court to declare dissolution of company void

[1] **651.**—(1) Where a company has been dissolved, the court may, on an application made for the purpose by the liquidator of the company or by any other person appearing to the court to be interested, make an order, on such terms as the court thinks fit, declaring the dissolution to have been void.

(2) Thereupon such proceedings may be taken as might have been taken if the company had not been dissolved.

(3) It is the duty of the person on whose application the order was made, within seven days after its making (or such further time as the court may allow), to deliver to the registrar of companies for registration an office copy of the order.

If the person fails to do so, he is liable to a fine and, for continued contravention, to a daily default fine.

(4) Subject to the following provisions, an application under this section may not be made after the end of the period of two years from the date of the dissolution of the company.

(5) An application for the purpose of bringing proceedings against the company—

    (*a*) for damages in respect of personal injuries (including any sum claimed by virtue of section 1(2)(*c*) of the Law Reform (Miscellaneous Provisions) Act 1934 (funeral expenses)), or

    (*b*) for damages under the Fatal Accidents Act 1976 or the Damages (Scotland) Act 1976,

may be made at any time; but no order shall be made on such an application if it appears to the court that the proceedings would fail by virtue of any enactment as to the time within which proceedings must be brought.

(6) Nothing in subsection (5) affects the power of the court on making an order under this section to direct that the period between the dissolution of the company and the making of the order shall not count for the purposes of any such enactment.

(7) In subsection (5)(*a*) "personal injuries" includes any disease and any impairment of a person's physical or mental condition.

NOTE
[1] As amended by the Companies Act 1989, s.141(1)–(3). See *ibid.*, subss. (4)–(5).

Registrar may strike defunct company off register

652.—(1) If the registrar of companies has reasonable cause to believe that a company is not carrying on business or in operation, he may send to the company by post a letter inquiring whether the company is carrying on business or in operation.

(2) If the registrar does not within one month of sending the letter receive any answer to it, he shall within 14 days after the expiration of that month send to the company by post a registered letter referring to the first letter, and stating that no answer to it has been received, and that if an answer is not received to the second letter within one month from its date, a notice will be published in the *Gazette* with a view to striking the company's name off the register.

(3) If the registrar either receives an answer to the effect that the company is not carrying on business or in operation, or does not within one month after sending the second letter receive any answer, he may publish in the *Gazette*, and send to the company by post, a notice that at the expiration of three months from the date of that notice the name of the company mentioned in it will, unless cause is shown to the contrary, be struck off the register and the company will be dissolved.

(4) If, in a case where a company is being wound up, the registrar has reasonable cause to believe either that no liquidator is acting, or that the affairs of the company are fully wound up, and the returns required to be made by the liquidator have not been made for a period of six consecutive months, the registrar shall publish in the *Gazette* and send to the company or the liquidator (if any) a like notice as is provided in subsection (3).

(5) At the expiration of the time mentioned in the notice the registrar may, unless cause to the contrary is previously shown by the company, strike its name off the register, and shall publish notice of this in the *Gazette*; and on the publication of that notice in the *Gazette* the company is dissolved.

(6) However—

    (*a*) the liability (if any) of every director, managing officer and member of the company continues and may be enforced as if the company had not been dissolved and

    (*b*) nothing in subsection (5) affects the power of the court to wind up a company the name of which has been struck off the register.

(7) A notice to be sent to a liquidator under this section may be addressed to him at his last known place of business; and a letter or notice to be sent under this section to a company may be addressed to the company at its

registered office or, if no office has been registered, to the care of some officer of the company.

If there is no officer of the company whose name and address are known to the registrar of companies, the letter or notice may be sent to each of the persons who subscribed the memorandum, addressed to him at the address mentioned in the memorandum.

Objection to striking off by person aggrieved

653.—(1) The following applies if a company or any member or creditor of it feels aggrieved by the company having been struck off the register.

(2) The court, on an application by the company or the member or creditor made before the expiration of 20 years from publication in the *Gazette* of notice under section 652, may, if satisfied that the company was at the time of the striking off carrying on business or in operation, or otherwise that it is just that the company be restored to the register, order the company's name to be restored.

(3) On an office copy of the order being delivered to the registrar of companies for registration the company is deemed to have continued in existence as if its name had not been struck off; and the court may by the order give such directions and make such provisions as seem just for placing the company and all other persons in the same position (as nearly as may be) as if the company's name had not been struck off.

Property of dissolved company to be bona vacantia

[1] **654.**—(1) When a company is dissolved, all property and rights whatsoever vested in or held on trust for the company immediately before its dissolution (including leasehold property, but not including property held by the company on trust for any other person) are deemed to be *bona vacantia* and—

    (*a*) accordingly belong to the Crown, or to the Duchy of Lancaster or to the Duke of Cornwall for the time being (as the case may be), and

    (*b*) vest and may be dealt with in the same manner as other *bona vacantia* accruing to the Crown, to the Duchy of Lancaster or to the Duke of Cornwall.

(2) Except as provided by the section next following, the above has effect subject and without prejudice to any order made by the court under section 651 or 653.

NOTE

[1] Applied (*mod.*) by the Building Societies Act 1986, Sched. 15, para. 57, with effect from 1st January 1988.

Effect on s. 654 of company's revival after dissolution

[1] **655.**—(1) The person in whom any property or right is vested by section 654 may dispose of, or of an interest in, that property or right notwithstanding that an order may be made under section 651 or 653.

(2) Where such an order is made—

    (*a*) it does not affect the disposition (but without prejudice to the order so far as it relates to any other property or right previously vested in or held on trust for the company), and

    (*b*) the Crown or, as the case may be, the Duke of Cornwall shall pay to the company an amount equal to—

        (i) the amount of any consideration received for the property or right, or interest therein, or

        (ii) the value of any such consideration at the time of the disposition,

or, if no consideration was received, an amount equal to the value of the property, right or interest disposed of, as at the date of the disposition.

(3) Where a liability accrues under subsection (2) in respect of any property or right which, before the order under section 651 or 653 was made,

had accrued as *bona vacantia* to the Duchy of Lancaster, the Attorney-General of the Duchy shall represent Her Majesty in any proceedings arising in connection with that liability.

(4) Where a liability accrues under subsection (2) in respect of any property or right which, before the order under section 651 or 653 was made, had accrued as *bona vacantia* to the Duchy of Cornwall, such persons as the Duke of Cornwall (or other possessor for the time being of the Duchy)

may appoint shall represent the Duke (or other possessor) in any proceedings arising out of that liability.

(5) This section applies in relation to the disposition of any property, right or interest on or after 22nd December 1981, whether the company concerned was dissolved before, on or after that day.

NOTE

[1] Applied (*mod.*) by the Building Societies Act 1986, Sched. 15, para. 57, with effect from 1st January 1988.

Crown disclaimer of property vesting as bona vacantia

[1] **656.**—(1) Where property vests in the Crown under section 654, the Crown's title to it under that section may be disclaimed by a notice signed by the Crown representative, that is to say the Treasury Solicitor, or, in relation to property in Scotland, the Queen's and Lord Treasurer's Remembrancer.

(2) The right to execute a notice of disclaimer under this section may be waived by or on behalf of the Crown either expressly or by taking possession or other act evincing that intention.

(3) A notice of disclaimer under this section is of no effect unless it is executed—

    (*a*) within 12 months of the date on which the vesting of the property under section 654 came to the notice of the Crown representative, or

    (*b*) if an application in writing is made to the Crown representative by any person interested in the property requiring him to decide whether he will or will not disclaim, within a period of three months after the receipt of the application or such further period as may be allowed by the court which would have had jurisdiction to wind up the company if it had not been dissolved.

(4) A statement in a notice of disclaimer of any property under this section that the vesting of it came to the notice of the Crown representatives on a specified date, or that no such application as above mentioned was received by him with respect to the property before a specified date, is sufficient evidence of the fact stated, until the contrary is proved.

(5) A notice of disclaimer under this section shall be delivered to the registrar of companies and retained and registered by him; and copies of it shall be published in the *Gazette* and sent to any persons who have given the Crown representative notice that they claim to be interested in the property.

(6) This section applies to property vested in the Duchy of Lancaster or the Duke of Cornwall under section 654 as if for references to the Crown and the Crown representative there were respectively substituted references to the Duchy of Lancaster and to the Solicitor to that Duchy, or to the Duke of Cornwall and to the Solicitor to the Duchy of Cornwall, as the case may be.

NOTE

[1] Applied (*mod.*) by the Building Societies Act 1986, Sched. 15, para. 57, with effect from 1st January 1988.

Effect of Crown disclaimer under s. 656

[1] **657.**—(1) Where notice of disclaimer is executed under section 656 as respects any property, that property is deemed not to have vested in the Crown under section 654.

(2) As regards property in England and Wales, section 178(4) and sections 179 to 182 of the Insolvency Act shall apply as if the property had been disclaimed by the liquidator under the said section 91 immediately before the dissolution of the company.

(3) As regards property in Scotland, the following four subsections apply.

(4) The Crown's disclaimer operates to determine, as from the date of the disclaimer, the rights, interests and liabilities of the company, and the property of the company, in or in respect of the property disclaimed; but it does not (except so far as is necessary for the purpose of releasing the company and its property from liability) affect the rights or liabilities of any other person.

(5) The court may, on application by a person who either claims an interest in disclaimed property or is under a liability not discharged by this Act in respect of disclaimed property, and on hearing such persons as it thinks fit, make an order for the vesting of the property in or its delivery to any person entitled to it, or to whom it may seem just that the property should be delivered by way of compensation for such liability, or a trustee for him, and on such terms as the court thinks just.

(6) On such a vesting order being made, the property comprised in it vests accordingly in the person named in that behalf in the order, without conveyance or assignation for that purpose.

(7) Part II of Schedule 20 has effect for the protection of third parties where the property disclaimed is held under a lease.

NOTE
[1] As amended by the Insolvency Act 1985, Sched. 6, para. 46 and the Insolvency Act 1986, Sched. 13, Pt. I. "Section 91" refers to the Insolvency Act 1985, now s.178 of the 1986 Act. Applied (*mod.*) by the Building Societies Act 1986, Sched. 15, para. 57 with effect from 1st January 1988.

Liability for rentcharge on company's land after dissolution
[1] **658.**—(1) Section 180 of the Insolvency Act shall apply to land in England and Wales which by operation of law vests subject to a rentcharge in the Crown or any other person on the dissolution of a company as it applies to land so vesting on a disclaimer under that section.

(2) In this section "company" includes any body corporate.

NOTE
[1] As amended by the Insolvency Act 1985, Sched. 6, para. 47 and the Insolvency Act 1986, Sched. 13, Pt. I. Applied (*mod.*) by the Building Societies Act 1986, Sched. 15, para. 57, with effect from 1st January 1988.

CHAPTER VII
MISCELLANEOUS PROVISIONS ABOUT WINDING UP

[Repealed by the Insolvency Act 1986, Sched. 12.]

[THE NEXT PAGE IS I 327]

Part XXI

Winding Up of Unregistered Companies

[Repealed by the Insolvency Act 1986, Sched. 12.]

[1] Part XXII

Bodies Corporate Subject, or Becoming Subject, to this Act (Otherwise than by Original Formation Under Part I)

NOTE
[1] For interpretation of "public company", "private company" etc., see s. 1(3) and the Companies Consolidation (Consequential Provisions) Act 1985, s.1.

Chapter I
Companies Formed or Registered under Former Companies Acts

Companies formed and registered under former Companies Acts
675.—(1) In its application to existing companies, this Act applies in the same manner—
  (*a*) in the case of a limited company (other than a company limited by guarantee), as if the company had been formed and registered under Part I of this Act as a company limited by shares,
  (*b*) in the case of a company limited by guarantee, as if the company had been formed and registered under that Part as a company limited by guarantee, and
  (*c*) in the case of a company other than a limited company, as if the company had been formed and registered under that Part as an unlimited company.
(2) But reference, express or implied, to the date of registration is to be read as the date at which the company was registered under the Joint Stock Companies Acts, the Companies Act 1862, the Companies (Consolidation) Act 1908, the Companies Act 1929, or the Companies Act 1948.

Companies registered but not formed under former Companies Acts
676.—(1) This Act applies to every company registered but not formed under the Joint Stock Companies Acts, the Companies Act 1862, the Companies (Consolidation) Act 1908, the Companies Act 1929, or the Companies Act 1948, in the same manner as it is in Chapter II of this Part declared to apply to companies registered but not formed under this Act.

(2) But reference, express or implied, to the date of registration is to be read as referring to the date at which the company was registered under the Joint Stock Companies Acts, the Companies Act 1862, the Companies (Consolidation) Act 1908, the Companies Act 1929, or the Companies Act 1948.

Companies re-registered with altered status under former Companies Acts

677.—(1) This Act applies to every unlimited company registered or re-registered as limited in pursuance of the Companies Act 1879, section 57 of the Companies (Consolidation) Act 1908, section 16 of the Companies Act 1929, section 16 of the Companies Act 1948 or section 44 of the Companies Act 1967 as it (this Act) applies to an unlimited company re-registered as limited in pursuance of Part II of this Act.

(2) But reference, express or implied, to the date of registration or re-registration is to be read as referring to the date at which the company was registered or re-registered as a limited company under the relevant enactment.

Companies registered under Joint Stock Companies Acts

678.—(1) A company registered under the Joint Stock Companies Acts may cause its shares to be transferred in manner hitherto in use, or in such other manner as the company may direct.

(2) The power of altering articles under section 9 of this Act extends, in the case of an unlimited company formed and registered under the Joint Stock Companies Acts, to altering any regulations relating to the amount of capital or to its distribution into shares, notwithstanding that those regulations are contained in the memorandum.

Northern Ireland and Irish companies

679. Nothing in sections 675 to 678 applies to companies registered in Northern Ireland or the Republic of Ireland.

CHAPTER II
COMPANIES NOT FORMED UNDER COMPANIES LEGISLATION, BUT AUTHORISED TO REGISTER

Companies capable of being registered under this Chapter

680.—(1) With the exceptions and subject to the provisions contained in this section and the next—

    (a) any company consisting of two or more members, which was in existence on 2nd November 1862, including any company registered under the Joint Stock Companies Acts, and

    (b) any company formed after that date (whether before or after the commencement of this Act), in pursuance of any Act of Parliament (other than this Act), or of letters patent, or being otherwise duly constituted according to law, and consisting of two or more members,

may at any time, on making application in the prescribed form, register under this Act as an unlimited company, or as a company limited by shares, or as a company limited by guarantee; and the registration is not invalid by reason that it has taken place with a view to the company's being wound up.

(2) A company registered in any part of the United Kingdom under the Companies Act 1862, the Companies (Consolidation) Act 1908, the Companies Act 1929 or the Companies Act 1948 shall not register under this section.

(3) A company having the liability of its members limited by Act of Parliament or letters patent, and not being a joint stock company, shall not register under this section.

(4) A company having the liability of its members limited by Act of Parliament or letters patent shall not register in pursuance of this section as an unlimited company or as a company limited by guarantee.

(5) A company that is not a joint stock company shall not register under this section as a company limited by shares.

Procedural requirements for registration

681.—(1) A company shall not register under section 680 without the assent of a majority of such of its members as are present in person or by proxy (in cases where proxies are allowed) at a general meeting summoned for the purpose.

(2) Where a company not having the liability of its members limited by Act of Parliament or letters patent is about to register as a limited company, the majority required to assent as required by subsection (1) shall consist of not less than three-fourths of the members present in person or by proxy at the meeting.

(3) In computing any majority under this section when a poll is demanded, regard is to be had to the number of votes to which each member is entitled according to the company's regulations.

(4) Where a company is about to register (under section 680) as a company limited by guarantee, the assent to its being so registered shall be accompanied by a resolution declaring that each member undertakes to contribute to the company's assets, in the event of its being wound up while he is a member, or within one year after he ceases to be a member, for payment of the company's debts and liabilities contracted before he ceased to be a member, and of the costs and expenses of winding up and for the adjustment of the rights of the contributories among themselves, such amount as may be required, not exceeding a specified amount.

(5) Before a company is registered under section 680, it shall deliver to the registrar of companies—

    (*a*) a statement that the registered office of the company is to be situated in England and Wales, or in Wales, or in Scotland (as the case may be),

    (*b*) a statement specifying the intended situation of the company's registered office after registration, and

    (*c*) in an appropriate case, if the company wishes to be registered with the Welsh equivalent of "public limited company" or, as the case may be, "limited" as the last words or word of its name, a statement to that effect.

(6) Any statement delivered to the registrar under subsection (5) shall be made in the prescribed form.

Change of name on registration

682.—(1) Where the name of a company seeking registration under section 680 is a name by which it is precluded from registration by section 26 of this Act, either because it falls within subsection (1) of that section or, if it falls within subsection (2), because the Secretary of State would not approve the company's being registered with that name, the company may change its name with effect from the date on which it is registered under this Chapter.

(2) A change of name under this section requires the like assent of the company's members as is required by section 681 for registration.

Definition of "joint stock company"

683.—(1) For purposes of this Chapter, as far as relates to registration of companies as companies limited by shares, "joint stock company" means a company—

    (*a*) having a permanent paid-up or nominal share capital of fixed

amount divided into shares, also of fixed amount, or held and transferable as stock, or divided and held partly in one way and partly in
the other, and
  (*b*) formed on the principle of having for its members the holders of
         those shares or that stock, and no other persons.
(2) Such a company when registered with limited liability under this Act
is deemed a company limited by shares.

Requirements for registration by joint stock companies
  684.—(1) Before the registration under section 680 of a joint stock company, there shall be delivered to the registrar of companies the following
documents—
  (*a*) a statement in the prescribed form specifying the name with which
         the company is proposed to be registered,
  (*b*) a list in the prescribed form showing the names and addresses of all
         persons who on a day named in the list (not more than six clear days
         before the day of registration) were members of the company, with
         the addition of the shares or stock held by them respectively (dis-
         tinguishing, in cases where the shares are numbered, each share by
         its number), and
  (*c*) a copy of any Act of Parliament, royal charter, letters patent, deed
         of settlement, contract of copartnery or other instrument constitut-
         ing or regulating the company.
  (2) If the company is intended to be registered as a limited company,
there shall also be delivered to the registrar of companies a statement in
the prescribed form specifying the following particulars—
  (*a*) the nominal share capital of the company and the number of shares
         into which it is divided, or the amount of stock of which it consists,
         and
  (*b*) the number of shares taken and the amount paid on each share.

Registration of joint stock company as public company
  685.—(1) A joint stock company applying to be registered under section
680 as a company limited by shares may, subject to—
  (*a*) satisfying the conditions set out in section 44(2)(*a*) and (*b*) (where
         applicable) and section 45(2) to (4) as applied by this section, and
  (*b*) complying with subsection (4) below,
apply to be so registered as a public company.
  (2) Sections 44 and 45 apply for this purpose as in the case of a private
company applying to be re-registered under section 43, but as if a reference
to the special resolution required by section 43 were to the joint stock company's resolution that it be a public company.
  (3) The resolution may change the company's name by deleting the word
"company" or the words "and company", or its or their equivalent in
Welsh ("cwmni", "a'r cwmni"), including any abbreviation of them.
  (4) The joint stock company's application shall be made in the form prescribed for the purpose, and shall be delivered to the registrar of companies together with the following documents (as well as those required by
section 684), namely—
  (*a*) a copy of the resolution that the company be a public company,
  (*b*) a copy of a written statement by an accountant with the appropriate
         qualifications that in his opinion a relevant balance sheet shows that
         at the balance sheet date the amount of the company's net assets
         was not less than the aggregate of its called-up share capital and
         undistributable reserves,
  (*c*) a copy of the relevant balance sheet, together with a copy of an
         unqualified report (by an accountant with such qualifications) in
         relation to that balance sheet,

(*d*) a copy of any valuation report prepared under section 44(2)(*b*) as applied by this section, and

(*e*) a statutory declaration in the prescribed form by a director or secretary of the company—

(i) that the conditions set out in section 44(2)(*a*) and (*b*) (where applicable) and section 45(2) to (4) have been satisfied, and

(ii) that, between the balance sheet date referred to in paragraph (*b*) of this subsection and the joint stock company's application, there has been no change in the company's financial position that has resulted in the amount of its net assets becoming less than the aggregate of its called-up share capital and undistributable reserves.

(5) The registrar may accept a declaration under subsection (4)(*e*) as sufficient evidence that the conditions referred to in that paragraph have been satisfied.

(6) In this section—

"accountant with the appropriate qualifications" means a person who would be qualified under section 389(1) for appointment as the company's auditor, if it were a company registered under this Act,

"relevant balance sheet" means a balance sheet prepared as at a date not more than seven months before the joint stock company's application to be registered as a public company limited by shares, and

"undistributable reserves" has the meaning given by section 264(3); and section 46 applies (with necessary modifications) for the interpretation of the reference in subsection (4)(*c*) above to an unqualified report by the accountant.

Other requirements for registration

686.—(1) Before the registration in pursuance of this Chapter of any company (not being a joint stock company), there shall be delivered to the registrar of companies—

(*a*) a statement in the prescribed form specifying the name with which the company is proposed to be registered,

(*b*) a list showing the names, addresses and occupations of the directors or other managers (if any) of the company,

(*c*) a copy of any Act of Parliament, letters patent, deed of settlement, contract of copartnery or other instrument constituting or regulating the company, and

(*d*) in the case of a company intended to be registered as a company limited by guarantee, a copy of the resolution declaring the amount of the guarantee.

(2) The lists of members and directors and any other particulars relating to the company which are required by this Chapter to be delivered to the registrar shall be verified by a statutory declaration in the prescribed form made by any two or more directors or other principal officers of the company.

(3) The registrar may require such evidence as he thinks necessary for the purpose of satisfying himself whether a company proposing to be registered is or is not a joint stock company as defined by section 683.

Name of company registering

687.—(1) The following applies with respect to the name of a company registering under this Chapter (whether a joint stock company or not).

(2) If the company is to be registered as a public company, its name must end with the words "public limited company" or, if it is stated that the company's registered office is to be situated in Wales, with those words or their equivalent in Welsh ("cwmni cyfyngedig cyhoeddus"); and those words or that equivalent may not be preceded by the word "limited" or its equivalent in Welsh ("cyfyngedig").

(3) In the case of a company limited by shares or by guarantee (not being a public company), the name must have "limited" as its last word (or, if the company's registered office is to be situated in Wales, "cyfyngedig"); but this is subject to section 30 (exempting a company, in certain circumstances, from having "limited" as part of the name).

(4) If the company is registered with limited liability, then any additions to the company's name set out in the statements delivered under section 684(1)(*a*) or 686(1)(*a*) shall form and be registered as the last part of the company's name.

Certificate of registration under this Chapter

688.—(1) On compliance with the requirements of this Chapter with respect to registration, the registrar of companies shall give a certificate (which may be signed by him, or authenticated by his official seal) that the company applying for registration is incorporated as a company under this Act and, in the case of a limited company, that it is limited.

(2) On the issue of the certificate, the company shall be so incorporated; and a banking company in Scotland so incorporated is deemed a bank incorporated, constituted or established by or under Act of Parliament.

(3) The certificate is conclusive evidence that the requirements of this Chapter in respect of registration, and of matters precedent and incidental to it, have been complied with.

(4) Where on an application by a joint stock company to register as a public company limited by shares the registrar of companies is satisfied that the company may be registered as a public company so limited, the certificate of incorporation given under this section shall state that the company is a public company; and that statement is conclusive evidence that the requirements of section 685 have been complied with and that the company is a public company so limited.

Effect of registration

689. Schedule 21 to this Act has effect with respect to the consequences of registration under this Chapter, the vesting of property, savings for existing liabilities, continuation of existing actions, status of the company following registration, and other connected matters.

Power to substitute memorandum and articles for deed of settlement

690.—(1) Subject as follows, a company registered in pursuance of this Chapter may by special resolution alter the form of its constitution by substituting a memorandum and articles for a deed of settlement.

(2) The provisions of sections 4 to 6 of this Act with respect to applications to the court for cancellation of alterations of the objects of a company and matters consequential on the passing of resolutions for such alterations (so far as applicable) apply, but with the following modifications—

(*a*) there is substituted for the printed copy of the altered memorandum required to be delivered to the registrar of companies a printed copy of the substituted memorandum and articles, and

(*b*) on the delivery to the registrar of the substituted memorandum and articles or the date when the alteration is no longer liable to be cancelled by order of the court (whichever is the later)—

(i) the substituted memorandum and articles apply to the company in the same manner as if it were a company registered under Part I with that memorandum and those articles, and

(ii) the company's deed of settlement ceases to apply to the company.

(3) An alteration under this section may be made either with or without alteration of the company's objects.

(4) In this section "deed of settlement" includes any contract of copartnery or other instrument constituting or regulating the company, not being an Act of Parliament, a royal charter or letters patent.

PART XXIII

OVERSEA COMPANIES

CHAPTER I
REGISTRATION, ETC.

Documents to be delivered to registrar
691.—(1) When a company incorporated outside Great Britain establishes a place of business in Great Britain, it shall within one month of doing so deliver to the registrar of companies for registration—
 (*a*) a certified copy of the charter, statutes or memorandum and articles of the company or other instrument constituting or defining the company's constitution, and, if the instrument is not written in the English language, a certified translation of it; and
 (*b*) a return in the prescribed form containing—
  (i) a list of the company's directors and secretary, containing the particulars specified in the next subsection,
  (ii) a list of the names and addresses of some one or more persons resident in Great Britain authorised to accept on the company's behalf service of process and any notices required to be served on it,
  (iii) a list of the documents delivered in compliance with paragraph (*a*) of this subsection, and
  (iv) a statutory declaration (made by a director or secretary of the company or by any person whose name and address are given in the list required by sub-paragraph (ii)), stating the date on which the company's place of business in Great Britain was established.

(2) The list referred to in subsection (1)(*b*)(i) shall contain the following particulars—
 (*a*) with respect to each director—
  (i) in the case of an individual, his present Christian name and surname and any former Christian name or surname, his usual residential address, his nationality and his business occupation (if any), or, if he has no business occupation but holds other directorships, particulars of any of them,
  (ii) in the case of a corporation, its corporate name and registered or principal office;
 (*b*) with respect to the secretary (or, where there are joint secretaries, with respect to each of them)—
  (i) in the case of an individual, his present Christian name and surname, any former Christian name and surname and his usual residential address,
  (ii) in the case of a corporation or a Scottish firm, its corporate or firm name and registered or principal office.
Where all the partners in a firm are joint secretaries of the company, the name and principal office of the firm may be stated instead of the particulars mentioned in paragraph (*b*).

Section 289(2) applies for the purposes of the construction of references above to present and former Christian names and surnames.

Registration of altered particulars

692.—(1) If any alteration is made in—

(*a*) the charter, statutes, or memorandum and articles of an oversea company or any such instrument as is mentioned above, or

(*b*) the directors or secretary of an oversea company or the particulars contained in the list of the directors and secretary, or

(*c*) the names or addresses of the persons authorised to accept service on behalf of an oversea company,

the company shall, within the time specified below, deliver to the registrar of companies for registration a return containing the prescribed particulars of the alteration.

(2) If any change is made in the corporate name of an oversea company, the company shall, within the time specified below, deliver to the registrar of companies for registration a return containing the prescribed particulars of the change.

(3) The time for delivery of the returns required by subsections (1) and (2) is—

(*a*) in the case of an alteration to which subsection (1)(*c*) applies, 21 days after the making of the alteration, and

(*b*) otherwise, 21 days after the date on which notice of the alteration or change in question could have been received in Great Britain in due course of post (if despatched with due diligence).

Obligation to state name and other particulars

[1] **693.** Every oversea company shall—

(*a*) conspicuously exhibit on every place where it carries on business in Great Britain the company's name and the country in which it is incorporated,

(*b*) cause the company's name and the country in which it is incorporated to be stated in legible characters in all bill-heads and letter paper, and in all notices and other official publications of the company, and

(*c*) if the liability of the members of the company is limited, cause notice of that fact to be stated in legible characters in all bill-heads, letter paper, notices and other official publications of the company in Great Britain, and to be affixed on every place where it carries on its business.

NOTE

[1] As amended by the Financial Services Act 1986, Sched. 17.

Regulation of oversea companies in respect of their names

694.—(1) If it appears to the Secretary of State that the corporate name of an oversea company is a name by which the company, had it been formed under this Act, would on the relevant date (defined below in subsection (3)) have been precluded from being registered by section 26 either—

(*a*) because it falls within subsection (1) of that section, or

(*b*) if it falls within subsection (2) of that section, because the Secretary of State would not approve the company's being registered with that name,

the Secretary of State may serve a notice on the company, stating why the name would not have been registered.

(2) If the corporate name of an oversea company is in the Secretary of State's opinion too like a name appearing on the relevant date in the index of names kept by the registrar of companies under section 714 or which should have appeared in that index on that date, or is the same as a name which should have so appeared, the Secretary of State may serve a notice

on the company specifying the name in the index which the company's name is too like or which is the same as the company's name.

(3) No notice shall be served on a company under subsection (1) or (2) later than 12 months after the relevant date, being the date on which the company has complied with—

(*a*) section 691 in this Part, or

(*b*) if there has been a change in the company's corporate name, section 692(2).

(4) An oversea company on which a notice is served under subsection (1) or (2)—

(*a*) may deliver to the registrar of companies for registration a statement in the prescribed form specifying a name approved by the Secretary of State other than its corporate name under which it proposes to carry on business in Great Britain, and

(*b*) may, after that name has been registered, at any time deliver to the registrar for registration a statement in the prescribed form specifying a name approved by the Secretary of State (other than its corporate name) in substitution for the name previously registered.

(5) The name by which an oversea company is for the time being registered under subsection (4) is, for all purposes of the law applying in Great Britain (including this Act and the Business Names Act 1985), deemed to be the company's corporate name; but—

(*a*) this does not affect references to the corporate name in this section, or any rights or obligations of the company, or render defective any legal proceedings by or against the company, and

(*b*) any legal proceedings that might have been continued or commenced against the company by its corporate name or its name previously registered under this section may be continued or commenced against it by its name for the time being so registered.

(6) An oversea company on which a notice is served under subsection (1) or (2) shall not at any time after the expiration of two months from the service of that notice (or such longer period as may be specified in that notice) carry on business in Great Britain under its corporate name.

Nothing in this subsection, or in section 697(2) (which imposes penalties for its contravention) invalidates any transaction entered into by the company.

(7) The Secretary of State may withdraw a notice served under subsection (1) or (2) at any time before the end of the period mentioned in subsection (6); and that subsection does not apply to a company served with a notice which has been withdrawn.

Service of documents on oversea company

695.—(1) Any process or notice required to be served on an oversea company is sufficiently served if addressed to any person whose name has been delivered to the registrar under preceding sections in this Part and left at or sent by post to the address which has been so delivered.

(2) However—

(*a*) where such a company makes default in delivering to the registrar the name and address of a person resident in Great Britain who is authorised to accept on behalf of the company service of process or notices, or

(*b*) if at any time all the persons whose names and addresses have been so delivered are dead or have ceased so to reside, or refuse to accept service on the company's behalf, or for any reason cannot be served,

a document may be served on the company by leaving it at, or sending it by post to, any place of business established by the company in Great Britain.

Office where documents to be filed

696.—(1) Any document which an oversea company is required to deliver to the registrar of companies shall be delivered to the registrar at the registration office in England and Wales or Scotland, according to where the company has established a place of business.

(2) If the company has established a place of business both in England and Wales and in Scotland, the document shall be delivered at the registration office both in England and Wales and in Scotland.

(3) References in this Part to the registrar of companies are to be construed in accordance with the above subsections.

(4) If an oversea company ceases to have a place of business in either part of Great Britain, it shall forthwith give notice of that fact to the registrar of companies for that part; and as from the date on which notice is so given the obligation of the company to deliver any document to the registrar ceases.

Penalties for non-compliance

697.—(1) If an oversea company fails to comply with any of sections 691 to 693 and 696, the company, and every officer or agent of the company who knowingly and wilfully authorises or permits the default, is liable to a fine and, in the case of a continuing offence, to a daily default fine for continued contravention.

(2) If an oversea company contravenes section 694(6), the company and every officer or agent of it who knowingly and wilfully authorises or permits the contravention is guilty of an offence and liable to a fine and, for continued contravention, to a daily default fine.

Definitions for this Chapter

698. For purposes of this Chapter—

"certified" means certified in the prescribed manner to be a true copy or a correct translation;

"director", in relation to an oversea company, includes shadow director; and

"secretary" includes any person occupying the position of secretary by whatever name called.

Channel Islands and Isle of Man companies

699.—(1) With the exceptions specified in subsection (3) below, the provisions of this Act requiring documents to be forwarded or delivered to or filed with the registrar of companies and applying to companies formed and registered under Part I apply also (if they would not otherwise) to an oversea company incorporated in the Channel Islands or the Isle of Man.

(2) Those provisions apply to such a company—

(*a*) if it has established a place of business in England and Wales, as if it were registered in England and Wales,

(*b*) if it has established a place of business in Scotland, as if it were registered in Scotland, and

(*c*) if it has established a place of business both in England and Wales and in Scotland, as if it were registered in both England and Wales and Scotland,

with such modifications as may be necessary and, in particular, apply in a similar way to documents relating to things done outside Great Britain as if they had been done in Great Britain.

¹ (3) The exceptions are—

section 6(1) (resolution altering company's objects),

section 18 (alteration of memorandum or articles by statute or statutory instrument),

section 242(1) (directors' duty to file accounts),

section 288(2) (notice to registrar of change of directors or secretary), and

section 380 (copies of certain resolutions and agreements to be sent to registrar within 15 days), so far as applicable to a resolution altering a company's memorandum or articles.

NOTE
[1] As amended by the Companies Act 1989, s. 23 and Sched. 10, para. 12.

[1] CHAPTER II

———

NOTE
[1] Substituted by the Companies Act 1989, s. 23 and Sched. 10, para. 13.

———

DELIVERY OF ACCOUNTS AND REPORTS

Preparation of accounts and reports by oversea companies
700.—(1) Every oversea company shall in respect of each financial year of the company prepare the like accounts and directors' report, and cause to be prepared such an auditors' report, as would be required if the company were formed and registered under this Act.

[1] (2) The Secretary of State may by order—
(*a*) modify the requirements referred to in subsection (1) for the purpose of their application to oversea companies,
(*b*) exempt an oversea company from those requirements or from such of them as may be specified in the order.

[1] (3) An order may make different provision for different cases or classes of case and may contain such incidental and supplementary provisions as the Secretary of State thinks fit.

(4) An order under this section shall be made by statutory instrument which shall be subject to annulment in pursuance of a resolution of either House of Parliament.

NOTE
[1] See S.I. 1990 No. 440.

Oversea company's financial year and accounting reference periods
701.—(1) Sections 223 to 225 (financial year and accounting reference periods) apply to an oversea company, subject to the following modifications.

(2) For the references to the incorporation of the company substitute references to the company establishing a place of business in Great Britain.

(3) Omit section 225(4) (restriction on frequency with which current accounting reference period may be extended).

Delivery to registrar of accounts and reports of oversea company
702.—(1) An oversea company shall in respect of each financial year of the company deliver to the registrar copies of the accounts and reports prepared in accordance with section 700.

If any document comprised in those accounts or reports is in a language other than English, the directors shall annex to the copy delivered a translation of it into English, certified in the prescribed manner to be a correct translation.

(2) In relation to an oversea company the period allowed for delivering accounts and reports is 13 months after the end of the relevant accounting reference period.

This is subject to the following provisions of this section.

(3) If the relevant accounting reference period is the company's first and is a period of more than 12 months, the period allowed is 13 months from the first anniversary of the company's establishing a place of business in Great Britain.

(4) If the relevant accounting period is treated as shortened by virtue of a notice given by the company under section 225 (alteration of accounting reference date), the period allowed is that applicable in accordance with the above provisions or three months from the date of the notice under that section, whichever last expires.

(5) If for any special reason the Secretary of State thinks fit he may, on an application made before the expiry of the period otherwise allowed, by notice in writing to an oversea company extend that period by such further period as may be specified in the notice.

(6) In this section "the relevant accounting reference period" means the accounting reference period by reference to which the financial year for the accounts in question was determined.

Penalty for non-compliance

703.—(1) If the requirements of section 702(1) are not complied with before the end of the period allowed for delivering accounts and reports, or if the accounts and reports delivered do not comply with the requirements of this Act, the company and every person who immediately before the end of that period was a director of the company is guilty of an offence and liable to a fine and, for continued contravention, to a daily default fine.

(2) It is a defence for a person charged with such an offence to prove that he took all reasonable steps for securing that the requirements in question would be complied with.

(3) It is not a defence in relation to a failure to deliver copies to the registrar to prove that the documents in question were not in fact prepared as required by this Act.

PART XXIV

THE REGISTRAR OF COMPANIES, HIS FUNCTIONS AND OFFICES

Registration offices

704.—(1) For the purposes of the registration of companies under the Companies Acts, there shall continue to be offices in England and Wales and in Scotland, at such places as the Secretary of State thinks fit.

(2) The Secretary of State may appoint such registrars, assistant registrars, clerks and servants as he thinks necessary for that purpose, and may make regulations with respect to their duties, and may remove any persons so appointed.

(3) The salaries of the persons so appointed continue to be fixed by the Secretary of State, with the concurrence of the Treasury, and shall be paid out of money provided by Parliament.

(4) The Secretary of State may direct a seal or seals to be prepared for the authentication of documents required for or in connection with the registration of companies; and any seal so prepared is referred to in this Act as the registrar's official seal.

(5) Wherever any act is by the Companies Acts directed to be done to or by the registrar of companies, it shall (until the Secretary of State otherwise directs) be done to or by the existing registrar of companies in England and Wales or in Scotland (as the case may be), or to or by such person as the Secretary of State may for the time being authorise.

(6) In the event of the Secretary of State altering the constitution of the existing registration offices or any of them, any such act shall be done to or by such officer and at such place with reference to the local situation of the registered offices of the companies to be registered as the Secretary of State may appoint.

Companies' registered numbers

705.—(1) The registrar of companies shall allocate to every company a number, which shall be known as the company's registered number; and he may in addition allocate to any such company a letter, which is then deemed for all purposes to be part of the registered number.

(2) "Company" here includes—

(*a*) an oversea company which has complied with section 691 (delivery of statutes to registrar of companies, etc.) and which does not appear to the registrar not to have a place of business in Great Britain, and

(*b*) any incorporated or unincorporated body to which any provision of this Act applies by virtue of section 718 (unregistered companies).

Size, durability, etc. of documents delivered to registrar

706.—(1) For the purpose of securing that documents delivered to the registrar of companies under the Companies Acts are of standard size, durable and easily legible, regulations made by the Secretary of State by statutory instrument may prescribe such requirements (whether as to size, weight, quality or colour of paper, size, type or colouring of lettering, or otherwise) as he may consider appropriate; and different requirements may be so prescribed for different documents or classes of documents.

(2) If under any such provision there is delivered to the registrar a document (whether an original document or a copy) which in the registrar's opinion does not comply with such requirements prescribed under this section as are applicable to it, the registrar may serve on any person by whom under that provision the document was required to be delivered (or, if there are two or more such persons, may serve on any of them) a notice stating his opinion to that effect and indicating the requirements so prescribed with which in his opinion the document does not comply.

(3) Where the registrar serves such a notice with respect to a document delivered under any such provision, then, for the purposes of any enactment which enables a penalty to be imposed in respect of any omission to deliver to the registrar of companies a document required to be delivered under that provision (and, in particular, for the purposes of any such enactment whereby such a penalty may be imposed by reference to each day during which the omission continues)—

(*a*) any duty imposed by that provision to deliver such a document to the registrar is to be treated as not having been discharged by the delivery of that document, but

(*b*) no account is to be taken of any days falling within the period mentioned in the following subsection.

(4) That period begins with the day on which the document was delivered to the registrar as mentioned in subsection (2) and ends with the 14th day after the date of service of the notice under subsection (2) by virtue of which subsection (3) applies.

(5) In this section any reference to delivering a document includes sending, forwarding, producing or (in the case of a notice) giving it.

Power of registrar to accept information on microfilm, etc.

707.—(1) The registrar of companies may, if he thinks fit, accept under any provision of the Companies Acts requiring a document to be delivered to him any material other than a document which contains the information in question and is of a kind approved by him.

(2) The delivery to the registrar of material so accepted is sufficient compliance with the provision in question.

(3) In this section any reference to delivering a document includes sending, forwarding, producing or (in the case of a notice) giving it.

Fees payable to registrar

708.—(1) The Secretary of State may by regulations made by statutory instrument require the payment to the registrar of companies of such fees as may be specified in the regulations in respect of—

(a) the performance by the registrar of such functions under the Companies Acts as may be so specified, including the receipt by him of any notice or other document which under those Acts is required to be given, delivered, sent or forwarded to him.

(b) the inspection of documents or other material kept by him under those Acts.

(2) A statutory instrument containing regulations under this section requiring the payment of a fee in respect of a matter for which no fee was previously payable, or increasing a fee, shall be laid before Parliament after being made and shall cease to have effect at the end of the period of 28 days beginning with the day on which the regulations were made (but without prejudice to anything previously done under the regulations or to the making of further regulations) unless in that period the regulations are approved by resolution of each House of Parliament.

In reckoning that period of 28 days no account is to be taken of any time during which Parliament is dissolved or prorogued or during which both Houses are adjourned for more than four days.

(3) A statutory instrument containing regulations under this section, where subsection (2) does not apply, is subject to annulment in pursuance of a resolution of either House of Parliament.

(4) Fees paid to the registrar under the Companies Acts shall be paid into the Consolidated Fund.

(5) It is hereby declared that the registrar may charge a fee for any services provided by him otherwise than in pursuance of an obligation on him by law.

Inspection of documents kept by registrar

709.—(1) Subject to the provisions of this section, any person may—

(a) inspect a copy of any document kept by the registrar of companies or, if the copy is illegible or unavailable, the document itself,

(b) require a certificate of the incorporation of any company, or a certified copy or extract of any other document or any part of any other document.

A certificate given under paragraph (b) may be signed by the registrar, or authenticated by his official seal.

(2), (3) [Repealed by the Financial Services Act 1986, Sched. 17.]

(4) [Repealed by the Insolvency Act 1986, Sched. 12.]

Additional provisions about inspection

710.—(1) No process for compelling the production of any document kept by the registrar shall issue from any court except with the leave of that court; and any such process if issued shall bear on it a statement that it is issued with leave of the court.

(2) A copy of, or extract from, any document kept and registered at any of the offices for the registration of companies in England and Wales or Scotland, certified in writing by the registrar (whose official position it is unnecessary to prove) to be a true copy, is in all legal proceedings admissible in evidence as of equal validity with the original document.

(3) Copies or extracts of documents or parts of documents furnished by the registrar under section 709 may, instead of being certified by him in writing to be true copies, be sealed with his official seal.

(4) [Repealed by the Insolvency Act 1986, Sched. 12.]

(5) For purposes of section 709 and this section, a copy is to be taken to be the copy of a document notwithstanding that it is taken from a copy or other reproduction of the original; and in both sections "document" includes any material which contains information kept by the registrar of companies for purposes of the Companies Acts.

Public notice by registrar of receipt and issue of certain documents

711.—(1) The registrar of companies shall cause to be published in the *Gazette* notice of the issue or receipt by him of documents of any of the following descriptions (stating in the notice the name of the company, the description of document and the date of issue or receipt)—
- (*a*) any certificate of incorporation of a company,
- (*b*) any document making or evidencing an alteration in a company's memorandum or articles,
- (*c*) any notification of a change among the directors of a company,
- (*d*) any copy of a resolution of a public company which gives, varies, revokes or renews an authority for the purposes of section 80 (allotment of relevant securities),
- (*e*) any copy of a special resolution of a public company passed under section 95(1), (2) or (3) (disapplication of pre-emption rights),
- (*f*) any report under section 103 or 104 as to the value of a non-cash asset,
- (*g*) any statutory declaration delivered under section 117 (public company share capital requirements),
- (*h*) any notification (given under section 122) of the redemption of shares,
- (*j*) any statement or notice delivered by a public company under section 128 (registration of particulars of special rights),
- ⁰ (*k*) any documents delivered by a company under section 242 (accounts and reports),
- (*l*) a copy of any resolution or agreement to which section 380 applies and which—
  - (i) states the rights attached to any shares in a public company, other than shares which are in all respects uniform (for purposes of section 128) with shares previously allotted, or
  - (ii) varies rights attached to any shares in a public company, or
  - (iii) assigns a name or other designation, or a new name or designation, to any class of shares in a public company,
- (*m*) any return of allotments of a public company,
- (*n*) any notice of a change in the situation of a company's registered office,
- (*p*) any copy of a winding-up order in respect of a company,
- (*q*) any order for the dissolution of a company on a winding up,
- (*r*) any return by a liquidator of the final meeting of a company on a winding up,

[1] (s)   any copy of a draft of the terms of a scheme delivered to the registrar of companies under paragraph 2(1) of Schedule 15A,

[1] (t)   any copy of an order under section 425(2) or section 427 in respect of a compromise or arrangement to which section 427A(1) applies.

[2] (2) In section 42 "official notification" means—

(a)   in relation to anything stated in a document of any of the above description, the notification of that document in the *Gazette* under this section, and

(b)   in relation to the appointment of a liquidator in a voluntary winding up, the notification of it in the *Gazette* under section 109 of the Insolvency Act;

and "officially notified" is to be construed accordingly.

NOTES

[0] As amended by the Companies Act 1989, s. 23 and Sched. 10, para. 14.

[1] Added by S.I. 1987 No. 1991.

[2] As amended by the Insolvency Act 1986, Sched. 13, Pt. I.

Removal of documents to Public Record Office

712.—(1) Where a company has been dissolved, whether under this Act or otherwise, the registrar may, at any time after the expiration of two years from the date of the dissolution, direct that any documents in his custody relating to that company may be removed to the Public Record Office; and documents in respect of which such a direction is given shall be disposed of in accordance with the enactments relating to that office and the rules made under them.

(2) In this section "company" includes a company provisionally or completely registered under the Joint Stock Companies Act 1844.

(3) This section does not extend to Scotland.

Enforcement of company's duty to make returns

713.—(1) If a company, having made default in complying with any provision of the Companies Acts which requires it to file with, deliver or send to the registrar of companies any return, account or other document, or to give notice to him of any matter, fails to make good the default within 14 days after the service of a notice on the company requiring it to do so, the court may, on an application made to it by any member or creditor of the company or by the registrar of companies, make an order directing the company and any officer of it to make good the default within such time as may be specified in the order.

(2) The court's order may provide that all costs of and incidental to the application shall be borne by the company or by any officers of it responsible for the default.

(3) Nothing in this section prejudices the operation of any enactment imposing penalties on a company or its officers in respect of any such default as is mentioned above.

Registrar's index of company and corporate names

714.—(1) The registrar of companies shall keep an index of the names of the following bodies—

(a)   companies as defined by this Act,

(b)   companies incorporated outside Great Britain which have complied with section 691 and which do not appear to the registrar of companies not to have a place of business in Great Britain,

(c)   incorporated and unincorporated bodies to which any provision of this Act applies by virtue of section 718 (unregistered companies),

(d)   limited partnerships registered under the Limited Partnerships Act 1907,

(e)   companies within the meaning of the Companies Act (Northern Ireland) 1960, (*f*) companies incorporated outside Northern Ireland which have complied with section 356 of that Act (which corresponds with section 691 of this Act), and which do not appear to the registrar not to have a place of business in Northern Ireland, and

(*g*) societies registered under the Industrial and Provident Societies Act 1965 or the Industrial and Provident Societies Act (Northern Ireland) 1969.

(2) The Secretary of State may by order in a statutory instrument vary subsection (1) by the addition or deletion of any class of body, except any within paragraph (*a*) or (*b*) of the subsection, whether incorporated or unincorporated; and any such statutory instrument is subject to annulment in pursuance of a resolution of either House of Parliament.

Destruction of old records

715.—(1) The registrar of companies may destroy any documents or other material which he has kept for over 10 years and which were, or were comprised in or annexed or attached to, the accounts or annual returns of any company.

(2) The registrar shall retain a copy of any document or other material destroyed in pursuance of subsection (1); and sections 709 and 710 apply in relation to any such copy as if it were the original.

Part XXV

Miscellaneous and Supplementary Provisions

Prohibition of partnerships with more than 20 members

716.—(1) No company, association or partnership consisting of more than 20 persons shall be formed for the purpose of carrying on any business that has for its object the acquisition of gain by the company, association or partnership, or by its individual members, unless it is registered as a company under this Act, or is formed in pursuance of some other Act of Parliament, or of letters patent.

[1] (2) However, this does not prohibit the formation—

(*a*) for the purpose of carrying on practice as solicitors, of a partnership consisting of persons each of whom is a solicitor;

(*b*) for the purpose of carrying on practice as accountants, of a partnership consisting of persons each of whom falls within either paragraph (*a*) or (*b*) of section 389(1) (qualifications of company auditors);

(*c*) for the purpose of carrying on business as members of a recognised stock exchange, of a partnership consisting of persons each of whom is a member of that stock exchange.

(3) The Secretary of State may by regulations in a statutory instrument provide that subsection (1) shall not apply to the formation (otherwise than as permitted by subsection (2)), for a purpose specified in the regulations, of a partnership of a description so specified.

(4) In this section "solicitor"—

(*a*) in relation to England and Wales, means solicitor of the Supreme Court, and

(*b*) in relation to Scotland, means a person enrolled or deemed enrolled as a solicitor in pursuance of the Solicitors (Scotland) Act 1980.

(5) Subsection (1) does not apply in relation to any body of persons for the time being approved for the purposes of the Marine and Aviation Insurance (War Risks) Act 1952 by the Secretary of State, being a body the objects of which are or include the carrying on of business by way of the re-insurance of risks which may be re-insured under any agreement for the purpose mentioned in section 1(1)(*b*) of that Act.

NOTE
[1] As amended by the Financial Services Act 1986, Sched. 16, para. 22 and the Companies Act 1989, Sched. 24.

Limited partnerships: limit on number of members

717.—[1] (1) So much of the Limited Partnerships Act 1907 as provides that a limited partnership shall not consist of more than 20 persons does not apply—

(a) to a partnership carrying on practice as solicitors and consisting of persons each of whom is a solicitor,

(b) to a partnership carrying on practice as accountants and consisting of persons each of whom falls within either paragraph (a) or (b) of section 389(1) of this Act (qualification of company auditors),

(c) to a partnership carrying on business as members of a recognised stock exchange and consisting of persons each of whom is a member of that exchange.

(2) The Secretary of State may by regulations in a statutory instrument provide that so much of section 4(2) of the Act of 1907 as provides that a limited partnership shall not consist of more than 20 persons shall not apply to a partnership (other than one permitted by subsection (1) of this section) carrying on business of a description specified in the regulations, being a partnership of a description so specified.

(3) In this section "solicitor" means the same as in section 716.

NOTE
[1] As amended by the Financial Services Act 1986, Sched. 16, para. 22 and the Companies Act 1989, Sched. 24.

Unregistered companies

718.—(1) The provisions of this Act specified in the first column of Schedule 22 (relating respectively to the matters specified in the second column of the Schedule) apply to all bodies corporate incorporated in and having a principal place of business in Great Britain, other than those mentioned in subsection (2) below, as if they were companies registered under this Act, but subject to any limitations mentioned in relation to those provisions respectively in the third column and to such adaptations and modifications (if any) as may be specified by regulations made by the Secretary of State.[1]

(2) Those provisions of this Act do not apply by virtue of this section to any of the following—

(a) any body incorporated by or registered under any public general Act of Parliament,

(b) any body not formed for the purpose of carrying on a business which has for its object the acquisition of gain by the body or its individual members,

(c) any body for the time being exempted by direction of the Secretary of State (or before him by the Board of Trade).

(3) Where against any provision of this Act specified in the first column of Schedule 22 there appears in the third column the entry "Subject to section 718(3)", it means that the provision is to apply by virtue of this section so far only as may be specified by regulations made by the Secretary of State[1] and to such bodies corporate as may be so specified.

(4) The provisions specified in the first column of the Schedule also apply in like manner in relation to any unincorporated body of persons entitled by virtue of letters patent to any of the privileges conferred by the Chartered Companies Act 1837 and not registered under any other public general Act of Parliament, but subject to the like exceptions as are provided for in the case of bodies corporate by paragraphs (b) and (c) of subsection (2).

(5) This section does not repeal or revoke in whole or in part any enactment, royal charter or other instrument constituting or regulating any body in relation to which those provisions are applied by virtue of this section, or restrict the power of Her Majesty to grant a charter in lieu of or supplementary to any such charter as above mentioned; but, in relation to any such body, the operation of any such enactment, charter or instrument is suspended in so far as it is inconsistent with any of those provisions as they apply for the time being to that body.

(6) The power to make regulations conferred by this section (whether regulations under subsection (1) or subsection (3)) is exercisable by statutory instrument subject to annulment in pursuance of a resolution of either House of Parliament.

NOTE
[1] See S.I. 1985 No. 680.

Power of company to provide for employees on cessation or transfer of business
719.—(1) The powers of a company include (if they would not otherwise do so apart from this section) power to make the following provision for the benefit of persons employed or formerly employed by the company or any of its subsidiaries, that is to say, provision in connection with the cessation or the transfer to any person of the whole or part of the undertaking of the company or that subsidiary.

(2) The power conferred by subsection (1) is exercisable notwithstanding that its exercise is not in the best interests of the company.

(3) The power which a company may exercise by virtue only of subsection (1) shall only be exercised by the company if sanctioned—

    (*a*) in a case not falling within paragraph (*b*) or (*c*) below, by an ordinary resolution of the company, or

    (*b*) if so authorised by the memorandum or articles, a resolution of the directors, or

    (*c*) if the memorandum or articles require the exercise of the power to be sanctioned by a resolution of the company of some other description for which more than a simple majority of the members voting is necessary, with the sanction of a resolution of that description;

and in any case after compliance with any other requirements of the memorandum or articles applicable to its exercise.

(4) Any payment which may be made by a company under this section may, if made before the commencement of any winding up of the company, be made out of profits of the company which are available for dividend.

Certain companies to publish periodical statement
720.—(1) Every company, being an insurance company or a deposit, provident or benefit society, shall before it commences business, and also on the first Monday in February and the first Tuesday in August in every year during which it carries on business, make a statement in the form set out in Schedule 23, or as near to it as circumstances admit.

(2) A copy of the statement shall be put up in a conspicuous place in the company's registered office, and in every branch office or place where the business of the company is carried on.

(3) Every member and every creditor of the company is entitled to a copy of the statement, on payment of a sum not exceeding $2\frac{1}{2}$ pence.

(4) If default is made in complying with this section, the company and every officer of it who is in default is liable to a fine and, for continued contravention, to a daily default fine.

(5) For purposes of this Act, a company which carries on the business of insurance in common with any other business or businesses is deemed an insurance company.

(6) In the case of an insurance company to which Part II of the Insurance Companies Act 1982 applies, this section does not apply if the company complies with provisions of that Act as to the accounts and balance sheet to be prepared annually and deposited by such a company.

(7) The Secretary of State may, by regulations in a statutory instrument (subject to annulment in pursuance of a resolution of either House of Parliament), alter the form in Schedule 23.

Production and inspection of books where offence suspected

721.—(1) The following applies if on an application made—

(a) in England and Wales, to a judge of the High Court by the Director of Public Prosecutions, the Secretary of State or a chief officer of police, or

(b) in Scotland, to one of the Lord Commissioners of Justiciary by the Lord Advocate,

there is shown to be reasonable cause to believe that any person has, while an officer of a company, committed an offence in connection with the management of the company's affairs and that evidence of the commission of the offence is to be found in any books or papers of or under the control of the company.

(2) An order may be made—

(a) authorising any person named in it to inspect the books or papers in question, or any of them, for the purpose of investigating and obtaining evidence of the offence, or

(b) requiring the secretary of the company or such other officer of it as may be named in the order to produce the books or papers (or any of them) to a person named in the order at a place so named.

(3) The above applies also in relation to any books or papers of a person carrying on the business of banking so far as they relate to the company's affairs, as it applies to any books or papers of or under the control of the company, except that no such order as is referred to in subsection (2)(b) shall be made by virtue of this subsection.

(4) The decision of a judge of the High Court or of any of the Lords Commissioners of Justiciary on an application under this section is not appealable.

Form of company registers, etc.

722.—(1) Any register, index, minute book or accounting records required by the Companies Acts to be kept by a company may be kept either by making entries in bound books or by recording the matters in question in any other manner.

(2) Where any such register, index, minute book or accounting record is not kept by making entries in a bound book, but by some other means, adequate precautions shall be taken for guarding against falsification and facilitating its discovery.

(3) If default is made in complying with subsection (2), the company and every officer of it who is in default is liable to a fine and, for continued contravention, to a daily default fine.

Use of computers for company records

723.—(1) The power conferred on a company by section 722(1) to keep a register or other record by recording the matters in question otherwise than by making entries in bound books includes power to keep the register or other record by recording those matters oherwise than in a legible form, so long as the recording is capable of being reproduced in a legible form.

(2) Any provision of an instrument made by a company before 12th February 1979 which requires a register of holders of the company's debentures to be kept in a legible form is to be read as requiring the register to be kept in a legible or non-legible form.

(3) If any such register or other record of a company as is mentioned in section 722(1), or a register of holders of a company's debentures, is kept by the company by recording the matters in question otherwise than in a legible form, any duty imposed on the company by this Act to allow inspection of, or to furnish a copy of, the register or other record or any part of it is to be treated as a duty to allow inspection of, or to furnish, a reproduction of the recording or of the relevant part of it in a legible form.

(4) The Secretary of State may by regulations in a statutory instrument[1] make such provision in addition to subsection (3) as he considers appropriate in connection with such registers or other records as are mentioned in that subsection, and are kept as so mentioned; and the regulations may make modifications of provisions of this Act relating to such registers or other records.

(5) A statutory instrument under subsection (4) is subject to annulment in pursuance of a resolution of either House of Parliament.

NOTE
[1] See S.I. 1985 No. 724.

724. [Repealed by the Insolvency Act 1986, Sched. 12.]

Service of documents
725.—(1) A document may be served on a company by leaving it at, or sending it by post to, the company's registered office.

(2) Where a company registered in Scotland carries on business in England and Wales, the process of any court in England and Wales may be served on the company by leaving it at, or sending it by post to, the company's principal place of business in England and Wales, addressed to the manager or other head officer in England and Wales of the company.

(3) Where process is served on a company under subsection (2), the person issuing out the process shall send a copy of it by post to the company's registered office.

Costs and expenses in actions by certain limited companies
726.—(1) Where in England and Wales a limited company is plaintiff in an action or other legal proceeding, the court having jurisdiction in the matter may, if it appears by credible testimony that there is reason to believe that the company will be unable to pay the defendant's costs if successful in his defence, require sufficient security to be given for those costs, and may stay all proceedings until the security is given.

(2) Where in Scotland a limited company is pursuer in an action or other legal proceedings, the court having jurisdiction in the matter may, if it appears by credible testimony that there is reason to believe that the company will be unable to pay the defender's expenses if successful in his defence, order the company to find caution and sist the proceedings until caution is found.

Power of court to grant relief in certain cases
727.—(1) If in any proceedings for negligence, default, breach of duty or breach of trust against an officer of a company or a person employed by a company as auditor (whether he is or is not an officer of the company) it appears to the court hearing the case that that officer or person is or may be liable in respect of the negligence, default, breach of duty or breach of trust, but that he has acted honestly and reasonably, and that having regard to all the circumstances of the case (including those connected with his appointment) he ought fairly to be excused for the negligence, default, breach of duty or breach of trust, that court may relieve him, either wholly or partly, from his liability on such terms as it thinks fit.

(2) If any such officer or person as above-mentioned has reason to apprehend that any claim will or might be made against him in respect of any

negligence, default, breach of duty or breach of trust, he may apply to the court for relief; and the court on the application has the same power to relieve him as under this section it would have had if it had been a court before which proceedings against that person for negligence, default, breach of duty or breach of trust had been brought.

(3) Where a case to which subsection (1) applies is being tried by a judge with a jury, the judge, after hearing the evidence, may, if he is satisfied that the defendant or defender ought in pursuance of that subsection to be relieved either in whole or in part from the liability sought to be enforced against him, withdraw the case in whole or in part from the jury and forthwith direct judgment to be entered for the defendant or defender on such terms as to costs or otherwise as the judge may think proper.

Enforcement of High Court orders

728. Orders made by the High Court under this Act may be enforced in the same manner as orders made in an action pending in that court.

Annual report by Secretary of State

729. The Secretary of State shall cause a general annual report of matters within the Companies Acts to be prepared and laid before both Houses of Parliament.

Punishment of offences

730.—(1) Schedule 24 to this Act has effect with respect to the way in which offences under this Act are punishable on conviction.

(2) In relation to an offence under a provision of this Act specified in the first column of the Schedule (the general nature of the offence being described in the second column), the third column shows whether the offence is punishable on conviction on indictment, or on summary conviction, or either in the one way or the other.

(3) The fourth column of the Schedule shows, in relation to an offence, the maximum punishment by way of fine or imprisonment under this Act which may be imposed on a person convicted of the offence in the way specified in relation to it in the third column (that is to say, on indictment or summarily), a reference to a period of years or months being to a term of imprisonment of that duration.

(4) The fifth column shows (in relation to an offence for which there is an entry in that column) that a person convicted of the offence after continued contravention is liable to a daily default fine; that is to say, he is liable on a second or subsequent summary conviction of the offence to the fine specified in that column for each day on which the contravention is continued (instead of the penalty specified for the offence in the fourth column of the Schedule).

(5) For the purpose of any enactment in the Companies Acts which provides that an officer of a company who is in default is liable to a fine or penalty, the expression "officer who is in default" means any officer of the company who knowingly and wilfully authorises or permits the default, refusal or contravention mentioned in the enactment.

Summary proceedings

[1] **731.**—(1) Summary proceedings for any offence under the Companies Acts may (without prejudice to any jurisdiction exercisable apart from this subsection) be taken against a body corporate at any place at which the body has a place of business, and against any other person at any place at which he is for the time being.

(2) Notwithstanding anything in section 127(1) of the Magistrates' Courts Act 1980, an information relating to an offence under the Companies Acts which is triable by a magistrates' court in England and Wales may be so tried if it is laid at any time within three years after the commission of the offence and within 12 months after the date on which

evidence sufficient in the opinion of the Director of Public Prosecutions or the Secretary of State (as the case may be) to justify the proceedings comes to his knowledge.

(3) Summary proceedings in Scotland for an offence under the Companies Acts shall not be commenced after the expiration of three years from the commission of the offence.

Subject to this (and notwithstanding anything in section 331 of the Criminal Procedure (Scotland) Act 1975), such proceedings may (in Scotland) be commenced at any time within 12 months after the date on which evidence sufficient in the Lord Advocate's opinion to justify the proceedings came to his knowledge or, where such evidence was reported to him by the Secretary of State, within 12 months after the date on which it came to the knowledge of the latter; and subsection (3) of that section applies for the purpose of this subsection as it applies for the purpose of that section.

(4) For purposes of this section, a certificate of the Director of Public Prosecutions, the Lord Advocate or the Secretary of State (as the case may be) as to the date on which such evidence as is referred to above came to his knowledge is conclusive evidence.

NOTE
[1] Extended by the Business Names Act 1985, s.7(6).

Prosecution by public authorities
732.—(1) In respect of an offence under any of sections 210, 324, 329, 447 to 451 and 455, proceedings shall not, in England and Wales, be instituted except by or with the consent of the appropriate authority.

(2) That authority is—
(*a*) for an offence under any of sections 210, 324 and 329, the Secretary of State or the Director of Public Prosecutions,
(*b*) for an offence under any of sections 447 to 451, either one of those two persons or the Industrial Assurance Commissioner, and
(*c*) for an offence under section 455, the Secretary of State.
[1] (3) Where proceedings are instituted under the Companies Acts against any person by the Director of Public Prosecutions or by or on behalf of the Secretary of State or the Lord Advocate, nothing in those Acts is to be taken to require any person to disclose any information which he is entitled to refuse to disclose on grounds of legal professional privilege.

NOTE
[1] Extended by the Business Names Act 1985, s.7(6).

Offences by bodies corporate
[1] **733.**—(1) The following applies to offences under any of sections 210, 216(3), 394A(1) and 447 to 451.

(2) Where a body corporate is guilty of such an offence and it is proved that the offence occurred with the consent or connivance of, or was attributable to any neglect on the part of any director, manager, secretary of other similar officer of the body, or any person who was purporting to act in any such capacity, he as well as the body corporate is guilty of that offence and is liable to be proceeded against and punished accordingly.

(3) Where the affairs of a body corporate are managed by its members, then in the case of an offence under section 210 or 216(3), subsection (2) above applies in relation to the acts and defaults of a member in connection with his functions of management as if he were a director of the body corporate.

(4) In this section "director", in relation to an offence under any of sections 447 to 451, includes a shadow director.

NOTE
[1] As amended by the Insolvency Act 1985, Sched. 6, para. 7, the Insolvency Act 1986, Sched. 13, Pt. I, and the Companies Act 1989. s. 123(3).

Criminal proceedings against unincorporated bodies

¹ **734.**—(1) Proceedings for an offence alleged to have been committed under section 394A(1) or any of sections 447 to 451 by an unincorporated body shall be brought in the name of that body (and not in that of any of its members), and for the purposes of any such proceedings, any rules of court relating to the service of documents apply as if that body were a corporation.

(2) A fine imposed on an unincorporated body on its conviction of such an offence shall be paid out of the funds of that body.

(3) In a case in which an unincorporated body is charged in England and Wales with such an offence, section 33 of the Criminal Justice Act 1925 and Schedule 3 to the Magistrates' Courts Act 1980 (procedure on charge of an offence against a corporation) have effect in like manner as in the case of a corporation so charged.

(4) In relation to proceedings on indictment in Scotland for such an offence alleged to have been committed by an unincorporated body, section 74 of the Criminal Procedure (Scotland) Act 1975 (proceedings on indictment against bodies corporate) has effect as if that body were a body corporate.

NOTE
¹ As amended by the Companies Act 1989, s. 123(4).

PART XXVI

INTERPRETATION

"Company", etc.

735.—(1) In this Act—
(a) "company" means a company formed and registered under this Act, or an existing company;
(b) "existing company" means a company formed and registered under the former Companies Acts, but does not include a company registered under the Joint Stock Companies Acts, the Companies Act 1862 or the Companies (Consolidation) Act 1908 in what was then Ireland;
(c) "the former Companies Acts" means the Joint Stock Companies Acts, the Companies Act 1862, the Companies (Consolidation) Act 1908, the Companies Act 1929 and the Companies Acts 1948 to 1983.

(2) "Public company" and "private company" have the meanings given by section 1(3).

(3) "The Joint Stock Companies Acts" means the Joint Stock Companies Act 1856, the Joint Stock Companies Acts 1856, 1857, the Joint Stock Banking Companies Act 1857 and the Act to enable Joint Stock Banking Companies to be formed on the principle of limited liability, or any one or more of those Acts (as the case may require), but does not include the Joint Stock Companies Act 1844.

(4) The definitions in this section apply unless the contrary intention appears.

Relationship of this Act to Insolvency Act

¹ **735A.**—(1) In this Act "the Insolvency Act" means the Insolvency Act 1986; and in the following provisions of this Act, namely, sections 375(1)(b), 425(6)(a), 460(2), 675, 676, 677, 699(1), 728 and Schedule 21, paragraph 6(1), the words "this Act" are to be read as including Parts I to VII of that Act, sections 411, 413, 414, 416 and 417 in Part XV of that Act, and also the Company Directors Disqualification Act 1986.

(2) In sections 704(5), 706(1), 707(1), 708(1)(a) and (4), 710(5), 713(1), 729 and 732(3) references to the Companies Acts include Parts I to VII of the Insolvency Act, sections 411, 413, 414, 416 and 417 in Part XV of that Act, and also the Company Directors Disqualification Act 1986.

(3) Subsections (1) and (2) apply unless the contrary intention appears.

NOTE
¹ Inserted by the Insolvency Act 1986, Sched. 13, Pt. II. As amended by the Companies Act 1989, Sched. 24.

"Holding company", "subsidiary" and "wholly-owned subsidiary"

736.—(1) For the purposes of this Act, a company is deemed to be a subsidiary of another if (but only if)—

(a) that other either—

   (i) is a member of it and controls the composition of its board of directors, or

   (ii) holds more than half in nominal value of its equity share capital, or

(b) the first-mentioned company is a subsidiary of any company which is that other's subsidiary.

The above is subject to subsection (4) below in this section.

(2) For purposes of subsection (1), the composition of a company's board of directors is deemed to be controlled by another company if (but only if) that other company by the exercise of some power exercisable by it without the consent or concurrence of any other person can appoint or remove the holders of all or a majority of the directorships.

(3) For purposes of this last provision, the other company is deemed to have power to appoint to a directorship with respect to which any of the following conditions is satisfied—

(a) that a person cannot be appointed to it without the exercise in his favour by the other company of such a power as is mentioned above, or

(b) that a person's appointment to the directorship follows necessarily from his appointment as director of the other company, or

(c) that the directorship is held by the other company itself or by a subsidiary of it.

(4) In determining whether one company is a subsidiary of another—

(a) any shares held or power exercisable by the other in a fiduciary capacity are to be treated as not held or exercisable by it,

(b) subject to the two following paragraphs, any shares held or power exercisable—

   (i) by any person as nominee for the other (except where the other is concerned only in a fiduciary capacity), or

   (ii) by, or by a nominee for, a subsidiary of the other (not being a subsidiary which is concerned only in a fiduciary capacity),

   are to be treated as held or exercisable by the other,

(c) any shares held or power exercisable by any person by virtue of the provisions of any debentures of the first-mentioned company or of a trust deed for securing any issue of such debentures are to be disregarded,

(d) any shares held or power exercisable by, or by a nominee for, the other or its subsidiary (not being held or exercisable as mentioned in paragraph (c)) are to be treated as not held or exercisable by the other if the ordinary business of the other or its subsidiary (as the case may be) includes the lending of money and the shares are held or the power is exercisable as above-mentioned by way of security only for the purposes of a transaction entered into in the ordinary course of that business.

(5) For purposes of this Act—

(a) a company is deemed to be another's holding company if (but only if) the other is its subsidiary, and

(b) a body corporate is deemed the wholly-owned subsidiary of another if it has no members except that other and that other's wholly-owned subsidiaries and its or their nominees.

(6) In this section "company" includes any body corporate.

"Called-up share capital"

737.—(1) In this Act, "called-up share capital", in relation to a company, means so much of its share capital as equals the aggregate amount of the calls made on its shares (whether or not those calls have been paid), together with any share capital paid up without being called and any share capital to be paid on a specified future date under the articles, the terms of allotment of the relevant shares or any other arrangements for payment of those shares.

(2) "Uncalled share capital" is to be construed accordingly.

(3) The definitions in this section apply unless the contrary intention appears.

"Allotment" and "paid up"

738.—(1) In relation to an allotment of shares in a company, the shares are to be taken for the purposes of this Act to be allotted when a person acquires the unconditional right to be included in the company's register of members in respect of those shares.

(2) For purposes of this Act, a share in a company is deemed paid up (as to its nominal value or any premium on it) in cash, or allotted for cash, if the consideration for the allotment or payment up is cash received by the company, or is a cheque received by it in good faith which the directors have no reason for suspecting will not be paid, or is a release of a liability of the company for a liquidated sum, or is an undertaking to pay cash to the company at a future date.

(3) In relation to the allotment or payment up of any shares in a company, references in this Act (except sections 89 to 94) to consideration other than cash and to the payment up of shares and premiums on shares otherwise than in cash include the payment of, or any undertaking to pay, cash to any person other than the company.

(4) For the purpose of determining whether a share is or is to be allotted for cash, or paid up in cash, "cash" includes foreign currency.

"Non-cash asset"

739.—(1) In this Act "non-cash asset" means any property or interest in property other than cash; and for this purpose "cash" includes foreign currency.

(2) A reference to the transfer or acquisition of a non-cash asset includes the creation or extinction of an estate or interest in, or a right over, any property and also the discharge of any person's liability, other than a liability for a liquidated sum.

"Body corporate" and "corporation"

740. References in this Act to a body corporate or to a corporation do not include a corporation sole, but include a company incorporated elsewhere than in Great Britain.

Such references to a body corporate do not include a Scottish firm.

"Director" and "shadow director"

741.—(1) In this Act, "director" includes any person occupying the position of director, by whatever name called.

(2) In relation to a company, "shadow director" means a person in accordance with whose directions or instructions the directors of the company are accustomed to act.

However, a person is not deemed a shadow director by reason only that the directors act on advice given by him in a professional capacity.

(3) For the purposes of the following provisions of this Act, namely—

    section 309 (directors' duty to have regard to interests of employees),

    section 319 (directors' long-term contracts of employment),

    section 320 to 322 (substantial property transactions involving directors), and

    sections 330 to 346 (general restrictions on power of companies to make loans, etc., to directors and others connected with them), (being provisions under which shadow directors are treated as directors), a body corporate is not to be treated as a shadow director of any of its subsidiary companies by reason only that the directors of the subsidiary are accustomed to act in accordance with its directions or instructions.

Expressions used in connection with accounts

[1] **742.**—(1) In this Act, unless a contrary intention appears, the following expressions have the same meaning as in Part VII (accounts)—

"annual accounts",

"accounting reference date" and "accounting reference period",

"balance sheet" and "balance sheet date",

"current assets",

"financial year", in relation to a company,

"fixed assets",

"parent company" and "parent undertaking",

"profit and loss account", and

"subsidiary undertaking".

(2) References in this Act to "realised profits" and "realised losses", in relation to a company's accounts, shall be construed in accordance with section 262(3).

NOTE

[1] Substituted by the Companies Act 1989, s. 23 and Sched. 10, para. 15.

"Employees' share scheme"

743. For purposes of this Act, an employees' share scheme is a scheme for encouraging or facilitating the holding of shares or debentures in a company by or for the benefit of—

(a) the *bona fide* employees or former employees of the company, the company's subsidiary or holding company or a subsidiary of the company's holding company, or

(b) the wives, husbands, widows, widowers or children or step-children under the age of 18 of such employees or former employees.

Expressions used generally in this Act

[1] **744.** In this Act, unless the contrary intention appears, the following definitions apply—

"agent" does not include a person's counsel acting as such;

"annual return" means the return to be made by a company under section 363 or 364 (as the case may be);

"articles" means, in relation to a company, its articles of association, as originally framed or as altered by resolution, including (so far as applicable to the company) regulations contained in or annexed to any enactment relating to companies passed before this Act, as altered by or under any such enactment;

"authorised minimum" has the meaning given by section 118;

"bank holiday" means a holiday under the Banking and Financial Dealings Act 1971;

"banking company" means a company which is authorised under the Banking Act 1987;

"books and papers" and "books or papers" include accounts, deeds, writings and documents;

"the Companies Acts" means this Act, the Insider Dealing Act and the Consequential Provisions Act;

"the Consequential Provisions Act" means the Companies Consolidation (Consequential Provisions) Act 1985;

"the court", in relation to a company, means the court having jurisdiction to wind up the company;

"debenture" includes debenture stock, bonds and any other securities of a company, whether constituting a charge on the assets of the company or not;

"document" includes summons, notice, order, and other legal process, and registers;

"equity share capital" means, in relation to a company, its issued share capital excluding any part of that capital which, neither as respects dividends nor as respects capital, carries any right to participate beyond a specified amount in a distribution;

"expert" has the meaning given by section 62;

"floating charge" includes a floating charge within the meaning given by section 462;

"the *Gazette*" means, as respects companies registered in England and Wales, the *London Gazette* and, as respects companies registered in Scotland, the *Edinburgh Gazette*;

"hire-purchase agreement" has the same meaning as in the Consumer Credit Act 1974;

"the Insider Dealing Act" means the Company Securities (Insider Dealing) Act 1985;

"insurance company" means the same as in the Insurance Companies Act 1982;

"joint stock company" has the meaning given by section 683;

"memorandum", in relation to a company, means its memorandum of association, as originally framed or as altered in pursuance of any enactment;

"number", in relation to shares, includes amount, where the context admits of the reference to shares being construed to include stock;

"officer", in relation to a body corporate, includes a director, manager or secretary;

"official seal", in relation to the registrar of companies, means a seal prepared under section 704(4) for the authentication of documents required for or in connection with the registration of companies;

"oversea company" means—

(*a*) a company incorporated elsewhere than in Great Britain which, after the commencement of this Act, establishes a place of business in Great Britain, and

(*b*) a company so incorporated which has, before that commencement, established a place of business and continues to have an established place of business in Great Britain at that commencement;

"place of business" includes a share transfer or share registration office;

"prescribed" means—

(*a*) as respects provisions of this Act relating to winding up, prescribed by general rules, and

(*b*) otherwise, prescribed by statutory instrument made by the Secretary of State;

"prospectus" means any prospectus, notice, circular, advertisement, or other invitation, offering to the public for subscription or purchase any shares in or debentures of a company;

[2] "prospectus issued generally" means a prospectus issued to persons who are not existing members of the company or holders of its debentures;

"the registrar of companies" and "the registrar" mean the registrar or other officer performing under this Act the duty of registration of companies in England and Wales or in Scotland, as the case may require;

"share" means share in the share capital of a company, and includes stock (except where a distinction between shares and stock is express or implied); and "undistributable reserves" has the meaning given by section 264(3).

NOTES
[1] As amended by the Insolvency Act 1985, Sched. 10, Pt. II, the Financial Services Act 1986, Sched. 17, Banking Act 1987, Sched. 6, para. 18 and Sched. 7, Pt. I, and the Companies Act 1989, s. 23 and Sched. 10, para. 16, and Sched. 24. See S.I. 1988 No. 1359.
[2] Repealed (*prosp.*) by the Financial Services Act 1986, Sched. 17.

PART XXVII

FINAL PROVISIONS

Northern Ireland
745.—(1) Except where otherwise expressly provided, nothing in this Act (except provisions relating expressly to companies registered or incorporated in Northern Ireland or outside Great Britain) applies to or in relation to companies so registered or incorporated.

(2) Subject to any such provision, and to any express provision as to extent, this Act does not extend to Northern Ireland.

Commencement
[1] **746.** This Act comes into force on 1st July 1985.

NOTE
[1] As amended by the Companies Act 1989, Sched. 24.

Citation
747. This Act may be cited as the Companies Act 1985.

SCHEDULES

Section 10

SCHEDULE 1

PARTICULARS OF DIRECTORS ETC. TO BE CONTAINED IN STATEMENT
UNDER SECTION 10

Directors

1.—(1) Subject as provided below, the statement under section 10(2) shall contain the following particulars with respect to each person named as director—
  (*a*) in the case of an individual, his present Christian name and surname, any former Christian name or surname, his usual residential address, his nationality, his business occupation (if any), particulars of any other directorships held by him, or which have been held by him and, in the case of a company subject to section 293, the date of his birth;
  (*b*) in the case of a corporation, its corporate name and registered or principal office.

2.—(1) It is not necessary for the statement to contain particulars of a directorship—
  (*a*) which has not been held by a director at any time during the five years preceding the date on which the statement is delivered to the registrar,
  (*b*) which is held by a director in a company which—
    (i) is dormant or grouped with the company delivering the statement, and
    (ii) if he also held that directorship for any period during those five years, was for the whole of that period either dormant or so grouped,
  (*c*) which was held by a director for any period during those five years in a company which for the whole of that period was either dormant or grouped with the company delivering the statement.
  [1] (2) For these purposes, "company" includes any body corporate incorporated in Great Britain; and—
  (*a*) section 250(3) applies as regards whether and when a company is or has been "dormant", and

(b) a company is treated as being or having been at any time grouped with another company if at that time it is or was a company of which that other is or was a wholly-owned subsidiary, or if it is or was a wholly-owned subsidiary of the other or of another company of which that other is or was a wholly-owned subsidiary.

NOTE
[1] As amended by the Companies Act 1989, s. 23 and Sched. 10, para. 17.

Secretaries

3.—(1) The statement shall contain the following particulars with respect to the person named as secretary or, where there are to be joint secretaries, with respect to each person named as one of them—
    (a) in the case of an individual, his present Christian name and surname, any former Christian name or surname and his usual residential address,
    (b) in the case of a corporation or a Scottish firm, its corporate or firm name and registered or principal office.
(2) However, if all the partners in a firm are joint secretaries, the name and principal office of the firm may be stated instead of the particulars otherwise required by this paragraph.

Interpretation

4. In paragraphs 1 and 3 above—
    (a) "Christian name" includes a forename.
    (b) "surname", in the case of a peer or a person usually known by a title different from his surname, means that title,
    (c) the reference to a former Christian name or surname does not include—
        (i) in the case of a peer or a person usually known by a British title different from his surname, the name by which he was known previous to the adoption of or succession to the title, or
        (ii) in the case of any person, a former Christian name or surname where that name or surname was changed or disused before the person bearing the name attained the age of 18 or has been changed or disused for a period of not less than 20 years, or
        (iii) in the case of a married woman, the name or surname by which she was known previous to the marriage.

Sections 23, 145, 146, 148   [1] SCHEDULE 2

NOTE
[1] As amended by the Companies Act 1989, Scheds. 10, para. 18, and 24.

INTERPRETATION OF REFERENCES TO
"BENEFICIAL INTEREST"

PART I
REFERENCES IN SECTIONS 23, 145, 146 AND 148

*Residual interests under pension and
employees' share schemes*

1.—(1) Where shares in a company are held on trust for the purposes of a pension scheme or an employees' share scheme, there is to be disregarded any residual interest which has not vested in possession, being an interest of the company or, as respects—
    section 23(4),
of any subsidiary of the company.
(2) In this paragraph, "a residual interest" means a right of the company or subsidiary in question ("the residual beneficiary") to receive any of the trust property in the event of—
    (a) all the liabilities arising under the scheme having been satisfied or provided for, or
    (b) the residual beneficiary ceasing to participate in the scheme, or
    (c) the trust property at any time exceeding what is necessary for satisfying the liabilities arising or expected to arise under the scheme.

(3) In sub-paragraph (2), references to a right include a right dependent on the exercise of a discretion vested by the scheme in the trustee or any other person; and references to liabilities arising under a scheme include liabilities that have resulted or may result from the exercise of any such discretion.

(4) For purposes of this paragraph, a residual interest vests in possession—

  (*a*) in a case within (*a*) of sub-paragraph (2), on the occurrence of the event there mentioned, whether or not the amount of the property receivable pursuant to the right mentioned in that sub-paragraph is then ascertained, and

  (*b*) in a case within (*b*) or (*c*) of that sub-paragraph, when the residual beneficiary becomes entitled to require the trustee to transfer to that beneficiary any of the property receivable pursuant to that right.

(5) [Repealed by the Companies Act 1989, Scheds. 10, para. 18(3), and 24.]

2.—(1) The following has effect as regards the operation of sections 144, 145 and 146 to 149 in cases where a residual interest vests in possession.

(2) [Repealed by the Companies Act 1989, Sched. 24.]

(3) Where by virtue of paragraph 1 of this Schedule any shares are exempt from section 144 or 145 at the time when they are issued or acquired but the residual interest in question vests in possession before they are disposed of or fully paid up, those sections apply to the shares as if they had been issued or acquired on the date on which that interest vests in possession.

(4) Where by virtue of paragraph 1 any shares are exempt from sections 146 to 149 at the time when they are acquired but the residual interest in question vests in possession before they are disposed of, those sections apply to the shares as if they had been acquired on the date on which that interest vests in possession.

(5) The above sub-paragraphs apply irrespective of the date on which the residual interest vests or vested in possession; but where the date on which it vested was before 26th July 1983 (the passing of the Companies (Beneficial Interests) Act 1983), they have effect as if the vesting had occurred on that date.

Employer's charges and other rights of recovery

3.—(1) Where shares in a company are held on trust, there are to be disregarded—

  (*a*) if the trust is for the purposes of a pension scheme, any such rights as are mentioned in the following sub-paragraph, and

  (*b*) if the trust is for the purposes of an employees' share scheme, any such rights as are mentioned in (*a*) of the sub-paragraph,

being rights of the company or, as respects section 23(4) of any subsidiary of the company.

(2) The rights referred to are—

  (*a*) any charge or lien on, or set-off against, any benefit or other right or interest under the scheme for the purpose of enabling the employer or former employer of a member of the scheme to obtain the discharge of a monetary obligation due to him from the member, and

  (*b*) any right to receive from the trustee of the scheme, or as trustee of the scheme to retain, an amount that can be recovered or retained under section 47 of the Social Security Pensions Act 1975 (deduction of premium from refund of contributions) or otherwise as reimbursement or partial reimbursement for any state scheme premium paid in connection with the scheme under Part III of that Act.

(3) [Repealed by the Companies Act 1989, Scheds. 10, para. 18(4), and 24.]

Trustee's right to expenses, remuneration, indemnity, etc.

4.—(1) Where a company is a trustee, there are to be disregarded any rights which the company has in its capacity as trustee including, in particular, any right to recover its expenses or be remunerated out of the trust property and any right to be indemnified out of that property for any liability incurred by reason of any act or omission of the company in the performance of its duties as trustee.

(2) As respects section 23(4), sub-paragraph (1) has effect as if references to a company included any body corporate which is a subsidiary of a company.

[1] (3) As respects sections 145, 146 and 148, sub-paragraph (1) above applies where a company is a personal representative as it applies where a company is a trustee.

NOTE

[1] Inserted by the Companies Act 1989, s. 23 and Sched. 10, para. 18(5).

Supplementary

5.—(1) The following applies for the interpretation of this Part of this Schedule.

(2) "Pension scheme" means any scheme for the provision of benefits consisting of or including relevant benefits for or in respect of employees or former employees; and "relevant benefits" means any pension, lump sum, gratuity or other like benefit given or to be given on retirement or on death or in anticipation of retirement or, in connection with past service, after retirement or death.

(3) In sub-paragraph (2) of this paragraph, and in paragraph 3(2)(*a*), "employer" and "employee" are to be read as if a director of a company were employed by it.

¹ Part II

NOTE
¹ Inserted by the Companies Act 1989, s. 23 and Sched. 10, para. 18(7).

References in Schedule 5

Residual interests under pension and employees' share schemes

6.—(1) Where shares in an undertaking are held on trust for the purposes of a pension scheme or an employees' share scheme, there shall be disregarded any residual interest which has not vested in possession, being an interest of the undertaking or any of its subsidiary undertakings.

(2) In this paragraph a "residual interest" means a right of the undertaking in question (the "residual beneficiary") to receive any of the trust property in the event of—
- (*a*) all the liabilities arising under the scheme having been satisfied or provided for, or
- (*b*) the residual beneficiary ceasing to participate in the scheme, or
- (*c*) the trust property at any time exceeding what is necessary for satisfying the liabilities arising or expected to arise under the scheme.

(3) In sub-paragraph (2) references to a right include a right dependent on the exercise of a discretion vested by the scheme in the trustee or any other person; and references to liabilities arising under a scheme include liabilities that have resulted or may result from the exercise of any such discretion.

(4) For the purposes of this paragraph a residual interest vests in possession—
- (*a*) in a case within sub-paragraph (2)(*a*), on the occurrence of the event there mentioned, whether or not the amount of the property receivable pursuant to the right mentioned in that sub-paragraph is then ascertained;
- (*b*) in a case within sub-paragraph (2)(*b*) or (*c*), when the residual beneficiary becomes entitled to require the trustee to transfer to that beneficiary any of the property receivable pursuant to that right.

Employer's charges and other rights of recovery

7.—(1) Where shares in an undertaking are held on trust, there shall be disregarded—
- (*a*) if the trust is for the purposes of a pension scheme, any such rights as are mentioned in sub-paragraph (2) below;
- (*b*) if the trust is for the purposes of an employees' share scheme, any such rights as are mentioned in paragraph (*a*) of that sub-paragraph.
being rights of the undertaking or any of its subsidiary undertakings.

(2) The rights referred to are—
- (*a*) any charge or lien on, or set-off against, any benefit or other right or interest under the scheme for the purpose of enabling the employer or former employer of a member of the scheme to obtain the discharge of a monetary obligation due to him from the member, and
- (*b*) any right to receive from the trustee of the scheme, or as trustee of the scheme to retain, an amount that can be recovered or retained under section 47 of the Social Security Pensions Act 1975 (deduction of premium from refund of pension contributions) or otherwise as reimbursement or partial reimbursement for any state scheme premium paid in connection with the scheme under Part III of that Act.

Trustee's right to expenses, remuneration, indemnity, etc.

8. Where an undertaking is a trustee, there shall be disregarded any rights which the undertaking has in its capacity as trustee including, in particular, any right to recover its expenses or

be remunerated out of the trust property and any right to be indemnified out of that property for any liability incurred by reason of any act or omission of the undertaking in the performance of its duties as trustee.

Supplementary

9.—(1) The following applies for the interpretation of this Part of this Schedule.

(2) "Undertaking", and "shares" in relation to an undertaking, have the same meaning as in Part VII.

(3) This Part of this Schedule applies in relation to debentures as it applies in relation to shares.

(4) "Pension scheme" means any scheme for the provision of benefits consisting of or including relevant benefits for or in respect of employees or former employees; and "relevant benefits" means any pension, lump sum, gratuity or other like benefit given or to be given on retirement or on death or in anticipation of retirement or, in connection with past service, after retirement or death.

(5) In sub-paragraph (4) of this paragraph and in paragraph 7(2) "employee" and "employer" shall be read as if a director of an undertaking were employed by it.

SCHEDULE 3

MANDATORY CONTENTS OF PROSPECTUS

[Repealed by the Financial Services Act 1986, Sched. 17.]

Sections 228, 230   [1] SCHEDULE 4

FORM AND CONTENT OF COMPANY ACCOUNTS

NOTE

[1] As amended by the Companies Act 1989, Scheds. 1, 10 para. 20, and 24.

[1] PART I

NOTE

[1] See the Patents, Designs and Marks Act 1986, Sched. 2, Pt. I, para. 1(2)(*k*).

GENERAL RULES
AND FORMATS

SECTION A
GENERAL RULES

1.—(1) Subject to the following provisions of this Schedule—
    (*a*) every balance sheet of a company shall show the items listed in either of the balance sheet formats set out below in section B of this Part; and
    (*b*) every profit and loss account of a company shall show the items listed in any one of the profit and loss account formats so set out;
in either case in the order and under the headings and sub-headings given in the format adopted.

(2) Sub-paragraph (1) above is not to be read as requiring the heading or sub-heading for any item to be distinguished by any letter or number assigned to that item in the format adopted.

2.—(1) Where in accordance with paragraph 1 a company's balance sheet or profit and loss account for any financial year has been prepared by reference to one of the formats set out in section B below, the directors of the company shall adopt the same format in preparing the

[THE NEXT PAGE IS I 363]

accounts for subsequent financial years of the company unless in their opinion there are special reasons for a change.

(2) Particulars of any change in the format adopted in preparing a company's balance sheet or profit and loss account in accordance with paragraph 1 shall be disclosed, and the reasons for the change shall be explained, in a note to the accounts in which the new format is first adopted.

3.—(1) Any item required in accordance with paragraph 1 to be shown in a company's balance sheet or profit and loss account may be shown in greater detail than required by the format adopted.

(2) A company's balance sheet or profit and loss account may include an item representing or covering the amount of any asset or liability, income or expenditure not otherwise covered by any of the items listed in the format adopted, but the following shall not be treated as assets in any company's balance sheet—

(*a*)   preliminary expenses;

(*b*)   expenses of and commission on any issue of shares or debentures; and

(*c*)   costs of research.

(3) In preparing a company's balance sheet or profit and loss account the directors of the company shall adapt the arrangement and headings and sub-headings otherwise required by paragraph 1 in respect of items to which an Arabic number is assigned in the format adopted, in any case where the special nature of the company's business requires such adaptation.

(4) Items to which Arabic numbers are assigned in any of the formats set out in section B below may be combined in a company's accounts for any financial year if either—

(*a*)   their individual amounts are not material to assessing the state of affairs or profit or loss of the company for that year; or

(*b*)   the combination facilitates that assessment;

but in a case within paragraph (*b*) the individual amounts of any items so combined shall be disclosed in a note to the accounts.

(5) Subject to paragraph 4(3) below, a heading or sub-heading corresponding to an item listed in the format adopted in preparing a company's balance sheet or profit and loss account shall not be included if there is no amount to be shown for that item in respect of the financial year to which the balance sheet or profit and loss account relates.

(6) Every profit and loss account of a company shall show the amount of the company's profit or loss on ordinary activities before taxation.

(7) Every profit and loss account of a company shall show separately as additional items—

(*a*)   any amount set aside or proposed to be set aside to, or withdrawn or proposed to be withdrawn from, reserves; and

(*b*)   the aggregate amount of any dividends paid and proposed.

4.—(1) In respect of every item shown in a company's balance sheet or profit and loss account the corresponding amount for the financial year immediately preceding that to which the balance sheet or profit and loss account relates shall also be shown.

(2) Where that corresponding amount is not comparable with the amount to be shown for the item in question in respect of the financial year to which the balance sheet or profit and loss account relates, the former amount shall be adjusted and particulars of the adjustment and the reasons for it shall be disclosed in a note to the accounts.

(3) Paragraph 3(5) does not apply in any case where an amount can be shown for the item in question in respect of the financial year immediately preceding that to which the balance sheet or profit and loss account relates, and that amount shall be shown under the heading or sub-heading required by paragraph 1 for that item.

5. Amounts in respect of items representing assets or income may not be set off against amounts in respect of items representing liabilities or expenditure (as the case may be), or vice versa.

SECTION B

THE REQUIRED FORMATS FOR ACCOUNTS

Preliminary

6. References in this Part of this Schedule to the items listed in any of the formats set out below are to those items read together with any of the notes following the formats which apply to any of those items, and the requirement imposed by paragraph 1 to show the items listed in any such format in the order adopted in the format is subject to any provision in those notes for alternative positions for any particular items.

7. A number in brackets following any item in any of the formats set out below is a reference to the note of that number in the notes following the formats.

8. In the notes following the formats—

  (*a*) the heading of each note gives the required heading or sub-heading for the item to which it applies and a reference to any letters and numbers assigned to that item in the formats set out below (taking a reference in the case of format 2 of the balance sheet formats to the item listed under "Assets" or under "Liabilities" as the case may require); and

  (*b*) references to a numbered format are to the balance sheet format or (as the case may require) to the profit and loss account format of that number set out below.

Balance Sheet Formats

Format 1

A. Called up share capital not paid (*1*)

B. Fixed assets

  I   Intangible assets
      1. Development costs
      2. Concessions, patents, licences, trade marks and similar rights and assets (*2*)
      3. Goodwill (*3*)
      4. Payments on account

  II   Tangible assets
      1. Land and buildings
      2. Plant and machinery
      3. Fixtures, fittings, tools and equipment
      4. Payments on account and assets in course of construction

  III   Investments
      1. Shares in group undertakings
      2. Loans to group undertakings
      3. Participating interests
      4. Loans to undertakings in which the company has a participating interest
      5. Other investments other than loans
      6. Other loans
      7. Own shares (*4*)

C. Current assets

  I   Stocks
      1. Raw materials and consumables
      2. Work in progress
      3. Finished goods and goods for resale
      4. Payments on account

  II   Debtors (*5*)
      1. Trade debtors
      2. Amounts owed by group undertakings
      3. Amounts owed by undertakings in which the company has a participating interest
      4. Other debtors
      5. Called-up share capital not paid (*1*)
      6. Prepayments and accrued income (*6*)

  III   Investments
      1. Shares in group undertakings
      2. Own shares (*4*)
      3. Other investments

  IV   Cash at bank and in hand

D. Prepayments and accrued income (*6*)

E. Creditors: amounts falling due within one year
    1.   Debenture loans (*7*)
    2.   Bank loans and overdrafts
    3.   Payments received on account (*8*)
    4.   Trade creditors
    5.   Bills of exchange payable
    6.   Amounts owed to group undertakings
    7.   Amounts owed to undertakings in which the company has a participating interest
    8.   Other creditors including taxation and social security (*9*)
    9.   Accruals and deferred income (*10*)

F. Net current assets (liabilities) (*11*)

G. Total assets less current liabilities

H. Creditors: amounts falling due after more than one year
    1.   Debenture loans (*7*)
    2.   Bank loans and overdrafts
    3.   Payments received on account (*8*)
    4.   Trade creditors
    5.   Bills of exchange payable
    6.   Amounts owed to group undertakings
    7.   Amounts owed to undertakings in which the company has a participating interest
    8.   Other creditors including taxation and social security (*9*)
    9.   Accruals and deferred income (*10*)

I. Provisions for liabilities and charges
    1.   Pensions and similar obligations
    2.   Taxation, including deferred taxation
    3.   Other provisions

J. Accruals and deferred income (*10*)

K. Capital and reserves

  I   Called-up share capital (*12*)

  II Share premium account

  III Revaluation reserve

  IV Other reserves
    1.   Capital redemption reserve
    2.   Reserve for own shares
    3.   Reserves provided for by the articles of association
    4.   Other reserves

  V Profit and loss account

Balance Sheet Formats

Format 2

ASSETS

A. Called-up share capital not paid (*1*)

B. Fixed assets

  I Intangible assets
    1.   Development costs
    2.   Concessions, patents, licences, trade marks and similar rights and assets (*2*)
    3.   Goodwill (*3*)
    4.   Payments on account

II   Tangible assets
1.   Land and buildings
2.   Plant and machinery
3.   Fixtures, fittings, tools and equipment
4.   Payments on account and assets in course of construction

III   Investments
1.   Shares in group undertakings
2.   Loans to group undertakings
3.   Participating interests
4.   Loans to undertakings in which the company has a participating interest
5.   Other investments other than loans
6.   Other loans
7.   Own shares (*4*)

C. Current assets

I   Stocks
1.   Raw materials and consumables
2.   Work in progress
3.   Finished goods and goods for resale
4.   Payments on account

II   Debtors (*5*)
1.   Trade debtors
2.   Amounts owed by group undertakings
3.   Amounts owed by undertakings in which the company has a participating interest
4.   Other debtors
5.   Called-up share capital not paid (*1*)
6.   Prepayments and accrued income (*6*)

III   Investments
1.   Shares in group undertakings
2.   Own shares (*4*)
3.   Other investments

IV   Cash at bank and in hand

D. Prepayments and accrued income (*6*)

LIABILITIES

A. Capital and reserves

I   Called-up share capital (*12*)

II   Share premium account

III   Revaluation reserve

IV   Other reserves
1.   Capital redemption reserve
2.   Reserve for own shares
3.   Reserves provided for by the articles of association
4.   Other reserves

V   Profit and loss account

B. Provisions for liabilities and charges
1.   Pensions and similar obligations
2.   Taxation including deferred taxation
3.   Other provisions

C. Creditors *(13)*
1. Debenture loans *(7)*
2. Bank loans and overdrafts
3. Payments received on account *(8)*
4. Trade creditors
5. Bills of exchange payable
6. Amounts owed to group undertakings
7. Amounts owed to undertakings in which the company has a participating interest
8. Other creditors including taxation and social security *(9)*
9. Accruals and deferred income *(10)*

D. Accruals and deferred income *(10)*

Notes on the balance sheet formats

(1) Called-up share capital not paid
(Formats 1 and 2, items A and C.II.5.)
This item may be shown in either of the two positions given in formats 1 and 2.

(2) Concessions, patents, licences, trade marks and similar rights and assets
(Formats 1 and 2, item B.I.2.)
Amounts in respect of assets shall only be included in a company's balance sheet under this item if either—
(a) the assets were acquired for valuable consideration and are not required to be shown under goodwill; or
(b) the assets in question were created by the company itself.

(3) Goodwill
(Formats 1 and 2, item B.I.3.)
Amounts representing goodwill shall only be included to the extent that the goodwill was acquired for valuable consideration.

(4) Own shares
(Formats 1 and 2, items B.III.7 and C.III.2.)
The nominal value of the shares held shall be shown separately.

(5) Debtors
(Formats 1 and 2, items C.II.1 to 6.)
The amount falling due after more than one year shall be shown separately for each item included under debtors.

(6) Prepayments and accrued income
(Formats 1 and 2, items C.II.6 and D.)
This item may be shown in either of the two positions given in formats 1 and 2.

(7) Debenture loans
(Format 1, items E.1 and H.1 and format 2, item C.1.)
The amount of any convertible loans shall be shown separately.

(8) Payments received on account
(Format 1, items E.3 and H.3 and format 2, item C.3.)
Payments received on account of orders shall be shown for each of these items in so far as they are not shown as deductions from stocks.

(9) Other creditors including taxation and social security
(Format 1, items E.8 and H.8 and format 2, item C.8.)
The amount for creditors in respect of taxation and social security shall be shown separately from the amount for other creditors.

(10) Accruals and deferred income
(Format 1, items E.9, H.9 and J and format 2, items C.9 and D.)

The two positions given for this item in format 1 at E.9 and H.9 are an alternative to the position at J but if the item is not shown in a position corresponding to that at J it may be shown in either or both of the other two positions (as the case may require).

The two positions given for this item in format 2 are alternatives.

(11) Net current assets (liabilities)
(Format 1, item F.)

In determining the amount to be shown for this item any amounts shown under "prepayments and accrued income" shall be taken into account wherever shown.

(12) Called-up share capital
(Format 1, item K.I and format 2, item A.I.)

The amount of allotted share capital and the amount of called-up share capital which has been paid up shall be shown separately.

(13) Creditors
(Format 2, items C.1 to 9.)

Amounts falling due within one year and after one year shall be shown separately for each of these items and their aggregate shall be shown separately for all of these items.

Profit and loss account formats

Format 1

(see note *(17)* below)

1. Turnover
2. Cost of sales *(14)*
3. Gross profit or loss
4. Distribution costs *(14)*
5. Administrative expenses *(14)*
6. Other operating income
7. Income from shares in group undertakings
8. Income from participating interests
9. Income from other fixed asset investments *(15)*
10. Other interest receivable and similar income *(15)*
11. Amounts written off investments
12. Interest payable and similar charges *(16)*
13. Tax on profit or loss on ordinary activities
14. Profit or loss on ordinary activities after taxation
15. Extraordinary income
16. Extraordinary charges
17. Extraordinary profit or loss
18. Tax on extraordinary profit or loss
19. Other taxes not shown under the above items
20. Profit or loss for the financial year

Profit and loss account formats

Format 2

1. Turnover
2. Change in stocks of finished goods and in work in progress
3. Own work capitalised
4. Other operating income
5. (*a*) Raw materials and consumables
    (*b*) Other external charges
6. Staff costs:
    (*a*) wages and salaries
    (*b*) social security costs
    (*c*) other pension costs

7. (*a*) Depreciation and other amounts written off tangible and intangible fixed assets
   (*b*) Exceptional amounts written off current assets
8. Other operating charges
9. Income from shares in group undertakings
10. Income from participating interests
11. Income from other fixed asset investments (*15*)
12. Other interest receivable and similar income (*15*)
13. Amounts written off investments
14. Interest payable and similar charges (*16*)
15. Tax on profit or loss on ordinary activities
16. Profit or loss on ordinary activities after taxation
17. Extraordinary income
18. Extraordinary charges
19. Extraordinary profit or loss
20. Tax on extraordinary profit or loss
21. Other taxes not shown under the above items
22. Profit or loss for the financial year

Profit and loss account formats

Format 3

(see note (*17*) below)

A. Charges
1. Cost of sales (*14*)
2. Distribution costs (*14*)
3. Administrative expenses (*14*)
4. Amounts written off investments
5. Interest payable and similar charges (*16*)
6. Tax on profit or loss on ordinary activities
7. Profit or loss on ordinary activities after taxation
8. Extraordinary charges
9. Tax on extraordinary profit or loss
10. Other taxes not shown under the above items
11. Profit or loss for the financial year

B. Income
1. Turnover
2. Other operating income
3. Income from shares in group undertakings
4. Income from participating interests
5. Income from other fixed asset investments (*15*)
6. Other interest receivable and similar income (*15*)
7. Profit or loss on ordinary activities after taxation
8. Extraordinary income
9. Profit or loss for the financial year

Profit and loss account formats

Format 4

A. Charges
1. Reduction in stocks of finished goods and in work in progress
2. (*a*) Raw materials and consumables
   (*b*) Other external charges
3. Staff costs:
   (*a*) wages and salaries
   (*b*) social security costs
   (*c*) other pension costs
4. (*a*) Depreciation and other amounts written off tangible and intangible fixed assets
   (*b*) Exceptional amounts written off current assets
5. Other operating charges
6. Amounts written off investments
7. Interest payable and similar charges (*16*)

8. Tax on profit or loss on ordinary activities
9. Profit or loss on ordinary activities after taxation
10. Extraordinary charges
11. Tax on extraordinary profit or loss
12. Other taxes not shown under the above items
13. Profit or loss for the financial year

B. Income
1. Turnover
2. Increase in stocks of finished goods and in work in progress
3. Own work capitalised
4. Other operating income
5. Income from shares in group undertakings
6. Income from participating interests
7. Income from other fixed asset investments (*15*)
8. Other interest receivable and similar income (*15*)
9. Profit or loss on ordinary activities after taxation
10. Extraordinary income
11. Profit or loss for the financial year

Notes on the profit and loss account formats

(*14*) *Cost of sales: distribution costs: administrative expenses*
(Format 1, items 2, 4 and 5 and format 3, items A.1, 2 and 3.)
> These items shall be stated after taking into account any necessary provisions for depreciation or diminution in value of assets.

(*15*) *Income from other fixed asset investments: other interest receivable and similar income*
(Format 1, items 9 and 10; format 2, items 11 and 12: format 3, items B.5 and 6: format 4, items B.7 and 8.)
> Income and interest derived from group undertakings shall be shown separately from income and interest derived from other sources.

(*16*) *Interest payable and similar charges*
(Format 1, item 12: format 2, item 14: format 3, item A.5: format 4, item A.7.)
> The amount payable to group undertakings shall be shown separately.

(*17*) *Formats 1 and 3*
> The amount of any provisions for depreciation and diminution in value of tangible and intangible fixed assets falling to be shown under items 7(*a*) and A.4(*a*) respectively in formats 2 and 4 shall be disclosed in a note to the accounts in any case where the profit and loss account is prepared by reference to format 1 or format 3.

PART II

ACCOUNTING PRINCIPLES AND RULES

SECTION A
ACCOUNTING PRINCIPLES

Preliminary

9. Subject to paragraph 15 below, the amounts to be included in respect of all items shown in a company's accounts shall be determined in accordance with the principles set out in paragraphs 10 to 14.

Accounting principles

10. The company shall be presumed to be carrying on business as a going concern.

11. Accounting policies shall be applied consistently within the same accounts and from one financial year to the next.

12. The amount of any item shall be determined on a prudent basis, and in particular—
(*a*) only profits realised at the balance sheet date shall be included in the profit and loss account; and

(*b*) all liabilities and losses which have arisen or are likely to arise in respect of the financial year to which the accounts relate or a previous financial year shall be taken into account, including those which only become apparent between the balance sheet date and the date on which it is signed on behalf of the board of directors in pursuance of section 233 of this Act.

13. All income and charges relating to the financial year to which the accounts relate shall be taken into account, without regard to the date of receipt or payment.

14. In determining the aggregate amount of any item the amount of each individual asset or liability that falls to be taken into account shall be determined separately.

Departure from the accounting principles

15. If it appears to the directors of a company that there are special reasons for departing from any of the principles stated above in preparing the company's accounts in respect of any financial year they may do so, but particulars of the departure, the reasons for it and its effect shall be given in a note to the accounts.

SECTION B
HISTORICAL COST ACCOUNTING RULES

Preliminary

16. Subject to section C of this Part of this Schedule, the amounts to be included in respect of all items shown in a company's accounts shall be determined in accordance with the rules set out in paragraphs 17 to 28.

Fixed assets

General rules

17. Subject to any provision for depreciation or diminution in value made in accordance with paragraph 18 or 19 the amount to be included in respect of any fixed asset shall be its purchase price or production cost.

18. In the case of any fixed asset which has a limited useful economic life, the amount of—
(*a*) its purchase price or production cost; or
(*b*) where it is estimated that any such asset will have a residual value at the end of the period of its useful economic life, its purchase price or production cost less that estimated residual value;
shall be reduced by provisions for depreciation calculated to write off that amount systematically over the period of the asset's useful economic life.

19.—(1) Where a fixed asset investment of a description falling to be included under item B.III of either of the balance sheet formats set out in Part I of this Schedule has diminished in value provisions for diminution in value may be made in respect of it and the amount to be included in respect of it may be reduced accordingly; and any such provisions which are not shown in the profit and loss account shall be disclosed (either separately or in aggregate) in a note to the accounts.

(2) Provisions for diminution in value shall be made in respect of any fixed asset which has diminished in value if the reduction in its value is expected to be permanent (whether its useful economic life is limited or not), and the amount to be included in respect of it shall be reduced accordingly; and any such provisions which are not shown in the profit and loss account shall be disclosed (either separately or in aggregate) in a note to the accounts.

(3) Where the reasons for which any provision was made in accordance with sub-paragraph (1) or (2) have ceased to apply to any extent, that provision shall be written back to the extent that it is no longer necessary; and any amounts written back in accordance with this sub-paragraph which are not shown in the profit and loss account shall be disclosed (either separately or in aggregate) in a note to the accounts.

Rules for determining particular fixed asset items

20.—(1) Notwithstanding that an item in respect of "development costs" is included under "fixed assets" in the balance sheet formats set out in Part I of this Schedule, an amount may only be included in a company's balance sheet in respect of development costs in special circumstances.

(2) If any amount is included in a company's balance sheet in respect of development costs the following information shall be given in a note to the accounts—

(*a*) the period over which the amount of those costs originally capitalised is being or is to be written off; and

(*b*) the reasons for capitalising the development costs in question.

21.—(1) The application of paragraphs 17 to 19 in relation to goodwill (in any case where goodwill is treated as an asset) is subject to the following provisions of this paragraph.

(2) Subject to sub-paragraph (3) below, the amount of the consideration for any goodwill acquired by a company shall be reduced by provisions for depreciation calculated to write off that amount systematically over a period chosen by the directors of the company.

(3) The period chosen shall not exceed the useful economic life of the goodwill in question.

(4) In any case where any goodwill acquired by a company is shown or included as an asset in the company's balance sheet the period chosen for writing off the consideration for that goodwill and the reasons for choosing that period shall be disclosed in a note to the accounts.

Current assets

22. Subject to paragraph 23, the amount to be included in respect of any current asset shall be its purchase price or production cost.

23.—(1) If the net realisable value of any current asset is lower than its purchase price or production cost the amount to be included in respect of that asset shall be the net realisable value.

(2) Where the reasons for which any provision for diminution in value was made in accordance with sub-paragraph (1) have ceased to apply to any extent, that provision shall be written back to the extent that it is no longer necessary.

Miscellaneous and supplementary provisions

Excess of money owed over value received as an asset item

24.—(1) Where the amount repayable on any debt owed by a company is greater than the value of the consideration received in the transaction giving rise to the debt, the amount of the difference may be treated as an asset.

(2) Where any such amount is so treated—

(*a*) it shall be written off by reasonable amounts each year and must be completely written off before repayment of the debt; and

(*b*) if the current amount is not shown as a separate item in the company's balance sheet it must be disclosed in a note to the accounts.

Assets included at a fixed amount

25.—(1) Subject to the following sub-paragraph, assets which fall to be included—

(*a*) amongst the fixed assets of a company under the item "tangible assets"; or

(*b*) amongst the current assets of a company under the item "raw materials and consumables";

may be included at a fixed quantity and value.

(2) Sub-paragraph (1) applies to assets of a kind which are constantly being replaced, where—

(*a*) their overall value is not material to assessing the company's state of affairs; and

(*b*) their quantity, value and composition are not subject to material variation.

Determination of purchase price or production cost

26.—(1) The purchase price of an asset shall be determined by adding to the actual price paid any expenses incidental to its acquisition.

(2) The production cost of an asset shall be determined by adding to the purchase price of the raw materials and consumables used the amount of the costs incurred by the company which are directly attributable to the production of that asset.

(3) In addition, there may be included in the production cost of an asset—

(*a*) a reasonable proportion of the costs incurred by the company which are only indirectly attributable to the production of that asset, but only to the extent that they relate to the period of production; and

(*b*) interest on capital borrowed to finance the production of that asset, to the extent that it accrues in respect of the period of production;

provided, however, in a case within paragraph (*b*) above, that the inclusion of the interest in determining the cost of that asset and the amount of the interest so included is disclosed in a note to the accounts.

(4) In the case of current assets distribution costs may not be included in production costs.

27.—(1) Subject to the qualification mentioned below, the purchase price or production cost of—

    (*a*) any assets which fall to be included under any item shown in a company's balance sheet under the general item "stocks"; and

    (*b*) any assets which are fungible assets (including investments);

may be determined by the application of any of the methods mentioned in sub-paragraph (2) below in relation to any such assets of the same class.

The method chosen must be one which appears to the directors to be appropriate in the circumstances of the company.

(2) Those methods are—

    (*a*) the method known as "first in, first out" (FIFO);

    (*b*) the method known as "last in, first out" (LIFO);

    (*c*) a weighted average price; and

    (*d*) any other method similar to any of the methods mentioned above.

(3) Where in the case of any company—

    (*a*) the purchase price or production cost of assets falling to be included under any item shown in the company's balance sheet has been determined by the application of any method permitted by this paragraph; and

    (*b*) the amount shown in respect of that item differs materially from the relevant alternative amount given below in this paragraph;

the amount of that difference shall be disclosed in a note to the accounts.

(4) Subject to sub-paragraph (5) below, for the purposes of sub-paragraph (3)(*b*) above, the relevant alternative amount, in relation to any item shown in a company's balance sheet, is the amount which would have been shown in respect of that item if assets of any class included under that item at an amount determined by any method permitted by this paragraph had instead been included at their replacement cost as at the balance sheet date.

(5) The relevant alternative amount may be determined by reference to the most recent actual purchase price or production cost before the balance sheet date of assets of any class included under the item in question instead of by reference to their replacement cost as at that date, but only if the former appears to the directors of the company to constitute the more appropriate standard of comparison in the case of assets of that class.

(6) For the purposes of this paragraph, assets of any description shall be regarded as fungible if assets of that description are substantially indistinguishable one from another.

Substitution of original stated amount where price or cost unknown

28. Where there is no record of the purchase price or production cost of any asset of a company or of any price, expenses or costs relevant for determining its purchase price or production cost in accordance with paragraph 26, or any such record cannot be obtained without unreasonable expense or delay, its purchase price or production cost shall be taken for the purposes of paragraphs 17 to 23 to be the value ascribed to it in the earliest available record of its value made on or after its acquisition or production by the company.

SECTION C

ALTERNATIVE ACCOUNTING RULES

Preliminary

29.—(1) The rules set out in section B are referred to below in this Schedule as the historical cost accounting rules.

(2) Those rules, with the omission of paragraphs 16, 21 and 25 to 28, are referred to below in this Part of this Schedule as the depreciation rules; and references below in this Schedule to the historical cost accounting rules do not include the depreciation rules as they apply by virtue of paragraph 32.

30. Subject to paragraphs 32 to 34, the amounts to be included in respect of assets of any description mentioned in paragraph 31 may be determined on any basis so mentioned.

Alternative accounting rules

31.—(1) Intangible fixed assets, other than goodwill, may be included at their current cost.

(2) Tangible fixed assets may be included at a market value determined as at the date of their last valuation or at their current cost.

(3) Investments of any description falling to be included under item B.III of either of the balance sheet formats set out in Part I of this Schedule may be included either—

(*a*) at a market value determined as at the date of their last valuation; or

(*b*) at a value determined on any basis which appears to the directors to be appropriate in the circumstances of the company;

but in the latter case particulars of the method of valuation adopted and of the reasons for adopting it shall be disclosed in a note to the accounts.

(4) Investments of any description falling to be included under item C.III of either of the balance sheet formats set out in Part I of this Schedule may be included at their current cost.

(5) Stocks may be included at their current cost.

Application of the depreciation rules

32.—(1) Where the value of any asset of a company is determined on any basis mentioned in paragraph 31, that value shall be, or (as the case may require) be the starting point for determining, the amount to be included in respect of that asset in the company's accounts, instead of its purchase price or production cost or any value previously so determined for that asset; and the depreciation rules shall apply accordingly in relation to any such asset with the substitution for any reference to its purchase price or production cost of a reference to the value most recently determined for that asset on any basis mentioned in paragraph 31.

(2) The amount of any provision for depreciation required in the case of any fixed asset by paragraph 18 or 19 as it applies by virtue of sub-paragraph (1) is referred to below in this paragraph as the adjusted amount, and the amount of any provision which would be required by that paragraph in the case of that asset according to the historical cost accounting rules is referred to as the historical cost amount.

(3) Where sub-paragraph (1) applies in the case of any fixed asset the amount of any provision for depreciation in respect of that asset—

(*a*) included in any item shown in the profit and loss account in respect of amounts written off assets of the description in question; or

(*b*) taken into account in stating any item so shown which is required by note (*14*) of the notes on the profit and loss account formats set out in Part I of this Schedule to be stated after taking into account any necessary provisions for depreciation or diminution in value of assets included under it;

may be the historical cost amount instead of the adjusted amount, provided that the amount of any difference between the two is shown separately in the profit and loss account or in a note to the accounts.

Additional information to be provided in case of departure from historical cost accounting rules

33.—(1) This paragraph applies where the amounts to be included in respect of assets covered by any items shown in a company's accounts have been determined on any basis mentioned in paragraph 31.

(2) The items affected and the basis of valuation adopted in determining the amounts of the assets in question in the case of each such item shall be disclosed in a note to the accounts.

(3) In the case of each balance sheet item affected (except stocks) either—

(*a*) the comparable amounts determined according to the historical cost accounting rules; or

(*b*) the differences between those amounts and the corresponding amounts actually shown in the balance sheet in respect of that item;

shall be shown separately in the balance sheet or in a note to the accounts.

(4) In sub-paragraph (3) above, references in relation to any item to the comparable amounts determined as there mentioned are references to—

(*a*) the aggregate amount which would be required to be shown in respect of that item if the amounts to be included in respect of all the assets covered by that item were determined according to the historical cost accounting rules; and

(*b*) the aggregate amount of the cumulative provisions for depreciation or diminution in value which would be permitted or required in determining those amounts according to those rules.

Revaluation reserve

34.—(1) With respect to any determination of the value of an asset of a company on any basis mentioned in paragraph 31, the amount of any profit or loss arising from that determination (after allowing, where appropriate, for any provisions for depreciation or diminution in value made otherwise than by reference to the value so determined and any adjustments of any such provisions made in the light of that determination) shall be credited or (as the case may be) debited to a separate reserve ("the revaluation reserve").

(2) The amount of the revaluation reserve shall be shown in the company's balance sheet under a separate sub-heading in the position given for the item "revaluation reserve" in format 1 or 2 of the balance sheet formats set out in Part I of this Schedule, but need not be shown under that name.

[1] (3) An amount may be transferred from the revaluation reserve—

    (*a*) to the profit and loss account, if the amount was previously charged to that account or represents realised profit, or

    (*b*) on capitalisation;

and the revaluation reserve shall be reduced to the extent that the amounts transferred to it are no longer necessary for the purposes of the valuation method used.

[2] (3A) In sub-paragraph (3)(*b*) "capitalisation", in relation to an amount standing to the credit of the revaluation reserve, means applying it in wholly or partly paying up unissued shares in the company to be allotted to members of the company as fully or partly paid shares.

[2] (3B) The revaluation reserve shall not be reduced except as mentioned in this paragraph.

(4) The treatment for taxation purposes of amounts credited or debited to the revaluation reserve shall be disclosed in a note to the accounts.

NOTES

[1] Substituted by the Companies Act 1989, Sched. 1, para. 6.
[2] Inserted by the Companies Act 1989, Sched. 1, para. 6.

PART III

NOTES TO THE ACCOUNTS

Preliminary

35. Any information required in the case of any company by the following provisions of this Part of this Schedule shall (if not given in the company's accounts) be given by way of a note to those accounts.

Disclosure of accounting policies

36. The accounting policies adopted by the company in determining the amounts to be included in respect of items shown in the balance sheet and in determining the profit or loss of the company shall be stated (including such policies with respect to the depreciation and diminution in value of assets).

[1] 36A. It shall be stated whether the accounts have been prepared in accordance with applicable accounting standards and particulars of any material departure from those standards and the reasons for it shall be given.

NOTE

[1] Inserted by the Companies Act 1989, Sched. 1, para. 7.

Information supplementing the balance sheet

37. Paragraphs 38 to 51 require information which either supplements the information given with respect to any particular items shown in the balance sheet or is otherwise relevant to assessing the company's state of affairs in the light of the information so given.

Share capital and debentures

38.—(1) The following information shall be given with respect to the company's share capital—

    (*a*) the authorised share capital; and

    (*b*) where shares of more than one class have been allotted, the number and aggregate nominal value of shares of each class allotted.

(2) In the case of any part of the allotted share capital that consists of redeemable shares, the following information shall be given—

    (*a*) the earliest and latest dates on which the company has power to redeem those shares;

(*b*)　whether those shares must be redeemed in any event or are liable to be redeemed at the option of the company or of the shareholder; and

(*c*)　whether any (and, if so, what) premium is payable on redemption.

39. If the company has allotted any shares during the financial year, the following information shall be given—

(*a*)　the reason for making the allotment;

(*b*)　the classes of shares allotted; and

(*c*)　as respects each class of shares, the number allotted, their aggregate nominal value, and the consideration received by the company for the allotment.

40.—(1) With respect to any contingent right to the allotment of shares in the company the following particulars shall be given—

(*a*)　the number, description and amount of the shares in relation to which the right is exercisable;

(*b*)　the period during which it is exercisable; and

(*c*)　the price to be paid for the shares allotted.

(2) In sub-paragraph (1) above "contingent right to the allotment of shares" means any option to subscribe for shares and any other right to require the allotment of shares to any person whether arising on the conversion into shares of securities of any other description or otherwise.

41.—(1) If the company has issued any debentures during the financial year to which the accounts relate, the following information shall be given—

(*a*)　the reason for making the issue;

(*b*)　the classes of debentures issued; and

(*c*)　as respects each class of debentures, the amount issued and the consideration received by the company for the issue.

(2) Particulars of any redeemed debentures which the company has power to reissue shall also be given.

(3) Where any of the company's debentures are held by a nominee of or trustee for the company, the nominal amount of the debentures and the amount at which they are stated in the accounting records kept by the company in accordance with section 221 of this Act shall be stated.

Fixed assets

42.—(1) In respect of each item which is or would but for paragraph 3(4)(*b*) be shown under the general item "fixed assets" in the company's balance sheet the following information shall be given—

(*a*)　the appropriate amounts in respect of that item as at the date of the beginning of the financial year and as at the balance sheet date respectively;

(*b*)　the effect on any amount shown in the balance sheet in respect of that item of—

(i)　any revision of the amount in respect of any assets included under that item made during that year on any basis mentioned in paragraph 31;

(ii)　acquisitions during that year of any assets;

(iii)　disposals during that year of any assets; and

(iv)　any transfers of assets of the company to and from that item during that year.

(2) The reference in sub-paragraph (1)(*a*) to the appropriate amounts in respect of any item as at any date there mentioned is a reference to amounts representing the aggregate amounts determined, as at that date, in respect of assets falling to be included under that item on either of the following bases, that is to say—

(*a*)　on the basis of purchase price or production cost (determined in accordance with paragraphs 26 and 27); or

(*b*)　on any basis mentioned in paragraph 31,

(leaving out of account in either case any provisions for depreciation or diminution in value).

(3) In respect of each item within sub-paragraph (1)—

(*a*)　the cumulative amount of provisions for depreciation or diminution in value of assets included under that item as at each date mentioned in sub-paragraph (1)(*a*);

(*b*)　the amount of any such provisions made in respect of the financial year;

(*c*)　the amount of any adjustments made in respect of any such provisions during that year in consequence of the disposal of any assets; and

(*d*)　the amount of any other adjustments made in respect of any such provisions during that year;

shall also be stated.

43. Where any fixed assets of the company (other than listed investments) are included under any item shown in the company's balance sheet at an amount determined on any basis mentioned in paragraph 31, the following information shall be given—

    (*a*)   the years (so far as they are known to the directors) in which the assets were severally valued and the several values; and

    (*b*)   in the case of assets that have been valued during the financial year, the names of the persons who valued them or particulars of their qualifications for doing so and (whichever is stated) the bases of valuation used by them.

44. In relation to any amount which is or would but for paragraph 3(4)(*a*) be shown in respect of the item "land and buildings" in the company's balance sheet there shall be stated—

    (*a*)   how much of that amount is ascribable to land of freehold tenure and how much to land of leasehold tenure; and

    (*b*)   how much of the amount ascribable to land of leasehold tenure is ascribable to land held on long lease and how much to land held on short lease.

Investments

45.—(1) In respect of the amount of each item which is or would but for paragraph 3(4)(*b*) be shown in the company's balance sheet under the general item "investments" (whether as fixed assets or as current assets) there shall be stated—

    (*a*)   how much of that amount is ascribable to listed investments; and

[1] (*b*)   how much of any amount so ascribable is ascribable to investments as respects which there has been granted a listing on a recognised investment exchange other than an overseas investment exchange within the meaning of the Financial Services Act 1986 and how much to other listed investments.

(2) Where the amount of any listed investments is stated for any item in accordance with sub-paragraph (1)(*a*), the following amounts shall also be stated—

    (*a*)   the aggregate market value of those investments where it differs from the amount so stated; and

    (*b*)   both the market value and the stock exchange value of any investments of which the former value is, for the purposes of the accounts, taken as being higher than the latter.

NOTE
[1] As amended by the Financial Services Act 1986, Sched. 16, para 23.

Reserves and provisions

46.—(1) Where any amount is transferred—

    (*a*)   to or from any reserves; or

    (*b*)   to any provisions for liabilities and charges; or

    (*c*)   from any provision for liabilities and charges otherwise than for the purpose for which the provision was established;

and the reserves or provisions are or would but for paragraph 3(4)(*b*) be shown as separate items in the company's balance sheet, the information mentioned in the following sub-paragraph shall be given in respect of the aggregate of reserves or provisions included in the same item.

(2) That information is—

    (*a*)   the amount of the reserves or provisions as at the date of the beginning of the financial year and as at the balance sheet date respectively;

    (*b*)   any amounts transferred to or from the reserves or provisions during that year; and

    (*c*)   the source and application respectively of any amounts so transferred.

(3) Particulars shall be given of each provision included in the item "other provisions" in the company's balance sheet in any case where the amount of that provision is material.

Provision for taxation

[1] 47. The amount of any provision for deferred taxation shall be stated separately from the amount of any provision for other taxation.

NOTE
[1] As amended by the Companies Act 1989, Sched. 1, para. 8.

Details of indebtedness

48.—(1) In respect of each item shown under "creditors" in the company's balance sheet there shall be stated—

    (a) the aggregate amount of any debts included under that item which are payable or repayable otherwise than by instalments and fall due for payment or repayment after the end of the period of five years beginning with the day next following the end of the financial year; and

    (b) the aggregate amount of any debts so included which are payable or repayable by instalments any of which fall due for payment after the end of that period;

and in the case of debts within paragraph (b) above the aggregate amount of instalments falling due after the end of that period shall also be disclosed for each such item.

(2) Subject to sub-paragraph (3), in relation to each debt falling to be taken into account under sub-paragraph (1), the terms of payment or repayment and the rate of any interest payable on the debt shall be stated.

(3) If the number of debts is such that, in the opinion of the directors, compliance with sub-paragraph (2) would result in a statement of excessive length, it shall be sufficient to give a general indication of the terms of payment or repayment and the rates of any interest payable on the debts.

(4) In respect of each item shown under "creditors" in the company's balance sheet there shall be stated—

    (a) the aggregate amount of any debts included under that item in respect of which any security has been given by the company; and

    (b) an indication of the nature of the securities so given.

(5) References above in this paragraph to an item shown under "creditors" in the company's balance sheet include references, where amounts falling due to creditors within one year and after more than one year are distinguished in the balance sheet—

    (a) in a case within sub-paragraph (1), to an item shown under the latter of those categories; and

    (b) in a case within sub-paragraph (4), to an item shown under either of those categories;

and references to items shown under "creditors" include references to items which would but for paragraph 3(4)(b) be shown under that heading.

49. If any fixed cumulative dividends on the company's shares are in arrear, there shall be stated—

    (a) the amount of the arrears; and

    (b) the period for which the dividends or, if there is more than one class, each class of them are in arrear.

Guarantees and other financial commitments

50.—(1) Particulars shall be given of any charge on the assets of the company to secure the liabilities of any other person, including, where practicable, the amount secured.

(2) The following information shall be given with respect to any other contingent liability not provided for—

    (a) the amount or estimated amount of that liability;

    (b) its legal nature; and

    (c) whether any valuable security has been provided by the company in connection with that liability and if so, what.

(3) There shall be stated, where practicable—

    (a) the aggregate amount or estimated amount of contracts for capital expenditure, so far as not provided for; and

    (b) the aggregate amount or estimated amount of capital expenditure authorised by the directors which has not been contracted for.

(4) Particulars shall be given of—

    (a) any pension commitments included under any provision shown in the company's balance sheet; and

    (b) any such commitments for which no provision has been made;

and where any such commitment relates wholly or partly to pensions payable to past directors of the company separate particulars shall be given of that commitment so far as it relates to such pensions.

(5) Particulars shall also be given of any other financial commitments which—

    (a) have not been provided for; and

    (b) are relevant to assessing the company's state of affairs.

(6) [Repealed by the Companies Act 1989, Sched. 24.]

Miscellaneous matters

51.—(1) Particulars shall be given of any case where the purchase price or production cost of any asset is for the first time determined under paragraph 28.

¹ (2) Where any outstanding loans made under the authority of section 153(4)(*b*), (*bb*) or (*c*) or section 155 of this Act (various cases of financial assistance by a company for purchase of its own shares) are included under any item shown in the company's balance sheet, the aggregate amount of those loans shall be disclosed for each item in question.

(3) The aggregate amount which is recommended for distribution by way of dividend shall be stated.

NOTE
¹ As amended by the Companies Act 1989, Sched. 1, para. 9.

Information supplementing the profit and loss account

52. Paragraphs 53 to 57 require information which either supplements the information given with respect to any particular items shown in the profit and loss account or otherwise provides particulars of income or expenditure of the company or of circumstances affecting the items shown in the profit and loss account.

Separate statement of certain items of income and expenditure

53.—(1) Subject to the following provisions of this paragraph, each of the amounts mentioned below shall be stated.

(2) The amount of the interest on or any similar charges in respect of—
   (*a*) bank loans and overdrafts, and loans made to the company (other than bank loans and overdrafts) which—
      (i) are repayable otherwise than by instalments and fall due for repayment before the end of the period of five years beginning with the day next following the end of the financial year; or
      (ii) are repayable by instalments the last of which falls due for payment before the end of that period; and
   (*b*) loans of any other kind made to the company.

This sub-paragraph does not apply to interest or charges on loans to the company from group undertakings, but, with that exception, it applies to interest or charges on all loans, whether made on the security of debentures or not.

(3) The amounts respectively set aside for redemption of share capital and for redemption of loans.

(4) The amount of income from listed investments.

(5) The amount of rents from land (after deduction of ground rents, rates and other outgoings).

This amount need only be stated if a substantial part of the company's revenue for the financial year consists of rents from land.

(6) The amount charged to revenue in respect of sums payable in respect of the hire of plant and machinery.

(7) [Repealed by the Companies Act 1989, Sched. 24.]

Particulars of tax

54.—(1) The basis on which the charge for United Kingdom corporation tax and United Kingdom income tax is computed shall be stated.

(2) Particulars shall be given of any special circumstances which affect liability in respect of taxation of profits, income or capital gains for the financial year or liability in respect of taxation of profits, income or capital gains for succeeding financial years.

(3) The following amounts shall be stated—
   (*a*) the amount of the charge for United Kingdom corporation tax;
   (*b*) if that amount would have been greater but for relief from double taxation, the amount which it would have been but for such relief;
   (*c*) the amount of the charge for United Kingdom income tax; and
   (*d*) the amount of the charge for taxation imposed outside the United Kingdom of profits, income and (so far as charged to revenue) capital gains.

These amounts shall be stated separately in respect of each of the amounts which is or would but for paragraphs 3(4)(*b*) be shown under the following items in the profit and loss account, that is to say "tax on profit or loss on ordinary activities" and "tax on extraordinary profit or loss".

Particulars of turnover

55.—(1) If in the course of the financial year the company has carried on business of two or more classes that, in the opinion of the directors, differ substantially from each other, there shall be stated in respect of each class (describing it)—

(a) the amount of the turnover attributable to that class; and

(b) the amount of the profit or loss of the company before taxation which is in the opinion of the directors attributable to that class.

(2) If in the course of the financial year the company has supplied markets that, in the opinion of the directors, differ substantially from each other, the amount of the turnover attributable to each such market shall also be stated.

In this paragraph "market" means a market delimited by geographical bounds.

(3) In analysing for the purposes of this paragraph the source (in terms of business or in terms of market) of turnover or (as the case may be) of profit or loss, the directors of the company shall have regard to the manner in which the company's activities are organised.

(4) For the purposes of this paragraph—

(a) classes of business which, in the opinion of the directors, do not differ substantially from each other shall be treated as one class; and

(b) markets which, in the opinion of the directors, do not differ substantially from each other shall be treated as one market;

and any amounts properly attributable to one class of business or (as the case may be) to one market which are not material may be included in the amount stated in respect of another.

(5) Where in the opinion of the directors the disclosure of any information required by this paragraph would be seriously prejudicial to the interests of the company, that information need not be disclosed, but the fact that any such information has not been disclosed must be stated.

Particulars of staff

56.—(1) The following information shall be given with respect to the employees of the company—

(a) the average number of persons employed by the company in the financial year; and

(b) the average number of persons so employed within each category of persons employed by the company.

(2) The average number required by sub-paragraph (1)(a) or (b) shall be determined by dividing the relevant annual number by the number of weeks in the financial year.

(3) The relevant annual number shall be determined by ascertaining for each week in the financial year—

(a) for the purposes of sub-paragraph (1)(a), the number of persons employed under contracts of service by the company in that week (whether throughout the week or not);

(b) for the purposes of sub-paragraph (1)(b), the number of persons in the category in question of persons so employed;

and, in either case, adding together all the weekly numbers.

(4) In respect of all persons employed by the company during the financial year who are taken into account in determining the relevant annual number for the purposes of sub-paragraph (1)(a) there shall also be stated the aggregate amounts respectively of—

(a) wages and salaries paid or payable in respect of that year to those persons;

(b) social security costs incurred by the company on their behalf; and

(c) other pension costs so incurred;

save in so far as those amounts or any of them are stated in the profit and loss account.

(5) The categories of persons employed by the company by reference to which the number required to be disclosed by sub-paragraph (1)(b) is to be determined shall be such as the directors may select, having regard to the manner in which the company's activities are organised.

Miscellaneous matters

57.—(1) Where any amount relating to any preceding financial year is included in any item in the profit and loss account, the effect shall be stated.

(2) Particulars shall be given of any extraordinary income or charges arising in the financial year.

(3) The effect shall be stated of any transactions that are exceptional by virtue of size or incidence though they fall within the ordinary activities of the company.

General

58.—(1) Where sums originally denominated in foreign currencies have been brought into account under any items shown in the balance sheet or profit and loss account, the basis on which those sums have been translated into sterling shall be stated.

(2) Subject to the following sub-paragraph, in respect of every item stated in a note to the accounts the corresponding amount for the financial year immediately preceding that to which the accounts relate shall also be stated and where the corresponding amount is not comparable, it shall be adjusted and particulars of the adjustment and the reasons for it shall be given.

[1] (3) Sub-paragraph (2) does not apply in relation to any amounts stated by virtue of any of the following provisions of this Act—

(a)   paragraph 13 of Schedule 4A (details of accounting treatment of acquisitions),

(b)   paragraphs 2, 8(3), 16, 21(1)(d), 22(4) and (5), 24(3) and (4) and 27(3) and (4) of Schedule 5 (shareholdings in other undertakings),

(c)   Parts II and III of Schedule 6 (loans and other dealings in favour of directors and others), and

(d)   paragraphs 42 and 46 above (fixed assets and reserves and provisions).

NOTE
[1] Sub-paragraphs (a)–(d) substituted by the Companies Act 1989, Sched. 1, para. 10.

PART IV

SPECIAL PROVISIONS WHERE THE COMPANY IS A PARENT COMPANY OR
SUBSIDIARY UNDERTAKING

Company's own accounts

Dealings with or interests in group undertakings

[1] 59. Where a company is a parent company or a subsidiary undertaking and any item required by Part I of this Schedule to be shown in the company's balance sheet in relation to group undertakings includes—

(a)   amounts attributable to dealings with or interests in any parent undertaking or fellow subsidiary undertaking, or

(b)   amounts attributable to dealings with or interests in any subsidiary undertaking of the company,

the aggregate amounts within paragraphs (a) and (b) respectively shall be shown as separate items, either by way of subdivision of the relevant item in the balance sheet or in a note to the company's accounts.

NOTE
[1] Substituted by the Companies Act 1989, Sched. 1, para. 11.

Guarantees and other financial commitments in favour of group undertakings

[1] 59A. Commitments within any of sub-paragraphs (1) to (5) of paragraph 50 (guarantees and other financial commitments) which are undertaken on behalf of or for the benefit of—

(a)   any parent undertaking or fellow subsidiary undertaking, or

(b)   any subsidiary undertaking of the company,

shall be stated separately from the other commitments within that sub-paragraph, and commitments within paragraph (a) shall also be stated separately from those within paragraph (b).

NOTE
[1] Substituted by the Companies Act 1989, Sched. 1, para. 11.

60.–70. [Repealed by the Companies Act 1989, Sched. 24.]

PART V

SPECIAL PROVISIONS WHERE THE COMPANY IS AN INVESTMENT COMPANY

71.—(1) Paragraph 34 does not apply to the amount of any profit or loss arising from a determination of the value of any investments of an investment company on any basis mentioned in paragraph 31(3).

(2) Any provisions made by virtue of paragraph 19(1) or (2) in the case of an investment company in respect of any fixed asset investments need not be charged to the company's profit and loss account provided they are either—

(a) charged against any reserve account to which any amount excluded by sub-paragraph (1) from the requirements of paragraph 34 has been credited; or

(b) shown as a separate item in the company's balance sheet under the sub-heading "other reserves".

(3) For the purposes of this paragraph, as it applies in relation to any company, "fixed asset investment" means any asset falling to be included under any item shown in the company's balance sheet under the subdivision "investments" under the general item "fixed assets".

72.—(1) Any distribution made by an investment company which reduces the amount of its net assets to less than the aggregate of its called-up share capital and undistributable reserves shall be disclosed in a note to the company's accounts.

(2) For purposes of this paragraph, a company's net assets are the aggregate of its assets less the aggregate of its liabilities (including any provision for liabilities or charges within paragraph 89); and "undistributable reserves" has the meaning given by section 264(3) of this Act.

73. A company shall be treated as an investment company for the purposes of this Part of this Schedule in relation to any financial year of the company if—

(a) during the whole of that year it was an investment company as defined by section 266 of this Act, and

(b) it was not at any time during that year prohibited under section 265(4) of this Act (no distribution where capital profits have been distributed, etc.) from making a distribution by virtue of that section.

74. [Repealed by the Companies Act 1989, Sched. 24.]

PART VI

SPECIAL PROVISIONS WHERE THE COMPANY HAS ENTERED INTO ARRANGEMENTS SUBJECT TO MERGER RELIEF

75. [Repealed by the Companies Act 1989, Sched. 24.]

PART VII

INTERPRETATION OF SCHEDULE

76. The following paragraphs apply for the purposes of this Schedule and its interpretation.

77.–81. [Repealed by the Companies Act 1989, Sched. 24.]

Historical cost accounting rules

82. References to the historical cost accounting rules shall be read in accordance with paragraph 29.

Leases

83.—(1) "Long lease" means a lease in the case of which the portion of the term for which it was granted remaining unexpired at the end of the financial year is not less than 50 years.

(2) "Short lease" means a lease which is not a long lease.

(3) "Lease" includes an agreement for a lease.

Listed investments

[1] 84. "Listed investment" means an investment as respects which there has been granted a listing on a recognised investment exchange other than an overseas investment exchange within the meaning of the Financial Services Act 1986 or on any stock exchange of repute outside Great Britain.

NOTE

[1] As amended by the Financial Services Act 1986, Sched. 16, para. 23.

Loans

85. A loan is treated as falling due for repayment, and an instalment of a loan is treated as falling due for payment, on the earliest date on which the lender could require repayment or (as the case may be) payment, if he exercised all options and rights available to him.

Materiality

86. Amounts which in the particular context of any provision of this Schedule are not material may be disregarded for the purposes of that provision.

[THE NEXT PAGE IS I 383]

Notes to the accounts

87. [Repealed by the Companies Act 1989, Sched. 24.]

Provisions

88.—(1) References to provisions for depreciation or diminution in value of assets are to any amount written off by way of providing for depreciation or diminution in value of assets.

(2) Any reference in the profit and loss account formats set out in Part I of this Schedule to the depreciation of, or amounts written off, assets of any description is to any provision for depreciation or diminution in value of assets of that description.

89. References to provisions for liabilities or charges are to any amount retained as reasonably necessary for the purpose of providing for any liability or loss which is either likely to be incurred, or certain to be incurred but uncertain as to amount or as to the date on which it will arise.

90.–92. [Repealed by the Companies Act 1989, Sched. 24.]

Scots land tenure

93. In the application of this Schedule to Scotland, "land of freehold tenure" means land in respect of which the company is the proprietor of the *dominium utile* or, in the case of land not held on feudal tenure, is the owner; "land of leasehold tenure" means land of which the company is the tenant under a lease; and the reference to ground-rents, rates and other outgoings includes feu-duty and ground annual.

Staff costs

94.—(1) "Social security costs" means any contributions by the company to any state social security or pension scheme, fund or arrangement.

(2) "Pension costs" includes any other contributions by the company for the purposes of any pension scheme established for the purpose of providing pensions for persons employed by the company, any sums set aside for that purpose and any amounts paid by the company in respect of pensions without first being so set aside.

(3) Any amount stated in respect of either of the above items or in respect of the item "wages and salaries" in the company's profit and loss account shall be determined by reference to payments made or costs incurred in respect of all persons employed by the company during the financial year who are taken into account in determining the relevant annual number for the purposes of paragraph 56(1)(*a*).

95. [Repealed by the Companies Act 1989, Sched. 24.]

[1] SCHEDULE 4A

NOTE
[1] Inserted by the Companies Act 1989, s. 5(2) and Sched. 2.

FORM AND CONTENT OF GROUP ACCOUNTS

General rules

1.—(1) Group accounts shall comply so far as practicable with the provisions of Schedule 4 as if the undertakings included in the consolidation ("the group") were a single company.

(2) In particular, for the purposes of paragraph 59 of that Schedule (dealings with or interests in group undertakings) as it applies to group accounts—

   (*a*) any subsidiary undertakings of the parent company not included in the consolidation shall be treated as subsidiary undertakings of the group, and

   (*b*) if the parent company is itself a subsidiary undertaking, the group shall be treated as a subsidiary undertaking of any parent undertaking of that company, and the reference to fellow-subsidiary undertakings shall be construed accordingly.

(3) Where the parent company is treated as an investment company for the purposes of Part V of that Schedule (special provisions for investment companies) the group shall be similarly treated.

2.—(1) The consolidated balance sheet and profit and loss account shall incorporate in full the information contained in the individual accounts of the undertakings included in the consolidation, subject to the adjustments authorised or required by the following provisions of this Schedule and to such other adjustments (if any) as may be appropriate in accordance with generally accepted accounting principles or practice.

(2) If the financial year of a subsidiary undertaking included in the consolidation differs from that of the parent company, the group accounts shall be made up—

(*a*) from the accounts of the subsidiary undertaking for its financial year last ending before the end of the parent company's financial year, provided that year ended no more than three months before that of the parent company, or

(*b*) from interim accounts prepared by the subsidiary undertaking as at the end of the parent company's financial year.

3.—(1) Where assets and liabilities to be included in the group accounts have been valued or otherwise determined by undertakings according to accounting rules differing from those used for the group accounts, the values or amounts shall be adjusted so as to accord with the rules used for the group accounts.

(2) If it appears to the directors of the parent company that there are special reasons for departing from sub-paragraph (1) they may do so, but particulars of any such departure, the reasons for it and its effect shall be given in a note to the accounts.

(3) The adjustments referred to in this paragraph need not be made if they are not material for the purpose of giving a true and fair view.

4. Any differences of accounting rules as between a parent company's individual accounts for a financial year and its group accounts shall be disclosed in a note to the latter accounts and the reasons for the difference given.

5. Amounts which in the particular context of any provision of this Schedule are not material may be disregarded for the purposes of that provision.

Elimination of group transactions

6.—(1) Debts and claims between undertakings included in the consolidation, and income and expenditure relating to transactions between such undertakings, shall be eliminated in preparing the group accounts.

(2) Where profits and losses resulting from transactions between undertakings included in the consolidation are included in the book value of assets, they shall be eliminated in preparing the group accounts.

(3) The elimination required by sub-paragraph (2) may be effected in proportion to the group's interest in the shares of the undertakings.

(4) Sub-paragraphs (1) and (2) need not be complied with if the amounts concerned are not material for the purpose of giving a true and fair view.

Acquisition and merger accounting

7.—(1) The following provisions apply where an undertaking becomes a subsidiary undertaking of the parent company.

(2) That event is referred to in those provisions as an "acquisition", and references to the "undertaking acquired" shall be construed accordingly.

8. An acquisition shall be accounted for by the acquisition method of accounting unless the conditions for accounting for it as a merger are met and the merger method of accounting is adopted.

9.—(1) The acquisition method of acconting is as follows.

(2) The identifiable assets and liabilities of the undertaking acquired shall be included in the consolidated balance sheet at their fair values as at the date of acquisition.

In this paragraph the "identifiable" assets or liabilities of the undertaking acquired means the assets or liabilities which are capable of being disposed of or discharged separately, without disposing of a business of the undertaking.

(3) The income and expenditure of the undertaking acquired shall be brought into the group accounts only as from the date of the acquisition.

(4) There shall be set off against the acquisition cost of the interest in the shares of the undertaking held by the parent company and its subsidiary undertakings the interest of the parent company and its subsidiary undertakings in the adjusted capital and reserves of the undertaking acquired.

For this purpose—

"the acquisition cost" means the amount of any cash consideration and the fair value of any other consideration, together with such amount (if any) in respect of fees and other expenses of the acquisition as the company may determine, and

"the adjusted capital and reserves" of the undertaking acquired means its capital and reserves at the date of the acquisition after adjusting the identifiable assets and liabilities of the undertaking to fair values as at that date.

(5) The resulting amount if positive shall be treated as goodwill, and if negative as a negative consolidation difference.

10.—(1) The conditions for accounting for an acquisition as a merger are—

(*a*) that at least 90 per cent. of the nominal value of the relevant shares in the undertaking acquired is held by or on behalf of the parent company and its subsidiary undertakings,

(*b*) that the proportion referred to in paragraph (*a*) was attained pursuant to an arrangement providing for the issue of equity shares by the parent company or one or more of its subsidiary undertakings,

(*c*) that the fair value of any consideration other than the issue of equity shares given pursuant to the arrangement by the parent company and its subsidiary undertakings did not exceed 10 per cent. of the nominal value of the equity shares issued, and

(*d*) that adoption of the merger method of accounting accords with generally accepted accounting principles or practice.

(2) The reference in sub-paragraph (1)(*a*) to the "relevant shares" in an undertaking acquired is to those carrying unrestricted rights to participate both in distributions and in the assets of the undertaking upon liquidation.

11.—(1) The merger method of accounting is as follows.

(2) The assets and liabilities of the undertaking acquired shall be brought into the group accounts at the figures at which they stand in the undertaking's accounts, subject to any adjustment authorised or required by this Schedule.

(3) The income and expenditure of the undertaking acquired shall be included in the group accounts for the entire financial year, including the period before the acquisition.

(4) The group accounts shall show corresponding amounts relating to the previous financial year as if the undertaking acquired had been included in the consolidation throughout that year.

(5) There shall be set off against the aggregate of—

(*a*) the appropriate amount in respect of qualifying shares issued by the parent company or its subsidiary undertakings in consideration for the acquisition of shares in the undertaking acquired, and

(*b*) the fair value of any other consideration for the acquisition of shares in the undertaking acquired, determined as at the date when those shares were acquired,

the nominal value of the issued share capital of the undertaking acquired held by the parent company and its subsidiary undertakings.

(6) The resulting amount shall be shown as an adjustment to the consolidated reserves.

(7) In sub-paragraph (5)(*a*) "qualifying shares" means—

(*a*) shares in relation to which section 131 (merger relief) applies, in respect of which the appropriate amount is the nominal value; or

(*b*) shares in relation to which section 132 (relief in respect of group reconstructions) applies, in respect of which the appropriate amount is the nominal value together with any minimum premium value within the meaning of that section.

12.—(1) Where a group is acquired, paragraphs 9 to 11 apply with the following adaptations.

(2) References to shares of the undertaking acquired shall be construed as references to shares of the parent undertaking of the group.

(3) Other references to the undertaking acquired shall be construed as references to the group; and references to the assets and liabilities, income and expenditure and capital and reserves of the undertaking acquired shall be construed as references to the assets and liabilities, income and expenditure and capital and reserves of the group after making the set-offs and other adjustments required by this Schedule in the case of group accounts.

13.—(1) The following information with respect to acquisitions taking place in the financial year shall be given in a note to the accounts.

(2) There shall be stated—

    (*a*) the name of the undertaking acquired or, where a group was acquired, the name of the parent undertaking of that group, and

    (*b*) whether the acquisition has been accounted for by the acquisition or the merger method of accounting;

and in relation to an acquisition which significantly affects the figures shown in the group accounts, the following further information shall be given.

(3) The composition and fair value of the consideration for the acquisition given by the parent company and its subsidiary undertakings shall be stated.

(4) The profit or loss of the undertaking or group acquired shall be stated—

    (*a*) for the period from the beginning of the financial year of the undertaking or, as the case may be, of the parent undertaking of the group, up to the date of the acquisition, and

    (*b*) for the previous financial year of that undertaking or parent undertaking;

and there shall also be stated the date on which the financial year referred to in paragraph (*a*) began.

(5) Where the acquisition method of accounting has been adopted, the book values immediately prior to the acquisition, and the fair values at the date of acquisition, of each class of assets and liabilities of the undertaking or group acquired shall be stated in tabular form, including a statement of the amount of any goodwill or negative consolidation difference arising on the acquisition, together with an explanation of any significant adjustments made.

(6) Where the merger method of accounting has been adopted, an explanation shall be given of any significant adjustments made in relation to the amounts of the assets and liabilities of the undertaking or group acquired, together with a statement of any resulting adjustment to the consolidated reserves (including the re-statement of opening consolidated reserves).

(7) In ascertaining for the purposes of sub-paragraph (4), (5) or (6) the profit or loss of a group, the book values and fair values of assets and liabilities of a group or the amount of the assets and liabilities of a group, the set-offs and other adjustments required by this Schedule in the case of group accounts shall be made.

14.—(1) There shall also be stated in a note to the accounts the cumulative amount of goodwill resulting from acquisitions in that and earlier financial years which has been written off.

(2) That figure shall be shown net of any goodwill attributable to subsidiary undertakings or businesses disposed of prior to the balance sheet date.

15. Where during the financial year there has been a disposal of an undertaking or group which significantly affects the figures shown in the group accounts, there shall be stated in a note to the accounts—

    (*a*) the name of that undertaking or, as the case may be, of the parent undertaking of that group, and

    (*b*) the extent to which the profit or loss shown in the group accounts is attributable to profit or loss of that undertaking or group.

16. The information required by paragraph 13, 14 or 15 above need not be disclosed with respect to an undertaking which—

    (*a*) is established under the law of a country outside the United Kingdom, or

    (*b*) carries on business outside the United Kingdom,

if in the opinion of the directors of the parent company the disclosure would be seriously prejudicial to the business of that undertaking or to the business of the parent company or any of its subsidiary undertakings and the Secretary of State agrees that the information should not be disclosed.

Minority interests

17.—(1) The formats set out in Schedule 4 have effect in relation to group accounts with the following additions.

(2) In the Balance Sheet Formats a further item headed "Minority interests" shall be added—

    (*a*) in Format 1, either after item J or at the end (after item K), and

    (*b*) in Format 2, under the general heading "LIABILITIES", between items A and B;

and under that item shall be shown the amount of capital and reserves attributable to shares in subsidiary undertakings included in the consolidation held by or on behalf of persons other than the parent company and its subsidiary undertakings.

(3) In the Profit and Loss Account Formats a further item headed "Minority interests" shall be added—

- (*a*) in Format 1, between items 14 and 15,
- (*b*) in Format 2, between items 16 and 17,
- (*c*) in Format 3, between items 7 and 8 in both sections A and B, and
- (*d*) in Format 4, between items 9 and 10 in both sections A and B;

and under that item shall be shown the amount of any profit or loss on ordinary activities attributable to shares in subsidiary undertakings included in the consolidation held by or on behalf of persons other than the parent company and its subsidiary undertakings.

(4) In the Profit and Loss Account Formats a further item headed "Minority interests" shall be added—

- (*a*) in Format 1, between items 18 and 19,
- (*b*) in Format 2, between items 20 and 21,
- (*c*) in Format 3, between items 9 and 10 in section A and between items 8 and 9 in section B, and
- (*d*) in Format 4, between items 11 and 12 in section A and between items 10 and 11 in section B;

and under that item shall be shown the amount of any profit or loss on extraordinary activities attributable to shares in subsidiary undertakings included in the consolidation held by or on behalf of persons other than the parent company and its subsidiary undertakings.

(5) For the purposes of paragraph 3(3) and (4) of Schedule 4 (power to adapt or combine items)—

- (*a*) the additional item required by sub-paragraph (2) above shall be treated as one to which a letter is assigned, and
- (*b*) the additional items required by sub-paragraphs (3) and (4) above shall be treated as ones to which an Arabic number is assigned.

Interests in subsidiary undertakings excluded from consolidation

18. The interest of the group in subsidiary undertakings excluded from consolidation under section 229(4) (undertakings with activities different from those of undertakings included in the consolidation), and the amount of profit or loss attributable to such an interest, shall be shown in the consolidated balance sheet or, as the case may be, in the consolidated profit and loss account by the equity method of accounting (including dealing with any goodwill arising in accordance with paragraphs 17 to 19 and 21 of Schedule 4).

Joint ventures

19.—(1) Where an undertaking included in the consolidation manages another undertaking jointly with one or more undertakings not included in the consolidation, that other undertaking ("the joint venture") may, if it is not—

- (*a*) a body corporate, or
- (*b*) a subsidiary undertaking of the parent company,

be dealt with in the group accounts by the method of proportional consolidation.

(2) The provisions of this Part relating to the preparation of consolidated accounts apply, with any necessary modifications, to proportional consolidation under this paragraph.

Associated undertakings

20.—(1) An "associated undertaking" means an undertaking in which an undertaking included in the consolidation has a participating interest and over whose operating and financial policy it exercises a significant influence, and which is not—

- (*a*) a subsidiary undertaking of the parent company, or
- (*b*) a joint venture dealt with in accordance with paragraph 19.

(2) Where an undertaking holds 20 per cent. or more of the voting rights in another undertaking, it shall be presumed to exercise such an influence over it unless the contrary is shown.

(3) The voting rights in an undertaking means the rights conferred on shareholders in respect of their shares or, in the case of an undertaking not having a share capital, on members, to vote at general meetings of the undertaking on all, or substantially all, matters.

(4) The provisions of paragraphs 5 to 11 of Schedule 10A (rights to be taken into account and attribution of rights) apply in determining for the purposes of this paragraph whether an undertaking holds 20 per cent. or more of the voting rights in another undertaking.

21.—(1) The formats set out in Schedule 4 have effect in relation to group accounts with the following modifications.

(2) In the Balance Sheet Formats the items headed "Participating interests", that is—

(*a*) in Format 1, item B.III.3, and

(*b*) in Format 2, item B.III.3 under the heading "ASSETS",

shall be replaced by two items, "Interests in associated undertakings" and "Other participating interests".

(3) In the Profit and Loss Account Formats, the items headed "Income from participating interests", that is—

(*a*) in Format 1, item 8,

(*b*) in Format 2, item 10,

(*c*) in Format 3, item B.4, and

(*d*) in Format 4, item B.6,

shall be replaced by two items, "Income from interests in associated undertakings" and "Income from other participating interests".

22.—(1) The interest of an undertaking in an associated undertaking, and the amount of profit or loss attributable to such an interest, shall be shown by the equity method of accounting (including dealing with any goodwill arising in accordance with paragraphs 17 to 19 and 21 of Schedule 4).

(2) Where the associated undertaking is itself a parent undertaking, the net assets and profits or losses to be taken into account are those of the parent and its subsidiary undertakings (after making any consolidation adjustments).

(3) The equity method of accounting need not be applied if the amounts in question are not material for the purpose of giving a true and fair view.

[1] SCHEDULE 5

NOTE

[1] Substituted by the Companies Act 1989, s. 6 and Sched. 3.

DISCLOSURE OF INFORMATION: RELATED UNDERTAKINGS

PART I

COMPANIES NOT REQUIRED TO PREPARE GROUP ACCOUNTS

Subsidiary undertakings

1.—(1) The following information shall be given where at the end of the financial year the company has subsidiary undertakings.

(2) The name of each subsidiary undertaking shall be stated.

(3) There shall be stated with respect to each subsidiary undertaking—

(*a*) if it is incorporated outside Great Britain, the country in which it is incorporated;

(*b*) if it is incorporated in Great Britain, whether it is registered in England and Wales or in Scotland;

(*c*) if it is unincorporated, the address of its principal place of business.

(4) The reason why the company is not required to prepare group accounts shall be stated.

(5) If the reason is that all the subsidiary undertakings of the company fall within the exclusions provided for in section 229, it shall be stated with respect to each subsidiary undertaking which of those exclusions applies.

Holdings in subsidiary undertakings

2.—(1) There shall be stated in relation to shares of each class held by the company in a subsidiary undertaking—

(*a*) the identity of the class, and

(*b*) the proportion of the nominal value of the shares of that class represented by those shares.

(2) The shares held by or on behalf of the company itself shall be distinguished from those attributed to the company which are held by or on behalf of a subsidiary undertaking.

Financial information about subsidiary undertakings

3.—(1) There shall be disclosed with respect to each subsidiary undertaking—
  (a) the aggregate amount of its capital and reserves as at the end of its relevant financial year, and
  (b) its profit or loss for that year.

(2) That information need not be given if the company is exempt by virtue of section 228 from the requirement to prepare group accounts (parent company included in accounts of larger group).

(3) That information need not be given if—
  (a) the subsidiary undertaking is not required by any provision of this Act to deliver a copy of its balance sheet for its relevant financial year and does not otherwise publish that balance sheet in Great Britain or elsewhere, and
  (b) the company's holding is less than 50 per cent. of the nominal value of the shares in the undertaking.

(4) Information otherwise required by this paragraph need not be given if it is not material.

(5) For the purposes of this paragraph the "relevant financial year" of a subsidiary undertaking is—
  (a) if its financial year ends with that of the company, that year, and
  (b) if not, its financial year ending last before the end of the company's financial year.

Financial years of subsidiary undertakings

4. Where the financial year of one or more subsidiary undertakings did not end with that of the company, there shall be stated in relation to each such undertaking—
  (a) the reasons why the company's directors consider that its financial year should not end with that of the company, and
  (b) the date on which its last financial year ended (last before the end of the company's financial year).

Instead of the dates required by paragraph (b) being given for each subsidiary undertaking the earliest and latest of those dates may be given.

Further information about subsidiary undertakings

5.—(1) There shall be disclosed—
  (a) any qualifications contained in the auditors' reports on the accounts of subsidiary undertakings for financial years ending with or during the financial year of the company, and
  (b) any note or saving contained in such accounts to call attention to a matter which, apart from the note or saving, would properly have been referred to in such a qualification,

in so far as the matter which is the subject of the qualification or note is not covered by the company's own accounts and is material from the point of view of its members.

(2) The aggregate amount of the total investment of the company in the shares of subsidiary undertakings shall be stated by way of the equity method of valuation, unless—
  (a) the company is exempt from the requirement to prepare group accounts by virtue of section 228 (parent company included in accounts of larger group), and
  (b) the directors state their opinion that the aggregate value of the assets of the company consisting of shares in, or amounts owing (whether on account of a loan or otherwise) from, the company's subsidiary undertakings is not less than the aggregate of the amounts at which those assets are stated or included in the company's balance sheet.

(3) In so far as information required by this paragraph is not obtainable, a statement to that effect shall be given instead.

Shares and debentures of company held by subsidiary undertakings

6.—(1) The number, description and amount of the shares in and debentures of the company held by or on behalf of its subsidiary undertakings shall be disclosed.

(2) Sub-paragraph (1) does not apply in relation to shares or debentures in the case of which the subsidiary undertaking is concerned as personal representative or, subject as follows, as trustee.

(3) The exception for shares or debentures in relation to which the subsidiary undertaking is concerned as trustee does not apply if the company, or any subsidiary undertaking of the company, is beneficially interested under the trust, otherwise than by way of security only for the purposes of a transaction entered into by it in the ordinary course of a business which includes the lending of money.

(4) Schedule 2 to this Act has effect for the interpretation of the reference in sub-paragraph (3) to a beneficial interest under a trust.

Significant holdings in undertakings other than subsidiary undertakings

7.—(1) The information required by paragraphs 8 and 9 shall be given where at the end of the financial year the company has a significant holding in an undertaking which is not a subsidiary undertaking of the company.

(2) A holding is significant for this purpose if—
  (*a*) it amounts to 10 per cent. or more of the nominal value of any class of shares in the undertaking, or
  (*b*) the amount of the holding (as stated or included in the company's accounts) exceeds one-tenth of the amount (as so stated) of the company's assets.

8.—(1) The name of the undertaking shall be stated.
(2) There shall be stated—
  (*a*) if the undertaking is incorporated outside Great Britain, the country in which it is incorporated;
  (*b*) if it is incorporated in Great Britain, whether it is registered in England and Wales or in Scotland;
  (*c*) if it is unincorporated, the address of its principal place of business.
(3) There shall also be stated—
  (*a*) the identity of each class of shares in the undertaking held by the company, and
  (*b*) the proportion of the nominal value of the shares of that class represented by those shares.

9.—(1) Where the company has a significant holding in an undertaking amounting to 20 per cent. or more of the nominal value of the shares in the undertaking, there shall also be stated—
  (*a*) the aggregate amount of the capital and reserves of the undertaking as at the end of its relevant financial year, and
  (*b*) its profit or loss for that year.
(2) That information need not be given if—
  (*a*) the company is exempt by virtue of section 228 from the requirement to prepare group accounts (parent company included in accounts of larger group), and
  (*b*) the investment of the company in all undertakings in which it has such a holding as is mentioned in sub-paragraph (1) is shown, in aggregate, in the notes to the accounts by way of the equity method of valuation.
(3) That information need not be given in respect of an undertaking if—
  (*a*) the undertaking is not required by any provision of this Act to deliver a copy of its balance sheet for its relevant financial year and does not otherwise publish that balance sheet in Great Britain or elsewhere, and
  (*b*) the company's holding is less than 50 per cent. of the nominal value of the shares in the undertaking.
(4) Information otherwise reuqired by this paragraph need not be given if it is not material.
(5) For the purposes of this paragraph the "relevant financial year" of an undertaking is—
  (*a*) if its financial year ends with that of the company, that year, and
  (*b*) if not, its financial year ending last before the end of the company's financial year.

Arrangements attracting merger relief

10.—(1) This paragraph applies to arrangements attracting merger relief, that is, where a company allots shares in consideration for the issue, transfer or cancellation of shares in another body corporate ("the other company") in circumstances such that section 130 of this Act (share premium account) does not, by virtue of section 131(2) (merger relief), apply to the premiums on the shares.
(2) If the company makes such an arrangement during the financial year, the following information shall be given—
  (*a*) the name of the other company,
  (*b*) the number, nominal value and class of shares allotted,
  (*c*) the number, nominal value and class of shares in the other company issued, transferred or cancelled, and
  (*d*) particulars of the accounting treatment adopted in the company's accounts in respect of the issue, transfer or cancellation.

(3) Where the company made such an arrangement during the financial year, or during either of the two preceding financial years, and there is included in the company's profit and loss account—

    (*a*) any profit or loss realised during the financial year by the company on the disposal of—

        (i) any shares in the other company, or

        (ii) any assets which were fixed assets of the other company or any of its subsidiary undertakings at the time of the arrangement, or

    (*b*) any part of any profit or loss realised during the financial year by the company on the disposal of any shares (other than shares in the other company) which was attributable to the fact that there were at the time of the disposal amongst the assets of the company which issued the shares, or any of its subsdidiary undertakings, such shares or assets as are described in paragraph (*a*) above,

then, the net amount of that profit or loss or, as the case may be, the part so attributable shall be shown, together with an explanation of the transactions to which the information relates.

(4) For the purposes of this paragraph the time of the arrangement shall be taken to be—

    (*a*) where as a result of the arrangement the other company becomes a subsidiary undertaking of the company, the date on which it does so or, if the arrangement in question becomes binding only on the fulfilment of a condition, the date on which that condition is fulfilled;

    (*b*) if the other company is already a subsidiary undertaking of the company, the date on which the shares are allotted or, if they are allotted on different days, the first day.

Parent undertaking drawing up accounts for larger group

11.—(1) Where the company is a subsidiary undertaking, the following information shall be given with respect to the parent undertaking of—

    (*a*) the largest group of undertakings for which group accounts are drawn up and of which the company is a member, and

    (*b*) the smallest such group of undertakings.

(2) The name of the parent undertaking shall be stated.

(3) There shall be stated—

    (*a*) if the undertaking is incorporated outside Great Britain, the country in which it is incorporated;

    (*b*) if it is incorporated in Great Britain, whether it is registered in England and Wales or in Scotland;

    (*c*) if it is unincorporated, the address of its principal place of business.

(4) If copies of the group accounts referred to in sub-paragraph (1) are available to the public, there shall also be stated the addresses from which copies of the accounts can be obtained.

Identification of ultimate parent company

12.—(1) Where the company is a subsidiary undertaking, the following information shall be given with respect to the compahy (if any) regarded by the directors as being the company's ultimate parent company.

(2) The name of that company shall be stated.

(3) If known to the directors, there shall be stated—

    (*a*) if that company is incorporated outside Great Britain, the country in which it is incorporated;

    (*b*) if it is incorporated in Great Britain, whether it is registered in England and Wales or in Scotland.

(4) In this paragraph "company" includes any body corporate.

Constructions of references to shares held by company

13.—(1) References in this Part of this Schedule to shares held by a company shall be construed as follows.

(2) For the purposes of paragraphs 2 to 5 (information about subsidiary undertakings)—

    (*a*) there shall be attributed to the company any shares held by a subsidiary undertaking, or by a person acting on behalf of the company or a subsidiary undertaking; but

    (*b*) there shall be treated as not held by the company any shares held on behalf of a person other than the company or a subsidiary undertaking.

(3) For the purposes of paragraphs 7 to 9 (information about undertakings other than subsidiary undertakings)—

    (*a*) there shall be attributed to the company shares held on its behalf by any person; but

    (*b*) there shall be treated as not held by a company shares held on behalf of a person other than the company.

(4) For the purposes of any of those provisions, shares held by way of security shall be treated as held by the person providing the security—

    (*a*)   where apart from the right to exercise them for the purpose of preserving the value of the security, or of realising it, the rights attached to the shares are exercisable only in accordance with his instructions, and

    (*b*)   where the shares are held in connection with the granting of loans as part of normal business activities and apart from the right to exercise them for the purpose of preserving the value of the security, or of realising it, the rights attached to the shares are exercisable only in his interests.

PART II

COMPANIES REQUIRED TO PREPARE GROUP ACCOUNTS

Introductory

14. In this Part of this Schedule "the group" means the group consisting of the parent company and its subsidiary undertakings.

Subsidiary undertakings

15.—(1) The following information shall be given with respect to the undertakings which are subsidiary undertakings of the parent company at the end of the financial year.

(2) The name of each undertaking shall be stated.

(3) There shall be stated—

    (*a*)   if the undertaking is incorporated outside Great Britain, the country in which it is incorporated;

    (*b*)   if it is incorporated in Great Britain, whether it is registered in England and Wales or in Scotland;

    (*c*)   if it is unincorporated, the address of its principal place of business.

(4) It shall also be stated whether the subsidiary undertaking is included in the consolidation and, if it is not, the reasons for excluding it from consolidation shall be given.

(5) It shall be stated with respect to each subsidiary undertaking by virtue of which of the conditions specified in section 258(2) or (4) it is a subsidiary undertaking of its immediate parent undertaking.

That information need not be given if the relevant condition is that specified in subsection (2)(*a*) of that section (holding of a majority of the voting rights) and the immediate parent undertaking holds the same proportion of the shares in the undertaking as it holds voting rights.

Holdings in subsidiary undertakings

16.—(1) The following information shall be given with respect to the shares of a subsidiary undertaking held—

    (*a*)   by the parent company, and

    (*b*)   by the group;

and the information under paragraphs (*a*) and (*b*) shall (if different) be shown separately.

(2) There shall be stated—

    (*a*)   the identity of each class of shares held, and

    (*b*)   the proportion of the nominal value of the shares of that class represented by those shares.

Financial information about subsidiary undertakings not included in the consolidation

17.—(1) There shall be shown with respect to each subsidiary undertaking not included in the consolidation—

    (*a*)   the aggregate amount of its capital and reserves as at the end of its relevant financial year, and

    (*b*)   its profit or loss for that year.

(2) That information need not be given if the group's investment in the undertaking is included in the accounts by way of the equity method of valuation or if—

    (*a*)   the undertaking is not required by any provision of this Act to deliver a copy of its balance sheet for its relevant financial year and does not otherwise publish that balance sheet in Great Britain or elsewhere, and

    (*b*)   the holding of the group is less than 50 per cent. of the nominal value of the shares in the undertaking.

(3) Information otherwise required by this paragraph need not be given if it is not material.

(4) For the purposes of this paragraph the "relevant financial year" of a subsidiary undertaking is—

    (*a*) if its financial year ends with that of the company, that year, and

    (*b*) if not, its financial year ending last before the end of the company's financial year.

Further information about subsidiary undertakings excluded from consolidation

18.—(1) The following information shall be given with respect to subsidiary undertakings excluded from consolidation.

(2) There shall be disclosed—

    (*a*) any qualifications contained in the auditors' reports on the accounts of the undertaking for financial years ending with or during the financial year of the company, and

    (*b*) any note or saving contained in such accounts to call attention to a matter which, apart from the note or saving, would properly have been referred to in such a qualification,

in so far as the matter which is the subject of the qualification or note is not covered by the consolidated accounts and is material from the point of view of the members of the parent company.

(3) In so far as information required by this paragraph is not obtainable, a statement to that effect shall be given instead.

Financial years of subsidiary undertakings

19. Where the financial year of one or more subsidiary undertakings did not end with that of the company, there shall be stated in relation to each such undertaking—

    (*a*) the reasons why the company's directors consider that its financial year should not end with that of the company, and

    (*b*) the date on which its last financial year ended (last before the end of the company's financial year).

Instead of the dates required by paragraph (*b*) being given for each subsidiary undertaking the earliest and latest of those dates may be given.

Shares and debentures of company held by subsidiary undertakings

20.—(1) The number, description and amount of the shares in and debentures of the company held by or on behalf of its subsidiary undertakings shall be disclosed.

(2) Sub-paragraph (1) does not apply in relation to shares or debentures in the case of which the subsidiary undertaking is concerned as personal representative or, subject as follows, as trustee.

(3) The exception for shares or debentures in relation to which the subsidiary undertaking is concerned as trustee does not apply if the company or any of its subsidiary undertakings is beneficially interested under the trust, otherwise than by way of security only for the purposes of a transaction entered into by it in the ordinary course of a business which includes the lending of money.

(4) Schedule 2 to this Act has effect for the interpretation of the reference in sub-paragraph (3) to a beneficial interest under a trust.

Joint ventures

21.—(1) The following information shall be given where an undertaking is dealt with in the consolidated accounts by the method of proportional consolidation in accordance with paragraph 19 of Schedule 4A (joint ventures)—

    (*a*) the name of the undertaking;

    (*b*) the address of the principal place of business of the undertaking;

    (*c*) the factors on which joint management of the undertaking is based; and

    (*d*) the proportion of the capital of the undertaking held by undertakings included in the consolidation.

(2) Where the financial year of the undertaking did not end with that of the company, there shall be stated the date on which a financial year of the undertaking last ended before that date.

Associated undertakings

22.—(1) The following information shall be given where an undertaking included in the consolidation has an interest in an associated undertaking.

(2) The name of the associated undertaking shall be stated.

(3) There shall be stated—

(a) if the undertaking is incorporated outside Great Britain, the country in which it is incorporated;

(b) if it is incorporated in Great Britain, whether it is registered in England and Wales or in Scotland;

(c) if it is unincorporated, the address of its principal place of business.

(4) The following information shall be given with respect to the shares of the undertaking held—

(a) by the parent company, and

(b) by the group;

and the information under paragraphs (a) and (b) shall be shown separately.

(5) There shall be stated—

(a) the identity of each class of shares held, and

(b) the proportion of the nominal value of the shares of that class represented by those shares.

(6) In this paragraph "associated undertaking" has the meaning given by paragraph 20 of Schedule 4A; and the information required by this paragraph shall be given notwithstanding that paragraph 22(3) of that Schedule (materiality) applies in relation to the accounts themselves.

Other significant holdings of parent company or group

23.—(1) The information required by paragraphs 24 and 25 shall be given where at the end of the financial year the parent company has a significant holding in an undertaking which is not one of its subsidiary undertakings and does not fall within paragraph 21 (joint ventures) or paragraph 22 (associated undertakings).

(2) A holding is significant for this purpose if—

(a) it amounts to 10 per cent. or more of the nominal value of any class of shares in the undertaking, or

(b) the amount of the holding (as stated or included in the company's individual accounts) exceeds one-tenth of the amount of its assets (as so stated).

24.—(1) The name of the undertaking shall be stated.

(2) There shall be stated—

(a) if the undertaking is incorporated outside Great Britain, the country in which it is incorporated;

(b) if it is incorporated in Great Britain, whether it is registered in England and Wales or in Scotland;

(c) if it is unincorporated, the address of its principal place of business.

(3) The following information shall be given with respect to the shares of the undertaking held by the parent company.

(4) There shall be stated—

(a) the identity of each class of shares held, and

(b) the proportion of the nominal value of the shares of that class represented by those shares.

25.—(1) Where the company has a significant holding in an undertaking amounting to 20 per cent. or more of the nominal value of the shares in the undertaking, there shall also be stated—

(a) the aggregate amount of the capital and reserves of the undertaking as at the end of its relevant financial year, and

(b) its profit or loss for that year.

(2) That information need not be given in respect of an undertaking if—

(a) the undertaking is not required by any provision of this Act to deliver a copy of its balance sheet for its relevant financial year and does not otherwise publish that balance sheet in Great Britain or elsewhere, and

(b) the company's holding is less than 50 per cent. of the nominal value of the shares in the undertaking.

(3) Information otherwise required by this paragraph need not be given if it is not material.

(4) For the purposes of this paragraph the "relevant financial year" of an undertaking is—

(a) if its financial year ends with that of the company, that year, and

(b) if not, its financial year ending last before the end of the company's financial year.

26.—(1) The information required by paragraphs 27 and 28 shall be given where at the end of the financial year the group has a significant holding in an undertaking which is not a subsidiary undertaking of the parent company and does not fall within paragraph 21 (joint ventures) or paragraph 22 (associated undertakings).

(2) A holding is significant for this purpose if—
- (*a*) it amounts to 10 per cent. or more of the nominal value of any class of shares in the undertaking, or
- (*b*) the amount of the holding (as stated or included in the group accounts) exceeds one-tenth of the amount of the group's assets (as so stated).

27.—(1) The name of the undertaking shall be stated.
(2) There shall be stated—
- (*a*) if the undertaking is incorporated outside Great Britain, the country in which it is incorporated;
- (*b*) if it is incorporated in Great Britain, whether it is registered in England and Wales or in Scotland;
- (*c*) if it is unincorporated, the address of its principal place of business.

(3) The following information shall be given with respect to the shares of the undertaking held by the group.
(4) There shall be stated—
- (*a*) the identity of each class of shares held, and
- (*b*) the proportion of the nominal value of the shares of that class represented by those shares.

28.—(1) Where the holding of the group amounts to 20 per cent. or more of the nominal value of the shares in the undertaking, there shall also be stated—
- (*a*) the aggregate amount of the capital and reserves of the undertaking as at the end of its relevant financial year, and
- (*b*) its profit or loss for that year.

(2) That information need not be given if—
- (*a*) the undertaking is not required by any provision of this Act to deliver a copy of its balance sheet for its relevant financial year and does not otherwise publish that balance sheet in Great Britain or elsewhere, and
- (*b*) the holding of the group is less than 50 per cent. of the nominal value of the shares in the undertaking.

(3) Information otherwise required by this paragraph need not be given if it is not material.
(4) For the purposes of this paragraph the "relevant financial year" of an outside undertaking is—
- (*a*) if its financial year ends with that of the parent company, that year, and
- (*b*) if not, its financial year ending last before the end of the parent company's financial year.

Arrangements attracting merger relief

29.—(1) This paragraph applies to arrangements attracting merger relief, that is, where a company allots shares in consideration for the issue, transfer or cancellation of shares in another body corporate ("the other company") in circumstances such that section 130 of this Act (share premium account) does not, by virtue of section 131(2) (merger relief), apply to the premiums on the shares.

(2) If the parent company made such an arrangement during the financial year, the following information shall be given—
- (*a*) the name of the other company,
- (*b*) the number, nominal value and class of shares allotted,
- (*c*) the number, nominal value and class of shares in the other company issued, transferred or cancelled, and
- (*d*) particulars of the accounting treatment adopted in the parent company's individual and group accounts in respect of the issue, transfer or cancellation, and
- (*e*) particulars of the extent to which and manner in which the profit or loss for the financial year shown in the group accounts is affected by any profit or loss of the other company, or any of its subsidiary undertakings, which arose before the time of the arrangement.

(3) Where the parent company made such an arrangement during the financial year, or during either of the two preceding financial years, and there is included in the consolidated profit and loss account—
- (*a*) any profit or loss realised during the financial year on the disposal of—
  - (i) any shares in the other company, or
  - (ii) any assets which were fixed assets of the other company or any of its subsidiary undertakings at the time of the arrangement, or
- (*b*) any part of any profit or loss realised during the financial year on the disposal of any shares (other than shares in the other company) which was attributable to the fact

that there were at the time of the disposal amongst the assets of the company which issued the shares, or any of its subsidiary undertakings, such shares or assets as are described in paragraph (*a*) above,
then, the net amount of that profit or loss or, as the case may be, the part so attributable shall be shown, together with an explanation of the transactions to which the information relates.

(4) For the purposes of this paragraph the time of the arrangement shall be taken to be—

(*a*) where as a result of the arrangement the other company becomes a subsidiary undertaking of the company in question, the date on which it does so or, if the arrangement in question becomes binding only on the fulfilment of a condition, the date on which that condition is fulfilled;

(*b*) if the other company is already a subsidiary undertaking of that company, the date on which the shares are allotted or, if they are allotted on different days, the first day.

Parent undertaking drawing up accounts for larger group

30.—(1) Where the parent company is itself a subsidiary undertaking, the following information shall be given with respect to that parent undertaking of the company which heads—

(*a*) the largest group of undertakings for which group accounts are drawn up and of which that company is a member, and

(*b*) the smallest such group of undertakings.

(2) The name of the parent undertaking shall be stated.

(3) There shall be stated—

(*a*) if the undertaking is incorporated outside Great Britain, the country in which it is incorporated;

(*b*) if it is incorporated in Great Britain, whether it is registered in England and Wales or in Scotland;

(*c*) if it is unincorporated, the address of its principal place of business.

(4) If copies of the group accounts referred to in sub-paragraph (1) are available to the public, there shall also be stated the addresses from which copies of the accounts can be obtained.

Identification of ultimate parent company

31.—(1) Where the parent company is itself a subsidiary undertaking, the following information shall be given with respect to the company (if any) regarded by the directors as being that company's ultimate parent company.

(2) The name of that company shall be stated.

(3) If known to the directors, there shall be stated—

(*a*) if that company is incorporated outside Great Britain, the country in which it is incorporated;

(*b*) if it is incorporated in Great Britain, whether it is registered in England and Wales or in Scotland.

(4) In this paragraph "company" includes any body corporate.

Construction of references to shares held by parent company or group

32.—(1) References in this Part of this Schedule to shares held by the parent company or the group shall be construed as follows.

(2) For the purposes of paragraphs 16, 22(4) and (5) and 23 to 25 (information about holdings in subsidiary and other undertakings)—

(*a*) there shall be attributed to the parent company shares held on its behalf by any person; but

(*b*) there shall be treated as not held by the parent company shares held on behalf of a person other than the company.

(3) References to shares held by the group are to any shares held by or on behalf of the parent company or any of its subsidiary undertakings; but there shall be treated as not held by the group any shares held on behalf of a person other than the parent company or any of its subsidiary undertakings.

(4) Shares held by way of security shall be treated as held by the person providing the security—

(*a*) where apart from the right to exercise them for the purpose of preserving the value of the security, or of realising it, the rights attached to the shares are exercisable only in accordance with his instructions, and

(*b*) where the shares are held in connection with the granting of loans as part of normal business activities and apart from the right to exercise them for the purpose of preserving the value of the security, or of realising it, the rights attached to the shares are exercisable only in his interests.

Sections 232, 233, 234 ¹ SCHEDULE 6

DISCLOSURE OF INFORMATION: EMOLUMENTS AND OTHER BENEFITS OF DIRECTORS AND OTHERS

NOTE
¹ As amended by the Companies Act 1989, s. 6(4) and Sched. 4.

---

¹ PART I

NOTE
¹ Inserted by the Companies Act 1989, s. 6(4) and Sched. 4, para. 3.

CHAIRMAN'S AND DIRECTORS' EMOLUMENTS, PENSIONS AND COMPENSATION FOR LOSS OF OFFICE

Aggregate amount of directors' emoluments

1.—(1) The aggregate amount of directors' emoluments shall be shown.

(2) This means the emoluments paid to or receivable by any person in respect of—
  (*a*) his services as a director of the company, or
  (*b*) his services while director of the company—
    (i) as director of any of its subsidiary undertakings, or
    (ii) otherwise in connection with the management of the affairs of the company or any of its subsidiary undertakings.

(3) There shall also be shown, separately, the aggregate amount within sub-paragraph (2)(*a*) and (*b*)(i) and the aggregate amount within sub-paragraph (2)(*b*)(ii).

(4) For the purposes of this paragraph the "emoluments" of a person include—
  (*a*) fees and percentages,
  (*b*) sums paid by way of expenses allowance (so far as those sums are chargeable to United Kingdom income tax),
  (*c*) contributions paid in respect of him under any pension scheme, and
  (*d*) the estimated money value of any other benefits received by him otherwise than in cash,
and emoluments in respect of a person's accepting office as director shall be treated as emoluments in respect of his services as director.

Details of chairman's and directors' emoluments

2. Where the company is a parent company or a subsidiary undertaking, or where the amount shown in compliance with paragraph 1(1) is £60,000 or more, the information required by paragraphs 3 to 6 shall be given with respect to the emoluments of the chairman and directors, and emoluments waived.

3.—(1) The emoluments of the chairman shall be shown.

(2) The "chairman" means the person elected by the directors to be chairman of their meetings, and includes a person who, though not so elected, holds an office (however designated) which in accordance with the company's constitution carries with it functions substantially similar to those discharged by a person so elected.

(3) Where there has been more than one chairman during the year, the emoluments of each shall be stated so far as attributable to the period during which he was chairman.

(4) The emoluments of a person need not be shown if his duties as chairman were wholly or mainly discharged outside the United Kingdom.

4.—(1) The following information shall be given with respect to the emoluments of directors.

(2) There shall be shown the number of directors whose emoluments fell within each of the following bands—

not more than £5,000,
more than £5,000 but not more than £10,000,
more than £10,000 but not more than £15,000,
and so on.

(3) If the emoluments of any of the directors exceeded that of the chairman, there shall be shown the greatest amount of emoluments of any director.

(4) Where more than one person has been chairman during the year, the reference in sub-paragraph (3) to the emoluments of the chairman is to the aggregate of the emoluments of each person who has been chairman, so far as attributable to the period during which he was chairman.

(5) The information required by sub-paragraph (2) need not be given in respect of a director who discharged his duties as such wholly or mainly outside the United Kingdom; and any such director shall be left out of account for the purposes of sub-paragraph (3).

5. In paragraphs 3 and 4 "emoluments" has the same meaning as in paragraph 1, except that it does not include contributions paid in respect of a person under a pension scheme.

Emoluments waived

6.—(1) There shall be shown—
   (a) the number of directors who have waived rights to receive emoluments which, but for the waiver, would have fallen to be included in the amount shown under paragraph 1(1), and
   (b) the aggregate amount of those emoluments.

(2) For the purposes of this paragraph it shall be assumed that a sum not receivable in respect of a period would have been paid at the time at which it was due, and if such a sum was payable only on demand, it shall be deemed to have been due at the time of the waiver.

Pensions of directors and past directors

7.—(1) There shall be shown the aggregate amount of directors' or past directors' pensions.

(2) This amount does not include any pension paid or receivable under a pension scheme if the scheme is such that the contributions under it are substantially adequate for the maintenance of the scheme; but, subject to this, it includes any pension paid or receivable in respect of any such services of a director or past director as are mentioned in paragraph 1(2), whether to or by him or, on his nomination or by virtue of dependence on or other connection with him, to or by any other person.

(3) The amount shown shall distinguish between pensions in respect of services as director, whether of the company or any of its subsidiary undertakings, and other pensions.

(4) References to pensions include benefits otherwise than in cash and in relation to so much of a pension as consists of such a benefit references to its amount are to the estimated money value of the benefit.

The nature of any such benefit shall also be disclosed.

Compensation to directors for loss of office

8.—(1) There shall be shown the aggregate amount of any compensation to directors or past directors in respect of loss of office.

(2) This amount includes compensation received or receivable by a director or past director for—
   (a) loss of office as director of the company, or
   (b) loss, while director of the company or on or in connection with his ceasing to be a director of it, of—
      (i) any other office in connection with the management of the company's affairs, or
      (ii) any office as director or otherwise in connection with the management of the affairs of any subsidiary undertaking of the company;
and shall distinguish between compensation in respect of the office of director, whether of the company or any of its subsidiary undertakings, and compensation in respect of other offices.

(3) References to compensation include benefits otherwise than in cash; and in relation to such compensation references to its amount are to the estimated money value of the benefit.

The nature of any such compensation shall be disclosed.

(4) References to compensation for loss of office include compensation in consideration for, or in connection with, a person's retirement from office.

Sums paid to third parties in respect of directors' services

9.—(1) There shall be shown the aggregate amount of any consideration paid to or receivable by third parties for making available the services of any person—

(*a*) as a director of the company, or

(*b*) while director of the company—

(i) as director of any of its subsidiary undertakings, or

(ii) otherwise in connection with the management of the affairs of the company or any of its subsidiary undertakings.

(2) The reference to consideration includes benefits otherwise than in cash; and in relation to such consideration the reference to its amount is to the estimated money value of the benefit.

The nature of any such consideration shall be disclosed.

(3) The reference to third parties is to persons other than—

(*a*) the director himself or a person connected with him or body corporate controlled by him, and

(*b*) the company or any of its subsidiary undertakings.

Supplementary

10.—(1) The following applies with respect to the amounts to be shown under paragraphs 1, 7, 8 and 9.

(2) The amount in each case includes all relevant sums paid by or receivable from—

(*a*) the company; and

(*b*) the company's subsidiary undertakings; and

(*c*) any other person,

except sums to be accounted for to the company or any of its subsidiary undertakings or, by virtue of sections 314 and 315 of this Act (duty of directors to make disclosure on company takeover; consequence of non-compliance), to past or present members of the company or any of its subsidiaries or any class of those members.

(3) The amount to be shown under paragraph 8 shall distinguish between the sums respectively paid by or receivable from the company, the company's subsidiary undertakings and persons other than the company and its subsidiary undertakings.

(4) References to amounts paid to or receivable by a person include amounts paid to or receivable by a person connected with him or a body corporate controlled by him (but not so as to require an amount to be counted twice).

11.—(1) The amounts to be shown for any financial year under paragraphs 1, 7, 8 and 9 are the sums receivable in respect of that year (whenever paid) or, in the case of sums not receivable in respect of a period, the sums paid during that year.

(2) But where—

(*a*) any sums are not shown in a note to the accounts for the relevant financial year on the ground that the person receiving them is liable to account for them as mentioned in paragraph 10(2), but the liability is thereafter wholly or partly released or is not enforced within a period of 2 years; or

(*b*) any sums paid by way of expenses allowance are charged to United Kingdom income tax after the end of the relevant financial year,

those sums shall, to the extent to which the liability is released or not enforced or they are charged as mentioned above (as the case may be), be shown in a note to the first accounts in which it is practicable to show them and shall be distinguished from the amounts to be shown apart from this provision.

12. Where it is necessary to do so for the purpose of making any distinction required by the preceding paragraphs in an amount to be shown in compliance with this Part of this Schedule, the directors may apportion any payments between the matters in respect of which these have been paid or are receivable in such manner as they think appropriate.

Interpretation

13.—(1) The following applies for the interpretation of this Part of this Schedule.

(2) A reference to a subsidiary undertaking of the company—

(*a*) in relation to a person who is or was, while a director of the company, a director also, by virtue of the company's nomination (direct or indirect) of any other undertaking, includes (subject to the following sub-paragraph) that undertaking, whether or not it is or was in fact a subsidiary undertaking of the company, and

(*b*) for the purposes of paragraphs 1 to 7 (including any provision of this Part of this Schedule referring to paragraph 1) is to an undertaking which is a subsidiary undertaking at the time the services were rendered, and for the purposes of paragraph 8 to a subsidiary undertaking immediately before the loss of office as director.

(3) The following definitions apply—

(a) "pension" includes any superannuation allowance, superannuation gratuity or similar payment,

(b) "pension scheme" means a scheme for the provision of pensions in respect of services as director or otherwise which is maintained in whole or in part by means of contributions, and

(c) "contribution", in relation to a pension scheme, means any payment (including an insurance premium) paid for the purposes of the scheme by or in respect of persons rendering services in respect of which pensions will or may become payable under the scheme except that it does not include any payment in respect of two or more persons if the amount paid in respect of each of them is not ascertainable.

(4) References in this Part of this Scheme to a person being "connected" with a director, and to a director "controlling" a body corporate, shall be construed in accordance with section 346.

Supplementary

14. This Part of this Schedule requires information to be given only so far as it is contained in the company's books and papers or the company has the right to obtain it from the persons concerned.

Part II

Loans, Quasi-loans and Other Dealings in Favour of Directors

15. The group accounts of a holding company, or if it is not required to prepare group accounts its individual accounts, shall contain the particulars required by this Schedule of—

(a) any transaction or arrangement of a kind described in section 330 entered into by the company or by a subsidiary of the company for a person who at any time during the financial year was a director of the company or its holding company, or was connected with such a director;

(b) an agreement by the company or by a subsidiary of the company to enter into any such transaction or arrangement for a person who was at any time during the financial year a director of the company or its holding company, or was connected with such a director; and

(c) any other transaction or arrangement with the company or a subsidiary of it in which a person who at any time during the financial year was a director of the company or its holding company had, directly or indirectly, a material interest.

16. The accounts prepared by a company other than a holding company shall contain the particulars required by this Schedule of—

(a) any transaction or arrangement of a kind described in section 330 entered into by the company for a person who at any time during the financial year was a director of it or of its holding company or was connected with such a director;

(b) an agreement by the company to enter into any such transaction or arrangement for a person who at any time during the financial year was a director of the company or its holding company or was connected with such a director; and

(c) any other transaction or arrangement with the company in which a person who at any time during the financial year was a director of the company or of its holding company had, directly or indirectly, a material interest.

17.—(1) For purposes of paragraphs 15(c) and 16(c), a transaction or arrangement between a company and a director of it or of its holding company, or a person connected with such a director, is to be treated (if it would not otherwise be so) as a transaction, arrangement or agreement in which that director is interested.

(2) An interest in such a transaction or arrangement is not "material" for purposes of those sub-paragraphs if in the board's opinion it is not so; but this is without prejudice to the question whether or not such an interest is material in a case where the board have not considered the matter.

"The board" here means the directors of the company preparing the accounts, or a majority of those directors, but excluding in either case the director whose interest it is.

18. Paragraphs 15 and 16 do not apply in relation to the following transactions, arrangements and agreements—

(*a*) a transaction, arrangement or agreement between one company and another in which a director of the former or of its subsidiary or holding company is interested only by virtue of his being a director of the latter;

(*b*) a contract of service between a company and one of its directors or a director of its holding company, or between a director of a company and any of that company's subsidiaries;

(*c*) a transaction, arrangement or agreement which was not entered into during the financial year and which did not subsist at any time during that year.

19. Paragraphs 15 and 16 apply whether or not—

(*a*) the transaction or arrangement was prohibited by section 330;

(*b*) the person for whom it was made was a director of the company or was connected with a director of it at the time it was made;

(*c*) in the case of a transaction or arrangement made by a company which at any time during a financial year is a subsidiary of another company, it was a subsidiary of that other company at the time the transaction or arrangement was made.

20. Neither paragraph 15(*c*) nor paragraph 16(*c*) applies in relation to any transaction or arrangement if—

(*a*) each party to the transaction or arrangement which is a member of the same group of companies (meaning a holding company and its subsidiaries) as the company entered into the transaction or arrangement in the ordinary course of business, and

(*b*) the terms of the transaction or arrangement are not less favourable to any such party than it would be reasonable to expect if the interest mentioned in that sub-paragraph had not been an interest of a person who was a director of the company or of its holding company.

21. Neither paragraph 15(*c*) nor paragraph 16(*c*) applies in relation to any transaction or arrangement if—

(*a*) the company is a member of a group of companies (meaning a holding company and its subsidiaries), and

(*b*) either the company is a wholly-owned subsidiary or no body corporate (other than the company or a subsidiary of the company) which is a member of the group of companies which includes the company's ultimate holding company was a party to the transaction or arrangement, and

(*c*) the director in question was at some time during the relevant period associated with the company, and

(*d*) the material interest of the director in question in the transaction or arrangement would not have arisen if he had not been associated with the company at any time during the relevant period.

The particulars required by this Part

22.—(1) Subject to the next paragraph, the particulars required by this Part are those of the principal terms of the transaction, arrangement or agreement.

(2) Without prejudice to the generality of sub-paragraph (1), the following particulars are required—

(*a*) a statement of the fact either that the transaction, arrangement or agreement was made or subsisted (as the case may be) during the financial year;

(*b*) the name of the person for whom it was made and, where that person is or was connected with a director of the company or of its holding company, the name of that director;

(*c*) in a case where paragraph 15(*c*) or 16(*c*) applies, the name of the director with the material interest and the nature of that interest;

(*d*) in the case of a loan or an agreement for a loan or an arrangement within section 330(6) or (7) of this Act relating to a loan—

    (i) the amount of the liability of the person to whom the loan was or was agreed to be made, in respect of principal and interest, at the beginning and at the end of the financial year;

    (ii) the maximum amount of that liability during that year;

    (iii) the amount of any interest which, having fallen due, has not been paid; and

    (iv) the amount of any provision (within the meaning of Schedule 4 to this Act) made in respect of any failure or anticipated failure by the borrower to repay the whole or part of the loan or to pay the whole or part of any interest on it;

(*e*) in the case of a guarantee or security or an arrangement within section 330(6) relating to a guarantee or security—

      (i) the amount for which the company (or its subsidiary) was liable under the guarantee or in respect of the security both at the beginning and at the end of the financial year;

     (ii) the maximum amount for which the company (or its subsidiary) may become so liable; and

    (iii) any amount paid and any liability incurred by the company (or its subsidiary) for the purpose of fulfilling the guarantee or discharging the security (including any loss incurred by reason of the enforcement of the guarantee or security); and

    (*f*) in the case of any transaction, arrangement or agreement other than those mentioned in sub-paragraphs (*d*) and (*e*), the value of the transaction or arrangement or (as the case may be) the value of the transaction or arrangement to which the agreement relates.

23. In paragraph 22(2) above, sub-paragraphs (*c*) to (*f*) do not apply in the case of a loan or quasi-loan made or agreed to be made by a company to or for a body corporate which is either—

    (*a*) a body corporate of which that company is a wholly-owned subsidiary, or

    (*b*) a wholly-owned subsidiary of a body corporate of which that company is a wholly-owned subsidiary, or

    (*c*) a wholly-owned subsidiary of that company,

if particulars of that loan, quasi-loan or agreement for it would not have been required to be included in that company's annual accounts if the first-mentioned body corporate had not been associated with a director of that company at any time during the relevant period.

Excluded transactions

24.—(1) In relation to a company's accounts for a financial year, compliance with this Part is not required in the case of transactions of a kind mentioned in the following sub-paragraph which are made by the company or a subsidiary of it for a person who at any time during that financial year was a director of the company or of its holding company, or was connected with such a director, if the aggregate of the values of each transaction, arrangement or agreement so made for that director or any person connected with him, less the amount (if any) by which the liabilities of the person for whom the transaction or arrangement was made has been reduced, did not at any time during the financial year exceed £5,000.

(2) The transactions in question are—

    (*a*) credit transactions,

    (*b*) guarantees provided or securities entered into in connection with credit transactions,

    (*c*) arrangements within subsection (6) or (7) of section 330 relating to credit transactions,

    (*d*) agreements to enter into credit transactions.

25. In relation to a company's accounts for a financial year, compliance with this Part is not required by virtue of paragraph 15(*c*) or 16(*c*) in the case of any transaction or arrangement with a company or any of its subsidiaries in which a director of the company or its holding company had, directly or indirectly, a material interest if—

    (*a*) the value of each transaction or arrangement within paragraph 15(*c*) or 16(*c*) (as the case may be) in which that director had (directly or indirectly) a material interest and which was made after the commencement of the financial year with the company or any of its subsidiaries, and

    (*b*) the value of each such transaction or arrangement which was made before the commencement of the financial year less the amount (if any) by which the liabilities of the person for whom the transaction or arrangement was made have been reduced,

did not at any time during the financial year exceed in the aggregate £1,000 or, if more, did not exceed £5,000 or 1 per cent. of the value of the net assets of the company preparing the accounts in question as at the end of the financial year, whichever is the less.

For this purpose a company's net assets are the aggregate of its assets, less the aggregate of its liabilities ("liabilities" to include any provision for liabilities or charges within paragraph 89 of Schedule 4).

26. Section 345 of this Act (power of Secretary of State to alter sums by statutory instrument subject to negative resolution in Parliament) applies as if the money sums specified in paragraph 24 or 25 above were specified in Part X.

Interpretation

27.—(1) The following provisions of this Act apply for purposes of this Part of this Schedule—

[1] (*a*) section 331(2) and (7), as regards the meaning of "guarantee" and "credit transaction";

   (*b*) section 331(9), as to the interpretation of references to a transaction or arrangement being made "for" a person;

   (*c*) section 340, in assigning values to transactions and arrangements, and

   (*d*) section 346, as to the interpretation of references to a person being "connected with" a director of a company.

(2) In this Part of this Schedule "director" includes a shadow director.

NOTE

[1] As amended by the Banking Act 1987, Sched. 7, Pt. I.

Part III

Other Transactions, Arrangements and Agreements

28. This Part of this Schedule applies in relation to the following classes of transactions, arrangements and agreements—

   (*a*) loans, guarantees and securities relating to loans, arrangements of a kind described in subsection (6) or (7) of section 330 of this Act relating to loans and agreements to enter into any of the foregoing transactions and arrangements;

   (*b*) quasi-loans, guarantees and securities relating to quasi-loans, arrangements of a kind described in either of those subsections relating to quasi-loans and agreements to enter into any of the foregoing transactions and arrangements;

   (*c*) credit transactions, guarantees and securities relating to credit transactions, arrangements of a kind described in either of those subsections relating to credit transactions and agreements to enter into any of the foregoing transactions and arrangements.

29.—(1) To comply with this Part of this Schedule, the accounts must contain a statement, in relation to transactions, arrangements and agreements made by the company or a subsidiary of it for persons who at any time during the financial year were officers of the company (but not directors or shadow directors), of—

   (*a*) the aggregate amounts outstanding at the end of the financial year under transactions, arrangements and agreements within sub-paragraphs (*a*), (*b*) and (*c*) respectively of paragraph 28 above, and

   (*b*) the numbers of officers for whom the transactions, arrangements and agreements falling within each of those sub-paragraphs were made.

(2) This paragraph does not apply to transactions, arrangements and agreements made by the company or any of its subsidiaries for an officer of the company if the aggregate amount outstanding at the end of the financial year under the transactions, arrangements and agreements so made for that officer does not exceed £2,500.

(3) Section 345 of this Act (power of Secretary of State to alter money sums by statutory instrument subject to negative resolution in Parliament) applies as if the money sum specified above in this paragraph were specified in Part X.

30. The following provisions of this Act apply for purposes of this Part—

[1] (*a*) section 331(2), (3) and (7), as regards the meaning of "guarantee", "quasi-loan" and "credit transaction", and

   (*b*) section 331(9), as to the interpretation of references to a transaction or arrangement being made "for" a person;
   and "amount outstanding" means the amount of the outstanding liabilities of the person for whom the transaction, arrangement or agreement was made or, in the case of a guarantee or security, the amount guaranteed or secured.

NOTE

[1] As amended by the Banking Act 1987 Sched. 17, Pt. I.

      [1] SCHEDULE 7

MATTERS TO BE DEALT WITH IN DIRECTORS' REPORT

NOTE

[1] As amended by the Companies Act 1989, s. 8(2) and Sched. 5.

PART I

MATTERS OF A GENERAL NATURE

Asset values

1.—(1) If significant changes in the fixed assets of the company or of any of its subsidiary undertakings have occurred in the financial year, the report shall contain particulars of the changes.

(2) If, in the case of such of those assets as consist in interests in land, their market value (as at the end of the financial year) differs substantially from the amount at which they are included in the balance sheet, and the difference is, in the directors' opinion, of such significance as to require that the attention of members of the company or of holders of its debentures should be drawn to it, the report shall indicate the difference with such degree of precision as is practicable.

Directors' interests

2.—(1) The information required by paragraphs 2A and 2B shall be given in the directors' report, or by way of notes to the company's annual accounts, with respect to each person who at the end of the financial year was a director of the company.

(2) In those paragraphs—
    (a) "the register" means the register of directors' interests kept by the company under section 325; and
    (b) references to a body corporate being in the same group as the company are to its being a subsidiary or holding company, or another subsidiary of a holding company, of the company.

2A.—(1) It shall be stated with respect to each director whether, according to the register, he was at the end of the financial year interested in shares in or debentures of the company or any other body corporate in the same group.

(2) If he was so interested, there shall be stated the number of shares in and amount of debentures of each body (specifying it) in which, according to the register, he was then interested.

(3) If a director was interested at the end of the financial year in shares in or debentures of the company or any other body corporate in the same group—
    (a) it shall also be stated whether, according to the register, he was at the beginning of the financial year (or, if he was not then a director, when he became one) interested in shares in or debentures of the company or any other body corporate in the same group, and
    (b) if he was so interested, there shall be stated the number of shares in and amount of debentures of each body (specifying it) in which, according to the register, he was then interested.

(4) In this paragraph references to an interest in shares or debentures have the same meaning as in section 324; and references to the interest of a director include any interest falling to be treated as his for the purposes of that section.

(5) The reference above to the time when a person became a director is, in the case of a person who became a director on more than one occasion, to the time when he first became a director.

2B.—(1) It shall be stated with respect to each director whether, according to the register, any right to subscribe for shares in or debentures of the company or another body corporate in the same group was during the financial year granted to, or exercised by, the director or a member of his immediate family.

(2) If any such right was granted to, or exercised by, any such person during the financial year, there shall be stated the number of shares in and amount of debentures of each body (specifying it) in respect of which, according to the register, the right was granted or exercised.

(3) A director's "immediate family" means his or her spouse and infant children; and for this purpose "children" includes step-children, and "infant", in relation to Scotland, means pupil or minor.

(4) The reference above to a member of the director's immediate family does not include a person who is himself or herself a director of the company.

Political and charitable gifts

3.—(1) The following applies if the company (not being the wholly-owned subsidiary of a company incorporated in Great Britain) has in the financial year given money for political purposes or charitable purposes or both.

(2) If the money given exceeded £200 in amount, there shall be contained in the directors' report for the year—

    (*a*) in the case of each of the purposes for which money has been given, a statement of the amount of money given for that purpose, and

    (*b*) in the case of political purposes for which money has been given, the following particulars (so far as applicable)—

        (i) the name of each person to whom money has been given for those purposes exceeding £200 in amount and the amount of money given,

        (ii) if money exceeding £200 in amount has been given by way of donation or subscription to a political party, the identity of the party and the amount of money given.

4.—(1) Paragraph 3 does not apply to a company which, at the end of the financial year, has subsidiaries which have, in that year, given money as mentioned above, but is not itself the wholly-owned subsidiary of a company incorporated in Great Britain.

(2) But in such a case there shall (if the amount of money so given in that year by the company and the subsidiaries between them exceeds £200) be contained in the directors' report for the year—

    (*a*) in the case of each of the purposes for which money has been given by the company and the subsidiaries between them, a statement of the amount of money given for that purpose, and

    (*b*) in the case of political purposes for which money has been given, the like particulars (so far as applicable) as are required by paragraph 3.

5.—(1) The following applies for the interpretation of paragraphs 3 and 4.

(2) A company is to be treated as giving money for political purposes, if directly or indirectly—

    (*a*) it gives a donation or subscription to a political party of the United Kingdom or any part of it; or

    (*b*) it gives a donation or subscription to a person who, to the company's knowledge, is carrying on, or proposing to carry on, any activities which can, at the time at which the donation or subscription was given, reasonably be regarded as likely to affect public support for such a political party as is mentioned above.

(3) Money given for charitable purposes to a person who, when it was given, was ordinarily resident outside the United Kingdom is to be left out of account.

(4) "Charitable purposes" means purposes which are exclusively charitable; and, as respects Scotland, "charitable" is to be construed as if it were contained in the Income Tax Acts.

Insurance effected for officers or auditors

[1] 5A. Where in the financial year the company has purchased or maintained any such insurance as is mentioned in section 310(3)(*a*) (insurance of officers or auditors against liabilities in relation to the company), that fact shall be stated in the report.

NOTE
[1] Inserted by the Companies Act 1989, s. 137(2).

Miscellaneous

6. The directors' report shall contain—
 (*a*) particulars of any important events affecting the company or any of its subsidiary undertakings which have occurred since the end of the financial year,
 (*b*) an indication of likely future developments in the business of the company and of its subsidiary undertakings, and
 (*c*) an indication of the activities (if any) of the company and its subsidiary undertakings in the field of research and development.

PART II

DISCLOSURE REQUIRED BY COMPANY ACQUIRING ITS OWN SHARES, ETC.

7. This Part of this Schedule applies where shares in a company—
 (*a*) are purchased by the company or are acquired by it by forfeiture or surrender in lieu of forfeiture, or in pursuance of section 143(3) of this Act (acquisition of own shares by company limited by shares), or
 (*b*) are acquired by another person in circumstances where paragraph (*c*) or (*d*) of section 146(1) applies (acquisition by company's nominee, or by another with company financial assistance, the company having a beneficial interest), or
 (*c*) are made subject to a lien or other charge taken (whether expressly or otherwise) by the company and permitted by section 150(2) or (4), or section 6(3) of the Consequential Provisions Act (exceptions from general rule against a company having a lien or charge on its own shares).

8. The directors' report with respect to a financial year shall state—
 (*a*) the number and nominal value of the shares so purchased, the aggregate amount of the consideration paid by the company for such shares and the reasons for their purchase;
 (*b*) the number and nominal value of the shares so acquired by the company, acquired by another person in such circumstances and so charged respectively during the financial year;
 (*c*) the maximum number and nominal value of shares which, having been so acquired by the company, acquired by another person in such circumstances or so charged (whether or not during that year) are held at any time by the company or that other person during that year;
 (*d*) the number and nominal value of the shares so acquired by the company, acquired by another person in such circumstances or so charged (whether or not during that year) which are disposed of by the company or that other person or cancelled by the company during that year;
 (*e*) where the number and nominal value of the shares of any particular description are stated in pursuance of any of the preceding sub-paragraphs, the percentage of the called-up share capital which shares of that description represent;
 (*f*) where any of the shares have been so charged the amount of the charge in each case; and
 (*g*) where any of the shares have been disposed of by the company or the person who acquired them in such circumstances for money or money's worth the amount or value of the consideration in each case.

PART III

DISCLOSURE CONCERNING EMPLOYMENT, ETC. OF DISABLED PERSONS

9.—(1) This Part of this Schedule applies to the directors' report where the average number of persons employed by the company in each week during the financial year exceeded 250.

(2) That average number is the quotient derived by dividing, by the number of weeks in the financial year, the number derived by ascertaining, in relation to each of those weeks, the number of persons who, under contracts of service, were employed in the week (whether throughout it or not) by the company, and adding up the numbers ascertained.

(3) The directors' report shall in that case contain a statement describing such policy as the company has applied during the financial year—
 (*a*) for giving full and fair consideration to applications for employment by the company made by disabled persons, having regard to their particular aptitudes and abilities,

(*b*) for continuing the employment of, and for arranging appropriate training for, employees of the company who have become disabled persons during the period when they were employed by the company, and

(*c*) otherwise for the training, career development and promotion of disabled persons employed by the company.

(4) In this Part—

(*a*) "employment" means employment other than employment to work wholly or mainly outside the United Kingdom, and "employed" and "employee" shall be construed accordingly; and

(*b*) "disabled person" means the same as in the Disabled Persons (Employment) Act 1944.

Part IV

Health, Safety and Welfare at Work of Company's Employees

10.—(1) In the case of companies of such classes as may be prescribed by regulations made by the Secretary of State, the directors' report shall contain such information as may be so prescribed about the arrangements in force in the financial year for securing the health, safety and welfare at work of employees of the company and its subsidiaries, and for protecting other persons against risks to health or safety arising out of or in connection with the activities at work of those employees.

(2) Regulations under this Part may—

(*a*) make different provision in relation to companies of different classes,

(*b*) enable any requirements of the regulations to be dispensed with or modified in particular cases by any specified person or by any person authorised in that behalf by a specified authority,

(*c*) contain such transitional provisions as the Secretary of State thinks necessary or expedient in connection with any provision made by the regulations.

(3) The power to make regulations under this paragraph is exercisable by statutory instrument subject to annulment in pursuance of a resolution of either House of Parliament.

(4) Any expression used in sub-paragraph (1) above and in Part I of the Health and Safety at Work etc. Act 1974 has the same meaning here as it has in that Part of that Act; section 1(3) of that Act applies for interpreting that sub-paragraph; and in sub-paragraph (2) "specified" means specified in regulations made under that sub-paragraph.

Part V

Employee Involvement

11.—(1) This Part of this Schedule applies to the directors' report where the average number of persons employed by the company in each week during the financial year exceeded 250.

(2) That average number is the quotient derived by dividing by the number of weeks in the financial year the number derived by ascertaining, in relation to each of those weeks, the number of persons who, under contracts of service, were employed in the week (whether throughout it or not) by the company, and adding up the numbers ascertained.

(3) The directors' report shall in that case contain a statement describing the action that has been taken during the financial year to introduce, maintain or develop arrangements aimed at—

(*a*) providing employees systematically with information on matters of concern to them as employees,

(*b*) consulting employees or their representatives on a regular basis so that the views of employees can be taken into account in making decisions which are likely to affect their interests,

(*c*) encouraging the involvement of employees in the company's performance through an employees' share scheme or by some other means,

(*d*) achieving a common awareness on the part of all employees of the financial and economic factors affecting the performance of the company.

(4) In sub-paragraph (3) "employee" does not include a person employed to work wholly or mainly outside the United Kingdom; and for the purposes of sub-paragraph (2) no regard is to be had to such a person.

EXEMPTIONS FOR SMALL AND MEDIUM-SIZED COMPANIES

NOTE
[1] Substituted by the Companies Act 1989, s. 13(3) and Sched. 6.

PART I

SMALL COMPANIES

Balance sheet

1.—(1) The company may deliver a copy of an abbreviated version of the full balance sheet, showing only those items to which a letter or Roman number is assigned in the balance sheet format adopted under Part I of Schedule 4, but in other respects corresponding to the full balance sheet.

(2) If a copy of an abbreviated balance sheet is delivered, there shall be disclosed in it or in a note to the company's accounts delivered—

(a) the aggregate of the amounts required by note (5) of the notes on the balance sheet formats set out in Part I of Schedule 4 to be shown separately for each item included under debtors (amounts falling due after one year), and

(b) the aggregate of the amounts required by note (13) of those notes to be shown separately for each item included under creditors in Format 2 (amounts falling due within one year or after more than one year).

(3) The provisions of section 233 as to the signing of the copy of the balance sheet delivered to the registrar apply to a copy of an abbreviated balance sheet delivered in accordance with this paragraph.

Profit and loss account

2. A copy of the company's profit and loss account need not be delivered.

Disclosure of information in notes to accounts

3.—(1) Of the information required by Part III of Schedule 4 (information to be given in notes to accounts if not given in the accounts themselves) only the information required by the following provisions need be given—

paragraph 36 (accounting policies),

paragraph 38 (share capital),

paragraph 39 (particulars of allotments),

paragraph 42 (fixed assets), so far as it relates to those items to which a letter or Roman number is assigned in the balance sheet format adopted,

paragraph 48(1) and (4) (particulars of debts),

paragraph 58(1) (basis of conversion of foreign currency amounts into sterling),

paragraph 58(2) (corresponding amounts for previous financial year), so far as it relates to amounts stated in a note to the company's accounts by virtue of a requirement of Schedule 4 or under any other provision of this Act.

(2) Of the information required by Schedule 5 to be given in notes to the accounts, the information required by the following provisions need not be given—

paragraph 4 (financial years of subsidiary undertakings),

paragraph 5 (additional information about subsidiary undertakings),

paragraph 6 (shares and debentures of company held by subsidiary undertakings),

paragraph 10 (arrangements attracting merger relief).

(3) Of the information required by Schedule 6 to be given in notes to the accounts, the information required by Part I (directors' and chairman's emoluments, pensions and compensation for loss of office) need not be given.

Directors' report

4. A copy of the directors' report need not be delivered.

PART II

MEDIUM-SIZED COMPANIES

Profit and loss account

5. The company may deliver a profit and loss account in which the following items listed in the profit and loss account formats set out in Part I of Schedule 4 are combined as one item under the heading "gross profit or loss"—

 Items 1, 2, 3 and 6 in Format 1;
 Items 1 to 5 in Format 2;
 Items A.1, B.1 and B.2 in Format 3;
 Items A.1, A.2 and B.1 to B.4 in Format 4.

Disclosure of information in notes to accounts

6. The information required by paragraph 55 of Schedule 4 (particulars of turnover) need not be given.

PART III

SUPPLEMENTARY PROVISIONS

Statement that advantage taken of exemptions

7.—(1) Where the directors of a company take advantage of the exemptions conferred by Part I or Part II of this Schedule, the company's balance sheet shall contain—

 (*a*) a statement that advantage is taken of the exemptions conferred by Part I or, as the case may be, Part II of this Schedule, and

 (*b*) a statement of the grounds on which, in the directors' opinion, the company is entitled to those exemptions.

(2) The statements shall appear in the balance sheet immediately above the signature required by section 233.

Special auditors' report

8.—(1) If the directors of a company propose to take advantage of the exemptions conferred by Part I or II of this Schedule, it is the auditors' duty to provide them with a report stating whether in their opinion the company is entitled to those exemptions and whether the documents to be proposed to be delivered in accordance with this Schedule are properly prepared.

(2) The accounts delivered shall be accompanied by a special report of the auditors stating that in their opinion—

 (*a*) the company is entitled to the exemptions claimed in the directors' statement, and

 (*b*) the accounts to be delivered are properly prepared in accordance with this Schedule.

(3) In such a case a copy of the auditors' report under section 235 need not be delivered separately, but the full text of it shall be reproduced in the special report; and if the report under section 235 is qualified there shall be included in the special report any further material necessary to understand the qualification.

(4) Section 236 (signature of auditors' report) applies to a special report under this paragraph as it applies to a report under section 235.

Dormant companies

9. Paragraphs 7 and 8 above do not apply where the company is exempt by virtue of section 250 (dormant companies) from the obligation to appoint auditors.

Requirements in connection with publication of accounts

10.—(1) Where advantage is taken of the exemptions conferred by Part I or II of this Schedule, section 240 (requirements in connection with publication of accounts) has effect with the following adaptations.

(2) Accounts delivered in accordance with this Schedule and accounts in the form in which they would be required to be delivered apart from this Schedule are both "statutory accounts" for the purposes of that section.

(3) References in that section to the auditors' report under section 235 shall be read, in relation to accounts delivered in accordance with this Schedule, as references to the special report under paragraph 8 above.

[THE NEXT PAGE IS I 401]

Section 258   [1] SCHEDULE 9

SPECIAL PROVISIONS FOR BANKING AND INSURANCE COMPANIES AND GROUPS

NOTE
[1] As amended by the Companies Act 1989, s. 18(3) and Scheds. 7 and 24.

---

1. [Repealed by the Companies Act 1989, Scheds. 7 and 24.]

[1] PART I

NOTE
[1] See the Patents, Designs and Marks Act 1986, Sched. 2, Pt. I, para. 1(2)(*k*).

FORM AND CONTENT OF ACCOUNTS

Balance sheet

2. The authorised share capital, issued share capital, liabilities and assets shall be summarised, with such particulars as are necessary to disclose the general nature of the assets and liabilities, and there shall be specified—
  (*a*) any part of the issued capital that consists of redeemable shares, the earliest and latest dates on which the company has power to redeem those shares, whether those shares must be redeemed in any event or are liable to be redeemed at the option of the company or of the shareholder and whether any (and, if so, what) premium is payable on redemption;
  (*b*) so far as the information is not given in the profit and loss account, any share capital on which interest has been paid out of capital during the financial year, and the rate at which interest has been so paid;
  (*c*) the amount of the share premium account;
  (*d*) particulars of any redeemed debentures which the company has power to re-issue.

3. There shall be stated under separate headings, so far as they are not written off,—
  (*a*) the preliminary expenses;
  (*b*) any expenses incurred in connection with any issue of share capital or debentures;
  (*c*) the amount of the discount allowed on any issue of shares or debentures;
  (*d*) any sums allowed by way of discount in respect of any debentures; and
  (*e*) the amount of the discount allowed on any issue of shares at a discount.

4.—(1) The reserves, provisions, liabilities and assets shall be classified under headings appropriate to the company's business:
Provided that—
  (*a*) where the amount of any class is not material, it may be included under the same heading as some other class; and
  (*b*) where any assets of one class are not separable from assets of another class, those assets may be included under the same heading.
(2) Fixed assets, current assets and assets that are neither fixed nor current shall be separately identified.
(3) The method or methods used to arrive at the amount of the fixed assets under each heading shall be stated.

5.—(1) The method of arriving at the amount of any fixed asset shall, subject to the next following sub-paragraph, be to take the difference between—
  (*a*) its cost or, if it stands in the company's books at a valuation, the amount of the valuation; and
  (*b*) the aggregate amount provided or written off since the date of acquisition or valuation, as the case may be, for depreciation or diminution in value;
and for the purposes of this paragraph the net amount at which any assets stood in the company's books on 1st July 1948 (after deduction of the amounts previously provided or written

[*Release 19: 1 - vi - 90.*]

off for depreciation or diminution in value) shall, if the figures relating to the period before that date cannot be obtained without unreasonable expense or delay, be treated as if it were the amount of a valuation of those assets made at that date and, where any of those assets are sold, the said net amount less the amount of the sales shall be treated as if it were the amount of a valuation so made of the remaining assets.

(2) The foregoing sub-paragraph shall not apply—

(a) to assets for which the figures relating to the period beginning with 1st July 1948 cannot be obtained without unreasonable expense or delay; or

(b) to assets the replacement of which is provided for wholly or partly—

(i) by making provision for renewals and charging the cost of replacement against the provision so made; or

(ii) by charging the cost of replacement direct to revenue; or

(c) to any listed investments or to any unlisted investments of which the value as estimated by the directors is shown either as the amount of the investments or by way of note; or

(d) to goodwill, patents or trade marks.

(3) For the assets under each heading whose amount is arrived at in accordance with sub-paragraph (1) of this paragraph, there shall be shown—

(a) the aggregate of the amounts referred to in paragraph (a) of that sub-paragraph; and

(b) the aggregate of the amounts referred to in paragraph (b) thereof.

(4) As respects the assets under each heading whose amount is not arrived at in accordance with the said sub-paragraph (1) because their replacement is provided for as mentioned in sub-paragraph (2)(b) of this paragraph, there shall be stated—

(a) the means by which their replacement is provided for; and

(b) the aggregate amount of the provision (if any) made for renewals and not used.

6. In the case of unlisted investments consisting in equity share capital of other bodies corporate (other than any whose values as estimated by the directors are separately shown, either individually or collectively or as to some individually and as to the rest collectively, and are so shown either as the amount thereof, or by way of note), the matters referred to in the following heads shall, if not otherwise shown, be stated by way of note or in a statement or report annexed:—

(a) the aggregate amount of the company's income for the financial year that is ascribable to the investments;

(b) the amount of the company's share before taxation, and the amount of that share after taxation, of the net aggregate amount of the profits of the bodies in which the investments are held, being profits for the several periods to which accounts sent by them during the financial year to the company related, after deducting those bodies' losses for those periods (or vice versa);

(c) the amount of the company's share of the net aggregate amount of the undistributed profits accumulated by the bodies in which the investments are held since the time when the investments were acquired after deducting the losses accumulated by them since that time (or vice versa);

(d) the manner in which any losses incurred by the said bodies have been dealt with in the company's accounts.

7. The aggregate amounts respectively of reserves and provisions (other than provisions for depreciation, renewals or diminution in value of assets) shall be stated under separate headings;

Provided that—

(a) this paragraph shall not require a separate statement of either of the said amounts which is not material; and

(b) the Secretary of State may direct that a separate statement shall not be required of the amount of provisions where he is satisfied that that is not required in the public interest and would prejudice the company, but subject to the condition that any heading stating an amount arrived at after taking into account a provision (other than as aforesaid) shall be so framed or marked as to indicate that fact.

8.—(1) There shall also be shown (unless it is shown in the profit and loss account or a statement or report annexed thereto, or the amount involved is not material)—

(a) where the amount of the reserves or of the provisions (other than provisions for depreciation, renewals or diminution in value of assets) shows an increase as compared with the amount at the end of the immediately preceding financial year, the source from which the amount of the increase has been derived; and

(b) where—

(i) the amount of the reserves shows a decrease as compared with the amount at the end of the immediately preceding financial year; or

   (ii) the amount at the end of the immediately preceding financial year of the provisions (other than provisions for depreciation, renewals or diminution in value of assets) exceeded the aggregate of the sums since applied and amounts still retained for the purposes thereof;

the application of the amounts derived from the difference.

(2) Where the heading showing the reserves or any of the provisions aforesaid is divided into sub-headings, this paragraph shall apply to each of the separate amounts shown in the sub-headings instead of applying to the aggregate amount thereof.

9. If an amount is set aside for the purpose of its being used to prevent undue fluctuations in charges for taxation, it shall be stated.

10.—(1) There shall be shown under separate headings—

   (*a*) the aggregate amounts respectively of the company's listed investments and unlisted investments;

   (*b*) if the amount of the goodwill and of any patents and trade marks or part of that amount is shown as a separate item in or is otherwise ascertainable from the books of the company, or from any contract for the sale or purchase of any property to be acquired by the company, or from any documents in the possession of the company relating to the stamp duty payable in respect of any such contract or the conveyance of any such property, the said amount so shown or ascertained as far as not written off or, as the case may be, the said amount so far as it is so shown or ascertainable and as so shown or ascertained, as the case may be;

   (*c*) the aggregate amount of any outstanding loans made under the authority of section 153(4)(*b*), (*bb*) or (*c*) or 155 of this Act;

   (*d*) the aggregate amount of bank loans and overdrafts and the aggregate amount of loans made to the company which—

      (i) are repayable otherwise than by instalments and fall due for repayment after the expiration of the period of five years beginning with the day next following the expiration of the financial year; or

      (ii) are repayable by instalments any of which fall due for payment after the expiration of that period;

   not being, in either case, bank loans or overdrafts;

   (*e*) the aggregate amount which is recommended for distribution by way of dividend.

(2) Nothing in head (*b*) of the foregoing sub-paragraph shall be taken as requiring the amount of the goodwill, patents and trade marks to be stated otherwise than as a single item.

[1] (3) The heading showing the amount of the listed investments shall be subdivided, where necessary, to distinguish the investments as repects which there has, and those as respects which there has not, been granted a listing on a recognised investment exchange other than an overseas investment exchange within the meaning of the Financial Services Act 1986.

(4) In relation to each loan falling within head (*d*) of sub-paragraph (1) of this paragraph (other than a bank loan or overdraft), there shall be stated by way of note (if not otherwise stated) the terms on which it is repayable and the rate at which interest is payable thereon:

Provided that if the number of loans is such that, in the opinion of the directors, compliance with the foregoing requirement would result in a statement of excessive length, it shall be sufficient to give a general indication of the terms on which the loans are repayable and the rates at which interest is payable thereon.

NOTE

[1] As amended by the Financial Services Act 1986, Sched. 16, para. 24.

---

11. Where any liability of the company is secured otherwise than by operation of law on any assets of the company, the fact that that liability is so secured shall be stated, but it shall not be necessary to specify the assets on which the liability is secured.

12. Where any of the company's debentures are held by a nominee of or trustee for the company, the nominal amount of the debentures and the amount at which they are stated in the books of the company shall be stated.

13.—(1) The matters referred to in the following sub-paragraphs shall be stated by way of note, or in a statement or report annexed, if not otherwise shown.

(2) The number, description and amount of any shares in the company which any person has an option to subscribe for, together with the following particulars of the option, that is to say—

(*a*) the period during which it is exercisable;

(*b*) the price to be paid for shares subscribed for under it.

(3) [Repealed by the Companies Act 1989, s. 18(3) and Scheds. 7 and 24.]

(4) Any distribution made by an investment company within the meaning of Part VIII of this Act which reduces the amount of its net assets to less than the aggregate of its called-up share capital and undistributable reserves.

For purposes of this sub-paragraph, a company's net assets are the aggregate of its assets less the aggregate of its liabilities; and "undistributable reserves" has the meaning given by section 264(3).

(5) The amount of any arrears of fixed cumulative dividends on the company's shares and the period for which the dividends or, if there is more than one class, each class of them are in arrear.

(6) Particulars of any charge on the assets of the company to secure the liabilities of any other person, including, where practicable, the amount secured.

(7) The general nature of any other contingent liabilities not provided for and, where practicable, the aggregate amount or estimated amount of those liabilities, if it is material.

(8) Where practicable the aggregate amount or estimated amount, if it is material, of contracts for capital expenditure, so far as not provided for and, where practicable, the aggregate amount or estimated amount, if it is material, of capital expenditure authorised by the directors which has not been contracted for.

(9) In the case of fixed assets under any heading whose amount is required to be arrived at in accordance with paragraph 5(1) of this Schedule (other than unlisted investments) and is so arrived at by reference to a valuation, the years (so far as they are known to the directors) in which the assets were severally valued and the several values, and, in the case of assets that have been valued during the financial year, the names of the persons who valued them or particulars of their qualifications for doing so and (whichever is stated) the bases of valuation used by them.

(10) If there are included amongst fixed assets under any heading (other than investments) assets that have been acquired during the financial year, the aggregate amount of the assets acquired as determined for the purpose of making up the balance sheet, and if during that year any fixed assets included under a heading in the balance sheet made up with respect to the immediately preceding financial year (other than investments) have been disposed of or destroyed, the aggregate amount thereof as determined for the purpose of making up that balance sheet.

(11) Of the amount of fixed assets consisting of land, how much is ascribable to land of freehold tenure and how much to land of leasehold tenure, and, of the latter, how much is ascribable to land held on long lease and how much to land held on short lease.

(12) If in the opinion of the directors any of the current assets have not a value, on realisation in the ordinary course of the company's business, at least equal to the amount at which they are stated, the fact that the directors are of that opinion.

(13) The aggregate market value of the company's listed investments where it differs from the amount of the investments as stated and the stock exchange value of any investments of which the market value is shown (whether separately or not) and is taken as being higher than their stock exchange value.

(14) If a sum set aside for the purpose of its being used to prevent undue fluctuations in charges for taxation has been used during the financial year for another purpose, the amount thereof and the fact that it has been so used.

(15) If the amount carried forward for stock in trade or work in progress is material for the appreciation by its members of the company's state of affairs or of its profit or loss for the financial year, the manner in which that amount has been computed.

(16) The basis on which foreign currencies have been converted into sterling where the amount of the assets or liabilities affected is material.

(17) The basis on which the amount, if any, set aside for United Kingdom corporation tax is computed.

(18) [Repealed by the Companies Act 1989, Sched. 24.]

Profit and loss account

14.—(1) There shall be shown—

(*a*) the amount charged to revenue by way of provision for depreciation, renewals or diminution in value of fixed assets;

(*b*) the amount of the interest on loans of the following kinds made to the company (whether on the security of debentures or not), namely, bank loans, overdrafts and loans which, not being bank loans or overdrafts,—

    (i) are repayable otherwise than by instalments and fall due for repayment before the expiration of the period of five years beginning with the day next following the expiration of the financial year; or

    (ii) are repayable by instalments the last of which falls due for payment before the expiration of that period;

and the amount of the interest on loans of other kinds so made (whether on the security of debentures or not);

  (c) the amount of the charge to revenue for United Kingdom corporation tax and, if that amount would have been greater but for relief from double taxation, the amount which it would have been but for such relief, the amount of the charge for United Kingdom income tax, and the amount of the charge for taxation imposed outside the United Kingdom of profits, income and (so far as charged to revenue) capital gains;

  (d) the amounts respectively set aside for redemption of share capital and for redemption of loans;

  (e) the amount, if material, set aside or proposed to be set aside to, or withdrawn from, reserves;

  (f) subject to sub-paragraph (2) of this paragraph, the amount, if material, set aside to provisions other than provisions for depreciation, renewals, or diminution in value of assets or, as the case may be, the amount, if material, withdrawn from such provisions and not applied for the purposes thereof;

  (g) the amounts respectively of income from listed investments and income from unlisted investments;

  (h) if a substantial part of the company's revenue for the financial year consists in rents from land, the amount thereof (after deduction of ground-rents, rates and other out-goings);

  (j) the amount, if material, charged to revenue in respect of sums payable in respect of the hire of plant and machinery;

  (k) the aggregate amount of the dividends paid and proposed.

(2) The Secretary of State may direct that a company shall not be obliged to show an amount set aside to provisions in accordance with sub-paragraph (1)(f) of this paragraph, if he is satisfied that that is not required in the public interest and would prejudice the company, but subject to the condition that any heading stating an amount arrived at after taking into account the amount set aside as aforesaid shall be so framed or marked as to indicate that fact.

(3) If, in the case of any assets in whose case an amount is charged to revenue by way of provision for depreciation or diminution in value, an amount is also so charged by way of provision for renewal thereof, the last-mentioned amount shall be shown separately.

(4) If the amount charged to revenue by way of provision for depreciation or diminution in value of any fixed assets (other than investments) has been determined otherwise than by reference to the amount of those assets as determined for the purpose of making up the balance sheet, that fact shall be stated.

15. The amount of any charge arising in consequence of the occurrence of an event in a preceding financial year and of any credit so arising shall, if not included in a heading relating to other matters, be stated under a separate heading.

16. [Repealed by the Companies Act 1989, Sched. 24.]

17.—(1) The following matters shall be stated by way of note, if not otherwise shown.

(2) The turnover for the financial year, except in so far as it is attributable to the business of banking or discounting or to business of such other class as may be prescribed for the purposes of this sub-paragraph.

(3) If some or all of the turnover is omitted by reason of its being attributable as aforesaid, the fact that it is so omitted.

(4) The method by which turnover stated is arrived at.

(5) A company shall not be subject to the requirements of this paragraph if it is neither a parent company nor a subsidiary undertaking and the turnover which, apart from this sub-paragraph, would be required to be stated does not exceed £1 million.

18.—(1) The following matters shall be stated by way of note, if not otherwise shown.

(2) If depreciation or replacement of fixed assets is provided for by some method other than a depreciation charge or provision for renewals, or is not provided for, the method by which it is provided for or the fact that it is not provided for, as the case may be.

(3) The basis on which the charge for United Kingdom corporation tax and United Kingdom income tax is computed.

(4) Any special circumstances which affect liability in respect of taxation of profits, income or capital gains for the financial year or liability in respect of taxation of profits, income or capital gains for succeeding financial years.

(5) [Repealed by the Companies Act 1989, Sched. 24.]

(6) Any material respects in which items shown in the profit and loss account are affected—
  (a) by transactions of a sort not usually undertaken by the company or otherwise by circumstances of an exceptional or non-recurrent nature; or
  (b) by any charge in the basis of accounting.

Supplementary provisions

[1] 18A.—(1) Accounting policies shall be applied consistently within the same accounts and from one financial year to the next.

(2) If it appears to the directors of a company that there are special reasons for departing from the principle stated in sub-paragraph (1) in preparing the company's accounts in respect of any financial year, they may do so; but particulars of the departure, the reasons for it and its effect shall be given in a note to the accounts.

18B. It shall be stated whether the accounts have been prepared in accordance with applicable accounting standards, and particulars of any material departure from those standards and the reasons for it shall be given.

18C.—(1) In respect of every item shown in the balance sheet or profit and loss account, or stated in a note to the accounts, there shall be shown or stated the corresponding amount for the financial year immediately preceding that to which the accounts relate, subject to sub-paragraph (3).

(2) Where the corresponding amount is not comparable, it shall be adjusted and particulars of the adjustment and the reasons for it shall be given in a note to the accounts.

(3) Sub-paragraph (1) does not apply in relation to an amount shown—
  (a) as an amount the source or application of which is required by paragraph 8 above (reserves and provisions),
  (b) in pursuance of paragraph 13(10) above (acquisitions and disposals of fixed assets),
  (c) by virtue of paragraph 13 of Schedule 4A (details of accounting treatment of acquisitions),
  (d) by virtue of paragraph 2, 8(3), 16, 21(1)(d), 22(4) or (5), 24(3) or (4) or 27(3) or (4) of Schedule 5 (shareholdings in other undertakings), or
  (e) by virtue of Part II or III of Schedule 6 (loans and other dealings in favour of directors and others).

NOTE
[1] Inserted by the Companies Act 1989, s. 18(3) and Sched. 7, para. 4.

Provisions where company is parent company or subsidiary undertaking

19.—(1) This paragraph applies where the company is a parent company.

(2) The aggregate amount of assets consisting of shares in, or amounts owing (whether on account of a loan or otherwise) from, the company's subsidiary undertakings, distinguishing shares from indebtedness, shall be set out in the balance sheet separately from all the other assets of the company, and the aggregate amount of indebtedness (whether on account of a loan or otherwise) to the company's subsidiary undertakings shall be so set out separately from all its other liabilities and—
  (a) the references in paragraphs 5, 6, 10, 13 and 14 of this Schedule to the company's investments (except those in paragraphs 13(10) and 14(4)) shall not include investments in its subsidiary undertakings required by this paragraph to be separately set out; and
  (b) paragraph 5, sub-paragraph (1)(a) of paragraph 14, and sub-paragraph (2) of paragraph 18 of this Schedule shall not apply in relation to fixed assets consisting of interests in the company's subsidiary undertakings.

(3) to (7) [Repealed by the Companies Act 1989, s. 18(3), Sched. 7, para. 5(4), and Sched. 24.]

[1] 20.—(1) This paragraph applies where the company is a subsidiary undertaking.

(2) The balance sheet of the company shall show—
  (a) the aggregate amount of its indebtedness to undertakings of which it is a subsidiary undertaking or which are fellow subsidiary undertakings, and
  (b) the aggregate amount of the indebtedness of all such undertakings to it,
distinguishing in each case between indebtedness in respect of debentures and otherwise.

(3) The balance sheet shall also show the aggregate amount of assets consisting of shares in fellow subsidiary undertakings.

NOTE

[1] Substituted by the Companies Act 1989, s. 18(3) and Sched. 7, para. 6.

21.–26. [Repealed by the Companies Act 1989, s. 18(3) and Scheds. 7, para. 7, and 24.]

Exceptions for certain companies

27.—(1) The following applies to a banking company (if not subject to the Banking Companies (Accounts) Regulations 1970) which satisfies the Secretary of State that it ought to have the benefit of this paragraph.

[THE NEXT PAGE IS I 407]

(2) The company shall not be subject to the requirements of paragraphs 2 to 18 of this Schedule other than—

    (*a*) as respects its balance sheet, those of paragraphs 2 and 3, paragraph 4 (so far as it relates to assets), paragraph 10 (except sub-paragraphs (1)(*d*) and (4)), paragraphs 11 and 12 and paragraph 13 (except sub-paragraphs (9), (10), (11), (13) and (14)); and

    (*b*) as respects its profit and loss account, those of sub-paragraph (1)(*h*) and (*k*) of paragraph 14, and paragraph 15.

(3) But, where in the company's balance sheet reserves or provisions (other than provisions for depreciation, renewals or diminution in value of assets) are not stated separately, any heading stating an amount arrived at after taking into account a reserve or such a provision shall be so framed or marked as to indicate that fact, and its profit and loss account shall indicate by appropriate words the manner in which the amount stated for the company's profit or loss has been arrived at.

(4) The company's accounts shall not be deemed, by reason only of the fact that they do not comply with any requirements from which the company is exempt by virtue of this paragraph, not to give the true and fair view required by this Act.

28.—(1) An insurance company shall not be subject to the following requirements of paragraphs 2 to 18 of this Schedule, that is to say—

    (*a*) as respects its balance sheet, those of paragraphs 4 to 8 (both inclusive), sub-paragraphs (1)(*a*) and (3) of paragraph 10 and sub-paragraphs (6), (7) and (9) to (13) (both inclusive) of paragraph 13;

    (*b*) as respects its profit and loss account, those of paragraph 14 (except sub-paragraph (1)(*b*), (*c*), (*d*) and (*k*)) and paragraph 18(2);

but, where in its balance sheet reserves or provisions (other than provisions for depreciation, renewals or diminution in value of assets) are not stated separately, any heading stating an amount arrived at after taking into account a reserve or such a provision shall be so framed or marked as to indicate that fact, and its profit and loss account shall indicate by appropriate words the manner in which the amount stated for the company's profit or loss has been arrived at:

Provided that the Secretary of State may direct that any such insurance company whose business includes to a substantial extent business other than insurance business shall comply with all the requirements of the said paragraphs 2 to 18 or such of them as may be specified in the direction and shall comply therewith as respects either the whole of its business or such part thereof as may be so specified.

(2) The accounts of a company shall not be deemed, by reason only of the fact that they do not comply with any requirement of paragraphs 2 to 18 from which the company is exempt by virtue of this paragraph, not to give the true and fair view required by this Act.

[1] 28A. Where a company is entitled to, and has availed itself of, any of the provisions of paragraphs 27 or 28 of this Schedule, section 235(2) only requires the auditors to state whether in their opinion the accounts have been properly prepared in accordance with this Act.

NOTE
[1] Inserted by the Companies Act 1989, s. 18(3) and Sched. 7, para. 10.

Interpretation

32.—(1) For the purposes of this Part of this Schedule, unless the context otherwise requires,—

    (*a*) the expression "provision" shall, subject to sub-paragraph (2) of this paragraph, mean any amount written off or retained by way of providing for depreciation, renewals or diminution in value of assets or retained by way of providing for any known liability of which the amount cannot be determined with substantial accuracy;

    (*b*) the expression "reserve" shall not, subject as aforesaid, include any amount written off or retained by way of providing for depreciation, renewals or diminution in value of assets or retained by way of providing for any known liability or any sum set aside for the purpose of its being used to prevent undue fluctuations in charges for taxation;

and in this paragraph the expression "liability" shall include all liabilities in respect of expenditure contracted for and all disputed or contingent liabilities.

(2) Where—

(*a*) any amount written off or retained by way of providing for depreciation, renewals or diminution in value of assets; or

(*b*) any amount retained by way of providing for any known liability;

is in excess of that which in the opinion of the directors is reasonably necessary for the purpose, the excess shall be treated for the purposes of this Part of this Schedule as a reserve and not as a provision.

[1] 33. For the purposes aforesaid, the expression "listed investment" means an investment as respects which there has been granted a listing on a recognised investment exchange other than an overseas investment exchange within the meaning of the Financial Services Act 1986, or on any stock exchange of repute outside Great Britain and the expression "unlisted investment" shall be construed accordingly.

NOTE
[1] As amended by the Financial Services Act 1986, Sched. 16, para. 24.

---

34. For the purposes aforesaid, the expression "long lease" means a lease in the case of which the portion of the term for which it was granted remaining unexpired at the end of the financial year is not less than 50 years, the expression "short lease" means a lease which is not a long lease and the expression "lease" includes an agreement for a lease.

35. For the purposes aforesaid, a loan shall be deemed to fall due for repayment, and an instalment of a loan shall be deemed to fall due for payment, on the earliest date on which the lender could require repayment or, as the case may be, payment if he exercised all options and rights available to him.

36. In the application of this Part of this Schedule to Scotland, "land of freehold tenure" means land in respect of which the company is the proprietor of the *dominium utile* or, in the case of land not held on feudal tenure, is the owner; "land of leasehold tenure" means land of which the company is the tenant under a lease; and the reference to ground-rents, rates and other outgoings includes a reference to feu-duty and ground annual.

[1] Part II

NOTE
[1] Inserted by the Companies Act 1989, s. 18(3) and Sched. 7, para. 13.

ACCOUNTS OF BANKING OR INSURANCE GROUP

Undertakings to be included in consolidation

1. The following descriptions of undertaking shall not be excluded from consolidation under section 229(4) (exclusion of undertakings whose activities are different from those of the undertakings consolidated)—

(*a*) in the case of a banking group, an undertaking (other than a credit institution) whose activities are a direct extension of or ancillary to banking business;

(*b*) in the case of an insurance group, an undertaking (other than one carrying on insurance business) whose activities are a direct extension of or ancillary to insurance business.

For the purposes of paragraph (*a*) "banking" means the carrying on of a deposit-taking business within the meaning of the Banking Act 1987.

General application of provisions applicable to individual accounts

2.—(1) In paragraph 1 of Schedule 4A (application to group accounts of provisions applicable to individual accounts), the reference in sub-paragraph (1) to the provisions of Schedule 4 shall be construed as a reference to the provisions of Part I of this Schedule; and accordingly—

    (*a*) the reference in sub-paragraph (2) to paragraph 59 of Schedule 4 shall be construed as a reference to paragraphs 19(2) and 20 of Part I of this Schedule; and

    (*b*) sub-paragraph (3) shall be omitted.

(2) The general application of the provisions of Part I of this Schedule in place of those of Schedule 4 is subject to the following provisions.

Treatment of goodwill

3.—(1) The rules in paragraph 21 of Schedule 4 relating to the treatment of goodwill, and the rules in paragraphs 17 to 19 of that Schedule (valuation of fixed assets) so far as they relate to goodwill, apply for the purpose of dealing with any goodwill arising on consolidation.

(2) Goodwill shall be shown as a separate item in the balance sheet under an appropriate heading; and this applies notwithstanding anything in paragraph 10(1)(*b*) or (2) of Part I of this Schedule (under which goodwill, patents and trade marks may be stated in the company's individual accounts as a single item).

Minority interests and associated undertakings

4. The information required by paragraphs 17 and 20 to 22 of Schedule 4A (minority interests and associated undertakings) to be shown under separate items in the formats set out in Part I of Schedule 4 shall be shown separately in the balance sheet and profit and loss account under appropriate headings.

Companies entitled to benefit of exemptions

5.—(1) Where a banking or insurance company is entitled to the exemptions conferred by paragraph 27 or 28 of Part I of this Schedule, a group headed by that company is similarly entitled.

(2) Paragraphs 27(4), 28(2) and 28A (accounts not to be taken to be other than true and fair; duty of auditors) apply accordingly where advantage is taken of those exemptions in relation to group accounts.

Information as to undertaking in which shares held as result of financial assistance operation

6.—(1) The following provisions apply where the parent company of a banking group has a subsidiary undertaking which—

    (*a*) is a credit institution of which shares are held as a result of a financial assistance operation with a view to its reorganisation or rescue, and

    (*b*) is excluded from consolidation under section 229(3)(*c*) (interest held with a view to resale).

(2) Information as to the nature and terms of the operation shall be given in a note to the group accounts and there shall be appended to the copy of the group accounts delivered to the registrar in accordance with section 242 a copy of the undertaking's latest individual accounts and, if it is a parent undertaking, its latest group accounts.

If the accounts appended are required by law to be audited, a copy of the auditors' report shall also be appended.

(3) If any document required to be appended is in a language other than English, the directors shall annex to the copy of that document delivered a translation of it into English, certified in the prescribed manner to be a correct translation.

(4) The above requirements are subject to the following qualifications—

    (*a*) an undertaking is not required to prepare for the purposes of this paragraph accounts which would not otherwise be prepared, and if no accounts satisfying the above requirements are prepared none need be appended;

    (*b*) the accounts of an undertaking need not be appended if they would not otherwise be required to be published, or made available for public inspection, anywhere in the world, but in that case the reason for not appending the accounts shall be stated in a note to the consolidated accounts.

(5) Where a copy of an undertaking's accounts is required to be appended to the copy of the group accounts delivered to the registrar, that fact shall be stated in a note to the group accounts.

(6) Subsections (2) to (4) of section 242 (penalties, etc. in case of default) apply in relation to the requirements of this paragraph as regards the delivery of documents to the registrar as they apply in relation to the requirements of subsection (1) of that section.

[1] PART III

_____

NOTE
[1] Inserted by the Companies Act 1989, s. 18(3) and Sched. 7, para. 13.

_____

ADDITIONAL DISCLOSURE: RELATED UNDERTAKINGS

1. Where accounts are prepared in accordance with the special provisions of this Part relating to banking companies or groups, there shall be disregarded for the purposes of—
   (*a*) paragraphs 7(2)(*a*), 23(2)(*a*) and 26(2)(*a*) of Schedule 5 (information about significant holdings in undertakings other than subsidiary undertakings: definition of 10 per cent. holding), and
   (*b*) paragraphs 9(1), 25(1) and 28(1) of that Schedule (additional information in case of 20 per cent. holding),
any holding of shares not comprised in the equity share capital of the undertaking in question.

[1] PART IV

_____

NOTE
[1] Inserted by the Companies Act 1989, s. 18(3) and Sched. 7, para. 13.

_____

ADDITIONAL DISCLOSURE: EMOLUMENTS AND OTHER BENEFITS OF DIRECTORS AND OTHERS

1. The provisions of this Part of this Schedule have effect with respect to the application of Schedule 6 (additional disclosure: emoluments and other benefits of directors and others) to a banking company or the holding company of such a company.

Loans, quasi-loans and other dealings

2. Part II of Schedule 6 (loans, quasi-loans and other dealings) does not apply for the purposes of accounts prepared by a banking company, or a company which is the holding company of a banking company, in relation to a transaction or arrangement of a kind mentioned in section 330, or an agreement to enter into such a transaction or arrangement, to which that banking company is a party.

Other transactions, arrangements and agreements

3.—(1) Part III of Schedule 6 (other transactions, arrangements and agreements) applies for the purposes of accounts prepared by a banking company, or a company which is the holding company of a banking company, only in relation to a transaction, arrangement or agreement made by that banking company for—
   (*a*) a person who was a director of the company preparing the accounts, or who was connected with such a director, or
   (*b*) a person who was a chief executive or manager (within the meaning of the Banking Act 1987) of that company or its holding company.
(2) References in that Part to officers of the company shall be construed accordingly as including references to such persons.
(3) In this paragraph "director" includes a shadow director.
(4) For the purposes of that Part as it applies by virtue of this paragraph, a company which a person does not control shall not be treated as connected with him.
(5) Section 346 of this Act applies for the purposes of this paragraph as regards the interpretation of references to a person being connected with a director or controlling a company.

¹ SCHEDULE 10

NOTE
¹ Substituted by the Companies Act 1989, s. 18(5) and Sched. 8.

DIRECTORS' REPORT WHERE ACCOUNTS PREPARED IN ACCORDANCE WITH SPECIAL PROVISIONS FOR BANKING OR INSURANCE COMPANIES OR GROUPS

Recent issues

1.—(1) This paragraph applies where a company prepares individual accounts in accordance with the special provisions of this Part relating to banking or insurance companies.

(2) If in the financial year to which the accounts relate the company has issued any shares or debentures, the directors' report shall state the reason for making the issue, the classes of shares or debentures issued and, as respects each class, the number of shares or amount of debentures issued and the consideration received by the company for the issue.

Turnover and profitability

2.—(1) This paragraph applies where a company prepares group accounts in accordance with the special provisions of this Part relating to banking or insurance groups.

(2) If in the course of the financial year to which the accounts relate the group carried on business of two or more classes (other than banking or discounting or a class prescribed for the purposes of paragraph 17(2) of Part I of Schedule 9) that in the opinion of the directors differ substantially from each other, there shall be contained in the directors' report a statement of—

(*a*) the proportions in which the turnover for the financial year (so far as stated in the consolidated accounts) is divided amongst those classes (describing them), and

(*b*) as regards business of each class, the extent or approximate extent (expressed in money terms) to which, in the opinion of the directors, the carrying on of business of that class contributed to or restricted the profit or loss of the group for that year (before taxation).

(3) In sub-paragraph (2) "the group" means the undertakings included in the consolidation.

(4) For the purposes of this paragraph classes of business which in the opinion of the directors do not differ substantially from each other shall be treated as one class.

Labour force and wages paid

3.—(1) This paragraph applies where a company prepares individual or group accounts in accordance with the special provisions of this Part relating to banking or insurance companies or groups.

(2) There shall be stated in the directors' report—

(*a*) the average number of persons employed by the company or, if the company prepares group accounts, by the company and its subsidiary undertakings, and

(*b*) the aggregate amount of the remuneration paid or payable to persons so employed.

(3) The average number of persons employed shall be determined by adding together the number of persons employed (whether throughout the week or not) in each week of the financial year and dividing that total by the number of weeks in the financial year.

(4) The aggregate amount of the remuneration paid or payable means the total amount of remuneration paid or payable in respect of the financial year; and for this purpose remuneration means gross remuneration and includes bonuses, whether payable under contract or not.

(5) The information required by this paragraph need not be given if the average number of persons employed is less than 100.

(6) No account shall be taken for the purposes of this paragraph of persons who worked wholly or mainly outside the United Kingdom.

(7) This paragraph does not apply to a company which is a wholly-owned subsidiary of a company incorporated in Great Britain.

¹ SCHEDULE 10A

NOTE
¹ Inserted by the Companies Act 1989, s. 21(2) and Sched. 9.

PARENT AND SUBSIDIARY UNDERTAKINGS: SUPPLEMENTARY PROVISIONS

Introduction

1. The provisions of this Schedule explain expressions used in section 258 (parent and subsidiary undertakings) and otherwise supplement that section.

Voting rights in an undertaking

2.—(1) In section 258(2)(*a*) and (*d*) the references to the voting rights in an undertaking are to the rights conferred on shareholders in respect of their shares or, in the case of an undertaking not having a share capital, on members, to vote at general meetings of the undertaking on all, or substantially all, matters.

(2) In relation to an undertaking which does not have general meetings at which matters are decided by the exercise of voting rights, the references to holding a majority of the voting rights in the undertaking shall be construed as references to having the right under the constitution of the undertaking to direct the overall policy of the undertaking or to alter the terms of its constitution.

Right to appoint or remove a majority of the directors

3.—(1) In section 258(2)(*b*) the reference to the right to appoint or remove a majority of the board of directors is to the right to appoint or remove directors holding a majority of the voting rights at meetings of the board on all, or substantially all, matters.

(2) An undertaking shall be treated as having the right to appoint to a directorship if—
    (*a*) a person's appointment to it follows necessarily from his appointment as director of the undertaking, or
    (*b*) the directorship is held by the undertaking itself.

(3) A right to appoint or remove which is exercisable only with the consent or concurrence of another person shall be left out of account unless no other person has a right to appoint or, as the case may be, remove in relation to that directorship.

Right to exercise dominant influence

4.—(1) For the purposes of section 258(2)(*c*) an undertaking shall not be regarded as having the right to exercise a dominant influence over another undertaking unless it has a right to give directions with respect to the operating and financial policies of that other undertaking which its directors are obliged to comply with whether or not they are for the benefit of that other undertaking.

(2) A "control contract" means a contract in writing conferring such a right which—
    (*a*) is of a kind authorised by the memorandum or articles of the undertaking in relation to which the right is exercisable, and
    (*b*) is permitted by the law under which that undertaking is established.

(3) This paragraph shall not be read as affecting the construction of the expression "actually exercises a dominant influence" in section 258(4)(*a*).

Rights exercisable only in certain circumstances or temporarily incapable of exercise

5.—(1) Rights which are exercisable only in certain circumstances shall be taken into account only—
    (*a*) when the circumstances have arisen, and for so long as they continue to obtain, or
    (*b*) when the circumstances are within the control of the person having the rights.

(2) Rights which are normally exercisable but are temporarily incapable of exercise shall continue to be taken into account.

Rights held by one person on behalf of another

6. Rights held by a person in a fiduciary capacity shall be treated as not held by him.

7.—(1) Rights held by a person as nominee for another shall be treated as held by the other.
(2) Rights shall be regarded as held as nominee for another if they are exercisable only on his instructions or with his consent or concurrence.

Rights attached to shares held by way of security

8. Rights attached to shares held by way of security shall be treated as held by the person providing the security—
   (*a*) where apart from the right to exercise them for the purpose of preserving the value of the security, or of realising it, the rights are exercisable only in accordance with his instructions, and
   (*b*) where the shares are held in connection with the granting of loans as part of normal business activities and apart from the right to exercise them for the purpose of preserving the value of the security, or of realising it, the rights are exercisable only in his interests.

Rights attributed to parent undertaking

9.—(1) Rights shall be treated as held by a parent undertaking if they are held by any of its subsidiary undertakings.
(2) Nothing in paragraph 7 or 8 shall be construed as requiring rights held by a parent undertaking to be treated as held by any of its subsidiary undertakings.
(3) For the purposes of paragraph 8 rights shall be treated as being exercisable in accordance with the instructions or in the interests of an undertaking if they are exercisable in accordance with the instructions of or, as the case may be, in the interests of any group undertaking.

Disregard of certain rights

10. The voting rights in an undertaking shall be reduced by any rights held by the undertaking itself.

Supplementary

11. References in any provision of paragraphs 6 to 10 to rights held by a person include rights falling to be treated as held by him by virtue of any other provision of those paragraphs but not rights which by virtue of any such provision are to be treated as not held by him.

Section 279   [1] SCHEDULE 11

NOTE
[1] As amended by the Companies Act 1989, Scheds. 10, para. 21, 24.

MODIFICATIONS OF PART VIII WHERE COMPANY'S ACCOUNTS PREPARED IN ACCORDANCE WITH
SPECIAL PROVISIONS FOR BANKING OR INSURANCE COMPANIES

1. Section 264 applies as if in subsection (2) for the words following "the aggregate of its liabilities" there were subsituted "("liabilities" to include any provision within the meaning of Part I of Schedule 9, except to the extent that that provision is taken into account in calculating the value of any asset of the company)".

2. Section 265 applies as if—
   (*a*) for subsection (2) there were substituted—
              "(2) In subsection (1)(*a*), "liabilities" includes any provision (within the meaning of Part I of Schedule 9) except to the extent that that provision is taken into account for the purposes of that subsection in calculating the value of any asset of the company", and
   (*b*) there were added at the end of the section—
              "(7) In determining capital and revenue profits and losses, an asset which is not a fixed asset or a current asset is treated as a fixed asset."

3. Section 269 does not apply.

4. Section 270 applies as if—
   (*a*) in subsection (2) the following were substituted for paragraph (*b*)—
   "(*b*) provisions (within the meaning of Part I of Schedule 9)";

5. Section 271 applies as if—
   (*a*) in subsection (2), immediately before paragraph (*a*) there were inserted "except where the company is entitled to avail itself, and has availed itself, of any of the provisions of paragraph 27 or 28 of Schedule 9", and

6. Sections 272 and 273 apply as if in section 272(3)—
   (*a*) for the references to section 226 and Schedule 4 there were substituted references to section 255 and Part I of Schedule 9, and
   (*b*) immediately before paragraph (*a*) there were inserted "except where the company is entitled to avail itself, and has availed itself, of any of the provisions of paragraph 27 or 28 of Schedule 9".

7. Section 275 applies as if—
   (*a*) for subsection (1) there were substituted—
   "(1) For purposes of section 263, any provision (within the meaning of Part I of Schedule 9), other than one in respect of any diminution of value of a fixed asset appearing on a revaluation of all the fixed assets of the company, or of all its fixed assets other than goodwill, is to be treated as a realised loss"; and
   (*b*) "fixed assets" were defined to include any other asset which is not a current asset.

SCHEDULE 12

[Repealed by the Company Directors Disqualification Act 1986, Sched. 4.]

Sections 324, 325, 326, 328 and 346   [1] SCHEDULE 13

NOTE
[1] As amended by the Companies Act 1989, Sched. 24.

PROVISIONS SUPPLEMENTING AND INTERPRETING SECTIONS 324 TO 328

PART I

RULES FOR INTERPRETATION OF THE SECTIONS
AND ALSO SECTION 346(4) AND (5)

1.—(1) A reference to an interest in shares or debentures is to be read as including any interest of any kind whatsoever in shares or debentures.

(2) Accordingly, there are to be disregarded any restraints or restrictions to which the exercise of any right attached to the interest is or may be subject.

2. Where property is held on trust and any interest in shares or debentures is comprised in the property, any beneficiary of the trust who (apart from this paragraph) does not have an interest in the shares or debentures is to be taken as having such an interest; but this paragraph is without prejudice to the following provisions of this Part of this Schedule.

3.—(1) A person is taken to have an interest in shares or debentures if—
- (*a*) he enters into a contract for their purchase by him (whether for cash or other consideration), or
- (*b*) not being the registered holder, he is entitled to exercise any right conferred by the holding of the shares or debentures, or is entitled to control the exercise of any such right.

(2) For purposes of sub-paragraph (1)(*b*), a person is taken to be entitled to exercise or control the exercise of a right conferred by the holding of shares or debentures if he—
- (*a*) has a right (whether subject to conditions or not) the exercise of which would make him so entitled, or
- (*b*) is under an obligation (whether or not so subject) the fulfilment of which would make him so entitled.

(3) A person is not by virtue of sub-paragraph (1)(*b*) taken to be interested in shares or debentures by reason only that he—
- (*a*) has been appointed a proxy to vote at a specified meeting of a company or of any class of its members and at any adjournment of that meeting, or

[THE NEXT PAGE IS I 417]

(*b*) has been appointed by a corporation to act as its representative at any meeting of a company or of any class of its members.

4. A person is taken to be interested in shares or debentures if a body corporate is interested in them and—

    (*a*) that body corporate or its directors are accustomed to act in accordance with his directions or instructions, or

    (*b*) he is entitled to exercise or control the exercise of one-third or more of the voting power at general meetings of that body corporate.

As this paragraph applies for the purposes of section 346(4) and (5), "more than one-half" is subsituted for "one-third or more".

5. Where a person is entitled to exercise or control the exercise of one-third or more of the voting power at general meetings of a body corporate, and that body corporate is entitled to exercise or control the exercise of any of the voting power at general meetings of another body corporate ("the effective voting power"), then, for purposes of paragraph 4(*b*), the effective voting power is taken to be exercisable by that person.

As this paragraph applies for the purposes of section 346(4) and (5), "more than one-half" is substituted for "one-third or more".

6.—(1) A person is taken to have an interest in shares or debentures if, otherwise than by virtue of having an interest under a trust—

    (*a*) he has a right to call for delivery of the shares or debentures to himself or to his order, or

    (*b*) he has a right to acquire an interest in shares or debentures or is under an obligation to take an interest in shares or debentures;

whether in any case the right or obligation is conditional or absolute.

(2) Rights or obligations to subscribe for shares or debentures are not to be taken, for purposes of sub-paragraph (1), to be rights to acquire, or obligations to take, an interest in shares or debentures.

This is without prejudice to paragraph 1.

7. Persons having a joint interest are deemed each of them to have that interest.

8. It is immaterial that shares or debentures in which a person has an interest are unidentifiable.

9. So long as a person is entitled to receive, during the lifetime of himself or another, income from trust property comprising shares or debentures, an interest in the shares or debentures in reversion or remainder or (as regards Scotland) in fee, are to be disregarded.

10. A person is to be treated as uninterested in shares or debentures if, and so long as, he holds them under the law in force in England and Wales as a bare trustee or as a custodian trustee, or under the law in force in Scotland, as a simple trustee.

[1] 11. There is to be disregarded an interest of a person subsisting by virtue of—

    (*a*) any unit trust scheme which is an authorised unit trust scheme within the meaning of the Financial Services Act 1986;

    (*b*) a scheme made under section 22 of the Charities Act 1960, section 11 of the Trustee Investments Act 1961 or section 1 of the Administration of Justice Act 1965; or

    (*c*) the scheme set out in the Schedule to the Church Funds Investment Measure 1958.

NOTE

[1] As amended by the Financial Services Act 1986, Sched. 16, para. 25.

12. There is to be disregarded any interest—

    (*a*) of the Church of Scotland General Trustees or of the Church of Scotland Trust in shares or debentures held by them;

    (*b*) of any other person in shares or debentures held by those Trustees or that Trust otherwise than as simple trustees.

"The Church of Scotland General Trustees" are the body incorporated by the order confirmed by the Church of Scotland (General Trustees) Order Confirmation Act 1921; and "the Church of Scotland Trust" is the body incorporated by the order confirmed by the Church of Scotland Trust Order Confirmation Act 1932.

13. Delivery to a person's order of shares or debentures in fulfilment of a contract for the purchase of them by him or in satisfaction of a right of his to call for their delivery, or failure

to deliver shares or debentures in accordance with the terms of such a contract or on which such a right falls to be satisfied, is deemed to constitute an event in consequence of the occurrence of which he ceases to be interested in them, and so is the lapse of a person's right to call for delivery of shares or debentures.

PART II

PERIODS WITHIN WHICH OBLIGATIONS IMPOSED BY SECTION 324 MUST BE FULFILLED

14.—(1) An obligation imposed on a person by section 324(1) to notify an interest must, if he knows of the existence of the interest on the day on which he becomes a director, be fulfilled before the expiration of the period of five days beginning with the day following that day.

(2) Otherwise, the obligation must be fulfilled before the expiration of the period of five days beginning with the day following that on which the existence of the interest comes to his knowledge.

15.—(1) An obligation imposed on a person by section 324(2) to notify the occurrence of an event must, if at the time at which the event occurs he knows of its occurrence and of the fact that its occurrence gives rise to the obligation, be fulfilled before the expiration of the period of five days beginning with the day following that on which the event occurs.

(2) Otherwise the obligation must be fulfilled before the expiration of a period of five days beginning with the day following that on which the fact that the occurrence of the event gives rise to the obligation comes to his knowledge.

16. In reckoning, for purposes of paragraphs 14 and 15, any period of days, a day that is a Saturday or Sunday, or a bank holiday in any part of Great Britain, is to be disregarded.

PART III

CIRCUMSTANCES IN WHICH OBLIGATION IMPOSED BY SECTION 324 IS NOT DISCHARGED

17.—(1) Where an event of whose occurrence a director is, by virtue of section 324(2)(*a*), under obligation to notify a company consists of his entering into a contract for the purchase by him of shares or debentures, the obligation is not discharged in the absence of inclusion in the notice of a statement of the price to be paid by him under the contract.

(2) An obligation imposed on a director by section 324(2)(*b*) is not discharged in the absence of inclusion in the notice of the price to be received by him under the contract.

18.—(1) An obligation imposed on a director by virtue of section 324(2)(*c*) to notify a company is not discharged in the absence of inclusion in the notice of a statement of the consideration for the assignment (or, if it be the case that there is no consideration, that fact).

(2) Where an event of whose occurrence a director is, by virtue of section 324(2)(*d*), under obligation to notify a company consists in his assigning a right, the obligation is not discharged in the absence of inclusion in the notice of a similar statement.

19.—(1) Where an event of whose occurrence a director is, by virtue of section 324(2)(*d*), under obligation to notify a company consists in the grant to him of a right to subscribe for shares or debentures, the obligation is not discharged in the absence of inclusion in the notice of a statement of—

    (*a*) the date on which the right was granted,

    (*b*) the period during which or the time at which the right is exercisable,

    (*c*) the consideration for the grant (or, if it be the case that there is no consideration, that fact), and

    (*d*) the price to be paid for the shares or debentures.

(2) Where an event of whose occurrence a director is, by section 324(2)(*d*), under obligation to notify a company consists in the exercise of a right granted to him to subscribe for shares or debentures, the obligation is not discharged in the absence of inclusion in the notice of a statement of—

    (*a*) the number of shares or amount of debentures in respect of which the right was exercised, and

    (*b*) if it be the case that they were registered in his name, that fact, and, if not, the name or names of the person or persons in whose name or names they were registered, together (if they were registered in the names of two persons or more) with the number or amount registered in the name of each of them.

20. In this Part, a reference to price paid or received includes any consideration other than money.

PART IV

PROVISIONS WITH RESPECT TO REGISTER OF DIRECTORS' INTERESTS
TO BE KEPT UNDER SECTION 325

21. The register must be so made up that the entries in it against the several names appear in chronological order.

22. An obligation imposed by section 325(2) to (4) must be fulfilled before the expiration of the period of three days beginning with the day after that on which the obligation arises; but in reckoning that period, a day which is a Saturday or Sunday or a bank holiday in any part of Great Britain is to be disregarded.

23. The nature and extent of an interest recorded in the register of a director in any shares or debentures shall, if he so requires, be recorded in the register.

24. The company is not, by virtue of anything done for the purposes of section 325 or this Part of this Schedule, affected with notice of, or put upon enquiry as to, the rights of any person in relation to any shares or debentures.

25. The register shall—
   (a) if the company's register of members is kept at its registered office, be kept there;
   (b) if the company's register of members is not so kept, be kept at the company's registered office or at the place where its register of members is kept;
and shall be open to the inspection of any member of the company without charge and of any other person on payment of 5 pence, or such less sum as the company may prescribe, for each inspection.

26.—(1) Any member of the company or other person may require a copy of the register, or of any part of it, on payment of 10 pence, or such less sum as the company may prescribe, for every 100 words or fractional part of 100 words required to be copied.

(2) The company shall cause any copy so required by a person to be sent to him within the period of 10 days beginning with the day after that on which the requirement is received by the company.

27. The company shall send notice in the prescribed form to the registrar of companies of the place where the register is kept and of any change in that place, save in a case in which it has at all times been kept at its registered office.

28. Unless the register is in such a form as to constitute in itself an index, the company shall keep an index of the names inscribed in it, which shall—
   (a) in respect of each name, contain a sufficient indication to enable the information entered against it to be readily found; and
   (b) be kept at the same place as the register;
and the company shall, within 14 days after the date on which a name is entered in the register, make any necessary alteration in the index.

29. The register shall be produced at the commencement of the company's annual general meeting and remain open and accessible during the continuance of the meeting to any person attending the meeting.

Section 362   SCHEDULE 14

OVERSEAS BRANCH REGISTERS

PART I

COUNTRIES AND TERRITORIES IN WHICH OVERSEAS BRANCH
REGISTER MAY BE KEPT

Northern Ireland
Any part of Her Majesty's dominions outside the United Kingdom, the Channel Islands or the Isle of Man

Bangladesh	India
Cyprus	Kenya
Dominica	Kiribati
The Gambia	Lesotho
Ghana	Malawi
Guyana	Malaysia

Malta

Nigeria

Pakistan

Republic of Ireland

Seychelles

Sierra Leone

Singapore

South Africa

Sri Lanka

Swaziland

Trinidad and Tobago

Uganda

Zimbabwe

PART II

GENERAL PROVISIONS WITH RESPECT TO OVERSEAS BRANCH REGISTERS

1.—(1) A company keeping an overseas branch register shall give to the registrar of companies notice in the prescribed form of the situation of the office where any overseas branch register is kept and of any change in its situation, and, if it is discontinued, of its discontinuance.

(2) Any such notice shall be given within 14 days of the opening of the office or of the change or discontinuance, as the case may be.

(3) If default is made in complying with this paragraph, the company and every officer of it who is in default is liable to a fine and, for continued contravention, to a daily default fine.

2.—(1) An overseas branch register is deemed to be part of the company's register of members ("the principal register").

(2) It shall be kept in the same manner in which the principal register is by this Act required to be kept, except that the advertisement before closing the register shall be inserted in a newspaper circulating in the district where the overseas branch register is kept.

3.—(1) A competent court in a country or territory where an overseas branch register is kept may exercise the same jurisdiction of rectifying the register as is under this Act exercisable by the court in Great Britain; and the offences of refusing inspection or copies of the register, and of authorising or permitting the refusal, may be prosecuted summarily before any tribunal having summary criminal jurisdiction.

(2) This paragraph extends only to those countries and territories where, immediately before the coming into force of this Act, provision to the same effect made by section 120(2) of the Companies Act 1948 had effect as part of the local law.

4.—(1) The company shall—

    (a) transmit to its registered office a copy of every entry in its overseas branch register as soon as may be after the entry is made, and

    (b) cause to be kept at the place where the company's principal register is kept a duplicate of its overseas branch register duly entered up from time to time.

Every such duplicate is deemed for all purposes of this Act to be part of the principal register.

(2) If default is made in complying with sub-paragraph (1), the company and every officer of it who is in default is liable to a fine and, for continued contravention, to a daily default fine.

(3) Where, by virtue of section 353(1)(b), the principal register is kept at the office of some person other than the company, and by reason of any default of his the company fails to comply with sub-paragraph (1)(b) above he is liable to the same penalty as if he were an officer of the company who was in default.

5. Subject to the above provisions with respect to the duplicate register, the shares registered in an overseas branch register shall be distinguished from those registered in the principal register; and no transaction with respect to any shares registered in an overseas branch register shall, during the continuance of that registration, be registered in any other register.

6. A company may discontinue to keep an overseas branch register, and thereupon all entries in that register shall be transferred to some other overseas branch register kept by the company in the same country or territory, or to the principal register.

7. Subject to the provisions of this Act, any company may, by its articles, make such provisions as it thinks fit respecting the keeping of overseas branch registers.

[1] 8. An instrument of transfer of a share registered in an overseas branch register (other than such a register kept in Northern Ireland) is deemed a transfer of property situated

outside the United Kingdom and, unless executed in a part of the United Kingdom, is exempt from stamp duty chargeable in Great Britain.

_____

NOTE
[1] Excluded by the Finance Act 1986, s.99(10)(*b*).

_____

PART III

PROVISIONS FOR BRANCH REGISTERS OF OVERSEA COMPANIES TO BE KEPT IN GREAT BRITAIN

9.—(1) If by virtue of the law in force in any country or territory to which this paragraph applies companies incorporated under that law have power to keep in Great Britain branch registers of their members resident in Great Britain, Her Majesty may by Order in Council direct that—

(*a*) so much of section 353 as requires a company's register of members to be kept at its registered office,

(*b*) section 356 (register to be open to inspection by members), and

(*c*) section 359 (power of court to rectify),

shall, subject to any modifications and adaptations specified in the Order, apply to and in relation to any such branch registers kept in Great Britain as they apply to and in relation to the registers of companies subject to those sections.

(2) The countries and territories to which this paragraph applies are—

(*a*) all those specified in Part I of this Schedule, plus the Channel Islands and the Isle of Man,

(*b*) Botswana, Zambia and Tonga, and

(*c*) any territory for the time being under Her Majesty's protection or administered by the government of the United Kingdom under the trusteeship system of the United Nations.

Section 363   SCHEDULE 15

CONTENTS OF ANNUAL RETURN OF A COMPANY HAVING A SHARE CAPITAL

1. The address of the registered office of the company.

2.—(1) If the register of members is, under the provisions of this Act, kept elsewhere than at the registered office of the company, the address of the place where it is kept.

(2) If any register of holders of debentures of the company or any duplicate of any such register or part of any such register is, under the provisions of this Act, kept, in England and Wales in the case of a company registered in England and Wales or in Scotland in the case of a company registered in Scotland, elsewhere than at the registered office of the company, the address of the place where it is kept.

3. A summary, distinguishing between shares issued for cash and shares issued as fully or partly paid up otherwise than in cash, specifying the following particulars—

(*a*) the amount of the share capital of the company and the number of shares into which it is divided;

(*b*) the number of shares taken from the commencement of the company up to the date of the return;

(*c*) the amount called up on each share;

(*d*) the total amount of calls received;

(*e*) the total amount of calls unpaid;

(*f*) the total amount of the sums (if any) paid by way of commission in respect of any shares or debentures;

(*g*) the discount allowed on the issue of any shares issued at a discount or so much of that discount as has not been written off at the date on which the return is made;

(*h*) the total amount of the sums (if any) allowed by way of discount in respect of any debentures since the date of the last return;

(*i*) the total number of shares forfeited;

(*j*) the total number of shares for which share warrants are outstanding at the date of the return and of share warrants issued and surrendered respectively since the date of the last return, and the number of shares comprised in each warrant.

4. Particulars of the total amount of the company's indebtedness in respect of all mortgages and charges (whenever created) of any description specified in section 396(1) or, in the case of a company registered in Scotland, section 410(4).

5. A list—
   (a) containing the names and addresses of all persons who, on the fourteenth day after the company's annual general meeting for the year, are members of the company, and of persons who have ceased to be members since the date of the last return or, in the case of the first return, since the incorporation of the company;
   (b) stating the number of shares held by each of the existing members at the date of the return, specifying shares transferred since the date of the last return (or, in the case of the first return, since the incorporation of the company) by persons who are still members and have ceased to be members respectively and the dates of registration of the transfers;
   (c) if the names are not arranged in alphabetical order, having annexed to it an index sufficient to enable the name of any person in the list to be easily found.

6. All such particulars with respect to persons who at the date of the return are the directors of the company and any person who at that date is the secretary of the company as are by this Act required to be contained with respect to directors and the secretary respectively in the register of the directors and secretaries of a company.

¹ SCHEDULE 15A

WRITTEN RESOLUTIONS OF PRIVATE COMPANIES

_____

NOTE
¹ Inserted by the Companies Act 1989, s. 114.

_____

PART I

EXCEPTIONS

1. Section 381A does not apply to—
   (a) a resolution under section 303 removing a director before the expiration of his period of office, or
   (b) a resolution under section 391 removing an auditor before the expiration of his term of office.

PART II

ADAPTATION OF PROCEDURAL REQUIREMENTS

Introductory

2.—(1) In this Part of this Schedule (which adapts certain requirements of this Act in relation to proceedings under section 381A)—
   (a) a "written resolution" means a resolution agreed to, or proposed to be agreed to, in accordance with that section, and
   (b) a "relevant member" means a member by whom, or on whose behalf, the resolution is required to be signed in accordance with that section.
(2) A written resolution is not effective if any of the requirements of this Part of this Schedule is not complied with.

Section 95 (disapplication of pre-emption rights)

3.—(1) The following adaptations have effect in relation to a written resolution under section 95(2) (disapplication of pre-emption rights), or renewing a resolution under that provision.
(2) So much of section 95(5) as requires the circulation of a written statement by the directors with a notice of meeting does not apply, but such a statement must be supplied to each relevant member at or before the time at which the resolution is supplied to him for signature.

(3) Section 95(6) (offences) applies in relation to the inclusion in any such statement of matter which is misleading, false or deceptive in a material particular.

Section 155 (financial assistance for purchase of company's own shares or those of holding company)

4. In relation to a written resolution giving approval under section 155(4) or (5) (financial assistance for purchase of company's own shares or those of holding company), section 157(4)(*a*) (documents to be available at meeting) does not apply, but the documents referred to in that provision must be supplied to each relevant member at or before the time at which the resolution is supplied to him for signature.

Sections 164, 165 and 167 (authority for off-market purchase or contingent purchase contract of company's own shares)

5.—(1) The following adaptations have effect in relation to a written resolution—
  (*a*) conferring authority to make an off-market purchase of the company's own shares under section 164(2),
  (*b*) conferring authority to vary a contract for an off-market purchase of the company's own shares under section 164(7), or
  (*c*) varying, revoking or renewing any such authority under section 164(3).

(2) Section 164(5) (resolution ineffective if passed by exercise of voting rights by member holding shares to which the resolution relates) does not apply; but for the purposes of section 381A(1) a member holding shares to which the resolution relates shall not be regarded as a member who would be entitled to attend and vote.

(3) Section 164(6) (documents to be available at company's registered office and at meeting) does not apply, but the documents referred to in that provision and, where that provision applies by virtue of section 164(7), the further documents referred to in that provision must be supplied to each relevant member at or before the time at which the resolution is supplied to him for signature.

(4) The above adaptations also have effect in relation to a written resolution in relation to which the provisions of section 164(3) to (7) apply by virtue of—
  (*a*) section 165(2) (authority for contingent purchase contract), or
  (*b*) section 167(2) (approval of release of rights under contract approved under section 164 or 165).

Section 173 (approval for payment out of capital)

6.—(1) The following adaptations have effect in relation to a written resolution giving approval under section 173(2) (redemption or purchase of company's own shares out of capital).

(2) Section 174(2) (resolution ineffective if passed by exercise of voting rights by member holding shares to which the resolution relates) does not apply; but for the purposes of section 381A(1) a member holding shares to which the resolution relates shall not be regarded as a member who would be entitled to attend and vote.

(3) Section 174(4) (documents to be available at meeting) does not apply, but the documents referred to in that provision must be supplied to each relevant member at or before the time at which the resolution is supplied to him for signature.

Section 319 (approval of directors' service contract)

7. In relation to a written resolution approving any such term as is mentioned in section 319(1) (director's contract of employment for more than five years), section 319(5) (documents to be available at company's registered office and at meeting) does not apply, but the documents referred to in that provision must be supplied to each relevant member at or before the time at which the resolution is supplied to him for signature.

Section 337 (funding of director's expenditure in performing his duties)

8. In relation to a written resolution giving approval under section 337(3)(*a*) (funding a director's expenditure in performing his duties), the requirement of that provision that certain matters be disclosed at the meeting at which the resolution is passed does not apply, but those matters must be disclosed to each relevant member at or before the time at which the resolution is supplied to him for signature.

Section 427A   [1] SCHEDULE 15B

PROVISIONS SUBJECT TO WHICH SS.425–427 HAVE EFFECT IN THEIR APPLICATION TO MERGERS AND
DIVISIONS OF PUBLIC COMPANIES

———

NOTE
[1] Inserted by S.I. 1987 No. 1991. Renumbered by the Companies Act 1989, s. 114(2).

———

Meeting of transferee company
  1. Subject to paragraphs 10(1), 12(4) and 14(2), the court shall not sanction a compromise
or arrangement under section 425(2) unless a majority in number representing three-fourths
in value of each class of members of every pre-existing transferee company concerned in the
scheme, present and voting either in person or by proxy at a meeting, agree to the scheme.

Draft terms of merger
  2.—(1) The court shall not sanction the compromise or arrangement under section 425(2)
unless—
  (*a*) a draft of the proposed terms of the scheme (from here on referred to as the "draft
      terms") has been drawn up and adopted by the directors of all the transferor and pre-
      existing transferee companies concerned in the scheme,
  (*b*) subject to paragraph 11(3), in the case of each of those companies the directors have
      delivered a copy of the draft terms to the registrar of companies and the registrar has
      published in the Gazette notice of receipt by him of a copy of the draft terms from
      that company, and
  (*c*) subject to paragraphs 10 to 14, that notice was so published at least one month before
      the date of any meeting of that company summoned under section 425(1) or for the
      purposes of paragraph 1.
  (2) Subject to paragraph 12(2), the draft terms shall give particulars of at least the following
matters—
  (*a*) in respect of each transferor company and transferee company concerned in the
      scheme, its name, the address of its registered office and whether it is a company
      limited by shares or a company limited by guarantee and having a share capital;
  (*b*) the number of shares in any transferee company to be allotted to members of any
      transferor company for a given number of their shares (from here on referred to as
      the "share exchange ratio") and the amount of any cash payment;
  (*c*) the terms relating to the allotment of shares in any transferee company;
  (*d*) the date from which the holding of shares in a transferee company will entitle the
      holders to participate in profits, and any special conditions affecting that entitlement;
  (*e*) the date from which the transactions of any transferor company are to be treated for
      accounting purposes as being those of any transferee company;

[THE NEXT PAGE IS I 423]

    (*f*) any rights or restrictions attaching to shares or other securities in any transferee company to be allotted under the scheme to the holders of shares to which any special rights or restrictions attach, or of other securities, in any transferor company, or the measures proposed concerning them;

    (*g*) any amount or benefit paid or given or intended to be paid or given to any of the experts referred to in paragraph 5 or to any director of a transferor company or pre-existing transferee company, and the consideration for the payment of benefit.

(3) Where the scheme is a case 3 Scheme the draft terms shall also—

    (*a*) give particulars of the property and liabilities to be transferred (to the extent these are known to the transferor company) and their allocation among the transferee companies;

    (*b*) make provision for the allocation among and transfer to the transferee companies of any other property and liabilities which the transferor company has or may subsequently acquire; and

    (*c*) specify the allocation to members of the transferor company of shares in the transferee companies and the criteria upon which that allocation is based.

Documents and information to be made available

3. Subject to paragraphs 10 to 14, the court shall not sanction the compromise or arrangement under section 425(2) unless—

    (*a*) in the case of each transferor company and each pre-existing transferee company the directors have drawn up and adopted a report complying with paragraph 4 (from here on referred to as a "directors' report");

    (*b*) where the scheme is a case 3 Scheme, the directors of the transferor company have reported to every meeting of the members or any class of members of that company summoned under section 425(1), and to the directors of each transferee company, any material changes in the property and liabilities of the transferor company between the date when the draft terms were adopted and the date of the meeting in question;

    (*c*) where the directors of a transferor company have reported to the directors of a transferee company such a change as is mentioned in sub-paragraph (*b*) above, the latter have reported that change to every meeting of the members or any class of members of that transferee company summoned for the purposes of paragraph 1, or have sent a report of that change to every member who would have been entitled to receive a notice of such a meeting;

    (*d*) a report complying with paragraph 5 has been drawn up on behalf of each transferor company and pre-existing transferee company (from here on referred to as an "expert's report");

    (*e*) the members of any transferor company or transferee company were able to inspect at the registered office of that company copies of the documents listed in paragraph 6(1) in relation to every transferor company and pre-existing transferee company concerned in the scheme during a period beginning one month before, and ending on, the date of the first meeting of the members or any class of members of the first-mentioned transferor or transferee company summoned either under section 425(1) or for the purposes of paragraph 1 and those members were able to obtain copies of those documents or any part of them on request during that period free of charge; and

    (*f*) the memorandum and articles of association of any transferee company which is not a pre-existing transferee company, or a draft thereof, has been approved by ordinary resolution of every transferor company concerned in the scheme.

Directors' report

4.—(1) The directors' report shall consist of—

    (*a*) the statement required by section 426, and

    (*b*) insofar as that statement does not contain the following matters, a further statement—

        (i) setting out the legal and economic grounds for the draft terms, and in particular for the share exchange ratio, and, where the scheme is a case 3 Scheme, for the criteria upon which the allocation to the members of the transferor company of shares in the transferee companies was based, and

        (ii) specifying any special valuation difficulties.

(2) Where the scheme is a case 3 Scheme the directors' report shall also state whether a report has been made to the transferee company under section 103 (non-cash consideration to be valued before allotment) and, if so, whether that report has been delivered to the registrar of companies.

Expert's report

5.—(1) Except where a joint expert is appointed under sub-paragraph (2) below, an expert's report shall consist of a separate written report on the draft terms to the members of one transferor company or pre-existing transferee company concerned in the scheme drawn up by a separate expert appointed on behalf of that company.

(2) The court may, on the joint application of all the transferor companies and pre-existing transferee companies concerned in the scheme, approve the appointment of a joint expert to draw up a single report on behalf of all those companies.

(3) An expert shall be independent of any of the companies concerned in the scheme, that is to say a person qualified at the time of the report to be appointed, or to continue to be, an auditor of those companies.

(4) However, where it appears to an expert that a valuation is reasonably necessary to enable him to draw up the report, and it appears to him to be reasonable for that valuation, or part of it, to be made (or for him to accept such a valuation) by another person who—

(a) appears to him to have the requisite knowledge and experience to make the valuation or that part of it; and

(b) is not an officer or servant of any of the companies concerned in the scheme or any other body corporate which is one of those companies' subsidiary or holding company or a subsidiary of one of those companies' holding company or a partner or employee of such an officer or servant,

he may arrange for or accept such a valuation, together with a report which will enable him to make his own report under this paragraph.

(5) The reference in sub-paragraph (4) above to an officer or servant does not include an auditor.

(6) Where any valuation is made by a person other than the expert himself, the latter's report shall state that fact and shall also—

(a) state the former's name and what knowledge and experience he has to carry out the valuation, and

(b) describe so much of the undertaking, property and liabilities as were valued by the other person, and the method used to value them, and specify the date of the valuation.

(7) An expert's report shall—

(a) indicate the method or methods used to arrive at the share exchange ratio proposed;

(b) give an opinion as to whether the method or methods used are reasonable in all the circumstances of the case, indicate the values arrived at using each such method and (if there is more than one method) give an opinion on the relative importance attributed to such methods in arriving at the value decided on;

(c) describe any special valuation difficulties which have arisen;

(d) state whether in the expert's opinion the share exchange ratio is reasonable; and

(e) in the case of a valuation made by a person other than himself, state that it appeared to himself reasonable to arrange for it to be so made or to accept a valuation so made.

(8) Each expert has the right of access to all such documents of all the transferor companies and pre-existing transferee companies concerned in the scheme, and the right to require from the companies' officers all such information, as he thinks necessary for the purpose of making his report.

Inspection of documents

[1] 6.—(1) The documents referred to in paragraph 3(e) are, in relation to any company,—

(a) the draft terms;

(b) the directors' report referred to in paragraph 4 above;

(c) the expert's report;

[2](d) the company's annual accounts, together with the relevant directors' report and auditors' report, for the last three financial years ending on or before the relevant date; and

[2](e) if the last of those financial years ended more than six months before the relevant date, an accounting statement in the form described in the following provisions.

[3] In paragraphs (d) and (e) "the relevant date" means one month before the first meeting of the company summoned under section 425(1) or for the purposes of paragraph 1.

[4] (2) The accounting statement shall consist of—

(a) a balance sheet dealing with the state of the affairs of the company as at a date not more than three months before the draft terms were adopted by the directors, and;

(b) where the company would be required to prepare group accounts if that date were the last day of a financial year, a consolidated balance sheet dealing with the state of affairs of the company and its subsidiary undertakings as at that date.

[4] (3) The requirements of this Act as to balance sheets forming part of a company's annual accounts, and the matters to be included in notes thereto, apply to any balance sheet required for the accounting statement, with such modifications as are necessary by reason of its being prepared otherwise than as at the last day of a financial year.

[4] (4) Any balance sheet required for the accounting statement shall be approved by the board of directors and signed on behalf of the board by a director of the company.

[4] (5) In relation to a company within the meaning of Article 3 of the Companies (Northern Ireland) Order 1986, the references in this paragraph to the requirements of this Act shall be construed as reference to the corresponding requirements of that Order.

NOTES
[1] As amended by the Companies Act 1989, s. 23 and Sched. 10, para. 22.
[2] Substituted by the Companies Act 1989, s. 23 and Sched. 10, para. 22(3).
[3] Inserted by the Companies Act 1989, s. 23 and Sched. 10, para. 22(4).
[4] Substituted by the Companies Act 1989, s. 23 and Sched. 10, para. 22(5).

Transferor company holding its own shares

7. The court shall not sanction under section 425(2) a compromise or arrangement under which any shares in a transferee company are to be allotted to a transferor company or its nominee in respect of shares in that transferor company held by it or its nominee.

Securities other than shares to which special rights are attached

8.—(1) Where any security of a transferor company to which special rights are attached is held by a person other than as a member or creditor of the company, the court shall not sanction a compromise or arrangement under section 425(2) unless under the scheme that person is to receive rights in a transferee company of equivalent value.

(2) Sub-paragraph (1) above shall not apply in the case of any such security where—
  (a) the holder has agreed otherwise; or
  (b) the holder is, or under the scheme is to be, entitled to have the security purchased by a transferee company involved in the scheme on terms which the court considers reasonable.

Date and consequences of the compromise or arrangement

9.—(1) The following provisions of this paragraph shall apply where the court sanctions a compromise or arrangement.

(2) The court shall in the order sanctioning the compromise or arrangement or in a subsequent order under section 427 fix a date on which the transfer or transfers to the transferee company or transferee companies of the undertaking, property and liabilities of the transferor company shall take place; and any such order which provide for the dissolution of the transferor company shall fix the same date for the dissolution.

(3) If it is necessary for the transferor company to take any steps to ensure that the undertaking, property and liabilities are fully transferred, the court shall fix a date, not later than six months after the date fixed under sub-paragraph (2) above, by which such steps must be taken and for that purpose may postpone the dissolution of the transferor company until that date.

(4) The court may postpone or further postpone the date fixed under sub-paragraph (3) above if it is satisfied that the steps there mentioned cannot be completed by the date (or latest date) fixed under that sub-paragraph.

Exceptions

10.—(1) The court may sanction a compromise or arrangement under section 425(2) notwithstanding that—
  (a) any meeting otherwise required by paragraph 1 has not been summoned by a pre-existing transferee company ("the relevant company"), and
  (b) paragraphs 2(1)(c) and 3(e) have not been complied with in respect of that company, if the court is satisfied that the conditions specified in sub-paragraph (2) below have been complied with.

(2) Subject to paragraphs 11(3) and 12(3), the conditions mentioned in sub-paragraph (1) above are—
  (a) that the publication of notice of receipt of the draft terms by the registrar of companies referred to in paragraph 2(1)(b) took place in respect of the relevant company at least one month before the date of any meeting of members of any transferor company concerned in the scheme summoned under section 425(1);

(b) that the members of the relevant company were able to inspect at the registered office of that company the documents listed in paragraph 6(1) in relation to every transferor company and transferee company concerned in the scheme during a period ("the relevant period") beginning one month before, and ending on, the date of any such meeting, and that they were able to obtain copies of those documents or any part of them on request during that period free of charge; and

(c) that one or more members of the relevant company, who together held not less than five per cent. of the paid-up capital of that company which carried the right to vote at general meetings of the company, would have been able during the relevant period to require that a meeting of each class of members be called for the purpose of deciding whether or not to agree to the scheme but that no such requisition had been made.

11.—(1) The following sub-paragraphs apply where the scheme is a case 3 scheme.

(2) Sub-paragraphs (a) to (d) of paragraph 3 shall not apply and sub-paragraph (e) of that paragraph shall not apply as regards the documents listed in paragraph 6(1)(b), (c) and (e), if all members holding shares in, and all persons holding other securities of, any of the transferor companies and pre-existing transferee companies concerned in the scheme on the date of the application to the court under section 425(1), being shares or securities which as at that date carry the right to vote in general meetings of the company, so agree.

(3) The court may by order direct in respect of any transferor company or pre-existing transferee company that the requirements relating to—

(a) delivering copies of the draft terms and publication of notice of receipt of the draft terms under paragraph 2(1)(b) and (c), or

(b) inspection under paragraph 3(e),

shall not apply, and may by order direct that paragraph 10 shall apply to any pre-existing transferee company with the omission of sub-paragraph (2)(a) and (b) of that paragraph.

(4) The court shall not make any order under sub-paragraph (3) above unless it is satisfied that the following conditions will be fulfilled—

(a) that the members of the company will have received or will have been able to obtain free of charge copies of the documents listed in paragraph 6(1) in time to examine them before the date of the first meeting of the members or any class of members of the company summoned under section 425(1) or for the purposes of paragraph 1;

(b) in the case of a pre-existing transferee company, where in the circumstances described in paragraph 10 no meeting is held, that the members of that company will have received or will have been able to obtain free of charge copies of those documents in time to require a meeting under paragraph 10(2)(c);

(c) that the creditors of the company will have received or will have been able to obtain free of charge copies of the draft terms in time to examine them before the date of the meeting of the members or any class of members of the company, or, in the circumstances referred to in paragraph (b) above, at the same time as the members of the company; and

(d) that no prejudice would be caused to the members or creditors of any transferor company or transferee company concerned in the scheme by making the order in question.

Transferee company or companies holding shares in the transferor company

12.—(1) Where the scheme is a case 1 scheme and in the case of every transferor company concerned—

(a) the shares in that company, and

(b) such securities of that company (other than shares) as carry the right to vote at general meetings of that company,

are all held by or on behalf of the transferee company, section 427A and this Schedule shall apply subject to the following sub-paragraphs.

(2) The draft terms need not give particulars of the matters mentioned in paragraph 2(2)(b), (c) or (d).

(3) Section 426 and sub-paragraphs (a) and (d) of paragraph 3 shall not apply, and sub-paragraph (e) of that paragraph shall not apply as regards the documents listed in paragraph 6(1)(b) and (c).

(4) The court may sanction the compromise or arrangement under section 425(2) notwithstanding that—

(a) any meeting otherwise required by section 425 or paragraph 1 has not been summoned by any company concerned in the scheme, and

(b) paragraphs 2(1)(c) and 3(e) have not been complied with in respect of that company,

if it is satisfied that the conditions specified in the following sub-paragraphs have been complied with.

(5) The conditions mentioned in the previous sub-paragraph are—

    (*a*) that the publication of notice of receipt of the draft terms by the registrar of companies referred to in paragraph 2(1)(*b*) took place in respect of every transferor company and transferee company concerned in the scheme at least one month before the date of the order under section 425(2) ("the relevant date");

    (*b*) that the members of the transferee company were able to inspect at the registered office of that company copies of the documents listed in paragraphs 6(1)(*a*), (*d*) and (*e*) in relation to every transferor company or transferee company concerned in the scheme during a period ("the relevant period") beginning one month before, and ending on, the relevant date and that they were able to obtain copies of those documents or any part of them on request during that period free of charge; and

    (*c*) that one or more members of the transferee company who together held not less than five per cent. of the paid-up capital of the company which carried the right to vote at general meetings of the company would have been able during the relevant period to require that a meeting of each class of members be called for the purpose of deciding whether or not to agree to the scheme but that no such requisition has been made.

13.—(1) Where the scheme is a case 3 scheme and—

    (*a*) the shares in the transferor company, and

    (*b*) such securities of that company (other than shares) as carry the right to vote at general meetings of that company,

are all held by or on behalf of one or more transferee companies, section 427A and this Schedule shall apply subject to the following sub-paragraphs.

(2) The court may sanction a compromise or arrangement under section 425(2) notwithstanding that—

    (*a*) any meeting otherwise required by section 425 has not been summoned by the transferor company, and

    (*b*) paragraphs 2(1)(*c*) and 3(*b*) and (*e*) have not been complied with in respect of that company,

if it is satisfied that the conditions specified in the following sub-paragraph have been complied with.

(3) The conditions referred to in the previous sub-paragraph are—

    (*a*) the conditions set out in paragraph 12(5)(*a*) and (*c*);

    (*b*) that the members of the transferor company and every transferee company concerned in the scheme were able to inspect at the registered office of the company of which they were members copies of the documents listed in paragraph 6(1) in relation to every such company during a period beginning one month before, and ending on, the date of the order under section 425(2) ("the relevant date"), and that they were able to obtain copies of those documents or any part of them on request during that period free of charge; and

    (*c*) that the directors of the transferor company have sent to every member who would have been entitled to receive a notice of the meeting (had it been called), and to the directors of each transferee company, a report of any material changes in the property and liabilities of the transferor company between the date when the draft terms were adopted and a date one month before the relevant date.

14.—(1) Where the scheme is a case 1 scheme and in the case of every transferor company concerned 90 per cent. or more (but not all) of—

    (*a*) the shares in that company, and

    (*b*) such securities of that company (other than shares) as carry the right to vote at general meetings of that company,

are held by or on behalf of the transferee company, section 427A and this Schedule shall apply subject to the following sub-paragraphs.

(2) The court may sanction a compromise or arrangement under section 425(2) notwithstanding that—

    (*a*) any meeting otherwise required by paragraph 1 has not been summoned by the transferee company, and

    (*b*) paragraphs 2(1)(*c*) and 3(*e*) have not been complied with in respect of that company,

if the court is satisfied that the conditions specified in the following sub-paragraph have been complied with.

(3) The conditions referred to in the previous sub-paragraph are the same conditions as those specified in paragraph 10(2), save that for this purpose the condition contained in paragraph 10(2)(*b*) shall be treated as referring only to the documents listed in paragraph 6(1)(*a*), (*d*) and (*e*).

Liability of transferee companies for the default of another

15.—(1) Where the scheme is a case 3 scheme, each transferee company shall be jointly and severally liable, subject to sub-paragraph (2) below, for any liability transferred to any other transferee company under the scheme to the extent that that other company has made default in satisfying that liability, but so that no transferee company shall be so liable for an amount greater than the amount arrived at by calculating the value at the time of the transfer of the property transferred to it under the scheme less the amount at that date of the liabilities so transferred.

(2) If a majority in number representing three-fourths in value of the creditors or any class of creditors of the transferor company present and voting either in person or by proxy at a meeting summoned under section 425(1) so agree, sub-paragraph (1) above shall not apply in respect of the liabilities of the creditors or that class of creditors.

SCHEDULE 16

ORDERS IN COURSE OF WINDING UP PRONOUNCED IN
VACATION (SCOTLAND)

[Repealed by the Insolvency Act 1986, Sched. 12.]

SCHEDULES 17–19

[Repealed by the Insolvency Act 1985, Sched. 10, Pt. II.]

[THE NEXT PAGE IS I 425]

SCHEDULE 20

VESTING OF DISCLAIMED PROPERTY; PROTECTION OF
THIRD PARTIES

PART I

[Repealed by the Insolvency Act 1985, Sched. 10, Pt. II.]

PART II

CROWN DISCLAIMER UNDER SECTION 656
(SCOTLAND ONLY)

5. The court shall not under section 657 make a vesting order, where the property disclaimed is held under a lease, in favour of a person claiming under the company (whether as sub-lessee or as creditor in a duly registered or, as appropriate, recorded heritable security over a lease), except on the following terms.

6. The person must by the order be made subject—
   (a) to the same liabilities and obligations as those to which the company was subject under the lease in respect of the property at the commencement of the winding up, or
   (b) (if the court thinks fit) only to the same liabilities and obligations as if the lease had been assigned to him at that date;
and in either event (if the case so requires) the liabilities and obligations must be as if the lease had comprised only the property comprised in the vesting order.

7. A creditor or sub-lessee declining to accept a vesting order on such terms is excluded from all interest in and security over the property.

8. If there is no person claiming under the company who is willing to accept an order on such terms, the court has power to vest the company's estate and interest in the property in any person liable (either personally or in a representative character, and either alone or jointly with the company) to perform the lessee's obligations under the lease, freed and discharged from all interests, rights and obligations created by the company in the lease or in relation to the lease.

9. For the purposes of paragraph 5 above, a heritable security is duly recorded if it is recorded in the Register of Sasines and is duly registered if registered in accordance with the Land Registration (Scotland) Act 1979.

SCHEDULE 21

EFFECT OF REGISTRATION UNDER SECTION 680

Interpretation

1. In this Schedule—
    "registration" means registration in pursuance of section 680 in Chapter II of Part XXII
        of this Act, and "registered" has the corresponding meaning, and
    "instrument" includes deed of settlement, contract of copartnery and letters patent.

Vesting of property

2. All property belonging to or vested in the company at the date of its registration passes to
and vests in the company on registration for all the estate and interest of the company in the
property.

Existing liabilities

3. Registration does not affect the company's rights or liabilities in respect of any debt or
obligation incurred, or contract entered into, by, to, with or on behalf of the company before
registration.

Pending actions at law

4.—(1) All actions and other legal proceedings which at the time of the company's registration are pending by or against the company, or the public officer or any member of it, may be
continued in the same manner as if the registration had not taken place.

(2) However, execution shall not issue against the effects of any individual member of the
company on any judgment, decree or order obtained in such an action or proceeding; but in
the event of the company's property and effects being insufficient to satisfy the judgment,
decree or order, an order may be obtained for winding up the company.

The company's constitution

5.—(1) All provisions contained in any Act of Parliament or other instrument constituting or regulating the company are deemed to be conditions and regulations of the company, in the same manner and with the same incidents as if so much of them as would, if the company had been formed under this Act, have been required to be inserted in the memorandum, were contained in a registered memorandum, and the residue were contained in registered articles.

(2) The provisions brought in under this paragraph include, in the case of a company registered as a company limited by guarantee, those of the resolution declaring the amount of the guarantee; and they include also the statement under section 681(5)(a), and any statement under section 684(2).

6.—(1) All the provisions of this Act apply to the company, and to its members, contributories and creditors, in the same manner in all respects as if it had been formed under this Act, subject as follows.

(2) Table A does not apply unless adopted by special resolution.

(3) Provisions relating to the numbering of shares do not apply to any joint stock company whose shares are not numbered.

(4) Subject to the provisions of this Schedule, the company does not have power—
   (a) to alter any provision contained in an Act of Parliament relating to the company,
   (b) without the sanction of the Secretary of State, to alter any provision contained in letters patent relating to the company.

(5) The company does not have power to alter any provision contained in a royal charter or letters patent with respect to the company's objects.

Capital structure

7. Provisions of this Act with respect to—
   (a) the registration of an unlimited company as limited,
   (b) the powers of an unlimited company on registration as a limited company to increase the nominal amount of its share capital and to provide that a portion of its share capital shall not be capable of being called up except in the event of winding up, and
   (c) the power of a limited company to determine that a portion of its share capital shall not be capable of being called up except in that event,
apply, notwithstanding any provisions contained in an Act of Parliament, royal charter or other instrument constituting or regulating the company.

Supplementary

8. Nothing in paragraphs 5 to 7 authorises a company to alter any such provisions contained in an instrument constituting or regulating the company as would, if the company had originally been formed under this Act, have been required to be contained in the memorandum and are not authorised to be altered by this Act.

9. None of the provisions of this Act (except section 461(3)) derogate from any power of altering the company's constitution or regulations which may, by virtue of any Act of Parliament or other instrument constituting or regulating it, be vested in the company.

Section 718

¹ SCHEDULE 22

PROVISIONS OF THIS ACT APPLYING TO UNREGISTERED COMPANIES

NOTE

¹ As amended by the Financial Services Act 1986, Sched. 16, para. 26, and Sched. 17, and the Companies Act 1989, ss. 71, 123(5), and Scheds. 10 and 24.

Provisions of this Act applied	*Subject-matter*	*Limitations and exceptions (if any)*
In Part I—		
section 18	Statutory and other amendments of memorandum and articles to be registered.	Subject to section 718(3).
section 35	Company's capacity; power of directors to bind it.	Subject to section 718(3).
section 36(4)	Binding effect of contract made for company before its formation.	Subject to section 718(3).
section 40	Official seal for share certificates, etc.	Subject to section 718(3).
section 42	Events affecting a company's status to be officially notified.	Subject to section 718(3).
In Part V—		
section 185(4)	Exemption from duty to prepare certificates where shares etc. issued to clearing house or nominee.	Subject to section 718(3).
section 186	Certificate as evidence of title.	Subject to section 718(3).
Part VII, with— Schedules 4 to 8 ... Schedule 9 (except sub-paragraphs (*a*) to (*d*) of paragraph 2, sub-paragraphs (*c*) (*d*) and (*e*) of paragraph 3 and sub-paragraph (1)(*c*) of paragraph 10), and Schedules 10 and 10A	Accounts and audit.	Subject to section 718(3).
In Part IX—		
section 287	Registered office.	Subject to section 718(3).
sections 288 to 290	Register of directors and secretaries.	—

In Part X, sections 343 to 347	Register to be kept of certain transactions not disclosed in accounts; other related matters.	Subject to section 718(3).
In Part XI—		
section 351(1), (2) and (5)(*a*)	Particulars of company to be given in correspondence.	Subject to section 718(3).
sections 363 (with Schedule 15) to 365	Annual return.	Subject to section 718(3).
sections 384 to 394A	Appointment, etc., of auditors.	Subject to section 718(3).
In Part XIV (except section 446)	Investigation of companies and their affairs; requisition of documents	—
Part XV	Effect of order imposing restrictions on shares.	To apply so far only as relates to orders under section 445.
In Part XXIV—		
sections 706, 708 to 710, 712 and 713	Miscellaneous provisions about registration.	Subject to section 718(3).
section 711	Public notice by registrar of companies with respect to certain documents.	
In Part XXV—		
section 720	Companies to publish periodical statement.	Subject to section 718(3).
section 721	Production and inspection of company's books.	
section 722	Form of company registers, etc.	
section 723	Use of computers for company records.	
section 725	Service of documents.	To apply so far only as these provisions have effect in relation to provisions applying by virtue of the foregoing provisions of this Schedule.
section 730, with Schedule 24	Punishment of offences; meaning of "officer in default".	
section 731	Summary proceedings.	
section 732	Prosecution by public authorities.	
Part XXVI	Interpretation.	To apply so far as requisite for the interpretation of other provisions applied by section 718 and this Schedule.

Section 720   SCHEDULE 23

FORM OF STATEMENT TO BE PUBLISHED BY CERTAIN COMPANIES UNDER
SECTION 720

*The share capital of the company is   , divided into   shares of   each.

The number of shares issued is

Calls to the amount of   pounds per share have been made, under which the sum of   pounds has been received.

The liabilities of the company on the 1st day of January (*or* July) were—
    Debts owing to sundry persons by the company.

        On judgment (in Scotland, in respect of which decree has been granted), £
        On specialty, £
        On notes or bills, £
        On simple contracts, £
        On estimated liabilities, £

The assets of the company on that day were—

        Government securities [*stating them*]
        Bills of exchange and promissory notes, £
        Cash at the bankers, £
        Other securities, £

                ————

NOTE
*If the company has no share capital the portion of the statement relating to capital and shares must be omitted.

Section 730

¹ SCHEDULE 24

PUNISHMENT OF OFFENCES UNDER THIS ACT

NOTE

¹ As amended by the Insolvency Act 1986, Sched. 12, the Company Directors Disqualification Act 1986, Sched. 4, the Financial Services Act 1986, Scheds. 16, para. 27, and 17, and the Companies Act 1989, ss. 63(8), 64(2), 119(2), 120(3), 122(2), 123(2) and 139(3), and Scheds. 10, para. 24, and 24.

Note: In the fourth and fifth columns of this Schedule, "the statutory maximum" means—
  (a) in England and Wales, the prescribed sum under section 32 of the Magistrates' Courts Act 1980 (c. 43), and
  (b) in Scotland, the prescribed sum under section 289B of the Criminal Procedure (Scotland) Act 1975 (c. 21).

Section of Act creating offence	General nature of offence	Mode of prosecution	Punishment	Daily default fine (where applicable)
6(3)	Company failing to deliver to registrar notice or other document, following alteration of its objects.	Summary.	One-fifth of the statutory maximum.	One-fiftieth of the statutory maximum.
18(3)	Company failing to register change in memorandum or articles.	Summary.	One-fifth of the statutory maximum.	One-fiftieth of the statutory maximum.
19(2)	Company failing to send to one of its members a copy of the memorandum or articles, when so required by the member.	Summary.	One-fifth of the statutory maximum.	
20(2)	Where company's memorandum altered, company issuing copy of the memorandum without the alteration.	Summary.	One-fifth of the statutory maximum for each occasion on which copies are so issued after the date of the alteration.	
28(5)	Company failing to change name on direction of Secretary of State.	Summary.	One-fifth of the statutory maximum.	One-fiftieth of the statutory maximum.
31(5)	Company altering its memorandum or articles, so ceasing to be exempt from having "limited" as part of its name.	Summary.	The statutory maximum.	One-tenth of the statutory maximum.
31(6)	Company failing to change name, on Secretary of State's direction, so as to have "limited" (or Welsh equivalent) at the end.	Summary.	One-fifth of the statutory maximum.	One-fiftieth of the statutory maximum.

Section of Act creating offence	General nature of offence	Mode of prosecution	Punishment	Daily default fine (where applicable)
32(4)	Company failing to comply with Secretary of State's direction to change its name, on grounds that the name is misleading.	Summary.	One-fifth of the statutory maximum.	One-fiftieth of the statutory maximum.
33	Trading under misleading name (use of "public limited company" or Welsh equivalent when not so entitled); purporting to be a private company.	Summary.	One-fifth of the statutory maximum.	One-fiftieth of the statutory maximum.
34	Trading or carrying on business with improper use of "limited" or "cyfyngedig".	Summary.	One-fifth of the statutory maximum.	One-fiftieth of the statutory maximum.
54(10)	Public company failing to give notice, or copy of court order, to registrar, concerning application to re-register as private company.	Summary.	One-fifth of the statutory maximum.	One-fiftieth of the statutory maximum.
80(9)	Directors exercising company's power of allotment without the authority required by section 80(1).	1. On indictment. 2. Summary.	A fine. The statutory maximum.	
88(5)	Officer of company failing to deliver return of allotments, etc., to registrar.	1. On indictment. 2. Summary.	A fine. The statutory maximum.	One-tenth of the statutory maximum.
95(6)	Knowingly or recklessly authorising or permitting misleading, false or deceptive material in statement by directors under section 95(5).	1. On indictment. 2. Summary.	Two years or a fine; or both. Six months or the statutory maximum; or both.	
110(2)	Making misleading, false or deceptive statement in connection with valuation under section 103 or 104.	1. On indictment. 2. Summary.	Two years or a fine; or both. Six months or the statutory maximum; or both.	
111(3)	Officer of company failing to deliver copy of asset valuation report to registrar.	1. On indictment. 2. Summary.	A fine. The statutory maximum.	One-tenth of the statutory maximum.
111(4)	Company failing to deliver to registrar copy of resolution under section 104(4), with respect to transfer of an asset as consideration for allotment.	Summary.	One-fifth of the statutory maximum.	One-fiftieth of the statutory maximum.
114	Contravention of any of the provisions of sections 99 to 104, 106.	1. On indictment. 2. Summary.	A fine. The statutory maximum.	

Section	General nature of offence	Mode of prosecution	Punishment	Daily default fine
117(7)	Company doing business or exercising borrowing powers contrary to section 117.	1. On indictment. 2. Summary.	A fine. The statutory maximum.	One-fiftieth of the statutory maximum.
122(2)	Company failing to give notice to registrar of reorganisation of share capital.	Summary.	One-fifth of the statutory maximum.	One-fiftieth of the statutory maximum.
123(4)	Company failing to give notice to registrar of increase of share capital.	Summary.	One-fifth of the statutory maximum.	One-fiftieth of the statutory maximum.
127(5)	Company failing to forward to registrar copy of court order, when application made to cancel resolution varying shareholders' rights.	Summary.	One-fifth of the statutory maximum.	One-fiftieth of the statutory maximum.
128(5)	Company failing to send to registrar statement or notice required by section 128 (particulars of shares carrying special rights).	Summary.	One-fifth of the statutory maximum.	One-fiftieth of the statutory maximum.
129(4)	Company failing to deliver to registrar statement or notice required by section 129 (registration of newly created class rights).	Summary.	One-fifth of the statutory maximum.	One-fiftieth of the statutory maximum.
141	Officer of company concealing name of creditor entitled to object to reduction of capital, or wilfully misrepresenting nature or amount of debt or claim, etc.	1. On indictment. 2. Summary.	A fine. The statutory maximum.	
142(2)	Director authorising or permitting non-compliance with section 142 (requirement to convene company meeting to consider serious loss of capital).	1. On indictment. 2. Summary.	A fine. The statutory maximum.	
143(2)	Company acquiring its own shares in breach of section 143.	1. On indictment. 2. Summary.	In the case of the company, a fine. In the case of an officer of the company who is in default, two years or a fine; or both. In the case of the company, the statutory maximum. In the case of an officer of the company who is in default, six months or the statutory maximum; or both.	

Section of Act creating offence	General nature of offence	Mode of prosecution	Punishment	Daily default fine (where applicable)
149(2)	Company failing to cancel its own shares, acquired by itself, as required by section 146(2); or failing to apply for re-registration as private company as so required in the case there mentioned.	Summary.	One-fifth of the statutory maximum.	One-fiftieth of the statutory maximum.
151(3)	Company giving financial assistance towards acquisition of its own shares.	1. On indictment.	Where the company is convicted, a fine. Where an officer of the company is convicted, two years or a fine; or both.	
		2. Summary.	Where the company is convicted, the statutory maximum. Where an officer of the company is convicted, six months or the statutory maximum; or both.	

Section	General nature of offence	Mode of prosecution	Punishment	Daily default fine
156(6)	Company failing to register statutory declaration under section 155.	Summary.	Where an officer of the company is convicted, six months or the statutory maximum; or both. The statutory maximum.	One-fiftieth of the statutory maximum.
156(7)	Director making statutory declaration under section 155, without having reasonable grounds for opinion expressed in it.	1. On indictment. 2. Summary.	Two years or a fine; or both. Six months or the statutory maximum; or both.	
169(6)	Default by company's officer in delivering to registrar the return required by section 169 (disclosure by company of purchase of own shares).	1. On indictment. 2. Summary.	A fine. The statutory maximum.	One-tenth of the statutory maximum.
169(7)	Company failing to keep copy of contract, etc., at registered office; refusal of inspection to person demanding it.	Summary.	One-fifth of the statutory maximum.	One-fiftieth of the statutory maximum.
173(6)	Director making statutory declaration under section 173 without having reasonable grounds for the opinion expressed in the declaration.	1. On indictment. 2. Summary.	Two years or a fine; or both. Six months or the statutory maximum; or both.	
175(7)	Refusal of inspection of statutory declaration and auditors' report under section 173, etc.	Summary.	One-fifth of the statutory maximum.	One-fiftieth of the statutory maximum.
176(4)	Company failing to give notice to registrar of application to court under section 176, or to register court order.	Summary.	One-fifth of the statutory maximum.	One-fiftieth of the statutory maximum.
183(6)	Company failing to send notice of refusal to register a transfer of shares or debentures.	Summary.	One-fifth of the statutory maximum.	One-fiftieth of the statutory maximum.
185(5)	Company default in compliance with section 185(1) (certificates to be made ready following allotment or transfer of shares, etc.).	Summary.	One-fifth of the statutory maximum.	One-fiftieth of the statutory maximum.
189(1)	Offences of fraud and forgery in connection with share warrants in Scotland.	1. On indictment. 2. Summary.	Seven years or a fine; or both. Six months or the statutory maximum; or both.	
189(2)	Unauthorised making of, or using or possessing apparatus for making, share warrants in Scotland.	1. On indictment. 2. Summary.	Seven years or a fine; or both.	

Section of Act creating offence	General nature of offence	Mode of prosecution	Punishment	Daily default fine (where applicable)
191(4)	Refusal of inspection or copy of register of debenture-holders, etc.	Summary.	Six months or the statutory maximum; or both. One-fifth of the statutory maximum.	One-fiftieth of the statutory maximum.
210(3)	Failure to discharge obligation of disclosure under Part VI; other forms of non-compliance with that Part.	1. On indictment. 2. Summary.	Two years or a fine; or both. Six months or the statutory maximum; or both.	
211(10)	Company failing to keep register of interests disclosed under Part VI; other contraventions of section 211.	Summary.	One-fifth of the statutory maximum.	One-fiftieth of the statutory maximum.
214(5)	Company failing to exercise powers under section 212, when so required by the members.	1. On indictment. 2. Summary.	A fine. The statutory maximum.	
215(8)	Company default in compliance with section 215 (company report of investigation of shareholdings on members' requisition).	1. On indictment. 2. Summary.	A fine. The statutory maximum.	
216(3)	Failure to comply with company notice under section 212; making false statement in response, etc.	1. On indictment. 2. Summary.	Two years or a fine; or both. Six months or the statutory maximum; or both.	
217(7)	Company failing to notify a person that he has been named as a shareholder; on removal of name from register, failing to alter associated index.	Summary.	One-fifth of the statutory maximum.	One-fiftieth of the statutory maximum.
218(3)	Improper removal of entry from register of interests disclosed; company failing to restore entry improperly removed.	Summary.	One-fifth of the statutory maximum.	For continued contravention of section 218(2) one-fiftieth of the statutory maximum.
219(3)	Refusal of inspection of register or report under Part VI; failure to send copy when required.	Summary.	One-fifth of the statutory maximum.	One-fiftieth of the statutory maximum.
221(5) or 222(4)	Company failing to keep accounting records (liability of officers).	1. On indictment. 2. Summary.	Two years or a fine; or both. Six months or the statutory maximum; or both.	
222(6)	Officer of company failing to secure compliance with, or intentionally causing default under section 222(5) (preservation of accounting records for requisite number of years).	1. On indictment. 2. Summary.	Two years or a fine; or both. Six months or the statutory maximum; or both.	

231(6)	Company failing to annex to its annual return certain particulars required by Schedule 5 and not included in annual accounts.	Summary.	One-fifth of the statutory maximum.	One-fiftieth of the statutory maximum.
2332(4)	Default by director or officer of a company in giving notice of matters relating to himself for purposes of Schedule 6 Part I.	Summary.	One-fifth of the statutory maximum.	
234(5)	Non-compliance with Part VII, as to directors' report and its content; directors individually liable.	1. On indictment. 2. Summary.	A fine. The statutory maximum.	
233(6)	Laying or delivery of unsigned balance sheet; circulating copies of balance sheet without signatures.	Summary.	One-fifth of the statutory maximum.	
238(5)	Failing to send company's annual accounts, directors' report and auditors' report to those entitled to receive them.	1. On indictment. 2. Summary.	A fine. The statutory maximum.	
241(2) or 242(2)	Director in default as regards duty to lay and deliver.	Summary.	The statutory maximum.	One-tenth of the statutory maximum.
245(1)	Company's individual accounts not in conformity with requirements of this Act; directors individually liable	1. On indictment. 2. Summary.	A fine. The statutory maximum.	
245(2)	Holding company's group accounts not in conformity with sections 229 and 230 and other requirements of this Act; directors individually liable	1. On indictment. 2. Summary.	A fine. The statutory maximum.	
239(3)	Company failing to supply copy of accounts and reports to shareholder on his demand.	Summary	One-fifth of the statutory maximum.	One-fiftieth of the statutory maximum.
240(6)	Failure to comply with requirements in connection with publication of accounts.	Summary.	One-fifth of the statutory maximum.	One-fiftieth of the statutory maximum.

Section of Act creating offence	General nature of offence	Mode of prosecution	Punishment	Daily default fine (where applicable)
288(4)	Default in complying with section 288 (keeping register of directors and secretaries, refusal of inspection).	Summary.	The statutory maximum.	One-tenth of the statutory maximum.
291(5)	Acting as director of a company without having the requisite share qualification.	Summary.	One-fifth of the statutory maximum.	One-fiftieth of the statutory maximum.
294(3)	Director failing to give notice of his attaining retirement age; acting as director under appointment invalid due to his attaining it.	Summary.	One-fifth of the statutory maximum.	One-fiftieth of the statutory maximum.
305(3)	Company default in complying with section 305 (directors' names to appear on company correspondence, etc.)	Summary.	One-fifth of the statutory maximum.	
306(4)	Failure to state that liability of proposed director or manager is unlimited; failure to give notice of that fact to person accepting office.	1. On indictment. 2. Summary.	A fine. The statutory maximum.	
314(3)	Director failing to comply with section 314 (duty to disclose compensation payable on takeover, etc.); a person's failure to include required particulars in a notice he has to give of such matters.	Summary.	One-fifth of the statutory maximum.	
317(7)	Director failing to disclose interest in contract.	1. On indictment. 2. Summary.	A fine. The statutory maximum.	
318(8)	Company default in complying with section 318(1) or (5) (directors' service contracts to be open to inspection); 14 days' default in complying with section 318(4) (notice to registrar as to where copies of contracts and memoranda are kept); refusal of inspection required under section 318(7).	Summary.	One-fifth of the statutory maximum.	One-fiftieth of the statutory maximum.

Section	Nature of offence	Mode of prosecution	Punishment	Daily default fine
323(2)	Director dealing in options to buy or sell company's listed shares or debentures.	1. On indictment. 2. Summary.	Two years or a fine; or both. Six months or the statutory maximum; or both.	
324(7)	Director failing to notify interest in company's shares; making false statement in purported notification.	1. On indictment. 2. Summary.	Two years or a fine; or both. Six months or the statutory maximum; or both.	
326(2), (3), (4), (5)	Various defaults in connection with company register of directors' interests.	Summary.	One-fifth of the statutory maximum.	Except in the case of section 326(5), one-fiftieth of the statutory maximum.
328(6)	Director failing to notify company that members of his family have, or have exercised, options to buy shares or debentures; making false statement in purported notification.	1. On indictment. 2. Summary.	Two years or a fine; or both. Six months or the statutory maximum; or both.	
329(3)	Company failing to notify investment exchange of acquisition of its securities by a director.	Summary.	One-fifth of the statutory maximum.	One-fiftieth of the statutory maximum.
342(1)	Director of relevant company authorising or permitting company to enter into transaction or arrangement, knowing or suspecting it to contravene section 330.	1. On indictment. 2. Summary.	Two years or a fine; or both. Six months or the statutory maximum; or both.	
342(2)	Relevant company entering into transaction or arrangement for a director in contravention of section 330.	1. On indictment. 2. Summary.	Two years or a fine; or both. Six months or the statutory maximum; or both.	
342(3)	Procuring a relevant company to enter into transaction or arrangement known to be contrary to section 330.	1. On indictment. 2. Summary.	Two years or a fine; or both. Six months or the statutory maximum; or both.	
343(8)	Company failing to maintain register of transactions, etc., made with and for directors and not disclosed in company accounts; failing to make register available at registered office or at company meeting.	1. On indictment. 2. Summary.	A fine. The statutory maximum.	
348(2)	Company failing to paint or affix name; failing to keep it painted or affixed.	Summary.	One-fifth of the statutory maximum.	In the case of failure to keep the name painted or affixed, one-fiftieth of the statutory maximum.
349(2)	Company failing to have name on business correspondence, invoices, etc.	Summary.	One-fifth of the statutory maximum.	One-fifth of the statutory maximum.

Section of Act creating offence	General nature of offence	Mode of prosecution	Punishment	Daily default fine (where applicable)
349(3)	Officer of company issuing business letter or document not bearing company's name.	Summary.	One-fifth of the statutory maximum.	
349(4)	Officer of company signing cheque, bill of exchange, etc. on which company's name not mentioned.	Summary.	One-fifth of the statutory maximum.	
350(1)	Company failing to have its name engraved on company seal.	Summary.	One-fifth of the statutory maximum.	
350(2)	Officer of company, etc., using company seal without name engraved on it.	Summary.	One-fifth of the statutory maximum.	
351(5)(a)	Company failing to comply with section 351(1) or (2) (matters to be stated on business correspondence, etc.)	Summary.	One-fifth of the statutory maximum.	
351(5)(b)	Officer or agent of company issuing, or authorising issue of, business document not complying with those subsections.	Summary.	One-fifth of the statutory maximum.	
351(5)(c)	Contravention of section 351(3) or (4) (information in English to be stated on Welsh company's business correspondence, etc.).	Summary.	One-fifth of the statutory maximum.	For contravention of section 351(3), one-fiftieth of the statutory maximum.
352(5)	Company default in complying with section 352 (requirement to keep register of members and their particulars).	Summary.	One-fifth of the statutory maximum.	One-fiftieth of the statutory maximum.
353(4)	Company failing to send notice to registrar as to place where register of members is kept.	Summary.	One-fifth of the statutory maximum.	One-fiftieth of the statutory maximum.
354(4)	Company failing to keep index of members.	Summary.	One-fifth of the statutory maximum.	One-fiftieth of the statutory maximum.
356(5)	Refusal of inspection of members' register; failure to send copy on requisition.	Summary.	One-fifth of the statutory maximum.	
363(3)	Company with share capital failing to make annual return.	Summary.	The statutory maximum.	One-tenth of the statutory maximum.
364(4)	Company without share capital failing to complete and register annual return in due time.	Summary.	The statutory maximum.	One-tenth of the statutory maximum.
365(3)	Company failing to complete and send annual return to registrar in due time.	Summary.	The statutory maximum.	One-tenth of the statutory maximum.

Section	General nature of offence	Mode of prosecution	Punishment	Daily default fine
366(4)	Company default in holding annual general meeting.	1. On indictment. 2. Summary.	A fine. The statutory maximum.	
367(3)	Company default in complying with Secretary of State's direction to hold company meeting.	1. On indictment. 2. Summary.	A fine. The statutory maximum.	
367(5)	Company failing to register resolution that meeting held under section 367 is to be its annual general meeting.	Summary.	One-fifth of the statutory maximum.	One-fiftieth of the statutory maximum.
372(4)	Failure to give notice, to member entitled to vote at company meeting, that he may do so by proxy.	Summary.	One-fifth of the statutory maximum.	
372(6)	Officer of company authorising or permitting issue of irregular invitations to appoint proxies.	Summary.	One-fifth of the statutory maximum.	
376(7)	Officer of company in default as to circulation of members' resolutions for company meeting.	1. On indictment. 2. Summary.	A fine. The statutory maximum.	
380(5)	Company failing to comply with section 380 (copies of certain resolutions etc. to be sent to registrar of companies).	Summary.	One-fifth of the statutory maximum.	One-fiftieth of the statutory maximum.
380(6)	Company failing to include copy of resolution to which section 380 applies in articles; failing to forward copy to member on request.	Summary.	One-fifth of the statutory maximum for each occasion on which copies are issued or, as the case may be, requested.	
382(5)	Company failing to keep minutes of proceedings at company and board meetings, etc.	Summary.	One-fifth of the statutory maximum.	One-fiftieth of the statutory maximum.
383(4)	Refusal of inspection of minutes of general meeting; failure to send copy of minutes on member's request.	Summary.	One-fifth of the statutory maximum.	One-fiftieth of the statutory maximum.
387(2)	Company failing to give Secretary of State notice of non-appointment of auditors.	Summary,	One-fifth of the statutory maximum.	
389A(2)	Officer of company making false, misleading or deceptive statement to auditors.	1. On indictment. 2. Summary.	2 years or a fine; or both; 6 months or the statutory maximum; or both.	
389A(3)	Subsidiary undertaking or its auditor failing to give information to auditors of parent company.	Summary.	One-fifth of the statutory maximum.	One-fiftieth of the statutory maximum.
389A(4)	Parent company failing to obtain from subsidiary undertaking information for purposes of audit.	Summary.	One-fifth of the statutory maximum.	One-fiftieth of the statutory maximum.

Section of Act creating offence	General nature of offence	Mode of prosecution	Punishment	Daily default fine (where applicable)
389(10)	Person acting as company auditor knowing himself to be disqualified; failing to give notice vacating office when he becomes disqualified.	1. On indictment. 2. Summary.	A fine. The statutory maximum.	One-tenth of the statutory maximum. One-fiftieth of the statutory maximum.
391(2)	Failing to give notice to registrar of removal of auditor.	Summary.	One-fifth of the statutory maximum.	
392(3)	Company failing to forward notice of auditor's resignation to registrar.	1. On indictment. 2. Summary.	A fine The statutory maximum.	One-tenth of the statutory maximum.
392A(5)	Directors failing to convene meeting requisitioned by resigning auditor.	1. On indictment. 2. Summary.	A fine. The statutory maximum.	
394A(1)	Person ceasing to hold office as auditor failing to deposit statement as to circumstances.	1. On indictment 2. Summary	A fine. The statutory maximum.	
394A(4)	Company failing to comply with requirements as to statement of person ceasing to hold office as auditor.	1. On indictment. 2. Summary.	A fine. The statutory maximum.	One-tenth of the statutory maximum.
399(3)	Company failing to send to registrar particulars of charge created by it, or of issue of debentures which requires registration.	1. On indictment. 2. Summary.	A fine. The statutory maximum.	One-tenth of the statutory maximum.
400(4)	Company failing to send to registrar particulars of charge on property acquired.	1. On indictment. 2. Summary.	A fine. The statutory maximum.	One-tenth of the statutory maximum.
402(3)	Authorising or permitting delivery of debenture or certificate of debenture stock, without endorsement on it of certificate of registration of charge.	Summary.	One-fifth of the statutory maximum.	
405(4)	Failure to give notice to registrar of appointment of receiver or manager, or of his ceasing to act.	Summary.	One-fifth of the statutory maximum.	One-fiftieth of the statutory maximum.
407(3)	Authorising or permitting omission from company register of charges.	1. On indictment. 2. Summary.	A fine. The statutory maximum.	
408(3)	Officer of company refusing inspection of charging instrument, or of register of charges.	Summary.	One-fifth of the statutory maximum.	One-fiftieth of the statutory maximum.

415(3)	Scottish company failing to send to registrar particulars of charge created by it, or of issue of debentures which requires registration.	1. On indictment. 2. Summary.	A fine. The statutory maximum.	One-tenth of the statutory maximum.
416(3)	Scottish company failing to send to registrar particulars of charge on property acquired by it.	1. On indictment. 2. Summary.	A fine. The statutory maximum.	One-tenth of the statutory maximum.
422(3)	Scottish company authorising or permitting omission from its register of charges.	1. On indictment. 2. Summary.	A fine. The statutory maximum.	
423(3)	Officer of Scottish company refusing inspection of charging instrument, or of register of charges.	Summary.	One-fifth of the statutory maximum.	One-fiftieth of the statutory maximum.
425(4)	Company failing to annex to memorandum court order sanctioning compromise or arrangement with creditors.	Summary.	One-fifth of the statutory maximum.	
426(6)	Company failing to comply with requirements of section 426 (information to members and creditors about compromise or arrangement.)	1. On indictment. 2. Summary.	A fine. The statutory maximum.	
426(7)	Director or trustee for debenture holders failing to give notice to company of matters necessary for purposes of section 426.	Summary.	One-fifth of the statutory maximum.	One-fiftieth of the statutory maximum.
427(5)	Failure to deliver to registrar office copy of court order under section 427 (company reconstruction or amalgamation).	Summary.	One-fifth of the statutory maximum.	One-fiftieth of the statutory maximum.
429(6)	Offeror failing to send copy of notice or making statutory declaration knowing it to be false, etc.	1. On indictment. 2. Summary.	Two years or a fine; or both; Six months or the statutory maximum; or both.	One-fiftieth of the statutory maximum.
430A(6)	Offeror failing to give notice of rights to minority shareholder.	1. On indictment. 2. Summary.	A fine. The statutory maximum.	
444(3)	Failing to give Secretary of State, when required to do so, information about interests in shares, etc.; giving false information.	1. On indictment. 2. Summary.	Two years or a fine; or both. Six months or the statutory maximum; or both.	
447(6)	Failure to comply with requirement to produce documents imposed by Secretary of State under section 447.	1. On indictment. 2. Summary.	A fine. The statutory maximum.	
448(7)	Obstructing the exercise of any rights conferred by a warrant or failing to comply with a requirement imposed under subsection (3)(d).	1. On indictment. 2. Summary.	A fine. The statutory maximum.	

Section of Act creating offence	General nature of offence	Mode of prosecution	Punishment	Daily default fine (where applicable)
449(2)	Wrongful disclosure of information or document obtained under section 447 or 448.	1. On indictment. 2. Summary.	Two years or a fine; or both. Six months or the statutory maximum; or both.	
450	Destroying or mutilating company documents; falsifying such documents or making false entries; parting with such documents or altering them or making omissions.	1. On indictment. 2. Summary.	Seven years or a fine; or both. Six months or the statutory maximum; or both.	
451	Making false statement or explanation in purported compliance with section 447.	1. On indictment. 2. Summary.	Two years or a fine; or both. Six months or the statutory maximum; or both.	
455(1)	Exercising a right to dispose of, or vote in respect of, shares whcih are subject to restrictions under Part XV; failing to give notice in respect of shares so subject; entering into agreement void under section 454(2), (3).	1. On indictment. 2. Summary.	A fine. The statutory maximum.	
455(2)	Issuing shares in contravention of restrictions of Part XV.	1. On indictment. 2. Summary.	A fine. The statutory maximum.	
458	Being a party to carrying on company's business with intent to defraud creditors, or for any fraudulent purpose.	1. On indictment. 2. Summary.	Seven years or a fine; or both. Six months or the statutory maximum; or both.	
461(5)	Failure to register office copy of court order under Part XVII altering, or giving leave to alter, company's memorandum.	Summary.	One-fifth of the statutory maximum.	One-fiftieth of the statutory maximum.

[THE NEXT PAGE IS I 447]

Section	General nature of offence	Mode of prosecution	Punishment	Daily default fine
651(3)	Person obtaining court order to declare company's dissolution void, then failing to register the order.	Summary.	One-fifth of the statutory maximum.	One-fiftieth of the statutory maximum.
697(1)	Oversea company failing to comply with any of sections 691 to 693 or 696.	Summary.	For an offence which is not a continuing offence, one-fifth of the statutory maximum. For an offence which is a continuing offence, one-fifth of the statutory maximum.	One-fiftieth of the statutory maximum.
697(2)	Oversea company contravening section 694(6) (carrying on business under its corporate name after Secretary of State's direction).	1. On indictment. 2. Summary.	A fine. The statutory maximum.	One-tenth of the statutory maximum.
703(1)	Oversea company failing to comply with requirements as to accounts and reports.	1. On indictment. 2. Summary.	A fine. The statutory maximum.	One-tenth of the statutory maximum.
720(4)	Insurance company etc. failing to send twice-yearly statement in form of Schedule 23.	Summary.	One-fifth of the statutory maximum.	One-fiftieth of the statutory maximum.
722(3)	Company failing to comply with section 722(2), as regards the manner of keeping registers, minute books and accounting records.	Summary.	One-fifth of the statutory maximum.	One-fiftieth of the statutory maximum.
Sched. 14, Pt. II, para. 1(3)	Company failing to give notice of location of overseas branch register, etc.	Summary.	One-fifth of the statutory maximum.	One-fiftieth of the statutory maximum.
Sched. 14, Pt. II, para. 4(2)	Company failing to transmit to its registered office in Great Britain copies of entries in overseas branch register, or to keep a duplicate of overseas branch register.	Summary.	One-fifth of the statutory maximum.	One-fiftieth of the statutory maximum.

SCHEDULE 25

COMPANIES ACT 1981, SECTION 38, AS ORIGINALLY ENACTED

Relief from section 56 in respect of group reconstructions

38.—(1) This section applies where the issuing company—

(*a*) is a wholly-owned subsidiary of another company ("the holding company"); and

(*b*) allots shares to the holding company or to another wholly-owned subsidiary of the holding company in consideration for the transfer to it of shares in another subsidiary (whether wholly-owned or not) of the holding company.

(2) Where the shares in the issuing company allotted in consideration for the transfer are issued at a premium, the issuing company shall not be required by section 56 of the 1948 Act to transfer any amount in excess of the minimum premium value to the share premium account.

(3) In subsection (2) above "the minimum premium value" means the amount (if any) by which the base value of the shares transferred exceeds the aggregate nominal value of the shares allotted in consideration for the transfer.

(4) For the purposes of subsection (3) above, the base value of the shares transferred shall be taken as—

(*a*) the cost of those shares to the company transferring them; or

(*b*) the amount at which those shares are stated in that company's accounting records immediately before the transfer;

whichever is the less.

(5) Section 37 of this Act shall not apply in a case to which this section applies.

[THE NEXT PAGE IS I 529]

[1,2] **Insolvency Act 1986**

(1986 c. 45)

An Act to consolidate the enactments relating to company insolvency and winding up (including the winding up of companies that are not insolvent, and of unregistered companies); enactments relating to the insolvency and bankruptcy of individuals; and other enactments bearing on those two subject matters, including the functions and qualification of insolvency practitioners, the public administration of insolvency, the penalisation and redress of malpractice and wrongdoing, and the avoidance of certain transactions at an undervalue.

[25th July 1986]

NOTES
[1] This Act replaces in all material respects the Insolvency Act 1985 formerly reprinted in *The Parliament House Book*.
[2] See also the Drug Trafficking Offences Act 1986, s.17 and the Criminal Justice Act 1988, s.86.

ARRANGEMENT OF SECTIONS

THE FIRST GROUP OF PARTS
COMPANY INSOLVENCY; COMPANIES WINDING UP

PART I

COMPANY VOLUNTARY ARRANGEMENTS

The proposal

PART II

ADMINISTRATION ORDERS

Making, etc. of administration order

[THE NEXT PAGE IS I 531]

PART III

RECEIVERSHIP

CHAPTER I

RECEIVERS AND MANAGERS (ENGLAND AND WALES)

[Not reprinted.]

CHAPTER II

RECEIVERS (SCOTLAND)

CHAPTER IX

DISSOLUTION OF COMPANIES AFTER WINDING UP

CHAPTER X

MALPRACTICE BEFORE AND DURING LIQUIDATION:
PENALISATION OF COMPANIES AND COMPANY OFFICERS;
INVESTIGATIONS AND PROSECUTIONS

Offences of fraud, deception, etc.

Penalisation of directors and officers

Investigation and prosecution of malpractice

PART V

WINDING UP OF UNREGISTERED COMPANIES

Schedule 7—Insolvency Practitioners Tribunal.
Schedule 8—Provisions capable of inclusion in company insolvency rules.
Schedule 9—Provisions capable of inclusion in individual insolvency rules.
Schedule 10—Punishment of offences under this Act.
Schedule 11—Transitional provisions and savings.
Schedule 12—Enactments repealed.
Schedule 13—Consequential amendments of Companies Act 1985.
Schedule 14—Consequential amendments of other enactments.

THE FIRST GROUP OF PARTS

COMPANY INSOLVENCY; COMPANIES WINDING UP

PART I

COMPANY VOLUNTARY ARRANGEMENTS

The proposal

Those who may propose an arrangement

1.—(1) The directors of a company (other than one for which an administration order is in force, or which is being wound up) may make a proposal under this Part to the company and to its creditors for a composition in satisfaction of its debts or a scheme of arrangement of its affairs (from here on referred to, in either case, as a "voluntary arrangement").

(2) A proposal under this Part is one which provides for some person ("the nominee") to act in relation to the voluntary arrangement either as trustee or otherwise for the purpose of supervising its implementation; and the nominee must be a person who is qualified to act as an insolvency practitioner in relation to the company.

(3) Such a proposal may also be made—

(*a*) where an administration order is in force in relation to the company, by the administrator, and

(*b*) where the company is being wound up, by the liquidator.

Procedure where nominee is not the liquidator or administrator

2.—(1) This section applies where the nominee under section 1 is not the liquidator or administrator of the company.

(2) The nominee shall, within 28 days (or such longer period as the court may allow) after he is given notice of the proposal for a voluntary arrangement, submit a report to the court stating—

(*a*) whether, in his opinion, meetings of the company and of its creditors should be summoned to consider the proposal, and

(*b*) if in his opinion such meetings should be summoned, the date on which, and time and place at which, he proposes the meetings should be held.

(3) For the purposes of enabling the nominee to prepare his report, the person intending to make the proposal shall submit to the nominee—

(*a*) a document setting out the terms of the proposed voluntary arrangement, and

(*b*) a statement of the company's affairs containing—

(i) such particulars of its creditors and of its debts and other liabilities and of its assets as may be prescribed, and

(ii) such other information as may be prescribed.

(4) The court may, on an application made by the person intending to make the proposal, in a case where the nominee has failed to submit the report required by this section, direct that the nominee be replaced as such by another person qualified to act as an insolvency practitioner in relation to the company.

Summoning of meetings

3.—(1) Where the nominee under section 1 is not the liquidator or administrator, and it has been reported to the court that such meetings as are mentioned in section 2(2) should be summoned, the person making the report shall (unless the court otherwise directs) summon those meetings for the time, date and place proposed in the report.

(2) Where the nominee is the liquidator or administrator, he shall summon meetings of the company and of its creditors to consider the proposal for such a time, date and place as he thinks fit.

(3) The persons to be summoned to a creditors' meeting under this section are every creditor of the company of whose claim and address the person summoning the meeting is aware.

Consideration and implementation of proposal

Decisions of meetings

4.—(1) The meetings summoned under section 3 shall decide whether to approve the proposed voluntary arrangement (with or without modifications).

(2) The modifications may include one conferring the functions proposed to be conferred on the nominee on another person qualified to act as an insolvency practitioner in relation to the company.

But they shall not include any modification by virtue of which the proposal ceases to be a proposal such as is mentioned in section 1.

(3) A meeting so summoned shall not approve any proposal or modification which affects the right of a secured creditor of the company to enforce his security, except with the concurrence of the creditor concerned.

(4) Subject as follows, a meeting so summoned shall not approve any proposal or modification under which—

 (*a*) any preferential debt of the company is to be paid otherwise than in priority to such of its debts as are not preferential debts, or

 (*b*) a preferential creditor of the company is to be paid an amount in respect of a preferential debt that bears to that debt a smaller proportion than is borne to another preferential debt by the amount that is to be paid in respect of that other debt.

However, the meeting may approve such a proposal or modification with the concurrence of the preferential creditor concerned.

(5) Subject as above, each of the meetings shall be conducted in accordance with the rules.

(6) After the conclusion of either meeting in accordance with the rules, the chairman of the meeting shall report the result of the meeting to the court, and, immediately after reporting to the court, shall give notice of the result of the meeting to such persons as may be prescribed.

(7) References in this section to preferential debts and preferential creditors are to be read in accordance with section 386 in Part XII of this Act.

Effect of approval

5.—(1) This section has effect where each of the meetings summoned under section 3 approves the proposed voluntary arrangement either with the same modifications or without modifications.

(2) The approved voluntary arrangement—

 (*a*) takes effect as if made by the company at the creditors' meeting, and

 (*b*) binds every person who in accordance with the rules had notice of, and was entitled to vote at, that meeting (whether or not he was present or represented at the meeting) as if he were a party to the voluntary arrangement.

(3) Subject as follows, if the company is being wound up or an administration order is in force, the court may do one or both of the following, namely—

(*a*) by order stay or sist all proceedings in the winding up or discharge the administration order;

(*b*) give such directions with respect to the conduct of the winding up or the administration as it thinks appropriate for facilitating the implementation of the approved voluntary arrangement.

(4) The court shall not make an order under subsection (3) (*a*)—

(*a*) at any time before the end of the period of 28 days beginning with the first day on which each of the reports required by section 4(6) has been made to the court, or

(*b*) at any time when an application under the next section or an appeal in respect of such an application is pending, or at any time in the period within which such an appeal may be brought.

Challenge of decisions

6.—(1) Subject to this section, an application to the court may be made, by any of the persons specified below, on one or both of the following grounds, namely—

(*a*) that a voluntary arrangement approved at the meetings summoned under section 3 unfairly prejudices the interests of a creditor, member or contributory of the company;

(*b*) that there has been some material irregularity at or in relation to either of the meetings.

(2) The persons who may apply under this section are—

(*a*) a person entitled, in accordance with the rules, to vote at either of the meetings;

(*b*) the nominee or any person who has replaced him under section 2(4) or 4(2); and

(*c*) if the company is being wound up or an administration order is in force, the liquidator or administrator.

(2) An application under this section shall not be made after the end of the period of 28 days beginning with the first day on which each of the reports required by section 4(6) has been made to the court.

(4) Where on such an application the court is satisfied as to either of the grounds mentioned in subsection (1), it may do one or both of the following, namely—

(*a*) revoke or suspend the approvals given by the meetings or, in a case falling within subsection (1)(*b*), any approval given by the meeting in question;

(*b*) give a direction to any person for the summoning of further meetings to consider any revised proposal the person who made the original proposal may make or, in a case falling within subsection (1)(*b*), a further company or (as the case may be) creditors' meeting to reconsider the original proposal.

(5) Where at any time after giving a direction under subsection (4)(*b*) for the summoning of meetings to consider a revised proposal the court is satisfied that the person who made the original proposal does not intend to submit a revised proposal, the court shall revoke the direction and revoke or suspend any approval given at the previous meetings.

(6) In a case where the court, on an application under this section with respect to any meeting—

(*a*) gives a direction under subsection (4)(*b*), or

(*b*) revokes or suspends an approval under subsection (4)(*a*) or (5),

the court may give such supplemental directions as it thinks fit and, in particular, directions with respect to things done since the meeting under any voluntary arrangement approved by the meeting.

(7) Except in pursuance of the preceding provisions of this section, an approval given at a meeting summoned under section 3 is not invalidated by any irregularity at or in relation to the meeting.

Implementation of proposal

7.—(1) This section applies where a voluntary arrangement approved by the meetings summoned under section 3 has taken effect.

(2) The person who is for the time being carrying out in relation to the voluntary arrangement the functions conferred—

(*a*) by virtue of the approval on the nominee, or

(*b*) by virtue of section 2(4) or 4(2) on a person other than the nominee, shall be known as the supervisor of the voluntary arrangement.

(3) If any of the company's creditors or any other person is dissatisfied by any act, omission or decision of the supervisor, he may apply to the court; and on the application the court may—

(*a*) confirm, reverse or modify any act or decision of the supervisor,

(*b*) give him directions, or

(*c*) make such other order as it thinks fit.

(4) The supervisor—

(*a*) may apply to the court for directions in relation to any particular matter arising under the voluntary arrangement, and

(*b*) is included among the persons who may apply to the court for the winding up of the company or for an administration order to be made in relation to it.

(5) The court may, whenever—

(*a*) it is expedient to appoint a person to carry out the functions of the supervisor, and

(*b*) it is inexpedient, difficult or impracticable for an appointment to be made without the assistance of the court,

make an order appointing a person who is qualified to act as an insolvency practitioner in relation to the company, either in substitution for the existing supervisor or to fill a vacancy.

(6) The power conferred by subsection (5) is exercisable so as to increase the number of persons exercising the functions of supervisor or, where there is more than one person exercising those functions, so as to replace one or more of those persons.

[1] PART II

NOTE

[1] See the Debtors (Scotland) Act 1987, s.93(4)(*c*).

ADMINISTRATION ORDERS

Making etc. of administration order

Power of court to make order

[1] **8.**—(1) Subject to this section, if the court—

(*a*) is satisfied that a company is or is likely to become unable to pay its debts (within the meaning given to that expression by section 123 of this Act), and

(*b*) considers that the making of an order under this section would be likely to achieve one or more of the purposes mentioned below,

the court may make an administration order in relation to the company.

(2) An administration order is an order directing that, during the period for which the order is in force, the affairs, business and property of the company shall be managed by a person ("the administrator") appointed for the purpose by the court.

(3) The purposes for whose achievement an administration order may be made are—

(*a*) the survival of the company, and the whole or any part of its undertaking, as a going concern;

(*b*) the approval of a voluntary arrangement under Part I;

(c) the sanctioning under section 425 of the Companies Act of a compromise or arrangement between the company and any such persons as are mentioned in that section; and

(d) a more advantageous realisation of the company's assets than would be effected on a winding up;

and the order shall specify the purpose or purposes for which it is made.

(4) An administration order shall not be made in relation to a company after it has gone into liquidation, nor where it is—

(a) an insurance company within the meaning of the Insurance Companies Act 1982, or

[2] (b) an authorised institution or former authorised institution within the meaning of the Banking Act 1987.

NOTES

[1] See the Banking Act 1987, ss.11(8) and 58(2).

[2] Substituted by the Banking Act 1987, Sched. 6, para. 25.

Application for order

9.—(1) An application to the court for an administration order shall be by petition presented either by the company or the directors, or by a creditor or creditors (including any contingent or prospective creditor or creditors), or by all or any of those parties, together or separately.

(2) Where a petition is presented to the court—

(a) notice of the petition shall be given forthwith to any person who has appointed, or is or may be entitled to appoint, an administrative receiver of the company, and to such other persons as may be prescribed, and

(b) the petition shall not be withdrawn except with the leave of the court.

[1] (3) Where the court is satisfied that there is an administrative receiver of the company, the court shall dismiss the petition unless it is also satisfied either—

(a) that the person by whom or on whose behalf the receiver was appointed has consented to the making of the order, or

(b) that, if an administration order were made, any security by virtue of which the receiver was appointed would—

   (i) be liable to be released or discharged under sections 238 to 240 in Part VI (transactions at an undervalue and preferences),

   (ii) be avoided under section 245 in that Part (avoidance of floating charges), or

   (iii) be challengeable under section 242 (gratuitous alienations) or 243 (unfair preferences) in that Part, or under any rule of law in Scotland.

(4) Subject to subsection (3), on hearing a petition the court may dismiss it, or adjourn the hearing conditionally or unconditionally, or make an interim order or any other order that it thinks fit.

(5) Without prejudice to the generality of subsection (4), an interim order under that subsection may restrict the exercise of any powers of the directors or of the company (whether by reference to the consent of the court or of a person qualified to act as an insolvency practitioner in relation to the company, or otherwise).

NOTE

[1] Amended (*prosp.*) by the Companies Act 1989, Sched. 16, para. 3(2).

Effect of application

[1] **10.**—(1) During the period beginning with the presentation of a petition for an administration order and ending with the making of such an order or the dismissal of the petition—

(a) no resolution may be passed or order made for the winding up of the company;

(b) no steps may be taken to enforce any security over the company's property, or to repossess goods in the company's possession under any hire-purchase agreement, except with the leave of the court and subject to such terms as the court may impose; and

(c) no other proceedings and no execution or other legal process may be commenced or continued, and no distress may be levied, against the company or its property except with the leave of the court and subject to such terms as aforesaid.

(2) Nothing in subsection (1) requires the leave of the court—

(a) for the presentation of a petition for the winding up of the company,

(b) for the appointment of an administrative receiver of the company, or

(c) for the carrying out by such a receiver (whenever appointed) of any of his functions.

(3) Where—

(a) a petition for an administration order is presented at a time when there is an administrative receiver of the company, and

(b) the person by or on whose behalf the receiver was appointed has not consented to the making of the order,

the period mentioned in subsection (1) is deemed not to begin unless and until that person so consents.

(4) References in this section and the next to hire-purchase agreements include conditional sale agreements, chattel leasing agreements and retention of title agreements.

(5) In the application of this section and the next to Scotland, references to execution being commenced or continued include references to diligence being carried out or continued, and references to distress being levied shall be omitted.

NOTE

[1] Amended (*prosp.*) by the Companies Act 1989, Sched. 24.

Effect of order

11.—(1) On the making of an administration order—

(a) any petition for the winding up of the company shall be dismissed, and

(b) any administrative receiver of the company shall vacate office.

(2) Where an administration order has been made, any receiver of part of the company's property shall vacate office on being required to do so by the administrator.

(3) During the period for which an administration order is in force—

(a) no resolution may be passed or order made for the winding up of the company;

(b) no administrative receiver of the company may be appointed;

(c) no other steps may be taken to enforce any security over the company's property, or to repossess goods in the company's possession under any hire-purchase agreement, except with the consent of the administrator or the leave of the court and subject (where the court gives leave) to such terms as the court may impose; and

(d) no other proceedings and no execution or other legal process may be commenced or continued, and no distress may be levied, against the company or its property except with the consent of the administrator or the leave of the court and subject (where the court gives leave) to such terms as aforesaid.

(4) Where at any time an administrative receiver of the company has vacated office under subsection (1)(b), or a receiver of part of the company's property has vacated office under subsection (2)—

(a) his remuneration and any expenses properly incurred by him, and

(b) any indemnity to which he is entitled out of the assets of the company,

shall be charged on and (subject to subsection (3) above) paid out of any property of the company which was in his custody or under his control at that time in priority to any security held by the person by or on whose behalf he was appointed.

(5) Neither an administrative receiver who vacates office under subsection (1)(*b*) nor a receiver who vacates office under subsection (2) is required on or after so vacating office to take any steps for the purpose of complying with any duty imposed on him by section 40 or 59 of this Act (duty to pay preferential creditors).

Notification of order

12.—(1) Every invoice, order for goods or business letter which, at a time when an administration order is in force in relation to a company, is issued by or on behalf of the company or the administrator, being a document on or in which the company's name appears, shall also contain the administrator's name and a statement that the affairs, business and property of the company are being managed by the administrator.

(2) If default is made in complying with this section, the company and any of the following persons who without reasonable excuse authorises or permits the default, namely, the administrator and any officer of the company, is liable to a fine.

Administrators

Appointment of administrator

13.—(1) The administrator of a company shall be appointed either by the administration order or by an order under the next subsection.

(2) If a vacancy occurs by death, resignation or otherwise in the office of the administrator, the court may by order fill the vacancy.

(3) An application for an order under subsection (2) may be made—

(*a*) by any continuing administrator of the company; or

(*b*) where there is no such administrator, by a creditors' committee established under section 26 below; or

(*c*) where there is no such administrator and no such committee, by the company or the directors or by any creditor or creditors of the company.

General powers

14.—(1) The administrator of a company—

(*a*) may do all such things as may be necessary for the management of the affairs, business and property of the company, and

(*b*) without prejudice to the generality of paragraph (*a*), has the powers specified in Schedule 1 to this Act;

and in the application of that Schedule to the administrator of a company the words "he" and "him" refer to the administrator.

(2) The administrator also has power—

(*a*) to remove any director of the company and to appoint any person to be a director of it, whether to fill a vacancy or otherwise, and

(*b*) to call any meeting of the members or creditors of the company.

(3) The administrator may apply to the court for directions in relation to any particular matter arising in connection with the carrying out of his functions.

(4) Any power conferred on the company or its officers, whether by this Act or the Companies Act or by the memorandum or articles of association, which could be exercised in such a way as to interfere with the exercise by the administrator of his powers is not exercisable except with the consent of the administrator, which may be given either generally or in relation to particular cases.

(5) In exercising his powers the administrator is deemed to act as the company's agent.

(6) A person dealing with the administrator in good faith and for value is not concerned to inquire whether the administrator is acting within his powers.

Power to deal with charged property, etc.

15.—(1) The administrator of a company may dispose of or otherwise exercise his powers in relation to any property of the company which is subject to a security to which this subsection applies as if the property were not subject to the security.

(2) Where, on an application by the administrator, the court is satisfied that the disposal (with or without other assets) of—

(*a*) any property of the company subject to a security to which this subsection applies, or

(*b*) any goods in the possession of the company under a hire-purchase agreement,

would be likely to promote the purpose or one or more of the purposes specified in the administration order, the court may by order authorise the administrator to dispose of the property as if it were not subject to the security or to dispose of the goods as if all rights of the owner under the hire-purchase agreement were vested in the company.

(3) Subsection (1) applies to any security which, as created, was a floating charge; and subsection (2) applies to any other security.

(4) Where property is disposed of under subsection (1), the holder of the security has the same priority in respect of any property of the company directly or indirectly representing the property disposed of as he would have had in respect of the property subject to the security.

(5) It shall be a condition of an order under subsection (2) that—

(*a*) the net proceeds of the disposal, and

(*b*) where those proceeds are less than such amount as may be determined by the court to be the net amount which would be realised on a sale of the property or goods in the open market by a willing vendor, such sums as may be required to make good the deficiency,

shall be applied towards discharging the sums secured by the security or payable under the hire-purchase agreement.

(6) Where a condition imposed in pursuance of subsection (5) relates to two or more securities, that condition requires the net proceeds of the disposal and, where paragraph (*b*) of that subsection applies, the sums mentioned in that paragraph to be applied towards discharging the sums secured by those securities in the order of their priorities.

(7) An office copy of an order under subsection (2) shall, within 14 days after the making of the order, be sent by the administrator to the registrar of companies.

(8) If the administrator without reasonable excuse fails to comply with subsection (7), he is liable to a fine and, for continued contravention, to a daily default fine.

(9) References in this section to hire-purchase agreements include conditional sale agreements, chattel leasing agreements and retention of title agreements.

Operation of s.15 in Scotland

16.—(1) Where property is disposed of under section 15 in its application to Scotland, the administrator shall grant to the disponee an appropriate document of transfer or conveyance of the property, and—

(*a*) that document, or

(*b*) where any recording, intimation or registration of the document is a legal requirement for completion of title to the property, ·that recording, intimation or registration,

has the effect of disencumbering the property of or, as the case may be, freeing the property from the security.

(2) Where goods in the possession of the company under a hire-purchase agreement, conditional sale agreement, chattel leasing agreement or retention of title agreement are disposed of under section 15 in its application to Scotland, the disposal has the effect of extinguishing, as against the disponee, all rights of the owner of the goods under the agreement.

General duties

17.—(1) The administrator of a company shall, on his appointment, take into his custody or under his control all the property to which the company is or appears to be entitled.

(2) The administrator shall manage the affairs, business and property of the company—

    (*a*) at any time before proposals have been approved (with or without modifications) under section 24 below, in accordance with any directions given by the court, and

    (*b*) at any time after proposals have been so approved, in accordance with those proposals as from time to time revised, whether by him or a predecessor of his.

(3) The administrator shall summon a meeting of the company's creditors if—

    (*a*) he is requested, in accordance with the rules, to do so by one-tenth, in value, of the company's creditors, or

    (*b*) he is directed to do so by the court.

Discharge or variation of administration order

18.—(1) The administrator of a company may at any time apply to the court for the administration order to be discharged, or to be varied so as to specify an additional purpose.

(2) The administrator shall make an application under this section if—

    (*a*) it appears to him that the purpose or each of the purposes specified in the order either has been achieved or is incapable of achievement, or

    (*b*) he is required to do so by a meeting of the company's creditors summoned for the purpose in accordance with the rules.

(3) On the hearing of an application under this section, the court may by order discharge or vary the administration order and make such consequential provision as it thinks fit, or adjourn the hearing conditionally or unconditionally, or make an interim order or any other order it thinks fit.

(4) Where the administration order is discharged or varied the administrator shall, within 14 days after the making of the order effecting the discharge or variation, send an office copy of that order to the registrar of companies.

(5) If the administrator without reasonable excuse fails to comply with subsection (4), he is liable to a fine and, for continued contravention, to a daily default fine.

Vacation of office

19.—(1) The administrator of a company may at any time be removed from office by order of the court and may, in the prescribed circumstances, resign his office by giving notice of his resignation to the court.

(2) The administrator shall vacate office if—

    (*a*) he ceases to be qualified to act as an insolvency practitioner in relation to the company, or

    (*b*) the administration order is discharged.

(3) Where at any time a person ceases to be administrator, the next two subsections apply.

(4) His remuneration and any expenses properly incurred by him shall be charged on and paid out of any property of the company which is in his custody or under his control at that time in priority to any security to which section 15(1) then applies.

(5) Any sums payable in respect of debts or liabilities incurred, while he was administrator, under contracts entered into or contracts of employment adopted by him or a predecessor of his in the carrying out of his or the predecessor's functions shall be charged on and paid out of any such property as is mentioned in subsection (4) in priority to any charge arising under that subsection.

For this purpose, the administrator is not be taken to have adopted a contract of employment by reason of anything done or omitted to be done within 14 days after his appointment.

Release of administrator

20.—(1) A person who has ceased to be the administrator of a company has his release with effect from the following time, that is to say—

(*a*) in the case of a person who has died, the time at which notice is given to the court in accordance with the rules that he has ceased to hold office;

(*b*) in any other case, such time as the court may determine.

(2) Where a person has his release under this section, he is, with effect from the time specified above, discharged from all liability both in respect of acts or omissions of his in the administration and otherwise in relation to his conduct as administrator.

(3) However, nothing in this section prevents the exercise, in relation to a person who has had his release as above, of the court's powers under section 212 in Chapter X of Part IV (summary remedy against delinquent directors, liquidators, etc.).

Ascertainment and investigation of company's affairs

Information to be given by administrator

21.—(1) Where an administration order has been made, the administrator shall—

(*a*) forthwith send to the company and publish in the prescribed manner a notice of the order, and

(*b*) within 28 days after the making of the order, unless the court otherwise directs, send such a notice to all creditors of the company (so far as he is aware of their addresses).

(2) Where an administration order has been made, the administrator shall also, within 14 days after the making of the order, send an office copy of the order to the registrar of companies and to such other persons as may be prescribed.

(3) If the administrator without reasonable excuse fails to comply with this section, he is liable to a fine and, for continued contravention, to a daily default fine.

Statement of affairs to be submitted to administrator

22.—(1) Where an administration order has been made, the administrator shall forthwith require some or all of the persons mentioned below to make out and submit to him a statement in the prescribed form as to the affairs of the company.

(2) The statement shall be verified by affidavit by the persons required to submit it and shall show—

(*a*) particulars of the company's assets, debts and liabilities;

(*b*) the names and addresses of its creditors;

(*c*) the securities held by them respectively;

(*d*) the dates when the securities were respectively given; and

(*e*) such further or other information as may be prescribed.

(3) The persons referred to in subsection (1) are—

(*a*) those who are or have been officers of the company;

(*b*) those who have taken part in the company's formation at any time within one year before the date of the administration order;

(*c*) those whose are in the company's employment or have been in its employment within that year, and are in the administrator's opinion capable of giving the information required;

(*d*) those who are or have been within that year officers of or in the employment of a company which is, or within that year was, an officer of the company.

In this subsection "employment" includes employment under a contract for services.

(4) Where any persons are required under this section to submit a statement of affairs to the administrator, they shall do so (subject to the next subsection) before the end of the period of 21 days beginning with the day after that on which the prescribed notice of the requirement is given to them by the administrator.

(5) The administrator, if he thinks fit, may—

(*a*) at any time release a person from an obligation imposed on him under subsection (1) or (2), or

(*b*) either when giving notice under subsection (4) or subsequently, extend the period so mentioned;

and where the administrator has refused to exercise a power conferred by this subsection, the court, if it thinks fit, may exercise it.

(6) If a person without reasonable excuse fails to comply with any obligation imposed under this section, he is liable to a fine and, for continued contravention, to a daily default fine.

Administrator's proposals

Statement of proposals

23.—(1) Where an administration order has been made, the administrator shall, within three months (or such longer period as the court may allow) after the making of the order—

(*a*) send to the registrar of companies and (so far as he is aware of their addresses) to all creditors a statement of his proposals for achieving the purpose or purposes specified in the order, and

(*b*) lay a copy of the statement before a meeting of the company's creditors summoned for the purpose on not less than 14 days' notice.

(2) The administrator shall also, within three months (or such longer period as the court may allow) after the making of the order, either—

(*a*) send a copy of the statement (so far as he is aware of their addresses) to all members of the company, or

(*b*) publish in the prescribed manner a notice stating an address to which members of the company should write for copies of the statement to be sent to them free of charge.

(3) If the administrator without reasonable excuse fails to comply with this section, he is liable to a fine and, for continued contravention, to a daily default fine.

Consideration of proposals by creditors' meeting

24.—(1) A meeting of creditors summoned under section 23 shall decide whether to approve the administrator's proposals.

(2) The meeting may approve the proposals with modifications, but shall not do so unless the administrator consents to each modification.

(3) Subject as above, the meeting shall be conducted in accordance with the rules.

(4) After the conclusion of the meeting in accordance with the rules, the administrator shall report the result of the meeting to the court and shall give notice of that result to the registrar of companies and to such persons as may be prescribed.

(5) If a report is given to the court under subsection (4) that the meeting has declined to approve the administrator's proposals (with or without modifications), the court may by order discharge the administration order and make such consequential provision as it thinks fit, or adjourn the hearing conditionally or unconditionally, or make an interim order or any other order that it thinks fit.

(6) Where the administration order is discharged, the administrator shall, within 14 days after the making of the order effecting the discharge, send an office copy of that order to the registrar of companies.

(7) If the administrator without reasonable excuse fails to comply with subsection (6), he is liable to a fine and, for continued contravention, to a daily default fine.

Approval of substantial revisions

25.—(1) This section applies where—

(*a*) proposals have been approved (with or without modifications) under section 24, and

(*b*) the administrator proposes to make revisions of those proposals which appear to him substantial.

(2) The administrator shall—

(*a*) send to all creditors of the company (so far as he is aware of their addresses) a statement in the prescribed form of his proposed revisions, and

(*b*) lay a copy of the statement before a meeting of the company's creditors summoned for the purpose on not less than 14 days' notice;

and he shall not make the proposed revisions unless they are approved by the meeting.

(3) The administrator shall also either—

(*a*) send a copy of the statement (so far as he is aware of their addresses) to all members of the company, or

(*b*) publish in the prescribed manner a notice stating an address to which members of the company should write for copies of the statement to be sent to them free of charge.

(4) The meeting of creditors may approve the proposed revisions with modifications, but shall not do so unless the administrator consents to each modification.

(5) Subject as above, the meeting shall be conducted in accordance with the rules.

(6) After the conclusion of the meeting in accordance with the rules, the administrator shall give notice of the result of the meeting to the registrar of companies and to such persons as may be prescribed.

Miscellaneous

Creditors' committee

26.—(1) Where a meeting of creditors summoned under section 23 has approved the administrator's proposals (with or without modifications), the meeting may, if it thinks fit, establish a committee ("the creditors' committee") to exercise the functions conferred on it by or under this Act.

(2) If such a committee is established, the committee may, on giving not less than seven days' notice, require the administrator to attend before it at any reasonable time and furnish it with such information relating to the carrying out of his functions as it may reasonably require.

Protection of interests of creditors and members

27.—(1) At any time when an administration order is in force, a creditor or member of the company may apply to the court by petition for an order under this section on the ground—

(*a*) that the company's affairs, business and property are being or have been managed by the administrator in a manner which is unfairly prejudicial to the interests of its creditors or members generally, or of some part of its creditors or members (including at least himself), or

(*b*) that any actual or proposed act or omission of the administrator is or would be so prejudicial.

(2) On an application for an order under this section the court may, subject as follows, make such order as it thinks fit for giving relief in respect of the matters complained of, or adjourn the hearing conditionally or unconditionally, or make an interim order or any other order that it thinks fit.

(3) An order under this section shall not prejudice or prevent—

(*a*) the implementation of a voluntary arrangement approved under section 4 in Part I, or any compromise or arrangement sanctioned under section 425 of the Companies Act; or

(*b*) where the application for the order was made more than 28 days after the approval of any proposals or revised proposals under section 24 or 25, the implementation of those proposals or revised proposals.

(4) Subject as above, an order under this section may in particular—

(*a*) regulate the future management by the administrator of the company's affairs, business and property;

(*b*) require the administrator to refrain from doing or continuing an act complained of by the petitioner, or to do an act which the petitioner has complained he has omitted to do;

(*c*) require the summoning of a meeting of creditors or members for the purpose of considering such matters as the court may direct;

(*d*) discharge the administration order and make such consequential provision as the court thinks fit.

(5) Nothing in section 15 or 16 is to be taken as prejudicing applications to the court under this section.

(6) Where the administration order is discharged, the administrator shall, within 14 days after the making of the order effecting the discharge, send an office copy of that order to the registrar of companies; and if without reasonable excuse he fails to comply with this subsection, he is liable to a fine and, for continued contravention, to a daily default fine.

PART III

RECEIVERSHIP

CHAPTER I

RECEIVERS AND MANAGERS (ENGLAND AND WALES)

. . . .

CHAPTER II

RECEIVERS (SCOTLAND)

Extent of this Chapter

50. This Chapter extends to Scotland only.

Power to appoint receiver

51.—(1) It is competent under the law of Scotland for the holder of a floating charge over all or any part of the property (including uncalled capital), which may from time to time be comprised in the property and undertaking of an incorporated company (whether a company within the meaning of the Companies Act or not) which the Court of Session has jurisdiction to wind up, to appoint a receiver of such part of the property of the company as is subject to the charge.

(2) It is competent under the law of Scotland for the court, on the application of the holder of such a floating charge, to appoint a receiver of such part of the property of the company as is subject to the charge.

(3) The following are disqualified from being appointed as receiver—

(*a*) a body corporate;

(*b*) an undischarged bankrupt; and

(*c*) a firm according to the law of Scotland.

(4) A body corporate or a firm according to the law of Scotland which acts as a receiver is liable to a fine.

(5) An undischarged bankrupt who so acts is liable to imprisonment or a fine, or both.

(6) In this section, "receiver" includes joint receivers.

Circumstances justifying appointment

52.—(1) A receiver may be appointed under section 51(1) by the holder of the floating charge on the occurrence of any event which, by the provisions of the instrument creating the charge, entitles the holder of the charge to make that appointment and, in so far as not otherwise provided for by the instrument, on the occurrence of any of the following events, namely—

(*a*) the expiry of a period of 21 days after the making of a demand for payment of the whole or any part of the principal sum secured by the charge, without payment having been made;

(*b*) the expiry of a period of two months during the whole of which interest due and payable under the charge has been in arrears;

(*c*) the making of an order or the passing of a resolution to wind up the company;

(*d*) the appointment of a receiver by virtue of any other floating charge created by the company.

(2) A receiver may be appointed by the court under section 51(2) on the occurrence of any event which, by the provisions of the instrument creating the floating charge, entitles the holder of the charge to make that appointment and, in so far as not otherwise provided for by the instrument, on the occurrence of any of the following events, namely—

(*a*) where the court, on the application of the holder of the charge, pronounces itself satisfied that the position of the holder of the charge is likely to be prejudiced if no such appointment is made;

(*b*) any of the events referred to in paragraphs (*a*) to (*c*) of subsection (1).

Mode of appointment by holder of charge

53.—(1) The appointment of a receiver by the holder of the floating charge under section 51(1) shall be by means of a validly executed instrument in writing ("the instrument of appointment"), a copy (certified in the prescribed manner to be a correct copy) whereof shall be delivered by or on behalf of the person making the appointment to the registrar of companies for registration within seven days of its execution and shall be accompanied by a notice in the prescribed form.

[1] (2) If any person without reasonable excuse makes default in complying with the requirements of subsection (1), he is liable to a fine and, for continued contravention, to a daily default fine.

(3) The instrument of appointment is validly executed—

(*a*) by a company, if it is executed in accordance with the provisions of section 36 of the Companies Act as if it were a contract, and

(*b*) by any other person, if it is executed in the manner required or permitted by the law of Scotland in the case of an attested deed.

(4) The instrument may be executed on behalf of the holder of the floating charge by virtue of which the receiver is to be appointed—

(*a*) by any person duly authorised in writing by the holder to execute the instrument, and

(*b*) in the case of an appointment of a receiver by the holders of a series of secured debentures, by any person authorised by resolution of the debenture-holders to execute the instrument.

(5) On receipt of the certified copy of the instrument of appointment in accordance with subsection (1), the registrar shall, on payment of the prescribed fee, enter the particulars of the appointment in the register of charges.

(6) The appointment of a person as a receiver by an instrument of appointment in accordance with subsection (1)—

(*a*) is of no effect unless it is accepted by that person before the end of the business day next following that on which the instrument of appointment is received by him or on his behalf, and

(*b*) subject to paragraph (*a*), is deemed to be made on the day on and at the time at which the instrument of appointment is so received, as evidenced by a written docquet by that person or on his behalf;

and this subsection applies to the appointment of joint receivers subject to such modifications as may be prescribed.

(7) On the appointment of a receiver under this section, the floating charge by virtue of which he was appointed attaches to the property then subject to the charge; and such attachment has effect as if the charge was a fixed security over the property to which it has attached.

NOTE
[1] Amended (*prosp.*) by the Companies Act 1989, Sched. 16, para. 3(3).

Appointment by court

54.—(1) Application for the appointment of a receiver by the court under section 51(2) shall be by petition to the court, which shall be served on the company.

(2) On such an application, the court shall, if it thinks fit, issue an interlocutor making the appointment of the receiver.

[1] (3) A copy (certified by the clerk of the court to be a correct copy) of the court's interlocutor making the appointment shall be delivered by or on behalf of the petitioner to the registrar of companies for registration, accompanied by a notice in the prescribed form, within seven days of the date of the interlocutor or such longer period as the court may allow.

If any person without reasonable excuse makes default in complying with the requirements of this subsection, he is liable to a fine and, for continued contravention, to a daily default fine.

(4) On receipt of the certified copy interlocutor in accordance with subsection (3), the registrar shall, on payment of the prescribed fee, enter the particulars of the appointment in the register of charges.

(5) The receiver is to be regarded as having been appointed on the date of his being appointed by the court.

(6) On the appointment of a receiver under this section, the floating charge by virtue of which he was appointed attaches to the property then subject to the charge; and such attachment has effect as if the charge were a fixed security over the property to which it has attached.

(7) In making rules of court for the purposes of this section, the Court of Session shall have regard to the need for special provision for cases which appear to the court to require to be dealt with as a matter of urgency.

NOTE
[1] Amended (*prosp.*) by the Companies Act 1989, Sched. 16, para. 3(3).

Powers of receiver

55.—(1) Subject to the next subsection, a receiver has a relation to such part of the property of the company as is attached by the floating charge by virtue of which he was appointed, the powers, if any, given to him by the instrument creating that charge.

(2) In addition, the receiver has under this Chapter the powers as respects that property (in so far as these are not inconsistent with any provision contained in that instrument) which are specified in Schedule 2 to this Act.

(3) Subsections (1) and (2) apply—

(*a*) subject to the rights of any person who has effectually executed diligence on all or any part of the property of the company prior to the appointment of the receiver, and

(*b*) subject to the rights of any person who holds over all or any part of the property of the company a fixed security or floating charge having priority over, or ranking *pari passu* with, the floating charge by virtue of which the receiver was appointed.

(4) A person dealing with a receiver in good faith and for value is not concerned to enquire whether the receiver is acting within his powers.

Precedence among receivers

56.—(1) Where there are two or more floating charges subsisting over all or any part of the property of the company, a receiver may be appointed under this Chapter by virtue of each such charge; but a receiver appointed by, or on the application of, the holder of a floating charge having priority of ranking over any other floating charge by virtue of which a receiver has been appointed has the powers given to a receiver by section 55 and Schedule 2 to the exclusion of any other receiver.

(2) Where two or more floating charges rank with one another equally, and two or more receivers have been appointed by virtue of such charges, the receivers so appointed are deemed to have been appointed as joint receivers.

(3) Receivers appointed, or deemed to have been appointed, as joint receivers shall act jointly unless the instrument of appointment or respective instruments of appointment otherwise provide.

(4) Subject to subsection (5) below, the powers of a receiver appointed by, or on the application of, the holder of a floating charge are suspended by, and as from the date of, the appointment of a receiver by, or on the application of, the holder of a floating charge having priority of ranking over that charge to such extent as may be necessary to enable the receiver second mentioned to exercise his powers under section 55 and Schedule 2; and any powers so suspended take effect again when the floating charge having priority of ranking ceases to attach to the property then subject to the charge, whether such cessation is by virtue of section 62(6) or otherwise.

(5) The suspension of the powers of a receiver under subsection (4) does not have the effect of requiring him to release any part of the property (including any letters or documents) of the company from his control until he receives from the receiver superseding him a valid indemnity (subject to the limit of the value of such part of the property of the company as is subject to the charge by virtue of which he was appointed) in respect of any expenses, charges and liabilities he may have incurred in the performance of his functions as receiver.

(6) The suspension of the powers of a receiver under subsection (4) does not cause the floating charge by virtue of which he was appointed to cease to attach to the property to which it attached by virtue of section 53(7) or 54(6).

(7) Nothing in this section prevents the same receiver being appointed by virtue of two or more floating charges.

Agency and liability of receiver for contracts

57.—(1) A receiver is deemed to be the agent of the company in relation to such property of the company as is attached by the floating charge by virtue of which he was appointed.

(2) A receiver (including a receiver whose powers are subsequently suspended under section 56) is personally liable on any contract entered into by him in the performance of his functions, except in so far as the contract otherwise provides, and on any contract of employment adopted by him in the carrying out of those functions.

(3) A receiver who is personally liable by virtue of subsection (2) is entitled to be indemnified out of the property in respect of which he was appointed.

(4) Any contract entered into by or on behalf of the company prior to the appointment of a receiver continues in force (subject to its terms) notwithstanding that appointment, but the receiver does not by virtue only of his appointment incur any personal liability on any such contract.

(5) For the purposes of subsection (2), a receiver is not to be taken to have adopted a contract of employment by reason of anything done or omitted to be done within 14 days after his appointment.

(6) This section does not limit any right to indemnity which the receiver would have apart from it, nor limit his liability on contracts entered into or adopted without authority, nor confer any right to indemnity in respect of that liability.

(7) Any contract entered into by a receiver in the performance of his functions continues in force (subject to its terms) although the powers of the receiver are subsequently suspended under section 56.

Remuneration of receiver

58.—(1) The remuneration to be paid to a receiver is to be determined by agreement between the receiver and the holder of the floating charge by virtue of which he was appointed.

(2) Where the remuneration to be paid to the receiver has not been determined under subsection (1), or where it has been so determined but is disputed by any of the persons mentioned in paragraphs (*a*) to (*d*) below, it may be fixed instead by the Auditor of the Court of Session on application made to him by—

(*a*) the receiver;

(*b*) the holder of any floating charge or fixed security over all or any part of the property of the company;

(*c*) the company; or

(*d*) the liquidator of the company.

(3) Where the receiver has been paid or has retained for his remuneration for any period before the remuneration has been fixed by the Auditor of the Court of Session under subsection (2) any amount in excess of the remuneration so fixed for that period, the receiver or his personal representatives shall account for the excess.

Priority of debts

59.—(1) Where a receiver is appointed and the company is not at the time of the appointment in course of being wound up, the debts which fall under subsection (2) of this section shall be paid out of any assets coming to the hands of the receiver in priority to any claim for principal or interest by the holder of the floating charge by virtue of which the receiver was appointed.

(2) Debts falling under this subsection are preferential debts (within the meaning given by section 386 in Part XII) which, by the end of a period of six months after advertisement by the receiver for claims in the *Edinburgh Gazette* and in a newspaper circulating in the district where the company carries on business either—

(i) have been intimated to him, or

(ii) have become know to him.

(3) Any payments made under this section shall be recouped as far as may be out of the assets of the company available for payment of ordinary creditors.

Distribution of moneys
60.—(1) Subject to the next section, and to the rights of any of the following categories of persons (which rights shall, except to the extent otherwise provided in any instrument, have the following order of priority), namely—

(*a*) the holder of any fixed security which is over property subject to the floating charge and which ranks prior to, or *pari passu* with, the floating charge;

(*b*) all persons who have effectually executed diligence on any part of the property of the company which is subject to the charge by virtue of which the receiver was appointed;

(*c*) creditors in respect of all liabilities, charges and expenses incurred by or on behalf of the receiver;

(*d*) the receiver in respect of his liabilities, expenses and remuneration, and any indemnity to which he is entitled out of the property of the company; and

(*e*) the preferential creditors entitled to payment under section 59,

the receiver shall pay moneys received by him to the holder of the floating charge by virtue of which the receiver was appointed in or towards satisfaction of the debt secured by the floating charge.

(2) Any balance of moneys remaining after the provisions of subsection (1) and section 61 below have been satisfied shall be paid in accordance with their respective rights and interests to the following persons, as the case may require—

(*a*) any other receiver;

(*b*) the holder of a fixed security which is over property subject to the floating charge;

(*c*) the company or its liquidator, as the case may be.

(3) Where any question arises as to the person entitled to a payment under this section, or where a receipt or a discharge of a security cannot be obtained in respect of any such payment, the receiver shall consign the amount of such payment in any joint stock bank of issue in Scotland in name of the Accountant of Court for behoof of the person or persons entitled thereto.

Disposal of interest in property
61.—(1) Where the receiver sells or disposes, or is desirous of selling or disposing, of any property or interest in property of the company which is subject to the floating charge by virtue of which the receiver was appointed and which is—

(*a*) subject to any security or interest of, or burden or encumbrance in favour of, a creditor the ranking of which is prior to, or *pari passu* with, or postponed to the floating charge, or

(*b*) property or an interest in property affected or attached by effectual diligence executed by any person,

and the receiver is unable to obtain the consent of such creditor or, as the case may be, such person to such a sale or disposal, the receiver may apply to the court for authority to sell or dispose of the property or interest in property free of such security, interest, burden, encumbrance or diligence.

(2) Subject to the next subsection, on such an application the court may, if it thinks fit, authorise the sale or disposal of the property or interest in question free of such security, interest, burden, encumbrance or diligence, and such authorisation may be on such terms or conditions as the court thinks fit.

(3) In the case of an application where a fixed security over the property or interest in question which ranks prior to the floating charge has not been met or provided for in full, the court shall not authorise the sale or disposal of the property or interest in question unless it is satisfied that the sale or disposal would be likely to provide a more advantageous realisation of the company's assets than would otherwise be effected.

(4) It shall be a condition of an authorisation to which subsection (3) applies that—

(*a*) the net proceeds of the disposal, and

(*b*) where those proceeds are less than such amount as may be determined by the court to be the net amount which would be realised on a sale of the property or interest in the open market by a willing seller, such sums as may be required to make good the deficiency.

shall be applied towards discharging the sums secured by the fixed security.

(5) Where a condition imposed in pursuance of subsection (4) relates to two or more such fixed securities, that condition shall require the net proceeds of the disposal and, where paragraph (*b*) of that subsection applies, the sums mentioned in that paragraph to be applied towards discharging the sums secured by those fixed securities in the order of their priorities.

(6) A copy of an authorisation under subsection (2) certified by the clerk of court shall, within 14 days of the granting of the authorisation, be sent by the receiver to the registrar of companies.

(7) If the receiver without reasonable excuse fails to comply with subsection (6), he is liable to a fine and, for continued contravention, to a daily default fine.

(8) Where any sale or disposal is effected in accordance with the authorisation of the court under subsection (2), the receiver shall grant to the purchaser or disponee an appropriate document of transfer or conveyance of the property or interest in question, and that document has the effect, or, where recording, intimation or registration of that document is a legal requirement for completion of title to the property or interest, then that recording, intimation or registration (as the case may be) has the effect, of—

(*a*) disencumbering the property or interest of the security, interest, burden or encumbrance affecting it, and

(*b*) freeing the property or interest from the diligence executed upon it.

(9) Nothing in this section prejudices the right of any creditor of the company to rank for his debt in the winding up of the company.

Cessation of appointment of receiver

62.—(1) A receiver may be removed from office by the court under subsection (3) below and may resign his office by giving notice of his resignation in the prescribed manner to such persons as may be prescribed.

(2) A receiver shall vacate office if he ceases to be qualified to act as an insolvency practitioner in relation to the company.

(3) Subject to the next subsection, a receiver may, on application to the court by the holder of the floating charge by virtue of which he was appointed, be removed by the court on cause shown.

(4) Where at any time a receiver vacates office—

(*a*) his remuneration and any expenses properly incurred by him, and

(*b*) any indemnity to which he is entitled out of the property of the company,

shall be paid out of the property of the company which is subject to the floating charge and shall have priority as provided for in section 60 (1).

(5) When a receiver ceases to act as such otherwise than by death he shall, and, when a receiver is removed by the court, the holder of the floating charge by virtue of which he was appointed shall, within 14 days of the cessation or removal (as the case may be) give the registrar of companies notice to that effect, and the registrar shall enter the notice in the register of charges.

If the receiver or the holder of the floating charge (as the case may require) makes default in complying with the requirements of this subsection, he is liable to a fine and, for continued contravention, to a daily default fine.

(6) If by the expiry of a period of one month following upon the removal of the receiver or his ceasing to act as such no other receiver has been appointed, the floating charge by virtue of which the receiver was appointed—

(*a*) thereupon ceases to attach to the property then subject to the charge, and

(*b*) again subsists as a floating charge;

and for the purposes of calculating the period of one month under this subsection no account shall be taken of any period during which an administration order under Part II of this Act is in force.

NOTE

Subs. (5) amended (*prosp.*) by the Companies Act 1989, Sched. 16, para. 3(3).

Powers of court

63.—(1) The court on the application of—

(*a*) the holder of a floating charge by virtue of which a receiver was appointed, or

(*b*) a receiver appointed under section 51,

may give directions to the receiver in respect of any matter arising in connection with the performance by him of his functions.

(2) Where the appointment of a person as a receiver by the holder of a floating charge is discovered to be invalid (whether by virtue of the invalidity of the instrument or otherwise), the court may order the holder of the floating charge to indemnify the person appointed against any liability which arises solely by reason of the invalidity of the appointment.

Notification that receiver appointed

64.—(1) Where a receiver has been appointed, every invoice, order for goods or business letter issued by or on behalf of the company or the receiver or the liquidator of the company, being a document on or in which the name of the company appears, shall contain a statement that a receiver has been appointed.

(2) If default is made in complying with the requirements of this section, the company and any of the following persons who knowingly and wilfully authorises or permits the default, namely any officer of the company, any liquidator of the company and any receiver, is liable to a fine.

Information to be given by receiver

65.—(1) Where a receiver is appointed, he shall—

(*a*) forthwith send to the company and publish notice of his appointment, and

(*b*) within 28 days after his appointment, unless the court otherwise directs, send such notice to all the creditors of the company (so far as he is aware of their addresses).

(2) This section and the next do not apply in relation to the appointment of a receiver to act—

(*a*) with an existing receiver, or

(*b*) in place of a receiver who has died or ceased to act,

except that, where they apply to a receiver who dies or ceases to act before they have been fully complied with, the references in this section and the next to the receiver include (subject to subsection (3) of this section) his successor and any continuing receiver.

(3) If the company is being wound up, this section and the next apply notwithstanding that the receiver and the liquidator are the same person, but with any necessary modifications arising from that fact.

(4) If a person without reasonable excuse fails to comply with this section, he is liable to a fine and, for continued contravention, to a daily default fine.

Company's statement of affairs

66.—(1) Where a receiver of a company is appointed, the receiver shall forthwith require some or all of the persons mentioned in subsection (3) below to make out and submit to him a statement in the prescribed form as to the affairs of the company.

(2) A statement submitted under this section shall be verified by affidavit by the persons required to submit it and shall show—

(a) particulars of the company's assets, debts and liabilities;

(b) the names and addresses of its creditors;

(c) the securities held by them respectively;

(d) the dates when the securities were respectively given; and

(e) such further or other information as may be prescribed.

(3) The persons referred to in subsection (1) are—

(a) those who are or have been officers of the company;

(b) those who have taken part in the company's formation at any time within one year before the date of the appointment of the receiver;

(c) those who are in the company's employment or have been in its employment within that year, and are in the receiver's opinion capable of giving the information required;

(d) those who are or have been within that year officers of or in the employment of a company which is, or within that year was, an officer of the company.

In this subsection "employment" includes employment under a contract for services.

(4) Where any persons are required under this section to submit a statement of affairs to the receiver they shall do so (subject to the next subsection) before the end of the period of 21 days beginning with the day after that on which the prescribed notice of the requirement is given to them by the receiver.

(5) The receiver, if he thinks fit, may—

(a) at any time release a person from an obligation imposed on him under subsection (1) or (2), or

(b) either when giving the notice mentioned in subsection (4) or subsequently extend the period so mentioned,

and where the receiver has refused to exercise a power conferred by this subsection, the court, if it thinks fit, may exercise it.

(6) If a person without reasonable excuse fails to comply with any obligation imposed under this section, he is liable to a fine and, for continued contravention, to a daily default fine.

Report by receiver

67.—(1) Where a receiver is appointed under section 51, he shall within three months (or such longer period as the court may allow) after his appointment, send to the registrar of companies, to the holder of the floating charge by virtue of which he was appointed and to any trustees for secured creditors of the company and (so far as he is aware of their addresses) to all such creditors a report as to the following matters, namely—

(a) the events leading up to his appointment, so far as he is aware of them;

(b) the disposal or proposed disposal by him of any property of the company and the carrying on or proposed carrying on by him of any business of the company;

(c) the amounts of principal and interest payable to the holder of the floating charge by virtue of which he was appointed and the amounts payable to preferential creditors; and

(d) the amount (if any) likely to be available for the payment of other creditors.

(2) The receiver shall also, within three months (or such longer period as the court may allow) after his appointment, either—

    (*a*) send a copy of the report (so far as he is aware of their addresses) to all unsecured creditors of the company, or

    (*b*) publish in the prescribed manner a notice stating an address to which unsecured creditors of the company should write for copies of the report to be sent to them free of charge,

and (in either case), unless the court otherwise directs, lay a copy of the report before a meeting of the company's unsecured creditors summoned for the purpose on not less than 14 days' notice.

(3) The court shall not give a direction under subsection (2) unless—

    (*a*) the report states the intention of the receiver to apply for the direction, and

    (*b*) a copy of the report is sent to the persons mentioned in paragraph (*a*) of that subsection, or a notice is published as mentioned in paragraph (*b*) of that subsection, not less than 14 days before the hearing of the application.

(4) Where the company has gone or goes into liquidation, the receiver—

    (*a*) shall, within seven days after his compliance with subsection (1) or, if later, the nomination or appointment of the liquidator, send a copy of the report to the liquidator, and

    (*b*) where he does so within the time limited for compliance with subsection (2), is not required to comply with that subsection.

(5) A report under this section shall include a summary of the statement of affairs made out and submitted under section 66 and of his comments (if any) on it.

(6) Nothing in this section shall be taken as requiring any such report to include any information the disclosure of which would seriously prejudice the carrying out by the receiver of his functions.

(7) Section 65(2) applies for the purposes of this section also.

(8) If a person without reasonable excuse fails to comply with this section, he is liable to a fine and, for continued contravention, to a daily default fine.

(9) In this section "secured creditor", in relation to a company, means a creditor of the company who holds in respect of his debt a security over property of the company, and "unsecured creditor" shall be construed accordingly.

Committee of creditors

68.—(1) Where a meeting of creditors is summoned under section 67, the meeting may, if it thinks fit, establish a committee ("the creditors' committee") to exercise the functions conferred on it by or under this Act.

(2) If such a committee is established, the committee may on giving not less than seven days' notice require the receiver to attend before it at any reasonable time and furnish it with such information relating to the carrying out by him of his functions as it may reasonably require.

Enforcement of receiver's duty to make returns, etc.

69.—(1) If any receiver—

    (*a*) having made default in filing, delivering or making any return, account or other document, or in giving any notice, which a receiver is by law required to file, deliver, make or give, fails to make good the default within 14 days after the service on him of a notice requiring him to do so; or

    (*b*) has, after being required at any time by the liquidator of the company so to do, failed to render proper accounts of his receipts and payments and to vouch the same and to pay over to the liquidator the amount properly payable to him, the court may, on an application made for the purpose, make an order directing the receiver to make good the default within such time as may be specified in the order.

(2) In the case of any such default as is mentioned in subsection (1)(*a*), an application for the purposes of this section may be made by any member or creditor of the company or by the registrar of companies; and, in the case of any such default as is mentioned in subsection (1)(*b*), the application shall be made by the liquidator; and, in either case, the order may provide that all expenses of and incidental to the application shall be borne by the receiver.

(3) Nothing in this section prejudices the operation of any enactments imposing penalties on receivers in respect of any such default as is mentioned in subsection (1).

Interpretation for Chapter II

70.—(1) In this Chapter, unless the contrary intention appears, the following expressions have the following meanings respectively assigned to them—

> "company" means an incorporated company (whether or not a company within the meaning of the Companies Act) which the Court of Session has jurisdiction to wind up;

> "fixed security", in relation to any property of a company, means any security, other than a floating charge or a charge having the nature of a floating charge, which on the winding up of the company in Scotland would be treated as an effective security over that property, and (without prejudice to that generality) includes a security over that property, being a heritable security within the meaning of the Conveyancing and Feudal Reform (Scotland) Act 1970;

> "instrument of appointment" has the meaning given by section 53(1);

> "prescribed" means prescribed by regulations made under this Chapter by the Secretary of State;

> "receiver" means a receiver of such part of the property of the company as is subject to the floating charge by virtue of which he has been appointed under section 51;

> "register of charges" means the register kept by the registrar of companies for the purposes of Chapter II of Part XII of the Companies Act;

> "secured debenture" means a bond, debenture, debenture stock or other security which, either itself or by reference to any other instrument, creates a floating charge over all or any part of the property of the company, but does not include a security which creates no charge other than a fixed security; and

> "series of secured debentures" means two or more secured debentures created as a series by the company in such a manner that the holders thereof are entitled *pari passu* to the benefit of the floating charge.

(2) Where a floating charge, secured debenture or series of secured debentures has been created by the company, then, except where the context otherwise requires, any reference in this Chapter to the holder of the floating charge shall—

(*a*) where the floating charge, secured debenture or series of secured debentures provides for a receiver to be appointed by any person or body, be construed as a reference to that person or body;

(*b*) where, in the case of a series of secured debentures, no such provision has been made therein but—

> (i) there are trustees acting for the debenture-holders under and in accordance with a trust deed, be construed as a reference to those trustees, and

> (ii) where no such trustees are acting, be construed as a reference to—

(*aa*) a majority in nominal value of those present or represented by proxy and voting at a meeting of debenture-holders at which the holders of at least one-third in nominal value of the outstanding debentures of the series are present or so represented, or

(*bb*) where no such meeting is held, the holders of at least one-half in nominal value of the outstanding debentures of the series.

(3) Any reference in this Chapter to a floating charge, secured debenture, series of secured debentures or instrument creating a charge includes, except where the context otherwise requires, a reference to that floating charge, debenture, series of debentures or instrument as varied by any instrument.

(4) References in this Chapter to the instrument by which a floating charge was created are, in the case of a floating charge created by words in a bond or other written acknowledgement, references to the bond or, as the case may be, the other written acknowledgement.

Prescription of forms, etc.; regulations

71.—(1) The notice referred to in section 62(5), and the notice referred to in section 65(1)(*a*) shall be in such form as may be prescribed.

(2) Any power conferred by this Chapter on the Secretary of State to make regulations is exercisable by statutory instrument; and a statutory instrument made in the exercise of the power so conferred to prescribe a fee is subject to annulment in pursuance of a resolution of either House of Parliament.

CHAPTER III

RECEIVERS' POWERS IN GREAT BRITAIN AS A WHOLE

Cross-border operation of receivership provisions

72.—(1) A receiver appointed under the law of either part of Great Britain in respect of the whole or any part of any property or undertaking of a company and in consequence of the company having created a charge which, as created, was a floating charge may exercise his powers in the other part of Great Britain so far as their exercise is not inconsistent with the law applicable there.

(2) In subsection (1) "receiver" includes a manager and a person who is appointed both receiver and manager.

[1] PART IV

NOTE
[1] Applied by the Building Societies Act 1986, Sched. 15, Pt. I, and applied (*mod.*) by *ibid.*, Pt. II. See the Criminal Justice (Scotland) Act 1987, s.35(4) and the Criminal Justice Act 1988, s.86(5).

WINDING UP OF COMPANIES REGISTERED UNDER THE COMPANIES ACTS

CHAPTER I

PRELIMINARY

Modes of winding up

Alternative modes of winding up

73.—(1) The winding up of a company, within the meaning given to that expression by section 735 of the Companies Act, may be either voluntary (Chapters II, III, IV and V in this Part) or by the court (Chapter VI).

(2) This Chapter, and Chapters VII to X, relate to winding up generally, except where otherwise stated.

Contributories

Liability as contributories of present and past members

74.—(1) When a company is wound up, every present and past member is liable to contribute to its assets to any amount sufficient for payment of its debts and liabilities, and the expenses of the winding up, and for the adjustment of the rights of the contributories among themselves.

(2) This is subject as follows—

(*a*) a past member is not liable to contribute if he has ceased to be a member for one year or more before the commencement of the winding up;

(*b*) a past member is not liable to contribute in respect of any debt or liability of the company contracted after he ceased to be a member;

(*c*) a past member is not liable to contribute, unless it appears to the court that the existing members are unable to satisfy the contributions required to be made by them in pursuance of the Companies Act and this Act;

(*d*) in the case of a company limited by shares, no contribution is required from any member exceeding the amount (if any) unpaid on the shares in respect of which he is liable as a present or past member;

(*e*) nothing in the Companies Act or this Act invalidates any provision contained in a policy of insurance or other contract whereby the liability of individual members on the policy or contract is restricted, or whereby the funds of the company are alone made liable in respect of the policy or contract;

(*f*) a sum due to any member of the company (in his character of a member) by way of dividends, profits or otherwise is not deemed to be a debt of the company, payable to that member in a case of competition between himself and any other creditor not a member of the company, but any such sum may be taken into account for the purpose of the final adjustment of the rights of the contributories among themselves.

(3) In the case of a company limited by guarantee, no contribution is required from any member exceeding the amount undertaken to be contributed by him to the company's assets in the event of its being wound up; but if it is a company with a share capital, every member of it is liable (in addition to the amount so undertaken to be contributed to the assets), to contribute to the extent of any sums unpaid on shares held by him.

Directors, etc. with unlimited liability

75.—(1) In the winding up of a limited company, any director or manager (whether past or present) whose liability is under the Companies Act unlimited is liable, in addition to his liability (if any) to contribute as an ordinary member, to make a further contribution as if he were at the commencement of the winding up a member of an unlimited company.

(2) However—

(*a*) a past director or manager is not liable to make such further contribution if he has ceased to hold office for a year or more before the commencement of the winding up;

(*b*) a past director or manager is not liable to make such further contribution in respect of any debt or liability of the company contracted after he ceased to hold office;

(*c*) subject to the company's articles, a director or manager is not liable to make such further contribution unless the court deems it necessary to require that contribution in order to satisfy the company's debts and liabilities, and the expenses of the winding up.

Liability of past directors and shareholders

76.—(1) This section applies where a company is being wound up and—

  (*a*) it has under Chapter VII of Part V of the Companies Act (redeemable shares; purchase by a company of its own shares) made a payment out of capital in respect of the redemption or purchase of any of its own shares (the payment being referred to below as "the relevant payment"), and

  (*b*) the aggregate amount of the company's assets and the amounts paid by way of contribution to its assets (apart from this section) is not sufficient for payment of its debts and liabilities, and the expenses of the winding up.

(2) If the winding up commenced within one year of the date on which the relevant payment was made, then—

  (*a*) the person from whom the shares were redeemed or purchased, and

  (*b*) the directors who signed the statutory declaration made in accordance with section 173(3) of the Companies Act for purposes of the redemption or purchase (except a director who shows that he had reasonable grounds for forming the opinion set out in the declaration),

are, so as to enable that insufficiency to be met, liable to contribute to the following extent to the company's assets.

(3) A person from whom any of the shares were redeemed or purchased is liable to contribute an amount not exceeding so much of the relevant payment as was made by the company in respect of his shares; and the directors are jointly and severally liable with that person to contribute that amount.

(4) A person who has contributed any amount to the assets in pursuance of this section may apply to the court for an order directing any other person jointly and severally liable in respect of that amount to pay him such amount as the court thinks just and equitable.

(5) Sections 74 and 75 do not apply in relation to liability accruing by virtue of this section.

(6) This section is deemed included in Chapter VII of Part V of the Companies Act for the purposes of the Secretary of State's power to make regulations under section 179 of that Act.

Limited company formerly unlimited

77.—(1) This section applies in the case of a company being wound up which was at some former time registered as unlimited but has re-registered—

  (*a*) as a public company under section 43 of the Companies Act (or the former corresponding provision, section 5 of the Companies Act 1980), or

  (*b*) as a limited company under section 51 of the Companies Act (or the former corresponding provision, section 44 of the Companies Act 1967).

(2) Notwithstanding section 74(2)(*a*) above, a past member of the company who was a member of it at the time of re-registration, if the winding up commences within the period of three years beginning with the day on which the company was re-registered, is liable to contribute to the assets of the company in respect of debts and liabilities contracted before that time.

(3) If no persons who were members of the company at that time are existing members of it, a person who at that time was a present or past member is liable to contribute as above notwithstanding that the existing members have satisfied the contributions required to be made by them under the Companies Act and this Act.

This applies subject to section 74(2)(*a*) above and to subsection (2) of this section, but notwithstanding section 74(2)(*c*).

(4) Notwithstanding section 74(2)(*d*) and (3), there is no limit on the

amount which a person who, at that time, was a past or present member of the company is liable to contribute as above.

Unlimited company formerly limited

78.—(1) This section applies in the case of a company being wound up which was at some former time registered as limited but has been re-registered as unlimited under section 49 of the Companies Act (or the former corresponding provision, section 43 of the Companies Act 1967).

(2) A person who, at the time when the application for the company to be re-registered was lodged, was a past member of the company and did not after that again become a member of it is not liable to contribute to the assets of the company more than he would have been liable to contribute had the company not been re-registered.

Meaning of "contributory"

79.—(1) In this Act and the Companies Act the expression "contributory" means every person liable to contribute to the assets of a company in the event of its being wound up, and for the purposes of all proceedings for determining, and all proceedings prior to the final determination of, the persons who are to be deemed contributories, includes any person alleged to be a contributory.

(2) The reference in subsection (1) to persons liable to contribute to the assets does not include a person so liable by virtue of a declaration by the court under section 213 (imputed responsibility for company's fraudulent trading) or section 214 (wrongful trading) in Chapter X of this Part.

(3) A reference in a company's articles to a contributory does not (unless the context requires) include a person who is a contributory only by virtue of section 76.

This subsection is deemed included in Chapter VII of Part V of the Companies Act for the purposes of the Secretary of State's power to make regulations under section 179 of that Act.

Nature of contributory's liability

80. The liability of a contributory creates a debt (in England and Wales in the nature of a specialty) accruing due from him at the time when his liability commenced, but payable at the time when calls are made for enforcing the liability.

Contributories in case of death of a member

81.—(1) If a contributory dies either before or after he has been placed on the list of contributories, his personal representatives, and the heirs and legatees of heritage of his heritable estate in Scotland, are liable in a due course of administration to contribute to the assets of the company in discharge of his liability and are contributories accordingly.

(2) Where the personal representatives are placed on the list of contributories, the heirs or legatees of heritage need not be added, but they may be added as and when the court thinks fit.

(3) If in England and Wales the personal representatives make default in paying any money ordered to be paid by them, proceedings may be taken for administering the estate of the deceased contributory and for compelling payment out of it of the money due.

Effect of contributory's bankruptcy

82.—(1) The following applies if a contributory becomes bankrupt, either before or after he has been placed on the list of contributories.

(2) His trustee in bankruptcy represents him for all purposes of the winding up, and is a contributory accordingly.

(3) The trustee may be called on to admit to proof against the bankrupt's estate, or otherwise allow to be paid out of the bankrupt's assets in due

course of law, any money due from the bankrupt in respect of his liability to contribute to the company's assets.

(4) There may be proved against the bankrupt's estate the estimated value of his liability to future calls as well as calls already made.

Companies registered under Companies Act, Part XXII, Chapter II

83.—(1) The following applies in the event of a company being wound up which has been registered under section 680 of the Companies Act (or previous corresponding provisions in the Companies Act 1948 or earlier Acts).

(2) Every person is a contributory, in respect of the company's debts and liabilities contracted before registration, who is liable—

(*a*) to pay, or contribute to the payment of, any debt or liability so contracted, or

(*b*) to pay, or contribute to the payment of, any sum for the adjustment of the rights of the members among themselves in respect of any such debt or liability, or

(*c*) to pay, or contribute to the amount of, the expenses of winding up the company, so far as relates to the debts or liabilities above-mentioned.

(3) Every contributory is liable to contribute to the assets of the company, in the course of the winding up, all sums due from him in respect of any such liability.

(4) In the event of the death, bankruptcy or insolvency of any contributory, provisions of this Act, with respect to the personal representatives, to the heirs and legatees of heritage of the heritable estate in Scotland of deceased contributories and to the trustees of bankrupt or insolvent contributories respectively, apply.

Chapter II

Voluntary Winding Up (Introductory and General)

Resolutions for, and commencement of, voluntary winding up

Circumstances in which company may be wound up voluntarily

84.—(1) A company may be wound up voluntarily—

(*a*) when the period (if any) fixed for the duration of the company by the articles expires, or the event (if any) occurs, on the occurrence of which the articles provide that the company is to be dissolved, and the company in general meeting has passed a resolution requiring it to be wound up voluntarily;

(*b*) if the company resolves by special resolution that it be wound up voluntarily;

(*c*) if the company resolves by extraordinary resolution to the effect that it cannot by reason of its liabilities continue its business, and that it is advisable to wind up.

(2) In this Act the expression "a resolution for voluntary winding up" means a resolution passed under any of the paragraphs of subsection (1).

(3) A resolution passed under paragraph (*a*) of subsection (1), as well as a special resolution under paragraph (*b*) and an extraordinary resolution under paragraph (*c*), is subject to section 380 of the Companies Act (copy of resolution to be forwarded to registrar of companies within 15 days).

Notice of resolution to wind up

85.—(1) When a company has passed a resolution for voluntary winding up, it shall, within 14 days after the passing of the resolution, give notice of the resolution by advertisement in the *Gazette*.

(2) If default is made in complying with this section, the company and every officer of it who is in default is liable to a fine and, for continued contravention, to a daily default fine.

For purposes of this subsection the liquidator is deemed an officer of the company.

Commencement of winding up

86. A voluntary winding up is deemed to commence at the time of the passing of the resolution for voluntary winding up.

Consequences of resolution to wind up

Effect on business and status of company

87.—(1) In case of a voluntary winding up, the company shall from the commencement of the winding up cease to carry on its business, except so far as may be required for its beneficial winding up.

(2) However, the corporate state and corporate powers of the company, notwithstanding anything to the contrary in its articles, continue until the company is dissolved.

Avoidance of share transfers, etc. after winding-up resolution

88. Any transfer of shares, not being a transfer made to or with the sanction of the liquidator, and any alteration in the status of the company's members, made after the commencement of a voluntary winding up, is void.

Declaration of solvency

Statutory declaration of solvency

89.—(1) Where it is proposed to wind up a company voluntarily, the directors (or, in the case of a company having more than two directors, the majority of them) may at a directors' meeting make a statutory declaration to the effect that they have made a full inquiry into the company's affairs and that, having done so, they have formed the opinion that the company will be able to pay its debts in full, together with interest at the official rate (as defined in section 251), within such period, not exceeding 12 months from the commencement of the winding up, as may be specified in the declaration.

(2) Such a declaration by the directors has no effect for purposes of this Act unless—

(*a*) it is made within the five weeks immediately preceding the date of the passing of the resolution for winding up, or on that date but before the passing of the resolution, and

(*b*) it embodies a statement of the company's assets and liabilities as at the latest practicable date before the making of the declaration.

(3) The declaration shall be delivered to the registrar of companies before the expiration of 15 days immediately following the date on which the resolution for winding up is passed.

(4) A director making a declaration under this section without having reasonable grounds for the opinion that the company will be able to pay its debts in full, together with interest at the official rate, within the period specified is liable to imprisonment or a fine, or both.

(5) If the company is wound up in pursuance of a resolution passed within five weeks after the making of the declaration, and its debts (together with interest at the official rate) are not paid or provided for in full within the period specified, it is to be presumed (unless the contrary is shown) that the director did not have reasonable grounds for his opinion.

(6) If a declaration required by subsection (3) to be delivered to the registrar is not so delivered within the time prescribed by that subsection, the company and every officer in default is liable to a fine and, for continued contravention, to a daily default fine.

Distinction between "members' " and "creditors' " voluntary winding up

90. A winding up in the case of which a directors' statutory ⟍
under section 89 has been made is a "members' voluntary ⟍
and a winding up in the case of which such a declaration has not b⟍
is a "creditors' voluntary winding up".

CHAPTER III

MEMBERS' VOLUNTARY WINDING UP

Appointment of liquidator

91.—(1) In a members' voluntary winding up, the company in general meeting shall appoint one or more liquidators for the purpose of winding up the company's affairs and distributing its assets.

(2) On the appointment of a liquidator all the powers of the directors cease, except so far as the company in general meeting or the liquidator sanctions their continuance.

Power to fill vacancy in office of liquidator

92.—(1) If a vacancy occurs by death, resignation or otherwise in the office of liquidator appointed by the company, the company in general meeting may, subject to any arrangement with its creditors, fill the vacancy.

(2) For that purpose a general meeting may be convened by any contributory or, if there were more liquidators than one, by the continuing liquidators.

(3) The meeting shall be held in manner provided by this Act or by the articles, or in such manner as may, on application by any contributory or by the continuing liquidators, be determined by the court.

General company meeting at each year's end

93.—(1) Subject to sections 96 and 102, in the event of the winding up continuing for more than one year, the liquidator shall summon a general meeting of the company at the end of the first year from the commencement of the winding up, and of each succeeding year, or at the first convenient date within three months from the end of the year or such longer period as the Secretary of State may allow.

(2) The liquidator shall lay before the meeting an account of his acts and dealings, and of the conduct of the winding up, during the preceding year.

(3) If the liquidator fails to comply with this section, he is liable to a fine.

Final meeting prior to dissolution

94.—(1) As soon as the company's affairs are fully wound up, the liquidator shall make up an account of the winding up, showing how it has been conducted and the company's property has been disposed of, and thereupon shall call a general meeting of the company for the purpose of laying before it the account, and giving an explanation of it.

(2) The meeting shall be called by advertisement in the *Gazette*, specifying its time, place and object and published at least one month before the meeting.

(3) Within one week after the meeting, the liquidator shall send to the registrar of companies a copy of the account, and shall make a return to him of the holding of the meeting and of its date.

(4) If the copy is not sent or the return is not made in accordance with subsection (3), the liquidator is liable to a fine and, for continued contravention, to a daily default fine.

(5) If a quorum is not present at the meeting, the liquidator shall, in lieu

of the return mentioned above, make a return that the meeting was duly summoned and that no quorum was present; and upon such a return being made, the provisions of subsection (3) as to the making of the return are deemed complied with.

(6) If the liquidator fails to call a general meeting of the company as required by subsection (1), he is liable to a fine.

Effect of company's insolvency

95.—(1) This section applies where the liquidator is of the opinion that the company will be unable to pay its debts in full (together with interest at the official rate) within the period stated in the directors' declaration under section 89.

(2) The liquidator shall—

(*a*) summon a meeting of creditors for a day not later than the 28th day after the day on which he formed that opinion;

(*b*) send notices of the creditors' meeting to the creditors by post not less than seven days before the day on which that meeting is to be held;

(*c*) cause notice of the creditors' meeting to be advertised once in the *Gazette* and once at least in two newspapers circulating in the relevant locality (that is to say the locality in which the company's principal place of business in Great Britain was situated during the relevant period); and

(*d*) during the period before the day on which the creditors' meeting is to be held, furnish creditors free of charge with such information concerning the affairs of the company as they may reasonably require;

and the notice of the creditors' meeting shall state the duty imposed by paragraph (*d*) above.

(3) The liquidator shall also—

(*a*) make out a statement in the prescribed form as to the affairs of the company;

(*b*) lay that statement before the creditors' meeting; and

(*c*) attend and preside at that meeting.

(4) The statement as to the affairs of the company shall be verified by affidavit by the liquidator and shall show—

(*a*) particulars of the company's assets, debts and liabilities;

(*b*) the names and addresses of the company's creditors;

(*c*) the securities held by them respectively;

(*d*) the dates when the securities were respectively given; and

(*e*) such further or other information as may be prescribed.

(5) Where the company's principal place of business in Great Britain was situated in different localities at different times during the relevant period, the duty imposed by subsection (2)(*c*) applies separately in relation to each of those localities.

(6) Where the company had no place of business in Great Britain during the relevant period, references in subsections (2)(*c*) and (5) to the company's principal place of business in Great Britain are replaced by references to its registered office.

(7) In this section "the relevant period" means the period of six months immediately preceding the day on which were sent the notices summoning the company meeting at which it was resolved that the company be wound up voluntarily.

(8) If the liquidator without reasonable excuse fails to comply with this section, he is liable to a fine.

Conversion to creditors' voluntary winding up

96. As from the day on which the creditors' meeting is held under section 95, this Act has effect as if—

(*a*) the directors' declaration under section 89 had not been made; a.
(*b*) the creditors' meeting and the company meeting at which it w.
resolved that the company be wound up voluntarily were the meetings mentioned in section 98 in the next Chapter;
and accordingly the winding up becomes a creditors' voluntary winding up.

CHAPTER IV

CREDITORS' VOLUNTARY WINDING UP

Application of this Chapter
97.—(1) Subject as follows, this Chapter applies in relation to a creditors' voluntary winding up.

(2) Sections 98 and 99 do not apply where, under section 96 in Chapter
III, a members' voluntary winding up has become a creditors' voluntary
winding up.

Meeting of creditors
98.—(1) The company shall—
(*a*) cause a meeting of its creditors to be summoned for a day not later
than the 14th day after the day on which there is to be held the company meeting at which the resolution for voluntary winding up is to
be proposed;
(*b*) cause the notices of the creditors' meeting to be sent by post to the
creditors not less than seven days before the day on which that
meeting is to be held; and
(*c*) cause notice of the creditors' meeting to be advertised once in the
Gazette and once at least in two newspapers circulating in the relevant locality (that is to say the locality in which the company's principal place of business in Great Britain was situated during the
relevant period).

(2) The notice of the creditors' meeting shall state either—
(*a*) the name and address of a person qualified to act as an insolvency
practitioner in relation to the company who, during the period
before the day on which that meeting is to be held, will furnish
creditors free of charge with such information concerning the company's affairs as they may reasonably require; or
(*b*) a place in the relevant locality where, on the two business days falling next before the day on which that meeting is to be held, a list of
the names and addresses of the company's creditors will be available
for inspection free of charge.

(3) Where the company's principal place of business in Great Britain was
situated in different localities at different times during the relevant period,
the duties imposed by subsections (1)(*c*) and (2)(*b*) above apply separately
in relation to each of those localities.

(4) Where the company had no place of business in Great Britain during
the relevant period, references in subsections (1)(*c*) and (3) to the company's principal place of business in Great Britain are replaced by references to its registered office.

(5) In this section "the relevant period" means the period of six months
immediately preceding the day on which were sent the notices summoning
the company meeting at which it was resolved that the company be wound
up voluntarily.

(6) If the company without reasonable excuse fails to comply with subsection (1) or (2), it is guilty of an offence and liable to a fine.

Directors to lay statement of affairs before creditors

99.—(1) The directors of the company shall—

(*a*) make out a statement in the prescribed form as to the affairs of the company;

(*b*) cause that statement to be laid before the creditors' meeting under section 98; and

(*c*) appoint one of their number to preside at that meeting;

and it is the duty of the director so appointed to attend the meeting and preside over it.

(2) The statement as to the affairs of the company shall be verified by affidavit by some or all of the directors and shall show—

(*a*) particulars of the company's assets, debts and liabilities;

(*b*) the names and addresses of the company's creditors;

(*c*) the securities held by them respectively;

(*d*) the dates when the securities were respectively given; and

(*e*) such further or other information as may be prescribed.

(3) If—

(*a*) the directors without reasonable excuse fail to comply with subsection (1) or (2); or

(*b*) any director without reasonable excuse fails to comply with subsection (1), so far as requiring him to attend and preside at the creditors' meeting,

the directors are or (as the case may be) the director is guilty of an offence and liable to a fine.

Appointment of liquidator

100.—(1) The creditors and the company at their respective meetings mentioned in section 98 may nominate a person to be liquidator for the purpose of winding up the company's affairs and distributing its assets.

(2) The liquidator shall be the person nominated by the creditors or, where no person has been so nominated, the person (if any) nominated by the company.

(3) In the case of different persons being nominated, any director, member or creditor of the company may, within seven days after the date on which the nomination was made by the creditors, apply to the court for an order either—

(*a*) directing that the person nominated as liquidator by the company shall be liquidator instead of or jointly with the person nominated by the creditors, or

(*b*) appointing some other person to be liquidator instead of the person nominated by the creditors.

Appointment of liquidation committee

101.—(1) The creditors at the meeting to be held under section 98 or at any subsequent meeting may, if they think fit, appoint a committee ("the liquidation committee") of not more than five persons to exercise the functions conferred on it by or under this Act.

(2) If such a committee is appointed, the company may, either at the meeting at which the resolution for voluntary winding up is passed or at any time subsequently in general meeting, appoint such number of persons as they think fit to act as members of the committee, not exceeding five.

(3) However, the creditors may, if they think fit, resolve that all or any of the persons so appointed by the company ought not to be members of the liquidation committee; and if the creditors so resolve—

(*a*) the persons mentioned in the resolution are not then, unless the court otherwise directs, qualified to act as members of the committee; and

(*b*) on any application to the court under this provision the court may, if it thinks fit, appoint other persons to act as such members in place of the persons mentioned in the resolution.

(4) In Scotland, the liquidation committee has, in addition to the powers and duties conferred and imposed on it by this Act, such of the powers and duties of commissioners on a bankrupt estate as may be conferred and imposed on liquidation committees by the rules.

Creditors' meeting where winding up converted under s.96

102. Where, in the case of a winding up which was, under section 96 in Chapter III, converted to a creditors' voluntary winding up, a creditors' meeting is held in accordance with section 95, any appointment made or committee established by that meeting is deemed to have been made or established by a meeting held in accordance with section 98 in this Chapter.

Cesser of directors' powers

103. On the appointment of a liquidator, all the powers of the directors cease, except so far as the liquidation committee (or, if there is no such committee, the creditors) sanction their continuance.

Vacancy in office of liquidator

104. If a vacancy occurs, by death, resignation or otherwise, in the office of a liquidator (other than a liquidator appointed by, or by the direction of, the court), the creditors may fill the vacancy.

Meetings of company and creditors at each year's end

105.—(1) If the winding up continues for more than one year, the liquidator shall summon a general meeting of the company and a meeting of the creditors at the end of the first year from the commencement of the winding up, and of each succeeding year, or at the first convenient date within three months from the end of the year or such longer period as the Secretary of State may allow.

(2) The liquidator shall lay before each of the meetings an account of his acts and dealings and of the conduct of the winding up during the preceding year.

(3) If the liquidator fails to comply with this section, he is liable to a fine.

(4) Where under section 96 a members' voluntary winding up has become a creditors' voluntary winding up, and the creditors' meeting under section 95 is held three months or less before the end of the first year from the commencement of the winding up, the liquidator is not required by this section to summon a meeting of creditors at the end of that year.

Final meeting prior to dissolution

106.—(1) As soon as the company's affairs are fully wound up, the liquidator shall make up an account of the winding up, showing how it has been conducted and the company's property has been disposed of, and thereupon shall call a general meeting of the company and a meeting of the creditors for the purpose of laying the account before the meetings and giving an explanation of it.

(2) Each such meeting shall be called by advertisement in the *Gazette* specifying the time, place and object of the meeting, and published at least one month before it.

(3) Within one week after the date of the meetings (or, if they are not held on the same date, after the date of the later one) the liquidator shall send to the registrar of companies a copy of the account, and shall make a return to him of the holding of the meetings and of their dates.

(4) If the copy is not sent or the return is not made in accordance with subsection (3), the liquidator is liable to a fine and, for continued contravention, to a daily default fine.

(5) However, if a quorum is not present at either such meeting, the liquidator shall, in lieu of the return required by subsection (3), make a return that the meeting was duly summoned and that no quorum was present; and

upon such return being made the provisions of that subsection as to the making of the return are, in respect of that meeting, deemed complied with.

(6) If the liquidator fails to call a general meeting of the company or a meeting of the creditors as required by this section, he is liable to a fine.

CHAPTER V

PROVISIONS APPLYING TO BOTH KINDS OF VOLUNTARY WINDING UP

Distribution of company's property

107. Subject to the provisions of this Act as to preferential payments, the company's property in a voluntary winding up shall on the winding up be applied in satisfaction of the company's liabilities *pari passu* and, subject to that application, shall (unless the articles otherwise provide) be distributed among the members according to their rights and interests in the company.

Appointment or removal of liquidator by the court

108.—(1) If from any cause whatever there is no liquidator acting, the court may appoint a liquidator.

(2) The court may, on cause shown, remove a liquidator and appoint another.

Notice by liquidator of his appointment

109.—(1) The liquidator shall, within 14 days after his appointment, publish in the *Gazette* and deliver to the registrar of companies for registration a notice of his appointment in the form prescribed by statutory instrument made by the Secretary of State.

(2) If the liquidator fails to comply with this section, he is liable to a fine and, for continued contravention, to a daily default fine.

Acceptance of shares, etc., as consideration for sale of company property

110.—(1) This section applies, in the case of a company proposed to be, or being, wound up voluntarily, where the whole or part of the company's business or property is proposed to be transferred or sold to another company ("the transferee company"), whether or not the latter is a company within the meaning of the Companies Act.

(2) With the requisite sanction, the liquidator of the company being, or proposed to be, wound up ("the transferor company") may receive, in compensation or part compensation for the transfer or sale, shares, policies or other like interests in the transferee company for distribution among the members of the transferor company.

(3) The sanction requisite under subsection (2) is—

    (*a*) in the case of a members' voluntary winding up, that of a special resolution of the company, conferring either a general authority on the liquidator or an authority in respect of any particular arrangement, and

    (*b*) in the case of a creditors' voluntary winding up, that of either the court or the liquidation committee.

(4) Alternatively to subsection (2), the liquidator may (with that sanction) enter into any other arrangement whereby the members of the transferor company may, in lieu of receiving cash, shares, policies or other like interests (or in addition thereto), participate in the profits of, or receive any other benefit from, the transferee company.

(5) A sale or arrangement in pursuance of this section is binding on members of the transferor company.

(6) A special resolution is not invalid for purposes of this section by reason that it is passed before or concurrently with a resolution for voluntary

winding up or for appointing liquidators; but, if an order is made within a year for winding up the company by the court, the special resolution is not valid unless sanctioned by the court.

Dissent from arrangement under s.110

111.—(1) This section applies in the case of a voluntary winding up where, for the purposes of section 110(2) or (4), there has been passed a special resolution of the transferor company providing the sanction requisite for the liquidator under that section.

(2) If a member of the transferor company who did not vote in favour of the special resolution expresses his dissent from it in writing, addressed to the liquidator and left at the company's registered office within seven days after the passing of the resolution, he may require the liquidator either to abstain from carrying the resolution into effect or to purchase his interest at a price to be determined by agreement or by arbitration under this section.

(3) If the liquidator elects to purchase the member's interest, the purchase money must be paid before the company is dissolved and be raised by the liquidator in such manner as may be determined by special resolution.

(4) For purposes of an arbitration under this section, the provisions of the Companies Clauses Consolidation Act 1845 or, in the case of a winding up in Scotland, the Companies Clauses Consolidation (Scotland) Act 1845 with respect to the settlement of disputes by arbitration are incorporated with this Act, and—

(*a*) in the construction of those provisions this Act is deemed the special Act and "the company" means the transferor company, and

(*b*) any appointment by the incorporated provisions directed to be made under the hand of the secretary or any two of the directors may be made in writing by the liquidator (or, if there is more than one liquidator, then any two or more of them).

Reference of questions to court

112.—(1) The liquidator or any contributory or creditor may apply to the court to determine any question arising in the winding up of a company, or to exercise, as respects the enforcing of calls or any other matter, all or any of the powers which the court might exercise if the company were being wound up by the court.

(2) The court, if satisfied that the determination of the question or the required exercise of power will be just and beneficial, may accede wholly or partially to the application on such terms and conditions as it thinks fit, or may make such other order on the application as it thinks just.

(3) A copy of an order made by virtue of this section staying the proceedings in the winding up shall forthwith be forwarded by the company, or otherwise as may be prescribed, to the registrar of companies, who shall enter it in his records relating to the company.

Court's power to control proceedings (Scotland)

113. If the court, on the application of the liquidator in the winding up of a company registered in Scotland, so directs, no action or proceeding shall be proceeded with or commenced against the company except by leave of the court and subject to such terms as the court may impose.

No liquidator appointed or nominated by company

114.—(1) This section applies where, in the case of a voluntary winding up, no liquidator has been appointed or nominated by the company.

(2) The powers of the directors shall not be exercised, except with the sanction of the court or (in the case of a creditors' voluntary winding up) so far as may be necessary to secure compliance with sections 98 (creditors'

meeting) and 99 (statement of affairs), during the period before the appointment or nomination of a liquidator of the company.

(3) Subsection (2) does not apply in relation to the powers of the directors—

    (*a*) to dispose of perishable goods and other goods the value of which is likely to diminish if they are not immediately disposed of, and

    (*b*) to do all such other things as may be necessary for the protection of the company's assets.

(4) If the directors of the company without reasonable excuse fail to comply with this section, they are liable to a fine.

Expenses of voluntary winding up
115. All expenses properly incurred in the winding up, including the remuneration of the liquidator, are payable out of the company's assets in priority to all other claims.

Saving for certain rights
116. The voluntary winding up of a company does not bar the right of any creditor or contributory to have it wound up by the court; but in the case of an application by a contributory the court must be satisfied that the rights of the contributories will be prejudiced by a voluntary winding up.

CHAPTER VI

WINDING UP BY THE COURT

Jurisdiction (England and Wales)

High Court and county court jurisdiction
117.—(1) The High Court has jurisdiction to wind up any company registered in England and Wales.

(2) Where the amount of a company's share capital paid up or credited as paid up does not exceed £120,000, then (subject to this section) the county court of the district in which the company's registered office is situated has concurrent jurisdiction with the High Court to wind up the company.

(3) The money sum for the time being specified in subsection (2) is subject to increase or reduction by order under section 416 in Part XV.

(4) The Lord Chancellor may by order in a statutory instrument exclude a county court from having winding-up jurisdiction, and for the purposes of that jurisdiction may attach its district, or any part thereof, to any other county court, and may by statutory instrument revoke or vary any such order.

In exercising the powers of this section, the Lord Chancellor shall provide that a county court is not to have winding-up jurisdiction unless it has for the time being jurisdiction for the purposes of Parts VIII to XI of this Act (individual insolvency).

(5) Every court in England and Wales having winding-up jurisdiction has for the purposes of that jurisdiction all the powers of the High Court; and every prescribed officer of the court shall perform any duties which an officer of the High Court may discharge by order of a judge of that court or otherwise in relation to winding up.

(6) For the purposes of this section, a company's "registered office" is the place which has longest been its registered office during the six months immediately preceding the presentation of the petition for winding up.

Proceedings taken in wrong court

118.—(1) Nothing in section 117 invalidates a proceeding by reason of its being taken in the wrong court.

(2) The winding up of a company by the court in England and Wales, or any proceedings in the winding up, may be retained in the court in which the proceedings were commenced, although it may not be the court in which they ought to have been commenced.

Proceedings in county court; case stated for High Court

119.—(1) If any question arises in any winding-up proceedings in a county court which all the parties to the proceedings, or which one of them and the judge of the court, desire to have determined in the first instance in the High Court, the judge shall state the facts in the form of a special case for the opinion of the High Court.

(2) Thereupon the special case and the proceedings (or such of them as may be required) shall be transmitted to the High Court for the purposes of the determination.

Jurisdiction (Scotland)

Court of Session and sheriff court jurisdiction

120.—(1) The Court of Session has jurisdiction to wind up any company registered in Scotland.

[1] (2) When the Court of Session is in vacation, the jurisdiction conferred on that court by this section may (subject to the provisions of this Part) be exercised by the judge acting as vacation judge.

(3) Where the amount of a company's share capital paid up or credited as paid up does not exceed £120,000, the sheriff court of the sheriffdom in which the company's registered office is situated has concurrent jurisdiction with the Court of Session to wind up the company; but—

(*a*) the Court of Session may, if it thinks expedient having regard to the amount of the company's assets to do so—
  (i) remit to a sheriff court any petition presented to the Court of Session for winding up such a company, or
  (ii) require such a petition presented to a sheriff court to be remitted to the Court of Session; and

(*b*) the Court of Session may require any such petition as above-mentioned presented to one sheriff court to be remitted to another sheriff court; and

(*c*) in a winding up in the sheriff court the sheriff may submit a stated case for the opinion of the Court of Session on any question of law arising in that winding up.

(4) For purposes of this section, the expression "registered office" means the place which has longest been the company's registered office during the six months immediately preceding the presentation of the petition for winding up.

(5) The money sum for the time being specified in subsection (3) is subject to increase or reduction by order under section 416 in Part XV.

NOTE

[1] As amended by the Court of Session Act 1988, Sched. 2.

Power to remit winding up to Lord Ordinary

121.—(1) The Court of Session may, by Act of Sederunt, make provision for the taking of proceedings in a winding up before one of the Lords Ordinary; and, where provision is so made, the Lord Ordinary has, for the purposes of the winding up, all the powers and jurisdiction of the court.

(2) However, the Lord Ordinary may report to the Inner House any matter which may arise in the course of a winding up.

Grounds and effect of winding-up petition

Circumstances in which company may be wound up by the court

122.—(1) A company may be wound up by the court if—

(a) the company has by special resolution resolved that the company be wound up by the court,

(b) being a public company which was registered as such on its original incorporation, the company has not been issued with a certificate under section 117 of the Companies Act (public company share capital requirements) and more than a year has expired since it was so registered,

(c) it is an old public company, within the meaning of the Consequential Provisions Act,

(d) the company does not commence its business within a year from its incorporation or suspends its business for a whole year,

(e) the number of members is reduced below two,

(f) the company is unable to pay its debts,

(g) the court is of the opinion that it is just and equitable that the company should be wound up.

(2) In Scotland, a company which the Court of Session has jurisdiction to wind up may be wound up by the court if there is subsisting a floating charge over property comprised in the company's property and undertaking, and the court is satisfied that the security of the creditor entitled to the benefit of the floating charge is in jeopardy.

For this purpose a creditor's security is deemed to be in jeopardy if the court is satisfied that events have occurred or are about to occur which render it unreasonable in the creditor's interests that the company should retain power to dispose of the property which is subject to the floating charge.

Definition of inability to pay debts

123.—(1) A company is deemed unable to pay its debts—

(a) if a creditor (by assignment or otherwise) to whom the company is indebted in a sum exceeding £750 then due has served on the company, by leaving 'it at the company's registered office, a written demand (in the prescribed form) requiring the company to pay the sum so due and the company has for three weeks thereafter neglected to pay the sum or to secure or compound for it to the reasonable satisfaction of the creditor, or

(b) if, in England and Wales, execution or other process issued on a judgment, decree or order of any court in favour of a creditor of the company is returned unsatisfied in whole or in part, or

(c) if, in Scotland, the *induciae* of a charge for payment on an extract decree, or an extract registered bond, or an extract registered protest, have expired without payment being made, or

(d) if, in Northern Ireland, a certificate of unenforceability has been granted in respect of a judgment against the company, or

(e) if it is proved to the satisfaction of the court that the company is unable to pay its debts as they fall due.

(2) A company is also deemed unable to pay its debts if it is proved to the satisfaction of the court that the value of the company's assets is less than the amount of its liabilities, taking into account its contingent and prospective liabilities.

(3) The money sum for the time being specified in subsection (1)(a) is subject to increase or reduction by order under section 416 in Part XV.

Application for winding up

124.—(1) Subject to the provisions of this section, an application to the court for the winding up of a company shall be by petition presented either by the company, or the directors, or by any creditor or creditors (including any contingent or prospective creditor or creditors), contributory or contributories, or by all or any of those parties, together or separately.

(2) Except as mentioned below, a contributory is not entitled to present a winding-up petition unless either—

(*a*) the number of members is reduced below two, or

(*b*) the shares in respect of which he is a contributory, or some of them, either were originally allotted to him, or have been held by him, and registered in his name, for at least six months during the 18 months before the commencement of the winding up, or have devolved on him through the death of a former holder.

(3) A person who is liable under section 76 to contribute to a company's assets in the event of its being wound up may petition on either of the grounds set out in section 122(1)(*f*) and (*g*), and subsection (2) above does not then apply; but unless the person is a contributory otherwise than under section 76, he may not in his character as contributory petition on any other ground.

This subsection is deemed included in Chapter VII of Part V of the Companies Act (redeemable shares; purchase by a company of its own shares) for the purposes of the Secretary of State's power to make regulations under section 179 of that Act.

[1] (4) A winding-up petition may be presented by the Secretary of State—

(*a*) if the ground of the petition is that in section 122(1)(*b*) or (*c*), or

(*b*) in a case falling within section 124A below.

(5) Where a company is being wound up voluntarily in England and Wales, a winding-up petition may be presented by the official receiver attached to the court as well as by any other person authorised in that behalf under the other provisions of this section; but the court shall not make a winding-up order on the petition unless it is satisfied that the voluntary winding up cannot be continued with due regard to the interests of the creditors or contributories.

NOTE

[1] As amended by the Companies Act 1989, s.60(2).

Petition for winding up on grounds of public interest

[1] **124A.**—(1) Where it appears to the Secretary of State from—

(*a*) any report made or information obtained under Part XIV of the Companies Act 1985 (company investigations, etc.),

(*b*) any report made under section 94 or 177 of the Financial Services Act 1986 or any information obtained under section 105 of that Act,

(*c*) any information obtained under section 2 of the Criminal Justice Act 1987 or section 52 of the Criminal Justice (Scotland) Act 1987 (fraud investigations), or

(*d*) any information obtained under section 83 of the Companies Act 1989 (powers exercisable for purpose of assisting overseas regulatory authorities),

that it is expedient in the public interest that a company should be wound up, he may present a petition for it to be wound up if the court thinks it just and equitable for it to be so.

(2) This section does not apply if the company is already being wound up by the court.

NOTE

[1] Inserted by the Companies Act 1989, s. 60(3).

Powers of court on hearing of petition

125.—(1) On hearing a winding-up petition the court may dismiss it, or adjourn the hearing conditionally or unconditionally, or make an interim order, or any other order that it thinks fit; but the court shall not refuse to make a winding-up order on the ground only that the company's assets have been mortgaged to an amount equal to or in excess of those assets, or that the company has no assets.

(2) If the petition is presented by members of the company as contributories on the ground that it is just and equitable that the company should be wound up, the court, if it is of opinion—

(a) that the petitioners are entitled to relief either by winding up the company or by some other means, and

(b) that in the absence of any other remedy it would be just and equitable that the company should be wound up,

shall make a winding-up order; but this does not apply if the court is also of the opinion both that some other remedy is available to the petitioners and that they are acting unreasonably in seeking to have the company wound up instead of pursuing that other remedy.

Power to stay or restrain proceedings against company

126.—(1) At any time after the presentation of a winding-up petition, and before a winding-up order has been made, the company, or any creditor or contributory, may—

(a) where any action or proceeding against the company is pending in the High Court or Court of Appeal in England and Wales or Northern Ireland, apply to the court in which the action or proceeding is pending for a stay of proceedings therein, and

(b) where any other action or proceeding is pending against the company, apply to the court having jurisdiction to wind up the company to restrain further proceedings in the action or proceeding;

and the court to which application is so made may (as the case may be) stay, sist or restrain the proceedings accordingly on such terms as it thinks fit.

(2) In the case of a company registered under section 680 of the Companies Act (pre-1862 companies; companies formed under legislation other than the Companies Acts) or the previous corresponding legislation, where the application to stay, sist or restrain is by a creditor, this section extends to actions and proceedings against any contributory of the company.

Avoidance of property dispositions, etc.

127. In a winding up by the court, any disposition of the company's property, and any transfer of shares, or alteration in the status of the company's members, made after the commencement of the winding up is, unless the court otherwise orders, void.

Avoidance of attachments, etc.

128.—(1) Where a company registered in England and Wales is being wound up by the court, any attachment, sequestration, distress or execution put in force against the estate or effects of the company after the commencement of the winding up is void.

(2) This section, so far as relates to any estate or effects of the company situated in England and Wales, applies in the case of a company registered in Scotland as it applies in the case of a company registered in England and Wales.

Commencement of winding up

Commencement of winding up by the court

129.—(1) If, before the presentation of a petition for the winding up of a company by the court, a resolution has been passed by the company for voluntary winding up, the winding up of the company is deemed to have commenced at the time of the passing of the resolution; and unless the court, on proof of fraud or mistake, directs otherwise, all proceedings taken in the voluntary winding up are deemed to have been validly taken.

(2) In any other case, the winding up of a company by the court is deemed to commence at the time of the presentation of the petition for winding up.

Consequences of winding-up order

130.—(1) On the making of a winding-up order, a copy of the order must forthwith be forwarded by the company (or otherwise as may be prescribed) to the registrar of companies, who shall enter it in his records relating to the company.

(2) When a winding-up order has been made or a provisional liquidator has been appointed, no action or proceeding shall be proceeded with or commenced against the company or its property, except by leave of the court and subject to such terms as the court may impose.

(3) When an order has been made for winding up a company registered under section 680 of the Companies Act, no action or proceeding shall be commenced or proceeded with against the company or its property or any contributory of the company, in respect of any debt of the company, except by leave of the court, and subject to such terms as the court may impose.

(4) An order for winding up a company operates in favour of all the creditors and of all contributories of the company as if made on the joint petition of a creditor and of a contributory.

[THE NEXT PAGE IS I581]

Investigation procedures

Company's statement of affairs

131.—(1) Where the court has made a winding-up order or appointed a provisional liquidator, the official receiver may require some or all of the persons mentioned in subsection (3) below to make out and submit to him a statement in the prescribed form as to the affairs of the company.

(2) The statement shall be verified by affidavit by the persons required to submit it and shall show—

(*a*) particulars of the company's assets, debts and liabilities;

(*b*) the names and addresses of the company's creditors;

(*c*) the securities held by them respectively;

(*d*) the dates when the securities were respectively given; and

(*e*) such further or other information as may be prescribed or as the official receiver may require.

(3) The persons referred to in subsection (1) are—

(*a*) those who are or have been officers of the company;

(*b*) those who have taken part in the formation of the company at any time within one year before the relevant date;

(*c*) those who are in the company's employment, or have been in its employment within that year, and are in the official receiver's opinion capable of giving the information required;

(*d*) those who are or have been within that year officers of, or in the employment of, a company which is, or within that year was, an officer of the company.

(4) Where any persons are required under this section to submit a statement of affairs to the official receiver, they shall do so (subject to the next subsection) before the end of the period of 21 days beginning with the day after that on which the prescribed notice of the requirement is given to them by the official receiver.

(5) The official receiver, if he thinks fit, may—

(*a*) at any time release a person from an obligation imposed on him under subsection (1) or (2) above; or

(*b*) either when giving the notice mentioned in subsection (4) or subsequently, extend the period so mentioned;

and where the official receiver has refused to exercise a power conferred by this subsection, the court, if it thinks fit, may exercise it.

(6) In this section—

"employment" includes employment under a contract for services; and

"the relevant date" means—

(*a*) in a case where a provisional liquidator is appointed, the date of his appointment; and

(*b*) in a case where no such appointment is made, the date of the winding-up order.

(7) If a person without reasonable excuse fails to comply with any obligation imposed under this section, he is liable to a fine and, for continued contravention, to a daily default fine.

(8) In the application of this section to Scotland references to the official receiver are to the liquidator or, in a case where a provisional liquidator is appointed, the provisional liquidator.

Investigation by official receiver

132.—(1) Where a winding-up order is made by the court in England and Wales, it is the duty of the official receiver to investigate—

(*a*) if the company has failed, the causes of the failure; and

(*b*) generally, the promotion, formation, business, dealings and affairs of the company,

and to make such report (if any) to the court as he thinks fit.

(2) The report is, in any proceedings, *prima facie* evidence of the facts stated in it.

Public examination of officers

133.—(1) Where a company is being wound up by the court, the official receiver or, in Scotland, the liquidator may at any time before the dissolution of the company apply to the court for the public examination of any person who—

(a) is or has been an officer of the company; or

(b) has acted as liquidator or administrator of the company or as receiver or manager or, in Scotland, receiver of its property; or

(c) not being a person falling within paragraph (a) or (b), is or has been concerned, or has taken part, in the promotion, formation or management of the company.

(2) Unless the court otherwise orders, the official receiver or, in Scotland, the liquidator shall make an application under subsection (1) if he is requested in accordance with the rules to do so by—

(a) one-half, in value, of the company's creditors; or

(b) three-quarters, in value, of the company's contributories.

(3) On an application under subsection (1), the court shall direct that a public examination of the person to whom the application relates shall be held on a day appointed by the court; and that person shall attend on that day and be publicly examined as to the promotion, formation or management of the company or as to the conduct of its business and affairs, or his conduct or dealings in relation to the company.

(4) The following may take part in the public examination of a person under this section and may question that person concerning the matters mentioned in subsection (3), namely—

(a) the official receiver;

(b) the liquidator of the company;

(c) any person who has been appointed as special manager of the company's property or business;

(d) any creditor of the company who has tendered a proof or, in Scotland, submitted a claim in the winding up;

(e) any contributory of the company.

Enforcement of s.133

134.—(1) If a person without reasonable excuse fails at any time to attend his public examination under section 133, he is guilty of a contempt of court and liable to be punished accordingly.

(2) In a case where a person without reasonable excuse fails at any time to attend his examination under section 133 or there are reasonable grounds for believing that a person has absconded, or is about to abscond, with a view to avoiding or delaying his examination under that section, the court may cause a warrant to be issued to a constable or prescribed officer of the court—

(a) for the arrest of that person; and

(b) for the seizure of any books, papers, records, money or goods in that person's possession.

(3) In such a case the court may authorise the person arrested under the warrant to be kept in custody, and anything seized under such a warrant to be held, in accordance with the rules, until such time as the court may order.

Appointment of liquidator

Appointment and powers of provisional liquidator

135.—(1) Subject to the provisions of this section, the court may, at any time after the presentation of a winding-up petition, appoint a liquidator provisionally.

(2) In England and Wales, the appointment of a provisional liquidator may be made at any time before the making of a winding-up order; and either the official receiver or any other fit person may be appointed.

(3) In Scotland, such an appointment may be made at any time before the first appointment of liquidators.

(4) The provisional liquidator shall carry out such functions as the court may confer on him.

(5) When a liquidator is provisionally appointed by the court, his powers may be limited by the order appointing him.

Functions of official receiver in relation to office of liquidator

136.—(1) The following provisions of this section have effect, subject to section 140 below, on a winding-up order being made by the court in England and Wales.

(2) The official receiver, by virtue of his office, becomes the liquidator of the company and continues in office until another person becomes liquidator under the provisions of this Part.

(3) The official receiver is, by virtue of his office, the liquidator during any vacancy.

(4) At any time when he is the liquidator of the company, the official receiver may summon separate meetings of the company's creditors and contributories for the purpose of choosing a person to be liquidator of the company in place of the official receiver.

(5) It is the duty of the official receiver—

(a) as soon as practicable in the period of 12 weeks beginning with the day on which the winding-up order was made, to decide whether to exercise his power under subsection (4) to summon meetings, and

(b) if in pursuance of paragraph (a) he decides not to exercise that power, to give notice of his decision, before the end of that period, to the court and to the company's creditors and contributories, and

(c) (whether or not he has decided to exercise that power) to exercise his power to summon meetings under subsection (4) if he is at any time requested, in accordance with the rules, to do so by one-quarter, in value, of the company's creditors;

and accordingly, where the duty imposed by paragraph (c) arises before the official receiver has performed a duty imposed by paragraph (a) or (b), he is not required to perform the latter duty.

(6) A notice given under subsection (5)(b) to the company's creditors shall contain an explanation of the creditors' power under subsection (5)(c) to require the official receiver to summon meetings of the company's creditors and contributories.

Appointment by Secretary of State

137.—(1) In a winding up by the court in England and Wales the official receiver may, at any time when he is the liquidator of the company, apply to the Secretary of State for the appointment of a person as liquidator in his place.

(2) If meetings are held in pursuance of a decision under section 136(5)(a), but no person is chosen to be liquidator as a result of those meetings, it is the duty of the official receiver to decide whether to refer the need for an appointment to the Secretary of State.

(3) On an application under subsection (1), or a reference made in pursuance of a decision under subsection (2), the Secretary of State shall either make an appointment or decline to make one.

(4) Where a liquidator has been appointed by the Secretary of State under subsection (3), the liquidator shall give notice of his appointment to the company's creditors or, if the court so allows, shall advertise his appointment in accordance with the directions of the court.

(5) In that notice or advertisement the liquidator shall—

(*a*) state whether he proposes to summon a general meeting of the company's creditors under section 141 below for the purpose of determining (together with any meeting of contributories) whether a liquidation committee should be established under that section, and

(*b*) if he does not propose to summon such a meeting, set out the power of the company's creditors under that section to require him to summon one.

Appointment of liquidator in Scotland
138.—(1) Where a winding-up order is made by the court in Scotland, a liquidator shall be appointed by the court at the time when the order is made.

(2) The liquidator so appointed (here referred to as "the interim liquidator") continues in office until another person becomes liquidator in his place under this section or the next.

(3) The interim liquidator shall (subject to the next subsection) as soon as practicable in the period of 28 days beginning with the day on which the winding-up order was made or such longer period as the court may allow, summon separate meetings of the company's creditors and contributories for the purpose of choosing a person (who may be the person who is the interim liquidator) to be liquidator of the company in place of the interim liquidator.

(4) If it appears to the interim liquidator, in any case where a company is being wound up on grounds including its inability to pay its debts, that it would be inappropriate to summon under subsection (3) a meeting of the company's contributories, he may summon only a meeting of the company's creditors for the purpose mentioned in that subsection.

(5) If one or more meetings are held in pursuance of this section but no person is appointed or nominated by the meeting or meetings, the interim liquidator shall make a report to the court which shall appoint either the interim liquidator or some other person to be liquidator of the company.

(6) A person who becomes liquidator of the company in place of the interim liquidator shall, unless he is appointed by the court, forthwith notify the court of that fact.

Choice of liquidator at meetings of creditors and contributories
139.—(1) This section applies where a company is being wound up by the court and separate meetings of the company's creditors and contributories are summoned for the purpose of choosing a person to be liquidator of the company.

(2) The creditors and the contributories at their respective meetings may nominate a person to be liquidator.

(3) The liquidator shall be the person nominated by the creditors or, where no person has been so nominated, the person (if any) nominated by the contributories.

(4) In the case of different persons being nominated, any contributory or creditor may, within seven days after the date on which the nomination was made by the creditors, apply to the court for an order either—

(*a*) appointing the person nominated as liquidator by the contributories to be a liquidator instead of, or jointly with, the person nominated by the creditors; or

(*b*) appointing some other person to be liquidator instead of the person nominated by the creditors.

Appointment by the court following administration or voluntary arrangement
140.—(1) Where a winding-up order is made immediately upon the discharge of an administration order, the court may appoint as liquidator of the company the person who has ceased on the discharge of the administration order to be the administrator of the company.

(2) Where a winding-up order is made at a time when there is a supervisor of a voluntary arrangement approved in relation to the company under Part I, the court may appoint as liquidator of the company the person who is the supervisor at the time when the winding-up order is made.

(3) Where the court makes an appointment under this section, the official receiver does not become the liquidator as otherwise provided by section 136(2), and he has no duty under section 136(5)(*a*) or (*b*) in respect of the summoning of creditors' or contributories' meetings.

Liquidation committees

Liquidation committee (England and Wales)
141.—(1) Where a winding-up order has been made by the court in England and Wales and separate meetings of creditors and contributories have been summoned for the purpose of choosing a person to be liquidator, those meetings may establish a committee ("the liquidation committee") to exercise the functions conferred on it by or under this Act.

(2) The liquidator (not being the official receiver) may at any time, if he thinks fit, summon separate general meetings of the company's creditors and contributories for the purpose of determining whether such a committee should be established and, if it is so determined, of establishing it.

The liquidator (not being the official receiver) shall summon such a meeting if he is requested, in accordance with the rules, to do so by one-tenth, in value, of the company's creditors.

(3) Where meetings are summoned under this section, or for the purpose of choosing a person to be liquidator, and either the meeting of creditors or the meeting of contributories decides that a liquidation committee should be established, but the other meeting does not so decide or decides that a committee should not be established, the committee shall be established in accordance with the rules, unless the court otherwise orders.

(4) The liquidation committee is not to be able or required to carry out its functions at any time when the official receiver is liquidator; but at any such time its functions are vested in the Secretary of State except to the extent that the rules otherwise provide.

(5) Where there is for the time being no liquidation committee, and the liquidator is a person other than the official receiver, the functions of such a committee are vested in the Secretary of State except to the extent that the rules otherwise provide.

Liquidation committee (Scotland)
142.—(1) Where a winding-up order has been made by the court in Scotland and separate meetings of creditors and contributories have been summoned for the purpose of choosing a person to be liquidator or, under section 138(4), only a meeting of creditors has been summoned for that purpose, those meetings or (as the case may be) that meeting may establish a committee ("the liquidation committee") to exercise the functions conferred on it by or under this Act.

(2) The liquidator may at any time, if he thinks fit, summon separate general meetings of the company's creditors and contributories for the purpose of determining whether such a committee should be established and, if it is so determined, of establishing it.

(3) The liquidator, if appointed by the court otherwise than under section 139(4)(*a*), is required to summon meetings under subsection (2) if he is requested, in accordance with the rules, to do so by one-tenth, in value, of the company's creditors.

(4) Where meetings are summoned under this section, or for the purpose of choosing a person to be liquidator, and either the meeting of creditors or the meeting of contributories decides that a liquidation committee should be established, but the other meeting does not so decide or decides that a

committee should not be established, the committee shall be established in accordance with the rules, unless the court otherwise orders.

(5) Where in the case of any winding up there is for the time being no liquidation committee, the functions of such a committee are vested in the court except to the extent that the rules otherwise provide.

(6) In addition to the powers and duties conferred and imposed on it by this Act, a liquidation committee has such of the powers and duties of commissioners in a sequestration as may be conferred and imposed on such committees by the rules.

The liquidator's functions

General functions in winding up by the court

143.—(1) The functions of the liquidator of a company which is being wound up by the court are to secure that the assets of the company are got in, realised and distributed to the company's creditors and, if there is a surplus, to the persons entitled to it.

(2) It is the duty of the liquidator of a company which is being wound up by the court in England and Wales, if he is not the official receiver—

    (*a*) to furnish the official receiver with such information,

    (*b*) to produce to the official receiver, and permit inspection by the official receiver of, such books, papers and other records, and

    (*c*) to give the official receiver such other assistance,

as the official receiver may reasonably require for the purposes of carrying out his functions in relation to the winding up.

Custody of company's property

144.—(1) When a winding-up order has been made, or where a provisional liquidator has been appointed, the liquidator or the provisional liquidator (as the case may be) shall take into his custody or under his control all the property and things in action to which the company is or appears to be entitled.

(2) In a winding up by the court in Scotland, if and so long as there is no liquidator, all the property of the company is deemed to be in the custody of the court.

Vesting of company property in liquidator

145.—(1) When a company is being wound up by the court, the court may on the application of the liquidator by order direct that all or any part of the property of whatsoever description belonging to the company or held by trustees on its behalf shall vest in the liquidator by his official name; and thereupon the property to which the order relates vests accordingly.

(2) The liquidator may, after giving such indemnity (if any) as the court may direct, bring or defend in his official name any action or other legal proceeding which relates to that property or which it is necessary to bring or defend for the purpose of effectually winding up the company and recovering its property.

Duty to summon final meeting

146.—(1) Subject to the next subsection, if it appears to the liquidator of a company which is being wound up by the court that the winding up of the company is for practical purposes complete and the liquidator is not the official receiver, the liquidator shall summon a final general meeting of the company's creditors which—

    (*a*) shall receive the liquidator's report of the winding up, and

    (*b*) shall determine whether the liquidator should have his release under section 174 in Chapter VII of this Part.

(2) The liquidator may, if he thinks fit, give the notice summoning the final general meeting at the same time as giving notice of any final distribution of the company's property but, if summoned for an earlier date, that meeting shall be adjourned (and, if necessary, further adjourned) until a date on which the liquidator is able to report to the meeting that the winding up of the company is for practical purposes complete.

(3) In the carrying out of his functions in the winding up it is the duty of the liquidator to retain sufficient sums from the company's property to cover the expenses of summoning and holding the meeting required by this section.

General powers of court

Power to stay or sist winding up

147.—(1) The court may at any time after an order for winding up, on the application either of the liquidator or the official receiver or any creditor or contributory, and on proof to the satisfaction of the court that all proceedings in the winding up ought to be stayed or sisted, make an order staying or sisting the proceedings, either altogether or for a limited time, on such terms and conditions as the court thinks fit.

(2) The court may, before making an order, require the official receiver to furnish to it a report with respect to any facts or matters which are in his opinion relevant to the application.

(3) A copy of every order made under this section shall forthwith be forwarded by the company, or otherwise as may be prescribed, to the registrar of companies, who shall enter it in his records relating to the company.

Settlement of list of contributories and application of assets

148.—(1) As soon as may be after making a winding-up order, the court shall settle a list of contributories, with power to rectify the register of members in all cases where rectification is required in pursuance of the Companies Act or this Act, and shall cause the company's assets to be collected, and applied in discharge of its liabilities.

(2) If it appears to the court that it will not be necessary to make calls on or adjust the rights of contributories, the court may dispense with the settlement of a list of contributories.

(3) In settling the list, the court shall distinguish between persons who are contributories in their own right and persons who are contributories as being representatives of or liable for the debts of others.

Debts due from contributory to company

149.—(1) The court may, at any time after making a winding-up order, make an order on any contributory for the time being on the list of contributories to pay, in manner directed by the order, any money due from him (or from the estate of the person who he represents) to the company, exclusive of any money payable by him or the estate by virtue of any call in pursuance of the Companies Act or this Act.

(2) The court in making such an order may—

    (*a*) in the case of an unlimited company, allow to the contributory by way of set-off any money due to him or the estate which he represents from the company on any independent dealing or contract with the company, but not any money due to him as a member of the company in respect of any dividend or profit, and

    (*b*) in the case of a limited company, make to any director or manager whose liability is unlimited or to his estate the like allowance.

(3) In the case of any company, whether limited or unlimited, when all the creditors are paid in full (together with interest at the official rate), any money due on any account whatever to a contributory from the company may be allowed to him by way of set-off against any subsequent call.

Power to make calls
150.—(1) The court may, at any time after making a winding-up order, and either before or after it has ascertained the sufficiency of the company's assets, make calls on all or any of the contributories for the time being settled on the list of the contributories to the extent of their liability, for payment of any money which the court considers necessary to satisfy the company's debts and liabilities, and the expenses of winding up, and for the adjustment of the rights of the contributories among themselves, and make an order for payment of any calls so made.

(2) In making a call the court may take into consideration the probability that some of the contributories may partly or wholly fail to pay it.

Payment into bank of money due to company
151.—(1) The court may order any contributory, purchaser or other person from whom money is due to the company to pay the amount due into the Bank of England (or any branch of it) to the account of the liquidator instead of to the liquidator, and such an order may be enforced in the same manner as if it had directed payment to the liquidator.

(2) All money and securities paid or delivered into the Bank of England (or branch) in the event of a winding up by the court are subject in all respects to the orders of the court.

Order on contributory to be conclusive evidence
152.—(1) An order made by the court on a contributory is conclusive evidence that the money (if any) thereby appearing to be due or ordered to be paid is due, but subject to any right of appeal.

(2) All other pertinent matters stated in the order are to be taken as truly stated as against all persons and in all proceedings except proceedings in Scotland against the heritable estate of a deceased contributory; and in that case the order is only *prima facie* evidence for the purpose of charging his heritable estate, unless his heirs or legatees of heritage were on the list of contributories at the time of the order being made.

Power to exclude creditors not proving in time
153. The court may fix a time or times within which creditors are to prove their debts or claims or to be excluded from the benefit of any distribution made before those debts are proved.

Adjustment of rights of contributories
154. The court shall adjust the rights of the contributories among themselves and distribute any surplus among the persons entitled to it.

Inspection of books by creditors, etc.
155.—(1) The court may, at any time after making a winding-up order, make such order for inspection of the company's books and papers by creditors and contributories as the court thinks just; and any books and papers in the company's possession may be inspected by creditors and contributories accordingly, but not further or otherwise.

(2) Nothing in this section excludes or restricts any statutory rights of a government department or person acting under the authority of a government department.

Payment of expenses of winding up
156. The court may, in the event of the assets being insufficient to satisfy the liabilities, make an order as to the payment out of the assets of the expenses incurred in the winding up in such order of priority as the court thinks just.

Attendance at company meetings (Scotland)

157. In the winding up by the court of a company registered in Scotland, the court has power to require the attendance of any officer of the company at any meeting of creditors or of contributories, or of a liquidation committee, for the purpose of giving information as to the trade, dealings, affairs or property of the company.

Power to arrest absconding contributory

158. The court, at any time either before or after making a winding-up order, on proof of probable cause for believing that a contributory is about to quit the United Kingdom or otherwise to abscond or to remove or conceal any of his property for the purpose of evading payment of calls, may cause the contributory to be arrested and his books and papers and moveable personal property to be seized and him and them to be kept safely until such time as the court may order.

Powers of court to be cumulative

159. Powers conferred by this Act and the Companies Act on the court are in addition to, and not in restriction of, any existing powers of instituting proceedings against a contributory or debtor of the company, or the estate of any contributory or debtor, for the recovery of any call or other sums.

Delegation of powers to liquidator (England and Wales)

160.—(1) Provision may be made by rules for enabling or requiring all or any of the powers and duties conferred and imposed on the court in England and Wales by the Companies Act and this Act in respect of the following matters—

(*a*) the holding and conducting of meetings to ascertain the wishes of creditors and contributories,

(*b*) the settling of lists of contributories and the rectifying of the register of members where required, and the collection and application of the assets,

(*c*) the payment, delivery, conveyance, surrender or transfer of money, property, books or papers to the liquidator,

(*d*) the making of calls,

(*e*) the fixing of a time within which debts and claims must be proved,

to be exercised or performed by the liquidator as an officer of the court, and subject to the court's control.

(2) But the liquidator shall not, without the special leave of the court, rectify the register of members, and shall not make any call without either that special leave or the sanction of the liquidation committee.

Enforcement or, and appeal from, orders

Orders for calls on contributories (Scotland)

161.—(1) In Scotland, where an order, interlocutor or decree has been made for winding up a company by the court, it is competent to the court, on production by the liquidators of a list certified by them of the names of the contributories liable in payment of any calls, and of the amount due by each contributory, and of the date when that amount became due, to pronounce forthwith a decree against those contributories for payment of the sums so certified to be due, with interest from that date until payment (at 5 per cent. per annum) in the same way and to the same effect as if they had severally consented to registration for execution, on a charge of six days, of a legal obligation to pay those calls and interest.

(2) The decree may be extracted immediately, and no suspension of it is competent, except on caution or consignation, unless with special leave of the court.

Appeals from orders in Scotland

162.—(1) Subject to the provisions of this section and to rules of court, an appeal from any order or decision made or given in the winding up of a company by the court in Scotland under this Act lies in the same manner and subject to the same conditions as an appeal from an order or decision of the court in cases within its ordinary jurisdiction.

[1] (2) In regard to orders or judgments pronounced by the judge acting as vacation judge—

(a) none of the orders specified in Part I of Schedule 3 to this Act are subject to review, reduction, suspension or stay of execution, and

(b) every other order or judgment (except as mentioned below) may be submitted to review by the Inner House by reclaiming motion enrolled within 14 days from the date of the order or judgment.

(3) However, an order being one of those specified in Part II of that Schedule shall, from the date of the order and notwithstanding that it has been submitted to review as above, be carried out and receive effect until the Inner House have disposed of the matter.

(4) In regard to orders or judgments pronounced in Scotland by a Lord Ordinary before whom proceedings in a winding up are being taken, any such order or judgment may be submitted to review by the Inner House by reclaiming motion enrolled within 14 days from its date; but should it not be so submitted to review during session, the provisions of this section in regard to orders or judgments pronounced by the judge acting as vacation judge apply.

(5) Nothing in this section affects provisions of the Companies Act or this Act in reference to decrees in Scotland for payment of calls in the winding up of companies, whether voluntary or by the court.

NOTE

[1] As amended by the Court of Session Act 1988, Sched. 2.

CHAPTER VII

LIQUIDATORS

Preliminary

Style and title of liquidators

163. The liquidator of a company shall be described—

(a) where a person other than the official receiver is liquidator, by the style of "the liquidator" of the particular company, or

(b) where the official receiver is liquidator, by the style of "the official receiver and liquidator" of the particular company;

and in neither case shall he be described by an individual name.

Corrupt inducement affecting appointment

164. A person who gives, or agrees or offers to give, to any member or creditor of a company any valuable consideration with a view to securing his own appointment or nomination, or to securing or preventing the appointment or nomination of some person other than himself, as the company's liquidator is liable to a fine.

Liquidator's powers and duties

Voluntary winding up

165.—(1) This section has effect where a company is being wound up voluntarily, but subject to section 166 below in the case of a creditors' voluntary winding up.

(2) The liquidator may—

(*a*) in the case of a members' voluntary winding up, with the sanction of an extraordinary resolution of the company, and

(*b*) in the case of a creditors' voluntary winding up, with the sanction of the court or the liquidation committee (or, if there is no such committee, a meeting of the company's creditors),

exercise any of the powers specified in Part I of Schedule 4 to this Act (payment of debts, compromise of claims, etc.).

(3) The liquidator may, without sanction, exercise either of the powers specified in Part II of that Schedule (institution and defence of proceedings; carrying on the business of the company) and any of the general powers specified in Part III of that Schedule.

(4) The liquidator may—

(*a*) exercise the court's power of settling a list of contributories (which list is *prima facie* evidence of the liability of the persons named in it to be contributories),

(*b*) exercise the court's power of making calls,

(*c*) summon general meetings of the company for the purpose of obtaining its sanction by special or extraordinary resolution or for any other purpose he may think fit.

(5) The liquidator shall pay the company's debts and adjust the rights of the contributories among themselves.

(6) Where the liquidator in exercise of the powers conferred on him by this Act disposes of any property of the company to a person who is connected with the company (within the meaning of section 249 in Part VII), he shall, if there is for the time being a liquidation committee, give notice to the committee of that exercise of his powers.

Creditors' voluntary winding up

166.—(1) This section applies where, in the case of a creditors' voluntary winding up, a liquidator has been nominated by the company.

(2) The powers conferred on the liquidator by section 165 shall not be exercised, except with the sanction of the court, during the period before the holding of the creditors' meeting under section 98 in Chapter IV.

(3) Subsection (2) does not apply in relation to the power of the liquidator—

(*a*) to take into his custody or under his control all the property to which the company is or appears to be entitled;

(*b*) to dispose of perishable goods and other goods the value of which is likely to diminish if they are not immediately disposed of; and

(*c*) to do all such other things as may be necessary for the protection of the company's assets.

(4) The liquidator shall attend the creditors' meeting held under section 98 and shall report to the meeting on any exercise by him of his powers (whether or not under this section or under section 112 or 165).

(5) If default is made—

(*a*) by the company in complying with subsection (1) or (2) of section 98, or

(*b*) by the directors in complying with subsection (1) or (2) of section 99,

the liquidator shall, within seven days of the relevant day, apply to the court for directions as to the manner in which that default is to be remedied.

(6) "The relevant day" means the day on which the liquidator was nominated by the company or the day on which he first became aware of the default, whichever is the later.

(7) If the liquidator without reasonable excuse fails to comply with this section, he is liable to a fine.

Winding up by the court

167.—(1) Where a company is being wound up by the court, the liquidator may—

    (*a*) with the sanction of the court or the liquidation committee, exercise any of the powers specified in Parts I and II of Schedule 4 to this Act (payment of debts; compromise of claims, etc.; institution and defence of proceedings; carrying on of the business of the company), and

    (*b*) with or without that sanction, exercise any of the general powers specified in Part III of that Schedule.

(2) Where the liquidator (not being the official receiver), in exercise of the powers conferred on him by this Act—

    (*a*) disposes of any property of the company to a person who is connected with the company (within the meaning of section 249 in Part VII), or

    (*b*) employs a solicitor to assist him in the carrying out of his functions,

he shall, if there is for the time being a liquidation committee, give notice to the committee of that exercise of his powers.

(3) The exercise by the liquidator in a winding up by the court of the powers conferred by this section is subject to the control of the court, and any creditor or contributory may apply to the court with respect to any exercise or proposed exercise of any of those powers.

Supplementary powers (England and Wales)

168.—(1) This section applies in the case of a company which is being wound up by the court in England and Wales.

(2) The liquidator may summon general meetings of the creditors or contributories for the purpose of ascertaining their wishes; and it is his duty to summon meetings at such times as the creditors or contributories by resolution (either at the meeting appointing the liquidator or otherwise) may direct, or whenever requested in writing to do so by one-tenth in value of the creditors or contributories (as the case may be).

(3) The liquidator may apply to the court (in the prescribed manner) for directions in relation to any particular matter arising in the winding up.

(4) Subject to the provisions of this Act, the liquidator shall use his own discretion in the management of the assets and their distribution among the creditors.

(5) If any person is aggrieved by an act or decision of the liquidator, that person may apply to the court; and the court may confirm, reverse or modify the act or decision complained of, and make such order in the case as it thinks just.

Supplementary powers (Scotland)

169.—(1) In the case of a winding up in Scotland, the court may provide by order that the liquidator may, where there is no liquidation committee, exercise any of the following powers, namely—

    (*a*) to bring or defend any action or other legal proceeding in the name and on behalf of the company, or

    (*b*) to carry on the business of the company so far as may be necessary for its beneficial winding up,

without the sanction or intervention of the court.

(2) In a winding up by the court in Scotland, the liquidator has (subject to the rules) the same powers as a trustee on a bankrupt estate.

Enforcement of liquidator's duty to make returns, etc.

170.—(1) If a liquidator who has made any default—

    (*a*) in filing, delivering or making any return, account or other document, or

    (*b*) in giving any notice which he is by law required to file, deliver, make or give, fails to make good the default within 14 days after the service on him of a notice requiring him to do so, the court has the following powers.

(2) On an application made by any creditor or contributory of the company, or by the registrar of companies, the court may make an order directing the liquidator to make good the default within such time as may be specified in the order.

(3) The court's order may provide that all costs of and incidental to the application shall be borne by the liquidator.

(4) Nothing in this section prejudices the operation of any enactment imposing penalties on a liquidator in respect of any such default as is mentioned above.

Removal; vacation of office

Removal, etc. (voluntary winding up)

171.—(1) This section applies with respect to the removal from office and vacation of office of the liquidator of a company which is being wound up voluntarily.

(2) Subject to the next subsection, the liquidator may be removed from office only by an order of the court or—

    (*a*) in the case of a members' voluntary winding up, by a general meeting of the company summoned specially for that purpose, or

    (*b*) in the case of a creditors' voluntary winding up, by a general meeting of the company's creditors summoned specially for that purpose in accordance with the rules.

(3) Where the liquidator was appointed by the court under section 108 in Chapter V, a meeting such as is mentioned in subsection (2) above shall be summoned for the purpose of replacing him only if he thinks fit or the court so directs or the meeting is requested, in accordance with the rules—

    (*a*) in the case of a members' voluntary winding up, by members representing not less than one-half of the total voting rights of all the members having at the date of the request a right to vote at the meeting, or

    (*b*) in the case of a creditors' voluntary winding up, by not less than one-half, in value, of the company's creditors.

(4) A liquidator shall vacate office if he ceases to be a person who is qualified to act as an insolvency practitioner in relation to the company.

(5) A liquidator may, in the prescribed circumstances, resign his office by giving notice of his resignation to the registrar of companies.

(6) Where—

    (*a*) in the case of a members' voluntary winding up, a final meeting of the company has been held under section 94 in Chapter III, or

    (*b*) in the case of a creditors' voluntary winding up, final meetings of the company and of the creditors have been held under section 106 in Chapter IV,

the liquidator whose report was considered at the meeting or meetings shall vacate office as soon as he has complied with subsection (3) of that section and has given notice to the registrar of companies that the meeting or meetings have been held and of the decisions (if any) of the meeting or meetings.

Removal, etc. (winding up by the court)

172.—(1) This section applies with respect to the removal from office and vacation of office of the liquidator of a company which is being wound up by the court, or of a provisional liquidator.

(2) Subject as follows, the liquidator may be removed from office only by an order of the court or by a general meeting of the company's creditors summoned specially for that purpose in accordance with the rules; and a provisional liquidator may be removed from office only by an order of the court.

(3) Where—

(*a*) the official receiver is liquidator otherwise than in succession under section 136(3) to a person who held office as a result of a nomination by a meeting of the company's creditors or contributories, or

(*b*) the liquidator was appointed by the court otherwise than under section 139(4)(*a*) or 140(1), or was appointed by the Secretary of State,

a general meeting of the company's creditors shall be summoned for the purpose of replacing him only if he thinks fit, or the court so directs, or the meeting is requested, in accordance with the rules, by not less than one-quarter, in value, of the creditors.

(4) If appointed by the Secretary of State, the liquidator may be removed from office by a direction of the Secretary of State.

(5) A liquidator or provisional liquidator, not being the official receiver, shall vacate office if he ceases to be a person who is qualified to act as an insolvency practitioner in relation to the company.

(6) A liquidator may, in the prescribed circumstances, resign his office by giving notice of his resignation to the court.

(7) Where an order is made under section 204 (early dissolution in Scotland) for the dissolution of the company, the liquidator shall vacate office when the dissolution of the company takes effect in accordance with that section.

(8) Where a final meeting has been held under section 146 (liquidator's report on completion of winding up), the liquidator whose report was considered at the meeting shall vacate office as soon as he has given notice to the court and the registrar of companies that the meeting has been held and of the decisions (if any) of the meeting.

Release of liquidator

Release (voluntary winding up)

173.—(1) This section applies with respect to the release of the liquidator of a company which is being wound up voluntarily.

(2) A person who has ceased to be a liquidator shall have his release with effect from the following time, that is to say—

(*a*) in the case of a person who has been removed from office by a general meeting of the company or by a general meeting of the company's creditors that has not resolved against his release or who has died, the time at which notice is given to the registrar of companies in accordance with the rules that that person has ceased to hold office;

(*b*) in the case of a person who has been removed from office by a general meeting of the company's creditors that has resolved against his release, or by the court, or who has vacated office under section 171(4) above, such time as the Secretary of State may, on the application of that person, determine;

(*c*) in the case of a person who has resigned, such time as may be prescribed;

(*d*) in the case of a person who has vacated office under subsection (6)(*a*) of section 171, the time at which he vacated office;

(*e*) in the case of a person who has vacated office under subsection (6)(*b*) of that section—

(i) if the final meeting of the creditors referred to in that subsection has resolved against that person's release, such time as the Secretary of State may, on an application by that person, determine, and

(ii) if that meeting has not resolved against that person's release, the time at which he vacated office.

(3) In the application of subsection (2) to the winding up of a company registered in Scotland, the references to a determination by the Secretary

of State as to the time from which a person who has ceased to be liquidator shall have his release are to be read as references to such a determination by the Accountant of Court.

(4) Where a liquidator has his release under subsection (2), he is, with effect from the time specified in that subsection, discharged from all liability both in respect of acts or omissions of his in the winding up and otherwise in relation to his conduct as liquidator.

But nothing in this section prevents the exercise, in relation to a person who has had his release under subsection (2), of the court's powers under section 212 of this Act (summary remedy against delinquent directors, liquidators, etc.).

Release (winding up by the court)

174.—(1) This section applies with respect to the release of the liquidator of a company which is being wound up by the court, or of a provisional liquidator.

(2) Where the official receiver has ceased to be liquidator and a person becomes liquidator in his stead, the official receiver has his release with effect from the following time, that is to say—

(a) in a case where that person was nominated by a general meeting of creditors or contributories, or was appointed by the Secretary of State, the time at which the official receiver gives notice to the court that he has been replaced;

(b) in a case where that person is appointed by the court, such time as the court may determine.

(3) If the official receiver while he is liquidator gives notice to the Secretary of State that the winding up is for practical purposes complete, he has his release with effect from such time as the Secretary of State may determine.

(4) A person other than the official receiver who has ceased to be a liquidator has his release with effect from the following time, that is to say—

(a) in the case of a person who has been removed from office by a general meeting of creditors that has not resolved against his release or who has died, the time at which notice is given to the court in accordance with the rules that that person has ceased to hold office;

(b) in the case of a person who has been removed from office by a general meeting of creditors that has resolved against his release, or by the court or the Secretary of State, or who has vacated office under section 172(5) or (7), such time as the Secretary of State may, on an application by that person, determine;

(c) in the case of a person who has resigned, such time as may be prescribed;

(d) in the case of a person who has vacated office under section 172(8)—

(i) if the final meeting referred to in that subsection has resolved against that person's release, such time as the Secretary of State may, on an application by that person, determine, and

(ii) if that meeting has not so resolved, the time at which that person vacated office.

(5) A person who has ceased to hold office as a provisional liquidator has his release with effect from such time as the court may, on an application by him, determine.

(6) Where the official receiver or a liquidator or provisional liquidator has his release under this section, he is, with effect from the time specified in the preceding provisions of this section, discharged from all liability both in respect of acts or omissions of his in the winding up and otherwise in relation to his conduct as liquidator or provisional liquidator.

But nothing in this section prevents the exercise, in relation to a person who has had his release under this section, of the court's powers under section 212 (summary remedy against delinquent directors, liquidators, etc.).

(7) In the application of this section to a case where the order for winding up has been made by the court in Scotland, the references to a determination by the Secretary of State as to the time from which a person who has ceased to be liquidator has his release are to such a determination by the Accountant of Court.

CHAPTER VIII

PROVISIONS OF GENERAL APPLICATION IN WINDING UP

Preferential debts

Preferential debts (general provision)

175.—(1) In a winding up the company's preferential debts (within the meaning given by section 386 in Part XII) shall be paid in priority to all other debts.

(2) Preferential debts—

(*a*)   rank equally among themselves after the expenses of the winding up and shall be paid in full, unless the assets are insufficient to meet them, in which case they abate in equal proportions; and

(*b*)   so far as the assets of the company available for payment of general creditors are insufficient to meet them, have priority over the claims of holders of debentures secured by, or holders of, any floating charge created by the company, and shall be paid accordingly out of any property comprised in or subject to that charge.

Preferential charge on goods distrained

176.—(1) This section applies where a company is being wound up by the court in England and Wales, and is without prejudice to section 128 (avoidance of attachments, etc.).

(2) Where any person (whether or not a landlord or person entitled to rent) has distrained upon the goods or effects of the company in the period of three months ending with the date of the winding-up order, those goods or effects, or the proceeds of their sale, shall be charged for the benefit of the company with the preferential debts of the company to the extent that the company's property is for the time being insufficient for meeting them.

(3) Where by virtue of a charge under subsection (2) any person surrenders any goods or effects to a company or makes a payment to a company, that person ranks, in respect of the amount of the proceeds of sale of those goods or effects by the liquidator or (as the case may be) the amount of the payment, as a preferential creditor of the company, except as against so much of the company's property as is available for the payment of preferential creditors by virtue of the surrender or payment.

Special managers

Power to appoint special manager

177.—(1) Where a company has gone into liquidation or a provisional liquidator has been appointed, the court may, on an application under this section, appoint any person to be the special manager of the business or property of the company.

(2) The application may be made by the liquidator or provisional liquidator in any case where it appears to him that the nature of the business or property of the company, or the interests of the company's creditors or contributories or members generally, require the appointment of another person to manage the company's business or property.

(3) The special manager has such powers as may be entrusted to him by the court.

(4) The court's power to entrust powers to the special manager includes power to direct that any provision of this Act that has effect in relation to the provisional liquidator or liquidator of a company shall have the like effect in relation to the special manager for the purposes of the carrying out by him of any of the functions of the provisional liquidator or liquidator.

(5) The special manager shall—

(*a*) give such security or, in Scotland, caution as may be prescribed;

(*b*) prepare and keep such accounts as may be prescribed; and

(*c*) produce those accounts in accordance with the rules to the Secretary of State or to such other persons as may be prescribed.

Disclaimer (England and Wales only)

Power to disclaim onerous property

178.—(1) This and the next two sections apply to a company that is being wound up in England and Wales.

(2) Subject as follows, the liquidator may, by the giving of the prescribed notice, disclaim any onerous property and may do so notwithstanding that he has taken possession of it, endeavoured to sell it, or otherwise exercised rights of ownership in relation to it.

(3) The following is onerous property for the purposes of this section—

(*a*) any unprofitable contract, and

(*b*) any other property of the company which is unsaleable or not readily saleable or is such that it may give rise to a liability to pay money or perform any other onerous act.

(4) A disclaimer under this section—

(*a*) operates so as to determine, as from the date of the disclaimer, the rights, interests and liabilities of the company in or in respect of the property disclaimed; but

(*b*) does not, except so far as is necessary for the purpose of releasing the company from any liability, affect the rights or liabilities of any other person.

(5) A notice of disclaimer shall not be given under this section in respect of any property if—

(*a*) a person interested in the property has applied in writing to the liquidator or one of his predecessors as liquidator requiring the liquidator or that predecessor to decide whether he will disclaim or not, and

(*b*) the period of 28 days beginning with the day on which that application was made, or such longer period as the court may allow, has expired without a notice of disclaimer having been given under this section in respect of that property.

(6) Any person sustaining loss or damage in consequence of the operation of a disclaimer under this section is deemed a creditor of the company to the extent of the loss or damage and accordingly may prove for the loss or damage in the winding up.

Disclaimer of leaseholds

179.—(1) The disclaimer under section 178 of any property of a leasehold nature does not take effect unless a copy of the disclaimer has been served (so far as the liquidator is aware of their addresses) on every person claiming under the company as underlessee or mortgagee and either—

(*a*) no application under section 181 below is made with respect to that property before the end of the period of 14 days beginning with the day on which the last notice served under this subsection was served; or (*b*) where such an application has been made, the court directs that the disclaimer shall take effect.

(2) Where the court gives a direction under subsection (1)(*b*) it may also, instead of or in addition to any order it makes under section 181, make such orders with respect to fixtures, tenant's improvements and other matters arising out of the lease as it thinks fit.

Land subject to rentcharge

180.—(1) The following applies where, in consequence of the disclaimer under section 178 of any land subject to a rentcharge, that land vests by operation of law in the Crown or any other person (referred to in the next subsection as "the proprietor").

(2) The proprietor and the successors in title of the proprietor are not subject to any personal liability in respect of any sums becoming due under the rentcharge except sums becoming due after the proprietor, or some person claiming under or through the proprietor, has taken possession or control of the land or has entered into occupation of it.

Powers of court (general)

181.—(1) This section and the next apply where the liquidator has disclaimed property under section 178.

(2) An application under this section may be made to the court by—

(*a*) any person who claims an interest in the disclaimed property, or

(*b*) any person who is under any liability in respect of the disclaimed property, not being a liability discharged by the disclaimer.

(3) Subject as follows, the court may on the application make an order, on such terms as it thinks fit, for the vesting of the disclaimed property in, or for its delivery to—

(*a*) a person entitled to it or a trustee for such a person, or

(*b*) a person subject to such a liability as is mentioned in subsection (2)(*b*) or a trustee for such a person.

(4) The court shall not make an order under subsection (3)(*b*) except where it appears to the court that it would be just to do so for the purpose of compensating the person subject to the liability in respect of the disclaimer.

(5) The effect of any order under this section shall be taken into account in assessing for the purpose of section 178(6) the extent of any loss or damage sustained by any person in consequence of the disclaimer.

(6) An order under this section vesting property in any person need not be completed by conveyance, assignment or transfer.

Powers of court (leaseholds)

182.—(1) The court shall not make an order under section 181 vesting property of a leasehold nature in any person claiming under the company as underlessee or mortgagee except on terms making that person—

(*a*) subject to the same liabilities and obligations as the company was subject to under the lease at the commencement of the winding up, or

(*b*) if the court thinks fit, subject to the same liabilities and obligations as that person would be subject to if the lease had been assigned to him at the commencement of the winding up.

(2) For the purposes of an order under section 181 relating to only part of any property comprised in a lease, the requirements of subsection (1) apply as if the lease comprised only the property to which the order relates.

(3) Where subsection (1) applies and no person claiming under the company as underlessee or mortgagee is willing to accept an order under section 181 on the terms required by virtue of that subsection, the court may, by order under that section, vest the company's estate or interest in the property in any person who is liable (whether personally or in a representa-

tive capacity, and whether alone or jointly with the company) to perform the lessee's covenants in the lease.

The court may vest that estate and interest in such a person freed and discharged from all estates, incumbrances and interests created by the company.

(4) Where subsection (1) applies and a person claiming under the company as underlessee or mortgagee declines to accept an order under section 181, that person is excluded from all interest in the property.

Execution, attachment and the Scottish equivalents

Effect of execution or attachment (England and Wales)

183.—(1) Where a creditor has issued execution against the goods or land of a company or has attached any debt due to it, and the company is subsequently wound up, he is not entitled to retain the benefit of the execution or attachment against the liquidator unless he has completed the execution or attachment before the commencement of the winding up.

(2) However—

(*a*) if a creditor has had notice of a meeting having been called at which a resolution for voluntary winding up is to be proposed, the date on which he had notice is substituted, for the purpose of subsection (1), for the date of commencement of the winding up;

(*b*) a person who purchases in good faith under a sale by the sheriff any goods of a company on which execution has been levied in all cases acquires a good title to them against the liquidator; and

(*c*) the rights conferred by subsection (1) on the liquidator may be set aside by the court in favour of the creditor to such extent and subject to such terms as the court thinks fit.

(3) For purposes of this Act—

(*a*) an execution against goods is completed by seizure and sale, or by the making of a charging order under section 1 of the Charging Orders Act 1979;

(*b*) an attachment of a debt is completed by receipt of the debt; and

(*c*) an execution against land is completed by seizure, by the appointment of a receiver, or by the making of a charging order under section 1 of the Act above-mentioned.

(4) In this section, "goods" includes all chattels personal; and "the sheriff" includes any officer charged with the execution of a writ or other process.

(5) This section does not apply in the case of a winding up in Scotland.

Duties of sheriff (England and Wales)

184.—(1) The following applies where a company's goods are taken in execution and, before their sale or the completion of the execution (by the receipt or recovery of the full amount of the levy), notice is served on the sheriff that a provisional liquidator has been appointed or that a winding-up order has been made, or that a resolution for voluntary winding up has been passed.

(2) The sheriff shall, on being so required, deliver the goods and any money seized or received in part satisfaction of the execution to the liquidator; but the costs of execution are a first charge on the goods or money so delivered, and the liquidator may sell the goods, or a sufficient part of them, for the purpose of satisfying the charge.

[1] (3) If under an execution in respect of a judgment for a sum exceeding £500 a company's goods are sold or money is paid in order to avoid sale, the sheriff shall deduct the costs of the execution from the proceeds of sale or the money paid and retain the balance for 14 days.

(4) If within that time notice is served on the sheriff of a petition for the winding up of the company having been presented, or of a meeting having

been called at which there is to be proposed a resolution for voluntary winding up, and an order is made or a resolution passed (as the case may be), the sheriff shall pay the balance to the liquidator, who is entitled to retain it as against the execution creditor.

(5) The rights conferred by this section on the liquidator may be set aside by the court in favour of the creditor to such extent and subject to such terms as the court thinks fit.

(6) In this section, "goods" includes all chattels personal; and "the sheriff" includes any officer charged with the execution of a writ or other process.

(7) The money sum for the time being specified in subsection (3) is subject to increase or reduction by order under section 416 in Part XV.

(8) This section does not apply in the case of a winding up in Scotland.

NOTE
[1] As amended by S.I. 1986 No. 1996.

Effect of diligence (Scotland)

185.—(1) In the winding up of a company registered in Scotland, the following provisions of the Bankruptcy (Scotland) Act 1985—

   (*a*) subsections (1) to (6) of section 37 (effect of sequestration on diligence); and

   (*b*) subsections (3), (4), (7) and (8) of section 39 (realisation of estate),

apply, so far as consistent with this Act, in like manner as they apply in the sequestration of a debtor's estate, with the substitutions specified below and with any other necessary modifications.

(2) The substitutions to be made in those sections of the Act of 1985 are as follows—

   (*a*) for references to the debtor, substitute references to the company;

   (*b*) for references to the sequestration, substitute references to the winding up;

   (*c*) for references to the date of sequestration, substitute references to the commencement of the winding up of the company; and

   (*d*) for references to the permanent trustee, substitute references to the liquidator.

(3) In this section, "the commencement of the winding up of the company" means, where it is being wound up by the court, the day on which the winding-up order is made.

(4) This section, so far as relating to any estate or effects of the company situated in Scotland, applies in the case of a company registered in England and Wales as in the case of one registered in Scotland.

Miscellaneous matters

Rescission of contracts by the court

186.—(1) The court may, on the application of a person who is, as against the liquidator, entitled to the benefit or subject to the burden of a contract made with the company, make an order rescinding the contract on such terms as to payment by or to either party of damages for the non-performance of the contract, or otherwise as the court thinks just.

(2) Any damages payable under the order to such a person may be proved by him as a debt in the winding up.

Power to make over assets to employees

187.—(1) On the winding up of a company (whether by the court or voluntarily), the liquidator may, subject to the following provisions of this section, make any payment which the company has, before the commencement of the winding up, decided to make under section 719 of the Companies Act (power to provide for employees or former employees on cessation or transfer of business).

(2) The power which a company may exercise by virtue only of that sec-

tion may be exercised by the liquidator after the winding up has commenced if, after the company's liabilities have been fully satisfied and provision has been made for the expenses of the winding up, the exercise of that power has been sanctioned by such a resolution of the company as would be required of the company itself by section 719(3) before that commencement, if paragraph (*b*) of that subsection were omitted and any other requirement applicable to its exercise by the company had been met.

(3) Any payment which may be made by a company under this section (that is, a payment after the commencement of its winding up) may be made out of the company's assets which are available to the members on the winding up.

(4) On a winding up by the court, the exercise by the liquidator of his powers under this section is subject to the court's control, and any creditor or contributory may apply to the court with respect to any exercise or proposed exercise of the power.

(5) Subsections (1) and (2) above have effect notwithstanding anything in any rule of law or in section 107 of this Act (property of company after satisfaction of liabilities to be distributed among members).

Notification that company is in liquidation

188.—(1) When a company is being wound up, whether by the court or voluntarily, every invoice, order for goods or business letter issued by or on behalf of the company, or a liquidator of the company, or a receiver or manager of the company's property, being a document on or in which the name of the company appears, shall contain a statement that the company is being wound up.

(2) If default is made in complying with this section, the company and any of the following persons who knowingly and wilfully authorises or permits the default, namely, any officer of the company, any liquidator of the company and any receiver or manager, is liable to a fine.

Interest on debts

189.—(1) In a winding up interest is payable in accordance with this section on any debt proved in the winding up, including so much of any such debt as represents interest on the remainder.

(2) Any surplus remaining after the payment of the debts proved in a winding up shall, before being applied for any other purpose, be applied in paying interest on those debts in respect of the periods during which they have been outstanding since the company went into liquidation.

(3) All interest under this section ranks equally, whether or not the debts on which it is payable rank equally.

(4) The rate of interest payable under this section in respect of any debt ("the official rate" for the purposes of any provision of this Act in which that expression is used) is whichever is the greater of—

   (*a*)   the rate specified in section 17 of the Judgments Act 1838 on the day on which the company went into liquidation, and

   (*b*)   the rate applicable to that debt apart from the winding up.

(5) In the application of this section to Scotland—

   (*a*)   references to a debt proved in a winding up have effect as references to a claim accepted in a winding up, and

   (*b*)   the reference to section 17 of the Judgments Act 1838 has effect as a reference to the rules.

Documents exempt from stamp duty

190.—(1) In the case of a winding up by the court, or of a creditors' voluntary winding up, the following has effect as regards exemption from duties chargeable under the enactments relating to stamp duties.

(2) If the company is registered in England and Wales, the following documents are exempt from stamp duty—

   (*a*)   every assurance relating solely to freehold or leasehold property, or to any estate, right or interest in, any real or personal property, which forms part of the company's assets and which, after the execution of the assurance, either at law or in equity, is or remains part of those assets, and

(b) every writ, order, certificate, or other instrument or writing relating solely to the property of any company which is being wound up as mentioned in subsection (1), or to any proceeding under such a winding up.

"Assurance" here includes deed, conveyance, assignment and surrender.

(3) If the company is registered in Scotland, the following documents are exempt from stamp duty—

(a) every conveyance relating solely to property which forms part of the company's assets and which, after the execution of the conveyance, is or remains the company's property for the benefit of its creditors,

(b) any articles of roup or sale, submission and every other instrument and writing whatsoever relating solely to the company's property, and

(c) every deed or writing forming part of the proceedings in the winding up.

"Conveyance" here includes assignation, instrument, discharge, writing and deed.

Company's books to be evidence
191. Where a company is being wound up, all books and papers of the company and of the liquidators are, as between the contributories of the company, *prima facie* evidence of the truth of all matters purporting to be recorded in them.

Information as to pending liquidations
192.—(1) If the winding up of a company is not concluded within one year after its commencement, the liquidator shall, at such intervals as may be prescribed, until the winding up is concluded, send to the registrar of companies a statement in the prescribed form and containing the prescribed particulars with respect to the proceedings in, and position of, the liquidation.

(2) If a liquidator fails to comply with this section, he is liable to a fine and, for continued contravention, to a daily default fine.

Unclaimed dividends (Scotland)
193.—(1) The following applies where a company registered in Scotland has been wound up, and is about to be dissolved.

(2) The liquidator shall lodge in an appropriate bank or institution as defined in section 73(1) of the Bankruptcy (Scotland) Act 1985 (not being a bank or institution in or of which the liquidator is acting partner, manager, agent or cashier) in the name of the Accountant of Court the whole unclaimed dividends and unapplied or undistributable balances, and the deposit receipts shall be transmitted to the Accountant of Court.

(3) The provisions of section 58 of the Bankruptcy (Scotland) Act 1985 (so far as consistent with this Act and the Companies Act) apply with any necessary modifications to sums lodged in a bank or institution under this section as they apply to sums deposited under section 57 of the Act first mentioned.

Resolutions passed at adjourned meetings
194. Where a resolution is passed at an adjourned meeting of a company's creditors or contributories, the resolution is treated for all purposes as having been passed on the date on which it was in fact passed, and not as having been passed on any earlier date.

Meetings to ascertain wishes of creditors or contributories

195.—(1) The court may—

(*a*) as to all matters relating to the winding up of a company, have regard to the wishes of the creditors or contributories (as proved to it by any sufficient evidence), and

(*b*) if it thinks fit, for the purpose of ascertaining those wishes, direct meetings of the creditors or contributories to be called, held and conducted in such manner as the court directs, and appoint a person to act as chairman of any such meeting and report the result of it to the court.

(2) In the case of creditors, regard shall be had to the value of each creditor's debt.

(3) In the case of contributories, regard shall be had to the number of votes conferred on each contributory by the Companies Act or the articles.

Judicial notice of court documents

196. In all proceedings under this Part, all courts, judges and persons judicially acting, and all officers, judicial or ministerial, of any court, or employed in enforcing the process of any court shall take judicial notice—

(*a*) of the signature of any officer of the High Court or of a county court in England and Wales, or of the Court of Session or a sheriff court in Scotland, or of the High Court in Northern Ireland, and also

(*b*) of the official seal or stamp of the several offices of the High Court in England and Wales or Northern Ireland, or of the Court of Session, appended to or impressed on any document made, issued or signed under the provisions of this Act or the Companies Act, or any official copy of such a document.

Commission for receiving evidence

197.—(1) When a company is wound up in England and Wales or in Scotland, the court may refer the whole or any part of the examination of witnesses—

(*a*) to a specified county court in England and Wales, or

(*b*) to the sheriff principal for a specified sheriffdom in Scotland, or

(*c*) to the High Court in Northern Ireland or a specified Northern Ireland County Court,

("specified" meaning specified in the order of the winding-up court).

(2) Any person exercising jurisdiction as a judge of the court to which the reference is made (or, in Scotland, the sheriff principal to whom it is made) shall then, by virtue of this section, be a commissioner for the purpose of taking the evidence of those witnesses.

(3) The judge or sheriff principal has in the matter referred the same power of summoning and examining witnesses, of requiring the production and delivery of documents, of punishing defaults by witnesses, and of allowing costs and expenses to witnesses, as the court which made the winding-up order.

These powers are in addition to any which the judge or sheriff principal might lawfully exercise apart from this section.

(4) The examination so taken shall be returned or reported to the court which made the order in such manner as that court requests.

(5) This section extends to Northern Ireland.

Court order for examination of persons in Scotland

198.—(1) The court may direct the examination in Scotland of any person for the time being in Scotland (whether a contributory of the company or not), in regard to the trade, dealings, affairs or property of any company in course of being wound up, or of any person being a contributory of the company, so far as the company may be interested by reason of his being a contributory.

(2) The order or commission to take the examination shall be directed to the sheriff principal of the sheriffdom in which the person to be examined is residing or happens to be for the time; and the sheriff principal shall summon the person to appear before him at a time and place to be specified in the summons for examination on oath as a witness or as a haver, and to produce any books or papers called for which are in his possession or power.

(3) The sheriff principal may take the examination either orally or on written interrogatories, and shall report the same in writing in the usual form to the court, and shall transmit with the report the books and papers produced, if the originals are required and specified by the order or commission, or otherwise copies or extracts authenticated by the sheriff.

(4) If a person so summoned fails to appear at the time and place specified, or refuses to be examined or to make the production required, the sheriff principal shall proceed against him as a witness or haver duly cited; and failing to appear or refusing to give evidence or make production may be proceeded against by the law of Scotland.

(5) The sheriff principal is entitled to such fees, and the witness is entitled to such allowances, as sheriffs principal when acting as commissioners under appointment from the Court of Session and as witnesses and havers are entitled to in the like cases according to the law and practice of Scotland.

(6) If any objection is stated to the sheriff principal by the witness, either on the ground of his incompetency as a witness, or as to the production required, or on any other ground, the sheriff principal may, if he thinks fit, report the objection to the court, and suspend the examination of the witness until it has been disposed of by the court.

Costs of application for leave to proceed (Scottish companies)

199. Where a petition or application for leave to proceed with an action or proceeding against a company which is being wound up in Scotland is unopposed and is granted by the court, the costs of the petition or application shall, unless the court otherwise directs, be added to the amount of the petitioner's or applicant's claim against the company.

Affidavits etc. in United Kingdom and overseas

200.—(1) An affidavit required to be sworn under or for the purposes of this Part may be sworn in the United Kingdom, or elsewhere in Her Majesty's dominions, before any court, judge or person lawfully authorised to take and receive affidavits, or before any of Her Majesty's consuls or vice-consuls in any place outside her dominions.

(2) All courts, judges, justices, commissioners and persons acting judicially shall take judicial notice of the seal or stamp or signature (as the case may be) of any such court, judge, person, consul or vice-consul attached, appended or subscribed to any such affidavit, or to any other document to be used for the purposes of this Part.

CHAPTER IX

DISSOLUTION OF COMPANIES AFTER WINDING UP

Dissolution (voluntary winding up)

201.—(1) This section applies, in the case of a company wound up voluntarily, where the liquidator has sent to the registrar of companies his final account and return under section 94 (members' voluntary) or section 106 (creditors' voluntary).

(2) The registrar on receiving the account and return shall forthwith register them; and on the expiration of three months from the registration of the return the company is deemed to be dissolved.

(3) However, the court may, on the application of the liquidator or any other person who appears to the court to be interested, make an order deferring the date at which the dissolution of the company is to take effect for such time as the court thinks fit.

(4) It is the duty of the person on whose application an order of the court under this section is made within seven days after the making of the order to deliver to the registrar an office copy of the order for registration; and if that person fails to do so he is liable to a fine and, for continued contravention, to a daily default fine.

Early dissolution (England and Wales)

202.—(1) This section applies where an order for the winding up of a company has been made by the court in England and Wales.

(2) The official receiver, if—

(*a*) he is the liquidator of the company, and

(*b*) it appears to him—

  (i) that the realisable assets of the company are insufficient to cover the expenses of the winding up, and

  (ii) that the affairs of the company do not require any further investigation,

may at any time apply to the registrar of companies for the early dissolution of the company.

(3) Before making that application, the official receiver shall give not less than 28 days' notice of his intention to do so to the company's creditors and contributories and, if there is an administrative receiver of the company, to that receiver.

(4) With the giving of that notice the official receiver ceases (subject to any directions under the next section) to be required to perform any duties imposed on him in relation to the company, its creditors or contributories by virtue of any provision of this Act, apart from a duty to make an application under subsection (2) of this section.

(5) On the receipt of the official receiver's application under subsection (2) the registrar shall forthwith register it and, at the end of the period of three months beginning with the day of the registration of the application, the company shall be dissolved.

However, the Secretary of State may, on the application of the official receiver or any other person who appears to the Secretary of State to be interested, give directions under section 203 at any time before the end of that period.

Consequence of notice under s.202

203.—(1) Where a notice has been given under section 202(3), the official receiver or any creditor or contributory of the company, or the administrative receiver of the company (if there is one) may apply to the Secretary of State for directions under this section.

(2) The grounds on which that application may be made are—

(*a*) that the realisable assets of the company are sufficient to cover the expenses of the winding up;

(*b*) that the affairs of the company do require further investigation; or

(*c*) that for any other reason the early dissolution of the company is inappropriate.

(3) Directions under this section—

(*a*) are directions making such provision as the Secretary of State thinks fit for enabling the winding up of the company to proceed as if no notice had been given under section 202(3), and

(*b*) may, in the case of an application under section 202(5), include a direction deferring the date at which the dissolution of the company is to take effect for such period as the Secretary of State thinks fit.

(4) An appeal to the court lies from any decision of the Secretary of State on an application for directions under this section.

(5) It is the duty of the person on whose application any directions are given under this section, or in whose favour an appeal with respect to an application for such directions is determined, within seven days after the giving of the directions or the determination of the appeal, to deliver to the registrar of companies for registration such a copy of the directions or determination as is prescribed.

(6) If a person without reasonable excuse fails to deliver a copy as required by subsection (5), he is liable to a fine and, for continued contravention, to a daily default fine.

Early dissolution (Scotland)

204.—(1) This section applies where a winding-up order has been made by the court in Scotland.

(2) If after a meeting or meetings under section 138 (appointment of liquidator in Scotland) it appears to the liquidator that the realisable assets of the company are insufficient to cover the expenses of the winding up, he may apply to the court for an order that the company be dissolved.

(3) Where the liquidator makes that application, if the court is satisfied that the realisable assets of the company are insufficient to cover the expenses of the winding up and it appears to the court appropriate to do so, the court shall make an order that the company be dissolved in accordance with this section.

(4) A copy of the order shall within 14 days from its date be forwarded by the liquidator to the registrar of companies, who shall forthwith register it; and, at the end of the period of three months beginning with the day of the registration of the order, the company shall be dissolved.

(5) The court may, on an application by any person who appears to the court to have an interest, order that the date at which the dissolution of the company is to take effect shall be deferred for such period as the court thinks fit.

(6) It is the duty of the person on whose application an order is made under subsection (5), within seven days after the making of the order, to deliver to the registrar of companies such a copy of the order as is prescribed.

(7) If the liquidator without reasonable excuse fails to comply with the requirements of subsection (4), he is liable to a fine and, for continued contravention, to a daily default fine.

(8) If a person without reasonable excuse fails to deliver a copy as required by subsection (6), he is liable to a finc and, for continued contravention, to a daily default fine.

Dissolution otherwise than under ss.202–204

205.—(1) This section applies where the registrar of companies receives—

    (*a*) a notice served for the purposes of section 172(8) (final meeting of creditors and vacation of office by liquidator), or

    (*b*) a notice from the official receiver that the winding up of a company by the court is complete.

(2) The registrar shall, on receipt of the notice, forthwith register it; and, subject as follows, at the end of the period of three months beginning with the day of the registration of the notice, the company shall be dissolved.

(3) The Secretary of State may, on the application of the official receiver or any other person who appears to the Secretary of State to be interested, give a direction deferring the date at which the dissolution of the company is to take effect for such period as the Secretary of State thinks fit.

(4) An appeal to the court lies from any decision of the Secretary of State on an application for a direction under subsection (3).

(5) Subsection (3) does not apply in a case where the winding-up order was made by the court in Scotland, but in such a case the court may, on an application by any person appearing to the court to have an interest, order that the date at which the dissolution of the company is to take effect shall be deferred for such period as the court thinks fit.

(6) It is the duty of the person—

(*a*) on whose application a direction is given under subsection (3);

(*b*) in whose favour an appeal with respect to an application for such a direction is determined; or

(*c*) on whose application an order is made under subsection (5),

within seven days after the giving of the direction, the determination of the appeal or the making of the order, to deliver to the registrar for registration such a copy of the direction, determination or order as is prescribed.

(7) If a person without reasonable excuse fails to deliver a copy as required by subsection (6), he is liable to a fine and, for continued contravention, to a daily default fine.

CHAPTER X

MALPRACTICE BEFORE AND DURING LIQUIDATION; PENALISATION OF
COMPANIES AND COMPANY OFFICERS; INVESTIGATIONS AND PROSECUTIONS

Offences of fraud, deception, etc.

Fraud, etc. in anticipation of winding up

206.—(1) When a company is ordered to be wound up by the court, or passes a resolution for voluntary winding up, any person, being a past or present officer of the company, is deemed to have committed an offence if, within the 12 months immediately preceding the commencement of the winding up, he has—

[1] (*a*) concealed any part of the company's property to the value of £500 or more, or concealed any debt due to or from the company, or

[1] (*b*) fraudulently removed any part of the company's property to the value of £500 or more, or

(*c*) concealed, destroyed, mutilated or falsified any book or paper affecting or relating to the company's property or affairs, or

(*d*) made any false entry in any book or paper affecting or relating to the company's property or affairs, or

(*e*) fraudulently parted with, altered or made any omission in any document affecting or relating to the company's property or affairs, or

(*f*) pawned, pledged or disposed of any property of the company which has been obtained on credit and has not been paid for (unless the pawning, pledging or disposal was in the ordinary way of the company's business).

(2) Such a person is deemed to have committed an offence if within the period above mentioned he has been privy to the doing by others of any of the things mentioned in paragraphs (*c*), (*d*) and (*e*) of subsection (1); and he commits an offence if, at any time after the commencement of the winding up, he does any of the things mentioned in paragraphs (*a*) to (*f*) of that subsection, or is privy to the doing by others of any of the things mentioned in paragraphs (*c*) to (*e*) of it.

(3) For purposes of this section, "officer" includes a shadow director.

(4) It is a defence—

(*a*) for a person charged under paragraph (*a*) or (*f*) of subsection (1) (or under subsection (2) in respect of the things mentioned in either of those two paragraphs) to prove that he had no intent to defraud, and (*b*)   for a person charged under paragraph (*c*) or (*d*) of subsection (1) (or under subsection (2) in respect of the things mentioned in either of those two paragraphs) to prove that he had no intent to conceal the state of affairs of the company or to defeat the law.

    (5) Where a person pawns, pledges or disposes of any property in circumstances which amount to an offence under subsection (1)(*f*), every person who takes in pawn or pledge, or otherwise receives, the property knowing it to be pawned, pledged or disposed of in such circumstances, is guilty of an offence.

    (6) A person guilty of an offence under this section is liable to imprisonment or a fine, or both.

    (7) The money sums specified in paragraphs (*a*) and (*b*) of subsection (1) are subject to increase or reduction by order under section 416 in Part XV.

NOTE

[1] As amended by S.I. 1986 No. 1996.

Transactions in fraud of creditors

    207.—(1) When a company is ordered to be wound up by the court or passes a resolution for voluntary winding up, a person is deemed to have committed an offence if he, being at the time an officer of the company.

    (*a*)   has made or caused to be made any gift or transfer of, or charge on, or has caused or connived at the levying of any execution against, the company's property, or

    (*b*)   has concealed or removed any part of the company's property since, or within two months before, the date of any unsatisfied judgment or order for the payment of money obtained against the company.

    (2) A person is not guilty of an offence under this section—

    (*a*)   by reason of conduct constituting an offence under subsection (1)(*a*) which occurred more than five years before the commencement of the winding up, or

    (*b*)   if he proves that, at the time of the conduct constituting the offence, he had no intent to defraud the company's creditors.

    (3) A person guilty of an offence under this section is liable to imprisonment or a fine, or both.

Misconduct in course of winding up

    208.—(1) When a company is being wound up, whether by the court or voluntarily, any person, being a past or present officer of the company, commits an offence if he—

    (*a*)   does not to the best of his knowledge and belief fully and truly discover to the liquidator all the company's property, and how and to whom and for what consideration and when the company disposed of any part of that property (except such part as has been disposed of in the ordinary way of the company's business), or

    (*b*)   does not deliver up to the liquidator (or as he directs) all such part of the company's property as is in his custody or under his control, and which he is required by law to deliver up, or

    (*c*)   does not deliver up to the liquidator (or as he directs) all books and papers in his custody or under his control belonging to the company and which he is required by law to deliver up, or

    (*d*)   knowing or believing that a false debt has been proved by any person in the winding up, fails to inform the liquidator as soon as practicable, or

    (*e*)   after the commencement of the winding up, prevents the production of any book or paper affecting or relating to the company's property or affairs.

    (2) Such a person commits an offence if after the commencement of the winding up he attempts to account for any part of the company's property by fictitious losses or expenses; and he is deemed to have committed that

offence if he has so attempted at any meeting of the company's creditors within the 12 months immediately preceding the commencement of the winding up.

(3) For purposes of this section, "officer" includes a shadow director.

(4) It is a defence—

  (a) for a person charged under paragraph (a), (b) or (c) of subsection (1) to prove that he had no intent to defraud, and

  (b) for a person charged under paragraph (e) of that subsection to prove that he had no intent to conceal the state of affairs of the company or to defeat the law.

(5) A person guilty of an offence under this section is liable to imprisonment or a fine, or both.

Falsification of company's books

209.—(1) When a company is being wound up, an officer or contributory of the company commits an offence if he destroys, mutilates, alters or falsifies any books, papers or securities, or makes or is privy to the making of any false or fraudulent entry in any register, book of account or document belonging to the company with intent to defraud or deceive any person.

(2) A person guilty of an offence under this section is liable to imprisonment or a fine, or both.

Material omissions from statement relating to company's affairs

210.—(1) When a company is being wound up, whether by the court or voluntarily, any person, being a past or present officer of the company, commits an offence if he makes any material omission in any statement relating to the company's affairs.

(2) When a company has been ordered to be wound up by the court, or has passed a resolution for voluntary winding up, any such person is deemed to have committed that offence if, prior to the winding up, he has made any material omission in any such statement.

(3) For purposes of this section, "officer" includes a shadow director.

(4) It is a defence for a person charged under this section to prove that he had no intent to defraud.

(5) A person guilty of an offence under this section is liable to imprisonment or a fine, or both.

False representations to creditors

211.—(1) When a company is being wound up, whether by the court or voluntarily, any person, being a past or present officer of the company—

  (a) commits an offence if he makes any false representation or commits any other fraud for the purpose of obtaining the consent of the company's creditors or any of them to an agreement with reference to the company's affairs or to the winding up, and

  (b) is deemed to have committed that offence if, prior to the winding up, he has made any false representation, or committed any other fraud, for that purpose.

(2) For purposes of this section, "officer" includes a shadow director.

(3) A person guilty of an offence under this section is liable to imprisonment or a fine, or both.

Penalisation of directors and officers

Summary remedy against delinquent directors, liquidators, etc.

212.—(1) This section applies if in the course of the winding up of a company it appears that a person who—

  (a) is or has been an officer of the company,

  (b) has acted as liquidator, administrator or administrative receiver of the company, or

(c) not being a person falling within paragraph (*a*) or (*b*), is or has been concerned, or has taken part, in the promotion, formation or management of the company,

has misapplied or retained, or become accountable for, any money or other property of the company, or been guilty of any misfeasance or breach of any fiduciary or other duty in relation to the company.

(2) The reference in subsection (1) to any misfeasance or breach of any fiduciary or other duty in relation to the company includes, in the case of a person who has acted as liquidator or administrator of the company, any misfeasance or breach of any fiduciary or other duty in connection with the carrying out of his functions as liquidator or administrator of the company.

(3) The court may, on the application of the official receiver or the liquidator, or of any creditor or contributory, examine into the conduct of the person falling within subsection (1) and compel him—

(a) to repay, restore or account for the money or property or any part of it, with interest at such rate as the court thinks just, or

(b) to contribute such sum to the company's assets by way of compensation in respect of the misfeasance or breach of fiduciary or other duty as the court thinks just.

(4) The power to make an application under subsection (3) in relation to a person who has acted as liquidator or administrator of the company is not exercisable, except with the leave of the court, after that person has had his release.

(5) The power of a contributory to make an application under subsection (3) is not exercisable except with the leave of the court, but is exercisable notwithstanding that he will not benefit from any order the court may make on the application.

Fraudulent trading

213.—(1) If in the course of the winding up of a company it appears that any business of the company has been carried on with intent to defraud creditors of the company or creditors of any other person, or for any fraudulent purpose, the following has effect.

(2) The court, on the application of the liquidator may declare that any persons who were knowingly parties to the carrying on of the business in the manner above-mentioned are to be liable to make such contribution (if any) to the company's assets as the court thinks proper.

Wrongful trading

214.—(1) Subject to subsection (3) below, if in the course of the winding up of a company it appears that subsection (2) of this section applies in relation to a person who is or has been a director of the company, the court, on the application of the liquidator, may declare that that person is to be liable to make such contribution (if any) to the company's assets as the court thinks proper.

(2) This subsection applies in relation to a person if—

(a) the company has gone into insolvent liquidation,

(b) at some time before the commencement of the winding up of the company, that person knew or ought to have concluded that there was no reasonable prospect that the company would avoid going into insolvent liquidation, and

(c) that person was a director of the company at that time;

but the court shall not make a declaration under this section in any case where the time mentioned in paragraph (*b*) above was before 28th April 1986.

(3) The court shall not make a declaration under this section with respect to any person if it is satisfied that after the condition specified in subsection (2)(*b*) was first satisfied in relation to him that person took every step with a view to minimising the potential loss to the company's creditors as

(assuming him to have known that there was no reasonable prospect that the company would avoid going into insolvent liquidation) he ought to have taken.

(4) For the purposes of subsections (2) and (3), the facts which a director of a company ought to know or ascertain, the conclusions which he ought to reach and the steps which he ought to take are those which would be known or ascertained, or reached or taken, by a reasonable diligent person having both—

(*a*) the general knowledge, skill and experience that may reasonably be expected of a person carrying out the same functions as are carried out by that director in relation to the company, and

(*b*) the general knowledge, skill and experience that that director has.

(5) The reference in subsection (4) to the functions carried out in relation to a company by a director of the company includes any functions which he does not carry out but which have been entrusted to him.

(6) For the purposes of this section a company goes into insolvent liquidation if it goes into liquidation at a time when its assets are insufficient for the payment of its debts and other liabilities and the expenses of the winding up.

(7) In this section "director" includes a shadow director.

(8) This section is without prejudice to section 213.

Proceedings under ss.213, 214

215.–(1) On the hearing of an application under section 213 or 214, the liquidator may himself give evidence or call witnesses.

(2) Where under either section the court makes a declaration, it may give such further directions as it thinks proper for giving effect to the declaration; and in particular, the court may—

(*a*) provide for the liability of any person under the declaration to be a charge on any debt or obligation due from the company to him, or on any mortgage or charge or any interest in a mortgage or charge on assets of the company held by or vested in him, or any person on his behalf, or any person claiming as assignee from or through the person liable or any person acting on his behalf, and

(*b*) from time to time make such further order as may be necessary for enforcing any charge imposed under this subsection.

(3) For the purposes of subsection (2), "assignee"—

(*a*) includes a person to whom or in whose favour, by the directions of the person made liable, the debt, obligation, mortgage or charge was created, issued or transferred or the interest created, but

(*b*) does not include an assignee for valuable consideration (not including consideration by way of marriage) given in good faith and without notice of any of the matters on the ground of which the declaration is made.

(4) Where the court makes a declaration under either section in relation to a person who is a creditor of the company, it may direct that the whole or any part of any debt owed by the company to that person and any interest thereon shall rank in priority after all other debts owed by the company and after any interest on those debts.

(5) Sections 213 and 214 have effect notwithstanding that the person concerned may be criminally liable in respect of matters on the ground of which the declaration under the section is to be made.

Restriction on re-use of company names

216.—(1) This section applies to a person where a company ("the liquidating company") has gone into insolvent liquidation on or after the appointed day and he was a director or shadow director of the company at any time in the period of 12 months ending with the day before it went into liquidation.

(2) For the purposes of this section, a name is a prohibited name in relation to such a person if—

> (*a*) it is a name by which the liquidating company was known at any time in that period of 12 months, or
>
> (*b*) it is a name which is so similar to a name falling within paragraph (*a*) as to suggest an association with that company.

(3) Except with leave of the court or in such circumstances as may be prescribed, a person to whom this section applies shall not at any time in the period of five years beginning with the day on which the liquidating company went into liquidation—

> (*a*) be a director of any other company that is known by a prohibited name, or
>
> (*b*) in any way, whether directly or indirectly, be concerned or take part in the promotion, formation or management of any such company, or
>
> (*c*) in any way, whether directly or indirectly, be concerned or take part in the carrying on of a business carried on (otherwise than by a company) under a prohibited name.

(4) If a person acts in contravention of this section, he is liable to imprisonment or a fine, or both.

(5) In subsection (3) "the court" means any court having jurisdiction to wind up companies; and on an application for leave under that subsection, the Secretary of State or the official receiver may appear and call the attention of the court to any matters which seem to him to be relevant.

(6) References in this section, in relation to any time, to a name by which a company is known are to the name of the company at that time or to any name under which the company carries on business at that time.

(7) For the purposes of this section a company goes into insolvent liquidation if it goes into liquidation at a time when its assets are insufficient for the payment of its debts and other liabilities and the expenses of the winding up.

(8) In this section "company" includes a company which may be wound up under Part V of this Act.

Personal liability for debts, following contravention of s.216

217.—(1) A person is personally responsible for all the relevant debts of a company if at any time—

> (*a*) in contravention of section 216, he is involved in the management of the company, or
>
> (*b*) as a person who is involved in the management of the company, he acts or is willing to act on instructions given (without the leave of the court) by a person whom he knows at that time to be in contravention in relation to the company of section 216.

(2) Where a person is personally responsible under this section for the relevant debts of a company, he is jointly and severally liable in respect of those debts with the company and any other person who, whether under this section or otherwise, is so liable.

(3) For the purposes of this section the relevant debts of a company are—

> (*a*) in relation to a person who is personally responsible under paragraph (*a*) of subsection (1), such debts and other liabilities of the company as are incurred at a time when that person was involved in the management of the company, and
>
> (*b*) in relation to a person who is personally responsible under paragraph (*b*) of that subsection, such debts and other liabilities of the company as are incurred at a time when that person was acting or was willing to act on instructions given as mentioned in that paragraph.

(4) For the purposes of this section, a person is involved in the manage-

ment of a company if he is a director of the company or if he is concerned, whether directly or indirectly, or takes part, in the management of the company.

(5) For the purposes of this section a person who, as a person involved in the management of a company, has at any time acted on instructions given (without the leave of the court) by a person whom he knew at that time to be in contravention in relation to the company of section 216 is presumed, unless the contrary is shown, to have been willing at any time thereafter to act on any instructions given by that person.

(6) In this section "company" includes a company which may be wound up under Part V.

Investigation and prosecution of malpractice

Prosecution of delinquent officers and members of company

218.—(1) If it appears to the court in the course of a winding up by the court that any past or present officer, or any member, of the company has been guilty of any offence in relation to the company for which he is criminally liable, the court may (either on the application of a person interested in the winding up or of its own motion) direct the liquidator to refer the matter to the prosecuting authority.

(2) "The prosecuting authority" means—

(*a*) in the case of a winding up in England and Wales, the Director of Public Prosecutions, and

(*b*) in the case of a winding up in Scotland, the Lord Advocate.

(3) If in the case of a winding up by the court in England and Wales it appears to the liquidator, not being the official receiver, that any past or present officer of the company, or any member of it, has been guilty of an offence in relation to the company for which he is criminally liable, the liquidator shall report the matter to the official receiver.

(4) If it appears to the liquidator in the course of a voluntary winding up that any past or present officer of the company, or any member of it, has been guilty of an offence in relation to the company for which he is criminally liable, he shall—

(*a*) forthwith report the matter to the prosecuting authority, and

(*b*) furnish to that authority such information and give to him such access to and facilities for inspecting and taking copies of documents (being information or documents in the possession or under the control of the liquidator and relating to the matter in question) as the authority requires.

[1] (5) Where a report is made to him under subsection (4), the prosecuting authority may, if he thinks fit, refer the matter to the Secretary of State for further enquiry; and the Secretary of State—

(*a*) shall thereupon investigate the matter reported to him and such other matters relating to the affairs of the company as appear to him to require investigation, and

(*b*) for the purpose of his investigation may exercise any of the powers which are exercisable by inspectors appointed under section 431 or 432 of the Companies Act to investigate a company's affairs.

(6) If it appears to the court in the course of a voluntary winding up that—

(*a*) any past or present officer of the company, or any member of it, has been guilty as above-mentioned, and

(*b*) no report with respect to the matter has been made by the liquidator to the prosecuting authority under subsection (4),

the court may (on the application of any person interested in the winding up or of its own motion) direct the liquidator to make such a report.

On a report being made accordingly, this section has effect as though the report had been made in pursuance of subsection (4).

NOTE
[1] As amended by the Companies Act 1989, s.78.

Obligations arising under s.218

219.—(1) For the purpose of an investigation by the Secretary of State under section 218(5), any obligation imposed on a person by any provision of the Companies Act to produce documents or give information to, or otherwise to assist, inspectors appointed as mentioned in that subsection is to be regarded as an obligation similarly to assist the Secretary of State in his investigation.

(2) An answer given by a person to a question put to him in exercise of the powers conferred by section 218(5) may be used in evidence against him.

(3) Where criminal proceedings are instituted by the prosecuting authority or the Secretary of State following any report or reference under section 218, it is the duty of the liquidator and every officer and agent of the company past and present (other than the defendant or defender) to give to that authority or the Secretary of State (as the case may be) all assistance in connection with the prosecution which he is reasonably able to give.

For this purpose "agent" includes any banker or solicitor of the company and any person employed by the company as auditor, whether that person is or is not an officer of the company.

(4) If a person fails or neglects to give assistance in the manner required by subsection (3), the court may, on the application of the prosecuting authority or the Secretary of State (as the case may be) direct the person to comply with that subsection; and if the application is made with respect to a liquidator, the court may (unless it appears that the failure or neglect to comply was due to the liquidator not having in his hands sufficient assets of the company to enable him to do so) direct that the costs shall be borne by the liquidator personally.

[1] PART V

WINDING UP OF UNREGISTERED COMPANIES

NOTE
[1] See the Criminal Justice (Scotland) Act 1987, s.35(4), and the Criminal Justice Act 1988, s.86(5).

Meaning of "unregistered company"

220.—(1) For the purposes of this Part, the expression "unregistered company" includes any trustee savings bank certified under the enactments relating to such banks, any association and any company, with the following exceptions—

(*a*) a railway company incorporated by Act of Parliament,

(*b*) a company registered in any part of the United Kingdom under the Joint Stock Companies Acts or under the legislation (past or present) relating to companies in Great Britain.

(2) On such day as the Treasury appoints by order under section 4(3) of the Trustee Savings Banks Act 1985, the words in subsection (1) from "any trustee" to "banks" cease to have effect and are hereby repealed.

Winding up of unregistered companies

221.—(1) Subject to the provisions of this Part, any unregistered company may be wound up under this Act; and all the provisions of this Act and the Companies Act about winding up apply to any unregistered company with the exceptions and additions mentioned in the following subsections.

(2) If an unregistered company has a principal place of business situated in Northern Ireland, it shall not be wound up under this Part unless it has a principal place of business situated in England and Wales or Scotland, or in both England and Wales and Scotland.

(3) For the purpose of determining a court's winding-up jurisdiction, an unregistered company is deemed—

(*a*) to be registered in England and Wales or Scotland, according as its principal place of business is situated in England and Wales or Scotland, or

(*b*) if it has a principal place of business situated in both countries, to be registered in both countries;

and the principal place of business situated in that part of Great Britain in which proceedings are being instituted is, for all purposes of the winding up, deemed to be the registered office of the company.

(4) No unregistered company shall be wound up under this Act voluntarily.

(5) The circumstances in which an unregistered company may be wound up are as follows—

(*a*) if the company is dissolved, or has ceased to carry on business, or is carrying on business only for the purpose of winding up its affairs;

(*b*) if the company is unable to pay its debts;

(*c*) if the court is of opinion that it is just and equitable that the company should be wound up.

(6) A petition for winding up a trustee savings bank may be presented by the Trustee Savings Banks Central Board or by a commissioner appointed under section 35 of the Trustee Savings Banks Act 1981 as well as by any person authorised under Part IV of this Act to present a petition for the winding up of a company.

On such day as the Treasury appoints by order under section 4(3) of the Trustee Savings Banks Act 1985, this subsection ceases to have effect and is hereby repealed.

(7) In Scotland, an unregistered company which the Court of Session has jurisdiction to wind up may be wound up by the court if there is subsisting a floating charge over property comprised in the company's property and undertaking, and the court is satisfied that the security of the creditor entitled to the benefit of the floating charge is in jeopardy.

For this purpose a creditor's security is deemed to be in jeopardy if the court is satisfied that events have occurred or are about to occur which render it unreasonable in the creditor's interests that the company should retain power to dispose of the property which is subject to the floating charge.

Inability to pay debts: unpaid creditor for £750 or more

222.—(1) An unregistered company is deemed (for the purposes of section 221) unable to pay its debts if there is a creditor, by assignment or otherwise, to whom the company is indebted in a sum exceeding £750 then due and—

(*a*) the creditor has served on the company, by leaving at its principal place of business, or by delivering to the secretary or some director, manager or principal officer of the company, or by otherwise serving in such manner as the court may approve or direct, a written demand in the prescribed form requiring the company to pay the sum due, and

(*b*) the company has for three weeks after the service of the demand neglected to pay the sum or to secure or compound for it to the creditor's satisfaction.

(2) The money sum for the time being specified in subsection (1) is subject to increase or reduction by regulations under section 417 in Part XV; but no increase in the sum so specified affects any case in which the winding-up petition was presented before the coming into force of the increase.

Inability to pay debts: debt remaining unsatisfied after action brought

223. An unregistered company is deemed (for the purposes of section 221) unable to pay its debts if an action or other proceeding has been instituted against any member for any debt or demand due, or claimed to be due, from the company, or from him in his character of member, and—

(*a*) notice in writing of the institution of the action or proceeding has been served on the company by leaving it at the company's principal place of business (or by delivering it to the secretary, or some director, manager or principal officer of the company, or by otherwise serving it in such manner as the court may approve or direct), and

(*b*) the company has not within three weeks after service of the notice paid, secured or compounded for the debt or demand, or procured the action or proceeding to be stayed or sisted, or indemnified the defendant or defender to his reasonable satisfaction against the action or proceeding, and against all costs, damages and expenses to be incurred by him because of it.

Inability to pay debts: other cases

224.—(1) An unregistered company is deemed (for purposes of section 221) unable to pay its debts—

(*a*) if in England and Wales execution or other process issued on a judgment, decree or order obtained in any court in favour of a creditor against the company, or any member of it as such, or any person authorised to be sued as nominal defendant on behalf of the company, is returned unsatisfied;

(*b*) if in Scotland the *induciae* of a charge for payment on an extract decree, or an extract registered bond, or an extract registered protest, have expired without payment being made;

(*c*) if in Northern Ireland a certificate of unenforceability has been granted in respect of any judgment, decree or order obtained as mentioned in paragraph (*a*);

(*d*) if it is otherwise proved to the satisfaction of the court that the company is unable to pay its debts as they fall due.

(2) An unregistered company is also deemed unable to pay its debts if it is proved to the satisfaction of the court that the value of the company's assets is less than the amount of its liabilities, taking into account its contingent and prospective liabilities.

Oversea company may be wound up though dissolved

225. Where a company incorporated outside Great Britain which has been carrying on business in Great Britain ceases to carry on business in Great Britain, it may be wound up as an unregistered company under this Act, notwithstanding that it has been dissolved or otherwise ceased to exist as a company under or by virtue of the laws of the country under which it was incorporated.

Contributories in winding up of unregistered company

226.—(1) In the event of an unregistered company being wound up, every person is deemed a contributory who is liable to pay or contribute to the payment of any debt or liability of the company, or to pay or contribute to the payment of any sum for the adjustment of the rights of members among themselves, or to pay or contribute to the payment of the expenses of winding up the company.

(2) Every contributory is liable to contribute to the company's assets all sums due from him in respect of any such liability as is mentioned above.

(3) In the case of an unregistered company engaged in or formed for working mines within the stannaries, a past member is not liable to contribute to the assets if he has ceased to be a member for two years or more either before the mine ceased to be worked or before the date of the winding-up order.

(4) In the event of the death, bankruptcy or insolvency of any contributory, the provisions of this Act with respect to the personal representatives,

to the heirs and legatees of heritage of the heritable estate in Scotland of deceased contributories, and to the trustees of bankrupt or insolvent contributories, respectively apply.

Power of court to stay, sist or restrain proceedings

227. The provisions of this Part with respect to staying, sisting or restraining actions and proceedings against a company at any time after the presentation of a petition for winding up and before the making of a winding-up order extend, in the case of an unregistered company, where the application to stay, sist or restrain is presented by a creditor, to actions and proceedings against any contributory of the company.

Actions stayed on winding-up order

228. Where an order has been made for winding up an unregistered company, no action or proceeding shall be proceeded with or commenced against any contributory of the company in respect of any debt of the company, except by leave of the court, and subject to such terms as the court may impose.

Provisions of this Part to be cumulative

229.—(1) The provisions of this Part with respect to unregistered companies are in addition to and not in restriction of any provisions in Part IV with respect to winding up companies by the court; and the court or liquidator may exercise any powers or do any act in the case of unregistered companies which might be exercised or done by it or him in winding up companies formed and registered under the Companies Act.

(2) However, an unregistered company is not, except in the event of its being wound up, deemed to be a company under the Companies Act, and then only to the extent provided by this Part of this Act.

[1] PART VI

NOTE
[1] Applied by the Building Societies Act 1986, Sched. 15, Pt. I, with effect from 1st January 1988.

MISCELLANEOUS PROVISIONS APPLYING TO COMPANIES WHICH ARE INSOLVENT OR IN LIQUIDATION

Office-holders

Holders of office to be qualified insolvency practitioners

230.—(1) Where an administration order is made in relation to a company, the administrator must be a person who is qualified to act as an insolvency practitioner in relation to the company.

(2) Where an administrative receiver of a company is appointed, he must be a person who is so qualified.

(3) Where a company goes into liquidation, the liquidator must be a person who is so qualified.

(4) Where a provisional liquidator is appointed, he must be a person who is so qualified.

(5) Subsections (3) and (4) are without prejudice to any enactment under which the official receiver is to be, or may be, liquidator or provisional liquidator.

Appointment to office of two or more persons

231.—(1) This section applies if an appointment or nomination of any person to the office of administrator, administrative receiver, liquidator or provisional liquidator—

(*a*) relates to more than one person, or

(*b*) has the effect that the office is to be held by more than one person.

(2) The appointment or nomination shall declare whether any act required or authorised under any enactment to be done by the adminis-

trator, administrative receiver, liquidator or provisional liquidator is to be done by all or any one or more of the persons for the time being holding the office in question.

Validity of office-holder's acts

232. The acts of an individual as administrator, administrative receiver, liquidator or provisional liquidator of a company are valid notwithstanding any defect in his appointment, nomination or qualifications.

Management by administrators, liquidators, etc.

Supplies of gas, water, electricity, etc.

233.—(1) This section applies in the case of a company where—

(*a*) an administration order is made in relation to the company, or

(*b*) an administrative receiver is appointed, or

(*c*) a voluntary arrangement under Part I, approved by meetings summoned under section 3, has taken effect, or

(*d*) the company goes into liquidation, or

(*e*) a provisional liquidator is appointed;

and "the office-holder" means the administrator, the administrative receiver, the supervisor of the voluntary arrangement, the liquidator or the provisional liquidator, as the case may be.

(2) If a request is made by or with the concurrence of the office-holder for the giving, after the effective date, of any of the supplies mentioned in the next subsection, the supplier—

(*a*) may make it a condition of the giving of the supply that the office-holder personally guarantees the payment of any charges in respect of the supply, but

(*b*) shall not make it a condition of the giving of the supply, or do anything which has the effect of making it a condition of the giving of the supply, that any outstanding charges in respect of a supply given to the company before the effective date are paid.

(3) The supplies referred to in subsection (2) are—

(*a*) a public supply of gas,

(*b*) a public supply of electricity,

(*c*) a supply of water by statutory water undertakers or, in Scotland, a water authority,

(*d*) a supply of telecommunication services by a public telecommunications operator.

(4) "The effective date" for the purposes of this section is whichever is applicable of the following dates—

(*a*) the date on which the administration order was made,

(*b*) the date on which the administrative receiver was appointed (or, if he was appointed in succession to another administrative receiver, the date on which the first of his predecessors was appointed),

(*c*) the date on which the voluntary arrangement was approved by the meetings summoned under section 3,

(*d*) the date on which the company went into liquidation,

(*e*) the date on which the provisional liquidator was appointed.

(5) The following applies to expressions used in subsection (3)—

(*a*) "public supply of gas" means a supply of gas by the British Gas Corporation or a public gas supplier within the meaning of Part I of the Gas Act 1986,

(*b*) "public supply of electricity" means a supply of electricity by a public electricity supplier within the meaning of Part I of the Electricity Act 1989,

(*c*) "water authority" means the same as in the Water (Scotland) Act 1980, and

(*d*) "telecommunication services" and "public telecommunications operator" mean the same as in the Telecommunications Act 1984, except that the former does not include services consisting in the conveyance of programmes included in cable programme services (within the meaning of the Cable and Broadcasting Act 1984).

NOTE

As amended by the Electricity Act 1989, Sched. 16, para. 35.

Getting in the company's property

234.—(1) This section applies in the case of a company where—

(*a*) an administration order is made in relation to the company, or

(*b*) an administrative receiver is appointed, or

(*c*) the company goes into liquidation, or

(*d*) a provisional liquidator is appointed;

and "the office-holder" means the administrator, the administrative receiver, the liquidator or the provisional liquidator, as the case may be.

(2) Where any person has in his possession or control any property, books, papers or records to which the company appears to be entitled, the court may require that person forthwith (or within such period as the court may direct) to pay, deliver, convey, surrender or transfer the property, books, papers or records to the office-holder.

(3) Where the office-holder—

(*a*) seizes or disposes of any property which is not property of the company, and

(*b*) at the time of seizure or disposal believes, and has reasonable grounds for believing, that he is entitled (whether in pursuance of an order of the court or otherwise) to seize or dispose of that property.

the next subsection has effect.

(4) In that case the office-holder—

(*a*) is not liable to any person in respect of any loss or damage resulting from the seizure or disposal except in so far as that loss or damage is caused by the office-holder's own negligence, and

(*b*) has a lien on the property, or the proceeds of its sale, for such expenses as were incurred in connection with the seizure or disposal.

Duty to co-operate with office-holder

235.—(1) This section applies as does section 234; and it also applies, in the case of a company in respect of which a winding-up order has been made by the court in England and Wales, as if references to the office-holder included the official receiver, whether or not he is the liquidator.

(2) Each of the persons mentioned in the next subsection shall—

(*a*) give to the office-holder such information concerning the company and its promotion, formation, business, dealings, affairs or property as the office-holder may at any time after the effective date reasonably require, and

(*b*) attend on the office-holder at such times as the latter may reasonably require.

(3) The persons referred to above are—

(*a*) those who are or have at any time been officers of the company,

(*b*) those who have taken part in the formation of the company at any time within one year before the effective date,

(*c*) those who are in the employment of the company, or have been in its employment (including employment under a contract for services) within that year, and are in the office-holder's opinion capable of giving information which he requires,

(*d*) those who are, or have within that year been, officers of, or in the employment (including employment under a contract for services) of, another company which is, or within that year was, an officer of the company in question, and

(*e*) in the case of a company being wound up by the court, any person who has acted as administrator, administrative receiver or liquidator of the company

(4) For the purposes of subsections (2) and (3), "the effective date" is whichever is applicable of the following dates—

(*a*) the date on which the administration order was made,

(*b*) the date on which the administrative receiver was appointed or, if he was appointed in succession to another administrative receiver, the date on which the first of his predecessors was appointed,

(*c*) the date on which the provisional liquidator was appointed, and

(*d*) the date on which the company went into liquidation.

(5) If a person without reasonable excuse fails to comply with any obligation imposed by this section, he is liable to a fine and, for continued contravention, to a daily default fine.

Inquiry into company's dealings, etc.

236.—(1) This section applies as does section 234; and it also applies in the case of a company in respect of which a winding-up order has been made by the court in England and Wales as if references to the office-holder included the official receiver, whether or not he is the liquidator.

(2) The court may, on the application of the office-holder, summon to appear before it—

(*a*) any officer of the company,

(*b*) any person known or suspected to have in his possession any property of the company or supposed to be indebted to the company, or

(*c*) any person whom the court thinks capable of giving information concerning the promotion, formation, business, dealings, affairs or property of the company.

(3) The court may require any such person as is mentioned in subsection (2)(*a*) to (*c*) to submit an affidavit to the court containing an account of his dealings with the company or to produce any books, papers or other records in his possession or under his control relating to the company or the matters mentioned in paragraph (*c*) of the subsection.

(4) The following applies in a case where—

(*a*) a person without reasonable excuse fails to appear before the court when he is summoned to do so under this section, or

(*b*) there are reasonable grounds for believing that a person has absconded, or is about to abscond, with a view to avoiding his appearance before the court under this section.

(5) The court may, for the purpose of bringing that person and anything in his possession before the court, cause a warrant to be issued to a constable or prescribed officer of the court—

(*a*) for the arrest of that person, and

(*b*) for the seizure of any books, papers, records, money or goods in that person's possession.

(6) The court may authorise a person arrested under such a warrant to be kept in custody, and anything seized under such a warrant to be held, in accordance with the rules, until that person is brought before the court under the warrant or until such other time as the court may order.

Court's enforcement powers under s.236

237.—(1) If it appears to the court, on consideration of any evidence obtained under section 236 or this section, that any person has in his possession any property of the company, the court may, on the application of the office-holder, order that person to deliver the whole or any part of the property to the office-holder at such time, in such manner and on such terms as the court thinks fit.

(2) If it appears to the court, on consideration of any evidence so obtained, that any person is indebted to the company, the court may, on the application of the office-holder, order that person to pay to the office-holder, at such time and in such manner as the court may direct, the whole or any part of the amount due, whether in full discharge of the debt or otherwise, as the court thinks fit.

(3) The court may, if it thinks fit, order that any person who if within the jurisdiction of the court would be liable to be summoned to appear before it under section 236 or this section shall be examined in any part of the United Kingdom where he may for the time being be, or in a place outside the United Kingdom.

(4) Any person who appears or is brought before the court under section 236 or this section may be examined on oath, either orally or (except in Scotland) by interrogatories, concerning the company or the matters mentioned in section 236(2)(*c*).

Adjustment of prior transactions (administration and liquidation)

238–241. [Not applicable to Scotland.]

[¹ **238.**—(1) This section applies in the case of a company where—
   (*a*) an administration order is made in relation to the company, or
   (*b*) the company goes into liquidation;
and "the office-holder" means the administrator or the liquidator, as the case may be.]

NOTE
¹ Not applicable to Scotland; but see s.245(1).

Gratuitous alienations (Scotland)
242.—(1) Where this subsection applies and—
   (*a*) the winding up of a company has commenced, an alienation by the company is challengeable by—
      (i) any creditor who is a creditor by virtue of a debt incurred on or before the date of such commencement, or
      (ii) the liquidator;
   (*b*) an administration order is in force in relation to a company, and alienation by the company is challengeable by the administrator.
(2) Subsection (1) applies where—
   (*a*) by the alienation, whether before or after 1st April 1986 (the coming into force of section 75 of the Bankruptcy (Scotland) Act 1985), any part of the company's property is transferred or any claim or right of the company is discharged or renounced, and
   (*b*) the alienation takes place on a relevant day.
(3) For the purposes of subsection (2)(*b*), the day on which an alienation takes place is the day on which it becomes completely effectual; and in that subsection "relevant day" means, if the alienation has the effect of favouring—
   (*a*) a person who is an associate (within the meaning of the Bankruptcy (Scotland) Act 1985) of the company, a day not earlier than five years before the date on which—
      (i) the winding up of the company commences, or
      (ii) as the case may be, the administration order is made; or
   (*b*) any other person, a day not earlier than two years before that date.
(4) On a challenge being brought under subsection (1), the court shall grant decree of reduction or for such restoration of property to the company's assets or other redress as may be appropriate; but the court shall not grant such a decree if the person seeking to uphold the alienation establishes—
   (*a*) that immediately, or at any other time, after the alienation the company's assets were greater than its liabilities, or
   (*b*) that the alienation was made for adequate consideration, or
   (*c*) that the alienation—
      (i) was a birthday, Christmas or other conventional gift, or
      (ii) was a gift made, for a charitable purpose, to a person who is not an associate of the company,

which, having regard to all the circumstances, it was reasonable for the company to make:

Provided that this subsection is without prejudice to any right or interest acquired in good faith and for value from or through the transferee in the alienation.

(5) In subsection (4) above, "charitable purpose" means any charitable, benevolent or philanthropic purpose, whether or not it is charitable within the meaning of any rule of law.

(6) For the purposes of the foregoing provisions of this section, an alienation in implementation of a prior obligation is deemed to be one for which there was no consideration or no adequate consideration to the extent that the prior obligation was undertaken for no consideration or no adequate consideration.

(7) A liquidator and an administrator have the same right as a creditor has under any rule of law to challenge an alienation of a company made for no consideration or no adequate consideration.

(8) This section applies to Scotland only.

Unfair preferences (Scotland)

243.—(1) Subject to subsection (2) below, subsection (4) below applies to a transaction entered into by a company, whether before or after 1st April 1986, which has the effect of creating a preference in favour of a creditor to the prejudice of the general body of creditors, being a preference created not earlier than six months before the commencement of the winding up of the company or the making of an administration order in relation to the company.

(2) Subsection (4) below does not apply to any of the following transactions—

(*a*) a transaction in the ordinary course of trade or business;

(*b*) a payment in cash for a debt which when it was paid had become payable, unless the transaction was collusive with the purpose of prejudicing the general body of creditors;

(*c*) a transaction whereby the parties to it undertake reciprocal obligations (whether the performance by the parties of their respective obligations occurs at the same time or at different times) unless the transaction was collusive as aforesaid;

(*d*) the granting of a mandate by a company authorising an arrestee to pay over the arrested funds or part thereof to the arrester where—

  (i) there has been a decree for payment or a warrant for summary diligence, and

  (ii) the decree or warrant has been preceded by an arrestment on the dependence of the action or followed by an arrestment in execution.

(3) For the purposes of subsection (1) above, the day on which a preference was created is the day on which the preference became completely effectual.

(4) A transaction to which this subsection applies is challengeable by—

(*a*) in the case of a winding up—

  (i) any creditor who is a creditor by virtue of a debt incurred on or before the date of commencement of the winding up, or

  (ii) the liquidator; and

(*b*) in the case of an administration order, the administrator.

(5) On a challenge being brought under subsection (4) above, the court, if satisfied that the transaction challenged is a transaction to which this section applies, shall grant decree of reduction or for such restoration of property to the company's assets or other redress as may be appropriate:

Provided that this subsection is without prejudice to any right or interest acquired in good faith and for value from or through the creditor in whose favour the preference was created.

(6) A liquidator and an administrator have the same right as a creditor has under any rule of law to challenge a preference created by a debtor.

(7) This section applies to Scotland only.

Extortionate credit transactions

244.—(1) This section applies as does section 238, and where the company is, or has been, a party to a transaction for, or involving, the provision of credit to the company.

(2) The court may, on the application of the office-holder, make an order with respect to the transaction if the transaction is or was extortionate and was entered into in the period of three years ending with the day on which the administration order was made or (as the case may be) the company went into liquidation.

(3) For the purposes of this section a transaction is extortionate if, having regard to the risk accepted by the person providing the credit—

(*a*) the terms of it are or were such as to require grossly exorbitant payments to be made (whether unconditionally or in certain contingencies) in respect of the provisions of the credit, or

(*b*) it otherwise grossly contravened ordinary principles of fair dealing;

and it shall be presumed, unless the contrary is proved, that a transaction with respect to which an application is made under this section is or, as the case may be, was extortionate.

(4) An order under this section with respect to any transaction may contain such one or more of the following as the court thinks fit, that is to say—

(*a*) provision setting aside the whole or part of any obligation created by the transaction,

(*b*) provision otherwise varying the terms of the transaction or varying the terms on which any security for the purposes of the transaction is held,

(*c*) provision requiring any person who is or was a party to the transaction to pay to the office-holder any sums paid to that person, by virtue of the transaction, by the company,

(*d*) provision requiring any person to surrender to the office-holder any property held by him as security for the purposes of the transaction,

(*e*) provision directing accounts to be taken between any persons.

(5) The powers conferred by this section are exercisable in relation to any transaction concurrently with any powers exercisable in relation to that transaction as a transaction at an undervalue or under section 242 (gratuitous alienations in Scotland).

Avoidance of certain floating charges

245.—(1) This section applies as does section 238, but applies to Scotland as well as to England and Wales.

(2) Subject as follows, a floating charge on the company's undertaking or property created at a relevant time is invalid except to the extent of the aggregate of—

(*a*) the value of so much of the consideration for the creation of the charge as consists of money paid, or goods or services supplied, to the company at the same time as, or after, the creation of the charge,

(*b*) the value of so much of that consideration as consists of the discharge or reduction, at the same time as, or after, the creation of the charge, of any debt of the company, and

(*c*) the amount of such interest (if any) as is payable on the amount falling within paragraph (*a*) or (*b*) in pursuance of any agreement under which the money was so paid, the goods or services were so supplied or the debt was so discharged or reduced.

(3) Subject to the next subsection, the time at which a floating charge is created by a company is a relevant time for the purposes of this section if the charge is created—

    (*a*) in the case of a charge which is created in favour of a person who is connected with the company, at a time in the period of two years ending with the onset of insolvency,

    (*b*) in the case of a charge which is created in favour of any other person, at a time in the period of 12 months ending with the onset of insolvency, or

    (*c*) in either case, at a time between the presentation of a petition for the making of an administration order in relation to the company and the making of such an order on that petition.

(4) Where a company creates a floating charge at a time mentioned in subsection (3)(*b*) and the person in favour of whom the charge is created is not connected with the company, that time is not a relevant time for the purposes of this section unless the company—

    (*a*) is at that time unable to pay its debts within the meaning of section 123 in Chapter VI of Part IV, or

    (*b*) becomes unable to pay its debts within the meaning of that section in consequence of the transaction under which the charge is created.

(5) For the purposes of subsection (3), the onset of insolvency is—

    (*a*) in a case where this section applies by reason of the making of an administration order, the date of the presentation of the petition on which the order was made, and

    (*b*) in a case where this section applies by reason of a company going into liquidation, the date of the commencement of the winding up.

(6) For the purposes of subsection (2)(*a*) the value of any goods or services supplied by way of consideration for a floating charge is the amount in money which at the time they were supplied could reasonably have been expected to be obtained for supplying the goods or services in the ordinary course of business and on the same terms (apart from the consideration) as those on which they were supplied to the company.

246. [Not applicable to Scotland.]

[1] Part VII

NOTE

[1] Applied by the Building Societies Act 1986, Sched. 15, Pt. I, with effect from 1st January 1988.

Interpretation for First Group of Parts

"Insolvency" and "go into liquidation"

247.—(1) In this Group of Parts, except in so far as the context otherwise requires, "insolvency", in relation to a company, includes the approval of a voluntary arrangement under Part I, the making of an administration order or the appointment of an administrative receiver.

(2) For the purposes of any provision in this Group of Parts, a company goes into liquidation if it passes a resolution for voluntary winding up or an order for its winding up is made by the court at a time when it has not already gone into liquidation by passing such a resolution.

"Secured creditor", etc.

248. In this Group of Parts, except in so far as the context otherwise requires—

    (*a*) "secured creditor", in relation to a company, means a creditor of the company who holds in respect of his debt a security over property of the company, and "unsecured creditor" is to be read accordingly; and

(*b*) "security" means—
  (i) in relation to England and Wales, any mortgage, charge, lien or other security, and
  (ii) in relation to Scotland, any security (whether heritable or moveable), any floating charge and any right of lien or preference and any right of retention (other than a right of compensation or set off).

"Connected" with a company

249. For the purposes of any provision in this Group of Parts, a person is connected with a company if—
  (*a*) he is a director or shadow director of the company or an associate of such a director or shadow director, or
  (*b*) he is an associate of the company;
and "associate" has the meaning given by section 435 in Part XVIII of this Act.

"Member" of a company

250. For the purposes of any provision in this Group of Parts, a person who is not a member of a company but to whom shares in the company have been transferred, or transmitted by operation of law, is to be regarded as a member of the company, and references to a member or members are to be read accordingly.

Expressions used generally

251. In this Group of Parts, except in so far as the context otherwise requires—
  "administrative receiver" means—
    (*a*) an administrative receiver as defined by section 29(2) in Chapter I of Part III, or
    (*b*) a receiver appointed under section 51 in Chapter II of that Part in a case where the whole (or substantially the whole) of the company's property is attached by the floating charge;
  "business day" means any day other than a Saturday, a Sunday, Christmas Day, Good Friday or a day which is a bank holiday in any part of Great Britain;
  "chattel leasing agreement" means an agreement for the bailment or, in Scotland, the hiring of goods which is capable of subsisting for more than three months;
  "contributory" has the meaning given by section 79;
  "director" includes any person occupying the position of director, by whatever name called;
  "floating charge" means a charge which, as created, was a floating charge and includes a floating charge within section 462 of the Companies Act (Scottish floating charges);
  "office copy", in relation to Scotland, means a copy certified by the clerk of court;
  "the official rate", in relation to interest, means the rate payable under section 189(4);
  "prescribed" means prescribed by the rules;
  "receiver", in the expression "receiver or manager", does not include a receiver appointed under section 51 in Chapter II of Part III;
  "retention of title agreement" means an agreement for the sale of goods to a company, being an agreement—
    (*a*) which does not constitute a charge on the goods, but
    (*b*) under which, if the seller is not paid and the company is wound up, the seller will have priority over all other creditors of the company as respects the goods or any property representing the goods;

"the rules" means rules under section 411 in Part XV; and

"shadow director", in relation to a company, means a person in accordance with whose directions or instructions the directors of the company are accustomed to act (but so that a person is not deemed a shadow director by reason only that the directors act on advice given by him in a professional capacity);

and any expression for whose interpretation provision is made by Part XXVI of the Companies Act, other than an expression defined above in this section, is to be construed in accordance with that provision.

. . . . . .

THE THIRD GROUP OF PARTS
MISCELLANEOUS MATTERS BEARING ON BOTH COMPANY AND INDIVIDUAL INSOLVENCY; GENERAL INTERPRETATION; FINAL PROVISIONS

[1] PART XII

NOTE
[1] Applied by the Building Societies Act 1986, Sched. 15, Pt. I, and applied (*mod.*) by *ibid.* Pt. II, with effect from 1st January 1988.

PREFERENTIAL DEBTS IN COMPANY AND INDIVIDUAL INSOLVENCY

Categories of preferential debts
386.—[1] (1) A reference in this Act to the preferential debts of a company or an individual is to the debts listed in Schedule 6 to this Act (money owed to the Inland Revenue for income tax deducted at source; VAT, car tax, betting and gaming duties; social security and pension scheme contributions; remuneration etc. of employees; levies on coal and steel production); and references to preferential creditors are to be read accordingly.

(2) In that Schedule "the debtor" means the company or the individual concerned.

(3) Schedule 6 is to be read with Schedule 3 to the Social Security Pensions Act 1975 (occupational pension scheme contributions).

NOTE
[1] As amended by S.I. 1987 No. 2093.

"The relevant date"
387.—(1) This section explains references in Schedule 6 to the relevant date (being the date which determines the existence and amount of a preferential debt).

(2) For the purposes of section 4 in Part I (meetings to consider company voluntary arrangement), the relevant date in relation to a company which is not being wound up is—

(a) where an administration order is in force in relation to the company, the date of the making of that order, and

(b) where no such order has been made, the date of the approval of the voluntary arrangement.

(3) In relation to a company which is being wound up, the following applies—

(a) if the winding up is by the court, and the winding-up order was made immediately upon the discharge of an administration order, the relevant date is the date of the making of the administration order;

(b) if the case does not fall within paragraph (a) and the company—
 (i) is being wound up by the court, and
 (ii) had not commenced to be wound up voluntarily before the date of the making of the winding-up order,

the relevant date is the date of the appointment (or first appointment) of a provisional liquidator or, if no such appointment has been made, the date of the winding-up order;

(*c*) if the case does not fall within either paragraph (*a*) or (*b*), the relevant date is the date of the passing of the resolution for the winding up of the company.

(4) In relation to a company in receivership (where section 40 or, as the case may be, section 59 applies), the relevant date is—

(*a*) in England and Wales, the date of the appointment of the receiver by debenture-holders, and

(*b*) in Scotland, the date of the appointment of the receiver under section 53(6) or (as the case may be) 54(5).

(5) For the purposes of section 258 in Part VIII (individual voluntary arrangements), the relevant date is, in relation to a debtor who is not an undischarged bankrupt, the date of the interim order made under section 252 with respect to his proposal.

(6) In relation to a bankrupt, the following applies—

(*a*) where at the time the bankruptcy order was made there was an interim receiver appointed under section 286, the relevant date is the date on which the interim receiver was first appointed after the presentation of the bankruptcy petition;

(*b*) otherwise, the relevant date is the date of the making of the bankruptcy order.

PART XIII

INSOLVENCY PRACTITIONERS AND THEIR QUALIFICATION

Restrictions on unqualified persons acting as liquidator, trustee in bankruptcy, etc.

Meaning of "act as insolvency practitioner"

388.—(1) A person acts as an insolvency practitioner in relation to a company by acting—

(*a*) as its liquidator, provisional liquidator, administrator or administrative receiver, or

(*b*) as supervisor of a voluntary arrangement approved by it under Part I.

(2) A person acts as an insolvency practitioner in relation to an individual by acting—

(*a*) as his trustee in bankruptcy or interim receiver of his property or as permanent or interim trustee in the sequestration of his estate; or

(*b*) as trustee under a deed which is a deed of arrangement made for the benefit of his creditors or, in Scotland, a trust deed for his creditors; or

(*c*) as supervisor of a voluntary arrangement proposed by him and approved under Part VIII; or

(*d*) in the case of a deceased individual to the administration of whose estate this section applies by virtue of an order under section 421 (application of provisions of this Act to insolvent estates of deceased persons), as administrator of that estate.

(3) References in this section to an individual include, except in so far as the context otherwise requires, references to a partnership and to any debtor within the meaning of the Bankruptcy (Scotland) Act 1985.

(4) In this section—

"administrative receiver" has the meaning given by section 251 in Part VII;

"company" means a company within the meaning given by section 735(1) of the Companies Act or a company which may be wound up under Part V of this Act (unregistered companies); and "interim trustee" and "permanent trustee" mean the same as in the Bankruptcy (Scotland) Act 1985.

(5) Nothing in this section applies to anything done by the official receiver.

Acting without qualification an offence

389.—(1) A person who acts as an insolvency practitioner in relation to a company or an individual at a time when he is not qualified to do so is liable to imprisonment or a fine, or to both.

(2) This section does not apply to the official receiver.

The requisite qualification, and the means of obtaining it

Persons not qualified to act as insolvency practitioners

¹ **390.**—(1) A person who is not an individual is not qualified to act as an insolvency practitioner.

(2) A person is not qualified to act as an insolvency practitioner at any time unless at that time—

    (*a*) he is authorised so to act by virtue of membership of a professional body recognised under section 391 below, being permitted so to act by or under the rules of that body, or

    (*b*) he holds an authorisation granted by a competent authority under section 393.

(3) A person is not qualified to act as an insolvency practitioner in relation to another person at any time unless—

    (*a*) there is in force at that time security or, in Scotland, caution for the proper performance of his functions, and

    (*b*) that security or caution meets the prescribed requirements with respect to his so acting in relation to that other person.

(4) A person is not qualified to act as an insolvency practitioner at any time if at that time—

    (*a*) he has been adjudged bankrupt or sequestration of his estate has been awarded and (in either case) he has not been discharged,

    (*b*) he is subject to a disqualification order made under the Company Directors Disqualification Act 1986, or

    (*c*) he is a patient within the meaning of Part VII of the Mental Health Act 1983 or section 125(1) of the Mental Health (Scotland) Act 1984.

NOTE
¹ For regulations see S.I. 1986 No. 1995, as amended by S.I. 1986 No. 2247.

Recognised professional bodies

391.—(1) The Secretary of State may by order declare a body which appears to him to fall within subsection (2) below to be a recognised professional body for the purposes of this section.

(2) A body may be recognised if it regulates the practice of a profession and maintains and enforces rules for securing that such of its members as are permitted by or under the rules to act as insolvency practitioners—

    (*a*) are fit and proper persons so to act, and

    (*b*) meet acceptable requirements as to education and practical training and experience.

(3) References to members of a recognised professional body are to persons who, whether members of that body or not, are subject to its rules in the practice of the profession in question.

The reference in section 390(2) above to membership of a professional body recognised under this section is to be read accordingly.

(4) An order made under subsection (1) in relation to a professional body may be revoked by a further order if it appears to the Secretary of State that the body no longer falls within subsection (2).

(5) An order of the Secretary of State under this section has effect from such date as is specified in the order; and any such order revoking a previous order may make provision whereby members of the body in question continue to be treated as authorised to act as insolvency practitioners for a specified period after the revocation takes effect.

Authorisation by competent authority
[1] **392.**—(1) Application may be made to a competent authority for authorisation to act as an insolvency practitioner.

(2) The competent authorities for this purpose are—
(a) in relation to a case of any description specified in directions given by the Secretary of State, the body or person so specified in relation to cases of that description, and
(b) in relation to a case not falling within paragraph (a), the Secretary of State.

(3) The application—
(a) shall be made in such manner as the competent authority may direct,
(b) shall contain or be accompanied by such information as that authority may reasonably require for the purpose of determining the application, and
(c) shall be accompanied by the prescribed fee;
and the authority may direct that notice of the making of the application shall be published in such manner as may be specified in the direction.

(4) At any time after receiving the application and before determining it the authority may require the applicant to furnish additional information.

(5) Directions and requirements given or imposed under subsection (3) or (4) may differ as between different applications.

(6) Any information to be furnished to the competent authority under this section shall, if it so requires, be in such form or verified in such manner as it may specify.

(7) An application may be withdrawn before it is granted or refused.

(8) Any sums received under this section by a competent authority other than the Secretary of State may be retained by the authority; and any sums so received by the Secretary of State shall be paid into the Consolidated Fund.

NOTE
[1] For regulations see S.I. 1986 No. 1995, as amended by S.I. 1986 No. 2247.

Grant, refusal and withdrawal of authorisation
[1] **393.**—(1) The competent authority may, on an application duly made in accordance with section 392 and after being furnished with all such information as it may require under that section, grant or refuse the application.

(2) The authority shall grant the application if it appears to it from the information furnished by the applicant and having regard to such other information, if any, as it may have—
(a) that the applicant is a fit and proper person to act as an insolvency practitioner, and
(b) that the applicant meets the prescribed requirements with respect to education and practical training and experience.

(3) An authorisation granted under this section, if not previously withdrawn, continues in force for such period not exceeding the prescribed maximum as may be specified in the authorisation.

(4) An authorisation so granted may be withdrawn by the competent authority if it appears to it—
(a) that the holder of the authorisation is no longer a fit and proper person to act as an insolvency practitioner, or
(b) without prejudice to paragraph (a), that the holder—
(i) has failed to comply with any provision of this Part or of any regulations made under this Part or Part XV, or

(ii) in purported compliance with any such provision, has furnished the competent authority with false, inaccurate or misleading information.

(5) An authorisation granted under this section may be withdrawn by the competent authority at the request or with the consent of the holder of the authorisation.

NOTE

[1] For regulations see S.I. 1986 No. 1995, as amended by S.I. 1986 No. 2247.

Notices

394.—(1) Where a competent authority grants an authorisation under section 393, it shall give written notice of that fact to the applicant, specifying the date on which the authorisation takes effect.

(2) Where the authority proposes to refuse an application, or to withdraw an authorisation under section 393(4), it shall give the applicant or holder of the authorisation written notice of its intention to do so, setting out particulars of the grounds on which it proposes to act.

(3) In the case of a proposed withdrawal the notice shall state the date on which it is proposed that the withdrawal should take effect.

(4) A notice under subsection (2) shall give particulars of the rights exercisable under the next two sections by a person on whom the notice is served.

Right to make representations

395.—(1) A person on whom a notice is served under section 394(2) may within 14 days after the date of service make written representations to the competent authority.

(2) The competent authority shall have regard to any representations so made in determining whether to refuse the application or withdraw the authorisation, as the case may be.

Reference to Tribunal

396.—(1) The Insolvency Practitioners Tribunal ("the Tribunal") continues in being; and the provisions of Schedule 7 apply to it.

(2) Where a person is served with a notice under section 394(2), he may—

(*a*) at any time within 28 days after the date of service of the notice, or

(*b*) at any time after the making by him of representations under section 395 and before the end of the period of 28 days after the date of the service on him of a notice by the competent authority that the authority does not propose to alter its decision in consequence of the representations,

given written notice to the authority requiring the case to be referred to the Tribunal.

(3) Where a requirement is made under subsection (2), then, unless the competent authority—

(*a*) has decided or decides to grant the application or, as the case may be, not to withdraw the authorisation, and

(*b*) within seven days after the date of the making of the requirement, gives written notice of that decision to the person by whom the requirement was made,

it shall refer the case to the Tribunal.

Action of Tribunal on reference

397.—(1) On a reference under section 396 the Tribunal shall—

(*a*) investigate the case, and

(*b*) make a report to the competent authority stating what would in their opinion be the appropriate decision in the matter and the reasons for that opinion,

and it is the duty of the competent authority to decide the matter accordingly.

(2) The Tribunal shall send a copy of the report to the applicant or, as the case may be, the holder of the authorisation; and the competent authority shall serve him with a written notice of the decision made by it in accordance with the report.

(3) The competent authority may, if he thinks fit, publish the report of the Tribunal.

Refusal or withdrawal without reference to Tribunal

398. Where in the case of any proposed refusal or withdrawal of an authorisation either—

(a) the period mentioned in section 396(2)(a) has expired without the making of any requirement under that subsection or of any representations under section 395, or

(b) the competent authority has given a notice such as is mentioned in section 396(2)(b) and the period so mentioned has expired without the making of any such requirement,

the competent authority may give written notice of the refusal or withdrawal to the person concerned in accordance with the proposal in the notice given under section 394(2).

PART XIV

PUBLIC ADMINISTRATION (ENGLAND AND WALES)

. . . . . .

PART XV

SUBORDINATE LEGISLATION

General insolvency rules

Company insolvency rules

[1] **411.**—(1) Rules may be made—

(a) in relation to England and Wales, by the Lord Chancellor with the concurrence of the Secretary of State, or

(b) in relation to Scotland, by the Secretary of State,

for the purpose of giving effect to Parts I to VII of this Act.

(2) Without prejudice to the generality of subsection (1), or to any provision of those Parts by virtue of which rules under this section may be made with respect to any matter, rules under this section may contain—

(a) any such provision as is specified in Schedule 8 to this Act or corresponds to provision contained immediately before the coming into force of section 106 of the Insolvency Act 1985 in rules made, or having effect as if made, under section 663(1) or (2) of the Companies Act (old winding-up rules), and

(b) such incidental, supplemental and transitional provisions as may appear to the Lord Chancellor or, as the case may be, the Secretary of State necessary or expedient.

(3) In Schedule 8 to this Act "liquidator" includes a provisional liquidator; and references above in this section to Parts I to VII of this Act are to be read as including the Companies Act so far as relating to, and to matters connected with or arising out of, the insolvency or winding up of companies.

(4) Rules under this section shall be made by statutory instrument subject to annulment in pursuance of a resolution of either House of Parliament.

(5) Regulations made by the Secretary of State under a power conferred by rules under this section shall be made by statutory instrument and, after being made, shall be laid before each House of Parliament.

(6) Nothing in this section prejudices any power to make rules of court.

NOTE

[1] For regulations see S.I. 1986 No. 1925.

412, 413. [Not applicable to Scotland.]

Fees orders

Fees orders (company insolvency proceedings)

414.—(1) There shall be paid in respect of—

(*a*) proceedings under any of Parts I to VII of this Act, and

(*b*) the performance by the official receiver or the Secretary of State of functions under those Parts,

such fees as the competent authority may with the sanction of the Treasury by order direct.

(2) That authority is—

(*a*) in relation to England and Wales, the Lord Chancellor, and

(*b*) in relation to Scotland, the Secretary of State.

(3) The Treasury may by order direct by whom and in what manner the fees are to be collected and accounted for.

(4) The Lord Chancellor may, with the sanction of the Treasury, by order provide for sums to be deposited, by such persons, in such manner and in such circumstances as may be specified in the order, by way of security for fees payable by virtue of this section.

(5) An order under this section may contain such incidental, supplemental and transitional provisions as may appear to the Lord Chancellor, the Secretary of State or (as the case may be) the Treasury necessary or expedient.

(6) An order under this section shall be made by statutory instrument and, after being made, shall be laid before each House of Parliament.

(7) Fees payable by virtue of this section shall be paid into the Consolidated Fund.

(8) References in subsection (1) to Parts I to VII of this Act are to be read as including the Companies Act so far as relating to, and to matters connected with or arising out of, the insolvency or winding up of companies.

(9) Nothing in this section prejudices any power to make rules of court; and the application of this section to Scotland is without prejudice to section 2 of the Courts of Law Fees (Scotland) Act 1895.

415. [Not applicable to Scotland.]

Specification, increase and reduction of money sums relevant in the operation of this Act

Monetary limits (companies winding up)

[1] **416.**—(1) The Secretary of State may by order in a statutory instrument increase or reduce any of the money sums for the time being specified in the following provisions in the first Group of Parts—

> section 117(2) (amount of company's share capital determining whether county court has jurisdiction to wind it up);
>
> section 120(3) (the equivalent as respects sheriff court jurisdiction in Scotland);
>
> section 123(1)(*a*) (minimum debt for service of demand on company by unpaid creditor);

section 184(3) (minimum value of judgment, affecting sheriff's duties
    on levying execution);

section 206(1)(*a*) and (*b*) (minimum value of company property con-
    cealed or fraudulently removed, affecting criminal liability of com-
    pany's officer).

(2) An order under this section may contain such transitional provisions
as may appear to the Secretary of State necessary or expedient.

(3) No order under this section increasing or reducing any of the money
sums for the time being specified in section 117(2), 120(3) or 123(1)(*a*) shall

[THE NEXT PAGE IS I 633]

be made unless a draft of the order has been laid before and approved by a resolution of each House of Parliament.

(4) A statutory instrument containing an order under this section, other than an order to which subsection (3) applies, is subject to annulment in pursuance of a resolution of either House of Parliament.

NOTE
[1] Amendments by orders made under this section are incorporated in the relevant provisions.

Money sum in s.222

417. The Secretary of State may by regulations in a statutory instrument increase or reduce the money sum for the time being specified in section 222(1) (minimum debt for service of demand on unregistered company by unpaid creditor); but such regulations shall not be made unless a draft of the statutory instrument containing them has been approved by resolution of each House of Parliament.

418. [Not applicable to Scotland.]

Insolvency practice

Regulations for purposes of Part XIII
[1] **419.**—(1) The Secretary of State may make regulations for the purpose of giving effect to Part XIII of this Act; and "prescribed" in that Part means prescribed by regulations made by the Secretary of State.

(2) Without prejudice to the generality of subsection (1) or to any provision of that Part by virtue of which regulations may be made with respect to any matter, regulations under this section may contain—

(*a*) provision as to the matters to be taken into account in determining whether a person is a fit and proper person to act as an insolvency practitioner;

(*b*) provision prohibiting a person from so acting in prescribed cases, being cases in which a conflict of interest will or may arise;

(*c*) provision imposing requirements with respect to—
  (i) the preparation and keeping by a person who acts as an insolvency practitioner of prescribed books, accounts and other records, and
  (ii) the production of those books, accounts and records to prescribed persons;

(*d*) provision conferring power on prescribed persons—
  (i) to require any person who acts or has acted as an insolvency practitioner to answer any inquiry in relation to a case in which he is so acting or has so acted, and
  (ii) to apply to a court to examine such a person or any other person on oath concerning such a case;

(*e*) provision making non-compliance with any of the regulations a criminal offence; and

(*f*) such incidental, supplemental and transitional provisions as may appear to the Secretary of State necessary or expedient.

(3) Any power conferred by Part XIII or this Part to make regulations, rules or orders is exercisable by statutory instrument subject to annulment by resolution of either House of Parliament.

(4) Any rule or regulation under Part XIII or this Part may make different provision with respect to different cases or descriptions of cases, including different provision for different areas.

NOTE
[1] See S.I. 1986 No. 1995.

Other order-making powers

420, 421. [Not applicable to Scotland.]

Recognised banks, etc.

422.—[1] (1) The Secretary of State may, by order made with the concurrence of the Treasury and after consultation with the Bank of England, provide that such provisions in the first Group of Parts as may be specified in the order shall apply in relation to authorised institutions and former authorised institutions within the meaning of the Banking Act 1987 with such modifications as may be so specified.

(2) An order under this section may make different provision for different cases and may contain such incidental, supplemental and transitional provisions as may appear to the Secretary of State necessary or expedient.

(3) An order under this section shall be made by statutory instrument subject to annulment in pursuance of a resolution of either House of Parliament.

NOTE
[1] As amended by the Banking Act 1987, Sched. 6, para. 25.

PART XVI

PROVISIONS AGAINST DEBT AVOIDANCE (ENGLAND AND WALES ONLY)

. . . . . .

PART XVII

MISCELLANEOUS AND GENERAL

Co-operation between courts exercising jurisdiction in relation to insolvency

426.—(1) An order made by a court in any part of the United Kingdom in the exercise of jurisdiction in relation to insolvency law shall be enforced in any other part of the United Kingdom as if it were made by a court exercising the corresponding jurisdiction in that other part.

(2) However, without prejudice to the following provisions of this section, nothing in subsection (1) requires a court in any part of the United Kingdom to enforce, in relation to property situated in that part, any order made by a court in any other part of the United Kingdom.

(3) The Secretary of State, with the concurrence in relation to property situated in England and Wales of the Lord Chancellor, may by order make provision for securing that a trustee or assignee under the insolvency law of any part of the United Kingdom has, with such modifications as may be specified in the order, the same rights in relation to any property situated in another part of the United Kingdom as he would have in the corresponding circumstances if he were a trustee or assignee under the insolvency law of that other part.

(4) The courts having jurisdiction in relation to insolvency law in any part of the United Kingdom shall assist the courts having the corresponding jurisdiction in any other part of the United Kingdom or any relevant country or territory.

(5) For the purposes of subsection (4) a request made to a court in any part of the United Kingdom by a court in any other part of the United Kingdom or in a relevant country or territory is authority for the court to which the request is made to apply, in relation to any matters specified in

the request, the insolvency law which is applicable by either court in relation to comparable matters falling within its jurisdiction.

In exercising its discretion under this subsection, a court shall have regard in particular to the rules of private international law.

(6) Where a person who is a trustee or assignee under the insolvency law of any part of the United Kingdom claims property situated in any other part of the United Kingdom (whether by virtue of an order under subsection (3) or otherwise), the submission of that claim to the court exercising jurisdiction in relation to insolvency law in that other part shall be treated in the same manner as a request made by a court for the purpose of subsection (4).

(7) Section 38 of the Criminal Law Act 1977 (execution of warrant of arrest throughout the United Kingdom) applies to a warrant which, in exercise of any jurisdiction in relation to insolvency law, is issued in any part of the United Kingdom for the arrest of a person as it applies to a warrant issued in that part of the United Kingdom for the arrest of a person charged with an offence.

(8) Without prejudice to any power to make rules of court, any power to make provision by subordinate legislation for the purpose of giving effect in relation to companies or individuals to the insolvency law of any part of the United Kingdom includes power to make provision for the purpose of giving effect in that part to any provision made by or under the preceding provisions of this section.

(9) An order under subsection (3) shall be made by statutory instrument subject to annulment in pursuance of a resolution of either House of Parliament.

(10) In this section "insolvency law" means—

(*a*) in relation to England and Wales, provision made by or under this Act or sections 6 to 10, 12, 15, 19(*c*) and 20 (with Schedule 1) of the Company Directors Disqualification Act 1986 and extending to England and Wales;

(*b*) in relation to Scotland, provision extending to Scotland and made by or under this Act, sections 6 to 10, 12, 15, 19(*c*) and 20 (with Schedule 1) of the Company Directors Disqualification Act 1986, Part XVIII of the Companies Act or the Bankruptcy (Scotland) Act 1985;

(*c*) in relation to Northern Ireland, provision made by or under the Bankruptcy Acts (Northern Ireland) 1857 to 1980, Part V, VI or IX of the Companies Act (Northern Ireland) 1960 or Part IV of the Companies (Northern (Ireland) Order 1978;

(*d*) in relation to any relevant country or territory, so much of the law of that country or territory as corresponds to provisions falling within any of the foregoing paragraphs;

and references in this subsection to any enactment include, in relation to any time before the coming into force of that enactment the corresponding enactment in force at that time.

(11) In this section "relevant country or territory" means—

(*a*) any of the Channel Islands or the Isle of Man, or

[1] (*b*) any country or territory designated for the purposes of this section by the Secretary of State by order made by statutory instrument.

NOTE
[1] See S.I. 1986 No. 2123.

Parliamentary disqualification

427.—(1) Where a court in England and Wales or Northern Ireland adjudges an individual bankrupt or a court in Scotland awards sequestration of an individual's estate, the individual is disqualified—

(*a*) for sitting or voting in the House of Lords,

(*b*) for being elected to, or sitting or voting in, the House of Commons, and

(*c*) for sitting or voting in a committee of either House

(2) Where an individual is disqualified under this section, the disqualification ceases—

(*a*) except where the adjudication is annulled or the award recalled or reduced without the individual having been first discharged, on the discharge of the individual, and

(*b*) in the excepted case, on the annulment, recall or reduction, as the case may be.

(3) No writ of summons shall be issued to any lord of Parliament who is for the time being disqualified under this section for sitting and voting in the House of Lords.

(4) Where a member of the House of Commons who is disqualified under this section continues to be so disqualified until the end of the period of six months beginning with the day of the adjudication or award, his seat shall be vacated at the end of that period.

(5) A court which makes an adjudication or award such as is mentioned in subsection (1) in relation to any lord of Parliament or member of the House of Commons shall forthwith certify the adjudication or award to the Speaker of the House of Lords or, as the case may be, to the Speaker of the House of Commons.

(6) Where a court has certified an adjudication or award to the Speaker of the House of Commons under subsection (5), then immediately after it becomes apparent which of the following certificates is applicable, the court shall certify to the Speaker of the House of Commons—

(*a*) that the period of six months beginning with the day of the adjudication or award has expired without the adjudication or award having been annulled, recalled or reduced, or

(*b*) that the adjudication or award has been annulled, recalled or reduced before the end of that period.

(7) Subject to the preceding provisions of this section, so much of this Act and any other enactment (whenever passed) and of any subordinate legislation (whenever made) as—

(*a*) makes provision for or in connection with bankruptcy in one or more parts of the United Kingdom, or

(*b*) makes provision conferring a power of arrest in connection with the winding up or insolvency of companies in one or more parts of the United Kingdom,

applies in relation to persons having privilege of Parliament or peerage as it applies in relation to persons not having such privilege.

Exemptions from Restrictive Trade Practices Act

428.—(1) No restriction in respect of any of the matters specified in the next subsection shall, on or after the appointed day, be regarded as a restriction by virtue of which the Restrictive Trade Practices Act 1976 applies to any agreement (whenever made).

(2) Those matters are—

(*a*) the charges to be made, quoted or paid for insolvency services supplied, offered or obtained;

(*b*) the terms or conditions on or subject to which insolvency services are to be supplied or obtained;

(*c*) the extent (if any) to which, or the scale (if any) on which, insolvency services are to be made available, supplied or obtained;

(*d*) the form or manner in which insolvency services are to be made available, supplied or obtained;

(*e*) the persons or classes of persons for whom or from whom, or the areas or places in or from which, insolvency services are to be made available or supplied or are to be obtained.

(3) In this section "insolvency services" means the services of persons acting as insolvency practitioners or carrying out under the law of Northern Ireland functions corresponding to those mentioned in section 388(1) or (2) in Part XIII, in their capacity as such; and expressions which are also used in the Act of 1976 have the same meaning here as in that Act.

Disabilities on revocation of administration order against an individual

[1] **429.**—(1) The following applies where a person fails to make any payment which he is required to make by virtue of an administration order under Part VI of the County Courts Act 1984.

(2) The court which is administering that person's estate under the order may, if it thinks fit—

(*a*) revoke the administration order, and

(*b*) make an order directing that this section and section 12 of the Company Directors Disqualification Act 1986 shall apply to the person for such period, not exceeding two years, as may be specified in the order.

(3) A person to whom this section so applies shall not—

(*a*) either alone or jointly with another person, obtain credit to the extent of the amount prescribed for the purposes of section 360(1)(*a*) or more, or

(*b*) enter into any transaction in the course of or for the purposes of any business in which he is directly or indirectly engaged,

without disclosing to the person from whom he obtains the credit, or (as the case may be) with whom the transaction is entered into, the fact that this section applies to him.

(4) The reference in subsection (3) to a person obtaining credit includes—

(*a*) a case where goods are bailed or hired to him under a hire-purchase agreement or agreed to be sold to him under a conditional sale agreement, and

(*b*) a case where he is paid in advance (whether in money or otherwise) for the supply of goods or services.

(5) A person who contravenes this section is guilty of an offence and liable to imprisonment or a fine, or both.

NOTE
[1] Subss. (1) and (2) not applicable to Scotland: see s.440(2)(*c*).

Provision introducing Schedule of punishments

430.—(1) Schedule 10 to this Act has effect with respect to the way in which offences under this Act are punishable on conviction.

(2) In relation to an offence under a provision of this Act specified in the first column of the Schedule (the general nature of the offence being described in the second column), the third column shows whether the offence is punishable on conviction on indictment, or on summary conviction, or either in the one way or the other.

(3) The fourth column of the Schedule shows, in relation to an offence, the maximum punishment by way of fine or imprisonment under this Act which may be imposed on a person convicted of the offence in the way specified in relation to it in the third column (that is to say, on indictment or summarily) a reference to a period of years or months being to a term of imprisonment of that duration.

(4) The fifth column shows (in relation to an offence for which there is an entry in that column) that a person convicted of the offence after continued contravention is liable to a daily default fine; that is to say, he is liable on a second or subsequent conviction of the offence to the fine specified in that column for each day on which the contravention is continued (instead of the penalty specified for the offence in the fourth column of the Schedule).

(5) For the purpose of any enactment in this Act whereby an officer of a company who is in default is liable to a fine or penalty, the expression

"officer who is in default" means any officer of the company who knowingly and wilfully authorises or permits the default, refusal or contravention mentioned in the enactment.

Summary proceedings

431.—(1) Summary proceedings for any offence under any of Parts I to VII of this Act may (without prejudice to any jurisdiction exercisable apart from this subsection) be taken against a body corporate at any place at which the body has a place of business, and against any other person at any place at which he is for the time being.

(2) Notwithstanding anything in section 127(1) of the Magistrates' Courts Act 1980, an information relating to such an offence which is triable by a magistrates' court in England and Wales may be so tried if it is laid at any time within three years after the commission of the offence and within 12 months after the date on which evidence sufficient in the opinion of the Director of Public Prosecutions or the Secretary of State (as the case may be) to justify the proceedings comes to his knowledge.

(3) Summary proceedings in Scotland for such an offence shall not be commenced after the expiration of three years from the commission of the offence.

Subject to this (and notwithstanding anything in section 331 of the Criminal Procedure (Scotland) Act 1975), such proceedings may (in Scotland) be commenced at any time within 12 months after the date on which evidence sufficient in the Lord Advocate's opinion to justify the proceedings came to his knowledge or, where such evidence was reported to him by the Secretary of State, within 12 months after the date on which it came to the knowledge of the latter; and subsection (3) of that section applies for the purpose of this subsection as it applies for the purpose of that section.

(4) For purposes of this section, a certificate of the Director of Public Prosecutions, the Lord Advocate or the Secretary of State (as the case may be) as to the date on which such evidence as is referred to above came to his knowledge is conclusive evidence.

Offences by bodies corporate

432.—(1) This section applies to offences under this Act other than those excepted by subsection (4).

(2) Where a body corporate is guilty of an offence to which this section applies and the offence is proved to have been committed with the consent or connivance of, or to be attributable to any neglect on the part of, any director, manager, secretary or other similar officer of the body corporate or any person who was purporting to act in any such capacity he, as well as the body corporate, is guilty of the offence and liable to be proceeded against and punished accordingly.

(3) Where the affairs of a body corporate are managed by its members, subsection (2) applies in relation to the acts and defaults of a member in connection with his functions of management as if he were a director of the body corporate.

(4) The offences excepted from this section are those under sections 30, 39, 51, 53, 54, 62, 64, 66, 85, 89, 164, 188, 201, 206, 207, 208, 209, 210 and 211.

Admissibility in evidence of statements of affairs, etc.

433. In any proceedings (whether or not under this Act)—

(*a*) a statement of affairs prepared for the purposes of any provision of this Act which is derived from the Insolvency Act 1985, and

(*b*) any other statement made in pursuance of a requirement imposed by or under any such provision or by or under rules made under this Act,

may be used in evidence against any person making or concurring in making the statement.

Crown application

434. For the avoidance of doubt it is hereby declared that provisions of this Act which derive from the Insolvency Act 1985 bind the Crown so far as affecting or relating to the following matters, namely—

(*a*) remedies against, or against the property of, companies or individuals;

(*b*) priorities of debts;

(*c*) transactions at an undervalue or preferences;

(*d*) voluntary arrangements approved under Part I or Part VIII, and

(*e*) discharge from bankruptcy.

PART XVIII

INTERPRETATION

Meaning of "associate"

435.—(1) For the purposes of this Act any question whether a person is an associate of another person is to be determined in accordance with the following provisions of this section (any provision that a person is an associate of another person being taken to mean that they are associates of each other).

(2) A person is an associate of an individual if that person is the individual's husband or wife, or is a relative, or the husband or wife of a relative, of the individual or of the individual's husband or wife.

(3) A person is an associate of any person with whom he is in partnership, and of the husband or wife or a relative of any individual with whom he is in partnership; and a Scottish firm is an associate of any person who is a member of the firm.

(4) A person is an associate of any person whom he employs or by whom he is employed.

(5) A person in his capacity as trustee of a trust other than—

(*a*) a trust arising under any of the second Group of Parts or the Bankruptcy (Scotland) Act 1985, or

(*b*) a pension scheme or an employee's share scheme (within the meaning of the Companies Act),

is an associate of another person if the beneficiaries of the trust include, or the terms of the trust confer a power than may be exercised for the benefit of, that other person or an associate of that other person.

(6) A company is an associate of another company—

(*a*) if the same person has control of both, or a person has control of one and persons who are his associates, or he and persons who are his associates, have control of the other, or

(*b*) if a group of two or more persons has control of each company, and the groups either consist of the same persons or could be regarded as consisting of the same persons by treating (in one or more cases) a member of either group as replaced by a person of whom he is an associate.

(7) A company is an associate of another person if that person has control of it or if that person and persons who are his associates together have control of it.

(8) For the purposes of this section a person is a relative of an individual if he is that individual's brother, sister, uncle, aunt, nephew, niece, lineal ancestor or lineal descendant, treating—

(*a*) any relationship of the half blood as a relationship of the whole blood and the stepchild or adopted child of any person as his child, and

(*b*) an illegitimate child as the legitimate child of his mother and reputed father;

and references in this section to a husband or wife include a former husband or wife and a reputed husband or wife.

(9) For the purposes of this section any director or other officer of a company is to be treated as employed by that company.

(10) For the purposes of this section a person is to be taken as having control of a company if—

(*a*) the directors of the company or of another company which has control of it (or any of them) are accustomed to act in accordance with his directions or instructions, or

(*b*) he is entitled to exercise, or control the exercise of, one third or more of the voting power at any general meeting of the company or of another company which has control of it;

and where two or more persons together satisfy either of the above conditions, they are to be taken as having control of the company.

(11) In this section "company" includes any body corporate (whether incorporated in Great Britain or elsewhere); and references to directors and other officers of a company and to voting power at any general meeting of a company have effect with any necessary modifications.

Expressions used generally

436. In this Act, except in so far as the context otherwise requires (and subject to Parts VII and XI)—

"the appointed day" means the day on which this Act comes into force under section 443;

"associate" has the meaning given by section 435;

"business" includes a trade or profession;

"the Companies Act" means the Companies Act 1985;

"conditional sale agreement" and "hire-purchase agreement" have the same meanings as in the Consumer Credit Act 1974;

"modifications" includes additions, alterations and omissions and cognate expressions shall be construed accordingly;

"property" includes money, goods, things in action, land and every description of property wherever situated and also obligations and every description of interest, whether present or future or vested or contingent, arising out of, or incidental to, property;

"records" includes computer records and other non-documentary records;

"subordinate legislation" has the same meaning as in the Interpretation Act 1978; and

"transaction" includes a gift, agreement or arrangement, and references to entering into a transaction shall be construed accordingly.

Part XIX

Final Provisions

Transitional provisions, and savings

437. The transitional provisions and savings set out in Schedule 11 to this Act shall have effect, the Schedule comprising the following Parts—

Part I: company insolvency and winding up (matters arising before appointed day, and continuance of proceedings in certain cases as before that day);

Part II: individual insolvency (matters so arising, and continuance of bankruptcy proceedings in certain cases as before that day);

Part III: transactions entered into before the appointed day and capable of being affected by orders of the court under Part XVI of this Act;

Part IV: insolvency practitioners acting as such before the appointed day; and

Part V: general transitional provisions and savings required consequentially on, and in connection with, the repeal and replacement by this Act and the Company Directors Disqualification Act 1986 of provisions of the Companies Act, the greater part of the Insolvency Act 1985 and other enactments.

Repeals

438. The enactments specified in the second column of Schedule 12 to this Act are repealed to the extent specified in the third column of that Schedule.

Amendment of enactments

439.—(1) The Companies Act is amended as shown in Parts I and II of Schedule 13 to this Act, being amendments consequential on this Act and the Company Directors Disqualification Act 1986.

(2) The enactments specified in the first column of Schedule 14 to this Act (being enactments which refer, or otherwise relate, to those which are repealed and replaced by this Act or the Company Directors Disqualification Act 1986) are amended as shown in the second column of that Schedule.

(3) The Lord Chancellor may by order make such consequential modifications of any provision contained in any subordinate legislation made before the appointed day and such transitional provisions in connection with those modifications as appear to him necessary or expedient in respect of—

(*a*) any reference in that subordinate legislation to the Bankruptcy Act 1914;

(*b*) any reference in that subordinate legislation to any enactment repealed by Part III or IV of Schedule 10 to the Insolvency Act 1985; or

(*c*) any reference in that subordinate legislation to any matter provided for under the Act of 1914 or under any enactment so repealed.

(4) An order under this section shall be made by statutory instrument subject to annulment in pursuance of a resolution of either House of Parliament.

Extent (Scotland)

440.—(1) Subject to the next subsection, provisions of this Act contained in the first Group of Parts extend to Scotland except where otherwise stated.

(2) The following provisions of this Act do not extend to Scotland—

(*a*) in the first Group of Parts—
  section 43;
  sections 238 to 241; and
  section 246;

(*b*) the second Group of Parts;

(*c*) in the third Group of Parts—
  sections 399 to 402,
  sections 412, 413, 415, 418, 420 and 421,
  sections 423 to 425, and
  section 429(1) and (2); and

(*d*) in the Schedules—
  Parts II and III of Schedule 11; and
  Schedules 12 and 14 so far as they repeal or amend enactments which extend to England and Wales only.

Extent (Northern Ireland)

441.—(1) The following provisions of this Act extend to Northern Ireland—

(*a*) sections 197, 426, 427 and 428; and

(*b*) so much of section 439 and Schedule 14 as relates to enactments which extend to Northern Ireland.

(2) Subject as above, and to any provision expressly relating to companies incorporated elsewhere than in Great Britain, nothing in this Act extends to Northern Ireland or applies to or in relation to companies registered or incorporated in Northern Ireland.

Extent (other territories)

442. Her Majesty may, by Order in Council, direct that such of the provisions of this Act as are specified in the Order, being provisions formerly contained in the Insolvency Act 1985, shall extend to any of the Channel Islands or any colony with such modifications as may be so specified.

Commencement

443. This Act comes into force on the day appointed under section 236(2) of the Insolvency Act 1985 for the coming into force of Part III of that Act (individual insolvency and bankruptcy), immediately after that Part of that Act comes into force for England and Wales.

Citation

444. This Act may be cited as the Insolvency Act 1986.

SCHEDULES

Sections 14, 42   SCHEDULE 1

POWERS OF ADMINISTRATOR OR ADMINISTRATIVE RECEIVER

1. Power to take possession of, collect and get in the property of the company and, for that purpose, to take such proceedings as may seem to him expedient.

2. Power to sell or otherwise dispose of the property of the company by public auction or private contract or, in Scotland, to sell, feu, hire out or otherwise dispose of the property of the company by public roup or private bargain.

3. Power to raise or borrow money and grant security therefor over the property of the company.

4. Power to appoint a solicitor or accountant or other professionally qualified person to assist him in the performance of his functions.

5. Power to bring or defend any action or other legal proceedings in the name and on behalf of the company.

6. Power to refer to arbitration any question affecting the company.

7. Power to effect and maintain insurances in respect of the business and property of the company.

8. Power to use the company's seal.

9. Power to do all acts and to execute in the name and on behalf of the company any deed, receipt or other document.

10. Power to draw, accept, make and endorse any bill of exchange or promissory note in the name and on behalf of the company.

11. Power to appoint any agent to do any business which he is unable to do himself or which can more conveniently be done by an agent and power to employ and dismiss employees.

12. Power to do all such things (including the carrying out of works) as may be necessary for the realisation of the property of the company.

13. Power to make any payment which is necessary or incidental to the performance of his functions.

14. Power to carry on the business of the company.

15. Power to establish subsidiaries of the company.

16. Power to transfer to subsidiaries of the company the whole or any part of the business and property of the company.

17. Power to grant or accept a surrender of a lease or tenancy of any of the property of the company, and to take a lease or tenancy of any property required or convenient for the business of the company.

18. Power to make any arrangement or compromise on behalf of the company.

19. Power to call up any uncalled capital of the company.

20. Power to rank and claim in the bankruptcy, insolvency, sequestration or liquidation of any person indebted to the company and to receive dividends, and to accede to trust deeds for the creditors of any such person.

21. Power to present or defend a petition for the winding up of the company.

22. Power to change the situation of the company's registered office.

23. Power to do all other things incidental to the exercise of the foregoing powers.

Section 55   SCHEDULE 2

POWERS OF A SCOTTISH RECEIVER (ADDITIONAL TO THOSE CONFERRED ON HIM BY THE INSTRUMENT OF CHARGE)

1. Power to take possession of, collect and get in the property from the company or a liquidator thereof or any other person, and for that purpose, to take such proceedings as may seem to him expedient.

2. Power to sell, feu, hire out or otherwise dispose of the property by public roup or private bargain and with or without advertisement.

3. Power to raise or borrow money and grant security therefor over the property.

4. Power to appoint a solicitor or accountant or other professionally qualified person to assist him in the performance of his functions.

5. Power to bring or defend any action or other legal proceedings in the name and on behalf of the company.

6. Power to refer to arbitration all questions affecting the company.

7. Power to effect and maintain insurances in respect of the business and property of the company.

8. Power to use the company's seal.

9. Power to do all acts and to execute in the name and on behalf of the company any deed, receipt or other document.

10. Power to draw, accept, make and endorse any bill of exchange or promissory note in the name and on behalf of the company.

11. Power to appoint any agent to do any business which he is unable to do himself or which can more conveniently be done by an agent, and power to employ and dismiss employees.

12. Power to do all such things (including the carrying out of works), as may be necessary for the realisation of the property.

13. Power to make any payment which is necessary or incidental to the performance of his functions.

14. Power to carry on the business of the company or any part of it.

15. Power to grant or accept a surrender of a lease or tenancy of any of the property, and to take a lease or tenancy of any property required or convenient for the business of the company.

16. Power to make any arrangement or compromise on behalf of the company.

17. Power to call up any uncalled capital of the company.

18. Power to establish subsidiaries of the company.

19. Power to transfer to subsidiaries of the company the business of the company or any part of it and any of the property.

20. Power to rank and claim in the bankruptcy, insolvency, sequestration or liquidation of any person or company indebted to the company and to receive dividends, and to accede to trust deeds for creditors of any such person.

21. Power to present or defend a petition for the winding up of the company.

22. Power to change the situation of the company's registered office.

23. Power to do all other things incidental to the exercise of the powers mentioned in section 55(1) of this Act or above in this Schedule.

Section 162   SCHEDULE 3

ORDERS IN COURSE OF WINDING UP PRONOUNCED IN VACATION (SCOTLAND)

PART I

ORDERS WHICH ARE TO BE FINAL

Orders under section 153, as to the time for proving debts and claims.
Orders under section 195 as to meetings for ascertaining wishes of creditors or contributories.
Orders under section 198, as to the examination of witnesses in regard to the property or affairs of a company.

PART II

ORDERS WHICH ARE TO TAKE EFFECT UNTIL MATTER DISPOSED OF BY INNER HOUSE

Orders under section 126(1), 130(2) or (3), 147, 227 or 228, restraining or permitting the commencement or the continuance of legal proceedings.
Orders under section 135(5), limiting the powers of provisional liquidators.
Orders under section 108, appointing a liquidator to fill a vacancy.
Orders under section 167 or 169, sanctioning the exercise of any powers by a liquidator, other than the powers specified in paragraphs 1, 2 and 3 of Schedule 4 to this Act.
Orders under section 158, as to the arrest and detention of an absconding contributory and his property.

Sections 165, 167   SCHEDULE 4

POWERS OF LIQUIDATOR IN A WINDING UP

PART I

POWERS EXERCISABLE WITH SANCTION

1. Power to pay any class of creditors in full.

2. Power to make any compromise or arrangement with creditors or persons claiming to be creditors, or having or alleging themselves to have any claim (present or future, certain or contingent, ascertained or sounding only in damages) against the company, or whereby the company may be rendered liable.

3. Power to compromise, on such terms as may be agreed—
   (*a*) all calls and liabilities to calls, all debts and liabilities capable of resulting in debts, and all claims (present or future, certain or contingent, ascertained or sounding only in damages) subsisting or supposed to subsist between the company and a contributory or alleged contributory or other debtor or person apprehending liability to the company, and
   (*b*) all questions in any way relating to or affecting the assets or the winding up of the company,

and take any security for the discharge of any such call, debt, liability or claim and give a complete discharge in respect of it.

PART II

POWERS EXERCISABLE WITHOUT SANCTION IN VOLUNTARY WINDING UP, WITH SANCTION IN WINDING UP BY THE COURT

4. Power to bring or defend any action or other legal proceeding in the name and on behalf of the company.

5. Power to carry on the business of the company so far as may be necessary for its beneficial winding up.

PART III

POWERS EXERCISABLE WITHOUT SANCTION IN ANY WINDING UP

6. Power to sell any of the company's property by public auction or private contract with power to transfer the whole of it to any person or to sell the same in parcels.

7. Power to do all acts and execute, in the name and on behalf of the company, all deeds, receipts and other documents and for that purpose to use, when necessary, the company's seal.

8. Power to prove, rank and claim in the bankruptcy, insolvency or sequestration of any contributory for any balance against his estate, and to receive dividends in the bankruptcy, insolvency or sequestration in respect of that balance, as a separate debt due from the bankrupt or insolvent, and rateably with the other separate creditors.

9. Power to draw, accept, make and indorse any bill of exchange or promissory note in the name and on behalf of the company, with the same effect with respect to the company's liability as if the bill or note had been drawn, accepted, made or indorsed by or on behalf of the company in the course of its business.

10. Power to raise on the security of the assets of the company any money requisite.

11. Power to take out in his official name letters of administration to any deceased contributory, and to do in his official name any other act necessary for obtaining payment of any money due from a contributory or his estate which cannot conveniently be done in the name of the company.
In all such cases the money due is deemed, for the purpose of enabling the liquidator to take out the letters of administration or recover the money, to be due to the liquidator himself.

12. Power to appoint an agent to do any business which the liquidator is unable to do himself.

13. Power to do all such other things as may be necessary for winding up the company's affairs and distributing its assets.

. . . . . .

Section 386   SCHEDULE 6

THE CATEGORIES OF PREFERENTIAL DEBTS

Category 1: Debts due to Inland Revenue

1. Sums due at the relevant date from the debtor on account of deductions of income tax from emoluments paid during the period of 12 months next before that date.
The deductions here referred to are those which the debtor was liable to make under section 204 of the Income and Corporation Taxes Act 1970 (pay as you earn), less the amount of the repayments of income tax which the debtor was liable to make during that period.

2. Sums due at the relevant date from the debtor in respect of such deductions as are required to be made by the debtor for that period under section 69 of the Finance (No. 2) Act 1975 (sub-contractors in the construction industry).

Category 2: Debts due to Customs and Excise

3. Any value added tax which is referable to the period of six months next before the relevant date (which period is referred to below as "the six-month period").

For the purposes of this paragraph—

    (*a*) where the whole of the prescribed accounting period to which any value added tax is attributable falls within the six-month period, the whole amount of that tax is referable to that period; and

    (*b*) in any other case the amount of any value added tax which is referable to the six-month period is the proportion of the tax which is equal to such proportion (if any) of the accounting reference period in question as falls within the six-month period;

and in sub-paragraph (*a*) "prescribed" means prescribed by regulations under the Value Added Tax Act 1983.

4. The amount of any car tax which is due at the relevant date from the debtor and which became due within a period of 12 months next before that date.

5. Any amount which is due—

    (*a*) by way of general betting duty or bingo duty, or

    (*b*) under section 12(1) of the Betting and Gaming Duties Act 1981 (general betting duty and pool betting duty recoverable from agent collecting stakes), or

    (*c*) under section 14 of, or Schedule 2 to, that Act (gaming licence duty),

from the debtor at the relevant date and which became due within the period of 12 months next before that date.

Category 3: Social security contributions

6. All sums which on the relevant date are due from the debtor on account of Class 1 or Class 2 contributions under the Social Security Act 1975 or the Social Security (Northern Ireland) Act 1975 and which became due from the debtor in the 12 months next before the relevant date.

7. All sums which on the relevant date have been assessed on and are due from the debtor on account of Class 4 contributions under either of those Acts of 1975, being sums which—

    (*a*) are due to the Commissioners of Inland Revenue (rather than to the Secretary of State or a Northern Ireland department), and

    (*b*) are assessed on the debtor up to 5th April next before the relevant date,

but not exceeding, in the whole, any one year's assessment.

Category 4: Contributions to occupational pension schemes, etc.

8. Any sum which is owed by the debtor and is a sum to which Schedule 3 to the Social Security Pensions Act 1975 applies (contributions to occupational pension schemes and state scheme premiums).

Category 5: Remuneration, etc., of employees

[1] 9. So much of any amount which—

    (*a*) is owed by the debtor to a person who is or has been an employee of the debtor, and

    (*b*) is payable by way of remuneration in respect of the whole or any part of the period of four months next before the relevant date,

as does not exceed so much as may be prescribed by order made by the Secretary of State.

10. An amount owed by way of accrued holiday remuneration, in respect of any period of employment before the relevant date, to a person whose employment by the debtor has been terminated, whether before, on or after that date.

11. So much of any sum owed in respect of money advanced for the purpose as has been applied for the payment of a debt which, if it had not been paid, would have been a debt falling within paragraph 9 or 10.

[1] 12. So much of any amount which—

    (*a*) is ordered (whether before or after the relevant date) to be paid by the debtor under the Reserve Forces (Safeguard of Employment) Act 1985, and

    (*b*) is so ordered in respect of a default made by the debtor before that date in the discharge of his obligations under that Act,

as does not exceed such amount as may be prescribed by order made by the Secretary of State.

---

[1] S.I. 1986 No. 1996.

Interpretation for Category 5

13.—(1) For the purposes of paragraphs 9 to 12, a sum is payable by the debtor to a person by way of remuneration in respect of any period if—

 (*a*) it is paid as wages or salary (whether payable for time or for piece work or earned wholly or partly by way of commission) in respect of services rendered to the debtor in that period, or

 (*b*) it is an amount falling within the following sub-paragraph and is payable by the debtor in respect of that period.

(2) An amount falls within this sub-paragraph if it is—

 (*a*) a guarantee payment under section 12(1) of the Employment Protection (Consolidation) Act 1978 (employee without work to do for a day or part of a day);

 (*b*) remuneration on suspension on medical grounds under section 19 of that Act;

 (*c*) any payment for time off under section 27(3) (trade union duties), 31(3) (looking for work, etc.) or 31A(4) (ante-natal care) of that Act; or

 (*d*) remuneration under a protective award made by an industrial tribunal under section 101 of the Employment Protection Act 1975 (redundancy dismissal with compensation).

14.—(1) This paragraph relates to a case in which a person's employment has been terminated by or in consequence of his employer going into liquidation or being adjudged bankrupt or (his employer being a company not in liquidation) by or in consequence of—

 (*a*) a receiver being appointed as mentioned in section 40 of this Act (debenture-holders secured by floating charge), or

 (*b*) the appointment of a receiver under section 53(6) or 54(5) of this Act (Scottish company with property subject to floating charge), or

 (*c*) the taking of possession by debenture-holders (so secured), as mentioned in section 196 of the Companies Act.

(2) For the purposes of paragraphs 9 to 12, holiday remuneration is deemed to have accrued to that person in respect of any period of employment if, by virtue of his contract of employment or of any enactment that remuneration would have accrued in respect of that period if his employment had continued until he became entitled to be allowed the holiday.

(3) The reference in sub-paragraph (2) to any enactment includes an order or direction made under an enactment.

15. Without prejudice to paragraphs 13 and 14—

 (*a*) any remuneration payable by the debtor to a person in respect of a period of holiday or of absence from work through sickness or other good cause is deemed to be wages or (as the case may be) salary in respect of services rendered to the debtor in that period, and

 (*b*) references here and in those paragraphs to remuneration in respect of a period of holiday include any sums which, if they had been paid, would have been treated for the purposes of the enactments relating to social security as earnings in respect of that period.

Category 6: Levies on coal and steel production

[1] 15A. Any sums due at the relevant date from the debtor in respect of—

 (*a*) the levies on the production of coal and steel referred to in Articles 49 and 50 of the E.C.S.C. Treaty, or

 (*b*) any surcharge for delay provided for in Article 50(3) of that Treaty and Article 6 of Decision 3/52 of the High Authority of the Coal and Steel Community.

———

NOTE

 [1] Inserted by S.I. 1987 No. 1093, without affecting any declaration on payment of dividend before 1st January 1988: *ibid.*, reg. 3(2).

———

Orders

16. An order under paragraph 9 or 12—

 (*a*) may contain such transitional provisions as may appear to the Secretary of State necessary or expedient;

 (*b*) shall be made by statutory instrument subject to annulment in pursuance of a resolution of either House of Parliament.

SCHEDULE 7

INSOLVENCY PRACTITIONERS TRIBUNAL

Panels of members

1.—(1) The Secretary of State shall draw up and from time to time revise—
   (a) a panel of persons who are barristers, advocates or solicitors, in each case of not less than seven years' standing, and are nominated for the purpose by the Lord Chancellor or the Lord President of the Court of Session, and
   (b) a panel of persons who are experienced in insolvency matters;
and the members of the tribunal shall be selected from those panels in accordance with this Schedule.

(2) The power to revise the panels includes power to terminate a person's membership of either of them, and is accordingly to that extent subject to section 8 of the Tribunals and Inquiries Act 1971 (which makes it necessary to obtain the concurrence of the Lord Chancellor and the Lord President of the Court of Session to dismissals in certain cases).

Remuneration of members

2. The Secretary of State may out of money provided by Parliament pay to members of the tribunal such remuneration as he may with the approval of the Treasury determine; and such expenses of the tribunal as the Secretary of State and the Treasury may approve shall be defrayed by the Secretary of State out of money so provided.

Sittings of tribunal

3.—(1) For the purposes of carrying out their functions in relation to any cases referred to them, the tribunal may sit either as a single tribunal or in two or more divisions.

(2) The functions of the tribunal in relation to any case referred to them shall be exercised by three members consisting of—
   (a) a chairman selected by the Secretary of State from the panel drawn up under paragraph 1(1)(a) above, and
   (b) two other members selected by the Secretary of State from the panel drawn up under paragraph 1(1)(b).

Procedure of tribunal

4.—(1) Any investigation by the tribunal shall be so conducted as to afford a reasonable opportunity for representations to be made to the tribunal by or on behalf of the person whose case is the subject of the investigation.

(2) For the purposes of any such investigation, the tribunal—
   (a) may by summons require any person to attend, at such time and place as is specified in the summons, to give evidence or to produce any books, papers and other records in his possession or under his control which the tribunal consider it necessary for the purposes of the investigation to examine, and
   (b) may take evidence on oath, and for the purpose administer oaths, or may, instead of administering an oath, require the person examined to make and subscribe a declaration of the truth of the matter respecting which he is examined;
but no person shall be required, in obedience to such a summons, to go more than 10 miles from his place of residence, unless the necessary expenses of his attendance are paid or tendered to him.

(3) Every person who—
   (a) without reasonable excuse fails to attend in obedience to a summons issued under this paragraph, or refuses to give evidence, or
   (b) intentionally alters, suppresses, conceals or destroys or refuses to produce any document which he may be required to produce for the purpose of an investigation by the Tribunal,
is liable to a fine.

(4) Subject to the provisions of this paragraph, the Secretary of State may make rules for regulating the procedure on any investigation by the tribunal.

(5) In their application to Scotland, sub-paragraphs (2) and (3) above have effect as if for any reference to a summons there were substituted a reference to a notice in writing.

Section 411   SCHEDULE 8

PROVISIONS CAPABLE OF INCLUSION IN COMPANY INSOLVENCY RULES

Courts

1. Provision for supplementing, in relation to the insolvency or winding up of companies, any provision made by or under section 117 of this Act (jurisdiction in relation to winding up).

2. Provision for regulating the practice and procedure of any court exercising jurisdiction for the purposes of Parts I to VII of this Act or the Companies Act so far as relating to, and to matters connected with or arising out of, the insolvency or winding up of companies, being any provision that could be made by rules of court.

[THE NEXT PAGE IS I 649]

Notices, etc.

3. Provision requiring notice of any proceedings in connection with or arising out of the insolvency or winding up of a company to be given or published in the manner prescribed by the rules.

4. Provision with respect to the form, manner of serving, contents and proof of any petition, application, order, notice, statement or other document required to be presented, made, given, published or prepared under any enactment or subordinate legislation relating to, or to matters connected with or arising out of, the insolvency or winding up of companies.

5. Provision specifying the persons to whom any notice is to be given.

Registration of voluntary arrangements

6. Provision for the registration of voluntary arrangements approved under Part I of this Act, including provision for the keeping and inspection of a register.

Provisional liquidator

7. Provision as to the manner in which a provisional liquidator appointed under section 135 is to carry out his functions.

Conduct of insolvency

8. Provision with respect to the certification of any person as, and as to the proof that a person is, the liquidator, administrator or administrative receiver of a company.

9. The following provision with respect to meetings of a company's creditors, contributories or members—
   (*a*) provision as to the manner of summoning a meeting (including provision as to how any power to require a meeting is to be exercised, provision as to the manner of determining the value of any debt or contribution for the purposes of any such power and provision making the exercise of any such power subject to the deposit of a sum sufficient to cover the expenses likely to be incurred in summoning and holding a meeting);
   (*b*) provision specifying the time and place at which a meeting may be held and the period of notice required for a meeting;
   (*c*) provision as to the procedure to be followed at a meeting (including the manner in which decisions may be reached by a meeting and the manner in which the value of any vote at a meeting is to be determined);
   (*d*) provision for requiring a person who is or has been an officer of the company to attend a meeting;
   (*e*) provision creating, in the prescribed circumstances, a presumption that a meeting has been duly summoned and held;
   (*f*) provision as to the manner of proving the decisions of a meeting.

10.—(1) Provision as to the functions, membership and proceedings of a committee established under section 26, 49, 68, 101, 141 or 142 of this Act.
   (2) The following provision with respect to the establishment of a committee under section 101, 141 or 142 of this Act, that is to say—
   (*a*) provision for resolving differences between a meeting of the company's creditors and a meeting of its contributories or members;
   (*b*) provision authorising the establishment of the committee without a meeting of contributories in a case where a company is being wound up on grounds including its inability to pay its debts; and
   (*c*) provision modifying the requirements of this Act with respect to the establishment of the committee in a case where a winding-up order has been made immediately upon the discharge of an administration order.

11. Provision as to the manner in which any requirement that may be imposed on a person under any of Parts I to VII of this Act by the official receiver, the liquidator, administrator or administrative receiver of a company or a special manager appointed under section 177 is to be so imposed.

12. Provision as to the debts that may be proved in a winding up, as to the manner and conditions of proving a debt and as to the manner and expenses of establishing the value of any debt or security.

13. Provision with respect to the manner of the distribution of the property of a company that is being wound up, including provision with respect to unclaimed funds and dividends.

14. Provision which, with or without modifications, applies in relation to the winding up of companies any enactment contained in Parts VIII to XI of this Act or in the Bankruptcy (Scotland) Act 1985.

Financial provisions

15. Provision as to the amount, or manner of determining the amount, payable to the liquidator, administrator or administrative receiver of a company or a special manager appointed under section 177, by way of remuneration for the carrying out of functions in connection with or arising out of the insolvency or winding up of a company.

16. Provision with respect to the manner in which moneys received by the liquidator of a company in the course of carrying out his functions as such are to be invested or otherwise handled and with respect to the payment of interest on sums which, in pursuance of rules made by virtue of this paragraph, have been paid into the Insolvency Services Account.

17. Provision as to the fees, costs, charges and other expenses that may be treated as the expenses of a winding up.

18. Provision as to the fees, costs, charges and other expenses that may be treated as properly incurred by the administrator or administrative receiver of a company.

19. Provision as to the fees, costs, charges and other expenses that may be incurred for any of the purposes of Part I of this Act or in the administration of any voluntary arrangement approved under that Part.

Information and records

20. Provision requiring registrars and other officers of courts having jurisdiction in England and Wales in relation to, or to matters connected with or arising out of, the insolvency or winding up of companies—
    (*a*) to keep books and other records with respect to the exercise of that jurisdiction, and
    (*b*) to make returns to the Secretary of State of the business of those courts.

21. Provision requiring a creditor, member or contributory, or such a committee as is mentioned in paragraph 10 above, to be supplied (on payment in prescribed cases of the prescribed fee) with such information and with copies of such documents as may be prescribed.

22. Provision as to the manner in which public examinations under sections 133 and 134 of this Act and proceedings under sections 236 and 237 are to be conducted, as to the circumstances in which records of such examinations or proceedings are to be made available to prescribed persons and as to the costs of such examinations and proceedings.

23. Provision imposing requirements with respect to—
    (*a*) the preparation and keeping by the liquidator, administrator or administrative receiver of a company, or by the supervisor of a voluntary arrangement approved under Part I of this Act, of prescribed books, accounts and other records;
    (*b*) the production of those books, accounts and records for inspection by prescribed persons;
    (*c*) the auditing of accounts kept by the liquidator, administrator or administrative receiver of a company, or the supervisor of such a voluntary arrangement; and
    (*d*) the issue by the administrator or administrative receiver of a company of such a certificate as is mentioned in section 22(3)(*b*) of the Value Added Tax Act 1983 (refund of tax in cases of bad debts) and the supply of copies of the certificate to creditors of the company.

24. Provision requiring the person who is the supervisor of a voluntary arrangement approved under Part I, when it appears to him that the voluntary arrangement has been fully implemented and that nothing remains to be done by him under the arrangement—
    (*a*) to give notice of that fact to persons bound by the voluntary arrangement, and
    (*b*) to report to those persons on the carrying out of the functions conferred on the supervisor of the arrangement.

25. Provision as to the manner in which the liquidator of a company is to act in relation to the books, papers and other records of the company, including provision authorising their disposal.

26. Provision imposing requirements in connection with the carrying out of functions under section 7(3) of the Company Directors Disqualification Act 1986 (including, in particular, requirements with respect to the making of periodic returns).

General

27. Provision conferring power on the Secretary of State to make regulations with respect to so much of any matter that may be provided for in the rules as relates to the carrying out of the functions of the liquidator, administrator or administrative receiver of a company.

28. Provision conferring a discretion on the court.

29. Provision conferring power on the court to make orders for the purpose of securing compliance with obligations imposed by or under section 22, 47, 66, 131, 143(2) or 235 of this Act or section 7(4) of the Company Directors Disqualification Act 1986.

30. Provision making non-compliance with any of the rules a criminal offence.

31. Provision making different provision for different cases or descriptions of cases, including different provisions for different areas.

. . . . . .

Section 430

SCHEDULE 10

PUNISHMENT OF OFFENCES UNDER THIS ACT

Note: In the fourth and fifth columns of this Schedule, "the statutory maximum" means—
   (*a*) in England and Wales, the prescribed sum under section 32 of the Magistrates' Courts Act 1980 (c. 43), and
   (*b*) in Scotland, the prescribed sum under section 289B of the Criminal Procedure (Scotland) Act 1975 (c. 21).

Section of Act creating offence	General nature of offence	Mode of prosecution	Punishment	Daily default fine (where applicable)
12(2)	Company and others failing to state in correspondence etc. that administrator appointed.	Summary.	One-fifth of the statutory maximum.	One-fiftieth of the statutory maximum.
15(8)	Failure of administrator to register office copy of court order permitting disposal of charged property.	Summary.	One-fifth of the statutory maximum.	One-fiftieth of the statutory maximum.
18(5)	Failure of administrator to register office copy of court order varying or discharging administration order.	Summary.	One-fifth of the statutory maximum.	One-fiftieth of the statutory maximum.
21(3)	Administrator failing to register administration order and give notice of appointment.	Summary.	One-fifth of the statutory maximum.	One-fiftieth of the statutory maximum.
22(6)	Failure to comply with provisions relating to statement of affairs, where administrator appointed.	1. On indictment. 2. Summary.	A fine. The statutory maximum.	One-tenth of the statutory maximum.
23(3)	Administrator failing to send out, register and lay before creditors statement of his proposals.	Summary.	One-fifth of the statutory maximum.	One-fiftieth of the statutory maximum.
24(7)	Administrator failing to file court order discharging administration order under s. 24	Summary.	One-fifth of the statutory maximum.	One-fiftieth of the statutory maximum.
27(6)	Administrator failing to file court order discharging administration order under s. 27.	Summary.	One-fifth of the statutory maximum.	One-fiftieth of the statutory maximum.
30	Body corporate acting as receiver.	1. On indictment. 2. Summary.	A fine. The statutory maximum.	

Section	Description of offence	Mode of prosecution	Punishment	Daily default fine
31	Undischarged bankrupt acting as receiver or manager.	1. On indictment. 2. Summary.	Two years or a fine, or both. Six months or the statutory maximum, or both.	One-fiftieth of the statutory maximum.
38(5)	Receiver failing to deliver accounts to registrar.	Summary.	One-fifth of the statutory maximum.	One-fiftieth of the statutory maximum.
39(2)	Company and others failing to state in correspondence that receiver appointed.	Summary.	One-fifth of the statutory maximum.	
43(6)	Administrative receiver failing to file office copy of order permitting disposal of charged property.	Summary.	One-fifth of the statutory maximum.	One-fiftieth of the statutory maximum.
45(5)	Administrative receiver failing to file notice of vacation of office.	Summary.	One-fifth of the statutory maximum.	One-fiftieth of the statutory maximum.
46(4)	Administrative receiver failing to give notice of his appointment.	Summary.	One-fifth of the statutory maximum.	One-fiftieth of the statutory maximum.
47(6)	Failure to comply with provisions relating to statement of affairs, where administrative receiver appointed.	1. On indictment. 2. Summary.	A fine. The statutory maximum.	One-tenth of the statutory maximum.
48(8)	Administrative receiver failing to comply with requirements as to his report.	Summary.	One-fifth of the statutory maximum.	One-fiftieth of the statutory maximum.
51(4)	Body corporate or Scottish firm acting as receiver.	1. On indictment. 2. Summary.	A fine. The statutory maximum.	
51(5)	Undischarged bankrupt acting as receiver (Scotland).	1. On indictment. 2. Summary.	Two years or a fine, or both. Six months or the statutory maximum, or both.	
53(2)	Failing to deliver to registrar copy of instrument of appointment of receiver.	Summary.	One-fifth of the statutory maximum	One-fiftieth of the statutory maximum.
54(3)	Failing to deliver to registrar the court's interlocutor appointing receiver.	Summary.	One-fifth of the statutory maximum.	One-fiftieth of the statutory maximum.
61(7)	Receiver failing to send to registrar certified copy of court order authorising disposal of charged property.	Summary.	One-fifth of the statutory maximum.	One-fiftieth of the statutory maximum.
62(5)	Failing to give notice to registrar of cessation or removal of receiver.	Summary.	One-fifth of the statutory maximum.	One-fiftieth of the statutory maximum.
64(2)	Company and others failing to state on correspondence etc. that receiver appointed.	Summary.	One-fifth of the statutory maximum.	One-fiftieth of the statutory maximum.
65(4)	Receiver failing to send or publish notice of his appointment.	Summary.	One-fifth of the statutory maximum.	One-fiftieth of the statutory maximum.

Section of Act creating offence	General nature of offence	Mode of prosecution	Punishment	Daily default fine (where applicable)
66(6)	Failing to comply with provisions concerning statement of affairs, where receiver appointed.	1. On indictment. 2. Summary.	A fine. The statutory maximum.	One-tenth of the statutory maximum.
67(8)	Receiver failing to comply with requirements as to his report.	Summary.	One-fifth of the statutory maximum.	One-fiftieth of the statutory maximum.
85(2)	Company failing to give notice in *Gazette* of resolution for voluntary winding up.	Summary.	One-fifth of the statutory maximum.	One-fiftieth of the statutory maximum.
89(4)	Director making statutory declaration of company's solvency without reasonable grounds for his opinion.	1. On indictment. 2. Summary.	Two years or a fine, or both. Six months or the statutory maximum, or both.	
89(6)	Declaration under section 89 not delivered to registrar within prescribed time.	Summary.	One-fifth of the statutory maximum.	One-fiftieth of the statutory maximum.
93(3)	Liquidator failing to summon general meeting of company at each year's end.	Summary.	One-fifth of the statutory maximum.	
94(4)	Liquidator failing to send to registrar a copy of account of winding up and return of final meeting.	Summary.	One-fifth of the statutory maximum.	One-fiftieth of the statutory maximum.
94(6)	Liquidator failing to call final meeting.	Summary.	One-fifth of the statutory maximum.	
95(8)	Liquidator failing to comply with s. 95, where company insolvent.	Summary.	The statutory maximum.	
98(6)	Company failing to comply with s. 98 in respect of summoning and giving notice of creditors' meeting.	1. On indictment. 2. Summary.	A fine. The statutory maximum.	
99(3)	Directors failing to attend and lay statement in prescribed form before creditors' meeting.	1. On indictment. 2. Summary.	A fine. The statutory maximum.	
105(3)	Liquidator failing to summon company general meeting and creditors' meeting at each year's end.	Summary.	One-fifth of the statutory maximum.	
106(4)	Liquidator failing to send to registrar account of winding up and return of final meetings.	Summary.	One-fifth of the statutory maximum.	One-fiftieth of the statutory maximum.
106(6)	Liquidator failing to call final meeting of company or creditors.	Summary.	One-fifth of the statutory maximum.	
109(2)	Liquidator failing to publish notice of his appointment.	Summary.	One-fifth of the statutory maximum.	One-fiftieth of the statutory maximum.
114(4)	Directors exercising powers in breach of s. 114, where no liquidator.	Summary.	The statutory maximum.	

Section	Description	Mode of prosecution	Punishment	Daily default fine
131(7)	Failing to comply with requirements as to statement of affairs, where liquidator appointed.	1. On indictment. 2. Summary.	A fine. The statutory maximum.	One-tenth of the statutory maximum.
164	Giving, offering etc. corrupt inducement affecting appointment of liquidator.	1. On indictment. 2. Summary.	A fine. The statutory maximum.	
166(7)	Liquidator failing to comply with requirements of s. 166 in creditors' voluntary winding up.	Summary.	The statutory maximum.	
188(2)	Default in compliance with s. 188 as to notification that the company being wound up.	Summary.	One-fifth of the statutory maximum.	
192(2)	Liquidator failing to notify registrar as to progress of winding up.	Summary.	One-fifth of the statutory maximum.	One-fiftieth of the statutory maximum.
201(4)	Failing to deliver to registrar office copy of court order deferring dissolution.	Summary.	One-fifth of the statutory maximum.	One-fiftieth of the statutory maximum.
203(6)	Failing to deliver to registrar copy of directions or result of appeal under s. 203.	Summary.	One-fifth of the statutory maximum.	One-fiftieth of the statutory maximum.
204(7)	Liquidator failing to deliver to registrar copy of court order for early dissolution.	Summary.	One-fifth of the statutory maximum.	One-fiftieth of the statutory maximum.
204(8)	Failing to deliver to registrar copy of court order deferring early dissolution.	Summary.	One-fifth of the statutory maximum.	One-fiftieth of the statutory maximum.
205(7)	Failing to deliver to registrar copy of Secretary of State's directions or court order deferring dissolution.	Summary.	One-fifth of the statutory maximum.	One-fiftieth of the statutory maximum.
206(1)	Fraud etc. in anticipation of winding up.	1. On indictment. 2. Summary.	Seven years or a fine, or both. Six months or the statutory maximum, or both.	
206(2)	Privity to fraud in anticipation of winding up; fraud, or privity to fraud, after commencement of winding up.	1. On indictment. 2. Summary.	Seven years or a fine, or both. Six months or the statutory maximum, or both.	
206(5)	Knowingly taking in pawn or pledge, or otherwise receiving, company property.	1. On indictment. 2. Summary.	Seven years or a fine, or both. Six months or the statutory maximum, or both.	
207	Officer of company entering into transaction in fraud of company's creditors.	1. On indictment. 2. Summary.	Two years or a fine, or both. Six months or the statutory maximum, or both.	

Section of Act creating offence	General nature of offence	Mode of prosecution	Punishment	Daily default fine (where applicable)
208	Officer of company misconducting himself in course of winding up.	1. On indictment. 2. Summary.	Seven years or a fine, or both. Six months or the statutory maximum, or both.	
209	Officer or contributory destroying, falsifying, etc. company's books.	1. On indictment. 2. Summary.	Seven years or a fine, or both. Six months or the statutory maximum, or both.	
210	Officer of company making material omission from statement relating to company's affairs.	1. On indictment. 2. Summary.	Seven years or a fine, or both. Six months or the statutory maximum, or both.	
211	False representation or fraud for purpose of obtaining creditors' consent to an agreement in connection with winding up.	1. On indictment. 2. Summary.	Seven years or a fine, or both. Six months or the statutory maximum, or both.	
216(4)	Contravening restrictions on re-use of name of company in insolvent liquidation.	1. On indictment. 2. Summary.	Two years or a fine, or both. Six months or the statutory maximum, or both.	
235(5)	Failing to co-operate with office-holder.	1. On indictment. 2. Summary.	A fine. The statutory maximum.	One-tenth of the statutory maximum.
... 389	Acting as insolvency practitioner when not qualified.	1. On indictment. 2. Summary.	Two years or a fine, or both. Six months or the statutory maximum, or both.	
429(5)	Contravening s. 429 in respect of disabilities imposed by county court on revocation of administration order.	1. On indictment. 2. Summary.	Two years or a fine, or both. Six months or the statutory maximum, or both.	
Sch. 7, para. 4(3).	Failure to attend and give evidence to Insolvency Practitioners Tribunal; suppressing, concealing, etc. relevant documents.	Summary.	Level 3 on the standard scale within the meaning given by section 75 of the Criminal Justice Act 1982.	

SCHEDULE 11

TRANSITIONAL PROVISIONS AND SAVINGS

PART I

COMPANY INSOLVENCY AND WINDING UP

Administration orders

1.—(1) Where any right to appoint an administrative receiver of a company is conferred by any debentures or floating charge created before the appointed day, the conditions precedent to the exercise of that right are deemed to include the presentation of a petition applying for an administration order to be made in relation to the company.

(2) "Administrative receiver" here has the meaning assigned by section 251.

Receivers and managers (England and Wales)

2.—(1) In relation to any receiver or manager of a company's property who was appointed before the appointed day, the new law does not apply; and the relevant provisions of the former law continue to have effect.

(2) "The new law" here means Chapter I of Part III, and Part VI, of this Act; and "the former law" means the Companies Act and so much of this Act as replaces provisions of that Act (without the amendments in paragraphs 15 to 17 of Schedule 6 to the Insolvency Act 1985, or the associated repeals made by that Act), and any provision of the Insolvency Act 1985 which was in force before the appointed day.

(3) This paragraph is without prejudice to the power conferred by this Act under which rules under section 411 may make transitional provision in connection with the coming into force of those rules; and such provision may apply those rules in relation to the receiver or manager of a company's property notwithstanding that he was appointed before the coming into force of the rules or section 411.

Receivers (Scotland)

3.—(1) In relation to any receiver appointed under section 467 of the Companies Act before the appointed day, the new law does not apply and the relevant provisions of the former law continue to have effect.

(2) "The new law" here means Chapter II of Part III, and Part VI, of this Act; and "the former law" means the Companies Act and so much of this Act as replaces provisions of that Act (without the amendments in paragraphs 18 to 22 of Schedule 6 to the Insolvency Act 1985 or the associated repeals made by that Act), and any provision of the Insolvency Act 1985 which was in force before the appointed day.

(3) This paragraph is without prejudice to the power conferred by this Act under which rules under section 411 may make transitional provision in connection with the coming into force of those rules; and such provision may apply those rules in relation to a receiver appointed under section 467 notwithstanding that he was appointed before the coming into force of the rules or section 411.

Winding up already in progress

4.—(1) In relation to any winding up which has commenced, or is treated as having commenced, before the appointed day, the new law does not apply, and the former law continues to have effect, subject to the following paragraphs.

(2) "The new law" here means any provisions in the first Group of Parts of this Act which replace sections 66 to 87 and 89 to 105 of the Insolvency Act 1985; and "the former law" means Parts XX and XXI of the Companies Act (without the amendments in paragraphs 23 to 52 of Schedule 6 to the Insolvency Act 1985, or the associated repeals made by that Act).

Statement of affairs

5.—(1) Where a winding up by the court in England and Wales has commenced, or is treated as having commenced, before the appointed day, the official receiver or (on appeal from a refusal by him) the court may, at any time on or after that day—

(*a*) release a person from an obligation imposed on him by or under section 528 of the Companies Act (statement of affairs), or

(*b*) extend the period specified in subsection (6) of that section.

(2) Accordingly, on and after the appointed day, section 528(6) has effect in relation to a winding up to which this paragraph applies with the omission of the words from "or within" onwards.

Provisions relating to liquidator

6.—(1) This paragraph applies as regards the liquidator in the case of a winding up by the court in England and Wales commenced, or treated as having commenced, before the appointed day.

(2) The official receiver may, at any time when he is liquidator of the company, apply to the Secretary of State for the appointment of a liquidator in his (the official receiver's) place; and on any such application the Secretary of State shall either make an appointment or decline to make one.

(3) Where immediately before the appointed day the liquidator of the company has not made an application under section 545 of the Companies Act (release of liquidators), then—

(*a*) except where the Secretary of State otherwise directs, sections 146(1) and (2) and 172(8) of this Act apply, and section 545 does not apply, in relation to any liquidator of that company who holds office on or at any time after the appointed day and is not the official receiver;

(*b*) section 146(3) applies in relation to the carrying out at any time after that day by any liquidator of the company of any of his functions; and

(*c*) a liquidator in relation to whom section 172(8) has effect by virtue of this paragraph has his release with effect from the time specified in section 174(4)(*d*) of this Act.

(4) Subsection (6) of section 174 of this Act has effect for the purposes of sub-paragraph (3)(*c*) above as it has for the purposes of that section, but as if the reference to section 212 were to section 631 of the Companies Act.

(5) The liquidator may employ a solicitor to assist him in the carrying out of his functions without the permission of the committee of inspection; but if he does so employ a solicitor he shall inform the committee of inspection that he has done so.

Winding up under supervision of the court

7. The repeals in Part II of Schedule 10 to the Insolvency Act 1985 of references (in the Companies Act and elsewhere) to a winding up under the supervision of the court do not affect the operation of the enactments in which the references are contained in relation to any case in which an order under section 606 of the Companies Act (power to order winding up under supervision) was made before the appointed day.

Saving for power to make rules

8.—(1) Paragraphs 4 to 7 are without prejudice to the power conferred by this Act under which rules made under section 411 may make transitional provision in connection with the coming into force of those rules.

(2) Such provision may apply those rules in relation to a winding up notwithstanding that the winding up commenced, or is treated as having commenced, before the coming into force of the rules or section 411.

Setting aside of preferences and other transactions

9.—(1) Where a provision in Part VI of this Act applies in relation to a winding up or in relation to a case in which an administration order has been made, a preference given, floating charge created or other transaction entered into before the appointed day shall not be set aside under that provision except to the extent that it could have been set aside under the law in force immediately before that day, assuming for this purpose that any relevant administration order had been a winding-up order.

(2) The references above to setting aside a preference, floating charge or other transaction include the making of an order which varies or reverses any effect of a preference, floating charge or other transaction.

PART II

INDIVIDUAL INSOLVENCY

[Not applicable to Scotland.]

PART III

TRANSITIONAL EFFECT OF PART XVI

[Not applicable to Scotland.]

PART IV

INSOLVENCY PRACTITIONERS

21. Where an individual began to act as an insolvency practitioner in relation to any person before the appointed day, nothing in section 390(2) or (3) prevents that individual from being qualified to act as an insolvency practitioner in relation to that person.

PART V

GENERAL TRANSITIONAL PROVISIONS AND SAVINGS

Interpretation for this Part

22. In this Part of this Schedule, "the former enactments" means so much of the Companies Act as is repealed and replaced by this Act, the Insolvency Act 1985 and the other enactments repealed by this Act.

General saving for past acts and events

23. So far as anything done or treated as done under or for the purposes of any provision of the former enactments could have been done under or for the purposes of the corresponding provision of this Act, it is not invalidated by the repeal of that provision but has effect as if done under or for the purposes of the corresponding provision; and any order, regulation, rule or other instrument made or having effect under any provision of the former enactments shall, insofar as its effect is preserved by this paragraph, be treated for all purposes as made and having effect under the corresponding provision.

Periods of time

24. Where any period of time specified in a provision of the former enactments is current immediately before the appointed day, this Act has effect as if the corresponding provision had been in force when the period began to run; and (without prejudice to the foregoing) any period of time so specified and current is deemed for the purposes of this Act—
   (a) to run from the date or event from which it was running immediately before the appointed day, and
   (b) to expire (subject to any provision of this Act for its extension) whenever it would have expired if this Act had not been passed;
and any rights, priorities, liabilities, reliefs, obligations, requirements, powers, duties or exemptions dependent on the beginning, duration or end of such a period as above mentioned shall be under this Act as they were or would have been under the former enactments.

Internal cross-references in this Act

25. Where in any provision of this Act there is a reference to another such provision, and the first-mentioned provision operates, or is capable of operating, in relation to things done or omitted, or events occurring or not occurring, in the past (including in particular past acts of compliance with any enactment, failures of compliance, contraventions, offences and convictions of offences), the reference to the other provision is to be read as including a reference to the corresponding provision of the former enactments.

Punishment of offences

26.—(1) Offences committed before the appointed day under any provision of the former enactments may, notwithstanding any repeal by this Act, be prosecuted and punished after that day as if this Act had not passed.

(2) A contravention of any provision of the former enactments committed before the appointed day shall not be visited with any severer punishment under or by virtue of this Act than would have been applicable under that provision at the time of the contravention; but where an offence for the continuance of which a penalty was provided has been committed under any provision of the former enactments, proceedings may be taken under this Act in respect of the continuance of the offence on and after the appointed day in the like manner as if the offence had been committed under the corresponding provision of this Act.

References elsewhere to the former enactments

27.—(1) A reference in any enactment, instrument or document (whether express or implied, and in whatever phraseology) to a provision of the former enactments (including the corresponding provision of any yet earlier enactment) is to be read, where necessary to retain for the enactment, instrument or document the same force and effect as it would have had but for the passing of this Act, as, or as including, a reference to the corresponding provision by which it is replaced in this Act.

(2) The generality of the preceding sub-paragraph is not affected by any specific conversion of references made by this Act, nor by the inclusion in any provision of this Act of a reference (whether express or implied, and in whatever phraseology) to the provision of the former enactments corresponding to that provision, or to a provision of the former enactments which is replaced by a corresponding provision of this Act.

Saving for power to repeal provisions in section 51

28. The Secretary of State may by order in a statutory instrument repeal subsections (3) to (5) of section 51 of this Act and the entries in Schedule 10 relating to subsections (4) and (5) of that section.

Saving for Interpretation Act 1978 ss.16, 17

29. Nothing in this Schedule is to be taken as prejudicing sections 16 and 17 of the Interpretation Act 1978 (savings from, and effect of, repeals); and for the purposes of section 17(2) of that Act (construction of references to enactments repealed and replaced, etc.), so much of section 18 of the Insolvency Act 1985 as is replaced by a provision of this Act is deemed to have been repealed by this Act and not by the Company Directors Disqualification Act 1986.

Section 438   SCHEDULE 12

ENACTMENTS REPEALED

[Repeals to Acts reprinted in *The Parliament House Book* have been given effect.]

Section 439(1)   SCHEDULE 13

CONSEQUENTIAL AMENDMENTS OF COMPANIES ACT 1985

[Amendments affecting *The Parliament House Book* have been given effect.]

[THE NEXT PAGE IS I 663]

Section 439(2)

SCHEDULE 14

[Amendments to Acts reprinted in *The Parliament House Book* have been given effect.]

Company Directors Disqualification Act 1986

(1986 c. 46)

An Act to consolidate certain enactments relating to the disqualification of persons from being directors of companies, and from being otherwise concerned with a company's affairs.

[25th July 1986]

ARRANGEMENT OF SECTIONS

Preliminary

Disqualification orders: general

1.—(1) In the circumstances specified below in this Act a court may, and under section 6 shall, make against a person a disqualification order, that is to say an order that he shall not, without leave of the court—

(a) be a director of a company, or
(b) be a liquidator or administrator of a company, or
(c) be a receiver or manager of a company's property, or
(d) in any way, whether directly or indirectly, be concerned or take part in the promotion, formation or management of a company,

for a specified period beginning with the date of the order.

(2) In each section of this Act which gives to a court power or, as the case may be, imposes on it the duty to make a disqualification order there is specified the maximum (and, in section 6, the minimum) period of disqualification which may or (as the case may be) must be imposed by means of the order.

(3) Where a disqualification order is made against a person who is already subject to such an order, the periods specified in those orders shall run concurrently.

(4) A disqualification order may be made on grounds which are or include matters other than criminal convictions, notwithstanding that the person in respect of whom it is to be made may be criminally liable in respect of those matters.

Disqualification for general misconduct in connection with companies

Disqualification on conviction of indictable offence

2.—(1) The court may make a disqualification order against a person where he is convicted of an indictable offence (whether on indictment or summarily) in connection with the promotion, formation, management or liquidation of a company, or with the receivership or management of a company's property.

(2) "The court" for this purpose means—

(*a*) any court having jurisdiction to wind up the company in relation to which the offence was committed, or

(*b*) the court by or before which the person is convicted of the offence, or

(*c*) in the case of a summary conviction in England and Wales, any other magistrates' court acting for the same petty sessions area;

and for the purposes of this section the definition of "indictable offence" in Schedule 1 to the Interpretation Act 1978 applies for Scotland as it does for England and Wales.

(3) The maximum period of disqualification under this section is—

(*a*) where the disqualification order is made by a court of summary jurisdiction, five years, and

(*b*) in any other case, 15 years.

Disqualification for persistent breaches of companies legislation

3.—(1) The court may make a disqualification order against a person where it appears to it that he has been persistently in default in relation to provisions of the companies legislation requiring any return, account or other document to be filed with, delivered or sent, or notice of any matter to be given, to the registrar of companies.

(2) On an application to the court for an order to be made under this section, the fact that a person has been persistently in default in relation to such provisions as are mentioned above may (without prejudice to its proof in any other manner) be conclusively proved by showing that in the five years ending with the date of the application he has been adjudged guilty (whether or not on the same occasion) of three or more defaults in relation to those provisions.

¹ (3) A person is to be treated under subsection (2) as being adjudged guilty of a default in relation to any provision of that legislation if—

(*a*) he is convicted (whether on indictment or summarily) of an offence consisting in a contravention of or failure to comply with that provision (whether on his own part or on the part of any company), or

(*b*) a default order is made against him, that is to say an order under any of the following provisions—

(i) section 242(4) of the Companies Act (order requiring delivery of company accounts),

(ii) section 713 of that Act (enforcement of company's duty to make returns),

(iii) section 41 of the Insolvency Act (enforcement of receiver's or manager's duty to make returns), or

(iv) section 170 of that Act (corresponding provision for liquidator in winding up),

in respect of any such contravention of or failure to comply with that provision (whether on his own part or on the part of any company).

(4) In this section "the court" means any court having jurisdiction to wind up any of the companies in relation to which the offence or other default has been or is alleged to have been committed.

(5) The maximum period of disqualification under this section is five years.

NOTE
[1] As amended by the Companies Act 1989, Sched. 10, para. 35(2).

Disqualification for fraud, etc., in winding up
4.—(1) The court may make a disqualification order against a person if, in the course of the winding up of a company, it appears that he—
  (*a*) has been guilty of an offence for which he is liable (whether he has been convicted or not) under section 458 of the Companies Act (fraudulent trading), or
  (*b*) has otherwise been guilty, while an officer or liquidator of the company or receiver or manager of its property, of any fraud in relation to the company or of any breach of his duty as such officer, liquidator, receiver or manager.

(2) In this section "the court" means any court having jurisdiction to wind up any of the companies in relation to which the offence or other default has been or is alleged to have been committed; and "officer" includes a shadow director.

(3) the maximum period of disqualification under this section is 15 years.

Disqualification on summary conviction
5.—(1) An offence counting for the purposes of this section is one of which a person is convicted (either on indictment or summarily) in consequence of a contravention of, or failure to comply with, any provision of the companies legislation requiring a return, account or other document to be filed with, delivered or sent, or notice of any matter to be given, to the registrar of companies (whether the contravention or failure is on the person's own part or on the part of any company).

(2) Where a person is convicted of a summary offence counting for those purposes, the court by which he is convicted (or, in England and Wales, any other magistrates' court acting for the same petty sessions area) may make a disqualification order against him if the circumstances specified in the next subsection are present.

(3) Those circumstances are that, during the five years ending with the date of the conviction, the person has had made against him, or has been convicted of, in total not less than three default orders and offences counting for the purposes of this section; and those offences may include that of which he is convicted as mentioned in subsection (2) and any other offence of which he is convicted on the same occasion.

(4) For the purposes of this section—
  (*a*) the definition of "summary offence" in Schedule 1 to the Interpretation Act 1978 applies for Scotland as for England and Wales, and
  (*b*) "default order" means the same as in section 3(3)(*b*).

(5) The maximum period of disqualification under this section is five years.

Disqualification for unfitness

Duty of court to disqualify unfit directors of insolvent companies
6.—(1) The court shall make a disqualification order against a person in any case where, on an application under this section, it is satisfied—
  (*a*) that he is or has been a director of a company which has at any time become insolvent (whether while he was a director or subsequently), and
  (*b*) that his conduct as a director of that company (either taken alone or taken together with his conduct as a director of any other company or companies) makes him unfit to be concerned in the management of a company.

(2) For the purposes of this section and the next, a company becomes insolvent if—

   (*a*) the company goes into liquidation at a time when its assets are insufficient for the payment of its debts and other liabilities and the expenses of the winding up,

   (*b*) an administration order is made in relation to the company, or

   (*c*) an administrative receiver of the company is appointed;

and references to a person's conduct as a director of any company or companies include, where that company or any of those companies has become insolvent, that person's conduct in relation to any matter connected with or arising out of the insolvency of that company.

(3) In this section and the next "the court" means—

   (*a*) in the case of a person who is or has been a director of a company which is being wound up by the court, the court by which the company is being wound up,

   (*b*) in the case of a person who is or has been a director of a company which is being wound up voluntarily, any court having jurisdiction to wind up the company,

   (*c*) in the case of a person who is or has been a director of a company in relation to which an administration order is in force, the court by which that order was made, and

   (*d*) in any other case, the High Court or, in Scotland, the Court of Session;

and in both sections "director" includes a shadow director.

(4) Under this section the minimum period of disqualification is two years, and the maximum period is 15 years.

Applications to court under s.6; reporting provisions

   7.—(1) If it appears to the Secretary of State that it is expedient in the public interest that a disqualification order under section 6 should be made against any person, an application for the making of such an order against that person may be made—

   (*a*) by the Secretary of State, or

   (*b*) if the Secretary of State so directs in the case of a person who is or has been a director of a company which is being wound up by the court in England and Wales, by the official receiver.

(2) Except with the leave of the court, an application for the making under that section of a disqualification order against any person shall not be made after the end of the period of two years beginning with the day on which the company of which that person is or has been a director became insolvent.

(3) If it appears to the office-holder responsible under this section, that is to say—

   (*a*) in the case of a company which is being wound up by the court in England and Wales, the official receiver,

   (*b*) in the case of a company which is being wound up otherwise, the liquidator,

   (*c*) in the case of a company in relation to which an administration order is in force, the administrator, or

   (*d*) in the case of a company of which there is an administrative receiver, that receiver

that the conditions mentioned in section 6(1) are satisfied as respects a person who is or has been a director of that company, the office-holder shall forthwith report the matter to the Secretary of State.

(4) The Secretary of State or the official receiver may require the liquidator, administrator or administrative receiver of a company, or the former liquidator, administrator or administrative receiver of a company—

   (*a*) to furnish him with such information with respect to any person's conduct as a director of the company, and

   (*b*) to produce and permit inspection of such books, papers and other records relevant to that person's conduct as such a director, as the Secretary of State or the official receiver may reasonably require for the purpose of determining whether to exercise, or of exercising, any function of his under this section.

NOTE
  [1] See the Banking Act 1987, s.85(1)(*e*).

Disqualification after investigation of company
  [1] **8.**—(1) If it appears to the Secretary of State from a report made by inspectors under section 437 of the Companies Act or section 94 or 177 of the Financial Services Act 1986, or from information or documents obtained under section 447 or 448 of the Companies Act or section 105 of the Financial Services Act 1986 or section 2 of the Criminal Justice Act 1987 or section 52 of the Criminal Justice (Scotland) Act 1987 or section 83 of the Companies Act 1989, that it is expedient in the public interest that a disqualification order should be made against any person who is or has been a director or shadow director of any company, he may apply to the court for such an order to be made against that person.

(2) The court may make a disqualification order against a person where, on an application under this section, it is satisfied that his conduct in relation to the company makes him unfit to be concerned in the management of a company.

(3) In this section "the court" means the High Court or, in Scotland, the Court of Session.

(4) The maximum period of disqualification under this section is 15 years.

NOTE
  [1] As amended by the Financial Services Act 1986, s.198(2), the Criminal Justice (Scotland) Act 1987, s.55(*b*), the Criminal Justice Act 1988, s.145(*b*) and the Companies Act 1989, s.79. See the Banking Act 1987, s.85(1)(*e*).

Matters for determining unfitness of directors
  9.—(1) Where it falls to a court to determine whether a person's conduct as a director or shadow director of any particular company or companies makes him unfit to be concerned in the management of a company, the court shall, as respects his conduct as a director of that company or, as the case may be, each of those companies, have regard in particular—

  (*a*) to the matters mentioned in Part I of Schedule 1 to this Act, and
  (*b*) where the company has become insolvent, to the matters mentioned in Part II of that Schedule;

and references in that Schedule to the director and the company are to be read accordingly.

(2) Section 6(2) applies for the purposes of this section and Schedule 1 as it applies for the purposes of sections 6 and 7.

(3) Subject to the next subsection, any reference in Schedule 1 to an enactment contained in the Companies Act or the Insolvency Act includes, in relation to any time before the coming into force of that enactment, the corresponding enactment in force at that time.

(4) The Secretary of State may by order modify any of the provisions of Schedule 1; and such an order may contain such transitional provisions as may appear to the Secretary of State necessary or expedient.

(5) The power to make orders under this section is exercisable by statutory instrument subject to annulment in pursuance of a resolution of either House of Parliament.

Other cases of disqualification

Participation in wrongful trading
  10.—(1) Where the court makes a declaration under section 213 or 214 of the Insolvency Act that a person is liable to make a contribution to a company's assets, then, whether or not an application for such an order is made by any person, the court may, if it thinks fit, also make a disqualification order against the person to whom the declaration relates.

(2) The maximum period of disqualification under this section is 15 years.

Undischarged bankrupts

11.—(1) It is an offence for a person who is an undischarged bankrupt to act as director of, or directly or indirectly to take part in or be concerned in the promotion, formation or management of, a company, except with the leave of the court.

(2) "The court" for this purpose is the court by which the person was adjudged bankrupt or, in Scotland, sequestration of his estates was awarded.

(3) In England and Wales, the leave of the court shall not be given unless notice of intention to apply for it has been served on the official receiver; and it is the latter's duty, if he is of opinion that it is contrary to the public interest that the application should be granted, to attend on the hearing of the application and oppose it.

Failure to pay under county court administration order

12.—(1) The following has effect where a court under section 429 of the Insolvency Act revokes an administration order under Part VI of the County Courts Act 1984.

(2) A person to whom that section applies by virtue of the order under section 429(2)(*b*) shall not, except with the leave of the court which made the order, act as director or liquidator of, or directly or indirectly take part or be concerned in the promotion, formation or management of, a company.

Consequences of contravention

Criminal penalties

13.—(1) If a person acts in contravention of a disqualification order or of section 12(2), or is guilty of an offence under section 11, he is liable—

   (*a*) on conviction on indictment, to imprisonment for not more than two years or a fine, or both; and

   (*b*) on summary conviction, to imprisonment for not more than six months or a fine not exceeding the statutory maximum, or both.

Offences by body corporate

14.—(1) Where a body corporate is guilty of an offence of acting in contravention of a disqualification order, and it is proved that the offence occurred with the consent or connivance of, or was attributable to any neglect on the part of a director, manager, secretary or other similar officer of the body corporate, or any person who was purporting to act in any such capacity he, as well as the body corporate, is guilty of the offence and liable to be proceeded against and punished accordingly.

(2) Where the affairs of a body corporate are managed by its members, subsection (1) applies in relation to the acts and defaults of a member in connection with his functions of management as if he were a director of the body corporate.

Personal liability for company's debts where person acts while disqualified

15.—(1) A person is personally responsible for all the relevant debts of a company if at any time—

   (*a*) in contravention of a disqualification order or of section 11 of this Act he is involved in the management of the company, or

   (*b*) as a person who is involved in the management of the company, he acts or is willing to act on instructions given without the leave of the court by a person whom he knows at that time to be the subject of a disqualification order or to be an undischarged bankrupt.

(2) Where a person is personally responsible under this section for the relevant debts of a company, he is jointly and severally liable in respect of those debts with the company and any other person who, whether under this section or otherwise, is so liable.

(3) For the purposes of this section the relevant debts of a company are—

    (*a*) in relation to a person who is personally responsible under paragraph (*a*) of subsection (1), such debts and other liabilities of the company as are incurred at a time when that person was involved in the management of the company, and

    (*b*) in relation to a person who is personally responsible under paragraph (*b*) of that subsection, such debts and other liabilities of the company as are incurred at a time when that person was acting or was willing to act on instructions given as mentioned in that paragraph.

(4) For the purposes of this section, a person is involved in the management of a company if he is a director of the company or if he is concerned, whether directly or indirectly, or takes part, in the management of the company.

(5) For the purposes of this section a person who, as a person involved in the management of a company, has at any time acted on instructions given without the leave of the court by a person whom he knew at that time to be the subject of a disqualification order or to be an undischarged bankrupt is presumed, unless the contrary is shown, to have been willing at any time thereafter to act on any instructions given by that person.

Supplementary provisions

Application for disqualification order

16.—(1) A person intending to apply for the making of a disqualification order by the court having jurisdiction to wind up a company shall give not less than 10 days' notice of his intention to the person against whom the order is sought; and on the hearing of the application the last-mentioned person may appear and himself give evidence or call witnesses.

(2) An application to a court with jurisdiction to wind up companies for the making against any person of a disqualification order under any of sections 2 to 5 may be made by the Secretary of State or the official receiver, or by the liquidator or any past or present member or creditor of any company in relation to which that person has committed or is alleged to have committed an offence or other default.

(3) On the hearing of any application under this Act made by the Secretary of State or the official receiver or the liquidator, the applicant shall appear and call the attention of the court to any matters which seem to him to be relevant, and may himself give evidence or call witnesses.

Application for leave under an order

17.—(1) As regards the court to which application must be made for leave under a disqualification order, the following applies—

    (*a*) where the application is for leave to promote or form a company, it is any court with jurisdiction to wind up companies, and

    (*b*) where the application is for leave to be a liquidator, administrator or director of, or otherwise to take part in the management of a company, or to be a receiver or manager of a company's property, it is any court having jurisdiction to wind up that company.

(2) On the hearing of an application for leave made by a person against whom a disqualification order has been made on the application of the Secretary of State, the official receiver or the liquidator, the Secretary of State, official receiver or liquidator shall appear and call the attention of the court to any matters which seem to him to be relevant, and may himself give evidence or call witnesses.

Register of disqualification orders

18.—(1) The Secretary of State may make regulations[1] requiring officers of courts to furnish him with such particulars as the regulations may specify of cases in which—

(*a*) a disqualification order is made, or

(*b*) any action is taken by a court in consequence of which such an order is varied or ceases to be in force, or

(*c*) leave is granted by a court for a person subject to such an order to do any thing which otherwise the order prohibits him from doing;

and the regulations may specify the time within which, and the form and manner in which, such particulars are to be furnished.

(2) The Secretary of State shall, from the particulars so furnished, continue to maintain the register of orders, and of cases in which leave has been granted as mentioned in subsection (1)(*c*), which was set up by him under section 29 of the Companies Act 1976 and continued under section 301 of the Companies Act 1985.

(3) When an order of which entry is made in the register ceases to be in force, the Secretary of State shall delete the entry from the register and all particulars relating to it which have been furnished to him under this section or any previous corresponding provision.

(4) The register shall be open to inspection on payment of such fee as may be specified by the Secretary of State in regulations.

(5) Regulations under this section shall be made by statutory instrument subject to annulment in pursuance of a resolution of either House of Parliament.

NOTE

[1] See S.I. 1986 No. 2067.

Special savings from repealed enactments

19. Schedule 2 to this Act has effect—

(*a*) in connection with certain transitional cases arising under sections 93 and 94 of the Companies Act 1981, so as to limit the power to make a disqualification order, or to restrict the duration of an order, by reference to events occurring or things done before those sections came into force.

(*b*) to preserve orders made under section 28 of the Companies Act 1976 (repealed by the Act of 1981), and

(*c*) to preclude any applications for a disqualification order under section 6 or 8, where the relevant company went into liquidation before 28th April 1986.

Miscellaneous and general

Admissibility in evidence of statements

20. In any proceedings (whether or not under this Act), any statement made in pursuance of a requirement imposed by or under sections 6 to 10, 15 or 19(*c*) of, or Schedule 1 to, this Act, or by or under rules made for the purposes of this Act under the Insolvency Act, may be used in evidence against any person making or concurring in making the statement.

Interaction with Insolvency Act

21.—(1) References in this Act to the official receiver, in relation to the winding up of a company or the bankruptcy of an individual, are to any person who, by virtue of section 399 of the Insolvency Act, is authorised to act as the official receiver in relation to that winding up or bankruptcy; and, in accordance with section 401(2) of that Act, references in this Act to an official receiver includes a person appointed as his deputy.

[1] (2) Sections 6 to 10, 15, 19(*c*) and 20 of, and Schedule 1 to, this Act are

deemed included in Parts I to VII of the Insolvency Act for the purposes of the following sections of that Act—

    section 411 (power to make insolvency rules);

    section 414 (fees orders);

    section 420 (orders extending provisions about insolvent companies to insolvent partnerships);

    section 422 (modification of such provisions in their application to recognised banks).

(3) Section 434 of that Act (Crown application) applies to sections 6 to 10, 15, 19(*c*) and 20 of, and Schedule 1 to, this Act as it does to the provisions of that Act which are there mentioned.

[2] (4) For the purposes of summary proceedings in Scotland, section 431 of that Act applies to summary proceedings for an offence under section 11 or 13 of this Act as it applies to summary proceedings for an offence under Parts I to VII of that Act.

NOTES

[1] As amended by the Companies Act 1989, Sched. 24.

[2] Inserted by the Companies Act 1989, s. 208.

Interpretation

22.—(1) This section has effect with respect to the meaning of expressions used in this Act, and applies unless the context otherwise requires.

(2) The expression "company"—

    (*a*) in section 11, includes an unregistered company and a company incorporated outside Great Britain which has an established place of business in Great Britain, and

    (*b*) elsewhere, includes any company which may be wound up under Part V of the Insolvency Act.

(3) Section 247 in Part VII of the Insolvency Act (interpretation for the first Group of Parts of that Act) applies as regards references to a company's insolvency and to its going into liquidation; and "administrative receiver" has the meaning given by section 251 of that Act.

(4) "Director" includes any person occupying the position of director, by whatever name called, and in sections 6 to 9 includes a shadow director.

(5) "Shadow director", in relation to a company, means a person in accordance with whose directions or instructions the directors of the company are accustomed to act (but so that a person is not deemed a shadow director by reason only that the directors act on advice given by him in a professional capacity).

(6) Section 740 of the Companies Act applies as regards the meaning of "body corporate"; and "officer" has the meaning given by section 744 of that Act.

(7) In references to legislation other than this Act—

    "the Companies Act" means the Companies Act 1985;

    "the Companies Acts" has the meaning given by section 744 of that Act; and

    "the Insolvency Act" means the Insolvency Act 1986;

and in sections 3(1) and 5(1) of this Act "the companies legislation" means the Companies Acts (except the Insider Dealing Act), Parts I to VII of the Insolvency Act and, in Part XV of that Act, sections 411, 413, 414, 416 and 417.

(8) Any reference to provisions, or a particular provision, of the Companies Acts or the Insolvency Act includes the corresponding provisions or provision of the former Companies Acts (as defined by section 735(1)(*c*) of the Companies Act, but including also that Act itself) or, as the case may be, the Insolvency Act 1985.

(9) Any expression for whose interpretation provision is made by Part XXVI of the Companies Act (and not by subsections (3) to (8) above) is to be construed in accordance with that provision.

Transitional provisions, savings, repeals
   23.—(1) The transitional provisions and savings in Schedule 3 to this Act have effect, and are without prejudice to anything in the Interpretation Act 1978 with regard to the effect of repeals.
   (2) The enactments specified in the second column of Schedule 4 to this Act are repealed to the extent specified in the third column of that Schedule.

Extent
   24.—(1) This Act extends to England and Wales and to Scotland.
   (2) Nothing in this Act extends to Northern Ireland.

Commencement
   [1] **25.** This Act comes into force simultaneously with the Insolvency Act 1986.

NOTE
   [1] 29th December 1986, by virtue of s.443 of that Act and S.I. 1986 No. 1924.

Citation
   26. This Act may be cited as the Company Directors Disqualification Act 1986.

SCHEDULES

Section 9   SCHEDULE 1

MATTERS FOR DETERMINING UNFITNESS OF DIRECTORS

PART I

MATTERS APPLICABLE IN ALL CASES

   1. Any misfeasance or breach of any fiduciary or other duty by the director in relation to the company.

   2. Any misapplication or retention by the director of, or any conduct by the director giving rise to an obligation to account for, any money or other property of the company.

   3. The extent of the director's responsibility for the company entering into any transaction liable to be set aside under Part XVI of the Insolvency Act (provisions against debt avoidance).

   [1] 4. The extent of the director's responsibility for any failure by the company to comply with any of the following provisions of the Companies Act, namely—
   (*a*)   section 221 (companies to keep accounting records);
   (*b*)   section 222 (where and for how long records to be kept);
   (*c*)   section 288 (register of directors and secretaries);
   (*d*)   section 352 (obligation to keep and enter up register of members);
   (*e*)   section 353 (location of register of members);
   (*f*)   sections 363 and 364 (company's duty to make annual return);
   (*g*)   section 365 (time for completion of annual return); and
   (*h*)   sections 399 and 415 (company's duty to register charges it creates).

   [2] 5. The extent of the director's responsibility for any failure by the directors of the company to comply with—
   (*a*)   section 226 or 227 of the Companies Act (duty to prepare annual accounts), or
   (*b*)   section 233 of that Act (approval and signature of accounts).

NOTES
   [1] Amended (*prosp.*) by the Companies Act 1989, s.139(4) and Sched. 16, para. 4.
   [2] Substituted by the Companies Act 1989, Sched. 10, para. 35(3).

PART II

MATTERS APPLICABLE WHERE COMPANY HAS BECOME INSOLVENT

6. The extent of the director's responsibility for the causes of the company becoming insolvent.

7. The extent of the director's responsibility for any failure by the company to supply any goods or services which have been paid for (in whole or in part).

8. The extent of the director's responsibility for the company entering into any transaction or giving any preference, being a transaction or preference—
   (a) liable to be set aside under section 127 or sections 238 to 240 of the Insolvency Act, or
   (b) challengeable under section 242 or 243 of that Act or under any rule of law in Scotland.

9. The extent of the director's responsibility for any failure by the directors of the company to comply with section 98 of the Insolvency Act (duty to call creditors' meeting in creditors' voluntary winding up).

10. Any failure by the director to comply with any obligation imposed on him by or under any of the following provisions of the Insolvency Act—
   (a) section 22 (company's statement of affairs in administration);
   (b) section 47 (statement of affairs to administrative receiver);
   (c) section 66 (statement of affairs in Scottish receivership);
   (d) section 99 (directors' duty to attend meeting; statement of affairs in creditors' voluntary winding up);
   (e) section 131 (statement of affairs in winding up by the court);
   (f) section 234 (duty of any one with company property to deliver it up);
   (g) section 235 (duty to co-operate with liquidator, etc.).

Section 19   SCHEDULE 2

SAVINGS FROM COMPANIES ACT 1981, ss.93,94,
AND INSOLVENCY ACT 1985, SCHEDULE 9

1. Sections 2 and 4(1)(b) do not apply in relation to anything done before 15th June 1982 by a person in his capacity as liquidator of a company or as receiver or manager of a company's property.

2. Subject to paragraph 1—
   (a) section 2 applies in a case where a person is convicted on indictment of an offence which he committed (and, in the case of a continuing offence, has ceased to commit) before 15th June 1982; but in such a case a disqualification order under that section shall not be made for a period in excess of five years.
   (b) that section does not apply in a case where a person is convicted summarily—
      (i) in England and Wales, if he had consented so to be tried before that date, or
      (ii) in Scotland, if the summary proceedings commenced before that date.

3. Subject to paragraph 1, section 4 applies in relation to an offence committed or other thing done before 15th June 1982; but a disqualification order made on the grounds of such an offence or other thing done shall not be made for a period in excess of five years.

4. The powers of a court under section 5 are not exercisable in a case where a person is convicted of an offence which he committed (and, in the case of a continuing offence, had ceased to commit) before 15th June 1982.

5. For purposes of section 3(1) and section 5, no account is to be taken of any offence which was committed, or any default order which was made, before 1st June 1977.

6. An order made under section 28 of the Companies Act 1976 has effect as if made under section 3 of this Act; and an application made before 15th June 1982 for such an order is to be treated as an application for an order under the section last mentioned.

7. Where—
   (a) an application is made for a disqualification order under section 6 of this Act by virtue of paragraph (a) of subsection (2) of that section, and
   (b) the company in question went into liquidation before 28th April 1986 (the coming into force of the provision replaced by section 6),

the court shall not make an order under that section unless it could have made a disqualification order under section 300 of the Companies Act as it had effect immediately before the date specified in sub-paragraph (*b*) above.

8. An application shall not be made under section 8 of this Act in relation to a report made or information or documents obtained before 28th April 1986.

Section 23(1) SCHEDULE 3

TRANSITIONAL PROVISIONS AND SAVINGS

1. In this Schedule, "the former enactments" means so much of the Companies Act, and so much of the Insolvency Act, as is repealed and replaced by this Act; and "the appointed day" means the day on which this Act comes into force.

[THE NEXT PAGE IS I675]

2. So far as anything done or treated as done under of for the purposes of any provision of the former enactments could have been done under or for the purposes of the corresponding provision of this Act, it is not invalidated by the repeal of that provision but has effect as if done under or for the purposes of the corresponding provision; and any order, regulation, rule or other instrument made or having effect under any provision of the former enactments shall, insofar as its effect is preserved by this paragraph, be treated for all purposes as made and having effect under the corresponding provision.

3. Where any period of time specified in a provision of the former enactments is current immediately before the appointed day, this Act has effect as if the corresponding provision had been in force when the period began to run; and (without prejudice to the foregoing) any period of time so specified and current is deemed for the purposes of this Act—

(a) to run from the date or event from which it was running immediately before the appointed day, and

(b) to expire (subject to any provision of this Act for its extension) whenever it would have expired if this Act had not been passed;

and any rights, priorities, liabilities, reliefs, obligations, requirements, powers, duties or exemptions dependent on the beginning, duration or end of such a period as above mentioned shall be under this Act as they were or would have been under the former enactments.

4. Where in any provision of this Act there is a reference to another such provision, and the first-mentioned provision operates, or is capable of operating, in relation to things done or omitted, or events occurring or not occurring, in the past (including in particular past acts of compliance with any enactment, failures of compliance, contraventions, offences and convictions of offences) the reference to the other provision is to be read as including a reference to the corresponding provision of the former enactments.

5. Offences committed before the appointed day under any provision of the former enactments may, notwithstanding any repeal by this Act, be prosecuted and punished after that day as if this Act had not passed.

6. A reference in any enactment, instrument or document (whether express or implied, and in whatever phraseology) to a provision of the former enactments (including the corresponding provision of any yet earlier enactment) is to be read, where necessary to retain for the enactment, instrument or document the same force and effect as it would have had but for the passing of this Act, as, or as including, a reference to the corresponding provision by which it is replaced in this Act.

Section 23(2)   SCHEDULE 4

Repeals

[Repeals to Acts reprinted in *The Parliament House Book* have been given effect.]

Financial Services Act 1986
(1986 c. 60)

An Act to . . . make new provision with respect to the official listing of securities, offers of unlisted securities, takeover offers and insider dealing; . . . and for connected purposes.

[7th November 1986]

ARRANGEMENT OF SECTIONS

Parts I to III

[Not reprinted.]

. . . . . .

PART IV

OFFICIAL LISTING OF SECURITIES

Official listing

142.—(1) No investment to which this section applies shall be admitted to the Official List of The Stock Exchange except in accordance with the provisions of this Part of this Act.

(2) Subject to subsections (3) and (4) below, this section applies to any investment falling within paragraph 1, 2, 4 or 5 of Schedule 1 to this Act.

(3) In the application of those paragraphs for the purposes of subsection (2) above—

(*a*) paragraphs 1, 4 and 5 shall have effect as if paragraph 1 did not contain the exclusion relating to building societies, industrial and provident societies or credit unions;

(*b*) paragraph 2 shall have effect as if it included any instrument falling within paragraph 3 issued otherwise than by the government of a member State or a local authority in a member State; and

(*c*) paragraphs 4 and 5 shall have effect as if they referred only to investments falling within paragraph 1.

(4) The Secretary of State may by order direct that this section shall apply also to investments falling within paragraph 6 of Schedule 1 to this Act or to such investments of any class or description.

(5) An order under subsection (4) above shall be subject to annulment in pursuance of a resolution of either House of Parliament.

(6) In this Part of this Act "the competent authority" means, subject to section 157 below, the Council of The Stock Exchange; and that authority may make rules (in this Act referred to as "listing rules") for the purposes of any of the following provisions.

(7) In this Part of this Act—

"issuer", in relation to any securities, means the person by whom they have been or are to be issued except that in relation to a certificate or other instrument falling within paragraph 5 of Schedule 1 to this

Act it means the person who issued or is to issue the securities to which the certificate or instrument relates;

"the Official List" means the Official List of The Stock Exchange;

"securities" means investments to which this section applies;

and references to listing are references to inclusion in the Official List in pursuance of this Part of this Act.

(8) Any functions of the competent authority under this Part of this Act may be exercised by any committee, sub-committee, officer or servant of the authority except that listing rules—

(a) shall be made only by the authority itself or by a committee or sub-committee of the authority; and

(b) if made by a committee or sub-committee, shall cease to have effect at the end of the period of 28 days beginning with the day on which they are made (but without prejudice to anything done under them) unless before the end of that period they are confirmed by the authority.

(9) Nothing in this Part of this Act affects the powers of the Council of The Stock Exchange in respect of investments to which this section does not apply and such investments may be admitted to the Official List otherwise than in accordance with this Part of this Act.

Applications for listing

143.—(1) An application for listing shall be made to the competent authority in such manner as the listing rules may require.

(2) No application for the listing of any securities shall be made except by or with the consent of the issuer of the securities.

(3) No application for listing shall be made in respect of securities to be issued by a private company or by an old public company within the meaning of section 1 of the Companies Consolidation (Consequential Provisions) Act 1985 or the corresponding Northern Ireland provision.

Admission to list

144.—(1) The competent authority shall not admit any securities to the Official List except on an application duly made in accordance with section 143 above and unless satisfied that—

(a) the requirements of the listing rules made by the authority for the purposes of this section and in force when the application is made; and

(b) any other requirements imposed by the authority in relation to that application,

are complied with.

(2) Without prejudice to the generality of the power of the competent authority to make listing rules for the purposes of this section, such rules may, in particular, require as a condition of the admission of any securities to the Official List—

(a) the submission to, and approval by, the authority of a document (in this Act referred to as "listing particulars") in such form and containing such information as may be specified in the rules; and

(b) the publication of that document;

or, in such cases as may be specified by the rules, the publication of a document other than listing particulars.

(3) The competent authority may refuse an application—

(a) if it considers that by reason of any matter relating to the issuer the admission of the securities would be detrimental to the interests of investors; or

(b) in the case of securities already officially listed in another member State, if the issuer has failed to comply with any obligations to which he is subject by virtue of that listing.

(4) The competent authority shall notify the applicant of its decision on the application within six months from the date on which the application is received or, if within that period the authority has required the applicant to furnish further information in connection with the application, from the date on which that information is furnished.

(5) If the competent authority does not notify the applicant of its decision within the time required by subsection (4) above it shall be taken to have refused the application.

(6) When any securities have been admitted to the Official List their admission shall not be called in question on the ground that any requirement or condition for their admission has not been complied with.

Discontinuance and suspension of listing

145.—(1) The competent authority may, in accordance with the listing rules, discontinue the listing of any securities if satisfied that there are special circumstances which preclude normal regular dealings in the securities.

(2) The competent authority may in accordance with the listing rules suspend the listing of any securities.

(3) Securities the listing of which is suspended under subsection (2) above shall nevertheless be regarded as listed for the purposes of sections 153 and 155 below.

(4) This section applies to securities included in the Official List at the coming into force of this Part of this Act as it applies to securities included by virtue of this Part.

General duty of disclosure in listing particulars

146.—(1) In addition to the information specified by listing rules or required by the competent authority as a condition of the admission of any securities to the Official List any listing particulars submitted to the competent authority under section 144 above shall contain all such information as investors and their professional advisers would reasonably require, and reasonably expect to find there, for the purpose of making an informed assessment of—

    (*a*) the assets and liabilities, financial position, profits and losses, and prospects of the issuer of the securities; and

    (*b*) the rights attaching to those securities.

(2) The information to be included by virtue of this section shall be such information as is mentioned in subsection (1) above which is within the knowledge of any person responsible for the listing particulars or which it would be reasonable for him to obtain by making enquiries.

(3) In determining what information is required to be included in listing particulars by virtue of this section regard shall be had—

    (*a*) to the nature of the securities and of the issuer of the securities;

    (*b*) to the nature of the persons likely to consider their acquisition;

    (*c*) to the fact that certain matters may reasonably be expected to be within the knowledge of professional advisers of any kind which those persons may reasonably be expected to consult; and

    (*d*) to any information available to investors or their professional advisers by virtue of requirements imposed under section 153 below or by or under any other enactment or by virtue of requirements imposed by a recognised investment exchange for the purpose of complying with paragraph 2(2)(*b*) of Schedule 4 to this Act.

Supplementary listing particulars

147.—(1) If at any time after the preparation of listing particulars for submission to the competent authority under section 144 above and before the commencement of dealings in the securities following their admission to the Official List—

    (*a*) there is a significant change affecting any matter contained in those particulars whose inclusion was required by section 146 above or by listing rules or by the competent authority; or

(*b*) a significant new matter arises the inclusion of information in respect of which would have been so required if it had arisen when the particulars were prepared,

the issuer of the securities shall, in accordance with listing rules made for the purposes of this section, submit to the competent authority for its approval and, if approved, publish supplementary listing particulars of the change or new matter.

(2) In subsection (1) above "significant" means significant for the purpose of making an informed assessment of the matters mentioned in section 146(1) above.

(3) Where the issuer of the securities is not aware of the change or new matter in question he shall not be under any duty to comply with subsection (1) above unless he is notified of it by a person responsible for the listing particulars; but it shall be the duty of any person responsible for those particulars who is aware of such a matter to give notice of it to the issuer.

(4) Subsection (1) above applies also as respects matters contained in any supplementary listing particulars previously published under this section in respect of the securities in question.

Exemptions from disclosure

148.—(1) The competent authority may authorise the omission from listing particulars or supplementary listing particulars of any information the inclusion of which would otherwise be required by section 146 above—

(*a*) on the ground that its disclosure would be contrary to the public interest;

(*b*) subject to subsection (2) below, on the ground that its disclosure would be seriously detrimental to the issuer of the securities; or

(*c*) in the case of securities which fall within paragraph 2 of Schedule 1 to this Act as modified by section 142 (3)(*b*) above and are of any class specified by listing rules, on the ground that its disclosure is unnecessary for persons of the kind who may be expected normally to buy or deal in the securities.

(2) No authority shall be granted under subsection (1)(*b*) above in respect of, and no such authority shall be regarded as extending to, information the non-disclosure of which would be likely to mislead a person considering the acquisition of the securities as to any facts the knowledge of which it is essential for him to have in order to make an informed assessment.

(3) The Secretary of State or the Treasury may issue a certificate to the effect that the disclosure of any information (including information that would otherwise have to be included in particulars for which they are themselves responsible) would be contrary to the public interest and the competent authority shall be entitled to act on any such certificate in exercising its powers under subsection (1)(*a*) above.

(4) This section is without prejudice to any powers of the competent authority under rules made by virtue of section 156(2) below.

Registration of listing particulars

149.—(1) On or before the date on which listing particulars or supplementary listing particulars are published as required by listing rules a copy of the particulars shall be delivered for registration to the registrar of companies and a statement that a copy has been delivered to him shall be included in the particulars.

(2) In subsection (1) above "the registrar of companies" means—

(*a*) if the securities in question are or are to be issued by a company incorporated in Great Britain, the registrar of companies in England and Wales or the registrar of companies in Scotland according to whether the company's registered office is in England and Wales or in Scotland;

(b) if the securities in question are or are to be issued by a company incorporated in Northern Ireland, the registrar of companies for Northern Ireland;

(c) in any other case, any of those registrars.

(3) If any particulars are published without a copy of them having been delivered as required by this section the issuer of the securities in question and any person who is knowingly a party to the publication shall be guilty of an offence and liable—

(a) on conviction on indictment, to a fine;

(b) on summary conviction, to a fine not exceeding the statutory maximum.

Compensation for false or misleading particulars

150.—(1) Subject to section 151 below, the person or persons responsible for any listing particulars or supplementary listing particulars shall be liable to pay compensation to any person who has acquired any of the securities in question and suffered loss in respect of them as a result of any untrue or misleading statement in the particulars or the omission from them of any matter required to be included by section 146 or 147 above.

(2) Where listing rules require listing particulars to include information as to any particular matter on the basis that the particulars must include a statement either as to that matter or, if such is the case, that there is no such matter, the omission from the particulars of the information shall be treated for the purposes of subsection (1) above as a statement that there is no such matter.

(3) Subject to section 151 below, a person who fails to comply with section 147 above shall be liable to pay compensation to any person who has acquired any of the securities in question and suffered loss in respect of them as a result of the failure.

(4) This section does not affect any liability which any person may incur apart from this section.

(5) References in this section to the acquisition by any person of securities include references to his contracting to acquire them or an interest in them.

[1] (6) No person shall by reason of being a promoter of a company or otherwise incur any liability for failing to disclose any information which he would not be required to disclose in listing particulars in respect of a company's securities if he were responsible for those particulars or, if he is responsible for them, which he is entitled to omit by virtue of section 148 above.

The reference above to a person incurring liability includes a reference to any other person being entitled as against that person to be granted any civil remedy or to rescind or repudiate any agreement.

NOTE
[1] As amended by the Companies Act 1989, s.197(1).

Exemption from liability to pay compensation

151.—(1) A person shall not incur any liability under section 150(1) above for any loss in respect of securities caused by any such statement or omission as is there mentioned if he satisfies the court that at the time when the particulars were submitted to the competent authority he reasonably believed, having made such enquiries (if any) as were reasonable, that the statement was true and not misleading or that the matter whose omission caused the loss was properly omitted and—

(a) that he continued in that belief until the time when the securities were acquired; or

(b) that they were acquired before it was reasonably practicable to bring a correction to the attention of persons likely to acquire the securities in question; or

(c) that before the securities were acquired he had taken all such steps as it was reasonable for him to have taken to secure that a correction was brought to the attention of those persons; or

(d) that he continued in that belief until after the commencement of dealings in the securities following their admission to the Official List and that the securities were acquired after such a lapse of time that he ought in the circumstances to be reasonably excused.

(2) A person shall not incur any liability under section 150(1) above for any loss in respect of securities caused by a statement purporting to be made by or on the authority of another person as an expert which is, and is stated to be, included in the particulars with that other person's consent if he satisfies the court that at the time when the particulars were submitted to the competent authority he believed on reasonable grounds that the other person was competent to make or authorise the statement and had consented to its inclusion in the form and context in which it was included and—

(a) that he continued in that belief until the time when the securities were acquired; or

(b) that they were acquired before it was reasonably practicable to bring the fact that the expert was not competent or had not consented to the attention of persons likely to acquire the securities in question; or

(c) that before the securities were acquired he had taken all such steps as it was reasonable for him to have taken to secure that that fact was brought to the attention of those persons; or

(d) that he continued in that belief until after the commencement of dealings in the securities following their admission to the Official List and that the securities were acquired after such a lapse of time that he ought in the circumstances to be reasonably excused.

(3) Without prejudice to subsections (1) and (2) above, a person shall not incur any liability under section 150(1) above for any loss in respect of any securities caused by any such statement or omission as is there mentioned if he satisfies the court—

(a) that before the securities were acquired a correction, or where the statement was such as is mentioned in subsection (2), the fact that the expert was not competent or had not consented had been published in a manner calculated to bring it to the attention of persons likely to acquire the securities in question; or

(b) that he took all such steps as it was reasonable for him to take to secure such publication and reasonably believed that it had taken place before the securities were acquired.

(4) A person shall not incur any liability under section 150(1) above for any loss resulting from a statement made by an official person or contained in a public official document which is included in the particulars if he satisfies the court that the statement is accurately and fairly reproduced.

(5) A person shall not incur any liability under section 150(1) or (3) above if he satisfies the court that the person suffering the loss acquired the securities in question with knowledge that the statement was false or misleading, of the omitted matter or of the change or new matter, as the case may be.

(6) A person shall not incur any liability under section 150(3) above if he satisfies the court that he reasonably believed that the change or new matter in question was not such as to call for supplementary listing particulars.

(7) In this section "expert" includes any engineer, valuer, accountant or other person whose profession, qualifications or experience give authority to a statement made by him; and references to the acquisition of securities include references to contracting to acquire them or an interest in them.

Persons responsible for particulars

152.—(1) For the purposes of this Part of this Act the persons responsible for listing particulars or supplementary listing particulars are—

    (*a*) the issuer of the securities to which the particulars relate;

    (*b*) where the issuer is a body corporate, each person who is a director of that body at the time when the particulars are submitted to the competent authority;

    (*c*) where the issuer is a body corporate, each person who has authorised himself to be named, and is named, in the particulars as a director or as having agreed to become a director of that body either immediately or at a future time;

    (*d*) each person who accepts, and is stated in the particulars as accepting, responsibility for, or for any part of, the particulars;

    (*e*) each person not falling within any of the foregoing paragraphs who has authorised the contents of, or any part of, the particulars.

(2) A person is not responsible for any particulars by virtue of subsection (1)(*b*) above if they are published without his knowledge or consent and on becoming aware of their publication he forthwith gives reasonable public notice that they were published without his knowledge or consent.

(3) Where a person has accepted responsibility for, or authorised, only part of the contents of any particulars, he is responsible under subsection (1)(*d*) or (*e*) above for only that part and only if it is included in (or substantially in) the form and context to which he has agreed.

(4) Where the particulars relate to securities which are to be issued in connection with an offer by (or by a wholly-owned subsidiary of), the issuer for, or an agreement for the acquisition by (or by a wholly-owned subsidiary of) the issuer of, securities issued by another person or in connection with any arrangement whereby the whole of the undertaking of another person is to become the undertaking of the issuer (of a wholly-owned subsidiary of the issuer or of a body corporate which will become such a subsidiary by virtue of the arrangement) then if—

    (*a*) that other person; and

    (*b*) where that other person is a body corporate, each person who is a director of that body at the time when the particulars are submitted to the competent authority and each other person who has authorised himself to be named, and is named, in the particulars as a director of that body,

is responsible by virtue of paragraph (*d*) of subsection (1) above for any part of the particulars relating to that other person or to the securities or undertaking to which the offer, agreement or arrangement relates, no person shall be responsible for that part under paragraph (*a*), (*b*) or (*c*) of that subsection but without prejudice to his being responsible under paragraph (*d*).

(5) Neither paragraph (*b*) nor paragraph (*c*) of subsection (1) above applies in the case of an issuer of international securities of a class specified by listing rules for the purposes of section 148(1)(*c*) above; and neither of those paragraphs nor paragraph (*b*) of subsection (4) above applies in the case of any director certified by the competent authority as a person to whom that paragraph should not apply by reason of his having an interest, or of any other circumstances, making it inappropriate for him to be responsible by virtue of that paragraph.

(6) In subsection (5) above "international securities" means any investment falling within paragraph 2 of Schedule 1 to this Act as modified by section 142(3)(*b*) above which is of a kind likely to be dealt in by bodies incorporated in or persons resident in a country or territory outside the United Kingdom, is denominated in a currency other than sterling or is otherwise connected with such a country or territory.

(7) In this section "wholly-owned subsidiary", in relation to a person other than a body corporate, means any body corporate that would be his wholly-owned subsidiary if he were a body corporate.

(8) Nothing in this section shall be construed as making a person responsible for any particulars by reason of giving advice as to their contents in a professional capacity.

(9) Where by virtue of this section the issuer of any shares pays or is liable to pay compensation under section 150 above for loss suffered in respect of shares for which a person has subscribed no account shall be taken of that liability or payment in determining any question as to the amount paid on subscription for those shares or as to the amount paid up or deemed to be paid up on them.

Obligations of issuers of listed securities

153.—(1) Listing rules may specify requirements to be complied with by issuers of listed securities and make provision with respect to the action that may be taken by the competent authority in the event of non-compliance, including provision—

(a) authorising the authority to publish the fact that an issuer has contravened any provision of the rules; and

(b) if the rules require an issuer to publish any information, authorising the authority to publish it in the event of his failure to do so.

(2) This section applies to the issuer of securities included in the Official List at the coming into force of this Part of this Act as it applies to the issuer of securities included by virtue of this Part.

Advertisements etc. in connection with listing applications

154.—(1) Where listing particulars are or are to be published in connection with an application for the listing of any securities no advertisement or other information of a kind specified by listing rules shall be issued in the United Kingdom unless the contents of the advertisement or other information have been submitted to the competent authority and that authority has either—

(a) approved those contents; or

(b) authorised the issue of the advertisement or information without such approval.

(2) An authorised person who contravenes this section shall be treated as having contravened rules made under Chapter V of Part I of this Act or, in the case of a person who is an authorised person by virtue of his membership of a recognised self-regulating organisation or certification by a recognised professional body, the rules of that organisation or body.

(3) Subject to subsection (4) below, a person other than an authorised person, who contravenes this section shall be guilty of an offence and liable—

(a) on conviction on indictment, to imprisonment for a term not exceeding two years or to a fine or to both;

(b) on summary conviction, to a fine not exceeding the statutory maximum.

(4) A person who in the ordinary course of a business other than investment business issues an advertisement or other information to the order of another person shall not be guilty of an offence under this section if he proves that he believed on reasonable grounds that the advertisement or information had been approved or its issue authorised by the competent authority.

[1] (5) Where information has been approved, or its issue has been authorised, under this section neither the person issuing it nor any person responsible for, or for any part of, the listing particulars shall incur any civil liability by reason of any statement in or omission from the information if that information and the listing particulars, taken together, would not be likely to mislead persons of the kind likely to consider the acquisition of the securities in question.

The reference above to a person incurring civil liability includes a reference to any other person being entitled as against that person to be granted any civil remedy or to rescind or repudiate any agreement.

NOTE
[1] Amended by the Companies Act 1989, s.197(2).

Fees

155. Listing rules may require the payment of fees to the competent authority in respect of applications for listing and the retention of securities in the Official List.

Listing rules: general provisions

156.—(1) Listing rules may make different provision for different cases.

(2) Listing rules may authorise the competent authority to dispense with or modify the application of the rules in particular cases and by reference to any circumstances.

(3) Listing rules shall be made by an instrument in writing.

(4) Immediately after an instrument containing listing rules is made it shall be printed and made available to the public with or without payment.

(5) A person shall not be taken to have contravened any listing rule if he shows that at the time of the alleged contravention the instrument containing the rule had not been made available as required by subsection (4) above.

(6) The production of a printed copy of an instrument purporting to be made by the competent authority on which is endorsed a certificate signed by an officer of the authority authorised by it for that purpose and stating—

    (*a*) that the instrument was made by the authority;

    (*b*) that the copy is a true copy of the instrument; and

    (*c*) that on a specified date the instrument was made available to the public as required by subsection (4) above,

shall be prima facie evidence or, in Scotland, sufficient evidence of the facts stated in the certificate.

(7) Any certificate purporting to be signed as mentioned in subsection (6) above shall be deemed to have been duly signed unless the contrary is shown.

(8) Any person wishing in any legal proceedings to cite an instrument made by the competent authority may require the authority to cause a copy of it to be endorsed with such a certificate as is mentioned in subsection (6) above.

Alteration of competent authority

157.—(1) The Secretary of State may by order transfer the functions as competent authority of the Council of The Stock Exchange to another body or other bodies either at the request of the Council or if it appears to him—

    (*a*) that the Council is exercising those functions in a manner which is unnecessary for the protection of investors and fails to take into account the proper interests of issuers and proposed issuers of securities; or

    (*b*) that it is necessary to do so for the protection of investors.

(2) The Secretary of State may by order transfer all or any of the functions as competent authority from any body or bodies to which they have been previously transferred under this section to another body or bodies.

(3) Any order made under subsection (1) above at the request of the Council shall be subject to annulment in pursuance of a resolution of either House of Parliament; and no other order shall be made under this section unless a draft of it has been laid before and approved by a resolution of each House of Parliament.

(4) An order under this section shall not affect anything previously done by any body ("the previous authority") in the exercise of functions which are transferred by the order to another body ("the new authority") and may contain such supplementary provisions as the Secretary of State thinks necessary or expedient, including provisions—

    (*a*) for modifying or excluding any provision of this Part of this Act in its application to any such functions;

    (*b*) for the transfer of any property, rights or liabilities relating to any such functions from the previous authority to the new authority;

    (*c*) for the carrying on and completion by the new authority of anything in process of being done by the previous authority when the order takes effect; and (*d*) for the substitution of the new authority for the previous authority in any instrument, contract or legal proceedings.

(5) If by virtue of this section the function of admission to or discontinuance or suspension of listing is exercisable otherwise than by the Council of The Stock Exchange, references in this Part of this Act to the competent authority admitting securities to the Official List or to discontinuing or suspending the listing of any securities shall be construed as references to the giving of directions to the Council of The Stock Exchange to admit the securities or to discontinue or suspend their listing; and it shall be the duty of the Council to comply with any such direction.

PART V

OFFERS OF UNLISTED SECURITIES

Preliminary

158.—(1) This Part of this Act applies to any investment—

(*a*) which is not listed, or the subject of an application for listing, in accordance with Part IV of this Act; and

(*b*) falls within paragraph 1, 2, 4 or 5 of Schedule 1 to this Act.

(2) In the application of those paragraphs for the purposes of subsection (1) above—

(*a*) paragraphs 4 and 5 shall have effect with the omission of references to investments falling within paragraph 3; and

(*b*) paragraph 4 shall have effect as if it referred only to instruments issued by the person issuing the investment to be subscribed for.

(3) In this Part of this Act—

"issuer", in relation to any securities, means the person by whom they have been or are to be issued except that in relation to a certificate or other instrument falling within paragraph 5 of Schedule 1 to this Act it means the person who issued or is to issue the securities to which the certificate or instrument relates;

"securities" means investments to which this section applies.

(4) For the purposes of this Part of this Act an advertisement offers securities if—

(*a*) it invites a person to enter into an agreement for or with a view to subscribing for or otherwise acquiring or underwriting any securities; or

(*b*) it contains information calculated to lead directly or indirectly to a person entering into such an agreement.

(5) In this Part of this Act "the registrar of companies", in relation to any securities, means—

(*a*) if the securities are or are to be issued by a company incorporated in Great Britain, the registrar of companies in England and Wales or the registrar of companies in Scotland according to whether the company's registered office is in England and Wales or in Scotland;

(*b*) if the securities are or are to be issued by a company incorporated in Northern Ireland, the registrar of companies for Northern Ireland;

(*c*) in any other case, any of those registrars.

(6) In this Part of this Act "approved exchange", in relation to dealings in any securities, means a recognised investment exchange approved by the Secretary of State for the purposes of this Part of this Act either generally or in relation to such dealings, and the Secretary of State shall give notice in such manner as he thinks appropriate of the exchanges which are for the time being approved.

Offers of securities on admission to approved exchange

[1] **159.**—(1) No person shall issue or cause to be issued in the United Kingdom an advertisement offering any securities on the occasion of their

admission to dealings on an approved exchange or on terms that they will be issued if admitted to such dealings unless—

    (*a*) a document (in this Part of this Act referred to as a "prospectus") containing information about the securities has been submitted to and approved by the exchange and delivered for registration to the registrar of companies; or

    (*b*) the advertisement is such that no agreement can be entered into in pursuance of it until such a prospectus has been submitted, approved and delivered as aforesaid.

(2) Subsection (1) above does not apply if a prospectus relating to the securities has been delivered for registration under this Part of this Act in the previous 12 months and the approved exchange certifies that it is satisfied that persons likely to consider acquiring the securities will have sufficient information to enable them to decide whether to do so from that prospectus and any information published in connection with the admission of the securities.

² (3) Subsection (1) above has effect subject to section 160A (exemptions) and section 161 (exceptions).

NOTES
  ¹ As amended by the Companies Act 1989, s.198(3) and Sched. 24.
  ² Inserted by the Companies Act 1989, s. 198(3) and Sched. 24.

Other offers of securities
  ¹ **160.**—(1) No person shall issue or cause to be issued in the United Kingdom an advertisement offering any securities which is a primary or secondary offer within the meaning of this section unless—

    (*a*) he has delivered for registration to the registrar of companies a prospectus relating to the securities and expressed to be in respect of the offer; or

    (*b*) the advertisement is such that no agreement can be entered into in pursuance of it until such a prospectus has been delivered by him as aforesaid.

(2) For the purposes of this section a primary offer is an advertisement issued otherwise than as mentioned in section 159(1) above inviting persons to enter into an agreement for or with a view to subscribing (whether or not in cash) for or underwriting the securities to which it relates or containing information calculated to lead directly or indirectly to their doing so.

(3) For the purposes of this section a secondary offer is any other advertisement issued otherwise than as mentioned in section 159(1) above inviting persons to enter into an agreement for or with a view to acquiring the securities to which it relates or containing information calculated to lead directly or indirectly to their doing so, being an advertisement issued or caused to be issued by—

    (*a*) a person who has acquired the securities from the issuer with a view to issuing such an advertisement in respect of them;

    (*b*) a person who, with a view to issuing such an advertisement in respect of them, has acquired the securities otherwise than from the issuer but without their having been admitted to dealings on an approved exchange or held by a person who acquired them as an investment and without any intention that such an advertisement should be issued in respect of them; or

    (*c*) a person who is a controller of the issuer or has been such a controller in the previous 12 months and who is acting with the consent or participation of the issuer in issuing the advertisement.

(4) For the purposes of subsection (3)(*a*) above it shall be presumed in the absence of evidence to the contrary that a person has acquired securities with a view to issuing an advertisement offering the securities if he issues it or causes it to be issued—

    (*a*) within six months after the issue of the securities; or (*b*) before the consideration due from him for their acquisition is received by the person from whom he acquired them.

(5) Subsection (1) above does not apply to a secondary offer if such a prospectus as is mentioned in that subsection has been delivered in accordance with that subsection in respect of an offer of the same securities made in the previous six months by a person making a primary offer or a previous secondary offer.

² (6) Subsection (1) above has effect subject to section 160A (exemptions) and section 161 (exceptions).

NOTES

¹ Amended by the Companies Act 1989, s.198(4) and Sched. 24.
² Substituted for former subss. 6–9 by the Companies Act 1989, s. 198(4).

Exemptions

¹ **160A.**—(1) The Secretary of State may by order exempt from sections 159 to 160 when issued in such circumstances as may be specified in the order—

(*a*) advertisements appearing to him to have a private character, whether by reason of a connection between the person issuing them and those to whom they are addressed or otherwise;

(*b*) advertisements appearing to him to deal with investments only incidentally;

(*c*) advertisements issued to persons appearing to him to be sufficiently expert to understand any risks involved;

(*d*) such other classes of advertisements as he thinks fit.

(2) The Secretary of State may by order exempt from sections 159 and 160 an advertisement issued in whatever circumstances which relates to securities appearing to him to be of a kind that can be expected normally to be bought or dealt in only by persons sufficiently expert to understand any risks involved.

(3) An order under subsection (1) or (2) may require a person who by virtue of the order is authorised to issue an advertisement to comply with such requirements as are specified in the order.

(4) An order made by virtue of subsection (1)(*a*), (*b*) or (*c*) or subsection (2) shall be subject to annulment in pursuance of a resolution of either House of Parliament; and no order shall be made by virtue of subsection (1)(*d*) unless a draft of it has been laid before and approved by a resolution of each House of Parliament.

NOTE

¹ Inserted by the Companies Act 1989, s. 198(1).

Exceptions

161.—(1) Sections 159 and 160 above do not apply to any advertisement offering securities if the offer is conditional on their admission to listing in accordance with Part IV of this Act and section 159 above does not apply to any advertisement offering securities if they have been listed in accordance with that Part in the previous 12 months and the approved exchange in question certifies that persons likely to consider acquiring them will have sufficient information to enable them to decide whether to do so.

(2) Neither of those sections applies to any such advertisement as is mentioned in section 58(2) above.

(3) Neither of those sections applies if other securities issued by the same person (whether or not securities of the same class as those to which the offer relates) are already dealt in on an approved exchange and the exchange certifies that persons likely to consider acquiring the securities to which the offer relates will have sufficient information to enable them to decide whether to do so having regard to the steps that have been taken to comply in respect of those other securities with the requirements imposed by the exchange for the purpose of complying with paragraph

2(2)(*b*) of Schedule 4 to this Act, to the nature of the securities to which the offer relates, to the circumstances of their issue and to the information about the issuer which is available to investors by virtue of any enactment.

(4) If it appears to the Secretary of State that the law of a country or territory outside the United Kingdom provides investors in the United Kingdom with protection at lease equivalent to that provided by Part IV of this Act or this Part of this Act in respect of securities dealt in on an exchange or exchanges in that country or territory he may by order specify circumstances in which those sections are not to apply to advertisements offering those securities.

(5) An order under subsection (4) above shall be subject to annulment in pursuance of a resolution of either House of Parliament.

[THE NEXT PAGE IS I 689]

Form and content of prospectus

162.—(1) A prospectus shall contain such information and comply with such other requirements as may be prescribed by rules made by the Secretary of State for the purposes of this section.

(2) Rules under this section may make provision whereby compliance with any requirements imposed by or under the law of a country or territory outside the United Kingdom is treated as compliance with any requirements of the rules.

(3) If it appears to the Secretary of State that an approved exchange has rules in respect of prospectuses relating to securities dealt in on the exchange, and practices in exercising any powers conferred by the rules, which provide investors with protection at least equivalent to that provided by rules under this section he may direct that any such prospectus shall be subject to the rules of the exchange instead of the rules made under this section.

General duty of disclosure in prospectus

163.—(1) In addition to the information required to be included in a prospectus by virtue of rules applying to it by virtue of section 162 above a prospectus shall contain all such information as investors and their professional advisers would reasonably require, and reasonably expect to find there, for the purpose of making an informed assessment of—

   (*a*) the assets and liabilities, financial position, profits and losses, and prospects of the issuer of the securities; and

   (*b*) the rights attaching to those securities.

(2) The information to be included by virtue of this section shall be such information as is mentioned in subsection (1) above which is within the knowledge of any person responsible for the prospectus or which it would be reasonable for him to obtain by making enquiries.

(3) In determining what information is required to be included in a prospectus by virtue of this section regard shall be had—

   (*a*) to the nature of the securities and of the issuer of the securities;

   (*b*) to the nature of the persons likely to consider their acquisition;

   (*c*) to the fact that certain matters may reasonably be expected to be within the knowledge of professional advisers of any kind which those persons may reasonably be expected to consult; and

   (*d*) to any information available to investors or their professional advisers by virtue of any enactment or by virtue of requirements imposed by a recognised investment exchange for the purpose of complying with paragraph 2(2)(*b*) of Schedule 4 to this Act.

Supplementary prospectus

164.—(1) Where a prospectus has been registered under this Part of this Act in respect of an offer of securities and at any time while an agreement in respect of those securities can be entered into in pursuance of that offer—

   (*a*) there is a significant change affecting any matter contained in the prospectus whose inclusion was required by rules applying to it by virtue of section 162 above or by section 163 above; or

   (*b*) a significant new matter arises the inclusion of information in respect of which would have been so required if it had arisen when the prospectus was prepared,

the person who delivered the prospectus for registration to the registrar of companies shall deliver to him for registration a supplementary prospectus containing particulars of the change or new matter.

(2) In subsection (1) above "significant" means significant for the purpose of making an informed assessment of the matters mentioned in section 163(1) above.

(3) Where the person who delivered the prospectus for registration is not aware of the change or new matter in question he shall not be under any duty to comply with subsection (1) above unless he is notified of it by a person responsible for the prospectus; but any person responsible for the prospectus who is aware of such a matter shall be under a duty to give him notice of it.

(4) Subsection (1) above applies also as respects matters contained in a supplementary prospectus previously registered under this section in respect of the securities in question.

Exemptions from disclosure

165.—(1) If in the case of any approved exchange the Secretary of State so directs, the exchange shall have power to authorise the omission from a prospectus or supplementary prospectus of any information the inclusion of which would otherwise be required by section 163 above—

  (a) on the ground that its disclosure would be contrary to the public interest;

  (b) subject to subsection (2) below, on the ground that its disclosure would be seriously detrimental to the issuer of the securities; or

  (c) in the case of securities which fall within paragraph 2 of Schedule 1 to this Act and are of any class specified by the rules of the exchange, on the ground that its disclosure is unnecessary for persons of the kind who may be expected normally to buy or deal in the securities.

(2) No authority shall be granted under subsection (1)(b) above in respect of, and no such authority shall be regarded as extending to, information the non-disclosure of which would be likely to mislead a person considering the acquisition of the securities as to any facts the knowledge of which it is essential for him to have in order to make an informed assessment.

(3) The Secretary of State or the Treasury may issue a certificate to the effect that the disclosure of any information (including information that would otherwise have to be included in a prospectus or supplementary prospectus for which they are themselves responsible) would be contrary to the public interest and the exchange shall be entitled to act on any such certificate in exercising its powers under subsection (1)(a) above.

Compensation for false or misleading prospectus

166.—(1) Subject to section 167 below, the person or persons responsible for a prospectus or supplementary prospectus shall be liable to pay compensation to any person who has acquired the securities to which the prospectus relates and suffered loss in respect of them as a result of any untrue or misleading statement in the prospectus or the omission from it of any matter required to be included by section 163 or 164 above.

(2) Where rules applicable to a prospectus by virtue of section 162 above require it to include information as to any particular matter on the basis that the prospectus must include a statement either as to that matter or, if such is the case, that there is no such matter, the omission from the prospectus of the information shall be treated for the purpose of subsection (1) above as a statement that there is no such matter.

(3) Subject to section 167 below, a person who fails to comply with section 164 above shall be liable to pay compensation to any person who has acquired any of the securities in question and suffered loss in respect of them as a result of the failure.

(4) This section does not affect any liability which any person may incur apart from this section.

(5) References in this section to the acquisition by any person of securities include references to his contracting to acquire them or an interest in them.

Exemption from liability to pay compensation

167.—(1) A person shall not incur any liability under section 166(1) above for any loss in respect of securities caused by any such statement or omission as is there mentioned if he satisfies the court that at the time when the prospectus or supplementary prospectus was delivered for registration he reasonably believed, having made such enquiries (if any) as were reasonable, that the statement was true and not misleading or that the matter whose omission caused the loss was properly omitted and—

(*a*) that he continued in that belief until the time when the securities were acquired; or

(*b*) that they were acquired before it was reasonably practicable to bring a correction to the attention of persons likely to acquire the securities in question; or

(*c*) that before the securities were acquired he had taken all such steps as it was reasonable for him to have taken to secure that a correction was brought to the attention of those persons; or

(*d*) that the securities were acquired after such a lapse of time that he ought in the circumstances to be reasonably excused;

but paragraph (*d*) above does not apply where the securities are dealt in on an approved exchange unless he satisfies the court that he continued in that belief until after the commencement of dealings in the securities on that exchange.

(2) A person shall not incur any liability under section 166(1) above for any loss in respect of securities caused by a statement purporting to be made by or on the authority of another person as an expert which is, and is stated to be, included in the prospectus or supplementary prospectus with that other person's consent if he satisfies the court that at the time when the prospectus or supplementary prospectus was delivered for registration he believed on reasonable grounds that the other person was competent to make or authorise the statement and had consented to its inclusion in the form and context in which it was included and—

(*a*) that he continued in that belief until the time when the securities were acquired; or

(*b*) that they were acquired before it was reasonably practicable to bring the fact that the expert was not competent or had not consented to the attention of persons likely to acquire the securities in question; or

(*c*) that before the securities were acquired he had taken all such steps as it was reasonable for him to have taken to secure that that fact was brought to the attention of those persons; or

(*d*) that the securities were acquired after such a lapse of time that he ought in the circumstances to be reasonably excused;

but paragraph (*d*) above does not apply where the securities are dealt in on an approved exchange unless he satisfies the court that he continued in that belief until after the commencement of dealings in the securities on that exchange.

(3) Without prejudice to subsections (1) and (2) above, a person shall not incur any liability under section 166(1) above for any loss in respect of any securities caused by any such statement or omission as is there mentioned if he satisfies the court—

(*a*) that before the securities were acquired a correction or, where the statement was such as is mentioned in subsection (2) above, the fact that the expert was not competent or had not consented had been published in a manner calculated to bring it to the attention of persons likely to acquire the securities in question; or

(*b*) that he took all such steps as it was reasonable for him to take to secure such publication and reasonably believed that it had taken place before the securities were acquired.

(4) A person shall not incur any liability under section 166(1) above for

any loss resulting from a statement made by an official person or contained in a public official document which is included in the prospectus or supplementary prospectus if he satisfies the court that the statement is accurately and fairly reproduced.

(5) A person shall not incur any liability under section 166(1) or (3) above if he satisfies the court that the person suffering the loss acquired the securities in question with knowledge that the statement was false or misleading, of the omitted matter or of the change or new matter, as the case may be.

(6) A person shall not incur any liability under section 166(3) above if he satisfies the court that he reasonably believed that the change or new matter in question was not such as to call for a supplementary prospectus.

(7) In this section "expert" includes any engineer, valuer, accountant or other person whose profession, qualifications or experience give authority to a statement made by him; and references to the acquisition of securities include references to contracting to acquire them or an interest in them.

Persons responsible for prospectus

168.—(1) For the purposes of this Part of this Act the persons responsible for a prospectus or supplementary prospectus are—

(a) the issuer of the securities to which the prospectus or supplementary prospectus relates;

(b) where the issuer is a body corporate, each person who is a director of that body at the time when the prospectus or supplementary prospectus is delivered for registration;

(c) where the issuer is a body corporate, each person who has authorised himself to be named, and is named, in the prospectus or supplementary prospectus as a director or as having agreed to become a director of that body either immediately or at a future time;

(d) each person who accepts, and is stated in the prospectus or supplementary prospectus as accepting, responsibility for, or for any part of, the prospectus or supplementary prospectus;

(e) each person not falling within any of the foregoing paragraphs who has authorised the contents of, or of any part of, the prospectus or supplementary prospectus.

(2) A person is not responsible under subsection (1)(a), (b) or (c) above unless the issuer has made or authorised the offer in relation to which the prospectus or supplementary prospectus was delivered for registration; and a person is not responsible for a prospectus or supplementary prospectus by virtue of subsection (1)(b) above if it is delivered for registration without his knowledge or consent and on becoming aware of its delivery he forthwith gives reasonable public notice that it was delivered without his knowledge or consent.

(3) Where a person has accepted responsibility for, or authorised, only part of the contents of any prospectus or supplementary prospectus he is responsible under subsection (1)(d) or (e) above for only that part and only if it is included in (or substantially in) the form and context to which he has agreed.

(4) Where a prospectus or supplementary prospectus relates to securities which are to be issued in connection with an offer by (or by a wholly-owned subsidiary of) the issuer for, or an agreement for the acquisition by (or by a wholly-owned subsidiary of) the issuer of, securities issued by another person or in connection with any arrangement whereby the whole of the undertaking of another person is to become the undertaking of the issuer (of a wholly-owned subsidiary of the issuer or of a body corporate which will become such a subsidiary by virtue of the arrangement) then if—

(a) that other person; and

(b) where that other person is a body corporate, each person who is a director of that body at the time when the prospectus or supplementary prospectus is delivered for registration and each other person who has authorised himself to be named, and is named, in the prospectus or supplementary prospectus as a director of that body,

is responsible by virtue of paragraph (*d*) of subsection (1) above for any part of the prospectus or supplementary prospectus relating to that other person or to the securities or undertaking to which the offer, agreement or arrangement relates, no person shall be responsible for that part under paragraph (*a*), (*b*) or (*c*) of that subsection but without prejudice to his being responsible under paragraph (*d*).

(5) Neither paragraph (*b*) nor paragraph (*c*) of subsection (1) above nor paragraph (*b*) of subsection (4) above applies in the case of any director if the prospectus or supplementary prospectus is subject to the rules of an approved exchange by virtue of section 162(3) above and he is certified by the exchange as a person to whom that paragraph should not apply by reason of his having an interest, or of any other circumstances, making it inappropriate for him to be responsible by virtue of that paragraph.

(6) In this section "wholly-owned subsidiary", in relation to a person other than a body corporate, means any body corporate that would be his wholly-owned subsidiary if he were a body corporate.

(7) Nothing in this section shall be construed as making a person responsible for any prospectus or supplementary prospectus by reason only of giving advice as to its contents in a professional capacity.

(8) Where by virtue of this section the issuer of any shares pays or is liable to pay compensation under section 166 above for loss suffered in respect of shares for which a person has subscribed no account shall be taken of that liability or payment in determining any question as to the amount paid on subscription for those shares or as to the amount paid up or deemed to be paid up on them.

Terms and implementation of offer

169.—(1) The Secretary of State may make rules—
- (*a*) regulating the terms on which a person may offer securities by an advertisement to which this Part of this Act applies; and
- (*b*) otherwise regulating his conduct with a view to ensuring that the persons to whom the offer is addressed are treated equally and fairly.

(2) Rules under this section may, in particular, make provision with respect to the giving of priority as between persons to whom an offer is made and with respect to the payment of commissioners.

(3) Section 162(2) above shall apply also to rules made under this section.

Advertisements by private companies and old public companies

170.—(1) No private company and no old public company shall issue or cause to be issued in the United Kingdom any advertisement offering securities to be issued by that company.

[1] (2) The Secretary of State may by order exempt from subsection (1) when issued in such circumstances as may be specified in the order—
- (*a*) advertisements appearing to him to have a private character, whether by reason of a connection between the person issuing them and those to whom they are addressed or otherwise;
- (*b*) advertisements appearing to him to deal with investments only incidentally;
- (*c*) advertisements issued to persons appearing to him to be sufficiently expert to understand any risks involved;
- (*d*) such other classes of advertisements as he thinks fit.

[1] (3) The Secretary of State may by order exempt from subsection (1) an advertisement issued in whatever circumstances which relates to securities appearing to him to be of a kind that can be expected normally to be

bought or dealt in only by persons sufficiently expert to understand any risks involved.

[1] (4) An order under subsection (2) or (3) may require a person who by virtue of the order is authorised to issue an advertisement to comply with such requirements as are specified in the order.

[2] (4A) An order made by virtue of subsection (2)(*a*), (*b*) or (*c*) or subsection (3) shall be subject to annulment in pursuance of a resolution of either House of Parliament; and no order shall be made by virtue of subsection (2)(*d*) unless a draft of it has been laid before and approved by a resolution of each House of Parliament.

(5) In this section "old public company" has the meaning given in section 1 of the Companies Consolidation (Consequential Provisions) Act 1985 or the corresponding Northern Ireland provision.

NOTES

[1] Substituted by the Companies Act 1989, s.199.
[2] Inserted by the Companies Act 1989, s. 199.

Contraventions

[1] **171.**—(1) An authorised person who—

(*a*) contravenes section 159 or 160 above or rules made under section 169 above;

(*b*) contravenes any requirement imposed by an order under section 160A or 170 above; or

(*c*) on behalf of a company issues or causes to be issued an advertisement which that company is prohibited from issuing by section 170 above,

shall be treated as having contravened rules made under Chapter V of Part I of this Act or, in the case of a person who is an authorised person by virtue of his membership of a recognised self-regulating organisation or certification by a recognised professional body, the rules of that organisation or body.

(2) Section 57 above shall apply to a company which issues or causes to be issued an advertisement in contravention of section 170 above as it applies to a person who issues an advertisement in contravention of that section.

(3) A person, other than an authorised person, who contravenes section 159 or 160, the rules made under section 169 or any requirement imposed by an order under section 160A or 170 above shall be guilty of an offence and liable—

(*a*) on conviction on indictment, to imprisonment for a term not exceeding two years or to a fine or to both;

(*b*) on summary conviction, to imprisonment for a term not exceeding six months or to a fine not exceeding the statutory maximum or to both.

(4) A person who in the ordinary course of a business other than investment issues an advertisement to the order of another person shall not be guilty of an offence under subsection (3) above in respect of a contravention of section 159 or 160 above if he proves that he believed on reasonable grounds that neither section 159 nor section 160 above applied to the advertisement or that one of those sections had been complied with in respect of the advertisement.

(5) Without prejudice to any liability under section 166 above, a person shall not be regarded as having contravened section 159 or 160 above by reason only of a prospectus not having fully complied with the requirements of this Part of this Act as to its form and content.

(6) Any contravention to which this section applies shall be actionable at the suit of a person who suffers loss as a result of the contravention subject to the defences and other incidents applying to actions for breach of statutory duty.

NOTE

[1] Amended by the Companies Act 1989, s.198(5).

Part VI

Takeover Offers

Takeover offers

172.—(1) The provisions set out in Schedule 12 to this Act shall be substituted for sections 428, 429 and 430 of the Companies Act 1985.

(2) Subsection (1) above does not affect any case in which the offer in respect of the scheme or contract mentioned in section 428(1) was made before the coming into force of this section.

Part VII

Insider Dealing

Information obtained in official capacity: public bodies etc.

173.—(1) In section 2 of the Company Securities (Insider Dealing) Act 1985 (abuse of information obtained by Crown servants in official capacity) for the word "Crown" wherever it occurs there shall be substituted the word "public".

(2) At the end of that section there shall be added—

"(4) 'Public servant' means—

(*a*) a Crown servant;

(*b*) a member, officer or servant of a designated agency, competent authority or transferee body (within the meaning of the Financial Services Act 1986);

(*c*) an officer or servant of a recognised self-regulating organisation, recognised investment exchange or recognised clearing house (within the meaning of that Act);

(*d*) any person declared by an order for the time being in force under subsection (5) to be a public servant for the purposes of this section.

(5) If it appears to the Secretary of State that the members, officers or employees of or persons otherwise connected with any body appearing to him to exercise public functions may have access to unpublished price sensitive information relating to securities, he may by order declare that those persons are to be public servants for the purposes of this section.

(6) The power to make an order under subsection (5) shall be exercisable by statutory instrument and an instrument containing such an order shall be subject to annulment in pursuance of a resolution of either House of Parliament."

Market makers, off-market dealers etc.

174.—(1) In subsection (1) of section 3 of the Company Securities (Insider Dealing) Act 1985 (actions not prohibited by sections 1 and 2 of that Act) at the end of paragraph (*c*) there shall be inserted the words "; or

(*d*) doing any particular thing in relation to any particular securities if the information—

(i) was obtained by him in the course of a business of a market maker in those securities in which he was engaged or employed, and

(ii) was of a description which it would be reasonable to expect him to obtain in the ordinary course of that business,

and he does that thing in good faith in the course of that business.".

(2) At the end of that subsection there shall be inserted—

" 'Market maker' means a person (whether an individual, partnership or company) who—

(a) holds himself out at all normal times in compliance with the rules of a recognised stock exchange as willing to buy and sell securities at prices specified by him; and

(b) is recognised as doing so by that recognised stock exchange.".

(3) The existing provisions of section 4 of that Act (off-market deals in advertised securities) shall become subsection (1) of that section and after that subsection there shall be inserted—

"(2) In its application by virtue of this section the definition of "market maker" in section 3(1) shall have effect as if the references to a recognised stock exchange were references to a recognised investment exchange (other than an overseas investment exchange) within the meaning of the Financial Services Act 1986.".

(4) In section 13 of that Act—

(a) in subsection (1) (which defines dealing in securities and provides that references to dealing on a recognised stock exchange include dealing through an investment exchange) the words from "and references" onwards shall be omitted; and

(b) for subsection (3) (definition of off-market dealer) there shall be substituted—

"(3) 'Off-market dealer' means a person who is an authorised person within the meaning of the Financial Services Act 1986.".

Price stabilisation

175. For section 6 of the Company Securities (Insider Dealing) Act 1985 (international bonds) there shall be substituted—

"Price stabilisation

6.—(1) No provision of section 1, 2, 4 or 5 prohibits an individual from doing anything for the purpose of stabilising the price of securities if it is done in conformity with rules made under section 48 of the Financial Services Act 1986 and—

(a) in respect of securities which fall within any of paragraphs 1 to 5 of Schedule 1 to that Act and are specified by the rules; and

(b) during such period before or after the issue of those securities as is specified by the rules.

(2) Any order under subsection (8) of section 48 of that Act shall apply also in relation to subsection (1) of this section.".

Contracts for differences by reference to securities

176. After subsection (1) of section 13 of the Company Securities (Insider Dealing) Act 1985 (definition of dealing in securities), there shall be inserted—

"(1A) For the purposes of this Act a person who (whether as principal or agent) buys or sells or agrees to buy or sell investments within paragraph 9 of Schedule 1 to the Financial Services Act 1986 (contracts for differences etc.) where the purpose of pretended purpose mentioned in that paragraph is to secure a profit or avoid a loss wholly or partly by reference to fluctuations in the value or price of securities shall be treated as if he were dealing in those securities.".

Investigations into insider dealing

177.—(1) If it appears to the Secretary of State that there are circumstances suggesting that there may have been a contravention of section 1, 2, 4 or 5 of the Company Securities (Insider Dealing) Act 1985, he may appoint one or more competent inspectors to carry out such investigations as are requisite to establish whether or not any such contravention has occurred and to report the results of their investigations to him.

(2) The appointment under this section of an inspector may limit the period during which he is to continue his investigation or confine it to particular matters.

[1] (2A) At any time during the investigation the Secretary of State may vary the appointment by limiting or extending the period during which the inspector is to continue his investigation or by confining the investigation to particular matters.

(3) If the inspectors consider that any person is or may be able to give information concerning any such contravention they may require that person—

(a) to produce to them any documents in his possession or under his control relating to the company in relation to whose securities the contravention is suspected to have occurred or to its securities;

(b) to attend before them; and

(c) otherwise to give them all assistance in connection with the investigation which he is reasonably able to give;

and it shall be the duty of that person to comply with that requirement.

(4) An inspector may examine on oath any person who he considers is or may be able to give information concerning any such contravention, and may administer an oath accordingly.

(5) The inspectors shall make such interim reports to the Secretary of State as they think fit or he may direct and on the conclusion of the investigation they shall make a final report to him.

[2] (5A) If the Secretary of State thinks fit, he may direct the inspector to take no further steps in the investigation or to take only such further steps as are specified in the direction; and where an investigation is the subject of such a direction, the inspectors shall make a final report to the Secretary of State only where the Secretary of State directs them to do so.

(6) A statement made by a person in compliance with a requirement imposed by virtue of this section may be used in evidence against him.

(7) A person shall not under this section be required to disclose any information or produce any document which he would be entitled to refuse to disclose or produce on grounds of legal professional privilege in proceedings in the High Court or on grounds of confidentiality as between client and professional legal adviser in proceedings in the Court of Session.

[3] (8) A person shall not under this section be required to disclose any information or produce any document in respect of which he owes an obligation of confidence by virtue of carrying on the business of banking unless—

(a) the person to whom the obligation of confidence is owed consents to the disclosure or production, or

(b) the making of the requirement was authorised by the Secretary of State.

(9) Where a person claims a lien on a document its production under this section shall be without prejudice to his lien.

[4] (10) In this section "document" includes information recorded in any form; and in relation to information recorded otherwise than in legible form the power to require its production includes power to require the production of a copy of the information in legible form.

[5] (11) A person who is convicted on a prosecution instituted as a result of an investigation under this section may in the same proceedings be ordered to pay the expenses of the investigation to such extent as may be specified in the order.

There shall be treated as expenses of the investigation, in particular, such reasonable sums as the Secretary of State may determine in respect of general staff costs and overheads.

NOTES

[1] Inserted by the Companies Act 1989, s. 74(2).

[2] Inserted by the Companies Act 1989, s. 74(3).

[3] Substituted by the Companies Act 1989, s. 74(4).

[4] As amended by the Companies Act 1989, s. 74(5).

[5] Inserted by the Companies Act 1989, s. 74(6).

Penalties for failure to co-operate with s.177 investigations

178.—(1) If any person—

(a) refuses to comply with any request under subsection (3) of section 177 above; or

(b) refuses to answer any question put to him by the inspectors appointed under that section with respect to any matter relevant for establishing whether or not any suspected contravention has occurred,

the inspectors may certify that fact in writing to the court and the court may inquire into the case.

(2) If, after hearing any witness who may be produced against or on behalf of the alleged offender and any statement which may be offered in defence, the court is satisfied that he did without reasonable excuse refuse to comply with such a request or answer any such question, the court may—

(a) punish him in like manner as if he had been guilty of contempt of the court; or

(b) direct that the Secretary of State may exercise his powers under this section in respect of him;

and the court may give a direction under paragraph (b) above notwithstanding that the offender is not within the jurisdiction of the court if the court is satisfied that he was notified of his right to appear before the court and of the powers available under this section.

(3) Where the court gives a direction under subsection (2)(b) above in respect of an authorised person the Secretary of State may serve a notice on him—

(a) cancelling any authorisation of his to carry on investment business after the expiry of a specified period after the service of the notice;

(b) disqualifying him from becoming authorised to carry on investment business after the expiry of a specified period;

(c) restricting any authorisation of his in respect of investment business during a specified period to the performance of contracts entered into before the notice comes into force;

(d) prohibiting him from entering into transactions of a specified kind or entering into them except in specified circumstances or to a specified extent;

(e) prohibiting him from soliciting business from persons of a specified kind or otherwise than from such persons; or

(f) prohibiting him from carrying on business in a specified manner or otherwise than in a specified manner.

(4) The period mentioned in paragraphs (a) and (c) of subsection (3) above shall be such period as appears to the Secretary of State reasonable to enable the person on whom the notice is served to complete the performance of any contracts entered into before the notice comes into force and to terminate such of them as are of a continuing nature.

(5) Where the court gives a direction under subsection (2)(b) above in the case of an unauthorised person the Secretary of State may direct that any authorised person who knowingly transacts investment business of a specified kind, or in specified circumstances or to a specified extent, with or on behalf of that unauthorised person shall be treated as having contravened rules made under Chapter V of Part I of this Act or, in the case of a person who is an authorised person by virtue of his membership of a recognised self-regulating organisation or certification by a recognised professional body, the rules of that organisation or body.

(6) A person shall not be treated for the purposes of subsection (2) above as having a reasonable excuse for refusing to comply with a request or answer a question in a case where the contravention or suspected contravention being investigated relates to dealing by him on the instructions or for the account of another person, by reason that at the time of the refusal—

(a) he did not know the identity of that other person; or

(b) he was subject to the law of a country or territory outside the United Kingdom which prohibited him from disclosing information relating to the dealing without the consent of that other person, if he might have obtained that consent or obtained exemption from the law.

(7) A notice served on a person under subsection (3) above may be revoked at any time by the Secretary of State by serving a revocation notice on him; and the Secretary of State shall revoke such a notice if it appears to him that he has agreed to comply with the relevant request or answer the relevant question.

(8) The revocation of such a notice as is mentioned in subsection (3)(a) above shall not have the effect of reviving the authorisation cancelled by the notice except where the person would (apart from the notice) at the time of the revocation be an authorised person by virtue of his membership of a recognised self-regulating organisation or certification by a recognised professional body; but nothing in this subsection shall be construed as preventing any person who has been subject to such a notice from again becoming authorised after the revocation of the notice.

(9) If it appears to the Secretary of State—

(a) that a person on whom he serves a notice under subsection (3) above is an authorised person by virtue of an authorisation granted by a designated agency or by virtue of membership of a recognised self-regulating organisation or certification by a recognised professional body; or

(b) that a person on whom he serves a revocation notice under subsection (7) above was such an authorised person at the time that the notice which is being revoked was served,

he shall serve a copy of the notice on that agency, organisation or body.

(10) The functions to which section 114 above applies shall include the functions of the Secretary of State under this section but any transfer of those functions shall be subject to a reservation that they are to be exercisable by him concurrently with the designated agency and so as to be exercisable by the agency subject to such conditions or restrictions as the Secretary of State may from time to time impose.

[THE NEXT PAGE IS I 699]

PART X

MISCELLANEOUS AND SUPPLEMENTARY

. . . . . .

Powers of entry

199.—[1] (1) A justice of the peace may issue a warrant under this section if satisfied on information on oath given by or on behalf of the Secretary of State that there are reasonable grounds for believing that an offence has been committed—

(*a*) under section 4, 47, 57, 130, 133 or 171(2) or (3) above, or

(*b*) section 1, 2, 4 or 5 of the Company Securities (Insider Dealing) Act 1985,

and that there are on any premises documents relevant to the question whether that offence has been committed.

(2) A justice of the peace may also issue a warrant under this section if satisfied on information on oath given by or on behalf of the Secretary of State, or by a person appointed or authorised to exercise powers under section 94, 106 or 177 above, that there are reasonable grounds for believing that there are on any premises documents whose production has been required under section 94, 105 or 177 above and which have not been produced in compliance with the requirement.

(3) A warrant under this section shall authorise a constable, together with any other person named in it and any other constables—

(*a*) to enter the premises specified in the information, using such force as is reasonably necessary for the purpose;

[2](*b*) to search the premises and take possession of any documents appearing to be such documents as are mentioned in subsection (1) or, as the case may be, in subsection (2) above or to take, in relation to any such documents, any other steps which may appear to be necessary for preserving them or preventing interference with them;

(*c*) to take copies of any such documents; and

(*d*) to require any person named in the warrant to provide an explanation of them or to state where they may be found.

(4) A warrant under this section shall continue in force until the end of the period of one month beginning with the day on which it is issued.

(5) Any documents of which possession is taken under this section may be retained—

(*a*) for a period of three months; or

[3](*b*) if within that period proceedings to which the documents are relevant are commenced against any person for any criminal offence, until the conclusion of those proceedings.

[4] (6) Any person who intentionally obstructs the exercise of any rights conferred by a warrant issued under this section or fails without reasonable excuse to comply with any requirement imposed in accordance with subsection (3)(*d*) above shall be guilty of an offence and liable—

(*a*) on conviction on indictment, to a fine;

(*b*) on summary conviction, to a fine not exceeding the statutory maximum. . . .

[5] (8) In the application of this section to Scotland for the references to a justice of the peace substitute references to a justice of the peace or a sheriff, and for references to information on oath substitute references to evidence on oath.

[6] (9) In this section "documents" includes information recorded in any form.

NOTES

[1] Substituted by the Companies Act 1989, s. 76(2).

[2] As amended by the Companies Act 1989, s. 76(3).

³ As amended by the Companies Act 1989, s. 76(4).
⁴ As amended by the Companies Act 1989, s. 76(5).
⁵ Substituted by the Companies Act 1989, s. 76(7).
⁶ As amended by the Companies Act 1989, s. 76(8) and Sched. 24.

False and misleading statements

200.—(1) A person commits an offence if—

(*a*) for the purposes of or in connection with any application under this Act; or

(*b*) in purported compliance with any requirement imposed on him by or under this Act,

he furnishes information which he knows to be false or misleading in a material particular or recklessly furnishes information which is false or misleading in a material particular. . . .

(5) A person guilty of an offence under subsection (1) above shall be liable—

(*a*) on conviction on indictment, to imprisonment for a term not exceeding two years or to a fine or to both;

(*b*) on summary conviction, to imprisonment for a term not exceeding six months or to a fine not exceeding the statutory maximum or to both. . . .

                    .   .   .   .   .   .

Offences by bodies corporate, partnerships and unincorporated associations

202.—(1) Where an offence under this Act committed by a body corporate is proved to have been committed with the consent or connivance of, or to be attributable to any neglect on the part of—

(*a*) any director, manager, secretary or other similar officer of the body corporate, or any person who was purporting to act in any such capacity; or

(*b*) a controller of the body corporate,

he, as well as the body corporate, shall be guilty of that offence and liable to be proceeded against and punished accordingly.

(2) Where the affairs of a body corporate are managed by the members subsection (1) above shall apply in relation to the acts and defaults of a member in connection with his functions of management as if he were a director of the body corporate.

(3) Where a partnership is guilty of an offence under this Act every partner, other than a partner who is proved to have been ignorant of or to have attempted to prevent the commission of the offence, shall also be guilty of that offence and be liable to be proceeded against and punished accordingly.

(4) Where an unincorporated association (other than a partnership) is guilty of an offence under this Act—

(*a*) every officer of the association who is bound to fulfil any duty of which the breach is the offence; or

(*b*) if there is no such officer, every member of the governing body other than a member who is proved to have been ignorant of or to have attempted to prevent the commission of the offence,

shall also be guilty of the offence and be liable to be proceeded against and punished accordingly.

Jurisdiction and procedure in respect of offences

203.—(1) Summary proceedings for an offence under this Act may, without prejudice to any jurisdiction exercisable apart from this section, be taken against any body corporate or unincorporated association at any place at which it has a place of business and against an individual at any place where he is for the time being.

(2) Proceedings for an offence alleged to have been committed under

this Act by an unincorporated association shall be brought in the name of the association (and not in that of any of its members) and for the purposes of any such proceedings any rules of court relating to the service of documents shall have effect as if the association were a corporation. . . .

(4) In relation to any proceedings on indictment in Scotland for an offence alleged to have been committed under this Act by an unincorporated association, section 74 of the Criminal Procedure (Scotland) Act 1975 (proceedings on indictment against bodies corporate) shall have effect as if the association were a body corporate. . . .

(6) A fine imposed on an unincorporated association on its conviction of an offence under this Act shall be paid out of the funds of the association.

Service of notices

204.—(1) This section has effect in relation to any notice, direction or other document required or authorised by or under this Act to be given to or served on any person other than the Secretary of State, the Chief Registrar of friendly societies or the Registrar of Friendly Societies for Northern Ireland.

(2) Any such document may be given to or served on the person in question—

(*a*) by delivering it to him;

(*b*) by leaving it at his proper address; or

(*c*) by sending it by post to him at that address.

(3) Any such document may—

(*a*) in the case of a body corporate, be given to or served on the secretary or clerk of that body;

(*b*) in the case of a partnership, be given to or served on any partner;

(*c*) in the case of an unincorporated association other than a partnership, be given to or served on any member of the governing body of the association;

(*d*) in the case of an appointed representative, be given to or served on his principal.

(4) For the purposes of this section and section 7 of the Interpretation Act 1978 (service of documents by post) in its application to this section, the proper address of any person is his last known address (whether of his residence or of a place where he carries on business or is employed) and also any address applicable in his case under the following provisions—

(*a*) in the case of a member of a recognised self-regulating organisation or a person certified by a recognised professional body who does not have a place of business in the United Kingdom, the address of that organisation or body;

(*b*) in the case of a body corporate, its secretary or its clerk, the address of its registered or principal office in the United Kingdom;

(*c*) in the case of an unincorporated association (other than a partnership) or a member of its governing body, its principal office in the United Kingdom.

(5) Where a person has notified the Secretary of State of an address or a new address at which documents may be given to or served on him under this Act that address shall also be his proper address for the purposes mentioned in subsection (4) above or, as the case may be, his proper address for those purposes in substitution for that previously notified.

. . . . . .

Interpretation

207.—(1) In this Act, except where the context otherwise requires—

. . .

"body corporate" includes a body corporate constituted under the law of a country or territory outside the United Kingdom;

. . .

"competent authority" means the competent authority for the purposes of Part IV of this Act;

. . .

"director", in relation to a body corporate, includes a person occupying in relation to it the position of a director (by whatever name called) and any person in accordance with whose directions or instructions (not being advice given in a professional capacity) the directors of that body are accustomed to act;

. . .

"group", in relation to a body corporate, means that body corporate, any other body corporate which is its holding company or subsidiary and any other body corporate which is a subsidiary of that holding company;

. . .

"listing particulars" has the meaning given in section 144(2) above;

. . .

"partnership" includes a partnership constituted under the law of a country or territory outside the United Kingdom;

"prescribed" means prescribed by regulations made by the Secretary of State;

. . .

"private company" has the meaning given in section 1(3) of the Companies Act 1985 or the corresponding Northern Ireland provision;

. . .

(2) In this Act "advertisement" includes every form of advertising, whether in a publication, by the display of notices, signs, labels or showcards, by means of circulars, catalogues, price lists or other documents, by an exhibition of pictures or photographic or cinematographic films, by way of sound broadcasting or television, by the distribution of recordings, or in any other manner; and references to the issue of an advertisement shall be construed accordingly.

(3) For the purposes of this Act an advertisement or other information issued outside the United Kingdom shall be treated as issued in the United Kingdom if it is directed to persons in the United Kingdom or is made available to them otherwise than in a newspaper, journal, magazine or other periodical publication published and circulating principally outside the United Kingdom or in a sound or television broadcast transmitted principally for reception outside the United Kingdom.

(4) The Independent Broadcasting Authority shall not be regarded as contravening any provision of this Act by reason of broadcasting an advertisement in accordance with the provisions of the Broadcasting Act 1981.

(5) In this Act "controller" means—

(a) in relation to a body corporate, a person who, either alone or with any associate or associates, is entitled to exercise, or control the exercise of, 15 per cent. or more of the voting power at any general meeting of the body corporate or another body corporate of which it is a subsidiary; and

(b) in relation to an unincorporated association—

(i) any person in accordance with whose directions or instructions, either alone or with those of any associate or associates, the officers or members of the governing body of the association are accustomed to act (but disregarding advice given in a professional capacity); and

(ii) any person who, either alone or with any associate or associates, is entitled to exercise, or control the exercise of, 15 per cent. or more of the voting power at any general meeting of the association;

and for the purposes of this subsection "associate", in relation to any person, means that person's wife, husband or minor child or step-child, any body corporate of which that person is a director, any person who is an employee or partner of that person and, if that person is a body corporate, any subsidiary of that body corporate and any employee of any such subsidiary.

(6) In this Act, except in relation to a unit trust scheme or a registered friendly society, "manager" means an employee who—

(*a*) under the immediate authority of his employer is responsible, either alone or jointly with one or more other persons, for the conduct of his employer's business; or

(*b*) under the immediate authority of his employer or of a person who is a manager by virtue of paragraph (*a*) above exercises managerial functions or is responsible for maintaining accounts or other records of his employer;

and, where the employer is not an individual, references in this subsection to the authority of the employer are references to the authority, in the case of a body corporate, of the directors, in the case of a partnership, of the partners and, in the case of an unincorporated association, of its officers or the members of its governing body.

(7) In this Act "insurance business", "insurance company" and "contract of insurance" have the same meanings as in the Insurance Companies Act 1982.

(8) Section 736 of the Companies Act 1985 (meaning of subsidiary and holding company) shall apply for the purposes of this Act.

(9) In the application of this Act to Scotland, reference to a matter being actionable at the suit of a person shall be construed as references to the matter being actionable at the instance of that person.

(10) For the purposes of any provision of this Act authorising or requiring a person to do anything within a specified number of days no account shall be taken of any day which is a public holiday in any part of the United Kingdom. . . . .

. . . . . .

Northern Ireland

209.—(1) This Act extends to Northern Ireland.

(2) Subject to any Order made after the passing of this Act by virtue of subsection (1)(*a*) of section 3 of the Northern Ireland Constitution Act 1973 the regulation of investment business, the official listing of securities and offers of unlisted securities shall not be transferred matters for the purposes of that Act but shall for the purposes of subsection (2) of that section be treated as specified in Schedule 3 to that Act.

. . . . . .

Commencement and transitional provisions

[1] **211.**—(1) This Act shall come into force on such day as the Secretary of State may by order appoint and different days may be appointed for different provisions or different purposes. . . . .

NOTE

[1] The following dates of commencement (so far as relevant) have been prescribed:

15th October 1986: ss.177, 178 (part), 179 (part), 199–203 (part), 207 (part), 209 (part) (S.I. 1986 No. 1940).

27th November 1986: s.212(1) (S.I. 1986 No. 2031).

18th December 1986: ss.174(1) and (2), 179 (remainder), 202–203 (remainder), 207 (remainder), 209 (remainder) (S.I. 1986 No. 2246).

12th January 1987: Pt. IV (except s.154(2)–(4)) (part), ss.173, 176, 178(10), 200(1)(*b*) and (5) (part) (S.I. 1986 No. 2246).

16th February 1987, Pt. IV (except s.154(2)–(4)) (remainder) (S.I. 1986 No. 2246).

30th April 1987: s.172 (S.I. 1986 No. 2246).

Short title, consequential amendments and repeals

212.—(1) This Act may be cited as the Financial Services Act 1986. . . .

[THE NEXT PAGE IS I 701]

Companies Act 1989

(1989 c. 40)

An Act to amend the law relating to company accounts; to make new provision with respect to the persons eligible for appointment as company auditors; to amend the Companies Act 1985 and certain other enactments with respect to investigations and powers to obtain information and to confer new powers exercisable to assist overseas regulatory authorities; to make new provision with respect to the registration of company charges and otherwise to amend the law relating to companies; to amend the Fair Trading Act 1973; to enable provision to be made for the payment of fees in connection with the exercise by the Secretary of State, the Director General of Fair Trading and the Monopolies and Mergers Commission of their functions under Part V of that Act; to make provision for safeguarding the operation of certain financial markets; to amend the Financial Services Act 1986; to enable provision to be made for the recording and transfer of title to securities without a written instrument; to amend the Company Directors Disqualification Act 1986, the Company Securities (Insider Dealing) Act 1985, the Policyholders Protection Act 1975 and the law relating to building societies; and for connected purposes.   [16th November 1989]

ARRANGEMENT OF SECTIONS

PART I

COMPANY ACCOUNTS

[Amends the Companies Act 1985.]

PART II

ELIGIBILITY FOR APPOINTMENT AS COMPANY AUDITOR

Introduction

PART III

INVESTIGATIONS AND POWERS TO OBTAIN INFORMATION

Amendments of the Companies Act 1985

. . . .

Amendments of the Financial Services Act 1986

. . . . . .

Amendments of other enactments

. . . . . .

Powers exercisable to assist overseas regulatory authorities

PART X

MISCELLANEOUS AND GENERAL PROVISIONS

Miscellaneous

. . . . . .

General

PART I

COMPANY ACCOUNTS

Introduction

Introduction
[1] **1.** The provisions of this Part amend Part VII of the Companies Act 1985 (accounts and audit) by—
  (*a*) inserting new provisions in place of sections 221 to 262 of that Act, and
  (*b*) amending or replacing Schedules 4 to 10 to that Act and inserting new Schedules.

NOTE
[1] The amendments made will be given effect in the text of the 1985 Act as they are brought into force.

PART II

ELIGIBILITY FOR APPOINTMENT AS COMPANY AUDITOR

Introduction

Introduction
24.—(1) The main purposes of this Part are to secure that only persons who are properly supervised and appropriately qualified are appointed company auditors, and that audits by persons so appointed are carried out properly and with integrity and with a proper degree of independence.

(2) A "company auditor" means a person appointed as auditor under Chapter V of Part XI of the Companies Act 1985; and the expressions "company audit" and "company audit work" shall be construed accordingly.

Eligibility for appointment

Eligibility for appointment
25.—(1) A person is eligible for appointment as a company auditor only if he—

(*a*) is a member of a recognised supervisory body, and

(*b*) is eligible for the appointment under the rules of that body.

(2) An individual or a firm may be appointed a company auditor.

(3) In the cases to which section 34 applies (individuals retaining only 1967 Act authorisation) a person's eligibility for appointment as a company auditor is restricted as mentioned in that section.

Effect of appointment of partnership
26.—(1) The following provisions apply to the appointment as company auditor of a partnership constituted under the law of England and Wales or Northern Ireland, or under the law of any other country or territory in which a partnership is not a legal person.

(2) The appointment is (unless a contrary intention appears) an appointment of the partnership as such and not of the partners.

(3) Where the partnership ceases, the appointment shall be treated as extending to—

(*a*) any partnership which succeeds to the practice of that partnership and is eligible for the appointment, and

(*b*) any person who succeeds to that practice having previously carried it on in partnership and is eligible for the appointment.

(4) For this purpose a partnership shall be regarded as succeeding to the practice of another partnership only if the members of the successor partnership are substantially the same as those of the former partnership; and a partnership or other person shall be regarded as succeeding to the practice of a partnership only if it or he succeeds to the whole or substantially the whole of the business of the former partnership.

(5) Where the partnership ceases and no person succeeds to the appointment under subsection (3), the appointment may with the consent of the company be treated as extending to a partnership or other person eligible for the appointment who succeeds to the business of the former partnership or to such part of it as is agreed by the company shall be treated as comprising the appointment.

Ineligibility on ground of lack of independence
27.—(1) A person is ineligible for appointment as company auditor of a company if he is—

(*a*) an officer or employee of the company, or

(*b*) a partner or employee of such a person, or a partnership of which such a person is a partner,

or if he is ineligible by virtue of paragraph (*a*) or (*b*) for appointment as company auditor of any associated undertaking of the company.

For this purpose an auditor of a company shall not be regarded as an officer or employee of the company.

(2) A person is also ineligible for appointment as company auditor of a company if there exists between him or any associate of his and the company or any associated undertaking a connection of any such description as may be specified by regulations made by the Secretary of State.

The regulations may make different provisions for different cases.

(3) In this section "associated undertaking," in relation to a company, means—

    (*a*) a parent undertaking or subsidiary undertaking of the company, or

    (*b*) a subsidiary undertaking of any parent undertaking of the company.

(4) Regulations under this section shall be made by statutory instrument which shall be subject to annulment in pursuance of a resolution of either House of Parliament.

Effect of ineligibility

28.—(1) No person shall act as a company auditor if he is ineligible for appointment to the office.

(2) If during his term of office a company auditor becomes ineligible for appointment to the office, he shall thereupon vacate office and shall forthwith give notice in writing to the company concerned that he has vacated it by reason of ineligibility.

(3) A person who acts as company auditor in contravention of subsection (1), or fails to give notice of vacating his office as required by subsection (2), is guilty of an offence and liable—

    (*a*) on conviction on indictment, to a fine, and

    (*b*) on summary conviction, to a fine not exceeding the statutory maximum.

(4) In the case of continued contravention he is liable on a second or subsequent summary conviction (instead of the fine mentioned in subsection (3)(*b*)) to a fine not exceeding one-tenth of the statutory maximum in respect of each day on which the contravention is continued.

(5) In proceedings against a person for an offence under this section it is a defence for him to show that he did not know and had no reason to believe that he was, or had become, ineligible for appointment.

Power of Secretary of State to require second audit

29.—(1) Where a person appointed company auditor was, for any part of the period during which the audit was conducted, ineligible for appointment to that office, the Secretary of State may direct the company concerned to retain a person eligible for appointment as auditor of the company—

    (*a*) to audit the relevant accounts again, or

    (*b*) to review the first audit and to report (giving his reasons) whether a second audit is needed;

and the company shall comply with such a direction within 21 days of its being given.

(2) If a second audit is recommended the company shall forthwith take such steps as are necessary to comply with the recommendation.

(3) Where a direction is given under this section, the Secretary of State shall send a copy of the direction to the registrar of companies; and the company shall within 21 days of receiving any report under subsection (1)(*b*) send a copy of it to the registrar of companies.

The provisions of the Companies Act 1985 relating to the delivery of documents to the registrar apply for the purposes of this subsection.

(4) Any statutory or other provisions applying in relation to the first audit shall apply, so far as practicable, in relation to a second audit under this section.

(5) If a company fails to comply with the requirements of this section, it is guilty of an offence and liable on summary conviction to a fine not exceeding the statutory maximum; and in the case of continued contravention it is liable on a second or subsequent summary conviction (instead of the fine mentioned above) to a fine not exceeding one-tenth of the statutory maximum in respect of each day on which the contravention is continued.

(6) A direction under this section is, on the application of the Secretary of State, enforceable by injunction or, in Scotland, by an order under section 45 of the Court of Session Act 1988.

(7) If a person accepts an appointment, or continues to act, as company auditor at a time when he knows he is ineligible, the company concerned may recover from him any costs incurred by it in complying with the requirements of this section.

Recognition of supervisory bodies and professional qualifications

Supervisory bodies

30.—(1) In this Part a "supervisory body" means a body established in the United Kingdom (whether a body corporate or an unincorporated association) which maintains and enforces rules as to—

(*a*) the eligibility of persons to seek appointment as company auditors, and

(*b*) the conduct of company audit work,

which are binding on persons seeking appointment or acting as company auditors either because they are members of that body or because they are otherwise subject to its control.

(2) In this Part references to the members of a supervisory body are to the persons who, whether or not members of the body, are subject to its rules in seeking appointment or acting as company auditors.

(3) In this Part references to the rules of a supervisory body are to the rules (whether or not laid down by the body itself) which the body has power to enforce and which are relevant for the purposes of this Part.

This includes rules relating to the admission and expulsion of members of the body, so far as relevant for the purposes of this Part.

(4) In this Part references to guidance issued by a supervisory body are to guidance issued or any recommendation made by it to all or any class of its members or persons seeking to become members which would, if it were a rule, fall within subsection (3).

(5) The provisions of Parts I and II of Schedule 11 have effect with respect to the recognition of supervisory bodies for the purposes of this Part.

Meaning of "appropriate qualification"

31.—(1) A person holds an appropriate qualification for the purposes of this Part if—

(*a*) he was, by virtue of membership of a body recognised for the purposes of section 389(1)(*a*) of the Companies Act 1985, qualified for appointment as auditor of a company under that section immediately before 1st January 1990 and immediately before the commencement of section 25 above,

(*b*) he holds a recognised professional qualification obtained in the United Kingdom, or

(*c*) he holds an approved overseas qualification and satisfies any additional educational requirements applicable in accordance with section 33(4).

(2) A person who, immediately before 1st January 1990 and immediately before the commencement of section 25 above, was qualified for appointment as auditor of a company under section 389 of the Companies Act 1985 otherwise than by virtue of membership of a body recognised for the purposes of section 389(1)(*a*)—

(*a*) shall be treated as holding an appropriate qualification for 12 months from the day on which section 25 comes into force, and

(*b*) shall continue to be so treated if within that period he notifies the Secretary of State that he wishes to retain the benefit of his qualification.

The notice shall be in writing and shall contain such information as the Secretary of State may require.

(3) If a person fails to give such notice within the time allowed he may apply to the Secretary of State, giving such information as would have been required in connection with a notice, and the Secretary of State may, if he is satisfied—

    (*a*) that there was good reason why the applicant did not give notice in time, and

    (*b*) that the applicant genuinely intends to practise as an auditor in Great Britain,

direct that he shall be treated as holding an appropriate qualification for the purposes of this Part.

(4) A person who—

    (*a*) began before 1st January 1990 a course of study or practical training leading to a professional qualification in accountancy offered by a body established in the United Kingdom, and

    (*b*) obtained that qualification on or after that date and before 1st January 1996,

shall be treated as holding an appropriate qualification if the qualification is approved by the Secretary of State for the purposes of this subsection.

(5) Approval shall not be given unless the Secretary of State is satisfied that the body concerned has or, as the case may be, had at the relevant time adequate arrangements to ensure that the qualification is, or was, awarded only to persons educated and trained to a standard equivalent to that required in the case of a recognised professional qualification.

(6) A person shall not be regarded as holding an appropriate qualification for the purposes of this Part except in the above cases.

Qualifying bodies and recognised professional qualifications

32.—(1) In this Part a "qualifying body" means a body established in the United Kingdom (whether a body corporate or an unincorporated association) which offers a professional qualification in accountancy.

(2) In this Part references to the rules of a qualifying body are to the rules (whether or not laid down by the body itself) which the body has power to enforce and which are relevant for the purposes of this Part.

This includes rules relating to—

    (*a*) admission to or expulsion from a course of study leading to a qualification,

    (*b*) the award or deprivation of a qualification, or

    (*c*) the approval of a person for the purposes of giving practical training or the withdrawal of such approval,

so far as relevant for the purposes of this Part.

(3) In this Part references to guidance issued by any such body are to any guidance which the body issues, or any recommendation it makes to all or any class of persons holding or seeking to hold a qualification, or approved or seeking to be approved by the body for the purpose of giving practical training, which would, if it were a rule, fall within subsection (2).

(4) The provisions of Parts I and II of Schedule 12 have effect with respect to the recognition for the purposes of this Part of a professional qualification offered by a qualifying body.

Approval of overseas qualifications

33.—(1) The Secretary of State may declare that persons who—

    (*a*) are qualified to audit accounts under the law of a specified country or territory outside the United Kingdom, or

    (*b*) hold a specified professional qualification in accountancy recognised under the law of a country or territory outside the United Kingdom,

shall be regarded for the purposes of this Part as holding an approved overseas qualification.

(2) A qualification shall not be so approved by the Secretary of State unless he is satisfied that it affords an assurance of professional competence equivalent to that afforded by a recognised professional qualification.

(3) In exercising the power conferred by subsection (1) the Secretary of State may have regard to the extent to which persons—

(a) eligible under this Part for appointment as a company auditor, or

(b) holding a professional qualification recognised under this Part,

are recognised by the law of the country or territory in question as qualified to audit accounts there.

(4) The Secretary of State may direct that a person holding an approved overseas qualification shall not be treated as holding an appropriate qualification for the purposes of this Part unless he holds such additional educational qualifications as the Secretary of State may specify for the purpose of ensuring that such persons have an adequate knowledge of the law and practice in the United Kingdom relevant to the audit of accounts.

(5) Different directions may be given in relation to different qualifications.

(6) The Secretary of State may if he thinks fit, having regard to the considerations mentioned in subsections (2) and (3), withdraw his approval of an overseas qualification in relation to persons becoming qualified as mentioned in subsection (1)(a), or obtaining such a qualification as is mentioned in subsection (1)(b), after such date as he may specify.

Eligibility of individuals retaining only 1967 Act authorisation

34.—(1) A person whose only appropriate qualification is that he retains an authorisation granted by the Board of Trade or the Secretary of State under section 13(1) of the Companies Act 1967 is eligible only for appointment as auditor of an unquoted company.

(2) A company is "unquoted" if, at the time of the person's appointment, no share or debentures of the company, or of a parent undertaking of which it is a subsidiary undertaking, have been quoted on a stock exchange (in Great Britain or elsewhere) or offered (whether in Great Britain or elsewhere) to the public for subscription or purchase.

(3) This section does not authorise the appointment of such a person as auditor of a company that carries on business as the promoter of a trading stamp scheme within the meaning of the Trading Stamps Act 1964.

(4) References to a person eligible for appointment as company auditor under section 25 in enactments relating to eligibility for appointment as auditor of a body other than a company do not include a person to whom this section applies.

Duties of recognised bodies

The register of auditors

35.—(1) The Secretary of State shall make regulations requiring the keeping of a register of—

(a) the individuals and firms eligible for appointment as company auditor, and

(b) the individuals holding an appropriate qualification who are responsible for company audit work on behalf of such firms.

(2) The regulations shall provide that each person's entry in the register shall give—

(a) his name and address, and

(b) in the case of a person eligible as mentioned in subsection (1)(a), the name of the relevant supervisory body,

together with such other information as may be specified by the regulations.

(3) The regulations may impose such obligations as the Secretary of State thinks fit—

   (*a*) on recognised supervisory bodies,

   (*b*) on persons eligible for appointment as company auditor, and

   (*c*) on any person with whom arrangements are made by one or more recognised supervisory bodies with respect to the keeping of the register.

(4) The regulations may include provision—

   (*a*) requiring the register to be open to inspection at such times and places as may be specified in the regulations or determined in accordance with them,

   (*b*) enabling a person to require a certified copy of an entry in the register, and

   (*c*) authorising the charging of fees for inspection, or the provision of copies, of such reasonable amount as may be specified in the regulations or determined in accordance with them;

and may contain such other supplementary and incidental provisions as the Secretary of State thinks fit.

(5) Regulations under this section shall be made by statutory instrument which shall be subject to annulment in pursuance of a resolution of either House of Parliament.

(6) The obligations imposed by regulations under this section on such persons as are mentioned in subsection (3)(*a*) or (*c*) are enforceable on the application of the Secretary of State by injunction or, in Scotland, by an order under section 45 of the Court of Session Act 1988.

Information about firms to be available to public

36.—(1) The Secretary of State shall make regulations requiring recognised supervisory bodies to keep and make available to the public the following information with respect to the firms eligible under their rules for appointment as a company auditor—

   (*a*) in relation to a body corporate, the name and address of each person who is a director of the body or holds any shares in it,

   (*b*) in relation to a partnership, the name and address of each partner,

and such other information as may be specified in the regulations.

(2) The regulations may impose such obligations as the Secretary of State thinks fit—

   (*a*) on recognised supervisory bodies,

   (*b*) on persons eligible for appointment as company auditor, and

   (*c*) on any person with whom arrangements are made by one or more recognised supervisory bodies with respect to the keeping of the information.

(3) The regulations may include provision—

   (*a*) requiring that the information be open to inspection at such times and places as may be specified in the regulations or determined in accordance with them,

   (*b*) enabling a person to require a certified copy of the information or any part of it, and

   (*c*) authorising the charging of fees for inspection, or the provision of copies, of such reasonable amount as may be specified in the regulations or determined in accordance with them;

and may contain such other supplementary and incidental provisions as the Secretary of State thinks fit.

(4) The regulations may make different provision in relation to different descriptions of information and may contain such other supplementary and incidental provisions as the Secretary of State thinks fit.

(5) Regulations under this section shall be made by statutory instrument which shall be subject to annulment in pursuance of a resolution of either House of Parliament.

(6) The obligations imposed by regulations under this section on such persons as are mentioned in subsection (2)(*a*) or (*c*) are enforceable on the application of the Secretary of State by injunction or, in Scotland, by an order under section 45 of the Court of Session Act 1988.

Matters to be notified to the Secretary of State

37.—(1) The Secretary of State may require a recognised supervisory or qualifying body—

(*a*) to notify him forthwith of the occurrence of such events as he may specify in writing and to give him such information in respect of those events as is so specified;

(*b*) to give him, at such times or in respect of such periods as he may specify in writing, such information as is so specified.

(2) The notices and information required to be given shall be such as the Secretary of State may reasonably require for the exercise of his functions under this Part.

(3) the Secretary of State may require information given under this section to be given in a specified form or verified in a specified manner.

(4) Any notice or information required to be given under this section shall be given in writing unless the Secretary of State specifies or approves some other manner.

Power to call for information

38.—(1) The Secretary of State may by notice in writing require a recognised supervisory or qualifying body to give him such information as he may reasonably require for the exercise of his functions under this Part.

(2) The Secretary of State may require that any information which he requires under this section shall be given within such reasonable time and verified in such manner as he may specify.

Compliance orders

39.—(1) If at any time it appears to the Secretary of State—

(*a*) in the case of a recognised supervisory body, that any requirement of Schedule 11 is not satisfied,

(*b*) in the case of a recognised professional qualification, that any requirement of Schedule 12 is not satisfied, or

(*c*) that a recognised supervisory or qualifying body has failed to comply with an obligation to which it is subject by virtue of this Part,

he may, instead of revoking the relevant recognition order, make an application to the court under this section.

(2) If on such application the court decides that the subsection or requirement in question is not satisfied or, as the case may be, that the body has failed to comply with the obligation in question it may order the supervisory or qualifying body in question to take such steps as the court directs for securing that the subsection or requirement is satisfied or that the obligation is complied with.

(3) The jurisdiction conferred by this section is exercisable by the High Court and the Court of Session.

Directions to comply with international obligations

40.—(1) If it appears to the Secretary of State—

(*a*) that any action proposed to be taken by a recognised supervisory or qualifying body, or a body established by order under section 46, would be incompatible with Community obligations or any other international obligations of the United Kingdom, or

(*b*) that any action which that body has power to take is required for the purpose of implementing any such obligations,

he may direct the body not to take or, as the case may be, to take the action in question.

(2) A direction may include such supplementary or incidental requirements as the Secretary of State thinks necessary or expedient.

(3) A direction under this section is enforceable on the application of the Secretary of State by injunction or, in Scotland, by an order under section 45 of the Court of Session Act 1988.

Offences

False and misleading statements

41.—(1) A person commits an offence if—

(*a*) for the purposes of or in connection with any application under this Part, or

(*b*) in purported compliance with any requirement imposed on him by or under this Part,

he furnishes information which he knows to be false or misleading in a material particular or recklessly furnishes information which is false or misleading in a material particular.

(2) It is an offence for a person whose name does not appear on the register of auditors kept under regulations under section 35 to describe himself as a registered auditor or so to hold himself out as to indicate, or be reasonably understood to indicate, that he is a registered auditor.

(3) It is an offence for a body which is not a recognised supervisory or qualifying body to describe itself as so recognised or so to describe itself or hold itself out as to indicate, or be reasonably understood to indicate, that it is so recognised.

(4) A person guilty of an offence under subsection (1) is liable—

(*a*) on conviction on indictment, to imprisonment for a term not exceeding two years or to a fine or both;

(*b*) on summary conviction, to imprisonment for a term not exceeding six months or to a fine not exceeding the statutory maximum or both.

(5) A person guilty of an offence under subsection (2) or (3) is liable on summary conviction to imprisonment for a term not exceeding six months or to a fine not exceeding level 5 on the standard scale or both.

Where a contravention of subsection (2) or (3) involves a public display of the offending description, the maximum fine that may be imposed is (in place of that mentioned above) an amount equal to level 5 on the standard scale multiplied by the number of days for which the display has continued.

(6) It is a defence for a person charged with an offence under subsection (2) or (3) to show that he took all reasonable precautions and exercised all due diligence to avoid the commission of the offence.

Offences by bodies corporate, partnerships and unincorporated associations

42.—(1) Where an offence under this Part committed by a body corporate is proved to have been committed with the consent or connivance of, or to be attributable to any neglect on the part of, a director, manager, secretary or other similar officer of the body, or a person purporting to act in any such capacity, he as well as the body corporate is guilty of the offence and liable to be proceeded against and punished accordingly.

(2) Where the affairs of a body corporate are managed by its members, subsection (1) applies in relation to the acts and defaults of a member in connection with his functions of management as to a director of a body corporate.

(3) Where an offence under this Part committed by a partnership is proved to have been committed with the consent or connivance of, or to be attributable to any neglect on the part of, a partner, he as well as the partnership is guilty of the offence and liable to be proceeded against and punished accordingly.

(4) Where an offence under this Part committed by an unincorporated association (other than a partnership) is proved to have been committed with the consent or connivance of, or to be attributable to any neglect on the part of, any officer of the association or any member of its governing body, he as well as the association is guilty of the offence and liable to be proceeded against and punished accordingly.

Time limits for prosecution of offences

43.—(1) An information relating to an offence under this Part which is triable by a magistrates' court in England and Wales may be so tried on an information laid at any time within 12 months after the date on which evidence sufficient in the opinion of the Director of Public Prosecutions or the Secretary of State to justify the proceedings comes to his knowledge.

(2) Proceedings in Scotland for an offence under this Part may be commenced at any time within 12 months after the date on which evidence sufficient in the Lord Advocate's opinion to justify the proceedings came to his knowledge or, where such evidence was reported to him by the Secretary of State, within 12 months after the date on which it came to the knowledge of the latter.

For the purposes of this subsection proceedings shall be deemed to be commenced on the date on which a warrant to apprehend or to cite the accused is granted, if the warrant is executed without undue delay.

(3) Subsection (1) does not authorise the trial of an information laid, and subsection (2) does not authorise the commencement of proceedings, more than three years after the commission of the offence.

(4) For the purposes of this section a certificate of the Director of Public Prosecutions, the Lord Advocate or the Secretary of State as to the date on which such evidence as is referred to above came to his knowledge is conclusive evidence.

(5) Nothing in this section affects proceedings within the time limits prescribed by section 127(1) of the Magistrates' Courts Act 1980 or section 331 of the Criminal Procedure (Scotland) Act 1975 (the usual time limits for criminal proceedings).

Jurisdiction and procedure in respect of offences

44.—(1) Summary proceedings for an offence under this Part may, without prejudice to any jurisdiction exercisable apart from this section, be taken against a body corporate or unincorporated association at any place at which it has a place of business and against an individual at any place where he is for the time being.

(2) Proceedings for an offence alleged to have been committed under this Part by an unincorporated association shall be brought in the name of the association (and not in that of any of its members), and for the purposes of any such proceedings any rules of court relating to the service of documents apply as in relation to a body corporate.

(3) Section 33 of the Criminal Justice Act 1925 and Schedule 3 to the Magistrates' Courts Act 1980 (procedure on charge of offence against a corporation) apply in a case in which an unincorporated association is charged in England and Wales with an offence under this Part as they apply in the case of a corporation.

(4) In relation to proceedings on indictment in Scotland for an offence alleged to have been committed under this Part by an unincorporated association, section 74 of the Criminal Procedure (Scotland) Act 1975 (proceedings on indictment against bodies corporate) applies as if the association were a body corporate.

(5) A fine imposed on an unincorporated association on its conviction of such an offence shall be paid out of the funds of the association.

Supplementary provisions

Fees

45.—(1) An applicant for a recognition order under this Part shall pay such fee in respect of his application as may be prescribed; and no application shall be regarded as duly made unless this subsection is complied with.

(2) Every recognised supervisory or qualifying body shall pay such periodical fees to the Secretary of State as may be prescribed.

(3) In this section "prescribed" means prescribed by regulations made by the Secretary of State, which may make different provision for different cases or classes of case.

(4) Regulations under this section shall be made by statutory instrument which shall be subject to annulment in pursuance of a resolution of either House of Parliament.

(5) Fees received by the Secretary of State by virtue of this Part shall be paid into the Consolidated Fund.

Delegation of functions of Secretary of State

46.—(1) The Secretary of State may by order (a "delegation order") establish a body corporate to exercise his functions under this Part.

(2) A delegation order has the effect of transferring to the body established by it, subject to such exceptions and reservations as may be specified in the order, all the functions of the Secretary of State under this Part except—

    (*a*) such functions under Part I of Schedule 14 (prevention of restrictive practices) as are excepted by regulations under section 47, and

    (*b*) his functions in relation to the body itself;

and the order may also confer on the body such other functions supplementary or incidental to those transferred as appear to the Secretary of State to be appropriate.

(3) Any transfer of the functions under the following provisions shall be subject to the reservation that they remain exercisable concurrently by the Secretary of State—

    (*a*) section 38 (power to call for information), and

    (*b*) section 40 (directions to comply with international obligations);

and any transfer of the function of refusing to approve an overseas qualification, or withdrawing such approval, on the grounds referred to in section 33(3) (lack of reciprocity) shall be subject to the reservation that the function is exercisable only with the consent of the Secretary of State.

(4) A delegation order may be amended or, if it appears to the Secretary of State that it is no longer in the public interest that the order should remain in force, revoked by a further order under this section.

(5) Where functions are transferred or resumed, the Secretary of State may by order confer or, as the case may be, take away such other functions supplementary or incidental to those transferred or resumed as appear to him to be appropriate.

(6) The provisions of Schedule 13 have effect with respect to the status, constitution and proceedings of a body established by a delegation order, the exercise by it of certain functions transferred to it and other supplementary matters.

(7) An order under this section shall be made by statutory instrument.

(8) An order which has the effect of transferring or resuming any functions shall not be made unless a draft of it has been laid before and approved by resolution of each House of Parliament; and any other description of order shall be subject to annulment in pursuance of a resolution of either House of Parliament.

Restrictive practices

47.—(1) The provisions of Schedule 14 have effect with respect to certain matters relating to restrictive practices and competition law.

(2) The Secretary of State may make provision by regulations as to the discharge of the functions under paragraphs 1 to 7 of that Schedule when a delegation order is in force.

(3) The regulations may—

(*a*) except any function from the effect of the delegation order,

(*b*) modify any of the provisions mentioned in subsection (2), and

(*c*) impose such duties on the body established by the delegation order, the Secretary of State and Director General of Fair Trading as appear to the Secretary of State to be appropriate.

(4) The regulations shall contain such provision as appears to the Secretary of State to be necessary or expedient for reserving to him the decision—

(*a*) to refuse recognition on the ground mentioned in paragraph 1(3) of that Schedule, or

(*b*) to exercise the powers conferred by paragraph 6 of that Schedule.

(5) For that purpose the regulations may—

(*a*) prohibit the body from granting a recognition order without the leave of the Secretary of State, and

(*b*) empower the Secretary of State to direct the body to exercise its powers in such manner as may be specified in the direction.

(6) Regulations under this section shall be made by statutory instrument which shall be subject to annulment in pursuance of a resolution of either House of Parliament.

Exemption from liability for damages

48.—(1) Neither a recognised supervisory body, nor any of its officers or employees or members of its governing body, shall be liable in damages for anything done or omitted in the discharge or purported discharge of functions to which this subsection applies, unless the act or omission is shown to have been in bad faith.

(2) Subsection (1) applies to the functions of the body so far as relating to, or to matters arising out of—

(*a*) such rules, practices, powers and arrangements of the body to which the requirements of Part II of Schedule 11 apply, or

(*b*) the obligations with which paragraph 16 of that Schedule requires the body to comply,

(*c*) any guidance issued by the body, or

(*d*) the obligations to which the body is subject by virtue of this Part.

(3) Neither a body established by a delegation order, nor any of its members, officers or employees, shall be liable in damages for anything done or omitted in the discharge or purported discharge of the functions exercisable by virtue of an order under section 46, unless the act or omission is shown to have been in bad faith.

Service of notices

49.—(1) This section has effect in relation to any notice, direction or other document required or authorised by or under this Part to be given to or served on any person other than the Secretary of State.

(2) Any such document may be given to or served on the person in question—

(*a*) by delivering it to him,

(*b*) by leaving it at his proper address, or

(*c*) by sending it by post to him at that address.

(3) Any such document may—

(*a*) in the case of a body corporate, be given to or served on the secretary or clerk of that body;

(*b*) in the case of a partnership, be given to or served on any partner;

(*c*) in the case of an unincorporated association other than a partnership, be given to or served on any member of the governing body of the association.

(4) For the purposes of this section and section 7 of the Interpretation Act 1978 (service of documents by post) in its application to this section, the proper address of any person is his last known address (whether of his residence or of a place where he carries on business or is employed) and also—

(*a*) in the case of a person who is eligible under the rules of a recognised supervisory body for appointment as company auditor and who does not have a place of business in the United Kingdom, the address of that body;

(*b*) in the case of a body corporate, its secretary or its clerk, the address of its registered or principal office in the United Kingdom;

(*c*) in the case of an unincorporated association (other than a partnership) or a member of its governing body, its principal office in the United Kingdom.

Power to make consequential amendments

50.—(1) The Secretary of State may by regulations make such amendments of enactments as appear to him to be necessary or expedient in consequence of the provisions of this Part having effect in place of section 389 of the Companies Act 1985.

(2) That power extends to making such amendments as appear to the Secretary of State necessary or expedient of—

(*a*) enactments referring by name to the bodies of accountants recognised for the purposes of section 389(1)(*a*) of the Companies Act 1985, and

(*b*) enactments making with respect to other statutory auditors provision as to the matters dealt with in relation to company auditors by section 389 of the Companies Act 1985.

(3) The provision which may be made with respect to other statutory auditors includes provision as to—

(*a*) eligibility for the appointment,

(*b*) the effect of appointing a partnership which is not a legal person and the manner of exercise of the auditor's rights in such a case, and

(*c*) ineligibility on the ground of lack of independence or any other ground.

(4) The regulations may contain such supplementary, incidental and transitional provision as appears to the Secretary of State to be necessary or expedient.

(5) The Secretary of State shall not make regulations under this section with respect to any statutory auditors without the consent of—

(*a*) the Minister responsible for their appointment or responsible for the body or person by, or in relation to whom, they are appointed, or

(*b*) if there is no such Minister, the person by whom they are appointed.

(6) In this section a "statutory auditor" means a person appointed auditor in pursuance of any enactment authorising or requiring the appointment of an auditor or auditors.

(7) Regulations under this section shall be made by statutory instrument which shall be subject to annulment in pursuance of a resolution of either House of Parliament.

Power to make provision in consequence of changes affecting accountancy bodies

51.—(1) The Secretary of State may by regulations make such amendments of enactments as appear to him to be necessary or expedient in consequence of any change of name, merger or transfer of engagements affecting—

(*a*) a recognised supervisory or qualifying body under this Part, or

(*b*) a body of accountants referred to in, or approved, authorised or otherwise recognised for the purposes of, any other enactment.

(2) Regulations under this section shall be made by statutory instrument which shall be subject to annulment in pursuance of a resolution of either House of Parliament.

Meaning of "associate"

52.—(1) In this Part "associate," in relation to a person, shall be construed as follows.

(2) In relation to an individual "associate" means—

(*a*) that individual's spouse or minor child or step-child,

(*b*) any body corporate of which that individual is a director, and

(*c*) any employee or partner of that individual.

(3) In relation to a body corporate "associate" means—

(*a*) any body corporate of which that body is a director,

(*b*) any body corporate in the same group as that body, and

(*c*) any employee or partner of that body or of any body corporate in the same group.

(4) In relation to a Scottish firm, or a partnership constituted under the law of any other country or territory in which a partnership is a legal person, "associate" means—

(*a*) any body corporate of which the firm is a director,

(*b*) any employee of or partner in the firm, and

(*c*) any person who is an associate of a partner in the firm.

(5) In relation to a partnership constituted under the law of England and Wales or Northern Ireland, or the law of any other country or territory in which a partnership is not a legal person, "associate" means any person who is an associate of any of the partners.

Minor definitions

53.—(1) In this Part—

"address" means—

(*a*) in relation to an individual, his usual residential or business address, and

(*b*) in relation to a firm, its registered or principal office in Great Britain;

"company" means any company or other body to which section 384 of the Companies Act 1985 (duty to appoint auditors) applies;

"director," in relation to a body corporate, includes any person occupying in relation to it the position of a director (by whatever name called) and any person in accordance with whose directions or instructions (not being advice given in a professional capacity) the directors of the body are accustomed to act;

"enactment" includes an enactment contained in subordinate legislation within the meaning of the Interpretation Act 1978;

"firm" means a body corporate or a partnership;

"group," in relation to a body corporate, means the body corporate, any other body corporate which is its holding company or subsidiary and any other body corporate which is a subsidiary of that holding company; and

"holding company" and "subsidiary" have the meaning given by section 736 of the Companies Act 1985;

"parent undertaking" and "subsidiary undertaking" have the same meaning as in Part VII of the Companies Act 1985.

(2) For the purposes of this Part a body shall be regarded as "established in the United Kingdom" if and only if—

(*a*) it is incorporated or formed under the law of the United Kingdom or a part of the United Kingdom, or (*b*) its central management and control is exercised in the United Kingdom;

and any reference to a qualification "obtained in the United Kingdom" is to a qualification obtained from such a body.

Index of defined expressions

54. The following Table shows provisions defining or otherwise explaining expressions used in this Part (other than provisions defining or explaining an expression used only in the same section)—

address	section 53(1)
appropriate qualification	section 31
associate	section 52
company	section 53(1)
company auditor, company audit and company audit work	section 24(2)
delegation order	section 46
director (of a body corporate)	section 53(1)
Director (in Schedule 14)	paragraph 1(1) of that Schedule
enactment	section 53(1)
established in the United Kingdom	section 53(2)
firm	section 53(1)
group (in relation to a body corporate)	section 53(1)
guidance	
–of a qualifying body	section 32(3)
–of a supervisory body	section 30(4)
holding company	section 53(1)
member (of a supervisory body)	section 30(2)
obtained in the United Kingdom	section 53(2)
parent undertaking	section 53(1)
purposes of this Part	section 24(1)
qualifying body	section 32(1)
recognised	
–in relation to a professional qualification	section 32(4) and Schedule 12
–in relation to a qualifying body	paragraph 2(1) of Schedule 12
–in relation to a supervisory body	section 30(5) and Schedule 11
rules	
–of a qualifying body	section 32(2)
–of a supervisory body	section 30(3)
subsidiary and subsidiary undertaking	section 53(1)
supervisory body	section 30(1)

PART III

INVESTIGATIONS AND POWERS TO OBTAIN INFORMATION

[1] *Amendments of the Companies Act 1985*

NOTE

[1] Amendments to the 1985 Act, ss.432, 434, 436–442, 447–453 and Scheds. 22 and 24 will be given effect in the text of the Act as they are brought into force.

[1] *Amendments of the Financial Services Act 1986*

NOTE

[1] Amendments affecting those provisions of the Act reprinted in *The Parliament House Book* (ss.177 and 199) will be given effect in the text of that Act as they are brought into force.

. . . .

[1] *Amendments of other enactments*

NOTE

[1] Amendments to the Insolvency Act 1986, s.218(5), and the Company Directors Disqualification Act 1986, s.8, will be given effect in the texts of those Acts as they are brought into force.

．　．　．　．　．　．

Powers exercisable to assist overseas regulatory authorities

Request for assistance by overseas regulatory authority

82.—(1) The powers conferred by section 83 are exercisable by the Secretary of State for the purpose of assisting an overseas regulatory authority which has requested his assistance in connection with inquiries being carried out by it or on its behalf.

(2) An "overseas regulatory authority" means an authority which in a country or territory outside the United Kingdom exercises—

(*a*) any function corresponding to—
   (i) a function under the Financial Services Act 1986 of a designated agency, transferee body or competent authority (within the meaning of that Act),
   (ii) a function of the Secretary of State under the Insurance Companies Act 1982, the Companies Act 1985 or the Financial Services Act 1986, or
   (iii) a function of the Bank of England under the Banking Act 1987, or

(*b*) any function in connection with the investigation of, or the enforcement of rules (whether or not having the force of law) relating to, conduct of the kind prohibited by the Company Securities (Insider Dealing) Act 1985, or

(*c*) any function prescribed for the purposes of this subsection by order of the Secretary of State, being a function which in the opinion of the Secretary of State relates to companies or financial services.

An order under paragraph (*c*) shall be made by statutory instrument which shall be subject to annulment in pursuance of a resolution of either House of Parliament.

(3) The Secretary of State shall not exercise the powers conferred by section 83 unless he is satisfied that the assistance requested by the overseas regulatory authority is for the purposes of its regulatory functions.

An authority's "regulatory functions" means any functions falling within subsection (2) and any other functions relating to companies or financial services.

(4) In deciding whether to exercise those powers the Secretary of State may take into account, in particular—

(*a*) whether corresponding assistance would be given in that country or territory to an authority exercising regulatory functions in the United Kingdom;

(*b*) whether the inquiries relate to the possible breach of a law, or other requirement, which has no close parallel in the United Kingdom or involves the assertion of a jurisdiction not recognised by the United Kingdom;

(*c*) the seriousness of the matter to which the inquiries relate, the importance to the inquiries of the information sought in the United Kingdom and whether the assistance could be obtained by other means;

(*d*) whether it is otherwise appropriate in the public interest to give the assistance sought.

(5) Before deciding whether to exercise those powers in a case where the overseas regulatory authority is a banking supervisor, the Secretary of State shall consult the Bank of England.

A "banking supervisor" means an overseas regulatory authority with respect to which the Bank of England has notified the Secretary of State, for the purposes of this subsection, that it exercises functions corresponding to those of the Bank under the Banking Act 1987.

(6) The Secretary of State may decline to exercise those powers unless the overseas regulatory authority undertakes to make such contribution towards the costs of their exercise as the Secretary of State considers appropriate.

(7) References in this section to financial services include, in particular, investment business, insurance and banking.

Power to require information, documents or other assistance

83.—(1) The following powers may be exercised in accordance with section 82, if the Secretary of State considers there is good reason for their exercise.

(2) The Secretary of State may require any person—

(a) to attend before him at a specified time and place and answer questions or otherwise furnish information with respect to any matter relevant to the inquiries,

(b) to produce at a specified time and place any specified documents which appear to the Secretary of State to relate to any matter relevant to the inquiries, and

(c) otherwise to give him such assistance in connection with the inquiries as he is reasonably able to give.

(3) The Secretary of State may examine a person on oath and may administer an oath accordingly.

(4) Where documents are produced the Secretary of State may take copies or extracts from them.

(5) A person shall not under this section be required to disclose information or produce a document which he would be entitled to refuse to disclose or produce on grounds of legal professional privilege in proceedings in the High Court or on grounds of confidentiality as between client and professional legal adviser in proceedings in the Court of Session, except that a lawyer may be required to furnish the name and address of his client.

(6) A statement by a person in compliance with a requirement imposed under this section may be used in evidence against him.

(7) Where a person claims a lien on a document, its production under this section is without prejudice to his lien.

(8) In this section "documents" includes information recorded in any form; and, in relation to information recorded otherwise than in legible form, the power to require its production includes power to require the production of a copy of it in legible form.

Exercise of powers by officer, &c.

84.—(1) The Secretary of State may authorise an officer of his or any other competent person to exercise on his behalf all or any of the powers conferred by section 83.

(2) No such authority shall be granted except for the purpose of investigating—

(a) the affairs, or any aspects of the affairs, of a person specified in the authority, or

(b) a subject-matter so specified,

being a person who, or subject-matter which, is the subject of the inquiries being carried out by or on behalf of the overseas regulatory authority.

(3) No person shall be bound to comply with a requirement imposed by a person exercising powers by virtue of an authority granted under this section unless he has, if required, produced evidence of his authority.

(4) A person shall not by virtue of an authority under this section be required to disclose any information or produce any documents in respect

of which he owes an obligation of confidence by virtue of carrying on the business of banking unless—

    (*a*) the imposing on him of a requirement with respect to such information or documents has been specifically authorised by the Secretary of State, or

    (*b*) the person to whom the obligation of confidence is owed consents to the disclosure or production.

In this subsection "documents" has the same meaning as in section 83.

(5) Where the Secretary of State authorises a person other than one of his officers to exercise any powers by virtue of this section, that person shall make a report to the Secretary of State in such manner as he may require on the exercise of those powers and the results of exercising them.

Penalty for failure to comply with requirement, &c.

85.—(1) A person who without reasonable excuse fails to comply with a requirement imposed on him under section 83 commits an offence and is liable on summary conviction to imprisonment for a term not exceeding six months or to a fine not exceeding level 5 on the standard scale, or both.

(2) A person who in purported compliance with any such requirement furnishes information which he knows to be false or misleading in a material particular, or recklessly furnishes information which is false or misleading in a material particular, commits an offence and is liable—

    (*a*) on conviction on indictment, to imprisonment for a term not exceeding two years or to a fine, or both;

    (*b*) on summary conviction, to imprisonment for a term not exceeding six months or to a fine not exceeding the statutory maximum, or both.

Restrictions on disclosure of information

86.—(1) This section applies to information relating to the business or other affairs of a person which—

    (*a*) is supplied by an overseas regulatory authority in connection with a request for assistance, or

    (*b*) is obtained by virtue of the powers conferred by section 83, whether or not any requirement to supply it is made under that section.

(2) Except as permitted by section 87 below, such information shall not be disclosed for any purpose—

    (*a*) by the primary recipient, or

    (*b*) by any person obtaining the information directly or indirectly from him,

without the consent of the person from whom the primary recipient obtained the information and, if different, the person to whom it relates.

(3) The "primary recipient" means, as the case may be—

    (*a*) the Secretary of State,

    (*b*) any person authorised under section 84 to exercise powers on his behalf, and

    (*c*) any officer or servant of any such person.

(4) Information shall not be treated as information to which this section applies if it has been made available to the public by virtue of being disclosed in any circumstances in which, or for any purpose for which, disclosure is not precluded by this section.

(5) A person who contravenes this section commits an offence and is liable—

    (*a*) on conviction on indictment, to imprisonment for a term not exceeding two years or to a fine, or both;

    (*b*) on summary conviction, to imprisonment for a term not exceeding three months or to a fine not exceeding the statutory maximum, or both.

Exceptions from restrictions on disclosure

87.—(1) Information to which section 86 applies may be disclosed—

(*a*) to any person with a view to the institution of, or otherwise for the purposes of, relevant proceedings,

(*b*) for the purpose of enabling or assisting a relevant authority to discharge any relevant function (including functions in relation to proceedings),

(*c*) to the Treasury, if the disclosure is made in the interests of investors or in the public interest,

(*d*) if the information is or has been available to the public from other sources,

(*e*) in a summary or collection of information framed in such a way as not to enable the identity of any person to whom the information relates to be ascertained, or

(*f*) in pursuance of any Community obligation.

(2) The relevant proceedings referred to in subsection (1)(*a*) are—

(*a*) any criminal proceedings,

(*b*) civil proceedings arising under or by virtue of the Financial Services Act 1986 and proceedings before the Financial Services Tribunal, and

(*c*) disciplinary proceedings relating to—

   (i) the exercise by a solicitor, auditor, accountant, valuer or actuary of his professional duties, or

   (ii) the discharge by a public servant of his duties.

(3) In subsection (2)(*c*)(ii) "public servant" means an officer or servant of the Crown or of any public or other authority for the time being designated for the purposes of that provision by order of the Secretary of State.

(4) The relevant authorities referred to in subsection (1)(*b*), and the relevant functions in relation to each such authority, are as follows—

Authority	*Functions*
The Secretary of State.	Functions under the enactments relating to companies, insurance companies or insolvency, or under the Financial Services Act 1986 or Part II, this Part or Part VII of this Act.
An inspector appointed under Part XIV of the Companies Act 1985 or section 94 or 177 of the Financial Services Act 1986.	Functions under that Part or that section.
A person authorised to exercise powers under section 44 of the Insurance Companies Act 1982, section 447 of the Companies Act 1985, section 106 of the Financial Services Act 1986 or section 84 of this Act.	Functions under that section.
An overseas regulatory authority.	Its regulatory functions (within the meaning of section 82 of this Act).
The Department of Economic Development in Northern Ireland or a person appointed or authorised by that Department.	Functions conferred on it or him by the enactments relating to companies or insolvency.
A designated agency within the meaning of the Financial Services Act 1986.	Functions under that Act or Part VII of this Act.
A transferee body or the competent authority within the meaning of the Financial Services Act 1986.	Functions under that Act.
The body administering a scheme under section 54 of the Financial Services Act 1986.	Functions under the scheme.
A recognised self-regulating organisation, recognised professional body, recognised investment exchange, recognised clearing house or recognised self-regulating organisation for friendly societies (within the meaning of the Financial Services Act 1986).	Functions in its capacity as an organisation, body, exchange or clearing house recognised under that Act.

Authority	Functions
The Chief Registrar of friendly societies, the Registrar of Friendly Societies for Northern Ireland and the Assistant Registrar of Friendly Societies for Scotland.	Functions under the Financial Services Act 1986 or the enactments relating to friendly societies or building societies.
The Bank of England.	Functions under the Banking Act 1987 and any other functions.
The Deposit Protection Board.	Functions under the Banking Act 1987.
A body established by order under section 46 of this Act.	Functions under Part II of this Act.
A recognised supervisory or qualifying body within the meaning of Part II of this Act.	Functions as such a body.
The Industrial Assurance Commissioner and the Industrial Assurance Commissioner for Northern Ireland.	Functions under the enactments relating to industrial assurance.
The Insurance Brokers Registration Council.	Functions under the Insurance Brokers (Registration) Act 1977.
The Official Receiver or, in Northern Ireland, the Official Assignee for company liquidations or for bankruptcy.	Functions under the enactments relating to insolvency.
A recognised professional body (within the meaning of section 391 of the Insolvency Act 1986).	Functions in its capacity as such a body under the Insolvency Act 1986.
The Building Societies Commission.	Functions under the Building Societies Act 1986.
The Director General of Fair Trading.	Functions under the Financial Services Act 1986.

(5) The Secretary of State may by order amend the Table in subsection (4) so as to—

(*a*) add any public or other authority to the Table and specify the relevant functions of that authority,

(*b*) remove any authority from the Table, or

(*c*) add functions to, or remove functions from, those which are relevant functions in relation to an authority specified in the Table;

and the order may impose conditions subject to which, or otherwise restrict the circumstances in which, disclosure is permitted.

(6) An order under this section shall be made by statutory instrument which shall be subject to annulment in pursuance of a resolution of either House of Parliament.

Exercise of powers in relation to Northern Ireland

88.—(1) The following provisions apply where it appears to the Secretary of State that a request for assistance by an overseas regulatory authority may involve the powers conferred by section 83 being exercised in Northern Ireland in relation to matters which are transferred matters within the meaning of the Northern Ireland Constitution Act 1973.

(2) The Secretary of State shall before deciding whether to accede to the request consult the Department of Economic Development in Northern Ireland, and if he decides to accede to the request and it appears to him—

(*a*) that the powers should be exercised in Northern Ireland, and

(*b*) that the purposes for which they should be so exercised relate wholly or primarily to transferred matters,

he shall by instrument in writing authorise the Department to exercise in Northern Ireland his powers under section 83.

(3) The following provisions have effect in relation to the exercise of powers by virtue of such an authority with the substitution for references to the Secretary of State of references to the Department of Economic Development in Northern Ireland—

(*a*) section 84 (exercise of powers by officer, &c.),

(*b*) section 449 of the Companies Act 1985, section 53 or 54 of the Building Societies Act 1986, sections 179 and 180 of the Financial Services Act 1986, section 84 of the Banking Act 1987 and sections 86 and 87 above (restrictions on disclosure of information), and

(*c*) section 89 (authority for institution of criminal proceedings);

and references to the Secretary of State in other enactments which proceed by reference to those provisions shall be construed accordingly as being or including references to the Department.

(4) The Secretary of State may after consultation with the Department of Economic Development in Northern Ireland revoke an authority given to the Department under this section.

(5) In that case nothing in the provisions referred to in subsection (3)(*b*) shall apply so as to prevent the Department from giving the Secretary of State any information obtained by virtue of the authority; and (without prejudice to their application in relation to disclosure by the Department) those provisions shall apply to the disclosure of such information by the Secretary of State as if it had been obtained by him in the first place.

(6) Nothing in this section affects the exercise by the Secretary of State of any powers in Northern Ireland—

(*a*) in a case where at the time of acceding to the request it did not appear to him that the circumstances were such as to require him to authorise the Department of Economic Development in Northern Ireland to exercise those powers, or

(*b*) after the revocation by him of any such authority;

and no objection shall be taken to anything done by or in relation to the Secretary of State or the Department on the ground that it should have been done by or in relation to the other.

Prosecutions

89. Proceedings for an offence under section 85 or 86 shall not be instituted—

(*a*) in England and Wales, except by or with the consent of the Secretary of State or the Director of Public Prosecutions;

(*b*) in Northern Ireland, except by or with the consent of the Secretary of State or the Director of Public Prosecutions for Northern Ireland.

Offences by bodies corporate, partnerships and unincorporated associations

90.—(1) Where an offence under section 85 or 86 committed by a body corporate is proved to have been committed with the consent or connivance of, or to be attributable to any neglect on the part of, a director, manager, secretary or other similar officer of the body, or a person purporting to act in any such capacity, he as well as the body corporate is guilty of the offence and liable to be proceeded against and punished accordingly.

(2) Where the affairs of a body corporate are managed by its members, subsection (1) applies in relation to the acts and defaults of a member in connection with his functions of management as to a director of a body corporate.

(3) Where an offence under section 85 or 86 committed by a partnership is proved to have been committed with the consent or connivance of, or to be attributable to any neglect on the part of, a partner, he as well as the partnership is guilty of the offence and liable to be proceeded against and punished accordingly.

(4) Where an offence under section 85 or 86 committed by an unincorporated association (other than a partnership) is proved to have been committed with the consent or connivance of, or to be attributable to any neglect on the part of, any officer of the association or any member of its governing body, he as well as the association is guilty of the offence and liable to be proceeded against and punished accordingly.

Jurisdiction and procedure in respect of offences

91.—(1) Summary proceedings for an offence under section 85 may, without prejudice to any jurisdiction exercisable apart from this section, be taken against a body corporate or unincorporated association at any place at which it has a place of business and against an individual at any place where he is for the time being.

(2) Proceedings for an offence alleged to have been committed under section 85 or 86 by an unincorporated association shall be brought in the name of the association (and not in that of any of its members), and for the purposes of any such proceedings any rules of court relating to the service of documents apply as in relation to a body corporate.

(3) Section 33 of the Criminal Justice Act 1925 and Schedule 3 to the Magistrates' Courts Act 1980 (procedure on charge of offence against a corporation) apply in a case in which an unincorporated association is charged in England and Wales with an offence under section 85 or 86 as they apply in the case of a corporation.

(4) In relation to proceedings on indictment in Scotland for an offence alleged to have been committed under section 85 or 86 by an unincorporated association, section 74 of the Criminal Procedure (Scotland) Act 1975 (proceedings on indictment against bodies corporate) applies as if the association were a body corporate.

(5) Section 18 of the Criminal Justice Act (Northern Ireland) 1945 and Schedule 4 to the Magistrates' Courts (Northern Ireland) Order 1981 (procedure on charge of offence against a corporation) apply in a case in which an unincorporated association is charged in Northern Ireland with an offence under section 85 or 86 as they apply in the case of a corporation.

(6) A fine imposed on an unincorporated association on its conviction of such an offence shall be paid out of the funds of the association.

PART IV

REGISTRATION OF COMPANY CHARGES

Introduction

Introduction
[1] **92.** The provisions of this Part amend the provisions of the Companies Act 1985 relating to the registration of company charges—
  (a) by inserting in Part XII of that Act (in place of sections 395 to 408 and 410 to 423) new provisions with respect to companies registered in Great Britain, and
  (b) by inserting as Chapter III of Part XXIII of that Act (in place of sections 409 and 424) new provisions with respect to oversea companies.

NOTE
[1] The amendments made will be given effect in the text of the 1985 Act as they are brought into force.

PART V

[1] OTHER AMENDMENTS OF COMPANY LAW

A company's capacity and related matters

NOTE
[1] New ss.3A, 4, 35–35B and 322A of the Companies Act 1985, and amendments to Scheds. 21 and 22, will be given effect in the text of that Act as they are brought into force.

. . . .

Charitable companies (Scotland)

112.—(1) In the following provisions (which extend to Scotland only)—

(*a*) "company" means a company formed and registered under the Companies Act 1985, or to which the provisions of that Act apply as they apply to such a company; and

(*b*) "charity" means a body established for charitable purposes only (that expression having the same meaning as in the Income Tax Acts).

(2) Where a charity is a company or other body corporate having power to alter the instruments establishing or regulating it as a body corporate, no exercise of that power which has the effect of the body ceasing to be a charity shall be valid so as to affect the application of—

(*a*) any property acquired by virtue of any transfer, contract or obligation previously effected otherwise than for full consideration in money or money's worth, or any property representing property so acquired,

(*b*) any property representing income which has accrued before the alteration is made, or

(*c*) the income from any such property as aforesaid.

(3) Sections 35 and 35A of the Companies Act 1985 (capacity of company not limited by its memorandum; power of directors to bind company) do not apply to the acts of a company which is a charity except in favour of a person who—

(*a*) gives full consideration in money or money's worth in relation to the act in question, and

(*b*) does not know that the act is not permitted by the company's memorandum or, as the case may be, is beyond the powers of the directors,

or who does not know at the time the act is done that the company is a charity.

(4) However, where such a company purports to transfer or grant an interest in property, the fact that the act was not permitted by the company's memorandum or, as the case may be, that the directors in connection with the act exceeded any limitation on their powers under the company's constitution, does not affect the title of a person who subsequently acquires the property or any interest in it for full consideration without actual notice of any such circumstances affecting the validity of the company's act.

(5) In any proceedings arising out of subsection (3) the burden of proving—

(*a*) that a person knew that an act was not permitted by the company's memorandum or was beyond the powers of the directors, or

(*b*) that a person knew that the company was a charity,

lies on the person making that allegation.

(6) Where a company is a charity and its name does not include the word "charity" or the word "charitable," the fact that the company is a charity shall be stated in English in legible characters—

(*a*) in all business letters of the company,

(*b*) in all its notices and other official publications,

(*c*) in all bills of exchange, promissory notes, endorsements, cheques and orders for money or goods purporting to be signed by or on behalf of the company,

(*d*) in all conveyances purporting to be executed by the company, and

(*e*) in all its bills of parcels, invoices, receipts and letters of credit.

(7) In subsection (6)(*d*) "conveyance" means any document for the creation, transfer, variation or extinction of an interest in land.

(8) Section 349(2) to (4) of the Companies Act 1985 (offences in connection with failure to include required particulars in business letters, &c.) apply in relation to a contravention of subsection (6) above.

[1] *De-regulation of private companies*

NOTE
[1] New ss.80A, 366A, 379A, 381A–381C and 382A of and Sched. 15A to the Companies Act 1985, and consequential amendments, will be given effect in the text of that Act as they are brought into force.

Power to make further provision by regulations
117.—(1) The Secretary of State may by regulations make provision enabling private companies to elect, by elective resolution in accordance with section 379A of the Companies Act 1985, to dispense with compliance with such requirements of that Act as may be specified in the regulations, being requirements which appear to the Secretary of State to relate primarily to the internal administration and procedure of companies.

(2) The regulations may add to, amend or repeal provisions of that Act; and may provide for any such provision to have effect, where an election is made, subject to such adaptations and modifications as appear to the Secretary of State to be appropriate.

(3) The regulations may make different provision for different cases and may contain such supplementary, incidental and transitional provisions as appear to the Secretary of State to be appropriate.

(4) Regulations under this section shall be made by statutory instrument.

(5) No regulations under this section shall be made unless a draft of the instrument containing the regulations has been laid before Parliament and approved by a resolution of each House.

Appointment and removal of auditors and related matters

Introduction
[1] **118.**—(1) The following sections amend the provisions of the Companies Act 1985 relating to auditors by inserting new provisions in Chapter V of Part XI of that Act.

(2) The new provisions, together with the amendment made by section 124, replace the present provisions of that Chapter except section 389 (qualification for appointment as auditor) which is replaced by provisions in Part II of this Act.

NOTE
[1] The amendments made will be given effect in the text of the 1985 Act as they are brought into force. Section 124 amends the Trade Union and Labour Relations Act 1974, s.11.

. . . . . .

[1] *Company records and related matters*

NOTE
[1] New ss.706–707A, 709–710A and 715A in the Companies Act 1985, and consequential amendments, will be given effect in the text of that Act as they are brought into force.

. . . . . .

[1] *Miscellaneous*

NOTE
[1] So far as not printed below, the following sections make miscellaneous amendments to the Companies Act 1985 which will be given effect in the text of that Act as they are brought into force.

. . . . . .

Company contracts and execution of documents by companies

130.— . . . (6) The Secretary of State may make provision by regulations applying sections 36 to 36C of the Companies Act 1985 (company contracts; execution of documents; pre-incorporation contracts, deeds and obligations) to companies incorporated outside Great Britain, subject to such exceptions, adaptations or modifications as may be specified in the regulations.

Regulations under this subsection shall be made by statutory instrument which shall be subject to annulment in pursuance of a resolution of either House of Parliament.

(7) Schedule 17 contains further minor and consequential amendments relating to company contracts, the execution of documents by companies and related matters.

. . . .

Orders imposing restrictions on shares

135.—(1) The Secretary of State may by regulations made by statutory instrument make such amendments of the provisions of the Companies Act 1985 relating to orders imposing restrictions on shares as appear to him necessary or expedient—

(*a*) for enabling orders to be made in a form protecting the rights of third parties;

(*b*) with respect to the circumstances in which restrictions may be relaxed or removed;

(*c*) with respect to the making of interim orders by a court.

(2) The provisions referred to in subsection (1) are section 210(5), section 216(1) and (2), section 445 and Part XV of the Companies Act 1985.

(3) The regulations may make different provision for different cases and may contain such transitional and other supplementary and incidental provisions as appear to the Secretary of State to be appropriate.

(4) Regulations under this section shall not be made unless a draft of the regulations has been laid before Parliament and approved by resolution of each House of Parliament.

. . . . . .

Application to declare dissolution of company void

141.— . . . (4) An application may be made under section 651(5) of the Companies Act 1985 as inserted by subsection (3) above (proceedings for damages for personal injury, &c.) in relation to a company dissolved before the commencement of this section notwithstanding that the time within which the dissolution might formerly have been declared void under that section had expired before commencement.

But no such application shall be made in relation to a company dissolved more than 20 years before the commencement of this section.

(5) Except as provided by subsection (4), the amendments made by this section do not apply in relation to a company which was dissolved more than two years before the commencement of this section.

"Subsidiary," "holding company" and "wholly owned subsidiary"

144.— . . . (4) Schedule 18 contains amendments and savings consequential on the amendments made by this section; and the Secretary of State may by regulations make such further amendments or savings as appear to him to be necessary or expedient.

(5) Regulations under this section shall be made by statutory instrument which shall be subject to annulment in pursuance of a resolution of either House of Parliament.

(6) So much of section 23(3) of the Interpretation Act 1978 as applies section 17(2)(*a*) of that Act (presumption as to meaning of references to enactments repealed and re-enacted) to deeds or other instruments or documents does not apply in relation to the repeal and re-enactment by this section of section 736 of the Companies Act 1985.

Minor amendments
145. The Companies Act 1985 has effect with the further amendments specified in Schedule 19.

PART VI

MERGERS AND RELATED MATTERS

. . . . . .

PART VII

FINANCIAL MARKETS AND INSOLVENCY

. . . . . .

PART VIII

[1] AMENDMENTS OF THE FINANCIAL SERVICES ACT 1986

NOTE
[1] Amendments affecting those sections of the 1986 Act printed in *The Parliament House Book* will be given effect in the text of that Act as they are brought into force.

. . . . . .

PART IX

TRANSFER OF SECURITIES

Transfer of securities
207.—(1) The Secretary of State may make provision by regulations for enabling title to securities to be evidenced and transferred without a written instrument.
In this section—
   (*a*) "securities" means shares, stock, debentures, debenture stock, loan stock, bonds, units of a collective investment scheme within the meaning of the Financial Services Act 1986 and other securities of any description;
   (*b*) references to title to securities include any legal or equitable interest in securities; and
   (*c*) references to a transfer of title include a transfer by way of security.
(2) The regulations may make provision—
   (*a*) for procedures for recording and transferring title to securities, and
   (*b*) for the regulation of those procedures and the persons responsible for or involved in their operation.
(3) The regulations shall contain such safeguards as appear to the Secretary of State appropriate for the protection of investors and for ensuring that competition is not restricted, distorted or prevented.

(4) The regulations may for the purpose of enabling or facilitating the operation of the new procedures make provision with respect to the rights and obligations of persons in relation to securities dealt with under the procedures.

But the regulations shall be framed so as to secure that the rights and obligations in relation to securities dealt with under the new procedures correspond, so far as practicable, with those which would arise apart from any regulations under this section.

(5) The regulations may include such supplementary, incidental and transitional provisions as appear to the Secretary of State to be necessary or expedient.

In particular, provision may be made for the purpose of giving effect to—

(*a*) the transmission of title to securities by operation of law;

(*b*) any restriction on the transfer of title to securities arising by virtue of the provisions of any enactment or instrument, court order or agreement;

(*c*) any power conferred by any such provision on a person to deal with securities on behalf of the person entitled.

(6) The regulations may make provision with respect to the persons responsible for the operation of the new procedures—

(*a*) as to the consequences of their insolvency or incapacity, or

(*b*) as to the transfer from them to other persons of their functions in relation to the new procedures.

(7) The regulations may for the purposes mentioned above—

(*a*) modify or exclude any provision of any enactment or instrument, or any rule of law;

(*b*) apply, with such modifications as may be appropriate, the provisions of any enactment or instrument (including provisions creating criminal offences);

(*c*) require the payment of fees, or enable persons to require the payment of fees, of such amounts as may be specified in the regulations or determined in accordance with them;

(*d*) empower the Secretary of State to delegate to any person willing and able to discharge them any functions of his under the regulations.

(8) The regulations may make different provision for different cases.

(9) Regulations under this section shall be made by statutory instrument; and no such regulations shall be made unless a draft of the instrument has been laid before and approved by resolution of each House of Parliament.

PART X

MISCELLANEOUS AND GENERAL PROVISIONS

Miscellaneous

. . . . . .

General

Repeals

212. The enactments mentioned in Schedule 24 are repealed to the extent specified there.

Provisions extending to Northern Ireland

213.—(1) The provisions of this Act extend to Northern Ireland so far as they amend, or provide for the amendment of, an enactment which so extends.

(2) So far as any provision of this Act amends the Companies Act 1985 or the Insolvency Act 1986, its application to companies registered or incorporated in Northern Ireland is subject to section 745(1) of the Companies Act 1985 or section 441(2) of the Insolvency Act 1986, as the case may be.

(3) In Part III (investigations and powers to obtain information), sections 82 to 91, (powers exercisable to assist overseas regulatory authorities) extend to Northern Ireland.

(4) Part VI (mergers and related matters) extends to Northern Ireland.

(5) In Part VII (financial markets and insolvency) the following provisions extend to Northern Ireland—

    (*a*) sections 154 and 155 (introductory provisions and definition of "market contract"),

    (*b*) section 156 and Schedule 21 (additional requirements for recognition of investment exchange or clearing house),

    (*c*) sections 157, 160, 162, and 166 to 169 (provisions relating to recognised investment exchanges and clearing houses),

    (*d*) sections 170 to 172 (power to extend provisions to other financial markets),

    (*e*) section 184 (indemnity for certain acts), and

    (*f*) sections 185 to 191 (supplementary provisions).

(6) Part VIII (amendments of Financial Services Act 1986) extends to Northern Ireland.

(7) Part IX (transfer of securities) extends to Northern Ireland.

Subject to any Order made after the passing of this Act by virtue of section 3(1)(*a*) of the Northern Ireland Constitution Act 1973, the transfer of securities shall not be a transferred matter for the purposes of that Act but shall for the purposes of section 3(2) be treated as specified in Schedule 3 to that Act.

(8) In Part X (miscellaneous and general provisions), this section and sections 214 to 216 (general provisions) extend to Northern Ireland.

(9) Except as mentioned above, the provisions of this Act do not extend to Northern Ireland.

Making of corresponding provision for Northern Ireland

214.—(1) An Order in Council under paragraph 1(1)(*b*) of Schedule 1 to the Northern Ireland Act 1974 (legislation for Northern Ireland in the interim period) which contains a statement that it is only made for purposes corresponding to the purposes of provisions of this Act to which this section applies—

    (*a*) shall not be subject to paragraph 1(4) and (5) of that Schedule (affirmative resolution of both Houses of Parliament), but

    (*b*) shall be subject to annulment in pursuance of a resolution of either House of Parliament.

(2) The provisions of this Act to which this section applies are—

    (*a*) Parts I to V, and

    (*b*) Part VII, except sections 156, 157, 169 and Schedule 21.

Commencement and transitional provisions

215.—(1) The following provisions of this Act come into force on Royal Assent—

    (*a*) in Part V (amendments of company law), section 141 (application to declare dissolution of company void);

    (*b*) in Part VI (mergers)—

        (i) sections 147 to 150, and

(ii) paragraphs 2 to 12, 14 to 16, 18 to 20, 22 to 25 of Schedule 20, and section 153 so far as relating to those paragraphs;

(c) in Part VIII (amendments of the Financial Services Act 1986), section 202 (offers of short-dated debentures);

(d) in Part X (miscellaneous and general provisions), the repeals made by Schedule 24 in sections 71, 74, 88 and 89 of, and Schedule 9 to, the Fair Trading Act 1973, and section 212 so far as relating to those repeals.

[1] (2) The other provisions of this Act come into force on such day as the Secretary of State may appoint by order made by statutory instrument; and different days may be appointed for different provisions and different purposes.

(3) An order bringing into force any provision may contain such transitional provisions and savings as appear to the Secretary of State to be necessary or expedient.

(4) The Secretary of State may also by order under this section amend any enactment which refers to the commencement of a provision brought into force by the order so as to substitute a reference to the actual date on which it comes into force.

NOTE
[1] The following dates of commencement (so far as relevant) have been prescribed:

16th November 1989: s. 141 (Companies Act 1989, s. 215).

25th January 1990: s. 216 (S.I. 1990 No. 98).

2nd February 1990: ss. 213–215 (remainder) S.I. 1990 No. 142).

21st February 1990: ss. 55–64, 65 (part), 66–74, 76, 78, 79, 82–86, 87 (part), 88–91, 209, 212 (part) and Sched. 24 (part) (S.I. 1990 No. 142).

1st March 1990: ss. 15, 24 (part), 30, 31 (part), 32–33, 37–40, 41 (part), 42–44 (part), 45, 47 (part), 48 (part), 49 (part), 50–51, 52–54 (part), 145 (part), 208, 212 (part) and Scheds. 11, 12, 14, 19 (art), and 24 (part) (S.I. 1990 Nos. 142, 355).

15th March 1990: ss. 197–199, 212 (part) and Sched. 24 (part) (S.I. 1990 No. 354).

1st April 1990: ss. 2–6, 7 (part), 8–10, 11 (part), 13–14, 16–22, 23 (part), 24 (part), (ss. 2–24 subject to S.I. 1990 No. 355, arts. 6–9 and Sched. 2), 113–114, 115 (subject to S.I. 1990 No. 355, art. 10 and Sched. 4), 116–117, 118 (subject to S.I. 1990 No. 355, art. 10 and Sched. 4), 119–123, 131 (subject to S.I. 1990 No. 355, art. 11), 132, 136 (subject to S.I. 1990 No. 355, art. 12), 137 (part, subject to S.I. 1990 No. 355, art. 13), 145 (part), 153 (part), 212 (part), and Scheds. 10 (part, subject to S.I. 1990 No. 355, Sched. 3), 19 (part), and 24 (part) (S.I. 1990 No. 355).

31st May 1990: ss. 134 (part), 212 (part) and Sched. 24 (part) (S.I. 1990 No. 713).

1st August 1990: s. 23 (part) and Sched. 10 (part, subject to S.I. 1990 No. 355, Sched. 3) (S.I. 1990 No. 355).

Short title
216. This Act may be cited as the Companies Act 1989.

[1] SCHEDULES

NOTE
[1] Schedules amending the Companies Act 1985 will be given effect in the text of that Act as they are brought into force.

. . . . . .

Section 30(5)   SCHEDULE 11

RECOGNITION OF SUPERVISORY BODY

PART I

GRANT AND REVOCATION OF RECOGNITION

Application for recognition of supervisory body

1.—(1) A supervisory body may apply to the Secretary of State for an order declaring it to be a recognised supervisory body for the purposes of this Part of this Act.

(2) Any such application—

(*a*) shall be made in such manner as the Secretary of State may direct, and

(*b*) shall be accompanied by such information as the Secretary of State may reasonably require for the purpose of determining the application.

(3) At any time after receiving an application and before determining it the Secretary of State may require the applicant to furnish additional information.

(4) The directions and requirements given or imposed under sub-paragraphs (2) and (3) may differ as between different applications.

(5) Any information to be furnished to the Secretary of State under this paragraph shall, if he so requires, be in such form or verified in such manner as he may specify.

(6) Every application shall be accompanied by a copy of the applicant's rules and of any guidance issued by the applicant which is intended to have continuing effect and is issued in writing or other legible form.

Grant and refusal of recognition

2.—(1) The Secretary of State may, on an application duly made in accordance with paragraph 1 and after being furnished with all such information as he may require under that

[THE NEXT PAGE IS I 733]

paragraph, make or refuse to make an order (a "recognition order") declaring the applicant to be a recognised supervisory body for the purposes of this Part of this Act.

(2) The Secretary of State shall not make a recognition order unless it appears to him, from the information furnished by the body and having regard to any other information in his possession, that the requirements of Part II of this Schedule are satisfied as respects that body.

(3) The Secretary of State may refuse to make a recognition order in respect of a body if he considers that its recognition is unnecessary having regard to the existence of one or more other bodies which maintain and enforce rules as to the appointment and conduct of company auditors and which have been or are likely to be recognised.

(4) Where the Secretary of State refuses an application for a recognition order he shall give the applicant a written notice to that effect specifying which requirements in the opinion of the Secretary of State are not satisfied or stating that the application is refused on the ground mentioned in sub-paragraph (3).

(5) A recognition order shall state the date on which it takes effect.

Revocation of recognition

3.—(1) A recognition order may be revoked by a further order made by the Secretary of State if at any time it appears to him—

- (*a*) that any requirement of Part II of this Schedule is not satisfied in the case of the body to which the recognition order relates ("the recognised body"),
- (*b*) that the recognised body has failed to comply with any obligation to which it is subject by virtue of this Part of this Act, or
- (*c*) that the continued recognition of the body is undesirable having regard to the existence of one or more other bodies which have been or are to be recognised.

(2) An order revoking a recognition order shall state the date on which it takes effect and that date shall not be earlier than three months after the day on which the revocation order is made.

(3) Before revoking a recognition order the Secretary of State shall give written notice of his intention to do so to the recognised body, take such steps as he considers reasonably practicable for bringing the notice to the attention of members of the body and publish it in such manner as he thinks appropriate for bringing it to the attention of any other persons who are in his opinion likely to be affected.

(4) A notice under sub-paragraph (3) shall state the reasons for which the Secretary of State proposes to act and give particulars of the rights conferred by sub-paragraph (5).

(5) A body on which a notice is served under sub-paragraph (3), any member of the body and any other person who appears to the Secretary of State to be affected may within three months after the date of service or publication, or within such longer time as the Secretary of State may allow, make written representations to the Secretary of State and, if desired, oral representations to a person appointed for that purpose by the Secretary of State; and the Secretary of State shall have regard to any representations made in accordance with this sub-paragraph in determining whether to revoke the recognition order.

(6) If in any case the Secretary of State considers it essential to do so in the public interest he may revoke a recognition order without regard to the restriction imposed by sub-paragraph (2) and notwithstanding that no notice has been given or published under sub-paragraph (3) or that the time for making representations in pursuance of such a notice has not expired.

(7) An order revoking a recognition order may contain such transitional provisions as the Secretary of State thinks necessary or expedient.

(8) A recognition order may be revoked at the request or with the consent of the recognised body and any such revocation shall not be subject to the restrictions imposed by sub-paragraphs (1) and (2) or the requirements of sub-paragraphs (3) to (5).

(9) On making an order revoking a recognition order the Secretary of State shall give the body written notice of the making of the order, take such steps as he considers reasonably practicable for bringing the making of the order to the attention of members of the body and publish a notice of the making of the order in such manner as he thinks appropriate for bringing it to the attention of any other persons who are in his opinion likely to be affected.

Part II

Requirements for Recognition

Holding of appropriate qualification

4.—(1) The body must have rules to the effect that a person is not eligible for appointment as a company auditor unless—

(a) in the case of an individual, he holds an appropriate qualification;

(b) in the case of a firm—

    (i) the individuals responsible for company audit work on behalf of the firm hold an appropriate qualification, and

    (ii) the firm is controlled by qualified persons (see paragraph 5 below).

(2) This does not prevent the body from imposing more stringent requirements.

(3) A firm which has ceased to comply with the conditions mentioned in sub-paragraph (1)(b) may be permitted to remain eligible for appointment as a company auditor for a period of not more than three months.

5.—(1) The following provisions explain what is meant in paragraph 4(1)(b)(ii) by a firm being "controlled by qualified persons".

(2) For this purpose references to a person being qualified are, in relation to an individual, to his holding an appropriate qualification, and in relation to a firm, to its being eligible for appointment as a company auditor.

(3) A firm shall be treated as controlled by qualified persons if, and only if—

(a) a majority of the members of the firm are qualified persons, and

(b) where the firm's affairs are managed by a board of directors, committee or other management body, a majority of the members of that body are qualified persons or, if the body consists of two persons only, at least one of them is a qualified person.

(4) A majority of the members of a firm means—

(a) where under the firm's constitution matters are decided upon by the exercise of voting rights, members holding a majority of the rights to vote on all, or substantially all, matters;

(b) in any other case, members having such rights under the constitution of the firm as enable them to direct its overall policy or alter its constitution.

(5) A majority of the members of the management body of a firm means—

(a) where matters are decided at meetings of the management body by the exercise of voting rights, members holding a majority of the rights to vote on all, or substantially all, matters at such meetings;

(b) in any other case, members having such rights under the constitution of the firm as enable them to direct its overall policy or alter its constitution.

(6) The provisions of paragraphs 5 to 11 of Schedule 10A to the Companies Act 1985 (rights to be taken into account and attribution of rights) apply for the purposes of this paragraph.

Auditors to be fit and proper persons

6.—(1) The body must have adequate rules and practices designed to ensure that the persons eligible under its rules for appointment as a company auditor are fit and proper persons to be so appointed.

(2) The matters which the body may take into account for this purpose in relation to a person must include—

(a) any matter relating to any person who is or will be employed by or associated with him for the purposes of or in connection with company audit work; and

(b) in the case of a body corporate, any matter relating to any director or controller of the body, to any other body corporate in the same group or to any director or controller of any such other body; and

(c) in the case of a partnership, any matter relating to any of the partners, any director or controller of any of the partners, any body corporate in the same group as any of the partners and any director or controller of any such other body.

(3) In sub-paragraph (2)(b) and (c) "controller", in relation to a body corporate, means a person who either alone or with any associate or associates is entitled to exercise or control the exercise of 15 per cent. or more of the rights to vote on all, or substantially all, matters at general meetings of the body or another body corporate of which it is a subsidiary.

Professional integrity and independence

7.—(1) The body must have adequate rules and practices designed to ensure—

(a) that company audit work is conducted properly and with integrity, and

(b) that persons are not appointed company auditor in circumstances in which they have any interest likely to conflict with the proper conduct of the audit.

(2) The body must also have adequate rules and practices designed to ensure that no firm is eligible under its rules for appointment as a company auditor unless the firm has arrangements to prevent—

(*a*)　individuals who do not hold an appropriate qualification, and

(*b*)　persons who are not members of the firm,

from being able to exert any influence over the way in which an audit is conducted in circumstances in which that influence would be likely to affect the independence or integrity of the audit.

Technical standards

8. The body must have rules and practices as to the technical standards to be applied in company audit work and as to the manner in which those standards are to be applied in practice.

Procedures for maintaining competence

9. The body must have rules and practices designed to ensure that persons eligible under its rules for appointment as a company auditor continue to maintain an appropriate level of competence in the conduct of company audits.

Monitoring and enforcement

10.—(1) The body must have adequate arrangements and resources for the effective monitoring and enforcement of compliance with its rules.

(2) The arrangements for monitoring may make provision for that function to be performed on behalf of the body (and without affecting its responsibility) by any other body or person who is able and willing to perform it.

Membership, eligibility and discipline

11. The rules and practices of the body relating to—

(*a*)　the admission and expulsion of members,

(*b*)　the grant and withdrawal of eligibility for appointment as a company auditor, and

(*c*)　the discipline it exercises over its members,

must be fair and reasonable and include adequate provision for appeals.

Investigation of complaints

12.—(1) The body must have effective arrangements for the investigation of complaints—

(*a*)　against persons who are eligible under its rules to be appointed company auditor, or

(*b*)　against the body in respect of matters arising out of its functions as a supervisory body.

(2) The arrangements may make provision for the whole or part of that function to be performed by and to be the responsibility of a body or person independent of the body itself.

Meeting of claims arising out of audit work

13.—(1) The body must have adequate rules or arrangements designed to ensure that persons eligible under its rules for appointment as a company auditor take such steps as may reasonably be expected of them to secure that they are able to meet claims against them arising out of company audit work.

(2) This may be achieved by professional indemnity insurance or other appropriate arrangements.

Register of auditors and other information to be made available

14. The body must have rules requiring persons eligible under its rules for appointment as a company auditor to comply with any obligations imposed on them by regulations under section 35 or 36.

Taking account of costs of compliance

15. The body must have satisfactory arrangements for taking account, in framing its rules, of the cost to those to whom the rules would apply of complying with those rules and any other controls to which they are subject.

Promotion and maintenance of standards

16. The body must be able and willing to promote and maintain high standards of integrity in the conduct of company audit work and to co-operate, by the sharing of information and otherwise, with the Secretary of State and any other authority, body or person having responsibility in the United Kingdom for the qualification, supervision or regulation of auditors.

Section 32(4)   SCHEDULE 12

RECOGNITION OF PROFESSIONAL QUALIFICATION

PART I

GRANT AND REVOCATION OF RECOGNITION

Application for recognition of professional qualification

1.—(1) A qualifying body may apply to the Secretary of State for an order declaring a qualification offered by it to be a recognised professional qualification for the purposes of this Part of this Act.
(2) Any such application—
  (*a*) shall be made in such manner as the Secretary of State may direct, and
  (*b*) shall be accompanied by such information as the Secretary of State may reasonably require for the purpose of determining the application.
(3) At any time after receiving an application and before determining it the Secretary of State may require the applicant to furnish additional information.
(4) The directions and requirements given or imposed under sub-paragraphs (2) and (3) may differ as between different applications.
(5) Any information to be furnished to the Secretary of State under this section shall, if he so requires, be in such form or verified in such manner as he may specify.
In the case of examination standards, the verification required may include independent moderation of the examinations over such period as the Secretary of State considers necessary.
(6) Every application shall be accompanied by a copy of the applicant's rules and of any guidance issued by it which is intended to have continuing effect and is issued in writing or other legible form.

Grant and refusal of recognition

2.—(1) The Secretary of State may, on an application duly made in accordance with paragraph 1 and after being furnished with all such information as he may require under that paragraph, make or refuse to make an order (a "recognition order") declaring the qualification in respect of which the application was made to be a recognised professional qualification for the purposes of this Part of this Act.
In this Part of this Act a "recognised qualifying body" means a qualifying body offering a recognised professional qualification.
(2) The Secretary of State shall not make a recognition order unless it appears to him, from the information furnished by the applicant and having regard to any other information in his possession, that the requirements of Part II of this Schedule are satisfied as respects the qualification.
(3) Where the Secretary of State refuses an application for a recognition order he shall give the applicant a written notice to that effect specifying which requirements, in his opinion, are not satisfied.
(4) A recognition order shall state the date on which it takes effect.

Revocation of recognition

3.—(1) A recognition order may be revoked by a further order made by the Secretary of State if at any time it appears to him—
  (*a*) that any requirement of Part II of this Schedule is not satisfied in relation to the qualification to which the recognition order relates, or
  (*b*) that the qualifying body has failed to comply with any obligation to which it is subject by virtue of this Part of this Act.

(2) An order revoking a recognition order shall state the date on which it takes effect and that date shall not be earlier than three months after the day on which the revocation order is made.

(3) Before revoking a recognition order the Secretary of State shall give written notice of his intention to do so to the qualifying body, take such steps as he considers reasonably practicable for bringing the notice to the attention of persons holding the qualification or in the course of studying for it and publish it in such manner as he thinks appropriate for bringing it to the attention of any other persons who are in his opinion likely to be affected.

(4) A notice under sub-paragraph (3) shall state the reasons for which the Secretary of State proposes to act and give particulars of the rights conferred by sub-paragraph (5).

(5) A body on which a notice is served under sub-paragraph (3), any person holding the qualification or in the course of studying for it and any other person who appears to the Secretary of State to be affected may within three months after the date of service or publication, or within such longer time as the Secretary of State may allow, make written representations to the Secretary of State and, if desired, oral representations to a person appointed for that purpose by the Secretary of State; and the Secretary of State shall have regard to any representations made in accordance with this subsection in determining whether to revoke the recognition order.

(6) If in any case the Secretary of State considers it essential to do so in the public interest he may revoke a recognition order without regard to the restriction imposed by sub-paragraph (2) and notwithstanding that no notice has been given or published under sub-paragraph (3) or that the time for making representations in pursuance of such a notice has not expired.

(7) An order revoking a recognition order may contain such transitional provisions as the Secretary of State thinks necessary or expedient.

(8) A recognition order may be revoked at the request or with the consent of the qualifying body and any such revocation shall not be subject to the restrictions imposed by sub-paragraphs (1) and (2) or the requirements of sub-paragraphs (3) to (5).

(9) On making an order revoking a recognition order the Secretary of State shal! give the qualifying body written notice of the making of the order, take such steps as he considers reasonably practicable for bringing the making of the order to the attention of persons holding the qualification or in the course of studying for it and publish a notice of the making of the order in such manner as he thinks appropriate for bringing it to the attention of any other persons who are in his opinion likely to be affected.

PART II

REQUIREMENTS FOR RECOGNITION

Entry requirements

4.—(1) The qualification must only be open to persons who have attained university entrance level or have a sufficient period of professional experience.

(2) In relation to a person who has not been admitted to a university or other similar establishment in the United Kingdom, attaining university entrance level means—

  (a) being educated to such a standard as would entitle him to be considered for such admission on the basis of—
    (i) academic or professional qualifications obtained in the United Kingdom and recognised by the Secretary of State to be of an appropriate standard, or
    (ii) academic or professional qualifications obtained outside the United Kingdom which the Secretary of State considers to be of an equivalent standard; or
  (b) being assessed on the basis of written tests of a kind appearing to the Secretary of State to be adequate for the purpose, with or without oral examination, as of such a standard of ability as would entitle him to be considered for such admission.

(3) The assessment, tests and oral examination referred to in sub-paragraph (2)(b) may be conducted by the qualifying body or by some other body approved by the Secretary of State.

Course of theoretical instruction

5. The qualification must be restricted to persons who have completed a course of theoretical instruction in the subjects prescribed for the purposes of paragraph 7 or have a sufficient period of professional experience.

Sufficient period of professional experience

6.—(1) The references in paragraphs 4 and 5 to a sufficient period of professional experience are to not less than seven years' experience in a professional capacity in the fields of finance, law and accountancy.

(2) Periods of theoretical instruction in the fields of finance, law and accountancy may be deducted from the required period of professional experience, provided the instruction—

    (a) lasted at least one year, and

    (b) is attested by an examination recognised by the Secretary of State for the purposes of this paragraph;

but the period of professional experience may not be so reduced by more than four years.

(3) The period of professional experience together with the practical training required in the case of persons satisfying the requirement in paragraph 5 by virtue of having a sufficient period of professional experience must not be shorter than the course of theoretical instruction referred to in that paragraph and the practical training required in the case of persons satisfying the requirement of that paragraph by virtue of having completed such a course.

Examination

7.—(1) The qualification must be restricted to persons who have passed an examination (at least part of which is in writing) testing—

    (a) theoretical knowledge of the subjects prescribed for the purposes of this paragraph by regulations made by the Secretary of State, and

    (b) ability to apply that knowledge in practice,

and requiring a standard of attainment at least equivalent to that required to obtain a degree from a university or similar establishment in the United Kingdom.

(2) The qualification may be awarded to a person without his theoretical knowledge of a subject being tested by examination if he has passed a university or other examination of equivalent standard in that subject or holds a university degree or equivalent qualification in it.

(3) The qualification may be awarded to a person without his ability to apply his theoretical knowledge of a subject in practice being tested by examination if he has received practical training in that subject which is attested by an examination or diploma recognised by the Secretary of State for the purposes of this paragraph.

(4) Regulations under this paragraph shall be made by statutory instrument which shall be subject to annulment in pursuance of a resolution of either House of Parliament.

Practical training

8.—(1) The qualification must be restricted to persons who have completed at least three years' practical training of which—

    (a) part was spent being trained in company audit work, and

    (b) a substantial part was spent being trained in company audit work or other audit work of a description approved by the Secretary of State as being similar to company audit work.

For this purpose "company audit work" includes the work of a person appointed as auditor under the Companies (Northern Ireland) Order 1986 or under the law of a country or territory outside the United Kingdom where it appears to the Secretary of State that the law and practice with respect to the audit of company accounts is similar to that in the United Kingdom.

(2) The training must be given by persons approved by the body offering the qualification as persons as to whom the body is satisfied, in the light of undertakings given by them and the supervision to which they are subject (whether by the body itself or some other body or organisation), that they will provide adequate training.

(3) At least two-thirds of the training must be given by a fully-qualified auditor, that is, a person—

    (a) eligible in accordance with this Part of this Act to be appointed as a company auditor, or

    (b) satisfying the corresponding requirements of the law of Northern Ireland or another member State of the European Economic Community.

The body offering the qualification

9.—(1) The body offering the qualification must have—

    (a) rules and arrangements adequate to ensure compliance with the requirements of paragraphs 4 to 8, and

(b) adequate arrangements for the effective monitoring of its continued compliance with those requirements.

(2) The arrangements must include arrangements for monitoring the standard of its examinations and the adequacy of the practical training given by the persons approved by it for that purpose.

Section 46(6)   SCHEDULE 13

SUPPLEMENTARY PROVISIONS WITH RESPECT TO DELEGATION ORDER

Introductory

1. The following provisions have effect in relation to a body established by a delegation order under section 46; and any power to make provision by order is to make provision by order under that section.

Status

2. The body shall not be regarded as acting on behalf of the Crown and its members, officers and employees shall not be regarded as Crown servants.

Name, members and chairman

3.—(1) The body shall be known by such name as may be specified in the delegation order.

(2) The body shall consist of such persons (not being less than eight) as the Secretary of State may appoint after such consultation as he thinks appropriate; and the chairman of the body shall be such person as the Secretary of State may appoint from amongst its members.

(3) The Secretary of State may make provision by order as to the terms on which the members of the body are to hold and vacate office and as to the terms on which a person appointed as chairman is to hold and vacate the office of chairman.

Financial provisions

4.—(1) The body shall pay to its chairman and members such remuneration, and such allowances in respect of expenses properly incurred by them in the performance of their duties, as the Secretary of State may determine.

(2) As regards any chairman or member in whose case the Secretary of State so determines, the body shall pay or make provision for the payment of—

(a) such pension, allowance or gratuity to or in respect of that person on his retirement or death, or

(b) such contributions or other payment towards the provision of such a pension, allowance or gratuity,

as the Secretary of State may determine.

(3) Where a person ceases to be a member of the body otherwise than on the expiry of his term of office and it appears to the Secretary of State that there are special circumstances which make it right for him to receive compensation, the body shall make a payment to him by way of compensation of such amount as the Secretary of State may determine.

Proceedings

5.—(1) The delegation order may contain such provision as the Secretary of State considers appropriate with respect to the proceedings of the body.

(2) The order may, in particular—

(a) authorise the body to discharge any functions by means of committees consisting wholly or partly of members of the body;

(b) provide that the validity of proceedings of the body, or of any such committee, is not affected by any vacancy among the members or any defect in the appointment of any member.

Fees

6.—(1) The body may retain fees payable to it.

(2) The fees shall be applied for meeting the expenses of the body in discharging its functions and for any purposes incidental to those functions.

(3) Those expenses include any expenses incurred by the body on such staff, accommodation, services and other facilities as appear to it to be necessary or expedient for the proper performance of its functions.

(4) In prescribing the amount of fees in the exercise of the functions transferred to it the body shall prescribe such fees as appear to it sufficient to defray those expenses, taking one year with another.

(5) Any exercise by the body of the powers to prescribe fees requires the approval of the Secretary of State; and the Secretary of State may, after consultation with the body, by order vary or revoke any regulations made by it prescribing fees.

Legislative functions

7.—(1) Regulations made by the body in the exercise of the functions transferred to it shall be made by instrument in writing, but not by statutory instrument.

(2) The instrument shall specify the provision of this Part of this Act under which it is made.

(3) The Secretary of State may by order impose such requirements as he thinks necessary or expedient as to the circumstances and manner in which the body must consult on any regulations it proposes to make.

8.—(1) Immediately after an instrument is made it shall be printed and made available to the public with or without payment.

(2) A person shall not be taken to have contravened any regulation if he shows that at the time of the alleged contravention the instrument containing the regulation had not been made available as required by this paragraph.

9.—(1) The production of a printed copy of an instrument purporting to be made by the body on which is endorsed a certificate signed by an officer of the body authorised by it for the purpose and stating—

   (a) that the instrument was made by the body,
   (b) that the copy is a true copy of the instrument, and
   (c) that on a specified date the instrument was made available to the public as required by paragraph 8,

is prima facie evidence or, in Scotland, sufficient evidence of the facts stated in the certificate.

(2) A certificate purporting to be signed as mentioned in sub-paragraph (1) shall be deemed to have been duly signed unless the contrary is shown.

(3) Any person wishing in any legal proceedings to cite an instrument made by the body may require the body to cause a copy of it to be endorsed with such a certificate as is mentioned in this paragraph.

Report and accounts

10.—(1) The body shall at least once in each year for which the delegation order is in force make a report to the Secretary of State on the discharge of the functions transferred to it and on such other matters as the Secretary of State may by order require.

(2) The Secretary of State shall lay before Parliament copies of each report received by him under this paragraph.

(3) The Secretary of State may, with the consent of the Treasury, give directions to the body with respect to its accounts and the audit of its accounts and it is the duty of the body to comply with the directions.

(4) A person shall not be appointed auditor of the body unless he is eligible for appointment as a company auditor under section 25.

Other supplementary provisions

11.—(1) The transfer of a function to a body established by a delegation order does not affect anything previously done in the exercise of the function transferred; and the resumption of a function so transferred does not affect anything previously done in exercise of the function resumed.

(2) The Secretary of State may by order make such transitional and other supplementary provision as he thinks necessary or expedient in relation to the transfer or resumption of a function.

(3) The provision that may be made in connection with the transfer of a function includes, in particular, provision—

(a) for modifying or excluding any provision of this Part of this Act in its application to the function transferred;

(b) for applying to the body established by the delegation order, in connection with the function transferred, any provision applying to the Secretary of State which is contained in or made under any other enactment;

(c) for the transfer of any property, rights or liabilities from the Secretary of State to that body;

(d) for the carrying on and completion by that body of anything in process of being done by the Secretary of State when the order takes effect;

(e) for the substitution of that body for the Secretary of State in any instrument, contract or legal proceedings.

(4) The provision that may be made in connection with the resumption of a function includes, in particular, provision—

(a) for the transfer of any property, rights or liabilities from that body to the Secretary of State;

(b) for the carrying on and completion by the Secretary of State of anything in process of being done by that body when the order takes effect;

(c) for the substitution of the Secretary of State for that body in any instrument, contract or legal proceedings.

12. Where a delegation order is revoked, the Secretary of State may by order make provision—

(a) for the payment of compensation to persons ceasing to be employed by the body established by the delegation order; and

(b) as to the winding up and dissolution of the body.

Section 47(1)   SCHEDULE 14

SUPERVISORY AND QUALIFYING BODIES: RESTRICTIVE PRACTICES

PART I

PREVENTION OF RESTRICTIVE PRACTICES

Refusal of recognition on grounds related to competition

1.—(1) The Secretary of State shall before deciding whether to make a recognition order in respect of a supervisory body or professional qualification send to the Director General of Fair Trading (in this Schedule referred to as "the Director") a copy of the rules and of any guidance which the Secretary of State is required to consider in making that decision together with such other information as the Secretary of State considers will assist the Director.

(2) The Director shall consider whether the rules or guidance have, or are intended or likely to have, to any significant extent the effect of restricting, distorting or preventing competition, and shall report to the Secretary of State; and the Secretary of State shall have regard to his report in deciding whether to make a recognition order.

(3) The Secretary of State shall not make a recognition order if it appears to him that the rules and any guidance of which copies are furnished with the application have, or are intended or likely to have, to any significant extent the effect of restricting, distorting or preventing competition, unless it appears to him that the effect is reasonably justifiable having regard to the purposes of this Part of this Act.

Notification of changes to rules or guidance

2.—(1) Where a recognised supervisory or qualifying body amends, revokes or adds to its rules or guidance in a manner which may reasonably be regarded as likely—

(a) to restrict, distort or prevent competition to any significant extent, or

(b) otherwise to affect the question whether the recognition order granted to the body should continue in force, it shall within seven days give the Secretary of State written notice of the amendment, revocation or addition.

(2) Notice need not be given under sub-paragraph (1) of the revocation of guidance not intended to have continuing effect or issued otherwise than in writing or other legible form, or of any amendment or addition to guidance which does not result in or consist of guidance which is intended to have continuing effect and is issued in writing or other legible form.

Continuing scrutiny by the Director General of Fair Trading

3.—(1) The Director shall keep under review the rules made or guidance issued by a recognised supervisory or qualifying body, and if he is of the opinion that any rules or guidance of such a body have, or are intended or likely to have, to any significant extent the effect of restricting, distorting or preventing competition, he shall report his opinion to the Secretary of State, stating what in his opinion the effect is or is likely to be.

(2) The Secretary of State shall send to the Director copies of any notice received by him under paragraph 2, together with such other information as he considers will assist the Director.

(3) The Director may report to the Secretary of State his opinion that any matter mentioned in such a notice does not have, and is not intended or likely to have, to any significant extent the effect of restricting, distorting or preventing competition.

(4) The Director may from time to time consider whether—

    (*a*)   any practices of a recognised supervisory or qualifying body in its capacity as such, or

    (*b*)   any relevant practices required or contemplated by the rules or guidance of such a body or otherwise attributable to its conduct in its capacity as such,

have, or are intended or likely to have, to any significant extent the effect of restricting, distorting or preventing competition and, if so, what that effect is or is likely to be; and if he is of that opinion he shall make a report to the Secretary of State stating his opinion and what the effect is or is likely to be.

(5) The practices relevant for the purposes of sub-paragraph (4)(*b*) in the case of a recognised supervisory body are practices engaged in for the purposes of, or in connection with, appointment as a company auditor or the conduct of company audit work by persons who—

    (*a*)   are eligible under its rules for appointment as a company auditor, or

    (*b*)   hold an appropriate qualification and are directors or other officers of bodies corporate which are so eligible or partners in, or employees of, partnerships which are so eligible.

(6) The practices relevant for the purposes of sub-paragraph (4)(*b*) in the case of a recognised qualifying body are—

    (*a*)   practices engaged in by persons in the course of seeking to obtain a recognised professional qualification from that body, and

    (*b*)   practices engaged in by persons approved by the body for the purposes of giving practical training to persons seeking such a qualification and which relate to such training.

Investigatory powers of the Director

4.—(1) The following powers are exercisable by the Director for the purpose of investigating any matter in connection with his functions under paragraph 1 or 3.

(2) The Director may by a notice in writing require any person to produce, at a time and place specified in the notice, to the Director or to any person appointed by him for the purpose, any documents which are specified or described in the notice and which are documents in his custody or under his control and relating to any matter relevant to the investigation.

(3) The Director may by a notice in writing require any person to furnish to the Director such information as may be specified or described in the notice, and specify the time within which and the manner and form in which any such information is to be furnished.

(4) A person shall not under this paragraph be required to produce any document or disclose any information which he would be entitled to refuse to produce or disclose on grounds of legal professional privilege in proceedings in the High Court or on the grounds of confidentiality as between client and professional legal adviser in proceedings in the Court of Session.

(5) Subsections (6) to (8) of section 85 of the Fair Trading Act 1973 (enforcement provisions) apply in relation to a notice under this paragraph as they apply in relation to a notice under subsection (1) of that section but as if, in subsection (7) of that section, for the words from "any one" to "the Commission" there were substituted "the Director".

Publication of Director's reports

5.—(1) The Director may, if he thinks fit, publish any report made by him under paragraph 1 or 3.

(2) He shall exclude from a published report, so far as practicable, any matter which relates to the affairs of a particular person (other than the supervisory or qualifying body concerned) the publication of which would or might in his opinion seriously and prejudicially affect the interests of that person.

Powers exercisable by the Secretary of State in consequence of report

6.—(1) The powers conferred by this section are exercisable by the Secretary of State if, having received and considered a report from the Director under paragraph 3(1) or (4), it appears to him that—

(*a*) any rules made or guidance issued by a recognised supervisory or qualifying body, or

(*b*) any such practices as are mentioned in paragraph 3(4),

have, or are intended or likely to have, to any significant extent the effect of restricting, distorting or preventing competition and that that effect is greater than is reasonably justifiable having regard to the purposes of this Part of this Act.

(2) The powers are—

(*a*) to revoke the recognition order granted to the body concerned,

(*b*) to direct it to take specified steps for the purpose of securing that the rules, guidance or practices in question do not have the effect mentioned in sub-paragraph (1), and

(*c*) to make alterations in the rules of the body for that purpose.

(3) The provisions of paragraph 3(2) to (5), (7) and (9) of Schedule 11 or, as the case may be, Schedule 12 have effect in relation to the revocation of a recognition order under sub-paragraph (2)(*a*) above as they have effect in relation to the revocation of such an order under that Schedule.

(4) Before the Secretary of State exercises the power conferred by sub-paragraph (2)(*b*) or (*c*) above he shall—

(*a*) give written notice of his intention to do so to the body concerned and take such steps (whether by publication or otherwise) as he thinks appropriate for bringing the notice to the attention of any other person who in his opinion is likely to be affected by the exercise of the power, and

(*b*) have regard to any representation made within such time as he considers reasonable by the body or any such other person.

(5) A notice under sub-paragraph (4) shall give particulars of the manner in which the Secretary of State proposes to exercise the power in question and state the reasons for which he proposes to act; and the statement of reasons may include matters contained in any report received by him under paragraph 4.

Supplementary provisions

7.—(1) A direction under paragraph 6 is, on the application of the Secretary of State, enforceable by injunction or, in Scotland, by an order under section 45 of the Court of Session Act 1988.

(2) The fact that any rules made by a recognised supervisory or qualifying body have been altered by the Secretary of State, or pursuant to a direction of the Secretary of State, under paragraph 6 does not preclude their subsequent alteration or revocation by that body.

(3) In determining for the purposes of this Part of this Schedule whether any guidance has, or is likely to have, any particular effect the Secretary of State and the Director may assume that the persons to whom it is addressed will act in conformity with it.

PART II

CONSEQUENTIAL EXEMPTIONS FROM COMPETITION LAW

Fair Trading Act 1973 (c. 41)

8.—(1) For the purpose of determining whether a monopoly situation within the meaning of the Fair Trading Act 1973 exists by reason of the circumstances mentioned in section 7(1)(*c*) of that Act (supply of services by or for group of two or more persons), no account shall be taken of—

    (*a*) the rules of or guidance issued by a recognised supervisory or qualifying body, or

    (*b*) conduct constituting such a practice as is mentioned in paragraph 3(4) above.

  (2) Where a recognition order is revoked there shall be disregarded for the purpose mentioned in sub-paragraph (1) any such conduct as is mentioned in that sub-paragraph which occurred while the order was in force.

  (3) Where on a monopoly reference under section 50 or 51 of the Fair Trading Act 1973 falling within section 49 of that Act (monopoly reference not limited to the facts) the Monopolies and Mergers Commission find that a monopoly situation within the meaning of that Act exists and—

    (*a*) that the person (or, if more than one, any of the persons) in whose favour it exists is—

        (i) a recognised supervisory or qualifying body, or

        (ii) a person of a description mentioned in paragraph 3(5) or (6) above, or

    (*b*) that any such person's conduct in doing anything to which the rules of such a body relate is subject to guidance issued by the body,

the Commission in making their report on that reference shall exclude from their consideration the question whether the rules or guidance of the body concerned, or the acts or omissions of that body in its capacity as such, operate or may be expected to operate against the public interest.

Restrictive Trade Practices Act 1976 (c. 34)

  9.—(1) The Restrictive Trade Practices Act 1976 does not apply to an agreement for the constitution of a recognised supervisory or qualifying body in so far as it relates to rules of or guidance issued by the body, and incidental matters connected therewith, including any term deemed to be contained in it by virtue of section 8(2) or 16(3) of that Act.

  (2) Nor does that Act apply to an agreement the parties to which consist of or include—

    (*a*) a recognised supervisory or qualifying body, or

    (*b*) any such person as is mentioned in paragraph 3(5) or (6) above,

by reason that it includes any terms the inclusion of which is required or contemplated by the rules or guidance of that body.

  (3) Where an agreement ceases by virtue of this paragraph to be subject to registration—

    (*a*) the Director shall remove from the register maintained by him under the Act of 1976 any particulars which are entered or filed in that register in respect of the agreement, and

    (*b*) any proceedings in respect of the agreement which are pending before the Restrictive Practices Court shall be discontinued.

  (4) Where a recognition order is revoked, sub-paragraphs (1) and (2) above shall continue to apply for a period of six months beginning with the day on which the revocation takes effect, as if the order were still in force.

  (5) Where an agreement which has been exempt from registration by virtue of this paragraph ceases to be exempt in consequence of the revocation of a recognition order, the time within which particulars of the agreement are to be furnished in accordance with section 24 of and Schedule 2 to the Act of 1976 shall be the period of one month beginning with the day on which the agreement ceased to be exempt from registration.

  (6) Where in the case of an agreement registered under the 1976 Act a term ceases to fall within sub-paragraph (2) above in consequence of the revocation of a recognition order and particulars of that term have not previously been furnished to the Director under section 24 of that Act, those particulars shall be furnished to him within the period of one month beginning with the day on which the term ceased to fall within that sub-paragraph.

Competition Act 1980 (c. 21)

  10.—(1) No course of conduct constituting any such practice as is mentioned in paragraph 3(4) above shall constitute an anti-competitive practice for the purposes of the Competition Act 1980.

  (2) Where a recognition order is revoked there shall not be treated as an anti-competitive practice for the purposes of that Act any such course of conduct as is mentioned in sub-paragraph (1) which occurred while the order was in force.

. . . . . .

Section 144(4)   SCHEDULE 18

"Subsidiary" and Related Expressions: Consequential Amendments and Savings

.   .   .   .   .   .

Companies Act 1985 (c. 6)

32.—(1) The following provisions have effect with respect to the operation of section 23 of the Companies Act 1985 (prohibition on subsidiary being a member of its holding company).

(2) In relation to times, circumstances and purposes before the commencement of section 144(1) of this Act, the references in section 23 to a subsidiary or holding company shall be construed in accordance with section 736 of the Companies Act 1985 as originally enacted.

(3) Where a body corporate becomes or ceases to be a subsidiary of a holding company by reason of section 144(1) coming into force, the prohibition in section 23 of the Companies Act 1985 shall apply (in the absence of exempting circumstances), or cease to apply, accordingly.

.   .   .   .   .   .

34. Section 293 of the Companies Act 1985 (age limit for directors) does not apply in relation to a director of a company if—

 (*a*) he had attained the age of 70 before the commencement of section 144(1) of this Act, and

 (*b*) the company became a subsidiary of a public company by reason only of the commencement of that subsection.

35. Nothing in section 144(1) affects the operation of Part XIIIA of the Companies Act 1985 (takeover offers) in relation to a takeover offer made before the commencement of that subsection.

36. For the purposes of section 719 of the Companies Act 1985 (power to provide for employees on transfer or cessation of business), a company which immediately before the commencement of section 144(1) was a subsidiary of another company shall not be treated as ceasing to be such a subsidiary by reason of that subsection coming into force.

37. For the purposes of section 743 of the Companies Act 1985 (meaning of "employees' share scheme"), a company which immediately before the commencement of section 144(1) was a subsidiary of another company shall not be treated as ceasing to be such a subsidiary by reason of that subsection coming into force.

38. In Schedule 25 to the Companies Act 1985 "subsidiary" has the meaning given by section 736 of that Act as originally enacted.

[THE NEXT PAGE IS I 1001]

Notes

Guidance Notes—The Companies Act 1985 (1987)

These notes, issued by the Companies Registration Office, are a guide to the main requirements of the Companies Act 1985. The winding up provisions of the Companies Act 1985 have been replaced by the Insolvency Act 1986 which is not covered. Throughout the notes the relevant provisions of the 1985 Act are indicated, but reference should be made at all times to the Act and to statutory instruments for fuller information.

Whilst every effort is made to ensure that the information given in this booklet is accurate, neither the Department of Trade and Industry nor the registrar of companies can accept responsibility for any errors or omissions.

CONTENTS

1. COMPANIES REGISTRATION OFFICES

Useful information

For companies registered in England and Wales the addresses are:

Companies Registration Office	London Search Room
Companies House	Companies House
Crown Way, Maindy	55–71 City Road
Cardiff	London
CF4 3UZ	EC1Y 1BB
Telephone: 0222 388588	Telephone: 01–253–9393

Cardiff and London public search rooms are open 9.30a.m.–4.00p.m. Monday to Friday except Bank Holidays. Last searches taken at 3.30p.m. for same day service. The fee for each microfiche record is £1.

Statutory forms and notes for guidance are available free of charge, on written request from the Stationery Section at Cardiff.

When telephoning, if you do not have the correct extension number, please give the switchboard operator the company number and brief details of your inquiry so that you can be put through to the right section.

If you are unable to visit either of the search rooms, write to the postal search section at Cardiff giving details of what you require. The cost of a microfiche record is £2 but if you want photocopies of particular documents, the fees vary. A leaflet is available on request.

For companies registered in Scotland the address is:

Companies Registration Office
102 George Street
Edinburgh
EH2 3DJ

Telephone numbers are as follows:

Charges section	031–225 5897
Default section	031–225 5779
Documents section	031–225 5777
New incorporations/names	031–225 5774
Public search	031–225 5774

The public search room is open 9.45a.m.–3.45p.m. Monday to Friday except Bank Holidays. The fee for each microfiche record is £1.

Statutory forms and notes for guidance are available free of charge from the stationery section.

When telephoning, if you do not have the correct extension number, please give the switchboard operator the company number and brief details of your inquiry so that you can be put through to the right section.

2. DIRECTORS' AND SECRETARIES DO'S AND DON'TS

Directors and secretaries

Public companies *must* have at least two directors and a private company *must* have at least one (section 282).

Every company *must* have a secretary. A sole director may not also act as the secretary (section 283(2)).

Any changes in the directors or secretaries or their particulars *must* be notified within 14 days to the appropriate Companies Registration Office on form 288.

Responsibility of directors/officers

The Companies Act provides for the imposition of penalties for failing to comply with the requirements of the Act. Directors and officers of a company are personally responsible if defaults occur, whether or not the preparation of returns etc. has been delegated to accountants or other parties.

Section 730 of and Schedule 24 to the Companies Act 1985 provide for a maximum fine of £2,000 for each offence of failing to file an annual return and for each offence of failing to file a set of accounts. On conviction after continued contravention, the maximum fine is £200 per day for each annual return and set of accounts. A director may also be disqualified from acting as a director or taking part in the formation or management of any company.

It is a criminal offence for an officer of the company to make false or misleading statements to an auditor (section 393).

Directors' report

The directors *must* make a report as part of the annual accounts. Details are given in Chapter 5 on Accounts.

Service contracts (contracts of employment)

The Registrar *must* be notified on form 318 if the directors' service contracts (or the memorandum setting out the terms of the contract if the contract is not in writing) are kept at any address other than the registered office address (section 318).

Disqualification of directors

The Secretary of State has the power to apply to the court for an order to disqualify a person from being a director or taking part in the promotion, formation or management of a company for up to five years if he has persistently been in default of the relevant requirements of the Act; or if he has been found guilty of three or more defaults in filing returns, accounts or other documents to the registrar within a period of five years (sections 295–299).

A public register of disqualified persons is open to inspection at the following addresses:

Companies Registration Office
Companies House, Crown Way, Maindy, Cardiff CF4 3UZ

The Insolvency Service
Atlantic House, Holborn Viaduct, London EC1N 2HD

London Search Room
Companies House, 55/71 City Road, London EC1Y 1BB

Companies Registration Office
102 George Street, Edinburgh EH2 3DJ.

Company secretaries' qualifications

The directors of a public company *must* take all reasonable steps to ensure that the secretary or each joint secretary of the company is a person who appears to have the knowledge and experience to fulfill all secretarial functions.

Section 286 of the Companies Act 1985 lists legal and other professional bodies whose members are suitable for appointment. However, the section allows directors flexibility to choose from other sources.

3. Auditors' Do's and Don'ts

Auditors' qualifications

An auditor *must* either be a member of one of the following recognised bodies:
    The Institute of Chartered Accountants in England and Wales;
    The Institute of Chartered Accountants of Scotland;
    The Chartered Association of Certified Accountants;
    The Institute of Chartered Accountants in Ireland;
or have been authorised by the Secretary of State (section 389).

Appointment and removal

Auditors *must* be appointed at each general meeting at which accounts are laid and can hold office until the end of the next such meeting. Automatic reappointment is no longer permitted. Where a company fails to appoint an auditor, the Secretary of State may appoint a person to fill the vacancy. An auditor may, under certain circumstances, be removed on or before the end of the term of office. Notification *must* be made to the registrar on form 386 within 14 days (sections 386 and 387).

Resignation

An auditor who resigns *must* deposit written notice of his resignation at the company's registered office. The notice should contain a statement as to whether or not there are circumstances connected with his resignation which should be brought to the attention of shareholders or creditors. If there are, the auditor *must* say what they are. A copy of his resignation and statement *must* be filed with the registrar within 14 days and sent by the company to everyone entitled to receive a copy of the company's accounts.

If a retiring auditor makes a statement, the auditor may call on the directors to hold an extraordinary meeting to receive and consider the explanation of the circumstances of his resignation (sections 390 and 391).

Powers in relation to subsidiaries

If a holding company has a subsidiary incorporated in Great Britain, it is the duty of that subsidiary and its auditors to give to the auditors of the holding company whatever information they may require (section 392).

4. COMPANY DO'S AND DON'TS

Definition: private and public company

A *private company* is any company which is not a public company. Any company which was registered as other than private under the definitions existing before 22nd December 1980 which has failed to comply with section 5 of the Companies Consolidation (Consequential Provisions) Act 1985 is liable to proceedings, as are its officers.

A public company is a limited company whose memorandum states that it is to be a public company and which was registered or re-registered on or after 22nd December 1980. It *must* have a minimum allotted capital of £50,000 (of which one quarter *must* be paid up on each share) and will be designated as "Public Limited Company" or "PLC" (section 1(3) and (4)).

Obligation to show certain information

Every company, including all oversea companies establishing a place of business in Great Britain, *must* either state the names of all directors, or none, (i.e. it cannot be selective) on all company business letters (section 305).

In addition every company *must* show its full registered name legibly on all
letterheadings;
notices and official publications;
bills of exchange, promissory notes, endorsements, cheques and orders
for money or goods signed by or on behalf of the company;
bills of parcels, invoices, receipts and letters of credit (section 349).
Companies are also required to show on business letters and order forms;
the place of registration indicated by any one of the following:
Registered in England and Wales
Registered in London
Registered in Wales
Registered in Cardiff
Registered in Scotland
Registered in Edinburgh,
together with the *registration number* of the company (shown on its certificate of incorporation), and if the company is exempt from using the word 'Limited' as part of its name, the fact that it is a limited company (section 351).

If a letterheading or order form shows more than one address, it is essential to indicate which is the registered office address.

A reference to capital is not obligatory, but if there is any reference to the amount of share capital on any company letterheading or order form, the reference *must* be to paid-up share capital.

If the company is exempt from using the word 'Limited', it may be omitted from the company name but must be included on the stationery, e.g. "Registered in England and Wales as a limited company".

Companies registered in Wales

If the memorandum of a company states that its registered office is in Wales it may register the following Welsh equivalents as the last word, or words, in its name:

"Cyfyngedig" ("Limited")—abbreviation "cyf"

"Cwmni Cyfyngedig Cyhoeddus"—abbreviation "C.C.C." ("Public Limited Company").

If a company uses these Welsh equivalents, the fact that the company is Limited or a Public Limited Company *must* be stated in English on all company stationery and *must* be displayed in every place where the company carries on business (section 351).

Company name outside business premises

Every company *must* paint or fix (and maintain legibly) its name in a prominent position, on the outside of every office or place of business (section 348).

Registered office

Every company *must* have a registered office address. Details of any changes in the situation of a company's registered office *must* be sent to the registrar on form 287 within 14 days (section 287).

Overseas branch register

A company having a share capital and whose objects comprise the transaction of business in any of the specified countries or territories can keep in that country or territory a branch register of members resident there (Schedule 14, Part I and section 362).

An overseas branch register is to be kept in the same manner as the company's principal register of members. The company *must* give notice to the registrar on forms 362 or 362a of the address of the office where any overseas branch register is kept. If the address changes or the register is discontinued, notice *must* be given within 14 days (Schedule 14, Part II).

Substantial interests in a public company

A public company *must* be informed, in writing within five days, when any person acquires or ceases to hold a 5 per cent. interest in its voting shares. Any significant change in the number of shares in which he/she is interested above 5 per cent. *must* also be notified. Notifications *must* include details of the shareholder's identity and the number of shares held (sections 198 to 202).

Certain family and corporate interests as well as group interests of people acting together *must* also be notified (sections 203 to 210).

Prospectus

A prospectus is a document containing an offer of shares or debentures for sale to the public.

A copy of every prospectus, signed and dated and accompanied by any consents or material contracts, *must* be filed with the registrar on or before the date of its publication.

A copy of any listing particulars prepared under Stock Exchange regulations *must* be filed with the registrar on or before the date of publication.

For administrative reasons, the Registrar for England and Wales requires two copies of each prospectus or listing particulars.

Company seal

Every company *must* have its name engraved in legible characters on its seal (section 350).

Change of name

A company can change its name by special resolution. The resolution *must* be sent to the registrar of companies with a registration fee of £40 (section 28).

When choosing a company name, companies are advised to refer to the notes for guidance on company names, available free of charge if you write to the stationery section of Companies Registration Offices at Cardiff or Edinburgh.

Mortgage debentures and other charges

Details of certain mortgages or charges created by a company, or existing on property acquired by a company, are required to be delivered within 21 days of the creation of the charge or the acquisition of the property (section 395).

All mortgage or charge documents should be sent marked "For the attention of Mortgage Section".

Prohibition on loans to directors

A company cannot normally make:

loans or quasi-loans, or

offer guarantees or security for loans, or

enter into credit transactions for directors of the company, or

people connected with them (section 330).

Exemptions:

Loans between members of a group of companies when a director of one company is also a director of another company.

Quasi-loans totalling not more than £1,000, if repayment is due within 2 months.

Credit transactions:

of not more than £5,000, or

entered into in the company's normal course of business, or

of a value not greater than and on terms no better than would have been offered to an unconnected person of the same financial standing.

Anything done for the purposes of the company or to enable the director to perform his duties. But the transaction or loan must:

not total more than £10,000,

and be approved in advance by the company in general meeting, or

be conditional on such approval being given at the next annual general meeting of the company.

A loan or quasi-loan not exceeding £50,000 made by a money-lending company in the course of its normal business and of any amount not greater than, and on terms no more favourable than, would be offered to any person of the same financial standing.

Loans totalling not more than £50,000 to purchase or improve the only or main director's home or in substitution for such a loan, provided that the loans are ordinarily made to employees of the company on no less favourable terms.

Resolutions

Certain types of resolutions passed *must* be filed with the registrar. They are, in the main, special and extraordinary resolutions and ordinary resolutions increasing capital, all of which *must* be filed within 15 days of being passed. The registrar requests that all resolutions are signed by an officer of the company (sections 123 and 380).

Alteration of memorandum of association

A company can alter its objects within the limits laid down in section 4 of the Companies Act 1985. To do this it *must* pass a special resolution, a copy of which *must* be sent to the registrar within 15 days, together with a printed copy of its altered memorandum (provided there is no application to the court to cancel the application).

An application to the court for the alteration *must* be made within 21 days and notice *must* be given immediately to the registrar on form 6.

An office copy of the court order cancelling or confirming the alteration *must* be sent to the registrar within 15 days of the order being made. If the alteration is confirmed, a printed copy of the altered memorandum *must* accompany the office copy court order (section 6).

When any alteration is made in the company's memorandum, other than under section 4 of the Companies Act 1985, a copy of the document making or showing the alteration *must* be sent to the registrar within 15 days with a printed copy of the altered memorandum (section 31).

Alteration of articles of association

A company can alter its articles of association by passing a special resolution specifying the alterations. A copy of the special resolution *must* be sent to the registrar within 15 days, together with a printed copy of the altered articles (section 9).

Adoption of new memorandum or articles

Resolutions to adopt a new memorandum or articles *must* have a revised copy attached to the resolution. In cases where new memorandum or articles are adopted, a printed copy *must* be sent to the registrar within 15 days.

Oversea companies

Companies incorporated outside Great Britain which have established a place of business in Great Britain are obliged to register certain documents with the registrar (Part XXIII, sections 691 to 699).

A company which has a place of business in both Scotland and England (or Wales) *must* register with both registrars and supply each with the relevant documents to be filed (with the exception of charges).

Further information about oversea companies may be obtained from Companies Registration Office.

Notifying a change in company status

The following changes in a company's status *must* be "officially notified":

the making of a winding up order in respect of the company or the appointment of a liquidator in a voluntary winding up of the company
any alteration of the company's memorandum or articles
any change relating to the company's directors
any change in the situation of the company's registered office (as regards service of any document on the company) (section 42).

"Officially notified"

An event is "officially notified" when a notice is published in the London or Edinburgh Gazette by the registrar of companies that he has received the relevant document relating to it.

In the case of the appointment of a liquidator in a voluntary winding up, the liquidator must publish notice of his appointment in the Gazette.

Defunct companies

The registrar has the power to strike companies off the register when he has reason to believe that they are not carrying on business or in operation (section 652).

The registrar will also consider striking a company off the register if he is asked to do so by the company officers or their legal representatives.

5. ACCOUNTS

Accounting requirements (see also Chapter 6 on disclosure exemptions)

Every company *must* keep accounting records, comprehensive enough to disclose with reasonable accuracy, the financial position of the company at any time.

Records *must* be kept of the daily receipt and payment of money, the assets, liabilities, stocktaking records at the end of the financial year and, except for retail sales, sufficient detail to enable the goods, buyers and sellers to be identified. These accounting records *must* be kept, in the case of a private company, for 3 years and in any other case for 6 years (sections 221 and 222).

The company's accounts *must* be prepared in accordance with formats laid down in Schedule 4 of the Companies Act 1985, and include:

a profit and loss account, or income and expenditure account, if appropriate.

a balance sheet dated the same as the profit and loss account.

an auditors' report.

a directors' report.

Every balance sheet of a company and every copy which is laid before the company in general meeting or delivered to the registrar, *must* be signed on behalf of the board by 2 directors of the company. If there is only one director it *must* be signed by that person. *The registrar will only accept a copy balance sheet if it bears original signatures* (sections 238 and 241).

Copies of balance sheets (except those laid before the company or delivered to the registrar) which are issued, circulated or published by a company can have copy signatures. However, the copy signatures *must* reproduce the exact style of the original signature, e.g. if the original signature was "John Ernest Brown", it is not sufficient to print "J.E. Brown" on the subsequent copies.

Directors' report

The directors' report *must* present a fair review of the development of the business of the company and any subsidiaries during the financial year ended with the balance sheet date and of their position at the end of it. It *must* also indicate the dividend, if any, the directors recommend and the amount they propose to carry to reserves (section 235(1)).

The directors' report *must* contain general matters concerning the company's organisation covering:

(*a*) The names of those who have been directors during the accounting reference period (section 235(2)).

(*b*) The principal activities of the company and its subsidiaries during the year and any significant changes (section 235(2)).

(*c*) Details of any significant changes in the fixed assets of the company or any of its subsidiaries (Schedule 7, Part I, paragraph 1).

(*d*) Any interests that the directors may have in shares or debentures of the company or its holding company's subsidiaries etc. This information may be given by way of notes to the company's accounts, instead of being in the directors' report (Schedule 7, Part I, paragraph 2).

(*e*) Details of any important matters affecting the company or any of its subsidiaries which have occurred since the year's end (Schedule 7, Part I, paragraph 6(*b*)).

(*f*) Any indication of likely developments in the business of the company and its subsidiaries (Schedule 7, Part I, paragraph 6(*a*)).

(*g*) An indication of the activities, if any, of the company and its subsidiaries in the field of research and development (Schedule 7, Part I, paragraph 6(*c*)).

(*h*) Details of contributions made by the company for political and/or charitable purposes if the total exceeds £200 in the accounting period (Schedule 7, Part I, paragraphs 3 to 5).

(*i*) Details of any shares in the company purchased or acquired:
by the company itself, or
by another person acting as the company's nominee, or
with financial assistance from the company, or
made subject to a lien or other charge (Schedule 7, Part II, paragraphs 7 to 8).

(*j*) When the average number of employees in each week during the financial year exceeds 250, the directors' report *must* include a statement on the policy of the company concerning the employment of disabled people. Details of the arrangements to keep employees in touch with the affairs of the company *must* also be included (Schedule 7, Part III, paragraph 9 and Part V, paragraph 11).

Disclosure of substantial contracts with directors and related persons

When a company prepares accounts, it *must* give details of any loans given, entered into, or agreed to be given or entered, by the company or any person who was at the time:
a director of the company or its holding company, or
connected with a director including:
spouses,
children or step-children,
associated corporate bodies (other than members of the same group of companies) (sections 232, 237(5), 330),
trustees of trusts for which any of these connected people are beneficiaries (Schedule 6, Part I), or
partners of any director or of any of the above categories of connected people (Schedule 6, Part II).

Duty to deliver a copy of the accounts

A company, *must* show the accounts for each accounting period to its members at a general meeting.

Every company *must* deliver a copy of its accounts to the registrar of companies unless throughout the accounting reference period the following conditions are satisfied:
the company is unlimited and is not a subsidiary of, or the holding company for, a limited company and it has not carried out business as a Trading Stamp Scheme promoter.

Time limits for submission

The accounts *must* be laid before the company and delivered to the registrar within the following time limits:

Private companies—within 10 months of the end of the accounting reference period.

Public companies—within 7 months of the end of the accounting reference period.

Companies with overseas interests outside the United Kingdom, the Channel Islands and the Isle of Man—can claim an extension of 3 months, i.e. private companies 13 months, public companies 10 months. To claim an extension, form 242 must be completed and delivered to the registrar before the end of the standard period allowed, i.e. before the end of 10 months (for a private company) or 7 months (for a public company).

New companies—if a newly incorporated company's first accounting reference period is more than 12 months as described above, the period for laying and delivering accounts will be reduced by the amount of time by which the accounting reference period exceeded 12 months, but will not be less than 3 months.

There are fines and other penalties for failing to lay or deliver accounts. Persistent default can result in directors being disqualified from taking part in the management of any company for up to 5 years.

New companies and their first accounting reference period

A new company's first accounting period begins on the date of its incorporation and *must* be for a period of more than 6 months but not more than 18 months.

Accounting reference date

Every newly formed company may notify the registrar on form 224 of the date on which its accounting reference period will end in each year, known as the company's accounting reference date. *If it does not notify a particular date to the registrar within 6 months of its incorporation, the accounting reference date will be 31 March* (section 224).

Changing the accounting reference date

In certain circumstances a company can change the accounting reference date by notifying the registrar on form 225(1) or 225(2).

Form 225(1) is for extending or shortening the current accounting reference period. Notice *must* be given before the end of the accounting period which *must not* exceed 18 months.

The accounting reference date cannot be extended more than once in 5 years unless the company is aligning its accounting reference date with that of a holding or subsidiary company. A company may shorten the current period as often as desired.

Form 225(2) is only for use by a company aligning its accounting reference date with that of its holding or subsidiary company. It can only be used in respect of the previous accounting reference period. The notice *must* be given before the end of the time allowed for laying and delivering accounts relating to the old accounting reference period (section 225).

Change of an accounting period other than a current or last one is not allowed.

6. DISCLOSURE EXEMPTIONS FOR SMALL, MEDIUM AND DORMANT COMPANIES

Small and medium companies

All companies *must* prepare full accounts for presentation to the members of the company. However, the following companies may deliver modified accounts to the registrar:

Small companies may submit only a shortened balance sheet and abbreviated notes relating to it, if they satisfy two of the following criteria in any one financial year (section 248(1)):

　turnover not exceeding £2,000,000
　balance sheet total not exceeding £975,000
　average number of employees not exceeding 50.

However, they *must* submit a directors' statement and a special auditors' report—see paragraph below on claiming exemptions.

Medium-sized companies may submit a modified profit and loss account which need not disclose turnover, a balance sheet and a directors' report if they satisfy two of the following criteria in any one financial year:

　turnover not exceeding £8,000,000
　balance sheet total not exceeding £3,900,000
　average number of employees not exceeding 250 (section 248(2)).

However, a directors' statement and special auditors' report *must* be submitted.

Claiming exemptions

To claim the accounting exemptions, a set of modified accounts *must* include:

a statement by the directors, immediately above their signatures on the balance sheet, that:

they rely on sections 247–249 of the Companies Act 1985 as entitling them to deliver modified accounts, and

they do so because the company is entitled to the benefit of those sections as a small or medium-sized company (Schedule 8, Part I, paragraph 9).

a special auditor's report, stating that in their opinion:

the directors are entitled to deliver modified accounts in respect of the financial year, as claimed in the directors' statement, and

any accounts comprised in the documents delivered as modified accounts are properly prepared in accordance with this schedule.

A copy of the auditors' report need not be delivered, but the full text of it *must* be reproduced in the special auditors' report (Schedule 8, Part I, paragraphs 10(1) and (2)).

The exemptions are *not* available to public companies, banking, insurance or shipping companies, and companies other than dormant companies which are members of a group included in any of these categories.

As the accounting exemptions are not mandatory, small and medium-sized companies may, if they wish, deliver full accounts to the registrar for filing.

Dormant companies

Provided no transactions take place (in any period) which should be included in a company's accounting records, the company is regarded as being dormant (sections 221 and 252).

A company can pass a special resolution at a general meeting when its accounts are presented (or before its first meeting if it is a newly-formed company) to exclude section 384 of the Companies Act from applying. It is then exempt from the obligation to appoint an auditor.

A dormant company is one which has passed a special resolution and which has filed a copy of it with the registrar. The company can then deliver accounts consisting merely of a balance sheet. This *must* state, above the directors' signatures, that the company was dormant throughout the financial year (sections 252 and 253).

If the company's status changes, the directors can appoint an auditor to serve until the end of the next general meeting. Alternatively, the company in general meeting can appoint an auditor.

Modified and dormant accounts are subject to the same time limits for submission as full accounts—see Chapter 5.

7. Company Meetings and Annual Returns

Annual general meetings

Every company *must* hold a general meeting as its annual general meeting (AGM) each calendar year and there *must not* be more than 15 months between AGM's.

As long as a company holds its first AGM within 18 months of its incorporation, it need not hold it in the year of its incorporation or the following year.

Failure to hold an AGM is an offence (section 366).

Annual Returns

Every company *must* make an annual return to the registrar, whether or not it is in business or operation.

The year to be covered by the annual return is governed by the date of the AGM and not by the date of the accounts laid before the meeting. The return *must* be filed within 42 days of the meeting. In the case of a company having a share capital, the return should be made up to the fourteenth day after the date of the AGM. If a company fails to hold an AGM, the annual return should be made up to a date 15 months plus 14 days after the last AGM or 31 December, whichever is the earlier. Failure to send a copy of the annual return to the registrar is an offence (section 365).

Notice of any change of registered office address must be given on form 287 within 14 days of the change. It is not sufficient merely to show the change on an annual return.

8. Dealing in Shares

Register of directors' interests

Every company *must* keep a register of any interests in which directors have shares, or debentures of, the company, its holding company or any subsidiaries. Interests of directors' spouses and children *must* also be stated (sections 324 and 325).

If this register is not held at the company's registered office, then a notification of the address at which it is kept (and any changes in that address) *must* be sent to the registrar on form 325. Use form 325a if the register is not kept in a legible form (i.e. on a computer) (Schedule 13, Part IV, paragraph 27).

If a company is listed on a Stock Exchange, it *must* notify the Stock Exchange if a director, director's spouse or child acquires or disposes of any of its shares or debentures. Notification *must* be made by the following day, unless that day is a Saturday, Sunday or Bank Holiday (section 329).

Financial assistance for the acquisition of shares

There are restrictions on companies giving assistance in the purchase of their shares (sections 155 to 158).

This is a subject which may require professional advice.

Purchase or redemption by a company of its own shares

There are restrictions on companies purchasing or redeeming their own shares (sections 155, 159 to 181, 380, 503, 504, 507, 519).

This is a subject which may require professional advice.

Members' (shareholders') register

Every company *must* have a members' register containing:

    The name and address of each member

    The date on which they were registered as a member

    The date on which they ceased to be a member

and if the company has a share capital:

    The number of shares held by each member together with details of the amount paid or considered to be paid.

Unless the work of making up the register is carried out at another office of the company, or is done by some other person on behalf of the company, the register *must* be kept at the company's registered office. If it is not, the registrar *must* be notified of the address at which it is kept or of any changes in that address on form 353. Use form 353a if the register is kept in non-legible form.

In any event, the register for a company registered in England and Wales must be kept in England and Wales. For a company registered in Scotland, the register must be kept in Scotland (sections 352 and 353).

9. PRINTING REQUIREMENTS

Resolutions, memorandum and articles of association

It is important that documents concerning resolutions, memorandum and articles are of good quality. The following *must* therefore be printed:

　　Articles of association (section 7(3))

　　Altered articles of association (section 18)

　　Altered memorandum of association (sections 6(1) and 18)

Most modern printing processes are acceptable. The print *must* be black on white paper of reasonable thickness (90gsm).

However, the following presentation of amendments to the memorandum and articles are acceptable:

If the amendment is small e.g., a change of name or a change in the nominal capital, a copy of the original document can be amended by rubber stamp, 'top copy' typing or in some other permanent manner (but not a hand written amendment);

An alteration of a few lines or a complete short paragraph may be similarly dealt with if the new version is permanently fixed to the original, covering the words to be amended;

If more substantial amendments are involved, the amended pages can be removed from a copy of the original, the amended text inserted and the pages securely fixed. The inserted material *must* be 'printed' as defined but need not be produced by the same process as the original.

In all cases the alterations *must* be validated by the seal or an official stamp of the company (section 350).

The following documents for registration *must* be either printed or a typed original in a layout approved by the registrar:

　　ordinary resolutions increasing the capital of any company.

　　special and extraordinary resolutions and agreements as specified in
　　section 380 of the Companies Act 1985.

The registrar is prepared to accept for registration such copy resolutions and agreements, if produced to an acceptable standard.

No document will be accepted if it is illegible. Where it is considered that a document, though legible, cannot be reproduced to an adequate standard for presentation to the public in microfiche or photocopy form, the registrar's practice is to seek the co-operation of the presentor in providing a clearer copy.

Statutory forms

Copies of all statutory forms are available from the stationery sections of the Companies Registration Offices. These forms show the format and style of type which will normally be acceptable to the registrar.

They are intended to take into account modern company secretarial practice and are designed with the intention of producing forms which are best suited for public inspection. They also include the experience gained by the registry in the preparation of bulk microfilm records and have been designed to ensure a high standard of legibility for reproduction of company records from microfilm back to hard paper copy. A list of all the forms prescribed under the Companies Act 1985 is given infra.

Although statutory forms can be obtained direct from the CRO's some people produce their own and for those wishing to do so, the followng advice is based upon the standards to which the registrar works:

Size

International A4 size should be used.

The layout *must be portrait and the dimensions are given below:*

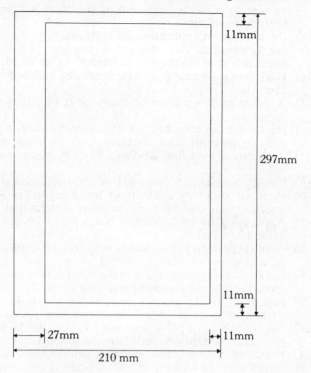

Colour
   Black print on white paper of no less than 90gsm.

Typeface
   Any plain typeface of medium or semibold appearance in either 10 point or elite (12 typewriter characters to the inch).
   Additionally, there is an increasing call for the information required to be filed at the Companies Registration Office to be produced in the form of Computer Output. The registrar has no objection, in principle, to this move towards mechanically completed forms. Because of other constraints in making the information available and the statutory duty for forms to follow as closely as possible the prescribed layout, he does need an opportunity to approve formally any draft layout.
   Only a top copy will be accepted, printed on plain paper and not on "listing paper". Computer stationery must be trimmed and burst and securely tagged together.
   If you require any help or advice on design and approval of forms under the Companies Act you should address your enquiries to the Forms Design Unit, Room 1.12, Companies House, Crown Way, Maindy, Cardiff CF4 3UZ.

10. LIST OF STATUTORY FORMS

  6 Notice of application to the court for cancellation of alteration to the objects of a company.
 10 Statement of first directors and secretary and intended situation of registered office.
 12 Statutory declaration of compliance with requirements on application for registration of a company.

30(5)(a) Declaration on application for the registration of a company exempt from the requirement to use the word "limited" or its Welsh equivalent.

30(5)(b) Declaration on application for registration under section 680 of the Companies Act 1985 of a company exempt from the requirement to use the word "limited" or its Welsh equivalent.

30(5)(c) Declaration on change of name omitting "limited" or its Welsh equivalent.

43(3) Application by a private company for re-registration as a public company.

43(3)(e) Declaration of compliance with requirements by a private company on application for re-registration as a public company.

49(1) Application by a limited company to be re-registered as unlimited.

49(8)(a) Members' assent to company being re-registered as unlimited.

49(8)(b) Form of statutory declaration by directors as to members' assent to re-registration of a company as unlimited.

51 Application by an unlimited company to be re-registered as limited.

53 Application by a public company for re-registration as a private company.

54 Notice of application made to the court for the cancellation of a special resolution regarding re-registration.

97 Statement of the amount or rate percent of any commission payable in connection with the subscription of shares.

117 Application by a public company for certificate to commence business and statutory declaration in support.

122 Notice of consolidation, division, sub-division, redemption or cancellation of shares, or conversion, re-conversion of stock into shares.

123 Notice of increase in nominal capital.

128(1) Statement of rights attached to allotted shares.

128(3) Statement of particulars of variation of rights attached to shares.

128(4) Notice of assignment of name or new name to any class of shares.

129(1) Statement by a company without share capital of rights attached to newly created class of members.

129(2) Statement by a company without share capital of particulars of variation of members' class rights.

129(3) Notice by a company without share capital of assignment of a name or other designation to a class of members.

139 Application by a public company for re-registration as a private company following a court order reducing capital.

147 Application by a public company for re-registration as a private company following cancellation of shares and reduction of nominal value of issued capital.

155(6)a Declaration in relation to assistance for the acquisition of shares.

155(6)b Declaration by the directors of a holding company in relation to assistance for the acquisition of shares.

157 Notice of application made to the court for the cancellation of a special resolution regarding financial assistance for the acquisition of shares.

169 Return by a company purchasing its own shares.

173 Declaration in relation to the redemption or purchase of shares out of capital.

176 Notice of application made to the court for the cancellation of a resolution for the redemption or purchase of shares out of capital.

190 Notice of place where a register of holders of debentures or a duplicate is kept or of any change in that place.

190a Notice of place for inspection of a register of holders of debentures which is kept in a non-legible form, or of any change in that place.

224 Notice of accounting reference date (to be delivered within 6 months of incorporation).

225(1) Notice of new accounting reference date given during the course of an accounting reference period.

225(2) Notice by an holding company or subsidiary company of a new accounting reference date given after the end of an accounting reference period.

242 Notice of claim to extension of period allowed for laying and delivering accounts—overseas business or interest.

266(1) Notice of intention to carry on business as an investment company.

266(3) Notice that a company no longer wishes to be an investment company.

287 Notice of change in situation of registered office.

288 Notice of change of directors or secretaries or their particulars.

318 Notice of place where copies of directors' service contracts and any memoranda are kept or of any change in that place.

325 Notice of place where register of directors' interests in shares etc. is kept or of any change in that place.

325a Notice of place for inspection of a register of directors' interests in shares which is kept in a non-legible form, or of any change in that place.

353 Notice of place where a register of members is kept or of any change in that place.

353a Notice of place for inspection of a register of members which is kept in a non-legible form, or of any change in that place.

362 Notice of a place where an overseas branch register is kept, or any change in that place, or of discontinuance of any such register.

362a Notice of place for inspection of any overseas branch register which is kept in a non-legible form, or of any change in that place.

363 Annual return of a company.

386 Notice of passing of resolution removing an auditor.

395 Particulars of a mortgage or charge. (Also for the use of a company incorporated outside Great Britain which has a place of business in England or Wales.)

397 Particulars for the registration of a charge to secure a series of debentures. (Also for the use of a company incorporated outside Great Britain which has a place of business in England or Wales.)

397a Particulars of an issue of secured debentures in a series. (Also for the use of a company incorporated outside Great Britain which has a place of business in England or Wales.)

398 Certificate of Registration in Scotland or Northern Ireland of a charge comprising property situate there.

400 Particulars of a mortgage or charge subject to which property has been acquired. (Also for the use of a company incorporated outside Great Britain which has a place of business in England or Wales.)

403a Declaration of satisfaction in full or in part of mortgage or charge. (Also for the use of a company incorporated outside Great Britain which has a place of business in England or Wales.)

403b	Declaration that part of the property or undertaking charged (a) has been released from the charge; (b) no longer forms part of the company's property or undertaking. (Also for the use of a company incorporated outside Great Britain which has a place of business in England or Wales.)
405(1)	Notice of appointment of receiver or manager.
405(2)	Notice of ceasing to act as receiver or manager.
428	Notice to non-assenting share holders.
429(4)	Notice to non-assenting share holders.
429dec	Statutory declaration relating to a notice to non-assenting shareholders.
430A	Notice to transferee company by non-assenting share holder.
*495(2)a	Notice to company of appointment of receiver or manager.
*495(3)a	Statement of affairs (including lists A–G + Sch I–V to List A).
*495(3)b	Statement of affairs (including lists A–G + Sch I–V to List A).
*497	Receiver or manager's abstract of receipts or payments.
600	Notice of appointment of a liquidator voluntary winding up (members or creditors).
600(a)	Notice of appointment of liquidator (members') (creditors') voluntary winding up.
680a	Application by a Joint stock company for registration under Part XXII of the Companies Act 1985 and declaration and related statements.
680b	Application by a company which is not a joint stock company for registration under part XXII of the Companies Act 1985 and Declaration and related statements.
684	Registration under Part XXII of the Companies Act 1985 list of members—existing joint stock company.
685	Declaration on application by a joint stock company for registration as a public company.
686	Registration under Part XXII of the Companies Act 1985 statutory declaration verifying list of members.
R7	Application by an old public company for re-registration as a public company.
R7a	Notice of application made to the court for the cancellation of a special resolution by an old public company not to be re-registered as a public company.
R8	Declaration by director or secretary on application by an old public company for re-registration as a public company.
R9	Declaration by an old public company that it does not meet the requirements for a public company.

Capital Forms

88(2)	Return of allotments of shares issued by way of capitalisation of reserves (bonus issues).
88(3)	Particulars of a contract related to shares allotted as fully or partly paid up otherwise than for cash.
PUC1	Statement on formation of a company to be incorporated with limited liability under the Companies Act 1985.
PUC2	Return of allotments of shares issued for cash.
PUC3	Return of allotments for shares issued wholly or in part for a consideration other than in cash.
PUC4	Claim for a credit or relief from capital duty under section 49(5) of the Finance Act 1973.
PUC5	Statement of amounts or further amounts paid or nil paid or partly paid shares (under Part V of the Finance Act 1973).
PUC6	Statement relating to a chargeable transaction of a capital company.

Scottish Forms

> 410 Particulars of a charge created by a company registered in Scotland. (Also for the use of a company incorporated outside Great Britain which has a place of business in Scotland.)
>
> 413 Particulars for the registration of a charge to secure a series of debentures (note 1). (Also for the use of a company incorporated outside Great Britain which has a place of business in Scotland.)
>
> 413a Particulars of an issue of debentures out of a series of secured Debentures (note 1). (Also for the use of a company incorporated outside Great Britain which has a place of business in Scotland.)
>
> 416 Particulars of a charge subject to which property has been acquired by a company registered in Scotland. (Also for the use of a company incorporated outside Great Britain which has a place of business in Scotland.)
>
> 419a Application for registration of a memorandum of satisfaction in full or in part of a registered charge. (Also for the use of a company incorporated outside Great Britain which has a place of business in Scotland.)
>
> 419b Application for registration of a memorandum of fact that part of the property charged:
> (a) has been released from the charge;
> (b) no longer forms part of the company's property. (Also for the use of a company incorporated outside Great Britain which has a place of business in Scotland.)
>
> 466 Particulars of an instrument of alteration to a floating charge created by a company registered in Scotland. (Also for the use of a company incorporated outside Great Britain which has a place of business in Scotland.)
>
> [1] 469 Notice to the registrar of appointment of a receiver by the holder of a floating charge.
>
> [1] 470 Notice to the registrar of appointment of a receiver by the court.
>
> [1] 478 Notice of ceasing to act as, or removal of, a receiver.
>
> [1] 481 Abstract of receiver's receipts and payments.
>
> [1] 482 Statement as to affairs of a company (including Lists A–G + Schedule I–V to List A).

NOTE
[1] These forms have been revoked by S.I. 1986 No. 2097, which came into force on 29th December 1986. However, the forms are still available for use under section 2(2) of the Instrument. This relates to any receiver appointed under section 467 of the Companies Act 1985 before 29th December 1986 or to any receiver or manager appointed before that date to whom Part XIX of the Act applies.

Oversea Company Forms

> 691 Return and declaration, delivered for registration by an oversea company.
>
> 692(1)(a) Return of alteration in the charter, statues, etc. of an oversea company.
>
> 692(1)(b) Return of alteration in the directors or secretary of oversea company or in their particulars.
>
> 692(1)(c) Return of alteration in the names or addresses of persons resident in Great Britain authorised to accept service on behalf of an oversea company.
>
> 692(2) Return of change in the corporate name of an oversea company.

694(a) Statement of name, other than a corporate name, which an oversea company proposes to carry on business in Great Britain.

694(b) Statement of name other than a corporate name under which an oversea company proposes to carry on business in Great Britain in substitution for name previously registered.

701(2) Notice of accounting reference date by an oversea company.

701(6)(a) Notice by an oversea company of new accounting reference date given during the course of an accounting reference period.

701(6)(b) Notice by an oversea company of new accounting reference date given after the end of an accounting reference period.

Statutory Instruments

Companies (Tables A to F) Regulations 1985

(S.I. 1985 No. 805)

[22nd May 1985]

The Secretary of State, in exercise of the powers conferred by section 454(2) of the Companies Act 1948, and now vested in him, of the powers conferred by sections 3 and 8 of the Companies Act 1985 and of all other powers enabling him in that behalf, hereby makes the following Regulations—

1. These Regulations may be cited as the Companies (Tables A to F) Regulations 1985 and shall come into operation on 1st July 1985.

2. The regulations in Table A and the forms in Tables B, C, D, E and F in the Schedule to these Regulations shall be the regulations and forms of memorandum and articles of association for the purposes of sections 3 and 8 of the Companies Act 1985.

3. The Companies (Alteration of Table A etc.) Regulations 1984 are hereby revoked.

SCHEDULE

TABLE A

REGULATIONS FOR MANAGEMENT OF A COMPANY LIMITED BY SHARES

INTERPRETATION

1. In these regulations—
   "the Act" means the Companies Act 1985 including any statutory modification or re-enactment thereof for the time being in force;
   "the articles" means the articles of the company;
   "clear days" in relation to the period of a notice means that period excluding the day when the notice is given or deemed to be given and the day for which it is given or on which it is to take effect;
   "executed" includes any mode of execution;
   "office" means the registered office of the company;
   "the holder" in relation to shares means the member whose name is entered in the register of members as the holder of the shares;
   "the seal" means the common seal of the company;
   "secretary" means the secretary of the company or any other person appointed to perform the duties of the secretary of the company, including a joint, assistant or deputy secretary;
   "the United Kingdom" means Great Britain and Northern Ireland.

Unless the context otherwise requires, words or expressions contained in these regulations bear the same meaning as in the Act but excluding any statutory modification thereof not in force when these regulations become binding on the company.

SHARE CAPITAL

2. Subject to the provisions of the Act and without prejudice to any rights attached to any existing shares, any share may be issued with such rights or restrictions as the company may by ordinary resolution determine.

3. Subject to the provisions of the Act, shares may be issued which are to be redeemed or are to be liable to be redeemed at the option of the company or the holder on such terms and in such manner as may be provided by the articles.

4. The company may exercise the powers of paying commissions conferred by the Act. Subject to the provision of the Act, any such commission may be satisfied by the payment of cash or by the allotment of fully or partly paid shares or partly in one way and partly in the other.

5. Except as required by law, no person shall be recognised by the company as holding any share upon any trust and (except as otherwise provided by the articles or by law) the company shall not be bound by or recognise any interest in any share except an absolute right to the entirety thereof in the holder.

SHARE CERTIFICATES

6. Every member, upon becoming the holder of any shares, shall be entitled without payment to one certificate for all the shares of each class held by him (and, upon transferring a part of his holding of shares of any class, to a certificate for the balance of such holding) or several certificates each for one or more of his shares upon payment for every certificate after the first of such reasonable sum as the directors may determine. Every certificate shall be sealed with the seal and shall specify the number, class and distinguishing numbers (if any) of the shares to which it relates and the amount or respective amounts paid up thereon. The company shall not be bound to issue more than one certificate for shares held jointly by several persons and delivery of a certificate to one joint holder shall be a sufficient delivery to all of them.

7. If a share certificate is defaced, worn-out, lost or destroyed, it may be renewed on such terms (if any) as to evidence and indemnity and payment of the expenses reasonably incurred by the company in investigating evidence as the directors may determine but otherwise free of charge, and (in the case of defacement or wearing-out) on delivery up of the old certificate.

LIEN

8. The company shall have a first and paramount lien on every share (not being a fully paid share) for all moneys (whether presently payable or not) payable at a fixed time or called in respect of that share. The directors may at any time declare any share to be wholly or in part exempt from the provisions of this regulation. The company's lien on a share shall extend to any amount payable in respect of it.

9. The company may sell in such manner as the directors determine any shares on which the company has a lien if a sum in respect of which the lien exists is presently payable and is not paid within 14 clear days after notice has been given to the holder of the share or to the person entitled to it in consequence of the death or bankruptcy of the holder, demanding payment and stating that if the notice is not complied with the shares may be sold.

10. To give effect to a sale the directors may authorise some person to execute an instrument of transfer of the shares sold to, or in accordance with the directions of, the purchaser. The title of the transferee to the shares shall not be affected by any irregularity in or invalidity of the proceedings in reference to the sale.

11. The net proceeds of the sale, after payment of the costs, shall be applied in payment of so much of the sum for which the lien exists as is presently payable, and any residue shall (upon surrender to the company for cancellation of the certificate for the shares sold and subject to a like lien for any moneys not presently payable as existed upon the shares before the sale) be paid to the person entitled to the shares at the date of the sale.

CALLS ON SHARES AND FORFEITURE

12. Subject to the terms of allotment, the directors may make calls upon the members in respect of any moneys unpaid on their shares (whether in respect of nominal value or premium) and each member shall (subject to receiving at least 14 clear days' notice specifying when and where payment is to be made) pay to the company as required by the notice the amount called on his shares. A call may be required to be paid by instalments. A call may, before receipt by the company of any sum due thereunder, be revoked in whole or part and payment of a call may be postponed in whole or part. A person upon whom a call is made shall remain liable for calls made upon him notwithstanding the subsequent transfer of the shares in respect whereof the call was made.

13. A call shall be deemed to have been made at the time when the resolution of the directors authorising the call was passed.

14. The joint holders of a share shall be jointly and severally liable to pay all calls in respect thereof.

15. If a call remains unpaid after it has become due and payable the person from whom it is due and payable shall pay interest on the amount unpaid from the day it became due and payable until it is paid at the rate fixed by the terms of allotment of the share or in the notice of the call or, if no rate is fixed, at the appropriate rate (as defined by the Act) but the directors may waive payment of the interest wholly or in part.

16. An amount payable in respect of a share on allotment or at any fixed date, whether in respect of nominal value or premium or as an instalment of a call, shall be deemed to be a call and if it is not paid the provisions of the articles shall apply as if that amount had become due and payable by virtue of a call.

17. Subject to the terms of allotment, the directors may make arrangements on the issue of shares for a difference between the holders in the amounts and times of payment of calls on their shares.

18. If a call remains unpaid after it has become due and payable the directors may give to the person from whom it is due not less than 14 clear days' notice requiring payment of the amount unpaid together with any interest which may have accrued. The notice shall name the place where payment is to be made and shall state that if the notice is not complied with the shares in respect of which the call was made will be liable to be forfeited.

19. If the notice is not complied with any share in respect of which it was given may, before the payment required by the notice has been made, be forfeited by a resolution of the directors and the forfeiture shall include all dividends or other moneys payable in respect of the forfeited shares and not paid before the forfeiture.

20. Subject to the provisions of the Act, a forfeited share may be sold, re-alloted or otherwise disposed of on such terms and in such manner as the directors determine either to the person who was before the forfeiture the holder or to any other person and at any time before sale, re-allotment or other disposition, the forfeiture may be cancelled on such terms as the directors think fit. Where for the purposes of its disposal a forfeited share is to be transferred to any person the directors may authorise some person to execute an instrument of transfer of the share to that person.

21. A person any of whose shares have been forfeited shall cease to be a member in respect of them and shall surrender to the company for cancellation the certificate for the shares forfeited but shall remain liable to the company for all moneys which at the date of forfeiture were presently payable by him to the company in respect of those shares with interest at the rate at which interest was payable on those moneys before the forfeiture or, if no interest was so payable, at the appropriate rate (as defined in the Act) from the date of forfeiture until payment but the directors may waive payment wholly or in part or enforce payment without any allowance for the value of the shares at the time of forfeiture or for any consideration received on their disposal.

22. A statutory declaration by a director or the secretary that a share has been forfeited on a specified date shall be conclusive evidence of the facts stated in it as against all persons claiming to be entitled to the share and the declaration shall (subject to the execution of an instrument of transfer if necessary) constitute a good title to the share and the person to whom the share is disposed of shall not be bound to see to the application of the consideration, if any, nor shall his title to the share be affected by any irregularity in or invalidity of the proceedings in reference to the forfeiture or disposal of the share.

TRANSFER OF SHARES

23. The instrument of transfer of a share may be in any usual form or in any other form which the directors may approve and shall be executed by or on behalf of the transferor and, unless the share is fully paid, by or on behalf of the transferee.

24. The directors may refuse to register the transfer of a share which is not fully paid to a person of whom they do not approve and they may refuse to register the transfer of a share on which the company has a lien. They may also refuse to register a transfer unless—
   (a) it is lodged at the office or at such other place as the directors may appoint and is accompanied by the certificate for the shares to which it relates and such other evidence as the directors may reasonably require to show the right of the transferor to make the transfer;
   (b) it is in respect of only one class of shares; and
   (c) it is in favour of not more than four transferees.

25. If the directors refuse to register a transfer of a share, they shall within two months after the date on which the transfer was lodged with the company send to the transferee notice of the refusal.

26. The registration of transfers of shares or of transfers of any class of shares may be suspended at such times and for such periods (not exceeding 30 days in any year) as the directors may determine.

27. No fee shall be charged for the registration of any instrument of transfer or other document relating to or affecting the title to any share.

28. The company shall be entitled to retain any instrument of transfer which is registered, but any instrument of transfer which the directors refuse to register shall be returned to the person lodging it when notice of the refusal is given.

TRANSMISSION OF SHARES

29. If a member dies the survivor or survivors where he was a joint holder, and his personal representatives where he was a sole holder or the only survivor of joint holders, shall be the only persons recognised by the company as having any title to his interest; but nothing herein contained shall release the estate of a deceased member from any liability in respect of any share which had been jointly held by him.

30. A person becoming entitled to a share in consequence of the death or bankruptcy of a member may, upon such evidence being produced as the directors may properly require, elect either to become the holder of the share or to have some person nominated by him registered as the transferee. If he elects to become the holder he shall give notice to the company to that effect. If he elects to have another person registered he shall execute an instrument of transfer of the share to that person. All the articles relating to the transfer of shares shall apply to the notice or instrument of transfer as if it were an instrument of transfer executed by the member and the death or bankruptcy of the member had not occurred.

31. A person becoming entitled to a share in consequence of the death or bankruptcy of a member shall have the rights to which he would be entitled if he were the holder of the share, except that he shall not, before being registered as the holder of the share, be entitled in respect of it to attend or vote at any meeting of the company or at any separate meeting of the holders of any class of shares in the company.

ALTERATION OF SHARE CAPITAL

32. The company may by ordinary resolution—
   (a) increase its share capital by new shares of such amount as the resolution prescribes;
   (b) consolidate and divide all or any of its share capital into shares of larger amount than its existing shares;
   (c) subject to the provisions of the Act, sub-divide its shares, or any of them, into shares of smaller amount and the resolution may determine that, as between the shares resulting from the sub-division, any of them may have any preference or advantage as compared with the others; and
   (d) cancel shares which, at the date of the passing of the resolution, have not been taken or agreed to be taken by any person and diminish the amount of its share capital by the amount of the shares so cancelled.

33. Whenever as a result of a consolidation of shares any members would become entitled to fractions of a share, the directors may, on behalf of those members, sell the shares representing the fractions for the best price reasonably obtainable to any person (including, subject to the provisions of the Act, the company) and distribute the net proceeds of sale in due proportion among those members, and the directors may authorise some person to execute an instrument of transfer of the shares to, or in accordance with the directions of, the purchaser. The transferee shall not be bound to see to the application of the purchase money nor shall his title to the shares be affected by any irregularity in or invalidity of the proceedings in reference to the sale.

34. Subject to the provisions of the Act, the company may by special resolution reduce its share capital, any capital redemption reserve and any share premium account in any way.

PURCHASE OF OWN SHARES

35. Subject to the provisions of the Act, the company may purchase its own shares (including any redeemable shares) and, if it is a private company, make a payment in respect of the redemption or purchase of its own shares otherwise than out of distributable profits of the company or the proceeds of a fresh issue of shares.

GENERAL MEETINGS

36. All general meetings other than annual general meetings shall be called extraordinary general meetings.

37. The directors may call general meetings and, on the requisition of members pursuant to the provisions of the Act, shall forthwith proceed to convene an extraordinary general meeting for a date not later than eight weeks after receipt of the requisition. If there are not within the United Kingdom sufficient directors to call a general meeting, any director or any member of the company may call a general meeting.

NOTICE OF GENERAL MEETINGS

38. An annual general meeting and an extraordinary general meeting called for the passing of a special resolution or a resolution appointing a person as a director shall be called by at least 21 clear days' notice. All other extraordinary general meetings shall be called by at least 14 clear days' notice but a general meeting may be called by shorter notice if it is so agreed—

(a) in the case of an annual general meeting, by all the members entitled to attend and vote thereat; and

(b) in the case of any other meeting by a majority in number of the members having a right to attend and vote being a majority together holding not less than 95 per cent. in nominal value of the shares giving that right.

The notice shall specify the time and place of the meeting and the general nature of the business to be transacted and, in the case of an annual general meeting, shall specify the meeting as such.

Subject to the provisions of the articles and to any restrictions imposed on any shares, the notice shall be given to all the members, to all persons entitled to a share in consequence of the death or bankruptcy of a member and to the directors and auditors.

39. The accidental omission to give notice of a meeting to, or the non-receipt of notice of a meeting by, any person entitled to receive notice shall not invalidate the proceedings at that meeting.

PROCEEDINGS AT GENERAL MEETINGS

40. No business shall be transacted at any meeting unless a quorum is present. Two persons entitled to vote upon the business to be transacted, each being a member or a proxy for a member or a duly authorised representative of a corporation, shall be a quorum.

41. If such a quorum is not present within half an hour from the time appointed for the meeting, or if during a meeting such a quorum ceases to be present, the meeting shall stand adjourned to the same day in the next week at the same time and place or such time and place as the directors may determine.

42. The chairman, if any, of the board of directors or in his absence some other director nominated by the directors shall preside as chairman of the meeting, but if neither the chairman nor such other director (if any) be present within 15 minutes after the time appointed for holding the meeting and willing to act, the directors present shall elect one of their number to be chairman and, if there is only one director present and willing to act, he shall be chairman.

43. If no director is willing to act as chairman, or if no director is present within 15 minutes after the time appointed for holding the meeting, the members present and entitled to vote shall choose one of their number to be chairman.

44. A director shall, notwithstanding that he is not a member, be entitled to attend and speak at any general meeting and at any separate meeting of the holders of any class of shares in the company.

45. The chairman may, with the consent of a meeting at which a quorum is present (and shall if so directed by the meeting), adjourn the meeting from time to time and from place to place, but no business shall be transacted at an adjourned meeting other than business which might properly have been transacted at the meeting had the adjournment not taken place. When a meeting is adjourned for 14 days or more, at least seven clear days' notice shall be given specifying the time and place of the adjourned meeting and the general nature of the business to be transacted. Otherwise it shall not be necessary to give any such notice.

46. A resolution put to the vote of a meeting shall be decided on a show of hands unless before, or on the declaration of the result of, the show of hands a poll is duly demanded. Subject to the provisions of the Act, a poll may be demanded—

(a) by the chairman; or

(*b*) by at least two members having the right to vote at the meeting; or

(*c*) by a member or members representing not less than one-tenth of the total voting rights of all the members having the right to vote at the meeting; or

(*d*) by a member or members holding shares conferring a right to vote at the meeting being shares on which an aggregate sum has been paid up equal to not less than one-tenth of the total sum paid up on all the shares conferring that right;

and a demand by a person as proxy for a member shall be the same as a demand by the member.

47. Unless a poll is duly demanded a declaration by the chairman that a resolution has been carried or carried unanimously, or by a particular majority, or lost, or not carried by a particular majority and an entry to that effect in the minutes of the meeting shall be conclusive evidence of the fact without proof of the number or proportion of the votes recorded in favour of or against the resolution.

48. The demand for a poll may, before the poll is taken, be withdrawn but only with the consent of the chairman and a demand so withdrawn shall not be taken to have invalidated the result of a show of hands declared before the demand was made.

49. A poll shall be taken as the chairman directs and he may appoint scrutineers (who need not be members) and fix a time and place for declaring the result of the poll. The result of the poll shall be deemed to be the resolution of the meeting at which the poll was demanded.

50. In the case of an equality of votes, whether on a show of hands or on a poll, the chairman shall be entitled to a casting vote in addition to any other vote he may have.

51. A poll demanded on the election of a chairman or on a question of adjournment shall be taken forthwith. A poll demanded on any other question shall be taken either forthwith or at such time and place as the chairman directs not being more than 30 days after the poll is demanded. The demand for a poll shall not prevent the continuance of a meeting for the transaction of any business other than the question on which the poll was demanded. If a poll is demanded before the declaration of the result of a show of hands and the demand is duly withdrawn, the meeting shall continue as if the demand had not been made.

52. No notice need be given of a poll not taken forthwith if the time and place at which it is to be taken are announced at the meeting at which it is demanded. In any other case at least seven clear days' notice shall be given specifying the time and place at which the poll is to be taken.

53. A resolution in writing executed by or on behalf of each member who would have been entitled to vote upon it if it had been proposed at a general meeting at which he was present shall be as effectual as if it had been passed at a general meeting duly convened and held and may consist of several instruments in the like form each executed by or on behalf of one or more members.

VOTES OF MEMBERS

54. Subject to any rights or restrictions attached to any shares, on a show of hands every member who (being an individual) is present in person or (being a corporation) is present by a duly authorised representative, not being himself a member entitled to vote, shall have one vote and on a poll every member shall have one vote for every share of which he is the holder.

55. In the case of joint holders the vote of the senior who tenders a vote, whether in person or by proxy, shall be accepted to the exclusion of the votes of the other joint holders; and seniority shall be determined by the order in which the names of the holders stand in the register of members.

56. A member in respect of whom an order has been made by any court having jurisdiction (whether in the United Kingdom or elsewhere) in matters concerning mental disorder may vote, whether on a show of hands or on a poll, by his receiver, *curator bonis* or other person authorised in that behalf appointed by that court, and any such receiver, *curator bonis* or other person may, on a poll, vote by proxy. Evidence to the satisfaction of the directors of the authority of the person claiming to exercise the right to vote shall be deposited at the office, or at such other place as is specified in accordance with the articles for the deposit of instruments of proxy, not less than 48 hours before the time appointed for holding the meeting or adjourned meeting at which the right to vote is to be exercised and in default the right to vote shall not be exercisable.

57. No member shall vote at any general meeting or at any separate meeting of the holders of any class of shares in the company, either in person or by proxy, in respect of any share held by him unless all moneys presently payable by him in respect of that share have been paid.

58. No objection shall be raised to the qualification of any voter except at the meeting or adjourned meeting at which the vote objected to is tendered, and every vote not disallowed at the meeting shall be valid. Any objection made in due time shall be referred to the chairman whose decision shall be final and conclusive.

59. On a poll votes may be given either personally or by proxy. A member may appoint more than one proxy to attend on the same occasion.

60. An instrument appointing a proxy shall be in writing, executed by or on behalf of the appointor and shall be in the following form (or in a form as near thereto as circumstances allow or in any other form which is usual or which the directors may approve)—

"   PLC/Limited

          I/We,   , of
                                                              , being a
member/members of the above-named company, hereby appoint
                                         of
                                 , or failing him,
      of   , as my/our proxy to vote in my/our name[s] and on my/our behalf at
      the   annual/extraordinary   general   meeting   of   the   company   to   be   held
      on   19   , and at any adjournment thereof.
      Signed on   19   ."

61. Where it is desired to afford members an opportunity of instructing the proxy how he shall act the instrument appointing a proxy shall be in the following form (or in a form as near thereto as circumstances allow or in any other form which is usual or which the directors may approve)—

"   PLC/Limited
          I/We,   , of
                                                              , being a
member/members of the above-named company, hereby appoint
                                         of
                                 , or failing him
      of   , as my/our proxy to vote in my/our name[s] and on my/our behalf at
      the   annual/extraordinary   general   meeting   of   the   company,   to   be   held
      on   19   , and at any adjournment thereof.

This form is to be used in respect of the resolutions mentioned below as follows:

      Resolution No. 1 *for *against
      Resolution No. 2 *for *against.

*Strike out whichever is not desired.

Unless otherwise instructed, the proxy may vote as he thinks fit or abstain from voting.

Signed this   day of   19   ."

62. The instrument appointing a proxy and any authority under which it is executed or a copy of such authority certified notarially or in some other way approved by the directors may—

    (a) be deposited at the office or at such other place within the United Kingdom as is specified in the notice convening the meeting or in any instrument of proxy sent out by the company in relation to the meeting not less than 48 hours before the time for holding the meeting or adjourned meeting at which the person named in the instrument proposes to vote; or

    (b) in the case of a poll taken more than 48 hours after it is demanded, be deposited as aforesaid after the poll has been demanded and not less than 24 hours before the time appointed for the taking of the poll; or

    (c) where the poll is not taken forthwith but is taken not more than 48 hours after it was demanded, be delivered at the meeting at which the poll was demanded to the chairman or to the secretary or to any director;

and an instrument of proxy which is not deposited or delivered in a manner so permitted shall be invalid.

63. A vote given or poll demanded by proxy or by the duly authorised representative of a corporation shall be valid notwithstanding the previous determination of the authority of the person voting or demanding a poll unless notice of the determination was received by the company at the office or at such other place at which the instrument of proxy was duly

deposited before the commencement of the meeting or adjourned meeting at which the vote is given or the poll demanded or (in the case of a poll taken otherwise than on the same day as the meeting or adjourned meeting) the time appointed for taking the poll.

NUMBER OF DIRECTORS

64. Unless otherwise determined by ordinary resolution, the number of directors (other than alternate directors) shall not be subject to any maximum but shall be not less than two.

ALTERNATE DIRECTORS

65. Any director (other than an alternate director) may appoint any other director, or any other person approved by resolution of the directors and willing to act, to be an alternate director and may remove from office an alternate director so appointed by him.

66. An alternate director shall be entitled to receive notice of all meetings of directors and of all meetings of committees of directors of which his appointor is a member, to attend and vote at any such meeting at which the director appointing him is not personally present, and generally to perform all the functions of his appointor as a director in his absence but shall not be entitled to receive any remuneration from the company for his services as an alternate director. But it shall not be necessary to give notice of such a meeting to an alternate director who is absent from the United Kingdom.

67. An alternate director shall cease to be an alternate director if his appointor ceases to be a director; but, if a director retires by rotation or otherwise but is reappointed or deemed to have been reappointed at the meeting at which he retires, any appointment of an alternate director made by him which was in force immediately prior to his retirement shall continue after his reappointment.

68. Any appointment or removal of an alternate director shall be by notice to the company signed by the director making or revoking the appointment or in any other manner approved by the directors.

69. Save as otherwise provided in the articles, an alternate director shall be deemed for all purposes to be a director and shall alone be responsible for his own acts and defaults and he shall not be deemed to be the agent of the director appointing him.

POWERS OF DIRECTORS

70. Subject to the provisions of the Act, the memorandum and the articles and to any directions given by special resolution, the business of the company shall be managed by the directors who may exercise all the powers of the company. No alteration of the memorandum or articles and no such direction shall invalidate any prior act of the directors which would have been valid if that alteration had not been made or that direction had not been given. The powers given by this regulation shall not be limited by any special power given to the directors by the articles and a meeting of directors at which a quorum is present may exercise all powers exercisable by the directors.

71. The directors may, by power of attorney or otherwise, appoint any person to be the agent of the company for such purposes and on such conditions as they determine, including authority for the agent to delegate all or any of his powers.

DELEGATION OF DIRECTORS' POWERS

72. The directors may delegate any of their powers to any committee consisting of one or more directors. They may also delegate to any managing director or any director holding any other executive office such of their powers as they consider desirable to be exercised by him. Any such delegation may be made subject to any conditions the directors may impose, and either collaterally with or to the exclusion of their own powers and may be revoked or altered. Subject to any such conditions, the proceedings of a committee with two or more members shall be governed by the articles regulating the proceedings of directors so far as they are capable of applying.

APPOINTMENT AND RETIREMENT OF DIRECTORS

73. At the first annual general meeting all the directors shall retire from office, and at every subsequent annual general meeting one-third of the directors who are subject to retirement by rotation or, if their number is not three or a multiple of three, the number nearest to one-third shall retire from office; but, if there is only one director who is subject to retirement by rotation, he shall retire.

74. Subject to the provisions of the Act, the directors to retire by rotation shall be those who have been longest in office since their last appointment or reappointment, but as between persons who became or were last reappointed directors on the same day those to retire shall (unless they otherwise agree among themselves) be determined by lot.

75. If the company, at the meeting at which a director retires by rotation, does not fill the vacancy the retiring director shall, if willing to act, be deemed to have been reappointed unless at the meeting it is resolved not to fill the vacancy or unless a resolution for the reappointment of the director is put to the meeting and lost.

76. No person other than a director retiring by rotation shall be appointed or reappointed a director at any general meeting unless—
    (*a*) he is recommended by the directors; or
    (*b*) not less than 14 nor more than 35 clear days before the date appointed for the meeting, notice executed by a member qualified to vote at the meeting has been given to the company of the intention to propose that person for appointment or reappointment stating the particulars which would, if he were so appointed or reappointed, be required to be included in the company's register of directors together with notice executed by that person of his willingness to be appointed or reappointed.

77. Not less than seven nor more than 28 clear days before the date appointed for holding a general meeting notice shall be given to all who are entitled to receive notice of the meeting of any person (other than a director retiring by rotation at the meeting) who is recommended by the directors for appointment or reappointment as a director at the meeting or in respect of whom notice has been duly given to the company of the intention to propose him at the meeting for appointment or reappointment as a director. The notice shall give the particulars of that person which would, if he were so appointed or reappointed, be required to be included in the company's register of directors.

78. Subject as aforesaid, the company may by ordinary resolution appoint a person who is willing to act to be a director either to fill a vacancy or as an additional director and may also determine the rotation in which any additional directors are to retire.

79. The directors may appoint a person who is willing to act to be a director, either to fill a vacancy or as an additional director, provided that the appointment does not cause the number of directors to exceed any number fixed by or in accordance with the articles as the maximum number of directors. A director so appointed shall hold office only until the next following annual general meeting and shall not be taken into account in determining the directors who are to retire by rotation at the meeting. If not reappointed at such annual general meeting, he shall vacate office at the conclusion thereof.

80. Subject as aforesaid, a director who retires at an annual general meeting may, if willing to act, be reappointed. If he is not reappointed, he shall retain office until the meeting appoints someone in his place, or if it does not do so, until the end of the meeting.

DISQUALIFICATION AND REMOVAL OF DIRECTORS

81. The office of a director shall be vacated if—
    (*a*) he ceases to be a director by virtue of any provision of the Act or he becomes prohibited by law from being a director; or
    (*b*) he becomes bankrupt or makes any arrangement or composition with his creditors generally; or
    (*c*) he is, or may be, suffering from mental disorder and either—
        (i) he is admitted to hospital in pursuance of an application for admission for treatment under the Mental Health Act 1983 or, in Scotland, an application for admission under the Mental Health (Scotland) Act 1960, or
        (ii) an order is made by a court having jurisdiction (whether in the United Kingdom or elsewhere) in matters concerning mental disorder for his detention or for the appointment of a receiver, *curator bonis* or other person to exercise powers with respect to his property or affairs; or
    (*d*) he resigns his office by notice to the company; or
    (*e*) he shall for more than six consecutive months have been absent without permission of the directors from meetings of directors held during that period and the directors resolve that his office be vacated.

REMUNERATION OF DIRECTORS

82. The directors shall be entitled to such remuneration as the company may by ordinary resolution determine and, unless the resolution provides otherwise, the remuneration shall be deemed to accrue from day to day.

DIRECTORS' EXPENSES

83. The directors may be paid all travelling, hotel, and other expenses properly incurred by them in connection with their attendance at meetings of directors or committees of directors or general meetings or separate meetings of the holders of any class of shares or of debentures of the company or otherwise in connection with the discharge of their duties.

DIRECTORS' APPOINTMENTS AND INTERESTS

84. Subject to the provisions of the Act, the directors may appoint one or more of their number to the office of managing director or to any other executive office under the company and may enter into an agreement or arrangement with any director for his employment by the company or for the provision by him of any services outside the scope of the ordinary duties of a director. Any such appointment, agreement or arrangement may be made upon such terms as the directors determine and they may remunerate any such director for his services as they think fit. Any appointment of a director to an executive office shall terminate if he ceases to be a director but without prejudice to any claim to damages for breach of the contract of service between the director and the company. A managing director and a director holding any other executive office shall not be subject to retirement by rotation.

85. Subject to the provisions of the Act, and provided that he has disclosed to the directors the nature and extent of any material interest of his, a director notwithstanding his office—
   (a) may be a party to, or otherwise interested in, any transaction or arrangement with the company or in which the company is otherwise interested;
   (b) may be a director or other officer of, or employed by, or a party to any transaction or arrangement with, or otherwise interested in, any body corporate promoted by the company or in which the company is otherwise interested; and
   (c) shall not, by reason of his office, be accountable to the company for any benefit which he derives from any such office or employment or from any such transaction or arrangement or from any interest in any such body corporate and no such transaction or arrangement shall be liable to be avoided on the ground of any such interest or benefit.

86. For the purposes of regulation 85—
   (a) a general notice given to the directors that a director is to be regarded as having an interest of the nature and extent specified in the notice in any transaction or arrangement in which a specified person or class of persons is interested shall be deemed to be a disclosure that the director has an interest in any such transaction of the nature and extent so specified; and
   (b) an interest of which a director has no knowledge and of which it is unreasonable to expect him to have knowledge shall not be treated as an interest of his.

DIRECTORS' GRATUITIES AND PENSIONS

87. The directors may provide benefits, whether by the payment of gratuities or pensions or by insurance or otherwise, for any director who has held but no longer holds any executive office or employment with the company or with any body corporate which is or has been a subsidiary of the company or a predecessor in business of the company or of any such subsidiary, and for any member of his family (including a spouse and a former spouse) or any person who is or was dependent on him, and may (as well before as after he ceases to hold such office or employment) contribute to any fund and pay premiums for the purchase or provision of any such benefit.

PROCEEDINGS OF DIRECTORS

88. Subject to the provisions of the articles, the directors may regulate their proceedings as they think fit. A director may, and the secretary at the request of a director shall, call a meeting of the directors. It shall not be necessary to give notice of a meeting to a director who is absent from the United Kingdom. Questions arising at a meeting shall be decided by a majority of votes. In the case of an equality of votes, the chairman shall have a second or casting vote. A director who is also an alternate director shall be entitled in the absence of his appointor to a separate vote on behalf of his appointor in addition to his own vote.

89. The quorum for the transaction of the business of the directors may be fixed by the directors and unless so fixed at any other number shall be two. A person who holds office only as an alternate director shall, if his appointor is not present, be counted in the quorum.

90. The continuing directors or a sole continuing director may act notwithstanding any vacancies in their number, but, if the number of directors is less than the number fixed as the quorum, the continuing directors or director may act only for the purpose of filling vacancies or of calling a general meeting.

91. The directors may appoint one of their number to be the chairman of the board of directors and may at any time remove him from that office. Unless he is unwilling to do so, the director so appointed shall preside at every meeting of directors at which he is present. But if there is no director holding that office, or if the director holding it is unwilling to preside or is not present within five minutes after the time appointed for the meeting, the directors present may appoint one of their number to be chairman of the meeting.

92. All acts done by a meeting of directors, or of a committee of directors, or by a person acting as a director shall, notwithstanding that it be afterwards discovered that there was a defect in the appointment of any director or that any of them were disqualified from holding office, or had vacated office, or were not entitled to vote, be as valid as if every such person had been duly appointed and was qualified and had continued to be a director and had been entitled to vote.

93. A resolution in writing signed by all the directors entitled to receive notice of a meeting of directors or of a committee of directors shall be as valid and effectual as if it had been passed at a meeting of directors or (as the case may be) a committee of directors duly convened and held and may consist of several documents in the like form each signed by one or more directors; but a resolution signed by an alternate director need not also be signed by his appointor and, if it is signed by a director who has appointed an alternate director, it need not be signed by the alternate director in that capacity.

94. Save as otherwise provided by the articles, a director shall not vote at a meeting of directors or of a committee of directors on any resolution concerning a matter in which he has, directly or indirectly, an interest or duty which is material and which conflicts or may conflict with the interests of the company unless his interest or duty arises only because the case falls within one or more of the following paragraphs—

    (*a*)   the resolution relates to the giving to him of a guarantee, security, or indemnity in respect of money lent to, or an obligation incurred by him for the benefit of, the company or any of its subsidiaries;

    (*b*)   the resolution relates to the giving to a third party of a guarantee, security, or indemnity in respect of an obligation of the company or any of its subsidiaries for which the director has assumed responsibility in whole or part and whether alone or jointly with others under a guarantee or indemnity or by the giving of security;

    (*c*)   his interest arises by virtue of his subscribing or agreeing to subscribe for any shares, debentures or other securities of the company or any of its subsidiaries, or by virtue of his being, or intending to become, a participant in the underwriting or sub-underwriting of an offer of any such shares, debentures, or other securities by the company or any of its subsidiaries for subscription, purchase or exchange;

    (*d*)   the resolution relates in any way to a retirement benefits scheme which has been approved, or is conditional upon approval, by the Board of Inland Revenue for taxation purposes.

For the purposes of this regulation, an interest of a person who is, for any purpose of the Act (excluding any statutory modification thereof not in force when this regulation becomes binding on the company), connected with a director shall be treated as an interest of the director and, in relation to an alternate director, an interest of his appointor shall be treated as an interest of the alternate director without prejudice to any interest which the alternate director has otherwise.

95. A director shall not be counted in the quorum present at a meeting in relation to a resolution on which he is not entitled to vote.

96. The company may by ordinary resolution suspend or relax to any extent, either generally or in respect of any particular matter, any provision of the articles prohibiting a director from voting at a meeting of directors or of a committee of directors.

97. Where proposals are under consideration concerning the appointment of two or more directors to offices or employments with the company or any body corporate in which the company is interested the proposals may be divided and considered in relation to each director separately and (provided he is not for another reason precluded from voting) each of the

directors concerned shall be entitled to vote and be counted in the quorum in respect of each resolution except that concerning his own appointment.

98. If a question arises at a meeting of directors or of a committee of directors as to the right of a director to vote, the question may, before the conclusion of the meeting, be referred to the chairman of the meeting and his ruling in relation to any director other than himself shall be final and conclusive.

SECRETARY

99. Subject to the provisions of the Act, the secretary shall be appointed by the directors for such term, at such remuneration and upon such conditions as they may think fit; and any secretary so appointed may be removed by them.

MINUTES

100. The directors shall cause minutes to be made in books kept for the purpose—
 (a) of all appointments of officers made by the directors; and
 (b) of all proceedings at meetings of the company, of the holders of any class of shares in the company, and of the directors, and of committees of directors, including the names of the directors present at each such meeting.

THE SEAL

101. The seal shall only be used by the authority of the directors or of a committee of directors authorised by the directors. The directors may determine who shall sign any instrument to which the seal is affixed and unless otherwise so determined it shall be signed by a director and by the secretary or by a second director.

DIVIDENDS

102. Subject to the provisions of the Act, the company may by ordinary resolution declare dividends in accordance with the respective rights of the members, but no dividend shall exceed the amount recommended by the directors.

103. Subject to the provisions of the Act, the directors may pay interim dividends if it appears to them that they are justified by the profits of the company available for distribution. If the share capital is divided into different classes, the directors may pay interim dividends on shares which confer deferred or non-preferred rights with regard to dividend as well as on shares which confer preferential rights with regard to dividend, but no interim dividend shall be paid on shares carrying deferred or non-preferred rights if, at the time of payment, any preferential dividend is in arrear. The directors may also pay at intervals settled by them any dividend payable at a fixed rate if it appears to them that the profits available for distribution justify the payment. Provided the directors act in good faith they shall not incur any liability to the holders of shares conferring preferred rights for any loss they may suffer by the lawful payment of an interim dividend on any shares having deferred or non-preferred rights.

104. Except as otherwise provided by the rights attached to shares, all dividends shall be declared and paid according to the amounts paid up on the shares on which the dividend is paid. All dividends shall be apportioned and paid proportionately to the amounts paid up on the shares during any portion or portions of the period in respect of which the dividend is paid; but, if any share is issued on terms providing that it shall rank for dividend as from a particular date, that share shall rank for dividend accordingly.

105. A general meeting declaring a dividend may, upon the recommendation of the directors, direct that it shall be satisfied wholly or partly by the distribution of assets and, where any difficulty arises in regard to the distribution, the directors may settle the same and in particular may issue fractional certificates and fix the value for distribution of any assets and may determine that cash shall be paid to any member upon the footing of the value so fixed in order to adjust the rights of members and may vest any assets in trustees.

106. Any dividend or other moneys payable in respect of a share may be paid by cheque sent by post to the registered address of the person entitled or, if two or more persons are the holders of the share or are jointly entitled to it by reason of the death or bankruptcy of the holder, to the registered address of that one of those persons who is first named in the register of members or to such person and to such address as the person or persons entitled may in writing direct. Every cheque shall be made payable to the order of the person or persons entitled or to such other person as the person or persons entitled may in writing direct and

payment of the cheque shall be a good discharge to the company. Any joint holder or other person jointly entitled to a share as aforesaid may give receipts for any dividend or other moneys payable in respect of the share.

107. No dividend or other moneys payable in respect of a share shall bear interest against the company unless otherwise provided by the rights attached to the share.

108. Any dividend which has remained unclaimed for 12 years from the date when it became due for payment shall, if the directors so resolve, be forfeited and cease to remain owing by the company.

ACCOUNTS

109. No member shall (as such) have any right of inspecting any accounting records or other book or document of the company except as conferred by statute or authorised by the directors or by ordinary resolution of the company.

CAPITALISATION OF PROFITS

110. The directors may with the authority of an ordinary resolution of the company—
   (*a*) subject as hereinafter provided, resolve to capitalise any undivided profits of the company not required for paying any preferential dividend (whether or not they are available for distribution) or any sum standing to the credit of the company's share premium account or capital redemption reserve;
   (*b*) appropriate the sum resolved to be capitalised to the members who would have been entitled to it if it were distributed by way of dividend and in the same proportions and apply such sum on their behalf either in or towards paying up the amounts, if any, for the time being unpaid on any shares held by them respectively, or in paying up in full unissued shares or debentures of the company of a nominal amount equal to that sum, and allot the shares or debentures credited as fully paid to those members, or as they may direct, in those proportions, or partly in one way and partly in the other: but the share premium account, the capital redemption reserve, and any profits which are not available for distribution may, for the purposes of this regulation, only be applied in paying up unissued shares to be allotted to members credited as fully paid;
   (*c*) make such provision by the issue of fractional certificates or by payment in cash or otherwise as they determine in the case of shares or debentures becoming distributable under this regulation in fractions; and
   (*d*) authorise any person to enter on behalf of all the members concerned into an agreement with the company providing for the allotment to them respectively, credited as fully paid, of any shares or debentures to which they are entitled upon such capitalisation, any agreement made under such authority being binding on all such members.

NOTICES

111. Any notice to be given to or by any person pursuant to the articles shall be in writing except that a notice calling a meeting of the directors need not be in writing.

112. The company may give any notice to a member either personally or by sending it by post in a prepaid envelope addressed to the member at his registered address or by leaving it at that address. In the case of joint holders of a share, all notices shall be given to the joint holder whose name stands first in the register of members in respect of the joint holding and notice so given shall be sufficient notice to all the joint holders. A member whose registered address is not within the United Kingdom and who gives to the company an address within the United Kingdom at which notices may be given to him shall be entitled to have notices given to him at that address, but otherwise no such member shall be entitled to receive any notice from the company.

113. A member present, either in person or by proxy, at any meeting of the company or of the holders of any class of shares in the company shall be deemed to have received notice of the meeting and, where requisite, of the purposes for which it was called.

114. Every person who becomes entitled to a share shall be bound by any notice in respect of that share which, before his name is entered in the register of members, has been duly given to a person from whom he derives his title.

115. Proof that an envelope containing a notice was properly addressed, prepaid and posted shall be conclusive evidence that the notice was given. A notice shall, unless the contrary is proved, be deemed to be given at the expiration of 48 hours after the envelope containing it was posted.

116. A notice may be given by the company to the persons entitled to a share in consequence of the death or bankruptcy of a member by sending or delivering it, in any manner authorised by the articles for the giving of notice to a member, addressed to them by name, or by the title of representatives of the deceased, or trustee of the bankrupt or by any like description at the address, if any, within the United Kingdom supplied for that purpose by the persons claiming to be so entitled. Until such an address has been supplied, a notice may be given in any manner in which it might have been given if the death or bankruptcy had not occurred.

WINDING UP

117. If the company is wound up, the liquidator may, with the sanction of an extraordinary resolution of the company and any other sanction required by the Act, divide among the members *in specie* the whole or any part of the assets of the company and may, for that purpose, value any assets and determine how the division shall be carried out as between the members or different classes of members. The liquidator may, with the like sanction, vest the whole or any part of the assets in trustees upon such trusts for the benefit of the members as he with the like sanction determines, but no member shall be compelled to accept any assets upon which there is a liability.

INDEMNITY

118. Subject to the provisions of the Act but without prejudice to any indemnity to which a director may otherwise be entitled, every director or other officer or auditor of the company shall be indemnified out of the assets of the company against any liability incurred by him in defending any proceedings, whether civil or criminal, in which judgment is given in his favour or in which he is acquitted or in connection with any application in which relief is granted to him by the court from liability for negligence, default, breach of duty or breach of trust in relation to the affairs of the company.

TABLE B

A PRIVATE COMPANY LIMITED BY SHARES

MEMORANDUM OF ASSOCIATION

1. The company's name is "The South Wales Motor Transport Company cyfyngedig".

2. The company's registered office is to be situated in Wales.

3. The company's objects are the carriage of passengers and goods in motor vehicles between such places as the company may from time to time determine and the doing of all such other things as are incidental or conducive to the attainment of that object.

4. The liability of the members is limited.

5. The company's share capital is £50,000 divided into 50,000 shares of £1 each.

We, the subscribers to this memorandum of association, wish to be formed into a company pursuant to this memorandum; and we agree to take the number of shares shown opposite our respective names.

Names and Addresses of Subscribers	Number of shares taken by each Subscriber
1. Thomas Jones, 138 Mountfield Street, Tredegar.	1
2. Mary Evans, 19 Merthyr Road, Aberystwyth.	1
Total shares taken	2

Dated   19 .

Witness to the above signatures,
Anne Brown, "Woodlands", Fieldside Road, Bryn Mawr.

TABLE C

A COMPANY LIMITED BY GUARANTEE AND NOT HAVING A SHARE CAPITAL

MEMORANDUM OF ASSOCIATION

1. The company's name is "The Dundee School Association Limited".

2. The company's registered office is to be situated in Scotland.

3. The company's objects are the carrying on of a school for boys and girls in Dundee and the doing of all such other things as are incidental or conducive to the attainment of that object.

4. The liability of the members is limited.

5. Every member of the company undertakes to contribute such amount as may be required (not exceeding £100) to the company's assets if it should be wound up while he is a member or within one year after he ceases to be a member, for payment of the company's debts and liabilities contracted before he ceases to be a member, and of the costs, charges and expenses of winding up, and for the adjustment of the rights of the contributories among themselves.

We, the subscribers to this memorandum of association, wish to be formed into a company pursuant to this memorandum.

Names and Addresses of Subscribers.

1. Kenneth Brodie, 14 Bute Street, Dundee.
2. Ian Davis, 2 Burns Avenue, Dundee.

Dated   19   .

Witness to the above signatures,
Anne Brown, 149 Princes Street, Edinburgh.

ARTICLES OF ASSOCIATION

PRELIMINARY

1. Regulations 2 to 35 inclusive, 54, 55, 57, 59, 102 to 108 inclusive, 110, 114, 116 and 117 of Table A, shall not apply to the company but the articles hereinafter contained and, subject to the modifications hereinafter expressed, the remaining regulations of Table A shall constitute the articles of association of the company.

INTERPRETATION

2. In regulation 1 of Table A, the definition of "the holder" shall be omitted.

MEMBERS

3. The subscribers to the memorandum of association of the company and such other persons as are admitted to membership in accordance with the articles shall be members of the company. No person shall be admitted a member of the company unless he is approved by the directors. Every person who wishes to become a member shall deliver to the company an application for membership in such form as the directors require executed by him.

4. A member may at any time withdraw from the company by giving at least seven clear days' notice to the company. Membership shall not be transferable and shall cease on death.

NOTICE OF GENERAL MEETINGS

5. In regulation 38 of Table A—
    (*a*) in paragraph (*b*) the words "of the total voting rights at the meeting of all the members" shall be substituted for "in nominal value of the shares giving that right" and
    (*b*) the words "The notice shall be given to all the members and to the directors and auditors" shall be substituted for the last sentence.

PROCEEDINGS AT GENERAL MEETINGS

6. The words "and at any separate meeting of the holders of any class of shares in the company" shall be omitted from regulation 44 of Table A.

7. Paragraph (*d*) of regulation 46 of Table A shall be omitted.

VOTES OF MEMBERS

8. On a show of hands every member present in person shall have one vote. On a poll every member present in person or by proxy shall have one vote.

DIRECTORS' EXPENSES

9. The words "of any class of shares or" shall be omitted from regulation 83 of Table A.

PROCEEDINGS OF DIRECTORS

10. In paragraph (*c*) of regulation 94 of Table A the word "debentures" shall be substituted for the words "shares, debentures or other securities" in both places where they occur.

MINUTES

11. The words "of the holders of any class of shares in the company" shall be omitted from regulation 100 of Table A.

NOTICES

12. The second sentence of regulation 112 of Table A shall be omitted.

13. The words "or of the holders of any class of shares in the company" shall be omitted from regulation 113 of Table A.

TABLE D

PART I

A PUBLIC COMPANY LIMITED BY GUARANTEE AND HAVING A SHARE CAPITAL

MEMORANDUM OF ASSOCIATION

1. The company's name is "Gwestai Glyndwr, cwmni cyfyngedig cyhoeddus".

2. The company is to be a public company.

3. The company's registered office is to be situated in Wales.

4. The company's objects are facilitating travelling in Wales by providing hotels and conveyances by sea and by land for the accommodation of travellers and the doing of all such other things as are incidental or conducive to the attainment of those objects.

5. The liability of the members is limited.

6. Every member of the company undertakes to contribute such amount as may be required (not exceeding £100) to the company's assets if it should be wound up while he is a member or within one year after he ceases to be a member, for payment of the company's debts and liabilities contracted before he ceases to be a member, and of the costs, charges and expenses of winding up, and for the adjustment of the rights of the contributories among themselves.

7. The company's share capital is £50,000 divided into 50,000 shares of £1 each.

We, the subscribers to this memorandum of association, wish to be formed into a company pursuant to this memorandum; and we agree to take the number of shares shown opposite our respective names.

Names and Addresses of Subscribers	Number of shares taken by each Subscriber
1. Thomas Jones, 138 Mountfield Street, Tredegar.	1
2. Andrew Smith, 19 Merthyr Road, Aberystwyth.	1
Total shares taken	2

Dated   19   .

Witness to the above signatures,
Anne Brown, "Woodlands", Fieldside Road, Bryn Mawr.

PART II

A PRIVATE COMPANY LIMITED BY GUARANTEE AND HAVING A SHARE CAPITAL

MEMORANDUM OF ASSOCIATION

1. The company's name is "The Highland Hotel Company Limited".

2. The company's registered office is to be situated in Scotland.

3. The company's objects are facilitating travelling in the Highlands of Scotland by providing hotels and conveyances by sea and by land for the accommodation of travellers and the doing of all such other things as are incidental or conducive to the attainment of those objects.

4. The liability of the members is limited.

5. Every member of the company undertakes to contribute such amount as may be required (not exceeding £100) to the company's assets if it should be wound up while he is a member or within one year after he ceases to be a member, for payment of the company's debts and liabilities contracted before he ceases to be a member, and of the costs, charges and expenses of winding up, and for the adjustment of the rights of the contributories among themselves.

6. The company's share capital is £50,000 divided into 50,000 shares of £1 each.

We, the subscribers to this memorandum of association, wish to be formed into a company pursuant to this memorandum; and we agree to take the number of shares shown opposite our respective names.

Names and Addresses of Subscribers	Number of shares taken by each Subscriber
1. Kenneth Brodie, 14 Bute Street, Dundee	1
2. Ian Davis, 2 Burns Avenue, Dundee.	1
Total shares taken	2

Dated   19   .

Witness to the above signatures,
Anne Brown, 149 Princes Street, Edinburgh.

PART III

A COMPANY (PUBLIC OR PRIVATE) LIMITED BY GUARANTEE AND HAVING A SHARE CAPITAL

ARTICLES OF ASSOCIATION

The regulations of Table A shall constitute the articles of association of the company.

TABLE E

AN UNLIMITED COMPANY HAVING A SHARE CAPITAL

MEMORANDUM OF ASSOCIATION

1. The company's name is "The Woodford Engineering Company".

2. The company's registered office is to be situated in England and Wales.

3. The company's objects are the working of certain patented inventions relating to the application of microchip technology to the improvement of food processing, and the doing of all such other things as are incidental or conducive to the attainment of that object.

We, the subscribers to this memorandum of association, wish to be formed into a company pursuant to this memorandum; and we agree to take the number of shares shown opposite our respective names.

Names and Addresses of Subscribers	Number of shares taken by each Subscriber
1. Brian Smith, 24 Nibley Road, Wotton-under-Edge, Gloucestershire.	3
2. William Green, 278 High Street, Chipping Sodbury, Avon.	5
Total shares taken	8

Dated   19 .

Witness to the above signatures,
Anne Brown, 108 Park Way, Bristol 8.

ARTICLES OF ASSOCIATION

1. Regulations 3, 32, 34 and 35 of Table A shall not apply to the company, but the articles hereinafter contained and, subject to the modification hereinafter expressed, the remaining regulations of Table A shall constitute the articles of association of the company.

2. The words "at least seven clear days' notice" shall be substituted for the words "at least 14 clear days' notice" in regulation 38 of Table A.

3. The share capital of the company is £20,000 divided into 20,000 shares of £1 each.

4. The company may by special resolution—
   (*a*) increase the share capital by such sum to be divided into shares of such amount as the resolution may prescribe;
   (*b*) consolidate and divide all or any of its share capital into shares of a larger amount than its existing shares;
   (*c*) subdivide its shares, or any of them, into shares of a smaller amount than its existing shares;
   (*d*) cancel any shares which at the date of the passing of the resolution have not been taken or agreed to be taken by any person;
   (*e*) reduce its share capital and any share premium account in any way.

TABLE F

A PUBLIC COMPANY LIMITED BY SHARES

MEMORANDUM OF ASSOCIATION

1. The company's name is "Western Electronics Public Limited Company".

2. The company is to be a public company.

3. The company's registered office is to be situated in England and Wales.

4. The company's objects are the manufacture and development of such descriptions of electronic equipment, instruments and appliances as the company may from time to time determine, and the doing of all such other things as are incidental or conducive to the attainment of that object.

5. The liability of the members is limited.

6. The company's share capital is £5,000,000 divided into 5,000,000 shares of £1 each.

We, the subscribers to this memorandum of association, wish to be formed into a company pursuant to this memorandum; and we agree to take the number of shares shown opposite our respective names.

Names and Addresses of Subscribers	Number of shares taken by each Subscriber
1. James White, 12 Broadmead, Birmingham	1
2. Patrick Smith, 145A Huntley House, London Wall, London EC2.	1
Total shares taken	2

Dated   19

Witness to the above signatures,
Anne Brown, 13 Hute Street, London WC2.

Act of Sederunt (Disqualification of Directors etc.) 1986

(S.I. 1986 No. 692)

[10th April 1986]

The Lords of Council and Session, under and by virtue of the powers conferred on them by section 32 of the Sheriff Courts (Scotland) Act 1971, and of all other powers enabling them in that behalf, do hereby enact and declare:—

Citation, commencement and interpretation
1.—(1) This Act of Sederunt may be cited as the Act of Sederunt (Disqualification of Directors etc.) 1986 and shall come into operation on 28th April 1986.
(2) This Act of Sederunt shall be inserted in the Books of Sederunt.
(3) In this Act of Sederunt—
"the 1985 Act" means the Insolvency Act 1985.

Disqualification of unfit directors of insolvent companies
2.—(1) Applications for a disqualification order under section 12(3) of the 1985 Act shall be made by summary application.
(2) In an application under sub-paragraph (1) which proceeds as undefended, evidence submitted in the form of affidavits shall be admissible in place of parole evidence.

(3) For the purposes of this paragraph—

(*a*) "affidavit" includes affirmation and statutory or other declaration; and

(*b*) an affidavit shall be treated as admissible if it is duly emitted before a notary public or any other competent authority.

Orders to comply with requirement for information or inspection

3.—(1) This paragraph applies to an application to the court under rule 4 of the Insolvent Companies (Reports on Conduct of Directors) (Scotland) Rules 1986.

(2) Subject to sub-paragraph (3), the application shall be made by summary application.

(3) Where an application has been made under section 12(3) of the 1985 Act for a disqualification order, the application under this paragraph may be made by minute in the proceedings in which that order is sought.

Declarator of liability to contribute to company's assets

4.—(1) This paragraph applies to an application by a liquidator under section 15(1) of the 1985 Act, for a declarator that a director, or former director, of a company which is in the course of being wound up, is liable to make a contribution to the assets of the company.

(2) Subject to sub-paragraph (3), the application shall be made by summary application.

(3) Where the company is being wound up by the court, the application may be made by minute in the winding-up proceedings.

Company Directors Disqualification 1986

(S.I. 1986 No. 2296)

[19th December 1986]

The Lords of Council and Session, under and by virtue of the powers conferred on them by section 32 of the Sheriff Courts (Scotland) Act 1971, and of all other powers enabling them in that behalf, do hereby enact and declare:—

Citation, commencement and interpretation

1.—(1) This Act of Sederunt may be cited as the Act of Sederunt (Company Directors Disqualification) 1986 and shall come into operation on 29th December 1986.

(2) This Act of Sederunt shall be inserted in the Books of Sederunt.

(3) In this Act of Sederunt—

"disqualification order" shall have the meaning assigned to it by section 1(1) of the Company Directors Disqualification Act 1986.

Revocation

2. The Act of Sederunt (Disqualification of Directors etc.) 1986 is hereby revoked.

Applications for disqualification orders

3.—(1) An application to the sheriff for a disqualification order or for leave of the court under the Company Directors Disqualification Act 1986 shall be made by summary application.

(2) In an application under sub-paragraph (1) which proceeds as unopposed, evidence submitted by way of affidavit shall be admissible in place of parole evidence.

(3) For the purposes of this paragraph—

(*a*) "affidavit" includes affirmation and statutory declaration; and

(*b*) an affidavit shall be treated as admissible if it is duly emitted before a notary public or any other competent authority.

Orders to furnish information or for inspection

4.—(1) Subject to sub-paragraph (2), an application for an order of the court under rule 4(2) of the Insolvent Companies (Reports on Conduct of Directors) (No. 2) (Scotland) Rules 1986 (order to furnish information, etc.) shall be made by summary application.

(2) Where an application has been made under the Company Directors Disqualification Act 1986 for a disqualification order, an application under this paragraph may be made by minute in the proceedings in which the disqualification order is sought.

Sheriff Court Company Insolvency Rules 1986

(S.I. 1986 No. 2297)

[19th December 1986]

The Lords of Council and Session, under and by virtue of the powers conferred on them by section 32 of the Sheriff Courts (Scotland) Act 1971, and of all other powers enabling them in that behalf, after consultation with the Sheriff Court Rules Council, do hereby enact and declare:—

Citation and commencement

1.—(1) This Act of Sederunt may be cited as the Act of Sederunt (Sheriff Court Company Insolvency Rules) 1986 and shall come into operation on 29th December 1986.

(2) This Act of Sederunt shall be inserted in the Books of Sederunt.

Revocation and transitional provision

2.—(1) The Act of Sederunt (Sheriff Court Liquidations) 1930 is hereby revoked.

(2) Notwithstanding paragraph (1), the Act of Sederunt (Sheriff Court Liquidations) 1930 shall continue to have effect in relation to proceedings commenced before the coming into operation of this Act of Sederunt.

Interpretation

3.—(1) In these rules—

"the Act of 1986" means the Insolvency Act 1986;

"the Insolvency Rules" means the Insolvency (Scotland) Rules 1986;

"registered office" means—

(*a*) the place specified, in the statement of the company delivered to the registrar of companies under section 10 of the Companies Act 1985, as the intended place of its registered office on incorporation; or

(*b*) where notice has been given by the company to the registrar of companies under section 287 of the Companies Act 1985 of a change of registered office, the place specified in the last such notice;

"sheriff clerk" has the meaning assigned to it in section 3(*f*) of the Sheriff Courts (Scotland) Act 1907.

(2) Unless the context otherwise requires, words and expressions used in these rules which are also used in the Act of 1986 or the Insolvency Rules have the same meaning as in that Act or those Rules.

Part I

Company Voluntary Arrangements

Lodging of nominee's report (Part 1, Chapter 2 of the Insolvency Rules)

4.—(1) This rule applies where the company is not being wound up, is not in liquidation and an administration order is not in force in respect of it.

(2) A report of a nominee, sent to the court under section 2(2) of the Act of 1986, shall be accompanied by a covering letter, lodged in the offices of the court and marked by the sheriff clerk with the date on which it is received.

(3) The report shall be placed before the sheriff for consideration of any direction which he may make under section 3(1) of the Act of 1986.

(4) An application by a nominee to extend the time within which he may lodge his report under section 2(2) of the Act of 1986 shall be made by letter addressed to the sheriff clerk, who shall place the matter before the sheriff for determination.

(5) The letter of application under paragraph (4) and a copy of the reply by the court shall be placed by the sheriff clerk with the nominee's report when it is subsequently lodged.

(6) A person who states in writing that he is a creditor, member or director of the company may, by himself or his agent, on payment of the appropriate fee, inspect the nominee's report lodged under paragraph (2).

Lodging of nominee's report (Part 1, Chapter 4 of the Insolvency Rules)

5.—(1) This rule applies where the company is being wound up, is in liquidation or there is an administration order in force in respect of it.

(2) Where a report of a nominee is sent to the court under section 2(2) of the Act of 1986, it shall be lodged in the process of the petition to wind up the company or the petition for an administration order which is in force in respect of it, as the case may be.

(3) Where the nominee is not the liquidator or administrator, the report shall be placed before the sheriff for consideration of any direction which he may make under section 3(1) of the Act of 1986.

(4) An application by a nominee to extend the time within which he may lodge his report under section 2(2) of the Act of 1986 shall be made by letter addressed to the sheriff clerk, who shall place the matter before the sheriff for determination.

(5) The letter of application under paragraph (4) and a copy of the reply by the court shall be placed by the sheriff clerk in the process of the petition to wind up the company or the petition for an administration order which is in force in respect of it, as the case may be.

(6) A person who states in writing that he is a creditor, member or director of the company may, by himself or his agent, on payment of the appropriate fee, inspect the nominee's report lodged under paragraph (2).

Applications to replace nominee

6. An application under section 2(4) of the Act of 1986 to replace a nominee who has failed to lodge a report under section 2(2) of the Act of 1986, shall be made—

(*a*) by petition where the company is not being wound up, is not in liquidation and an administration order is not in force in respect of it; or

(*b*) by note in the process of the petition to wind up the company or the petition for an administration order which is in force in respect of it, as the case may be,

and shall be intimated and served as the court shall direct.

Report of meetings to approve arrangement

7. The report of the result of a meeting to be sent to the court under section 4(6) of the Act of 1986 shall be sent to the sheriff clerk who shall cause it to be lodged—

    (*a*) in a case to which rule 4 applies, with the nominee's report lodged under that rule; or

    (*b*) in a case to which rule 5 applies, in the process of the petition to wind up the company or the petition for an administration order which is in force in respect of it, as the case may be.

Abstracts of supervisor's receipts and payments and notices of completion of arrangement

8. An abstract of receipts and payments prepared by a supervisor to be sent to the court under rule 1.21(2) of the Insolvency Rules or a notice of completion of the arrangement (together with a copy of the supervisor's report) to be sent to the court under rule 1.23(3) of those Rules shall be sent to the sheriff clerk, who shall cause it to be lodged—

    (*a*) in a case to which rule 4 applies, with the nominee's report lodged under that rule; or

    (*b*) in a case to which rule 5 applies, in the process of the petition to wind up the company or the petition for an administration order which is in force in respect of it, as the case may be.

Form of certain applications

9.—(1) This rule applies to applications under any of the following provisions of the Act of 1986 and the Insolvency Rules:—

    (*a*) section 6 (to challenge a decision in relation to an arrangement);

    (*b*) section 7(3) (to challenge actings of a supervisor);

    (*c*) section 7(4)(*a*) (by supervisor for directions);

    (*d*) section 7(5) (to appoint a supervisor);

    (*e*) rule 1.21(5) (to dispense with sending abstracts or reports or to vary dates on which obligation to send abstracts or reports arises);

    (*f*) rule 1.23(4) (by supervisor to extend period for sending notice of implementation of arrangement); and

    (*g*) any other provision relating to company voluntary arrangements not specifically mentioned in this Part.

(2) An application shall be made—

    (*a*) in a case to which rule 4 applies, by petition; or

    (*b*) in a case to which rule 5 applies, by note in the process of the petition to wind up the company or the petition for an administration order which is in force in respect of it, as the case may be.

Part II

Administration Orders

Petitions for administration orders

10.—(1) A petition for an administration order shall include averments in relation to—

    (*a*) the petitioner and the capacity in which he presents the petition, if other than the company;

    (*b*) whether it is believed that the company is, or is likely to become, unable to pay its debts and the grounds of that belief;

    (*c*) which of the purposes specified in section 8(3) of the Act of 1986 is expected to be achieved by the making of an administration order;

    (*d*) the company's financial position, specifying (so far as known) assets and liabilities, including contingent and prospective liabilities;

(e) any security known or believed to be held by creditors of the company, whether in any case the security confers power on the holder to appoint a receiver, and whether a receiver has been appointed;

(f) so far as known to the petition, whether any steps have been taken for the winding up of the company, giving details of them;

(g) other matters which, in the opinion of the petitioner, will assist the court in deciding whether to grant an administration order;

(h) whether a report has been prepared under rule 2.1 of the Insolvency Rules (independent report on affairs of the company), and, if not, an explanation why not; and

(i) the person proposed to be appointed as administrator, giving his name and address and that he is qualified to act as an insolvency practitioner in relation to the company.

(2) There shall be produced with the petition—

(a) any document instructing the facts relied on, or otherwise founded on, by the petitioner; and

(b) where a report has been prepared under rule 2.1 of the Insolvency Rules, a copy of that report.

Notice of petition

11. Notice of the petition on the persons to whom notice is to be given under rule 2.2 of the Insolvency Rules shall be made in such manner as the court shall direct.

Form of certain applications and appeals where administration order in force

12.—(1) An application or appeal under any of the following provisions of the Act of 1986 or the Insolvency Rules shall be made by note in the process of the petition for an administration order which is in force:—

(a) section 13(2) (application for appointment to fill a vacancy in office of administrator);

(b) section 14(3) (application by administrator for directions);

(c) section 15(2) (application by administrator for power to dispose of property subject to a security);

(d) section 18(1) (application by administrator for discharge or variation of administration order);

(e) section 19(1) (application for removal from office of administrator);

(f) section 22(5) (application for release from, or extension of time for, obligation to submit statement of affairs);

(g) section 27(1) (application for protection of interest of creditors and members);

(h) rule 2.6(2) (appeal against decision of administrator as to expenses of submitting statement of affairs);

(i) rule 2.16(3) (application by administrator for increase of remuneration); and

(j) any other application under a provision relating to administration orders not specifically mentioned in this Part.

(2) An application by an administrator to extend the period for sending an abstract of his receipts and payments under rule 2.17(2) of the Insolvency Rules shall be made by motion in the process of the petition.

Report of administrator's proposals

13.—(1) A report of the meeting to approve the administrator's proposals to be sent to the court under section 24(4) of the Act of 1986 shall be sent to the sheriff clerk, who shall cause it to be lodged in the process of the petition.

(2) Where the report lodged under paragraph (1) discloses that the meeting has declined to approve the administrator's proposals, the court shall appoint a special diet for determination by the sheriff of any order he may make under section 24(5) of the Act of 1986.

Abstracts of administrator's receipts and payments

14. An abstract of receipts and payments of an administrator to be sent to the court under rule 2.17(1) of the Insolvency Rules shall be sent to the sheriff clerk, who shall cause it to be lodged in the process of the petition.

PART III

RECEIVERS

Petitions to appoint receivers

15.—(1) A petition to appoint a receiver for a company shall include averments in relation to—

(*a*) any floating charge and the property over which it is secured;

(*b*) so far as known to the petitioner whether any petition for an administration order has been made in respect of the company, giving details of it;

(*c*) other matters which, in the opinion of the petitioner, will assist the court in deciding whether to appoint a receiver; and

(*d*) the person proposed to be appointed as receiver, giving his name and address and that he is qualified to act as a receiver.

(2) There shall be produced with the petition any document instructing the facts relied on, or otherwise founded on, by the petitioner.

Intimation, service and advertisement

16.—(1) Intimation, service and advertisement of the petition shall be made in accordance with the following provisions of this rule unless the court otherwise directs.

(2) There shall be included in the order for service, a requirement to serve—

(*a*) upon the company; and

(*b*) where a petition for an administration order has been presented, on that petitioner and any respondent to that petition.

(3) Subject to paragraph (5), service of a petition on the company shall be effected as its registered office—

(*a*) by registered or recorded delivery post addressed to the company; or

(*b*) by sheriff officer—

(i) leaving the citation in the hands of a person who, after due inquiry, he has reasonable grounds for believing to be a director, other officer or responsible employee of the company or authorised to accept service on behalf of the company; or

(ii) if there is no such person as is mentioned in head (i) present, depositing it in the registered office in such a way that it is likely to come to the attention of such a person attending at that office.

(4) Where service is effected in accordance with paragraph (3)(*b*)(ii), the sheriff officer thereafter shall send a copy of the petition and citation by ordinary first class post to the registered office of the company.

(5) Where service cannot be effected at the registered office of the company or the company has no registered office—

(*a*) service may be effected at the last known principal place of business of the company in Scotland or at some place in Scotland at which the company carries on business, by leaving the citation in the hands of such a person as is mentioned in paragraph (3)(*b*)(i) or by depositing it as specified in paragraph (3)(*b*)(ii); and

(*b*) where the citation is deposited as is specified in paragraph (3)(*b*)(ii), the sheriff officer thereafter shall send a copy of the petition and citation by ordinary first class post to such place mentioned in sub-paragraph (*a*) of this paragraph in which the citation was deposited.

(6) The petition shall be advertised forthwith—

(*a*) once in the *Edinburgh Gazette*; and

(*b*) once in one or more newspapers as the court shall direct for ensuring that it comes to the notice of the creditors of the company.

(7) The advertisement under paragraph (6) shall state—

(*a*) the name and address of the petitioner;

(*b*) the name and address of the solicitor for the petitioner;

(*c*) the date on which the petition was presented;

(*d*) the precise order sought;

(*e*) the period of notice; and

(*f*) that any person who intends to appear in the petition must lodge answers to the petition within the period of notice.

(8) The period of notice within which answers to the petition may be lodged and after which further consideration of the petition may proceed shall be eight days after such intimation, service and advertisement as the court may have ordered.

Form of certain applications where receiver appointed

17.—(1) An application under any of the following sections of the Act of 1986 shall be made by petition or, where the receiver was appointed by the court, by note in the process of the petition for appointment of a receiver:—

(*a*) section 61(1) (by receiver for authority to dispose of interest in property);

(*b*) section 62 (for removal or resignation of receiver);

(*c*) section 63(1) (by receiver for directions);

(*d*) section 69(1) (to enforce receiver to make returns, etc.); and

(*e*) any other section relating to receivers not specifically mentioned in this Part.

(2) An application under any of the following provisions of the Act of 1986 or the Insolvency Rules shall be made by motion in the process of the petition:—

(*a*) section 67(1) or (2) (by receiver to extend time for sending report); and

(*b*) rule 3.9(2) (by receiver to extend time for sending abstract of receipts and payments).

PART IV

WINDING UP BY THE COURT OF COMPANIES REGISTERED UNDER THE COMPANIES ACTS AND OF UNREGISTERED COMPANIES

Petitions to wind up a company

18.—(1) A petition to wind up a company under the Act of 1986 shall include—

(*a*) particulars of the petitioner, if other than the company;

(*b*) in respect of the company—

(i) the registered name;

(ii) the address of the registered office and any change of that address within the last six months so far as known to the petitioner;

(iii) a statement of the nature and objects, the amount of its capital (nominal and issued) and indicating what part is called up, paid up or credited as paid, and the amount of the assets of the company so far as known to the petitioner;

(*c*) a narrative of the facts on which the petitioner relies and any particulars required to instruct the title of the petitioner to present the petition;

(*d*) the name and address of the person to be appointed as interim liquidator and a statement that he is qualified to act as an insolvency
practitioner in relation to the company; and

(*e*) a crave setting out the orders applied for, including any intimation,
service and advertisement and any appointment of an interim liquidator.

(2) There shall be lodged with the petition any document—

(*a*) instructing the title of the petitioner; and

(*b*) instructing the facts relied on, or otherwise founded on, by the petitioner.

Intimation, service and advertisement

19.—(1) Intimation, service and advertisement shall be in accordance
with the following provisions of this rule unless the court—

(*a*) summarily dismisses the petition; or

(*b*) otherwise directs.

(2) There shall be included in the order for intimation and service, a
requirement—

(*a*) to intimate on the walls of the court;

(*b*) where the petitioner is other than the company, to serve upon the
company;

(*c*) where the company is being wound up voluntarily and a liquidator
has been appointed, to serve upon the liquidator;

(*d*) where a receiver has been appointed for the company, to serve upon
the receiver;

(*e*) where the company is—

(i) a recognised bank or licensed institution within the meaning of
the Banking Act 1979; or

(ii) an institution to which sections 16 and 18 of that Act apply as if
it were licensed,

and the petitioner is not the Bank of England, to serve upon the
Bank of England.

(3) Subject to paragraph (5), service of a petition on the company shall
be executed at its registered office—

(*a*) by registered or recorded delivery post addressed to the company;
or

(*b*) by sheriff officer—

(i) leaving the citation in the hands of a person who, after due
inquiry, he has reasonable grounds for believing to be a director, other officer or responsible employee of the company or
authorised to accept service on behalf of the company; or

(ii) if there is no such person as is mentioned in head (i) present,
depositing it in the registered office in such a way that it is likely
to come to the attention of such a person attending at that
office.

(4) Where service is effected in accordance with paragraph (3)(*b*)(ii), the
sheriff officer thereafter shall send a copy of the petition and citation by
ordinary first class post to the registered office of the company.

(5) Where service cannot be effected at the registered office or the company has no registered office—

(*a*) service may be effected at the last known principal place of business
of the company in Scotland or at some place in Scotland at which
the company carries on business, by leaving the citation in the hands
of such a person as is mentioned in paragraph (3)(*b*)(i) or by depositing it as specified in paragraph (3)(*b*)(ii); and

(*b*) where the citation is deposited as is specified in paragraph (3)(*b*)(ii),
the sheriff officer thereafter shall send a copy of the petition and the
citation by ordinary first class post to such place mentioned in sub-
paragraph (*a*) of this paragraph in which the citation was deposited.

(6) The petition shall be advertised forthwith—

(*a*) once in the *Edinburgh Gazette*; and

(*b*) once in one or more newspapers as the court shall direct for ensuring that it comes to the notice of the creditors of the company.

(7) The advertisement under paragraph (6) shall state—

(*a*) the name and address of the petitioner and, where the petitioner is the company, the registered office;

(*b*) the name and address of the solicitor for the petitioner;

(*c*) the date on which the petition was presented;

(*d*) the precise order sought;

(*e*) where a provisional liquidator has been appointed, his name, address and the date of his appointment;

(*f*) the period of notice; and

(*g*) that any person who intends to appear in the petition must lodge answers to the petition within the period of notice.

(8) The period of notice within which answers to the petition may be lodged and after which further consideration of the petition may proceed shall be eight days after such intimation, service and advertisement as the court may have ordered.

Lodging of caveats

20.—(1) A company, debenture holder, holder of a floating charge, receiver, shareholder of a company or other person claiming an interest, apprehensive that a petition to wind up that company may be presented and wishing to be heard by the court before an order for intimation, service and advertisement is pronounced, may lodge a caveat with the sheriff clerk.

(2) A caveat shall endure for 12 months on the expiry of which a new caveat may be lodged.

(3) Where a caveat has been lodged and has not expired, no order may be pronounced without the person lodging the caveat having been given an opportunity to be heard by the court.

Substitution of creditor or contributory for petitioner

21.—(1) This rule applies where a petitioner—

(*a*) is subsequently found not entitled to present the petition;

(*b*) fails to make intimation, service and advertisement as directed by the court;

(*c*) consents to withdraw the petition or to allow it to be dismissed or refused;

(*d*) fails to appear when the petition is called for hearing; or

(*e*) appears, but does not move for an order in terms of the prayer of the petition.

(2) The court may, on such terms as it considers just, sist as petitioner in room of the original petitioner any creditor or contributory who, in the opinion of the court, is entitled to present a petition.

(3) An application by a creditor or contributory to be sisted under paragraph (2)—

(*a*) may be made at any time before the petition is dismissed or refused; and

(*b*) shall be made by note in the process of the petition, and if necessary the court may continue the cause for a specified period to allow a note to be presented.

Advertisement of appointment of liquidator

22. Where a liquidator is appointed by the court, the court may order that the liquidator shall advertise his appointment once in one or more newspapers as the court shall direct for ensuring that it comes to the notice of creditors of the company.

Provisional liquidators

23.—(1) An application to appoint a provisional liquidator under section 135 of the Act of 1986 may be made—

(a) by the petitioner, in the crave of the petition or subsequently by note in the process of the petition; or

(b) by a creditor or contributory of the company, the company, Secretary of State or a person entitled under any enactment to present a petition to wind up the company, in a note in the process of the petition.

(2) The petition or note, as the case may be, shall include averments in relation to—

(a) the grounds on which it is proposed that a provisional liquidator should be appointed;

(b) the name and address of the person to be appointed as provisional liquidator and that he is qualified to act as an insolvency practitioner in relation to the company; and

(c) whether, to the knowledge of the applicant, there is a receiver for the company or a liquidator has been appointed for the voluntary winding up of the company.

(3) Where the court is satisfied that sufficient grounds exist for the appointment of a provisional liquidator, it shall, on making the appointment, specify the functions to be carried out by him in relation to the affairs of the company.

(4) The applicant shall send a certified copy of the interlocutor appointing a provisional liquidator forthwith to the person appointed.

(5) On receiving a certified copy of his appointment on an application by note, the provisional liquidator shall intimate his appointment forthwith—

(a) once in the *Edinburgh Gazette*; and

(b) once in one or more newspapers as the court shall direct for ensuring that it comes to the notice of creditors of the company.

(6) An application for discharge of a provisional liquidator shall be by note in the process of the petition.

Applications and appeals in relation to a statement of affairs

24.—(1) An application under section 131(5) of the Act of 1986 for—

(a) release from an obligation imposed under section 131(1) or (2) of the Act of 1986; or

(b) an extension of time for the submission of a statement of affairs,

shall be made by note in the process of the petition.

(2) A note under paragraph (1) shall be served on the liquidator or provisional liquidator, as the case may be.

(3) The liquidator or provisional liquidator may lodge answers to the note or lodge a report of any matters which he considers should be drawn to the attention of the court.

(4) Where the liquidator or provisional liquidator lodges a report under paragraph (3), he shall send a copy of it to the noter forthwith.

(5) Where the liquidator or provisional liquidator does not appear, a certified copy of the interlocutor pronounced by the court disposing of the note shall be sent by the noter forthwith to him.

(6) An appeal under rule 4.9(6) of the Insolvency Rules against a refusal by the liquidator of an allowance towards the expense of preparing a statement of affairs shall be made by note in the process of the petition.

Appeals against adjudication of claims

25.—(1) An appeal under section 49(6) of the Bankruptcy (Scotland) Act 1985, as applied by rule 4.16 of the Insolvency Rules, by a creditor or contributory of the company against a decision of the liquidator shall be made by note in the process of the petition.

(2) A note under paragraph (1) shall be served on the liquidator.

(3) On receipt of the note served on him under this rule, the liquidator forthwith shall send to the court the claim in question and a copy of his adjudication for lodging in process.

(4) After the note has been disposed of, the court shall return the claim and the adjudication to the liquidator together with a copy of the interlocutor.

Appointment of liquidator by the court

26.—(1) An application to appoint a liquidator under section 139(4) of the Act of 1986 shall be made by note in the process of the petition.

(2) Where the court appoints a liquidator under section 138(5) of the Act of 1986, the sheriff clerk shall send a certified copy of the interlocutor pronounced by the court to the liquidator forthwith.

Removal of liquidator

27. An application by a creditor of the company for removal of a liquidator or provisional liquidator from office under section 172 of the Act of 1986 or for an order under section 171(3) of the Act of 1986 directing a liquidator to summon a meeting of creditors for the purpose of removing him shall be made by note in the process of the petition.

Applications in relation to remuneration of liquidator

28.—(1) An application by a liquidator under rule 4.34 of the Insolvency Rules shall be made by note in the process of the petition.

(2) An application by a creditor of the company under rule 4.35 of the Insolvency Rules shall be made by note in the process of the petition.

(3) A note under paragraph (2) shall be served on the liquidator.

Application to appoint a special manager

29.—(1) An application under section 177 of the Act of 1986 by a liquidator or provisional liquidator for the appointment of a special manager shall be made by note in the process of the petition.

(2) The cautioner, for the caution to be found by the special manager within such time as the court shall direct, may be—

(*a*) a private person, if approved by the court; or

(*b*) a guarantee company, chosen from a list of such companies prepared for this purpose annually by the accountant of court and approved by the Lord President of the Court of Session.

(3) A bond of caution certified by the noter under rule 4.70(4) of the Insolvency Rules shall be delivered to the sheriff clerk by the noter, marked as received by him and transmitted forthwith by him to the accountant of court.

(4) On receipt of the bond of caution, the sheriff clerk shall issue forthwith to the person appointed to be special manager a certified copy of the interlocutor appointing him.

(5) An application by a special manager to extend the time within which to find caution shall be made by motion.

Other applications

30. An application under the Act of 1986 or rules made under that Act in relation to a winding up by the court not specifically mentioned in this Part shall be made by note in the process of the petition.

PART V

GENERAL PROVISIONS

Application
31. This Part applies to Parts I to IV of these rules.

Intimation, service and advertisement of notes and appeals
32. An application by note, or an appeal, to the court under these rules shall be intimated, served and, if necessary, advertised as the court shall direct.

Affidavits
33. The court may accept as evidence an affidavit lodged in support of a petition or note.

Notices, reports and other documents sent to the court
34. Where, under the Act of 1986 or rules made under that Act—
  (*a*) notice of a fact is to be given to the court;
  (*b*) a report is to be made, or sent, to the court; or
  (*c*) some other document is to be sent to the court;
it shall be sent or delivered to the sheriff clerk of the court, who shall cause it to be lodged in the appropriate process.

Failure to comply with rules
35.—(1) The court may, in its discretion, relieve a party from the consequences of any failure to comply with the provisions of a rule shown to be due to mistake, oversight or other cause, which is not wilful non-observance of the rule, on such terms and conditions as the court considers just.
  (2) Where the court relieves a party from the consequences of failure to comply with a rule under paragraph 1, the court may pronounce such interlocutor as may be just so as to enable the cause to proceed as if the failure to comply with the rule had not occurred.

PART VI

APPEALS

Appeals to the sheriff principal or Court of Session
36.—(1) Where an appeal to the sheriff principal or the Court of Session is competent, it shall be taken by note of appeal which shall—
  (*a*) be written by the appellant or his solicitor on—
      (i) the interlocutor sheet or other written record containing the interlocutor appealed against; or
      (ii) a separate document lodged with the sheriff clerk;
  (*b*) be as nearly as may be in the following terms:— "The (*petitioner, noter, respondent or other party*) appeals to the Sheriff Principal [*or* Court of Session]"; and
  (*c*) be signed by the appellant or his solicitor and bear the date on which it is signed.
  (2) Such an appeal shall be marked within 14 days of the date of the interlocutor appealed against.
  (3) Where the appeal is to the Court of Session, the note of appeal shall specify the name and address of the solicitor in Edinburgh who will be acting for the appellant.
  (4) On an appeal being taken, the sheriff clerk shall within four days—

(*a*) transmit the process—
    (i) where the appeal is to sheriff principal, to him; or
    (ii) where the appeal is to the Court of Session, to the deputy principal clerk of session; and

(*b*) send written notice of the appeal to any other party to the cause and certify in the interlocutor sheet, or other written record containing the interlocutor appealed against, that he has done so.

(5) Failure of the sheriff clerk to give notice under paragraph 4(*b*) shall not invalidate the appeal.